BRITISH PHILOSOPHY IN THE NINETEENTH CENTURY

THE OXFORD HANDBOOK OF

BRITISH PHILOSOPHY IN THE NINETEENTH CENTURY

Edited by

W. J. MANDER

OXFORD

UNIVERSITY PRESS

OXFORD
UNIVERSITY PRESS

Great Clarendon Street, Oxford, OX2 6DP,
United Kingdom

Oxford University Press is a department of the University of Oxford.
It furthers the University's objective of excellence in research, scholarship,
and education by publishing worldwide. Oxford is a registered trade mark of
Oxford University Press in the UK and in certain other countries

Published in the United States of America by Oxford University Press
198 Madison Avenue, New York, NY 10016, United States of America

British Library Cataloguing in Publication Data
Data available

Library of Congress Control Number: 2013943251

ISBN 978-0-19-959447-4

Printed and bound in Great Britain by
CPI Group (UK) Ltd, Croydon, CR0 4YY

Contents

PART III SCIENCE AND PHILOSOPHY

PART IV ETHICAL, SOCIAL, AND POLITICAL THOUGHT

PART V RELIGIOUS PHILOSOPHY

PART VI THE PRACTICE OF PHILOSOPHY

Notes on Contributors

James W. Allard is Professor of Philosophy, Emeritus, at Montana State University. He is the editor, with Guy Stock, of *F. H. Bradley: Writings on Logic and Metaphysics* and the author of *The Logical Basis of Bradley's Metaphysics*.

Leslie Armour is Fellow of the Royal Society of Canada. Since 1997 he has been Research Professor of Philosophy at the Dominican University College, Ottawa, and Emeritus Professor of Philosophy at the University of Ottawa. He has taught philosophy and held administrative posts at various universities in California, Ohio, Montana, and Ontario, and was educated at the University of British Columbia (BA, 1952) and the University of London (PhD, 1956.) His books include *Infini Rien: Pascal's Wager and the Human Paradox*; *Being and Idea: Developments of Some Themes in Spinoza and Hegel*; *The Rational & The Real*; *Logic & Reality*; *The Concept of Truth*; and *The Idea of Canada and the Crisis of Community*. He wrote *The Faces of Reason: An Essay in Philosophy and Culture in English Canada, 1850–1950* with Elizabeth Trott; *The Conceptualization of the Inner Life* with Edward T. Bartlett III; and *Inference and Persuasion* with Richard Feist.

Pierfrancesco Basile is Lecturer in Philosophy at the University of Berne, Switzerland. His publications include two books, *Experience and Relations: An Examination of Francis Herbert Bradley's Conception of Reality* (1999) and *Leibniz, Whitehead and the Metaphysics of Causation* (2009), as well as several essays on issues in Spinoza's metaphysics, process thought, British Idealism, and early analytic philosophy.

David Boucher is Professor of Political Theory and International Relations at Cardiff University, Distinguished Research Associate at the University of Joannesburg, and Director of the Collingwood and British Idealism Centre. He has published widely, including *The Social and Political Thought of R. G. Collingwood* (1989), *Political Theories of International Relations* (1998), *The Limits of Ethics in International Relations* (2009), and, with Andrew Vincent, *British Idealism and Political Theory* (2001) and *British Idealism: A Guide for the Perplexed* (2011).

John Hedley Brooke was the first Andreas Idreos Professor of Science and Religion at Oxford University, Director of the Ian Ramsey Centre, and Fellow of Harris Manchester College. Following retirement in 2006, he has spent time as a 'Distinguished Fellow' at the Institute of Advanced Study, University of Durham. Until recently he was President of the International Society for Science and Religion.

Stuart Brown was formerly Professor of Philosophy at the Open University and is now Professor Emeritus. His interests range over the history of modern and recent philosophy and he has written on many philosophers, Leibniz in particular. He has been actively involved, as editor and contributor, with several dictionaries of philosophy and philosophers from the seventeenth to the twentieth century.

Barbara Caine is Professor of History and the Head of the School of Philosophical and Historical Inquiry at the University of Sydney. She has written extensively on the history of feminism. Her publications include *Victorian Feminists* (Oxford, 1992); *English Feminism c1780–1980* (Oxford 1998); *Bombay to Bloomsbury: A Biography of the Stracheys* (Oxford, 2005); and *Gendering European History* (co-authored with Glenda Sluga, University of Leicester Press, 2000).

Steffen Ducheyne is Research Professor at the Free University of Brussels (VUB), Belgium. His main area of research is the history of scientific methodology with a particular interest in Newton's natural philosophy and the interaction between science and philosophy from the seventeenth to the nineteenth century.

Phillip Ferreira is Professor of Philosophy at Kutztown University of Pennsylvania. He is the author of many articles on British Idealism as well as *Bradley and the Structure of Knowledge* (SUNY Press, 1999).

Mark Francis is Professor in the Department of Philosophy and Political Science at the University of Canterbury, Christchurch, New Zealand. He has been Fowler Hamilton Senior Research Fellow at Christ Church, Oxford, and Rutherford Scholar at Trinity College, Cambridge. His publications include *Herbert Spencer and the Invention of Modern Life* (Cornell University Press, 2007); 'Social Darwinism and the Construction of Institutionalized Racism in Australia', *Journal of Australian Studies*, 50/1 (1996); and *Governors and Settlers: Images of Authority in the British Colonies, 1820–1860* (Cambridge Commonwealth Series, 1992). He is currently engaged in research projects on non-Darwinian evolutionary psychology and on the history of philosophy.

David Godden (PhD McMaster University, 2004) is Assistant Professor of Philosophy at Old Dominion University, with research interests in epistemology, the theory of rationality, reasoning and argument, the theory of evidence, the history and philosophy of logic, and twentieth-century analytic philosophy. His article 'Psychologism in the Logic of John Stuart Mill: Mill on the Subject Matter and Foundations of Ratiocinative Logic' appeared in *History and Philosophy of Logic* (2005). He has published on a wide variety of topics including psychologism, Quine's holism, corroborative evidence, common knowledge, presumption and argumentation schemes, and his work has appeared in journals such as *Synthese*, *Argumentation*, *Ratio Juris*, *Philosophy & Rhetoric*, and *Informal Logic*.

Gordon Graham is Henry Luce III Professor of Philosophy and the Arts at Princeton Theological Seminary, where he is also Director of the Center for the Study of Scottish Philosophy. He was formerly Regius Professor of Moral Philosophy at the University of Aberdeen and is founding editor of the *Journal of Scottish Philosophy*. He is the editor of *Scottish Philosophy After the Enlightenment: A History of Scottish Philosophy*, volume ii (OUP, forthcoming).

Jeremy Gray is Professor of the History of Mathematics at the Open University, and Honorary Professor at the University of Warwick, where he lectures on the history of mathematics.

Gary Hatfield is Adam Seybert Professor in Moral and Intellectual Philosophy at the University of Pennsylvania. He has published extensively on the history of modern philosophy and the history and philosophy of psychology from the medieval period into the twentieth century, including *The Natural and the Normative: Theories of Spatial Perception from Kant to Helmholtz* (1990), *Descartes and the Meditations* (2003), and *Perception and Cognition: Essays in the Philosophy of Psychology* (2009). He recently co-edited a volume with Sarah Allred, entitled *Visual Experience: Sensation, Cognition, and Constancy* (2012).

Jenny Keefe has been Assistant Professor of Philosophy at the University of Wisconsin-Parkside since 2008. Her research interests include British Idealism and Scottish philosophy. She is the author of articles on J. F. Ferrier's philosophy and the editor of *James Frederick Ferrier: Selected Writings* (2011).

Anthony Kenny is one of Britain's most distinguished academics and philosophers. He has been Pro-Vice-Chancellor of the University of Oxford, Master of Balliol College, and President of the British Academy. He is particularly well known for his work on Aristotle, Aquinas, Descartes, and Wittgenstein. He has also published acclaimed books on the philosophy of mind and action and the philosophy of religion.

David Leopold is University Lecturer in Political Theory, University of Oxford, and John Milton Fellow, Mansfield College, Oxford. He has research interests in contemporary political philosophy and the history of political thought (especially nineteenth-century European political thought). His publications include *The Young Karl Marx: German Philosophy, Modern Politics, and Human Flourishing* (Cambridge, 2007).

W. J. Mander is Lecturer in Philosophy at Oxford University, where he is also Fellow of Harris Manchester College. He is the author of *British Idealism: A History* (OUP, 2011).

Dale E. Miller is Professor of Philosophy at Old Dominion University. He is the author of *John Stuart Mill: Moral, Social and Political Thought* (Polity, 2010). He is the co-editor of several collections: *John Stuart Mill and the Art of Life* (Oxford, 2011, with Ben Eggleston and David Weinstein); *Morality, Rules and Consequences* (Edinburgh, 2000, with Brad Hooker and Elinor Mason); and *The Cambridge Companion to Utilitarianism* (forthcoming from Cambridge, with Ben Eggleston).

John Offer is Professor of Social Theory and Policy at the University of Ulster, Coleraine, N. Ireland. He has published widely on Spencer, including *Herbert Spencer: Political Writings* (Cambridge University Press, 1994) and *Herbert Spencer and Social Theory* (Palgrave Macmillan, 2010). He has also written *An Intellectual History of British Social Policy* (Policy Press, 2006), and is Chair of the Editorial Board of *Sociology*.

Michael Ruse is Lucyle T. Werkmeister Professor of Philosophy and the Director of the Program in the History and Philosophy of Science at Florida State University. He is the author or editor of many books on Darwin and his revolution, including the *Cambridge Encyclopedia of Darwin and Evolutionary Thought*.

Philip Schofield is Professor of the History of Legal and Political Thought in the Faculty of Laws, University College London. He is Director of the Bentham Project and General Editor of the new authoritative edition of *The Collected Works of Jeremy Bentham*, which is being published by Oxford University Press.

Bart Schultz is Senior Lecturer in Philosophy and Director of the Civic Knowledge Project at the University of Chicago. His book *Henry Sidgwick: Eye of the Universe* (Cambridge, 2004) won the American Philosophical Society's prestigious Jacques Barzun Prize in Cultural History for 2004. Other publications include *Essays on Henry Sidgwick* (Cambridge, 1992) and *Utilitarianism and Empire* (Lexington, 2005). He has also designed and implemented a precollegiate philosophy programme, Winning Words, which won the American Philosophical Association's 2012 PDC Prize for Excellence and Innovation in Philosophy Programming.

Alan P. F. Sell (University of Wales Trinity Saint David) is a widely published philosopher-theologian and ecumenist, who lectures and examines at home and abroad.

Avital Simhony is Associate Professor in the School of Politics and Global Studies at Arizona State University. She is the co-editor of *The New Liberalism: Reconciling Liberty and Community* (CUP, 2001) and has published articles in journals such as *Collingwood and British Idealism Studies*, *Hegel Bulletin*, *History of Political Thought*, *Journal of Political Ideologies*, *Political Theory*, *Political Studies*, and *Utilitas*.

William Sweet is Professor of Philosophy and Director of the Centre for Philosophy, Theology, and Cultural Traditions, at St Francis Xavier University, Antigonish, NS, Canada. A Past President of the Canadian Philosophical Association and a member of the Steering Committee of the Fédération Internationale des Sociétés de Philosophie, he is the author and/or editor of some thirty books including *Idealism and Rights* (1997), *Bernard Bosanquet and the Legacy of British Idealism* (2007), *The Moral, Social and Political Philosophy of the British Idealists* (2009), *Responses to the Enlightenment* (2012, with Hendrik Hart), and *Migrating Texts and Traditions* (2012). He is an editor of the journal *Collingwood and British Idealism Studies*, and of the *Biographical Encyclopedia of British Idealism* (2010) and *The Collected Works of Bernard Bosanquet* (2001).

James Vigus is Lecturer in English at Queen Mary, University of London. He is also Co-Director of the Dr Williams's Centre for Dissenting Studies, Queen Mary. Previously a postdoctoral research fellow in Jena and Munich, he works on the reception of German thought in British Romanticism; his publications include the monograph *Platonic Coleridge* (2009) and a critical edition of Henry Crabb Robinson's *Essays on Kant, Schelling, and German Aesthetics* (2010). He is currently working on a collaborative edition of Robinson's *Reminiscences* and *Diary*.

Andrew Vincent, FRHistS, FLSW, is Honorary Professor, Cardiff University, and Emeritus Professor of Political Theory, Sheffield University. He is a widely respected theorist specializing in political philosophy, ideologies, human rights, and philosophical idealism. Recent publications include: *The Politics of Human Rights* (2010), *British Idealism: A Guide for the Perplexed* (with David Boucher, 2011), and *Comparative Political Thought: Theorizing Practices* (with Michael Freeden, 2012).

Ralph Waller is the Principal of Harris Manchester College Oxford and Director of the Farmington Institute. He is also Pro-Vice-Chancellor of the University of Oxford. He is the author of *John Wesley: A Personal Portrait* (SPCK, 2003).

CHAPTER 1

....

INTRODUCTION

....

W. J. MANDER

THE Edwardian mind reacted so harshly against the age that preceded it that not until the second half of the twentieth century was the Victorian world able to reassert itself as a legitimate domain of academic interest. Nor has this rehabilitation even been complete, since to the majority of English-speaking historians of philosophy the term 'nineteenth-century philosophy' indicates the great systems of *Continental* thought—Hegel, Kierkegaard, Schopenhauer, Nietzsche—rather than the *British* tradition which, with exception of isolated names like Mill or Newman, to this day remains almost entirely unknown. The current volume seeks to redress that situation and urge that the renewed levels of attention and scholarship which contemporary philosophers have applied to British philosophy of the seventeenth and eighteenth centuries should be extended also to the work of the nineteenth.

With its earnest yet pragmatic anti-intellectualism focused largely on commerce and respectability, it is sometimes thought that the Victorian mind produced little philosophy of any note. But as the chapters of this volume make very apparent that could not be further from the truth. The nineteenth century was a time of intense intellectual activity, in which critical advances inspired in equal measures both anxious doubt and creative expansion, and nowhere is this more evident than in the work of its philosophers. Conceding this, it is sometimes thought that such philosophy as may be found in the nineteenth century is simply *irrelevant* to the contemporary subject; its problems, methods, and language quite unlike anything today. For (it is argued) the analytic discipline in which most English-language philosophers now work grew precisely out of the sharp break with the past that occurred at the beginning of the twentieth century, and which we associate with the names of Russell, Moore, and Wittgenstein. But to make this charge is to confuse familiarity with relevance. Certainly nineteenth-century philosophy is conducted in an outdated idiom and subject to a set of different assumptions which make it seem opaque at first sight, but in truth this is no more than might be said of the philosophy of the seventeenth and eighteenth centuries; the difference is simply that their central place in the philosophy curriculum has served to make these earlier schemes of thought almost second nature to us. As each of the essays in this volume shows, once we find our way beneath its veneer of obscurity, the relevance of nineteenth-century philosophy comes out very clearly. Often, indeed, we find its philosophers to be addressing the same problems as concern us today.

The following introductory chapter briefly surveys the century's philosophical developments, contextualizing the chapters that follow. One point which emerges both from that survey and the chapters themselves should be noted at the very start. We can only approach the past from the perspective of our present understanding, and hence modern subject classifications have been used to parcel up the various discussions. That results in a certain distortion, however, for our conception of where these divisions and boundaries lie was not necessarily shared in the nineteenth century, with the result that their theories and arguments often refuse to confine themselves to the neat boxes in which we would now attempt to house them.

Logic and Scientific Method

The technical innovations of Frege, Russell, and Whitehead were so striking that modern logicians tend to regard their subject as newborn in the twentieth century, lumping together everything that went before (from Aristotelian syllogistic until the discovery of predicate calculus) as simply 'traditional logic'. This completely whitewashes an interesting developmental story, however. In particular it ignores the fact that technical logic in Britain in the nineteenth century, emerging from its moribund status in the preceding era, experienced a rebirth which, even if it was not simply incorporated into the modern discipline, included developments that laid important foundations for what was to follow.

At the beginning of the nineteenth century the study of formal logic in Britain was at a very low ebb indeed, having degenerated into little more than informal scientific methodology and the most rudimentary teaching of Aristotle. The person who did most to bring about a change in this state of affairs was **Richard Whately** (1787–1863). Without pretending to originality, his clear and accurate presentation of logic as a purely formal science of syllogistic reasoning made his 1826 *Elements of Logic* perfectly suited as a textbook. Moreover, himself a theologian who rose ultimately to become Archbishop of Dublin, Whately was able to offer a clear motivation for its study:

> Those who are engaged in, or designated for the Sacred Ministry, and all others who are sensible that the cause of true Religion is not a concern of the Ministry alone, should remember that this is no time to forego any of the advantages which that cause may derive from an active and judicious cultivation of the faculties.... Among the enemies of the Gospel now, are to be found men not only of learning and of ingenuity, but of *cultivated argumentative powers*, and not unversed in the principles of Logic. If the advocates of our Religion think proper to disregard this help, they will find, on careful inquiry, that *their opponents do not*.[1]

Sharing his conception of the subject as purely formal, but not his belief that it found its last word in Aristotle, **William Hamilton** (1788–1856) first came to public attention in 1833 as a critic of certain aspects of Whately's work, but it was not until 1846 that he set out the innovation for which he is best-known, the quantification of the predicate.[2] Arguing that

---

[1] Whately (1827), Preface, pp. 28–9.
[2] Even then the matter was only set out sketchily in an appendix to his edition of the works of Thomas Reid.

in affirmative as well as in negative judgements the predicate may be either distributed or undistributed, so that (for example) 'All As are B' can be read as either 'All As are all Bs' or 'All As are some Bs' and the overall number of valid syllogisms thereby increased from twenty-four to thirty-six, the historical importance of Hamilton's innovation lay more than anything else in the spur it gave to subsequent studies, such as those of **Augustus de Morgan** (1806–71). Much of de Morgan's published work arose out of his acrimonious dispute with Hamilton about who first discovered the quantification of the predicate doctrine and, more importantly, about its precise nature and significance, although for his broader contribution to the subject as a whole de Morgan should equally be remembered for his opening up of the *logic of relations*, and for the laws which bear his name relating the operators *and*, *not*, and *or*.[3]

The pioneering work of **George Boole** (1815–64) moved formal logic further from traditional philosophy in the direction of mathematics, locating a fundamental similarity between the symbolic systems of algebra and those that might be used to express thought more generally, thereby permitting logical propositions to be expressed in the form of algebraic equations and deductions to be performed mathematically. This method, now known as Boolean algebra and familiar to many as the foundation of computer science, he demonstrated by reference to a variety of historical theological arguments and—of more interest to modern readers—by application to probability theory. Boole's work was taken up by figures like **W. S. Jevons** (1835–82), **John Venn** (1834–1923), and **Lewis Carroll** (Charles Dodgson) (1832–98) but only joined with the deep influence of Frege were these advances able to contribute to the great flowering of logic that emerged in Cambridge in the early twentieth century due to Russell and Whitehead.

The nineteenth century also saw important developments in inductive logic which, without even the excuse of a 'modern canon' against which they may be found wanting, have become almost as neglected as those in formal logic. Thomas Kuhn is famous for having urged philosophers to remember their history of science.[4] But ironically he and they had forgotten not just their history of *science*, but their history of the *philosophy of science*, for they could have learned the very same lesson from **William Whewell** (1794–1866), whose philosophy of the inductive sciences grew out of his magisterial *History of the Inductive Sciences, from the Earliest to the Present Times* (1837). Whewell claimed to be 'renovating' Bacon's inductive method, but such allegiance as he had to the classical empiricist tradition was augmented by a vital debt to the philosophy of Kant, whose thinking he did much to introduce into Britain, albeit in highly modified form. For Whewell all knowledge requires, as well as 'fact' or 'experience', the presence of some organizing 'idea' or 'principle'—he takes these terms very broadly—two elements whose roles, if they can be distinguished, can never be separated. Neither innate nor unrepresentative of the world in the manner of Kant's categories, the role which Whewell's ideas play in induction is a creative one; that of providing the conceptual framework that 'colligates' the facts into an explanatory system. Novel prediction, consilience (when an induction, obtained from one class of facts, coincides with an induction, obtained from another different class), and the progressive unification or simplification of diverse phenomena may all be used to test for truth, but most curiously of all

---

[3] 'The negation of a conjunction is the disjunction of the negations' and 'The negation of a disjunction is the conjunction of the negations'.

[4] Kuhn (1962), ch. 1.

Whewell argues that the process of scientific progress arrives in the end at necessary truths, thereby rejecting any fundamental distinction between induction and deduction.

Though less influenced by historical reflections and hopeful of distilling a timelessly valid scientific method, **John Stuart Mill** (1806–73) agreed with Whewell in regarding induction as the sole legitimate procedure for the extension of knowledge. But fully aware of Hume's critique he offers no justificatory defence of its use beyond the fact that it is spontaneous and unavoidable; something done all the time by all of us. Indeed, reflecting the conclusion arrived at in the twentieth century by such figures as Nelson Goodman and Peter Strawson, he concludes that, rather than consider the standing of induction *in general*, the proper task of philosophy should be to determine the criteria for good or bad inductions *in particular*. It is in this context that we need to understand Mill's famous canons of induction, his five principles for identifying those instances of genuine causality which we may (as later philosophers have put it) 'project' into the future.

However, Mill and Whewell disagreed profoundly over the correct understanding of what was involved in inductive inference, entering into an important dispute with one another, which extended over many years from the first edition of Mill's *System of Logic* in 1843 until Whewell's *On the Philosophy of Discovery* in 1860. Essentially a difference of opinion about the sense in which inductive inference can 'advance' beyond what is empirically given, an important part of the discussion focused around the illustrative example of Kepler's discovery that the planet Mars moves in an ellipse. Mill allowed that Kepler had to bring in the concept of 'lying on an ellipse' in order to characterize rightly the data, but insisted on its presence somehow within that observational data since, by his lights, any move beyond the given must be deemed illegitimate. For Whewell, by contrast, the notion of an 'ellipse' is a new one imposed upon the data by a creative act of the mind, 'colligating' the observed facts, and guaranteeing that the inference is more than simply a union or collection of particulars. Contra Mill, he insists that there can be no mechanical 'inductive logic' with canons parallel to those of formal logic, or rather to put the same point slightly differently, that the real work of scientific discovery lies in the reduction of complex phenomena into their underlying patterns of similarity and difference, a distillation from experience which is impossible without the admixture of creative organizing ideas.

Although Mill championed inductive logic, his view that all knowledge proceeds from particular experience pushed him into developing important ideas about the apparent counterexamples to that position, that is, about a priori knowledge. Holding that all genuine inference proceeds from particular to particular, with general statements serving merely as a summary or 'register' of such inferences, he rejects syllogism as not properly a species of inference at all, while mathematical and geometrical truths he treats as highly generalized empirical claims about the physical world, with the consequent and unsettling implication that they are both fallible and contingent.

During the last quarter of the nineteenth century British philosophy experienced something of a revolution, as an idealism heavily indebted to Kant and Hegel appeared on the scene and rapidly came to dominate, first in Oxford and Glasgow and then in the country at large.[5] Dismissed by its opponents as the last gasp of an outmoded system which even in Germany had succumbed to a more modern empiricism—it was quipped that Oxford is the

---

[5] Mander (2011).

place to which bad German philosophers go when they die[6]—in truth the turn to idealism in Britain represented something new and vital. The Idealists did much to revitalize and professionalize the study of philosophy. Nowhere is this more apparent than in their logic which originates in **T. H. Green** (1836–82), but was most developed in **F. H. Bradley** (1846–1924) and **Bernard Bosanquet** (1848–1923). If Idealism is today one of the most neglected parts of the century's thinking, its logic is the most neglected part of a neglected system. The reason for this lies in its great difference from either species of logic so far considered but, as Ferreira's essay makes clear, once the initial hurdle of unfamiliarity is passed they reveal themselves to be logicians of very great acuity. In Idealist hands logic is no longer a purely formal discipline confining itself solely to the interrelations between ideas but becomes instead the science of knowledge (or true thinking) as forms of judgement and inference are analysed and assessed for their ability to express reality itself. Guided by a holistic metaphysics, logic shifts from a subject whose essence lies in sharp distinctions into one characterized everywhere by fluidity. Implying more than they are able to say, terms have indistinct edges, while the lines between different types of judgement—even between judgement and inference—become blurred, as everywhere the chief criterion of adequacy for any analysis that may be proposed becomes how coherent, comprehensive, and systematic a conceptual scheme it allows us to build. Not even the great distinction between inductive and deductive logic can stand, argued the Idealists, when both come before the same measure of their contribution to the coherent explanation of experience as a whole. The contrast becomes a relative difference of emphasis. For Bradley all inference rests ultimately on universals, and for this reason he was clear in his rejection of Mill's conception of induction, although he seems unaware how close his own line brings him to Whewell.

METAPHYSICS

During the first half of the nineteenth century the two chief metaphysical systems which dominated British philosophy were both national and traditional. On the one hand there was the Scottish or Common Sense school which took its lineage from Thomas Reid's response to David Hume. Work in this tradition continued throughout the nineteenth century, but in terms of influence the greatest figure was William Hamilton who from the 1830s to the 1850s was held in extremely high regard (a level of reputation that in hindsight seems most curious). Though allowing that our grasp of the world functions in accordance with certain basic and native regulatory principles of 'common sense', unlike Reid Hamilton argued that this brought us to a position that was more like *faith* than *knowledge*. He urged a 'natural' or direct realism of perception according to which we have unmediated access to both the self and the not-self, although here again he disagreed with Reid, insisting that our access is only to things not separated from us by space or time, with the consequences that we can know the light-rays which come from physical objects but not the physical objects themselves, and that we can entertain only present memory

---

[6] Webb (1933), p. 97—a fate some other versions of the joke assign to *good* German philosophers—Wace (1888), p. 275.

images but not the past itself. Fully conversant with German philosophy, perhaps the most significant thing about Hamilton's philosophy was the way in which he attempted to combine his native common-sense tradition with more Kantian ways of thinking in what he called the Philosophy of the Conditioned. The 'relativity of knowledge', he argues, limits what we can ever know to that which is conditioned by our own finite faculties of cognition, but this is something which falls always between two exclusive and contradictory extremes. Though clearly taking as its source the antinomies of pure reason, Hamilton's theory here varies from its Kantian origin in that, rather than accept the legitimacy of both opposing arguments and hence the self-contradictory nature of reality—its utter discrepancy with our reason—he argues that one side must be true. We just don't know which. Thus the proper lesson to be drawn is simply one of the limitation on our knowledge.

The other great tradition, the English or Empirical school, was equally venerable in that it traced its lineage back to the sensory and psychological tradition of Bacon and Locke. These ideas it took forward principally through the work of John Stuart Mill. Mill espoused a psychologically focused doctrine in which the only items of which we have direct awareness are our own mind-dependent sensations, anything beyond that to be arrived at by inductive reasoning. This famously led him to a phenomenalist conception of physical reality as consisting in permanent possibilities of sensation.[7]

Hamilton's attempt to combine Reid's natural realism with a Kantian doctrine of the relativity of knowledge has been judged inconsistent by many scholars, including Mill himself,[8] whose disagreement called forth what became in fact his most substantial foray into metaphysics, *An Examination of Hamilton's Philosophy* (1865). In this work Mill is quite unsparing in his criticisms of Hamilton, and contemporary scholars have almost all judged Mill the victor. But events at the time might be read to tell a different story, for in the second half of the century metaphysical speculation found new life, and to no small extent it was Hamilton's work that encouraged this.[9] British philosophy entered what might be thought of as a golden age of independent constructive metaphysics,[10] as the following three examples illustrate.

The philosophy of **James Frederick Ferrier** (1808–64) represents a substantially new coinage. Against the faith of the Scottish school in the natural power of mind, which philosophy can only confuse, and against the faith of the Empirical school in science, which philosophy can only serve, Ferrier represents a renewed belief in the power of philosophy itself both to diagnose error and to move constructively beyond it. An a priori project reliant solely on non-contradiction and set out in something akin to geometrical form, his final work, the *Institutes of Metaphysics* (1854), has polarized opinion, seeming to some readers a falling-away from the heights of the tradition which nurtured him, and to others a confident new dawn of fresh philosophical speculation. Against his somewhat implausible (and not unpolitical) insistence that his philosophy was but a development of the Scottish tradition, the influences that more readily spring to mind are Spinoza and Hegel (though ostensibly he rejects both). Ferrier was in large part responsible for the rehabilitation of Berkeley,

---

[7] Mill (1875), ch. XI, p. 233.

[8] Mill (1875), ch. III.

[9] Madden (1985), p. 839.

[10] If we include the constructive work of such figures as J. M. E. McTaggart, Samuel Alexander, and A. N. Whitehead, this period might be said to last until the 1920s.

and it is with idealism he begins, recasting the fundamental unit of apprehension as always subject-plus-object. He argues that we can be ignorant only of what could be known, and that since all knowledge consists of some subject in synthesis with some object[11] not only is it impossible to know either a subject-in-itself or a thing-in itself, but it makes no sense either to suppose that this is something lying outside our knowledge. Ferrier is here criticizing both Kant and Hamilton's agnostic doctrine of the unconditioned. In doing so he ushers in a new and strong anti-realism, for which contribution the Idealists who followed him gave explicit acknowledgement.

Another metaphysician now even more ignored, though likewise highly regarded in his day, was **Shadworth Hodgson** (1832–1912). But contemporary esteem and influence on subsequent thinkers are not the only criteria for inclusion in a history of philosophy,[12] and since such histories have an inevitable tendency to narrow canons, inclusion of a figure like Hodgson reminds us of the great diversity and originality of philosophical work to be found in the nineteenth century. One of the last 'lay' philosophers, as the first president of the Aristotelian Society Hodgson was also significant in the process of the professionalization of philosophy. Much of his thought was set out in his series of annual presidential addresses to the society, but it was in the four-volume *Metaphysic of Experience* (1898) that it found its fullest expression. Like many nineteenth-century writers Hodgson's verbose style itself won him no friends, but he illustrates how elaborate constructive work in philosophy was not simply the preserve of 'rationalists'. For taking Hume's method as far as it is possible to go, his close attention to the detailed texture of actual experience results in a detailed constructive system which anticipates both phenomenology and radical empiricism.

At the opposite end of the spectrum of both fame and influence, F. H. Bradley's metaphysics was no less original, and where previous scholarship has often viewed Bradley simply as a disciple of Hegel, Basile in his contribution notes that more recent studies—without, of course, denying the importance of Hegel—have given us a much broader picture; drawing attention both to his divergences from Hegel (e.g. the refusal simply to *identify* thought and reality) and to the influence of other figures (e.g. Herbart and Leibniz). It has been noted already how Idealist logic is grounded in holistic metaphysics and a crucial argument behind that holism lay in Bradley's famous denial of the reality of relations, both the centre of his own system and the claim that spurred Russell and Moore to formulate their own alternative conception of reality. The thesis that relational experience is self-defeating has two important consequences. If reality itself is non-contradictory then such defects must be ones which we have added, implying the existence of a more basic and uncorrupted species of experience, which Bradley calls 'Feeling', while on the other side, the power of thought to diagnose its own error points to a higher form of experience beyond it, which he terms 'the Absolute'. It is important to realize that if in both of these cases we pass beyond thought, we never pass beyond experience and hence Bradley's position remains squarely within the Idealist fold. Bradley declines to call the Absolute 'God', unlike Ferrier and Hodgson both of whose systems make explicit room for the divine, but in this era the impulse to metaphysics cannot well be separated from the impulse to religion

---

[11] To think of either without the other, he said, was like trying to think of a stick with only one end (Caird 1893, vol. i, p. 133).

[12] The first would rule out Hume, who was long held in higher regard as a *historian*, and the second would exclude Berkeley, who probably never won any actual *disciples*.

and even Bradley himself admits that 'with certain persons, the intellectual effort to understand the universe is a principal way of thus experiencing the Deity'.[13] He is most likely thinking of himself here.

SCIENCE AND PHILOSOPHY

Natural science came of age in the nineteenth century, and in the attempt to discern the philosophical significance of this development two new and controversial ideas stand out: the emerging sense that scientific thinking alone was able to yield truth, and the growing realization that it was a method which could be extended from the physical world to the human sphere.

Perhaps the earliest of nineteenth-century philosophies systematically to address these notions was that of Auguste Comte, who found British followers in such figures as John Stuart Mill, George Eliot, and Harriet Martineau. A key thinker here was **George Henry Lewes** (1817–78), an eclectic thinker whose literary reputation has tended to eclipse his philosophical work. His popular *Biographical History of Philosophy* was much influenced by Comte's thinking and became one of the chief routes by which the ideas of positivism were introduced into Britain. From the uncompromisingly critical rationale of that first book, written as an attempt to '[show] by Argument, what History shows by Facts,—that to attempt to construct a science of Metaphysics is to attempt an impossibility'[14] he gradually moved to the more moderate stance of attacking its method rather than its subject matter, arguing 'that metaphysical problems have, rationally, no other difficulties than those which beset all problems; and, when scientifically treated, they are capable of solutions not less satisfactory and certain than those of physics'.[15] This empirical metaphysics is best illustrated in his efforts to develop a theory of mind upon wholly physical lines most notable today for their early anticipation of the notion of 'emergence'. Another cognate writer, whose philosophical reputation also became buried under his literary fame, was **Leslie Stephen** (1832–1904). Again like Lewes, the scientifically grounded agnosticism to which his reading of Comte and Mill brought him was one was expressed largely through his work on the history of philosophy, such as his *History of English Thought in the Eighteenth Century* (1876) and *The English Utilitarians* (1900).

Though unwilling to classify himself as a positivist and largely ignorant of Comte's system, **Herbert Spencer** (1820–1903) was a member of the Comtist circle which introduced those ideas into Britain, and his thinking was of sufficiently similar stamp that many at the time regarded him as a positivist. Few philosophers have met with such extremes of fortune as Spencer, who from being perhaps the most debated of all Victorian thinkers has fallen into a near complete disregard from which he has yet to recover. His thought displays three characteristic marks of its time. First, although prefaced with a species of philosophical agnosticism derived from Mansel, it confidently moves forward under the assumption that everything from material reality, to psychology, to ethics, to sociology can be explained

---

[13] Bradley (1897), p. 5.   [14] Lewes (1892), p. 342: 1846 preface to *Second Series*.
[15] Lewes (1874), p. 5.

'scientifically'. Second, it offers a unified synoptic view of everything; his ten-volume *synthetic philosophy* grew to become the work of a lifetime. Thirdly, it is deeply optimistic. For Spencer the key to understanding is 'evolution'; it being a fundamental law of matter that wherever homogeneity is acted on by external forces it produces difference and variety, generating a vast evolutionary scheme which manifests itself throughout the physical, biological, and social worlds. These ideas on evolution were arrived at in advance of Darwin and Wallace, and applied to biology as but an instance of a cosmic scheme, and although Spencer coined the phrase 'survival of the fittest',[16] his evolution was in fact Lamarckian (although he did later allow a small role for natural selection).

For all that it may have been preceded and out-popularized by Spencer's evolutionary system, **Charles Darwin's** (1809–82) theory of evolution by natural selection was a creation of incomparably greater significance. Given that it is a theory which in the present day is commonly thought to have profound implications for wide range of domains, it is important to look carefully at its influence on the philosophy of its time for, although it was recognized from the first as vitally important, attitudes towards the theory were quite different from those which hold today—and different too, it must be said, from the way in which many today have sought to portray them. That it challenged orthodox religious belief can hardly be denied, but if it undermined the cosy dovetailed alliance between science and religion that characterized the work of such eighteenth-century figures as Paley, it was replaced not by simple opposition, but by a complex of differing reactions—ranging from those who concluded that science and religion had nothing to do with each other at all, to those who welcomed the theory with open arms as revealing precisely *how* God had performed his miracle of creation. The great problems, of course, were the continuity between man and nature, and the apparent lack of purpose (and especially moral direction) in the scheme. But important though these points were in fostering debate they should not be allowed more space than a careful weighing of the evidence bears, for it is well to record that if Darwin himself lost his faith it was for reasons other than his own theory (such as the doctrine of eternal damnation), and by the end of the nineteenth century mainstream theological opinion had very largely accommodated itself to the new theory. One of its greatest supporters was Frederick Temple who went on to become Archbishop of Canterbury.

That ideas of evolution might be used to ground an ethics free from religious support inspired many to create systems of evolutionary ethics, such as that developed by Leslie Stephens in his *The Science of Ethics* (1882). But if both Spencer and Darwin's evolutionary theories had ethical import, as Ruse shows in his essay, their cases and merits were very different. For Spencer evolutionary forces tended towards complexity and differentiation, concepts of cooperation and justice evolving naturally as part of the progressive development of social frameworks. This tended to generate an ethic which, while it finds a place for sympathetic moral sense, took its main root in liberal individualism; moral progress is won when individual creativity is subject to as few restrictions as possible. (And despite his talk of the 'social organism' Spencer remained at root an individualist, as the later Idealist Henry Jones showed.[17]) In the hands of subsequent 'social Darwinists' this became the view that laissez-faire systems encouraging unfettered competition were the chief route to moral

---

[16] Spencer (1864), vol. i, p. 444.   [17] Jones (1883).

health and progress. Yet against this simplistic conflation of 'is' and 'ought' Henry Sidgwick and T. H. Huxley spoke out strongly. The latter, for example, wrote,

> the practice of that which is ethically best—what we call goodness or virtue—involves a course of conduct which, in all respects, is opposed to that which leads to success in the cosmic struggle for existence. In place of ruthless self-assertion it demands self-restraint; in place of thrusting aside, or treading down, all competitors, it requires that the individual shall not merely respect, but shall help his fellows; its influence is directed, not so much to the survival of the fittest, as to the fitting of as many as possible to survive. It repudiates the gladiatorial theory of existence. It demands that each man who enters into the enjoyment of the advantages of a polity shall be mindful of his debt to those who have laboriously constructed it; and shall take heed that no act of his weakens the fabric in which he has been permitted to live. Laws and moral precepts are directed to the end of curbing the cosmic process and reminding the individual of his duty to the community, to the protection and influence of which he owes, if not existence itself, at least the life of something better than a brutal savage.[18]

As the result of such criticism the reputation of Spencer's ethics sank very low, but the grand speculations of that system could not be further in temperament from the contributions of Darwin himself, whose own small-scale suggestions about how moral instincts might come about and what evolutionary advantage they might confer have proved far more attractive and fruitful to contemporary evolutionary theorists.

It can thus be seen that the reaction to evolutionary theory was very complex, and this is particularly well illustrated by reference to Idealism, which came to dominate the philosophical scene at the same time as Darwinianism was gaining currency. Fully committed by their Hegelianism to a universe which, in all departments of its being, was best understood in developmental or evolutionary terms, at one level Darwin seemed an ally to the Idealists, and equally to be approved of was the manner in which his system cut away the ground from any dualist or super-naturalist conception of the universe. Reality was one whole governed by a single set of laws. However, where Hegelian evolution was teleological or purposive, evolution by natural selection seemed thoroughly causal and blind, and so the Idealists were never able to embrace Darwinism without qualification. However, whether it was best rejected (Green), admitted as a lower or partial expression of a truth more adequately explained by philosophy (Bosanquet and Jones), or interpreted in such a way as to fall fundamentally in harmony with Hegelian development (Ritchie) was a point of ongoing debate and disagreement among them.

There is one last aspect of scientific development in the nineteenth century which deserves special mention. In the seventeenth century natural science emerged as a distinct discipline, in part bringing to the table new subjects and methods of inquiry, in part taking over work which had once been regarded as 'philosophical', and in a somewhat similar process during the nineteenth century psychology came into being as an autonomous academic discipline, separate from but closely connected to philosophy. Hatfield argues in his essay that in Britain, the disciplinary practice of psychology came into being considerably before it acquired any institutional foothold or clear self-understanding, either of its own nature or of its relations to philosophical thinking about the mind. The long British tradition of mental philosophy which took in both the Associationist and the Common Sense schools made

---

[18] Huxley (1894b), p. 82.

it possible for many to regard the emergence of experimental psychology not as the arrival of a new discipline but simply as the supplementation of new methods of working, while for others the new approach only heightened the need of philosophy proper to distinguish itself from such merely empirical distractions; just one part of a general opposition between philosophical and scientific thinking which Hatfield argues lasted well into the twentieth century.

ETHICAL, SOCIAL, AND POLITICAL THOUGHT

For much of the nineteenth century the landscape of ethical philosophy was dominated by two theories, utilitarianism and intuitionism.[19] Both approaches are actively discussed today. However, the nineteenth-century incarnations of the former are much more familiar than those of the latter because, while modern discussions of utility commonly look to the nineteenth century, those of intuitionism tend instead to refer to early twentieth-century figures. Nineteenth-century utilitarianism, however, cannot be properly appreciated except against a backdrop of the position to which it was opposed. Intuitionism originated in the eighteenth century—in the work of Thomas Reid (1710–96) and Richard Price (1723–91)—and was developed in the nineteenth century by figures including William Whewell, William Hamilton, H. L. Mansel, James Martineau, and Henry Calderwood. The utilitarianism–intuitionism debate was often a cover for further issues. For example, John Stuart Mill's criticism of Whewell's moral intuitionism was that, because necessary truths are always true, it implied that morality could not progress which made it a position allied to reactionism in politics and superstition in religion; something a 'radical' such as himself was duty-bound to resist. But the distance between the camps was not always as great as they thought. Dale Miller argues in his contribution for Mill that not *all* intuition was rejected. Taking this rapprochement even further, Henry Sidgwick, whilst rejecting common-sense or intuitive morality in favour of what he took to be its implicit ground in utilitarianism, nonetheless came to think of the basis for that ground as ultimately intuitive, albeit fallible—utilitarianism 'on an intuitional basis' he called it[20]—thereby rejecting not just the notion that the first principles of morality might be necessary truths, but also the view of his utilitarian predecessors that they were empirical inductions. Their certainty he thought made that impossible.

There can be no doubt however that the most famous ethical doctrine to emerge from the nineteenth century was utilitarianism and, while earlier antecedents can be found in figures like Hume and there have been important further advances in the second half of the twentieth century, the line of thinking from Bentham and James Mill through John Stuart Mill to Henry Sidgwick still represents the classical development of this doctrine. Neither probing deeply into psychological theory nor into the foundations of ethics, it was to **Jeremy Bentham** (1748–1832) a plain truth of observation that human beings are motivated solely by pleasure and pain and plain pragmatic sense that right action should seek 'the greatest happiness of the greatest number'; a phrase whose discovery in 1769 he was right to regard

[19] Schneewind (1965).   [20] Sidgwick (1901), Preface, p. xx.

as the 'Eureka moment' that determined his philosophy (whether, as he recalled, he first found it in the work of Joseph Priestley or whether, as modern scholarship has argued, it may be traced to an English translation of Beccaria's *Dei delitti e delle pene*).[21] Subservient to no authority, it was the legal and political ramifications of the principle that most exercised him, as he reflected on how best to defeat the 'sinister interests' that must otherwise flourish as leaders, no less self-interested than anyone else, put their own greatest happiness above that of the community. Though it might on a superficial look seem otherwise, his celebrated criticism of the natural rights tradition ('nonsense upon stilts') is not in fact contra-rights, but rather contra-metaphysics; a protest against the empty bolstering of an essentially self-evident ethical truth. For rights can have no existence independently of governments or laws that secure them, and moral claims are obscured rather than strengthened by being made to dress up in the borrowed clothes of rights.

In the shadow of his larger-than-life friend and collaborator, **James Mill** (1773–1836) has not received the attention his philosophical work deserves. Making good the theoretical foundations over which Bentham had taken little concern, his *Analysis of the Phenomena of the Human Mind* (1829) sets out in greater detail than had ever been done before the doctrine of associationism which lay behind both their empiricism and their hedonism, reducing the vast theatre of mind to the play of basic sensory elements under the play of the pleasure–pain principle. Although he wrote widely on a variety of topics, including character, education, and economics, James Mill's current standing rests largely on his 1820 *Essay on Government* in which he argues that a society fashioned upon utilitarian principles must be a representative democracy, in which elected members have identical interests with those they represent; for only thus can it guard against the abuse of power that must otherwise occur when power is concentrated in the hands of a few. The essay itself is remembered today perhaps as much for the prolonged dispute it occasioned with the essayist and historian **T. B. Macaulay** (1800–59) who took issue with Mill's claim that political rulers are chiefly determined by their selfish personal interests.

Together Bentham and his spokesman Mill made a formidable team, founding in 1824 the *Westminster Review,* and inspiring a group of philosophers set on reshaping society, and known to history as the 'philosophical radicals'. They included such figures as David Ricardo (1772–1823), Joseph Hume (1777–1855), Henry Brougham (1788–1868), John Austin (1790–1859), George Grote (1794–1871), John Arthur Roebuck (1802–79), Charles Buller (1806–48), and William Molesworth (1810–55) and together they did much to shape and bring about reform in early Victorian Britain. But with respect to the future of *philosophy*, there can be no denying that their greatest influence was on James's own son, John Stuart Mill, who later in life described his own education as 'a course of Benthamism'.[22] His *Utilitarianism* and *On Liberty* have become the definitive statements of the classical utilitarian tradition, attracting volumes of critical attention, but it is important to acknowledge too that the younger Mill extended and even to some measure subverted the views of his teachers. Rejecting any simplistic hedonism, Mill's great contribution was to broaden the goal of morality, allowing that happiness has within it many parts and departments—some earning their place only by association with others—and that pleasure must be assessed by its quality as well as just quantity. (Although the break here should not be overstressed, for in this

---

[21] Burns (2005).   [22] Mill (1924), ch. III, p. 54.

last, rarely recognized is the role of his own father who, contrary to Bentham's notorious dictum that 'pushpin is as good as poetry', argued that senses and consequent pleasures formed a hierarchy from the most sensual up to the most intellectual.[23]) It is sometimes thought that there exists some kind of tension between Mill's advocacy of individual liberty and his moral philosophy in which the many outweigh the few but, for Mill, liberty is the supreme utility, allowing individuals to satisfy their own preferences and vital for personal development. (And here, interestingly, we see Mill picking up from his father's work the psychological topic of the formation of character, which in his *System of Logic* he christened 'ethology',[24] and which continued to play throughout nineteenth-century educational writing.)

Notwithstanding its importance in its own era and its currently high profile, it should be noted that for most of the intervening period the reputation of utilitarian ethics has been very much lower, and for the explanation of this fact we must look to a third ethical and political tradition that flourished in nineteenth-century Britain, the school of Idealism— whose chief standard-bearers, Green, Bradley, and Bosanquet we have already met. Criticized by such figures as Thomas Carlyle (who was no philosopher, but whose views no history of philosophy can afford to ignore) and John Grote (1813–66), utilitarian philosophy met with challenge from the outset, but at the hands of the Idealists this became a far more focused and sophisticated attack. Defeated by its own psychology, utilitarianism (it was charged) is unable to provide us with any coherent or achievable goal at which to aim our lives. In conceiving of pleasures as mental states, that is, subjective and transitory feelings, it reduces the good life to nothing but a series of such 'perishing particulars'.[25] The 'self' which strives after this good evaporates into a sequence of instantaneous and heterogeneous 'satisfactions'. The attempt may be made to give more unity and coherence to this postulated ideal by suggesting we aim at a 'sum' of pleasures, but the pleasures *of a lifetime* cannot be summed until we are dead and past enjoying them. We might seek instead to maximize the pleasures *of the moment*, but if our target is as much pleasure as possible, we must all fail to reach it since no one can experience an infinity of pleasures, while if we aim for as much pleasure as we can get, trivially everyone all of the time achieves that, at least by the lights of the hedonist psychology upon which the theory rests.[26] With these and other criticisms the Idealists devastated the utilitarian tradition, casting it into a neglect that long outlasted their own period of dominance.

Now, of course, it is the turn of Idealist ethics to sit in the shade. One factor that explains this neglect—the point that perhaps most sharply distinguishes their moral and social thought from what occurred before, and what went after—is its unashamedly metaphysical basis. Turning their backs on the question 'what actions should we do?' for the rather older question 'what kind of people should we be?', the Idealists urged that ethical life aims at self-realization, but this framework requires a metaphysical theory of the true nature of the self and, rejecting the individualist and atomic conception of selfhood defended by figures like Mill and Spencer, they urged that man is a properly social creature, who

[23] James Mill (1869), ch. 1, p. 8. By their intellectual superiority and consequent value in life Mill ranked sensations in the following increasing order: (1) Sensations of Organic life, (2) Taste, (3) Smell, (4) Touch, (5) Hearing, (6) Sight.

[24] Mill (1843), Bk. VI, ch. v.

[25] Bradley (1927), p. 96.

[26] Bradley (1927), pp. 97–8.

correspondingly finds his greatest fulfilment in social life. As his most fundamental form of life is found in community, so his greatest good is not individual but common. How to articulate such a position without wholly subsuming the life of the individual into that of the collective became one of the chief tasks and problems of the Idealist school.

Their social conception of the individual led to a moral conception of the political and we find a continuity between ethical and political philosophy in Idealist thought, placing it in sharp difference from moderns conceptions of political science as the art of structuring communal life in the absence of shared culture or value. Idealist political philosophy reached its height at the turn of the century, but following two world wars and the hostile reaction they engendered towards any theory which appeared to exalt institutions at the expense of individuals, it suffered a massive reversal of fortune from which it has still not fully recovered. But as both the chapters by Vincent and Simhony demonstrate, recent scholarship has gone a long way towards correcting this picture. The state was never for the Idealists something that could be set in opposition to individuals, for it had no purpose beyond the freedom and fulfilment of individuals and if (like the utilitarians they so criticized) the Idealists rejected natural rights it was because they saw rights as moral structures which exist only for the sake of the good, with the consequence that there can be no right to act contrary to one's own good or that of one's society.

There is irony in the fact that at the same time as the Idealists in Oxford and Glasgow were so effectively destroying the reputation of utilitarian philosophy it was finding its most able exponent in Cambridge, in the figure of **Henry Sidgwick** (1838–1900). Sidgwick made a number of advances. Where classical utilitarianism looked to questions of legislation, Sidgwick championed it as a system of personal morality, and he recognized clearly that its aggregative calculus stood in need of a further supplementary principle of distribution, most plausibly an egalitarian one.[27] But perhaps his most important advance was to break clearly from the psychological egoism with which utilitarianism had always been associated. To Bentham and James Mill it was axiomatic that we desire only pleasure, while John Stuart Mill, even if he had eventually come to see that happiness was something best not pursued directly but found along the way,[28] was unable to free himself from the thought that 'desiring a thing and finding it pleasant [are] ... in strictness of language, two different modes of naming the same psychological fact.'[29] But Sidgwick was clear that while it was possible to desire pleasure, in point of fact people do desire much else besides.[30] For all his efforts, however, he was unable to reform utilitarianism to his own satisfaction. In particular, unable to share the confidence of the Idealists that the pursuit of personal and public good necessarily coincide, his ethics came to rest upon a fundamental dualism which he was unable to reconcile harmoniously except on the hypothesis that the universe was subject to divine moral governance. At a personal level, unable ever to satisfy himself on such religious questions, he found himself pushed into an interest in spiritualism. In this (it should be noted) he was far from alone among late nineteenth-century thinkers in Britain.[31]

---

[27] Sidgwick (1901), pp. 416–17.
[28] Mill (1924), ch. IV, p. 120.
[29] Mill (1972), ch. 4, p. 36.
[30] Sidgwick (1901), Bk I, ch. IV.
[31] Of related interest, both Mander and Brooke in this volume note the contemporary importance of Tait and Stewart's work, *The Unseen Universe* (1875).

Philosophy does not proceed in a vacuum, and the nineteenth century was a period of very rapid social change, which inevitably shaped its intellectual development also. Two areas which illustrate this very well are the growth and development of socialism and that of feminism. If the nineteenth century appears to us in retrospect a period of political stability and steady progress, that was not how it seemed at the time. The ever-developing forces of industrialization and modernization generated immense social tension as pressures grew year on year for a more inclusive and egalitarian form of society; pressures whose occasional explosion into social disturbance—the Peterloo massacre, the Tolpuddle martyrs, the Sheffield outrages—created also a constant fear of social collapse or revolution. It was from these origins that British socialism emerged, beginning with the pioneering efforts of Robert Owen, and continuing through the development of trades unions, the Chartist movement, and the formation of groups such as the Christian Socialists. The role in this story of the most celebrated of all nineteenth-century socialists, **Karl Marx** (1818–83) has been ignored by past scholarship, which has treated him as a Continental thinker with Continental concerns who just happened to live in London. But as Leopold shows in his chapter that is far from the truth. Fully meriting his place in a history of nineteenth-century British philosophy, Marx was much engaged in British socialism, influenced in particular by Robert Owen (his own socialism he was proud to think of as descended from Owen's), as well as being himself an important influence on British socialists who followed him such as Hyndman, Belfort Bax, and William Morris.

Another undeservedly neglected part of the history of social and political philosophy in nineteenth-century Britain is feminist thinking; for although the long intellectual effort to diagnose, analyse, and counter the forces which oppress women in political, social, and family life is not one which has much engaged historians of nineteenth-century philosophy, it was in fact a vital period for the emergence of feminist philosophy. As Caine demonstrates in her essay, the tale to be told is a complex one. We find many different voices, from the radical **Mary Wollstonecraft** (1759–97) through the more conservative **Josephine Butler** (1828–1906) to the activism of **Millicent Fawcett** (1847–1929). Drawing upon a variety of traditions, including that of rights and nonconformist religion, contributions were sparked by different issues (such as women's education, married women's property rights, suffrage, and the sexual double standard) and not always in agreement; there was for example disagreement between these for whom the case for women's inclusion in society lay in the lack of difference and those for whom it lay in the intrinsic difference and consequent moral quality they could bring to bear. From all this variety, however, there emerges a new perspective as the previously silenced speak out and in doing so highlight the limitations of the previous conversation.

RELIGIOUS PHILOSOPHY

Unlike today where, except with respect to certain specific topics, philosophy is pursued quite independently of religious questions, there are but few parts of nineteenth-century philosophy which may be adequately understood without an appreciation of their religious context and implications. However, that context is diverse and complicated, for while there occurred a growth in 'religiosity', as compared with the preceding century, matters became at the same time more complex and contentious than ever before.

A vital spur to the growth of religion was the Evangelical movement. Evangelicalism was not a system to produce its own philosophy, but it did prompt it, most notably in the work of **S. T. Coleridge** (1772–1834). Probably no one did more in the first third of the nineteenth century than Coleridge to counter the Evangelical emphasis on feeling and the Bible and, defending traditional Anglicanism and the idea of the Church, to reassert the place of reason in religion. While Coleridge's poetical star has remained consistently high, his philosophical reputation has met with a more varied fortune. Lauded in his day as a great Christian philosopher who broke from deterministic or necessitarian materialism in order to make room for a kind of faith which was intellectually robust but at the same time profoundly spiritual, there can be no doubt that his writings did contribute greatly to the reawakening of serious religious thought in Britain, but lack of system, charges of misunderstanding the Kantian ideas he employed in that task (especially his curious distinction between reason and understanding), not to mention accusations of outright plagiarism, all served to undermine that status. But as Vigus argues in his contribution, it is possible to take a more sympathetic reading and think of Coleridge as one who, fully aware of the limitations of a system in which religious ideas could claim to be no more than 'regulative', cultivates those 'hints' which Kant dropped into a more positive direction, for example developing thoughts from the *Critique of Judgement* about the faculty of Imagination. These post-Kantian reflections were of course laid on top of an earlier deep-set Platonism. Plato's works, Coleridge suggested, are 'preparatory exercises' for the mind, leading it beyond appearances to a higher logic—that of ideas.[32]

But Evangelicalism and conservative Anglicanism were not the only religious forces at work in the nineteenth century; a strong alternative to them both making itself felt in the Dissenting tradition, most particularly in Unitarianism. With roots in such figures as Richard Price (1723–91) and Joseph Priestley (1733–1804) this intellectually robust lineage reached its apex in the thought of **James Martineau** (1805–1900). Breaking away from the associationist, hedonist, and necessitarian legacy that hitherto characterized Unitarian thought and in which he had been educated, Martineau was another key figure in the introduction into Britain of Kantian ideas, but if (contra the egoistic consequentialism of Bentham) he embraced an ethic of conscientious allegiance to duty, he could sign up to neither the autonomy of ethics nor the view that God's existence was only a 'practical postulate'. For Martineau conscience is an immediate encounter with an external 'higher than ourselves', the ground of our direct and personal knowledge of God. Martineau's case for the existence of God was not just ethical but metaphysical also, though the epistemology remained intuitive. Opposing all materialism, as well as Spencer's (and others') retreat into the 'unknowable', Martineau suggests that there can be no understanding of causality except that which we find in our own case, that is, as a species of volition or willing. From this point the progressive unification of causal forces under scientific law encourages him to posit an eternal will on whom the world depends for its existence, that is, to posit the existence of God. Nationally Martineau was a figure of great repute during his long career—he would in 1866 have been appointed to the chair of philosophy at University College London, had it not been for the lobbying of parties determined to resist religious influence in that institution—but soon after his death that repute went into a sharp decline, from which it has yet to recover.

---

[32] Coleridge (1917), 30 April 1830, p. 82.

For all that interest in religious matters experienced a time of growth, as the century progressed a variety of factors including biblical criticism, philosophical criticism, the advance of science, and increased knowledge of other cultures and religions all came together to put more and more pressure on traditional religious belief, making that growth an uneasy one and culminating in what has been called the Victorian 'crisis of faith'. Falling between such thinkers such as the mathematician William Kingdom Clifford who urged that it was morally wrong for belief to go beyond evidence and the engineer William Froude who protested that no honest mind could be certain of any dogma, the painful vice in which many Victorians found themselves is all too apparent.[33] Nor was the concern merely personal, for in ways which to modern thinking now seems very strange, there was a genuine and widespread belief that morality depends upon religion, and hence that a weakening of traditional faith might precipitate moral and social disaster. This period of religious uncertainty produced a variety of different reactions of philosophical note.

One early response can be seen in the thought of **John Henry Newman** (1801–90) who attempted to defend the certainty of faith even in the absence of perfect logical demonstration. Although his *Essay in Aid of a Grammar of Assent*, which contains his final reflections on the matter, was not published until 1870, most its ideas go back to the *Oxford Sermons* of 1843 before his conversion to Catholicism. Writing from within a faith position, rather than as one who suspends belief, Newman's concern is with the real way in which people come to believe in God, rather than with abstract philosophical constructions never employed by anyone. Such faith he argues is not only rational, but something absolute. This point he makes by drawing a contrast between assent and inference. Assent is unconditional, while in inference one proposition is held depending on another. Moreover assent is certain, while inference is only probable. In arguing that unconditional assent does not require demonstration, Newman insists that religious belief is no different from everyday belief. (We all believe unconditionally that 'Great Britain is an island' though we none of us have, and it would be absurd to demand, conclusive proof of the matter.) For critics this might seem a desperate leap into blind faith but Newman is not suggesting that belief formation be allowed wholly without intellectual licence; simply that instead of formal proofs we must look to what he calls the *illative sense*, the way people actually reason. Influenced by antecedent beliefs and personal measures, this is largely a question of the convergence of probabilities and although assent is intellectual, it does also involve emotion and will; it is a response of the whole person. Looking to Newman's own application of this sense we see that for him traditional arguments (such as that from design) played but a small role, and more dominant were the history of the Church and fact of conscience which he suggests, 'vaguely reaches forward to something beyond self, and dimly discerns a sanction higher than self for its decisions, as is evidenced in that keen sense of obligation'.[34] This last links him to Martineau.

Philosophy of religion in Scotland took a somewhat different course, often influenced by local religious politics,[35] as the common-sense tradition of Reid and Hamilton provided the

---

[33] 'it is wrong always, everywhere, and for anyone, to believe anything upon insufficient evidence' Clifford (1877), p. 295. Froude: 'More strongly than I believe anything else I believe this—that [in] no subject whatever...is my mind (or as far as I can tell the mind of any human being) capable of arriving at an absolutely certain conclusion', Harper (1933), pp. 119–20.

[34] Newman (1979), p. 99.

[35] As both Sell and Brown in this volume point out, the Scottish chairs were often a matter of intense local politics.

intellectual backdrop for a sequence of ethical theists — including such figures as Alexander Campbell Fraser (1819–1914), James Iverach (1839–1922), James Orr (1844–1913), and Robert Macintosh (1858–1933). Perhaps chief among these was Robert Flint (1838–1910) who, unwilling to base faith on mere feeling, was determined to demonstrate the rationality of belief in God. Though no single argument for God's existence is logically conclusive, he argued, they all stem from a unified theistic perspective and together amass a cumulative power which critics attempt to evade by dividing them.

> They are naturally and, as it were, organically related; they support and strengthen one another. It is therefore an arbitrary and illegitimate procedure to separate them any further than may be necessary for the purpose of clear and orderly exposition. It is sophistry to attempt to destroy them separately by assailing each as if it had no connection with the other, and as if each isolated fragmentary argument were bound to yield as large a conclusion as all the arguments combined. A man quite unable to break a bundle of rods firmly bound together may be strong enough to break each rod separately. But before proceeding to deal with the bundle in that way, he may be required to establish his right to untie it, and to decline putting forth his strength upon it as it is presented to him.[36]

For those unpersuaded that reason could take them to an absolute or even to a modest conviction alternative routes were needed, and developing the ideas of Hamilton, **H. L. Mansel** (1820–71) sought refuge in a doctrine of the limitations of human reason; rather in the manner of Kant, denying knowledge to make room for faith. His Bampton lectures on *The Limits of Religious Thought* (1858) were immensely popular at the time, but historically more important for the way in which they unwittingly laid the foundations for something more sceptical. Although substantially the same doctrine occurs with the 'unknowable' of Spencer's *First Principles* (1862) the name by which this position ultimately became known, 'agnosticism', was in fact coined at about the same time by **Thomas Henry Huxley** (1825–95) for whom it became a methodological principle that in matters of intellect: 'do not pretend conclusions are certain that are not demonstrated or demonstrable'. [37] Less negative than they tend to be today, it has been argued that the majority of nineteenth-century agnostic thinkers were far from hostile to religion, their scepticism leaving room for a neo-Kantian God behind nature.[38] For some few however the only option was outright atheism. But in taking this path, figures such as Richard Carlile (1790–1843), George Grote (1794–1871), G. J. Holyoake (1817–1906), and Charles Bradlaugh (1833–91) were the exception rather than the rule.

The century saw one further move with respect to religious philosophy. If most nineteenth-century thinkers concerned with religion sought to find ways in which philosophical reason might be accommodated with traditional religious belief, the Idealists took the opposite course of modifying religious faith to make it fit with philosophical reason. If advances in biblical scholarship and in natural science made the traditional doctrines of religion no longer tenable, that was no reason to throw in the towel, for as John Caird put it, the project of rational criticism, once begun, must be carried through to the end—'If you begin with reason and criticism you must go on with them…the wounds of reason can only be healed by reason.'[39] To the Idealists, philosophy was able to show that traditional religious doctrines were the partial expressions of deeper philosophical truths—a project in natural theology which they played out in a series of imaginative Gifford Lectures—but even these truths they portrayed as ancillary to

---

[36] Flint (1877), pp. 74–5.   [37] Huxley (1894a), p. 246.   [38] Lightman (1990), p. 303.
[39] John Caird (1898), p. 189.

the true heart of religion, which was ethical. As Sweet demonstrates in his contribution, within this umbrella there was room for a variety of different positions. Absolute idealism portrayed the universe as a unitary spiritual whole whose maximally coherent and comprehensive grasp encompasses the whole of reality while its main rival, personal idealism (which owed a keen debt to Martineau), stressed the metaphysical autonomy of distinct minds. The majority of Idealists were explicitly religious, but even those who ostensibly opposed religion remained deeply spiritual in their philosophy. Bradley and Bosanquet may have thought of God as but an appearance, but the Absolute plays in their philosophical systems much the same role as God. Similarly, the personal idealist **J. M. E. McTaggart** (1866–1925), though openly atheistic, was led as much by his mystical experience as by his reason to posit a universe in which, behind the appearance of time, reality consists in a community of immortal spirits bound together by relations of loving perception—a sort of communitarian version of the beatific vision.

THE PRACTICE OF PHILOSOPHY

It was during the course of the nineteenth century that philosophy became the professional academic discipline that we know today, and it is this vital transition which forms the subject of Stuart Brown's contribution. It is important to realize that this transition cannot simply be relegated to the level of 'interesting history' for it affects the body of philosophy itself. For example, today original philosophy is found in professional journals or monographs written for other professionals. In the nineteenth century, by contrast, it was written in literary reviews of other works intended for a general lay audience.[40] Again, debate now found in papers and replies or in published symposia, was then often conducted through privately circulated pamphlets (such as those of the Metaphysical Society[41]) and through further editions of already published works. The range of sources in which philosophy found outlet was greater than today—in her discussion of feminist literature, for instance, Caine draws attention to the importance of *novels*—but all such organs placed their own constraints. Another interesting aspect of the professionalization process which should not go unrecorded is the emergence of textbooks and histories of philosophy, such as those (already noted) of G. H. Lewes and Leslie Stephen, and of the Idealists. Part of the growing sense of self-awareness of an autonomous discipline, these new forms of writing became very influential and changed the very nature of reader's encounter with philosophy.

Looking back on the nineteenth century, Bosanquet suggested that in a culture where philosophical speculation had become stagnant it was inevitable that it sought to find release elsewhere, in literature and poetry.[42] This volume casts doubt on his first suggestion that Victorian philosophy made no room for creation, but his second is very important and

---

[40] For example, *Edinburgh Review* (founded 1802), *Quarterly Review* (founded 1809), *Westminster Review* (founded 1823).

[41] The Metaphysical Society founded by Sir James Knowles was a philosophical debating club which ran from 1869 to 1880. Its members included such figures as J. R. Seeley, T. H. Huxley, John Tyndall, Henry Sidgwick, James Martineau, Mark Pattison, Alexander Campbell Fraser, W. K. Clifford, Leslie Stephen, A. J. Balfour, and Shadworth Hodgson. For further details, see Brown (1947).

[42] Bosanquet (1889), pp. 91–6.

raises the question of the relationship between the poetic and the philosophic imagination. Few philosophers today would define their work in relation to poetry, where, as it has
recently been put, the barricades between the two are vigilantly maintained.[43] But to the
nineteenth century there was a deep affinity between both their methods and their aims and
there was nothing odd about looking to poetry for philosophical ideas. In the penultimate
paper of the collection Leslie Armour traces this connection from Coleridge, for whom 'No
man was ever yet a great poet, without being at the same time a profound philosopher',[44]
through to Idealists such as Edward Caird for whom 'the highest truth of philosophy is a
rational and self-conscious poetry, as the highest poetry may be described as an irrational
and unconscious philosophy'.[45]

REFERENCES

Bosanquet, B. (1889) 'The Part Played by Aesthetic in the Development of Modern Philosophy',
    Proceedings of the Aristotelian Society, 1, pp. 77–97.
Bradley, F. H. (1927) *Ethical Studies*, Oxford: Clarendon Press [1st published 1876].
Bradley, F. H. (1897) *Appearance and Reality*, Oxford: Clarendon Press [1st published 1876].
Brown, Alan Willard (1947) *The Metaphysical Society: Victorian Minds in Crisis, 1869–1880*,
    New York: Columbia University Press.
Burns, J. H. (2005) 'Happiness and Utility: Jeremy Bentham's Equation', *Utilitas*, 17/1, pp. 46–61.
Caird, E. (1865) 'Plato and the Other Companions of Socrates' *North British Review*, 43,
    pp. 351–84.
Caird, E. (1893) *The Evolution of Religion*, Glasgow: James MacLehose.
Caird, J. (1898) *University Addresses*, Glasgow: James MacLehose.
Clifford W. K. (1877) 'The Ethics of Belief', *Contemporary Review*, 29, pp. 289–309.
Coleridge, S. T. (1906) *Biographia Literaria*, London: Everymans library [1st published 1817].
Coleridge, S. T. (1917) *The Table Talk and Omniana of Samuel Taylor Coleridge*,
    London: George Bell.
Eagleton, T. (2007) *The Meaning of Life*, Oxford: Oxford University Press.
Flint, R. (1877) *Theism*, London: William Blackwood.
Harper, G. H. (1933) *Cardinal Newman and William Froude: A Correspondence*, Baltimore: Johns
    Hopkins Press.
Huxley, T. H. (1894a) 'Agnosticism', in *Collected Essays*, London: Macmillan, vol. v, pp. 209–62
    [1st published 1889].
Huxley, T. H. (1894b) 'Evolution and Ethics', in *Collected Essays*, London: Macmillan, vol. ix,
    pp. 46–116 [1st published 1893].
Jones, Henry (1883) 'The Social Organism', in A. Seth and R. B. Haldane (eds.), *Essays in
    Philosophical Criticism*, London: Longmans Green, pp. 187–213.
Kuhn, T. (1962) *The Structure of Scientific Revolutions*, Chicago: Chicago University Press.
Lewes, G. H. (1874) *Problems of Life and Mind*, London: Trübner, *First Series*, vol. i.
Lewes, G. H. (1892) *Biographical History of Philosophy*, London: George Routledge [1st
    published 1846].

[43] Eagleton (2007), p. 5.   [44] Coleridge (1906), ch. xv, p. 171.
[45] Edward Caird (1865) p. 352.

Lightman, B. (1990) 'Robert Elsmere and the Agnostic Crises of Faith', in Richard Helmstadter and Bernard Lightman (eds.), *Victorian Faith in Crisis: Essays on Continuity and Change in Nineteenth Century Religious Belief*, Houndmills: Macmillan, pp. 283–311.

Madden, E. H. (1985) 'Sir William Hamilton, Critical Philosophy, and the Commonsense Tradition', *Review of Metaphysics*, 38/4, pp. 839–66.

Mander, W. J. (2011) *British Idealism, a History*, Oxford: Oxford University Press.

Mill, James (1869) *Analysis of the Phenomena of the Human Mind*, London: Longmans.

Mill, J. S. (1843) *A System of Logic*, London: Longmans.

Mill, J. S. (1972) *Utilitarianism*, London: Everymans Library [1st published 1863].

Mill, J. S. (1875) *An Examination of Sir William Hamilton's Philosophy*, 5th edn., London: Longmans [1st published 1865].

Mill, J. S. (1924) *Autobiography*, Oxford: Oxford World's Classics [1st published 1873].

Newman, J. H. (1979) *Essay in Aid of a Grammar of Assent*, Notre Dame, Ill.: University of Notre Dame Press [1st published 1870].

Schneewind, J. B. (1965), 'Moral Problems and Moral Philosophy in the Victorian Period', *Victorian Studies*, 9, suppl., pp. 29–46

Sidgwick, H. (1901) *Methods of Ethics*, 6th edn., London: Macmillan [1st published 1874].

Spencer, H. (1864) *Principles of Biology*, London: Williams and Norgate.

Wace, Henry (1888) 'Robert Elsmere and Christianity', *Quarterly Review*, 167, pp. 273–302.

Webb, C. C. J. (1933) *A Study of Religious Thought in England*, Oxford: Clarendon Press.

Whately, R. (1827) *Elements of Logic*, 2nd edn., London: J. Mawman [1st published 1826].

PART I

LOGIC AND SCIENTIFIC METHOD

CHAPTER 2

....

EARLY
NINETEENTH-CENTURY LOGIC

....

JAMES W. ALLARD

In 1808, when Britain was in the midst of the Napoleonic Wars, an unsigned review of
Laplace's *Traité de Méchanique Céleste* written by John Playfair, a Scottish geologist and
mathematician, appeared in the *Edinburgh Review*. In the course of praising Laplace,
Playfair commented on the inferiority of English mathematicians in comparison with their
Continental counterparts. He traced the source of the problem to English public institutions, in particular the two English universities. Of Oxford he wrote, 'In one of these, where
the dictates of Aristotle are still listened to as infallible decrees, and where the infancy of
science is mistaken for its maturity, the mathematical sciences have never flourished' (1808,
283). This was Playfair's only sentence about Oxford, but it was one of a number of asides
disparaging Oxford in *Edinburgh Review* articles during the early nineteenth century. In
subsequent articles the tone of these remarks grew more caustic. In 1809 the reviewer of
Richard Edgeworth's *Essays on Professional Education* wrote, 'An infinite quantity of talent is
annually destroyed in the Universities of England, by the miserable jealousy and littleness of
ecclesiastical instructors' (quoted in Green 1986, 633). To these and other 'sarcastic sneers
and allusions... keen reproaches and bold accusations' (1810a, 10), Oxford's reply was delivered in a polemical masterpiece by the formidable Edward Copleston, a fellow and tutor at
Oriel College, soon to become provost of Oriel, and a leading figure among the Noetics. 'It
is time', Copleston wrote, 'to raise the voice of injured freedom and insulted honor' (1810a,
4) so that the public will cease to be taught that Oxford is inhabited by 'either gloomy bigots,
lazy monks, or ignorant pretenders to learning and science' (1810a, 10).

Copleston responded in detail and with great force to the particular remarks about
Oxford made in three *Edinburgh Review* articles, but his larger aim was to defend Oxford
education in the Classics as the proper education for a gentleman, as a liberal education. It
is an education, he wrote, that 'enlarges the mind, excites its faculties, and calls those limbs
and muscles into freer exercise, which, by too constant a use in one direction... acquire
an illiberal air' (1810a, 111–12). Such an education, Copleston argued, is to be found in
the study of Classical literature and, of course, this was just the sort of education Oxford
provided. He vigorously denied that Aristotle's *Physics* was taught as science at Oxford, but
he strongly defended the importance of Aristotle's deductive logic. 'As an engine of science',

Copleston said, 'it is not, and never was, proposed' (1810a, 26). Its value, he asserted, is that it enables students to state their reasoning in the most bare and elementary form and so to cut short wrangling (1810a, 22). Logic, he concluded, is an essential component of a liberal education.

Copleston preceded this forceful defence, continued through two further exchanges with his Scottish critics, by calling on Oxford to clean its own house and to teach Aristotle's logic properly. This call is found in Copleston's devastating criticism of a short book on logic, *Logic Made Easy*, by a fellow supporter of educational reform at Oxford, Henry Kett. Kett thought that logic was unduly difficult for students to master because most logic books were either too concise, too technical, lacked examples and applications, or were written in Latin (1809, pp. iii–iv). So by borrowing haphazardly and inconsistently from others writers, Kett provided what he thought to be the needed book, one that would make logic easy. This was too much for Copleston whose pamphlet *The Examiner Examined, or Logic Vindicated* shredded Kett's book page by page. Copleston criticized Kett's account of definitions and of propositions, he noted Kett's 'blunders' about major, minor, and middle terms, and he commented on Kett's 'mutilation' of the rules for structuring syllogisms. When he came to Kett's 4th rule, 'That syllogism is faulty, in which the middle term is not distributed in the premises, but is distributed in the conclusion: for the middle term is not proved to agree with either the major on the minor' (Kett 1809, 61), Copleston snorted, 'The Middle term in the conclusion!!! How very easy logic is now made!' (Copleston 1809, 23). These confusions may do Mr Kett no harm, Copleston continued, 'But if a candidate were to give this account of things in the Schools, he would be *plucked*' (1809, 23). Though very harsh, Copleston's pamphlet was more than a criticism of Kett. It was also a vehicle for Copleston's views on logic and its role in education, views he hinted he might develop more fully later (1809, 55). Although he went on to become dean of Chester and bishop of Llandaff, Copleston never wrote his book on logic. But he shared his views on logic with his pupil and later lifelong friend, Richard Whately, in their long walks and talks together, and Whately incorporated them into his book, *Elements of Logic*. This was the book that began the revival of the study of formal logic in nineteenth-century Britain.

In what follows I will mention some seventeenth- and eighteenth-century criticisms of formal logic and sketch the case Copleston made for formal logic in the face of them. I will then describe how Whately defined logic and set forth its contents. Next I will discuss some responses to Whately's book including Sir William Hamilton's review of it, a review that established Hamilton as the foremost British logician of his time. I will conclude by considering Hamilton's attempt to bring logic to completion by qualifying not only the subjects but also the predicates of propositions.

I

By the early nineteenth century formal logic in Britain had endured, in the words of Sir William Hamilton, a century and a half of 'perversion and neglect' (Hamilton 1853a, 121). The decline of formal logic was a component of the scientific revolution and the initial charge against it was that it was not useful for science. Critics of formal logic claimed that the new science required a new logic, a logic of induction rather than of deduction.

The most prominent spokesperson for this view was Francis Bacon, who in his *Novum Organum* complained that logic as it had been practised 'does more to entrench errors than to reveal the truth' (2004, 55). He called for 'a form of *Induction* other than the one in use hitherto' (2004, 163), one that would not be 'useless for discovering sciences' (2004, 69). His rejection of formal logic was seconded by John Locke who thought that formal logic was no help in finding those ideas whose perceived agreement would enlarge knowledge (1975, 668–70, 679). But Locke went beyond Bacon in claiming that formal logic was of no great use in education and was often more prone to error than the natural forms of reasoning it was intended to replace (1975, 677–8). It was, he said, 'a captious and fallacious use of doubtful words' of 'little advantage' to the young (1989, 240–1). Locke pointed out that 'a great many natural defects in the understanding [are] capable of amendment' and that these are 'overlooked and wholly neglected' by logic (1996, 168). His alternative, set forth most fully in his posthumously published *Of the Conduct of the Understanding*, was a set of recommendations on improving one's intellectual faculties. In the eighteenth century, these recommendations became the core of a new form of logic, facultative logic. The goal of this form of logic was to identify rules for forming habits of mind conducive to finding truth, evaluating evidence, and forming well-grounded opinions (Buickerood 1985, 159–63). The two significant British eighteenth-century logics, Isaac Watt's *Logick: Or, the Right Use of Reason in the Enquiry after Truth* (1725) and William Duncan's *Elements of Logic* (1748), are devoted to this sort of development of the faculties. Both treat formal logic in a cursory way as one component of such development. As a result, logic as a subject of study was losing its formal content and formal logic was becoming much less central in education.

Coupled with being edged out by facultative logic, formal logic was subject to a number of criticisms about its adequacy as an analysis of correct reasoning. It was strongly criticized in the eighteenth century by the Scottish philosophers Thomas Reid, Lord Kames, and George Campbell. Henry Home, Lord Kames, compared Aristotle's logic to 'a bubble made of soap-water for amusing children; a beautiful figure with splendid colours; fair on the outside, empty within. It has for more than two thousand years been the hard fate of Aristotle's followers, Ixion like, to embrace a cloud for a goddess' (1778, 308). Nor was this simply an exercise in Kames's powers of description. His complaint was that the conclusion of a syllogism was not inferred from its major premise, but 'included in it' (1778, 306). Unfortunately, Kames did not explain the distinction between being inferred from and included in or what fault failing to draw it involved. But one way of understanding it was explained by his Scottish contemporary George Campbell. Campbell argued that because the conclusion of a valid syllogism is contained in its major premise valid syllogisms commit the sophism of begging the question (1963, 62–7). This was the complaint made famous by Mill and it continues to hound syllogistic logic.

Although Kames did not provide, as Campbell did, a considered evaluation of syllogistic reasoning, he did something more valuable for the development of logic. As the editor of *Sketches of the History of Man*, Kames asked Thomas Reid to contribute an essay on Aristotle's logic. Reid's *A Brief Account of Aristotle's Logic*, as might be expected, treated Aristotle's *Organon* insightfully but very critically. Perhaps his most important criticism challenged the adequacy of Aristotle's account of logical form. Reid maintained that it was inadequate because many mathematical propositions lack subject–predicate form. As he put it, 'They express some relation which one quantity bears to another, and on that account must have three terms. The quantities compared make two, and the relation between them is a third' (2004, 128–9). If this is the case, then inferences featuring these propositions as premises and conclusions are not Aristotelian syllogisms. To use Reid's example, 'A is equal to B, B is equal to C, therefore A is equal to C' is not an Aristotelian syllogism and the rules for evaluating syllogisms fail to apply to it. It follows from this that Aristotle's account of logical form is at best incomplete. This simply stated criticism identified the key issue in the nineteenth-century development of logic.

During this century and a half of 'perversion and neglect' of formal logic, the teaching of it suffered. It was hardly taught in the Scottish universities or at Trinity College Dublin, and at Cambridge it had become, in the words of Sir William Hamilton, 'a muddy scantling of metaphysic, psychology, *and* dialectic' (1853a, 124). The only British university in which the study of formal logic survived was Oxford and its condition there was not good. Although Oxford candidates for degrees were required to know sufficient logic to take part in traditional disputations, the administration of these exercises and the system of instruction they were designed to test were widely regarded as unsatisfactory and even the reforms of the early nineteenth century did little to change this as far as the teaching of logic was concerned (Whately 1826, p. xiv; Sutherland 1986, 469–72). Formal logic had come to its historical nadir. In the early years of the nineteenth century, as Richard Whately remarked, 'a Treatise on Logic would have been regarded in much the same light as one on Chiromancy or Astrology' (1854, 92).

There was, however, one hopeful sign. The most commonly used Oxford logic text, Henry Aldrich's 1691 *Artis Logicae Compendium*, contained what appears to be the only formally adequate post-medieval account of the syllogism prior to the nineteenth century (Ashworth 1974, 237). The *Compendium* was available in two different versions during the eighteenth century and from 1817 on it was also available in an abridged version, *Artis Logicae Rudimenta* (Howell 1971, 42–3, 58). Even though logic was not Aldrich's main interest—he was far better known as an architect—his logic in one form or another was in continuous use at Oxford from the time of its publication well into the nineteenth century. Aldrich organized his book around three operations of mind: simple apprehension, judgement, and discourse.[1] He correlated these mental operations with their linguistic expressions: terms, propositions, and syllogisms respectively. Each of them has a corresponding defect—indistinctness for terms, falsity for propositions, and incorrectness for reasoning—and it is the function of logic to remedy these defects. Aldrich discussed these mental operations and their associated defects in the three main parts of the book. The most important part is the account of reasoning.[2] Allowing that Aldrich is not always a reliable guide in logic, Ivor Thomas describes his treatment of the syllogism as 'a small miracle'. Aldrich defines major and minor terms in the Philoponian way and correctly lists the result as twenty-four valid moods in four figures with 232 invalid ones.[3] 'To come on

---

[1] For a discussion of the origin of this way of organizing logic texts, see Ashworth 1985, pp. xli–xlii.
[2] For further discussion of Aldrich, see Howell 1971, 42–60.
[3] Aristotle treated the major term in first-figure syllogisms as the term with the widest extension and in second- and third-figure syllogisms (where the major term is not always the one with the widest extension) as the term mentioned first. In order to have a definition common to all three figures, John Philoponus proposed defining the major term as the predicate of the conclusion. In the seventeenth century this became the usual definition (Kneale and Kneale 1984, 68–71).

these few pages after the logical rags and tatters of the previous two centuries', Thomas remarks, 'is to be presented with a creation of *haute couture*' (I. Thomas 1964, 310–11). Aldrich also offered the start of a defence of formal logic against the criticisms of the advocates of inductive logic. He thought, contra Bacon, that logic was not concerned with scientific discovery. Its use is to be found in communication. 'The duty of logic', as he saw it, is 'to aid the person who wishes either to teach or learn the inventions which they call the liberal arts'.[4]

What made this defence of moment in early nineteenth-century Britain was the formation of a new conception of a liberal education. In Georgian Britain a liberal education was the mark of a gentleman, a sociable person with proper character and proper manners (Rothblatt 1976, 23–6). A university degree was not necessary and might even interfere with this sort of liberal education. A degree required training in logic and logic was thought to induce wrangling, the very opposite of sociability (Rothblatt 1976, 78–80).[5] In the early nineteenth century, however, the Georgian conception of a liberal education was evolving into a somewhat different conception. In this newer conception a person with a liberal education had a properly trained mind. This emphasized the importance of logic, at least of the Lockean facultative variety, because that was its goal as well. In such an education, the importance of the study of a particular subject matter could be measured by its role in developing one's faculties (Rothblatt 1976, 131–2). If it could be shown that formal logic played an important role in doing this, then its place in a liberal education was assured.

This, of course, was exactly what Copleston claimed formal logic did. He insisted that it has 'no necessary or natural connection' to the progress of science (1810b, 19). Its purpose lies in regulating the language by means of which we communicate our opinions and our reasons for holding them. Copleston admitted that logic is not sufficient to ensure effective communication, but he continued, 'without Logic it cannot be done' (1809, 52). From this he concluded that logic is necessary for a liberal education. This is the view of logic presented at full length in Whately's *Elements of Logic*, published in 1826 as an expanded version of Whately's article on logic in the *Encyclopaedia Metropolitana*. Even though Whately was the sole author, he dedicated the book to Copleston and acknowledged Copleston's contribution to it. 'I am indebted to you', Whately wrote, 'as having contributed remarks, explanations, and illustrations, relative to the most important point, to so great an amount that I can hardly consider myself as the Author of more than half of such portions of the treatise as are not borrowed from former publications' (1826, p. iii).[6] It was through Whately's book that Copleston's ideas on logic reached a wider audience.

---

[4] Translated and quoted in Howell 1971, 50, from the *Conclusio* of the shorter version of the *Compendium* (1696).

[5] Cf. Locke's comment '[B]e sure not to let your son be bred up in the art and formality of disputing … unless instead of an able man, you desire to have him an insignificant wrangler, opinionater in discourse, and priding himself on contradicting others' (1989, 241).

[6] Whately also acknowledged the help he received from one of his students, John Henry Newman, who, Whately wrote, 'actually composed a considerable portion of the work as it now stands, from manuscripts not designed for publication, and who is the original author of several pages' (1826, p. viii).

II

In *Elements of Logic* Whately contributed three crucial things to the revival of logic.[7] He limited the subject matter of logic to reasoning, he insisted that logic is formal, and he provided an account of logical form. The first of these contributions is his definition of logic as 'an analysis of the process of the mind in Reasoning' (1826, 1). This is often taken to be the traditional way of understanding logic. This appearance is reinforced a few pages later by Whately's comment that 'as far as the main principles of the science [of logic] are concerned, [it] properly commences and ends with Aristotle' (1826, 6). But there is more innovation here than meets the eye. Aristotle did not define logic and its content was traditionally taken from his *Organon*, a post-Aristotelian grouping of texts. Its subject matter had generally, but not always, included the theory of the syllogism. It had also usually included the categories of being from the *Categories* and the methods for inventing dialectical arguments from the *Topics*. In early modern logic those who included the methods from the *Topics* in the subject matter of logic often rationalized their decision by adding to the three commonly recognized mental operations of concern to logic, simple apprehensive, judgement, and correct reasoning, a fourth operation, ordering. Ordering had its linguistic counterpart in a doctrine of method, the concern of which was the listing of subjects or topics from which arguments could be constructed. Arnauld and Nicole's *Port Royal Logic* (also known as *Logic or the Art of Thinking*), for example, was organized around these four operations. Even though Aldrich did not recognize ordering as one of the distinctly logical operations of mind, his *Compendium* contained a short discussion of method. By restricting logic to the art of reasoning Whately eliminated method, marginalized the categories of being, and considered the operations of simple apprehension and judgement only insofar as they are of concern to an analysis of reasoning. His memorable description of Copleston's education in logic is also a description of what Whately achieved with Copleston's aid.

> Mr. Copleston...having received no instruction in [logic], and having no living help to apply to, collected and read all the books he could meet with that professed to treat of it. The far greater part of what he had thus to wade through, he found to be either ingenious trifling, or matter irrelevant to science. But from the chaos of loose materials, mingled with rubbish, he formed in his own mind a coherent, and intelligible, and valuable system, carefully separating and preserving every particle of gold found mingled with the worthless clay and sand that was to be washed away. (Whately 1854, 95)

Whately found gold in the analysis of reasoning.

Whately's second contribution to the revival of logic is his insistence that the process of reasoning is to be understood formally. There are two parts to this. First, Whately takes reasoning to be 'the act of proceeding from one judgment to *another* founded upon it' (1826, 55). But he immediately adds 'Language affords the *signs* by which these operations of mind are expressed and communicated' (1826, 55). From this he concludes that logic '*is entirely conversant about language*' (1826, 56 n.). Consequently, for Whately 'an analysis of the process of the mind reasoning' is not a psychological analysis but rather an analysis of a

---

[7] I have taken the second and third of these items from Merrill 1990, 3.

relationship between of acts of judgements and their linguistic counterparts, propositions. By confining logic to language he effectively distinguishes between the act of reasoning and its content and limits logic to its content.

Second, Whately refines the subject matter of logic further by considering the objection that logic fails to deal with the indistinctness of terms and the nature of the evidence for propositions. He replies that this could only be done by a system of universal knowledge and that such a system requires far more than logic or any other single discipline can provide. 'To find fault with Logic for not performing this', he remarks, 'is as if one should object to the science of Optics for not giving sight to the blind' (1826, 12–13). Concerns about the indistinctness of terms and the nature of evidence, he continues, are '*not* in the process of reasoning itself (which alone is the appropriate province of Logic), but in the subject-matter about which it is employed' (1826, 13). In this respect he thinks logic is like arithmetic. It is concerned with numerical relationships, irrespective of the items numerated. Likewise logic deals with the relationships between propositions without considering the subject matter of those propositions. Logic, Whately claims, can 'pronounce on the validity of a regularly-constructed argument, equally well, though arbitrary symbols may have been substituted for the terms' (1826, 14). The validity of an argument for Whately 'is manifest from the *mere force of the expression, i.e.,* without considering the *meaning of the terms*' (1826, 88). One could, in other words, 'substitute arbitrary unmeaning symbols for the significant terms' (1826, 35) in an argument and determine its validity by means of those symbols alone. Logic for Whately is thus the formal analysis of the content of the act of reasoning.[8]

There is a bit more to this than might be immediately apparent. For reasons that will soon appear, Whately thinks that the act of reasoning is a particular process, one that stated 'regularly and at full length' is a syllogism. A syllogism, in his view, 'is not a particular *kind of argument*', but a 'peculiar *form* of expression in which every argument may be stated' (1826, 24). His belief that logic is concerned with the only such process allows him to reply to many of the critics of formal logic against whom, as Mill commented, he carries on a 'running fire' (Mill 1978, 7). He replies ad hominem to the objection implicit in Campbell that all valid syllogisms are circular. According to Whately, Campbell is objecting to his own reasoning and so is in the position of the woodman who chopped off the branch on which he was standing (1826, 32–3).[9] He also replies to those who proposed to replace deductive logic with inductive logic. He does this by distinguishing between two meanings of the term 'induction'. It can refer either to the process of collecting facts or the process of deducing conclusions from those facts (1826, 208). The former is the process of collecting instances relevant to a particular inquiry (1826, 209–10). This indeed enlarges knowledge, but it is not, Whately claims, a process of inference. The latter, on Whately's analysis, is a syllogism incompletely expressed, an enthymeme (1826, 209). The conjunction of propositions listing the relevant property of the cases examined forms the minor premise of the syllogism. The major premise in its general form is the proposition that 'what belongs to the individual or individuals we have examined belongs to the whole class under which they come' (1826, 209). Induction, as a process of inference, Whately concludes, is a formal deductive inference and not an alternative kind of reasoning.

---

[8] For Whately's conception of logical form, see Merrill 1990, 3–9.

[9] Whately added the analogy in the 5th edition of the *Elements* (1834, 36).

This reply to Campbell also allows Whately to respond to one of Locke's criticisms, that formal logic is more prone to error than natural forms of reasoning. Contra Locke, Whately claims that natural forms of reasoning are deductive inferences. To Locke's other criticism, that logic is useless in education, Whately replies as Copleston does, that it is useful for a liberal education. If we examine the occupations of gentlemen, Whately writes, we find that their practitioners are engaged in both physical and mental activity. The mental activity invariably involves reasoning, the drawing of conclusions from premises. The theory which enables one to do this well is a component of all occupations and is thereby 'an essential part of a liberal education' (1826, pp. x–xi).

Whately's third contribution to logic is his account of the logical form of inferences. As already mentioned, he thinks that all inferences, stated 'regularly and at full length', have the form of syllogisms whose validity can be tested using Aristotle's *dictum de omni et nullo*. He develops this view on the basis of an analysis of propositions and terms. According to this analysis, a proposition is an indicative sentence containing two terms connected by a copula. Each of the terms signifies an object of simple apprehension. The copula is a sign of the act of judgement. It signifies that one of these terms, the predicate, is affirmed or denied either as a whole or in part of the other, which is the subject (1826, 57). If the predicate of a proposition is said of the whole subject, of all of it, the proposition is universal, but if it is said of only part of the subject, of some of it, the proposition is particular. The subjects but not the predicates of propositions are quantified. Propositions can also be either affirmative or negative. Combining these distinctions of quantity and quality yields the four familiar forms of Aristotelian propositions: universal affirmative (since medieval times abbreviated as 'A'), universal negative (abbreviated as 'E'), particular affirmative (abbreviated as 'I'), and particular negative (abbreviated as 'O'). Syllogisms are composed of three such propositions, two of them as premises, the third as the conclusion. Each syllogism contains exactly three terms, each of which occurs in two propositions.

Whately follows Aldrich in recognizing four figures of categorical syllogisms and in recognizing twenty-four valid moods and 232 invalid ones. Of the twenty-four valid moods Whately neglects five because they draw particular conclusions when universal conclusions could be drawn. He lists the remaining nineteen valid moods using their Latin names. I have capitalized the letters abbreviating the forms of the premises as Whately does in the following list of valid moods.

(1st figure) bArbArA, cElArEnt, dArII, fErIOque
(2nd figure) cEsArE, cAmEstrEs, fEstInO, bArOkO
(3rd figure) dArAptI, dIsAmIs, dAtIsI, fElAptOn, bOkArdO, fErIsO
(4th figure) brAmAntIp, cAmEnEs, dImArIs, fEsApO, frEsIsOn (1826, 98)

This is not quite Aristotle's account because it accepts the existence of a fourth figure, but it shares the formal sophistication of Aristotle's account, a sophistication only recently appreciated.[10]

Whately claims that all and only valid syllogisms are instances of Aristotle's *dictum de omni et nullo*, 'whatever is predicated (*i.e.*, affirmed or denied) universally, of any class of

---

[10]   E.g. Corcoran 1974.

things, may be predicated, in like manner, (viz., affirmed or denied) of any thing compre-hended in that class' (1826, 31–2).[11] Whately takes this maxim to apply immediately only to first-figure syllogisms, but he argues that other categorical syllogisms can be reduced to this class by the appropriate conversions of their premises. Once this has been done, it is possi-ble to test the validity of any categorical syllogism using the maxim. Whately completes his account by arguing that sorites and both forms of hypothetical syllogisms, the conditional and the disjunctive, can be appropriately reduced and tested by the *dictum*. Whately's claim that all arguments are syllogisms whose validity can be tested by the *dictum* is the third of his contributions to the development of nineteenth-century logic.

Whately's three logical claims were, however, only part of the reason for the success of his book. Its popularity was also due to its witty, up-to-date style, and clever organization. It had the added virtue of applying logic to theological issues. In the first edition there are notes on Hume's argument against the existence of miracles and there are further notes in later editions.[12] In the fourth edition Whately added an appendix analysing a portion of Paley's argument from design (1831, 374–84). The *Elements* went through nine editions during Whately's lifetime and many more after his death. It was widely used as a textbook in both Britain and America, and it stimulated a number of other books that abridged, com-mented on, or criticized it.[13] In 1864 Alexander Campbell Fraser wrote that 'logic is at pre-sent, in a great measure the consequence of Whately, more used as an organ and test of a liberal education, and philosophical discipline is more generally required of all candidates for the offices of life, than at any time since the decline of the study in the seventeenth cen-tury' (1864, 5). Augustus De Morgan rightly called Whately the 'restorer of logical study in England' (1966, 247).

III

There were others besides Whately thinking about logic in early nineteenth-century Britain. Mineralogist Richard Kirwan had published his *Logick* in 1807 as part of a series of works on various sciences, but only a small part of that book covered formal logic. In the 1820s Samuel Taylor Coleridge was working on a manuscript of a logic inspired by Kant, but it was brilliant and idiosyncratic in Coleridge's best manner and it was not published in entirety until 1981. More significant for the development of logic was the Scottish philosopher Sir William Hamilton. Hamilton established his reputation in the late 1820s and early 1830s with three striking articles in the *Edinburgh Review*. The first two attempted to fuse Scottish common-sense philosophy with the philosophy of Kant. The third was a review of recent books on logic, among them Whately's *Elements*.

---

[11] The *dictum* is derived from Aristotle's *Prior Analytics*, 24b25–30.

[12] Details are kept to a minimum, probably because Whately treated that argument at length in his only other significant philosophical publication, *Historic Doubts Relative to Napoleon Buonaparte*. In this once-popular essay Whately used Hume's reasons for doubting miracles to doubt the existence of Napoleon.

[13] For its reception, see Van Evra (2008), an article to which I am indebted.

Although Hamilton's review covered ten books, he properly concentrated on Whately's *Elements* because it had inspired most of the other works under review. In his learned, pedantic, and forceful review Hamilton agreed with Whately that logic is a formal science (1853a, 121). Having said that, however, he went on to identify what he thought to be Whately's insufficiencies. These, he wrote, included Whately's claim that the history of logic ends with Aristotle, his definitions of certain logical terms, such as 'categorical' and 'hypothetical', his treatment of modality as formal rather than as Hamilton thought material, and his account of induction. The review exhibited a remarkable grasp of the history of logic and established Hamilton as the foremost British authority on logic. It also contained one line of reasoning that contained Hamilton's main contribution to logic. It challenged Whately's account of the logical form of propositions.

Hamilton did this in the course of criticizing Whately's theory of induction. Hamilton agreed with Whately that the term 'induction' is ambiguous. Unlike Whately, however, Hamilton thought it had not two but three meanings: the empirical investigation of facts, the material inference of a universal judgement from particular observed facts, and the formal inference of a universal judgement from particular judgements (1853a, 157). Hamilton agreed that the first was not properly the subject matter of logic, but he claimed that Whately had conflated the second and third. This, Hamilton thought, had led him to treat inductive inferences as enthymemes with their common major premise, 'what belongs to the individual or individuals we have examined belongs to the whole class under which they come', suppressed. But this, Hamilton claimed, is an extralogical postulate. It concerns material rather than formal reasoning. Hamilton then proceeded to sketch a formal theory of induction. Hamilton claimed that the mind can link reason and consequence in only two ways: from a whole to its parts or from parts to a whole. The former is deductive reasoning, the latter inductive. Because 'knowledge commences with the apprehension of singulars' (1853a, 160), deductive inference presupposes inductive inference and as a consequence logic must vindicate both. Hamilton then sketched how the two processes are the reverses of each other. Here is his example.

Inductive	*Deductive*
x, y, z are A	B is A
x, y, z are (whole) B	x, y, z are (under) B
Therefore, B is A	Therefore, x, y, z are A

The reversal is that the conclusion of the inductive argument is the first premise of the deductive argument. Because knowledge begins with the apprehension of singulars, this is a way of representing the dependence of deduction on induction.

But there is a further difference to be noted. The inductive argument appears to be a third-figure syllogism with a universal rather than a particular conclusion and so, by traditional analysis, invalid. What saves it, as Hamilton points out, is that the copula is ambiguous. In the first premise of the inductive argument, the predicate A *contains* the subject, x, y, z, while in the second, the subject, x, y, z, *constitutes* the predicate. Both patterns are valid and exhibit the pattern found in syllogisms that are valid by inspection. In syllogisms of this kind, the predicate of the major premise is the subject of the minor premise. The pattern is more easily seen when the syllogisms are rewritten as follows (1853a, 161–2).

Inductive	*Deductive*
A contains x, y, z	A contains B
x, y, z, constitute B	B contains x, y, z
Therefore, A contains B	Therefore, A contains x, y, z

The importance of this treatment of induction is that the second premise of the inductive argument in effect states that x, y, and z are all of B. But to say this is to apply the quantitative word 'all' to the predicate 'B' because, to use Hamilton's way of expressing it, x, y, and z are all B. This quantifies the predicate of one of the premises of a syllogism. Hamilton later pointed out that his treatment of induction in this review proceeded on his belief that predicates could be quantified (1853c, 646).

Although Hamilton later and with great urgency claimed priority in this discovery, several of his lesser known contemporaries also challenged this aspect of Whately's view of logical form. The earliest was George Bentham, Jeremy Bentham's nephew.[14] This was embarrassing for Hamilton because Bentham's book was included among the list of titles reviewed in Hamilton's *Edinburgh Review* article. When George Bentham discovered Whately's *Elements*, he had already begun his distinguished career as a botanist but was for financial reasons editing his uncle's unpublished logic papers. Bentham's book, *Outline of a New System of Logic*, published in 1827, is a running commentary on Whately's *Elements* that develops some ideas Bentham borrowed from his uncle. Bentham thought that by excluding method Whately had defined logic too narrowly. As a result of his study of botany, Bentham's interests inclined him towards method and he was particularly interested in the method of division, especially as exemplified in biological classifications. He used the method of division to classify propositions. A proposition, he claimed, consists of two terms, one a subject, the other a predicate, with a copula expressing one of three relations between the terms: identity, diversity, or subalternation (1827, 127–8). The terms can refer either to individuals or to 'collective entities' and when they refer to 'collective entities' their identity can be universal or partial. The identity is universal if it holds between any individual referred to by one collective term and any individual referred to by the other, as for example, in the identity between equilateral and equiangular triangles. The identity can be partial in two ways. It can hold between any individual referred to by one term and any of one part only of the individuals referred to by the other, as, for example between horses and quadrupeds. It can also be partial if it holds between any of one part only of one term and any of one part only of the other, as for example, between quadrupeds and swimming animals. To regard subject–predicate relations in this way is to quantify the predicate, something that Bentham explicitly did. Allowing the addition of a quantifier, either 'all' and 'some', to the predicates of A, E, I, and O propositions, turned these four forms into eight. But Bentham realized some of these forms are equivalent and that there are only five possible relations between the terms in them (1827, 129–35). Moreover, he did not use his discovery to enlarge the number of valid syllogisms. Instead he proposed some rules for evaluating syllogisms, showed how they could be applied to traditionally valid forms of argument, and proposed scrapping traditional distinctions of mood and syllogism in favour of his rules (1827, 154–62). Unfortunately, the press that published *Outline of a New System of Logic*

---

[14] In what follows, I am heavily indebted to McOuat and Varma 2008.

went bankrupt after only sixty copies of the book had been sold. The book was virtually unnoticed until a contributor to *The Athenaeum* mentioned Bentham as having preceded Hamilton in quantifying the predicate (Warlow 1850).[15]

A second person who considered the quantification of the predicate was Thomas Solly (1816–75). Like Bentham, Solly had read Whately, and was dissatisfied with some parts of Whately's work, particularly his confining logic to a study of language (Solly 1839, 11–15). Solly's *Syllabus of Logic*, published in 1839, introduces the valid moods of the syllogism with an account of Kant's view of the understanding. Solly distinguishes transcendental from formal logic by assigning to the former but not the latter a concern with the pure conception of an object in general. He thinks this is important for formal logic because transcendental logic requires judgements to have certain characteristics and explains some of their features (1839, 8–9, 127–9).[16] In his examination of the logical forms of judgement, Solly acknowledges that the predicates of judgements can be quantified. But, for transcendental reasons, he denies that this is a real possibility and he does not consider it further (1839, 45–50). The formal interest of Solly's work is not here, however, but in the use of mathematical methods for showing syllogisms to be valid, although he did not attempt to use these to expand the number of valid syllogisms. As a result, the mathematical development of the quantification of the predicate was better carried on by another logician working at this time, Augustus De Morgan.

De Morgan's *First Notions*, later chapter 1 of his *Formal Logic*, was published in 1839 and by 1846 he was developing what he called a 'numerically definite syllogism', a form of reasoning that involved introducing numerical quantifiers (e.g. 'most') into logic. While he was doing this, he wrote to Hamilton asking for a clarification of Hamilton's doctrine of the quantification of the predicate.[17] Hamilton responded with the prospectus for his announced, but never published, work on logic and with some additional notes. De Morgan did not find them helpful but added a note acknowledging Hamilton in his 1846 paper 'On the Structure of the Syllogism'. He sent an offprint to Hamilton in 1847, at which point Hamilton wrote to De Morgan accusing him of plagiarism and an acrimonious controversy began. The initial issue was Hamilton's accusation, but the controversy soon spread to logical matters.

IV

Prior to the controversy, the work of Solly and De Morgan was not well known. Even Hamilton was unaware of it, perhaps because of his antipathy to mathematics.[18] His own essays, however, were widely known, and in 1836 on the strength of them he was elected

---

[15] Warlow's letter produced a flurry of further letters including one by Hamilton. The source for Warlow's hard-to-locate letter is given in Van Evra 1992, 406 n.–7 n.

[16] In what follows I am heavily indebted to Panteki 1993.

[17] For a careful discussion of the controversy, see Heath 1966.

[18] In his *Edinburgh Review* article, 'On the Study of Mathematics, as an Exercise of Mind', Hamilton claimed that the study of mathematics incapacitates the mind and disposes it to blind credulity or irrational scepticism (1853b, 275). This article was a response to William Whewell's *Thoughts on the Study of Mathematics as a Part of a Liberal Education*.

to the Chair of Logic and Metaphysics at the University of Edinburgh. In this capacity Hamilton alternated a year of lecturing on metaphysics with a year of lecturing on logic. His lectures on logic, written during the term in 1837–8 (1866a, pp. ix–xi), give a systematic presentation of his view of logic. But while he continued to deliver these lectures with only a few additions about his later views, he began supplementing them with additional lectures that developed his views further. In the course of doing so Hamilton arrived at his most important result, that the predicates of premises and conclusions of syllogisms could be quantified (1853c, 646). If this is so, the proposition 'all A is B' expresses two different propositions, 'All A is all B' and 'All A is some B'. He claimed that by taking these forms into account he could enlarge the number of valid syllogisms from twenty-four to thirty-six. This was his discovery of the quantification of the predicate, which he claimed helped complete logic by placing 'the keystone in the Aristotelic arch' (1866b, 251). Tragically, however, Hamilton suffered a stroke in 1844 that left him partially paralysed. In 1846 he announced his discovery of the quantification of the predicate, published a prospectus for an essay he was preparing for on it, and listed some of the theses his essay would contain.[19] But he was not able to complete the essay and his doctrine of the quantification of the predicate has to be reconstructed from his scattered publications, his posthumously published lectures and notes, and from some of his controversial writings. Prior to most of these publications, however, Hamilton's views about logic had been accepted by two respected Oxford writers, William Thomson and Henry Longueville Mansel. Thomson incorporated his own version of the quantification of the predicate into his 1842 *Outline of the Necessary Laws of Thought* while Mansel defended Hamilton's view of logic as a formal science of the necessary laws of thought. Mansel did this in the notes to his edition of Aldrich, in his *Prolegomena Logica*, and in his essays (especially 1873), and he took Hamilton's part in the controversy with De Morgan.

Hamilton's doctrine is a development of the view of logic found in his *Lectures on Logic*. These posthumously published lectures do not make pleasant reading. Hamilton emerges from them as a repetitious, pedantic lecturer, given to introducing extraneous material, and anxious to display his truly extraordinary knowledge of the minutiae of the history of logic. Moreover, he insists on using his own peculiar vocabulary and often quotes other authors at length.[20] His claims to have improved logic have generally not been well regarded by his critics, among them John Stuart Mill.[21] However, in company with Hamilton's other nineteenth-century critics, Mill was not able to give a satisfactory interpretation of Hamilton's doctrine of the quantification of the predicate and it is here that Hamilton made his contribution to the development of logic.

Hamilton's doctrine concerns the logical form of judgements. A judgement for Hamilton is the recognition of 'the relation of congruence or of confliction, in which two concepts, two individual things, or a concept and an individual, compared together, stand to each other' (1866a, 226). Unlike Whately, who attached quantities only to the subjects of

---

[19] The announcement appeared as an appendix in his edition of *The Works of Thomas Reid* and it is partially reprinted in Hamilton 1853c, 646–7, and in 1866b, 251–4, but without the paragraph in which he announced that his purpose was to 'formally establish [his] right of authorship' for the discovery (1846, 1).

[20] Especially Wilhelm Traugott Krug 1806 and Wilhelm Esser 1830.

[21] For Mill's often devastating criticisms, see his 1979, 301–429.

propositions, Hamilton thinks that both subjects and predicates have quantities. Both quantities, he argues, must be present in thought, but he admits that the quantity of the predicate is usually elided in speech. But given his postulate that it is allowable to state 'explicitly in language all that is implicitly contained in thought' (1866a, 114), he concludes that the quantity of the proposition may be expressed in language as well. If the logical quantities 'all' and 'some' are added to predicates, then the four Aristotelian forms, A, E, I, and O become eight forms.[22] I have added in parenthesis Hamilton's designations of them (1866b, 287):

   1. All A is all B.   (toto-total)
   2. All A is some B.   (toto-partial)
   3. Some A is all B.   (parti-total)
   4. Some A is some B.   (parti-partial)
   5. Any A is not any B.   (toto-total)
   6. Any A is not some B.   (toto-partial)
   7. Some A is not any B.   (parti-total)
   8. Some A is not some B.   (parti-partial)[23]

Contrary to what Hamilton says, these forms of speech are not in ordinary use and it is not immediately clear what they mean. One suggestion is to take them as Bentham did, as relations between the extensions of the terms 'A' and 'B'. The difficulty with this suggestion is that there are only five such relations, not eight as in Hamilton's list (Bednarowski 1955-6, 217-19). A further difficulty is that Hamilton claimed, falsely, that he had shown propositions to be equations. This is false because 'All humans are mortal' would only be an equation if it contained singular terms flanking an 'is' of identity and it does not. These points suggest that a more adequate interpretation of his doctrine is needed.

In developing a better interpretation it is helpful to consider De Morgan's criticisms of Hamilton.[24] De Morgan found the following four problems with Hamilton's doctrine. First, Hamilton's (1), 'All A is all B', is seems equivalent to 'Every A is B and every B is A'. But this is a compound rather than a simple proposition. It is not a relation between a subject and a predicate. Second, Hamilton's (8), 'Some A is not some B', on De Morgan's interpretation means 'Some of the A's are not some of the B's'. Contradicting it requires asserting that there is only one A and one B and they are identical, but this proposition is not in Hamilton's system and it cannot be contradicted by any one of the other propositions in Hamilton's system. Moreover, and this is De Morgan's third criticism, (8) cannot be contradicted by any combination of propositions in Hamilton's system. Fourth, Hamilton's (1), 'All A is all B', is, on De Morgan's interpretation, compounded from (2) and (3). This is because (2), 'All A is some B', is equivalent to 'Every A is B' and (3), 'Some A is all B', is equivalent to 'every

---

[22] Hamilton treated universal judgements as having existential import and he recognized the ambiguity of the word 'some', which can mean 'some, perhaps all' or 'some, not all'. He thought logic should take account of both meanings of 'some' (1866b, 281-5).

[23] As I. M. Bocheński points out, this is an elaboration of the medieval doctrine of the exponibles (n.d., 262, 234-6), a fact marginally acknowledged by Hamilton and his editors (1866b, 263 n.–264 n.).

[24] I am heavily indebted to Fogelin 1992a and 1992b in what follows.

B is A'. So (1) asserts the conjunction of (2) and (3) (De Morgan 1966, 257–8). If there is to be a successful interpretation of Hamilton's system, it will need to respond to De Morgan's criticisms.

Far and away the best interpretation, that of Robert Fogelin, interprets Hamilton's propositions as containing quantifiers that range over identities and non-identities. Given two non-empty classes, A and B, Hamilton's (2), 'All A is some B', can be read as asserting that any member of A is identical with something that is a member of B (Fogelin 1992a, 154). The fact that on this interpretation propositions assert identity and deny identity perhaps explains why Hamilton thought of propositions as equations. This interpretation also makes sense of one of Hamilton's diagrams in which lines are drawn between the pairs (1,8), (2,7), (3,6), and (4,5). Hamilton didn't explain these lines, but his terms for them suggest that the pairs stand in contradictory opposition. If this is the case, then propositions 2–7 can be rewritten as follows:

2. All A is B.   (toto-partial)
3. All B is A.   (parti-total)
4. Some A is B.   (parti-partial)
5. No A is B.   (toto-total)
6. Some B is not A.   (toto-partial)
7. Some A is not B.   (parti-total) (Fogelin 1992a, 150–1)

None of De Morgan's criticisms apply to these propositions. They apply to Hamilton's first and last propositions.

The difficulty is to construe the first and last propositions so that they are contradictories. The correct way would seem to be

1. Anything that is an A is identical with anything that it is a B.   (toto-total)
8. Something that is an A is not identical with something that is a B.   (parti-partial)
                                                          (Fogelin, 1992b, 167)

This responds to De Morgan's first and fourth criticisms because 'All A is All B' is no longer a compound proposition and hence it is not compounded from propositions already in the system. It also responds to De Morgan's second and third criticisms because the contradictory of 'Some A is not some B' is 'All A is all B' (Fogelin 1992a, 150–1).

Fogelin's interpretation has the further virtue of explaining a number of other claims that Hamilton makes. In particular, it explains why Hamilton thought he could reduce the general laws for evaluating categorical syllogisms from three to one, simplify the conversion of propositions from three forms to one, simple conversion, and show that figure was inessential in evaluating syllogisms. Even more important, Hamilton claimed that he had expanded the number of valid moods from twenty-four to thirty-six and this too can be supported on this interpretation. For example,

Some P is not any M.
Some S is not some M.
Therefore, some S is not some P.

On Fogelin's interpretation this is equivalent to

> Some P is not M.
> Some S is M.
> Therefore, there is at least one S and at least one P that are not identical.

This is a valid, non-Aristotelian syllogism (Fogelin 1992b, 166–7). Hamilton was thus correct in criticizing Whately's account of logical form and expanding the number of available logical forms.

But while he succeed in enlarging Whately's account of valid logical forms of inference, Hamilton clearly failed to complete logic. In quantifying over identities and non-identities he expanded logic in a non-Aristotelian way that suggested further expansions. In addition, he failed to reply satisfactorily to Reid's claim that most mathematical reasoning is not syllogistic. Hamilton replied to Reid by citing the work of two 'zealous thick-headed logicians' (1853b, 279 n.), Christianus Herlinus and Conradus Dasypodius, who, he claimed, had reduced the demonstrations in the first six books of Euclid to syllogisms (1863, 702). As Ian Mueller shows, however, demonstrating even the first proposition in Euclid's *Elements* requires at least the resources of first-order predicate logic (1974, 38–43). This is particularly relevant to Hamilton's reply to Reid because as Herlinus and Dasypodius reconstruct the demonstration it requires the inference that things equal to the same thing are equal to each other. This was just the inference Reid cited to show that mathematical reasoning is not syllogistic.[25]

The irony of the situation is that neither Hamilton nor his advocates were able to clarify his doctrine so that his critics could understand it. As a result, Hamilton did not convince his contemporaries that he had discovered valid, non-Aristotelian forms of inference. But he did suggest to them that formal logic might not be complete. His claim to discoveries in logic led to his controversy with De Morgan who eventually replied constructively to Reid's criticism by developing an abstract, non-Aristotelian form of the copula, 'X stands in relation L to Y', to handle relational inferences (1966, 252). De Morgan's controversy with Hamilton in turn stimulated George Boole, whose logic was innovative in a much more profound way (Boole 1952, 47). De Morgan and Boole in their separate ways showed that neither Aristotle nor Hamilton had completed logic and opened the door to more extensive expansions. Much of this was made possible by Whately who not only defined logic in a coherent way, but conjoined his definition with a clear and simple thesis about logical form that could be challenged. Hamilton's importance in the history of logic is that he was the first significant British philosopher to rise to the challenge.[26]

---

[25] For a discussion of Hamilton's reply to Reid, see Merrill 1990, 10–23.

[26] I did the initial research for this paper while I was a Visiting Scholar at Harris Manchester College. I very much appreciate the hospitality of the college and the support and advice I received from W. J. Mander and Sue Killoran.

BIBLIOGRAPHY

Aldrich, Henry. [1691] 1696. *Artis Logicae Compendium*. Oxford: E Theatro Sheldoniano.

Arnauld, Antoine, and Pierre Nicole. [1662] 1996. *Logic or the Art of Thinking*. 5th edn. Trans. Jill Vance Buroker. Cambridge: Cambridge University Press.

Ashworth, E. J. 1974. *Language and Logic in the Post-Medieval Period*. Dordrecht: D. Reidel.

Ashworth, E. J. 1985. Introduction. In Robert Sanderson, *Logicae Artis Compendium*, pp. xi–lv. Bologna: CLUEB.

Bacon, Francis. [1620] 2004. *The 'Instauratio Magna' Part II: 'Novum Organum' and Associated Texts*. Ed. and trans. Graham Rees and Maria Wakely. *The Oxford Francis Bacon*, vol. xi. Oxford: Clarendon Press.

Bednarowski, W. 1955–6. Hamilton's Quantification of the Predicate. *Proceedings of the Aristotelian Society* 56: 217–40.

Bentham, George. 1827. *Outline of a New System of Logic*. London: Hunt and Clarke.

Bocheński, I. M. n.d. *A History of Formal Logic*. 2nd edn. Trans. Ivor Thomas. New York: Chelsea.

Boole, George. [1847] 1952. *The Mathematical Analysis of Logic*. In Boole, *Studies in Logic and Probability*, 45–119. London: Watts.

Buickerood, James G. 1985. The Natural History of the Understanding: Locke and the Rise of Facultative Logic in the Eighteenth Century. *History and Philosophy of Logic* 6: 157–90.

Campbell, George. [1776] 1963. *The Philosophy of Rhetoric*. Ed. Lloyd F. Bitzer. Carbondale, Ill.: Southern Illinois University.

Coleridge, Samuel Taylor. 1981. *Logic*. Ed. J. R. de J. Jackson. *The Collected Works of Samuel Taylor Coleridge*, vol. xiii. Princeton: Princeton University Press.

Copleston, Edward. 1809. *The Examiner Examined*. Oxford: Printed for the Author.

Copleston, Edward. 1810a. *A Reply to the Calumnies of the Edinburgh Review Against Oxford, Containing an Account of Studies Pursued in That University*. Oxford: Printed for the Author.

Copleston, Edward. 1810b. *A Second Reply to the Edinburgh Review*. Oxford: Printed for the Author.

Corcoran, John. 1974. Aristotle's Natural Deduction System. In Corcoran (ed.), *Ancient Logic and Its Modern Interpretations*, 85–131. Dordrecht: Kluwer.

De Morgan, Augustus. [1847] 1926. *Formal Logic*. Ed. A. E. Taylor. London: Open Court. Citations to this edition use the pagination of the original edition.

De Morgan, Augustus. [1846–68] 1966. *On the Syllogism and Other Logical Writings*. Ed. Peter Heath. London: Routledge and Kegan Paul.

Duncan, William. 1748. *The Elements of Logic*. London: Printed for R. Dodsley.

Esser, Wilhelm. 1830. *System der Logik*. Münster: Theissingschen Buchhandlung.

Fogelin, Robert J. [1976] 1992a. Hamilton's Quantification of the Predicate. *Philosophical Quarterly* 26: 217–28. Repr. in Fogelin, *Philosophical Interpretations*, 149–65. New York: Oxford University Press.

Fogelin, Robert J. [1976] 1992b. Hamilton's Theory of Quantifying the Predicate—A Correction. *Philosophical Quarterly* 26: 352–3. Repr. in Fogelin, *Philosophical Interpretations*, 166–8. New York: Oxford University Press.

Fraser, Alexander Campbell. 1864. *Archbishop Whately and the Restoration of the Study of Logic*. London: Macmillan.

Green, V. H. H. 1986. Reformers and Reform in the University. In *The History of the University of Oxford*, v. *The Eighteenth Century*, ed. L. S. Sutherland and L. G. Mitchell, 607–37. Oxford: Clarendon Press.

Hamilton, William. 1846. Preparing for Publication. In *The Works of Thomas Reid*, ed. Sir William Hamilton, following 914, separately numbered 1–5. Edinburgh: MacLachlan and Stewart.

Hamilton, William. [1833] 1853a. Logic. In Reference to the Recent English Treatises on that Science. *Edinburgh Review* 56: 194–238. Repr. with additional notes in Hamilton, *Discussions on Philosophy and Literature, Education and University Reform*, 2nd edn., 120–73. London: Longman, Brown, Green and Longmans.

Hamilton, William. [1836] 1853b. On the Study of Mathematics, as an Exercise of Mind. In Hamilton, *Discussions on Philosophy and Literature, Education and University Reform*, 2nd edn., 257–312. London: Longman, Brown, Green and Longmans.

Hamilton, William. 1853c. Of Syllogism, Its Kinds, Canons, Notations, &c. In Hamilton, *Discussions on Philosophy and Literature, Education and University Reform*, 2nd edn., 646–71. London: Longman, Brown, Green and Longmans.

Hamilton, William. [1846] 1863. *The Works of Thomas Reid*, 6th edn., vol. ii. Ed. Sir William Hamilton. Edinburgh: MacLachlan and Stewart.

Hamilton, William. 1866a. *Lectures on Logic*, vol. i. 2nd edn., rev. edn. Ed. H. L. Mansel and John Veitch. Edinburgh: William Blackwood, 1866.

Hamilton, William. 1866b. *Lectures on Logic*, vol. ii. 2nd edn., rev. edn. Ed. H. L. Mansel and John Veitch. Edinburgh: William Blackwood, 1866.

Heath, Peter. 1966. Introduction. In Augustus De Morgan, *On the Syllogism and Other Logical Writings*, pp. vii–xxxi. London: Routledge and Kegan Paul.

Herlinus, Christianus and Conradus Dasypodius. 1566. *Analyseis Geometricae Sex Librorum Euclidis*. Strasbourg: Rihelius.

Howell, Wilbur Samuel. 1971. *Eighteenth Century British Logic and Rhetoric*. Princeton: Princeton University Press.

Kames, Henry Home, Lord Kames. 1778. *Sketches of the History of Man*, 2nd edn., vol. iii. Edinburgh: W. Creech.

Kett, Henry. 1809. *Logic Made Easy*. Oxford: Oxford University Press.

Kirwan, Richard. 1807. *Logick*. 2 vols. London: Payne and Mackinley.

Kneale, William, and Martha Kneale. [1962] 1984. *The Development of Logic*. Repr. with corrections. Oxford: Clarendon Press.

Krug, Wilhelm Traugott. 1806. *Denklehre oder Logik*. Königsberg: Goebbels und Unzer.

Locke, John. [1690] 1975. *An Essay concerning Human Understanding*. Ed. Peter H. Nidditch. Oxford: Clarendon Press.

Locke, John. [1693] 1989. *Some Thoughts Concerning Education*. Ed. John W. and Jean S. Yolton. Oxford: Clarendon Press.

Locke, John. [1706] 1996. *Of the Conduct of the Understanding*. In Locke, *Some Thoughts Concerning Education* and *Of the Conduct of the Understanding*, 163–227. Ed. Ruth W. Grant and Nathan Tarcov. Indianapolis: Hackett.

McOuat, Gordon R., and Charissa S. Varma. 2008. Bentham's Logic. In Dov M. Gabbay and John Woods (eds.), *Handbook of the History of Logic*, iv. *British Logic in the Nineteenth Century*, 1–32. Amsterdam: Elsevier.

Mansel, Henry Longueville. [1851] 1860. *Prolegomena Logica*, 2nd edn. Oxford: Henry Hammans.

Mansel, Henry Longueville. 1862. *Artis Logicae Rudimenta, from the Text of Aldrich with Notes and Marginal References*, 4th edn. Oxford: H. Hammans.

Mansel, Henry Longueville. [1851] 1873. Recent Extensions of Formal Logic. In Mansel, *Letters, Lectures and Reviews*, 37–76. Ed. Henry W. Chandler. London: John Murray.

Merrill, Daniel D. 1990. *Augustus De Morgan and the Logic of Relations*. Dordrecht: Kluwer.

Mill, John Stuart. [1828] 1978. Whately's Elements of Logic. In *Essays on Philosophy and the Classics*, 3–35. Ed. J. M. Robson. *The Collected Works of John Stuart Mill*, vol. xi. Toronto: Toronto University Press.

Mill, John Stuart. [1865] 1979. *An Examination of Sir William Hamilton's Philosophy*. Ed. J. M. Robson. *The Collected Works of John Stuart Mill*, vol. ix. Toronto: Toronto University Press.

Mueller, Ian. 1974. Greek Mathematics and Greek Logic. In John Corcoran (ed.), *Ancient Logic and Its Modern Interpretations*, 35–70. Dordrecht: D. Reidel.

Panteki, M. 1993. Thomas Solly (1816–1875): An Unknown Pioneer of the Mathematization of Logic in England, 1839. *History and Philosophy of Logic* 14: 133–69.

Playfair, Thomas. 1808. Review of P. S. La Place, *Traité de Méchanique Céleste*. *Edinburgh Review* 11: 249–84.

Reid, Thomas. [1778] 2004. *A Brief Account of Aristotle's Logic*. In *Thomas Reid on Logic, Rhetoric, and the Fine Arts*, 97–149. Ed. Alexander Broadie. University Park, Pa.: Pennsylvania State University Press.

Rothblatt, Sheldon. 1976. *Tradition and Change in English Liberal Education*. London: Faber and Faber.

Solly, Thomas. 1839. *A Syllabus of Logic*. Cambridge: J. & J. J. Deighton.

Sutherland, L. S. 1986. The Curriculum. In *The History of the University of Oxford*, v. *The Eighteenth Century*, ed. L. S. Sutherland and L. G. Mitchell, 469–91. Oxford: Clarendon Press.

Thomas, Ivor. 1964. Medieval Aftermath: Oxford Logic and Logicians of the Seventeenth Century. In *Oxford Studies Presented to Daniel Callus, Oxford Historical Society*, NS 16: 297–311. Oxford: Clarendon Press.

Thomson, William. [1842] 1860. *An Outline of the Necessary Laws of Thought*, 5th edn. London: Longman, Green, Longman, and Roberts. (The original title was *Outline of the Laws of Thought*.)

Van Evra, James W. 1992. Review of George Bentham, *Outline of a New System of Logic*. (Bristol: Thoemmes Antiquarian Books, 1990). *Modern Logic* 2: 405–9.

Van Evra, James W. 2008. Richard Whately and Logical Theory. In Dov M. Gabbay and John Woods (eds.), *Handbook of the History of Logic*, iv. *British Logic in the Nineteenth Century*, 75–91. Amsterdam: Elsevier.

Warlow, W. 1850. Quantification of the Predicate. In Miscellanea. *The Athenaeum*, 1208 (21 Dec), 1351.

Watts, Isaac. 1725. *Logick: Or, the Right Use of Reason in the Enquiry after Truth*. London: Printed for John Clark, Richard Hett, Emanuel Matthews, and Richard Ford.

Whately, Richard. [1819] 1859. *Historic Doubts Relative to Napoleon Buonaparte*, 13th edn. London: John W. Parker.

Whately, Richard. 1826. *Elements of Logic*. London: J. Mawman.

Whately, Richard. [1826] 1831. *Elements of Logic*. 4th edn. London: B. Fellowes.

Whately, Richard. [1826] 1834. *Elements of Logic*. 5th edn. London: B. Fellowes.

Whately, Richard. 1854. Reminiscences of Bishop Copleston. In *Remains of the Late Edward Copleston D.D., Bishop of Llandaff*, 1–96. London: J. W. Parker, 1854.

Whewell, William. 1835. *Thoughts on the Study of Mathematics as a Part of a Liberal Education*. Cambridge: J. and J. J. Deighton.

CHAPTER 3

....

MILL'S *SYSTEM OF LOGIC*

....

DAVID GODDEN

INTRODUCTION

....

JOHN STUART MILL'S (1806–73) *A System of Logic*, first published in 1843 and going through a total of eight editions over the next three decades, appeared at a pivotal juncture in the history of logic. Prior to the nineteenth century logic had suffered a great decline, coinciding with the scientific and metaphysical achievements of the Enlightenment. Generally it was felt that logic, whose methods and systems of proof had made no advancement since Aristotle's syllogism, was incapable of advancing knowledge. By contrast, by the time of the *Logic*'s eighth edition in 1872, it was well known that the syllogism was incapable of representing the truth-preserving structure of many valid arguments. Moreover, while the conception of logic as a formal calculus can be traced back to Leibniz (1646–1716), significant advancements in the techniques for formalizing logical structure occurred in the time of Mill's *Logic*.[1] Yet, the *Logic* was—and remained—uninfluenced by these developments, holding fast to the idea that the syllogism embodied the form of all valid reasoning. Indeed, as Scarre notes (1989, p. 1), Mill, in a letter to John Elliot Cairnes (5 December 1871), complained that his contemporaries Jevons, Boole, De Morgan, and Hamilton 'have a mania for encumbering questions with useless complications, and with a notation implying the existence of greater precision in the data than the questions admit of'. Rather than this 'mania', Mill preferred that 'scientific deductions should be made as simple and as easily intelligible

---

[1] George Bentham's (1800–84) *Outline of a New System of Logic* (1827) proposed quantifying the predicates of categorical statements as well as their subjects. DeMorgan's (1806–71) *Formal Logic* (1847) introduced a logic of relations, on which the copula of categorical statements is only one relation, and such that the validity of the *Barbara* syllogism, for example, is explained as a particular instance of the transitivity of a relation. Boole's (1815–64) *Mathematical Analysis of Logic* (1847) offered an algebraic formalization of syllogistic logic, which was developed in his *Laws of Thought* (1854). Finally, in removing many of the mathematical elements from the Boolean symbolism, Jevons's (1835–82) *Pure Logic* (1864) offered the logicist thesis that mathematics is logical in nature. Indeed 1879 would see the publication of Frege's (1848–1925) *Begriffschrift* which offered a fully articulated quantified predicate calculus.

For a developed discussion of these themes see Gray's 'Some British Logicians' (this volume). See also Thiel (1982), Peckhaus (1999), Simons (2003), and Gabbay and Woods (2004), to whom the preceding summary is indebted.

as they can be made without ceasing to be scientific' (*CW* xvii. 1862–3).[2] Thus, the significance of the *System of Logic* should not be sought in its contribution to logical techniques or systems. Instead, its significance is best sought in a meta-logical context.

One way to approach the project of Mill's *Logic* is to understand it as an exposition of an empiricist account of the nature, structure, and foundations of inferential knowledge. Here at least one of Mill's targets was the rationalistic view that some substantive truths can be known by reason alone, and that a priori knowledge is required if truths deemed necessary can be known at all. This view Mill identified as perhaps the single greatest source of error in the natural as well as the moral sciences.

> The notion that truths external to the mind may be known by intuition or consciousness, independently of observation and experience, is, I am persuaded, in these times, the great intellectual support of false doctrines and bad institutions. By the aid of this theory, every inveterate belief and every intense feeling, of which the origin is not remembered, is enabled to dispense with the obligation of justifying itself by reason, and is erected into its own all-sufficient voucher and justification. (*CW* i. 233)

As Mill describes in his *Autobiography*, the *Logic* offers a reply to such theories by providing a detailed account of those domains of knowledge, whether abstract or scientific, founded solely on empiricist principles.

> In attempting to clear up the real nature of the evidence of mathematical and physical truths, the *System of Logic* met the intuition philosophers on ground on which they had previously been deemed unassailable; and gave its own explanation, from experience and association, of that peculiar character of what are called necessary truths, which is adduced as proof that their evidence must come from a deeper source than experience. (*CW* i. 233)

A second way to contextualize the *Logic* is to situate it in the development of Mill's meta-logical theories concerning the nature, and the epistemic foundation and utility, of demonstrative reasoning. The problem which captured Mill's attention here is that deduction, if valid, must be non-ampliative and hence is seemingly incapable of advancing knowledge.

> It is universally allowed that a syllogism is vicious [i.e. invalid] if there be anything more in the conclusion than was assumed in the premises. But this is, in fact, to say that nothing ever was, or can be, proved by syllogism, which was not known, or assumed to be known, before. (*CW* vii. 183)

In the *Logic*, Mill took issue both with those who, in the face of this problem, inconsistently continued 'to represent the syllogism as the correct analysis of what the mind actually performs in discovering and proving the larger half of the truths, whether of science or daily life, which we believe', and again with those who, as a consequence of this view, were 'led to impute uselessness and frivolity to the syllogistic theory itself, on the ground of the *petitio principii* which they allege to be inherent in every syllogism' (*CW* vii. 183). Mill sought to resolve this dilemma by presenting a corrected account of the relationship between syllogistic and inductive reasoning.

---

[2] References to the Toronto edition of Mill's *Collected Works* (Mill 1963–91) will be given in the form *CW*, followed by volume and page numbers.

Epistemological and Metaphysical Background[3]

For Mill, 'Every consistent scheme of philosophy requires as its starting-point, a theory respecting the sources of human knowledge, and the objects which the human faculties are capable of taking cognizance of' (*CW* x. 125). Placing himself within the 'School of Experience', Mill's theories on these points are empiricist in their epistemology, and phenomenalist in their metaphysics (cf. McRae 1973, p. xxii).

Epistemically, he claimed, 'all knowledge consists of generalizations from experience.... There is no knowledge *a priori*; no truths cognizable by the mind's inward light, and grounded on intuitive evidence. Sensation, and the mind's consciousness of its own acts, are not only the exclusive sources, but the sole materials of our knowledge' (*CW* x. 125). This empiricism involves a standard internalist and foundationalist account of the structure of justification.

> Truths are known to us in two ways: some are known directly, and of themselves; some through the medium of other truths. The former are the subject of Intuition, or Consciousness; the latter, of Inference. The truths known by intuition are the original premises from which all others are inferred. Our assent to the conclusion being grounded on the truth of the premises, we could never arrive at any knowledge by reasoning, unless something could be known antecedently to all reasoning. (*CW* vii. 6–7)

While the *Logic* treats of inference and thereby of derived truths, the original premises of inference are items of which we are directly conscious. These, for Mill, are objects of pure consciousness (e.g. sensations), from which we must infer truths about the external world.

> [O]f the outward world, we know and can know absolutely nothing, except the sensations which we experience from it. (*CW* vii. 62)
>
> Of nature, or anything whatever external to ourselves, we know...nothing, except the facts which present themselves to our senses, and such other facts as may, by analogy, be inferred from these. (*CW* x. 125)

Mill's empiricist epistemology readily gives rise to a phenomenalist metaphysics. 'Existence, so far as Logic is concerned about it, has reference only to phenomena; to actual, or possible, states of external or internal consciousness in ourselves or others' (*CW* vii. 604). Yet, the existing world is not limited to the present contents of our collective consciousness. Unperceived things are also properly said to exist, though for Mill such claims assert only counterfactual conditionals to the effect that were we in the right circumstances we would have certain perceptual experiences. We must infer the existence of unperceived objects by linking their existence to some known (i.e. directly perceived) thing using an inductive law of succession of coexistence (*CW* vii. 605–6). Objects, then, are really 'permanent

---

[3] For an extended overview of these topics, see Skorupski (1994), Donner and Fumerton (2001), and Fumerton (2009), to whom the discussion offered here is indebted.

possibilities of sensation'. 'The existence, therefore, of a phenomenon, is but another word for its being perceived, or for the inferred possibility of perceiving it' (*CW* vii. 605).

> I believe that Calcutta exists, though I do not perceive it, and that it would still exist if every percip-
> ient inhabitant were suddenly to leave the place, or be struck dead. But when I analyse the belief,
> all I find in it is, that were these events to take place, the Permanent Possibility of Sensation which
> I call Calcutta would still remain; that if I were suddenly transported to the banks of the Hoogly,
> I should still have the sensations which, if now present, would lead me to affirm that Calcutta
> exists here and now. We may infer, therefore, that both philosophers and the world at large, when
> they think of matter, conceive it really as a Permanent Possibility of Sensation. (*CW* ix. 184)

In attempting to set the sciences, including putative a priori sciences, on this foundation, Mill provided an account of all knowledge as a posteriori. Only in this way, Mill felt, could one rightly understand the actual inferential structure of knowledge and the proper function of the syllogism. To appreciate this point and to place Mill's *Logic* in the theoretical context in which it was developed, it is best to begin with a review of some standard empiricist critiques of syllogistic inference, and of Whately's defence of the syllogism and its epistemic utility.

WHATELY AND THE REVIVAL OF LOGIC IN THE BRITISH TRADITION[4]

Up until the adoption of Whately's (1787–1863) *Elements of Logic* (1826), the standard logic text at Oxford was Aldrich's (1647–1710) *Artis Logicae Compendium* (1691). Beginning with Aristotle's definition of the syllogism as 'Discourse such that something being asserted, something necessarily follows from it' (*Prior Analytics* 24b18; *Topics* 100a25–7), Aldrich conceived of logic as the art of reasoning—a body of prescriptive rules designed to prevent indistinctness in apprehension, falsity in judgement, and inconclusiveness in discourse (or inference). At the time, such a conception was quite standard. For example, the *Port Royal Logic* (1662) characterized logic as the 'art of thinking', defining it as 'the art of conducting reason well in knowing things, as much to instruct ourselves about them as to instruct oth-ers' (Arnauld and Nicole 1996, p. 23).

Yet by the seventeenth century, this scholastic conception of syllogistic logic as the art of proper reasoning had fallen into disrepute from criticisms by Enlightenment human-ists. While it was acknowledged that reasoning could be represented (or, perhaps more accurately, reconstructed) syllogistically, the idea that Aristotelian logic could advance knowledge was rejected. If the conclusions of valid syllogisms follow necessarily from their premises, then those conclusions cannot assert anything beyond what is already stated in their premises. Hence, syllogistic validity seems only explained as a kind of *petitio principii*, and syllogistic reasoning is thereby entirely incapable of producing or justifying new knowl-edge. Thus in the *Advancement of Learning* (1605), Bacon (1561–1626) wrote:

---

[4] For an extended discussion of this topic, see James W. Allard's 'Early Nineteenth-Century Logic' (this volume). The discussion offered here is heavily indebted to Van Evra (1984), and George and Van Evra (2002).

> For as water ascends no higher than the level of the first spring, so knowledge derived from Aristotle will at most arise no higher again than the knowledge of Aristotle. And therefore, though a scholar must have faith in his master, yet a man well instructed must judge for himself. (1900, p. 20; cf. Van Evra 1984, p. 6)

While our knowledge without Aristotle might be comparatively dwarfed, to see further one must judge for oneself, and in order to judge for oneself one requires new means of judgement and inference.

More harshly, Locke (1632–1704), in the *Essay Concerning Human Understanding* (1690), ridiculed the idea that Aristotle's syllogism provides the only means for inferential knowledge.

> If syllogisms must be taken for the only proper instrument of reason and means of knowledge, it will follow, that before Aristotle there was not one man that did or could know any thing by reason, and that since the invention of syllogisms there is not one of ten thousand that doth.
>
> But God has not been so sparing to men to make them barely two-legged creatures, and left it to Aristotle to make them rational. (IV.xvii.4; 1975, p. 671)

Rather, according to Locke, syllogistic reasoning is only subsequent to knowledge, rather than advancing it into the territory of the unknown.

> A man knows first, and then his is able to prove syllogistically.…Syllogism, at best, is but the art of fencing with the little knowledge we have, without making any addition to it. (IV.xvii. 6; 1975, p. 679)[5]

In place of the syllogism, Locke recommended 'native rustic reason', or a common-sense employment of our common-sense reasoning abilities.

> [N]ative rustick reason…is likelier to open a way to, and add to the common stock of mankind, rather than any scholastic proceeding.…For beaten tracts lead these sort of cattle…whose thoughts reach only to imitation, *non quo eundum est, sed quo itur* [not where we ought to go, but where we have been]. (IV.xvii.6–7; 1975, pp. 679–80)

WHATELY'S *ELEMENTS OF LOGIC*

Whately's *Elements of Logic* (1827) sought to rehabilitate the study and practice of logic from the 'common-sense' theorists,[6] by challenging the idea at the centre of the Enlightenment

---

[5] Previously, Descartes (1596–1650) had drawn a similar conclusion, in his *Discourse on Method* (1637), finding that the syllogism does not contribute to learning or the advancement of knowledge by providing a theory of evidence, but rather by explaining what is already known.

> I observed with regard to logic that syllogisms and most of its other techniques are of less use for learning things than for explaining to others the things one already knows or even…for speaking without judgement about matters of which one is ignorant. (1985, p. 119; cf. Van Evra 1984, p. 7)

[6] In the Preface (pp. xii–xiv) to the edition of the *Elements* which appeared in the *Encyclopaedia Metropolitana* edition studied by Mill, Whately characterizes the common sense championed by the critics of logic as 'an exercise of the judgment unaided by any Art or system of rules; such as we must necessarily employ in numberless cases of daily occurrence' (as quoted in Mill, *CW* xi. 6).

critique that logic is merely *an* art of reasoning—that there are alternative, non-syllogistic ways of reasoning correctly. Rather, according to Whately, 'in every instance in which we *reason*…a certain process takes place in the mind, which is one and the same in all cases, provided it be correctly conducted' (1975, p. 18). This has important consequences for logic as a normative and theoretical discipline. Whately wrote:

> Logic has usually been considered by these objectors as professing to furnish a *peculiar* method of reasoning, instead of a method of analyzing that mental process which must *invariably* take place in all correct reasoning.…For Logic, which is, as it were, the Grammar of Reasoning, does not bring forward the regular Syllogism as a distinct mode of argumentation…but as the form to which *all* correct reasoning may be ultimately reduced; and which, consequently, serves the purpose (when we are employing Logic as an *art*) of a test to try the validity of any argument. (1975, pp. 11–12)

For Whately, just as it is a mistake to think that there can be intelligible but ungrammatical sentences, so is it a mistake to think that there can be correct but non-syllogistic inferences. In this way, logic is not merely the art of reasoning, but it is also the science on which the art is based. 'Logic,' begins the *Elements*, 'in the most extensive sense which the name can with propriety be made to bear, may be considered as the Science, and also the Art, of Reasoning.' As the art of reasoning logic 'investigates the principles on which argumentation is conducted, and furnishes the [practical] rules to secure the mind from error in its deductions', while as a science logic involves 'an analysis of the process of the mind in Reasoning' (1975, p. 1).[7,8]

---

[7] Two points here merit comment. First, Whately's definition of logic as the art and science of reasoning seems not to reject or emend a scholastic account, but rather to return to it. Consider St Thomas Aquinas's definition, offered in his commentaries on Aristotle's *Posterior Analytics*: 'Logic is the science and art which directs the act of the reason, by which a man in the exercise of his reason is enabled to proceed without error, confusion, or unnecessary difficulty' (quoted in Hebermann et al., 1913, p. 324). Secondly, in taking logic to be the art and science of reasoning, Whately accepted the then unquestioned view that reasoning is the subject matter of logic. As Hume (1711–76) had claimed in the *Treatise* (1739), 'the sole end of logic is to explain the principles and operations of our reasoning faculty and the nature of our ideas' (1978, p. xv). Problematically, such a view readily leads to psychologism (see section 'Psychologism in Mill').

[8] Competent reasoners need neither be (i) 'conscious of this process [by which reasoning proceeds] in his own mind', nor (ii) 'competent to explain the principles on which it proceeds' (1975, p. 18). Indeed, Whately agrees with Locke that people reasoned correctly before Aristotle described the valid forms of the syllogism. But this does not show that their reasoning was other than syllogistic, or that there are a variety of ways by which people may reason correctly. Rather, it shows that the practice of reasoning exists separately from the theory of it. For Whately, 'the practice [of correct reasoning] not only may exist independently of the theory, but *must* have preceded the theory' (1975, p. 18) since it is these processes which form the subject matter of the theory (i.e, the science of logic) itself. So, as McKerrow (Whately, 1975, p. viii) observes, by Whately's account Aristotle did not *invent* the syllogism, he merely discovered the principles of syllogistic reasoning and expressed them in the form of rules.

Indeed, for Whately there is a single principle on which all reasoning is based: Aristotle's *dictum de omni et nullo*.

> All reasoning whatever, then, rests on the one simple principle laid down by Aristotle, that 'what is predicated, either affirmatively or negatively, of a term distributed, may be predicated in a like manner (i.e. affirmatively or negatively) of anything contained under that term'. (1975, p. 45; cf. pp. 31 ff.)

Whately on Induction

Crucially then, Whately rejected induction as a legitimate form of reasoning. 'Induction', he observed (1975, p. 208 ff.) ambiguously indicates two distinct activities: (i) the process of inquiry of collecting facts so as to obtain or evaluate premises for reasoning, and (ii) the process of inferring conclusions from those facts. Yet, as a process of inference, Whately claimed, induction is always an enthymematic deduction—a syllogism with the major premise suppressed—and thus not a uniquely legitimate form of reasoning. On the other hand, as a process of information acquisition, induction is not a form or reasoning at all, and thus not within the domain of logic. Rather, Whately (1975, p. 211) called this process *investigation*, and described it as the '*Inductive process*; which is that by which we gain, properly, *new truths*, and which is not connected with Logic'. While investigation has epistemic functions such as knowledge acquisition and premise evaluation, it is not a part of logic.

Whately on the Province of Logic

Whately responded to the criticism that logic can make no contribution to the advancement of knowledge by considering the province of reasoning (1975, pp. 205 ff.). Logic is the study of reasoning as it applies to all subject matters, but it is not the task of logic to provide us with information concerning any particular subject matter. Thus logic is concerned with validity only (whether the conclusion *follows fairly from* the premises), not soundness (which includes whether the premises are *fairly laid down*) (1975, p. 210).

Whately admitted that there is such a thing as 'logical discovery', whereby the mind becomes aware, through the process of demonstration, of knowledge to which it was previously entitled (being justified by knowledge consciously held), but of which it had not been explicitly aware prior to demonstration. Whately illustrated logical discovery by comparing it to a man discovering a vein of metal ore, of which he was previously unaware, running through his land. According to Whately, while the man already possessed the mineral deposits since they always belonged to him, for practical purposes they are new possessions to him since prior to his discovery of them he could make no use of them (1975, pp. 224–5). In this way, logic does indeed advance our knowledge, though it is incapable of discovering new truths which is the province of investigation not reasoning.

MILL'S EARLY WORK ON LOGIC AND RECEPTION OF WHATELY

Mill's Early Readings in Logic

Not only did Whately's *Elements* provide the basis for Mill's first published work on logic, but it also inspired his *System of Logic* and informed many of its basic views. Mill's logical upbringing, as with all his early education, occurred at the direction and frequently at the hands of his father. At the age of 12, Mill tells us in his *Autobiography*, his father had him read Aristotle's *Organon*, as well as several seventeenth-century scholastic logic texts, and Hobbes's 'Computatio sive Logica'. These texts became the subject of extended and intensive discussion during their walks together, where, Mill tells us,

> It was his [father's] invariable practice, whatever studies he exacted from me, to make me as far as possible understand and feel the utility of them: and this he deemed peculiarly fitting in the case of the syllogistic logic, the usefulness of which had been impugned by so many writers of authority. (*CW* i. 21)

Of his resulting 'early [and] practical familiarity with the school logic', Mill reflected, 'I know of nothing, in my education, to which I think myself more indebted for whatever capacity of thinking I have attained' (*CW* i. 23).

In 1825 Mill joined the 'Society for Students of Mental Philosophy' whose meetings involved the careful reading and thorough, open discussion of a variety of systematic treatises on a wide range of topics. In 1827 they turned to scholastic logic.

> Our first text book was Aldrich, but being disgusted with its superficiality, we reprinted one of the most finished among the many manuals of the school logic, which my father, a great collector of such books, possessed, the *Manuductto ad Logicam* of the Jesuit Du Trieu. After finishing this, we took up Whately's *Logic*, then first republished from the *Encyclopaedia Metropolitana*, and finally the 'Computatio sive Logica' of Hobbes. These books, dealt with in our manner, afforded a wide range for original metaphysical speculation: and most of what has been done in the First Book of my *System of Logic*, to rationalize and correct the principles and distinctions of the school logicians, and to improve the theory of the Import of Propositions, had its origin in these discussions... From this time I formed the project of writing a book on Logic, though on a much humbler scale than the one I ultimately executed. (*CW* i. 125)

Mill's Review of Whately's *Elements*

Mill's first published work on logic was an extensive review of the *Elements* appearing in the *Westminster Review* in 1828. Although it took issue with Whately on several significant points—including Whately's realist and essentialist account of classification and definition, which conflicted with Mill's own nominalism (*CW* xi. 20 ff.)—Mill's review is generally flattering. To begin, Mill found that Whately's 'vindication of the utility of logic is conclusive: his explanation of its distinguishing character and peculiar objects, of the purposes to which it is and is not applicable, and the mode of its application, leave scarcely anything to be desired' (*CW* xi. 3–4).

Crucially, in 1828 Mill accepted many of Whately's central views. Principal among these was Mill's acceptance of the view that logic is the art and science of reasoning. Additionally, Mill accepted that all reasoning is properly syllogistic. Consequently, induction is not a form of reasoning at all.

> Syllogistic reasoning is not a *kind* of reasoning, for *all* correct reasoning is syllogistic: and to *reason by induction* is a recommendation which implies as thorough a misconception of the meaning of the two words, as if the advice were, to *observe by syllogism*. (*CW* xi. 15)

Hence the rules of the syllogism provide correct norms for all reasoning. Mill further accepted the *dictum de omni et nullo* as the universal principle of all reasoning (*CW* xi. 17).

And, in response to those who advocated the common-sense method of rational analysis and evaluation, Mill replied:

> When all is done which has here been supposed [by the common-sense theorist], the argument is actually reduced to a series of syllogisms: so that the all-sufficiency of common-sense amounts only to this, that, if the man of common-sense *makes use of the same means* which logic supplies, he may attain the same end. (*CW* xi. 10)[9,10]

Yet, despite his sympathies for Whately's project and perspective, Mill was deeply puzzled about how logic could be informative. He found it a paradox as yet unexplained on philosophical principles

> that mankind may correctly apprehend and fully assent to a general proposition, yet remain for ages ignorant of myriads of truths which are embodied in it, and which, in fact, are but so many particular cases of that which, as a general truth, they have long known. (*CW* xi. 34)

Even in 1828, Mill seemed unconvinced by Whately's explanation of logic's informativeness as 'logical discovery': an account which assigns to logic a merely cognitive—rather than a properly epistemic—function.

THE *SYSTEM OF LOGIC*

The Great Paradox

It was not until the early 1830s, when he (*CW* i. 189) returned to the 'great paradox of the discovery of new truths by general reasoning', that Mill came to feel that Whately had explained away, rather than explained, the epistemic function of logic. While agreeing that 'all reasoning was resolvable into syllogisms', Mill further noted that 'in every syllogism the

---

[9] This reply echoes Whately's observation that 'each [man] gives the preference to unassisted Common-Sense only in those cases where he himself has nothing else to trust to, and invariably resorts to the rules of art wherever he possesses the knowledge of them' (quoted in Mill, *CW* xi. 7).

[10] Similarly, while Mill recognized that syllogistic analysis will not aid in the evaluation of arguments whose faults lie in their premises (*CW* xi. 30–1), he found that syllogistic analysis seems to render many of the formal fallacies transparently invalid. '[W]hat higher compliment can be paid to the doctrine of the syllogism', he wrote (*CW* xi. 11), 'than to say that the same fallacy, in the form of a syllogism, deceives nobody, which [quoting Dugald Stewart's (1753–1828) *Elements of the Philosophy of the Human Mind* (1792/1827)] "may deceive half the world if *diluted* in a quarto volume." '

conclusion is actually contained and implied in the premises'. The paradox involves not only the logical problem of how conclusions, being contained in their premises, could express any new content or truth, but also the cognitive mystery of how 'the theorems of geometry, so different to all appearance from, the definitions and axioms, could be all contained in these [definitions and axioms]' (*CW* i. 189).

It was in rereading Dugald Stewart's (1753–1828) *Elements of the Philosophy of the Human Mind* (vol. ii, 1814) that Mill found the catalyst for his resolution of this 'great paradox'. There, as Mill tells us in his *Autobiography*,

> I came upon an idea of his [Stewart's] respecting the use of axioms in ratiocination, which I did not remember to have before noticed, but which now, in meditating on it, seemed to me not only true of axioms, but of all general propositions whatever, and to be the key of the whole perplexity. From this germ grew the theory of the Syllogism propounded in the second Book of the *Logic*; which I immediately fixed by writing it out. (*CW* i. 189–91)

While Mill does not reveal what specific idea in Stewart inspired his treatment of ratiocination in the *Logic*, we might surmise that it was Stewart's views about the probative role of general axioms in demonstrative reasoning.

> It was long ago remarked by Locke, of the axioms of geometry, as stated by Euclid, that although the proposition be at first enunciated in *general* terms, and afterwards appealed to, in its *particular* applications, as a principle *previously* examined and admitted, yet that the truth is not less evident in the latter case than in the former. He observes farther, that it is in some of its particular applications, that the truth of every axiom is originally perceived by the mind, and, therefore, that the general proposition, so far from being the *ground* of our assent to the truths which it comprehends, is only a verbal generalization of what, in particular instances, has already been acknowledged as true. (Stewart 1821, p. 23 [vol. ii, ch. i, §1])

Accepting this picture effectively reverses the epistemic priority of general claims and the particular claims which are deduced from them. The growth of knowledge occurs not in the ratiocinative process of deriving theorems from axioms, but rather in establishing the axioms (i.e. general premises and principles of ratiocination) themselves. And this, consistently with Mill's empiricism, can only happen through experience of the particulars. Stewart wrote:

> [I]n all our reasonings about the established order of the universe, experience is our sole guide, and knowledge is to be acquired only by ascending from particulars to generals; whereas the syllogism leads us invariably from universals to particulars, the truth of which instead of being a *consequence* of the universal proposition, is *implied* and *presupposed* in the very terms of its enunciation. The syllogistic art, therefore, it has been justly concluded, can be of no use in extending our knowledge of nature. (Stewart 1821, p. 154 [vol. ii, ch. iii, §2])

These ideas bear a remarkable resemblance to key elements of the theory of the syllogism found in Mill's *Logic*, and stand in stark contrast to the picture Mill accepted from Whately in 1828. Although the *Logic* retains Whately's general definition of logic as the art and science of reasoning, its views on the foundation and utility of, and relationship between, ratiocination and induction are dramatically changed. Siding with Stewart rather than Whately, the *Logic* explains the epistemic foundation of syllogistic reasoning as irreducibly based on the cogent induction of general premises, and the function of the syllogism as evaluative, rather than representative or epistemic.

Real Versus Apparent Inference

To understand Mill's theory of ratiocination in the *Logic*, it is best to begin with his distinctions between real and apparent inference and real versus verbal propositions. For Mill, the requirement that logic be capable of advancing knowledge is a demand that logic should have an epistemic function—it must contain real inferences 'in which we set out from known truths, to arrive at others really distinct from them' (*CW* vii. 162). Real inferences, for Mill, are ampliative—their conclusions assert more information than what is contained in their premises.

By contrast, an apparent inference 'occurs when the proposition ostensibly inferred from another, appears on analysis to be merely a repetition of the same, or part of the same, assertion, which was contained in the first' (*CW* vii. 158).

> In all these cases there is not really any inference; there is in the conclusion no new truth, nothing but what was already asserted in the premises, and obvious to whoever apprehends them. The fact asserted in the conclusion is either the very same fact, or part of the fact, asserted in the original proposition. (*CW* vii. 160)

Corresponding to the distinction between real and apparent inference is Mill's distinction between real and verbal propositions—a distinction which Mill takes to correspond to Kant's distinction between synthetic and analytic judgements (*CW* vii. 116 fn.). Verbal propositions 'in which the predicate is of the essence of the subject (that is, in which the predicate connotes the whole or part of what the subject connotes, but nothing besides) answer no purpose but that of unfolding the whole or some part of the meaning of the name, to those who did not previously know it' (*CW* vii. 113). Technically, verbal propositions are not truth-apt: they are 'not, strictly speaking, susceptible of truth or falsity, but only of conformity or disconformity to usage or convention; and all the proof they are capable of, is proof of usage' (*CW* vii. 109). Real propositions, by contrast,

> predicate of a thing some fact not involved in the signification of the name by which the proposition speaks of it; some attribute not connoted by the name. Such are...all general or particular propositions in which the predicate connotes any attribute not connoted by the subject. All these, if true, add to our knowledge: they convey information, not already involved in the names employed. (*CW* vii. 115–16)

The upshot of this picture is that the sciences, including putatively a priori sciences such as logic and mathematics, must contain real propositions if they are to be at all informative or true. Furthermore, if they are capable of advancing knowledge, they must involve real, rather than merely apparent, inferences whose conclusions are real propositions. Yet deduction, whose validity is explained in terms of its monotinicity, is clearly a case of merely apparent inference. Thus, if knowledge can be advanced through inference not only must the role of deduction be reconceived, but there must be another kind of inference capable of doing the required epistemic lifting.

MILL'S ACCOUNT OF RATIOCINATIVE LOGIC

Ratiocination, for Mill, is 'all reasoning by which, from general propositions previously admitted, other propositions equally or less general are inferred' (*CW* vii. 166).

Mill held, albeit mistakenly, that all valid ratiocination can be represented syllogistically, and that by a series of merely verbal transformations of the propositions comprising them, any syllogism can be represented in the first figure. Indeed, Mill claimed that all valid syllogisms can ultimately be represented as one of the following four: affirmative syllogisms as either *Barbara* or *Darii*, and negative syllogisms as either *Clarent* or *Ferio* (*CW* vii. 168; see Table 3.1).

Mill on the Fundamental Principle of Ratiocination

By the time of the *Logic* Mill had abandoned the Whatelian *dictum de omni et nullo* as the fundamental principle of the syllogism, rejecting both realist (Platonist) and conceptualist (conventionalist) accounts of it. On a realist view (whereby universals are substances or real, abstract entities), the *dictum* is a real proposition—a 'fundamental law of the universe' expressing the 'intercommunity of nature' (*CW* vii. 174). Yet accepting that universals are not the objects of our experience, they are not real, and such a view is thus inconsistent with Mill's empiricism. By contrast, on a nominalist account (whereby universals are nothing more than collections of particular objects), consistent with his own empiricism, the *dictum* 'merely amounts to the identical [i.e. verbal] proposition, that whatever is true of certain objects, is true of each of those objects' (*CW* vii. 175). It thus becomes not an axiom but a definition explaining 'in a circuitous and paraphrastic manner, the meaning of the word *class*' (*CW* vii. 175).

For Mill, since ratiocination is a mode of acquiring real knowledge, ratiocinative reasoning must be comprised of real, and not merely verbal, propositions. The terms of a syllogism's major premise are connotative names, denoting objects and connoting attributes. Thus the premise asserts of the two attributes connoted that they either always or never coexist together (*CW* vii. 177).

As such, Mill held the fundamental principle of ratiocination is the transitivity of coexistence. The validity of affirmative syllogisms is based on the principle that 'things which

Table 3.1 The four forms of valid syllogism

Affirmative			Negative		
Every B is C			No B is C		
All A	}	is B,	All A	}	is B,
Some A			Some A		
therefore,			therefore,		
All A	}	is C.	No A is	}	C.
Some A			Some A is not		

coexist with the same thing, coexist with one another' while valid negative syllogisms are underwritten by the principle that 'a thing which coexists with another thing, with which other a third thing does not coexist, is not coexistent with that third thing' (*CW* vii. 178). Importantly for Mill, these principles are real and have the character of universally true laws of nature.

> These axioms manifestly relate to facts, and not to conventions; and one or the other of them is the ground of the legitimacy of every argument in which facts and not conventions are the matter treated of. (*CW* vii. 178)

Resolving the Great Paradox

While it is Mill's position, then, that valid ratiocination both involves, and relies upon, real propositions, the question remains as to whether ratiocination constitutes real inference or whether it is merely apparent. While Mill granted as 'irrefragable' the view that 'no reasoning from general to particulars can ... prove anything: since from a general principle we cannot infer any particulars, but those which the principle itself assumes as known' (*CW* vii. 184), he rejected both the common-sense theorist's conclusion that syllogistic reasoning is therefore useless or frivolous and Whately's view that the syllogism is 'the correct analysis of what the mind actually performs in discovering or proving [the majority of our beliefs]' (*CW* vii. 183). Here, indeed, Mill finally rejected Whately's explanation of the epistemic function of ratiocination as 'logical discovery' whereby entire sciences like geometry 'can be "wrapt up" in a few definitions and axioms' (*CW* vii. 185).

The key to Mill's resolution, as inspired by Stewart, is found in his explanation of the epistemic foundation of general propositions, and hence of the epistemic status of a syllogism's major premise. Mill thought that the only view consistent with his own empiricism is that we come to know generalities through knowing their particulars: 'all experience begins with individual cases, and proceeds from them to generals' (*CW* vii. 163). When discussing the justification of the major premise in a syllogism, Mill wrote:

> [W]hence do we derive our knowledge of that general truth? Of course from observation. Now, all which man can observe are individual cases. From these all general truths must be drawn, and into these they may again be resolved; for a general truth is but an aggregate of particular truths; a comprehensive expression, by which an indefinite number of individual facts are affirmed or denied at once. (*CW* vii. 186)

This view embraces Stewart's point that, while the truth of a particular proposition may, logically speaking, be a consequence of the truth of a general proposition which encompasses it, it is not an epistemic consequence. Rather, epistemically speaking, the truth of the particular is presupposed in the assertion of the general and hence must be known prior to it.[11]

---

[11] To object, even empiricists should grant that general claims may be known by means other than through knowing each particular instance, as for example one might come to know general truths by testimony or authority and thereby legitimately infer to the particulars.

Because general truths are not known prior to the particulars they encompass, they are not justification-conferring in ratiocination. Instead, Mill characterized general claims as 'registers of inferences already made'. Because of this, ratiocination is not a form of real inference and by itself it is incapable of advancing knowledge even in Whately's cognitive sense of 'logical discovery'. Rather, ratiocination is itself dependent on another kind of inference whereby the truth of its major premises—indeed all general truths—are known: namely, induction. And, it is only in this sense that ratiocination is a mode of acquiring real knowledge.

> All inference is from particulars to particulars: General propositions are merely registers of such inferences already made, and short formulae for making more: The major premise of a syllogism, consequently, is a formula of this description: and the conclusion is not an inference drawn *from* the formula, but an inference drawn *according to* the formula: the real logical antecedent, or premise, being the particular facts from which the general proposition was collected by induction. (*CW* vii. 193)

And thus Mill resolved the great paradox. In doing so, he accepted Stewart's view that general truths do not, properly speaking, supply any epistemic grounds in ratiocination. Rather, general truths supply formulae in accordance with which we may reason. But the proper grounds for such reasoning are to be found in the particular truths already known and presupposed by general claims. Furthermore, the epistemic validity and utility of ratiocination depends on the validity of induction through which knowledge of general claims is achieved.

The Proper Function of the Syllogism

In concluding that ratiocination does not confer justification but instead depends on induction for its epistemic foundation and utility, Mill also abandoned the Whatelian view that the syllogism analyses 'that mental process which must invariably take place in all correct reasoning' (1975, pp. 11–12). Indeed, the syllogism does not correctly represent inference at all.

> [T]hough there is always a process of reasoning or inference where a syllogism is used, the syllogism is not a correct analysis of that process of reasoning or inference; which is, on the contrary, (when not a mere inference from testimony) an inference from particulars to particulars. (*CW* vii. 196)

Rather, 'the syllogism is not the form in which we necessarily reason, but a test of reasoning: a form into which we may translate any reasoning, with the effect of exposing all the points at which any unwarranted inference can have got in' (*CW* ix. 390).

> The value, therefore, of the syllogistic form, and of the rules for using it correctly, does not consist in their being the form and the rules according to which our reasonings are necessarily, or even usually, made; but in their furnishing us with a mode in which those reasonings may always be represented, and which is admirably calculated, if they are inconclusive, to bring their inconclusiveness to light. An induction from particulars to generals, followed by a syllogistic process from those generals to other particulars, is a form in which we may always state our reasonings if we please. It is not a form in which we *must* reason, but it is a form in which we *may* reason, and into which it is indispensable to throw our reasoning, when there is any doubt of its validity. (*CW* vii. 198)

MILL ON INDUCTION

For Mill, then, induction is the very core of logic. Induction 'consists in inferring from some individual instances in which a phenomenon is observed to occur, that it occurs in all instances…which *resemble* the former, in…the material circumstances' (*CW* vii. 306). In being 'a process of inference…[that] proceeds from the known to the unknown' (*CW* vii. 288), induction is the sole form of real inference. Clearly, this is a far cry from Mill's view of 1828 that induction is an entirely illegitimate form of reasoning, as misconceived as 'observation by syllogism'. Quite the opposite: 'What Induction is…and what conditions render it legitimate, cannot but be deemed the main question of the science of logic—the question which includes all others' (*CW* vii. 283).

Given this agenda, Mill's treatment of induction is, perhaps, disappointing. It is frequently observed, for example, that Mill failed to recognize, let alone address, the sceptical problems of induction (Skorupski 1994, p. 100; Scarre 1998, p. 116).[12] Instead, Mill seems to have simply taken it for granted that induction is a cogent and justification-conferring, albeit defeasible, form of inference, when rightly conducted.

> Assuredly, if induction by simple enumeration were an invalid process, no process grounded on it would be valid; just as no reliance could be placed on telescopes, if we could not trust our eyes. But though a valid process, it is a fallible one, and fallible in very different degrees: if therefore we can substitute for the more fallible forms of the process, an operation grounded on the same process in a less fallible form, we shall have effected a very material improvement. And this is what scientific induction does. (*CW* vii. 567–8)

The Ground of Induction

Since induction provides the only proper epistemic grounds for ratiocination, a central task for Mill's *Logic* is to articulate some adequate account of the ground of the cogency of inductive inference. Unsurprisingly, Mill found the uniformity principle [UP]—'that the course of nature is uniform; that the universe is governed by general laws'—to be 'our warrant for all inferences from experience' and 'the fundamental principle, or general axiom, of induction' (*CW* vii. 306–7). For Mill, our acceptance of this 'universal fact' is justifiable experientially and inductively.[13]

> And, if we consult the actual course of nature, we find that the assumption is warranted. The universe, so far as known to us, is so constituted, that whatever is true in any one case is true in all cases of a certain description; the only difficulty is, to find what description. (*CW* vii. 306)

---

[12] Scarre (1998, p. 117) excuses this, claiming that the problems of induction were not well known in Mill's time. 'But the fact is that there was nowhere a lively interest in this sceptical problem of induction before the Green and Grose edition of Hume's work in 1874—and by that date Mill was dead.'

[13] On this point, Scarre (1998, p. 117) justifiably complains: 'Characteristically, he [Mill] also held that it is experience which *justifies* the belief in uniformity, and thus unwittingly exposed himself to the objection that he was proposing an inductive justification of the very principle which he takes to warrant our inductive practice.'

Yet, despite being the warrant licensing all inductive inference, UP is 'itself an instance of induction': it is a general truth whose justification is reached inductively. Indeed, Mill tells us, it is one of the one of the last inductions we naturally make, and one which is 'founded on' many lesser, but prior, generalizations.

> We should never have thought of affirming that all phenomena take place according to general laws, if we had not first arrived, in the case of a great multitude of phenomena, at some knowledge of the laws themselves; which could be done no otherwise than by induction. (*CW* vii. 307)

Thus, although UP is the 'ultimate major premise of all induction', it is the source of cogency in any particular inductive inference only in the same sense that the major (i.e. universal) premise of any syllogism establishes its conclusion: 'not contributing at all to prove it, but being a necessary condition of its being proved' (*CW* vii. 308).

Moreover, the rigorously articulated and analysed form of induction employed in science and studied by logicians is parasitic on a kind of 'spontaneous' induction performed naturally by all human beings.

> Many of the uniformities existing among phenomena are so constant, and so open to observation, as to force themselves upon involuntary recognition. Some facts are so perpetually and familiarly accompanied by certain others, that mankind learnt, as children learn, to expect the one where they found the other, … It will appear, I think, … that there is no logical fallacy in this mode of proceeding; but we may see already that any other mode is rigorously impractical: since it is impossible to frame any scientific method of induction, or test of the correctness of inductions, unless on the hypothesis that some inductions deserving of reliance have already been made. (*CW* vii. 318–19)

In the final analysis, then, Mill seems to have embraced a naïve naturalism about the primitive cogency of induction. Although an inferential, rather than a basic, mode of knowledge, induction is nevertheless a primitive or basic *source* of justification. Rather than to discover and articulate any deeper justificatory foundation of induction than induction itself, the proper task of the logician is to supply a set of criteria or tests which can be used to distinguish good from bad inductive inferences.

> Why is a single instance, in some cases, sufficient for a complete induction, while in others, myriads of concurring instances, without a single exception known or presumed, go such a very little way towards establishing an universal proposition? Whoever can answer this question knows more of the philosophy of logic than the wisest of the ancients, and has solved the problem of induction. (*CW* vii. 314)

Laws of Causation as Principles of Induction

The answer to this question, Mill felt, is to be found in the laws of causation. The uniformity of nature occurs along axes of simultaneity and succession, and the law describing nature's successive uniformity Mill called the Law of Universal Causation: 'The truth that every fact which has a beginning has a cause, is coextensive with human experience' (*CW* vii. 325).

Yet, Mill recognized that nature's uniformity was neither simple nor uniform. Rather, 'what is called the uniform course of nature, is, that it is itself a complex fact, compounded of all the separate uniformities which exist in respect to single phenomena' (*CW* vii. 315). Thus, the task of the logician is to discover those particular uniformities which obtain in nature, and to ascertain those conditions which give rise to the occurrence of some one of them rather than to any of the others. It is only by knowing these individual causes, and the laws which govern them, that the logician will ever be able to distinguish those cases in which a single instance is sufficient for a complete induction—because the causal law instantiated is known—from those where myriads of concurring instances go nowhere to establishing a universal proposition—because whatever causal laws are at work are unknown. Knowledge of the laws of causation, then, is the only solution to the problem of induction, according to Mill. Thus the principal task of the inductive logician is no different from that of the natural scientist—to ascertain and articulate those causal laws of the universe.

Mill's Methods

Yet, causes, insofar as we ordinarily experience them, are complex and indistinct. To the end of identifying those aspects of our experience which possess genuine causal efficacy, Mill offered a series of Baconian methods of experimental inquiry, or canons of induction (*CW* vii. 389 ff.). The *method of agreement* seeks to identify operative causes by varying antecedent conditions so as to isolate exactly those conditions which are common to (i.e. agree with) all cases in which the phenomenon in question (i.e. effect) obtains. The process is one of elimination since 'Whatever circumstance can be excluded, without prejudice to the phenomenon, or can be absent notwithstanding its presence, is not connected with it in the way of causation' (*CW* vii. 390). The *method of difference* proceeds by holding antecedent conditions constant save for some single feature, while seeking variety (i.e. difference) in the obtaining of the effect. Here, those invariant antecedent conditions are eliminated as causally ineffectual, while the cause is isolated using the principle that 'Whatever antecedent condition cannot be excluded without preventing the phenomenon, is the cause, or a condition, of that phenomenon' (*CW* vii. 391). These first two methods can be combined in the *joint method of agreement and difference*, which Mill identified as his third canon. The final two methods rely on the results of previous inductions. In the *method of residues*, known chains of cause and effect are used to explain certain features of a complex event, leaving a residue to be explained. This residue serves to isolate a set of (remaining) antecedent conditions which are supposed to be the causes of the (remaining) effects. Finally there is the *method of concomitant variations*, which relies on the principle that correlation is a sign of causation. When two phenomena co-vary, either one is the cause of the other or they share some common cause.

Mill Versus Whewell on Induction[14]

One of the most significant debates to arise out of Mill's *Logic* was his debate with William Whewell (1794–1866) concerning the nature and methods of induction. Mill's progress on the *Logic* had stalled for several years following his resolution of the 'great paradox'. Having

---

[14] For a detailed discussion of Whewell's philosophy of science, see Ducheyne's contribution of that title (this volume). For a detailed discussion of the Mill–Whewell debate, see Ducasse (1951), Strong (1955), Snyder (1997), and Forster (2009), to whom, as well as Scarre (1998), the discussion offered here is indebted.

placed induction at the centre of logic, and the discovery of the laws of causation at the centre of induction, Mill felt that he required a better understanding of scientific methodology and examples of its practice. One place Mill found this was in Whewell's newly published *History of the Inductive Sciences* (vol. i, 1837) (*CW* i. 215). In the preface to the first edition of the *Logic*, Mill tells us that 'without the aid derived from the facts and ideas contained in … [the *History*], the corresponding portion of this work would probably not have been written' (*CW* vol. vii, p. cxiii). Further, while Mill was rewriting the *Logic* prior to its first publication, Whewell's *Philosophy of the Inductive Sciences* (vol. i, 1840) appeared, providing Mill with a representative of 'the German, or *a priori* view of human knowledge, and of the knowing faculties' (*CW* i. 231–3; cf. Scarre 1998, p. 115) against which he could present his own empiricist views. As Passmore later observed, 'Whewell's existence saved Mill the trouble of inventing him' (1957, p. 18; cf. Snyder 1997, p. 161).

Holding a chair in moral philosophy at Cambridge (indeed, soon to become master of Trinity College), and being a pre-eminent historian of science, Whewell presented a formidable opponent for Mill. As Reverend Sydney Smith (1771–1845) once remarked of Whewell, 'Science is his forte; omniscience his foible' (quoted in Scarre 1998, p. 115). Whewell's reply to Mill's criticisms, *Of Induction, with especial reference to Mr. J. Stuart Mill's System of Logic*, appeared in 1849, to which Mill responded with some extensive revisions to the third edition to his *Logic* in 1851. The discussion offered here will identify two points of their debate: first, Whewell's criticism of Mill's experimental methods, and second on Whewell's view that induction involves the *colligation* of facts.

Mill and Whewell agreed that the experimental techniques of the sciences, being best suited for discovering the laws of nature, provide the best available paradigms for inductive methods. Yet, Whewell criticized Mill's canons claiming that they did not accurately describe the experimental procedures actually employed in science (McRae 1973, p. xlvi).

> Who will tell us which of the methods of inquiry those historically real and successful inquiries exemplify? Who will carry these formulae through the history of the sciences, as they have really grown up; and show us that these four methods have been operative in their formation; or that any light is thrown upon the steps of their progress by reference to these formulae? (Whewell 1860, pp. 263–4; as quoted by Mill, *CW* vii. 430)

Because of this, Mill took Whewell to claim that the canons are not a vehicle of discovery or advancement of knowledge.

Mill's strategy in responding to these criticisms echoes Whately's response to the 'common-sense' criticism that syllogistic inference does not represent the actual practices of ordinary reasoners. Firstly, just as the practice of ratiocination is, as Whately claimed, separate from, and prior to, the theory of the syllogism, so, Mill claimed, are experimental practices separate from and prior to the theory (i.e. canons) of induction. Secondly, theory is related to practice not descriptively, but normatively. The canons do not seek to represent the activity of inquiry, but rather to articulate a set of rules to which the practice must accord if it is to succeed. Contrary to Whately, though, these rules do not describe a procedure which must be followed, but instead supply a set of conditions in terms of which inductive practices can be reconstructed in evaluation.

> The business of inductive logic is to provide rules and models (such as the syllogism and its rules are for ratiocination) to which if inductive arguments conform, those arguments are

conclusive, and not otherwise. This is what the four methods profess to be, and what I believe they are universally considered to be by experimental philosophers, who had practised all of them long before any one sought to reduce the practice to theory.... In saying that no discoveries were ever made by the four methods, he [i.e. Whewell] affirms that none were ever made by observation and experiment; for assuredly if any were, it was by processes reducible to one or other of those methods. (*CW* vii. 430–1)

The second point of contention between Mill and Whewell divides their philosophies more deeply. To whatever extent canons of induction are sufficient to reveal the secret machinery of nature, Mill steadfastly held that laws thereby discovered are not only universal, 'coextensive with the entire field of successive phenomena' (*CW* vii. 325), but also objective, holding 'independently of all considerations respecting the ultimate mode of production of phenomena, and of every other question regarding the nature of "things in themselves"' (*CW* vii. 327). For Mill, the nature's regularities are 'out there' and that is where we find them.

While Mill and Whewell agreed as to the nature of induction, they disagreed as to how it is achieved. Specifically, they disagreed about what, if anything, is contributed by the mind itself in the inductive process beyond what is found 'out there' among the phenomena.

For Whewell, all knowledge involves a combination of facts and ideas, and as such the mind actively supplies essential components to knowledge. In induction this involves something Whewell called the *colligation* of facts—or the bringing together of particular facts under some general conception which unites them. Importantly, this general conception, necessary for every induction, is not in the phenomena, or facts, themselves; rather it is supplied by the mind.[15]

> The particular facts are not merely brought together, but there is a new element added to the combination by the very act of thought by which they are combined. There is a Conception of the mind introduced in the general proposition, which did not exist in any of the observed facts.... The facts are known, but they are insulated and unconnected, till the discoverer supplies from his own store a principle of connexion. The pearls are there, but they will not hang together till someone provides the string. (Whewell 1858, pp. 72–3)

In induction, the colligatory step is followed by a generalizing step in which the colligated property is projected over the entire class of phenomena including the unobserved instances. This generalizing step permits predictions which can be tested in future observations to confirm the hypothesis (Snyder 1997, pp. 170 ff.).

Of Whewell's colligation, Mill tells us that he 'would gladly transfer all that portion of [Whewell's] book into [his] own pages' (*CW* vii. 294) except that it does not belong to the process of induction, properly understood. Rather, for Mill, colligation has a cognitive function in the description of facts—where facts may be organized, perhaps fictitiously, according to many different unifying principles—but not an epistemic function in their

---

[15] Snyder (1997, pp. 173 ff.) distinguishes a special kind of induction, discovery (or 'discoverer's induction') where the uniting principle is not already apparent, and claims that it is only in discovery that the colligating principle must be newly supplied by the mind. Technically this is correct, since the generalizing principle might already be known. But, for Whewell this knowledge could have only been the result of some previous colligation—in other words, the generalizing conception is already known because it has previously been supplied by the mind.

explanation or prediction—whose success depends on the truth of the principles being applied, in other words, their actually being 'out there'.

> A conception implies, and corresponds to, something conceived: and though the conception itself is not in the facts, but in our mind, yet if it is to convey any knowledge relating to them, it must be a conception *of* something which really is in the facts, some property which they actually possess, and which they would manifest to our senses, if our senses were able to take cognizance of it. (*CW* vii. 295)

Because induction, for Mill, properly applies only to explanation and prediction, Whewell's colligation plays no role in it (*CW* vii. 299). Specifically, the principles relied on in induction are not supplied by the mind, but rather are found 'out there' among the phenomena.

> No one ever disputed that in order to reason about anything we must have a conception of it; or that when we include a multitude of things under a general expression, there is implied in the expression a conception of something common to those things. But it by no means follows that the conception is necessarily pre-existent, or constructed by the mind out of its own materials. If the facts are rightly classed under the conception, it is because there is in the facts themselves something of which the conception is itself a copy; and which if we cannot directly perceive, it is because of the limited power of our organs, and not because the thing itself is not there. (*CW* vii. 296)

MILL ON THE SCIENCE OF NUMBER

In view of Mill's empiricism and his position that induction provides the epistemic foundation for ratiocination, his account of putatively a priori sciences merits attention, as it remains a site of controversy.

Mill considered the laws of mathematics (arithmetic, algebra, and geometry) to be real, rather than verbal, propositions, comprising the most general laws of nature, specifically concerning the relation of resemblance among phenomena (*CW* vii. 607). Number terms are connotative names, denoting physical phenomena (collections or aggregates of things) and connoting some physical property of those phenomena, specifically the 'characteristic manner in which the agglomeration is made up of, and may be separated into, parts' (*CW* vii. 610–11). Because of this, Mill, in a passage that echoes Whately,[16] claimed

> All numbers must be numbers of something: there are no such things as numbers in the abstract. *Ten* must mean ten bodies, or ten sounds, or ten beatings of the pulse. But though numbers must be numbers of something, they may be numbers of anything. Propositions, therefore, concerning numbers, have the remarkable peculiarity that they are propositions concerning all things whatever; all objects, all existences of every kind, known to our experience. (*CW* vii. 254–5)

---

[16] Whately (1975, pp. 13–14), writes: 'All numbers … must be numbers of some things, whether coins, persons, measures or anything else; but to introduce into the science [of arithmetic] any notice of the things respecting which calculations are made, would be evidently irrelevant, and would destroy its scientific character: we proceed therefore with arbitrary signs representing numbers in the abstract.'

As such, Mill held that physical facts are asserted in the definitions of number terms.

> Two, for instance, denotes all pairs of things, and twelve all dozens of things, connoting what makes them pairs, or dozens; and that which makes them so is something physical; since it cannot be denied that two apples are physically distinguishable from three apples, two horses from one horse, and so forth: that they are a different visible and tangible phenomenon. (*CW* vii. 610)

Importantly, because number terms denote physical phenomena, Mill thought that all mathematical inference requires the additional *hypothesis* of identity—in other words, that *things* behave like *units*—'that 1=1; that all numbers are numbers of the same or equal units' even though Mill concedes that this is never, in fact, true (*CW* vii. 258, 259).

Mathematical propositions are thus real, not verbal, and assert empirical claims about the physical world. An arithmetical proposition, for example, 'affirms that a certain aggregate might have been formed by putting together certain other aggregates, or by withdrawing certain portions of some aggregate; and that, by consequence, we might reproduce those aggregates from it, by reversing the process' (*CW* vii. 611).

Arithmetic operates as though it were a deductive science because of the universal generality of its basic axioms. According to Mill, these are only two: the transitivity of identity (*CW* vii. 610) and the addition and subtraction postulates (*CW* vii. 258). The remaining basic mathematical truths, he claims, derive from these by *reductio* (*CW* vii. 258). Like particular arithmetical truths, these basic axioms are real propositions, known by induction. For example, in considering the epistemic ground for the axiom *the sum of equals are equals* (which he considered equivalent to the metaphysical principle *Whatever is made up of parts, is made up of the parts of those parts*), Mill wrote:

> This truth, obvious to the senses in all cases which can be fairly referred to their decision, and so general as to be coextensive with nature itself, being true of all sorts of phenomena, (for all admit of being numbered,) must be considered an inductive truth, or law of nature, of the highest order. And every arithmetical operation is an application of this law, or of other laws capable of being deduced from it. This is our warrant for all calculations. (*CW* vii. 613)

Similarly, Mill claimed, 'Every theorem in geometry is a law of external nature, and might have been ascertained by generalizing from observation and experiment' (*CW* vii. 616).

Because of this, mathematics involves real inferences: 'there is in every step of an arithmetical or algebraical calculation a real induction, a real inference of facts from facts; and that what disguises the induction is simply its comprehensive nature, and the consequent extreme generality of the language' (*CW* vii. 254).

While this empirical view that mathematical truths have the same status and foundation of laws of nature has the disquieting consequence that mathematical truths are only justifiable, and are therefore refutable, a posteriori, Kitcher (1998) notes that it confers the significant benefit of explaining what he calls the 'mathematical structure of reality'. Nature behaves arithmetically because arithmetic describes 'permanent possibilities of rearrangement' (1998, p. 69).

Psychologism in Mill[17]

That Mill held both logic and mathematics to be synthetic and a posteriori is beyond dispute. By contrast, Mill scholarship remains divided on the point of whether his account is psychologistic. Minimally, psychologistic accounts of some domain assert that the truths of that (ostensibly non-psychological) domain are dependent upon, if not completely determined by, facts about human psychology. One recognizable version of psychologism holds that logical laws are a subset of psychological laws, and thus that the foundation of logic is ineliminably psychological. Such a position might result from the metaphysical view that reasoning and inference are psychological processes, and that in studying them the subject matter of logic is itself psychological.

In accepting Whately's definition of logic as the art and science of reasoning, and in understanding reasoning as a mental process (*CW* vii. 4), Mill seems committed to the psychologistic view that the subject matter of logic is psychological in nature. 'Logic', Mill tells us, '…is the science of the operations of the understanding which are subservient to the estimation of evidence: both the process itself of advancing from known truths to unknown, and all other intellectual operations in so far as auxiliary to this' (*CW* vii. 12). Yet, while its subject matter is psychological, logic as an art has a prescriptive, rather than a descriptive, relationship to mental processes. 'Logic is not the science of belief, but the science of proof, or evidence. Insofar as belief professes to be founded on proof, the office of logic is to supply a test for ascertaining whether or not the belief is well grounded' (*CW* vii. 9).

Perhaps then, the prescriptive norms of logic do not depend on psychology. Yet, instead Mill seems to hold that the art of reasoning is grounded in the science of it. For Mill, the art of logic provides 'the rules, grounded on that analysis [of the mental process which takes place whenever we reason] for conducting the process correctly' (*CW* vii. 4). Indeed, in the *Examination* (1865/1867) Mill writes that the science of reasoning is required for the *justification* of logical rules:

> I conceive it to be true that logic is not the theory of thought as thought, but of valid thought; not of thinking, but of correct thinking. It is not a science distinct from, and coordinate with, psychology. So far as it is a science at all, it is a part, or branch, of psychology; differing from it, on the one hand as a part differs from the whole, and on the other, as an art differs from a science. Its theoretic grounds are wholly borrowed from psychology, and include as much of that science as is required to justify the rules of the art. (*CW* ix. 359)

For example, Mill describes the principle of non-contradiction as being founded on the introspective observations concerning psychological facts.

> I consider it to be, like other axioms, one of the first and most familiar generalizations from experience. The original foundation of it I take to be, that belief and disbelief are two different mental states, excluding one another. (*CW* vii. 277)

---

[17] For survey of psychologism in nineteenth-century logic see Brockhaus (1991) and Kusch (1995). For an extended discussion of psychologism in Mill, see Godden (2005).

It would seem, then, that, even when understood as the science of proof or evidence, psychological facts have a role not only in describing the subject matter of logic, but in formulating, grounding, and justifying logical norms and principles.

Frege's Arguments Against Mill's Psychologism

Regardless of whether we now find Mill's account to be psychologistic or merely empiricist, a seminal criticism of this account, due to Gottlob Frege (1848–1925), identifies it as psychologistic. Frege specifically addressed Mill's account of number in his 1884 *Grundlagen* (*Foundations of Arithmetic*, 1980), and later in his 1894 review of Edmund Husserl's *Philosophy of Arithmetic* (1972).

Some of the concerns motivating Frege's attack apply even if Mill's account is only empiricist. Even this would have the unpalatable consequence that arithmetical truths would be knowable only a posteriori and their justification would necessarily involve contingent, physical facts. Yet Frege also found that Mill's account makes the truths of arithmetic dependent upon psychological facts such as perception and abstraction.

While Frege recognized that simple arithmetical theorems (e.g. 7+5=12) and laws (e.g., the associativity of addition) are 'amply established by the countless applications made of them every day' (1980, p. 2), his logicist position claims that such observations play no part in the demonstration of such laws and truths, which are instead established by definitions and derivation from logical truths.[18] Similarly, definitions of arithmetical terms do not involve reference to facts—numbers are *not* numbers *of things*, but are instead concepts.

Frege's criticisms of Mill's 'gingerbread or pebble arithmetic' (1980, p. vii) are frequently caustic and dismissive. He accused Mill of holding a 'naïve' conception of number, according to which numbers are either aggregates of things, or properties of aggregates.

> The most naïve opinion is that according to which a number is something like a heap, a swarm in which the things are contained lock, stock and barrel. Next comes the conception of a number as a property of a heap, aggregate, or whatever else one might call it. Thereby one feels the need for cleansing the objects of their particularities. The present attempt belongs to those which undertake this cleansing in the psychological washtub. (1972, p. 323)

Each naïve opinion, according to Frege, yields incoherencies and false consequences, as well as confuses the origin of a concept in the mind with its meaning (1980, p. vii) and the application of a proposition or concept with its meaning (1980, p. 13).

Naïve conceptions of number are wrecked on the three reefs, Frege claimed: (i) the identity and distinguishability of numerical units, (ii) the numbers zero and one, and (iii) large numbers (1972, p. 330). Though the second and third reefs lie downstream of the first, it is convenient to start with them. The general problem is that no observed facts or entities (whether psychological or physical) seem to correspond to numbers or arithmetical truths. Frege asserted that 'no one...has ever seen or touched o pebbles' (1980, p. 11), and

---

[18] As Goldfarb writes 'Clearly, we would not be able to arrive at correct mathematical arguments if our inkblots were constantly to change. Yet that does not imply that mathematics presupposes the physical laws of inkblots, that those laws would figure in the justifications of mathematical laws' (2001, p. 34).

he wonders '[what observed or physical fact] is asserted in the definition of the number 777864' (1980, p. 9). Worse still, 'If numbers are presentations, then the limited nature of our powers of presentation must also carry along with it a limitation of the domain of numbers' (1972, p. 334). As to the thesis that the truths of addition are contingent on the way objects combine, Frege chastised: 'What a mercy, then, that not everything in the world is nailed down; for if it were we should not be able to bring off this separation, and 2 + 1 would not be 3' (1972, p. 334). Frege further rejected Mill's contention that the identity 1 = 1 could be false 'on the ground that one pound weight does not always weigh precisely the same as another'; consequently, whatever the truth-makers for propositions like '1 = 1' are, they are not (combinations of) things in the world (1980, p. 13).

The primary wrecking-point of naïve conceptions of number, Frege claimed, is their failure to comprehend identity and difference. This failure yields a convoluted account of numerical units, and hence of the number one and indeed any individual number. In trying to comprehend a naïve justification of the truth '1 + 1 + 1 = 3', Frege wrote:

> If we try to produce the number [three] by putting together distinct objects, the result is an agglomeration in which the objects contained remain still in possession of precisely those properties which serve to distinguish them from one another; and that is not the number. But if we try to do it the other way, by putting together identicals, the result runs perpetually together into one and we never reach a plurality. (1980, p. 50)

Psychological logicians attempt to overcome this difficulty by employing the mind to abstract away the properties of concrete objects which distinguish them. Yet, Frege held, such an attempt not only makes the truths of arithmetic dependent on the success of cognitive operations, it entirely fails to solve the problem since the partially abstracted particulars will remain either distinguishable (and hence not like numerical units) or identical (and hence not combinable) (1972, p. 325 ff.).[19] 'Inattention', Frege ridiculed, '... [has become] an exceedingly effective logical power; whence, presumably, the absentmindedness of scholars' (1972, p. 324).

Despite these differences, Frege and Mill shared what Goldfarb (2001, p. 28) has called a *universalist conception* of logic, whereby logical laws are universal truths (cf. Skorupski 1998a, p. 44). For Mill, logical truths have the same scope and justification as laws of nature, while for Frege their scope is much broader and their justification categorically different.

---

[19] See Kessler (1980) for an argument which draws upon contemporary, formalized mereology to show that Frege's criticisms can be overcome in a way consistent with Mill's basic empiricism. Roughly on Kessler's model, rather than conceive of a number as a property of an aggregate, 'a number is to be understood as a special sort of relation which holds between aggregates and properties that pick out parts of those aggregates' (p. 69).

Sympathetically, Kitcher (1998, pp. 64 ff.) contends that treating numbers as mereological sums rather than as abstract properties is not only consistent with Mill's nominalism and his view that 'attributions of number to agglomerations always carry with them some way in which the agglomeration is supposed to be divided up into parts' (cf. *CW* vii. 610), but that it also avoids Frege's central criticism that naturalized accounts of number fail to comprehend the identity and difference of numerical units.

For Frege, the laws of logic are the laws of Thought—'laws of the laws of nature'—which hold between judgements some of which express the laws of nature (1980, p. 99).

CONCLUSION

Importantly, just as developments in logical techniques within and following the time of Mill's *Logic* rendered its account of the structure of deduction antiquated, a similar fate affected its empiricist meta-logic and account of the deductive sciences. As Goldfarb (2001, pp. 26 ff.) describes, the universalist conception of logic shared by Mill and Frege was replaced with the contemporary, Tarski-Quine schematic conception. On the schematic conception, logic is not about the world—neither the world of concrete particulars nor the world of abstract universals. Rather, 'the subject matter of logic consists of logical properties of sentences and logical relations among sentences' (Goldfarb 2001, p. 26). Logic, on this conception, is a properly formal science. Its formuale are schemata, or logical forms, which are representations of the structural (e.g. truth-functional, quantificational, relational) composition of sentences using logical signs. Schemata are not about anything; they have no semantic content and hence are neither true nor false. When interpreted, the elements of the schemata are supplied with a subject matter, or semantic content; interpreted formulae thereby receive a truth-value. '[O]ne schema *implies* another, that is, the second schema is a *logical consequence* of the first, if and only if every interpretation that makes the first schema true also makes the second true' (Goldfarb 2001, p. 26). Although Mill never conceived of logic as a purely formal science, it would likely not have been satisfactory to him, since he required that logic contain both real propositions and real inferences if it was to be capable of advancing knowledge.

In summary, this chapter has offered an overview of Mill's *System of Logic* (1843/72) by situating its development in the context of some of the meta-logical themes and disputes characteristic of the nineteenth century as well as his empiricism. Mill's early views on the nature and utility of syllogistic reasoning were significantly shaped by Whately's (1827) *Elements of Logic*. While aspects of the *Elements* remain in the *Logic*, Mill came to hold that not only must induction be a genuine form of inference but indeed that 'all [real] inference is from particulars to particulars'. Having been inspired by Stewart, Mill concluded that the only account of the foundation ratiocination consistent with his own empiricism and capable of solving the 'great paradox' of the informativeness of deduction was that ratiocination depends on the cogency of induction, since all general claims, including the major premises of all syllogisms, are 'registers of inferences already made'. The proper task of the inductive logician is no different than that of the natural scientist, namely the discovery of the true causal laws of the universe. These, contrary to Whewell, are properly understood to be found 'out there', among the phenomena, and are not supplied by the mind through colligation. Only through the knowledge of causes can one know which inferences from the particular and known to the general and unknown are legitimate because the relation in question rightly instantiates some causal law. This empiricist approach to the epistemic foundations of logic led Mill to offer a naturalized account of putatively a priori disciplines such as the science of number, which in turn attracted Frege's criticisms of the *Logic* as psychologistic.

REFERENCES

Arnauld, A., and Nicole, P., [1662] 1996, *Logic, or the Art of Thinking*, 5th edn. [1863], ed. and trans. J. V. Buroker, Cambridge: Cambridge UP.

Bacon, F., 1900, *Advancement of Learning* [1605] *and Novum Organum* [1620], New York: Colonial Press.

Brockhaus, R., 1991, 'Realism and Psychologism in 19th Century Logic', *Philosophy and Phenomenological Research*, 51: 493–524.

Descartes, R., [1637] 1985, *Discourse on Method*, in *The Philosophical Writings of Descartes*, vol. i, trans. J. Cottingham, R. Stoothoff, and D. Murdoch, Cambridge: Cambridge UP.

Donner, W., and Fumerton, R., 2001, 'John Stuart Mill', in S. M. Emmanuel (ed.), *The Blackwell Guide to Modern Philosophers: From Descartes to Nietzsche*, Oxford: Blackwell, pp. 343–69.

Ducasse, C. T. 1951, 'Whewell's Philosophy of Scientific Discovery I & II', *Philosophical Review*, 60/1: 56–69, 60/2: 213–34.

Forster, M. 2009, 'The Debate between Whewell and Mill on the Nature of Scientific Induction', in D. M. Gabbay, S. Hartmann, and J. Woods (eds.), *Handbook of the History of Logic*, x. *Inductive Logic*, Amsterdam: North Holland (Elsevier), pp. 93–115.

Frege, G., [1884] 1980, *The Foundations of Arithmetic*, trans. J. L. Austin, 2nd edn., Evanston, Ill.: Northwestern UP.

Frege, G., [1894] 1972, 'Review of Dr. E. Husserl's *Philosophy of Arithmetic*', trans. E. W. Kluge, *Mind*, 81: 321–37.

Fumerton, R., 2009, 'Mill's Logic, Metaphysics and Epistemology', in W. Donner and R. Fumerton, *Mill*, Oxford: Wiley-Blackwell, pt. 2, pp. 145–95.

Gabbay, D. M., and Woods, J. (eds.), 2004, *Handbook of the History of Logic*, iii. *The Rise of Modern Logic: From Leibniz to Frege*, Amsterdam: North Holland (Elsevier).

George, R., and Van Evra, J., 2002, 'The Rise of Modern Logic', in D. Jacquette (ed.), *A Companion to Philosophical Logic*, Oxford: Blackwell, pp. 35–48.

Godden, D., 2005, 'Psychologism in the Logic of John Stuart Mill: Mill on the Subject Matter and Foundations of Logic', *History and Philosophy of Logic*, 26: 115–43.

Goldfarb, W., 2001, 'Frege's Conception of Logic', in J. Floyd and S. Shieh (eds.), *Future Pasts: The Analytic Tradition in Twentieth-Century Philosophy*, Oxford: Oxford UP, pp. 25–41.

Hebermann, C. G., Pace, E. A., Pallen, C. B., Shanan, T. J., and Wynne, J. W. (eds.), 1913, *The Catholic Encyclopedia*, vol. ix, New York: Encyclopedia Press Inc.

Hume, D., [1739] 1978. *A Treatise of Human Nature*, 2nd edn., ed. L. A. Shelby-Bigge, Oxford: Clarendon Press.

Kessler, G., 1980, 'Frege, Mill, and the Foundations of Arithmetic', *Journal of Philosophy*, 77: 65–79.

Kitcher, P., 1998, 'Mill, Mathematics, and the Naturalist Tradition', in Skorupski (1998b), pp. 57–111.

Kusch, M., 1995, *Psychologism: A Case Study in the Sociology of Philosophical Knowledge*, New York: Routledge.

Locke, J., [1690] 1975, *An Essay Concerning Human Understanding*, ed. P. H. Nidditch, Oxford: Clarendon Press.

McRae, R. F., 1973, 'Introduction', in J. M. Robson (ed.), *The Collected Works of John Stuart Mill*, vii. *A System of Logic Ratiocinative and Inductive: Being a Connected View of the Principles of Evidence and the Methods of Scientific Investigation, Books 1–3*, Toronto: University of Toronto Press and London: Routledge and Kegan Paul, pp. xxi–xlviii.

Mill, J. S., 1963–91, *The Collected Works of John Stuart Mill (CW)*, 33 vols., ed. J. M. Robson, Toronto: University of Toronto Press.

Passmore, J., 1957, *A Hundred Years of Philosophy*, London: Gerald Duckworth & Co.

Peckhaus, V., 1999, '19th Century Logic between Philosophy and Mathematics', *Bulletin of Symbolic Logic*, 5: 433–50.

Scarre, G., 1989, *Logic and Reality in the Philosophy of John Stuart Mill*, London: Kluwer Academic Publishers.

Scarre, G., 1998, 'Mill on Induction and Scientific Method', in Skorupski (1998b), pp. 112–38.

Simons, P., 2003, 'Logic: Revival and Reform', in T. Baldwin (ed.), *The Cambridge History of Philosophy 1970–1945*, Cambridge: Cambridge University Press, pp. 119–27.

Skorupski, J., 1989, *John Stuart Mill*, London: Routledge.

Skorupski, J., 1994, 'J. S. Mill, Logic and Metaphysics', in C. L. Ten (ed.), *The Nineteenth Century: Routledge History of Philosophy*, vii, New York: Routledge, pp. 98–121.

Skorupski, J., 1998a, 'Mill on Language and Logic', in Skorupski (1998b), pp. 35–56.

Skorupski, J. (ed.), 1998b, *The Cambridge Companion to Mill*, Cambridge: Cambridge University Press.

Snyder, L., 1997, 'The Mill–Whewell Debate: Much Ado about Induction', *Perspectives on Science*, 5: 159–98.

Stewart, D., 1821, *Elements of the Philosophy of the Human Mind*, vol. ii, Boston: Wells & Lilly.

Strong, E. W., 1955, 'William Whewell and John Stuart Mill: Their Controversy about Scientific Knowledge', *Journal of the History of Ideas*, 16: 209–31.

Thiel, C., 1982, 'From Leibniz to Frege: Mathematical Logic Between 1679 and 1879', *Studies in Logic and the Foundations of Mathematics*, 104: 755–70.

Van Evra, J., 1984, 'Richard Whately and the Rise of Modern Logic', *History and Philosophy of Logic*, 5: 1–18.

Whately, R., [1827] 1975, *Elements of Logic*, 2nd edn., introd. R. W. McKerrow, Delmar, NY: Scholar's Facsimiles & Reprints.

Whewell, W., 1858, *Novum Organon Renovatum (Being the Second Part of the Philosophy of the Inductive Sciences)*, 3rd edn., London: John W. Parker & Son.

Whewell W., [1860] 1971, *On the Philosophy of Discovery: Chapters Historical and Critical*, facs. edn., New York: Burt Franklin.

CHAPTER 4

WHEWELL'S PHILOSOPHY OF SCIENCE[1]

STEFFEN DUCHEYNE

INTRODUCTION

BEYOND any doubt, William Whewell (1794–1866), the Master at Trinity College, Cambridge, was one of the protagonists in the Victorian debate on science and its methods (Snyder 2011).[2] He was so because he developed a systematic and original position on the nature, development, and methodology of science by reforming Baconian inductivism (Snyder 1999; 2006, chs. 1 and 3).[3] The Victorian debate on 'defining science' did not occur in a void: science was debated 'in a framework that included values—religious, moral, and political' (Yeo 1993, p. 5).[4] It is therefore not at all surprising that Whewell conceived of his

[1] The author is indebted to William J. Mander and Laura J. Snyder for their comments and suggestions. The author is also grateful to the Master and Fellows of Trinity College, Cambridge for their permission to quote from the Whewell Papers and especially to Jonathan Smith, chief librarian at Wren Library, and his staff for their kind assistance during my research stay in Cambridge. In this chapter I occasionally draw upon material from Ducheyne 2009a, 2010a, 2010b, and 2011.

[2] For some basic biographical information on Whewell, see Cannon 1964; Robson and Cannon 1984; and Yeo 2009. For an overview of Whewell's intellectual activities, see Becher 1991 and Ruse 1991. On Whewell and natural theology, see Brooke 1977 and 1991; Ruse 1977; and Yeo 1979. On Whewell and mathematics, see Becher 1981 and Williams 1991. On Whewell and economy, see Henderson 1996. On the Mill–Whewell debate, see Snyder 1997a and 2006, and Buchdahl 1991. On Whewell's own reservations against J. S. Mill's inductive logic, see *PD*, pp. 238–91.

[3] Whewell called Bacon 'the supreme Legislator of the modern Republic of Science' (*PD*, p. 126). However, Bacon 'could only divine how sciences might be constructed; we can trace, in their history, how their construction has taken place' (*NOR*, p. iii).

[4] With respect to the rapport which Whewell envisioned between philosophy of science and theology, it might be pointed out that in his *Bridgewater Treatise* (1833) he argued that induction, contrary to deduction, is conducive to the belief in a deity (*CW* ix. 332–3) and that in *On the Philosophy of Discovery* (1860) he had provided a 'theological deduction' of the Fundamental Ideas (*PD*, pp. 354–75, esp. 363); Ducheyne 2009a, pp. 339–44, 353–6). Whewell's theological deduction of the Fundamental Ideas not only served the purpose of ontologically justifying them (Butts 1965a, pp. 177–9), it also paved the way

philosophical views on scientific method as instrumental in renovating society, politics, and morality (Snyder 2006, pp. 4, 8).

In order to establish 'a new method of pursuing the philosophy of human knowledge', Whewell turned to '*a connected and systematic survey of the whole range of Physical Science and its History*', in other words, the 'most certain and stable' portion of knowledge which we have obtained over the centuries (*PIS* i. 7–8). He undertook this survey in his two major works, the *History of the Inductive Sciences* (3 vols., 1837, 1847, 1857) and *The Philosophy of the Inductive Sciences* (2 vols., 1840, 1847). According to Whewell, these two works are closely interconnected, as they 'resulted simultaneously from the same examination of the principal writers on science in all ages, and may serve to supplement each other' (*HIS* i. 16).[5] In line with what he wrote on the construction of science, Whewell presented his *Philosophy* as inductively obtained from the History of Science. For Whewell the task of the Philosophy of Science was twofold:

> THE PHILOSOPHY OF SCIENCE [. . .] would imply nothing less than a complete insight *into the essence and conditions of all real knowledge*,[6] and an *exposition of the best methods for the discovery of new truths.* We must narrow and lower this conception, in order to mould it into a form in which we may make it the immediate object of our labours with good hope of success; yet still it may be a rational and useful undertaking, to endeavour to make some advance towards such a Philosophy, even according to the most ample conception of it which we can form. (*PIS* i. 1 [italics added])

He carried out these two tasks in the first and second volume of the *Philosophy* respectively. The second volume of his *Philosophy* was later published as two separated works: *Novum Organum Renovatum* (1858), which focused on Whewell's own views on scientific method, and *On the Philosophy of Discovery* (1860), which was based on Book XII of the *Philosophy*, 'Review of Opinions on the Nature of Knowledge, and the Method of Seeking it', but contained several additions.[7] The Philosophy of Science which he developed had to meet two

for establishing that *scientific progress* went hand in hand with man's *spiritual progress*, essentially because man's scientific ideas were those according to which God had created and continued to contemplate the natural world (Yeo 1979; Belsey 1974). In this context, Cantor has rightly stressed that 'for Whewell progress was not a purely secular concept; instead progress in our knowledge of the physical world was analogous to moral progress and strengthened our conviction in the latter' (Cantor 1991, p. 82). Additionally, Whewell recorded that 'No philosophy of science can be complete which is not also a philosophy of the universe; and no philosophy of the universe can satisfy thoughtful men, which does not include a reference to the power by which the universe came to be what it is' (*PD*, p. 354). With respect to the induction of causes, he pointed out that in '*contemplating the series of Causes which are themselves the effects or other causes, we are necessarily led to assume a Supreme Cause*' (*NOR*, p. 247, cf. pp. 251–6).

⁵ In a letter to Richard Jones on 6 October 1834, Whewell wrote: 'I write at the same time two Books, one of history, and one of philosophy, and when I find myself, in the course of my historical researches, becoming metaphysical and transcendental, I open *Book two*, in which all these things fall into their places' (*CW* xvi. 193).

⁶ In the context of this fragment, 'real knowledge' refers to empirical knowledge obtained by scientific inquiry.

⁷ When discussing Whewell's methodology, I shall rely on *Novum Organum Renovatum*. I shall omit further discussion of the final book of *Novum Organon Renovatum* which concerns the language of science and the construction of clear and well-defined technical terms (*NOR*, pp. 257–370). The significance of this aspect of Whewell's Philosophy of Science was motivated by his conviction that

important desiderata, which Whewell himself had imposed: it needed to show, first of all, *that science establishes necessary truths*, an idea which, as we will see, he had borrowed from Kant, and, secondly, *that progress in science is possible*, an insight which he had derived from his studies of the development of science.

WHEWELL ON IDEAS IN SCIENCE

In this section I shall focus on how Whewell tackled the first task he had set on the agenda for the Philosophy of Science, in other words, *getting a grasp on the nature and conditions of scientific knowledge*. The quintessence of the position which he developed in order to accomplish this task consisted in a specific epistemological stance, which he dubbed the 'Fundamental Antithesis of Philosophy'—which in fact is '*an antithesis of inseparable elements*' (*PIS* ii. 651).[8] Given its centrality in Whewell's thought more generally and given its repercussions for his Philosophy of Science more particularly, I shall start by explaining Whewell's famous antithesis and its corollaries.[9] 'The simplest and most idiomatic expression of the antithesis to which I refer', Whewell wrote, 'is that in which we oppose to each other THINGS and THOUGHTS.' In clarifying his position, he added: 'Our Thoughts are something which belongs to ourselves; something which takes place within us; they are what *we* think; they are actions of our minds. Things, on the contrary, are something different from ourselves and independent of us; something which is without us; they *are*; we see them, touch them, and thus we know that they exist; but we do not make them by seeing or touching them, as we make our *Thoughts* by thinking them; we are passive, and *Things* act upon our organs of perception' (*PIS* i. 17). 'In all cases,' Whewell continued, 'Knowledge implies a combination of Thoughts and Things. Without this combination, it would not be Knowledge. Without Thoughts, there could be no connexion; without Things, there could be no reality. Thoughts and Things are so intimately combined in our Knowledge, that we do not look upon them as distinct. One single act of the mind involves both; and their contrast disappears in their union' (*PIS* i. 18, cf. 54).[10] This antithesis of thoughts and things '*makes objective reality a corrective of our subjective imperfections in the pursuit of knowledge*' (*PIS* ii. 667). Correspondingly, the progress of science consists in the establishment of ideas which are better attuned to the relevant facts than previous ones.

As a corollary to his antithesis, Whewell came to accept that both theories and facts are closely interwoven and required for the establishment of knowledge: 'in Theory the Ideas

---

technical terms 'record' discoveries (*HIS* i. 8): 'only the persons who succeed in making great alterations in the language of science, are not those who make names arbitrarily and as an exercise of ingenuity, but those who have much new knowledge to communicate; so that the vehicle is commended to general reception by the value of what it contains' (*NOR*, p. 293). The terms they introduce express theoretical relations (*NOR*, p. 269).

[8] The latter quote is taken from Whewell's 1844 essay 'On the Fundamental Antithesis of Philosophy' (*PIS* ii. 647–68).

[9] In Aphorism IV to Book I of *Novum Organon Renovatum*, Whewell considered the antithesis as 'the foundation of the Philosophy of Science' (*NOR*, p. 5).

[10] This quote might strike the reader as an echo of Kant. I shall go into more detail on Kant's potential influence on Whewell in the section 'Whewell and Kant'.

are considered as distinct from the Facts: in Facts, though Ideas may be involved, they are not, in our apprehension, separated from the sensations. In a Fact the Ideas are applied so readily and familiarly, and incorporated with the sensations so entirely, that we do not see *them*, we see *through them*' (*PIS* i. 40). In this context, Whewell declared that 'a True Theory is a Fact; a Fact is a familiar Theory' (*PIS* i. 40) and that we should consider Theory as a conscious inference and fact as an unconscious inference (*PIS*, i. 42). Hereby, he was anticipated the theory-ladenness of observation.

Given the Fundamental Antithesis of Philosophy, it also follows that both sensations and ideas are requisite in knowledge acquisition (*PIS* i. 24–7). One of the prominent goals of Whewell's *Philosophy of the Inductive Sciences* (1840) was to show the place which Ideas have in the progress of science and in the discovery of new truths about the natural world. As each branch of science progresses, a core Fundamental Idea is rendered explicit. Some ideas are peculiar to one branch, others are common to more. For example, in the development of mechanics the Ideas of Force, Matter, and Cause are quintessential; in chemistry, the Ideas Chemical Affinity and Substance occupy centre stage; in crystallography, we have the Idea of Symmetry; in the Classificatory Sciences, the Idea of Resemblance and Natural Affinity; in electricity, the Idea of Polarity, and so on.[11] According to Whewell, the progress of science was only possible by the fruitful combination of both metaphysics and experience: 'the metaphysical is a necessary part of the inductive movement', as he declared (*PIS*, vol. i, p. ix). Consequently, the progress of science has its place in observation, in the application of Ideas, which regulate our active operations of the mind, and in the union of the two.[12] Great discoverers are distinguished from barren speculators 'not by having *no* metaphysics in their heads, but by having *good* metaphysics while their adversaries had bad; and by binding their metaphysics to their physics, instead of keeping the two asunder' (*PIS*, vol. i, p. x).

Fundamental Ideas are at the heart of Whewell's philosophy of knowledge and it is important to understand their role. It should be noted that Whewell used the word 'Idea' in a rather unconventional manner:

> But it may suffice to observe that we use the word *Ideas*, in the manner already explained, to express that element, supplied by the mind itself, which must be combined with Sensation in order to produce knowledge. *For us, Ideas are not Objects of Thought, but rather Laws of Thought. Ideas are not synonymous with Notions; they are Principles which give our Notions whatever they contain of truth.* (*PIS* i. 29 [italics added])

Note that, when dealing with the Fundamental Ideas in terms of 'Laws of Thought', Whewell was not referring to the Law of Identity, the Law of Non-Contradiction, and the like; rather, according to him, the Fundamental Ideas are the conditions under which we experience the world (or the conditions under which we can obtain proper knowledge within a specified domain of science). They are conditions 'without which the external world can neither be observed nor conceived' (*PIS* i. 76) and they 'necessarily impose their conditions upon that

---

[11] See, furthermore, Whewell's classification scheme on *PIS* ii. 117.

[12] Later in his *On the Philosophy of Discovery* (1860) Whewell wrote: 'They [i.e. the Fundamental Ideas] are not proved in the course of scientific investigations, but brought to light as such investigations showed their necessity. They are not the results, but *the conditions of experimental sciences*. [. . .] They are not the consequences of knowledge, acquired from without, but *the internal condition of our being able to know*' (*PD*, pp. 349–50 [italics added]).

knowledge of which observation supplies the material' (*PIS* i. 79). The goal of *The Philosophy of the Inductive Sciences* was 'not merely to prove that there *are* such Fundamental Ideas or Laws of mental activity, but to enumerate those of them which are involved in the existing sciences' (*PD*, p. 489). Whewell considered the Ideas of Space and Time as *intuitions*: we necessarily conceive events occurring in space and time (*PIS* i. 89–91, 128–9). These ideas are conditions impressed upon our knowledge by the constitution of the mind itself. With respect to the Idea of Cause, Whewell similarly remarked that it is 'a relation or condition under which events are apprehended, which relation is not given by observation, but supplied by the mind itself' (*PIS* i. 176). Apart from these intuitions, Whewell allowed for Fundamental Ideas that are specific within a particular branch of science; he also allowed that new Fundamental Ideas could be disclosed in the course of the history of science.

For Whewell proper scientific knowledge is *necessary and universal*. In contrast to contingent truths, necessary truths are those 'in which we not only learn that the proposition *is* true, but see that it *must be* true; in which the negation of the truth is not only false, but impossible; in which we cannot, even by an effort of imagination, or in a supposition, conceive the reverse of that which is asserted' (*PIS* i. 55 ff.).[13] Where do necessary truths derive their necessity from? As Whewell argued, their necessity cannot derive from observations alone, for 'how numerous, they may be, they can show nothing with regard to the infinite number of cases in which the experiment has not been made' (*PIS* i. 63). If certain truths are necessary and universal, 'this universality flows from the *ideas* which we apply to our experience, and which are, as we have seen, the real sources of necessary truth' (*PIS* i. 64). But how exactly do ideas render scientific truths necessary? In this context, Whewell developed a twofold answer which can be summarized as follows: scientific truths derive their necessity from certain axioms (*interpretative necessity*), while the necessity of these axioms in its turn follows from the necessity of the Fundamental Ideas which they disclose (*constitutive necessity*).[14] I shall provide an example to convey more clearly what is involved. The example is taken from 'On the Nature of the Truth of the Laws of Motion' (1834) (*PIS* ii. 573–94). In his 1834 paper Whewell's focus is on mechanics. Since mechanics studies the causes, in other words, the forces, of motions, the truth and necessity of the laws of motion depends 'upon the way in which we can and do reason concerning causes' (*PIS* ii. 574). According to Whewell, the Axioms of Causation are the following:

Axiom I.—Every change is produced by a cause.

Axiom II.—Causes are measured by their effects.

---

[13] In *On the Philosophy of Induction* (1860), Whewell observed: 'The necessity of such Axioms is seen, but it is not seen at first. It becomes clearer and clearer to each person, and clear to one person after another, as the human mind dwells more and more steadily on the several subjects of speculation. *There are scientific truths which are seen by intuition, but this intuition is progressive*' (*PD*, p. 344, cf. pp. 347–453).

[14] The reader should be aware that the twofold distinction between constitutive and interpretative necessity is reflective of my own account of Whewell's notion of necessity. Other alternatives can readily be found in the scholarly literature: Walsh 1962; Butts 1965a, 1965b; Fisch 1985a; Snyder 1994; and Morrison 1997. In Ducheyne 2009a I have argued for my own account and defended it against the alternatives.

Axiom III.—Action is always accompanied by an equal and opposite Reaction. (*PIS* ii. 574–6, cf. 177–85)

These axioms are necessarily true according to 'our notions of material causation' and are 'the universal and necessary rules of causation' (*PIS* ii. 591). The Axioms of Causation are necessary because they give a partial description of the constitutively necessary conditions of human perception. In other words, what they describe is *constitutively necessary* of our nature as experiential beings with respect to our reasoning on cause and effect. The negation of the Axioms of Causation is inconceivable. Note that they disclose, but do not fully reveal, the Idea of Cause (*PIS* i 73); they are 'exhibitions of the Idea of Cause under various aspects' (*PIS* i. 248). The laws of motion in their turn derive their necessary status from their being interpretations of the Axioms of Causation, in other words, they are formally 'derived from *à priori* reasonings' (*PIS* ii. 594), but empirically determined by observation. Each of the laws of motion corresponds to and is based on the forms of the Axioms of Causation. For instance, in order to derive the second law of motion, which essentially states that force is measured by the accelerative effect it produces, from the Axiom 'causes are measured by their effect', we need to know, for one thing, how we should measure the accelerative effect. In other words, according to Whewell, the laws of motion are established by giving empirical content to the Axioms of Causation (*PIS* ii. 591). They are interpretations because they instantiate the form of the Axiom and because they concretize the general terms 'cause' and 'effect' into their empirical counterparts. The laws of motion have both an empirical part, which can be denied without self-contradiction, and a necessary part, which cannot be denied without self-contradiction. While the form of the laws of motion is derived from the Axioms of Causation, their matter derives from experience—and this is what 'being an interpretation of an Axiom' amounts to:

> The form, and even the language of these laws is of necessity what it is; but the interpreta-tion and application of them is not possible without reference to fact. We may imagine many rules according to which bodies might move (for many sets of rules, different from the existing ones, are, so far as we can see, possible) and we would still have to assert—that velocity could not change without a cause—that change of action is proportional to the force which produces it,—and that action is and reaction are equal and opposite. The truth of these assertions is involved in these notions of causation and matter, which the very attempt to know anything concerning the relations of matter and motion presupposes. (*PIS* v. 588)

By the time Whewell had finished his *History* in 1837, he came to generalize this account to other domains of science which have progressed according to other Fundamental Ideas. The overarching idea was that the laws arrived at in all other sciences were also necessary, because they derive their form from the Axioms of their corresponding Fundamental Idea, and empirical, because they are interpretations, concretizations, or 'modifications' of their corresponding Axioms. Whewell did not go into any detail as to how scientific laws in other branches of science can be seen as interpretations of their corresponding axioms. He con-cluded the first volume of the *Philosophy* as follows:

> We have been employed up to the present stage of this work in examining the materials of knowledge, namely, Facts and Ideas; and we have dwelt particularly upon the latter element; inasmuch as the consideration of it is, on various accounts, and especially at the present time, by far the most important. We have now to proceed to the remainder of our task;—to determine the processes by which those materials may actually be made to constitute knowledge. (*PIS* i. 708)

Before we turn to how Whewell tackled the second task for the Philosophy of Science, in other words, *explicating the best precepts for the discovery of new truths*,[15] I shall discuss the exact nature of Kant's influence on Whewell.

WHEWELL AND KANT

Given the prima facie resemblance between Whewell's doctrine of Fundamental Ideas and Kant's position, it has often been debated in the scholarly literature whether Whewell was influenced by Kant. In defence of such influence, Robert E. Butts has claimed that Whewell 'owes his theory of science to Kant' (Butts 1994, p. 278), which is somewhat of an overstatement in view of what follows. Menachem Fisch, on the other hand, has denied a substantial significance of Kant on Whewell's philosophy and has pointed out that in Whewell's notebook we cannot find any of the questions raised in the *Critique* (Fisch 1991, p. 105). Laura J. Snyder has correctly pointed out that there are important differences between Kant's transcendental philosophy and Whewell's antithetical philosophy. Most notably, she has pointed out that 'Whewell did not follow Kant in distinguishing between the a priori components of knowledge provided by intuition (*Sinnlichkeit*), the Understanding (*Verstand*), and the faculty of Reason (*Vernunft*)', that 'many of Whewell's Fundamental Ideas function not as conditions of experience but as conditions for having knowledge within their respective sciences', and that 'Whewell did not attempt to give an exhaustive list of these Fundamental Ideas; rather, he believed that there are others which will emerge in the course of the development of science' (Snyder 2006, p. 44). These points are well taken—although Whewell did distinguish between intuitions and Fundamental Ideas pertaining only to particular branches of science—and on the basis of them Snyder has concluded that 'Kant was not explicitly on Whewell's mind as he strove to develop an epistemology that could incorporate both empirical and ideal elements of knowledge' (Snyder 2006, p. 46). While I am in agreement with Snyder's insightful observations, I disagree with the conclusion she wishes to draw from them.

Whether or not Kant influenced Whewell's thought is not contingent on the fact whether or not Whewell was an orthodox Kantian. Whewell was surely not 'the English Kant'. Moreover, Whewell himself asserted that he departed in significant ways from Kant's project (Snyder 2006, pp. 45–6). However, as we will see, Kant was relevant for Whewell *with respect to the sorts of epistemological questions he put on the agenda*. More precisely, Whewell's epistemological position developed in close dialogue with Kantian philosophy and should be seen as an answer to the bridging problem that could not, according to Whewell, be answered by Kant (Ducheyne 2011). The bridging problem consisted in showing how a priori principles could give rise to physics by means of intermediary concepts—Whewell's Axioms, which partially disclose Fundamental Ideas, served exactly this purpose.

Whewell's inclination towards Kantian philosophy and his familiarity with it can easily be gathered from several of his notebooks which were written between *c*.1830 and 1833, i.e. the

---

[15] Whewell denied in clear terms that an 'Art of Discovery' was possible: 'The practical results of the Philosophy of Science must be rather classification and analysis of what has been done, than precept and method for future doing' (*NOR*, p. v).

period in which Whewell was working out the basics of his epistemology (Butts 1965a). In notebook five, he left notes on Kant's *Kritik der praktischen Vernunft* (WP, R.18.17[5], pp. 181, 183, 184). In notebook six, Whewell also drew on Kant's *Kritik der reinen Vernuft*, as is clear from the following statement:

> The conditions of our perceptions, in consequence of w[ch] we apprehend objects as existing in space and time, are capable, as we have seen, of giving truth to extensive and important sciences, that is, systematically arranged trains of speculative truth. But these conditions of our perception show themselves in another way, in which indeed, they operate ↓by↓[16] far ↓the↓most extensively; and which, indeed, for various reasons, we mightmay consider as the primary use of this part of our internal constitution. The apprehension of things as existing and occurring in space and time, regulates every action of every principal creature. (WP, R.18.17[6], p. 13; cf. WP, R.18.17[7], p. 43)

He noted, furthermore, that 'the German system' has 'not merely a tie connecting the impressions which we progressively receive, but a constitution of the active faculties which makes the impressions impossible without the connexion' (WP, R.18.17[9], p. 11). He also stressed that in order to know we must perceive and conceive. Knowledge implies both passive as well as active thought: 'collection of impressions' and 'the operations of the reason' (WP, R.18.17[8], fo. 19r). The actions of the mind work on impressions provided by the senses (WP, R.18.17[8], fo. 36v). Whewell noted that by using language 'we do not expose our impressions only, but expose them modified and transformed by the operations of our thoughts' (WP, R.18.17[7], p. 23), so that human minds are 'perpetually exercising a formative and productive power' (WP, R.18.17[7], p. 24), which is 'exercised upon the rude material' (WP, R.18.17[7], p. 41). Such a priori principles, which 'are part of the original furniture of the common or unsystematic reason' (WP, R.18.17[7], p. 14) and which spell out the '↓universal↓ and familiar modes of contemplating objects' (WP, R.18.17[7], p. 18), have been brought to light and systematized during the course of human history. According to Whewell, 'sound and real physical science consists in apprehending a general fact of observation by means of ↓distinct↓ ideas' (WP, R.18.17[7], p. 61). Whewell warned that he did not use the term 'idea' in its customary sense and noted that 'the ideas of which I have to speak are general notions of relation, connexion, dependence, by which ↓such↓ conceptions are combined with one another' (WP, R.18.17[7], p. 61). Such ideas or conceptions involve 'an act of the mind by which it gives a certain unity ↓to each↓ of the groups of things so seemed'; furthermore, '[t]his act may be expressed by saying that we *conceive* the objects as one, and the faculty of the mind may be called conception' (WP, R.18.17[8], fo. 15r; cf. WP, R.18.17[10], p. 3). In other words, 'the perceptions of this faculty of perceiving acts, are bound together by conceptions which give them unity' (WP, R.18.17[8], fo. 16r, cf. fo. 32v). In his early notebooks, Whewell sought to unravel 'the general fundamental convictions and laws' underlying human reasoning and science (WP, R.18.17[6], p. 12). His aim was to show how these laws or principles gave rise to sound scientific knowledge:

> Our object is to ascertain the ↓general↓ laws which govern the formation and progress of knowledge in the largest sense; And the course which we purpose to follow leads us to examine

---

[16] Words between downward arrows designate words that were inserted above the line in the original manuscripts.

their ↓laws↓ in the first place, as they have operated in those branches of human knowledge which more peculiarly termed *Sciences*, and in which the certainty and progressive character of our knowledge are most striking and incontestable. [. . .] Science may be ↑for our purpose↑[17] described as *speculative knowledge of general truths*. (WP, R.18.17[6], p. 84)

On space and time Whewell noted that 'all things are presented to our apprehension under the conditions of space and time' (WP, R.18.17[7], p. 12). Space and time are intuitions. When using the word 'intuition' he used it as an equivalent to 'the German word *Anschauung*' (WP, R.18.17[8], fo. 67v). He noted that '[s]pace is not a notion obtained by experience' (WP, R.18.17[8], fo. 38v) and that 'the existence of space as a real and necessary condition of all objects as perceived' (WP, R.18.17[8], fo. 42r, cf. fo. 58v). On time he wrote: 'Time is a necessary condition in the presentation to our minds of all occurrences' (WP, R.18.17[8], fo. 56v). Space, time, causation (and 'the like') express relations between our impressions (WP, R.18.17[7], pp. 16, 18).[18] The concept of cause is not derived from experience (WP, R.18.17[9], p. 6). He wrote the following on Kant's account of the idea of cause:

> While this series of disputes was going on in Scotland [Whewell is referring here to Hume, Stewart, and Brown], a great metaphysical genius ↓in Germany↓ was evolving his solution of the same problem. Kant's speculations originate, as he informs us, in the trains of thought to which Hume's writings gave rise, and the Critik [*sic*] der Reinen Vernunft, an examination of the pure Reason was published in 1781, with the view of showing the true nature of our knowledge. [. . .] According to Kant, causality is a condition of our experiences; a connexion in events is requisite to our apprehending them as events; [. . .]. The ↓relation↓ of causation is a condition of our thinking of things, as the relations of space are a condition of our seeing them. (WP, R.18.17[9], p. 10)

These conditions 'reside in the constitution of the mind' (WP, R.18.17[8], fo. 41v) and are the 'conditions of experience'[19] (WP, R.18.17[8], fo. 43r).

In notebook nine, Whewell set out to find an answer to the following paradox: if mechanics has empirical content how can it be necessary (cf. Yeo 1993, pp. 13–14)? In other words, '[i]n the phraseology usual among German writers' his aim was 'to prove the possibility of the science of mechanics' (WP, R.18.17[9], p. 2).[20] However, according to Whewell, the Kantian account of the idea of cause, which is 'indispensably true as far as it goes', 'requires further explanation' (WP, R.18.17[9], p. 12). The notion of cause must be expressed 'in the form of propositions in order that they may form a foundation for our reasonings' (WP, R.18.17[9], p. 12). In other words, we must be able 'to lay down certain Axioms, or Definitions which may be seen as Axioms, in order that we may have such a structure of Demonstration concerning causation *in any of its modifications*' (WP, R.18.17[9], p. 12 [italics added]). Whewell

---

[17] Words between upward arrows designate words that were inserted below the line in the original manuscripts.

[18] In a letter to Richard Jones, 21 August 1834, Whewell used the term 'ideal relations' (WP, Add. Ms. c. 51[175], fo. 1v).

[19] Whewell also used the following terms: 'Conditions of Inductivity' (WP, R.18.17[11], fos. 1r, 30r), 'Regulative & Interpretative Conceptions' (WP, R.18.17[13], fo. c.75r), and 'the conditions of our receptivity' (WP, R.18.17[11], fo. 75v).

[20] In an earlier notebook dating back to 1827, Whewell recorded the following on Kant's *Kritik der reinen Vernunft*: 'The object of this celebrated work is *to show the possibility of knowledge i.e. of universal and necessary truths*' (WP, R.19[14], fo. 2r [emphasis added]).

drew close analogy between the axioms of mechanics and the axioms of geometry: 'The axioms of ↓mechanics↓ do, in fact, flow from our idea of cause, as necessarily as the axioms of geometry ↓do↓ from our intuition of space' (WP, R.18.17⁹, p. 32). He then continued to show that the statement 'that *everything which happens must have a cause*' is a partial expression of our idea of cause,[21] but that 'we still have to show *how it enters into the construction of the mechanical sciences*' (WP, R.18.17⁹, p. 32 [italics added]). Whewell's solution consisted in uncovering the Axioms of Causation which serve as general intermediate forms and to which empirical content could be given.

Whewell clearly took over the idea of Kant that scientific knowledge derives from a priori principles. Nevertheless, he was dissatisfied with Kant's failure to show how these a priori principles enter into the construction of science. In other words, according to Whewell, Kant had failed to provide bridging principles between the a priori principles and scientific laws which have empirical content. Whewell, who took Kant's philosophy as a point of departure for his doctrine of Fundamental Ideas, was unsatisfied with Kant's philosophy of science because it did not show how 'modifications' (in the sense of concretizations) of a priori principles resulted in empirical laws. Therefore, he tried to transform and go beyond the Kantian project. Kant was definitively on Whewell's mind when he was in the midst of elaborating his doctrine of Fundamental Ideas, for it provided an important philosophical point of departure for him.

WHEWELL ON THE CONSTRUCTION OF SCIENCE

In order to have science, both ideas as well as facts are required: 'When our Conceptions are clear and distinct, when our Facts are certain and sufficiently numerous, and when the Conceptions, being suited to the nature of the Facts, are applied to them so as to produce an exact and universal accordance, we attain knowledge of a precise and comprehensive kind, which we may term *Science*' (NOR, pp. 27–8). Whewell stated that in the construction of science six consecutive processes ought to be distinguished: (1) Decomposition and Observation of Facts, (2) Measurement of Phenomena, (3) Explication of Conceptions, (4) Induction of Laws of Phenomena, (5) Induction of Causes, (6) Application and Verification of Inductive Discoveries (NOR, p. 143). A discussion of (6) will be undertaken in the section 'Whewell on Confirmation'.

Processes (1) and (2) are closely connected. Step (1) refers to the process whereby we 'resolve the complex appearances which nature offers to us, and the mixed and manifold modes of looking at these appearances which rise in our thoughts, into limited, definite and clearly-understood portions' (NOR, p. 56).[22] Step (2) consists in measuring the partial

---

[21] He noted: 'This Axiom expresses only a result, a consequence, ↓a derivative↓ of our idea of cause, a portion of the convictions which accompany it. The Axiom may be requisite in the exposition of our knowledge, but the idea itself is the foundation of the knowledge' (WP, R.18.17⁹, p. 14).

[22] On this matter, Whewell recorded that 'We are not able, nor need we endeavour, to exclude Ideas from our Facts; but we may be able to discern, with perfect distinctness, the Ideas which we include' (NOR, p. 54).

facts obtained in step (1) according to '*Number, Place, Figure, Motion*' (*NOR*, p. 50).[23] Step (3) consists in the process, during which '*Conceptions* are *made more clear* in themselves' (*NOR*, p. 29).[24] When our conceptions are explicated, they are 'carefully *unfolded*, so as to bring clear into view the elements of truth with which they are marked from their ideal origin' (*NOR*, p. 31). This process typically occurs in debates on how specific technical terms should be defined (for instance, the definition of uniform force). Establishing scientific definitions should always occur 'by the light of facts' (*NOR*, p. 45): 'To unfold our Conceptions by the means of Definitions, has never been serviceable to science, except when it has been associated with the immediate *use* of the Definitions' (*NOR*, p. 37). Steps (4)–(5) are examples of properly methodized Colligations of Facts: induction refers to '*a True Colligation of Facts by means of an exact and appropriate Conception*' (*NOR*, p. 70). Colligations of Facts occur when conceptions '*bind together the Facts*' (*NOR*, p. 29), by which Whewell sought to emphasize that, in contrast with simple enumerative induction, the inductive act introduces a new conception 'which did not exist in any of the observed facts' (*NOR*, p. 72). Hypotheses have an important heuristic role in the establishment of Colligations of Facts. In Aphorism VIII to Book II, Whewell wrote: '*The Conceptions by which Facts are bound together, are suggested by the sagacity of discovers. This sagacity cannot be taught. It commonly succeeds by guessing; and this success seems to consist in framing several* tentative hypotheses, *and selecting the right one. But a supply of appropriate hypotheses cannot be constructed by rule, nor without inventive talent*' (*NOR*, p. 59, cf. pp. 78–83).[25] Even wrong hypotheses can eventually lead to the discovery of truth: 'To try wrong guesses is, with most persons, the only way to hit upon the right ones' (*NOR*, p. 79). According to Whewell, inductions are more than the sum of facts which are colligated: 'there is a New Element added to the combination by the very act of thought by which they are combined' (*NOR*, p. 72, cf. p. 108) or, in other words, 'there is some Conception *superinduced* upon the Facts' (*NOR*, p. 74)—in this respect, Whewell's account of induction differed radically from that of his opponent J. S. Mill (Snyder 1997a and 2006; Buchdahl 1991). According to Whewell, the notion of 'superinduction' explains why inductive inferences are ampliative—in contrast to deductive ones which are strictly truth-preserving. Inductions can result in Laws of Phenomena or in Laws of Causes (*NOR*, pp. 118–28, 247–51). The former always precede the latter. Whewell, furthermore, divided the process of induction into three successive steps: the Selection of the (Fundamental) Idea involved, the Construction of the Conception, in other words, a specific modification of the Fundamental Idea involved, and the Determination of the Magnitudes, in other words, deducing the quantitative consequences of a Conception under consideration (*NOR*, pp. 186–94).

How does a Conception, which initially has a clear conjectural status, become a well-established theory? We shall address this question in the following section.

---

[23] See, furthermore, Whewell's discussion of the Methods of Observation (*NOR*, pp. 145–63).

[24] See, furthermore, Whewell's discussion of the Methods of Acquiring clear Scientific Ideas (*NOR*, pp. 164–85).

[25] Given his insistence on hypotheses and guesses, Whewell came to criticize Newton's *hypotheses non fingo* (*PD*, pp. 182–3; cf Aphorisms X–XI to Book II in *NOR*, p. 70).

WHEWELL ON CONFIRMATION

Hypotheses are tentative conceptions of which we seek to investigate their truth. 'The framing of hypotheses', Whewell remarked, 'is, for the inquirer after truth, not the end, but the beginning of the work' (*NOR*, p. 80). In line with his extensive research on the history of science, Whewell conceived of confirmation as a long-term process. Proper testing and confirmation of a hypothesis is a gradual process which takes decades, if not centuries. Equivalently, the falsification of a hypothesis requires the work of many generations of scientists. With respect to the hypothesis of celestial vortices, Whewell pointed out that 'Before it has disappeared, it has been modified so as to have all palpable falsities squeezed out of it, and subsidiary provisions added, in order to reconcile it with the phenomena. It has, in short, been penetrated, infiltrated, and metamorphosed by the surrounding medium of truth, before the merely arbitrary and erroneous residuum has been finally ejected out of the body of permanent and certain knowledge' (*PD*, p. 503).[26] Just as facts are decomposed in the context of establishing a hypothesis, its verification requires its decomposition into 'a number of small steps, of which almost any one falls within the reach of common talents and industry'. 'Of these portions,' Whewell continued, 'each may appear by itself narrow and easy; and yet they are so woven together, by hypothesis and conjunction, that the truth of the parts necessarily assures us of the truth of the whole' (*NOR*, p. 104).

It has often been argued that Whewell's account of verification was hypothetico-deductive.[27] According to the hypothetico-deductive model of confirmation, a hypothesis is accepted or considered as truthful if its empirically testable consequences are confirmed by experience.[28] It is important to realize that standard hypothetico-deductivism (H-D), does *not* impose any constraints on the sorts of hypotheses that are allowable for empirical testing: any old hypothesis qualifies for empirical testing. There are two compelling reasons not to read Whewell as endorsing H-D in any simplistic or unqualified form: first of all, Whewell *imposed constraints on the sorts of hypotheses that qualify for empirical testing*, and, secondly, *his notion of empirical success is more sophisticated than the simple verification of the deductive consequences of a hypothesis*.

Haphazardly framed hypotheses, in other words, hypotheses which are no way based on or inferable from the data at hand, cannot pass as candidates for empirical testing, according to Whewell (Snyder 1997a, pp. 167–76; 1997b, pp. 585–8, p. 598; 2006, pp. 171–5). In this context, Whewell pointed out the following:

> Some hypotheses are necessary, in order to connect the facts which are observed; some new principle of unity must be applied to the phenomena, *before induction can be attempted*. What is requisite, is, *that the hypothesis should be close to the facts, and not connected with them by*

[26] This quote comes from Whewell's 1851 paper 'Of the Transformation of Hypotheses in the History of Science', which is appended to *On the Philosophy of Discovery* (*PD*, pp. 492–503).

[27] Whewell's work certainly contains passages which suggest a hypothetico-deductive reading (esp. *NOR*, pp. 67–8). However, in light of what follows, Whewell cannot be straightforwardly read as such. For hypothetico-deductive readings of Whewell, see e.g. Butts 1977; Laudan 1981, pp. 163–80; and Wettersten 1994.

[28] Useful discussion of the hypothetico-deductive model of confirmation is provided in Nola and Irzik 2005, ch. 8.

other arbitrary and untried facts; and that the philosopher should be ready to resign it as soon as the facts refuse to confirm it. (*NOR*, p. 193 [italics added])

Although, as we have said, we can give few precise directions for this cardinal process, the Selection of the Idea, in speculating on phenomena, yet there is one Rule which may have its use: it is this:– *The idea and the facts must be homogeneous*: the elementary Conceptions, into which the facts have been decomposed, must be of the same nature as the Idea by which we attempt to collect them into laws. (*PIS* ii. 387)

In similar vein, Whewell stressed that, in finding formulae by which the laws of nature are expressed, scientists have been guided 'in the selection of their formula, by some *Hypothesis respecting the mode of connection of the facts*' (*NOR*, p. 200 [italics added]). Whether Whewell's constraints provide well-defined, sufficient, and necessary conditions for filtering out potentially true hypotheses is a different matter, but it is clear that he sought to impose constraints on the conditions under which hypotheses qualify for empirical testing.

Whewell's articulation of empirical success is also more complex than H-D. According to H-D, empirical success only requires that the deductive consequences of a hypothesis are confirmed. Whewell insisted that such was insufficient to count as empirical success. Accordingly, he insisted on mainly two *evidential virtues* that hypotheses might acquire in the process of empirical testing: prediction and consilience of inductions. Aphorism XII to Book II of *Novum Organon Renovatum* states: '*It is a test of true theories not only to account for, but to predict phenomena*' (*NOR*, p. 70). Accordingly, when a hypothesis predicts known phenomena which were previously unpredictable and, especially, when it predicts formerly unknown ones, the evidence for that hypothesis increases. With respect to the former, Whewell argued that the 'prediction of results, *even of the same kind* as those which have been observed, in new cases, is a proof of real success in our inductive processes' (*NOR*, p. 87 [italics added]). With respect to the latter, Whewell pointed out that 'the evidence in favour of our induction is of a much higher and more forcible character when it enables to explain and determine cases of a *kind different* from those which were contemplated in the formation of our hypotheses' (*NOR*, pp. 87–8). This is referred to by Whewell as Consilience of Inductions or the 'jumping together' of two different classes of phenomena (Butts 1977, 1994; Fisch 1985b; Harper 1989; Laudan 1981, pp. 163–80; Snyder 2005). An example of this is provided in Proposition IV of Book III of Newton's *Principia*. In this proposition Newton demonstrated that the fall of terrestrial bodies and the orbiting of the Moon are both produced by the Earth's inverse-square centripetal force (Ducheyne 2009b, pp. 240–4). Consilience of Inductions, which leads to 'progressive *Simplification of the Theory* as it is extended to new cases' (*NOR*, p. 95), is the sort of evidence that belongs only to 'the best established theories which the history of science contains' (*NOR*, p. 88)—by which Whewell had in mind the theory of universal gravitation and the wave theory in optics (*HIS* ii. 310, 328, 341, 429, 459, 464).

Whewell, furthermore, emphasized that applications or extensions of a theory have evidential significance: '*When the theory of any subject is established, the observations and experiments which are made in applying the science to use and to instruction, supply a perpetual verification of the theory*' (*NOR*, p. 233). Such applications and extensions have evidential significance not only because they repeat certain experiments and have the potential of correcting certain observations, but also because they oftentimes concern facts 'not included in the original induction, and apparently of a different kind' (*NOR*, p. 236). In doing so, we also refine the theory at hand: 'we suppose the theory, not only to be tested, but also to be *corrected* when it is found to be imperfect' (*NOR*, p. 235).

WHEWELL'S METHODOLOGICAL DEVELOPMENT: A ROLE FOR TIDOLOGY

According to Richard Yeo, Whewell was essentially a meta-scientist or looker-on-science, in other words, he created for himself 'a role as the critic and reviewer, adjudicator and legislator of science' (Yeo 1993, p. 8). Yeo stressed that Whewell's contributions in mineralogy and tidology 'were important, but neither met his own criteria for truly significant advances in science, and they did not compare with those of leading men of science he counted among his friends' (Yeo 1993, p. 54). Menachem Fisch has equally dismissed the importance of Whewell's tidal studies for his philosophical-methodological views (Fisch 1991, pp. 58–9). Joan Richards's opinion on the matter is closely aligned with Yeo's for she claims that Whewell 'was more an observer [of science] than a participant [in science]' (Richards 1996, p. 235).

To claim, however, that Whewell was primarily an observer of science and not a participant is simply unfair in light of his numerous scientific papers on the tides (Reidy 2008, pp. 126–7; Snyder 2006, pp. 150–1, and 2011, pp. 169–79; Ducheyne 2010b). Primarily between 1833 and 1840 Whewell was actively involved in the study of the tides.[29] Moreover, Michael S. Reidy has stressed the importance of Whewell's tidal researches for the methodological views he developed in his *Philosophy of the Inductive Sciences*: 'His early work on tidology also taught him valuable lessons concerning the discovery process, including the difficulty of connecting facts with theory, the disparate ways of testing those theories, and the proper methods of data analysis and representation' (Reidy 2008, p. 14, cf. p. 155). Additionally, Reidy has called attention to the connection between Whewell's tidal research and his discussion of the 'Special Methods of Induction Applicable to Quantity' (Reidy 2008, pp. 182, 220, 245).[30] In the remainder of this chapter I shall focus on the interplay between Whewell's philosophy of science and his tidology, while focusing on confirmation.[31] More precisely, I shall show that Whewell's preference for equilibrium-theory, which has baffled previous interpreters (Ruse 1991, p. 96; 1976, pp. 235–6), was motivated by his own methodological considerations on what counts as a useful hypothesis.

With respect to the theoretical apparatus required to tackle the problems of the tides, Whewell noted that there were two different approaches available: *equilibrium theory* as developed by Newton and especially Bernouilli who 'have assumed the form of the fluid

---

[29] For an overview, see Ducheyne 2010b, pp. 31–4.

[30] In his monograph, Reidy did not show, however, that Whewell's views on scientific methodology changed over time in view of his tidal research, neither did he engage much in Whewell's Philosophy of Science. Before Whewell had turned to tidology, his views on methodology were very rudimentary (Ducheyne 2010b, pp. 29–30).

[31] For a detailed treatment, see Ducheyne 2010b. My claim is not that Whewell's Philosophy of Science simply derives from his tidal studies, but rather that tidology provided him with a concrete means to develop, test, and refine his methodological views. Whewell's Philosophy of Science and tidology constantly interacted and it is hard to tell cause from effect.

spheroid, under the influence of the sun and moon, to be the form of equilibrium' (Whewell 1834, p. 16) and *oscillatory theory* as developed by Laplace who has treated 'the tides as a problem of the oscillations', while supposing the whole globe to be covered with water of a uniform depth (Whewell 1833, p. 147). With respect to the former option, he noted that the waters of the seas cannot be considered at rest 'and therefore the form of the surfaces is not that of equilibrium' (Whewell 1833, p. 218) and that Laplace's theory is undoubtedly 'the correct view of the real operation of the forces; but it does not appear that in this way he has obtained any consequences to which NEWTON's mode of considering the subject did not lead with equal certainty and greater simplicity' (Whewell 1833, p. 147).[32] Although mathematicians, including Laplace, have tried to show that *some* laws of fact agree with the measurements predicted by theory, no one has so far shown that 'the *general course* of the effects produced upon the tides, by the changes of position and distance of the heavenly bodies is such as, according to the mathematical reasoning, it should be' (Whewell 1834, p. 17).

Whewell was quite aware that the standard equilibrium theory was 'not the true theory, but a very inaccurate and insufficient substitute for it, which we are compelled to adopt in consequence of the extremely imperfect state of the mathematical science of hydrodynamics', since the 'tides are a problem of motion, not of equilibrium of fluids; and we can never fully explain the circumstances of the phenomena till the problem has been solved in its genuine form' (Whewell 1836, p. 134). Nevertheless, using an incorrect, though *clearly conceived* working-hypothesis, which is at least to some degree based on observation, could be useful to suggest a better one (Whewell to Airy, 18 January 1843, *CW* xvi. 307). In 1834 he wrote: 'The laws of the tides, thus empirically obtained, may be used either as tests of the extant theories, or as suggestions for the improvement of those portions of mathematical hydraulics on which the true theory must depend' (Whewell 1834, p. 19).

Whewell never thought that Laplace's account was appealing since it involved laborious computations, but worse, the hypothesis on which his solution was based affected the results 'so as to make them differ altogether from those of the real case' (Whewell 1834, p. 35). Whewell noted that '[t]ide tables were never, I believe, calculated upon Laplace's theory, and thus never fairly brought to the test' (WP, R.18.13², fo. 278v). Furthermore, Laplace's theory rested on 'arbitrary hypotheses' (Whewell 1836, p. 134): it rested on the supposition that the Earth was uniformly covered with water—by contrast, Newton's theory left the depth of the oceans open; it did not enable us to collect from it anything about the depth of the motion and hence did not take into account the existence of continents; and, finally, it remained unclear what the mechanical principle was by which the tides were dependent on the depth of the ocean (Whewell to Lyell, 5 March 1835, *CW*, xvi. 207). Laplace also introduced the precarious assumption that in a system of bodies, in which periodical forces act, the state of the system is periodical like the forces (*HIS* ii. 92, 195). Later, in a letter to Airy in 1843, Whewell added that Laplace's theory thus required 'some general conjectural reasoning to bridge over the gap between the mathematical hypothesis and the case of nature' (Whewell to Airy, 2 March 1843, *CW* xvi. 311). Laplace's hypothesis was not 'close to the facts'—it simply explained the form and depth of the seabed away, instead of attempting to account for such factors—nor did it make any predictions about new phenomena (*HIS* ii. 191). Laplace had *accounted* for some observations at Brest, but he had not *predicted new data*. As we have

---

[32] On Laplace's tidal research, see Reidy 2008, pp. 50–6.

seen, a fruitful hypothesis should not only be able to explain the facts we hitherto observed, but also foretell phenomena which have not yet been observed.

By contrast, equilibrium theory, which is a corollary to the law of universal gravitation, which was considered by Whewell as one of the most stringently tested and best confirmed theories available, rests on the assumption that 'a fluid will always tend to the condition of equilibrium, though the circumstances of the case prevent its ever reaching that condition; a very just and reasonable assumption' (Whewell to Airy, 18 January 1843, *CW* xvi. 307; WP, R.18.13², fo. 280r). So while equilibrium theory supposed a *tendency* towards equilibrium (*HIS* ii. 195)—a tendency that is disturbed by additional parameters—Laplace's theory assumed an unrealistic idealization: that the Earth is uniformly covered by a world ocean. Whewell was, however, doubtful whether equilibrium theory alone could provide the correct theoretical apparatus for tidal phenomena: he believed that equilibrium theory '*in conjunction with the laws of waves*, so far as we knew those waves' could result in a truer theory (Whewell to Airy, 22 February 1843, *CW* xvi. 309).

Looking back on what has been surveyed in this chapter, it becomes apparent that Whewell's Philosophy of Science developed as a rich mixture of various traditions and practices, which squares rather nicely with the polymath that he was.

References

The following abbreviations are used throughout the text and notes:

CW	*Collected Works of William Whewell*, ed. and introd. Richard Yeo, 16 vols. Bristol: Thoemmes, 2001.
HIS i–iii	*History of the Inductive Sciences*, in *CW*, i–iii.
NOR	*Novum Organum Renovatum*, in *CW*, vi.
PD	*On the Philosophy of Discovery*, in *CW*, vii.
PIS i–ii	*The Philosophy of the Inductive Sciences*, in *CW*, iv–v.
WP	Whewell Papers, Wren Library, Trinity College, University of Cambridge.

Becher, H. W. (1981). 'William Whewell and Cambridge Mathematics'. *Historical Studies in the Physical Sciences*, 11: 1–49.

Becher, H. W. (1991). 'William Whewell's Odyssey: From Mathematics to Moral Philosophy', in Fisch and Schaffer (1991), 1–30.

Belsey, A. (1974). 'Interpreting Whewell'. *Studies in History and Philosophy of Science*, 5: 49–58.

Brooke, J. H. (1977). 'Natural Theology and the Plurality of Worlds: Observations on the Brewster–Whewell Debate'. *Annals of Science*, 34: 221–86.

Brooke, J. H. (1991). 'Indications of a Creator: Whewell as Apologist and Priest', in Fisch and Schaffer (1991), 149–73.

Buchdahl, G. (1991). 'Deductivist versus Inductivist Approaches in the Philosophy of Science as Illustrated by Some Controversies Between Whewell and Mill', in Fisch and Schaffer (1991), 311–34.

Butts, R. E. (1965a). 'Necessary Truths in Whewell's Theory of Science'. *American Philosophical Quarterly*, 2: 161–81.

Butts, R. E. (1965b). 'On Walsh's Reading of Whewell's View of Necessity'. *Philosophy of Science*, 32: 175–81.

Butts, R. E. (1977). 'Consilience of Inductions and the Problem of Conceptual Change in Science', in R. G. Colodny (ed.), *Logic, Laws and Life: Some Philosophical Complications*. Pittsburgh: Pittsburgh University Press, 71–88.

Butts, R. E. (1994). 'Induction as Unification: Kant, Whewell, and Recent Developments', in P. Parrini (ed.), *Kant and Contemporary Epistemology*. Dordrecht: Kluwer, 273–89.

Cannon, W. F. (1964). 'William Whewell: Contributions to Science and Learning'. *Notes and Records of the Royal Society*, 19: 176–91.

Cantor, G. N. (1991). 'Between Rationalism and Romanticism: Whewell's Historiography of the Inductive Sciences', in Fisch and Schaffer (1991), 67–86.

Ducheyne, S. (2009a). 'Whewell, Necessity and the Inductive Sciences'. *South African Journal of Philosophy*, 28: 333–58.

Ducheyne, S. (2009b). 'Understanding (in) Newton's Argument of Universal Gravitation'. *Journal of General Philosophy of Science*, 40: 227–58.

Ducheyne, S. (2010a). 'Fundamental Questions and Some New Answers on Philosophical, Contextual and Scientific Whewell: Some Reflections on Recent Whewell Scholarship and the Progress Made Therein'. *Perspectives on Science*, 18: 242–72.

Ducheyne, S. (2010b). 'Whewell's Tidal Researches: Scientific Practise and Philosophical Methodology'. *Studies in History and Philosophy of Science*, 41A: 26–40.

Ducheyne, S. (2011). 'Kant and Whewell on Bridging Principles between Metaphysics and Physics'. *Kant Studien*, 102: 22–45.

Fisch, M. (1985a). 'Necessary and Contingent Truth in William Whewell's Antithetical Theory of Knowledge'. *Studies in History and Philosophy of Science*, 16: 275–314.

Fisch, M. (1985b). 'Whewell's Consilience of Inductions: An Evaluation'. *Philosophy of Science*, 52: 239–55.

Fisch, M. (1991). *William Whewell, Philosopher of Science*. Oxford: Clarendon Press.

Fisch, M., and S. Schaffer (eds.) (1991). *William Whewell, A Composite Portrait*. Oxford, Clarendon Press.

Harper, W. (1989). 'Consilience and Natural Kind Reasoning', in J. R. Brown and J. Mittelstrass (eds.), *An Intimate Relation: Studies in the History and Philosophy of Science*. Dordrecht: Kluwer, 115–52.

Henderson, J. P. (1996). *Early Mathematical Economy: William Whewell and the British Case*. Lanham, Md.: Rowman and Littlefield.

Laudan, L. (1981). *Science and Hypothesis*. Dordrecht: Kluwer.

Morrison, M. (1977). 'Whewell on the Ultimate Problem of Philosophy', *Studies in History and Philosophy of Science*, 28: 417–37.

Nola, R., and G. Irzik (2005). *Philosophy, Science, Education and Culture*. Dordrecht: Springer.

Reidy, M. S. (2008). *Tides of History, Ocean Science and Her Majesty's Navy*. Chicago: University of Chicago Press.

Richards, J. (1996). 'Observing Science in Early Victorian England: Recent Scholarship on Whewell'. *Perspectives on Science*, 4: 231–47.

Robson, R., and W. F. Cannon (1984). 'William Whewell, F.R.S. (1794–1866)'. *Notes and Records of the Royal Society of London*, 19: 168–91.

Ruse, M. (1976). 'The Scientific Methodology of W. Whewell'. *Centaurus*, 20: 227–57.

Ruse, M. (1977). 'William Whewell and the Argument from Design'. *Monist*, 60: 244–68.

Ruse, M. (1991). 'William Whewell: Omniscientist', in Fisch and Schaffer (1991), 87–116.

Snyder, L. J. (1994). 'It's All Necessarily So: William Whewell on Scientific Truth'. *Studies in History and Philosophy of Science*, 25: 785–807.

Snyder, L. J. (1997a). 'The Mill–Whewell Debate: Much Ado about Induction'. *Perspectives on Science*, 5: 159–298.

Snyder, L. J. (1997b). 'Discoverers' Induction'. *Philosophy of Science*, 64: 580–604.

Snyder, L. J. (1999). 'Renovating the *Novum Organum*: Bacon, Whewell and Induction', *Studies in History and Philosophy of Science*, 30A: 531–57.

Snyder, L. J. (2005). 'Consilience, Confirmation, and Realism', in P. Achinstein (ed.), *Scientific Evidence: Philosophical Theories and Applications*. Baltimore, Md.: Johns Hopkins University Press, 129–48.

Snyder, L. J. (2006). *Reforming Philosophy: A Victorian Debate on Science and Society*. Chicago: University of Chicago Press.

Snyder, L. J. (2011). *The Philosophical Breakfast Club: Four Remarkable Friends Who Transformed Science and Changed the World*. New York: Broadway.

Walsh, H. T. (1962). 'Whewell on Necessity'. *Philosophy of Science*, 29: 139–45.

Wettersten, J. (1994). 'Discussion: William Whewell: Problems of Induction vs. Problems of Rationality'. *British Journal for the Philosophy of Science*, 45: 716–42.

Wettersten, J. (2005). *Whewell's Critics: Have They Prevented Him from Doing Good?* New York and Amsterdam: Rodopi.

Whewell, W. (1833). 'Essay towards a First Approximation to a Map of Cotidal Lines'. *Philosophical Transactions of the Royal Society*, 123: 147–236.

Whewell, W. (1834). 'On the Empirical Laws of the Tides in the Port of London, With Some Reflexions on the Theory'. *Philosophical Transactions of the Royal Society of London*, 124: 15–45.

Whewell, W. (1836). 'Researches on the Tides.—Fifth Series, On the Solar Inequality and on the Diurnal Inequality of the Tides at Liverpool'. *Philosophical Transactions of the Royal Society of London*, 126: 131–47.

Williams, P. (1991). 'Passing on the Torch: Whewell's Philosophy and the Principles of English University Education', in Fisch and Schaffer (1991), 117–47.

Yeo, R. (1979). 'William Whewell, Natural Theology and the Philosophy of Science in Mid Nineteenth Century Britain'. *Annals of Science*, 36: 493–516.

Yeo, R. (1989). 'Reviewing Herschel's Discourse'. *Studies in History and Philosophy of Science*, 20: 541–52.

Yeo, R. (1993). *Defining Science: William Whewell, Natural Knowledge and Public Debate in Early Victorian Britain*. Cambridge: Cambridge University Press.

Yeo, R. (2009). 'Whewell, William (1794–1866)', in L. Goldman (ed.), *Oxford Dictionary of National Biography* (online edition, May 2009). Oxford: Oxford University Press. <http://www.oxforddnb.com/view/article/29200>; accessed 12 April 2012].

CHAPTER 5

....

SOME BRITISH LOGICIANS

....

JEREMY GRAY

This chapter considers the work of Augustus De Morgan, George Boole, Stanley Jevons, Charles Dodgson (Lewis Carroll), John Venn, and, more briefly Hugh MacColl.

1. LOGIC, PHILOSOPHY, AND MATHEMATICS

....

LOGIC, like time, is a subject that can very profitably be left alone but was very seldom studied with profit. Many writers in the eighteenth and early nineteenth centuries dismissed it as a subject essentially opened and closed by Aristotle, and requiring only polishing and fresh exposition. Kant, in his *Logic* (1974, 23) said that logic 'has not gained much in *content* since Aristotle's times, and indeed it cannot, due to its nature'. But there were tensions that should have been apparent. The Aristotelian syllogistic logic was offered as the paradigm of simple logical arguments, and longer arguments were supposed to be compounded of syllogisms. But the paradigm of extended reasoning from simple premises was Euclid's *Elements*, which is not only not written in this language—which should surely have caused some alarm— but cannot be unless extravagantly rewritten. Indeed, it might be impossible. To give two examples, Stanley Jevons pointed out that the statement that '*All* equilateral triangles are *all* equiangular triangles' could appear in syllogistic form only as 'All equilateral triangles are equiangular', which does not even say the same thing. De Morgan gave this example of a non-syllogistic form of reasoning: 'A man is an animal, so the head of a man is the head of an animal'.

Moreover, the general understanding of Aristotelian logic was incompatible with the progress of knowledge, as Kant had underlined in opposition to Leibniz. On the traditional view of logic the syllogism adds nothing to our store of knowledge. If we know that all men are mortal, and if we know that Socrates is a man, then we know that he too will die. We may not have been consciously aware of the fact, but we cannot claim it as a piece of new knowledge. It follows that all knowledge is in the premises—but what are they and how can we know them? If they are only logical truths that cannot be otherwise and are entirely independent of the world, then all our knowledge is a gigantic tautology. Kant had argued for a novel kind of starting point, the synthetic a priori truths that, by being synthetic were about the world but by being a priori could not be otherwise, were fit for philosophical purpose. Science, on the other hand, offered only probable assertions, a weak and perhaps hopelessly inadequate kind of knowledge, subject to endless revision, hedged about with uncertainty, and quite often to be rejected as false after a time. The special status of scientific claims was not to be handled by logic, but by other kinds of philosophy, by discussion of probabilities, and in other ad hoc ways.

And was logic part of philosophy anyway? Was there anything a philosopher could say about it, or was it simply a necessary aspect of philosophical behaviour? If no one would willingly peddle a bad argument—and to be sure logic could expose certain kinds of invalid arguments—then a check on one's logic, or one's opponent's, would only reveal a flaw of the most basic kind. It was likely that substantial disagreements on substantial issues would not be traced back to errors of logic, but other kinds of presuppositions, uses of key terms, and so forth. No wonder that Kant dismissed Aristotelian logic as to all appearances a closed and completed body of doctrine (*Critique of Pure Reason*, B viii).

But there were questions to be asked about logic, if not about the nature of inference, then about its context. Deductions took true statements as input, and if valid produced true statements as output: what, precisely, was truth doing here? Did it matter if the statements were about non-existent objects, unicorns, perhaps? If we replace 'All men are mortal' by 'All men are foolish' why does it not still follow that Socrates was a fool? Presumably logic says that if we assent to the claims that all men are X and Socrates is a man, then we must assent to the claim that Socrates is X? But what are we doing deducing the mortality, or the foolishness, of Socrates from a claim about all men? Should we not examine Socrates, determine on some other grounds that he is mortal but not a fool, and add him to the list of mortal men while keeping off the list of foolish ones? In which case, how can we assent to the initial major premiss, which now follows from something about Socrates and cannot be said to precede or imply it?

What are we to make of the palpable inability of people to think straight most of the time? This happens often enough for it to be impossible to say that our minds, or our brains, are thinking machines. The deductions of logic have a normative character: they are accounts of how people ought to think, not how they do think. We can imagine that the brain, like the rest of the body, tries and fails, but it can be asked where the normative character of logic comes from.

The relation of logic to mathematics is also a vexed one, and that is where the English story in the nineteenth century is centred. As many historians have commented, mathematics in Britain was concentrated in Cambridge, which was with a few exceptions where the only significant research in the subject was done in the entire century, and in the opening decades when Whewell dominated Cambridge the Cambridge view was that mathematics was a (even, the) fit subject for the education of gentlemen, but not a creative or a research subject. Such a view, markedly out of line with the view in France or the states of Germany, stunts even teaching, since the whole reason for doing mathematics is reduced to admiring the achievements of Euclid and Newton, and then to admiring only their more accessible results, under the cover of a claim that it is a training for the mind. Such a claim could of course be made about theology, philosophy, or any other intellectual discipline, but only mathematics looked adequately uncontroversial and to have a secure place for authority. It may even be that the very backwardness of British mathematics throughout most of the nineteenth century contributed to the turn towards the investigation of logic. Although there were logicians in France and Germany the inquiring mind in Britain was under no temptation, because it had no opportunity, to take up advanced mathematics.

2. Augustus De Morgan

Even in such a deliberately impoverished environment people can find problems to chew on, and, as is well known, the Cambridge environment did generate some controversies out of which grew some contributions. William Frend objected strongly to the very idea of negative numbers and to algebra that talked about $a - b$: what could it mean, he wanted to know, when $a = 3$ and $b = 5$? (see Pycior 1983, 123). This is a question that deserves an answer, even if Frend's belief that it cannot be answered and algebra must therefore be restricted to the point of uselessness is not worth a moment's thought, and in due course it brought forth some answers. Peacock's doctrine of the equivalence of forms took the view that the rules of ordinary algebra were formal and arbitrary, but needed to agree with the rules of arithmetic when numbers were substituted for letters. What he called the principle of the permanence of equivalent forms asserts (*A Treatise on Algebra*, 1830, 104):

> Whatever form is Algebraically equivalent to another, when expressed in general symbols, must be true, whatever those symbols denote.
>
> Conversely, if we discover an equivalent form in Arithmetical Algebra or any other subordinate science, when the symbols are general in form though specific in their nature, the same must be an equivalent form, when the symbols are general in their nature as well as in their form.

Finding himself unable to comply with the Test Act, which required those teaching at Oxford or Cambridge to subscribe to the Thirty-Nine Articles of the Church of England, De Morgan debarred himself from teaching in Cambridge and instead took up a position at the newly founded University of London. A fluent writer, a natural controversialist, an original but not a profound thinker, he saw no reason to reduce mathematics to a pastime for gentlemen on their ways to careers in the Church or law, even if in his teaching he had little opportunity to teach the brightest students (Sylvester, Jevons, and Todhunter passed through, but the London syllabus was elementary and Cambridge was the intended generation of students who took mathematics seriously). But nor did he sit back and let the Cambridge professors write the story.

De Morgan's initial reaction to Peacock's algebra was shock. In his review of *A Treatise on Algebra*, he wrote: 'it seemed to us something like symbols bewitched, and running about the world in search of meaning' (1835, 311), as well it might to someone accustomed to think of algebra as nothing more than a disguised way of reasoning with numbers. On that view, the truth of the distributive law, $a(b + c) = ab + ac$ follows from the fact that it is always true when numbers are substituted for a, b, and c. What he feared he saw in Peacock's work was meaningless symbols with, accordingly, no rhyme or reason for the rules they might be said to obey.

In due course he calmed down, and saw that indeed one might specify rules for symbols, but never gave up on the belief that in the end the symbols had to mean something. He remained close to Peacock's way of thinking of algebra as but a step removed from arithmetic, and as a result had, for a time, little to say about it. Then, in 1844, a year after his friend William Rowan Hamilton (the mathematician) had published his novel algebra of quaternions, De Morgan took up the task that Hamilton had thereby abandoned and tried to develop an algebra of triplets. The aim was to find a rule for multiplying triples of numbers that obeyed all the usual rules of algebra, and while this cannot be done, De Morgan's attempts do show a willingness to contemplate more arbitrary rules for the manipulation of symbols.

He next turned away from arithmetic to formalize another activity: logic. Now the symbols would be given rules appropriate to their intended interpretation in inferences. He published repeatedly on the subject, and had no qualms about repeating himself extensively, which makes it both difficult and perhaps unnecessary to trace the evolution of his thought. In fact, it seems best to regard him as someone capable of scattered insights but not of extended periods of originality, and, as we shall see, he cannot be regarded as a clear expositor. Indeed, it must be said that De Morgan's exposition is descriptive rather than explanatory, and later accounts are suddenly augmented with symbols from earlier accounts without explanation. The contrast with Boole is marked, and it is no wonder that Boole is remembered where De Morgan has slipped into history.

His critique of syllogistic logic in his (1851) or his more accessible (1860) requires us first of all to review the theory of propositions as it then stood. There were four types, denoted A, E, I, and O (De Morgan 1860, 14). Type A asserts 'All X are Y', as in 'All sheep are mammals'. Type E asserts 'No X are Y', as in 'No sheep are reptiles'. Type I asserts 'Some X are Y', as in 'Some sheep are edible'. Type O asserts 'Some X are not Y', as in 'Some sheep are not edible'. In 1850 De Morgan objected to the letters on the grounds that they should be compound. Type A, for example, which was known as the universal affirmative sentence because it affirmed something about all X, should in his view have had a name like AB, where A stood for affirming and B for universal. Likewise there should be a symbol for negating, E, and one for particular (rather than universal) propositions, such as N. Then instead of A, E, I, and O we would have, respectively, AB, EB, AN, and EN. It might be unfair to criticize De Morgan for not using N for negation, because this notation was not intended for public consumption, but we shall see that his eventual notation was still clumsy. However, it was worth noting that he was right that these propositions did two things, not one: they crudely quantified Xs into all or some, and then they asserted something of Xs and Ys.

This suggested to De Morgan that he devise a notation that captured both aspects of a proposition. He wrote $X)$ or $(X$ to denote all X; the notation was intended to suggest that all X have been contained by the bracket. To express the idea of 'some X' he reversed the bracket and wrote $)X$ or $X($. Now, to write 'All sheep are mammals' he let X denote the class of sheep and Y that of mammals. This gave him $X)$ for all sheep and $)Y$ for some mammals. To express the relationship between these two classes, he now juxtaposed the symbols, obtaining $X))Y$; he could equally well have obtained $X)Y($. He then introduced dots, primarily to express negation but also to make expressions easier to read. So, he could write the above expression as $X) \cdot \cdot)Y$, because he regarded double negation as affirmation. He explained that the awkward sentence 'All sheep are some mammals' was intended to convey that all sheep are mammals but there may or may not be mammals that are not sheep.

Before we deal with the account of negation, it should be noted that De Morgan seems to have assumed that his classes were never empty. This also means that the opposite class to X, consisting of all the objects (in a given context) that are not X, is not empty. De Morgan denoted this class by x. 'Let every name which belongs to the whole universe be excluded as needless' he wrote, in (1860, 12), which, in this context, excludes the empty set. The result is that some of his claims are incorrect.

Let us first note the problems caused by the words 'all' and 'some', which De Morgan attempted to address, although, unlike Boole, he failed to provide illustrative examples that would certainly have helped (we shall return to this point, but presently let us understand De Morgan's notation). The positive propositions are Type A, 'All X are Y', as in 'All sheep are mammals' and Type I, which asserts 'Some X are some Y', as in 'Some sheep are edible'. These De Morgan wrote respectively as $X))Y$, as we have just seen, and X ()Y, and in set-theoretic notation we would write $X \subseteq Y$ and $X \cap Y \neq \emptyset$. That leaves $X)(Y$ and X ((Y. With these propositions, we shall find that De Morgan offered verbal equivalents that are not only not grammatical English but at best difficult to understand and at worst ambiguous. I shall say that these glosses are in 'near-English'.

The expression $X)(Y$, which says in words that 'All X are all Y', was glossed by De Morgan as 'Some things are not either (all) Xs or (all) Ys', which is baffling at first sight. The clear meaning is that every X is a Y and every Y is an X, that is, in our set-theoretic notation, $X = Y$, and as already noted this is how Jevons interpreted his example of a proposition that escapes syllogistic logic. But De Morgan inferred (tacitly appealing to his avoidance of the empty set) that there will be non Xs and non Ys and so some objects that are neither X not Y, so the correct set-theoretic translation is $x \cap y \neq \emptyset$.

The expression X ((Y says in words that 'Some Xs are all Ys', or 'Every Y is an X' (and perhaps there are some Xs that are not Ys), and was glossed that way by De Morgan. In our set-theoretic notation it says $Y \subseteq X$.

Simple negation was symbolized by a $\cdot$. But what an expression with a negation in it says is not clear. If a statement of Type A, and so of the form $X))Y$, is wrong, there is some X that is not a Y, so it is the particular negation that forms Type O. This De Morgan wrote as $X (\cdot (Y$.

Similarly, we should get Type E as the negation of Type I. Type I expressions are of the form X ()Y, and they say that some Xs are (all) Ys, so their negation, written $X) \cdot (Y$, is that no X is a Y, or, in our set-theoretic notation that $X \cap Y = \emptyset$ or $x \cup y = 1$. In the convoluted near-English of De Morgan the negation translates as 'All Xs are not all Ys', which may be said to mean that no X is a Y.

We notice that in each case the brackets are turned round and a $\cdot$ inserted between them, so De Morgan's symbolic notation is tidy, but his interpretations are obscure.

We now try this observation on the expressions $X)(Y$ and X ((Y. The negation of $X)(Y$ should be $X (\cdot)Y$, which says 'Some Xs are not some Ys'. Now, we interpreted $X)(Y$ as $x \cap y \neq \emptyset$, so its negation is $x \cap y = \emptyset$ or $X \cup Y = 1$.

The negation of X ((Y should be $X) \cdot)Y$, which says 'All Xs are not some Ys', which is quite unclear in English. As the negation of 'All Xs are some Ys' it ought to say that 'Some Xs are not Ys' but it is arguably synonymous with 'All Xs are not any Ys' which would say that 'Every X is not a Y' or 'All Xs are ys'. We shall interpret it in our set-theoretic notation as saying that $Y \not\subseteq X$.

Table 5.1 De Morgan's simple forms and their set-theoretic equivalents

De Morgan's form	Set-theoretic equivalent
X))Y	$X \subseteq Y$
X)(Y	$x \cap y \neq \emptyset$
X ()Y	$X \cap Y \neq \emptyset$
X ((Y	$Y \subseteq X$
X)·)Y	$Y \not\subseteq X$
X) · (Y	$X \cap Y = \emptyset$ or $x \cup y = 1$
X (·)Y	$X \cup Y = 1$ or $x \cap y = \emptyset$
X (·(Y	$X \not\subseteq Y$

Table 5.2 De Morgan's simple forms involving contraries and their set-theoretic equivalents

De Morgan's form	Set-theoretic equivalent
X))Y	$X \subseteq Y$
X) · (y	$X \cap y = \emptyset$
x(·)Y	$x \cup Y = 1$
x((y	$y \subseteq x$
X ()Y	$X \cap Y \neq \emptyset$
X (·(y	$X \not\subseteq y$
x)·)Y	$Y \not\subseteq x$
x)(y	$X \cap Y \neq \emptyset$

We list these results in Table 5.1, again using De Morgan's device of introducing lower-case letters to denote contraries, or complements, as they would later be called. So x stood for all the things that are not Xs. Of course, in ordinary discussions the contrary of X is usually easy to understand: in the right context men and women are contraries, as are adults and children, or humans and mammals, or mammals and other animals. There is a tacit understanding of all the things we are talking about when we single out the class of Xs, and the ones that remain fill out precisely the class x. But in any abstract setting, as the earlier conversational examples illustrate, this needs to be made precise, and we shall see how De Morgan did this shortly, but grant him for the moment something like a universe of discourse. So $X))y$ says 'All Xs are (some) ys' or 'All Xs are non-Ys' or 'No X is a Y'. We have introduced the symbol 1 to stand for everything under discussion, which De Morgan called the universe.

Note that, as De Morgan intended, lines 4 and 5 are a pair of opposites, as are lines 3 and 6, lines 2 and 7, and lines 1 and 8.

The convoluted and at times ambiguous near-English expressions were briefly analysed by De Morgan. He traced the ambiguity back to a problem with 'all' and 'some'. He took the four types of statement he had given by universal or particular, affirmation or negation, and wrote them as follows:

- *A* (universal affirmation) *X*))*Y*, which says 'All *X*s are some *Y*s'
- *E* (universal negation) *X*) · (*Y*, which says 'All *X*s are not (all) *Y*s'
- *I* (particular affirmative) *X* ()*Y*, which says 'Some *X*s are some *Y*s'
- *O* (particular negation) *X* (·(*Y*, which says 'Some *X*s are not (all) *Y*s'.

As De Morgan pointed out, this illustrates a problem with the words 'all', 'some', and 'any', and the word 'all' in parentheses should be replaced with the word 'any'. This makes it clearer that *E* says 'No *X* is a *Y*' and that *O* says 'Some *X*s are not *Y*s'.

De Morgan now made use of the contraries, and wrote down the thirty-two expressions obtained from the above eight on replacing *X*))*Y*, by *X*))*y*, *x*))*Y*, and *x*))*y*, which he sorted out into eight families each consisting of four identical propositions. Two of these are listed in Table 5.2 to show what can be done.

De Morgan defended his new symbolism (1860, 14) on the grounds that his symbols were clearer than the corresponding statements in English and easier to use, challenging any doubters to decide, immediately and with a demonstration, which, if either, of the following sentences was true: 1) All Englishmen who do not take snuff are to be found among Europeans who do not use tobacco, and 2) All Englishmen who do not use tobacco are to be found among Europeans who do not take snuff. Indeed, the ability to sort out such sentences on logical grounds was, arguably, the only defence for teaching logic at all. So he now had to demonstrate the power of his new notation, and after all, no notation is worth learning if it does not repay the time spent learning it with time saved using it.

De Morgan chose to cover pages of his (1860) with equivalent forms of his own notation, thus essentially displaying the algebra of the symbols ')' and '·', replete with a dictionary in the language of the syllogism and the standard forms of syllogistic reasoning. For example, conversion reads a proposition backwards, converting *X*))*Y* into *Y* ((*X*, which turns 'All *X*s are *Y*s' into 'some *Y*s are *X*s'. He also applied it to the syllogism in all of its forms. For example, the expression *X*))*Y*))*Z* implied *X*))*Z*. The traditional term for a collection of propositions, the major term of each being the minor term of the next is a sorites, and these are inferences, he reminded his readers, when all terms are universal and each intermediate term enters once totally and once partially, or when one and only one of those conditions is broken just once.

There is no point in a new notation if it does not do any work. In the present case, it should make deduction easier. To this end, De Morgan introduced his erasure rule (1851, 87). From 'All *X* are *Y*' and 'Some *Z*s are not *Y*, or *X*))*Y* and *Y*)·)*Z*, the reader deduces 'Some *Z*s are not *X*s'. In De Morgan's notation, this looks like *X*))*Y*)·)*Z* implies *X*)·)*Z*, which is obtained by erasing)*Y*) from the previous expression. As he put it: 'Erase the symbols of the middle term, the remaining terms shew the inference' (quoted in Hobart and Richards 2008, 300). Or, removing the letters)))·) gives)·).

He also introduced his transformation rule, which involves negation. He wrote 'To use the contrary of a term without altering the import of the proposition, alter the curvature of its parenthesis and annex or withdraw a negative point' (1851, 92) (quoted in Hobart and Richards 2008, 302). So 'All *X*s are some *Y*s', written as *X*))*Y*, says the same as 'All *X*s are not

Table 5.3 Examples for De Morgan's transformation rule

De Morgan's form	Set-theoretic equivalent
X (·(Y	$X \nsubseteq Y$
X ()y	$X \cap y \neq \emptyset$
x)·)y	$X \nsubseteq Y$
x)(Y	$X \cap y \neq \emptyset$

some ys', which is written X).)y. In this way repeated use of the transformation rule gave De Morgan these logical equivalences:

$$X (\cdot (Y = X \, ()y = x)\cdot)y = x)(Y.$$

We can check these as shown in Table 5.3.

In his symbolism, the conclusion is obtained by erasing all the intermediate terms and their quantities, and allowing that double negation is affirmation. Thus, to give his first example,

$$X))Y) \cdot (Z \, ()T) \cdot (U (\cdot)V))W \text{ gives } X)\cdot)W.$$

To understand this, we must read the initial proposition as saying $X))Y$ and $Y) \cdot (Z$ and $Z \, ()T$ and $T) \cdot (U$ and $U (\cdot)V$ and $V))W$, which in words is 'All Xs are Ys and no Y is a Z and some Z s are Ts and no T is a U and everything is either U or V and all V s are W s'. From this we apparently deduce $X)\cdot)W$, or 'All Xs are not some Ws', which set theoretically is $x \nsubseteq w$, and, happily for us, correct (for example, let $X = \{x'\}$, $Y = \{x',y'\}$, $Z = \{u',w',t'\}$, $T = \{y',t'\}$, $U = \{u',w'\}$, $V = \{x',y',w',t'\}$, and $W = V$, so $x = \{y',u',w',t'\}$ and $w = \{u'\}$).

Let us work through this more slowly than De Morgan did. From $X))Y$ and $Y) \cdot (Z$ the erasure rule gives us $X) \cdot (Z$. This is correct set-theoretically, as are all the remaining deductions.

From $X) \cdot (Z$ and $Z \, ()T$ erasure gives us $X)\cdot)T$.

From $X)\cdot)T$ and $T) \cdot (U$ erasure gives us $X) \cdot \cdot(U$, which by double negation is the same as $X)(U$.

From $X)(U$ and $U (\cdot)V$ erasure gives us $X)\cdot)V$.

From $X)\cdot)V$ and $V))W$ erasure gives us $X)\cdot)W$.

We shall now dispense with the near-English glosses and pass straight to set-theoretic expressions when necessary.

Where De Morgan departed from the syllogism was when he used what he called 'strengthened propositions' (1860, §30). 'A particular proposition', he wrote, 'is strengthened into a universal which affirms it (and more, may be) by altering one of the quantities: thus)·) is affirmed in (·) and in) · ('. To see what this means, insert an X and a Y in)·), to get $X)\cdot)Y$ or

$x \not\subseteq y$. Now do the same to (·), and get X (·)Y, or $X \cup Y = 1$, and do the same to) · (to get X) · (Y, or $X \cap Y = \emptyset$. In each case the original proposition, call it B, is implied by the one it is affirmed in, which we shall call B'.

Now, if propositions A and B together imply C, and B' implies B, then we can infer that A and B' together imply C. So if we take an argument and replace a particular proposition by one it is affirmed in, B', we obtain a new valid argument. However, if the original argument was in syllogistic form, but the new one is not, then this means that De Morgan's battery of arguments includes ones that cannot be expressed syllogistically, and this is indeed the case.

Consider the example (in Hobart and Richards 2008, 310) X) · (Y and Y))Z imply by erasure that X)·)Z. This translates set-theoretically into $X \cap Y = \emptyset$ and $Y \subseteq Z$, from which we validly deduce $Z \subseteq X$ using the fact that in De Morgan's work we have $Y \neq \emptyset$. But verbally, this translates into 'No X is a Y' and 'Every Y is a Z', from which we cannot infer that 'Some Xs are Zs'. But X)·)Z does not say 'Some Xs are Zs'; it says that 'All Xs are not some Zs', or that some X is not a Z, or that $X \cup z \neq \emptyset$.

These do not say the same thing, but they play the same role in De Morgan's eliminative strategy. He had therefore to explain how his algebra did not describe the rules of syllogistic logic without making his algebra absurd, which he did by making a vague analogy with complex numbers (see Hobart and Richards 2008, 312).

Elsewhere, De Morgan gave an early account of the logic of relations. As Grattan-Guinness has pointed out (2000, 32) it is remarkable that no one before him seems to have pointed out that expressions of the form 'Jack is taller than Jill' cannot be handled in syllogistic logic, and in opening up this part of logic De Morgan made arguably his most important contribution. That said, as Grattan-Guinness remarks (2000, 33), De Morgan's best paper on the subject 'is a ramble even by his standards', and he singles out two key passages. De Morgan glossed X.. LY as signifying that Xs stand in relation L to Ys, or, as he put it, X is 'some one of the objects of thought which stand to Y in the relation L' or 'X is one of the Ls of Y'. The first key idea is that of the contrary of a relation, so if X..LY and l is the contrary of L then X.LY and X.lY signify that Xs are not in the relation L to Ys. Thus, if L is the relation 'less than' then.L and l signify the relation 'not less than'. De Morgan also discussed compound relations. For example, the relations L for 'less than' and M for 'relatively prime to' may form the compound LM signifying 'less than and relatively prime to'. De Morgan wrote X..LMY and X..$L(MY)$ to signify 'X is one of the Ls of one of the Ms of Y'. The concept of the converse of a relation is illustrated by the example 'X is an ancestor of Y' and its converse 'Y is a descendant of X'; De Morgan denoted the converse of a relation L by L^{-1} to signify 'Y is one of the Ls of X', and he noted that $(LM)^{-1} = L^{-1}M^{-1}$. Quantification was handled by upper and lower primes, so X..$LM'Y$ signifies 'X is an L of every M of Y', and L.., M signifies 'X is an L of none but Ms of Y'. He called a relation L convertible when it provides its own converse, so X..LY implies Y.. LX, and he conjectured in his (1860, 225) that every convertible relation L is reducible to the form LL^{-1}. A relationship L was said to be transitive when X..LY and Y..LZ together imply X.. LZ. But after this useful labelling exercise, De Morgan did not do much to develop a theory of relations, a task much better handled by Charles Sanders Peirce in his (1870) and subsequent papers.

This extension of the usual copula 'is' to what De Morgan called the abstract copula brought predictable criticism from a reviewer of the *Formal Logic*, who charged that De Morgan had left formal logic for material implication, by which he meant that 'is' obeys purely logical rules but the new copulas require an understanding of what the symbolized word in the relation actually means. De Morgan replied that on the contrary until now formal logicians had been confused about the copula 'is'. It was its formal property of transitivity that permitted the deduction of 'All Xs are Zs' from 'All Xs are Ys' and 'All Ys are Zs', and this was a property that 'is' shared with some other relations (such as 'less than') but not others. In his best polemical style he added 'Historically speaking, the copula has been material to this day.'

De Morgan did not appreciate the riches that lay before him and was unable to walk away from his relationship with the syllogism. He recast the syllogism in the form of a compounding of relations, he noted that from X..LY and Y..MZ one could deduce X..LMY, and he recognized that he had brought the topic of relations to the surface, but he did not appreciate what he had done and he could not build on it. Despite the unwieldy and at times downright unreadable sentences that glossed his formal remarks, he did not see that developing the symbolism might be a fruitful direction to take. He noted that there were many similarities with his logic and ordinary algebra and he sometimes devised his notation accordingly; he was clear that some sort of logic, in the form of axioms, must underpin any sort of algebra, but he was not systematic enough or insightful enough to force his contemporaries to reckon with what he had done. For all his vigour and his often high opinion of himself and his originality, De Morgan could not shake off the limitations of his intellectual milieu, and his analysis of logic ended here.

Finally, mention ought to be made of the eponymous laws. In his *Formal Logic* (1847, 115–16) De Morgan had introduced a notation for compound propositions:

> Thus P, Q, R being certain names, if we wish to give a name to everything which is all three, we may join them thus, P QR: if we wish to give a name to everything which is either of the three (one or more of them) we may write P, Q, R: if we want to signify anything that is either both P and Q, or R, we have P Q, R. The contrary of P QR is p, q, r; that of P, Q, R is pqr.

This is likely to be the first occurrence of De Morgan's laws in the work of De Morgan, although verbal statements go back to medieval logicians. The second of the laws is also found in Jevons, *The Principles of Science* (1874, 87).

3 GEORGE BOOLE

Boole's *Mathematical Analysis of Logic* (1847), although it first acknowledges recent debates between Hamilton and De Morgan, gets going with this remark about logic: 'If it was lawful to regard it from *without*, as connecting itself through the medium of Number with the intuitions of Space and Time, it was lawful also to regard it from *within*, as based upon facts of another order which have their abode in the constitution of the Mind.'[1] His way of extending British symbolical algebra to logic was much more forceful and clear than De Morgan's, because it was much less attached to the syllogism. It also reflects his experience dealing with problems in the calculus via a formal study of operators. Boole regarded algebra, even in the setting of differential equations, as an activity in which

---

[1] (Boole 1847, 1).

symbols were dealt with according to stated laws of combination, without reference to any meaning they might have. He further suggested that while this was the standard procedure in mathematics, it had largely, even exclusively, concerned itself with quantities and magnitudes, and he now wished to break with this limitation and extend mathematical analysis of this kind to logic. As he put it (Boole 1847, 4): 'We might justly assign it as the definitive character of a true Calculus, that it is a method resting upon the employment of Symbols, whose laws of combination are known and general, and whose results admit of a consistent interpretation.' Logic would be amenable to this treatment because of 'the existence in our minds of general notions, our ability to conceive of a class, and to designate its individual members by a common name'. And he immediately went on (Boole 1847, 4–5): 'The theory of Logic is thus intimately connected with that of Language.' So he saw his work as a step towards a philosophical language, one that, for better or worse, he chose not to pursue.

In Boole's view, the basic mental operations are subject to 'peculiar laws' and relations, that, however obvious they might appear, and while 'probably they are noticed for the first time in this Essay' could not be otherwise or the 'entire mechanism of reasoning [...]' would be vitally changed' (Boole 1847, 6). Inevitably, Boole was led to discuss the relation between logic, as a branch of philosophy, and mathematics. The Scottish philosopher Sir W. Hamilton was at the time in a public argument with De Morgan in which he contended that the study of mathematics was simultaneously dangerous and useless. Philosophy, he contended, was the science of real existence and real causes, it answers the question 'why?', whereas mathematics is credulous in its premises. To this, Boole suggested that while he might agree with those who contended that such a philosophy was impossible, he was willing to grant that 'the problem which has baffled the efforts of ages, is not a hopeless one' (Boole 1847, 13), but he felt compelled to assert that on this view of the nature of philosophy, 'Logic forms no part of it', and logic should be classified instead with mathematics, because logic, like geometry, could be given axiomatic foundations.

Boole then developed a symbolic calculus which he presented in an extended setting six years later in his *Laws of Thought* (1854), and though he carefully pointed out that this work was not a republication of the old one, being much more general and wider in its applications, it overlaps with it to a great extent.

Capital letters X, Y, Z, said Boole, represent individual members of classes, so X applies to every member of one class. Lower-case letters x, y, z are symbols operating on classes, so x selects from that subject all the Xs that it contains. Boole called these symbols elective because of the nature of the operation they represent, and spoke of expressions in them as elective functions and equations between them as elective equations. There is a universe, denoted 1, which is the 'subject understood', which we may take to be the context, everything that is presently under discussion. These rather murky definitions are then illustrated with the example

$$x = x\,(1),$$

'the meaning of either term being the selection from the Universe of all the Xs which it contains, and the result of the operation being in common language, the class X, i.e. the class of which each member is an X' (1847, 15–16).

Things improve when the symbol xy is explained as such individuals as are both Xs and Ys. If a class is divided into two parts and written $u + v$ then Boole gave a quick verbal argument to show that

$$x(u + v) = xu + xv.$$

The symbol '+' had not been defined, and it is not clear if the division is into disjoint parts. More verbal arguments gave these rules and

$$xy = yx$$
$$x^2 = x, \text{ and so } x^n = x$$

for any positive integer n. In a footnote Boole further deduced that

$$+^n = +,$$

which, he said, 'is the known property of that symbol'.

Boole then translated the four A, E, I, O premisses of a syllogism into his symbolic language, so I, some Xs are Ys, was written

$$v = xy,$$

it being assumed that v did not select nothing. He summarized his results in a helpful table on p. 25, which has the incidental effect of making it clear how substantial is his move into a symbolic algebra, because it demonstrates the possibility of reasoning with the symbols alone, and leaving their verbal equivalents behind. Indeed, the rest of the book is devoted to extending the range of verbal statements that can be expressed in this fashion and then indicating how a symbolic calculus could be developed to handle them. So in a chapter entitled 'Properties of Elective Functions', we get Maclaurin's theorem applied to an arbitrary elective function $\varphi(x)$, with the result that

$$\varphi(x) = \varphi(1)x + \varphi(0)(1 - x),$$

where $\varphi(0)$ and $\varphi(1)$ are called the moduli of the function $\varphi(x)$. The result is promptly extended to functions of two (and by implication any number of) variables. The next chapter is entitled 'On the Solution of Elective Equations'.

This short book was far from being precise, and its examples of reasoning unlikely to persuade anyone skilful in verbal arguments to spend the time learning the symbolism. His later and ultimately much more influential book, *An Investigation into the Laws of Thought, on Which are Founded the Mathematical Theories of Logic and Probability* (1854), therefore went over that ground again before proceeding further.[2]

---

[2] Boole was not the first to use the phrase 'the laws of thought' as the title of a book, an honour that may belong to *Outline of the Laws of Thought* by William Thomson, Archbishop of York (London, 1842). De Morgan had also spoken of producing an 'algebra of the laws of thought', at the start of his (1851).

As he now saw it, the principal difficulty in distilling a science of logic from the multiplicity of truths one could easily summon up was in identifying the fundamental ones from
which all others could be derived. As he pointed out later, not only could the syllogisms of
traditional logic be analysed into simpler forms, and therefore should not be regarded as
basic, there were logically valid deductions that could not be put in syllogistic form.

Boole again viewed language as a system of signs, such as words. He introduced his fundamental ideas (1854, 27) this way:

> All the operations of Language, as an instrument of reasoning, may be conducted by a system
> of signs composed of the following elements, viz.:
>
> 1st. Literal symbols, as x, y, & c., representing things as subjects of our conceptions.
>
> 2nd. Signs of operation, as $+$, $-$, $\times$ standing for those operations of the mind by which the
> conceptions of things are combined or resolved so as to form new conceptions involving the
> same elements.
>
> 3rd. The sign of identity, $=$.
>
> And these symbols of Logic are in their use subject to definite laws, partly agreeing with and
> partly differing from the laws of the corresponding symbols in the science of Algebra.

Appellative or descriptive signs could be either nouns or adjectives because they named
either things or some quality of things. Concatenation of symbols produced a sign naming
the things with all the properties of the concatenated parts (so, in his helpful example, if x
stands for sheep and y for white, then xy stands for white sheep). Their laws of combination
were commutative, $xy = yx$, 'like the symbols of algebra' (1854, 31). But in the logical case
it was also true that $x^2 = x$. The symbol '$+$' he introduced to stand for the exclusive 'or', on
the grounds that that was, in strictness, how the words 'and' and 'or' were used in ordinary
language[3] (1854, 32–3) and the symbol '$-$' to stand for taking complements, so if (to give
his example) x stands for all men, and y for Asiatics, then $x - y$ stands for all men except
Asiatics.

The analysis of complements led him to introduce a universe of discourse, the class consisting of all objects under discussion (1854, 42), which he denoted by the symbol '1', and the
class Nothing by the symbol '0'. These were chosen (1854, 57) because the only numbers that
satisfy the equation $x^2 = x$ are 0 and 1. So '1 $- x$', represents all the objects under consideration which are not x. This duly led Boole to the proposition (1854, 49) that:

> That axiom of metaphysicians which is termed the principle of contradiction, and which
> affirms that it is impossible for any being to possess a quality, and at the same time not to pos-
> sess it, is a consequence of the fundamental law of thought, whose expression is $x^2 = x$.
>
> Let us write this equation in the form whence we have
>
> $$x - x^2 = 0$$
> $$x(1 - x) = 0;$$
>
> both these transformations being justified by the axiomatic laws of combination and transpo-
> sition (1854, ch. II. 13).

Boole next attempted to show that his symbolism was useful in carrying out certain kinds
of logical argument, by indicating how some verbal arguments can be translated into his

---

[3] Boole seems not to have noticed that this was not how he symbolized 'and'.

symbolic form. For this he had to create a theory of elimination (just as we eliminate reference to men from the famous syllogism to deduce the mortality of Socrates), and he hoped to do this by following the analogy with the solution of algebraic equations that he had often stressed when setting up his system. In this he was not very successful. He was led, via an obscure concept of division, to devise a symbol for 'all, some, or none', in order to cope with the fact that logical equations can have indefinite solutions ('some men are foolish'). Boole's choice for this symbol was 0/0. For example (1854, 105), he expressed the statement 'No men are perfect' as

$$y = v(1-x)$$

where y represents men, v is an indefinite class, and x perfect beings. He eliminated v and arrived at $yx = 0$, which states that 'perfect men do not exist'. From this he wrote

$$x = \frac{0}{y} = \frac{0}{0}(1-y)$$

'No perfect beings are men' and

$$1 - x = y + \frac{0}{0}(1-y)$$

'Imperfect beings are all men with an indefinite remainder of beings, which are not men'.

First, Boole dealt with what he called primary or concrete propositions, which are assertions about facts. Then he turned to what he called secondary propositions, those that relate propositions to other propositions. He turned them into primary propositions by the device of interpreting the proposition 'If the proposition X is true then the proposition Y is true' as saying that the time during which X is true is time during which Y is true. So (1854, 165) Boole introduced the convention that x represents the act of mind by which we concentrate on the portion of time for which X is true (and stipulated that this is what it means to say x denotes the time for which X is true). He could then write the proposition 'X is true' as $x = 1$, the contrary proposition 'X is false' as $x = 0$, and the proposition 'If X is true then Y is true' as $x = vy$.

To demonstrate the fertility and generality of his method, Boole examined theological arguments from Plato, Clarke, and Spinoza. He concluded that Spinoza's *Ethics* was imperfect, and that it is 'impossible, therefore, by the mere processes of Logic, to deduce the whole of the conclusions of the first book of the *Ethics* from the axioms and definitions which are prefixed to it' (1854, 213). Boole felt that his examination of theology compelled the view that it was futile to establish entirely a priori the existence of an Infinite Being, and it was better to fall back on the argument by design.

In chapter XV Boole was dismissive of syllogistic reasoning. He found that 'it is not a science, but a collection of scientific truths, too incomplete to form a system of themselves' (1854, 241). When it was regarded as a method of elimination, he felt it was imperfect: all elimination could be carried out by means of syllogisms but only after the original statements had been re-expressed using non-syllogistic methods. And while syllogistic reasoning always eliminates, Boole felt that reasoning need not always do so. Instead, he advocated organizing Logic so that it was derived from a set of simple axioms, such as Leibniz's principle of contradiction (1854, 240).

Boole then moved into an extensive discussion of probability before returning, at the very end of his book, to discuss some of the philosophical issues his analysis of logic had raised. Following Whewell, whom he cited, he argued that the fundamental concepts of science are 'neither, as I conceive, intellectual products independent of experience nor mere copies of external things' (1854, 406); they have necessary antecedents in experience and also require some power of abstraction for their formation. He recognized that his laws of thought led him to admit that they were of a different kind from natural or scientific laws. External nature conformed to (correct) laws inexorably, but the mind frequently violated the laws of thought, which could therefore be 'the laws of right reasoning only' (1854, 408). But that was enough to show that the human mind has the capacity to ascend from particular facts to the general propositions of science. Finally, Boole contended that the laws of thought are the same kind as the laws of the acknowledged processes of mathematics. But he did not claim that mathematics was a mere part of logic, still less that mathematics could be regarded as all of knowledge (that would exalt the faculty of reasoning over those of observation, reflection, and judgement).

Boole's achievement was not, therefore, what Russell said it was in his oft-cited aphorism 'Pure mathematics was discovered by George Boole in his work published in 1854'.[4] But nor did it languish in obscurity in its day, as some historians have suggested.[5] Both views may be different ways of exaggerating its originality. In fact, it was read, in Britain at least, but with difficulty, by a handful of authors.

4. Jevons and Venn

William Stanley Jevons had his interest in logic awakened by De Morgan when Jevons studied under him at University College London. He left there, however, without taking his degree in order to embark on a career in business, and shortly took a job working in the Australian Mint, returning in 1859 to complete his education.[6]

He published his short *Pure Logic, or the Logic of Quality Apart from Quantity* in 1864. He acknowledged that 'in a considerable degree this system is founded on that of Prof. Boole, as stated in his admirable and highly original Mathematical Analysis of Logic', which he footnoted as '*Investigation of the Laws of Thought* 1854'. Pure logic, he then explained, is about the sameness or difference of things. For a reason which he did not make clear Jevons wished to play down the mathematical aspects of his work, perhaps from a feeling that the relationship between the two needed more clarity than he could give it. So he explained (1864, 7) that the letters *A, B, C*, etc. and the marks +,0, and = that he would use were 'in no way mysterious symbols'. Terms like *A*, for example, were merely convenient abbreviations for ordinary terms of language such as 'red' or 'The Lords Commissioners'. This ambiguous presentation is dwarfed by the next one: '+ is merely a mark, substituted for the sake of clearness, for the conjunctions *and, either, or* &c of common language.' Happily, 'the mark = is

---

[4] Russell (1901/1963, 59).
[5] A trickle of problems even passed through the *Educational Times*, so the topic had some currency.
[6] Jevons's main work was on economics. He died by drowning just before his 47th birthday.

merely the copula *is* ', and 'the meaning of 0 whatever it may be may also be expressed in words'.

Matters get no better when we learn (1864, 14) that when 'several names are placed together side by side, the meaning of the joint term is sometimes the sum of the meaning of the separate terms'. Set aside the worrying 'sometimes', what is the sum of the various meanings? Is it the same as their product, or is that different? No examples are given to aid the perplexed. We learn that $AB = BA$, that $AA = A$, and that $ABCD = ABC\,D.BCD = A.BB.C$ $C.DD$, although the dot is not explained, because, by what Jevons called the law of simplicity $AA = A$, we have $BB = B$, $CC = C$, and $DD = D$. Two pages later it is explained that if $A = B$ then $AC = BC$, and still we cannot be sure that the juxtaposition of symbols A and B, written AB, produces the class of objects that are both A and B.

On p. 25 we are introduced to plural terms, of which the first example is *B or C*, and allowed to write them as $B + C$, so we may now suspect that AB after all means things that are both A and B. But we may pursue a new ambiguity, because it is not clear if + denotes the inclusive or the exclusive 'or', and Boole has, as we saw, used the exclusive 'or'. However, we may write $A(B + C) = AB + AC$, and $A + A = A$, so we infer the inclusive 'or' is intended. It is therefore correct to say that Jevons replaced Boole's exclusive 'or' with the inclusive 'or', which makes the system more flexible and abolishes the problem of understanding expressions of the form $x + y$ when x and y have elements in common, which is particularly acute in the case when $x = y$.

Jevons introduced negation on (1864, 31), and explained that *notA* is the negative term signifying the absence of the quality or set of qualities of A. We then learn that if $A = BC$ then $notA = B.notC + notB.C + notB.notC$. Moreover, 'the negative of a negative term is the corresponding positive term', so 'What is *notnotA* is *A*', and for convenience (and following De Morgan without saying so) *notA* will be written a. On the next page we are told that 'It is is the nature of thought and things that *a thing cannot both have and not have the same quality.*' Contradictory terms are those that have no meaning, and are marked with a 0, so Jevons wrote $Aa = Aa0$ and for brevity $Aa = 0$, and informed his readers that 'The term 0, meaning *excluded from thought*, obeys the law of terms $0.0 = 0$, $0 + 0 = 0$'. We learn that $A = AB + Ab$, and are warned not to interpret this to mean that 'Virtue is either black or not-black', which is absurd, because we must attend to the ambiguity between 'Coloured but not black' and 'Not coloured'. This should have prompted Jevons to reflect on the universe of discourse, and what is meant by *not = A*, but it did not.

Jevons then collected his rules together in one place, made a few more remarks about them, and then compared them with the four basic propositions A, E, I, and O of syllogistic logic. For this, after rightly protesting at the difficulties with the word 'some' in most expositions of logic, he introduced a new symbol, U, not necessarily the same on each occurrence, so that he could write

- A: every A is B, $A = UB$ or $A = AB$
- E: no A is B, $A = Ub$ or $A = Ab$
- I: some A is B, $UA = UB$ or $CA = DB$
- O: some A is not B, $UA = Ub$ or $CA = Db$

The point of all of this was to reduce complicated logical arguments to the exercise of straightforward algebra, without the contrivance of Boole's symbol 0/0, and this was bound to fail since Jevons has done nothing except prefer the inclusive to the exclusive 'or', which does nothing to eliminate the inherent limitations of this form of algebra. But Jevons had a graver problem than Boole did with negation, because, as he admitted, it is not clear on his system what *notB* means even when the meaning of *B* is clear. This led him to the brink of confusion on p. 65, when in an extensive footnote he argued that

> Every logical term must have its contrary.
>   That is to say:—Whatever quality we treat as present we may also treat as absent. Thus there is no boundary to the universe of logic. No term can be proposed wide enough to cover its whole sphere; for the contrary of any term must add a sphere of indefinite magnitude. Let *U* be the universe; then *u* is not included in *U*. Nor will special terms limit the universe.

He then recoiled and admitted that 'this subject needs more consideration'.

The explicit disagreements with Boole at the end are the most useful and interesting parts of the book. One interesting disagreement between the two is that whereas Boole had seen his mathematical logic as new form of mathematics that was not restricted to the study of quantity, Jevons saw 'the Mathematics as rather derivatives of Logic' (1864, 5).

The method of elimination was a particular problem, and it was much refined by Jevons's attempt to mechanize the process. After some ten years of work, he exhibited a logical machine at the Royal Society of London in 1870 (see the description in the *Philosophical Transactions of the Royal Society*, 1870 and in Jevons, *The Principles of Science*, 1874). It became known as Jevons's logical piano.

Boole's advocate among subsequent British authors was John Venn, who in 1881 published his *Symbolic Logic*, a book of some 578 pages. Early on (pp. xix–xx) he remarked that

> It may almost be doubted whether any human being, provided he had received a good general education, was ever seriously baffled in any problem, either of conduct or of thought (examinations and the like of course excluded) by what could strictly be called a merely logical difficulty.... The question is rather this:—Do we ever fail to get at a conclusion, when we have the data perfectly clear before us, not from prejudice or oversight but from sheer inability to see our way through a train of logical reasoning?

After noting that this was the habitual problem of the mathematician, to have the data, in the form of equations, but be unable to solve them, he went on:

> It is almost needless to say that there is nothing resembling this in logic; the difficulties which persistently baffle us here, when we really take pains to understand the point in dispute, being philosophical rather than logical.

That being so, one may wonder what occupies so many pages, and the only answer is an extremely leisurely exposition of what Boole had already said. Grattan-Guinness notes a mere four pages in the book on the logic of relations, and there are some useful disparagements of the syllogism, but it is hard to see anything significantly new here. Except, perhaps, for the eponymous Venn diagram. These, as their author noted elsewhere (see Edwards 2004: 4), were initially an adaptation of diagrams Euler had used for a similar purpose. But even Venn could not find a way of drawing diagrams to this purpose for more than four classes (recently it has been shown that it can be done, see Edwards 2004). Lewis Carroll accomplished something similar with two diagrams for five classes in his *Symbolic Logic*.

5. Lewis Carroll

One should never take Lewis Carroll too seriously, even when he was Charles Dodgson, lecturer in mathematics at Christ Church, Oxford, but a good joke often has a serious point to it, and his typically concerned the empty set. Even if the elementary steps in a formal argument are set up to refer to sets that are neither empty nor the universe, they can rapidly lead to empty sets, and the consequences are counter-intuitive.

Let it be granted that all animals are either vicious or harmless, and no animal is both. Russell was to propose that the way to understand sentences like 'The present King of France is bald' is that it is false, because it should be construed as saying 'There is a King of France, and he is bald', but there is no King of France, so the statement is incorrect. Very well, applied to the non-existent unicorn we deduce that it is false that it is vicious, which makes it true that it is harmless, and also, by the same argument, that it is false that it is harmless, and so it must be vicious.

In a paradox more linguistic than logical, Carroll (or rather his character the King in *Through the Looking-Glass*) likewise professed himself impressed that somebody could see *nobody*:

> The King remarked in a fretful tone. 'To be able to see Nobody! And at that distance, too!

The most substantial part of his *Symbolic Logic* was the Appendix addressed to teachers, where he endeavoured to clear up some obscurities that might confuse a student but which should not confuse a teacher unless the intention was to confuse the student. The first of these was the existential import of statements. He began with a statement of Type I, that is, 'Some Xs are Ys'. The question is whether this entails the statement that there is at least one X, and Carroll took the view that this was for the writer, like Humpty-Dumpty, to decide. The criteria for deciding are that what is proposed is consistent with itself and the accepted facts of logic. If these statements assert the existence of at least one X then a fortiori statements of Type A ('All Xs are Ys') assert the existence of at least one X. Now Carroll considered the universal negation, Type E, 'All Xs are not all Ys', and showed that this must be taken not to assert. He argued as follows: Suppose it does assert, then the statement 'No XY are Z' asserts that some things exist that are both X and Y, so we may say 'Some X are Y'. Consider now the statement 'Some XY are Z'. It too implies that 'Some X are Y', but the statements 'No XY are Z' and 'Some XY are Z' are contraries, only one can be true, but either way we deduce that 'Some X are Y' is true. So it is always true that 'Some X are Y', which is absurd. This shows that if statements of Types I and A assert, then statements of Type E cannot.

Carroll next considered that statements of Type I do not assert, but those of Type A do assert, and deduced that then statements of Type E do assert. But he rejected it on the grounds that it fitted the rules of life too badly. He asked his readers to contemplate a club in which it was said that some members were millionaires, even when it has no members, but into which no one convicted seven times of forgery can be admitted, a statement that implies that such people do exist. This is indeed an unusual use of language.

There remained one other consistent view, which was that no statements of Types I, A, or E assert, and rather makes remarks along the lines of 'If there are any Xs, then some are Ys', and so forth. But Carroll indicated that this too was not how ordinary language construed things (1896, 167–8). He imagined a school in which class 1, the highest class, required all the boys to learn French, Greek, and Latin, where boys in class 2 all learn only Greek, and boys in class 3 all learn only Latin, but in which there are boys only in classes 2 and 3 but not yet in class 1. Such a school, on this construal of assertion, could claim that 'If there are any boys doing French then all of them are doing Greek' and also 'If there are any boys doing French then all of them are doing Latin', which would imply that 'If any boys are doing Latin then some of them are doing Greek', which is an invalid argument (there are boys doing Latin, and none of them are doing Greek).

Carroll therefore took the view that the only worthwhile way forward was to say that statements of Types I and A assert, but those of Type E do not.

Next, Carroll turned to negation, which we have already seen tends to produce statements that are not in understandable English. He proposed that for every attribute there be a contrary attribute, so that everything in a given universe that is not an X is a *notX*, and that every statement of the form 'Some (or all) Xs are-not Ys' be read as saying 'Some (or all) Xs are *notYs*'.

6. Hugh MacColl

The last logician to be considered in this article fits no better in here than he did into Britain or the community of logicians in his lifetime. Hugh MacColl was born in Argyllshire in 1837, and his first language was Gaelic. After some years working as a schoolteacher he emigrated permanently to Boulogne in France, eventually becoming a French citizen. His innovative contributions to logic were largely rejected by Jevons, and MacColl seems to have little impact on British readers, although Christine Ladd-Franklin had a high opinion of his work on universal propositions.

As we have seen, particular problems in logic concern propositions about non-existing objects. As noted, Russell's approach was to regard all statements about such as objects as false (except, of course, those saying that the non-existent object does not exist). This is unsatisfactory on two counts. First, to say that 'Hamlet disliked his mother' and 'Hamlet disliked daytime TV' are both false because Hamlet does not exist is to miss more interesting ways in which they are false for different reasons. Second, there are many occasions when one wants to reason about objects that may or may not exist. At present, the status of Goldbach's conjecture (which claims that every even integer is the sum of two primes) is unresolved. The even integer that is the smallest counterexample to this conjecture either exists or it does not, let us suppose that it is under intense scrutiny and more and more is discovered about it. If finally it can be shown to exist, even if it can only be shown to lie below some enormous number and well beyond our ability to compute, then we would say that all our claims about it were true. If the intense scrutiny results in a proof that no such number exists and Goldbach's conjecture is false, do we want to say that all the statements made about it were false?

Consider now implication $A \to B$. When we construe this as material implication, we say that the implication is valid if both A and B are true or A is false, so $A \to B$ holds if and only if $notA \vee B$ holds, or, equivalently $A \wedge notB$ does not hold. This strikes many people as an odd thing to say about the relationship between two statements that have no meanings in common. MacColl, in a disagreement with Russell over this point, considered the example of a man who is not red-haired. It is true that he is a doctor and he is not red-haired, but no one would say that he is red-haired therefore he is a doctor (at least in the absence of some social prejudice).

MacColl's way round this was to construe the connective modally: A implies B in the sense of strict implication if it is impossible that A and $not - B$. Unfortunately it is not possible to pursue this and MacColl's interest in language further in this essay. For an account of MacColl's work, and an interpretation of MacColl's modal logic as what is called modal logic T, see Rahman and Redmond (2008) and the references cited there.

7. CONCLUSIONS

The British line of research into logic begun by De Morgan and Boole did not immediately lead to a powerful school of logicians. Undoubtedly, one reason for this in the strictly British setting is the fragmentary organization of mathematics in Britain, with Cambridge at its head. But in that setting it did little worse than invariant theory or even (shockingly) analysis. As noted, Boole's work was taken up by Jevons, by Venn, who was not first rate but kept the subject alive, and by Lewis Carroll. By 1900 it had reached Whitehead and Russell, where it joined with other influences to be sure, but the flowering of logic cannot be denied. Internationally, the situation was also propitious. Through Jevons it passed to Schröder in Germany. It was taken up directly by C. S. Peirce. It was eventually to reach Poland. There would be no difficulty in listing branches of mathematics which did no better for their first fifty years, and it represents an area of research in which the British were pioneers.

But it must also be said that it failed to deliver any strong new ways of thinking. It may have helped to display the limitations of the syllogism, but it never suggested that anyone with a substantial problem of an intellectual kind would be advised to write it in xs and ys. The problems that were put up for such analysis remained patently contrived if sometimes charming, mere puzzles that, what is more, the apparatus did little to simplify. The failure at the time of Venn diagrams to deal with more than four types of object (five if one uses Carroll's trick of two simultaneous diagrams), and the failure of the algebra as well, says two things. First, that should anybody have had six classes of objects to look at simultaneously (accused bribers with a previous record, extenuating circumstances, who are female, over 18, and with access to expensive lawyers, perhaps) is probably not going to be helped by a mastery of *The Laws of Thought*. Second, that there was not a fruitful source of such problems requiring this kind of analysis anyway.

Despite the irritating lack of clarity on some issues, such as empty sets, there was a body of ideas worth respecting, but the best idea was left fallow. The study of relations, which Pierce took up and which must have impressed his British readers, was indeed productive. Taken that way, there was at least a language for analysing mathematics and for obtaining interesting results. By not going in that direction, a generation of British logicians deprived themselves of a rich connection to mathematics.

Nor, until Russell and Whitehead, and therefore not until the generation influenced by Frege, did the British dig deep into the very idea of logic. They were tidying up, superficially rewriting, logical arguments; they were not asking questions about what logic is and what its reach might be.

Nor, until MacColl, did they begin to engage with language. It was clear to them that syllogistic logic could never be the language of classical mathematics; but the awfulness of the verbal expressions used by De Morgan, and the inadequacies of Boole's eliminative processes and his use of 0/0, did nothing to suggest that an analysis of logic could usefully be extended to other kinds of reasoning.

Perhaps that would have been too much to ask. Enough that later generations got round to these tasks. But the question would then be: why remember these British pioneers? Why, in particular, remember Boole? The answer is clear: Boolean algebra has become the language of computer engineers. Hardware and software designers use it all the time, and the whole world relies on it as a result. The normative aspect of human reasoning, submerged as it often is by cognitive short cuts of various kinds that have or had some evolutionary value, is precisely what we want of our computers. That this reasoning is amenable to algebra was a significant, lasting discovery that, when its time came, enabled the design of these machines. The forerunner was not Jevons's logical piano, although they pointed up the need, but Marquand's electronic circuits.[7]

REFERENCES

Boole, G., 1847. *Mathematical Analysis of Logic*, Cambridge and London.

Boole, G., 1854. *An Investigation into the Laws of Thought, on Which are Founded the Mathematical Theories of Logic and Probability*, London: Walton & Maberly.

Carroll, L. 1896. *Symbolic Logic*, London: Macmillan.

De Morgan, A., 1835. A Review of George Peacock, *A Treatise on Algebra*, *Quarterly Journal of Mathematics* 9: 311.

De Morgan, A., 1847. *Formal Logic*, London: Taylor and Walton.

De Morgan, A., 1851. 'On the Symbols of Logic, etc', *Trans. Cam. Phil. Soc.* 79–127.

De Morgan, A., 1860. *Syllabus of a Proposed System of Logic*, London: Walton & Maberly.

Edwards, A. W. F., 2004. *Cogwheels of the Mind*, Baltimore, Md.: Johns Hopkins University Press.

Gardner, M., 1983. *Logic Machines and Diagrams*. 2nd edn., Brighton, Harvester Press.

Grattan-Guinness, I., 2000. *The Search for Mathematical Roots*, Princeton: Princeton University Press.

Hobart, M. E., and Richards, J. L., 2008. 'De Morgan's Logic', in J. Woods and D. M. Gabby (eds.), *Handbook of the History of Logic*, Amsterdam: Elsevier, iv. 283–329.

Jacquette, D., 2008. 'Boole's Logic', in J. Woods and D. M. Gabbay (eds.), *Handbook of the History of Logic*, Amsterdam: Elsevier, iv. 332–79.

Jevons, W. S., 1864. *Pure Logic, or the Logic of Quality Apart from Quantity*, London: E. Stanford.

---

[7] As described, for example, in Gardner (1983).

Jevons, W. S., 1874. *The Principles of Science*, New York: Macmillan.

Kant, I., 1929. *Critique of Pure Reason*, trans. N. K. Smith, London: Macmillan.

Kant, I., 1974. *Logic*, trans. with introd., R. S. Hartman and W. Schwarz, New York: Dover.

Peacock, G., 1830. *A Treatise on Algebra*, Cambridge: Deighton.

Peirce, C. S., 1870. 'Description of a Notation for the Logic of Relatives, Resulting from an Amplification of the Conceptions of Booles Calculus of Logic', *Memoirs of the American Academy of Arts and Sciences*, 9: 317–78. In *Collected Papers*, ed. C. Hartshorne and P. Weiss (eds.), i. 27–98.

Pycior, H. M., 1983. 'Augustus De Morgan's Algebraic Work: The Three Stages', *ISIS* 74: 211–26.

Rahman, S. and Redmond, J., 2008. 'Hugh MacColl and the Birth of Logical Pluralism', in J. Woods and D. M. Gabbay (eds.), *Handbook of the History of Logic*, Amsterdam: Elsevier, iv. 535–606.

Russell, B., 1901/1963. 'Mathematics and the Metaphysicians'; repr. in *Mysticism and Logic*. London: Unwin.

Venn, J., 1881. *Symbolic Logic*. London: Macmillan.

CHAPTER **6**

....

IDEALIST LOGIC

....

PHILLIP FERREIRA

FOR most readers, the term 'idealist logic' has little meaning. Idealist logical theory is rarely mentioned in the standard histories.[1] And, despite its importance for English-speaking philosophy during the late nineteenth and early twentieth centuries, few are aware of its doctrines.

We shall consider the central claims of this logic in this chapter. However, we should understand that, though many contributed to its development, three names stand out. These are T. H. Green, F. H. Bradley, and Bernard Bosanquet. (All were Oxford-trained Englishmen.) And, despite the contributions by others, in terms of influence on the larger philosophical community, these writers are the most important.[2] But how did these idealist logicians understand their subject matter? F. H. Bradley tells us that

> [Logic's] direct purpose is...to set out the general essence of the main types of inference and judgment, and, with regard to each of these, to explain its special merits and defects. The measure here to be applied is the idea of perfect truth...The degree in which various types each succeed and fail in their common end, gives to each of them its respective place and its rank in the whole body. Such an exposition is in my view the main purpose of Logic.[3]

We might immediately note that this conception of 'logic' is much broader than what we understand by the term today. By contemporary standards, idealist logic must be seen as an enterprise that embraces, not just the analysis of propositions within a framework of established rules of inference, but also much of 'epistemology' or the 'theory of knowledge'.

---

[1] Consider Kneale and Kneale (1962). Other than a brief discussion of Kant, there is no account of 'idealist logic'. The names Green, Bradley, and Bosanquet are found neither in the bibliography nor the index. By contrast, see Adamson (1911).

[2] Other contributors would include: J. F. Ferrier (St Andrews), Edward Caird (Glasgow, Oxford), R. L. Nettleship (Oxford), H. W. B. Joseph (Oxford), H. H. Joachim (Oxford).

[3] Bradley (1922), p. 600.

Historical

T. H. Green was Fellow and tutor at Balliol College, Oxford from 1860 to the time of his death in 1882. He was also appointed Whyte's professor of moral philosophy in 1878. Green's influence, both as a tutor and a university lecturer, was enormous. Bernard Bosanquet, the most prolific of the idealist logicians, studied with Green while an undergraduate at Balliol; and we have good evidence that F. H. Bradley, too, attended Green's lectures.[4] While Green's contribution to logical theory is seldom discussed, we find in his 'Lectures on Logic' (1874–5) many of the themes that would dominate the work of later writers. Although Green never undertook the classification of judgement forms, he was the first in this school to argue for the systematic nature of thought, and to criticize the syllogism for its failure in this regard.

Green's work is of value, too, for making clear the relation between German and British idealism. Although Bradley and Bosanquet only occasionally make reference to their German predecessors, Green openly acknowledges this intellectual debt. Green lectured extensively on Kant; and in his work we can easily trace this influence. Of course, the effect of German idealism should not be overestimated. Green was also a great scholar of classical empiricism; and his 'Introduction' to Hume's *Treatise on Human Nature* has been seen by many as the definitive critique of that school.[5] As a student of John Stuart Mill's thought, Green had few peers. Though the history of idealist logic is yet to be written, when it is, the work of T. H. Green will likely hold a significant place.

Certainly, the best known of the British idealists is F. H. Bradley; and it is generally believed that his 1883 *Principles of Logic* stood at the centre of the new logic that developed in the late nineteenth century. Although Green's lectures pre-date Bradley's book, the account of inference that we find in Bradley's logical treatise, was, according to one writer, without precedent.[6] *The Principles of Logic* was, however, controversial—and for several reasons. In the idealist camp it caused concern as it seemed to reject much of the Hegelianism of Bradley's earlier work in moral theory.[7] Some were concerned for different reasons, though. Bernard Bosanquet believed that, while correct in its essential doctrine, Bradley's work contained serious inconsistencies. Indeed, Bosanquet argued in his *Knowledge and Reality* (1885), that the doctrine of 'floating ideas'—the view that we could entertain concepts without affirming them to be continuous with the larger reality—was problematic. Not only did it conflict with Bradley's general definition of judgement, it led to an account of hypothetical assertion as 'pure supposal'.[8] This was the idea that we could, without an appeal to the judgement's conditioning context, derive genuine logical results. (This claim shall be considered later.) Such a 'reactionary view', Bosanquet claimed, could not be reconciled with the larger agenda of Bradley's book.[9]

---

[4] Keene (1999), pp. xv, xvi.

[5] I refer here to the 'General Introduction' and 'Introduction II' of the Green and Gross edition of Hume. These were republished in vol. i of Green's *Works*. See Green (1910), i. 1–371.

[6] Bosanquet (1920), p. 115.

[7] Bradley (1876).

[8] See Bosanquet (1885), pp. 39–58. See also Bosanquet (1911), i. 278–9.

[9] Bosanquet believed that Bradley was at times unduly influenced by the work of Christian Sigwart, and R. H. Lotze. See e.g. Bosanquet (1885), pp. 21–46, also 214 ff.

Knowledge and Reality appeared to have an enormous effect on Bradley. Certainly in everything he wrote after 1885, there was no trace of 'floating ideas' or 'pure supposal'. And in future years Bradley would regularly refer readers to Bosanquet's work—particularly his *Logic or the Morphology of Knowledge* (1888). We shall return to Bosanquet's discussion of these matters momentarily. First, however, I would like to briefly describe Bradley's ongoing work in logical theory.

Bradley's most famous work, *Appearance and Reality*, appeared in 1893. While it was devoted to 'first principles', many of the ideas discussed in his earlier work on logic were considered there as well. Bradley was always of the mind that logic should be treated as a 'special science' with appeal to metaphysical argument only as was absolutely necessary. However, in *Appearance and Reality*, this restraint was set aside and he provided a fuller justification for the assumptions of his *Principles of Logic*.

The next major publication from Bradley was his *Essays on Truth and Reality* (1914). In this work Bradley brought together a number of articles that were concerned not so much with the nature of judgement and inference (the principal topics of logic) as with the nature and test of of truth. These criteria he identified as 'coherence' and 'comprehensiveness'. Also of great importance was an essay called 'Floating Ideas and the Imaginary'.[10] In this essay Bradley clarified many of the ambiguities surrounding his earlier account of hypothetical judgement and the role of supposition in our larger experience.

In 1922, two years before his death, Bradley reissued his *Principles of Logic*.[11] This second edition contained not only extensive notes appended to the chapters, but also twelve 'Terminal Essays'. At more than 130 pages, they constituted a restatement of his views on subjects discussed almost forty years earlier. These 'Essays' provide the final statement of Bradley's position, and can be read independently of the original text.

Bernard Bosanquet's career was closely intertwined with that of Bradley. We have already mentioned the effect that *Knowledge and Reality* had on the author of the *Principles of Logic*. But the influence did not end there. There are many references to Bosanquet's *Logic* in Bradley's writings; and in the second edition of the *Principles of Logic* we are told that for the 'correct view' readers should consult the work of 'Dr. Bosanquet'. But some mention should be made of Bosanquet's other works. For the purposes of this essay, I would mention three: *The Essentials of Logic* (1895); *The Principle of Individuality and Value* (1912); and his last work, *Implication and Linear Inference* (1920).

In his *Essentials of Logic* Bosanquet summarizes the major points of *Logic or the Morphology of Knowledge.* And, though intended as a general introduction to the subject, it provides a comprehensive overview of the doctrine that was developed in detail a decade earlier. *The Principle of Individuality and Value* is (like Bradley's *Appearance and Reality*) typically seen as a work on metaphysics. However, in this volume Bosanquet takes great pains to explicate the doctrine of the 'concrete universal'—an idea that he sees as at the foundation of judgement and inference. The work is particularly noteworthy for its explanation of the logical foundation of value.

A largely ignored work, Bosanquet's *Implication and Linear Inference* not only examines the theory of inference as developed by Bradley and himself, it also discusses how this

---

[10] Bradley (1914), pp. 28–64.   [11] Bradley (1914), pp. 28–64.

theory differs from its competitors. Bosanquet describes numerous opposing doctrines (including traditional syllogism, empirical induction, and modern symbolic logic) as cases of 'linear' inference.[12] This linear form of inference was seen by him as both inaccurate as a descriptive account of reasoning, and a normative failure. There is probably no work in the literature that more succinctly explains the idealist doctrine of systematic inference, and it, along with the new material found in the second edition of Bradley's *Principles of Logic*, should be seen as a major contribution to idealist logical theory.

Philosophical

Green's 'Lectures on Logic' divides into two parts; these are titled 'The Logic of the Formal Logicians' and 'The Logic of J. S. Mill'.[13] In the first, Green focuses on three ideas that he finds common to both Sir William Hamilton and H. Mansel. These are (i) the doctrine of eliminative abstraction; (ii) the presentative–representative distinction; and (iii) the idea of formal inference through an independent middle term. We shall be limited here to (i) and (ii).

'The Logic of the Formal Logicians'

(i) The doctrine of eliminative abstraction assumes that objects and events come to us in perception as individual and concrete. On this theory, concepts are formed by attending to the similarities between these presented objects while ignoring their differences. A concept consists of a group of isolated similarities (or 'marks') that are fixed through naming. For example, I might examine a number of animals that resemble one another in various ways, and by noticing what they have in common, come to possess concepts of individual animals such as 'cow', 'horse', 'whale', and 'human being'. I might then perform a similar act of abstraction on the concepts thus obtained. For example, while holding before the mind the concepts 'cow', 'horse', 'whale' (and possibly others) I might notice similarities such as 'backboned', 'warm-blooded', and 'gives live birth to its young'. And it is by grasping the similarities between these animal concepts and giving them a name—'mammal'—that I arrive at an even more general idea. This activity can be repeated almost indefinitely. Thus as concepts become broader (or more 'denotative') they are understood to be 'emptier' because containing fewer internal marks.

But Green tells us, a careful reflection upon our experience shows that this is not how our concepts are formed; and if this were an accurate account, then the more we thought, the further we would get from reality. On Green's view this is backwards; and this is because as I examine the various creatures that come to be called 'mammals' I simultaneously apprehend both what they have in common and how they are different. Hence the concept 'mammal', while it certainly contains the marks just mentioned ('warm-blooded', 'back-boned', etc.), contains as well the differences that the various creatures exhibit ('swims in the ocean', 'rational-biped', 'cloven-hoofed', etc.). According to Green, the more comprehensive the

---

[12] Bosanquet's most direct account of symbolic logic is found in Bosanquet (1911), ii. 40 ff.
[13] Green (1910), ii. 158–306.

concept—that is, the greater the number of entities it refers to—the richer it becomes. And the actual concept 'mammal' will be found to exhibit the systematic unity between *both* sameness and difference.

(ii) Green also attacks the distinction presupposed by the doctrine of eliminative abstraction—the belief that objects are, prior to the activity of thought, 'presented' as wholly concrete and individual. On this theory, when thought goes to work on concrete perception, what results (concepts) are abstract 'representations' of what came before. However, according to Green, this theory fails to provide an accurate account of perceptual experience in that it does not recognize that the characteristics of specificity and particularity are not given or presented; rather, they are the *result* of thought's activity. On Green's view, to recognize something as a specific 'this' and not 'that' requires that we place it within a fuller context. That is, we must discover its precise place within the larger system of experience. And so far as thought ceases to engage in this activity, it will fail to apprehend that particularity; what is presented will appear, just to the extent that the contextualizing activity of thought is suppressed, as an abstract kind.

The rejection of eliminative abstraction and the presentative–representative distinction led to what was known as the doctrine of the 'concrete universal'. On this view, an experiential content may function as both particular and universal at once.[14] Contents that are 'run through' (i.e. brought into systematic relation) by thought are seen as particulars, while concepts that effect this systematic union function as universals. And what is at one level a unifying concept (or universal) may function at another as a particular because it falls under a more comprehensive notion. For example, though the individual marks that fall under the concept 'cow' may be particulars in relation to that idea, the concept 'cow' also functions as a particular since it is contained within the larger idea 'mammal'.

The importance of this doctrine for idealist logical theory cannot be overstated. When we consider the theory of inference developed by later writers, we should always understand that the view of the relation between thought and reality as articulated by Green was, though stated somewhat differently, at the heart of their analyses.[15]

'The Logic of J. S. Mill'

At more than one hundred pages, Green's discussion of Mill's *System of Logic* is the most comprehensive of the idealist authors. And, while Green acknowledges Mill's desire to arrive at a more adequate theory of inference, he claims that, in the end, Mill falls back on an associationist account.[16] Since we shall consider this doctrine later, I will only say here that Green's influence on those who followed appears to be considerable.

---

[14] Green (1910), ii. 189 ff.

[15] For example, much confusion has arisen over the terms 'relation' and 'relational'. Green often used these terms to refer to the synthetic and unifying function of thought; Bradley used them to indicate analysis and division. Both, however, saw synthesis and analysis as inseparable; and both were committed to the doctrine of the systematic (concrete) universal. Green (1910), ii. 184; Bradley (1922), pp. 470–1.

[16] Green (1910), ii. 277 ff.

The General Nature of Judgement

The judgement (and not the isolated idea) is, for Bradley and Bosanquet, the most basic unit of thought. And, while judgement does not exhaust our experience, we may say that—so far as we are conscious of objects and events—the activity of judgement is present. Of course, judgement contains ideas; but ideas cannot exist prior to or outside of judgement. And the judgement is, despite its internal division into subject, copula, and predicate, best understood as a *single* idea.[17] 'The wolf eats the lamb' should not, we are told, be seen as containing the isolated ideas of 'wolf' and 'lamb' which are then joined by the copula idea 'eats'. The judgement is better viewed as a single, though internally diverse, concept.[18]

But what for these writers is the essence of judgement? Judgement, we are told, consists in the 'affirmation of an ideal content to a reality beyond the act'.[19] And in describing the judgement as 'ideal' we should understand it to be an activity of *thought*; it is, we should say, the thinking 'elaboration' or 'extension' of reality as sensuously presented. But let us continue by considering a simple categorical assertion. In the judgement 'The pan is hot' what is meant is (i) that 'the ideal content S' ('the pan') is, though thought by me, still real; and (ii) that it forms a *continuous tissue* with the experiential content P ('hot') which, though thought by me, is also an aspect of the real universe. The copula, on this analysis, merely indicates the continuity of the asserted contents with one another and their conditioning ground—reality as a whole.[20] But with this definition we have identified a fundamental feature of judgement. The judgement, so far as 'ideal-not-real', is liable to error.

But we must at this point consider the structure of judgement more closely. We must notice that, on the idealist analysis, there are two senses in which we can construe the terms 'logical subject' and 'logical predicate'. What both Bradley and Bosanquet see as the *ultimate* subject in every judgement is 'reality as a whole'. Hence, every judgement takes the form: 'Reality is such that S is P' (where 'S is P' is the explicit content being asserted). But if we take reality as a whole as the ultimate subject, this forces us to see the content as judged (what is stated by the proposition) as a *complex predicate term*.[21]

This characterization will require some qualification when we consider hypothetical and counter-factual assertion; but before tackling these difficulties we must arrive at a more refined understanding of judgement in general; and to this end we should understand that, while reality as a whole constitutes the *ultimate* subject of every judgement, there is also a 'special' (or 'logical') subject and predicate. These are often, though not always, the grammatical subject and predicate of the proposition. Still, we are warned against seeing the grammatical structure as unambiguously representing the deeper logical form. Consider, for example, 'A is simultaneous with B', 'C is to the east of D', and 'E is equal to F'. We are told that it is 'unnatural' to view A, C, or E, as they appear in these propositions as the only rightful subjects.[22] Indeed, the structure of the actual judgement might be better expressed by

---

[17]   Bradley (1922), pp. 11–13. See also Bosanquet (1895), pp. 98–100 and 112–26.

[18]   The special subject should not be seen as a particular devoid of universal content. Both subject and predicate terms are, on this view, 'systematic universals'. The wholly individual subject can only be the 'ultimate subject' (reality-as-a-whole). See Bosanquet (1911) i. 255 ff.; Bradley (1922), pp. 628 ff., 659–61.

[19]   Bradley (1922), p. 10; but see p. 30 n. 10. See also Bosanquet (1911), i. 68–9.

[20]   Bosanquet (1895), pp. 99–100. See also Bradley (1922), pp. 21–7.

[21]   Bradley (1922), pp. 11–12, 622–6.

[22]   Bradley (1922), p. 13.

seeing the grammatical predicates functioning as subjects as in 'B is simultaneous with A', 'A and B are synchronous', and 'C and D lie east and West'. Grammatical form is, on this view, a mere schematic of an underlying conceptual structure which the proposition may or may not accurately characterize.

Before considering the several basic judgement forms, I would offer a further comment on the general nature of judgement. Given that the goal of judgement is to characterize the subject by the predicate, and given that reality as a whole is always seen as the ultimate subject, the success or failure of any act of predication (i.e. judgement) resides with the judgement's ability to get that reality within its own four corners. To put the point differently, we are, on this theory, trying always to see the universe whole and complete.[23] However, some judgements are more up to the task than others; that is, some judgements succeed to a far greater degree to grasp their true or ultimate subject (reality-as-a-whole). And this gives rise to the idea of a scale of judgement forms.

There are, then, three basic judgement types considered by the idealist logicians. These are (in order of adequacy): (i) the 'individual' (or 'perceptive') judgement; (ii) the hypothetical judgement; and (iii) the disjunctive judgement. A fourth (iv), the negative judgement, may be seen as a variation that, while it applies to each, finds its fullest expression in disjunction. But let us consider these judgement types in turn.

The Individual Judgement

The 'individual' (or 'perceptive') judgement is the categorical assertion of traditional logic.[24] And it is called 'categorical' because it purports to be about fact. 'The grass is green', 'This rock is heavy', and 'It is cold today' are examples. These judgements all qualify the contents of perception (directly or indirectly) with various adjectives; and they both analyse and extend what is given in our immediate sensuous awareness.

In his *Principles of Logic*, Bradley breaks up individual judgements into three classes.[25] These he calls 'analytic judgements of sense', 'synthetic judgements of sense', and an unnamed 'third class'. His analysis may be briefly described as follows: (i) an analytic judgement of sense takes what is directly before me in perception and identifies within it various qualities. If I assert 'This road is narrow' while focused on a given section of tarmac, I am analysing the contents of sense as consisting of two different contents; these we may call 'roadness' and 'narrowness'. These would constitute the special subject and special predicate as described earlier. And in such a judgement I am affirming a *continuity of content* between the larger reality (the ultimate subject) and the 'roadness' and 'narrowness' that is currently before me. (ii) In a synthetic judgement of sense—such as 'This road leads to London'—I am overtly

---

[23] It should be noted that the ideas in judgement are not, according to the idealist authors, psychical images. Although a specific image usually accompanies an idea, that image is a fragmentary symbol of the reality of which the idea is a partial apprehension. For example, the fuller meaning of 'horse' could never be exhausted by a given image (or finite series of images). Still we utilize imagery in an effort to make concrete to ourselves the meaning of our terms. See Bradley (1922), pp. 71, 76–7; also Bosanquet (1911), i. 68–73, and (1920), pp. 141 ff.

[24] See Bosanquet (1911), i. 88–9. Bradley (1922), pp. 44–8, also 622-3.

[25] Bradley (1922), pp. 15–19; see, however, p. 108 n. 7.

extending the given perceptual content. That is, I am reaching beyond what is immediately before me (at least, that is, if the city of London is not currently within my perceptual awareness). However, the basic structure of judgement is always present. That is, I am still affirming that the road that I see is continuous with something I do not currently see ('London'); and I am affirming as well that these experiential contents are all part of the larger reality. (iii) The 'third class' of individual judgements consists of those assertions that purport to be about given fact, but which find their special subject and predicate absent from my direct awareness. For example, I might assert 'London is a great centre of commerce' while located somewhere in North America. Still, what takes place in such a judgement is the assertion of a continuity of content between what I presently perceive and objects and events that are absent from my perceptual awareness. It is important to understand, though, that when we speak of 'given perception' we are not referring to a 'concept-free' sensuous experience. The contents of given perception are understood as already conceptually laden, and hence we must not give too much importance to the fact that certain contents are currently part of perceptual awareness while others are not.

But these divisions, while they may be a useful way of viewing our individual (perceptive) judgements, do not get to what is most characteristic of them. First, we must understand that, on this theory, the individual judgement has direct existential import; it would be false should its terms not exist. And second, the special subject and predicate in these judgements stand in an essentially conjunctive relation both to one another and their conditioning context. For example, in 'This road leads to London' there is nothing about 'this road' that necessarily contains a 'leading to London'. Indeed, the special subject 'this road' (at least as I have grasped it) might have attached to it a special predicate such as 'leads to Manchester' or 'heads out to the countryside'.

Now it is this conjunctive relation between special subject and predicate that, on the idealist analysis, betrays its weakness. In the real universe there are precise conditions that unite subject and predicate. However, these conditions are largely absent from the individual (perceptive) assertion. Precisely *why* 'this road' leads to London, and precisely why London has a road such as this leading into it is simply not part of—or at least not a significant part of—my awareness. However, this calls into question the categorical status of such judgements.

We must remember that a categorical assertion purports to be about fact. However, on the idealist analysis, the implicit claim of the categorical judgement cannot be maintained. We are given three reasons for this.[26] First the (purportedly) categorical assertion is *incomplete*. Much of what makes 'this road' a specific and unique road is simply not before me when I judge. But if I am to grasp its factual character—that it is *this* road and not another— its *full* nature needs to be present. Second, in being incomplete the categorical assertion also *distorts* its object. The road as it actually exists contains relations of content to other realities, and these relations are an integral part of its character. However, these relations my judgement has arbitrarily altered; thus the true nature of the object—its nature as categorical fact—remains obscure. And finally, while I intend to characterize the object before me in its full specificity, I fail to do so. I grasp only an abstract fragment of what in reality is perfectly concrete and wholly individual. Though I *mean* this and only this road leads to the one and

---

[26]   Bradley (1922), pp. 59–73.

only London, what I actually manage to grasp in any individual (perceptive) judgement is 'rounded-off'. Thus it fails to uniquely designate its object.

But it is this fact that leads both Bradley and Bosanquet to condemn the individual (categorical) assertion as 'conditional'. And they say this because its truth is dependent upon conditions that fall *outside* its boundaries. But it is just this externality of conditioning context that makes the judgement subject to falsification to an extent that other judgements are not. Consider 'John is happy'. This is a judgement that might, when made at a given time, be true. However, since there are specific conditions—conditions that are largely unknown—that unite special subject and predicate, it cannot be asserted without qualification.[27] Should I assert 'John is happy' in an unqualified sense I would find that it is sometimes false. (John might have just lost his job and or become seriously ill.) But this betrays a fundamental weakness in the individual assertion.

The Hypothetical Judgement

The hypothetical judgement is of great importance for the idealist logicians as it marks the first line of advance beyond the individual assertion. It also assumes great importance because it is the principal judgement of science. And, while it is sometimes difficult to locate the precise line where the individual judgement becomes hypothetical there is, nevertheless, a clear distinction between the two types.

At the heart of this distinction is what Bosanquet likes to call the 'relativity' of knowledge. Whereas the individual judgement apprehends an essentially conjunctive relation between its terms, the hypothetical judgement goes further; it takes as its first task the discovery of necessary relations between experiential contents. But let us begin by considering how both Bradley and Bosanquet understand these hypothetical assertions.

We must first differentiate between the collective judgement and the universal affirmative. Consider 'All the exams have been marked'. This assertion would, despite its grammatical form, be an individual judgement in that it asserts 'this exam, and this exam, and this exam etc. have been marked'. Not only are the exams of a definite (though possibly unknown) number, the terms stand in an essentially conjunctive relation to one another. However, in 'All men are mortal' we mean something quite different. Here we are asserting—not that we have examined all men and have found each to be mortal—rather, we are asserting that 'If man, then mortal'. That is, we are asserting that whenever and wherever the condition 'human being' is found, so too will there exist the condition of 'mortality'. Hence the true universal affirmative, in being hypothetical, goes well beyond observed cases. It asserts that there is a *universal connection of content*—a connection of content that will always hold—between special subject and predicate. But more than this, the hypothetical judgement presupposes that we have within our grasp much of the ground upon which these terms are combined.

Although the precise nature of hypothetical judgement was the source of considerable controversy, it was generally agreed that the hypothetical assertion does not necessarily claim for the grammatical subject existence in the real universe. It says that *if* 'such and such'

---

[27] Bradley (1922), pp. 104–7.

exists, then 'so and so' will invariably be found along with it. Indeed, it is sometimes the case in hypothetical judgement that the grammatical subject *cannot* exist in the real universe. However, the judgement may, nevertheless, possess truth, and, on the idealist analysis, truth of a rather high sort. But let us consider why this is.

We must not lose sight of the fact that the *ultimate* subject in every judgement is, on this theory, 'reality as a whole'. Hence, the proper formulation of the hypothetical assertion is 'Reality is such that if p then q'. But if reality is the ultimate subject in all judgement, and if all judgement has the capacity to be 'true or false', exactly what, it might be asked, is being asserted in the hypothetical judgement? The answer that must *sometimes* be given is 'a latent quality of the real'. Consider the following examples: 'If you ask him for permission, he will refuse', or 'All trespassers will be prosecuted'. We should understand that in both cases there is something in the real universe that (a) makes the judgement true or false; and (b) allows the consequent to follow from the antecedent, even though that antecedent *as stated* might not—and may never—exist. But what could the 'latent condition' be in these cases?

In the first example we have an aspect of the subject's character; in the second case, a deci-sion—perhaps a legal restriction or public policy—that demands the prosecution of tres-passers should they come into being and be caught. But what the idealist logic insists upon is this: hypothetical judgements are never 'mere supposals'. And this brings us to an important point in the analysis of hypothetical assertion. While we may 'suppose' anything at all, when we *judge*, we must return to the domain of the real universe.[28] As Bosanquet tells us:

> An ultimate ground [in hypothetical judgement] must be actual; it is the fact which is judged in hypothetical judgment. We may of course freely suppose or imagine *a* system, as complex as we please; but if we proceed to *judge* about the consequences or results of such a system, it must thus be related to these consequences within some further system; and this further sys-tem must be actual. In other words, you can only suppose an antecedent, you cannot suppose a consequent; the consequent must be judged, not supposed; and in judging the consequent you assert the underlying ground to be actual.[29]

There seem to be, then, three possibilities. We may (i) engage in 'pure supposal'; we may (ii) make hypothetical assertions that are 'counter-factual' (but still grounded in reality); or we may (iii) make universal affirmative assertions in hypothetical form.

In pure supposal (which is not, on this analysis, 'judgement' at all) we engage in a kind of imaginative exercise; and a pure supposal that took the form of 'if p then q' would consist in little more than the unpacking of postulated relations between terms in that imaginative domain.[30] As for counter-factual assertion it would have (if a genuine judgement) the char-acteristics described in our previous examples. That is, the grammatical subject as indicated by the antecedent term would not be the true logical subject. And we could assert of that subject (the 'latent quality' of the real) certain consequences only on the assumption that this subject and that which follows from it fall within the larger system of real objects and events.

But let us consider 'All fires are hot' or 'All men are mortal'. These assertions mean 'If fire, then hot' and 'If human, then mortal'. And, on the idealist analysis these judgements—even

---

[28] Bosanquet (1911), ii. 10–11. See Bradley (1922), pp. 110–13 esp. n. 40; see too pp. 634–40.
[29] Bosanquet (1911), i. 272.
[30] Bosanquet (1911), i. 269 ff.

if the condition named by the antecedent does not currently exist—are still grounded in fact, and what makes the consequent follow from the antecedent is just the larger reality in which they occur. While it is not evident in the explicit grammatical proposition, the claim here is that the ground—or at least some of the ground—that unites special subject and predicate has become explicit. And the hypothetical, unlike the individual, judgement, claims to have brought its conditions into the conceptual space of the judgement. That is, it purports to show (to some degree) that fire is *necessarily* connected to heat. And, while this necessity may not be 'fully visible', it is the claim of hypothetical assertion that we have sufficient warrant to claim that the consequent flows from the antecedent everywhere and always. Whereas the individual (or perceptive) judgement is 'conditional'—in other words, special subject and predicate come together on the basis of conditions that are largely unknown and external to the assertion—the hypothetical judgement is 'condition*ed*'. That is, the larger reality, in which heat follows from fire, has been made (partially) explicit and is now part of the conceptual content of the assertion.

We might note, too, that as the conditions that bring the antecedent and consequent of hypothetical assertions together become more expansive they approach what Bosanquet and Bradley call 'reciprocity'. While we, following the conditions of ordinary linguistic usage, are not inclined to say 'If drowned, then dead' implies 'If dead, then drowned' (death may have come about in some other way), as our grasp of the ground between 'drowned' and 'dead' expands, it can reach a point where we might safely make this inference. This is because the kind of death that is actually *implied* by 'drowned' is 'death by water suffocation'.[31] And if this sort of systematic awareness works its way into our judgement ('If drowned then dead') the reciprocal inference would seem quite natural.

In summary, we should note that the hypothetical assertion, though in one sense more abstract than the individual judgement (it is quite narrow and focused), is, in another sense, more concrete. And this is because it has brought into its explicit grasp (even if imperfectly) the conditions that unite antecedent and consequent.

The Disjunctive Judgement

There is probably no aspect of the idealist logical theory that stands further from our contemporary view than the account of disjunctive judgement. And this is because the disjunctive judgement is seen as being a complex form of assertion in which two things occur. First, the results of the abstract hypothetical are, so to speak, brought 'back to earth'. That is, they are seen as having concrete application in this or that domain of experience. And second, the data of the individual judgement are now seen as unified within a limited system.

But let us consider an example: 'The signal light is either red or green'. To follow the idealists here we must understand that this is a complex act of cognition that contains the following assertions. 'There is a signal light'; 'This signal light shows some colour'; 'If it shows red, it does not show green'; and 'If it does not show red, it shows green'.[32] The judgement

---

[31] E.g. Bosanquet (1911), i. 248–53, 272. See, too, Bradley (1922), pp. 697–8.

[32] While this is a simple example (from Bosanquet), it should be noted that the hypothetical assertions that are internal to the disjunction may be of a very high order. For example, the law-like statements of the empirical sciences may also become part of the disjunctive judgement. See Bosanquet (1911), i. 322 ff., and (1895), pp. 123–5.

is categorical in that it asserts the real existence of its special subject. But more than this, the disjunctive judgement exhibits its special subject (the signal light) as a 'system' or an 'identity-in-difference'. It shows us that there is an object (or an event) that has internal to itself certain differences, and that these differences stand to one another in quite specific relations. Although there can exist 'false' or 'partial' disjunctions, the true disjunctive judgement must be, on this analysis, both exclusive and exhaustive.[33] It must be exclusive in the sense that 'If A is B, then it is not C'. And 'If it is C, it is not B'. And, while there may be any number of disjuncts (B, C, D, E, etc.), this relation of exclusivity must stand. But so too, for the idealists, must the true disjunctive judgement be exhaustive. It must cover all the differences that fall under the identity that is predicated.

But what is the point of the disjunctive judgement? It is in disjunctive judgement that both categorical (individual) and hypothetical assertion reach their fulfilment. The conjunctive relations that characterized our individual judgements have, with the help of hypothetical assertion, made explicit their previously unknown conditions; and the abstract and narrow hypothetical judgements have, through their application to perceptive (individual) assertion, been concretized and distributed into the larger system of objects and events. As we read:

> The disjunction seems to complete the system of judgments, including all the others in itself.... For disjunction in itself implies a kind of individuality which is beyond mere fact, and mere abstract truth though allied to both.[34]

And here we come to the essential point. As already stated, the goal of knowledge on the idealist analysis is to see the world 'whole and complete'. Of course, this is not something that can be immediately achieved. It requires a building-up of our experience. We take this fragment, and then that, and progressively weave these together so as to arrive at a systematic and comprehensive grasp of the universe. (We can, of course, only progressively—and never fully—achieve this end.) Individual judgements constitute the initial stage; and from these we rise to the more specialized mode of hypothetical assertion—the mode in which we discover the law-like relations between the various contents which we first experience as disconnected and discrete. But it is in the disjunctive assertion that we finally achieve the systematic union of abstract hypothesis and individual fact. It is here that we grasp things both in their identity and their difference; that is, as an integrated system.

The Negative Judgement

I would begin by saying that, for the idealist writers, there is no such thing as 'pure negation'. The negative judgement, while it denies that this or that content (identified by the special predicate) belongs to the special subject, must be seen as 'relative'. That is, in denying that a given content attaches to the subject, it says *some other* content prevents this attachment from occurring. In 'My car is not blue' I am implicitly claiming that it is red, or white, or silver (or whatever). In other words, all negation asserts that there exists a contrary predicate

---

[33] Bosanquet (1895), pp. 123–7. Bradley (1922), pp. 137–8 n. 1, also 602–3.
[34] Bosanquet (1895), p. 126. Bradley (1922), pp. 110–11 n. 40, also 426–7 n. 24.

(known or unknown) that repels that which is explicitly identified in the negative judge-ment.[35] And whether negation occurs in individual, hypothetical, or disjunctive judgement it always has this function. Consider this example from Bosanquet:

> If you ask me, 'Are you going to Victoria, London Chatham and Dover Station?' and I answer 'I am going to Victoria, London Brighton and South Coast', that will not be satisfactory to you, unless you happen to know beforehand that these stations are so arranged that if you are at one you are not at the other. They might be a single station used by different companies, and called indifferently by the name of either. To make it clear that the suggestion and the answer are incompatible, I must say, 'I am *not* going to Victoria, London Chatham and Dover', and I may add or not add, 'I *am* going to Victoria, London Brighton and South Coast'.[36]

Establishing exclusivity, then, is the basic function of negation; and it attempts this in all types of judgement. As suggested earlier, through negation we are ultimately striving towards the exhaustiveness of disjunctive assertion. But how does negation achieve this? The judgement 'The signal light is not green' could, of course, be made under conditions that tell us little about its positive nature. However, when we combine this negative asser-tion with 'The signal light shows some colour' and 'The signal light is *either* red or green' we come to possess knowledge of exactly which contrary predicate repels green. If we know that the light is either green or red, and we know that it is not green, there is no alterna-tive other than its being red. We may summarize, then, by saying that negation progres-sively assumes a positive role in our experience, because, in order to grasp what the nature of anything is, we must at the same time know what stands against it. And it is the nega-tive judgement, functioning within the context of disjunction, that allows us to achieve this understanding.

Systematic Inference

Given that most judgements are themselves the result of reasoning—instances of mediated knowledge—it is a short step to an understanding of inference. Hence, let us consider the general nature of inference as described by F. H. Bradley.

> Every inference combines two elements; it is in the first place a process, and in the second a result. The process is an operation of synthesis; it takes its *data* and by ideal construc-tion combines them into a whole. The result is the perception of a new relation within that unity.[37]

Inference is, then, an 'ideal construction' that unifies data or premises. What is most dis-tinctive about this theory, however, is that, in this unification, something *new* is brought to light. What is new may be only a deepened grasp of the relations between the terms of our premises; or it may be an entirely new aspect of those terms.[38] But what we discover in our conclusion is understood as not having been manifest in the premises with which we began. We should notice, too, that with this new element, the *meanings* of the terms of the premises (at least as understood by us) have changed; they have been expanded, enlarged, or (at least)

---

[35] Bosanquet (1911), i. 279 ff.; Bradley (1922), pp. 662–7.   [36] Bosanquet (1895), p. 130.
[37] Bradley (1922), p. 256.   [38] Bosanquet (1920), pp. 118 ff.; also Bradley (1922), pp. 598–601.

more tightly integrated with one another and the larger reality. It should be emphasized here that this process is not, according to the idealists, an arbitrary one—an expression of subjective fancy. In whatever direction the process moves—if it is a genuine inference—its movement is dictated by the nature of the object. And to emphasize this point Bradley came to describe inference the 'ideal self-development of the object'.[39]

But let us consider the meaning of this phrase. When it is said that inference is 'ideal', we should understand that it involves the activity of thought. However, as mentioned earlier, that inference is a thinking activity should not be taken as meaning that it is not constrained or limited. Indeed, we are told that the movement of inference (if it be inference) is one that the *object itself* determines. And the idea here is that in our inferential constructs we must, so far as possible, follow the lines of relevant content. That is, we must look to the proximate and determining context of our judgements so as to let it draw out the fuller meaning of our terms. And the point to be emphasized is this: The actual data (or premises) with which we begin are always immersed in a larger whole; and it is on this basis that we may gradually incorporate aspects of that whole into the explicit data of the conclusion. This is what keeps the movement of thought 'on track' in its inferential development.[40]

But let us consider some examples in which the fuller meaning of our terms in judgement is parasitic upon the whole; and let us consider how this whole provides the material for the object's self-development. Consider: 'City A is due north of City B'; 'City B is due east of City C'; hence, 'City A is north-east of City C'. We may see here how our conclusion meets the conditions stated.[41] That 'City A is north-east of City C' (our inferred conclusion) is, in a very real sense, not contained in our initial premises; certainly there is nothing about either premise by itself that suggests this. However, when we put these premises together—along with the whole within which such judgements must occur—a new fact emerges. So the judgement 'City A is north-east of City C' was not overtly 'in' the premises at all. However, it was 'in' the premises in the sense that the larger system of spatial relations which is presupposed by those premises contains all that is required to support the conclusion.[42] We may notice as well that the meaning of our terms has, through inferential development, changed. We now understand 'City A' to mean (amongst other things) 'a city north-east of C'; and 'City B' to mean (amongst other things) 'a city south of A but west of C'.

Consider also these examples: 'A ton of coal costs thirty shillings; this is a half-ton hence it costs fifteen shillings'; or 'Given a machine that can fly at two hundred miles an hour, it can fly from London to Edinburgh in two hours'.[43] That the conclusions follow from the premises here, no one would question. And, while one might be able to generate a number of 'suppressed premises' so as to force either of these arguments into syllogistic form, it would be wholly unnatural to do so. Both our inference to the cost of a half a ton of coal, and the flying time between London and Edinburgh follow on this theory—not because the data found in the conclusion is already contained within the premises—but because the *partial* system stated by the premises (what was described earlier as the 'special object') is asserted within the *whole* system that is their ground. And it is only because of the *immanence* of the whole within the partial system that the conclusion can, in each of these cases, be drawn.

[39] Bradley (1922), pp. 493 ff. and 597–601.   [40] Bradley (1922), pp. 437–42, also 597 ff.
[41] Bradley (1922), pp. 394 ff.   [42] Bradley (1922), pp. 223–4.
[43] Bosanquet (1920), pp. 4, 25.

This is what both Bradley and Bosanquet referred to as the 'double nature' of the object—a double nature that, on the idealist view, lies behind all logical implication.

This conception of inference as the ideal self-development of the object does constitute, it was admitted, something of a 'paradox' or 'puzzle'.[44] And what makes it a puzzle has to do with the fact that our conclusion is both 'in' our premises and 'not in' our premises at the same time. As Bradley writes:

> The general solution of the problem raised by the essence of inference is found, I think, so far as logic is concerned, in the double nature of the object. Every inference...both starts with and is confined to a special object. Now this object, like all objects, is taken, we may say, as referred to Reality, the real Universe; or, to speak more correctly, the object is taken as in one with this Reality. Hence the object not only is itself, but is also contained as an element in a whole; and it *is* itself, we must add, only as being so contained. And the difference of the object from, and its essential identity with a whole beyond itself—a whole which logic takes as a system both ideal and real—is the key (so far as logic is concerned) to this puzzle of self-development. On the one side the special object advances to a result beyond the beginning, and yet its progress throughout is nothing beyond the intrinsic development of its proper being. For that which mediates and necessitates its advance is implied within its own self.[45]

We should understand that what Bradley tells us here, presupposes the metaphysics of absolute idealism. That inference is capable of giving us something new, comes about only because our special object is understood as being connected to the larger reality— the reality which, in the end, makes the special object what it is. Cut the connections of content between special object and the whole, and the threads on which inference proceeds disappear. And if we should assume (contra idealism) that the world just is a collection of essentially discrete objects and events, the basis of inference must be understood in a very different fashion. Rather than belonging to the object itself, we must see it as located within the mind of individual finite subjects. But, as we shall consider later, this was seen as taking away from our inferences any claim to objectivity and necessity.

A brief word is, perhaps, in order here on deduction and induction. All inferences, on the idealist view, share the characteristics just outlined. However, some inferences emphasize the analytic (deductive) aspect, some the synthetic (inductive). We are inclined to call inferences that look to the interior of some previously apprehended whole 'deductive', while our synthetic construction of such wholes we typically describe as 'inductive'. But, again, it is, on this theory, a matter of emphasis.[46]

But let us consider how, for Bradley and Bosanquet, what we would call an ordinary inductive inference would proceed. And to begin we must remember that, like any other inference, it is an ideal construction. There is a process and a result; and the result is often (though not always) what we have identified as the hypothetical judgement. Consider that we routinely make individual judgements that bring experiential contents together in a conjunctive manner. 'This water boils when heated to 212 degrees Fahrenheit.'

---

[44] Bosanquet (1895), p. 137; Bradley (1922), p. 599.
[45] Bradley (1922), pp. 599–600.
[46] Bosanquet (1911), i. 91–5, 183–4; also ii. 119 ff. See Bradley (1922), pp. 470–1; Green (1910), ii. 288–90.

In the beginning we recognize only a loose relation between water, heat, and boiling. However, each time we experience water boiling at a given temperature our larger perceptual-conceptual universe is altered; and with every successive experience of water, heat, and boiling the meaning of these contents expands, incorporating subtle differences of context.

For example, I might notice that the time it takes for water to boil varies according to the container in which it is placed. I may also notice that, while water will always boil if sufficiently heated, the temperature that is required varies with geographical location. Sometimes (e.g. when visiting my mountain retreat) it boils a bit sooner and at a slightly lower temperature than when I am at my beachfront home. Progressively, then, certain conditions are seen as relevant to the relation between heat and water's boiling while certain others are not. For example, while at one point I might judge 'Water boils when heated to 212 degrees Fahrenheit in an aluminum kettle', my collective experience will eventually cause me to drop what is an irrelevant condition in the relation between water, heat, and boiling. And as this process continues, I shall eventually be led to assert 'Water boils when heated to 212 degrees Fahrenheit under one atmosphere of pressure'. But what supports this inference?

We should understand that the judgement being made is one that contains a wealth of experiential content. And it is just this accumulated content—along with the larger reality—that constitute what are called 'the conditions' of the judgement. Although I must acknowledge that there could be some factor which is essential to the unity of these contents that I remain unaware of (and which could, if they became known, force me to modify my assertion), I would still feel confident in my judgement to the degree that my experience as a whole supports it. Stated differently, it is to the degree that my judgement ('Water boils at 212 degrees Fahrenheit under one atmosphere of pressure') coheres with my fuller conceptual-perceptual universe that I take it as true.[47]

We may also notice that the sheer number of times water is experienced as boiling when heated to a given temperature is ultimately irrelevant to the connection of content expressed by my judgement. While it might *practically* require a good number of occurrences to establish my awareness of what are the conditions that effect this connection of content, once those conditions are understood, additional experiences are unnecessary. This point may be put differently by stating that it is not the increasing strength of 'mental habit' that effects this connection of contents; rather, it is an apprehension of the larger system of conditions provided by reality as a whole.

But how do I know that what I have previously experienced is a reliable guide to the future, and that my limited awareness of the larger reality justifies such inferences? The idealists argued that, if I were to deny the principle 'Once true, always true' (or, less accurately, 'The future will resemble the past') I would be denying one of the fundamental conditions upon which experience maintains itself. And if that principle were to go, then nothing would be left standing.[48] But let us consider this all-important idea in greater detail.

---

[47] Bradley (1914), pp. 209–18; also Bradley (1897), pp. 480–1; and Bosanquet (1911), ii. 157 ff.
[48] Bosanquet (1920), pp. 2–6, also 16–20. Also Bosanquet (1912), pp. 174–84.

Logical Stability and Degrees of Truth

Every inference results, of course, in a judgement. But, as already discussed, our judgements are of differing value. Some (e.g. the lowly individual judgement) exhibit little 'stability'. They are true at one time and place, and false at another. Others (e.g. certain hypothetical and disjunctive judgements) may be fully supported by the system of which they are expressions. But what makes for this difference?

Our individual (or perceptive) assertions, we have learned, are dependent for their truth on conditions of which we are largely ignorant. Hence we may say that their incorporation of the fuller system of reality is relatively slight. But since so little of the larger reality is incorporated within the individual judgement's boundaries, its falsification does not have a great effect on the system of experience as a whole. The situation is, however, very different when it comes to the higher level judgements. If the judgement 'Water boils at 212 degrees Fahrenheit at one atmosphere of pressure' were shown to be false, it would take down with it enormous tracts of experience. We would be forced to revise, not just many of our ordinary beliefs about water and how we should interact with it, but a massive amount of scientific understanding as well. Hence, we would say that this judgement has a much greater purchase on, or engagement with, reality as a whole. And it is just this larger engagement that provides the judgement with its greater level of *logical stability*. This notion of logical stability—which may be described as its coherence and comprehensiveness—also constitutes the judgement's 'degree of truth'.[49]

On this theory there are many judgements whose entanglement with reality goes even further. There are some judgements which, if they could (*per impossibile*) be shown to be false, would take down with them the basis of any and every experience. Of course, it was the identification of such judgements that marked the foundation of modern idealism. Kant's 'transcendental deduction' of the categories as found in his *Critique of Pure Reason* takes on just this task; and so too does Hegel's *Science of Logic*. Both writers, through transcendental arguments, attempted to establish that there are certain concepts (and judgements derived from those concepts) that are conditions of any actual or possible experience.

Now neither Bradley nor Bosanquet were inclined to identify categorial concepts. However, their general logical method may also be described as 'transcendental'. We are often told by them that it is 'this or nothing'.[50] But when we encounter this claim what is meant is that if you deny the principle in question, you deny the very basis upon which intelligible experience proceeds. And when we realize that we cannot engage in wholesale denial without being ensnared in self-contradiction, the principle in question must be allowed to stand.[51]

There are, however, two aspects of this doctrine that deserve special notice. One we have already considered. This is the idea that logical stability—the measure of a judgement's 'necessity'—can be a matter of degree. The other point is that our ordinary conceptions regarding logical contingency and necessity are often confused. While it is obvious that

---

[49] Green (1910), ii. 294–5; Bradley (1914), pp. 202–18; Bradley (1922), pp. 685–9; Bosanquet (1911), i. 272 ff.

[50] Bosanquet (1920), pp. 2–6, 17–20. Also Bosanquet (1912), p. 49, and (1911), i. 272 ff.; Bradley (1914), pp. 219–44.

[51] Bosanquet (1920), pp. 3 ff.; Bradley (1897), pp. 488–9.

some judgements are necessarily false (because they directly deny the basis upon which they are made), we are told that there are others that are equally false, though their falsehood is not immediately apparent. Bosanquet provides numerous examples. Consider: 'There is no truth'. Here is an assertion of the first type. In order to be true, it must be false, which is to say it is self-contradictory. However, Bosanquet also argued that a judgement like 'There is no moral experience' is of a similar nature.

We are told that, while we can easily see that 'There is no truth' contradicts itself, the assertion 'There is no morality' usually slips by as 'contingent' because we cannot easily grasp its self-defeating character. In 'There is no truth' our attention is focused on a very narrow range of content; and it is just this narrowness that makes for easy insight into its logical character. The case is, however, different with 'There is no moral experience'. Given the judgement's broad range and complex content, our initial inclination is to think that it could be asserted, while still leaving much of our experience intact. But, we are told, this is not the case. When the fuller meaning of 'moral experience' is thought through, we realize that the wholesale denial of that experience would tear down its own basis as well.[52] And it is only by treating the notion 'moral experience' in an excessively abstract and truncated fashion that we might be led to think otherwise. Indeed, Bosanquet even tells us that what initially appears as the more 'contingent' assertion, often carries greater logical force. We read that

> The proof of everything that is proved is ultimately one and the same, namely that if it is to be denied, nothing can be affirmed. And as it is impossible to deny everything, a proposition so guaranteed must be allowed to stand. Now a certainty thus grounded is really in the spirit of logic greater in proportion as the whole experience is fuller and more coherent; for the difficulty of denying everything obviously becomes enhanced as everything becomes a more completely apprehended cosmos with a fuller self-maintenance.[53]

But this idea also carries forward into the notions of logical possibility and impossibility. Consider the judgement 'There is a chimpanzee who is a great philosopher'. Many would argue that there is some 'possible world' in which this judgement is true (though admittedly false in our own). But, for the idealists, this claim rests on a confusion. When the fuller meaning of these contents ('chimpanzee' and 'philosopher') are thought through, we find that they cannot be coherently combined. At some point in our grasp of their meaning we would see that they, and the larger reality that is their condition, would openly repel one another.[54] And if we think otherwise, it is because we have only a limited understanding of our terms.

Linear or Non-Systematic Inference

The theory of inference outlined earlier came to be described as 'systematic' and 'non-linear'. What I would now like to do is briefly examine what were considered erroneous accounts

---

[52] See e.g. Bosanquet (1920), pp. 92–3.   [53] Bosanquet (1912), p. 49.
[54] Bosanquet (1912), pp. 49–50; Bradley (1922), pp. 699 ff.

of inference. Hence we shall briefly consider what were at the time the most significant of these: the theory of the association of ideas and the traditional syllogism.

The Theory of the Association of Ideas

First, then, let us consider Bradley's attack on associationism, as this was the principal account of reasoning provided by the 'school of experience' (Bradley's disparaging term for the empiricist tradition). The theory's essentials are these: (i) Through the appearance of 'impressions' (or faded impressions which have become 'ideas') in relations of contiguous or sequential conjunction, associative bonds develop within the mind of the experiencing subject; (ii) the strength of the associative bond is directly related to the frequency and regularity of these conjunctive relations; ideas that appear together without exception are called (by Mill) 'indissoluble associations', and carry with them a sense of necessity; (iii) ideas that possess less than this degree of associative force provide conviction in proportion to our experience of the frequency of their conjunctive regularity. That is, if B follows A only in two out of three appearances of A, we would come to believe that there was a 'two-thirds' chance of B following A in the future; (iv) associative bonds (mental habits) develop through repeated conjunctive regularity over time; and when at some point one term of the association appears by itself, the other is 'inferred' by the force of the established mental habit. For example, having experienced 'fire' followed by 'heat' many times, an association would develop (possibly an indissoluble association). Hence, upon any subsequent appearance of fire, I would conclude that it must be hot, even if heat is not currently experienced. According to the associationist theory, all our factual inferences are of this general type.

Bradley's critique can be summarized as follows: (a) the doctrine of associationism requires that we accept without explanation or defence, the claim that there exists a 'storehouse of ideas' in which previously existing impressions (having become 'less lively' ideas) are maintained; it is unclear how this could be (on the metaphysical assumptions of empiricism), yet it is required by the theory. (b) The mechanism of association is—as described—incoherent; and this is because what is said to 'call up' or 'revivify' previously existing impressions (now stored ideas) is the relation of *similarity* (or resemblance). However, similarity (resemblance) is a relation that requires two (or more) terms. And no account is given of how a presently existing term (the given impression) can be similar to a past, but stored, idea. To stand in the relation of similarity *both* terms must be present; but if both are present, then the one idea before my mind does not 'call up' an absent idea; what is said to be 'called up' must already be present. And finally (c) the associationist doctrine throws to the winds any defensible criterion of rationality. Given that different subjects could develop radically different associations between experiential contents, and given that it is the established set of associative bonds that constitutes for any judging subject the standard of 'right reason', there could exist, on this theory, a plurality of criteria as to what constitutes 'rationality'. Hence, the theory of associationism opens the door to a radically subjectivist account of knowledge.[55]

---

[55] Bradley (1922), pp. 299 ff.; also Bosanquet (1911), ii. 14–16. See too Green (1910), ii. 275–6.

Syllogistic Inference

Both Bradley and Bosanquet spend considerable time criticizing syllogistic logic and the linear conception of inference it presupposes. Their claim is that, while the syllogism might point to cases of genuine inference, it cannot on its own terms explain the basis of those inferences. And this is largely because syllogism views reasoning (inferring) as a process that subsumes data 'borrowed from elsewhere' under the general rule of the major premise.[56]

For example, in 'All men are mortal', 'Socrates is a man', therefore, 'Socrates is mortal' we see the conclusion resting upon the minor premise with its middle term 'man'. This is the link that allows the attribution of the major's predicate (mortality) to the minor's subject (Socrates). But, according to both Bradley and Bosanquet, the syllogism (in whatever mood and figure) contains a distorted conception of inference. The fundamental problem is described by Bosanquet when he writes:

> On the traditional theory of the syllogism, and according to any or all of the maxims which have been suggested as its ground, its terms are marks or properties which affect each other, so far as the technical purpose of the reasoning is concerned, only as indicators of each other's presence and absence. If the predicate of the conclusion in Barbara is modified from the predicate of the major premise, because it is affected by the change of the subject, the argument is vitiated. The rules forbid you to regard the argument as the construction of a system in which by their combination the terms throw a new light on one another.... Each term must preserve its independent being, as if enclosed in a bracket, and can only react on others by indicating the consequences of its presence or absence in respect of the presence or absence of the others.[57]

The sentence that requires our closest attention here is this: 'The rules forbid you to regard the argument as the construction of a system....' Here we find the crux of the matter. Genuine inference, according to the idealists, is *systematic*. But the rules of syllogism (or any 'linear' account of inference) preclude a system from developing. In treating the subject and predicate of propositions as isolated and independent kernels of thought—and insisting that their meaning remain fixed— syllogism remains blind to the actual (i.e. systematic) nature of inference. In our example, 'man' and 'mortality' reside in the major premise like collections of objects found together in a drawer. And the minor premise suggests that, if we look closely at the collection labelled 'man', we shall find as one of its members this thing called 'Socrates'. But since Socrates lies within the collection 'man', and since 'man' lies within the drawer alongside of 'mortality', we may view Socrates as lying in the drawer as well. This is the nature of the relation between terms that syllogism postulates—a relation that interprets inference according to the idea of class inclusion or exclusion. But what, on the idealist view, are its shortcomings?

We may first notice that the syllogism cannot 'particularize the predicate'.[58] That is, syllogistic theory keeps thought locked in a circle of ideas and precludes it from grasping the concrete nature of its object. The terms in judgement are, according to syllogism, essentially abstract and general. Typically (though not always) understood as derived by the process

---

[56] Bosanquet (1920), p. 24; Bradley (1922), pp. 285–7, also 525 ff.

[57] Bosanquet (1920), pp. 24–5.

[58] Bosanquet (1920), p. 22 ff.; Bradley (1922), 432–40, also 602 ff.; Green (1910), ii. 188–9, also 275.

of eliminative abstraction, when reassembled in the conclusion they retain their abstract generality and, more importantly, their self-contained character as found in the premises. But this failure to modify the terms in the conclusion is, on the idealist analysis, a failure to understand the true movement of inference. As we have seen, for both Bradley and Bosanquet, 'true deduction' (what syllogism purports to be but isn't) brings terms together in the conclusion in such a way that they take on a new significance. Having become united within a system, they begin to exhibit new aspects of identity with and difference from one another and their conditioning context. And it is just their becoming placed *in situ*, that brings to the fore their concrete character.[59]

As the idealists saw it, a thing is what it is by holding a precise place in the universe as a whole; and it is the work of systematic thinking to make this place explicit. But this is just what the syllogistic conception of inference, by insisting upon the fixed nature of its terms, precludes. By demanding that the meaning of terms remain fixed and independent, the concretization of thought (particularization of the predicate) is made impossible.

We may note too that syllogistic inference can provide for its premises and conclusion no substantive justification. While the premises of the syllogism might provide the appearance of support for the conclusion, they themselves (on most interpretations) are ultimately indefensible. When we ask what justifies either the syllogistic major or minor, we may appeal to an earlier set of premises (a 'chain of belief'); however, these premises must either reach back indefinitely or terminate in a (purportedly) 'self-evident' truth.[60] The isolated self-evident truth is, however, notoriously problematic. What one individual sees as self-evidently true, another may see as wholly contingent or even false. Hence what is required here—but what syllogism cannot provide—is a justification of premises that does not make a dogmatic appeal to self-evidence. As we have seen, on the idealist account, any adequate justification of premises (or data) can arise only by an appeal to 'experience as a whole'. Unless we can show that the denial of the premise (or premises) undercuts the basis upon which it is made, the syllogistic chain must remain 'in the air' and without logical support.

Bradley and Bosanquet spend a good deal of time explaining how the problems associated with the linear conception of inference also plague most accounts of inductive inference. Consider that when we arrive at a belief like 'All fires are hot' we treat that belief exactly like a major premise in a syllogism. For example, if I come to believe 'All fires are hot' (because their conjunctive regularity has formed in me a mental habit), my inference to 'This is a fire so it too will be hot', like syllogism, subsumes particulars under a general rule.[61] There is no systematic integration of data here. Hence induction, at least as ordinarily conceived, is linear in nature as well.

We may conclude this brief account of linear inference by saying that the idealists saw it as both descriptively false and normatively inadequate. Descriptively the theory is false because it fails entirely to appreciate the natural flow of argument.[62] In our ordinary arguments, we most often begin with descriptions of various conditions; and once those conditions are accepted,

[59] Bosanquet (1912), pp. 55–60. Green (1910), ii. 188–9, 275 ff.; Bradley (1922), pp. 603 ff.

[60] Bosanquet (1920), pp. 23–4, and 158–9. Bradley (1922), pp. 654–70; also Bradley (1897), pp. 480–4. Also Bradley (1914), pp. 204 ff.

[61] Bosanquet (1920), pp. 49–50, 59. Bradley (1922), pp. 352–4. The particular here is the recognition that 'This is a fire'.

[62] Bosanquet (1920), p. 50 ff. Also Bradley (1922), pp. 394 ff.

they force upon us conclusions that we cannot—without inconsistency—deny. Normatively, the doctrine fails because it can articulate no exhaustive standard by which our inferences can be evaluated. This is painfully obvious in associative theories where what constitutes the standard of correctness in inference is simply what has already been psychologically established. But syllogism (and any theory resembling it) has a similar difficulty. We might condemn an inference as invalid because it violates the principles of syllogism. However, unless the moods and figures of syllogistic reasoning can be shown to be both necessary and exhaustive, their ability to arbitrate between valid and invalid reasoning is called into question.

But this objection equally applies to any system of 'formal' logic. Since, on the idealist view, inference proceeds upon an identity of content between premises (or data) and their conditioning ground (the larger reality), it is impossible to specify an exhaustive list of 'rules of inference'.[63] And perhaps it is this point that explains why the idealist conception of logic has for so many years been ignored.

Select Bibliography

Adamson, Robert (1911), *A Short History of Logic*, Edinburgh: William Blackwood and Sons.

Bosanquet, Bernard (1885), *Knowledge and Reality*, London: Swan Sonneschein and Co.

Bosanquet, Bernard (1895), *The Essentials of Logic*, London: Macmillan and Co.

Bosanquet, Bernard (1911), *Logic or the Morphology of Knowledge*, 2nd edn. [1st pub. 1888], 2 vols., Oxford: Clarendon Press.

Bosanquet, Bernard (1912), *The Principle of Individuality and Value*, London: Macmillan and Co.

Bosanquet, Bernard (1920), *Implication and Linear Inference*, London: Macmillan and Co.

Bradley, Francis Herbert (1876). *Ethical Studies*, London: H. S. King and Co. [2nd edn., Oxford: Clarendon Press, 1922].

Bradley, Francis Herbert (1883), *The Principles of Logic*, London: Kegan, Paul, Trench and Co.

Bradley, Francis Herbert (1897), *Appearance and Reality*, 2nd edn. [1st pub. 1893], London: Swann Sonnenschein and Co.

Bradley, Francis Herbert (1914), *Essays on Truth and Reality*, Oxford: Clarendon Press.

Bradley, Francis Herbert (1922), *The Principles of Logic*, 2nd edn., Oxford: Clarendon Press [includes new material, including 'Twelve Terminal Essays'].

Caird, Edward (1887), *A Critical Account of the Philosophy of Kant*, Glasgow: James Maclehose.

Ferrier, James Frederick (1854), *The Institutes of Metaphysics*, Edinburgh: William Blackwood and Sons.

Green, Thomas Hill (1893), *Prolegomena to Ethics*, Oxford: Clarendon Press.

Green, Thomas Hill ([1885–8] 1910), *Collected Works*, in 3 vols., 2nd edn., London: Longmans, Green and Co.

Joachim, H. H. (1906), *The Nature of Truth*, Oxford: Oxford University Press.

Joseph, H. W. B. ([1906] 1916), *Introduction to Logic*, 2nd edn., Oxford: Clarendon Press.

Keene, Carol (1999), *A Pluralistic Approach to Philosophy*, Bristol: Thoemmes Press.

Kneale, William, and Kneale, Martha (1962). *The Development of Logic*, Oxford: Clarendon Press.

Nettleship, R. L. (1897), *Philosophical Fragments and Remains*, in 2 vols., London: Macmillan.

---

[63] Bradley (1922), pp. 521, also 618–19. See Bosanquet (1920), pp. 163–4.

PART II

METAPHYSICS

CHAPTER 7

··

HAMILTON, SCOTTISH COMMON SENSE, AND THE PHILOSOPHY OF THE CONDITIONED

··

GORDON GRAHAM

It is widely agreed that eighteenth-century Scotland was remarkable for its philosophical fertility. From the early years of the century almost to its close, a line of notable philosophers engaged each other in debate on many of the main topics of philosophy, and in the course of it wrote books that have remained important texts in the history of the subject. The philosophers were not alone. They were simply the most prominent group within a larger community of intellectuals engaged in social, historical, literary, and scientific inquiry.

For the most part, this intellectual activity took place in three locations, and centred on four small university colleges—two in Aberdeen, one in Edinburgh, and another in Glasgow. (Scotland's most ancient university—St Andrews—seems to have played little part in this intellectual ferment.) For most of the century, the University of Edinburgh was renowned for its medical sciences, while Glasgow was especially notable for its philosophical prowess. Francis Hutcheson assumed the Glasgow Chair of Moral Philosophy in 1726. His student Adam Smith later occupied the same chair, in which he was succeeded by Thomas Reid. Though Hutcheson was venerated as the 'Father' of this remarkable line, it was Reid who came to be identified as the founder of a distinctive philosophical school—'the Scottish School of Common Sense'. The name was derived from Reid's *Inquiry into the Human Mind upon the Principles of Common Sense*, completed while he was still at Aberdeen.

Another key contributor to this philosophical ferment was David Hume. Though he never held a university post, despite applications to Glasgow and Edinburgh, Hume provided the single most important stimulus to the philosophical debates of the period. Just as on the continent of Europe he awakened Immanuel Kant from his 'dogmatic slumbers', so in his native land the sceptical conclusions of his *Treatise of Human Nature* became a challenge to the holders of university chairs, and the esteem in which Reid's *Inquiry* was held resulted primarily from the belief that it contained a conclusive answer to Hume.

With Reid's demise in 1796, philosophical leadership passed to Edinburgh where Dugald Stewart held the Chair of Moral Philosophy. Stewart's personal learning and international prestige sustained the 'School' but added nothing innovative to it. His successor Thomas

Brown found more to praise in Hume than Reid, of whom he was highly critical. But though a popular lecturer, he did little to displace the pre-eminence of Common Sense, which became a dull philosophical orthodoxy. The same situation prevailed at the University of Glasgow, where philosophy fell into a period of relative intellectual decline. No one of the stature of Hutcheson, Smith, or Reid arose to take their place, or even anyone with the equivalent of Stewart's prestige or Brown's popularity. 'The dry instruction of the class-room', James McCosh recalls, was 'solid, but not inspiriting. The course of instruction was substantial, but very narrow, and the professors were bitterly opposed to enlarging it' (McCosh 1896: 27). Yet out of these inauspicious circumstances, almost from nowhere, another intellectual giant appeared to emerge—William Hamilton.

I

Sir William Hamilton was born in Glasgow, where his father was Regius professor of anatomy and botany at the university (and Thomas Reid's family physician). He attended schools in both Scotland and England, before matriculating at the University of Glasgow in 1803. Reid's Common Sense School was the dominant philosophy and Hamilton took classes in logic with Professor George Jardine, noted for his student-centred educational methods, and in moral philosophy with Professor James Mylne, Reid's successor in the Chair of Moral Philosophy. He rapidly made a powerful impression, being so intellectually gifted (as well as remarkably handsome) and, by the votes of his fellow students, was awarded honours in both classes. It was as an undergraduate that he began to collect the books that came to comprise his outstanding personal library of almost ten thousand volumes.

In the year after his graduation from Glasgow, Hamilton took up the study of medicine, and though he soon abandoned the idea of a medical career, his knowledge of physiology later stood him in good stead in his exchanges with phrenologists. The following year (1807), his outstanding academic record at Glasgow enabled him to follow in the footsteps of Adam Smith (among others) by winning a Snell Exhibition at Balliol College, Oxford. These scholarships, founded in 1677 and reserved for Scottish students, were intended to enable gifted Glasgow graduates to continue their studies at a more advanced level. At Oxford the study of Aristotle was in the ascendant, and Hamilton's philosophical work thereafter was strongly influenced by his knowledge and admiration of Aristotle. Once again he shone academically. He graduated with a first-class arts degree in 1811, having chosen to be examined on an unprecedented number of texts. In place of his earlier medical ambitions, he took up the study of law and became a member of the Scottish Bar in 1813. In 1816 his legal investigations enabled him to claim the baronetcy of the ancient family of Hamilton of Preston. This had been in abeyance since the death of Sir Robert Hamilton of Preston in 1701. Hamilton became the 9th Baron and was thereafter always referred to as Sir William.

In 1817 and 1820 Hamilton made two key visits to Germany. He became fluent in German and read extensively, thus becoming the first Scottish (and British) philosopher of any consequence to engage with the immensely influential German philosophical movement that Kant had inaugurated. This third strand in his intellectual formation gave Hamilton a unique orientation. His grounding in Common Sense philosophy in Glasgow left him with an enduring admiration for Thomas Reid. His study of Aristotle at Oxford resulted in a great facility in logic, and a deep belief in its importance. His two visits to Germany abroad gave him an unrivalled textual knowledge of Kant's philosophy as well as Schelling's (though not of Hegel's it seems). The combination was to prove critical in the development of the Scottish philosophical tradition in the nineteenth century. It drew widespread attention to his writings in England and the continent of Europe, and gave them immense authority in the universities of Canada and the United States.

Hamilton's enthusiasm for philosophy greatly exceeded his interest in the law. Accordingly when the Chair of Moral Philosophy in the University of Edinburgh was rendered vacant by the unexpected death of Thomas Brown in 1820, he applied for it. Though his application was unsuccessful, a year later he was appointed to the Chair of Civil History. This was a peculiar position. No students were required to attend his lectures (on history and literature), and the salary (which relied on a local beer tax) was discontinued after a time. Unsurprisingly Hamilton relinquished the chair, but he continued his intellectual work, and his best-known essay, the 'Philosophy of the Unconditioned', appeared in the *Edinburgh Review* in this period. It was one of a series of articles (originally published anonymously) that constituted the basis of a successful application for the Chair of Logic and Metaphysics at Edinburgh, to which he was appointed in 1836.

He held the chair for the next twenty years, and exercised an enormous intellectual influence over several generations of Scottish intellectuals. His copiously annotated edition of the *Collected Works of Thomas Reid* appeared in 1846, accompanied by over three hundred pages of 'supplementary dissertations', and his *Review* essays were republished (with additions) in 1852–3 under the title *Discussions in Philosophy, Literature and Education*. By this time, paralysis had seriously crippled him, though it left his mind unimpaired. With the help of his wife, he completed a nine-volume edition of the *Collected Works of Dugald Stewart*, published in 1854–5 (though the accompanying *Memoir* of Stewart was never finished), and was able to continue teaching until very shortly before his death in 1856. In 1859 the first of four volumes of lectures appeared, edited by his two greatest philosophical admirers, Henry Mansel at Oxford and John Veitch in Glasgow. In the same year Mansel published *The Limits of Religious Thought*, the text of his Bampton Lectures delivered in Oxford a year earlier. These were essentially an elaboration of Hamilton's philosophy in defence of religion, and the Christian faith in particular. Ten years later (1869) Veitch published a full-scale biography of Hamilton, which included a lengthy appendix by Noah Porter, president of Yale.

II

The academic prestige and intellectual admiration William Hamilton enjoyed during his lifetime, and retained for some decades after his death, contrasts very sharply with his subsequent relegation to the status of a minor philosophical figure. Thomas Carlyle, who knew him before he obtained a university post, speaks of him in glowing terms. Alexander Campbell Fraser, his student and successor in the Edinburgh Chair of Logic, describes Hamilton as 'perhaps the most learned Scot that ever lived' (Fraser 1904: 62). Fraser rated his personal intellectual debt to Hamilton above any other, and he was by no means alone. James McCosh, who also attended Hamilton's lectures, notes that 'every year a larger or less number [of students] ... rejoiced to find that he awakened independent thought within them, and were ready to acknowledge ever afterwards that they owed more to him than to...all the other professors under whom they studied' (McCosh 1875: 428). In the introduction to their edition of these lectures, Mansel and Veitch declare that in Hamilton 'speculative accomplishments [and] profound philosophical learning...were conjoined in an equal degree by no other man of his time' (Hamilton 1859: p. ix). Nor was this simply the result of Hamilton's personal impressiveness. His writings were held in the highest regard by those who never met him. Noah Porter, in his appendix to Veitch's *Memoir*, records the astonishing impact that Hamilton's *Edinburgh Review* articles had on philosophy in the United States where he came to be regarded as 'the greatest writer and teacher among living Englishmen [*sic!*]' (Veitch 1869: 424). And as late as 1870, John Clark Murray published an *Outline* of Hamilton's philosophy which was intended, and for some years served, as the standard philosophical text for the universities of Canada.

Hamilton's 'profound philosophical learning' was never called in question, even by those who were highly critical of his philosophy. It was not long after Hamilton's death, however, that deeper doubts arose about the true value of his 'speculative accomplishments'. The debate had been under way for some time. In 1854, while Hamilton was still alive, Henry Calderwood, one of his students and later professor of moral philosophy at Edinburgh, published a highly critical volume, though he noted in the preface that he differed from Hamilton 'to a degree which is painful to one who has been indebted to the instructions of that distinguished philosopher' (Calderwood 1854: p. vi). Philosophical criticism took on a much more strident tone, however, with the publication of John Stuart Mill's *An Examination of Sir William Hamilton's Philosophy* (1865). Though written with a close regard to conventional niceties, and in acknowledgement of Hamilton's learning, Mill's criticism is severe.

> It is much to be regretted that Sir W Hamilton did not write the history of philosophy, instead of choosing, as the direct object of his intellectual exertions, philosophy itself. He possessed a knowledge of the materials such as no one, probably, for many generations, will take the trouble of acquiring again; and the erudition of philosophy is emphatically one of the things which it is good that a few should acquire for the benefit of the rest.... A man who had done it so thoroughly as Sir W Hamilton, should have made his contemporaries and successors, once for all, partakers of the benefit; and rendered it unnecessary for anyone to do it again... This, which no one but himself could have done, he has left undone; and has given us, instead, a contribution to mental philosophy which has been more than equalled by many not superior to him in powers, and wholly destitute of erudition. (Mill 1865/1884: 343-4)

Mill, of course, was approaching Hamilton's philosophical endeavours from a philosophical position shaped by empirical science and associationist theories of mind. But Hamilton came under fire from the opposite end of the philosophical spectrum also. In the same year as Mill's *Examination*, James Hutcheson Stirling, an early Absolute Idealist and author of *The Secret of Hegel*, published *Sir William Hamilton: Being the Philosophy of Perception, an Analysis*. Stirling was no less severe than Mill.

> I seem to myself to have discovered in Hamilton a certain vein of disingenuousness that, cruelly unjust to individuals, has probably caused the retardation of general British philosophy, by, perhaps, a generation. (Stirling 1865: p. v)

It was Mill's rather than Stirling's book that called forth the most vigorous responses from Hamilton's admirers. In 1866 there appeared H. L. Mansel's *The Philosophy of the Conditioned*, subtitled 'Comprising some Remarks on Sir William Hamilton's Philosophy and on Mr J. S. Mill's Examination of that Philosophy'. 'It was natural to expect beforehand', Mansel tells us, that Mill's *Examination*

> would contain a sharp and vigorous assault on the principle doctrines of that philosophy. And this expectation has been amply fulfilled. But there was also reason to expect, from the ability and critical power displayed in Mr Mill's previous writings, that his assault, whether successful or not in overthrowing his enemy, would at least be guided by a clear knowledge of that enemy's position and purposes; that his dissent would be accompanied by an intelligent apprehension, and an accurate statement of the doctrines dissented from. In this expectation, we regret to say, we have been disappointed. Not only is Mr Mill's attack on Hamilton's philosophy, with the exception of some minor details, unsuccessful; but we are compelled to add, that with regard to the three fundamental doctrines of that philosophy...Mr Mill has, throughout his criticism, altogether missed the meaning of the theories he is attempting to assail. (Mansel 1866: 62–3)

The same criticism was made in another book published in the same year and with a similar title—James McCosh's *An Examination of Mr J. S. Mill's Philosophy*. The book was written before McCosh moved to Princeton and during his tenure of the Chair of Logic and Metaphysics at Belfast. Though a student and admirer of Hamilton, McCosh was not among his disciples. Yet he reaches the same conclusion about Mill.

> I am sure Mr Mill means to be a just critic of his rival. But from having attached himself to a narrow and exclusive school of philosophy and of history, he is scarcely capable of comprehending, he is certainly utterly incapable of appreciating, some of Hamilton's profounder discussions. (McCosh 1866: 11)

John Veitch, Hamilton's amanuensis in his declining years, who subsequently held philosophy chairs at St Andrews and Glasgow, makes a similar complaint in the volume on *Hamilton* that he contributed several years later to William Knight's prestigious *Blackwood's Philosophical Classics* series.

> [T]he critic so lauded in his hour, while making here his little acutenesses, has the essential defect of misconceiving his author on every essential of his philosophy....Mr Mill...has entirely misconceived the doctrine of the Unconditioned...missed the point of the argument against Cousin...confused the Infinite and the Indefinite...entirely misunderstood the distinction between immediate and Mediate knowledge. As for Hamilton's main logical doctrines, Mill's examination is for the most part simple caricature....This method of criticism is convenient and cheap, but it is fruitless of anything but the semblance of victory. (Veitch 1882: 31–2)

Somewhat ironically, the charge that Mansel, McCosh, and Veitch bring against Mill—an inability to understand a different way of thinking—is precisely the charge Mill brings against Hamilton. The concluding chapter of the *Examination* is in fact devoted to recounting several lengthy examples of 'Sir W. Hamilton's inability to enter into the very mind of another thinker' (1865/1884: 352).

The highly combative tone of these exchanges is striking to the modern reader. It has a certain fittingness in the discussion of Hamilton, since he himself generally adopted the same tone, most notably in his ferocious criticisms of Thomas Brown in the *Edinburgh Review* article on 'The Philosophy of Perception'.[1] But in part, it is simply characteristic of the period; Brown's criticisms of Reid, after all, to which Hamilton was responding, were not much less strident. In any event the debate died down fairly soon. Hamilton himself was not there to take part, H. L. Mansel, probably his most intellectually distinguished exponent, died in 1871, and Mill just two years after that. Most importantly, perhaps, the field divided between Absolute Idealists who abandoned any appeal to the 'Principles of Common Sense' and those who saw empirical psychology as a more likely source of solutions to problems in the philosophy of mind. Veitch contended in 1882 that 'the tide has turned' (in favour of Hamilton), but in retrospect this looks like wishful thinking. Indeed, it is a measure of Mill's ultimate victory in this debate that, before long, philosophers came to have so little interest in the works of Hamilton, that the *Examination* is the least-read part of Mill's own work, and quite unknown to even the most enthusiastic admirers of, for example, *Utilitarianism*, *On Liberty*, and *The Subjection of Women*.

III

The verdict of history with respect to Hamilton seems to be certain; no one now would rank him alongside Descartes, Leibniz, Hume, and Kant, as his inclusion in the *Blackwood's Philosophical Classics* series does. Indeed, such a comparison would strike contemporary philosophers as absurd. But just how absurd is it? Is Hamilton a justly or an unjustly neglected thinker? In order to answer this question something must first be said about the philosophical context in which he was working. Leaving aside for present purposes the question of his contribution to formal logic,[2] the relevant context was one dominated by a near obsession with the topics of knowledge and scepticism, and with their relation to the viability of religious belief. The principal sceptical challenge to the possibility of knowledge and the rationality of belief in the Christian God had been given its most influential articulation by Hume, especially in the *Treatise* and the *Dialogues*. Thanks in large part to Victor Cousin, who was first to coin the expression *Philosophie écossaise* (the title of a work never translated into English), it came to be widely believed that there were two major answers to this challenge—the Scottish and the German. The first—which appealed to the principle of Common Sense—owed its origins to the careful moral psychology of Thomas Reid. The second—which invoked the concept of 'transcendental apperception'—arose from the philosophical genius of Immanuel Kant.

---

[1] Hamilton on Brown: 'It is always unlucky to stumble on the threshold' (Hamilton 1853: 69). At one point Mansel says of Mill *almost exactly* what Hamilton says of Brown: 'It is always unfortunate to make a stumble on the threshold' (Mansel 1866: 90).

[2] Hamilton's logic is dealt with in another essay in this *Handbook*. Suffice to say here that his accomplishments in logic were no less hotly disputed. On the one hand, he was heralded as 'the one who has at length arisen, able to recognize and complete the plan of the mighty builder, Aristotle' (Baynes 1850: 2). On the other, Mill devotes a chapter of his *Examination* to 'Sir William Hamilton's Supposed Improvements in Formal Logic', the title of which gives advance notice of his conclusion.

On the face of it the two answers were wholly independent of each other. Reid knew nothing of Kant, and Kant, in the *Prolegomena*, famously discounted any philosophical appeal to common sense as 'the last refuge of the stalest windbag', possibly because he relied on second-hand accounts that put Reid on a level with less sophisticated exponents of Common Sense such as Beattie and Oswald. Yet, from quite early on, some commentators saw an affinity between these two answers to Hume, and strove to articulate it. Reid's *Inquiry* first appeared in German in 1782, just a year after the *Critique of Pure Reason*, and the translator's preface detects important points of similarity between the two (see Kuehn 1987: ch. 10). In 1813, James Mackintosh, a graduate of Aberdeen, published an essay in the *Edinburgh Review* in which he contended that Kant and Reid were concerned with 'the same ultimate laws of thought which mark the boundaries of reason' and that their differences were more of style than of substance (see Burns 2009: 118–19).

Cousin's contribution to this debate lay in his attempt to weave together versions of the two answers, along with other philosophical schools, into an 'eclecticism' that would combine their strengths and discard their weaknesses. It was this attempt that provided the subject matter of Hamilton's first important essay—'The Philosophy of the Unconditioned'—a lengthy review of Cousin's *Cours de philosophie*, published in Paris in 1828. The essay attracted wide attention, and admiration, in large part because it displayed evident first-hand knowledge of German philosophy, at that time still largely unknown in Scotland and Britain more widely. Moreover, to those who read it correctly, the essay used that knowledge to articulate and defend a more sophisticated version of Reid's philosophical position.

Hamilton identifies four logical possibilities—a 'philosophy of the conditioned' (his version of Common Sense), Kant's transcendental Idealism, Schelling's mysticism, and Cousin's electicism. He articulates the first, which he means to defend, as follows.

> The conditioned is the mean between two extremes—two inconditionates, exclusive of each other, neither of which can be conceived as possible, but of which, on the principles of contradiction and the excluded middle, one must be admitted as necessary. On this opinion, therefore, reason is shown to be weak, but not deceitful. The mind is not represented as conceiving two propositions subversive of each other, as equally possible; but only, as unable to understand as possible, either of two extremes; one of which, however, on the ground of their mutual repugnance, it is compelled to recognize as true. We are thus taught the salutary lesson, that the capacity of thought is not to be constituted into the measure of existence; and are warned from recognizing the domain of our knowledge as necessarily co-extensive with the horizon of our faith. And by a wonderful revelation, we are thus, in the very consciousness of our inability to conceive aught above the relative and finite, inspired with a belief in the existence of something unconditioned beyond the sphere of all comprehensible reality. (1853: 15)

The two 'inconditionates' that Hamilton has in mind are the Infinite and the Absolute. The Absolute is that which admits of no further division or analysis, and the Infinite is that which admits of unlimited division. Though the two terms are often thrown together as though they meant the same (as in Mill's *Examination*), as Hamilton uses them they are opposites. The 'Infinite' and 'the Absolute' are mutually exclusive, but they also exhaust the possibilities; either reality is without limit, or it is not. It follows that we know that one must be true, and yet we cannot know which one. This necessary combination of affirmation and ignorance means that all human knowledge must fall, and be content to fall, between the two, while at the same time acknowledging 'a belief in the existence of something unconditioned beyond the sphere of all comprehensible reality'.

This argument about the necessary either/or of the Absolute and the Infinite reveals the degree to which Hamilton's thought was influenced by Kant's 'antinomies', whose point is also to show the inescapable limits of the human mind's endeavours. But how does Hamilton's assertion differ, precisely, from the Kantian postulation of world of unknowable 'things-in-themselves'? And in what relation, if any, does the 'mean' which this 'philosophy of the conditioned' commends stand to Reid's 'Principles of Common Sense'? Hamilton's answer to the first of these questions follows almost immediately. 'Kant has shown clearly that the idea of the unconditioned can have no objective reality—that it conveys no knowledge—and that it involves the most insoluble contradictions' (1853: 17). So far so good, but a problem arises, Hamilton argues, because of a distinction Kant draws between Reason (*Vernunft*) and Understanding (*Verstand*). *Vernunft*, supposedly, gives us access to the Unconditioned, while *Verstand* give us access to the Conditioned. This lends a spuriously positive character to the Unconditioned, which, Hamilton contends, should be defined purely negatively—as 'containing nothing even conceivable'. Given Kant's distinction, however, Understanding is 'shown to be weak', but Reason is then shown to be 'deceitful'.

> The imperfection and partiality of Kant's analysis are betrayed in its consequences. His doctrine leads to absolute scepticism. Speculative reason, on Kant's own admission, is an organ of mere delusion. The idea of the unconditioned, about which it is conversant, is shown to involve insoluble contradictions, and yet to be the legitimate product of intelligence. Hume has well observed, 'that it matters not whether we possess a false reason, or no reason at all.' If the light that leads us astray, be a light from heaven' what are we to believe? If our intellectual nature be perfidious in one revelation, it must be deceitful in all.... Kant annihilated the older metaphysic, but the germ of a more visionary doctrine of the absolute, than any of those refuted, was contained in the bosom of his own philosophy. He had slain the body, but had not exorcised the spectre of the absolute; and this spectre has continued to haunt the schools of Germany even to the present day. (1853: 25)

'If our intellectual nature be perfidious in one revelation, it must be deceitful in all.' This is the link with Reid, whose philosophical response to Hume rests chiefly on an affirmation of the reliability of our faculties. Reid is, in fact, the principal subject of Hamilton's second *Review* essay, occasioned by the publication of a French edition of *Reid's Works*, translated by Jouffroy and Royer-Collard, his two leading proponents in France. Hamilton takes the opportunity presented by this review to make his most blistering attack on Thomas Brown, Dugald Stewart's successor in the Chair of Moral Philosophy at Edinburgh. Brown's well-known criticisms of Reid, Hamilton argues, are a result of the fact that 'he has completely misapprehended Reid's philosophy, even in its fundamental position'.

The fault is not entirely Brown's however. Reid failed to articulate his central insight adequately, and a large part of the point of Hamilton's essay is to make good this deficiency. There are, he holds, two major errors in Reid's analysis of the human mind. First, like Kant, he drew a distinction where he ought not to have done—between consciousness and perception. According to Hamilton, consciousness is not a faculty of the mind comparable to perception, imagination, memory, and so on, but simply the generic name for all of these. We can certainly draw a logical distinction between seeing and our awareness that we are seeing. But it is a profound mistake to confuse this with a psychological distinction, because it is in fact psychologically impossible to be conscious that we are seeing (a horse, say) without at the same time being conscious what it is (a horse) that we are seeing.

This first error is not a very grave one. It is of significance chiefly because it misleads people like Brown.

> Reid's erroneous analysis of consciousness is not perhaps of so much importance in itself, as from causing confusion in its consequences. Had he employed this term as tantamount to immediate knowledge in general, whether of self or not, and thus distinctly expressed what he certainly taught, that mind and matter are both equally known to us as existent and in themselves; Dr Brown could hardly have so far misconceived his doctrine, as actually to lend him the very opinion which his whole philosophy was intended to refute, viz. That an immediate and consequently a real, knowledge of external things is impossible. (1853: 52)

The second error (by Hamilton's account) is much more significant. Reid's 'superstitious horror of the ideal theory' led him to deny what seems incontestable—that memory and imagination 'are of necessity, mediate and representative'.

> There exists, therefore, a distinction of knowledge—as immediate, intuitive, or presentative, and as mediate or representative. The former is logically simple, as only contemplative; the latter is logically complex, as both representative and contemplative of the representation.... Representative knowledge is purely subjective, for its object known is always ideal; presentative may be either subjective or objective, for its one object may be either ideal or material... Considered in relation to each other: immediate knowledge is complete, as all-sufficient in itself; mediate incomplete, as realized only through the other. (1853: 53)

Perception tells us about the world around us; imaginary objects are in the mind only, and in this sense these objects of knowledge are purely subjective. Accordingly, and *pace* Reid, knowledge can be of mental 'ideas' as well as external 'objects'. On the basis of this emendation of Reid, Hamilton endorses what he calls 'Natural Realism'. At its heart lies a conviction in the 'veracity of consciousness'. In precisely the same spirit as Reid, Hamilton writes:

> As we did not create ourselves, and are not even in the secret of our creation, we must take our existence, our knowledge *upon trust*: and that philosophy is the only true, because in it alone *can* truth be realized, which does not revolt against the *authority* of our natural *beliefs*. (1853: 63, emphasis original)

The watchword of the Natural Realist is 'The facts of consciousness, the whole facts, and nothing but the facts', and an inescapable fact is this: in any act of consciousness we are aware, and cannot but be aware, of a distinction between 'Ego' and 'Non-ego'. We apprehend this distinction immediately as a fact of consciousness. The Absolute Idealist denies this distinction and holds that Ego and Non-ego are ultimately identical. The subjective Idealist believes that Non-ego is simply a manifestation of Ego, while the Materialist believes the opposite—that Ego is a manifestation, or a product, of Non-ego. The 'Hypothetical Realist'—or 'Cosmothetic Idealist'—tries to straddle these divisions by supposing that Ego (the contents of mind) somehow mediately represents Non-ego. Hypothetical Realism, Hamilton declares, 'although the most inconsequent of all systems has been embraced, under various forms, by the immense majority of philosophers' (1853: 56).

> The scheme of Natural Realism (which it is Reid's honour to have been the first, among not forgotten philosophers, virtually and intentionally, at least, to embrace) is...the only system

on which the truth of consciousness and the possibility of knowledge can be vindicated; whilst the Hypothetical Realist, in his effort to be 'wise above knowledge,' like the dog in the fable, loses the substance, in attempting to realize the shadow. (1853: 68)

IV

Is Hamilton's Natural Realism truly the solution to the problems that haunted philosophers since Hume? Despite their adulation, his admirers did not suppose, any more than his detractors, that he had said the final word on these matters. The question, rather, was whether his philosophy in some important way advanced matters, or whether it was in reality an unholy concoction of radically disparate elements. For Mill 'after all the experience we have had of the facility with which Sir W Hamilton forgets in one part of his speculations what he has thought in another' (Mill 1865/84: 222), it was clearly the latter. Hutcheson Stirling shares the same opinion, and in general Hamilton's critics allege that what he presents as a unified position that overcomes the defects in Kant and Reid, is in fact an unstable vacillation between the two. The contrary appearance, it is also alleged, is secured in large part by an impressive, but ultimately redundant, structure of complex logical analysis, and the employment of quasi-technical terms that serve no useful purpose.

Both Mill and Stirling find it relatively easy to assemble seemingly contradictory pronouncements in Hamilton. They give the impression, though, that their deep lack of sympathy with him inclines them to search these out a little too avidly. Mansel, in his defence of Hamilton, replies in some detail with respect to some of the passages they quote, and finds them much less contradictory.[3] But the most valuable service he performs is to set out a version of 'the philosophy of the conditioned' that abstracts from the rhetorical and terminological excesses of Hamilton's prose and thus allows a clearer view of its basic aims and a more dispassionate assessment of the degree to which it accomplishes them.

To begin with, Mansel dispels some of the unfamiliarity attaching to the terms 'Conditioned' and 'Unconditioned'. A philosophy of the Unconditioned is any philosophy that seeks to base human knowledge on an incontrovertible foundation that transcends the vagaries and contingencies of human understanding. The quest for such a philosophy—the pursuit of the Unconditioned—is as old as Plato and so no novelty of Hamilton's invention. Yet this recurrent ambition is as fruitless as it is familiar. We cannot reach beyond the limits of our understanding, which is the same as saying that everything we know must be 'conditioned' by those limits. We know that we do not know everything; we know that knowledge grows; the implication of both these propositions is that ignorance is a necessary concomitant of knowledge.

We also know that our knowledge is conditioned by many different things—the language we speak, for one, but also the way our minds work. Our experience of the world is of a

---

[3] 'It is curious', he writes in a note, 'that the very passage which Mr Mill cites as proving that Hamilton, in spite of his professed phenomenalism, was an unconscious noumenalist, is employed by Mr Stirling to prove that, in spite of his professed presentationism, he was an unconscious representationalist' (Mansel 1866: 85).

certain kind because we are creatures of time and place, and it is on that experience, necessarily, that our knowledge depends.

> Conditioned existence is existence in time: to attain to a philosophy of the unconditioned, we must rise to existence out of time. The attempt may be made in two ways, and in two only. Either we may endeavour to conceive an absolutely first moment in time … or we may endeavour to conceive time as an unlimited duration, containing an infinite series [that forms] an unconditioned whole … [T]hese two systems may be regarded as the type of all subsequent attempts. Both, however, alike aim at an object which is beyond positive conception. … Time, as the universal condition of human consciousness, clings round the very conception which strives to destroy it … [T]o conceive an infinite succession of conditioned existences … we must add moment to moment for ever—a process that would require an eternity to complete. Wherever, therefore, I stop in my addition, I do not positively conceive the terms which lie beyond. I apprehend them only as a series of unknown *somethings* of which I may believe *that* they are, but am unable to say *what* they are.
>
> The cardinal point, then, of Sir W Hamilton's philosophy, expressly announced as such by himself, is the absolute necessity, under any system of philosophy whatever, of acknowledging the existence of a sphere of belief beyond the limits of the sphere of thought. (Mansel 1866: 49–51, emphasis original)

To say that our knowledge is conditioned in this way is not to say that it is relative, as this is normally understood. The conditions under which we know do not determine the truth of what we know, but impose a certain limit. This limit is not coextensive with what we can know, however, only with what we can come to know unaided. Indeed, Mansel's own main interest—articulated at length in his Bampton Lectures—is to make 'the philosophy of the conditioned' a structure within which to identify the need for, and proper province of, knowledge courtesy of divine revelation. It is a theme on which Hamilton touches, as his reference to a 'wonderful revelation' suggests, and (though not many were convinced, perhaps) it purports to distinguish the philosophy of the conditioned from the radical agnosticism of Herbert Spencer, for whom all talk of 'ultimate reality' is pointless. The issue is not one to be examined here, however. For present purposes, it is enough to notice that the conception of 'unknown somethings' is purely negative; without divine revelation, it is impossible to say anything about what these 'somethings' are. In this respect it differs from the more positive Kantian notion. Of the noumena that lie beyond our knowledge of phenomena, we are supposed to be able to say at least, that they are 'things-in-themselves'.

The question now arises, however, as to how our 'knowledge' is related to reality. It is easy to say that Mansel and Hamilton are not relativists, but if scientific knowledge truly is inescapably conditioned by our creaturehood, how do we know that the phenomena of our experience reflect an objectively existing world?

> The key to all this is not difficult to find. It is simply that *objective existence* does not mean existence *per se*; and that a *phenomenon* does not mean a mere mode of mind. Objective existence is existence *as an object*, in perception, and therefore in relation; and a phenomenon may be material, as well as mental. The thing *per se* may be only the unknown cause of what we directly know; but what we directly know is something more than our sensations. In other words, the phenomenal effect is material as well as the cause, and is, indeed, that form which our primary conceptions of matter are derived. Matter does not cease to be matter when modified by its contact with mind, as iron does not cease to be iron when smelted and forged. (Mansel 1866: 82–3, emphasis original)

A key sentence here is this: 'The thing *per se* may be only the unknown cause of what we directly know; but what we directly know is something more than our sensations.' If we do not know the cause of our sensations, can we know anything more than our sensations? Hamilton, Mansel, and Reid say 'Yes'. Mill and Brown (and Locke) say 'No'.

What reason is there to side with the Common Sense theorists on this point? Reid's answer is that there is an unshakeable conviction on the part of all human beings, which, while rarely expressed as a doctrine, is nonetheless embodied in the structure of their languages and in their daily practice, namely, that whatever the causal connection between mind and matter, we do directly perceive, and hence can truly know about, the objects that constitute the world around us. None of the parties to this debate disputes that such a conviction is indeed so widespread as to be accurately called 'Universal'. The crucial question, is: what is the status of this conviction? Is it properly called knowledge? Or is it simply a matter of belief? The Common Sense School takes the conviction to be authoritative, and is thus ready to call it knowledge, just because it is so firmly lodged in human thought, and so indispensable to human practice. But how can conviction, however strong, show that the belief of which we are convinced is true? Surely people have had many deeply held convictions that have subsequently proved false—the once universal belief that the Sun goes round the Earth, for instance.

It is precisely on this point that Hamilton is supposed to have made an important advance. Whereas Reid's affirmation of the principles of Common Sense rested on essentially contingent grounds—this is just the way the human mind works—Hamilton aims to support Natural Realism by drawing on a version of Kant in the amendment of Reid. The crucial conviction, he holds, is necessitated by the structure of consciousness.

> When I concentrate my attention in the simplest act of perception, I return from my observation with the most irresistible conviction of two facts, or rather, two branches of the same fact; that I am—and that something different from me exists. In this act I am conscious of myself as a perceiving subject, and of an external reality as the object perceived; and I am conscious of both existences in the same indivisible moment of intuition. The knowledge of the subject does not precede nor follow the knowledge of the object;—neither determines, neither is determined, by the other.... Such is the fact of perception revealed in consciousness, and as it determines mankind in general in their equal assurance of the reality of an external world, and of the existence of their own minds. (1866: 54–5)

This passage makes it possible to detect the point at which the philosophies of Hamilton and Mill pass by each other. Here is Mill.

> The proof that any of the alleged Universal Beliefs, or Principles of Common Sense are affirmations of consciousness, supposes two things; that the beliefs exist, and that they cannot possibly have been acquired. The first is in most cases undisputed, but the second is a subject of inquiry which often taxes the utmost resources of psychology. Locke was therefore right in believing that 'the origin of our ideas' is the main stress of the problem of mental science, and the subject which must be first considered in forming the theory of the Mind.... [W]e cannot study the original elements of mind in the facts of our present consciousness. Those original elements can only come to light as residual phenomena, by a previous study of the modes of generation of the mental facts which are confessedly not original.... This mode of ascertaining the original elements of mind I call the psychological, as distinguished from the simply

introspective mode. It is the known and approved method of physical science, adapted to the necessities of psychology.

That we cannot imagine a time at which we had no knowledge of Extension, is no evidence that there has not been such a time. (Mill 1865/84: 184–6)

As this last sentence reveals, Mill takes Hamilton's contentions about the *structure* of consciousness to be contentions about the *history* of consciousness, and as his critics pointed out, this is indeed a misunderstanding. Hamilton nowhere makes any claims about 'what Consciousness told us at the time when its revelations were in their pristine purity' (1865/84: 182). To suppose that he does is to reject Reid's most basic insight from the start, and thus invite this question from the Natural Realist: how would 'a study of the modes of generation of the mental facts', such as Mill supposes psychology to be, be possible without a prior exercise of consciousness? We can only assemble, arrange, and theorize facts that we have first been able to ascertain. How does Mill imagine we are to ascertain the facts his study requires, unless we hold it to be incontestably true that our acts of consciousness give us access to facts that are not of our own manufacture?

From the perspective of Hamilton and Mansel, Mill inevitably slides back into some version of sterile Lockean 'sensationalism'. All we have access to are mental sensations. The Hypothetical Realist declares these to be the product of an objective world we cannot access. Mill, it seems, does not even go this far. By his account the only intelligible conception of 'matter' is 'a Permanent Possibility of Sensation', which, he thinks, 'includes the whole meaning attached to [the concept] by the common world' (1865/84: 243). However, Possibility, even if it is permanent, is not Reality, from which it would appear to follow that mental sensations are all in all. If so, we are back to a version of 'the ideal theory' that wholly vindicates Reid's 'superstitious horror'.

V

The reason that Mill misses the mark in his criticisms of Hamilton has a deeper source. Hamilton, successfully or unsuccessfully, is attempting to do something that lies at the heart of Common Sense philosophy—namely establish a philosophical conception of mind and matter that avoids the errors of both sensationalism and materialism. Reid's *Inquiry into the Human Mind upon the Principles of Common Sense*, and everything that took a lead from it, aimed to construe the relation between the mental and the material worlds properly, by doing justice to the facts of both. In this sense it seeks a middle ground between the traditional dichotomy of mind and matter. For Mill, however, this is a necessarily fruitless endeavour since there is no middle ground. The 'laws of the mind', he tells us, are either 'the laws of association according to one class of thinkers, [or] the Categories of the Understanding according to another' (1865/84: 183). If we pursue the former, then the future lies with empirical associationist psychology. If we pursue the latter there is (so to speak) heavy duty metaphysics to be done. The speciousness of any 'middle ground' is revealed by the fact that it generates neither empirical psychology or Idealist metaphysics. This is precisely the charge Mill brings against Hamilton.

> In the mode he practices of ascertaining [the primary facts of consciousness], there is nothing
> for science to do. For, to call them so because in his opinion he himself, and those who agree
> with him, cannot get rid of the belief in them, does not seem exactly a scientific process. It is,
> however, characteristic of what I have called the introspective, in contradistinction to the psy-
> chological, method of metaphysical inquiry. (1865/84: 189)

Whatever the justice of this charge, Mill is here reflecting an increasingly widespread opinion of his time—that the project of Reid's *Inquiry* was at bottom unscientific, and in the
hands of some of its proponents even anti-scientific. As this opinion gathered strength, the
established philosophers in Scotland increasingly abandoned 'the Scottish School', though
'anti-scientific' meant different things to different critics. James Frederick Ferrier, professor of moral philosophy at St Andrews from 1845 to 1864, was especially strident is his
denunciation of Reid on whom, he thought, Hamilton had wasted his exceptional talents.
Since Common Sense was necessarily unphilosophical, 'the philosophy of Common Sense'
was a contradiction in terms. The associationist psychology favoured by Mill was expressly
advocated, and considerably advanced, by his friend Alexander Bain, founder of the journal *Mind*, who was appointed Regius professor of logic at the newly united University of
Aberdeen in 1860. This empiricist criticism was not endorsed but it was matched with
another from those of a more metaphysical cast of mind. In broadly the same period,
Edward Caird held the Chair of Moral Philosophy at Glasgow, and assumed a leading role in
a new generation of Scottish philosophers attracted to the Absolute Idealism of Hegel. For
them, the appeal to Common Sense was no better than Samuel Johnson's method of 'refuting' Berkeley's immaterialism by kicking a stone.

The combined effect of these rather different criticisms was the same. When Andrew Seth
devoted his Balfour Lectures at Edinburgh in 1884 to a 'critical review of Scottish philosophy' he began with the observation that while 'there is a savour of superfluity in discours-
ing on Scottish philosophy to a Scottish audience [this] is perhaps hardly so much the case as
might be supposed. The thread of national tradition, it is tolerably well known, has been but
loosely held of late by many of our best Scottish students of philosophy' (Seth 1885: 1–2).

This fact was also noted, and lamented, by James McCosh. In an essay comparing Scottish
and German philosophy, he writes: 'In the land of its birth [the Scottish philosophy] is not
particularly strong at the present time, being opposed by the materialism of Bain and the
Hegelianism...of Prof Edward Caird of Glasgow' (McCosh 1882: 327). For McCosh this
was a matter of regret because 'The great merit of the Scottish Philosophy', he tells us,

> lies in the large body of truth which it has—if not discovered—at least settled on a foundation
> which can never be moved. It has added very considerably to our knowledge of the human
> mind, bringing out to view the characteristics of mental as distinguished from material action.
> (McCosh 1875: 9)

Hamilton was the last and 'most learned of all the Scottish metaphysicians' (McCosh
1875: 415) but he had in fact 'departed so far from the true Scottish school' (1875: 420) as
to be a significant cause of its demise. Whereas 'the Scottish school has never been slow
to profit by the discoveries of science', Hamilton's enthusiasm for German philosophy had
led him into 'abstractions and erudition' (1875: 420). Though McCosh was highly critical of
Mill, Mill makes a similar point in fact when he observes in a footnote that 'The signs of Sir
W Hamilton's want of familiarity with the physical sciences meet us in every corner of his
works' (Mill 1865/84: 342).

For McCosh, as for many others at this time, 'it has been the great error and sin of speculative philosophy that it has been expending its strength in building in one age ingenious
theories which the next age takes down' (McCosh 1875: 430). He makes this remark in his
essay on Hamilton, having noted Hamilton's approbation of Lessing's well-known dictum
'Did the Almighty, holding in his right hand Truth, and in his left Search after truth, deign
to tender me the one I might prefer,—in all humility, but without hesitation, I would request
Search after Truth'. Such a search, McCosh asserts, must derive its value from the value of the
truth that it actually finds.

McCosh's contention might be taken as obvious, and yet there is reason to think that at
this point, and despite all the differences between them, both Mill and McCosh are judging
Hamilton in the light of a criterion that is in fact alien to (what we might call) his intellectual ambition. This becomes more apparent if we turn to the place where Hamilton quotes
Lessing. It follows a quote from Cousin.

> Since the metaphysic of Locke crossed the channel [says Cousin]...Sensationalism has
> reigned in France without contradiction with an authority of which there is no parallel in the
> whole history of philosophy. It is a fact, marvellous but incontestable, that from the time of
> Condillac, there has not appeared among us any philosophical work, at variance with his doc-
> trine, which has produced the smallest impression on the public mind. Condillac thus reigned
> in peace...Discussion had ceased: his disciples had only to develop the words of their mas-
> ter: philosophy seemed accomplished.

Hamilton then remarks:

> Nor would such a result have been desirable, *had the one exclusive opinion been true*, as it was
> false—innocent, as it was corruptive. If the accomplishment of philosophy is simply a ces-
> sation of discussion—if the result of speculation be a paralysis of itself; the consummation
> of knowledge is the condition of intellectual barbarism...In *action* is...the perfection of our
> being; knowledge is only precious, as it may afford a stimulus to the exercise of our powers,
> and the condition of their more complete activity. Speculative truth is, therefore, subordinate
> to speculation itself...On this ground...we rest the pre-eminent utility of metaphysical spec-
> ulations. That they comprehend all the sublimest objects of our theoretical and moral inter-
> est...[and are] almost exclusively conducive to the highest education of our noblest powers.
> (1853: 39–41, emphasis added)

'Speculative truth is, therefore, subordinate to speculation itself'. This is precisely the
reverse of McCosh's view of the matter, and it explains why physical science figures so
little in Hamilton's intellectual reflection. In so far as science (perhaps properly) aims
to secure proven results, its success means the end of discussion. What is true, and has
been demonstrated to be true, is not up for debate. Hamilton's principle also explains
the important distinction he goes on to draw between 'the march of the intellect' and
'the march of science'. The former is 'no inseparable concomitant of the latter' and 'the
cultivation of the individual is not to be rashly confounded with the progress of the
species' (1853: 47). Plato and Aristotle, for example, whom Hamilton cites, represent
the highest standards by which 'the march of the intellect' is to be measured, and their
works can still serve to stimulate that march in those who study them. But neither can
now be attributed with having established 'results' by which modern science continues
to benefit.

The intellectual ambition that animates Mill (and in effect is endorsed by McCosh) aspires to the production of truth that will prove beneficial (in a broad sense) to human kind and thereby advance 'the march of science'. The intellectual ambition that Hamilton espouses in the passages quoted, aims to provide the stimulus to the mind that will serve 'the highest education of our noblest powers'. In short, Hamilton is engaged in a different enterprise.

VI

This is not the place in which to examine the interesting and important question of the relative merits of these rival conceptions of philosophy.[4] The relevance of the distinction in the present context, however, is not merely to identify an important source of Mill's misunderstanding of Hamilton. It also throws a different light on the Scottish philosophical tradition, and Hamilton's place within it.

According to Hutcheson Stirling, perception 'constitutes the middle-point of the entire movement named Scotch Philosophy, and the reason lies in the general object of that movement's originator, Reid' (Stirling 1865: 2). Stirling is here concurring with an idea that had become a commonplace by the mid-nineteenth century. Moreover it was a commonplace that Hamilton did much to confirm. In effect his three *Edinburgh Review* articles constituted his major philosophical work, and the essay in which he has most to say about Reid was explicitly entitled 'The Philosophy of Perception'. Furthermore, though ostensibly the review of an edition of Reid's *complete* works, it focuses almost exclusively on themes from the *Inquiry*, and their (alleged) misinterpretation by Brown. And, despite its reference to the 'sublimest objects of moral interest', it touches only in the briefest way on the topics of freedom of the will and personal identity. Nor does it make any reference to Reid's *Essays on the Active Powers*.

In this way, unintentionally perhaps, Hamilton gave unwitting support to Stirling's highly truncated conception of the 'Scotch Philosophy'. If we take McCosh's magisterial survey as our guide, the origin is to be found, not in Reid as Stirling says, but in Carmichael, Turnbull, and especially, Francis Hutcheson. Hutcheson, certainly, was concerned with the human mind, but he has little to say about perception, and his interests are almost entirely on the 'moral' side. Nor is it plausible to say that in succeeding years, debate came to focus ever more closely on knowledge and perception. Adam Smith, Adam Ferguson, and Henry Home (Lord Kames) must all figure in the story of its development, and none of them was primarily concerned with perception. Even David Hume, whose *Treatise* undoubtedly prompted the enduring concern with scepticism about belief in an external world, ranged much more widely, and his *Natural History of Religion* is as properly regarded as integral to his conception of philosophy as his *Enquiry concerning Human Understanding*. Even if we regard his role as that of stimulus to, rather than exponent of, 'the Scotch Philosophy', his moral philosophy was as much part of that stimulus as his metaphysics. Stirling, and others, understood Scottish philosophy as they did because they took Reid's *Inquiry* to be its cardinal text.

---

[4] I address this question, in a limited way, in Graham (2007).

The late nineteenth century certainly saw the disappearance of Scottish philosophy, if not its demise. In 1902 Henry Laurie published a book with the title *Scottish Philosophy in Its National Development*. It took the story beyond Hamilton, and included a brief chapter on 'Recent Developments'. On inspection, however, these 'developments' are mostly retrospective reflections, such as those of Seth and McCosh, or else self-conscious departures like Caird's Hegelianism. When intellectual historians eventually recovered an interest in the Scottish philosophical tradition, especially in its eighteenth-century manifestation, quite a different picture emerged. In one of the earliest of these studies, *Man and Society* (1945), Gladys Bryson takes Adam Ferguson to be Scottish philosophy's clearest exemplar, and wonders, in fact, whether Reid should figure in it at all.

Adam Ferguson was professor of moral philosophy at Edinburgh from 1764 to 1785. His best known work *An Essay on the History of Civil Society* (1767) went into many editions and translations, and for a time was no less influential than Reid's *Inquiry*. Like his contemporaries, Ferguson thought of himself as engaged in 'moral science', a term characteristic of the period in fact. However, this 'science' is not in the business of producing new knowledge. Indeed, when it comes to the study of our moral nature, Ferguson expressly admits to what Mill regards as a fault: '[W]hoever pretends to tell us of anything new, or that is not of our own minds, has mistaken his subject, or would mislead us from it.' Moral education is necessarily self-education. 'Questions may be stated, and a method proposed; but ... to succeed in the study of mind, every reader must perform the work for himself ... The learner of moral wisdom is himself the witness to be cited in evidence of the truth' (Ferguson 2007: 101).

Ferguson's account of the 'study of mind' fits Hamilton's 'march of the intellect', but not 'the march of science'. Moreover, Ferguson expressly holds that such study is practically valuable because it enables us to make greater use of our powers. 'Whoever is successful in the study of his own nature, as he may lay the foundations of a happy choice in the exercise of his will, so he may lay the foundations of power also, in applying the laws of his nature to the command of himself' (Ferguson 2007: 100). In the light of this remark, it is not difficult to suppose that he would have wholeheartedly concurred with Hamilton's belief that the purpose of philosophy is 'the highest education of our noblest powers'.

It would, of course, be no less distorting to make Ferguson Scottish philosophy's 'key' author instead of Reid. But the fact is that his conception of moral philosophy as a 'normative' science for the purposes of civic education, is widely endorsed—by Hutcheson, Smith, and Reid, as well as by less well-known figures such as Turnbull and Beattie. In the *Essays on the Active Powers*, Reid draws a distinction between the 'theory of morals' and 'our knowledge of our duty', the second being no less a part of philosophy than the former, and more important. In the *Theory of Moral Sentiments*, Adam Smith draws a very similar distinction. 'In treating of the principles of morals', he says, 'there are two questions to be considered. First, wherein does virtue consist? ... And secondly, by what power or faculty in the mind is it, that this character, whatever it be, is recommended to us?' (Smith 1759: VII.i.2). The first of these questions is of practical, and educational importance. The second 'though of the greatest importance in speculation, is of none in practice' (VII.iii.Introd.3). Hume, of course, stands apart from all these other thinkers since for him there can be no *knowledge* of duty or virtue.

The point of these references to Ferguson, Reid, and Smith is to locate Hamilton in a different and more encompassing understanding of the nature of the Scottish philosophical tradition and its intellectual aspirations. His distinction between 'the march of the intellect' and 'the march of science', it is true, is not always very evident in his own writings, and if his commitment was to the first rather than the second this is not easy to reconcile with his highly combative tone, in which it seems truth and error are the only things that matter. On the other hand, to see him as standing in this tradition explains why Mill could dismiss Hamilton's 'speculative accomplishments' so convincingly, because he did so in a world determined to model the study of mind on the study of matter. At the same time it explains the powerful sense of indebtedness among the gifted students who leapt to Hamilton's defence, and many of whom became teachers of philosophy themselves.

McCosh describes America in the latter decades of the nineteenth century as a place where 'the glow, left behind for a time by the sun of Hamilton as it set, has faded into shadow' (McCosh 1878: 192). It is plausible to think that Hamilton's sun did not merely set. A number of intellectual trends militated against his philosophy, and justly or unjustly, this enabled Mill's *Examination* to eclipse it so completely that it requires a considerable effort to recover a sense of why it once shone so very brightly.

BIBLIOGRAPHY

Baynes, T. S. (1850), *An Essay on the New Analytic of Logical Forms: With an Historical Appendix*, London.

Bryson, Gladys (1945), *Man and Society: The Scottish Inquiry of the Eighteenth Century*, Princeton.

Burns, J. H. (2009), 'Scottish Kantians: An Exploration', *Journal of Scottish Philosophy* 7/2: 115–31.

Calderwood, Henry (1854), *The Philosophy of the Infinite with Special Reference to the Theories of Sir William Hamilton and M. Cousin*, Edinburgh and London.

Ferguson, Adam (2007), *Selected Philosophical Writings*, ed. Eugene Heath, Exeter.

Fraser, Alexander Campbell (1904), *Biographia Philosophia*, Edinburgh and London.

Graham, Gordon (2007), 'The Ambition of Scottish Philosophy', *The Monist* 90/2 (April 2007), 154–69.

Hamilton, Sir William (1853), *Discussions on Philosophy and Literature, Education and University Reform*, 2nd edn., London and Edinburgh.

Hamilton, Sir William (1859), *Lectures on Metaphysics and Logic*, vol. i, ed. H. L. Mansel and J. Veitch, Edinburgh and London.

Kuehn, Manfred (1987), *Scottish Common Sense in Germany, 1768–1800*, Montreal and Kingston.

Laurie, Henry (1902), *Scottish Philosophy in Its National Development*, Glasgow.

McCosh, James (1866), *An Examination of Mr J S Mill's Philosophy; being a Defence of Fundamental Truth*; 2nd edn. London and New York, 1880; repr. Memphis, Tenn., 2010.

McCosh, James (1875), *The Scottish Philosophy, Biographical, Expository, Critical, From Hutcheson to Hamilton*, London.

McCosh, James (1878), 'Contemporary Philosophy: Historical', *Princeton Review* 1: 192–206.

McCosh, James (1882), 'The Scottish Philosophy, as Contrasted with the German', *Princeton Review* 2: 326–44.

McCosh, James (1896), *The Life of James McCosh: A Record Chiefly Autobiographical* (with William Milligan Sloane), New York.

Mansel, H. L. (1866), *The Philosophy of the Conditioned*, London and New York.

Mill, John Stuart (1865/84), *An Examination of Sir William Hamilton's Philosophy and of the Principle Philosophical Questions Discussed in His Writings*, 2 vols. in 1, New York.

Reid, Thomas (1764/1997), *An Inquiry into the Human Mind on the Principles of Common Sense*, ed. Derek R. Brookes, Edinburgh.

Reid, Thomas (1788/2010), *Essays on the Active Powers of Man*, ed. Knud Haakonssen and James A Harris, Edinburgh.

Seth, Andrew (1885), *Scottish Philosophy: A Comparison of the Scottish and German Answers to Hume*, Edinburgh and London.

Smith, Adam (1759/2002), *The Theory of Moral Sentiments* ed. Knud Haakonssen, Cambridge.

Stirling, James H. (1865), *Sir William Hamilton: Being the Philosophy of Perception, an Analysis*, London.

Veitch, John (1869) *Memoir of Sir William Hamilton, Bart.*, Edinburgh and London.

Veitch, John (1882), *Hamilton*, Edinburgh and London.

CHAPTER 8

···

J. F. FERRIER'S *INSTITUTES OF METAPHYSIC*

···

JENNY KEEFE

I. INTRODUCTION

···

JAMES FREDERICK FERRIER was the professor of moral philosophy at the University of St Andrews between 1845 and his death in 1864. He wrote several articles on philosophy and other topics from the 1830s to the 1850s. In his work we see an abandonment of a science of mind and a foreshadowing of the idealism that was to dominate British philosophy until the beginning of the twentieth century. He provides an idealist metaphysics which he develops from his rejection and revision of aspects of common-sense philosophy as well as from a defence of Berkeley's idealism. His major work, the *Institutes of Metaphysic*, was published in 1854 and here he attempts to provide a complete system of metaphysics.

George Davie is the most significant modern commentator on Ferrier and can be credited with not only writing some of the best accounts of Scottish thought[1] but also with ensuring that many Scottish thinkers, especially Ferrier, have not fallen into total obscurity. In his last work on Ferrier, *Ferrier and the Blackout of the Scottish Enlightenment*, he contends that the *Institutes* marks an intellectual breakdown in his thought. He believes that his pamphlet on the Disruption, 'Observations on Church and State', which was published six years earlier, signals the start of an intellectual decline which eventually culminates with the *Institutes*. Davie views this work as not only substandard and contradictory but also as an abandonment and a betrayal of Ferrier's earlier, Hegelian revision of Scottish philosophy. He says:

> The difficulty that occupied me was how to make sense of the apparent contradictions between Ferrier's early philosophy in his *Blackwood's* articles and his later philosophy as contained in the *Institutes of Metaphysic* some fourteen years afterwards...Ultimately, I have come to the firm conclusion that what Ferrier calls the 'New' Scottish philosophy—that is, the *Institutes*—is not merely irreconcilable with his version of the 'Old' Scottish philosophy, but is a contradictory and irreconcilable position.[2]

---

[1] Most notably Davie (1961).   [2] Davie (2003), p. i.

Given that the *Institutes* are the fullest and most mature version of Ferrier's philosophy, Davie's assessment is damning. And he is not alone in this respect. Ferrier's contemporary, the Revd John Cairns says that rather than accept the conclusions of the *Institutes* it would be 'Better [to] abolish the study of metaphysics altogether, than to degrade [it] into a mere arena of dialectical exercises'.[3] Yet, there are also more positive reviews by some of his contemporaries. Alexander Campbell Fraser says that the *Institutes* takes the reader 'over the arctic wastes of abstract thought as happily as if we were on a journey through the regions of poetry or romance'.[4] And John Stuart Mill says: 'His fabric of speculation is so effectively constructed, and imposing, that it almost ranks as a work of art. It is the romance of logic.'[5] Nevertheless, the *Institutes* was not successful when it was published and it has not been since. The question remains why this should be so. Is it because the *Institutes* are, as Davie concludes, nothing more than 'a bottle of smoke' or is this book a forgotten metaphysical masterpiece?[6] As is often the case, the answer lies somewhere between these extremes. Davie is undoubtedly right that Ferrier's philosophy coincides with the end of the Scottish Enlightenment; unlike many figures of that period, Ferrier is evidently no empiricist and he is openly against the central task of the Enlightenment: to develop a science of man. Yet, this is not an abandonment of an earlier project but rather a central theme of his complete works of philosophy. In his earliest articles on philosophy he argued that the self, unlike any other object a scientist may study, is at once the subject and object of her study. Thus, in making the self an object the scientist must deprive it of self-consciousness,[7] which must always remain with herself. Given that the object of her study is missing its distinguishing feature, it follows that any such science is fundamentally flawed from the outset. So Ferrier rejects the Baconian model and suggests that philosophy should instead mirror self-consciousness and be the systematic observation of phenomena. Philosophy thereby becomes an extension of what every person naturally does.[8] In the *Institutes* Ferrier sets out his metaphysical system and attempts to produce what his earlier works called for: a systematic form of consciousness.

II. THE ROMANCE OF LOGIC

The *Institutes* consists of a series of propositions, followed by a number of observations and explanations as well as counter-propositions which are supposed to represent the prevailing and mistaken views of his philosophical contemporaries and predecessors. It is divided into three main sections: the Epistemology, the Agnoiology, and the Ontology. The structure is deliberate and a consequence of his view that it is not possible to ascertain what is before what can and cannot be known has been determined.

---

[3] Cairns (1856), p. 30.

[4] Fraser (1856), p. 288.

[5] Letter to Sir John McNeill, 5 December 1854, in Mill (1972), pp. 246, 247.

[6] In reference to Ferrier's *Institutes*, ch. 5 of Davie (2003) is named 'A Bottle of Smoke'.

[7] Ferrier uses the word consciousness, however, he means self-consciousness: the awareness of the self that accompanies all cognition.

[8] See 'An Introduction to a Philosophy of Consciousness', in Ferrier (2001), iii. 46–90 and 196–7.

It begins with a single proposition, and then, via progressive demonstrations, he deduces the rest of his system. He hopes to diminish the role of contingent truth in philosophy and build his system from a single, primary, axiomatic proposition by applying the criterion of contradiction. He criticizes the fact that Thomas Reid and the Common Sense school were content with contingencies, and argues that metaphysics should be exclusively concerned with necessity. Yet, he believes that a proper account of the laws of intelligence in which those things that can be, cannot be, and are knowable and known, are revealed, will be in accordance with a form of common-sense philosophy. He says: 'Novel, and somewhat startling, as this doctrine may seem, it will be found, on reflection, to be the only one which is consistent with the dictates of an enlightened common sense.'[9] Indeed, it is only here in his later works that he presents his work as a form of common-sense philosophy; this is not something he is concerned with in his earlier publications.

He dismisses the role of induction in the determination of the necessary truths of reason and argues that a system which possesses truth but which is not deductively reasoned is not appropriately scientific and thereby lacks philosophical rigour. Thus, he rejects Baconian induction in favour of deduction and asserts that each demonstration in his system 'professes to be as strict as any demonstration in Euclid'.[10] He says that the *Institutes* cannot be considered to be viable unless it conforms to these strict terms:

> if there be any one premiss or any one conclusion which is not as certain as that two and two make four, the whole scheme falls to pieces, and must be given up, root and branch. Everything is perilled on the pretension that the scheme is rigidly demonstrated throughout; for a philosophy is not entitled to exist, unless it can make good this claim.[11]

His rejection of inductive reasoning in favour of deduction led some of his critics to accuse him of producing a system akin to Spinoza's pantheism. Ferrier rejects such attacks, saying: 'I owe no fealty to Spinoza. I preach none of his opinions. Indeed, I am not charged with anything of his except a method, which he has in common with all rigorous reasoners.'[12] In preferring deduction over induction he departs from the favoured methodology of the Common Sense school. Yet, he does not strictly adhere to the conditions he places upon philosophy and in his attempt to derive absolute existence, he fails to solely utilize deduction in the production of necessary truths. In fact, the *Institutes* are not 'rigidly demonstrated throughout'; contingent, reflective experience, abstractive induction, and a presupposition in the existence of a world which is independent from Ferrier's own mind all feature in his system.

In the 'Introduction' he outlines the purpose and nature of philosophy. He believes that philosophy is essentially corrective. He says:

---

[9] Ferrier (2001), i. 434 (the Thoemmes edition is a reprint of J. F. Ferrier, *Institutes of Metaphysic* (3rd edn., Edinburgh: Blackwood, 1875)).

[10] Ferrier (2001), i. 30.

[11] Ferrier (2001), i. 30.

[12] Ferrier (1856), p. 14. This short book was written following his failure to acquire the Chair of Logic and Metaphysics at the University of Edinburgh and in here he defends the *Institutes* and expands upon some of his ideas. It is a polemical work, replete with acerbic attacks on Edinburgh Town Council and those that campaigned against his philosophy on the basis that it was overly 'German' (viz., Hegelian) and not sufficiently 'Scottish' (that is to say, too far removed from Reid's common-sense philosophy).

philosophy exists only to correct the inadvertencies of man's ordinary thinking. She has no other mission to fulfil; no other object to overtake; no other business to do. If man naturally thinks aright, he need not be taught to think aright…The original dowry, then, of man, is inadvertency and error. This assumption is the ground and only justification of the existence of philosophy.[13]

This assumption is directly at odds with Reid's view, according to which man is essentially truth-acquiring rather than prone to error. Reid thinks that the constitution of the mind controls the excesses of philosophy, whereas Ferrier thinks that philosophy is the discipline through which the mind comes to know itself. For Reid a clearly constructed rational mind is a natural endowment, which checks and corrects philosophical error. But, for Ferrier, a clearly constructed rational mind is what we end up with if we philosophize well; philosophy transforms our natural, error-prone minds into well-formed critically thinking things. Therefore, in his conception of the purpose of philosophy, Ferrier clearly separates himself from his common-sense predecessors.

He asserts that philosophy is the systematic pursuit of reasoned truth. More specifically, the ultimate end of philosophy is truth and the proximate end is reason; but of the two ends, the existence of the latter is mandatory in order for a system to be described as a philosophical system. This is because it is possible that truth may be outwith our reach, whereas reason is achievable. He adds that philosophical systems which are reasoned but untrue possess some worth because, at the very least, they exercise our reasoning powers. Moreover, he believes that the pursuit of reason will eventually result in the acquisition of truth. On the other hand, he says that a system that is true but which is not reasoned 'is not philosophy at all' and that 'it has no scientific worth'.[14] He also maintains that if philosophers ensure that all of their philosophical systems are reasoned systems, there will be a greater level of clarity in philosophy and so a proper discourse between philosophers can take place. And he argues that a failure to do this has meant that philosophers have not been engaged in the same activity as each other and have not attempted to answer the same questions; he compares this to 'one man…playing at chess, [whilst] his adversary is playing against him at billiards'.[15]

He observes that in both philosophy and science there is a discrepancy between truth and feeling. For example, it is well known that the earth moves at an incredible velocity in space. However, during ordinary life, when a person is lying still, she *feels* that she *is* still although she *knows* that she is not.[16] Ferrier believes that a similar dichotomy between what a person knows and feels is applicable in philosophy. Thus, the principles which express what a person feels she knows about cognition and truth are the apparent and erroneous principles of common sense. The true and real principles of philosophy can only be settled by undermining what people think that they know and by determining what they actually do know. He

---

[13] Ferrier (2001), i. 32, 33.

[14] Ferrier (2001), i. 3.

[15] Ferrier (2001), i. 8.

[16] Ferrier (2001), i. 65. If we consider the theory of relativity, Ferrier's example is shown to be flawed. It is not sufficient to ask if a person lying in a room is moving because whether she is or not is relative; in relation to the room she is still, but in relation to the sun she is moving. Yet, it should be noted that the discrepancy argument was received wisdom in Ferrier's day and Einstein's theory of relativity did not come to popular attention until the beginning of the twentieth century.

argues that the erroneous conclusions of apparent thinking have been wrongly endorsed as the basis of a legitimate philosophy by the common-sense philosophers.

But arguably Ferrier misunderstands the Scottish school because Reid and the common-sense philosophers do not try to expose a new set of philosophical truths which consists of statements such as 'I exist', 'there is an external world', and so on. Rather, the importance is located in the implicit assent to these beliefs in every human action. However, the question remains whether or not such principles can perform a useful role in the field of metaphysics. Ferrier describes them as 'good for nothing in science, however indispensable they may be in life'.[17] He accepts that such things may be true but he thinks that they are of no philosophical interest because they merely state what everyone already knows. It is not possible to attribute certainty to an unreasoned philosophy and so, although it might be true, it has no educational quality and cannot be taught or learnt. Thus, a system which is true but unreasoned, whatever it is, it is not a system of philosophy.

According to Ferrier, the canon of philosophy is to

> *Affirm* nothing but what is enforced by reason as a necessary truth—that is, as a truth the supposed reversal of which would involve a contradiction; and *deny* nothing, unless its affirmation involves a contradiction—that is, contradicts some necessary truth or law of reason. Let this rule be strictly adhered to, and all will go on well in philosophy.[18]

He believes that a perpetual inability to implement this canon is one of the main failures of existing philosophy. A result of this is that the necessary truths of reason have not been properly distinguished from contingent truths and contradictions. He argues that unearthing the necessary truths of reason will make us reassess the 'inadvertencies and errors' of our ordinary thought because 'Each deliverance…of ordinary thinking contradicts some necessary law or truth of all reason'.[19]

Accordingly, in the *Institutes* he wants to distinguish the necessary truths of knowledge and existence from contingent truths and he thinks that applying the principle of non-contradiction[20] is the way to achieve this. One of his main motivations is a desire to provide a firmer ground for truth. He says:

> [the demonstrated truths of philosophy] appeal not to the feelings of men, but simply to their catholic reason. The mind may fall away from them; but they can never fall away. Human passion cannot obscure them; human weakness cannot infect them; but, when once established, they enjoy for ever an immunity from all those mutations to which the truths of mere contingency are exposed.[21]

Philosophy's inability to clearly distinguish between the necessary and contingent conditions of knowledge is responsible for what he describes as the 'errors of representationism' and the 'insufficiency of Berkleianism'.[22] And he believes that a failure to employ the

---

[17] Ferrier, (1856), p.11.

[18] Ferrier (2001), i. 29.

[19] Ferrier (2001), i. 39.

[20] Ferrier refers to the 'law of contradiction', also known as the 'principle/law of Non-contradiction'. I will employ the latter in order to avoid confusion.

[21] Ferrier (2001), i. 543.

[22] Ferrier (2001), i. 394–9.

principle of non-contradiction is a philosophical oversight present in both German and Scottish philosophy. He criticizes Kant, the German Idealists, and the Scottish philosophers for such a lack of clarity. Such criticisms add credence to the view that Ferrier's own philosophy is neither inherently 'German' nor 'Scottish' but is rather an eclectic combination of elements from both traditions. Indeed, his implementation of the principle of non-contradiction is a striking way in which his philosophy is an unusual hybrid of British and German philosophy. The Irish philosopher William Graham attacks British philosophers who invoke the principle of non-contradiction in opposition to Hegel's notion of the Absolute when he says:

> it would be not less absurd to maintain that the Law of Contradiction must be vindicated, at all hazards, against the Absolute, on the ground that if its authority be once impugned, it is, so to speak, all over with us in the world of thought. This appeal to consequences is not either the German or the French way of dealing with the most abstract question in Metaphysics, though I believe something remarkably like this line of argument and mode of defence is adopted by several English writers in favour of the Law of Contradiction as against the Absolute of Hegel, when it is supposed by them that two such 'mighty opposites' are arrayed against each other in Hegel's system.[23]

Graham refers mostly to Mill but also to Sir William Hamilton and Henry Longueville Mansel's use of the principle of non-contradiction to counter idealism, yet Ferrier employs this very principle in order to develop a system of idealism.

III. Everything Which I, Or Any Intelligence, Can Apprehend, Is Steeped Primordially in *Me*

The first main section of the *Institutes* is the Epistemology. And the centrality of epistemology in his system of metaphysics is fitting given that he was the first philosopher to employ the term to refer to the study of knowledge. In the Epistemology we see the development of his idealist conception of knowledge upon which he bases the remainder of his system. His account of knowledge forms the most crucial part of his system; the laws of thought are primary and they determine his entire metaphysics.

He asserts that before it is possible to determine what exists, we must first find out what we *can* know. He says:

> It is clear that we cannot declare *what is*—in other words, cannot get a footing on ontology until we have ascertained *what is known*—in other words, until we have exhausted all the details of a thorough and systematic epistemology. It may be doubtful whether we can get a footing on ontology even then. But, at any rate, we cannot pass to the problem of absolute existence, except through the portals of the solution to the problem of knowledge.[24]

---

[23] W. Graham (1872), pp. xi, xii.   [24] Ferrier (2001), i. 49.

There is a Cartesian assumption behind Ferrier's assertion that a philosophical inquiry must first determine the extent and nature of knowledge before it can proceed to an assessment of what is known; the manner and methods of knowledge are primary and precede the mind's grasp of things external to it. His focus on the relation between knowing and being links his philosophical system with Hegel's philosophy; a similarity which critics such as Cairns drew attention to in order to imply that Ferrier's philosophy was not Scottish enough. Yet, Ferrier denies that this is so, asserting that his system is the reverse of Hegel's. He says:

> If Hegel follows (as I do) the demonstrative method, I own I cannot see it, and would feel much obliged to any one who would point this out, and make it clear. In other respects, my method is diametrically opposed to his: he begins with the consideration of Being; my whole design compels me to begin with the consideration of Knowing.[25]

He begins his Epistemology with the following proposition, which he describes as 'The Primary Law or Condition of all Knowledge': 'Along with whatever any intelligence knows; it must, as the ground or condition of its knowledge, have some cognisance of *itself*.'[26] The presence of the ego signifies the existence of *some* knowledge and conversely when the ego is absent, knowledge is impossible. In this way, self-consciousness is the feature which is common to, and thereby links, all knowledge. In his earlier articles 'An Introduction to the Philosophy of Consciousness' he set out the agenda for philosophy by arguing that self-consciousness is the peculiar and defining feature of human beings and as such should be the primary focus of philosophy. And he supports a change in philosophy from the Enlightenment model of a science of man to a systematic form of consciousness. In the *Institutes* he tries to produce a philosophy which fits this revised model; the primary proposition maintains that consciousness is the condition of knowledge and the remainder of his system derives from this source. The *Institutes* are his systematic consciousness. Thus, there is a continuity of both content and intention from his articles on consciousness in the late 1830s to the *Institutes* in the mid-1850s.

Ferrier intends for the *Institutes* to be a purely deductive account of truth. Consequently, it is notable that he seeks the information of experience at crucial parts of his philosophy. At the very beginning of the Epistemology he must abandon Spinoza's method in the instance of his primary proposition, which bears more resemblance to Kant's appeal to the transcendental unity of apperception. He says:

> Strictly speaking, the proposition cannot be demonstrated, because, being itself the absolute starting-point, it cannot be deduced from any antecedent data; but it may be explained in such a way as to leave no doubt as to its axiomatic character. It claims all the stringency of a geometrical axiom, and its claims, it is conceived, are irresistible...Can *I* know without knowing that it is *I* who know? No, truly. But if a man, in knowing anything, must always know that he knows it, he must always be self-conscious. And therefore reason establishes our first proposition as a necessary truth—as an axiom, the denial of which involves a contradiction, or is, in plain words, nonsense.[27]

His explanation of self-conscious knowing is derived from the *experience* of a knowing subject, namely himself. A universal truth is inferred from the observation of a particular

---

[25] Ferrier (1856), p. 14.   [26] Ferrier (2001), i. 79.   [27] Ferrier (2001), i. 88, 89.

individual's experience; in other words, introspection of the experience of knowing leads Ferrier to observe that the ego is present in every instance of knowledge. However, by making use of subjective experience in this instance, it follows that Ferrier cannot be sure that the deductive demonstration which forms the remainder of the *Institutes* derives from indubitable premises. It is not clear that Ferrier's attempt to explain rather than demonstrate his primary proposition rationally establishes this as the primary axiom of knowledge. In this way his system does not adequately conform to the strict regulations that he asserts all philosophical systems must possess; his primary proposition contradicts his contention that 'everything is perilled on the pretension that the scheme is rigidly demonstrated throughout'.

Moreover, the distinction between Ferrier's primary proposition and one of Reid's principles of common sense is slight. If Ferrier's primary proposition is discovered by the experience of introspection, it is unclear how this may be distinguished from one of the principles of common sense suggested by Reid. In fact, there is no difference between Reid's principles of common sense and Ferrier's primary proposition. His whole system is developed from a truth which derives from ordinary thinking. The difference with Ferrier's system is that the primary proposition, or self-evident principle, is not the focus of his philosophy; it is his starting point. His main interest is what can be demonstrated *from* this principle. Yet, if the primary proposition is self-evident, then an argument which follows from this premise to a conclusion would not serve to establish it as something which is otherwise not known. Ferrier could argue that, although he appeals to the evidence of experience to establish his primary proposition, the remainder of the *Institutes* follows a wholly deductive method. Yet, under the terms of the strict conditions he places upon philosophy, the primary proposition is not properly established. In his defence, he may require the evidence of experience to produce the primary proposition but he also applies the principle of non-contradiction to the proposition so that it may be shown to be a necessary truth. Hence, he reveals that the self-evident and contingent primary proposition is an essential condition of cognition.

Also, we may question whether Ferrier is correct to posit this particular proposition as *the* primary datum of consciousness. For example, Fraser regards the *Institutes* as an interesting exposition of *one* of the truths of human intelligence, which is that human knowledge is relative. Implicit in this assessment is the accusation that Ferrier overlooks other essential truths of human intelligence. And, if we agree with Ferrier that his primary proposition is axiomatic, we may yet argue that there are other necessary truths which are equally valid and could form the basis of his system. What he fails to show is why the primary proposition of the *Institutes* is the only primary datum of consciousness.

According to Ferrier's primary proposition, whatever a person knows is herself in synthesis with thoughts and things. Thus, a self-conscious subject-*with*-object is the minimum unit of cognition. Mansel objects to the idealist principle at the centre of Ferrier's epistemology and argues that the primary proposition of the *Institutes* is problematic. He argues that if you accept, as Ferrier does, that matter per se is a contradiction,[28] then you are led into an infinite regress. He says:

---

[28] Indeed, this is one of the propositions Ferrier derives from his primary proposition. See Ferrier (2001), vol. i (section I, proposition IV).

According to Professor Ferrier, the apprehension of matter *per se* is a contradiction. I can only apprehend myself-as-apprehending-matter. But this second self is, *ex hypothese*, equally incapable of apprehending matter *per se*. It can only apprehend it under the same condition as the first, namely, by apprehending itself along with it. I cannot therefore apprehend myself as apprehending matter; but I must apprehend myself as apprehending myself-as-apprehending-matter. But the third self, again, is under the same law as the second. Wheel within wheel, *ego* within *ego*, the process continues *ad infinitum*.[29]

In response to Mansel, Ferrier draws a distinction between *inchoate* and *completed* apprehension. He says that in the expression 'I apprehend myself apprehending matter' the word 'apprehend' is an example of completed apprehension, whereas the word 'apprehending' merely refers to inchoate apprehension. He maintains that apprehension may only be described as completed when it refers to a synthesis between a self and the objective part of cognition. On the other hand, inchoate apprehension refers to the objective part of cognition. Consequently, inchoate apprehension does not refer to something which is really conceivable, it is only the objective aspect of what can be conceived. According to Ferrier, the subjective and objective aspects of a subject-*with*-object synthesis cannot be actually abstracted from one another; when we think of the subjective aspect of the synthesis we focus on that but the object of thought remains subject-*with*-object rather than the subject per se. Neither the ego per se nor matter per se is knowable; each may only be known in conjunction with the other. He argues that the object and the subject can be distinguished in cognition but they cannot be separated. In this way we can refer to the subject or the object yet we can never truly conceive of either of them abstracted from the other; it is impossible to conceive a thing out of relation to a mind, and a mind out of relation to thoughts and things is inconceivable. Both the objective and the subjective part may be known but they cannot be known out of relation to each other. The smallest unit which may be known, as it is in itself, is a union of subject with object. The things, which are commonly referred to as the subject and the object, are simply the *phenomena* of knowledge. The subjective phenomenon is the universal and necessary part of knowledge, whereas the objective phenomenon constitutes the particular and contingent part of knowledge. In the *Institutes* Ferrier reiterates his objection to the psychologist's attempt to analyse cognition that he makes in his 1847 article 'Reid and the Philosophy of Common Sense'. He argues that it is nonsensical to examine subjects and objects because the union of subject-*with*-object is the minimum unit of cognition. Therefore, it is not possible to assert, in the example of perception, that there is knowledge of matter per se. In Ferrier's account, neither knowledge of nor the denial of the existence of matter can occur out of relation to oneself. He accepts that consciousness presents the perceiving agent with both herself and the thing perceived. However, he does not believe we can deduce from this basic fact of consciousness the mutual independence of subject and object. He says: 'The objective part of the object of knowledge, though distinguishable, is not separable in cognition from the subjective part, or the ego; but the objective part and the subjective part do together constitute the unit or *minimum* of knowledge.'[30] Further, he denies that his primary proposition leads to an infinite regress. He says:

---

[29] Mansel (1855), pp. 41, 42. A similar criticism is made in Davie (2003), pp. 39–42.
[30] Ferrier (2001), i. 105.

All that is necessary, in the eye of reason, to constitute knowledge is, that, in every cognition, there shall be a point of unity and a point (or points) of diversity…But this law is fulfilled so soon as the ego turns round *once* upon itself (performs *one* act of self-duplication). It then apprehends itself, together with the other element of cognition, whatever that may be, which is not itself. And no more than this single self-duplication, or reflection on self, seems to be necessary, either for the constitution of the object, or for the performance of the act of knowledge.[31]

By employing the principle of economy he asserts that reason does not assume more than is necessary because no more than a single self-conscious self is required by reason.

After the primary proposition, and by using the method of deduction, he works through twenty-two propositions. And the key argument of the Epistemology, which follows from his assertion that consciousness is the condition of knowledge, is that a union of subject-*with*-object is the minimum unit of cognition. He says that this union is the *absolute* in cognition. Thus Ferrier's idealism is at the centre of his philosophical system. He says: 'Everything which I, or any intelligence, can apprehend, is steeped primordially in *me*; and it ever retains, and ever must retain, the flavour of that original impregnation.'[32] The absolute in human knowledge is a self, which knows itself in synthesis with thoughts or things.

Ferrier's second section, his theory of ignorance which he calls the Agnoiology, is possibly the most interesting and unique aspect of his philosophy given that ignorance is a topic which has received scant attention in the history of philosophy. Nevertheless, in the context of the structure of his metaphysics it is essentially an extension of his epistemology. Here he reiterates his central argument that matter per se is fundamentally inconceivable as well as his idealist account of cognition. He points out that minds and things-in-themselves are neither the objects of knowledge nor the objects of ignorance. And, in this way he criticizes figures such as Sir William Hamilton and Kant who allow for ignorance of the unconditioned or noumenal world. In Ferrier's view it is nonsensical to say that we cannot know the unknowable. As a privation of knowledge ignorance must involve the lack of possible knowledge. It is not possible to know minds-in-themselves or things-in-themselves; therefore, they cannot be things that persons are ignorant of. Instead, they are the inconceivable.

IV. Absolute Being

After his Epistemology and Agnoiology Ferrier sets out his theory of being in the final section of the *Institutes*: the Ontology. And it is here that the significance of his earlier sections becomes apparent. He contends that the laws of existence are in accordance with the laws of knowledge.[33] In the Ontology he argues that absolute existence must be either that which is the object of knowledge, that which is the object of ignorance, or that which is neither the object of knowledge nor ignorance. The first two options are equivalent, as laid out in

---

[31] Ferrier (1856), p. 57.

[32] Ferrier (2001), i. 120.

[33] John Haldane observes that the connection which Ferrier makes between knowledge and what is known, as well as his rejection of empiricism and his emphasis on self-consciousness, anticipates the philosophy of some modern writers, including Thomas Nagel, Michael Dummett and Hilary Putnam. See Haldane (2001), p. xii.

his Epistemology and Agnoiology; according to Ferrier, the object of either knowledge or ignorance must be some subject in synthesis with some object. The third option, that which is neither the object of knowledge nor ignorance, is equivalent to the unknowable and he calls this the contradictory; he describes it as 'that which the laws of all reason prevent from being known on any terms by any intelligence'.[34] In keeping with his previous two sections, the contradictory includes subjects-in themselves and things-in-themselves; both of which are unknowable by all intelligences. He concludes that absolute existence cannot be the contradictory and he asserts that this is a conclusion that even sceptics must allow. He emphasizes that sceptics are not concerned with existential questions, and would not doubt that *something* exists. Hence, a philosopher is not required to demonstrate existence per se. In response to his critics he says:

> the necessity of thinking—*that* is the necessity by which nonsense cannot fill the universe. Sheer nonsense and absurdity cannot be either known or conceived, by any intelligence, to fill the universe, and therefore they do not fill it. I am as much entitled to argue from knowledge to existence as any other philosopher is.[35]

Given this, we cannot accept that the contradictory exists and are therefore led to conclude that that which has absolute existence must be the object of either knowledge or ignorance. Therefore, his definition of absolute existence is in accordance with and is demonstrated from his primary proposition that consciousness is the necessary condition of knowledge.

The absolute existence, which a given individual can be cognizant of, is herself apprehending things via the senses. The absolute in human cognition is both contingent and necessary in its character. The mode of apprehension by which a person apprehends things is her senses but it is conceivable that there are other intelligences that apprehend things in a different way than she does. Therefore, the senses are the contingent conditions of cognition and are an accidental component of absolute existence. On the other hand, everything that exists must consist of some self in synthesis with thoughts or things. He says: 'every Absolute Existence must consist of the two terms—ego and non-ego—subject and object—universal and particular; in other words, of a self, and something or other (be it what it may) in union with a self'.[36] Consequently, a subject in conjunction with an object is the necessary condition of cognition and as such, it is the essential component of absolute existence. The union of subject-*with*-object is the necessary condition of cognition but within this union, there is both a necessary and a contingent part. The subject is necessary because in a given individual's cognition of absolute existence it is always her*self* in synthesis with varying, and thereby contingent, thoughts or things.

Despite praising Ferrier's literary abilities and saying that he anticipated the *Institutes* 'with more sympathy and higher expectations, than almost any philosophical book that has recently appeared',[37] Fraser believes that the conclusions of the *Institutes* are disappointing and that the substance of the book fails to reflect the genius of the style. He asserts that human beings do and must believe in 'seeming contradictions' and to disregard all such beliefs in favour of a consistent ontology creates a false philosophical system which dismisses faith in favour of reason. He differentiates between ontologists and

---

[34] Ferrier (2001), i. 459.   [35] Ferrier (1856), p. 35.   [36] Ferrier (2001), i. 518.
[37] Fraser (1856), p. 288.

philosophers; the former, such as Ferrier, are akin to sophists and have a love of intelligence, whereas philosophers, such as himself, are concerned with love and faith. Fraser makes a distinction between a philosophy of rationalism and a philosophy of faith. He asserts that the former type of philosophy, of which he counts Ferrier's *Institutes* as a prime example, leads to scepticism because the contradictory tendency of human knowledge leads to the rejection of all truth. On the other hand, the faith-led philosophers resolve the problem by reconciling the apparently contradictory nature of human knowledge with faith in an unknown. Fraser is right in saying that Ferrier's metaphysics does not include faith in an unknown. Indeed, he rejects Kant's noumena and Hamilton's unconditioned as contradictory precisely because they are unknowable. But this need not be viewed as leading to scepticism. In Ferrier's view, reality is not beyond our cognition and he thinks that those who believe that it is not only violate the laws of thought but also allow for the possibility of scepticism. In this respect he echoes Berkeley who rejected Locke's substratum on similar grounds; if we say reality is beyond our grasp, an opening is presented for the sceptic who can then deny the existence of that unknowable world. Yet Fraser's central difficulty with Ferrier's ontology concerns its scope. Unlike Ferrier, he does not believe that a proper ontology is attainable. He contends that the flawed and finite nature of our reason reveals that we cannot attribute universal laws to all reason. And he believes that this is demonstrated by propositions of faith, such as those which concern immensity, eternity, and causation, and which suggest that there is a Supreme Being who does not conform to our limited understanding of existence. Ferrier rejects Fraser's argument and says that the imperfection of human reason does not necessitate that there are no universal laws that apply to all intelligence:

> when we say, that the Supreme Being *knows* and *exists*, we must mean by these words something analogous (however small and imperfectly understood the analogy may be), to what we mean when we employ the same words in reference to ourselves, or in any other relation. Language would have no meaning unless this were admitted.[38]

In addition, he points out that there is at least one universal law which everyone agrees on: the principle of non-contradiction. Therefore, the argument that there are no such universal laws is shown to be incorrect; if it is conceded that there is one such law, it follows that there may be others. As regards his supposed omission of important propositions such as those regarding immensity and eternity, he asserts that rather than being at odds with his system '"Immensity" and "Eternity" are mere expressions of nonsense, unless an intelligence (or subject) is conceived of along with them'.[39] He allows that the validity of the *Institutes* depends on 'the legitimacy of extending to *all* knowledge and *all* reason certain necessary laws of our knowledge and our reason'[40] and he contends that Fraser attempts to undermine the *Institutes* by arguing the opposite by saying that necessary laws cannot be extended to all knowledge and reason. But he finds this to be a small victory because he himself accepts that unless this underlying principle is accepted, his system cannot work. He believes that a contrary presupposition underlies Fraser's own theory and thereby his objections to Ferrier's philosophy. Unless they are agreed on this primary point Ferrier believes that there can be no genuine dispute between himself and Fraser.

---

[38] Ferrier (1856), p. 47.   [39] Ferrier (1856), p. 50.   [40] Ferrier (1856), p. 42.

Ferrier's interest is the laws of cognition not the extent of knowledge or ignorance and so it is perfectly consistent with his account that other non-human conscious agents have greater or lesser capacities for knowledge. Nonetheless, Ferrier's response to Fraser reveals that his metaphysics is anthropomorphic; all intelligences, including a supreme intelligence, are subject to the same laws as finite beings. Mansel recognizes the difficulty that this presents for verifying Ferrier's account:

> a theory of knowing which shall be valid for other than human intelligences can only be constructed by one who has himself been emancipated from the conditions of human thought. Till this is accomplished, an unacknowledged anthropomorphism pervades the whole of our speculations: we conceive other intelligences only by first identifying them with our own...I have generalized the *Ego* and named it Pan: I have gazed on the image of my own mind, and in that microcosm I have symbolized the Universe.[41]

But if Mansel is right this means that any universal law, known or otherwise and pertaining to not only philosophy but also nature and logic, must in some sense be anthropomorphic. In making any universal claim the particular is generalized. Ferrier accepts as a given that there are universal laws that govern existence, including human existence, and he is by no means unusual in this respect. Problematic anthropomorphism consists in saying that the knowledge of other agents is exactly like it is for humans. Ferrier does not say this; instead he merely says that all cognition consists of some subject in synthesis with some object. This is not to say that all knowledge is the same as his knowledge because the only subject–object synthesis that Ferrier can actually conceive of is his own. All he is saying is that when such a synthesis exists, then it is a knowledge relation. In response to an accusation of anthropomorphism by his correspondent George Makgill, Ferrier says:

> You cannot charge me with anthropomorphism without being guilty of it yourself. Don't you see that 'the Beyond' all human thought and knowledge is itself *a category* of human thought? There is much *naïveté* in the procedure of you cautious gentry who would keep scrupulously *within* the length of your tether: as if the conception of a *without* that tether was not a mode of thinking...the anthropomorphist and the anti-anthropomorphist are both of necessity anthropomorphists, and for my part I maintain that the anti-man is the bigger anthropomorphist of the two.[42]

This response could easily be directed at Mansel. For Ferrier, a simple yet frequently overlooked truism of the laws of cognition is that thought cannot be surpassed. This means that as thinkers all persons are essentially anthropomorphic and it is also why his epistemology renders things-in-themselves as nonsensical; for Ferrier, philosophy should be exclusively concerned with the thinkable.

According to Ferrier, the absolute in cognition is equivalent to the absolute in existence. Cairns highlights the strong correlation between knowing and being in Ferrier's *Institutes* when he says: 'It is hard to say whether at present the title of professor Ferrier's work ought to stand "Knowing *and* Being" or Knowing = Being.'[43] And perhaps this indicates a serious

---

[41]   Mansel (1855), pp. 42–4.
[42]   Ferrier, Letter to George Makgill of Kemback, 1851, in Haldane (1899), pp. 82–3.
[43]   Cairns (1856), p. 11.

problem with Ferrier's philosophy, namely, that he wrongly assumes that the laws of existence correspond to the laws of knowledge. Although he shows that a cognitive act always
includes a subject in synthesis with an object, it is not clear that we can derive an existential
subject-*with*-object from this. We may question if it is possible to deduce what really exists
from what is known. However, Ferrier does not equate what exists with what is known by
human beings. Instead he equates what exists with what is and can be known, or in other
words, the actual and possible objects of knowledge and ignorance. In this way some entities
which absolutely exist may be forever unknowable by finite human beings, yet they are still
knowable per se.

By equating the objects of knowledge and ignorance, Ferrier is led to the conclusion that
absolute existence must consist of some subject in synthesis with some object. And in this
respect he revises the philosophy of Hamilton. In his biography of Schelling Ferrier outlines
the implications of Hamilton's philosophy of the unconditioned. He says:

> Hamilton's opinion is grounded on the assumption that whatever man knows he knows only
> in relation, that is, only in relation to his own faculties of knowledge. He can, therefore, appre-
> hend only relative or conditioned truth. The unconditioned (truth in itself) is beyond his
> grasp. But it is plain that this argument proves too much, it proves that the unconditioned
> truth is equally beyond the grasp of Omniscience; because it is surely manifest that omnisci-
> ence can know things only in relation to itself; and therefore Omniscience is just as incompe-
> tent as man is to apprehend the unconditioned, if this must be apprehended out of all relation
> to intelligence.[44]

In the *Institutes* he agrees with Hamilton by saying that all knowledge or ignorance must
be in relation to a self but he differs from him in the respect that he denies the existence
of unconditioned truth because he does not want to allow that the Supreme Being is subject to the same constraints as finite beings. For Ferrier, absolute existence must involve
some subject in synthesis with some object. Therefore truth is restricted to the conditioned. The unconditioned is both unknowable as well as inconceivable because it is the
contradictory.

He concludes the *Institutes* with the proposition that there is only one *necessary* absolute existence, namely, a supreme mind in synthesis with the universe. He argues that
reason dictates that there must be a supreme mind to prevent the universe from being
contradictory. This is because objects per se are contradictory. Therefore, the universe,
which is the sum total of the objective part of knowledge, must be in conjunction with
some subject in order to provide it with existence. Yet, for Ferrier to consider a universe,
which does not include his own finite absolute existence, he is obliged to employ abstraction. Shadworth H. Hodgson outlines this as follows: 'it can only be done by abstracting,
for the purpose of thought, from a fact which can never be actually absent, the presence of
self-consciousness or reflection'.[45] However, according to Ferrier's idealism, the thought of
a Supreme Being in synthesis with the world is not an abstract thought; rather it is subject
to the same rules as any other knowledge relation; it forms the objective aspect of Ferrier's
own, finite subject-*with*-object synthesis. Finite beings in union with the universe can

---

[44] Ferrier (2001), vol. iii, 'Biography of Schelling', pp. 551–2.
[45] Hodgson (1878), ii. 255.

only provide a contingent absolute existence; it is contingent because the universe is rendered contradictory prior to and following the presence of such beings. Therefore, he argues that reason shows that there must be a supreme mind eternally in union with the universe. He says:

> we are compelled, by the most stringent necessity of thinking, to conceive a supreme intelligence as the ground and essence of the Universal Whole. Thus the postulation of the Deity is not only permissible, it is unavoidable. Every mind thinks, and *must* think of God (however little conscious it may be of the operation which it is performing), whenever it thinks of anything as lying beyond all human observation, or as subsisting in the absence or annihilation of all finite intelligences.[46]

So, yet again, he employs the principle of economy; he maintains that reason only requires one intelligence to be infinitely in union with the world in order to save it from contradiction. His argument may also be applied in reverse; the belief in a universe which exists independently of our own finite existence, is essential to having a belief that there are other minds, including the supreme mind. Ferrier depends upon the world to construct his idea of God and depends upon a supreme mind to construct his idea of the world; each is necessarily in synthesis with the other. He effectively says that in order to believe in a world independent of ourselves, we *must* believe in God and that in order to believe in God we *must* believe in an independent world. Berkeley's idealism has been criticized for being similarly circular, although he is perhaps less vulnerable than Ferrier because as an empiricist he also employs the teleological argument in favour of the existence of God. In the *Institutes* the existence of God is not provided as a reason to believe in the world beyond Ferrier's own cognition but it is essential for the existence of the world prior to the existence of human beings. In going beyond his own experience he can conceive of what such existence involves but he cannot know it. Therefore, the existence of such a world cannot be demonstrated.

He argues that thinking is the basis upon which the universe is not contradictory. Therefore, absolute existence, prior to and following the thought of a given individual, can only be demonstrated if it can be shown that thought extends beyond the given individual. Unless Ferrier can demonstrate that there are other minds besides his own, all he can deduce is that 'sheer nonsense and absurdity cannot be either known or conceived' by his own intelligence. However, his account is problematic when he attempts to prove the existence of other minds. Cairns observes this difficulty when he says:

> let him shew either that other minds are not to me external objects of thought—or that, consistently with his principles, they can remain in existence except as a contradiction, when I who think of them are withdrawn, or even think of them no longer. It will not do to say that his first principle requires only *some* self to be present in all thought, but not *my* self. *I am the only self that can begin to apply the principle*, as Professor Ferrier acknowledges. I must treat every other as a not-self in relation to me; and thus the existence of any other self apart from my thought is inconceivable.[47]

Absolute existence in Ferrier's account consists of an intelligence in synthesis with the universe. However, the only absolute existence he knows is that of his own mind in synthesis

---

[46] Ferrier (2001), i. 524.   [47] Cairns (1856), p. 18. Davie and Mansel make similar criticisms.

with the universe, which seems to allow for the possibility of solipsism. He concedes that any one individual can only know her own experience of absolute existence. But, despite this, he says that from this knowledge it is possible, via analogy, to conceive of several absolute existences, which are constituted by other minds in union with the universe. He says:

> every man is ignorant (in the strict sense of having no experience) of all absolute existences except this—his own individual case. But a man is not ignorant of all absolute existences except himself and his own presentations, in the sense of having no conception of them. He can conceive them as conceivable, that is to say, as non-contradictory. He has given to him, in his own case, the type or pattern by means of which he can conceive of other cases of absolute existence. Hence he can affirm, with the fullest assurance, that he is surrounded by absolute existences constituted like himself, although it is impossible that he can ever know them as they know themselves, or as he knows himself.[48]

It is arguable that Ferrier can satisfactorily assert from a conception of other minds in union with the universe that there *are* other absolute existences divorced from his own knowledge of absolute existence. He can easily conceive of his mind in union with some object, which he has not yet experienced. For example, he can conceive that there is a tree, which he has not perceived. The *thought* of such a tree in union with his mind has absolute existence but that does not necessitate that the *perception* of a tree in union with his mind has absolute existence. Although he has the experience of some trees in union with his mind, which provides 'the type or pattern' for his mind in union with all trees, the thought of a tree does not have to correspond to a perceived tree that may form a union with his mind. Similarly, Ferrier can conceive of other minds in union with the universe but that does not necessarily imply that this conception corresponds to knowledge of minds in union with the universe. He may assert that the thought of other minds in union with the universe, in synthesis with his own mind, has absolute existence but it is not possible to deduce from this that there *are* other minds in synthesis with the universe.

Ferrier's account of absolute existence directly derives from his own experience of knowing. He argues that '[oneself] must form a part of everything which any intelligence can conceive'.[49] Therefore, he cannot remove himself from the equation. Consequently, in order to say that there are other minds in synthesis with the universe, he must also say that his own mind is in union with this synthesis. However, he cannot assert this because, as he himself acknowledges, 'every man is ignorant (in the strict sense of having no experience) of all absolute existences except this—his own individual case'. He maintains that the object of knowledge or ignorance is a synthesis of subject-*with*-object. However, the object of other minds in synthesis with the universe has an additional feature, which is Ferrier's mind in union with this synthesis, or, in other words, a second-order synthesis. He argues that this is not problematic when he says:

> although I cannot cogitate things *plus* another self without taking my own self into account as well, yet I can perfectly well understand how such a case (to wit, a case of objects *plus* another

---

[48] Ferrier (2001), i. 519, 520.   [49] Ferrier (2001), i. 514.

subject) should take place without my having anything to do with it. There is no necessity whatever for *me* to take into account any other self, when I am cognisant of things *plus* my individual me; and therefore there is no necessity for another self to take *me* into account, when he is cognisant of himself and the things by which he is surrounded.[50]

In this way he shows that in the conception of other absolute existences, nothing essential is added to or subtracted from the necessary structure; there remains *some* self in synthesis with *some* object. Nonetheless, this does not sufficiently resolve the difficulty. All Ferrier can assert by reason is that, if there are other subjects, they will adhere to the laws of knowledge as he himself does.

Moreover, when he maintains that there are other absolute existences besides those he experiences, he utilizes abstractive induction and infers a general law from the intro-spection of his own particular experience. Thus, he again abandons his strictly deductive method. Ferrier tries to resolve this difficulty by saying: 'What is possible at all is possible to any extent. *My* consciousness is both possible and actual, and therefore *other* conscious-nesses are possible; and, by a very easy and reasonable determination of the mind, I can admit them to be actual.'[51] This argument appears inadequate. It is not clear that Ferrier can determine the actual from the conceivable. He argues that a 'reasonable determination of the mind' is all that is required to convert a number of possible consciousnesses into an actual number of consciousnesses. However, it is not apparent that reason requires him to believe in other absolute existences; in fact, holding such a belief is a matter of inference. Reason would require a mind to believe in other absolute existences if there was a pre-liminary belief in an independent world. Yet, if this is the case, Ferrier again confirms that the *Institutes* do not wholly derive from his primary proposition. Moreover, even if he can account for other absolute existences, he can only identify them as belonging to persons in the world as a result of experience. Davie points out that when Ferrier connects minds with bodies he utilizes experience rather than deduction; he says:

> he can't prove the point that he is making without diverging from the deductive system and introducing experienced fact—the fact of experienced bodies and how they connect with their imagined minds. Ferrier is here contradicting his thesis that the *Institutes* contains nothing but necessary truths. In other words he has admitted a contingent truth as essential.[52]

V. CONCLUSION

Ferrier's metaphysics as set out in the *Institutes* do not adhere to the strict standards that he himself demands of a philosophical system; in particular, his move from knowing to being is problematic. Nevertheless, his theories of knowledge and ignorance provide a compel-ling idealist account of the laws of cognition. Moreover, there is not a marked change in the philosophy of Ferrier from his early articles on consciousness to the *Institutes*. The former are perhaps better, and more clearly and elegantly express his ideas, whereas the *Institutes* suffers from its odd and inaccessible style. However, in the *Institutes* we see a continuation of

---

[50] Ferrier (2001), i. 319.   [51] Ferrier (2001), i. 317.   [52] Davie (2003), p. 50.

beliefs from his early published works: idealism, systematic consciousness, and a rejection of things-in-themselves. Ultimately, Ferrier's work was published a few decades too soon. Later in the nineteenth century absolute idealism was the dominant type of philosophy throughout Britain yet Ferrier offers an anti-Enlightenment system at a time when Scottish philosophy was very much entrenched in the shadow of its influential Enlightenment philosopher: Thomas Reid.

BIBLIOGRAPHY

Cairns, Revd J. C. (1856) *An Examination of Professor Ferrier's 'Theory of Knowing and Being'*, Edinburgh: Thomas Constable and Co.

Davie, G. (1961) *The Democratic Intellect*, Edinburgh: Edinburgh University Press.

Davie, G. (1994) *A Passion for Ideas: Essays on the Scottish Enlightenment*, vol. ii, Edinburgh: Polygon.

Davie, G. (2001) *The Scotch Metaphysics: A Century of Enlightenment in Scotland*, London: Routledge.

Davie, G. (2003) *Ferrier and the Blackout of the Scottish Enlightenment*, Edinburgh: Edinburgh Review.

Ferreira, Phillip (2006) 'James Frederick Ferrier', in A. C. Grayling, Naomi Goudler, and Andrew Pyle (eds.), *Continuum Encyclopedia of British Philosophy*, London: Thoemmes Continuum, 2006, ii. 1085–7.

Ferrier, J. F. (1848) Observations on Church and State: *The Duke of Argyll's Essay on the Ecclesiastical History of Scotland*, Edinburgh: William Blackwood and Sons.

Ferrier, J. F. (1856) *Scottish Philosophy: The Old and the New*, Edinburgh: Sunderland and Knox.

Ferrier, J. F. (2001) *Philosophical Works of James Frederick*, 3 vols.: i. *Institutes of Metaphysic*; ii. *Lectures on Greek Philosophy*; iii. *Philosophical Remains*, Bristol: Thoemmes Press.

Fraser, A. C. (1856) 'Ferrier's Theory of Knowing and Being', in *Essays in Philosophy*, Edinburgh: W. P. Kennedy.

Graham, G. (2003) 'The Nineteenth-Century Aftermath', in A. Broadie (ed.), *The Cambridge Companion to the Scottish Enlightenment*, Cambridge : Cambridge University Press. ch. 17.

Graham, W. (1872) *Idealism: An Essay, Metaphysical and Critical*, London: Longmans, Green and Co..

Haldane, E. S. (1899) *James Frederick Ferrier*, Edinburgh and London: Oliphant Anderson & Ferrier.

Haldane, J. (2001) 'Introduction', in Ferrier (2001), vol. i.

Haldane, J. (2007) 'Introduction to "Dissolving Hume's Paradox: Of Knowledge of Mind and Self" James Frederick Ferrier', *Journal of Scottish Philosophy*, 5/1 (Spring 2007), 1–6.

Hodgson, S. H. (1878) *The Philosophy of Reflection*, vol. ii, London: Longmans, Green and Co.

Jaffro, L. (2010) ' "Reid said the business, but Berkeley did it.": Ferrier interprète de l'immatérialisme', *Revue philosophique de la France et de l'étranger*, 135/1: 135–49.

Keefe, J. (2007a) 'Ferrier, Common Sense and Consciousness', *Journal of Scottish Philosophy*, 5/2 (Fall), 169–85.

Keefe, J. (2007b) 'James Ferrier and the Theory of Ignorance', *The Monist*, 90/2 (Apr.), 297–309.

Keefe, J. (2007c) 'The Return to Berkeley', *British Journal for the History of Philosophy*, 15/1, (Feb.), 101–13.

Laurie, H. (1902) *Scottish Philosophy in its National Development*, Glasgow: James MacLehose and Sons.

McCosh, J. (1875) *The Scottish Philosophy, Biographical, Expository, Critical, From Hutcheson to Hamilton*, London: MacMillan and Co.

Mansel, H. L. (1855) *Psychology: The Test of Moral and Metaphysical Psychology*, an inaugural lecture delivered in Magdalen College, Oxford; Oxford: Graham and London: Whittaker and Co..

Mayo, B. (1969) 'The Moral and the Physical Order: A Reappraisal of James Frederick Ferrier', inaugural lecture, University of St Andrews.

Metz, R. (1938) *A Hundred Years of British Philosophy*, London and New York: MacMillan Company.

Mill, J. S. (1972) *Collected Works of John Stuart Mill*, xiv. *The Later Letters of John Stuart Mill 1849–1873*, Toronto: University of Toronto Press.

Muirhead, J. H. (1931) *The Platonic Tradition in Anglo-Saxon Philosophy*, London: George Allen & Unwin Ltd.

Segerstedt, T. T. (1935) *The Problem of Knowledge in Scottish Philosophy (Reid—Stewart—Hamilton—Ferrier)*, Lund: Gleerup.

Seth, A. (1885) *Scottish Philosophy: A Comparison of the Scottish and German Answers to Hume*, Edinburgh and London: William Blackwood and Sons.

Seth, J. (1912) *English Philosophers and Schools of Philosophy*, London: J. M. Dent & Sons Ltd.

Sorley, W. R. (1920) *A History of English Philosophy*, Cambridge: Cambridge University Press.

Thomson, A. (1985) *Ferrier of St Andrews: An Academic Tragedy*, Edinburgh: Scottish Academic Press.

Waddington, M. M. (1919) *The Development of British Thought from 1820 to 1890 with Special Reference to German Influences*, Toronto: J. M. Dent & Sons, Ltd.

CHAPTER 9

··

THE PHILOSOPHY OF SHADWORTH HODGSON

··

W. J. MANDER

In philosophy no less than any other field, canons self-reinforce their own narrowness and it is always well to remind ourselves from time to time how much of genuine quality, of contemporaneous influence, and of enduring philosophical interest there is to be found just outside their bounds. Our standard histories extract but a fragment. With such thoughts in mind we may examine the work of Shadworth Hollway Hodgson, an esteemed nineteenth-century figure whose work has now all but disappeared from view.

Born at Boston in Lincolnshire on 25 December 1832, Hodgson was educated at Rugby and Corpus Christi College, Oxford, from which he graduated in 1854. He married the following year, but only three years later his wife died in childbirth and with her his infant son. The tragedy determined the course of his life, as he turned to philosophy for consolation and it became more and more his absorbing interest, until in the end he devoted his whole life to the subject. Of independent means, he never held nor sought any academic post, nor did he have any other profession, but was rather an independent scholar. An early member of Sir James Knowles's Metaphysical Society which ran from 1869 to 1880, he was a joint founder of the Aristotelian Society which followed it, and whose first president he was from 1880 to 1894. (He was followed by Bernard Bosanquet, at this point in his life, another 'lay' philosopher.) He was also, in 1901, one of the founding fellows of the British Academy.[1]

Common enough in the days of Mill, by the end of the nineteenth century the intellectual centre of gravity had shifted back to the universities, and such independent scholars were the exception. Hodgson's anomalous position had two interesting effects. One concerns the range of his sources. Unhampered by teaching duties he read very widely, with a knowledge of contemporary French, German, and Italian philosophy as well as British, of ancient philosophy (both Greek and Latin) as well as modern, and of Eastern systems (both Hindu and Buddhist) as well as Western ones. This breadth can be seen in his library, which has been preserved, although the matter is just as visible in his writings. The second point is the

---

[1] For further biographical details, see Carr (1911–12), 326–33; Carr (1928–9), 361–5; Dunstan (1942), 362–3.

extent of those writings which, given the time at his disposal, are absolutely voluminous: several lengthy books and a string of articles—many, such as his annual presidential addresses, long enough to be considered books in their own right.[2] While his views did not radically change over his lifetime, they did evolve, and culminate in his four-volume *The Metaphysic of Experience* (1898)—a complete and detailed system of original metaphysical speculation. While never dismissing his earlier books, this was his chief work, and the one by which he desired his philosophy to be judged. Accordingly it will be the central focus of this chapter.

Though respected in his day—William James held him in very high regard, he was made an honorary Fellow of his old Oxford College, and he was awarded an honorary LLD from Edinburgh University—his work won him no disciples and little critical attention. In this he was partly himself to blame; his style and expansiveness did him no favours. But the problem was partly too his immense *originality*, as he tried to introduce a type of philosophical work without parallel in the century. Before his death on 13 June 1912, he himself expressed disappointment that his philosophy had not met with a better reception, and arguably it has never really received the critical attention which it deserves.

I

Philosophy aims at the knowledge of Being,[3] Hodgson informs us, but since conscious experience is the only medium by which Being is known to us,[4] it follows that the proper method of philosophy—or 'Metaphysic'[5] as he calls it—is that of 'the subjective analysis of experience'.[6] Each term of this characterization may be probed further. Since consciousness is both our only point of contact with reality and our only tool for its investigation, philosophy can be nothing but the interrogation of consciousness by consciousness, and it is in this sense *subjective*;[7] in contrast to an objective approach which distinguishes sharply between knowing and being, between our perceptions or ideas and the wholly different order we call their objects.[8] The lens must be turned on itself. The method is one of *analysis* because it is in the first place descriptive, an appeal to experience alone, just as it is experienced, uncoloured by any kind of foreign assumption or interpretation. Failure wholly to eliminate extraneous intellectual processing had been, Hodgson thought, the downfall of all previous philosophies, for completely to free oneself from every presumption is an extremely difficult thing to do. We must get clear about just *what* it is we meet with in consciousness before we can ever move on to inquire into its

---

[2] The author of four substantial monographs—*Time and Space: A Metaphysical Essay* (1865); *The Theory of Practice: An Ethical Inquiry*, 2 vols. (1870); *The Philosophy of Reflection*, 2 vols. (1878) (hereafter PR); *The Metaphysic of Experience*, 4 vols. (1898) (hereafter *ME*)—a sequence of fourteen presidential addresses, and over fifty articles, a rough estimate of Hodgson's lifetime output comes in at around 5,988 published pages. In the footnotes, works by Hodgson will be referred to by title and date throughout.

[3] *ME* i. 7, 9.

[4] *ME* i. 7.

[5] *ME* i. 9.

[6] *ME* i. 10.

[7] *ME* i. 7.

[8] *ME* i. 13.

origins or conditions of possibility.[9] Behind such a proposal lies the thought that we may distinguish between two quite different sorts or grades of *experience*.[10] At our point of departure there is the everyday sort of experience identified by Hodgson as 'the common-sense view of things in general',[11] the acquisition of a now long-forgotten schooling which, once we stop to examine it closely, our philosophy uncovers to be full of unsuspected assumptions and preconceptions. Purged of these we find underneath a pure philosophical experience ('the stream or content of actual consciousness as it occurs in consciousness'[12]) which, properly described, organized, and analysed, we may regard as the underlying explanation of our more familiar starting point. [13] That we could aim to become 'perfectly receptive, with regard to experience [and] bring with us no bias of our own',[14] that there really exists such an experiential core antecedent to and independent of our conceptual interpretation, is a point which, for all his reading of Kant and Hegel, Hodgson seems never to have questioned.

We understand this method better if we compare it with two others, the empirical and the phenomenological. The method of appealing solely to experience is, notes Hodgson, one that has always specially recommended itself to the English, but the fact that he regards Descartes and Kant as equal contributors with Bacon to the 'subjective tendency' in philosophy[15] should make us hesitate to catalogue him unproblematically as belonging to the classical empiricist tradition. Philosophy's effort to reproduce in a pure, reasoned, and systematic form the conceptually tainted phenomena of common sense is similar in many ways to that of empirical science, Hodgson acknowledges. But, like common sense itself, empiricism is an objective approach with an interest only in the facts known—that is, already separated from our knowing of them[16]—and for this reason it is every bit as blind as common sense to the many ways in which it unthinkingly moves beyond what is actually given in experience.

Empiricism takes our experience to be of some portion of a world of empirical objects, qualities, and events and takes ourselves to be real persons experiencing them, but in both points it assumes more than it has a right to do, for all that is found directly in the ultimate datum of consciousness is a complex of contents of varied kinds: colours, sounds, odours, shapes, tactile qualities, memories, imaginations, emotional feelings, pleasures and pains, desires, thoughts, and volitions.[17] Though so familiar it takes great effort to discount it, the distinction between subject and object is not given, argues Hodgson, but something inferred that does not in fact arise until a much later stage of the analysis. Empiricism, in its Humean form at least, makes another unconscious assumption, when it treats our impressions as separate, 'as if they came raining in upon us like hailstones'.[18] For Idealists such as

---

[9] 'In appealing to experience we must appeal to experience alone, without a priori assumptions of any kind; and in analysing experience we must analyse it as it is actually experienced, and in all the modes which it includes' (*ME* i. 12). 'Experience, alone, without assumptions, is the ultimate source of all our knowledge under this head' (*ME* i. 43).

[10] 'Reorganisation of Philosophy' (1886), 9.

[11] *ME* i. 15.

[12] 'Reorganisation of Philosophy', 9.

[13] *ME* i. 17,109

[14] 'The Metaphysical Method in Philosophy' (1884a), 56.

[15] *ME* i. 11.

[16] *ME* i. 17–19.

[17] *ME* i. 39.

[18] *PR* i. 11.

T. H. Green the difficulties of mental atomism led them to recognize the unifying work of conceptual understanding right at the heart of experience, but as Hodgson saw it there was no need to introduce thought to stitch back together the separated elements of experience for, in truth, they were given from the beginning in unity.[19] Classical empiricism overreaches itself yet again in its widespread assumption that the lowest data of experience are sensations rather than perceptions, something Hodgson rejects on the grounds that sense impressions are inferred entities hypothesized from a psychological point of view rather than the very thing observed to enter into our experience.[20]

But if Hume went wrong, the solution is not to abandon his method and look instead to some rationalist or a priori mode of working, but rather to stick even more faithfully to his precepts than he did himself. And, while in the specific points just detailed, Hodgson's position is distinguished from that of classical empiricism, empiricism itself is a large school and it will not go unnoticed that the method and viewpoint he proposes is markedly similar to the position called *radical empiricism* which William James outlined in his 1904 essay 'A World of Pure Experience'. Such an empiricism, states James, must neither admit any element that is not directly experienced, nor exclude any element that is directly experienced, one consequence of which is that the relations that connect experiences must themselves be experienced relations.[21] It is thus no surprise to find that William James was in fact one of Hodgson's most vocal supporters. He first met Shadworth Hodgson in the summer of 1880 whilst travelling in Europe, a relationship which they continued both in correspondence and in person (especially during James's extended Europe sabbatical in 1882–3).[22] His encounter with Hodgson was a vital influence on his own brand of empiricism. Further points of influence of Hodgson on James's work will be noted later.

Another methodology with which we find a striking similarity is that of phenomenology, and several commentators have seen in Hodgson a close anticipation of Husserl.[23] Hodgson's directive to discard all assumptions and stick to 'experience alone'[24] performs similar work to Husserl's *phenomenological reduction (epoché)* in which one 'brackets' or suspends all questions of existence or origin in order to arrive at the pure essence of consciousness.[25] Nor is this parallel accidental. Husserl was very aware of James's pioneering work, and there is evidence that he knew and was influenced by Hodgson's also.[26]

II

One aspect of Hodgson's analysis of pure experience that was particularly influential on both James and Husserl was his strikingly original account of time perception. We think naturally of ourselves as experiencing a flow of time in which the long not-yet becomes momentarily actual before passing for ever into the no-more, but stopping to reflect more carefully we realize that notions of future and past, even the notion of succession itself, can

---

[19] *PR* ii. 15.   [20] *ME* i. 78–9.   [21] James (1904), p. 534.
[22] Perry (1935), i. 617. See chs. xxxviii and xxxix for further details.   [23] Spicker (1971).
[24] *ME* i. 18, 12.   [25] See Husserl (1973).   [26] Anderson and Grush (2009), pp. 296–9.

be but inferences we make from all that is ever actually given us[27]—the present moment.[28] Although even this is problematic; for we often think of the present as the boundary line which divides the future from the past, but an abstract mathematical instant of time (like a mathematical point of space) carries in itself no content at all, and without content it is nothing for us. It cannot enter into our experience.[29] Instead we must stick to what Hodgson calls 'the empirical present' which covers a *portion* of time, or strictly, not time itself—for there is no experience of time in itself—but rather extended contents or processes in time.

For Hodgson this extended empirical present is always carved up into two sections, a part felt as coming or growing stronger and a part felt as receding or growing fainter.[30] But since we can hardly perceive what has not yet happened or what has now ceased, that experience must be accounted for in terms of some rudimentary type of memory, 'memory in its lowest terms',[31] whereby the immediate past is retained into the present. Hodgson was keen to stress that this retention is different from ordinary memory, for as C. D. Broad once acutely observed there is a world of difference between seeing a second hand move and noticing that the minute hand has moved.[32] But at bottom Hodgson's point remains that we perceive the world not so much as it comes upon us but as it takes its leave from us.

It is natural to ask as to the dimensions of Hodgson's empirical present. But here he disappoints. As with other dimensions of experience (like size or intensity) for which there obtain thresholds below which perception is impossible, with time too Hodgson insists that there must exist a *minima sensibilia* shorter than which no state of consciousness could exist at all.[33] But what that minimum might be he does not venture to suggest. On the issue of upper limits he is just as disconcertingly vague. The empirical present of any single experience lasts from the moment of its rising into consciousness to the moment of its disappearance out of consciousness. But since our total awareness will contain many such contents of different overlapping durations, not all beginning or ceasing together, with an eye to the whole of our experience it is impossible to lay down any fixed duration to the limits of presentness.[34]

The puzzle of time perception that Hodgson is addressing in putting forward his account was hardly new. It can be traced back to the Scottish Common Sense school and before them to the British Empiricists,[35] but in its late nineteenth-century context it must also be seen as an alternative kind of response to T. H. Green's influential discussion of time perception which undergirds the prevailing Idealist school. Green insisted that no sequence of conscious events could ever deliver consciousness of a sequence of events, and that to

---

[27] 'The divisions of pure time and of pure space are given only by changes in sensation, and without these divisions of pure time and of pure space we should have no consciousness whatever of time in lengths of duration, or of space in its configurations or relative positions of points, lines, or surfaces' (*PR* i. 43).

[28] *ME* i. 35–6.

[29] *ME* i. 35.

[30] *PR* i. 250, 253.

[31] *ME* i. 59, 70.

[32] Broad (1923), p. 351.

[33] *ME* i. 93.

[34] *ME* i. 37.

[35] Anderson and Grush (2009), pp. 281–93.

experience the passing of time successive states of experience need to be brought together in one consciousness; past, present, and future held together in one timeless experience itself falling outside of them altogether.[36] Hodgson separates himself from any such a priori model,[37] insisting that the relations between our experiences are themselves of a piece with relata experienced. Hodgson's account of time perception particularly impressed William James. Although the term he gave it—the 'specious present'—was in fact borrowed from elsewhere,[38] the notion which he puts forward in his 1890 masterpiece, *The Principles of Psychology*, of the present as 'saddle-back' 'with a certain breadth of its own on which we sit perched, and from which we look in two directions into time'[39] was, with acknowledgement and substantial quotation, taken directly from Hodgson. It has been argued that Hodgson's account also influenced Husserl's understanding of time consciousness[40] as a complex structure made up of *retentions* (immediate memories of what has just past), *original impressions* (awareness of what is happening at that instant), and *protentions* (immediate anticipations of what is to come). The doctrine of the specious present no longer enjoys the success it once had in the early part of the twentieth century, but that success was considerable, and we should not forget Hodgson's place in the story.

III

Simply to say that for Hodgson philosophy proceeds by unprejudiced description of immediate experience is to leave out what he regarded as the most distinctive feature of his philosophy; his great discovery. The point follows directly from his analysis of time perception.

For Hodgson, when we experience anything our field of awareness includes also that which was experienced a fraction of a second before as, from the instant of its first appearance in consciousness, each item begins to recede into the past of our retention.[41] This means that all conscious experience displays a double aspect,[42] each content of experience becoming immediately a 'retained object' in the field of awareness which characterizes the moment of consciousness which immediately follows it. Consciousness may be thought of as formed out of a content perceived and the perceiving of it—aspects Hodgson calls *whatness* and *thatness*[43]—and in reflective experience (he hypothesizes) these become separated; the *whatness* occurs in real time but its *thatness* is grasped only in retrospect.[44] As time flows on, act and object separate, and the percept is perceived as earlier than the perceiving, though still present to it. Of course, we don't explicitly to ourselves distinguish these two

---

[36] 'a consciousness of events as a related series . . . cannot properly be said to be developed out of, a mere series of related events, of successive modifications of body and soul . . . No one and no number of a series of related events can be the consciousness of the series as related', Green (1883), §16.

[37] 'Perception of Change and Duration' (1900), p. 243.

[38] For details see Anderson and Grush (2009), pp. 295–6.

[39] James (1890), p. 574.

[40] Anderson and Grush (2009), pp. 299–306; see Husserl (1990).

[41] *ME* i. 77.

[42] *ME* i. 75.

[43] *ME* i. 61.

[44] *ME* i. 74.

sides to experience and so to us the whole seems but one self-conscious unit; what Hodgson terms a 'process-content'.

This theory of 'the reflective character of consciousness'[45] was something Hodgson lighted on early in his career and progressively refined over the years, until finally in *Metaphysic of Experience* it appears as part of the phenomena of time perception, but Hodgson was in no doubt from the very first that it was an insight of fundamental importance. For as he put it in his 1878 *Philosophy of Reflection*,

> Reflection is the foundation of metaphysic because, being the moment of distinguishing the objective and subjective aspects of phenomena, it gives us our notion of *existence* as well as cognition, and that in the largest sense of the term existence, so that we cannot speak or even frame a notion of anything beyond it.[46]

Consciousness as knowledge or awareness is prior to consciousness as a state of being, since the former is the only evidence we have for the latter, but even if it provides us with the very first rudiments of the subjective–objective distinction, the duality of reflective consciousness is not that of subject and object, for the latter contrast is one which emerges only gradually, thinks Hodgson.[47] Moreover, if one and the same process-content may be thought of as both reflecting and existing, as displaying both the subjective aspect of knowing and the objective aspect of being, this is not to be read in any Hegelian sense.[48] Rather Hodgson invites us to take the contrast in terms of the phenomenology of time perception, as one and the same consciousness displaying apparent motion in two opposite directions in time. In reflecting mode it is a prolongation of felt moments from the present stretching out into the past, while as existent it presents itself as at the head of a wave ever moving forwards into the future.[49]

IV

The raw material isolated, Hodgson's next task—which occupies him for the whole of the first volume of his *Metaphysic of Experience*—is to explain how, on its basis, we arrive at our common-sense experience of the world. The complex construction is one with many steps, but it may be briefly outlined as follows.

All of our experiences are temporal, but some—those of sight and touch—are also spatial. Neither of these on its own can give us a complete grasp of space, however, for both are but

---

[45] *PR* i. 149; *ME* i, ch. II, §5. 'This notion of "reflective perception" has been the underlying key behind all our previous works, but only in this last has it now been fully expressed' (*ME* i. 107–8).

[46] *PR* i. 6.

[47] He makes a great deal of the fact that he does not take this distinction as ultimate, but this is less distinctive than he thinks. His claim that Idealists take it as ultimate (*ME*, vol. i, p. ix) seems wilful in its misunderstanding of the Hegelian idealist position which regards the subject–object distinction as one both *arrived at* and subsequently *transcended*.

[48] Hodgson sharply repudiated this charge when it was made by Stout ('Reflective Consciousness' (1894), p. 212).

[49] *ME* i. 84.

'surface sensations' conveying to us only two 'dimensions'.[50] But what they cannot do alone they may achieve together, for visual and tactile extension are very different. Wherever we see some object, we see at the same time always spatial extension around it, but the amount of surface actually touched at any one time is very limited and the sensation tells us nothing of extension beyond the surface actually touched. The two revelations are so different that it might never occur to us to unify them were it not for the fact that they are experienced simultaneously. Combining them together, however—something revealed most graphically in the experience of grasping one hand with the other at the same time as seeing what we are doing[51]—we come up with the more fully fledged notion of a space whose sensible surfaces in fact enclose a further 'dimension' of space; depth, as we might put it, in addition to length and breadth. Hodgson's account of space perception invites comparison with Berkeley who thought also that vision needs complementation by touch to give a full idea of space, but unlike Hodgson Berkeley thinks there is nothing inadequate about the purely tactile grasp of space.[52]

Advance from experience of a *spatial* world to experience of an *external* one, occurs as we notice that within the compass of our awareness there is one ever-present and central element, that which we later come to refer to as *our body*. If the paradigm type of sense experience may be thought of as extension which is both seen and felt, occasions of seen but unfelt extension may be accounted for by reference to that constant mass, that is, in terms of their distance from our body.[53] This gives us the thought of an extended world *external* to our physical body. Since we may reach out to touch such distant items, the conception we have arrived at here is also one of moveable objects, which furnishes us with the further notion of body in general as opposed to mere space; making this also the idea of a *material* world.[54]

At this stage experience may have crystallized itself into a material world, but there is no sense yet of subject and object, not even of perception distinct from object perceived.[55] These further structures emerge only gradually in stages, suggests Hodgson.[56] To begin with, the experience of disappointed expectation leads us to distinguish between *presentation* and *representation*. He gives the example of a child who returns from dinner in the hope of continuing to play with his favourite dog only to find it gone. The disappointment forces the child to recognize that the dog has a double existence, in his representations and in his presentation, the latter of which has just failed to match the former.[57] Whatever else may vanish from the field of presentation, our body is always there, and for this reason we connect the ever-available set of representations specifically with our body, suggests Hodgson.[58] Arriving in this fashion at a partition between two streams, one a fainter copy of the other, to which it sometimes corresponds and sometimes fails to match, the two orders are denominated 'knowledge' and 'reality' respectively.[59]

---

[50] 'Reality' (1903–4), 64 / *ME* i. 209. It is clear that this is not the usual sense of 'dimension'.

[51] *ME* i. 256.

[52] Berkeley (1709), §§45–54.

[53] *ME* i. 270. The parallel case of felt but unseen extension (e.g. the wind) is explained in terms of particles too small for our bodies to grasp (*ME* i. 272).

[54] *ME* i. 273–4.

[55] *ME* i. 299.

[56] *ME* i. 310.

[57] *ME* i. 311.

[58] *ME* i. 313.

[59] *ME* i. 336.

The next step is to pass from the recognition that one mode of consciousness, pure representation, is seated in the body, to the further recognition that presentations and representations are *both* located in the body, and directly dependent on it.[60] The key element in this transition is *desire*, a naturally occurring state, which as a mode of representation we refer to our body.[61] Desire is always for something absent and its fulfilment or satisfaction always takes the form of some presentation; we are given or presented with that which we were wanting or hoping for. But since the representation and the desire are recognized as located in the body, so too (we conclude) must be the perception which is continuous with and which displaces them.[62] How could the presentation satisfy the desire unless it were co-located with it? To return to the earlier example, if the child's desire for its canine playmate has been located in its body, how could a perception that the dog has now returned satisfy that desire unless it too were located in one and the same body?

This is a puzzling result in that it leaves the world of presented objects dually located, both external to the body and present within the body, but before we can address that puzzle it is necessary to take something of a sidestep and think about *why* things appear as they do. In order to do this we need to introduce Hodgson's notion of a *real condition*. Again the key concept needed here is desire. Without desire we would have no interest in things, we would never ask ourselves how they may be obtained or avoided, and we should never find ourselves asking why they occur or fail to occur. We would rest for ever in the de facto order of actual experience. 'Were it not for that fence,' thinks the child, 'I could get at those gooseberries,' thereby locating the real condition that obstructs his desire.[63] But in supposing that certain items depend upon others for their existence, that they would not occur but for those others, we move beyond the merely given, and hence the real conditions which we introduce in this way to render intelligible the perceived course of nature are themselves intellectual constructs and not immediately perceived realities; although since it is explicitly one of hypothesis and empirical confirmation the extension is (Hodgson argues) justified by experience.[64] Through instantiating relations of dependence between elements of experience, the notions of *real condition* and *conditionate* do duty in Hodgson's philosophy for the more usual idea of cause and effect, but Hodgson avoids all talk of production or generation and stresses that by this device we may account only for the existence and not the nature of things.[65] A real condition is something on the existence or continuance of which something else comes into or continues in existence, and without which it would not do so. But carrying no implication that they resemble each other or that the nature of the one *explains* the nature of the other, and calling for its justification nothing beyond observed uniformity, Hodgson regards the relation as an empirically respectable account of efficient causation.[66]

[60] *ME* i. 365.

[61] *ME* i. 366.

[62] *ME* i. 368.

[63] *ME* i. 380.

[64] *ME* i. 377. To fully appreciate this it is necessary to understand both Hodgson's view of concepts and his understanding of inductive inference. For Hodgson 'Concepts are percepts modified by attention and comparison' ('Unseen World' (1887), p. 9). 'By Induction I understand that method of enquiry which studies the order of Real Conditioning and its laws, by means of hypothesis founded on experience, prediction of consequences, and verification by subsequent experiment or observation' (*ME* i. 120).

[65] *ME* i. 327; 'The Conceptions of Cause and Real Condition' (1900–1a).

[66] 'The Conceptions of Cause and Real Condition', p. 54.

We find many examples of real conditioning within our experiences—for example, the tolling of the bell I see may be judged a real condition of the sound which I hear[67]—but we make a significant advance if we ask about the real condition of the stream of conscious perceptions and representations that our reasoning has located in the body. For on further reflection we see that the body provides not just the location, but the real condition also of our mental life. Ample evidence tells us that our consciousness as an existent depends for its existence on the neuro-cerebral workings of our body, while the fact that the one need in no way resemble the other makes the association easier for us to draw.[68] In consequence Hodgson argues that it is only in so far as we thus find the real condition of consciousness that we arrive at the idea of ourselves as a distinct and permanent psychological *subject* of consciousness;[69] although elsewhere a more modest conclusion is advanced, namely that the 'self' which we all take ourselves to be can be understood in either of two ways, *psychologically*, as the neuro-cerebral system which really conditions our inner life, or *philosophically* as the set of process-contents thus conditioned.[70] Since the postulation of any specifically immaterial Mind, Soul, or Ego does nothing more than repeat the phenomena to be accounted for, whilst grandly labelling it 'substance',[71] we ought properly to conclude that the only permanent subject to be admitted is the physical body. But Hodgson's result here must not be misunderstood; if 'there is no longer a mind' in the sense of 'an immaterial substance, with its several distinct and ultimate faculties' there is still 'a single broad and ever broadening stream of consciousness'.[72]

We were left with the puzzle that presented objects appeared to have two locations, both external to the body and co-located with it, but this conundrum finds an answer if we ask further about the real conditions of our experience. Specifically why do our experiences occur in the order and combinations they do? The perceptions themselves can supply no answer to this question, but reflection on our tactile experience provides a vital clue, for while other sensations tell us about the world at one degree removed, as it were, in touch we actually enter right into the world we learn of. The products of vision, smell, or hearing—colours, shapes, odours, sounds, and so forth—we attribute to the objects thus perceived, but with the modality of touch this easy ascription becomes compromised, for our tactile sense speaks to us only when our own body comes into contact with whatever it is we are sensing. But when it does so, referring them back to what we thus appreciate is the real condition of their occurrence, the deliverances of tactile sense we are forced to locate in our body, as the sensations of touch and pressure. And since the same quality may not exist in two material objects at once, the resultant anomaly we resolve by taking the sensations as indications of further properties—hardness and resistance—in the object itself.[73] The intuitive sense that in touch we both feel the surface of an object and the state of our own fingers makes sense only if sensation is accompanied by a sort of replica of itself in the actual object, something which is both the object of our sensation and the real condition of our sensing

[67] *ME* i. 388.
[68] *ME* i. 416; 'Relation of Philosophy to Science' (1884b), p. 39.
[69] *ME* i. 371.
[70] 'Reality' (1903–4), p. 79; *ME* i. 448.
[71] *ME* i. 420.
[72] *PR* i. 101.
[73] *ME* i. 4–5; 'The Conscious Being' (1900–1b), pp. 223–4; 'Reorganisation of Philosophy' (1886), p. 22.

it. The puzzling dual-location turns out in fact to be the locations of two different phenomena: one experienced, the other merely inferred. Realism asserts itself, as we conclude that our experiences are in fact representations of a real world outside of our own bodies.

Reviewing this complex reconstruction of our everyday experience, the exercise invites comparison with the constructions of external reality attempted by such figures as David Hume or Bertrand Russell. Like them its very status is a complex matter; it offers as much revision as it does description, and as much justification as it does analysis, while its reconstructions display a degree of speculative imagination not easy to square with its official methodology, and it remains unclear whether the steps set out are ones that Hodgson supposes were actually taken either in the history of the individual or of the species, or whether the narrative device is simply one for setting out the underlying rational structure of our experience.

V

A further puzzle about the reconstruction set out in *Metaphysic of Experience* concerns its author. Often Hodgson writes in semi-Hegelian mode of *our experience itself* as evolving under its own necessity,[74] at other times he presents its reconstruction as something *we*, its subjects, engage in. Yet this second way of thinking is problematic for him, since a crucial element to his claim that the only real conditions of consciousness are material, is to reject the idea of genuinely mental agency. It was on just this subject of 'automaton theory'—the question of whether or not consciousness is an effective agent in its own right—that the correspondence between Hodgson and William James first began. James started out as an automatist but subsequently came round to a belief in agency, while the evolution of Hodgson's opinion took the exact opposite course.[75] Despite his earliest intuitions to the contrary, by the end he regarded the impotence of mind as introspectively obvious.

> In consciousness as a perceiving, or as a thinking, or as a willing, there is literally no suggestion of agency at all, I mean no suggestion that consciousness itself perceives, thinks, or wills. By itself it is a perceiving, a thinking, and a willing; these are so many modes of it. By itself it is not a perceiver, or a thinker, or a will; it is a changing content, or a process-content...[76]

Though scarcely ever actually held, this doctrine that matter affects consciousness while consciousness cannot affect matter, is a position regularly encountered in books on the philosophy of mind under the name 'epiphenomenalism'. Indeed on Hodgson's scheme, states of consciousness not only do not cause material events, they may not even cause other conscious states. The passivity of mind is a key point in his thinking. He describes

---

[74] The analysis proceeds, for example, he tells us 'with the view of seeing what further features it contains, and must inevitably disclose to percipients' (*ME* i. 307).

[75] Perry (1935), i. 615 ff.

[76] *ME* i. 377. In a similar vein he argues, 'we have positively no proof at all that it possesses agency of any kind. It clearly possesses none when considered as content simply, and the agency which it seems to have, when considered as the function of a conscious being, is not its own, but the agency of the conscious being whose function it is' ('Unseen World' (1887), p. 15).

it as 'the great crucial and fundamental question which divides philosophers at the present day, and prevents the acceptance of any group of ideas or doctrines, however small, as a common and universally admitted basis'.[77] In his stance he takes himself to differ from idealism which he insists errs, in all its forms, by attributing creative agency or power to the self. In this criticism Hodgson rather betrays his want of sympathetic understanding for idealism. If Idealists do think that mind in some fashion 'makes' nature, this is certainly not (on any serious system of idealism) as one item among others in the causal order.

Since it is the conscious self that we habitually take as the free yet responsible self which acts, to refuse to attribute to it any causal agency has clear implications for the notion of human freedom, of which Hodgson gives a lengthy and careful examination in volume iv of *The Metaphysic of Experience*. Freedom is not to be found in any sort of indeterminist retreat from the universality of natural law, for action originated *ex nihilo* is exactly the same as *chance*, and no possible basis for moral responsibility.[78] It is only slightly better to think of freedom as lack of constraint by external forces for this is always a matter of degree, since nothing could be *wholly* a conduit for external forces or ever act *wholly* free from the system in which it finds itself.[79] Hodgson argues that there is no freedom except where there is deliberation, however brief, and choice between presented alternatives,[80] and thus free will may become pushed out altogether either by a motive so strong as to blind us to alternatives, or by a choice so regularly exercised that it becomes simply fixed or habitual, for in neither of these cases are we left with any room for deliberation.[81] The process of deliberation is crucial. We are not creatures who simply translate into action our antecedently strongest motives, rather we are creatures who consider our actions, and that is a process whose operation can often alter what would otherwise have happened without it. That this process is reducible to the lawlike functioning of the brain is no worry to Hodgson: 'just as water does not cease to be water because it can be theoretically analysed into oxygen and hydrogen, so the real and active Self does not cease to be a real and active Self because it can be theoretically analysed into brain and consciousness'.[82] Hodgson's thoroughgoing compatibilist analysis does not perhaps do justice to our most worrying intuitions about the question of moral responsibility, but our sense of being free, he accounts for as the combined experience that we are deliberating and still ignorant of the eventual outcome of that process.[83] Our sense of freedom is most fundamentally the sense of not yet knowing what we are in the process of deciding.

There is one last point about Hodgson's philosophy of mind deserving of our attention. With consciousness solidly grounded in the material world, the last thing we might expect is a doctrine of immortality, but surprisingly Hodgson offers a speculative hypothesis that would allow for its possibility. Utilizing the reasonable-enough thought that material reality contains regions and mechanisms as yet wholly unknown to us, Hodgson hypothesizes that cerebral base that grounds our conscious life, might at the same time in some wholly unknown ethereal region of reality generate a new and corresponding organism, capable of carrying on after the body and carrying with it traces of its past life. (To

---

[77] *ME*, vol. i, preface, p. xi.   [78] *ME* iv. 131.   [79] *ME* iv. 126–8.
[80] *ME* iv. 143, 150.   [81] *ME* iv. 153–4.   [82] *ME* iv. 158.
[83] *ME* iv. 160, 162, 179.

illustrate: we might imagine that our computer, by means of a link to some external hard drive quite unknown to us, is generating a copy of itself and its history just in case it ever gets destroyed.)[84]The species of survival which Hodgson offers is of course physical and speculative. Far from an irrelevance, this seemingly remote possibility of survival was one to which Hodgson himself attached the deepest significance, and it is impossible at this point not to recall the personal tragedy that began his philosophical career.[85] But if the appeal to para-science in support of such things seems odd to us, it needs to be placed in historical context. During the last quarter of the nineteenth century and first quarter of the twentieth there was a great deal of interest in scientific research into psychical phenomena.[86] Of more interest perhaps to modern readers is to note the sense of personal identity employed here. In so far as what 'survives' on this suggestion is in effect a copy of the structure or information in a brain, the conception is close to contemporary *functionalist* conceptions of mind.

VI

Looking over Hodgson's metaphysical system it would be easy to think that we have the measure of it, but that would be too comfortable. Hodgson has often been dismissed because he has been assumed somewhat unoriginal. We have already seen this is certainly not so methodologically. But neither is it the case in terms of his metaphysical doctrine. A good way to appreciate this is to reflect upon his complex relations to both materialism and idealism.

It would be simple enough to suppose Hodgson a materialist, but that will not quite do. Certainly consciousness is not for him some extra entity or substance, so his position is not dualism in any Cartesian sense, but neither does the fact that he regards matter as the real condition of consciousness mean that he thinks mental life identical with or reducible to matter. Given the nature of real conditioning, matter may be that without which consciousness would not *exist* but he holds it utterly unable to explain the *nature* of consciousness. The fundamental difference between consciousness and matter, between knowing and being, remains. Neither may we cling to some sort of materialism by holding that matter is the *only* type of being. For Hodgson argues that just as the existence of consciousness must rest on a real condition other than itself, viz. matter, so too must matter be regarded as the result of a further real condition, not itself material. Matter, he insists, cannot be regarded as something self-existent or eternal, for it is essentially composite, and as such

---

[84] *ME* iv. 392–5. The model Hodgson appeals to here is that suggested by Tait and Stewart (1875): a controversial attempt to use developments in contemporary science as the basis for a new theory of immortality. For further details, see the essay by John Brooke in this volume.

[85] Carr (1928–9), pp. 363–4.

[86] Illustrative of this, we may note the Society for Psychical Research which was founded in 1882 and whose presidents included such eminent figures Henry Sidgwick, Balfour Stewart, Arthur Balfour, William James, Frederic Myers, and Sir Oliver Lodge. Philosophical interest in psychic phenomena continued through to C. D. Broad, but few philosophers now pay such matters any attention.

there must be some real condition that brings and keeps its parts together. Since all we are acquainted with is consciousness and matter, we are forced to conclude that all around us there exists an infinite unseen world upon which the material universe depends for its origin and continued existence.[87] Science may be materialist, but speculative philosophy exposes the utter impossibility of taking materialism as the last word about the universe at large.

The dominant philosophy of Hodgson's own day was idealism, but he was equally emphatic that his position was not idealist either. He allowed that the idealist was able to marshal strong arguments for his view, but felt able to resist them, and it is worth following two of his replies for they are revealing. It is true (Hodgson admits) that consciousness is the only kind of reality that we ever in fact encounter. All other modes of existence are inferred. But this point, he argues, need not worry us for the inferences beyond consciousness are sound and, besides, consciousness as knowing has no agency whatsoever about it and it is quite impossible to account for the entire universe in terms of something without any agency at all.[88]

A stronger argument for idealism would urge that if consciousness is the only species of existence that we ever actually encounter then surely it defines whatever we can possibly mean by 'existence'. And interestingly Hodgson goes a surprisingly long way towards conceding this point. He admits that 'Perceivability is the mark by which we render definite our idea of existence generally. It gives its general idea, the *sine qua non* basis of our thought of it'.[89] A clearer statement of idealism it might be hard to find. Hodgson resists the charge, however, arguing that even if the root conception of 'being' is that expressed in Berkeley's *esse* is *percipi* dictum, it does not follow that that root *exhausts* what we mean by the term. He further urges that as our analysis of experience develops, although we never escape the primary meaning of existence as experience, we can add more depth to it such that in its fullest articulation it has an import quite different from that of idealism. Specifically he isolates four different increasingly articulated notions of 'reality': (i) Something simply in consciousness, (ii) Something which has a definite place in perception, or objective thought, (iii) Something which has existence independently of whether it is perceived or unperceived, thought of or not thought of, at any given time, and (iv) Something which has efficacy as a real condition.[90] He uses in particular the distinction between the first and the fourth senses to draw the sting from Berkeley's philosophy, which would seem to imply that things no longer exist when unperceived. To adequately respond to Berkeley's charge, replies Hodgson, we need to distinguish between the content or nature of a thing and the real conditions or causes of its existence. Contentwise we must say with Berkeley that *esse* is *percipi*, but nothing in that admission itself requires us to follow him in the further causal claim that the existence of a thing depends upon its being perceived. What a thing is, even that it is, is something given by perception, but we need not conclude from that fact the further position that it depends for existence on perception.[91] We see more clearly Hodgson's separation between these two senses of 'being' in his account of the root temptation to idealism. This he traces back to his own groundbreaking analysis of reflective awareness. It is in failure properly to appreciate the distinction between consciousness as knowing and consciousness as a

---

[87] ME i. 409, iv. 363–71.   [88] ME iv. 377.   [89] *ME* iv. 375.
[90] *ME* i. 457–8.   [91] 'Two Senses of Reality' (1883), p. 38.

real existent that the error of idealism arises; consciousness may be a real existent as well as a knowing, but it cannot contain the real conditions of its own existence.[92]

Hodgson's response to idealism is less strong than he imagines and based upon a rather simplistic grasp of that position. He resists a relatively crude understanding of idealism which treats objects of knowledge as the causal products of knowing (in the sense perhaps that objects of imagination are products of that creative faculty), but in allowing that the base meaning of 'existence' from which thought never escapes is given in perception, he places himself within a conceptual framework to which any other notion of being, however different it may seem, must in the end be judged but an elaboration or extension of that first or original sense. And that seems to be the very heart of idealism. The idealist holds that there is no conception of *being itself*, only being *as experienced*.

VII

The doctrine of the Unseen World might seem a largely empty and redundant addition to Hodgson's system, but gives him one further result of vital significance—the existence of God. In view of the fact that the former mode of arriving at answers suggests only the power of God, whereas the latter mode suggests to us his goodness, Hodgson follows Kant in thinking that 'the idea of God, as the great Object of Religion, is an idea of the practical not of the speculative reason'.[93] It is our conscience which gives us the key to the Unseen World.[94] But if at its heart belief in God is ethical rather than theoretical, theory may none-theless be called in to support the mode of inference by which we arrive at it. For if our prac-tical reasoning generates a belief in the Unseen World, suggests Hodgson, it is also true that that act of reasoning is itself conditioned by the brain which, as a part of the material sphere, is in its turn conditioned by the same Unseen World that the inference leads us to. While we might fear that it emerges unsupported under its own steam, in fact, our faith derives its origin ultimately, through Matter, from the very thing that it is we come to believe in; and in this sense (Hodgson claims) it 'has all the validity which from the nature of the case is possible'.[95]

BIBLIOGRAPHY

Anderson, H. K., and Grush, R. (2009) 'A Brief History of Time-Consciousness: Historical Precursors to James and Husserl', *Journal of the History of Philosophy*, 47, pp. 277–307.

Berkeley, G. (1709) *An Essay towards a New Theory of Vision* (Dublin: Pepyat).

Broad, C. D. (1923) *Scientific Thought* (London: Routledge and Kegan Paul).

Carr, H. Wildon (1911–12) 'Obituary: Shadworth Hollway Hodgson', *Proceedings of the Aristotelian Society*, NS 12, pp. 326–33.

Carr, H. Wildon (1928–9) 'The Fiftieth Session: A Retrospect', *Proceedings of the Aristotelian Society*, NS 29, pp. 359–86.

---

[92] *ME* iv. 380–2.   [93] *ME* iii. 221.   [94] *ME* iii. 333–4.   [95] *ME* iv. 337.

Dunstan, W. R. (1942) 'Our Quest for Philosophy and What Came of It', *Hibbert Journal*, 40, pp. 361–8.

Green, T. H. (1883) *Prolegomena to Ethics* (Oxford: Clarendon Press).

Hodgson, S. H. (1865) *Time and Space: A Metaphysical Essay* (London: Longman, Green, Longman, Roberts and Green).

Hodgson, S. H. (1870) *The Theory of Practice: An Ethical Inquiry* (London: Longmans, Green, Reader, and Dyer).

Hodgson, S. H. (1878) *The Philosophy of Reflection* (London: Longmans, Green).

Hodgson, S. H. (1883) 'The Two Senses of Reality: An Address' (privately printed).

Hodgson, S. H. (1884a) 'The Metaphysical Method in Philosophy', *Mind*, os 9, pp. 48–72.

Hodgson, S. H. (1884b) '*The Relation of Philosophy to Science*: An Address' (London: Williams and Norgate).

Hodgson, S. H. (1886) 'The Reorganisation of Philosophy: An Address' (London: Williams and Norgate).

Hodgson, S. H. (1887) 'The Unseen World: An Address' (London: Williams and Norgate).

Hodgson, S. H. (1894) 'Reflective Consciousness' *Mind*, NS 3, pp. 208–21.

Hodgson, S. H. (1898) *The Metaphysic of Experience* (London: Longmans, Green).

Hodgson, S. H. (1900) 'Perception of Change and Duration—A Reply', *Mind*, 9, pp. 240–3.

Hodgson, S. H. (1900–1a) 'The Conceptions of Cause and Real Condition', *Proceedings of the Aristotelian Society*, NS 1, pp. 45–56.

Hodgson, S. H. (1900–1b) 'The Conscious Being', *Proceedings of the Aristotelian Society*, NS 1, pp. 220–6.

Hodgson, S. H. (1903–4) 'Reality', *Proceedings of the Aristotelian Society*, NS 4, pp. 53–86.

Husserl, E. (1973) *Logical Investigations*, trans. J. N. Findlay (London: Routledge) [1st published 1913].

Husserl, E. (1990) *On the Phenomenology of the Consciousness of Internal Time (1893–1917)*, trans. J. B. Brough (Dordrecht: Kluwer) [1st published 1928].

James, W. (1890) *The Principles of Psychology* (Boston: Henry Holt).

James, W. (1904) 'A World of Pure Experience', *Journal of Philosophy, Psychology and Scientific Methods*, 1, pp. 533–43 and 561–70.

Perry, R. B. (1935) *Thought and Character of William James* (London: Oxford University Press).

Reck, A. J. (1982) 'Hodgson's Metaphysics of Experience', in J. Sallis (ed.), *Philosophy and Archaic Experience* (Pittsburgh: Duquesne University Press), pp. 29–47.

Spicker, S. (1971) 'Shadworth Hodgson's Reduction as an Anticipation of Husserl's Phenomenological Psychology', *Journal of the British Society for Phenomenology*, 2, pp. 57–73.

Tait, P. G., and Stewart, B. (1875) *The Unseen Universe, or Physical Speculations On A Future State* (London: Macmillan).

CHAPTER 10

BRADLEY'S METAPHYSICS

PIERFRANCESCO BASILE

Metaphysics is the finding of bad reasons for what we believe upon instinct, but to find these reasons is no less an instinct.

F. H. Bradley, *Aphorisms*

1. Introduction: Metaphysics and Human Nature

ARISTOTLE famously begins his *Metaphysics* by pointing to the intimate connection holding between human nature and metaphysical speculation: 'All men', he says, 'by nature desire to know' (*Met.* 980a21). This epistemic urge takes on different forms, before culminating in the metaphysician's grasp of the ultimate causes (*aitiai*) of all things. Once this point has been reached, which happens once we have come to grasp the nature of the Deity and how anything else is dependent upon it, human nature reaches fulfilment. A life of contemplation is the highest life a human being can aspire to. It is the one most fitting for beings endowed with reason. As a student in Oxford and later as a lifelong fellow of that university, Francis Herbert Bradley[1] must have had many occasions to meditate upon the significance of Aristotle's conception of the ideal human life. He too defines metaphysics as 'the study of first principles' (*AR* 1), in other words, as an inquiry into ultimate reasons or causes. But he denies that a life of contemplation has any claim to superiority over other forms of life. To believe this would be to indulge in 'a most deplorable error, the superstition that the mere intellect is the highest side of our nature, and the false idea that in the intellectual world work done on higher subjects is for that reason higher work' (*AR* 5–6).

Why do human beings engage in metaphysics? On the Aristotelian view, speculation is propelled by our natural tendency to achieve full completion. We are rational beings, and we strive to become philosophers in much the same way in which a seed strives to mature

---

[1] Cf. Taylor (1925) and Mure (1961) for biographical information.

into a full-grown plant. Bradley does not deny that the metaphysician seeks self-realization. Nevertheless, he thinks that speculation aims at satisfying not solely our reason, but also what he terms our 'mystical side' (*AR* 6). As he explains:

> All of us...are led beyond the region of ordinary facts. Some in one way and some in others, we seem to touch and have communion with what is beyond the visible world. In various manners we find something higher, which both supports and humbles, both chastens and transports us. (*AR* 5)

Thus, the ultimate roots of metaphysics are religious. In the absence of a sense of communion with a greater power, no one will ever be persuaded that there is any worth in the enterprise, however strong the arguments that may be adduced in its support.

At the same time, it would be impossible to dissuade a mind infected with the mystical germ from pursuing speculative studies. 'The man whose nature is such that by one path alone his chief desire will reach consummation', Bradley says, 'will try to find it on that path, whatever it may be' (*AR* 6). Given this understanding of the source of metaphysics, it is not surprising Bradley should display very little patience with Kantian scruples concerning its possibility. There is no way to prove that metaphysics is impossible, he argues, except by holding a theory of the relation between thought and reality that is itself metaphysical in nature (*AR* 1–2; see also his critique of Kant in *AR* 127–32).

Bradley provides the most detailed articulation of his metaphysics in *Appearance and Reality* (1893). His world view is further defended and developed in an important 'Appendix' added to the second edition (1897) of that work, as well as in shorter pieces collected in *Essays on Truth and Reality* (1914) and *Collected Essays* (1935). The latter was published posthumously by the Oxford idealist Harold Joachim and contains the unfinished paper 'Relations', which is Bradley's very last word on this fundamental issue. Important metaphysical pronouncements occur in two earlier masterpieces, *Ethical Studies* (1876) and *Principles of Logic* (1883). Given the specific focus of these books, however, one does not find here any detailed elaboration of his metaphysical outlook.

Bradley's 'Absolute Idealism', as his theory is usually called, is a combination of substance-monism, the view that reality is a single cosmic Individual, and metaphysical idealism. Given Bradley's standard association with Hegelianism, the term 'idealism' may be taken to stand for the claim that thought and reality are one and the same, as if Bradley wished to understand reality after the fashion of Hegel's Absolute Idea, as a system of interrelated categories. This is, however, a view Bradley forcefully rejects:

> a lingering scruple still forbids us to believe that reality can ever be purely rational. It may come from a failure in my metaphysics, or from a weakness of the flesh which continues to blind me, but the notion that existence could be the same as understanding strikes as cold and ghost-like as the dreariest materialism. (*PL* 591)

This chapter will show how Bradley's non-Hegelian brand of idealism manages to provide a reconciliation of the logical and the mystical sides of our nature. But the best place to enter his metaphysics is its other cardinal thesis, substance-monism.

2. Metaphysics as the Analysis
of Experience

Bradley's argument for substance-monism is developed in chapter III of Book I of *Appearance and Reality*. Put at its simplest, it runs as follows: pluralism is the view that reality consists of many interrelated beings; since the concept of relation is a contradictory one, pluralism cannot be true. Hence, reality must be conceived as a single Individual, after the fashion of Parmenides and Spinoza. How did the concept of relation come to play such a significant role in Bradley's philosophy?

Bradley is largely indebted to another great Oxford thinker, Thomas Hill Green. In the first book of his *Prolegomena to Ethics* (1883), Green argues in a Kantian fashion that the manifold of sensations is brought to a unity by the relating activity of a transcendental Ego. And since we all live in the same world, Green concludes, the synthesis must be performed by an all-encompassing Consciousness of which we are just partial manifestations. Whilst the significance of Green's metaphysics for Bradley's own has been widely noticed by commentators,[2] little or no attention has been paid to the philosophy of another thinker who helped Bradley shape his thought, Johann Friedrich Herbart. Herbart is a forgotten thinker today; if at all, he is remembered for his pedagogical rather than for his metaphysical works. But he was a major presence in early nineteenth-century German philosophy, where his system was one of the few serious alternatives to post-Kantian Idealism. Most importantly, Herbart's theory of reality is both praised and criticized by Bradley in the course of his anti-relational argument. This provides sufficient justification for taking a careful look at his thought.

In his metaphysical writings Herbart argues that this very special kind of inquiry must begin with an analysis of ordinary experience. The world as concretely experienced (*die Erfahrungswelt*) is the only world of which we have immediate certainty. This is why it should be the metaphysician's starting point, independently of the question of its ultimate ontological status, which is the object of metaphysics to ascertain. Eventually, Herbart's analysis leads to the discovery that the world of experience has a conceptual structure, as Kant and Green had taught too. But it also leads to the recognition that this structure is riddled with contradictions. Herbart, who thinks of himself as renewing the Eleatic tradition of Parmenides and Zeno, sees contradictions in the notions of 'thing', 'causation', 'change', 'space', 'time', and even the 'self'. However, the metaphysician cannot be satisfied by these results, for they are purely sceptical. The way to achieve a fuller grasp of the nature of reality, Herbart argues, is by showing how the contradictions that have been discovered in the structure of experience can be amended (Herbart 1993, 30; 1883–93, iv. 16).

One example will make Herbart's method clear. Consider our concept of a thing. We ordinarily think of a thing as being qualified by its sensible properties; for example, we say of an apple that it is red, sweet, and hard. If we abstain from any supposition as to the existence of non-empirical realities, all we have in our hands is a collection of sensible qualities. What do we mean when we proffer such a judgement as 'This apple is red'? More precisely, what

---

[2] See e.g. Hylton (1990, 21–43).

is here the meaning of the 'is'? Given that all there is to the actually experienced apple are its sensible properties, we can't appeal to the notion of *inherence*, for this comes with a distinction between the sensible properties on the one hand and a non-empirical *substratum* or subject of predication on the other. Hence, all we can possibly mean is that the apple is identical with its redness, identical with its sweetness, identical with any of its other perceptible qualities. But since these qualities are different from one another (sweetness ≠ redness), we are led to the absurd conclusion that the apple *is* and *is not* identical with itself; from 'A is (=) b', 'A is (=) c', and 'b ≠ c', one can derive 'A ≠ A', which is a violation of the Law of Identity (Herbart 1883–93, iv. 99–102).

The problem of accounting for the unity of the thing is not new, as it also arises in the philosophies of Green, Hume, and Hegel.[3] Herbart's originality lies in the way he uses it to secure a positive metaphysical conclusion. Reasoning like a sixth-century Eleatic thinker, he argues that the contradictions he has found in the concepts of thing, change, time, etc. cumulatively show that genuine being—whatever truly *is*—must be *simple*, i.e. devoid of all internal complexity; *absolute*, i.e. such that its nature is not determined by way of negation with other things; *non-extended*, i.e. existing neither through a slice of time nor a portion of space. Then, he raises the question as to the number of beings. It is here that he departs from the Eleatic tradition. Should we think of reality as a single being or as a plurality of beings? Contrary to the teaching of Parmenides, Herbart chooses the latter option, on the ground that it is the only ontological assumption capable of resolving the paradoxes of ordinary experience. Thus, Parmenides' Reality gets fragmented into a plurality of Reals, each of which has all the properties of Eleatic being (Herbart 1883–93, iv. 77 ff.).

To see how Herbart's solution works, consider the contradiction in the concept of a thing. Granting that b ≠ c, one could derive (3) 'A ≠ A', from (1) 'A is (=) b', and (2) 'A is (=) c'. But the Theory of Reals now puts us in a position to argue that in (1) and (2) A is *considered from different points of view*. In (1) 'A is b', the subject of which the sensible quality b is predicated is not A, but A taken in conjunction with other Reals, say, B and C; analogously, in (2) 'A is c', A is viewed as a member of a different group, say, in conjunction with D and E. Thus, no contradiction arises for different and incompatible predicates are not ascribed to A *sic et simpliciter*, but only under different conditions. The A which *is* b, is not A, but A together with B and C; and the A which *is* c, is A together with D and E. The subjects of predication in (1) and (2) are distinct; yet, since A is a constituent of both of them, the two judgements preserve a common reference.

A comparison with Leibniz's notion of a 'well-founded phenomenon' might help to clarify Herbart's crucial notion of a 'point of view'. What makes the perceptual judgement 'This apple is red' true (assuming that it is true) is that our experience of a red apple has as its noumenal backing a group of simple substances, of which A is a member. The very same A also enters as a member of the group of substances that grounds our experience of a sweet apple, an experience that gets recorded in the judgement 'This apple is sweet'. Thus, both Herbart and Leibniz agree that our experiences are imperfect ways of apprehending certain complexes of more basic metaphysical entities.

But Leibniz's monads do actually form groups of a stronger or weaker union. What makes my body *my* body, for example, is that the dominant monad which is my individual soul

---

[3] Green (1883, §62). Westphal (1998) discusses Hume's and Hegel's treatment of this problem.

perceives the monads constituting my body in a peculiarly distinct way. There is no direct causal connection here, but the *epistemic* link between my soul and the monads in the body is nonetheless real. Furthermore, each monad perceives all other monads, but the epistemic connection between my soul and the monads of my body is incomparably *stronger* than the connection between my soul and the monads in other people's bodies. On the contrary, Herbart's Reals are wholly unrelated to one another. They are brought into relation in the act of judgement *only* by an external observer. This is why Herbart refers to our points of view (*Ansichten*) as 'contingent' (*zufällig*). Although there are realities corresponding to them, they are not ontologically necessitated.[4]

3. Against Unrelated Many: Bradley's Critique of Herbart

There are many points of commonality between the metaphysics of Bradley and Herbart. Both begin their inquiries with an examination of ordinary experience and with the alleged discovery of the self-contradictory nature of its basic conceptual structures. Chapter 1 of *Appearance and Reality* features a critique of the distinction between primary and secondary qualities. But the main object of this discussion is to bring home the very Herbartian point that we can't begin our inquiry by assuming a dualistic theory of reality (*AR* 19). Rather, we should take the world in the way it comes to us in ordinary, pre-philosophical experience and reach for a metaphysical conclusion only in a second stage, by developing the implications of the contradictions we discover therein. Furthermore, the categories rejected by Herbart as self-contradictory correspond to the categories rejected by Bradley in the course of his analysis of appearances in the later chapters of Book I of *Appearance and Reality*, although the contradictions are not always exposed in the same way.

All this does not prevent Bradley from being deeply unsatisfied with Herbart's theory of Reals. As against this, he argues as follows:

> I rest my argument upon this, that if there are no differences, there are no qualities, since all must fall into one. But, if there is any difference, then that implies a relation...And this is the point on which all seems to turn, Is it possible to think of qualities without thinking of distinct characters? Is it possible to think of these without some relation between them, either explicit, or else unconsciously supplied by the mind that tries only to apprehend? Have qualities without relation any meaning for thought? For myself, I am sure that they have none. (*AR* 29–30)

How does this argument work? In the first place, Bradley notes, the notion of a plurality of simples is inconsistent with the Principle of the Identity of Indiscernibles. Herbart's Reals are atoms of pure being; as such, they are indistinguishable from one another and therefore identical. Secondly, Bradley reinforces this critique by appealing to the converse of the Identity of Indiscernibles, the Principle of the Dissimilarity of the Distinct. If there is

---

[4] A brief but helpful account of Herbart's theory is provided by Latta (1898, 184–6); cf. also Moosherr (1898) and Langley (1913).

a plurality of beings, they will be different from one another. Determinacy of content is not just a matter of what a thing *is*, however, but also of what a thing excludes or *is not*. Hence, if the Reals are many, they must be related, not totally self-contained as Herbart believes. Given the crucial role of the Principle of the Identity of Indiscernibles in this argument, one would expect Bradley to comment upon it extensively. But the only discussion occurs in his *Logic*, where he claims that the principle is a necessary presupposition of our reasoning: '[I]t is because the…content *seems* the same, that we *therefore* assume it to be really identical' (*PL* 587–8; cf. also 72, 287–94).

Having rejected the theory of Reals, the problem remains of how to make sense of our contradictory experience. Significantly enough, it is out of a discussion of the notion of a thing that Bradley's argument in support of monism begins to unfold in chapter II of *Appearance and Reality*. Granted that the unity of the thing cannot be explained either in terms of the notion of *identity* or the notion of *inherence*, it remains to be investigated whether its unity could be explained in terms of the concept of *relation*. A thing could be nothing over and above the set of its properties, held into a unity by a common relational tie. Bradley takes a lump of sugar as his example:

> Sugar is, of course, not the mere plurality of its different adjectives; but why should it be more than its properties in relation? When 'white', 'hard', 'sweet', and the rest coexist in a certain way, that is surely the secret of the thing. The qualities are, and are in relation. (*AR* 20)

In this way, the stage is set for Bradley's notorious anti-relational argument in chapter III of his metaphysical masterpiece.

4. RELATIONS AS ONTOLOGICAL TIES: BRADLEY'S ANTI-RELATIONAL ARGUMENT

Do relations have unifying power? Consider a relational statement such as 'Socrates is taller than Plato'. Now, so Bradley's reasoning goes, there are two ways of taking the relation *being taller than*. One way is to take it as an independent reality, existing besides *Socrates* and *Plato*. But if we hold this view of the nature of the relation, we are immediately caught into an infinite regress. For *being taller than* now becomes itself a third term whose connection with *Socrates* and *Plato* stands in need of an explanation. More generally, if *A* stands in the relation *R* to *B*, what links *A* and *R*? We now need a further relation *R1*, holding between *A* and *R*, to explain this connection. In this way, a vicious regress is launched.

This is Bradley's own way of phrasing his notorious 'chain argument':

> The relation C has been admitted different from A and B, and no longer is predicated of them. Something, however, seems to be said of this relation C, and said, again, of A and B…If so, it would appear to be another relation, D, in which C, on one side, and, on the other side, A and B, stand. But such a makeshift leads at once to the infinite process. (*AR* 21)

Bradley has been severely criticized for having advanced this argument. In *An Outline of Philosophy*, Bertrand Russell writes that 'Bradley conceives a relation as something just as substantial as its terms, and not radically different in kind' (Russell 1927, 263). And Charles Dunbar Broad has remarked: 'Charity bids us avert our eyes from the pitiable spectacle of a great philosopher using an argument that would disgrace a child or savage' (Broad 1933, 85). Bradley's occasional obscurities notwithstanding, it is difficult to understand how such critics could have failed to see that Bradley is only concerned with outlining the implications of the conception of a relation as a substantial item, rather than endorsing it.[5]

The alternative to conceiving of a relation as a third term is to deny that it possesses full ontological independency. If Socrates is taller than Plato, this is because the relation has an *internal foundation* in the nature of the terms between which it holds. After all, it is because Socrates is of a certain height X and Plato of a certain height Y that the former is taller than the latter. But to hold this view is to conceive of each related term as having two distinct sides, since *Socrates* and *Plato* are more than their respective heights. Thus, each term is implicitly conceived as itself a *relational complex*. This immediately reopens the original problem as to relations' relating power. Let A stand in the relation R to B. If R requires a foundation in their terms, then A is really made up of two parts, A1 and A2; these now need to be related by a further relation R1. Again, an infinite regress arises, although this time it breaks up within each term, instead of between each term and their relation.

Here is Bradley's statement of his 'internal diversity argument':

> If we call its diverse aspects a and *a*, then A is partly each of these. As a it is the difference on which the distinction is based, while as *a* it is the distinctness that results from connection. A is really both somehow together as A(a-*a*). But... *without* the use of a relation it is impossible to predicate this variety of A. And, on the other hand, *with* an internal relation A's unity disappears, and its contents are dissipated in an endless process of distinction. (*AR* 31)

It is important to emphasize that Bradley's regresses are parts of a single line of argument. The failure to read them in context has been a major source of misunderstanding. Broad's complaint that Bradley has disgraced himself by conceiving of relations as if they were things arises from focusing solely upon Bradley's chain argument. There is also a widespread notion that Bradley's metaphysics is built upon the thesis that all relations are internal. This charge will be discussed later on in Section 6. However, it is easy to see how such an interpretation could have arisen by limiting one's attention to the internal diversity argument. As the passage just quoted shows, Bradley calls 'internal' those relations that are grounded in the natures of their terms (by contrast, 'external' relations lack any such foundation, as in the chain argument). Taken by itself, the passage does indeed suggest that Bradley is criticizing relations *on the assumption* that they are internal. But if one looks at the argument in its entirety, one immediately sees that Bradley's aim is to show that both types of relations— external as well as internal—are involved with a vicious circularity.

Thus, Bradley's actual conclusion is that relations, *however conceived*, are no ontological ties. This discloses a deeper reason why Bradley thinks that *inherence* can't provide a solution to the problem of the unity of the thing, besides the already-mentioned fact that this notion carries with it the idea of a non-empirical substratum. This is that *inherence* is itself a

---

[5] There is some irony in the fact that Bradley thought other philosophers were guilty of the mistake of reifying relations. Cf. his critique of Huxley in *PL* 96.

relation. As such, we are now in a position to see, it couldn't possibly connect the predicates with their subject.

As against the entire line of argument, the objection could be raised that relations' relating power is no real mystery; relations relate, and there is nothing more that needs to be said upon this issue. But it shouldn't be difficult to see that this response fails to meet Bradley's challenge. His argument pivots upon the question: do relations have a foundation in their terms? This question is a wholly intelligible one and does therefore deserve an answer. But if the answer is 'No', the regress associated with the chain argument is launched; if 'Yes', the regress associated with the internal diversity argument threatens. One could construe Bradley's argument as an open one. Are there other ways of understanding a relation besides those he considers? But if one reads the argument this way, the burden of proof shifts upon the critic's shoulders. He stands now under an obligation to show that his understanding of relations is immune from regresses of a Bradleyan type.

Another way of countering the argument is to acknowledge that it works, while denying that it proves what Bradley takes it to prove. In such works as a *Pluralistic Universe* (1909) and *Essays in Radical Empiricism* (1912), William James argued that Bradley's regresses show that we are incapable of *reconstructing* the unity of the experienced world in thought, not that actually experienced relations fail to connect. This reply overlooks that within Bradley's philosophy the distinction between *real relations* and *relations as they are grasped in thought* is a spurious one. Like Kant, he believes the basic structures of the experienced world to be intellectual in nature. But even granting the validity of the distinction, James's objection has very little force. James believed in the reality of connecting relations because he thought he could experience them. As he has it, it is a 'statement of fact' that 'the relations between things, conjunctive as well as disjunctive, are just a matter of direct particular experience, neither more nor less so than the things themselves' (James 1912, p. x). But why couldn't Bradley experience relations that way too? James's contention sounds too much like the mere assertion that he *knows* that relations relate.[6]

5. Unity and Harmony: The Road to Monism

Bradley's anti-relational argument is stronger than most of his best-known critics suppose.[7] What are its most important metaphysical implications? One main conclusion Bradley draws is that the concept of a relation is self-contradictory. The idea of a relation is the idea of

---

[6] Sprigge (1993) is an in-depth discussion of the relationship between the two thinkers. On this issue, cf. also Ferreira (1999, 209–31).

[7] Commentators disagree as to the argument's actual strength. Mander (1994, 84–111) apparently endorses it as it stands. Wollheim (1969, 114) and Basile (1999, 49) are sceptical about the possibility of making sense of the notion that a related term breaks up in two parts when the term is a quality (say, a certain shade of redness) instead of a person, as in the example considered here. Sprigge (1993, 393–434) regards the argument as basically sound, although not in the exact form in which Bradley presents it. Sprigge (1983, 162–224 and 232–49) is a resolute attempt to put it in a better shape.

a link, yet this link proves unable to connect anything. As Bradley explains in the 'Appendix' to the second edition of *Appearance and Reality*, however, the contradiction in question is not so much formal as dynamic. The paradox of relational thought is that it attempts to do something it cannot do, in other words, unify their terms without effacing their individualities. Given any two terms,

> Thought can of itself supply no internal bond by which to hold them together, nor has it any internal diversity by which to maintain them apart. It must therefore seek barely to identify them, though they are different, or somehow to unite both diversities where it has no ground of distinction and union. (*AR* 565)

This is as clear a statement of Bradley's difficulty as one could possibly wish. To identify different terms is to violate the Law of Identity, while to keep them apart is to have lost the unity in which they are originally given.

Bradley's favourite way of stating his view of the ontological status of relations is by saying that they are 'unreal'. But how can relations be at the same time self-contradictory and unreal? It is as if Bradley had picked up relations and examined them, but only to deny that the very things he had focused his attention upon exist at all! In order to understand Bradley's claim properly, it is necessary to consider the role played by the principle of non-contradiction in his philosophy. According to Bradley, the principle states that 'Ultimate Reality is such that it does not contradict itself' (*AR* 136). Thus, the principle is not solely recognized as the basic principle of reason; it is also ontologically interpreted as furnishing a criterion of ultimate reality. To claim that relations are unreal is not to say that they are wholly non-existent; it means that they fail to satisfy this ultimate ontological standard.

However, a doubt might arise as to the legitimacy of interpreting the principle ontologically instead of as purely logically. Scepticism might be prompted by the difficulty of understanding what kind of property we are ascribing to the real (as opposed to a system of concepts) when we say that it is 'coherent' or 'harmonious'. As James Ward put it in a critical review of *Appearance and Reality*, 'coherence' and 'harmony' are 'merely logical terms improperly transferred in an ontological sense' (Ward 1894, 111). Consider Bradley's defence of the principle by means of the Aristotelian elenchus: 'the principle is proved absolute by the fact that, either in endeavouring to deny it, or even to doubt it, we tacitly assume its validity' (*AR* 31; cf. *Met.* 1006a12–15). What this line of argument shows is that we are bound to respect the principle as long as we reason and speak meaningfully. But does this also suffice to prove that *reality* is coherent? Unfortunately, Bradley does not elaborate on this important point and simply equates the absoluteness involved with the fact that we can't renounce the principle as long as we speak and reason with the absoluteness involved in the fact that reality must be rational.

Be that as it may, the implications of Bradley's claim that the relational form of thought is contradictory are momentous. Since all basic concepts in terms of which we make sense of reality (space, time, change, causation, the self, etc.) are relational, they too can be rejected as metaphysically flawed. Again, this does not mean that relational experiences do not exist at all, which would be an absurd claim to make. Our own stream of thought is one such prolonged temporal and changing experience; surely, we need no proof that it exists. What Bradley denies is that such experiences could exist apart from a larger overarching Reality, and that this is relational in nature.

Bradley's critique of relations needs to be considered in the context of his analysis of the world of ordinary experience. The previous discussion of the concept of a thing has shown that the possibility of interpreting the experienced world as being real stands or falls with the power of relations—which of that world are the basic structures—to link several qualities (or, more generally, distinct terms) into one. Now that relations have been shown to be unequal to this metaphysical task, it becomes clear that the world's foundation cannot lie in itself. The world must derive its unity from a more fundamental source. How is this ultimate ground to be conceived? The anti-relational argument provides crucial information. If relations are self-contradictory and plurality is meaningless without relations (this is the lesson of Bradley's critique of Herbart), then ultimate reality must be a single Individual. At the same time, the world of ordinary experience can't be ontically distinct from the ultimately real, like a veil behind which the latter hides, for this would yield a relational theory of reality. Hence, the only option open is to conceive the experienced world pan-theistically, as one of the modes *through* which absolute Reality exists, as well as pan-*en*-theistically, as existing *within* it.

At the end of chapter III—after only thirty pages of a book of over five hundred—almost all of the basic elements of Bradley's world view are already in place. Reality is a harmonious, non-temporal, non-spatial, uncreated, changeless Individual, beyond which there is nothing and within which all things exist. But if Reality is harmonious and appearances are contradictory, why don't they infect the whole with contradiction? Bradley's answer is that our experiences are rearranged when absorbed within the Absolute. They exist there in a transmuted, altered form. (Cf. *AR* 123, 204.)

6. The Axiom of Internal Relations: The Russell–Moore Legacy

Before considering how Bradley provides the final touch to his system by arguing that Reality is experience—thereby denying that it could ever be what Hegel took it to be, a system of interrelated categories—it will be good to consider in what terms his metaphysics was discussed by Russell and George Edward Moore. Indeed nobody was as successful as they were in shaping the later reception of his philosophy.

Russell repeatedly charges Bradley with the accusation that his monism is based upon the 'axiom of internal relations'. What does this axiom say? In what is arguably Russell's most extended discussion of the axiom, the paper 'On the Nature of Truth', he equates it with the statement that 'every relation is grounded in the nature of the related terms' (1906–7: 37). This is a fair rendering of Bradley's use of the term 'internal', as this occurs in his internal diversity argument. When Russell actually begins to argue against the axiom, however, this gets suddenly reinterpreted as the much stronger thesis that relations can be reduced to properties of their terms. And this is surely a different usage of the term 'internal' than Bradley's rather innocent one.

How could relations be reconceptualized as properties? According to Russell, one way is by holding the view that relations are separate properties of their terms. On this view, which Russell ascribes to Leibniz, the relational fact *A is greater than B* is the conjunction of the two non-relational facts *A is of size X* & *B is of size Y*. As Russell points out, however, this account provides an incomplete analysis of relational complexes, for a full explication of *A is greater than B* would require the further specification that *X is greater than Y*. As an alternative, one may want to conceive of a relation as a property of the complex formed by its terms. But this view, which Russell now ascribes to Bradley, fails to account for asymmetrical relations. For example, such a theory cannot explain the difference between *A is greater than B* and *B is greater than A*. The only way to explain this distinction is by specifying the *order* in which A and B enter into the complexes of which *greater than* is predicated. Once again, this requires making use of a relation. Russell's overall conclusion is that relations cannot be eliminated from one's basic ontology. Hence, and in spite of the many significant differences in their metaphysics, Leibniz and Bradley were wrong in condemning relations as unreal.[8]

This is not the place to discuss the adequacy of Russell's interpretation of Leibniz's philosophy,[9] but it should be already evident that his argument fails as a critique of Bradley's. As we have seen, Bradley rejects the notion of *inherence* because he thinks that the subject/predicate pattern is itself relational. But how could someone holding this view also think that relations are reducible to properties? Furthermore, Bradley *explicitly* denies that relations can be reduced to properties in an important footnote towards the end of chapter III. One main purpose of this footnote, one should also notice, is to clarify what is involved— and, most importantly, what is *not* involved—in Bradley's anti-relational argument. Bradley writes:

> The relation is not the adjective of one term for, if so, it does not relate. Nor for the same reason is it the adjective of each term taken apart, for then again there is no relation between them. Nor is the relation their common property, for then what keeps them apart? (*AR* 32 n.)

The reasoning is condensed, but its overall drift is clear enough. Consider the statement 'A stands in the relation *R* to *B*'. According to Bradley, we can't analyse this as the ascription of a relational property *standing-in-the relation-R-to-B* to a subject A, for we have the problem of explaining the connection between the two. Nor can we dissolve the relation *R* into two distinct predicates of A and B, for this would yield two distinct, separate facts, say *A is b* and *B is d*, instead of the original unity represented by *A in the relation R to B*. Lastly, one cannot interpret the relation *R* as a property of a compound subject, say (*A-B*), for then what connects (without identifying) A and B within this new complex? The overall conclusion is that a relation can't be reduced to a predicate of either *one* of the related terms, or of *both taken singly*, or of *both taken together*. But if this is what Bradley is arguing in this passage—and no alternative interpretation seems to be available—then one is faced with a paradoxical situation. For it now turns out that Russell not solely fails to do justice to Bradley's position, he also attacks it by means of arguments virtually identical to those Bradley himself had used to enable his reader to get a better hold of his anti-relational argument!

How could Russell's blatant misunderstanding be explained? Here, one can solely speculate. By the time he wrote his book on Leibniz in 1900, Russell had matured the conviction that metaphysics is based upon logic (Russell 1900, 50). On this view, to get the logic wrong

---

[8] Cf. also Russell (1903, §§212–16) where the two alternatives are referred to respectively as the 'monadistic' and the 'monistic' theory of relations.

[9] Leibniz's theory of relations is briefly discussed in Mates (1986, 215–18), more extensively in Mugnai (1992).

is to get the metaphysics wrong. It is therefore understandable that Russell might have tried to refute the main types of metaphysical systems by showing that they were based upon mistaken logical assumptions. The danger is that one's reading of other philosophers might turn out to be 'ideologically' motivated. The basic interpretative scheme is set up in advance, independently of any careful consideration of what the philosopher under consideration actually said. Be that as it may, Bradley protested against Russell's misinterpretation, pointing out that he never held the view that relations are properties but the quite different one that they exist within a larger non-relational unity:

> This is the doctrine for which I have now for so many years contended. Relations exist only in and through a whole which can not in the end be resolved into relations and terms. 'And', 'together' and 'between', are all in the end senseless apart from such a whole. The opposite view is maintained (as I understand) by Mr. Russell... But for myself, I am unable to find that Mr. Russell has ever really faced the question. (*PL* 96)

Could Russell have failed to know of this and other similar explanations on the part of Bradley? This is hardly credible. Still Bradley's timely clarifications did not prevent Russell from repeating the self-congratulatory story that he had liberated philosophy from the pernicious implications of the axiom of internal relations even long after Bradley's death.[10] And unfortunately for Bradley's reputation, Russell's story was uncritically believed by later generations of philosophers.[11]

The other main source of the widespread conviction that Bradley's views are based upon the axiom of internal relations is Moore's 'External and Internal Relations' (1919). Moore understands the term 'internal' in a way that differs from both Bradley's and Russell's. For according to Moore, a relation is internal if it is essential to the nature of its terms. Thus, if A stands in the relation R to B, and R is internal in Moore's sense, then A would cease to be itself if it were to cease standing in the relation R to B. Moore thinks this view is so obviously false that it doesn't even require to be refuted. Accordingly, his only concern is to explain why Bradley could have been so confused as to believe it.

Like Russell's, Moore's critique is based upon what is in itself a sound logical insight. Moore observes that it is plainly true that (1) if something A has a certain relational property P, then whatever has not P is not A. Quite another thing, however, is to argue that (2) if something A has a certain relational property P, it couldn't have failed to have that property. As it happened, Aristotle was the author of the *Metaphysics*, so that nobody who failed to write that book could be Aristotle. Nevertheless, this doesn't imply that Aristotle necessarily had to write that book. According to Moore, Bradley holds that all relations are necessary to a term's being what it is because he confounds the two kinds of statement. Hence, all of a thing's relations are fallaciously turned into necessary properties.

The distinction so agreeably tickles our sense of subtlety and Moore's overall interpretation is so well thought out that one is actually tempted to believe that he must be right. But at least two very prosaic points need here to be considered. The first is whether Bradley ever held the doctrine of internal relations in Moore's sense. Bradley himself rejected this reading

---

[10] See e.g. Russell (1959, 55–61), which reproduces a significant part of Russell (1906–7).

[11] Virtually all books on Bradley include some discussion of Russell's criticisms, but see Candlish (2007) for a very careful reconstruction and balanced evaluation of the debate between the two philosophers.

of his metaphysics: 'As to what has been called the axiom of internal relations, I can only repeat that "internal relations," thought truer by far than "external," are, in my opinion, not true in the end' (*ETR* 312). Bradley's point can be paraphrased by saying that an interpretation of reality in terms of internal relations is less distorting than an interpretation in terms of external relations. This is because the latter suggests a view of the universe as a plurality of dissociated items, whereas the former depicts reality as a closely knit system, thereby approximating to Bradley's actual conception of reality as a unified, non-relational whole.

The second question is whether there is any evidence of Bradley's committing the fallacy with which Moore charges him. As a variety of interpreters has noticed, the texts do not seem to lend any support to Moore's accusation. Not surprisingly, the only commentator who is willing to endorse Moore's critique is as fierce an enemy of metaphysics (and of Bradley's in particular) as Alfred Jules Ayer.[12] Obviously, it is one thing to provide an intelligible reconstruction of how things *might* have gone, quite another to discover how they actually went. But in their treatment of past philosophers, Moore and Russell overlooked this distinction, mistaking their own rationalizations for actual facts. The belief that metaphysics—and perhaps all philosophy—ultimately reduces to logic might help explain (but not justify) why they made themselves guilty of such a trivial error.

7. Leibniz's Shadow: Bradley on Absolute Experience

Bradley's official argument in support of his idealism, the view that Reality is experience, is provided in chapter xiv of *Appearance and Reality*. Here, we are asked to perform a simple thought-experiment. Can we conceive of non-experienced things? Bradley writes:

> I can myself conceive of nothing else than the experienced. Anything, in no sense felt or perceived, becomes to me quite unmeaning. And as I cannot try to think of it without realizing either that I am not thinking at all, or that I am thinking of it against my will as being experienced, I am driven to the conclusion that for me experience is the same as reality. (*AR* 145)

Here Bradley seems to be gesturing—but no more than gesturing—at Bishop Berkeley's argument to the effect that non-experienced realities are unthinkable and therefore impossible. But if this is what Bradley has in mind (the passage is not as clear as one would wish it to be), then Bradley's reasoning would be open to the sort of objections that are usually raised against Berkeley's. Specifically, the argument involves confusion between thinking of an *object* and thinking of *our idea of an object*. For I need to have an idea of an object (say, a tree) in order to be able to think it. But this does not imply that a representation of myself as thinking that object is also part of that idea's representational content.

It is true that, where thought is associated with visual images, a tree cannot be represented except as viewed from a certain perspective, as if perceived by a subject standing in some spatial relation to the imagined object. Nevertheless, visual imageries are neither a necessary

---

[12] Ayer (1971, 158). However, Ayer too fails to provide the required textual evidence.

nor a sufficient condition of thought, although they can accompany it. (The former point is forcefully brought home by Descartes's example of our idea of a chiliagon in the *Meditations*; the latter by Wittgenstein's remark that the very same visual image can be used to convey more than one meaning, which shows that *by itself* an image conveys none, in other words, has no specific *ideatum*.)

But even granting the argument's validity, it would seem that it fails to secure the conclusion Bradley is aiming at. First, the argument would only show that there cannot be anything which is not an object of thought, while Bradley's conclusion is that the Absolute *is* itself experience. Thus, there is a gap here between *epistemological* idealism (nothing can exist independently of a perceiving subject) and *metaphysical idealism* (what is, *is* experiential in nature) that remains unclosed. Secondly, if valid, the argument would only show that nothing can possibly exist that is not an object of *my* experience. Hence, its immediate conclusion is *solipsism*, rather than Bradley's view that whatever is experienced is experienced *within* the Absolute. There might be ways of bridging these gaps.[13] But it is notable that Bradley never tried to do this. Thus, rather than charging him with a paralogism that wouldn't in any case provide him with what he needs, it is better to consider if there are other ways of understanding how he might have arrived at his idealistic conclusion.

One way to do this is by following an indirect route, turning first to Bradley's doctrine of 'immediate experience' or 'feeling'. As we have seen, Bradley's metaphysics begins with an analysis of ordinary experience's relational structures. However, there must be more to ordinary experience than mere form. Bradley denies that the sensuous contents that constitute the *material* side of our experience can be conceived as mental items of the like of Hume's atomic impressions of sensation. He forcefully rejects all attempts at reconstructing the unity of the phenomenal field by appealing to alleged laws of association. But if not in the form of a plurality, how are the contents of human experience originally given? Bradley's answer is that they must be thought of as constituting a 'many-in-one', a sensuous unity not yet broken by perception and reflection. Such a whole is ordinary experience's *transcendental* foundation, its ever-present background (*ETR* 161). Can we interpret the relation between immediate and ordinary experience *psychologically*, as if they were two temporally successive stages in the actual development of human consciousness? Bradley is not interested in this question, presumably because he regards it as lying outside the proper scope of philosophy.

The notion that ordinary experience emerges from within a confused mass of experiential contents marks an improvement upon the traditional depiction of human consciousness as made up of elementary sensations in much the same way in which a wall is made up of bricks. Nevertheless, it has its own difficulties. For in order for feeling to be able to perform the transcendental function Bradley assigns to it, feeling must be both *complex* and *non-relational*. There is a clear division of tasks between the two experiential levels. Feeling must be *complex*, because it furnishes ordinary experience with its very materials. But it must also be *non-relational*, because it is ordinary experience that places such contents into relational grids. Thus, we are left with the notion of feeling as containing unrelated differences. This is by itself a difficult idea. But it is also one Bradley would seem to be scarcely

---

[13] Mander (1996b) is an attempt. See also Candlish (2007, 33–45) on the ambiguities involved in Bradley's official argument for idealism.

entitled to in light of his rejection of the notion of an unrelated many in his critique of Herbart's metaphysics.

In order to see how all this bears upon the larger question of the intrinsic nature of reality, one has to consider Bradley's treatment of the notion of the self. In his view, there cannot be a subject without an object. Since self and not-self, subject and object, are correlative and can't therefore be divorced from one another, they form a relational structure that, as such, can only develop *within* the larger whole of feeling. The self is, as Bradley says, 'one of the results gained by transcending the first...form of experience' (*AR* 525). But *whose* experience, then, is immediate experience? Bradley answers this question in terms of the notion of a finite centre. This is to be viewed as the *metaphysical point* in which all of a person's experiences unfold. However, such a centre is neither a self (as we have just seen) nor can it properly be called a 'soul' (*AR* 529), for according to Bradley a soul's life must be capable of enduring for a significant amount of time, while the experiences unfolding within a finite centre might be as brief as a momentary occurrence, breaking into existence, as it were, like a light flashing in the dark. Bradley also thinks that finite centres are not *themselves* in time, although there obviously is a temporal quality to the experiences unfolding within them. Most importantly, and puzzling as it might seem on a first hearing, Bradley denies that a finite centre is in any deep metaphysical sense a reality *distinct* from its experiences. There is nothing more to the centre than the stream of its experiences—each is a quantum of flowing feeling.

Unfortunately, Bradley provides no systematic treatment of the doctrine of finite centres. Its content must be gathered from remarks scattered in several places in his writings. But it is evident that this doctrine very closely approximates to Leibniz's theory of monads, a fact that was noticed by an early commentator such as Thomas Stearns Eliot: 'I suggest that from the "pluralism" of Leibniz there is only a step to the "absolute zero" of Bradley and that Bradley's Absolute dissolves at a touch into its constituents' (Eliot [1916] 1964, 200).[14] Eliot's insight puts us in a position to appreciate how Bradley uses the metaphysics of finite centres as an intermediate step towards his Absolute Idealism. For if one starts with the doctrine that there are many monad-like entities of the kind described by Bradley, that is, *purely experiential beings*, one can appeal to the anti-relational argument to conclude that they are aspects of a larger unified totality in which their contents are (somehow) rearranged and merged. And from here, it is indeed just a short step to the further conclusion that the larger totality, being the repository and gathering point of all finite experiences, is itself an experience.

This interpretation receives substantial support from Bradley's texts. At one point in *Appearance and Reality*, Bradley makes a polemical remark against the metaphysics of Rudolph Hermann Lotze.[15] According to Bradley, Lotze is guilty of oscillating between a pluralistic theory of monads and a monistic theory in which the monads are preserved but conceived as aspects of a larger totality. 'The attentive reader of Lotze'—Bradley writes— 'must...have found it hard to discover why individual selves [monads] with him are more

---

[14] Later readers of Bradley seem to have lost sight of the Leibnizian strand in his philosophy. It is recovered in the interpretations of McHenry (1992, 28–37), Sprigge (1993, 522–32), and Basile (2004); see also the brief but penetrating comments in Allard and Stock (1994, 111–13).

[15] See Basile (2009, 41–9) for a brief account of Lotze's metaphysics as developed in Lotze (1887). Cf. also Latta (1898, 190–7).

than phenomenal adjectives' (*AR* 118 n.). What needs to be recognized, he argues, is that 'relations...are fatal to the monads' independence. The substances clearly become adjectival, and mere elements within an all-comprehending whole' (*AR* 117–88).

In the same context Bradley also expresses his conviction that the future course of philosophy will witness a resurgence of interest in monadism: 'Monadism, on the whole, will increase and will add to the difficulties which already exist' (*AR* 118–19). This forecast is not as wrong as it might look at first sight, for philosophers like Ward, John Ellis McTaggart, Alfred North Whitehead, and Herbert Wildon Carr did try to infuse new life in the idea of the psychic monad as the ultimate constituent of reality.[16] But this passage strongly suggests that Bradley considers monadism (rather than, say, materialism or orthodox Hegelianism) to be the most serious alternative to his Absolute Idealism. Hence, it would have been reasonable for him to argue for the superiority of Absolute Idealism by showing that monadism fails, but that what is good in it can be preserved within a monistic framework.[17] The following formulation is revelatory: 'The Universe', Bradley says, '...is one Experience which appears in finite centres' (*ETR* 410). This is the step Bradley thinks Lotze should have wholeheartedly taken. Finite centres are denied full substantiality while being preserved as the focal points through which the Absolute shines.

8. Conclusion: Mysticism, Logic, and Human Life

As we have seen at the very beginning of this article, Bradley defines metaphysics as an attempt to satisfy the mystical as well as the logical side of our nature. But what's so mystical about the view that Reality is one Experience that appears in finite centres? The mystical strain in Bradley's philosophy emerges most fully in chapter xv of *Appearance and Reality*, where Bradley outlines the metaphysical implications of the theory of judgement he had argued for in the *Logic*.

According to Bradley's theory, judgement is the mental act that ascribes an ideal content to reality as a whole. On this view, the general form of judgement is 'Reality is such that *P*', where *P* is not a single idea, but a whole proposition. The perceptual judgement 'This apple is red', for example, is only superficially about an apple; its real subject is reality as a whole, and what is predicated of it is not 'redness', but the entire propositional content expressed by 'This apple is red'. What the judgement says, in other words, is that the fact of there being here and now a red apple holds of reality. It is important to realize that the sense in which the terms 'subject' and 'predicate' are used in Bradley's theory differs radically from the sense in which they are used in current logical books (and by Russell as well). Bradley's theory of

---

[16] See respectively Ward (1911), McTaggart (1921 and 1927), Carr (1922 and 1930), Whitehead ([1929] 1978).

[17] The same strategy is at play in Bradley's anti-relational argument; after all, as Latta (1898, 185) also acknowledges, Herbart's theory of Reals is a monadology of sorts and Bradley uses it as a stepping stone to reach his monistic conclusion.

judgement is not a theory of propositions, but of *mental acts*. Hence, 'subject' and 'predicate' do not refer to elements that can be distinguished within the proposition. Rather, the entire proposition entertained in the act of judgement is the predicate. A specific sort of mental operation, judgement, ascribes this ideal predicate to a non-ideal subject of predication, reality as a whole.

Bradley had tried to avoid all metaphysical speculations in the *Logic*. But the logical problem naturally turns metaphysical as soon as one asks the question as to the nature of truth. Like Aquinas, Bradley holds to the conception of truth as *adaequatio intellectus et rei*. However, this has startling consequences when taken together with his theory of judgement. For in this theory the intellectual side of this equation is an ideal content the mind has generated by way of *abstraction*, whereas the thing thought is striving to be adequate to is *reality as a whole*. These two poles—one *real*, the other *ideal*—are so different from one another than one wonders how they could come to achieve the required agreement. And indeed, Bradley argues in *Appearance and Reality*, such an agreement cannot possibly be achieved.

The problem lies in the *partiality* of the predicated ideal content, which captures only some of the aspects of the real. As Bradley views things, in order to realize full agreement the ideal content would have to be so enlarged as to include all that it leaves out. And this is, of course, an impossible requirement to satisfy. The roots of the impossibility are not practical (it is not that it would take an infinite amount of time to complete the predicated ideal content), but lie in the very nature of thought as an 'ideal' thing. The partiality of the ideal content is a function of its abstractness. Hence, the only way thought has to bridge the gap is to renounce all abstractedness, thereby becoming the concrete reality it is aiming at.

But how could *thought* become *real*, without *ipso facto* ceasing to be thought? This question discloses the paradoxical nature of thought, for it makes clear that thought's quest for truth is at the same time a striving towards self-destruction. However, thought's 'suicide' is a 'happy' one, as Bradley colourfully puts it, for a true thought would be such as to be identical with the Absolute. Hence, thought's dissolution can be compared to that of a river running into the sea, or of a lover who loses himself in love (*AR* 173). One renounces oneself, but only to become part of a richer life. Bradley writes: 'Every flame of passion, chaste or carnal, would still burn in the Absolute unquenched and unabridged, a note absorbed in the harmony of its higher bliss' (*AR* 172). It is at this point that Bradley's metaphysics achieves mystical overtones. For it is now evident that the philosopher's search, if successful, would be nothing less than an *itinerarium mentis in Deum*.

Bradley's Absolute cannot be identified with the God of the Judaeo-Christian tradition, which is distinct from the created world (the very notion of creation makes little sense within Bradley's monistic metaphysics). Still, it can be called 'God' in a very important and orthodox sense, although Bradley himself declined to do so (*AR* 447). This becomes clear as soon as one further develops the implication of his account of truth as requiring the identity of thought and reality. Since truth cannot be achieved except at the cost of dissolution, Bradley reasons, each particular thought can be regarded as more or less true, according to how close it comes to realizing that paradoxical identification. Contrary to a widespread prejudice whose origin can be traced back to Russell's early attack on idealism, Bradley never held a 'coherence theory' of truth. It is not solely that

Bradley's is an identity theory. It is also that 'coherence' as understood in standard logical textbooks does not even suffice as a criterion for Bradley. The standard for measuring *degrees* of truth (as opposed to establishing whether a thesis is true or false in a black-or-white sense) is the Absolute's harmonious character. And 'harmony' includes absence of logical contradiction ('coherence') as well as the 'inclusiveness' of the predicated content.[18]

At the same time, the identity theory of truth enables Bradley to argue that different existents can be regarded as more or less 'real' according to how close they come to realizing the Absolute's perfection. This notion of reality as having degree also fits nicely with Bradley's doctrine of finite centres, for their ontological ranking could now be made dependent upon their comparative capacity to grasp the surrounding world in a coherent and complete fashion. In this way, the idea of a great chain of being is rehabilitated, its top being occupied by the Absolute—that 'of-which-nothing-greater-can-be-conceived', as in Anselm's formula. Thus, Bradley's Absolute turns out to be one more version of a very traditional understanding of the Deity. Bradley's is even a reactionary conception, if one considers the tremendous impact of Darwinism upon nineteenth-century culture generally. For the implication of that theory is that, if there is a hierarchy of beings, this is not written once for all in the very nature of things, like Bradley believes; rather, it is a precarious achievement of natural history.[19]

While the theological side of Bradley's metaphysics did not raise the attention of later analytic philosophers, it did attract the polemical wits of thinkers who conceived of themselves less as professionals engaged in putting philosophy on the secure path of science than as humanists concerned with assessing the implications of different metaphysical beliefs for human life. Within the pragmatist camp, William James rejected Bradley's God as unhelpful; from his perspective, there is little point in believing in a Deity with which one can't enter into an I–Thou relationship and which can't therefore offer any active support in the face of ordinary human struggles.[20] Another great pragmatist, John Dewey, rejected Bradley's Absolute as yet another self-delusory attempt to escape the seriousness of life by projecting our human ideals of harmony and pacification in a supra-empirical realm, instead of actually striving to ameliorate the world we live in.[21] In spite of his critique of Aristotle's ideal of a contemplative life, there is little doubt that Bradley still conceives of metaphysics as an eminently *theoretical* enterprise. But how just are these charges? This is an important question that must be left for the reader to ponder.

---

[18] See e.g. Russell (1906–7, 136); Bradley's reply is in *ETR*, 202.

[19] Allard (2005, 1–23) discusses the intimate connection between the rise of Darwinism and the origin of British Idealism. Ward (1911) and Whitehead ([1929] 1978) are attempts at developing a conception of the Deity compatible with evolutionary theory. Bradley does not deny evolution but downgrades it to an 'appearance' of the unchanging Reality (*AR* 442).

[20] According to James (1907, esp. chs.IV and VIII), belief in the Absolute is damaging to our moral and psychical health, since it encourages us to take 'moral holidays' rather than helping us to sustain the 'strenuous mood'.

[21] Dewey (1929, 59–61).

REFERENCES

Allard, J. W. (2005), *The Logical Foundations of Bradley's Metaphysics: Judgment, Inference, and Truth* (Cambridge: Cambridge University Press).

Allard, J. W., and Stock, G. (eds.) (1994), *F. H. Bradley: Writings on Logic and Metaphysics* (Oxford: Clarendon Press).

Aristotle (1894), *Metaphysics (Met.)*, in *The Complete Works of Aristotle*, ii, ed. J. Barnes, trans. W. D. Ross (Princeton: Princeton University Press), 1552–1867.

Ayer, A. J. (1971), *Russell and Moore: The Analytical Heritage* (London: Macmillan).

Baldwin, T. (1990), *G. E. Moore* (London: Routledge).

Basile, P. (1999), *Experience and Relations: An Examination of F. H. Bradley's Conception of Reality* (Berne: Paul Haupt).

Basile, P. (2004), 'Why Did Bradley Matter to Whitehead? Some Questions Concerning Bradley's Doctrine of Finite Centres', *Bradley Studies*, 10: 15–32.

Basile, P. (2009), *Leibniz, Whitehead and the Metaphysics of Causation* (Basingstoke and New York: Palgrave Macmillan).

Bradley, F. H. (1883), *Principles of Logic (PL)* (Oxford: Clarendon Press, 2nd edn.1922, corr. edn. 1928).

Bradley, F. H. (1893), *Appearance and Reality: A Metaphysical Essay (AR)* (London: George Allen and Unwin; 2nd edn. 1897).

Bradley, F. H. (1914), *Essays on Truth and Reality (ETR)* (Oxford: Clarendon Press).

Bradley, F. H. (1935), *Collected Essays (CE)* (Oxford: Clarendon Press).

Bradley, F. H. (1999), *The Collected Works of F. H. Bradley*, 12 vols., ed. and introd. W. J. Mander and C. A. Keene (Bristol: Thoemmes).

Bradley, J. (ed.) (1996), *Philosophy after F. H. Bradley* (Bristol: Thoemmes).

Broad, C. D. (1933), *Examination of McTaggart's Philosophy*, vol. i (Cambridge: Cambridge University Press).

Candlish, S. (1989), 'The Truth about F. H. Bradley', *Mind* 98: 331–48.

Candlish, S. (2007), *The Russell/Bradley Dispute and Its Significance for Twentieth Century Philosophy* (Basingstoke & New York: Palgrave Macmillan).

Carr, H. W. (1922), *A Theory of Monads: Outlines of the Philosophy of the Principle of Relativity* (London: Macmillan).

Carr, H. W. (1930), *Cogitans Cogitata* (Los Angeles: The Favill Press).

Dewey, J. (1929), *Experience and Nature* (New York: Dover).

Eliot, T. S. ([1916] 1964), *Knowledge and Experience in the Philosophy of F. H. Bradley* (London: Faber).

Ferreira, P. (1999), *Bradley and the Structure of Knowledge* (Albany, NY: State University of New York Press).

Green, T. H. (1883), *Prolegomena to Ethics*, ed. A. C. Bradley (Oxford: Clarendon Press).

Herbart, J. F. (1993), *Lehrbuch zur Einleitung in die Philosophie*, ed. W. Enckmann (Hamburg: Meiner).

Herbart, J. F. (1883–93), *Sämtliche Werke*, 13 vols., ed. v. G. Hartenstein (Leipzig: Leopold Voss).

Hylton, P. (1990), *Russell, Idealism, and the Emergence of Analytic Philosophy* (Oxford: Clarendon Press).

James, W. (1907), *Pragmatism: A New Name for Some Old Ways of Thinking* (New York: Longmans, Green and Co.).

James, W. (1909), *A Pluralistic Universe* (New York: Longmans, Green and Co.).

James, W. (1912), *Essays in Radical Empiricism* (New York: Longmans, Green and Co.).

Langley, G. H. (1913), 'The Metaphysical Method of Herbart', *Mind*, 22: 62–75.

Latta, R. (1898), 'Introduction', in Leibniz (1898), 1–211.

Leibniz, G. W. (1898), *The Monadology and Other Philosophical Writings*, trans., introd., and notes by R. Latta (Oxford: Clarendon Press).

Lotze, R. H. (1887), *Metaphysics, in Three Books, Ontology, Cosmology and Psychology*, trans. B. Bosanquet et al. (2nd edn., Oxford: Clarendon Press).

McHenry, L. B. (1992), *Whitehead and Bradley: A Comparative Analysis* (Albany, NY: State University of New York Press).

McTaggart, J. M. E. (1921), *The Nature of Existence*, vol. i (Cambridge: Cambridge University Press).

McTaggart, J. M. E. (1927), *The Nature of Existence*, vol. ii, ed. C. D. Broad (Cambridge: Cambridge University Press).

Mander, W. (1994), *An Introduction to Bradley's Metaphysics* (Oxford: Clarendon Press).

Mander, W. (ed.) (1996a), *Perspectives on the Logic and Metaphysics of F. H. Bradley* (Bristol: Thoemmes).

Mander W. (ed.) (1996b), 'The Role of the Self in Bradley's Argument for Idealism', in Mander (1996a), 61–74.

Manser, A., and Stock, G. (eds.) (1984), *The Philosophy of F. H. Bradley* (Oxford: Clarendon Press).

Mates, B. (1986), *The Philosophy of Leibniz: Metaphysics and Language* (New York and Oxford: Oxford University Press).

Moore, G. E. (1919), 'External and Internal Relations', *Proceedings of the Aristotelian Society*, 20: 40–62; repr. in Moore (1922), 276–309.

Moore, G. E. (1922), *Philosophical Studies* (London: Routledge).

Moosherr, T. (1898), *Eine Einleitung in das Studium der theoretischen Philosophie Herbarts* (Basel: Bürgin).

Mugnai, M. (1992), *Leibniz's Theory of Relations* (Stuttgart: Meiner).

Mure, G. R. G. (1961), 'F. H. Bradley: Towards a Portrait', *Encounter*, 16: 28–35.

Roberts, G. W. (1979), *Bertrand Russell Memorial Volume* (London: George Allen & Unwin).

Russell, B. (1900), *A Critical Exposition of the Philosophy of Leibniz* (Cambridge: Cambridge University Press).

Russell, B. (1903), *The Principles of Mathematics* (Cambridge: Cambridge University Press).

Russell, B. (1906–7), 'On the Nature of Truth', *Proceedings of the Aristotelian Society*, 7: 28–49.

Russell, B. (1927), *An Outline of Philosophy* (London: George Allen and Unwin).

Russell, B. (1959), *My Philosophical Development* (London: George Allen and Unwin).

Sprigge, Timothy (1983), *The Vindication of Absolute Idealism* (Edinburgh: Edinburgh University Press).

Sprigge, Timothy (1993) *James and Bradley: American Truth and British Reality* (Chicago and La Salle, Ill.: Open Court).

Stock, G. (ed.) (1998), *Appearance versus Reality* (Oxford: Clarendon Press).

Taylor, A. (1925), 'F. H. Bradley', *Mind*, 34: 1–12.

Ward, J. (1894), 'Critical Notice', *Mind*, 3: 109–25.

Ward, J. (1911), *The Realm of Ends or Pluralism and Theism: The Gifford Lectures Delivered in the University of St. Andrews in the Years 1907-1910* (Cambridge: Cambridge University Press).

Westphal, K. (1998), *Hegel, Hume und die Identität wahrnehmbarer Dinge* (Frankfurt am Main: Klostermann).

Whitehead, A. N. ([1929] 1978), *Process and Reality*, ed. and corrected by D. R. Griffin and D. W. Sherburne (New York: Free Press).

Wollheim, R. (1969), *F. H. Bradley* (Harmondsworth: Penguin).

PART III

SCIENCE AND PHILOSOPHY

CHAPTER 11

···

EVOLUTION AND RELIGION

···

JOHN HEDLEY BROOKE

DURING his five-year voyage on HMS *Beagle* Charles Darwin experienced an earth-quake. Entering the harbour of Concepción in March 1835, he discovered a city in deso-lation. Where there had been a cathedral there was now a 'grand pile of ruins' (Darwin [1845] 1910: 298). For some, the image of a cathedral in ruins provides an apt symbol of the effect Darwin's science would eventually have on nineteenth-century religious thought. When Sigmund Freud later referred to three revolutions that had transformed human self-understanding, he had in mind the decentring, deflating consequences of Copernican astronomy, the further humbling of humanity as a consequence of Darwin's science, and his own demonstration that humans were no longer masters of their own subconscious minds (Freud 1922: 240–1).

It has been observed, correctly, that only in retrospect did the displacement of the Earth from the centre of the cosmos amount to a diminution of human significance (Danielson 2009). In Renaissance Europe, to confer the status of a planet on the Earth was to elevate its inhabitants. The centre of the cosmos, according to Aristotelian philosophy, was the place to which all earthly matter fell. In Galileo's estimate it was the sink of all refuse in the universe. To place it among the planets was to promote it. For the astronomer Johannes Kepler, it was to place it where humans could at last take their rightful place as true citizens of the heavens (Kepler 1965: 45–6). Both Galileo and Kepler would have been surprised by Freud's judge-ment on the Copernican innovation. In their science they had surpassed that of the ancient astronomers, elevating further the stature of the human mind. Darwin, by contrast, would not have been surprised to find himself among those who, by putting men and women in their place, had humbled them. In one of his early notebooks, he declared that 'man in his arrogance thinks himself a great work worthy the interposition of a deity, more humble & I believe truer to consider him created from animals' (Brooke 1985: 66).

The affirmation of continuity between humans and their animal progenitors was the sin-gle most shocking feature of Darwin's science, as it had been of earlier concepts of evolution. Potentially damaging implications for religious belief were famously crystallized in anec-dotes. Apes in the London zoo allegedly asked 'Am I my keeper's brother?' Darwin came close to saying that those who opposed his theory by snarling and baring their teeth only confirmed thereby their canine origins. Darwin became a household name in part because of pervasive cartoons depicting him with simian hair and tail (Browne 2002: 373–81). The rich legacy of anecdote still conjures up images of a simple dichotomy—a glaring conflict between science and religion. For the Tory politician Benjamin Disraeli, speaking at the Oxford Diocesan Society in November 1864, the question was simple: 'Is man an ape or an angel?' Amid the cheers he declared himself on the side of the angelic (Desmond and Moore 1991: 460–1; Browne 2002: 250). Oxford had earlier witnessed what would become the most enduring symbol of the victory of science over reactionary religion. This was the encounter between Darwin's 'bulldog' Thomas Huxley and the bishop of Oxford, Samuel Wilberforce, at the 1860 meeting of the British Association for the Advancement of Science. Having impudently baited Huxley by enquiring whether he preferred to think of himself having an ape for an ancestor on his grandmother's or grandfather's side, the bishop suffered a stinging riposte when Huxley declared that he would rather have an ape for an ancestor than a man who used his authority and great gifts to obscure the truth. Inflated into what has become widely known as the 'great debate', the story stands as a foundation myth of scientific professionalism (Livingstone 2009).

It will be necessary to return to this anecdote because there is much that needs correction in popular perceptions of the Darwinian revolution. However, it would be absurd to suggest that Darwin's *On the Origin of Species* (1859) was not a profoundly disturbing revelation. For many conservative religious thinkers there really was (and in some constituencies still is) a contradiction between the biblical doctrine that humans had been created in the image of God and what they perceived to be the degrading doctrine of our derivation from brutes. For Victorian thinkers on the brink of losing their Christian faith, Darwin's staggering vision of a long, tortuous, bloodstained trail of evolution could be the last straw, as it was for Samuel Butler (Turner 1974: 168–78). Irrespective of religious sensibilities, there were concerns for the stability of society if moral values were relativized by the assumption that they, too, had evolved.

The idea of evolution had been a subject of intense public debate before Darwin published his theory of natural selection. The transformation of living forms proposed by the French naturalist Jean-Baptiste Lamarck had been publicized by Darwin's geological mentor Charles Lyell even as he repudiated the idea. Ironically, it was through reading Lyell's refutation of Lamarck in the second volume of his *Principles of Geology* (1830–3) that Herbert Spencer became a convert to evolutionary thinking (Dean 2004: 1285). Fifteen years before Darwin's *Origin*, the anonymous *Vestiges of the Natural History of Creation* (1844) had created a sensation with its propagation of a *law* of development that had supposedly regulated the transmutation of species and the eventual emergence, rather than direct creation, of humankind. The identity of the author, Scottish publisher Robert Chambers, was a well-guarded secret and the subject of so much speculation that his evolutionary thesis enjoyed great notoriety during the 1840s. The quality of the supporting evidence left much to be desired and T. H. Huxley, who was to be Darwin's fervent advocate, was one of the book's severest critics. But the public controversies that raged over *Vestiges* had already raised many of the religious questions that would resurface in the 1860s in the Darwinian debates: whether, for example, a naturalistic account of human development would inevitably lead to a materialistic understanding of the human mind and whether scientific knowledge could continue to be seen as spiritually edifying if it called into question traditional arguments for design. In a long, vituperative review of *Vestiges*, Darwin's Cambridge teacher Adam Sedgwick had vilified the book as a work of 'gross credulity and rank infidelity', which if true would reduce morality to 'moonshine' (Gillispie 1959: 165).

From James Secord's meticulous study of popular reactions to *Vestiges* (Secord 2000), it is clear that Darwin's achievement was to project the science of evolution to a higher level where it could be taken seriously by those Darwin described as sound naturalists. This had been made possible by twenty-five years of reflection on the fossil record, on the staggering extent of extinction, the geographical distribution of species, the resemblances between embryos of disparate forms, and the plasticity of nature in the hands of domestic breeders who could produce such a repertoire of fancy pigeons that even a well-trained ornithologist might mistake them for distinct species. Darwin's argument was that in a relentless struggle for limited resources, even minor variations among individuals could confer advantage on those who possessed them, allowing them to produce more offspring and so transmit their variant characteristics to subsequent generations. Given aeons of time, the gradual accumulation of slight variations could eventuate in new species, their disadvantaged progenitors having been successively displaced. It was a thesis that had been beset with difficulties, as Darwin was the first to acknowledge (Darwin 1859: 171–206, 235–42). But, by unifying what would otherwise be a collection of disparate phenomena, and by adducing an extraordinary range of supportive evidence, Darwin introduced unprecedented rigour into the discussion of biological evolution. His was the science that persuaded an intelligentsia that the successive modification of living forms had been a historical reality.

In charting the consequences for religious reflection, it will be convenient, first, to present an overview of the broad cultural shifts to which Darwin's science contributed. This will serve to identify issues that were to feature in popular religious debate and in theological reconstruction. Secondly, a finer brush will be used to examine selected issues in a more nuanced manner and to sample the more engaging theological options.

1. Evolution and Religion in Broad Perspective

At least four cultural shifts can be associated with Darwin's scientific achievement. To attribute them to Darwin alone would be a mistake. But Darwin's advocacy of evolution by natural selection was more than merely a symbol of them. In developing his theory Darwin forged new resources and a new vocabulary for discussing the appearance of design and adaptation in nature (Beer 1983). The shifts are the deepening of divisions on how scientific and religious beliefs were to be related and possibly integrated; the gradual, and often painful, adjustment to the continuity Darwin proposed between humans and their animal ancestors; the eventual elimination of references to a Creator and to the supernatural in technical scientific publications; and the gradual displacement of a genre of apologetic literature that had sought to harmonize biblical exegesis with the latest science.

The Divisiveness of Darwinism

From the moment Darwin published his *Origin*, the prospects for achieving consensus on the relations between science and religion rapidly receded. The divisiveness of his vision was immediately apparent in the reactions of his Cambridge mentors, botanist John Henslow and geologist Adam Sedgwick. Having earlier vent his spleen on *Vestiges*, Sedgwick now reproached Darwin for a view of nature in which there appeared to be no place for design or purpose. The idea of 'final cause', which Sedgwick and the Cambridge philosopher William Whewell saw as fundamental to explanation in the life sciences, constituted a precious link between the material and the moral that Sedgwick accused Darwin of having ignored (Sedgwick 1859). Smarting from Sedgwick's reproach, Darwin could later take comfort from the quite different reaction of Henslow, who in May 1860 seized an opportunity to put Sedgwick in his place:

> I got up...and stuck up for Darwin as well as I could, refusing to allow that he was guided by any but truthful motives, and declaring that he himself believed he was exalting & not debasing our views of a Creator, in attributing to him a power of imposing laws on the Organic World by which to do his work, as effectually as his laws imposed upon the inorganic had done it in the Mineral Kingdom. (Henslow 1860)

The more closely one examines the religious responses to Darwinian evolution, the more one is struck by their diversity (Brooke 2009a). One of the most radical came from the Oxford theologian and Professor of Geometry Baden Powell, whose contribution to *Essays and Reviews* (1860) effectively argued that the best way to relate the discourses of science and religion was not to relate them. It was the attempts to do so that had led to the steady retreat of religious authority in the face of scientific progress. To avoid further embarrassment, Powell recommended a separation of their respective magisteria. Scientists should be granted authority over the interpretation of the physical world, reserving for religion a jurisdiction over moral issues. Darwin's naturalism was enlisted by Powell to reinforce his message. Darwin's 'masterly volume' would soon 'bring about an entire revolution of opinion in favour of the grand principle of the self-evolving powers of nature' (Powell [1860] 1861: 139; Corsi 1988: 227).

For many religious commentators this was to cede too much to the sciences. To have two distinct and autonomous domains was even unattractive to some leaders of scientific opinion. In North America, Louis Agassiz resisted Darwin's theory, having developed a philosophy of nature in which 'the intervention of a Creator is displayed in the most striking manner, in every stage of the history of the world' (Roberts 1988: 34). By contrast, Agassiz's Harvard colleague Asa Gray, a committed Presbyterian, did more than anyone in North America to promote Darwin's theory, delighting Darwin by his insistence that belief in natural selection was compatible with a Christian natural theology (Gray 1860a, 1860b).

Such divisions can be found in many institutions and contexts. At Princeton, the Presbyterian theologian Charles Hodge drew a very different conclusion from Gray, arguing that, while the idea of evolution was not intrinsically atheistic, the specifically Darwinian mechanism of natural selection effectively was. In his *What is Darwinism?* (1874) Hodge considered that the randomness of the variations on which Darwin relied, and the accidents and contingencies that affected evolutionary outcomes, evacuated the concept of a designed creation (Livingstone 1987: 102–5). And yet, another Princeton theologian, James McCosh, had little difficulty in integrating Darwinism with his Christian faith. In his first book, *The Method of Divine Government, Physical and Moral* (1850) McCosh had argued that God governs the world both by law and through a combination of laws that produced what he described as 'fortuities' (Moore 1979: 246). This was a view commensurate with Darwin's understanding of 'chance' events as those arising from the intersection of otherwise independent causal chains. After assimilating Darwin's theory and cautiously appraising the mechanism of natural selection, McCosh saw no reason to reject either on the ground that accident and contingency lay outside divine jurisdiction. If evolution was God's method of creation, the prevalence of accident could not be accidental. Events that it was tempting to ascribe to 'chance' were still the result of designed laws and were instrumental in introducing novelty in an evolving universe. As with so many sympathetic commentators on Darwin, McCosh nevertheless stopped short of permitting a fully naturalistic account of human capacities and their origins (Moore 1979: 248).

The concept of evolution, Darwin's in particular, would continue to be divisive in Christendom (Brooke 2012). Any hope of achieving consensus in the construction of a theology of nature was henceforth hard to sustain. This is not to suggest that there had been a united view on the relations between science and religion earlier in the century. It is sometimes assumed that the *Natural Theology* (1802) of William Paley was paradigmatic in this respect. Certainly it can be helpful for didactic purposes to contrast Paley's static universe, in which creatures had been pre-adapted to their conditions of life, with the dynamic historical orientation that Darwin brought to his science. But by the 1830s, when the *Bridgewater Treatises* on natural theology were published, Paley's text was already obsolete.

By then, the earth sciences had disclosed a far longer and more complex history for the world in which species had come and gone. This had obliged the Oxford geologist William Buckland to argue that, while it could still be said that the Creator had created every species it was possible to create, they had not coexisted simultaneously (Rupke 1983: 158–9, 172–3). Another *Bridgewater Treatise* author, the physiologist Peter Mark Roget, went beyond Paley by introducing higher-level organizing principles. Roget eschewed a utilitarian appeal to individual structures and their functions, appealing instead to archetypal patterns discernible across an entire range of vertebrates. He could then argue that the taxonomic classes represented 'parts of one general plan' that 'emanated from the same Creator' (Topham 2010: 105). That additions had been made to creation in a pattern of progressive complexity, rather than the whole completed *ab initio*, was another resource available to apologists who took their inspiration from the French palaeontologist Georges Cuvier. To add to the diversification, in the *Bridgewater Treatise* of William Whewell (1833) we find a greater emphasis on the *laws* of nature and the beneficial consequences of their combination. This was an emphasis that Darwin himself appreciated, citing Whewell at the front of the *Origin* to advertise a Christian precedent for extending his naturalism:

> But with regard to the material world, we can at least go so far as this—we can perceive that events are brought about not by insulated interpositions of Divine power, exerted in each particular case, but by the establishment of general laws. (Darwin 1859: frontispiece)

For Whewell the laws were indicative of a lawmaker, as they had been for many natural philosophers since the seventeenth century. The critical point, however, is the diversification within natural theology to which Jonathan Topham, among others, has drawn attention (Topham 2010; Brooke 1994; McGrath 2011: 108–42). Accordingly, a contrast with the post-Darwinian period cannot be complete. Yet there is a difference. Although the *Bridgewater Treatises* functioned more as politically safe vehicles for the popularization of science than as sophisticated apologias for Christianity, they conveyed a continuing sense of compatibility between scientific knowledge and religious belief. They did not convince everyone. Adrian Desmond has drawn attention to the medical reformers and political radicals in London who were willing to lampoon the 'Bilgewater treatises' (Desmond 1989: 20; 116–17). Nevertheless, inferences from nature to nature's God were still pervasive while Darwin was developing his theory. One reason why the theory proved so disturbing was that, if substantiated, the life sciences could no longer supply the unequivocal support to religious belief that, in the English-speaking world, had so long, and by so many, been taken for granted.

Naturalizing Humanity

In Darwin's *Origin*, 'man' as a product of evolution was conspicuous by his absence. One brief sentence captured the promise that 'light will be thrown on the origin of man and his history' (Darwin 1859: 488). The fulfilment of that promise represents a second cultural shift that accompanied the discussion of human evolution (both biological and social) during the second half of the nineteenth century. Readjusting to the repositioning of humanity in a long line of nature's products was painful to many. It was not a great problem for Darwin himself, who tended to elevate animal capacities rather than diminish those of humans. A striking example occurs in his *Descent of Man* (1871), in the specific context of religious belief. Here Darwin enlists the behaviour of his dog to illuminate the origins of religion. One summer day, the dog had barked at the swaying of a parasol in the breeze. Darwin reasoned that the dog had reasoned that there must be an invisible intruder on its territory. How easy it would have been, Darwin suggested, for early humans to populate the invisible realm with spirits (Darwin [1871] 1906: 145).

Darwin's legacy extended far beyond the text and parameters of the *Origin*. When speculating about the origins of religion, or the evolution of the moral sense, he rendered *Homo sapiens* the subject of naturalistic explanation. In so doing he deeply disturbed the presuppositions of those, including his wife Emma, whose religious faith was anchored, at least in part, in moral absolutes. Distilling the essence of a long discussion, Darwin wrote of the 'moral sense or conscience' as 'a highly complex sentiment—originating in the social instincts, largely guided by the approbation of our fellow-men, ruled by reason, self-interest, and in later times by deep religious feelings, and confirmed by instruction and habit' (Darwin [1871] 1906: 203). As a stimulus to the development of the social virtues, the 'praise and blame of our fellow men' was given special emphasis, allowing a further instance of continuity with the animal kingdom. His proto-religious dog made another appearance: 'it appears that even dogs appreciate encouragement, praise, and blame' (Darwin [1871] 1906: 201). Because the foundation stone of morality was that one should 'do unto others as ye would they should do unto you', Darwin considered it 'hardly possible to exaggerate the importance during rude times of the love of praise and the dread of blame' (Darwin [1871] 1906: 202). In this respect, self-interest had played a crucial role in the emergence of cooperative beings. Emma Darwin spoke for many of her generation when she confided to her son, Frank, that 'your father's opinion that *all* morality has grown up by evolution is painful to me' (Darwin 1958: 93).

The shift in sensibility required by Darwin's alignment of humanity with the animals was too painful even for some of his most esteemed scientific colleagues. Optimistically, Darwin once described his geological mentor, Charles Lyell, as an 'entire convert' to his views from having been 'our chief maintainer of the immutability of species' (Brooke 2009b: 256). Yet Lyell could never bring himself to believe that the capacities of the human mind could be ascribed simply to the action of natural selection. He remained resistant to 'going the whole orang', as he had once put it (Bartholomew 1973), worried that Darwin was deifying natural selection, and commended an analogy between the freedom of human volition and that of its ultimate source in the Deity (Lyell 1860). Even the co-founder of the theory of natural selection, Alfred Russel Wallace, dismayed Darwin when he took steps to protect the human spirit. As with Lyell, Wallace pointed to human attributes that he considered inexplicable on the basis of natural selection. A pronounced aesthetic sense, mathematical ability, and a gift for musical appreciation were so unevenly distributed among humankind that it was difficult to explain them on the basis of advantages they might have conferred during earlier stages of human evolution (Kottler 1974). Wallace lost Darwin when he upheld the reality of a spirit agency guiding the course of evolution, his scientific reputation suffering from his apparent credulity when examining paranormal phenomena associated with spiritualist mediums (Turner 1974: 68–103). Yet, for all his idiosyncrasy, Wallace shows how difficult it was to readjust to an all-embracing scientific naturalism. Still writing in the first decade of the twentieth century, he paradoxically enlisted the Darwinian theory to support his proposal that humans are unique and that similarly intelligent beings are unlikely to be found on other worlds. One of his contentions in an appendix added in 1904 to *Man's Place in the Universe* (1903) was that, on Darwinian principles, the course of evolution on Earth had been shaped by so many accidents and contingencies that, even if there were other planets with similar physical and chemical preconditions for life, the chances of an evolutionary process eventuating in close analogues of human beings would be extremely remote (Crowe 1986: 530–1).

Changing the Culture of Science

During Darwin's lifetime, there was a discernible change within the culture of science. By the end of the century, despite critiques of Darwinism from those who favoured more Lamarckian models of evolution, references to the activity of a Creator, or to that of any supernatural agent, disappeared from technical scientific texts (Bowler 1990: 167–76). This was not yet the case at mid-century when Darwin was composing his *Origin*. Indeed, he himself retained references to a Creator, adding to their number in the second edition of 1860. Though he regretted it later, he even used biblical language when referring to the life breathed into the first living forms (Brooke 2009b: 264–7). The deliberate exclusion of theological language from technical science was a result of the successful expansion of naturalism in several scientific disciplines. In the physical sciences, the development of Laplace's nebular hypothesis for the origins of the solar system displaced Newton's explicitly theistic account of the system's beauty. Particularly among the German monists of the mid-nineteenth century, the laws of thermodynamics were interpreted to imply a closed, law-bound universe, impervious to transcendent manipulation (Gregory 1977). Darwinian evolution was, nevertheless, a richer, albeit controversial, resource for those who wielded the new, severer criteria for what should count as serious, professional science. The shift can be detected in Darwin himself during the 1860s. It was only in the later editions of the *Origin* that he would confidently assert that explanations going beyond the natural simply could not *count* as science.

It is not difficult to see why evolutionary theory might encourage a severer kind of natu-ralism. Already by the late 1830s, Darwin was developing a monistic understanding of the human mind: 'Oh you Materialist!' he had chided himself in March 1838, as he speculated that love of the deity was an effect of the brain's organization (Kohn 1989: 224). The very fact that he was positing material connections between species bound together by a common genealogy contrasted with idealist philosophies of nature such as that embraced by Louis Agassiz who could write that 'there will be no *evidence* of God's working in nature until nat-uralists have shown that the whole creation is the *expression of thought* and not the *product of physical agents*' (Roberts 1988: 34). In Darwin's theory of 'descent with modification', spe-cies were derived materially from pre-existing species. It was not long before his champion, T. H. Huxley, was arguing for the physical basis of life.

It would be wrong to streamline this cultural shift within science. There were physical sci-entists critical of the hypothetical character of natural selection and who were not won over to a complete ontological naturalism. Crosbie Smith has drawn attention to a group of north British physicists who, far from deserting a theistic philosophy of nature, saw theological meaning in their thermodynamics (Smith 1998: 110–11). For William Thomson (later Lord Kelvin), the impress of a Scottish voluntarist theology can, according to Smith, be seen *in* his thermodynamics. The principle of energy *conservation* accorded with the principle that only God could create and destroy the energy in the universe, while the principle of energy *dissipation* chimed with a world held in Scripture to be transitory. Attempts were made by scientists to construct theologies of nature in which there was still permeability between the mundane and the transcendent. A striking example is enshrined in *The Unseen Universe* (1875), authored by two physicists, Balfour Stewart and Peter Guthrie Tait, who reconciled science and Christianity to their satisfaction by postulating an eternal, ethereal, invisible universe intimately connected to the visible. Vibrations accompanying human thought would be stored in this unseen realm, in which energy dissipated from the visible world could accumulate and be returned in the form of apparent miracles. Their book enjoyed enormous popularity, scoring a seventeenth edition by 1901 (Noakes 2004: 1912).

Popular science and an elite scientific culture are not, however, the same thing; and it is precisely such extravagant metaphysical schemes that were purged by those content to base their science on the properties of matter and the laws it obeyed. The tensions between elite and popular science were heightened in Belfast in 1874 when the physicist John Tyndall delivered his Presidential Address to the British Association for the Advancement of Science. Incensed by the reluctance of Catholic colleges in Ireland to introduce science into their curricula, Tyndall went on the offensive. Men of science, he announced, would wrest from theology the entire domain of cosmological theory. Darwin had shown how it could be done. Tyndall even admonished Darwin for not pressing his naturalism to the limit. He took exception to Darwin's seeming prevarication over the ultimate origin of life. And in this context we see the demands of a severe methodological naturalism placed before a pub-lic, many of whom found the tone patronizing and belligerent:

> We need clearness and thoroughness here. Two courses and two only are possible. Either let us open our doors freely to the conception of creative acts, or abandoning them let us radically change our notions of matter. (Tyndall [1874] 1879: 191)

Tyndall would not have described himself as a materialist, a creed he considered too restrictive to do justice to the creative faculties of the human mind, the origins of which still spoke of a mystery that he wrote with a capital 'M'. The world, he wrote, 'embraces not only a Newton, but a Shakespeare—not only a Boyle, but a Raphael—not only a Kant, but a Beethoven—not only a Darwin, but a Carlyle' (Tyndall [1874] 1879: 202–3). In claiming for science an 'unrestricted right of search', he was nevertheless adamant that in conventional, dualistic, matter/spirit ontologies, matter in its supposed passivity had been much maligned. His 'Belfast Address' seriously damaged the prospects for Darwin's science among the Irish clergy, both Catholic and Protestant (O'Leary 2009; Livingstone 1999), his triumphalist version of the history of science having much in common with John William Draper's influential *History of the Conflict between Religion and Science* (1875).

Changing the Culture of Biblical Interpretation

Darwin's science became the subject of public controversy at just the time the Christian churches had to cope with new approaches to the study of the Bible. Literal readings of the Genesis creation narratives had been compromised earlier through new disclosures from the earth sciences. Decades before Darwin published, it had ceased to be credible that animal pain and suffering had first entered the world as a consequence of human sin. Animal species had become extinct long before humans had appeared. During the first half of the nineteenth century, however, many attempts had been made to find ways of harmonizing science and Scripture, treating the six Genesis 'days', for example, as shorthand for geological epochs. The goal was to preserve the authority of the Bible without rejecting the latest science. By 1860, this hermeneutic practice was under increasing strain, threatened both by the historical sciences and by the application of historical methods to biblical sources (Barton and Wilkinson 2009).

Darwin was perfectly aware that his understanding of human origins would create difficulties for conservative exegetes. As early as January 1860, the clerical naturalist Leonard Jenyns informed him that he doubted whether the image of man as an even '*greatly improved orang*' would find general acceptance: 'I am not one of those in the habit of mixing up questions of science and scripture, but I can hardly see what sense or meaning is to be attached to *Gen*: 2.7. & yet more to vv. 21. 22, of the same chapter, giving an account of the creation of *wo*man,—if the human species at least has not been created independently of other animals' (Brooke 2009b: 268).

The challenge of having to find new meanings in Scripture if Darwin were correct was compounded by the challenge of how to deal with the claim, publicized in *Essays and Reviews* (1860), that the biblical authors had been ordinary men of their time, fallible on matters, such as scientific detail, of which they were ignorant. *Essays and Reviews* arguably created a greater furore in the Anglican Church than Darwin's *Origin of Species*, not least because Oxford clergy were among those urging that the Bible should be read like any other book. Samuel Wilberforce was more vitriolic in denouncing it than he was in his reaction to Darwin. From one of the essays, that of Charles Goodwin, it is clear that the harmonization programme was reaching a crisis state even before the full impact of Darwin was felt. Looking back over sixty years of harmonizing strategies, Goodwin declared that repeated attempts to reconcile Genesis with geology had led to failure. In retrospect, it had been a misguided strategy and one that had imposed on scientists a burden they should not have been asked to carry. Goodwin pointedly identified problems with each of the harmonizing schemes. Both William Buckland in Oxford and Adam Sedgwick in Cambridge had been forced to abandon their earlier claim that geology provided proof of a universal flood. A rough concordance between the order of creation in Genesis and the order discernible from the fossil record might be affirmed; but there was dissonance in the details. Goodwin observed that in Genesis birds preceded reptiles, whereas in geology reptiles came first. The alternative strategy of protecting the literal 'days' by expanding the time between an initial chaos and the first day of creation proved unsustainable with advances in stratigraphy that undermined belief in the almost simultaneous creation of all living things. Critically, the point on which Goodwin rested his case was the discord *between* the various attempts to preserve scientific authority for the Bible. The 'trenchant manner' in which 'theological geologists overthrow one another's theories' spoke volumes and was a sure indication that the authority of Scripture should be reserved for its moral jurisdiction not for any scientific provenance. 'No one contends', he wrote in conclusion, that the Bible 'can be used as a basis of astronomical or geological teaching'. Straining to bring it into accord with scientifically established facts was to 'despoil it of its consistency and grandeur, both of which may be preserved if we recognize in it, not an authentic utterance of Divine knowledge, but a human utterance, which it has pleased Providence to use in a special way for the education of mankind' (Goodwin [1860] 1861: 253). In that contrast lies the hermeneutic shift to which Darwin contributed.

Again, however, there is the danger of streamlining a complex process of readjustment. There were Christian commentators, favourably disposed towards the idea of evolution, who continued in the harmonizing mode. In general terms it was not impossible to achieve a limited rapprochement. After all, the Genesis text did not say 'Let there be man...' but 'Let us make man'. Again, if one were looking for some general congruence, one might observe that Genesis describes life appearing in stages, which is what evolutionary science described in detail. George Frederick Wright was an influential proponent of theistic evolution in America, who saw no problem with the Genesis account: 'the language of Genesis may properly be regarded as the language of theistic evolution'. And he pointed to the biblical phrase 'Let the earth bring forth' as an implicit avowal of organic evolution (Roberts 1988: 148).

The safer and more sophisticated option was for Christian evolutionists to search for deeper spiritual meanings in biblical texts that were now understood to convey neither historical nor scientific facts concerning the technicalities of creation. This was the influential approach of Samuel Driver who, in an Oxford sermon of 1883, created space for a non-literal reading of his Genesis text by emphasizing the many different literary genres in the Bible, including allegory, poetry, and parable (Rogerson 2009: 85–7). To subscribe to a theory of evolution did nothing to detract from a Creation narrative, the purpose of which was to underline the dependence of all that exists on an ulterior transcendent power, and so to warn against idolatry. A few years later, it was possible for F. W. Farrar to report not only the widespread acceptance of Darwin's science by the scientific fraternity, but also the acceptance by leading theologians that there was 'nothing in it contrary to the creeds of the Catholic faith'. Farrar had been asked to be a pall-bearer and to preach a funeral sermon when Darwin was buried in Westminster Abbey. In *The Bible, Its Meaning and Supremacy* (1887), he insisted that the first chapter of Genesis was still of transcendent value. In a few lines it 'corrected the idolatry, the polytheism, the atheism, the pantheism, the ditheism, the agnosticism, the pessimism of millions of mankind' (Farrar 1887: 155). Within a few years, in 1896, Frederick Temple, who was known for his support of biological evolution, became Archbishop of Canterbury, symbolizing its assimilation by the Anglican Establishment.

2. Refining the Narratives

In many popular accounts of the Darwinian revolution there is a degree of caricature that needs correction if the engagement of theology with evolutionary motifs, whether in cosmology or biology, is to be properly grasped. For example, the so-called 'great debate' between Huxley and Bishop Wilberforce has been the subject of extensive historical revisionism (Brooke 2001 and 2011; Gilley 1981; Frank James 2005; Livingstone 2009; Lucas 1979). In the *Life and Letters of Thomas Henry Huxley* (1900), Leonard Huxley never claimed that his father had been the victor. In his view a large proportion of the audience of several hundred in the Oxford Museum would have sided with the bishop. Indeed at least one convert to Darwin's theory, the naturalist Henry Baker Tristram, was de-converted as he witnessed the exchange. Wilberforce was confident that there were eminent scientists, notably Charles Lyell and Richard Owen, who would be on his side. When he reviewed the *Origin of Species* for the *Quarterly Review*, he successfully identified the weakest points in Darwin's argument—for example the paucity of intermediate forms in the fossil record (Wilberforce [1860] 1874). Darwin found the review scientifically worthless but described it as 'uncommonly clever': it 'quizzes me in splendid style' (Darwin 1860a). Much of the bishop's critique was devoted to philosophical, not overtly theological, objections. He was not alone in observing that Darwin frequently spoke of natural selection as a 'hypothesis' that only 'might' or 'could' explain the salient data. Darwin's science was to be a remarkable vindication of a hypothetico-deductive methodology in the life sciences, but Wilberforce was correct in recognizing a departure from the hallowed strictures of Baconian induction. Both Huxley and the botanist Joseph Hooker separately sought to ingratiate themselves with Darwin by claiming that it was they who, at Oxford, had inflicted humiliation on the bishop. A report in the *Athenaeum* gave a less partisan view: Wilberforce and Huxley had 'each found foemen worthy of their steel, and made their charges and counter-charges very much to their own satisfaction and the delight of their respective friends'. Darwin valued the publicity but it is not clear that the skirmish at the British Association left any significant mark in the decades that followed. It largely disappeared from view until some thirty years later when, with the deaths of Darwin, Hooker, and Huxley, recollections of the event were woven into a mythology of scientific heroism (Frank James 2005).

This does not mean that Wilberforce was theologically more receptive to evolution than one might infer from the anecdotes. He was careful to avoid—indeed prided himself on avoiding—two theological mistakes. He did not fire biblical proof-texts against Darwin's science. Nor did he try to bring biblical exegesis into harmony with the latest scientific knowledge, recognizing, as did the illustrious scientist James Clerk Maxwell, that this was a strategy likely to backfire, given the provisional, often transient, character of scientific hypotheses (Wilberforce [1860] 1874: 92). But for Wilberforce there was ultimately a barrier. His recalcitrance introduces the first of the theological issues that now require closer examination.

The Divine Image in Humankind

This, for Wilberforce, was the problem: 'Man's derived supremacy over the earth; man's power of absolute speech; man's gift of reason; man's free will and responsibility; man's fall and...redemption; the incarnation of the Eternal Son; the indwelling of the Eternal Spirit,— all are equally and utterly irreconcilable with the degrading notion of the brute origin of him who was created in the image of God and redeemed by the Eternal Son' (Wilberforce [1860] 1874: 94). Humans were made in the image of God. It was for humans that Jesus Christ had died. There was a dignity to be respected and preserved.

And yet, had Wilberforce not overreacted by leaving no room for manoeuvre? It was surely possible to argue that, irrespective of origins, humans did have capacities that had advanced beyond those of their simian relatives. Darwin had never said that humans were nothing but apes. Attributes such as rationality, free will, self-consciousness, moral sensibility, imagination, the capacity to pursue a quest for truth, and the potential for self-improvement, were not deleted from humanity by virtue of their having progressively evolved from animal precursors. An aesthetic response to the beauties of nature and, for some, a grateful responsiveness to a supposed Creator of that beauty still remained facets of human experience. Darwin had been no stranger to them. In his *Journal of Researches*, he had reflected on the sublimity of the Brazilian forests and the desolate landscape of the Tierra del Fuego, both 'temples filled with the varied production of the God of Nature'. No one could 'stand in these solitudes unmoved, and not feel that there is more in man than the mere breath of his body' (Darwin [1845] 1910: 473).

The critical question for theologians sympathetic to Darwin was whether the 'more in man' was simply the emergent product of a 'natural' process devised by the Creator to make complex beings with spiritual capacities; or whether a special, additional act of creation had taken place at a crucial juncture to insert a distinctively human 'soul' into a hominid form. Whereas a comprehensive methodological naturalism favoured the former, Roman Catholic theology in particular has preferred the latter. A precedent was set for that dualistic response by an early convert to evolution who was also a convert to Roman Catholicism. St George Jackson Mivart, a pupil of Thomas Huxley, was to become an irritant to the inner Darwin circle by constructing an account of evolution at variance with Darwin's own (Brooke and Cantor 1998: 255–62). Whereas Darwin had depicted lines of evolutionary *divergence* from common ancestors, Mivart saw evolutionary processes repeatedly *converging* on similar anatomical forms. It was as if there was an inherent drive towards particular evolutionary goals that could itself be ascribed to a Creator. Mivart's defence of theistic evolution was accompanied in his *Genesis of Species* (1871) by a tenacious critique of natural selection that Darwin considered biased and unfair. Mivart was duly rebuked in a new chapter for the sixth edition of the *Origin* (Brooke 2009b: 271–2). In two respects, however, he illustrates a form of mediation between theology and evolution that was to be repeated in many different contexts. If the seemingly directionless manner in which natural selection worked on random variations could be qualified, and if in the narrative of evolution the human soul could still be seen as a late product of divine interposition, a degree of accommodation was achievable (Gregory 1986: 378–83; Moore 1979: 117–22, 233). In retrospect it is easy to censure religious thinkers who developed deviant models of theistic evolution; but the status of natural selection as the primary mechanism of evolutionary change was controversial among evolutionary biologists themselves for many decades to come (Bowler 1983 and 2001).

The Rise and Fall of *Homo sapiens*

Critics of Christianity living in a post-Darwinian universe rejoiced in the fact that man had risen, not fallen. What could be saved of the fundamental doctrine of the 'fall' in the light of human evolution? For Evangelical Christians this was, and for many has remained, a sticking point. It would, however, be misleading to imagine that no reinterpretation was possible of the Genesis story of Adam and Eve and their fall from grace. Much ink was spilled in the nineteenth century on the question whether Adam and Eve had to be individual historical figures or whether they could stand as symbols for all humankind. Literacy in evolutionary biology undoubtedly encouraged the more existential interpretations of a myth that, by liberal theologians, was seen as capturing the self-centred and selfish propensities in all humankind—propensities that led inexorably to a sense of alienation from a transcendent 'Other' to whom all were answerable. There was even a sense in which evolutionary biology underwrote the propriety of a discourse in which sinfulness was both real and redescribable in terms of vestigial animality. Self-centredness, according to Huxley, had been a condition of victory in the struggle for existence. As an inheritance it was nothing less than the 'reality at the bottom of the doctrine of original sin' (Huxley [1893/4] 1947: 49). In his *Theology of an Evolutionist* (1897), one of America's outstanding representatives of theological liberalism, Lyman Abbott, saw no reason to demur.

Concepts of evolution, especially when applied to cultural development, were a valuable resource for liberal theologies. For example, they facilitated the construction of replies to radical biblical critics. To see in Scripture the gradual evolution of religious sensibilities, and to apply a concept of 'progressive revelation', allowed one to jettison older notions of biblical inspiration without discarding a privileged role for the Bible. It could be seen as providing a unique, historical record of spiritual ascent—away from a vengeful, tribal deity towards a more refined understanding of God. Liberal theologians could see themselves as completing the work of evolutionary biologists by documenting, through Scripture, the spiritual evolution of humankind. This superimposition of the spiritual on the biological was to take many forms and was sometimes the subject of elaborate, metaphysical synthesis, as in the works of Henri Bergson and, moving further into the twentieth century, the Jesuit anthropologist Pierre Teilhard de Chardin (Haught 2003: 152–3, 162–75). Teilhard's vision, though sufficiently heterodox to bring censorship from his Catholic superiors, integrated a Christology into his synthesis by presenting the character of Christ as exemplar and prefigurement of the highest ideal to which humankind could aspire in its evolutionary movement. Such schemes were often too metaphysical for their scientific critics; but, as late as 1962, one of the twentieth century's greatest geneticists, Theodosius Dobzhansky, volunteered an account of the rise and fall of *Homo sapiens* that was both biologically informed and faithful to his Eastern Orthodox Christianity:

> The meaning of the acquisition of self-awareness in human evolution is expressed beautifully in the biblical symbol of the Fall of Man. Self-awareness is a blessing and a curse. Through self-awareness man attained the status of a person in the existential sense: he became conscious of himself and of his environment...Self-awareness and foresight brought, however, the awesome gifts of freedom and responsibility Man knows that he is accountable for his acts: he has acquired the knowledge of good and evil. This is a dreadfully heavy load to carry. No other animal has to withstand anything like it. There is a tragic discord in the soul of man.
> (Dobzhansky 1962: 338)

The Discord of Suffering

No subject has been closer to the heart of religious reflection than that of human suffering. No subject has been as intractable for philosophical theodicies as the discord between images of a benevolent, merciful God and the pervasive realities of pain and disease—between concepts of a caring Providence and the prevalence of natural disasters. How might a new understanding of an evolving creation bear on attempts to rationalize the seeming cruelty and indifference of nature? This is a question that Darwin himself considered. When reflecting on the reasons that led him to abandon Christianity, scepticism arising from his science was rarely given prominence. It is true that his commitment to explanation by natural laws militated against belief in miracles. It is also true, as his cousin Emma predicted before their marriage, that the critical mindset required for rigorous work in the sciences would and did contribute to his rejection of revelation. But, from his *Autobiography*, we learn that the most compelling reasons for his eventual agnosticism had derived not from his theory of natural selection but from moral revulsion against certain Christian teachings, notably the doctrine of eternal damnation for those who could not bring themselves to believe the tenets of an orthodox faith. Though Emma believed that Charles was rejecting a caricature of the Christian faith, he knew that his grandfather, Erasmus Darwin, his unbelieving father, Robert, and his atheist brother, Erasmus, would be among the damned. And this was a 'damnable doctrine' (Darwin 1958: 87). Adding weight to his renunciation was the classic difficulty: the 'very old argument from the existence of suffering against the existence of an intelligent first cause seems to me a strong one' (Darwin 1958: 90). He was no stranger to suffering himself. Dogged by an illness that often left him incapacitated, he witnessed the death of his beloved daughter Annie at the tender age of 10. There was cruelty and bitterness in the loss.

For Darwin himself, to understand the world as an evolving system lent grandeur to one's perception of nature. It did also have a bearing on the issue of suffering. The presence of so much suffering told against the existence of an intelligent first cause, whereas it 'agrees well with the view that all organic beings have been developed through variation and natural selection' (Darwin 1958: 90). He had often used metaphors from the battlefield when describing the competitive struggle for existence. There was a 'concealed war' in nature whose works were often cruel and wasteful (Desmond and Moore 1991: 293–4). From Darwin's perspective more sense could be made of pain and suffering from the vantage of his evolutionary vista than from within a traditional theism. He recognized that Christian theologians had sometimes rationalized suffering by suggesting that it served for moral improvement; but his challenge could not be so easily met: 'the number of men in the world is as nothing compared with that of all other sentient beings, and these often suffer greatly without any moral improvement' (Darwin 1958: 90). Darwin's student in the study of animal behaviour, George Romanes, would crystallize the difficulty in his *Thoughts on Religion* (1896) when he contrasted the nature of the Mind behind the general order of nature, as inferred from biological phenomena, with that conceived by the most highly developed form of religion. More than contrast, there was actually a 'contradiction which can be only be overcome by supposing, either that Nature conceals God, while man reveals Him, or that Nature reveals God while man misrepresents Him' (Romanes 1896: 83).

Romanes vacillated between theism and agnosticism, as did Darwin in his later years when he confessed to many fluctuations of belief, the agnosticism gradually prevailing over his earlier theistic conviction that it was impossible to conceive 'that this grand and wondrous universe, with our conscious selves, arose through chance' (Francis Darwin 1887: i. 304 and 312–13). One reason, perhaps, why there could be such vacillation was that if one presupposed the existence of a benevolent Creator, there was a sense in which the metaphysics of a naturalistic account of evolution might have something to offer those seeking a theodicy. There was a current in Darwin's thinking deeply averse to implicating God directly for particular instances of suffering and indeed for what he saw as the more devilish features of creation. To have the Creator create through intermediate processes, rather than each species by separate fiat, might distance the deity from direct responsibility for what Darwin once called a 'long succession of vile molluscous animals' (Brooke 1985: 47). If, as his theorizing seemed to suggest, living forms, including humans, were the result of 'designed laws with the details left to chance' (Darwin 1860b), then the world in which human intelligence had been possible was a world in which the preconditions of that possibility were such that less congenial outcomes were also possible. Darwin did not develop this train of thought into a formal theodicy, but hints of it can be detected in his correspondence with Asa Gray. It also featured briefly in a letter to Mary Boole of 1866: 'It has always appeared to me more satisfactory to look at the immense amount of pain and suffering in this world, as the inevitable result of the natural sequence of events, i.e. general laws, rather than from the direct intervention of God' (Darwin 1866). The laws could be justified in that they had permitted what Darwin earlier described as the 'highest good we can conceive', namely the 'creation of the higher animals' (Brooke 1985: 47). He stopped short of a formal theodicy because, as in his note to Mary Boole, he acknowledged that to exonerate an 'omniscient deity' in this way was 'not logical'. As Elliott Sober has remarked, one could still ask why omniscience had not devised laws with less destructive consequences (Sober 2011: 127).

But if Darwin did not develop a theodicy, his theory was occasionally appropriated for that purpose, and along the lines he had intimated. For Asa Gray it was one of the advantages of Darwin's science that it had something of real value to give to the theologian:

> Darwinian teleology has the special advantage of accounting for the imperfections and failures as well as for successes. It not only accounts for them, but turns them to practical account. It explains the seeming waste as being part and parcel of a great economical process. Without the competing multitude, no struggle for life; and without this, no natural selection and survival of the fittest, no continuous adaptation to changing surroundings, no diversification and improvement, leading from lower up to higher and nobler forms. So the most puzzling things of all to the old-school teleologists are the *principia* of the Darwinian. (Gray 1963: 311)

Gray's argument for a Darwinian theodicy has appealed more to scientifically minded than mainstream theologians. It still finds currency in Francisco Ayala's depiction of Darwin's theory as a 'gift' to both science and religion (Ayala 2007). Gray's reference to a single 'great economical process' is, however, a pointer to a subtle respect in which Darwin's synthesis could be construed more generally as a gift to religion. This was in its unification of the history of creation. Instead of a multiplicity of separate acts of creation, there was parsimony in the Darwinian image of a single branching tree. There was also a sense in which Darwin's science could be used to proclaim the unity of the human species since all races were united by common descent. This was a positive attraction for those campaigning against polygenism—against multiple-origin theories of humankind, which not only threatened conservative accounts of original sin and its transmission, but which also, in some minds, sanctioned pro-slavery policies that were deeply abhorrent to Darwin, Wallace, and Gray (Desmond and Moore 2009). Theologians commenting on evolution today (for example McGrath 2011: 188) still tend to assume a singularity of process, the existence of a single overarching narrative. Yet among their forebears were religious thinkers who, in the light of Darwin's science, and especially in the light of human suffering, were willing to consider more fragmented, multivalent models. The Jesuit modernist George Tyrrell would be one example. Darwin had made it impossible to think of nature as a single great machine. A better image, Tyrrell argued, was that of an artist's canvas on which many creative strokes can be discerned. Like Darwin, Tyrrell found it hard to see some single overriding cosmic purpose working itself out through nature. Terrible natural disasters with their attendant suffering could not be slotted into an all-embracing goal-directed process. But if the universe were conceived as a canvas, or even a keyboard, then each picture or each melody might have an independent worth in itself (Brooke and Cantor 1998: 163–4).

Images of the Deity

If theories of evolution led to a questioning of what it meant for humankind to be made in the image of God, Tyrrell's conception of the deity as an artist shows that images of the divine were themselves under scrutiny in the aftermath of the Darwinian debates. Two common conceptions were clearly under threat. The image of a deity who had repeatedly intervened in nature to conjure new species into existence lost its provenance. So did the image of an artisan God who, in William Paley's famous argument, had fashioned each living thing, and contrived each part of every living thing, as a skilled watchmaker puts together a watch.

The loss of the divine conjuror was, for many of Darwin's converts, no great sacrifice. And Christian clergymen were among the earliest converts. In response to Darwin's argument in the *Origin*, Charles Kingsley reported his inclination to believe that it was 'as noble a conception of Deity, to believe that he created primal forms capable of self development... as to believe that He required a fresh act of intervention to supply the lacunas which he himself had made'. He delighted Darwin by implying that he found the former the 'loftier thought'— a response that, with Kingsley's permission, Darwin included in his second edition (Brooke 2009b: 265–6). There were echoes here of a much earlier debate in the philosophy of religion when Gottfried Leibniz had suggested that Newton's image of an intervening deity, who periodically reformed the solar system, was seriously demeaning (Alexander 1956).

As for the image of the divine watchmaker, it simply had to be sacrificed if Darwin's account of species formation and transformation was correct. The perfecting action of natural selection, as advantageous variations accumulated over countless generations, created an appearance of meticulous design that was, however, illusory. More critically, Darwin stressed the randomness of the variations on which natural selection worked. In his *Variation in Animals and Plants under Domestication* (1868) he introduced an analogy directed against Asa Gray's tentative proposal that variations had been providentially led in propitious directions. A man might build a house from a pile of stones, of different shapes and sizes, found at the foot of a precipice. Surely, Darwin asked, one would not say that the stones had the shapes they had in order that the man could build his house? So it was with the variations occurring in the individual members of a species. Because they were randomly distributed, many of them deleterious, it was surely implausible to argue that they had been produced with a prospective end in view? Gray's response shows the degree to which religious minds could be thrown on the defence (Gray 1868). In a letter of 25 May 1868, he conceded the force of Darwin's sceptical analogy: 'I found your stone-house argument unanswerable in substance (for the notion of design must after all rest mostly on faith, and on accumulation of adaptations).' William James would say of the 1870s that this had been a time when 'Darwin opened our minds to the power of chance happenings' (James [1907] 1975: 57). Chance events, understood in the sense of lying at the intersection of otherwise independent causal chains, need not rule out references to design. But an antithesis between chance and design reverberated throughout the post-Darwinian controversies and it is hard to deny that apologias of the Paley type suffered as a consequence.

If, with Gray, one acknowledged that design was now to be perceived through the eye of faith, were models for the Creator other than Paley's watchmaker possible? As we have already seen, the image of the divine legislator could survive in a reform of natural theology. Despite his misgivings, Darwin toyed with the notion of 'designed laws'. Even Huxley complained that there had been too great a song and dance about the notion of design. It was open to those who wished to defend a Designer to locate the design in an original configuration of the universe containing, as it were, the seeds of its future evolution. In that respect, Huxley exclaimed, Darwin's theory had no more to do with theism than had the first book of Euclid. The doctrine of evolution was neither 'Anti-theistic nor Theistic'. A 'wider teleology' than that of Paley was not proscribed (Huxley 1887: 201–2).

For Christian apologists, Huxley's image of a distant designer was simply too remote to be edifying. Paradoxically, Darwinian evolution was invoked by some to promote a compensating image—that of an active deity immanent in the whole of creation. If static, mechanistic models of nature had favoured models of divine transcendence, Darwin's dynamic, evolving universe with its inherent creativity offered the better symbols of divine participation in the world. So argued the Oxford Anglo-Catholic theologian Aubrey Moore in his contribution to *Lux Mundi*, a collection of original theological essays, circulating around 1890, which reaffirmed the centrality to Christianity of the doctrine of Incarnation, of God's participation in the suffering of the world in the person of Jesus Christ. Accordingly, Moore made clear his opposition to semi-deistic images of God that implied his absence from the world except when intervening:

> The one absolutely impossible conception of God, in the present day, is that which represents him as an occasional visitor. Science has pushed the deist's God further and further away, and at the moment when it seemed as if He would be thrust out all together, Darwinism appeared, and, under the disguise of a foe, did the work of a friend.... Either God is everywhere present in nature, or He is nowhere. (Moore [1889] 1890: 82)

Embracing Huxley's conception of a 'wider teleology' in nature, Moore argued for a return to the Christian doctrine of 'direct Divine agency, the immanence of Divine power in nature from end to end, the belief in a God in whom not only we, but all things have their being' (Moore [1889] 1890: 82). The uniform operation of natural laws was itself an indication of a continual divine agency in the world. But it was certainly not a proof. Moore conceded that natural laws were susceptible of alternative, even atheistic, interpretations. Their efficacy could confirm a pre-existing theistic belief but was unlikely to induce theistic convictions in the mind of a sceptic. In a letter to Frederick Dixey of March 1888, Moore had written that 'We really *bring to* Nature much that we afterwards find *verified in* Nature, and I don't feel sure that Paley knew this' (England 2001: 280). The eye of faith would see God working through nature. Others, who did not share Christian belief, would see only the laws.

That Darwin could be presented as a friend to the Christian doctrine of God may still come as a surprise. For a Christian intelligentsia in the last decades of the nineteenth century, a science of evolution could, however, be a liberating force, allowing one to distance oneself from popular but reactionary frames of reference. It has been suggested by Richard England that, towards the close of the century, a small group of highly cultured scientists in Oxford, which included the Christian evolutionary biologists Edward Poulton and Frederick Dixey, was encouraged in the defence of natural selection by the openness to Darwin's science evinced by Aubrey Moore (England 2001). The image of a God who worked *in* and *through* nature, rather than occasionally and coercively from without, would continue to find favour among proponents of theistic evolution during the first half of the twentieth century, even if Moore's stark choice between a God who was everywhere or nowhere was to receive finer tuning, particularly in the process theologies of nature inspired by the philosophy of Alfred North Whitehead. In the contemporary theology of the Catholic scholar John Haught, which is more sensitive than most to the exigencies of evolutionary science, the doctrine of Providence ceases to denote either a micro-managing deity or a Creator's blueprint for the world: 'The new evolutionary accounts of nature invite us to recapture the often obscured portrait of a self-humbling, suffering God who is anything but a divine controller or designer of the cosmos' (Haught 2003: 81).

From Ernst Haeckel in the 1860s to Richard Dawkins and Daniel Dennett today, there has been a recurring tendency to inflate Darwin's science into a world view antithetical to such religious modes of thought and to institutional religion in particular. The use of Darwinism for attacking religious beliefs and sensibilities has undoubtedly added to the difficulties faced by members of religious denominations seeking guidance on how to evaluate the underlying science. In Darwin's day, the impact of his science could be shattering and it would be incorrect to imply otherwise. The young William James recorded that day after day he had experienced a feeling of horrible dread. It seemed that the foundations of morality had collapsed, the freedom of the will fallen victim to scientific determinism. And yet, as Bernard Lightman has recently stressed, advocates of a naturalistic world view did not have it all their own way. Their critics were legion (Lightman 2009). Indeed, as the century closed, James himself would write of religion, its resilience, and the fortitude it brought to religious believers, in a manner that testifies against a common historiography in which nineteenth-century science, and that of Darwin in particular, had driven religion to the wall:

> Every sort of energy and endurance, of courage and capacity for handling life's evils, is set free in those who have religious faith. For this reason the strenuous type of character will on the battle-field of human history always outwear the easy-going type, and religion will drive irreligion to the wall. (William James 1999)

In a Darwinian universe, it was the religious who were best fitted to survive.

References

Alexander, H. G. (1956). *The Leibniz–Clarke Correspondence*. Manchester: Manchester University Press.

Ayala, Francisco (2007). *Darwin's Gift to Science and Religion*. Washington: Joseph Henry Press.

Bartholomew, Michael (1973). 'Lyell and Evolution: An Account of Lyell's Response to the Prospect of an Evolutionary Ancestry for Man', *British Journal for the History of Science* 6: 261–303.

Barton, Stephen, and David Wilkinson (eds.) (2009). *Reading Genesis after Darwin*. Oxford: Oxford University Press.

Beer, Gillian (1983). *Darwin's Plots*. London: Routledge & Kegan Paul.

Bowler, Peter (1983). *The Eclipse of Darwinism*. Baltimore: Johns Hopkins University Press.

Bowler, Peter (1990). *Charles Darwin*. Oxford: Blackwell.

Bowler, Peter (2001). *Reconciling Science and Religion*. Chicago: University of Chicago Press.

Brooke, John Hedley (1985). 'The Relations between Darwin's Science and His Religion', in John Durant (ed.), *Darwinism and Divinity*. Oxford: Blackwell, 40–75.

Brooke, John Hedley (1994). 'Between Science and Theology: The Defence of Teleology in the Interpretation of Nature, 1820–1876', *Journal for the History of Modern Theology* 1: 47–65.

Brooke, John Hedley (2001). 'The Wilberforce–Huxley Debate: Why Did It Happen?', *Science and Christian Belief* 13: 127–41.

Brooke, John Hedley (2009a). 'Darwin and Victorian Christianity', in Jonathan Hodge and Gregory Radick (eds.), *The Cambridge Companion to Darwin*. 2nd edn. Cambridge: Cambridge University Press, 197–218.

Brooke, John Hedley (2009b). ' "Laws impressed on matter by the Creator?": The *Origin* and the Question of Religion', in Michael Ruse and Robert Richards (eds.), *The Cambridge Companion to the 'Origin of Species'*. Cambridge: Cambridge University Press, 256–74.

Brooke, John Hedley (2011). 'Samuel Wilberforce, Thomas Huxley, and Genesis', in Michael Lieb, Emma Mason and Jonathan Roberts (eds.), *The Oxford Handbook of the Reception History of the Bible*. Oxford: Oxford University Press, 397–412.

Brooke, John Hedley (2012). 'Christian Darwinians', in Andrew Robinson (ed.), *Darwinism and Natural Theology: Evolving Perspectives*. Newcastle upon Tyne: Cambridge Scholars Press, 47–67.

Brooke, John Hedley, and Geoffrey Cantor (1998). *Reconstructing Nature: The Engagement of Science and Religion*. Edinburgh: T & T Clark.

Browne, Janet (2002). *Charles Darwin: The Power of Place*. London: Jonathan Cape.

Corsi, Pietro (1988). *Science and Religion: Baden Powell and the Anglican Debate, 1800–1860*. Cambridge: Cambridge University Press.

Crowe, Michael (1986). *The Extra-Terrestrial Life Debate 1750–1900*. Cambridge: Cambridge University Press.

Danielson, Dennis (2009). '[The Myth] that Copernicanism demoted Humans from the Center of the Cosmos', in Ronald Numbers (ed.), *Galileo Goes to Jail and Other Myths about Science and Religion*. Cambridge, Mass.: Harvard University Press, 50–8.

Darwin, Charles ([1845] 1910). *Journal of Researches*. Henry Colburn 1839, rev. edn. 1845; London: Ward Lock & Co.

Darwin, Charles (1859). *On the Origin of Species by Means of Natural Selection*. London: Murray.

Darwin, Charles (1860a). Letter to Asa Gray, 22 July 1860, in *The Correspondence of Charles Darwin*, ed. Frederick Burkhardt. Cambridge: Cambridge University Press, 1993, viii. 298–9.

Darwin, Charles (1860b). Letter to Asa Gray, 22 May 1860, in *Darwin Correspondence*, ed. Burkhardt. Cambridge: Cambridge University Press, 1993, viii. 223–4.

Darwin, Charles (1866). Letter to Mary Boole. Letter 5307, Darwin Correspondence Project. University of Cambridge: <www.darwinproject.ac.uk/home>.

Darwin, Charles ([1871] 1906). *The Descent of Man*. London: Murray.

Darwin, Charles (1958). *The Autobiography of Charles Darwin*, ed. Nora Barlow. London: Collins.

Darwin, Francis (1887). *The Life and Letters of Charles Darwin*, 3 vols. London: Murray.

Dean, Dennis (2004). 'Charles Lyell', in Bernard Lightman (ed.), *The Dictionary of Nineteenth-Century British Scientists*. Bristol: Thoemmes Continuum, iii. 1281–7.

Desmond, Adrian (1989). *The Politics of Evolution*. Chicago: University of Chicago Press.

Desmond, Adrian, and James Moore (1991), *Darwin*. London: Michael Joseph.

Desmond, Adrian, and James Moore (2009). *Darwin's Sacred Cause: Race, Slavery and the Quest for Human Origins*. London: Allen Lane.

Dobzhansky, Theodosius (1962). *Mankind Evolving*. New Haven: Yale University Press.

England, Richard (2001). 'Natural Selection, Teleology, and the Logos: From Darwin to the Oxford Neo-Darwinists, 1859–1909', *Osiris* 16: 270–87.

Farrar, Frederick (1887). *The Bible, Its Meaning and Supremacy*. London: Longmans, Green and Co.

Freud, Sigmund (1922). *Introductory Lectures on Psycho-Analysis*, trans. Joan Riviere. London: Allen and Unwin.

Gilley, Sheridan (1981). 'The Huxley–Wilberforce Debate: A Reconsideration', in Keith Robbins (ed.), *Religion and Humanism*. Oxford: Blackwell, 325–40.

Gillispie, Charles (1959). *Genesis and Geology*. New York: Harper.

Goodwin, Charles ([1860] 1861). 'Mosaic Cosmogony', in Frederick Temple et al., *Essays and Reviews*. London: Longman, 207–53.

Gray, Asa (1860a). 'The Origin of Species by Means of Natural Selection', in Gray, *Darwiniana*, ed. A. Hunter Dupree. Cambridge, Mass.: Harvard University Press, 1963, 7–50.

Gray, Asa (1860b). 'Natural Selection not Inconsistent with Natural Theology', in Gray, *Darwiniana*, ed. Dupree. Cambridge, Mass.: Harvard University Press, 1963, 72–145.

Gray, Asa (1868). Letter to Charles Darwin, 25 May 1868, in *Darwin Correspondence*, ed. Frederick Burkhardt. Cambridge: Cambridge University Press, 2008, xvi. 536–7.

Gray, Asa (1963). 'Evolutionary Teleology', in *Darwiniana*, ed. Dupree. Cambridge, Mass.: Harvard University Press, 293–320.

Gregory, Frederick (1977). *Scientific Materialism in Nineteenth-Century Germany*. Dordrecht: Reidel.

Gregory, Frederick (1986). 'The Impact of Darwinian Evolution on Protestant Theology in the Nineteenth Century', in David Lindberg and Ronald Numbers (eds.), *God and Nature*. Berkeley and Los Angeles: University of California Press, 369–90.

Haught, John (2003). *Deeper than Darwin*. Boulder, Colo.: Westview Press.

Henslow, John (1860). Letter to Joseph Hooker, 10 May 1860, in *Darwin Correspondence*, ed. Burkhardt. Cambridge: Cambridge University Press, 1993, viii. 200–1.

Huxley, Thomas (1887). 'On the Reception of the "Origin of Species"', in Francis Darwin, *The Life and Letters of Charles Darwin*, 3 vols. London: Murray, ii. 179–204.

Huxley, Thomas ([1893/4] 1947). 'Evolution and Ethics: Prolegomena to the Romanes Lecture', in *Evolution and Ethics 1893–1943, by T. H. Huxley and Julian Huxley*. London: Pilot Press, 33–60.

James, Frank (2005). 'An "Open Clash between Science and the Church"? Wilberforce, Huxley and Hooker on Darwin at the British Association, Oxford, 1860', in David Knight and Matthew Eddy (eds.), *Science and Beliefs*. Aldershot: Ashgate, 171–93.

James, William (1999). *The Will to Believe and Other Essays in Popular Philosophy.* New York: Longmans, Green & Co.

James, William ([1907] 1975). *Pragmatism*, in *The Collected Works of William James.* Cambridge, Mass.: Harvard University Press.

Kepler, Johannes (1965). *Conversation with Galileo's Sidereal Messenger* (1610), trans. Edward Rosen. New York: Johnson Reprint Corporation.

Kohn, David (1989). 'Darwin's Ambiguity: The Secularization of Biological Meaning', *British Journal for the History of Science* 22: 215–39.

Kottler, Malcolm (1974). 'Alfred Russel Wallace, the Origin of Man, and Spiritualism', *Isis* 65: 145–92.

Lightman, Bernard (2009). *Evolutionary Naturalism in Victorian Britain.* Farnham: Ashgate, Variorum Series.

Livingstone, David (1987). *Darwin's Forgotten Defenders.* Grand Rapids, Mich.: Eerdmans.

Livingstone, David (1999). 'Science, Region, and Religion: The Reception of Darwinism in Princeton, Belfast, and Edinburgh', in Ronald Numbers and John Stenhouse (eds.), *Disseminating Darwinism.* Cambridge: Cambridge University Press, 7–38.

Livingstone, David (2009). '[The Myth] that Huxley Defeated Wilberforce in their Debate over Evolution and Religion', in Numbers (ed.), *Galileo Goes to Jail.* Cambridge, Mass.: Harvard University Press, 152–60.

Lucas, John (1979). 'Wilberforce and Huxley: A Legendary Encounter', *Historical Journal* 22: 313–30.

Lyell, Charles (1860). Letter to Charles Darwin, 19 June 1860, in *Darwin Correspondence*, ed. Burkhardt. Cambridge: Cambridge University Press, 1993, viii. 260.

McGrath, Alister (2011). *Darwinism and the Divine.* Chichester: Wiley-Blackwell.

Moore, Aubrey ([1889] 1890). 'The Christian Doctrine of God', in *Lux Mundi*, ed. Charles Gore. New York: United States Book Company, 47–90.

Moore, James (1979). *The Post-Darwinian Controversies.* Cambridge: Cambridge University Press.

Noakes, Richard (2004). 'Balfour Stewart', in Lightman (ed.), *The Dictionary of Nineteenth-Century British Scientists.* Bristol: Thoemmes, iii. 1909–13.

O'Leary, Don (2009). 'From the *Origin* to *Humani Generis*: Ireland as a Case-Study', in Louis Caruana (ed.), *Darwin and Catholicism.* London: T & T Clark, 13–26.

Powell, Baden ([1860] 1861). 'On the Study of the Evidences of Christianity', in Temple et al., *Essays and Reviews.*London: Longman, 94–144.

Roberts, Jon (1988). *Darwinism and the Divine in America* (Madison: University of Wisconsin Press).

Rogerson, John (2009). 'What Difference did Darwin Make? The Interpretation of Genesis in the Nineteenth Century', in Barton and Wilkinson 2009: 75–91.

Romanes, George (1896). *Thoughts on Religion.* London: Longmans, Green and Co.

Rupke, Nicolaas (1983). *The Great Chain of History.* Oxford: Oxford University Press.

Secord, James (2000). *Victorian Sensation.* Chicago: University of Chicago Press.

Sedgwick, Adam (1859). Letter to Charles Darwin, 24 November 1859, in *Darwin Correspondence*, ed. Frederick Burkhardt. Cambridge: Cambridge University Press, 1991, vii. 396–8.

Smith, Crosbie (1998). *The Science of Energy.* London: Athlone Press.

Sober, Elliott (2011). *Did Darwin Write the Origin Backwards?* Amherst NY: Prometheus Books.

Topham, Jonathan (2010). 'Biology in the Service of Natural Theology: Paley, Darwin, and the *Bridgewater Treatises*', in Denis Alexander and Ronald Numbers (eds.), *Biology and Ideology from Descartes to Dawkins.* Chicago: University of Chicago Press, 88–113.

Turner, Frank (1974). *Between Science and Religion*. New Haven: Yale University Press.

Tyndall, John ([1874] 1879). 'The Belfast Address', in *Fragments of Science: Essays, Addresses, and Reviews by John Tyndall*. London: Longmans, Green, and Co., ii. 137–203.

Wilberforce, Samuel ([1860] 1874). 'Darwin's Origin of Species', in *Essays Contributed to the Quarterly Review*. London: Murray, i. 52–103.

CHAPTER 12

....

EVOLUTION AND ETHICS IN VICTORIAN BRITAIN

....

MICHAEL RUSE

WHY EVOLUTION AND ETHICS?

THE place to start the discussion of evolution and ethics in the second half of the nineteenth century is with the collapse of Christianity around the middle of that century. I exaggerate of course. With the influx of major intellects like John Henry Newman, Catholicism was infused with new thinking that was still paying large dividends in the 1960s at the Second Vatican Council. Protestants too were searching for and finding new understandings and revival of thought. It would have come as a major shock to someone like Charles Hodge, principal of Princeton Theological Seminary, to learn that Christianity was collapsing. Indeed, one could make the opposite case. There are parts of the world still today—notably the American South and Midwest—where Christianity thrives as never before. But it is an exaggeration and not an outright untruth. By around 1850, many people in Great Britain, Europe, and the northern parts of the United States were finding increasingly that the Christian religion did not speak to their needs and indeed had little or no appeal to them (Vidler 1961; Chadwick 1966, 1970).

There were a number of reasons for this. First and most obviously there were the more intellectual or conceptual factors. For some decades now, scholars (particularly in Germany) had been looking at the biblical texts with a critical eye, examining their authenticity and veracity with respect to modern literary standards. So-called 'Higher Criticism' had a devastating effect, as increasingly it became apparent that the sacred writings of the religion—the Jewish Old Testament and the Christian New Testament—were very humanly composed books and less and less plausibly dictations taken down from on high. Particularly for Protestants, who had made the word of the Bible the central plank of their devotions, finding that the scriptures were not what they were once thought had a truly corrosive effect.

Combined with this were other factors, for instance an increasing sense that much that was claimed and demanded in the name of Christianity was simply not tenable. For instance, Charles Darwin—the English naturalist who will figure greatly in this discussion—lost his faith primarily because he could not reconcile his love of his father and of his brother—both acknowledged freethinkers—with gloomy predictions that those who reject the divinity of Christ are doomed to eternal damnation (Pallen and Pearn 2013). For educated people, who had been taught to think for themselves, the insistence that there were to be such constraints on the direction of such thinking was enough to drive them from the Christian faith. Probably also the rise of science played a role here, although one should be careful. Few in the nineteenth century showed a simple link between science and the loss of faith. The common pattern was that, having lost faith, people turned to science rather than vice versa (Budd 1977).

Paralleling the intellectual factors leading to the decline of Christianity were various social factors. The nineteenth century in Britain, Europe, and particularly the northern parts of the United States, increasingly saw a move away from the countryside and into the cities. Society was changing. No longer did people grow, live, and die within small, rural communities, where the squire and the clergyman—not only from the same class but often from the same family—led the way and set the norms. Now people were growing up in large cities, working as anonymous units in large factories, where the authority figures were distant and rather hostile. Where the culture was very different from that of their grandparents. A census of churchgoing in England and Wales in 1851 found that more than half of the population stayed home on Sundays. Now people were looking in their leisure time, not for church-based activities, but for more secular activities. It is no surprise that it is around this time we start to see the growth of organized, professional sports. It was not just that people were finding Christianity to be wrong but more it was increasingly becoming irrelevant (Hoppen 1998).

Yet, as every thoughtful commentator noted, matters could not be left there. Christianity was seen as having provided an essential support to the social fabric, particularly in the ways in which it prescribed moral and social mores. Often, almost paradoxically, those who led the way against Christianity as a satisfactory belief system were, in order to provide ongoing moral and social training, at the front of those insisting on Bible readings in secular education (Desmond 1997). The empire-building Victorians were not too much given to existential worrying, but one hears the cry of Nietzsche: 'God is dead'. Frederic Myers, poet and classicist, knew his audience when he wrote on the death of the novelist George Eliot (in 1880).

> I remember how, at Cambridge, I walked with her once in the Fellows' Garden of Trinity, on an evening of rainy May; and she, stirred somewhat beyond her wont, and taking as her text the three words which have been used so often as the inspiring trumpet-calls of men—the words *God, Immortality, Duty*—pronounced, with terrible earnestness, how inconceivable was the *first*, how unbelievable the *second*, and yet how peremptory and absolute the *third*. Never perhaps, have sterner accents affirmed the sovereignty of impersonal and unrecompensing Law. I listened, and night fell; her grave, majestic countenance turned toward me like a sibyl's in the gloom; it was as though she withdrew from my grasp, one by one, the two scrolls of promise, and left me the third scroll only, awful with inevitable fates. And when we stood at length and parted amid that columnar circuit of the forest trees, beneath the last twilight of starless skies, I seemed to be gazing, like Titus at Jerusalem, on vacant seats and empty halls—on a sanctuary with no Presence to hallow it, and heaven left lonely of a God. (Myers 1881, 62)

Increasingly, people turned to possible religion substitutes, especially as substitutes for the moral guidance that the Christian religion was believed to offer. It was nigh inevitable that evolution offered itself as an attractive alternative. It was after all, just like Christianity, a story of origins. It was also seen to be a story, just like Christianity, that had the arrival of humankind as the culmination and meaning of everything. It was also seen as something that could substitute at the social level (Ruse 2005). It is in the second half of the nineteenth century that we see the growth of the great natural history museums. Often consciously modelled on medieval churches—for instance the Royal Ontario Museum in Toronto, Canada, is an almost-perfect facsimile of the Norman-style Durham Cathedral in the north of England—these were places where families could go in their leisure time (particularly on Sundays) and see wonderful panoramas of the evolutionary chain. Panoramas going from the simple up to the complex and ultimately to humankind, fleshed out (to use an inappropriate metaphor) by all of those wonderful fossil dinosaur finds being brought back from the American and Canadian West.

Above all, evolution was seen as something that could offer moral directives for this new age, just as Christianity had offered moral directives for older ages.

HERBERT SPENCER

Speaking purely scientifically, Charles Darwin was and is the key figure in the history of evolutionary thinking (Ruse 1999, 2013). This is thanks to his great work, *On the Origin of Species*, published in 1859, where he introduced his theory of evolution through natural selection. Drawing on ideas of the Reverend Thomas Robert Malthus, Darwin noted that many more organisms are born than can possibly survive and reproduce. There will consequently be a struggle for existence and more importantly for reproduction. All natural populations carry reserves of heritable variation. There will thus be a natural winnowing or selection, as only some organisms get through to parent future generations. Most importantly the successful, or the 'fitter', will be different (with respect to the heritable variation) from the unsuccessful, or the 'unfit', and this will lead to ongoing change. Significantly, this change will not be random but will be of a kind that aids the winners in their success. One therefore gets the development of what are known as 'adaptations', design-like features such as the hand and the eye, those very items at the centre of the argument from design. In his later book on our own species, the *Descent of Man*, published in 1871, Darwin had much to say about morality and its evolution. This must however wait until later, for at the time, both with respect to morality specifically and to evolution generally, Darwin took somewhat of a back seat to his fellow Englishman Herbert Spencer. It was the latter whose thinking about evolution and ethics dominated the discussions of the second half of the nineteenth century, and so therefore it is appropriate to begin with him (Richards 1987).

Although this was not a phrase that the Victorians themselves used, today this kind of thinking is often labelled 'Social Darwinism' (Hofstadter 1944). As we shall see, if any label is to be used it would better be 'Social Spencerianism'. But by any name, what is it that we are talking about? There is a popular view about the nature of this traditional evolutionary ethics; but, although there is certainly truth in this view, the full story is somewhat more complex (Ruse 2009). The popular belief is that evolutionary ethicists took the Darwinian process of evolutionary change and transferred it directly into the social world. Since Darwinism focuses on a struggle for existence with the subsequent success of but a few, the fit, it is therefore thought that evolutionary ethics consists of transfers of the struggle to society, combined with exhortations to approve of such a transfer and to facilitate its success. In other words, it is thought that traditional evolutionary ethics endorses what is known as a laissez-faire view of society, where government restrictions are kept to a bare minimum, and where natural forces (meaning natural social and economic forces) are allowed full and unfettered scope. In short, the popular view is that Social Darwinism is little more than a relabelling of nineteenth-century liberalism, the creed of the Manchester businessman. It is little wonder, therefore, that this philosophy, if we may so call it, found much favour amongst the industrialists of North America—notably the founder of Standard Oil, John D. Rockefeller I, and the no-less-important and influential founder of US steel, Andrew Carnegie.

We can certainly find strong endorsement of laissez-faire economic principles in the writings of Herbert Spencer. His first book, *Social Statics*, published in 1851, was virtually a textbook on the subject. He was against all kinds of government interference, even arguing with that if shipowners need lighthouses to avoid wrecking, then it is for them to provide them rather than any central authority!

> We must call those spurious philanthropists, who, to prevent present misery, would entail greater misery upon future generations. All defenders of a Poor Law must, however, be classed among such. That rigorous necessity which, when allowed to act on them, becomes so sharp a spur to the lazy and so strong a bridle to the random, these pauper's friends would repeal, because of the wailing it here and there produces. Blind to the fact that under the natural order of things, society is constantly excreting its unhealthy, imbecile, slow, vacillating, faithless members, these unthinking, though well-meaning, men advocate an interference which not only stops the purifying process but even increases the vitiation—absolutely encourages the multiplication of the reckless and incompetent by offering them an unfailing provision, and *discourages* the multiplication of the competent and provident by heightening the prospective difficulty of maintaining a family. (Spencer 1851, 323–4)

However, at once we find that matters are a little more complex than this, not the least being that, when he wrote *Social Statics*, Spencer was only in the process of becoming an evolutionist. Moreover, as and when he did become an evolutionist, he was never a very enthusiastic Darwinian evolutionist. Spencer thought that the main cause of evolutionary change is so-called Lamarckism, the inheritance of acquired characteristics, and although it was he who gave natural selection its alternative name of the 'survival of the fittest', he always thought selection had but a minor role (Spencer 1862). Indeed, Spencer was of the opinion that by the time we come to humankind, selection has practically fallen away entirely and is no longer very significant in developmental processes (Spencer 1852). The Malthusian struggle leads to greater effort and with this comes improvement of features. Combining this conclusion with the very Victorian belief that organisms have only a limited quantity of vital bodily fluid, which can go either into making offspring or bigger and better brain cells, Spencer concluded that humankind, at least English and Scottish humankind—like everyone else, including Darwin, he was troubled by the reckless proliferation of the Irish—has reached a point of low reproduction and major intellectual capacity.

It is certainly true that Spencer thought that what we should be doing is promoting evolutionary workings, and there is certainly a carry-through from those earlier views about the need for harsh, near-libertarian measures to keep society functioning properly, but to him the key to understanding evolution—indeed the key to understanding virtually everything—was the very popular nineteenth-century notion of progress (Spencer 1857). As with the emergence of intellectually gifted humankind, Spencer saw everything in a state of upward rise—in biology, the monad to man, as they used to say—and this was bound up with the way in which he saw things developing. The Spencerian mark of upward rise is a move from simplicity to complexity, or what he liked to call a move from homogeneity to heterogeneity. In society (and Spencer was a great enthusiast for analogies between the organic and social), Spencer saw progress as involving a move from a simple, pre-urban society to the sophisticated societies that, by mid-century, he saw around him. Such societies, in line with Adam Smith's enthusiasm for the division of labour, had many different roles for many different people. They were vibrant, successful, and above all diverse and complex.

From this it all followed naturally that Spencerian moral directives lead to the production of the very kind of world within which he and his fellow Victorians were living! What is interesting, although perhaps to be expected, is that where and when Spencer saw conflict as standing in the way of the production of this kind of world, then in the name of evolution he opposed it. Towards the end of the nineteenth century, Britain and Germany in particular started to engage in the horrendous arms race that ended in the second decade of the twentieth century in the fields of Belgium and northern France. Although he saw the virtues of war in the early stages of societal development, Spencer was always opposed to this kind of potentially destructive activity in industrialized societies, thinking that competition between states too often led away from such things as free trade and the greater success of Victorian industrialism. Probably reflecting Quaker influences in his childhood, Spencer could not see that bigger and better arms production was the end point of human excellence. He made himself very unpopular by his strong opposition to the jingoism surrounding the Boer War.

Influence

To the modern reader, Spencer's writings—and there were many and almost invariably of great length—are the sorts of things that give the Victorians a bad name. They are tedious and repetitious in the extreme, jargon laden to the point of despair. But they spoke to the times and were picked up enthusiastically, not just in Britain, but all around the world. Whenever one hears about the spread of evolutionary ideas, although the name of Darwin is usually invoked, even casual inspection rapidly reveals that it is Spencer's thinking that is making its way forward. Nowhere did this happen with greater enthusiasm than in the United States of America. Moreover here, indeed, we do find those who exemplify the traditional reading of Social Darwinism, meaning unfettered enthusiasm for laissez-faire social and economic policies. It is a harsh world out there, nature gives nothing willingly, and thus we must labour without end to supply our needs, and slackers who do not pull their weight cannot be tolerated. This is the repeated theme of the Yale sociologist William Graham Sumner. 'Man is born under the necessity of sustaining the existence he has received by an onerous struggle against nature, both to win what is essential to his life and to ward off what is prejudicial to it. He is born under a burden and a necessity. Nature holds what is essential to him, but she offers nothing gratuitously. He may win for his use what she holds, if he can' (Sumner 1914, 17). This kind of thinking is also to be found in more popular culture, often in fictional form. There have been few American novels to rival the success of Jack London's story, *The Call of the Wild* (1903), about a domestic dog transplanted to the Canadian North and its subsequent struggles and eventual success. In itself, it is a thrilling story, but a major part of its appeal is the naked depiction of nature red in tooth and claw, combined with the author's obvious enthusiasm for such a state of affairs. The physical world is tough, but the battle ultimately comes down to strife for supremacy among one's fellows. Morality thus defined—Thrasymachus would have felt at home here—is a social phenomenon, with the rules governing behaviours between individuals of the same type.

Reinforcing the claim that an evolutionary approach to ethics came into being as a substitute or alternative for the more traditional Christian ethics is this very way in which evolutionary ethics was supposed to speak to the needs of modern, urban, industrial society. Laissez-faire, division of labour, free trade. But nothing is ever entirely new, and evolutionists of all people should expect that the new owes much to the old. By intention or otherwise, we fully expect that evolutionary ethics would take on some of the more prominent aspects of traditional ethics. One of the best known, one might say notorious, features of Christian ethics is the way that shared norms, most prominently the Love Commandment—you should love your neighbour as yourself—get such very different interpretations in different hands. In the First World War, good Christian pastors in Germany prayed to the Lord to smite the English and preserve the Germans, whereas good Christian vicars in England prayed to the Lord to smite the Germans and preserve the English! Today, in America, we find Christians differing bitterly over birth control, abortion, homosexuality, and capital punishment.

Likewise, traditional evolutionary ethicists of the Spencerian ilk differed in their understanding of the norms promoted by the evolutionary process. The co-discoverer of natural selection, Alfred Russel Wallace, moved from materialism (translated into evolution) in his youth to spiritualism (translated into evolution) in middle and old age. What caused human features was thus naturalistic at first and anything but at second. Yet the form of those features was unchanged. He was ever an ardent socialist (as a young man he had heard and been much impressed by the Scottish mill owner Robert Owen), and for all of his long life he promoted such socialism in the name of evolution (Wallace 1900, 1905). Analogously, the exiled Russian prince Peter Kropotkin (1902) argued for anarchy, maintaining that there is a naturally evolved sentiment promoting 'mutual aid' amongst all organisms, including humans. If biology is given free run, there will be no need of oppressive, centralized governments. At the other end of the spectrum, amongst those who warmed to some form of laissez-faire economic policy, not all were keen on the dark visions warmly embraced by people like Sumner. Industrialists like Andrew Carnegie were always much keener to stress the success of the successful in the struggle than the failure of the unsuccessful (Russett 1976). This of course was self-promotion, because they themselves were the best exemplifications of what could happen if nature worked right! It is for this reason that when Carnegie turned to philanthropy, he promoted the foundation of public libraries. Such institutions were places where poor-but-gifted children could go and better themselves, thereby rising in and improving the social system.

Philosophers talking about morality like to distinguish two levels, namely the level of action or prescription—often known as normative or substantive ethics—and the level of justification—often known as meta-ethics. Thus far, we have been considering normative ethics. What should one do? Turn now to matters of meta-ethics. Why should one do what one should do? We have already in our hands the foundation endorsed by Spencer and his followers (Sumner, Carnegie, and a host of lesser-known enthusiasts across the globe). To a person, they saw the evolutionary process as upwardly rising, as progressive, showing increased value down through the ages. Humans are the apotheosis of the process. It is clear that 'the possession of social power in any society or in any generation, produces social movement, with expansion, reiterated new achievement, social hope and enthusiasm, with all that we call progress; and that this movement is so directed that degradation is behind it' (Sumner 1914, 150).

In Spencerian terminology, we humans are the paradigm or touchstone of heterogeneity. We are the most valued, and therefore all action flows from and is justified by this undoubted fact. Humans are at the top of the ladder and morally it is our duty to preserve our status and perhaps even to improve it. 'The problem is not to account for degradation, because if we relax our efforts we shall fall back into it. The problem is how to maintain the effort and develop the power so as to keep up the movement away from it' (Sumner 1914, 150). Although Spencer was no leader in this respect, more than one sympathizer took up the call for improvement, arguing moral duties point towards the need to direct human breeding. So-called 'eugenicists', who looked back to the work of Spencer's contemporary and Darwin's cousin, Francis Galton, argued strenuously that unless we make conscious efforts to control unbridled sexual licence, humankind is doomed (Kevles 1985). I note without commenting on the paradox that Social Darwinism has now evolved to the point where, far from enthusiastic embrace of laissez-faire, we are in the murky world where the state is urged to interfere in the most intimate of human desires and actions. Spencer spotted this and it was a factor in his unease with the practice.

Criticisms

The decline and fall of Spencerian-type ethics was great and rapid. There were many reasons, not all entirely to be laid at the feet of Spencer himself. Eugenics, for instance, suffered greatly in reputation when the Third Reich took up selective breeding and culling with unseemly enthusiasm and ghastly consequences. However, there was quite enough explicit criticism to have ruined Spencer's reputation for the whole of the twentieth century. Most famously, at the beginning of the twentieth century, the Cambridge philosopher G. E. Moore (1903) was withering in his critique. He argued that Spencer's ethics is the classic case of committing the so-called 'naturalistic fallacy', where one tries illicitly to explain non-natural moral claims in terms of natural phenomena. Moore argued that any attempt to understand morality (speaking now at the substantive level) in terms of the facts of evolution is bound to come crashing down.

As has often been pointed out, in major respects what Moore was offering was a version of the kind of argument to be found in David Hume (1739–40), who complained that too often people talk in terms of matters of fact ('is' statements) and then switch without acknowledgement to talk about matters of value ('ought' statements). Moore's direct inspiration however was his own teacher, the Cambridge philosopher Henry Sidgwick. This major figure waged a long and strenuous battle against the sort of thinking represented by Herbert Spencer. In the very first issue of today's most prestigious of philosophical journals, *Mind*, Sidgwick (1876) argued with devastating force against Spencer's ethical argumentation. He took apart Spencer's claims about substantive ethics, and came close to ridiculing

Spencer's thinking about justification. Specifically, Sidgwick argued that there is absolutely no reason to think that more complex things, particularly complex societies, are going to be in any significant respect better than less complex things, including less complex societies. The Spencerian move from homogeneity to heterogeneity is at best vacuous and worst pernicious.

> [T]he most prominent characteristic of the advanced development of any organism is the specialization—or, as Mr Spencer calls it, 'differentiation'—of the functions of its different parts. Obviously the more this is effected, the more 'definite coherent heterogeneity' will be realised in the organism and in its relations to its environment. But obviously too, this involves *pro tanto* a proportionally less degree of variety and complexity in the life of each individual member of the society whose functions are thus specialised; and their life becoming narrow and monotonous must become according to our present hypothesis, less happy. This result has often been noticed by observers of the minute sub-division of labour which is a feature of our industrial progress. (Sidgwick 1876, 60–1)

In any case, there is no real reason to think of evolution as progressive, and certainly not progressive in any sense that points to an increase in value. In other words, any foundations that Spencer promoted were being read into the evolutionary process rather than directly out of it. There is simply no reason to turn to evolution for philosophical insight about the nature of morality.

Sidgwick's thinking was paralleled a few years later by Darwin's great supporter Thomas Henry Huxley (grandfather of the novelist Aldous Huxley). Huxley was close to Spencer, and indeed it was probably Spencer rather than Darwin who first convinced him of the truth of evolution. It is not surprising therefore that it took some time for Huxley to make an open and public break with his friend. However, pressure was building right through the 1870s, because by then Huxley was deeply involved in science education as well as being a consultant for the government on technical and scientific matters. He was therefore strongly committed to the virtues of the state and of central planning, very much in opposition to the laissez-faire views that always hovered over Spencer (T. H. Huxley 1871). Somewhat amusingly, in retirement the aged Huxley moved to the seaside resort of Eastbourne—a town that is the butt of many jokes about its being the last earthly residence of middle-class Britons before moving on to (we hope) higher things—where he cultivated a garden of which he was clearly intensely proud. Anything further from an unplanned 'state of nature' it would be hard to imagine.

By this closing phase of his life, Huxley had come right out in opposition to Spencerian-type thinking about morality. The garden figures prominently in the prolegomenon to a lecture given in 1893, 'Evolution and Ethics', where Huxley made virtually the same points hammered in by Sidgwick. (One should say that, although Sidgwick may have been first, Huxley's thinking was far clearer and more direct. There is little surprise that to this day, it is he who is always quoted as the great opponent of Social Darwinism.) At the substantive level, Huxley denied absolutely that evolution gives us any insights into proper action. More Darwinian than Spencer, Huxley pointed to the adaptations evolution has produced to help organisms succeed in the struggle for existence. The lion and tiger are superbly equipped carnivores, but no one would suggest that they are a model for human action. As Huxley pointed out, too often people pick and choose among adaptations in order to make their case. Circular arguments run rife, as people read in precisely the conclusions that they hope to extract. In fact, of course, the products of evolution are not even neutral. The aggression and force are precisely the attributes that a decent morality repudiates. Evolution in major respects is anti-moral.

The aged Huxley did not have a great deal of time for progress either. Earlier, he had been an enthusiast for the idea. But by the final decades of the nineteenth century, undoubtedly weighed down by his own periodic, crushing depressions as well as tragedies (the loss of children) in his family life, it was becoming more and more clear that building Jerusalem was going to take a lot more time and effort than possessed by the Victorians. The poverty and crime and dirt of the great cities showed that, heterogeneous though they may have been, only the morally blind could judge them perfect or even very far advanced in the respects that really matter. This anti-progress sentiment was picked up by the novelist H. G. Wells, who trained under Huxley as a biology teacher. The famous early novel *The Time Machine* (1895) tells of two future races, descended from today's humans. There are the above-ground-living Eloi, beautiful but stupid, and there are the below-ground-living Morlocks, intelligent but ugly and evil (they farm the Eloi for food). Degeneration was the theme of the day, and it is no wonder that Huxley, like Sidgwick, concluded that evolutionary progress is chimerical, at most a frail reed on which to base one's ethical prescriptions.

CHARLES DARWIN

Given the combined assault of philosophy and biology, the approach taken by Spencer and his followers towards questions of morality represented for many years the epitome of the way not to answer questions of great significance to humankind. Huxley's grandson Julian Huxley (the older brother of Aldous Huxley), author of a revealing book *Religion without Revelation* (1927), tried to reinvigorate the Spencerian approach, finding in evolution moral norms to replace those of conventional religion (J. S. Huxley 1943). At once, Moore's student C. D. Broad swung into action, bringing critical guns to bear. And once again, the journal *Mind* was the forum used to attack evolutionary ethics (Broad 1944). Well to the second half of the last century, Herbert Spencer on ethics was taken to be platonic form of how not to do philosophy. It was not just that his thinking was wrong but that somehow it was intellectually unclean. Rather like the philosophical equivalent of making a bad smell at a vicarage tea party.

And yet, today there is a vigorous philosophical movement determined to relate moral thinking and action to our evolutionary biology (Ruse 2009)! Obviously, we cannot be at the end of the story about evolution and ethics in the second half of the nineteenth century. Why should we be, for thus far we have ignored almost entirely the very large elephant in the room, namely Charles Darwin himself? Let us therefore turn to his thinking, specifically to his *Descent of Man* where, as noted, he had much to say about ethics. As we do so, observe that this attention is in itself significant, contrasting very much with the treatment of religion which is cursory and dismissive. Following David Hume, Darwin regarded religion as somewhat of a by-product of human nature and without cognitive significance (Ruse 2008). Ethics was different. Darwin, like his fellow Victorians, took the subject very seriously indeed and consequently his discussion was detailed and thoughtful.

And different. To see this, let us divide the discussion into three parts. First, let us ask: What was Darwin's thinking about morality? Second, let us ask: What was the scientific backing that Darwin gave to his thinking? Third, with an eye to the present as much as to the past, let us ask: What philosophical implications might be drawn either by Darwin himself or by his contemporaries?

Darwin on Morality

In one sense, Darwin's thinking was fairly conventional. The most popular mid-Victorian ethical theory was utilitarianism, the moral philosophy that elevates above all others the so-called 'greatest happiness principle'. 'You ought to promote the greatest happiness, and the least unhappiness, for the greatest number of people.' Sidgwick subscribed to a form of utilitarianism and before him there was John Stuart Mill, whose famous essay on the topic appeared in 1863. Mill was not the first to hold this philosophy. Jeremy Bentham was a famous precursor and there were others in the eighteenth century, including (and perhaps historically relevantly) Darwin's grandfather and fellow evolutionist Erasmus Darwin. In the words of the earlier Darwin, the progress of evolution 'is analogous to the improving excellence observable in every part of the creation such as the progressive increase of the wisdom and happiness of its inhabitants' (E. Darwin 1794–6, 509).

Charles Darwin gave the philosophy a little bit of a biological twist. 'The term, general good, may be defined as the term by which the greatest possible number of individuals can be reared in full vigour and health, with all their faculties perfect, under the conditions to which they are exposed' (Darwin 1871, i. 98). But, to be candid, Darwin did not show much interest in exploring precisely what his position might mean in practical terms. One suspects he thought no explicit statement was needed for the obvious answers—answers couched in terms acceptable to an upper-middle-class Englishman, one with liberal inclinations. We know that Darwin was filled with a hatred of slavery, and that unlike many of his countrymen he supported the northern states in the Civil War. This said, Darwin was strongly in favour of capitalism and regarded with great trepidation proposals that working men should be allowed to form unions. In his opinion, and that of his family and class, this would have violated sound economics, not to mention being an unwanted intrusion on the liberties of the owners of factories and similar industrial enterprises. To a Swiss correspondent he wrote about 'the rule insisted on by all our Trades-Unions, that all workmen,—the good and bad, the strong and weak,—sh[oul]d all work for the same number of hours and receive the same wages. The unions are also opposed to piece-work,—in short to all competition. I fear that Cooperative Societies, which many look at as the main hope for the future, likewise exclude competition. This seems to me a great evil for the future progress of mankind.' Adding, perhaps with more hope than conviction: 'Nevertheless under any system, temperate and frugal workmen will have an advantage and leave more offspring than the drunken and reckless.'[1]

Where Darwin did start to show crucial and inventive insight was in his understanding that the underlying key to morality, particularly considered at the biological level, is some

---

[1] This is from a letter, as yet unpublished by the Darwin Correspondence Project, from Darwin to Heinrich Fick, a law professor at the University of Zurich, on 26 July 1872. See Weikert (1995) for a full transcription.

element of natural sociability. Most particularly, it has to be adaptive that we humans feel that we should get on with our fellows and that we have the ability to do so.

> It has often been assumed that animals were in the first place rendered social, and that they feel as a consequence uncomfortable when separated from each other, and comfortable whilst together; but it is a more probable view that these sensations were first developed, in order that those animals which would profit by living in society, should be induced to live together, in the same manner as the sense of hunger and the pleasure of eating were, no doubt, first acquired in order to induce animals to eat. The feeling of pleasure from society is probably an extension of the parental or filial affections, since the social instinct seems to be developed by the young remaining for a long time with their parents; and this extension may be attributed in part to habit, but chiefly to natural selection. With those animals which were benefited by living in close association, the individuals which took the greatest pleasure in society would best escape various dangers, whilst those that cared least for their comrades, and lived solitary, would perish in greater numbers. With respect to the origin of the parental and filial affections, which apparently lie at the base of the social instincts, we know not the steps by which they have been gained; but we may infer that it has been to a large extent through natural selection. (Darwin 1871, i. 80)

Note incidentally, an important point that will be mentioned again shortly, that not only is it natural selection that causes all of this, but that the most crucial point seems to stem from 'parental and filial affections'.

Darwin realized that one had to go beyond this, and here he showed his background training and reading. As a young man he met and then read the works of James Mackintosh, Scottish lawyer and ethical philosopher, and had read Archdeacon Paley on moral philosophy when at Cambridge (Darwin 1969). So Darwin knew much about the basic moves needed for a full philosophical understanding of morality. In particular, Darwin was fully aware that morality is not just unreflective action, but at some level relies on conscious deliberation leading to action. In more modern language, one can say that Darwin appreciated that we have first-order desires, and then there are second-order reflections and thinking about these desires, leading to actions to tackle problems. This is much bound up with the notion of conscience. Darwin had read Hume on animal reasoning and, from his earliest years, particularly from his earliest years as an evolutionist (that is to say the late 1830s), he saw a continuity between apes and humans. But he realized and stressed in the *Descent of Man* that it is the ability to reflect at second-order level that distinguishes moral beings, like humans, from mere unreflective animals. 'The following proposition seems to me in a high degree probable—namely, that any animal whatever, endowed with well-marked social instincts, would inevitably acquire a moral sense or conscience, as soon as its intellectual powers had become as well, or nearly as well developed, as in man' (1871, i. 71–2).

To be honest, one might suspect that with all of this worrying about reflecting rather than getting on with things, Darwin is starting to sound rather more Germanic and British, that is to say more Kantian than Humean. Not much room here for a philosophy that calmly decrees that 'reason is the slave of passions'! Kant obsessed about reasoning and reflection, and it seems that nothing good can come from brute emotion. As it happens, Darwin did read Kant's *Metaphysics of Morals* a year or two before he wrote the *Descent of Man*, and, sounding rather like George Eliot at her most earnest, actually quoted one of Kant's more purple passages on the subject of morality. 'Duty! Wondrous thought, that workest neither by fond insinuation, flattery, nor by any threat, but merely by holding up thy naked law in the soul, and so extorting for thyself always reverence, if not always obedience; before whom all appetites are dumb, however secretly they rebel; whence thy original?' (1871, i. 70). In truth, however, unlike the novelist, Darwin was never really that attracted to Kant's philosophy. Apart, from anything else, for the sage of Königsberg, the key to understanding morality is that it has a kind of necessity, stemming from the conditions of rational beings living together. To put the matter in a jocular fashion but no less truthfully, if we were to find intelligent beings living socially on Andromeda, then for Kant they would be thinking and behaving in just the ways that one would expect of late eighteenth-century Germans living on the far reaches of the Baltic, revealing their Pietist childhoods.

Darwin showed his empiricist leanings by stating bluntly that had evolution gone otherwise, we might think that killing each other is the highest moral duty.

> It may be well first to premise that I do not wish to maintain that any strictly social animal, if its intellectual faculties were to become as active and as highly developed as in man, would acquire exactly the same moral sense as ours. In the same manner as various animals have some sense of beauty, though they admire widely-different objects, so they might have a sense of right and wrong, though led by it to follow widely different lines of conduct. If, for instance, to take an extreme case, men were reared under precisely the same conditions as hive-bees, there can hardly be a doubt that our unmarried females would, like the worker-bees, think it a sacred duty to kill their brothers, and mothers would strive to kill their fertile daughters; and no one would think of interfering.... The one course ought to have been followed, and the other ought not; the one would have been right and the other wrong; ... (Darwin 1871, i. 73–4)

There is still controversy among Darwin scholars about the extent to which Darwin was indebted to Hume directly. In the case of religion, we can trace influences with some confidence; the situation in morality is rather more complex. Direct influence or otherwise, Darwin was with the British empiricists all of the way. For him, as for Hume, not to mention Adam Smith and Edmund Burke, the key notion was always that of 'sympathy'—a kind of moral feeling or sentiment that one has for others. 'The aid which we feel impelled to give to the helpless is mainly an incidental result of the instinct of sympathy, which was originally acquired as part of the social instincts, but subsequently rendered...more tender and more widely diffused' (Darwin 1871, i. 86). Likewise: 'Nor could we check our sympathy, even at the urging of hard reason, without deterioration in the noblest part of our nature. The surgeon may harden himself whilst performing an operation, for he knows that he is acting for the good of his patient' (i. 169). For what it is worth, Hume also used surgery as a place where sympathy has a rough time operating.

The Evolution of Morality

Turn now to our second question, about how Darwin thought morality comes about. Darwin's chief mechanism of natural selection is the causal focal point here. On the surface, the discussion was fairly straightforward. Those humans or proto-humans who were moral, that is to say who had a moral sentiment or sense of sympathy towards their fellow humans, were ahead of the game when it came to survival and reproduction. Morality therefore is a straightforward adaptation just like hands and eyes. The fact that morality involves thinking and behaviour does not make it exceptional or peculiar. Darwin always recognized that adaptations go beyond the purely physical or morphological, and involve action and a certain amount of thought. However, obviously, there has to be more to the story than this. How can morality evolve and persist given the possibility of cheating or of avoiding one's duty? Darwin himself put the matter bluntly:

> It is extremely doubtful whether the offspring of the more sympathetic and benevolent parents, or of those who were the most faithful to their comrades, would be reared in greater numbers than the children of selfish and treacherous parents of the same tribe. He who was ready to sacrifice his life, as many a savage has been, rather than betray his comrades, would often leave no offspring to inherit his noble nature. The bravest men, who were always willing to come to the front in war, and who freely risked their lives for others, would on an average perish in larger numbers than other men. Therefore it seems scarcely possible (bearing in mind that we are not here speaking of one tribe being victorious over another) that the number of men gifted with such virtues, or that the standard of their excellence, could be increased through natural selection, that is, by the survival of the fittest. (Darwin 1871, i. 163)

Darwin grasped the nettle, giving this problem his fullest attention. For a start, he suggested that an important modifying factor might have been what is today known as 'reciprocal altruism'. You scratch my back and I'll scratch yours (Trivers 1971). 'In the first place, as the reasoning powers and foresight of the members became improved, each man would soon learn that if he aided his fellow-men, he would commonly receive aid in return. From this low motive he might acquire the habit of aiding his fellows; and the habit of performing benevolent actions certainly strengthens the feeling of sympathy which gives the first impulse to benevolent actions. Habits, moreover, followed during many generations probably tend to be inherited' (Darwin 1871, i. 163–4). But then Darwin went on to suggest—let us be more precise, apparently to suggest—that sometimes natural selection can work at the level of the group rather than the individual. It is in this way that it can bring about adaptations like morality. 'But there is another and much more powerful stimulus to the development of the social virtues, namely, the praise and the blame of our fellow-men. The love of approbation and the dread of infamy, as well as the bestowal of praise of blame, are primarily due, as we have seen in the third chapter, to the instinct of sympathy; and this instinct no doubt was originally acquired, like all the other social instincts, through natural selection' (i. 164).

He then elaborated:

> To do good unto others—to do unto others as ye would they should do unto you,—is the foundation-stone of morality. It is, therefore, hardly possible to exaggerate the importance during rude times of the love of praise and the dread of blame. A man who was not impelled by any deep, instinctive feeling, to sacrifice his life for the good of others, yet was roused to such actions by a sense of glory, would by his example excite the same wish for glory in other men, and would strengthen by exercise the noble feeling of admiration. He might thus do far more good to his tribe than by begetting offspring with a tendency to inherit his own high character. (Darwin 1871, i. 165)

It is thus that morality comes into being. One should add as one final point of clarification that although, perhaps naturally, Darwin's discussion focused on the biological, he did not want to argue that morality is only a matter of biology. At some level culture can come into play. 'But as man gradually advanced in intellectual power, and was enabled to trace the more remote consequences of his actions; as he acquired sufficient knowledge to reject baneful customs and superstitions; as he regarded more and more, not only the welfare, but the happiness of his fellow-men; as from habit, following on beneficial experience, instruction and example, his sympathies became more tender and widely diffused, so as to extend to the men of all races, to the imbecile, maimed, and other useless members of society, and finally to the lower animals,—so would the standard of his morality rise higher and higher' (i. 103). Today's best-known evolutionist, Harvard ant specialist and sociobiologist Edward O Wilson (1978), has argued that although culture is important in determining many of the ways in which we think and act, nevertheless this is all done on a bedrock or mattress of biology. This is Charles Darwin's position entirely.

Family Selection

We cannot leave the scientific discussion just yet. There is a major problem that needs our attention. Can it really be that selection works for the group at the expense of the individual? (In today's terminology, such selection is known as 'group selection', as opposed to 'individual selection'.) It will be useful at this point to pull back for a moment and to put the discussion in bigger context, in particular by mentioning thinking on this subject today. I do this not with the Whiggish intent of showing that Darwin was right (or wrong) judged by today's thinking, but rather to warn that it is difficult to discuss Darwin in a disinterested fashion given the heated discussion that still rages. The fact is that from Darwin down until the 1960s, with some few exceptions everyone thought that group selection can and does work often, especially in the social realm. For instance, the ethologist Konrad Lorenz (1966) argued that the reason why dogs do not fight to the death is because the survival of the loser benefits the species as a whole. Then opinion swung strongly the other way, with individual selection reigning supreme. Partly this was because individual selection unaided proved so very powerful; partly this was because of problems that seemed insoluble on the group perspective. Above all there was the problem that worried Darwin: cheaters. If everyone in a group is helping everyone else, at their own expense—you must add this caveat otherwise individual selection explains all—then a cheater who fails to help others is ahead, because it has its own help and that of others! And so the cheaters will win out in the struggle and soon everyone will be a cheater and group benefits have collapsed.

For most professional evolutionists today, this kind of reasoning is still definitive. When the just-mentioned Edward O. Wilson published a paper endorsing a group perspective, in immediate response almost 150 working evolutionists signed letters arguing against him (Nowak, Tarnita, and Wilson 2010; Pennisi 2011). In the non-scientific community however there is still considerable sympathy for group selection, and this does rather colour the picture painted of Darwin. I will make the case that Darwin was always an individual selectionist but it should be realized that while I will have the scientists with me, most philosophers and other students of the humanities would disagree strongly. It is idle to speculate too extensively on why there should be this divide between scientists and humanists—it is certainly not a divide over the nature of evolution itself—but it does reveal very different attitudes to the workings of nature. Speaking now of philosophers, particularly those in the analytic tradition, there has always been a wariness about Darwinism, perhaps because it was so enthusiastically picked up by the American pragmatists, who saw in the relativism and utility of selection the very idea at the centre of their own philosophy. Leading analytic philosophers like Bertrand Russell hated pragmatism, thinking it both epistemologically inadequate and socially dangerous. He did not have much more time for Darwin, although as a student of Sidgwick (he attended lectures on ethics) the real object of attack was Herbert Spencer and Darwin was a victim of guilt by association. Thinking the struggle for existence a sinister influence over the twentieth century, Russell showed empathy with a like antagonism that runs through the thinking of Ludwig Wittgenstein, who saw all evolutionary speculations in the Social Darwinian terms encountered in Europe in his youth. Darwin or Spencer, they are all equally culpable (Cunningham 1996). This understanding is true also of people like Karl Popper and Hannah Arendt (Beatty 2001).

Such uneasiness is found still today among many prominent analytic philosophers (Ruse 2012). There is an outright hostility to Darwin's ideas that not even an understandable distaste for the fundamentalist atheistic rhetoric of too many of his present-day supporters can quite explain. Even those prepared to accept Darwinism as a scientific theory however often want to ameliorate the harsh message of individual selection, wanting to see the world as a warmer, more holistic entity. God may not exist, but something must be done to soften the harsh message of the greatest cheerleader for individual selection. 'In a universe of blind physical forces and genetic replication, some people are going to get hurt, other people are going to get lucky, and you won't find any rhyme or reason in it, nor any justice. The universe we observe has precisely the properties we should expect if there is, at bottom, no design, no purpose, no evil and no good, nothing but blind, pitiless indifference' (Dawkins 1995, 133). Perhaps so, but at least group selection makes the passage through this vale of tears a little easier. (A recent book, giving a very different take on the analysis here, showing some ambivalence towards the whole Darwinian enterprise and certainly a strong commitment to group selection, is *Did Darwin Write the Origin Backwards?* by the distinguished philosopher Elliott Sober (Sober 2010).)

Against this background, picking up again on Darwin, we find that although his *Mind* article was mainly directed against Spencer, Sidgwick did not hesitate to take a swipe at Darwin on this score. He quoted Darwin himself on the ways in which cheaters might be expected to benefit at the expense of the rest of us, and took this as a refutation of Darwin's thinking. In the Darwinian world, the tribe can never take precedence. 'We require therefore some further explanation of the tendency of human character to take this particular line of change. For it will hardly do to reply that a tribe which manifested this tendency would necessarily flourish: the chances are so very much against the production of a tribe in which the individuals accidentally combine to maintain an individually unprofitable variation in one special direction' (Sidgwick 1876, 65).

This was very far from being a new challenge for Darwin. He had long worried about the individual–group selection problem (Ruse 1980). When he first discovered natural selection, and most particularly when he wrote about it in the *Origin of Species*, he stressed that ultimately it is the individual that counts. It is always one against all, and any evidence to the contrary must therefore be explained away. '[A]s more individuals are produced than can possibly survive, there must in every case be a struggle for existence, either one individual with another of the same species, or with the individuals of distinct species, or with the physical conditions of life' (Darwin 1859, 63). Quite why Darwin was so strong on this matter has been a matter of some debate. No doubt, from the first he saw the cheaters problem. However, one suspects strongly that he was influenced by his family and social background. He was the upper-middle-class son and grandson of industrialists. For Darwin, life is a battle where some win and some lose and that is all there is to it. It is surely interesting and pertinent to note that Alfred Russel Wallace always inclined to a group selection perspective and challenged Darwin repeatedly on this score. Wallace was, remember, an ardent socialist. Not so Darwin, whose family's motto—had not Erasmus Darwin already staked claim with *E conchis omnia*, or 'Everything from shells'—might have been taken straight from Adam Smith. 'It is not from the benevolence of the butcher, the brewer, or the baker that we expect our dinner, but from their regard to their own interest' (Smith 1976, 2A, 26–7).

Convictions are one thing and arguments another. Some cases that apparently support group selection got short shrift. Darwin simply dismissed them as by-products of the evolutionary process, where selection basically was not involved. Wallace made much of the sterility of hybrids like the mule, arguing that the lack of fertility is of benefit to the parental species. It is not in the interests of either horses or donkeys to have offspring that are not of their own species, and therefore natural selection promotes sterility for the benefit of the respective species. Darwin, to the contrary, simply argued that the mule's sterility is a by-product of normal physiological processes. It is sterile, not because of natural selection, but because the parental respective contributions to fertility simply don't mesh together in a working fashion.

But not all phenomena supposedly supporting group selection could be dismissed this readily. No one was going to say that the organization of the social insects—particularly the hymenoptera: the ants, bees, wasps—are by-products of natural selection. They work far too efficiently as groups for this to be so. The sterility of the workers had to be explained in terms of natural selection. Darwin was not so much worried about the production, at the physiological level, of sterility or that the sterile nest members might have features distinctive to them. He pointed out that breeders regularly castrate animals or kill them before they reproduce, and yet this does not pose a major problem to the breeding of desirable features in the non-reproducers. One simply goes back to the breeding stock and produces more offspring with the needed features. But why should sterility be produced in the first place? It seems that its only purpose can be the good of the group rather than for the individual. Darwin of course was hampered by not having an understanding of modern genetics. Today we (who think individual selection rules supreme) explain phenomena like this in terms of the ways in which sterile organisms share the same units of heredity, the genes, with their fertile relatives (Ruse 2006). Inasmuch as the relatives reproduce, the sterile organisms are doing so by proxy as it were. It is therefore an adaptation when sterile workers aid their fertile relatives to reproduce more than they otherwise would.

However, Darwin grasped the basic idea. He argued that, at some level, one has to think of the whole social insect unit, the nest or the hive, as an individual. Natural selection can work on it. This is not group selection as traditionally understood. For Darwin, as for today's evolutionists, interrelatedness was the crucial factor. One does not get organisms working together unless they are at some level part of a family. So if you want to say that Darwin endorsed some kind of family selection, then this is probably legitimate. At a personal level, Darwin would have seen this as no big extension. He himself was deeply embedded in family—and help given to a family member was part of the expected routine of life. He married a first cousin and it is clear that the union was welcomed by his father and hers because it kept the huge family fortune firmly within the interrelated group. Thus it is important to note that family selection was not group selection in the sense of organisms aiding unrelated species members. Darwin was always against this. (Remember how Darwin spoke of the 'extension of the parental or filial affections'.)

But surely, as we've already seen, when it came to humans Darwin had to admit that a form of group selection was operative? It was not the only factor. Apart from anything else, note the very peculiar fact that more than half of the *Descent of Man* is given over to an extended discussion of sexual selection. This is the secondary form of selection, with competition within species for mates—either through male combat (the antlers of the deer) or female choice (the tail feathers of the peacock). It is the epitome of individual selection and Darwin discusses it and then applies it directly to our own species—that is why men are big and strong and intelligent and women are (one still blushes to say) beings only half developed—and was invoked to counter Wallace who argued that many human characteristics cannot be explained by natural selection (with which Darwin agreed) and must be explained by spirit forces (with which Darwin emphatically disagreed). We have seen that Darwin also promoted a form of reciprocal altruism, and this is certainly something which benefits the individual rather than the group.

But he does seem to agree that the tribe can be the unit of selection. The key question then becomes: What is a tribe? Darwin is not quite as explicit on this subject as one might have wished, a function probably of the fact that although he was certainly not going to accept Wallace's views on the causal importance of spirits, it was a paper on human evolution that Wallace published in 1864 (before spiritualism) that inspired much of Darwin's thinking. In particular, in the context of human intelligence, Wallace wrote explicitly of selection between tribes. 'Tribes in which such mental and moral qualities were predominant, would therefore have an advantage in the struggle for existence over other tribes in which they were less developed, would live and maintain their numbers, while the others would decrease and finally succumb' (Wallace 1864, p. clxii). The debt is obvious. The trouble is that for Wallace it would not matter at all if a tribe were simply a group of unrelated individuals. He was fine with this. But what of Darwin who clearly, whatever the case here, had individualistic tendencies. Has he just accepted Wallace or has he taken over the language without truly making his own position clear? Does 'tribe' mean 'family'?

For Darwin, a tribe is certainly not a species. In the *Descent*, Darwin makes it clear that selection works for the tribe against the species. 'It is no argument against savage man being a social animal, that the tribes inhabiting adjacent districts are almost always at war with each other; for the social instincts never extend to all the individuals of the same species' (Darwin 1871, i. 85). But are the members interrelated? Darwin suggests that tribe members think they are. He quotes Spencer on the origin of religion, where tribe members think that 'names or nicknames given from some animal or other object to the early progenitors or founders of a tribe, are supposed after a long interval to represent the real progenitor of the tribe; and such animal or object is then naturally believed still to exist as a spirit, is held sacred, and worshipped as a god' (i. 66). Then, when talking of the members of one tribe being absorbed into another, Darwin refers to the historian of ancient law Henry Maine and his claim that after a while these absorbed members believe that 'they are the co-descendants of the same ancestors' (i. 159). Most pertinently, talking of superior intelligence and of how it leads to the invention of useful artifacts—although Darwin follows Wallace in suggesting that this intelligence and its consequences could be a very significant adaptive advantage in the struggle to survive and reproduce—he links the discussion right in with the point he made in the *Origin* about transmission of adaptations via close relatives.

> In a tribe thus rendered more numerous there would always be a rather better chance of the birth of other superior and inventive members. If such men left children to inherit their mental superiority, the chance of the birth of still more ingenious members would be somewhat better, and in a very small tribe decidedly better. Even if they left no children, the tribe would still include their blood-relations; and it has been ascertained by agriculturists that by preserving and breeding from the family of an animal, which when slaughtered was found to be valuable, the desired character has been obtained. (i. 161)

The tribe is starting to look very much like an extended family, and to gild the lily let us go back to Sidgwick's *Mind* article. Darwin read it and was much intrigued by it, somewhat irritated perhaps. He never wrote publicly about the article, but, in an as-yet-unpublished letter to his son George, Darwin took up the matter, making it very clear that, as far as he was concerned, tribes are not groups of unrelated individuals. They are akin to the nests or groups that we find in the social insects.

> To G. H. Darwin 27 April [1876]
> Down Beckenham Kent
> Ap.
> 27 th
> My dear George
> I send 'Mind'—it seems an excellent periodical—Sidgwicks article has interested me much.—
> It is wonderfully clear & makes me feel what a muddle-headed man I am.—I do not agree on one point, however, with him. He speaks of moral men arising in a tribe, accidentally, i.e. by so-called spontaneous variation; but I have endeavoured to show that such men are created by love of glory, approbation &c &c.—
> However they appear the tribe as a tribe will be successful in the battle of life, like a hive of bees or nest of ants.
> We are off to London directly, but I am rather bad. Leonard comes home on May 10 th!! Plans changed.

To sum up Darwin's thinking about the evolution of morality. It is natural, it is essentially biological, and it is produced by natural selection. It is in other words an adaptation. The claim here is that Darwin worked at the individual selection end of the spectrum rather than at the group selection end. If this be so, then we should understand Darwin as seeing the world as an empty place, without meaning or succour, but where nature's laws nevertheless come together to make for sentiments that promote group harmony and interests. For Richard Dawkins (2007), obviously, this is the other side of the coin to atheism. In Darwin's case, it is rather more complex. One can take an individual selectionist perspective and still believe in a god. Although he was not putting things in evolutionary terms, this was surely the position of Adam Smith with his famous reference to the 'Invisible Hand'. It was probably Darwin's also at the time of the writing of the *Origin*. By the *Descent*, he had become an agnostic (never an atheist); but his view of the world was always more cultural and social than Dawkins's bleaker, more metaphysical vision. It is in those terms that we should think about Darwin's thoughts on morality, those of a successful Victorian, rather than as a Nietzschian bellow of anger, defiance, and despair against a dead god.

Is This Relevant to Philosophy?

We come to the third and final question. What about the philosophical juice to be extracted from all this? For all that Darwin had read and continued to read works by and on philosophers, he was not a philosopher and his interests were not those of the philosopher. We should not expect to find, and we do not in fact find, a full and clarifying discussion about the philosophical implications of his scientific thinking on morality. Nevertheless we tease out a fair amount. We have already seen at the substantive level that he endorsed a form of utilitarianism. As it happens, Sidgwick was rather critical of Darwin on this matter, arguing that reproduction and the like is certainly not normally associated with happiness or things of worth. Savages have more offspring than Englishmen, sort of argumentation. I am not sure that Darwin would have been terribly troubled by this. He would probably have been happy to accept some of the emendations the Sidgwick would have made. Darwin would simply have insisted that, although obviously we don't normally think that reproduction is the only cause of human happiness, if happiness is not some level intimately involved in reproduction, the human species would have long gone extinct. For all of the somewhat commercial factors that led to his marriage to his first cousin, Emma Wedgwood, that it was long, fruitful, and incredibly happy obviously influenced his thinking here.

What about justification? What about questions at the meta-ethical level? Darwin simply does not speak to these matters nor would he have thought that he was obligated to do so. Yet, we can certainly glean a fair amount about where he did stand on these issues. As noted, although he was a progressionist, he was certainly not a progressionist in the Spencerian mode, thinking that there is a metaphysical force driving life up the scale until it reaches humankind (Ruse 1996). Darwin certainly did not see evolution as offering a justification for moral behaviour in this sort of way. He did think that evolution shows why some types of behaviour are sensible or otherwise. He was no full-blooded eugenicist, but like most of his fellows he thought that allowing the weaker members of society to breed more than the stronger members is a very bad thing. But this was not a matter of justifying the overall moral sentiment.

Ultimately, the simple and obvious answer is that Darwin thought that morality is natural and that that is an end to matters. As just noted, by the time he was writing the *Descent of Man*, Darwin did not believe in a God of any kind. So there was no divine backing to his thinking about morality. Would Darwin perhaps have accepted non-natural causes to explain morality, in the sort of way that someone like G. E. Moore accepted? It is impossible to say; but his rather pragmatic, empiricist attitude leads one to think that he would have thought them irrelevant and redundant. Does this then mean that Darwin thought that there were no justificatory factors, and that he was in today's terms a moral non-realist? Was Darwin an ethical sceptic, in the sense that he denied justification at all? Probably this is the best interpretation, although Darwin himself would have been very uncomfortable if one laid things out in stark terms. Darwin thought that morality was real and important. That was his starting point. He had no intention whatsoever of undermining morality. He just wanted to explain it as a natural phenomenon and leave it at that. And perhaps in Darwin's case that is what we should do also.

CONCLUSION

That seems to have been much the end of things in the nineteenth century. We know now that, for better or for worse, most of the discussion was moulded by drive to promote or augment the thinking of Spencer or to criticize it. Few, if any, took Darwin's thinking and used it to further philosophical discussion. Across the Channel in Germany, Frederick Nietzsche was certainly aware of the importance of providing naturalistic accounts of morality. He wrote:

> Fortunately I learned early to separate theological prejudice from moral prejudice and ceased to look for the origin of evil *behind* the world. A certain amount of historical and philological schooling, together with an inborn fastidiousness of taste in respect to psychological questions in general, soon transformed my problem into another one: under what conditions did man devise these value judgments good and evil? *and what value do they themselves possess?* Have they hitherto hindered or furthered human prosperity? Are they a sign of distress, of impoverishment, or the degeneration of life? Or is there revealed in them, on the contrary, the plenitude, force, and will of life, its courage, certainty future? ... We need a *critique* of moral values, *the value of these values themselves must first be called in question*—and for that there is needed a knowledge of the conditions and circumstances in which they grew, under which they evolved and changed. (Nietzsche 1887, Prologue, 3)

However, Nietzsche did not really follow this through in any greater detail and (like most people) he rather ran Darwin together with Spencer and, combining it with a general dislike of things English, had little good to say about Darwin and his thinking. And, even if we today see philosophical links between Darwin and Nietzsche, the German's intuitions were probably right. Culturally the two men are worlds apart.

The leitmotif of the general story about Charles Darwin and his thinking is one of delayed respect and appreciation. In his day, everyone praised Darwin for having given a definitive argument for the fact of evolution. Very few accepted his mechanism of natural selection in any great degree. It was not until the coming of Mendelian genetics in the twentieth century that people slowly realized that natural selection was the major force for evolutionary change. Today, although there are many qualifications, few professional evolutionists would argue with Darwin's enthusiasm for natural selection (Ruse and Travis 2009). It is seen as the major force for evolutionary change. It is not surprising that Darwin's thinking about morality rather reflects this overall history. Darwin put forward a case for the evolution of morality and most people agreed with him that morality is in some sense part of the overall human story. However, few took much interest in his thinking about the significance of natural selection. But in the last fifty years, with the triumph of natural selection generally, there has been a revived appreciation of Darwin's own theorizing on morality (Ruse 2009).

Today there is considerable interest, both in the actual ways in which morality might have evolved—the individual–group selection question is once again being debated—and about the implications that a naturally caused morality might have for our thinking on the big philosophical questions about ethics. On the one hand, at the substantive title level, many feel (contra Sidgwick) that a Darwinian approach throws considerable light on the ways in which we feel morally. Interestingly, some of the most fertile thinking in this direction has come from those who reject utilitarianism. For instance, the late John Rawls who promoted a form of neo-Kantianism, arguing that fairness is the key to morality, always saw evolutionary thinking as meshing with his position.

> In arguing for the greater stability of the principles of justice I have assumed that certain psychological laws are true, or approximately so. I shall not pursue the question of stability beyond this point. We may note however that one might ask how it is that human beings have acquired a nature described by these psychological principles. The theory of evolution would suggest that it is the outcome of natural selection; the capacity for a sense of justice and the moral feelings is an adaptation of mankind to its place in nature. As ethologists maintain, the behavior patterns of a species, and the psychological mechanisms of their acquisition, are just as much its characteristics as are the distinctive features of its bodily structures; and these patterns of behavior have an evolution exactly as organs and bones do. It seems clear that for members of species which lives in stable social groups, the ability to comply with fair cooperative arrangements and to develop the sentiments necessary to support them is highly advantageous, especially when individuals have a long life and are dependent on one another. These conditions guarantee innumerable occasions when mutual justice consistently adhered to is beneficial to all parties. (1971, 502–3)

Following on this almost-canonical work, others have explored the Darwinian implications in greater and greater details, often bringing to their aid the techniques and findings of modern game theory (Skyrms 1998, 2004).

On the other hand, at the meta-ethical level, equally many feel that Darwinism speaks to the pertinent issues. In particular, both non-realist and realists claim the support of Darwin—although sometimes, frankly, the differences seem more terminological than ontological. If Darwin is right, then (whatever your take on the individual–group selection controversy), in some basic sense morality is natural, meaning that it is tied in with human nature. One response to this is to say that you simply don't need any more (Ruse 1986). Morality is an adaptation like sexual desire, and there is no more to it than that. It exists purely to get us through life and on to the next generation and if it is successful that is all that needs to be said. It is subjective. Of course, you may think it is more—perhaps you have to think it is more if it is to work—but all such thoughts are without basis. 'Morality is an illusion put in place by your genes to make you a social cooperator' (Callebaut 1993, 437, in conversation with Michael Ruse). As noted, this is probably Darwin's position although he would never have put things this crudely and if challenged would probably have felt decidedly uncomfortable. It is not necessary to explore in too much detail every aspect of vital bodily functions.

Others agree that there is nothing 'out there', in the sense of objective non-natural properties (as suggested by Moore), but still think that Kant is not quite dead, and that morality has some real foundation in fact because of what we are and what we are bound to be as rational animals. And then, perhaps outlandishly (although not so much so if you think of the influence of the ultimate naturalist Aristotle), it has been suggested that a Darwinian approach meshes nicely with a Thomistic natural-law approach, and morality is seen as something natural, but where nature is something designed and made by God. So it is very real after all (Ruse 2010). Now is not the time to go in detail into these ongoing controversies, and certainly not to make judgements. It is enough to point to the continued relevance of Darwin's thinking.

To conclude. The second half of the nineteenth century saw considerable interest and debate in Britain about the relationship between evolution and ethics. The debate is interesting in its own right, throwing much light on the concerns of the later Victorians. Also the debate is interesting and relevant for the use that we might make of the ideas today. One hopes scholars will dig yet more deeply and broadly into these fascinating and ever-pertinent controversies.

References

Beatty, J., 2001. Hannah Arendt and Karl Popper: Darwinism, Historical Determinism, and Totalitarianism. In R. S. Singh, C. B. Krimbas, D. B. Paul, and J. Beatty (eds.), *Thinking About Evolution: Historical, Philosophical, and Political Perspectives*, pp. 62–76. Cambridge: Cambridge University Press.

Broad, C. D., 1944. Critical Notice of Julian Huxley's *Evolutionary Ethics. Mind* 53: 344–67.

Budd, S., 1977. *Varieties of Unbelief: Atheists and Agnostics in English Society 1850–1960.* London: Heinemann.

Callebaut, W., 1993. *Taking the Naturalistic Turn.* Chicago: University of Chicago Press.

Chadwick, O., 1966. *The Victorian Church. Part I.* London: A. and C. Black.

Chadwick, O., 1970. *The Victorian Church. Part II.* London: A. and C. Black.

Cunningham, S., 1996. *Philosophy and the Darwinian Legacy.* Rochester, NY: University of Rochester Press.

Darwin, C., 1859. *On the Origin of Species by Means of Natural Selection, or the Preservation of Favoured Races in the Struggle for Life.* London: John Murray.

Darwin, C., 1871. *The Descent of Man, and Selection in Relation to Sex.* London: John Murray.

Darwin, C., 1969. *Autobiography.* New York: Norton.

Darwin, E., 1794–6. *Zoonomia; or, the Laws of Organic Life.* London: J. Johnson.

Dawkins, R., 1995. *A River Out of Eden.* New York: Basic Books.

Dawkins, R., 2007. *The God Delusion.* New York: Houghton, Mifflin, Harcourt.

Desmond, A., 1997. *Huxley: Evolution's High Priest.* London: Michael Joseph.

Hofstadter, R., 1944. *Social Darwinism in American Thought,* rev. edn., Boston: Beacon Press.

Hoppen, K. T., 1998. *The Mid-Victorian Generation, 1846–1886 (The New Oxford History of England).* Oxford: Oxford University Press.

Hume, D., [1739–40] 1940. *A Treatise of Human Nature.* Oxford: Oxford University Press.

Huxley, J. S., 1927. *Religion without Revelation.* London: Ernest Benn.

Huxley, J. S., 1943. *Evolutionary Ethics.* Oxford: Oxford University Press.

Huxley, T. H., 1871. Administrative Nihilism. Reprinted in *Methods and Results,* pp. 251–89. London: Macmillan.

Huxley, T. H. [1893] 2009. *Evolution and Ethics,* ed. and introd. Michael Ruse. Princeton: Princeton University Press.

Kevles, D. J., 1985. *In the Name of Eugenics: Genetics and the Uses of Human Heredity.* New York: Knopf.

Kropotkin, P., [1902] 1955. *Mutual Aid.* Boston: Extending Horizons Books.

London, J., 1903. *The Call of the Wild.* New York: Macmillan.

Lorenz, K., 1966. *On Aggression.* London: Methuen.

Mill, J. S., 1863. *Utilitarianism.* London: Parker, Son, and Bourn.

Moore, G. E., 1903. *Principia Ethica.* Cambridge: Cambridge University Press.

Myers, F. W. H., 1881. George Eliot. *Century Magazine* 23: 57–64.

Nietzsche, F., 1887. *Zur Genealogie der Moral: Eine Streitschrift* [On the Genealogy of Morality: A Polemic]. Leipzig: Neumann.

Nowak, M. A., C. E. Tarnita, and E. O. Wilson, 2010. The Evolution of Eusociality. *Nature* 466: 1057–62.

Paley, W., [1785] 1819. *The Principles of Moral and Political Philosophy*. London: Rivington.

Pallen, M., and A. Pearn, 2013. Darwin and Religion. In M. Ruse (ed.), *The Cambridge Encyclopedia of Darwin and Evolutionary Thought*, pp. 211–17. Cambridge: Cambridge University Press.

Pennisi, E. 2011. Researchers Challenge E. O. Wilson Over Evolutionary Theory. <http://news. sciencemag.org/2011/03/researchers-challenge-e.-o.-wilson-over-evolutionary-theory? ref=hp>.

Rawls, J., 1971. *A Theory of Justice*. Cambridge, Mass.: Harvard University Press.

Richards, R. J., 1987. *Darwin and the Emergence of Evolutionary Theories of Mind and Behavior*. Chicago: University of Chicago Press.

Ruse, M., 1980. Charles Darwin and Group Selection. *Annals of Science* 37: 615–30.

Ruse, M., 1986. *Taking Darwin Seriously: A Naturalistic Approach to Philosophy*. Oxford: Blackwell.

Ruse, M., 1996. *Monad to Man: The Concept of Progress in Evolutionary Biology*. Cambridge, Mass.: Harvard University Press.

Ruse, M., 1999. *The Darwinian Revolution: Science Red in Tooth and Claw*. 2nd edn., Chicago: University of Chicago Press.

Ruse, M., 2005. *The Evolution–Creation Struggle*. Cambridge, Mass.: Harvard University Press.

Ruse, M., 2006. *Darwinism and Its Discontents*. Cambridge: Cambridge University Press.

Ruse, M., 2008. *Charles Darwin*. Oxford: Blackwell.

Ruse, M, (ed.) 2009. *Philosophy after Darwin: Classic and Contemporary Readings*. Princeton: Princeton University Press.

Ruse, M., 2010. *Science and Spirituality: Making Room for Faith in the Age of Science*. Cambridge: Cambridge University Press.

Ruse, M., 2012. Philosophy's Strain of Unevolved Thinking. *Chronicle of Higher Education*, 26 November.

Ruse, M. (ed.) 2013. *The Cambridge Encyclopedia of Darwin and Evolutionary Thought*. Cambridge: Cambridge University Press.

Ruse, M., and J. Travis (eds.), 2009. *Evolution: The First Four Billion Years*. Cambridge, Mass.: Harvard University Press.

Russett, C. E., 1976. *Darwin in America: The Intellectual Response, 1865–1912*. San Francisco: Freeman.

Sidgwick, H., 1876. The Theory of Evolution in Its Application to Practice. *Mind* 1: 52–67.

Skyrms, B., 1998. *Evolution of the Social Contract*. Cambridge: Cambridge University Press.

Skyrms, B., 2004. *The Stag Hunt and the Evolution of the Social Contract*. Cambridge: Cambridge University Press.

Smith, A., 1976. *The Glasgow Edition of the Works and Correspondence of Adam Smith*, ed. R. H. Cambell and A. S. Skinner. Oxford: Clarendon Press.

Sober, E., 2010. *Did Darwin Write the* Origin *Backwards? Philosophical Essays on Darwin's Theory*. Buffalo, NY: Prometheus.

Spencer, H., 1851. *Social Statics; Or the Conditions Essential to Human Happiness Specified and the First of Them Developed*. London: J. Chapman.

Spencer, H., 1852. A Theory of Population, Deduced from the General Law of Animal Fertility. *Westminster Review* 1: 468–501.

Spencer, H., 1857. Progress: Its Law and Cause. *Westminster Review* 67: 244–67.

Spencer, H., 1862. *First Principles*. London: Williams and Norgate.

Sumner, W. G., 1914. *The Challenge of Facts and Other Essays*. New Haven: Yale University Press.

Trivers, R. L., 1971. The Evolution of Reciprocal Altruism. *Quarterly Review of Biology* 46: 35–57.

Vidler, A. R., 1961. *The Church in an Age of Revolution, 1789 to the Present Day.* Harmondsworth: Penguin.

Wallace, A. R., 1864. The Origin of Human Races and the Antiquity of Man Deduced from the Theory of Natural Selection. *Journal of the Anthropological Society of London* 2, pp. clvii–clxxxvii.

Wallace, A. R., 1900. *Studies: Scientific and Social.* London: Macmillan.

Wallace, A. R., 1905. *My Life: A Record of Events and Opinions.* London: Chapman and Hall.

Weikert, R., 1995. A Recently Discovered Letter on Social Darwinism. *Isis* 86: 609–11.

Wilson, E. O., 1978. *On Human Nature.* Cambridge, Mass.: Harvard University Press.

CHAPTER 13

HERBERT SPENCER

JOHN OFFER

SPENCER's publications blended natural and social science-minded theory with philosophically significant conceptual innovation. Spencer regarded philosophy as ultimately 'an empirical enquiry, scientific in spirit' but characterized by a 'greater generality' (Passmore, 1968: 42; see also Haines, 1992). In this spirit he adopted the generic title 'A System of Synthetic Philosophy' for many of his publications. The ten-volume 'System' provided new interpretations of the subject matter of the sciences, including biology, psychology, sociology, and ethics, founded on a quasi-Kantian epistemological contrast between the 'unknowable' and the 'knowable'.[1] A universal theory of 'evolution' was his primary concern, not a priori relations (he distinguished between a 'cosmogony' and an 'organon', 1904, ii. 489). Spencer's theory was and remains philosophically interesting, and established him as a significant intellectual force. It is discussed in the first section of this chapter. Embedded within the theory were new interpretations of concepts such as 'society', 'mind', 'organism', and 'environment': Spencer was jumping disciplinary fences by the mid-1850s, opening out 'a new world of promise' as the economist Alfred Marshall noted (1925: 517). Thus the second section considers individuals and social life in his psychology and sociology and the third section his naturalistic approach to ethics. Spencer's support for freedom and beneficence, and of 'justice' as the state's sole proper concern, initially followed from general 'laws of life', but onwards from *First Principles* of 1862 (volume i of his 'System') it was underpinned by his full evolutionary theory. To describe Spencer as a 'liberal utilitarian' (Weinstein, 1998) marginalizes his multi-layered approach. His political and moral ideas developed over five decades, from an essay on poor law reform (1836), through *The Proper Sphere of Government* (1843), *Social Statics* (1851), the part of the *Principles of Sociology* on 'Political Institutions' (1882), and *The Man versus The State* (1884), to the second volume of the *Principles of Ethics* in 1893 (all, except 'Political Institutions' and the *Ethics*, outside the 'System'). Wiltshire rashly dismissed the science-based aims of the 'System' as a 'rationalization' of his political ideas (1978: 1), though many of them did pre-date it. In addition to *First Principles*, the 'System' (planned in the late 1850s) comprises *Principles of Biology*

---

[1] In its first decades *Mind* exhibited a complementary eclecticism, accommodating Spencer and his critics.

(2 vols., 1864 and 1867), a revised version of *Principles of Psychology* (first version, 1855) in two volumes (1870 and 1872), *Principles of Ethics* (2 vols.,1892 and 1893), and *Principles of Sociology* (3 vols., 1877, 1882, and 1896). The *Ethics* was the finale, elucidating 'a basis for a right rule of life, individual and social' (1904, ii. 314).[2]

Spencer was born in Derby in 1820 and died in Brighton in 1903. He was educated within the Derby family circle until 1833 and then by his uncle Thomas Spencer, a Cambridge graduate and Church of England clergyman whose parish was Hinton Charterhouse, south of Bath. Spencer did not attend university, opting for an engineering career in the construction of railways just as they began to recontour the landscape. Derby was a centre of scientific enthusiasm and innovation, in the inner circle of which his father George was comfortable. Here religious dissent and science were complementary: Erasmus Darwin's legacy may well have been decisive. His deistic evolutionary perspective embraced biology and geology, and a developmental associationist psychology (Elliott, 2003: 28). His conception of the mutability of animate life including patterns of human life challenged orthodoxy and nourished a scientific culture with utilitarian ends, associated with reform, political, religious, and moral. Unitarians were prominent in the scientific and educational networks familiar to George Spencer, noted as a teacher and educationalist specializing in geometry, who shaped his son's intellectual growth. His son's inclinations and education favoured science and mathematics. Thomas, himself evangelically inclined, wrote on ecclesiastical, social, and economic reform, both ruffling feathers in the Church and galvanizing his nephew. Edward Miall, editor of *The Nonconformist* and known to Thomas, acted as midwife to Spencer's first significant publication, twelve 'Letters', reissued as *The Proper Sphere of Government*.

Thus Spencer was raised in a milieu where Nonconformity, practical science, and economics went hand in hand, on which new light is shed by research into 'Christian political economics' (Hilton, 1988; Waterman, 1991). Christian political economics imprinted itself on Spencer. In the late eighteenth century ideological concerns may be discerned around the Christian idea of atonement which fused enlightenment rationalism with anxiety over human destiny. In 1798 Malthus's *Essay on the Principle of Population* offered a bracing antidote to the misplaced optimism, so it was argued, of William Paley's *Principles of Moral and Political Philosophy* of 1785, which had voiced a Christian utilitarianism in which man need display no intelligence and nature set no tests. Scarcity, starvation, war, and atheism bothered Malthus, who understood existing society as nevertheless essentially orderly, with natural laws as God's laws. His objective was to 'replace the doctrine that human life is a state of discipline and trial for eternity with the less familiar theory that it is, rather, "the mighty process of God…for the creation and formation of mind"' (Waterman, 1991: 98). Inequality was a precondition of intellectual and spiritual development. Richard Whately, later Archbishop of Dublin, shared this outlook. Whately treated reason/science and faith/theology as complementary spheres, and argued that God had not 'made Man too prolific, or the earth too barren'. It was rather that having made man rational, God had placed him in just the sort of ecological trap to stimulate rational thought…For though Malthus had

---

[2] The project was foreshadowed in his 'Progress' essay (1857a). Books additional to ones noted include *Education* (1861), *The Study of Sociology* (1873), and *An Autobiography* (2 vols., 1904). Care is needed over variations in the editions of Spencer's books. Spencer studies have been helped by Perrin's bibliography (1993). Laland and Brown (2002: 42) misattribute to Spencer *The Ascent of Man* of 1894 by Henry Drummond.

shown that man has a *tendency* to overpeople the world, in order to do so he would have to behave like the savage he is not' (Hilton, 1988: 79, quoting from Whately, 1832). Malthus was unveiling not the difficult case of the problem of evil, but God's wisdom. Later, Spencer cited Whately often: a popular author, Whately probably influenced him more than is credited (Offer, 2010).

Formal education completed, in the 1840s Spencer combined journalism with peripatetic employment on engineering and administrative tasks associated with railway construction. By 1848 he was in London, initially as a sub-editor with *The Economist*. A new acquaintance, John Chapman, published Spencer's *Social Statics* (in December 1850, not 1851 as dated). From 1852 essays appeared in the *Westminster Review* and elsewhere. A legacy from Thomas in 1853 freed him to concentrate on his own writing, including the *Psychology*. In the capital contacts with radical minds abounded and, cultural venues at his fingertips, friendships blossomed with George Henry Lewes, Thomas Henry Huxley, Marian Evans (George Eliot), and John Tyndall.[3] By 1857 he was on cordial terms with John Stuart Mill. The outline he sketched for *First Principles* and the whole 'System' (of which parts were to be issued serially) secured an additional set of names as subscribers, including Joseph Dalton Hooker, Charles Darwin, Sir John Herschel, Henry Buckle, Charles Kingsley, Charles Babbage, and David Masson. In America the popular-science writer, Edward Livingston Youmans, enthusiastically promoted Spencer. *First Principles* reached a global readership.

Contemporaries often regarded Spencer as a 'positivist', but he objected to the implied association with Comte. Comte's positivist philosophy was familiar in intellectual life, often as mediated by Lewes and Harriet Martineau. Spencer insisted in his *Autobiography* that he knew no more than Comte's name until spring 1852 when he read, in French, the 'Exposition' of his *Philosophie positive* in Marian Evans's copy (1904: i. 359). Early in 1854 he sampled Harriet Martineau's new abridged translation, already having read Lewes's outline of Comte in *The Leader* (1904: i. 445), but not 'the biological or psychological divisions' (1904: i. 446). In 1851 he did, though, read Lewes's *Biographical History of Philosophy* in its original four-volume form, which covered Comte (1904: i. 378; Taylor, 2007: 18). Spencer used the 'social organism' idea in 1843 and in *Social Statics* (written between 1848 and 1850), ahead of any knowledge of Comte. Spencer's essay 'The Social Organism' (1860) clarified the distinctive properties of his own conception. In 1864 he wrote to Lewes: 'If you believe that I was acquainted with Comte's ideas before *Social Statics* was written, you may suppose that I derived the notion of a social organism (which is the only point of community between us) from him; but if you do not suppose this, I do not see what grounds you have for the assumption that I am here in any way indebted to Comte' (1904: ii. 487).[4]

ON EVOLUTION

Some discussion of Spencer's understanding of 'evolution' is essential. It was finally defined as 'an integration of matter and concomitant dissipation of motion; during which the matter

---

[3] From 1864 Spencer, together with Huxley, Tyndall, Hooker, and five others, all science-minded, formed the 'X Club' to discuss shared causes (see Barton, 1990, 1998; Jenson, 1970; MacLeod, 1970).

[4] On Comte and Spencer, see Eisen, 1967; Jones, 1970; Wright, 1986; Pearce, 2010.

passes from a relatively indefinite, incoherent homogeneity to a relatively definite, coherent heterogeneity; and during which the retained motion undergoes a parallel transformation' (1900: 367). This definition did not preclude a reverse process of dissolution, for, as Spencer made clear in the first edition of *First Principles*: 'Just in the same way that a city, already multiform in its variously arranged structures of various architecture, may be made more multiform by an earthquake, which leaves part of it standing and overthrows other parts in different ways and degrees, and yet is at the same time reduced from definite arrangement to indefinite arrangement; so may organized bodies be made for a time more multiform by changes which are nevertheless disorganizing changes.... it is the absence of definiteness which distinguishes the multiformity of regression from the multiformity of progression' (1862: 178–9). Likewise, when social ties fracture, 'the combined actions of citizens lapse into uncombined actions. Those general forces which restrained individual doings, having disappeared, the only remaining restraints are those separately exercised by individuals on each other... the movement of parts replaces the movement of wholes' (1862: 352).

Spencer's theory of evolution depicts the physical 'laws' underpinning the features which *all* change exhibits, whether in the solar system or our cognitions.[5] These phenomena result from 'the persistence of force' in its forms as matter and motion. Force persists, unchanging in quantity but ever-changing in form. Force 'transcends human knowledge and conception—is an unknown and unknowable power, which we are obliged to recognize as without limit in space and without beginning or end in time' (1889: p. xi).

Spencer was not propounding a simple linear idea of progressive change: the rhythm of motion 'is a necessary characteristic of all motion'. It followed that 'throughout that re-arrangement of parts which constitutes Evolution, we must nowhere expect to see the change from one position of things to another, effected by continuous movement in the same

---

[5] The definition's abstractness masks the full scope of the theory. Spencer provided a more informative summary for Collins's *Epitome*, which the following account further abridges. In the universe, in particular instances and in general, matter and motion are unceasingly redistributed. The redistribution constitutes evolution when there is a predominant integration of matter and dissipation of motion, and dissolution when the opposite occurs. Evolution is *simple* when integration, or the forming of a coherent aggregate, arises if the parts are in identical circumstances. Evolution is *compound* when other, secondary, changes ensue from the different circumstances of different parts of the aggregate. What was relatively homogeneous thus becomes relatively heterogeneous, a transformation found in the whole and in its inorganic and organic details (meaning each organism and the aggregate of organisms, and also mind, society, and 'all products of social activity', 1889: p. ix). Integration is combined with differentiation, and produces a heterogeneity which possesses an increasing relative definiteness. Redistribution of the matter making up an evolving aggregate is accompanied by a redistribution of its retained motion, itself becoming more definitely heterogeneous. The change that is evolution is inevitable since an original homogeneity is always relative, not absolute; any part on which a force falls subdivides and differentiates that force, creating a 'multiplication of effects', in which any one change leads to diverse effects. Unlike units become separated and like units brought together; segregation thus arises. Equilibration results for an evolving aggregate when the forces opposed to it are balanced by the forces it opposes to them. In inorganic bodies this is a state of rest; in organic bodies it is death. Thereafter, the countercharge of unbalanced forces, dissolution, commences. Thus there is a 'rhythm of evolution and dissolution, completing itself during short periods in small aggregates and in the vast aggregates distributed through space completing itself in periods which are immeasurable by human thought' (1889: pp. x–xi). 'The persistence of force' in its forms as matter and motion, unchanging in quantity but ever-changing in form accounts for what there is. Force is an 'unknowable power' (1889: p. xi).

direction...we shall everywhere find a periodicity of action and reaction—a backward and forward motion, of which progress is a differential result' (1862: 334). Spencer's theory thus specifies the fundamental dynamics operating in all that there is. It is less about mechanisms of how specific changes originate than the morphology of change itself. However qualified, though, some *sense of* direction to change characterizes Spencerian evolution. His early idea of 'progress' itself evolved into 'evolution', but the idea largely remained pre-Darwinian.

First Principles earned Spencer the reputation of a serious thinker. Its theory structures the ensuing subject-specific volumes of the *System*. His publications before 1862 are not strictly 'evolutionary', though, as in *Social Statics*, he considered progressive development assured. In essays of the 1850s, especially 'The development hypothesis' and 'Manners and fashion', he explored ideas later absorbed into his theory of evolution.[6]

Freeman rightly emphasized that a 'lumping together of the evolutionary theories of Spencer and Darwin is...unwarranted, for the theories of Darwin and Spencer were unrelated in their origins, markedly disparate in their logical structures, and differed decisively in the degree to which they depended on the supposed mechanism of Lamarckian inheritance and recognized "progress" as "inevitable"' (1974: 9).[7] It should be added that Spencer claimed without foundation that Darwin's demonstration of 'natural selection' justified his own theory (1904: ii. 50). Darwin's idea of natural selection as a mechanism of species change was itself agnostic in relation to pivotal Spencerian hypotheses about heterogeneity and integration. Nevertheless, the temporal conjunction of their work was mutually reinforcing to their reputations, and it whipped up a swell against creationist accounts of order and change. John Dewey perceived the paradoxical significance of their independence: 'it was a tremendous piece of luck for both the Darwinian and Spencerian theories that they happened so nearly to coincide in the time of their promulgation. Each got the benefit not merely of the disturbance and agitation aroused by the other, but of psychological and logical reinforcement, as each blended into and fused with the other in the minds of readers and students' (1904: 39).[8]

Spencer retrospectively identified stages in the gestation of his theory: first, reading Charles Lyell's *Principles of Geology* in 1840, and accepting, contrary to Lyell, Lamarck's mechanism of organic change, understood as 'progressive modifications, physically caused

---

[6] Note too that the 1892 edition of *Social Statics* is abridged and revised, designed to align it with the theory of evolution and qualify the analysis of the status of women; that the first edition of the *Principles of Psychology* pre-dated *First Principles*; and that the first edition of *First Principles* was recast and extended in the second edition, with further changes up to the sixth and final edition of 1900.

[7] Describing Spencer as a 'Social Darwinist' is common but misleading. Hofstadter (1944) gave it currency. For important criticisms of the expression see G. M. Hodgson (2006) and Leonard (2009).

[8] From 1890 Spencer was engaged in controversy with August Weismann whose theory of the 'germ plasm' and heredity posed a huge and in the event decisive threat to Spencer's Lamarckian doctrine of the 'inheritance of acquired characteristics'. In 1891, the philosophically minded politician A. J. Balfour pinpointed the wider threat to Spencer was the doctrine upset, Balfour already himself sensing that the demise of the doctrine was unavoidable:

> his Ethics, his Psychology, and his Anthropology would all tumble to the ground without it. Yet this doctrine has for many years been questioned by a great English authority [Darwin], and...it has been directly controverted by one of the most eminent living German biologists...Weisman's [*sic*] conclusions are largely based on the extreme difficulty of conceiving any possible theory of heredity by which the transmission of acquired qualities could be accounted for; on the relative simplicity and plausibility of his own theory of heredity, according to which the transmission would be impossible; and on the absence of any conclusive proof that the transmission has ever taken place. (1892: 46–7; on Balfour, see Jacyna, 1980)

and inherited' (1904: i. 177); second, the 'doctrine of individuation', a feature of progress encountered in Coleridge's essay *The Theory of Life* while preparing *Social Statics*; third, the concept of a 'physiological division of labour', found in Henri Milne-Edwards's work on general zoology in 1851; fourth, also from 1851 and discovered in W. B. Carpenter's *Principles of Physiology*, the Estonian embryologist K. E. Von Baer's description of individual development as a change from the homogeneous to the heterogeneous, an idea Spencer applied to all change and elevated as the law of all progress. By 1857 Spencer also knew that science was 'possessed by the general doctrine of the "Conservation of Force", as it was then called'—he cites in particular the earlier publication of Sir William Grove's *The Correlation of Physical Forces* (1904: ii. 13). His 1850s essays applied these ideas in diverse contexts, with the first edition of his *Principles of Psychology* concerned especially with mental organization. Spencer noted that by 1857 'evolution' was replacing 'progress' in his writing (1904: i. 503; indeed it appears in 'Manners and Fashion' in 1854).[9]

A glance at other likely sources of inspiration complements Spencer's post hoc account. Robert Chambers, in his *Vestiges of Creation*, claimed change and progress evident throughout creation: 'The system of nature assures us that benevolence is a leading principle in the divine mind. But that system is at the same time deficient in a means of making this benevolence of invariable operation...the economy of nature, beautifully arranged and vast in its extent as it is, does not satisfy even man's idea of what might be; he feels that, if this multiplicity of theatres for the exemplification of such phenomena as we see on earth were to go on for ever unchanged, it would not be worthy of the Being capable of creating it' (1844: 385).[10] Chambers considered his book 'the first attempt to connect the natural sciences into a history of creation' (1844: 388).

George Combe's *Moral Philosophy* (1840) took the study of brain and character by phrenology as a guide for conduct. Spencer's first adult essays were phrenological, and he is likely to have encountered Combe's ideas. Indeed Combe,[11] like Spencer, had had close contact with Chapman, and Combe's earlier *The Constitution of Man* of 1828 had circulated widely (Taylor, 2007: 33).[12] According to Combe in *Moral Philosophy*, 'man is obviously progressive in the evolution of his mental powers...and the development of the brain also appears to improve with time, exercise, and the amelioration of social institutions' (1846: 57). Combe trusted in an era of enlightenment, optimistic that to the degree man 'shall evolve a correct knowledge of the elements of external nature, and of his own constitution...will his means of acting wisely, and advantageously for his own happiness, be augmented' (1846: 58). Chambers and Combe complemented Spencer's emphasis on liberty, progress, and faculty exercise in *Social Statics*, in turn laying foundations for *First Principles*.

New philosophical reflection on Christian faith, life's meaning, and the foundations of knowledge also touched Spencer in the 1850s, helping further to contour *First Principles*.

---

[9] The word 'evolution' was *not* 'added in' when Spencer revised the article for his *Essays*.

[10] On Chambers see Secord (2000).

[11] In 1831, Whately's interest in phrenology led to a 'personal acquaintance' with Combe (Gibbon, 1878: i: 264–76, at 264).

[12] Sources variously identify 1827 and 1828 as the date of first publication of *The Constitution of Man*. Combe himself gave 9 June 1828 in the sixth edition of 1845. Spencer makes no mention of Combe, but the broad contents of *Constitution* are highly likely to have been familiar: Young found 'no evidence that Spencer read it' (1970: 158).

Science, however, remained his key to interpreting the world: through Huxley and the physicist John Tyndall he tapped into the latest thinking. On psychic and social evolution as 'materialist', he rejected explicitly descriptions of his position. That evolution would yield a better future for mankind was a view never abandoned, though treated with caution late in his life.

First Principles had indeed begun with the idea of the 'unknowable' to counter any impression of a 'purely materialistic interpretation of things'. Spencer anticipated that his ensuing explanation of the order of phenomena manifested in the universe, through the doctrine of evolution, would show that the 'ultimate mystery' must be left unsolved. However, while the essential part of the book affirmed no 'metaphysical or theological beliefs', providentialist controversy surrounded 'the agnostic view which I set forth as a preliminary' (1904: ii: 75–6). An absurd misconception resulted: preliminaries and substance confused, readers, having 'inspected the portico…turned their backs on the building' (1899: 554). Among Spencer's sources in discussing the 'Unknowable', also characterized as the 'Inscrutable Power', 'Unseen Reality', and 'Unknown Cause' (1862: 108, 117, 123), were the intuitionalist philosophers Sir William Hamilton and Henry Mansel. Mansel had delivered the Bampton Lectures at Oxford in 1858, his *Limits of Religious Thought* justifying a place for a personal God beyond knowledge, which Spencer rejected. Spencer absorbed from both the ideas of psychological limits to our understanding and an absolute beyond them.[13] He concluded that the existence of the external world was indubitable, as was the 'unknowable': 'At the same time that by the laws of thought we are rigorously prevented from forming a conception of absolute existence; we are by the laws of thought equally prevented from ridding ourselves of the consciousness of absolute existence: this consciousness being…. the obverse of our self-consciousness' (1862: 96). (For Spencer, the 'unknowable' was not Humean scepticism. It covered such matters as that Space was in itself incomprehensible (Spencer, 1873a: 225–34), as he argued against the Kantian criticisms which Shadworth Hodgson directed at him (1872).) We cannot see the 'unknowable' as merely the negation of knowledge; it is part of our consciousness: 'A known cannot be thought of apart from an unknown; nor can an unknown be thought of apart from a known. And by consequence neither can become more distinct without giving greater distinctness to the other' (1862: 107–8). Spencer accepted that evolution and its interpretation possess a 'relativity which…characterizes all our knowledge' (1900: 514). Others had held this doctrine (Mill, Lewes, Bain, Huxley, Mansel, Hamilton, and Kant), but he contends that his version avoids self-refutation: 'the existence of a non-relative is not only a positive deliverance of consciousness, but a deliverance transcending in certainty all others whatever; and is one without which the doctrine of relativity cannot be framed in thought' (1873a: 260). The coexistence of subject and object, he adds, is a deliverance of consciousness which precedes all reasoning.[14]

---

[13] Hamilton, Mansel, and Spencer are discussed in Francis, 2007: ch. 10. While grappling with Hamilton's Scottish metaphysics, Spencer was approached for a testimonial by Alexander Campbell Fraser, a candidate to succeed to Hamilton's Edinburgh chair (he was successful). Spencer had not until then read Fraser, the result was 'a break-down' in health (1904: i. 483).

[14] Spencer's general position possessed some parallels with Schopenhauer's division between 'will' and 'idea'. In Spencer's 'Unseen Reality' may be detected a very thin causeway by which his philosophical outlook made contact with phenomenologists, such as Husserl, for whom ' "reality in itself", the "objective world out-there", is without significance, unsignified, meaningless apart from man's conscious attention to it' (Roche, 1973: 13). C. U. M. Smith draws a comparison between Spencer and Heidegger (1983: 9–11).

Philosophically informed responses commonly found Spencer's *First Principles* taken as a whole his Achilles' heel. For the American idealist Josiah Royce, the Spencerian description of evolution 'renders it possible, of course, to conceive the formula . . . to fit any special case that may arise. But what one misses is any guide, in the formula, for the precise definition of types of cases *in advance of such special adjustments*.' A permanently useful generalization must be such as to define for us not merely 'something abstract enough to be true whatever happens'. For Royce, the law of gravitation and the theory of energy 'are not formulas such as: . . . "Everything changes" ' (1904: 113–14). What we require is 'not that the philosopher should tell us (truly enough) that evolution involves both shrinkings and swellings, both mixings and sortings, both variety and order,—but that he should show us *how* these various tendencies are, in the various types of evolutionary process, kept in that peculiar balance and unity which, each time, constitutes an evolution' (1904: 114–15).

Without unambiguous criteria for relating key concepts to phenomena the theory was vulnerable to criticism as a cumbrous redescription of the world, in principle unfalsifiable. Huxley had once said, half-jokingly, 'Spencer's idea of a tragedy is a deduction killed by a fact' (in Spencer 1904: i. 403). Malcolm Guthrie too, in three books on Spencer (1879, 1882, and 1884), found the cosmic philosophy unpersuasive: 'constructed of terms which had no fixed and definite meaning, which were in fact merely symbols of symbolic conceptions, conceptions themselves symbolic because they were not understood—and the moment we begin to put them to use as having definite values they landed us forthwith in alternative contradictions' (1884: p. vii). '(F)ormidable if measured by bulk', was Spencer's retort (1904: ii. 358). However, Spencer did participate in an exchange with T. E. Cliffe Leslie (see Black, 2002). Leslie questioned Spencer's insistence that increasing heterogeneity characterizes evolution with some examples showing the reverse. Leslie also suggested that, contrary to a 'differentiation' between political and industrial functions, a man is now 'a merchant in the morning and a legislator at night; in mercantile business one year, and the next perhaps head of the navy, like Mr. Goschen or Mr. W. H. Smith' (1879: 408–9).

Spencer's replies to Leslie appear in the final edition of *First Principles* (1900). On the heterogeneity point Spencer argues that integration, or 'amalgamation', is occurring, not increasing homogeneity, with the integration then triggering differentiation and heterogeneity. Spencer insists that if one language supplants another this is not itself evidence of 'any tendency towards homogeneity in the proper sense' (1900: 526)—the surviving language would continue the theoretically predicted tendency to heterogeneity. While Spencer may display internal consistency here in his own 'technical' use of 'heterogeneity' and with his suggestion that the dying language would thus be undergoing 'dissolution', the question is begged whether this conceptual apparatus is, except in a self-serving sense, a clear or fruitful interpretation of events. Spencer's response to Leslie's allegation of declining differentiation between industrial and political functions is handled in a cognate fashion. The process of evolution anywhere depends upon surrounding conditions: the progress of a social organism towards more heterogeneous and more definite structures of a certain type depends upon stability in the associated circumstances (1900: 528). New conditions lead to structural transition. There is 'a mixture of structures causing apparent confusion of traits. . . . during the metamorphoses undergone by a society in which the militant activities and structures are dwindling while the industrial are growing, the old and new arrangements must be mingled in a perplexing way' (1900: 529). Leslie's concern is thus misplaced. There is a shift towards 'militant' social relations and even 'dissolution'. Again, though, the necessary criteria for holding to distinctions consistently and objectively seem compromised: the application of the distinctions seems in principle arbitrary, serving, 'in a perplexing way', authorial fiat.

Spencer also introduced a concession: even if the law of evolution is inapplicable to certain 'detached groups' of social phenomena, 'it would not follow that it does not hold of social processes and products in their totality. The law is a law of the transformation of aggregates' (1900: 531). The concession, though, contradicts his general position that evolution, through the processes of integration and differentiation leading to a change towards definiteness in heterogeneity, 'is exhibited in the totality of things *and in all its divisions and sub-divisions down to the minutest*' (1889: p. ix, emphasis added). Spencer in fact applied his law to such 'detached' phenomena as the develoment of printing technology (1873b: 126–32).

Spencer's responses to Leslie suggest evasions of difficulties and a self-defeating resort to conceptual 'malleability' or plasticity: a theory that is compatible with the occurrence of anything and everything explains nothing. William James, who studied Spencer closely, declared *First Principles* 'almost a museum of blundering reason', with terms of 'vagueness and ambiguity incarnate' (1911: 26, 27). J. A. Hobson thought it his book 'most open to the onslaughts of destructive logic' (1904: 13). The mathematician Thomas Penyngton Kirkman translated 'evolution' as 'a change from a nohowish untalkaboutable all-likeness, to a somehowish and in-general-talkaboutable not-all-likeness, by continuous somethingelse-ifications and sticktogetherations' (Kirkman, 1876: 292). In response, Spencer missed the point: 'a formula expressing all orders of changes in their general course... could not possibly be framed in any other than words of the highest abstractness' (1900: 520–1).

It was the interpretation of the 'persistence of force', in relation to social life in particular, that especially vexed William James, who detected a discordant miscellany of unanalysed functions in the text. General vagueness bred the special vagueness of 'social force': 'what on earth is "social force"? Sometimes he identifies it with "social activity" (showing the latter to be proportionate to the amount of food eaten), sometimes with the work done by human beings and their steam-engines, and shows it to be due ultimately to the sun's heat'. On how a 'social force' acting as a stimulus to change could be identified precisely Spencer was silent. James asks if 'a leader,... a discovery, a book, a new idea, or a national insult' count as 'social forces', emphasizing 'that the greatest of "forces" of this kind need embody no more "physical force" than the smallest'. 'The measure of greatness here', James thought, 'is the effect produced on the environment, not a quantity antecedently absorbed from physical nature. Mr. Spencer himself is a great social force; but he ate no more than an average man, and his body, if cremated, would disengage no more energy. The effects he exerts are of the nature of *releases*,—his words pull triggers in certain kinds of brain' (1911: 29).

In about 1857, Tyndall had alerted Spencer to the implication of Clausius' Second Law of Thermodynamics that the perfect equilibrium of forces in the universe would be death. Spencer henceforth drew out the process of equilibration in social life into the remote future, but his grasp of 'force' was flawed in this respect also.[15] The First Law of Thermodynamics did not assure 'growth' in any ordinary meaning of the word, and the Second Law 'was not... particularly helpful for Spencer's theory' (Taylor, 2007: 66). In 1923 Bertrand Russell advised Beatrice Webb, then reflecting on Spencer (whom she had known since her

---

[15] Sir Peter Medawar (1969) provides an analysis based on natural science of problems in Spencer on 'evolution' and 'force'.

childhood), that he might well have been upset: 'The law says that everything tends to uniformity and a dead level, diminishing (not increasing) heterogeneity. Energy is only useful when unevenly concentrated, and the law says that it tends to become evenly diffused. This law used to worry optimists about the time when Spencer was old' (in Webb, 1926: 78).[16]

Nevertheless, *First Principles* was a watershed in Spencer's thought (although the 'Progress' essay of 1857 was an early sea trial of ideas). Beforehand his analysis was based on 'laws of life', formulated for social life in the equal freedom principle (discussed in the section 'On Ethics'), and for all organic life in terms of the process of adaptation by organisms to their circumstances, with characteristics thereby acquired inherited by offspring. Articulated comprehensively in *Social Statics*, these 'laws', most writers on Spencer have agreed, were teleological. That is, there is a specific end towards which the laws lead. Providence ensured they operated throughout nature in a progressive direction; however, man could and did so act as to 'pervert' these laws of life thereby engendering 'evil', stagnation, and regression (Spencer's use of 'law' in descriptive and prescriptive senses can be problematic). Real controversy comes with the Spencer of *First Principles* and the 'System': is the 'mature' theory of evolution teleological?

In early editions (including the 1870 edition), Spencer proposed that from deductions based on the persistence of force we may infer 'a gradual advance towards harmony between man's mental nature and the conditions of his existence.... Evolution can end only in the establishment of the greatest perfection and the most complete happiness' (1862: 486), but the final edition excised the reference to perfection and happiness. The contingency of perfection is underlined. Moreover, in the *Sociology*, he cautioned against necessitarian optimism: 'Evolution does not imply a latent tendency to improve, everywhere in operation. There is no uniform ascent from lower to higher, but only an occasional production of a form, which in virtue of greater fitness for more complex conditions, becomes capable of a longer life of a more varied kind' (1896: 599). Social progress is 'divergent and re-divergent. Each divergent product gives origin to a new set of differentiated products' (1896: 325). In *Social Statics*, though, 'civilization' had been 'a development of man's latent capabilities under the action of favourable circumstances; *which favourable circumstances, mark, were certain some time or other to occur*' (1851: 415, italics added).

By the completion of the 'System' Spencer's explanatory framework, in which physical properties ultimately unify and determine the processes of inorganic and organic evolution, is in principle no longer teleological, but nor is it entirely agnostic over direction. Evolution possesses direction at least in morphological terms, given surrounding conditions. The theory is intended to be foundational science, freed from natural theology. Moreover, according to the evidence, in Spencer's view, social evolution is still likely to deliver human happiness, at least in the long run, though, in practice the message was nuanced. In his essay 'The Americans' Spencer assured his readers that 'Nature leads men by purely personal motives to fulfil her ends: Nature being one of our expressions for the Ultimate Cause of things, and the end, remote when not proximate, being the highest form of human life' (1883: 491). For Spencer, therefore, according to David Wiltshire, evolution is good, 'always invested with an aura of beneficence. The definition of "right" conduct as "conduct tending to increase life"

---

[16] On Russell's wider critical reaction to Spencer and its shaping of his own thought, see Cunningham, 1994.

(in other words conduct tending to facilitate evolution) entails the assumption that the evolutionary consummation is devoutly to be wished' (1978: 193).

However, the interpretation just outlined of the structure of Spencer's theory might still be challenged as 'immanentist', a variant of teleology. Some elaboration is needed to show that it does not confuse the distinction between the causes and the processes of change. Valerie Haines argues that in Spencer's theory *organic* evolution is the logical core: the general theory must be regarded as 'a generalization and respecification, in ultimate terms, of his theory of organic evolution. As the core of his system, . . . the theory of organic evolution determines the explanatory form of Spencer's theory of social evolution' (1988: 474). In particular it was, she believes, Von Baer's idea of epigenesis, of a *process* of development from homogeneity to heterogeneity, which formed Spencer's core argument, *coupled with*, as the *mechanism of change*, the Lamarckian inheritance of acquired characteristics.

I agree with Haines on two points: that Spencer had a theory of the *cause* of change in organic, human, and social life before *First Principles*, and that this Lamarckian theory was Spencer's effective mechanism of change, with a place accorded to some version of Darwin's natural selection as well, in and after *First Principles*. However, Haines's account of Spencer on organic and social evolution in and after *First Principles* is misleading: what are, in Spencer's own estimation, the most fundamental propositions of *First Principles* are described by Haines as merely generalizations from and a 'respecification in ultimate terms' (1988: 474) of his pre-*First Principles* Von Baerian ideas of the *process* of change. In fact, though, the propositions *materially supplemented* his understanding of the Von Baerian process of organic change with elements which Haines's approach here downplays, including the persistence of force, equilibration, integration, and rhythm of motion. Indeed, the whole larger 'envelope' in which the *causes* of change (Lamarckian and Darwinian) operate is now made explicit, according to Spencer, through the more general processes detailed in the *Principles of Biology*, involving 'force' and its manifestations. Hence Lamarckian adaptation is, in *First Principles*, renamed 'direct equilibration' and natural selection 'indirect equilibration'. Also, in the *Biology*, Spencer argues that it is an implication if not a deduction from first principles that the changes in an organism arising from a new equilibrium being established between it and its surroundings, 'must also be transmitted . . . from one generation to another':

> For if an organism A, has, by any peculiar habit or condition of life, been modified into the form A^1, it follows inevitably, that all the functions of A^1, reproductive function included, must be in some degree different from the functions of A. . . . It involves a denial of the persistence of force to say that A may be changed into A^1, and may yet beget offspring exactly like those it would have begotten had it not been so changed'. (1894: i. 255–6)

The 'persistence of force' here is not a *process* confused with the *cause or causes* of change but a reference to the framework of principles of change and equilibration within which such causes occur, and in what process. Haines's interpretation, however, overlooks Spencer's claim to have 'deduced' from his general law of evolution his biological mechanism(s) to explain actual changes. In fact, Spencer's theory of evolution did not generalize biological theories but gave an independent account of the processes and causes resulting 'in the growing complexity of the cosmos. The theories of biological evolution put forward by both Lamarck and Darwin did not inspire this overarching vision but were incorporated as parts of it' (Taylor, 1992: 84–5).

Spencer, then, believed he had connected the mechanisms and processes of change to his fundamental principles of evolution. The question resurfaces, however, given this more complete account of Spencer's position, of whether change is in fact occurring in the manner of a strong immanentist 'conspiracy'.[17] In this connection it may be noted that Spencer does emphasize that evolutionary change in particular functionings and structures depends upon 'conditions' (including the 're-adjustments' of moving equilibria disturbed by 'rhythm' or 'dissolution'). This feature makes a non-nuanced immanentist interpretation of *First Principles* difficult to sustain. Nevertheless, for Spencer the *whole* environment of a biological organism or an individual human being—an environment having the laws of force ultimately shaping its own changing nature—is also regarded as an active or 'direct' agent engendering change in an organism, rather than as an unfreighted, external, and self-acting 'test' of the viability of changes produced otherwise in the organism. Even operating as an 'indirect' agent in Spencer's usage the environment is still so shaped (Spencer also interpreted Darwin's 'variations' as the result of 'secondary and tertiary perturbations and deviations' (1894: i. 443–4).[18]) The mechanisms of change themselves, renamed as 'direct' and 'indirect' 'equilibration', convey baggage derived from the natural history of first principles at work in the relevant environments. I doubt, though, that to these features can be attributed more than a weak or contingent immanentism (he did distinguish 'legitimate' from 'illegitimate' teleology (1881b: 82–3) in reply to Sidgwick (1880)).[19] Contributing to the interpretative difficulties, however, is that Spencer did not perhaps always separate processes 'like the development of the embryo, where the outcome is genetically programmed at the outset, and ones like the evolution of a species or the socialization of infants, where the form of the outcome is in no sense innately determined right from the beginning' (Peel, 1971: 135). Even so, Spencer perceived the essential distinction, distinguishing between, for instance, the 'origin' and 'development' of harmony in music (Offer, 2010: ch. 8).

The flaws in *First Principles* are widely though not universally accepted. While the law of evolution is typically regarded as a 'rather fruitless cosmic cliché' (Young, 1967: 379), Robert Carneiro praises Spencer for originating 'the first precise, rigorous, and systematic concept of evolution' (1972: 427), the basis of 'a profound and universal transformation' (1981: 613). However, if few believe Spencer's theory of evolution can be rehabilitated, a familiarity with it assists in reviewing his more lasting impact on the specific themes now discussed.

ON SOCIETY

Spencer contributed very influentially to the conceptual development of psychology and sociology, as recognized by, among others, Douglas Spalding, Hughlings Jackson, Wilhelm Dilthey, Georg Simmel, Émile Durkheim, and Ferdinand Tönnies. Spencer's psychology interpreted individuals as possessing neither a fixed nature nor infinite malleability. He shifted

---

[17] The passage quoted earlier from Spencer's essay 'The Americans' (1883) might well appear to lend *some* limited support to this position.

[18] On this important contrast between the positions of Darwin and Spencer, see Alland (1974: 466) responding to Carneiro, 1973.

[19] Spencer explains the difference between a legitimate and an illegitimate teleology as that, while the one explains the existence of something 'as having gradually arisen by furthering the end, the other gives no explanation of its existence other than that it was put there to further the end' (1881b: 83).

the focus of study on to the continuity of psychological phenomena, and the relation between a being and its environment. So-called innate properties were an inheritance passed on from the accumulated adaptation to circumstances (including the presence of others) of previous generations, to which was added the product of the individual's own adaptation. Psychical evolution was essentially of a piece with physical evolution. Neural activity and conscious-ness were parallel tracks,[20] evolving through the adaptation of an individual to the environ-ment (including the presence of others) in union with their inheritance of acquired mental characteristics (physical and psychic) from previous generations; this process of change locks together and determines the form and content of both consciousness and the parallel neu-ral structures and associated nervous discharges.[21] So constituted, individuals in turn shape their environment (including the presence of others). Spencer's psychological understanding is driven by a biological determinism which eliminates much of what for us, in a conventional sense, would be considered as 'the social aspects of human mental development' (Rylance, 2000: 223). Whilst everyone is at liberty to do what he or she desires to do (supposing no external hindrances), no one is at liberty 'to desire or not to desire' (1881a: i. 500). This per-spective underlies his sociology. The scope for individuals to reason and act is constrained by their psychical character at a point in time. Nevertheless, his efforts to understand of 'society' and social life have proved key steps in the growth of sociology, especially his distinctive idea of the 'social organism', an often misunderstood innovation to clarify relationships between 'the individual' and 'the social' and a focus of later philosophical controversy. His philosophy of society as advanced in his eponymous essay of 1860, is the subject of this section.

For Spencer, societies are natural growths arising out of the gradual course of the 'divi-sion of labour', not arranged by 'direct interposition of Providence' (1860: 266). Plato and Hobbes were mistaken in considering societies as 'made', not growths (1860: 269–72; 1884: 136–7). Physiological science reveals 'real parallelisms' between a social body and organisms (1860: 269), facilitating a more fruitful approach. There are, however, apparent differences. First, there is no continuous mass of living tissue in a society. Since some organ-isms, though, have bodies of differentiated parts 'dispersed through an undifferentiated jelly' ministering to its life (1860: 274), 'the citizens who make up a community may be con-sidered as highly vitalized units surrounded by substances of lower vitality, from which they draw their nutriment' (1860: 275). Second, whereas the individuals in a social organism are capable of mobility, the living parts of an individual organism are mostly fixed in their rela-tive positions. Yet this disagreement is partial only: 'while citizens are locomotive in their private capacities, they are fixed in their public capacities'. The third difference, however, is not qualified: 'while in the body of an animal only a special tissue is endowed with feel-ing, in a society all the members are endowed with feeling' (1860: 276).[22] This is of supreme

---

[20] In a letter to Harald Höffding Spencer explained that the subjective states were the *obverse* of the physical states: 'the psychical action is the obverse of the physical action which initiates it, and again of the physical action which it initiates' (in Duncan, 1911: 180).

[21] Spencer responded to Sidgwick (1873) that consciousness did not arise at a specific stage of nervous action but is attributable when conduct is coherent, leading us to 'speak of it as intelligent' (Spencer, 1873a: 240).

[22] Spencer notes, though, that for some lower animals such sensitiveness can exist in all parts, and further that the members of a society vary in 'feeling': 'The classes engaged in laborious occupations are less susceptible, intellectually and emotionally, than the rest; and especially less so than the classes of highest mental culture.'

significance: 'while, in individual bodies, the welfare of all other parts is rightly subservient to the welfare of the nervous system, whose pleasurable or painful activities make up the good or ill of life; in bodies-politic the same thing does not hold (1860: 276–7)'. Corporate life in societies must serve the lives of the parts. This is vital to the idea of a social organism.

Societies, then, can be viewed as organisms.[23] To understand Spencer on this point it is important to note that he was wrestling simultaneously with practice-based yet conceptual problems in biology over the puzzling 'compound individuality' then predicated of certain organisms (Elwick, 2003).[24] In a related slightly earlier essay on 'Transcendental Physiology', he speculated on physiological structures beyond specimens populating the anatomy laboratory. The focus was on the *forms* of organisms and their physiologies, and their modification by the forces associated with the exercise of functions. This essay announced 'laws of development and function which hold not of particular kinds or classes of organisms, but of all organisms: laws, some of which have not, we believe, been hitherto enunciated' (1857b: 63). The essay compared physiological and social phenomena: 'the general principles of development and structure displayed in organized bodies are displayed in societies also'. Both display a mutual dependence of parts. In Spencer's 'new' physiology, sociology and physiology will 'more or less interpret each other'. Relations of cause and effect in 'the social organism' may lead 'to the search for analogous ones in the individual organism; and may so elucidate what might else be inexplicable'. Moreover, laws of growth and function 'disclosed by the pure physiologist, may occasionally give us the clue to certain social modifications otherwise difficult to understand' (1857b: 102). Insights into 'life' and 'mind' need no foundations in an extra-natural source. Nature provides the transcendental organization reason might conjecture.[25]

Spencer's idea of the 'social organism' thus had a nuanced conceptual foundation. A society was stipulated to be essentially a unique organism, 'not comparable to any particular type of individual organism, animal or vegetal' (1893: 580). Objections that the organic analogy, 'correctly' drawn, would indicate that government should design society short-changed his position. Spencer's general theory of evolution embraced both individualism and organicism, not self-evidently in a form which involved contradiction. As Taylor has observed, 'Greater individuation did not preclude the possibility of, or need for, strong central control, but it defined the form that such control could take'. Extensive state action was incompatible with 'the greater individuation of the social organism's component parts', but within its 'proper sphere of protecting liberty' government was necessary (2007: 101). Spencer thus considered his friend T. H. Huxley's 'Administrative nihilism' ill-informed in proclaiming

[23] Spencer concludes by admitting that he has not discussed what he calls the 'different types of social organization', or 'social metamorphoses'. The distinction between 'militant' and 'industrial' types of society and change from one to the other were explored later in *First Principles* and the *Principles of Sociology*.

[24] In the 1870s Huxley circumvented difficulties of description by introducing the concepts of zooids and metamerism.

[25] The idea of 'transcendental physiology' had also figured in *Social Statics*: morality 'is essentially one with physical truth—is, in fact, a species of transcendental physiology. That condition of things dictated by the law of equal freedom—that condition in which the individuality of each may be unfolded without limit, save the like individualities of others—that condition towards which ... mankind are progressing, is a condition towards which the whole creation tends' (1851: 436).

that, if resemblances between the body physiological and the body politic 'are any indication, not only of what the latter is, and how it has become what it is, but of what it ought to be, and what it is tending to become, I cannot but think that the real force of the analogy is totally opposed to the negative view of State function' (Huxley, 1871: 65).

Spencer's defence emphasized that social satisfactions are created out of individual actions, and by 'spontaneous cooperation', omitted by Huxley but which fulfils men's 'sympathetic interests' (1871: 432–3).[26] Where peaceful 'industrial' social relations have evolved, the distinction between legitimate 'negative' and illegitimate 'positive' regulation becomes paramount (1871: 419–20): 'were the restraining action of the State prompt, effective, and costless to those aggrieved, the pleas put in for positive regulation would nearly all disappear' (1871: 437).[27] He opposed a laissez-faire policy 'in the sense which the phrase commonly suggests', urging instead 'a more active control of the kind distinguishable as negatively regulative'. When state action is excluded from other spheres 'it may become more efficient within its proper sphere' (1871: 438).

The discussion of the 'social organism' in the later *Principles of Sociology* sets the concept in the context of 'super-organic' evolution.[28] Although super-organic evolution has come about out of organic evolution, Spencer distinguishes it in the first volume of 1876 as including the processes and products implying 'the co-ordinated actions of many individuals' (1893: 4). Super-organic features are clearly most evolved in human societies. The factors of 'super-organic' evolution are the units themselves and their conditions—intrinsic (physical and psychical) and external (climate, for instance). Both sets of conditions interact. There are also derived factors: as social life develops, it transforms its environment and the actions and reactions between the community and its members, and it reacts to other communities. There are distinctively super-organic products, 'the potency of which can scarcely be over-estimated' (1893: 12), such as culture, tools, language, and knowledge. These factors all affect action and reaction, and modify each other: accompanying social life are 'actions and reactions between the community and each member of it, such that either affects the other in nature. The control exercised by the aggregate over its units, tends ever to mould their activities and sentiments and ideas into congruity with social requirements; and these activities, sentiments, and ideas, in so far as they are changed by changing circumstances, tend to re-mould the society into congruity with themselves' (1893: 11).

Spencer regards a society as an entity because it has relatively permanent arrangements which are coordinated rather than accidental. We apply the idea of society 'only where

[26] Spencer also refers to these interests as 'altruism'. 'Egoistic' and 'altruistic' feelings 'amply suffice to originate and carry on all the activities which constitute healthy national life' (1871: 437).

[27] In 'The Filiation of Ideas' of 1899, Spencer judged that this rejoinder emphasized more than hitherto the truth that 'war has been the cause of the development of centralized governmental structures, which become coercive in proportion as war is the dominant social activity; while growth of that decentralized co-operation characterizing sustaining structures, becomes more marked as war ceases to be chronic' (in Duncan, 1911: 568).

[28] The concept of the 'super-organic' goes back to Spencer's 'Classification of the Sciences' essay of 1864 in which sociology is classed as a 'concrete' science, one that deals with an aggregate (a society) and pluralities of aggregates (societies). Each social aggregate presents 'multitudinous phenomena, simultaneous and successive, that are held together as parts of one combination' (1864: 100), and such an aggregate is 'super-organic' as distinct from 'organic' (1864: 102; see also the second edition of *First Principles* onwards (1867: 522)).

some constancy in the distribution of parts has resulted from settled life' (1893: 436). By the 'political institutions' division of the *Sociology*, 'cooperation' had superseded and subsumed 'co-ordination': 'A society, in the sociological sense, is formed only when, besides juxtaposition there is cooperation.' Cooperation cannot exist without a society, and is that for which a society exists. It may achieve something which no man may accomplish singly, or it may be 'an apportioning of different activities to different persons, who severally participate in the benefits of one another's activities' (1891: 244). A society grows and develops structures with the changes in the parts 'mutually determined, and the changed actions of the parts…mutually dependent' (1893: 439). A unified 'mankind' was not in prospect: 'in relation to its component individuals, each social aggregate stands for the species. Mankind survives not through arrangements which refer to it as a whole, but by survival of its separate societies; each of which struggles to maintain its existence' (1893: 598).[29]

Exchange develops, permitting specialization: 'This division of labour, first dwelt on by political economists as a social phenomenon, and thereupon recognized by biologists as a phenomenon of living bodies is that which in the society makes it a living whole' (1893: 440). Language substitutes for the directly physical cooperation of a biological organism. Given distance, each 'unit' has had to continue to possess a brain, and thus 'consciousness is diffused throughout the aggregate: all the units possess the capacities for happiness and misery' (1893: 449). This feature of the 'social' organism is a contrast 'fundamentally affecting our idea of the ends to be achieved by social life' (1893: 448). It permits a 'catallaxy'[30] of interactions and transactions, made viable by a government ensuring observance of agreements and reward in proportion to merit (the equal freedom principle): 'the welfare of the aggregate, considered apart from that of the units, is not an end to be sought. The society exists for the benefit of its members; not its members for the benefit of the society. It has ever to be remembered that great as may be the efforts made for the prosperity of the body politic, yet the claims of the body politic are nothing in themselves, and become something only in so far as they embody the claims of its component individuals' (1893: 449–50).[31] However, Spencer's denial of freedom of will in his *Psychology* seems to eclipse scope for *genuinely deliberative* agency innovation by the 'units'; despite appearances, such change is produced by (evolving) mental heredities as modified by contact with present conditions (Offer, 2003).

Spencer also identifies the growth of structures and functions within the social organism as in accord with his evolutionary theory. 'Changes of structures', Spencer declares, 'cannot appear without changes of functions' (1893: 473). There are 'systems of organs', with a primary differentiation between 'organs' focused on outer and inner relations as between 'warriors' and 'slaves'. Spencer, however, does not directly address the nature of the connection between such super-organic 'systems' and spontaneous cooperation. Peel recognized the potential problem here: 'A dangerous distinction is set up between events, the particular doings of men, on the one hand, and the stuff of social change, on the other, to which they are epiphenomenal. The

---

[29] Spencer here undermines Ritchie's implication that he saw mankind as an organism (1900: 78).

[30] Whately described economics as 'catallactics' but Spencer uses neither 'catallaxy' nor 'catallactics', though he is referring to what 'catallaxy' denotes. On Whately and economics, see Rashid, 1977. On Whately, Mises, and Hayek, and the distinction between 'sociologics' and 'catallactics' see Zafirovski, 2003.

[31] This situation can at best pertain to a small degree in a society where 'militant' social forms predominate.

evolution of structures and functions thus becomes "reified"' (1971: 162). Yet while Spencer's conception of all change in social life (including spontaneous cooperation) is idiosyncratically sclerotic, for reasons grounded in his understanding of psychology and psychical and physical adaptation, the doings of men are not in this context 'epiphenomenal', and the structures and functions are not 'reified' as in principle external to men's doings. The structures and functions arise out of the cooperative doings, and then shape them further, and these modifications modify afresh the structures and functions. Changes to structures and functions are the outcome of a 'natural' process of adaptation between men and circumstances, in which men themselves and the circumstances may alter (his rejection of 'artificial' legislative provision remains). It is a neglected point of some significance that no contradiction in principle arises when Spencer twins his altruistic 'spontaneous co-operation' or catallaxy 'model' of interaction with social structures and functions *conceived as mutable* (G. H. Smith, 1981; Perrin, 1995; T. Gray, 1996: 233).

Much contemporary criticism of Spencer's 'social organism' echoed Huxley's reservations. It was often connected with idealist criticism of his ethics and is considered in the next section.

ON ETHICS

The discussion of Spencer on evolution in general and the evolution of individuals, psychically and socially, has paved the way for a consideration of the *Principles of Ethics*. This begins with a section on 'the data of ethics' first published independently in 1879. Spencer maintains that conduct of ethical significance is part of conduct in general. Conduct in animals and humans evolves, becoming more adapted to ends. From gregariousness springs passive and active cooperation, permitted initially by a sympathetic 'pro-altruistic sentiment of justice' (1910: ii. 29). Without the sentiment any cooperation must be unprofitable and collapse. Once cooperation is established, ideas of 'justice' emerge in the course of civilization. 'Justice' for Spencer in social life involves more than a simple pre-social connection between conduct and its consequences for ill or good. Conduct is unjust if its consequences infringe the like liberty to act of others (1910: ii. 45–6). Spencer considers that the liberty which accords with 'justice' has been compromised when a society is under external threat or governed by coercion but flourishes with peaceful cooperation, a point at the heart of his contrast between 'militant' and 'industrial' types of social relation (in a society the two were not mutually exclusive). His idea of 'justice', or 'equal freedom', represented an 'absolute' ethic, against which the 'relative' practices of existing societies could be assessed.[32] The role of the state was to protect 'justice'. Within this proper sphere of action government has a crucial role to play. If it fails, social advance will be reversed. Government action *outside* of its 'proper sphere' will protect people 'artificially' from the consequences of non-adaptation, and increase the suffering when protection ceases. It will also punish those who have already adapted through adding to the taxation they face. The fundamental character of individuals cannot be changed 'artificially', it must adapt naturally to circumstances, which include

---

[32] Spencer included a response (1910: i. 271–9) to Sidgwick's critique of the relevance of 'absolute ethics' to the real world in which we live in *The Methods of Ethics* (1877).

surrounding society. One objective of Spencer's social theory, unlike Comte's, was to show the incoherence of social engineering.

'Justice' in social life was necessary, but in high civilized life it is augmented by the further altruism of voluntary private beneficence, both negative (not enforcing 'justice' if it would cause disproportionate hardship) and positive (giving aid and care beyond what 'justice' required when disruption to adaptation was small). Justice was the sphere of the state, beneficence that of private citizens. Compulsory beneficence, lacking knowledge of personal circumstances, was vetoed again as slowing adaptation through the taxation it necessitated, and encouraging a failure to adapt in recipients. To seek directly a 'higher' or 'common' good ignored the complexity, and social and individual relativity, of 'good' or 'happiness' (1910: i. 170). Spencer's emphases on the need for prompt, accessible, and free administration of 'justice', and on beneficence engendered by fellow feeling, remain seldom noted (see Offer, 2006).

For Spencer, conduct, moral consciousness, and sociality were evolving (as was a 'moral sense' (1910, i: 322)). Not all adaptations survived. Since conditions could change, the 'fitness' of any practice was in present conditions inevitably contingent (on the element of Darwinian 'selectionism' in Spencer on social evolution see Offer (2010: ch. 5)). Spencer regarded his moral thought as utilitarian, but distinctive because grounded in a 'science of right conduct'. Happiness was to be found not directly but proximately, by acting in accord with rules disclosed by evolutionary science. In *Utilitarianism*, John Stuart Mill had presented *Social Statics* as offering a 'disproof of the pretensions of utility'. In the 1863 printing, at Spencer's request, Mill included a Note recording that Spencer regarded himself as a utilitarian. Not in the Note was Spencer's gnomic remark to Mill: 'If not a Utilitarian in the direct sense, I am still a Utilitarian in the transcendental sense' (in Duncan, 1911: 108).

Much contemporary criticism of the *Ethics* concerned 'justice'. Lester Frank Ward charged Spencer with being 'utterly blind' to 'the most conspicuous fact in society, that under an unregulated or "competitive" régime there is very little relation between "benefits" and "merits" or "fitness"'. It fell to the state to effect in part such a correspondence: 'the essence of the idea of "justice", in the human sense, is the proportioning of benefits to merits, which "Nature's methods" do not secure' (1894: 87). Spencer declared 'unjust' the private ownership of land but, disinclined to countenance a sudden change, he was chastised for inconsistency by Henry George (1892). In this context Henry Sidgwick alighted on the inadequacy of Spencer's 'single formula' of justice:

> When we are inquiring into what compensation is justly due to persons whose rights have admittedly been encroached upon, supposing the encroachments have been sanctioned by law and custom and complicated by subsequent exchange, it is evident that the Law of Equal Freedom cannot help us; we want some quite different principle of Distributive or Reparative justice. (1892: 379)

Sidgwick identified a genuine lacuna in Spencer's thought. Ward, though, suggested no alternative to an open-ended organization or catallaxy compatible with a liberal outlook (see J. N. Gray, 1995: 67–8), and neglects the part of Spencer's conception of justice whereby an individual is allowed to take the rewards of or suffer the consequences of their conduct, provided others have the same freedom (1910: ii. 15, 45). According to Spencer himself wage levels in some mills flout this principle and amount to slavery (1896: 515–16). He credits trade unions with preventing employers from 'doing unfair things' (1896: 542). Indeed, the principle appears to suggest equal work and equal rewards are linked. There remain, though, disputes in Spencer studies over the precise form of his idea of justice.[33]

Another kind of reaction questioned Spencer's attempted derivation of ethics from his theory of evolution. The American Unitarian James Bixby found 'The data of ethics' to be 'in blank contradiction to our moral consciousness. The idea of duty is granted only an "illusive independence"'. In Spencer's analysis our moral ideas are not what we individually reason as right 'but what preceding generations thought most useful' (1882: 305; see also Benn, 1880). Bixby hammered home the point: by 'subtle operations of heredity' our ancestors' ideas

> as to what was conducive to their happiness have not only smuggled themselves into our brains, but have assumed a sacred authority. As the suggestion of a companion may take possession of the brain of a delirious person... so do the experiences of past generations as to the pleasurable and the painful obsess our brains with their illusory convictions of self-evident right and solemn duty. Not only is our general idea of duty an illusion, but our special ethical ideas are hallucinations. (1882: 305)[34]

Idealist social thought, associated with T. H. Green, Bernard Bosanquet, and David George Ritchie, developed cognate criticism (Harris, 1992). However, Spencer knew the chasm between his thought and idealism (Gaus, 2001; Lewis, 1995). Bosanquet signed the letter of congratulation to Spencer in 1896 to mark the completion of his 'System'; a year before, however, he criticized Spencer sharply (Bosanquet, 1895; see also MacBriar, 1987: 126). As Vincent remarks, 'Bosanquet contrasted what he called the ethical individual against the Spencerian atomic individual' (1984: 353). Idealists reconfigured 'the social organism', holding that it was in the membership of society, with a 'general will' and conceived of as a 'moral organism', a higher mode of life, that individuals became meaningful: society was the genesis of the moral self, or as Green put it 'without society, no persons' (1883: sect. 288).[35] For F. H. Bradley the idea of the individual was accompanied 'in every fibre' by 'relations of community' (1876: 155). Moral action demanded a sense of a permanent, higher good, realizable only in a society. James Seth argued that 'moral life' cannot be identified 'with the life of nature, or...be interpreted in its terms'. Freedom, or willpower, was vital to ethical life, and, something natural science cannot recognize, it required 'a different interpretation of Evolution as applied to human character and conduct'. Self-conscious evolution was 'essentially different from unconscious evolution' (1889: 350). Henry Calderwood objected to the continuum joining 'human' and 'animal' ethics'.[36] In the lives of even higher vertebrates we

---

[33] David Miller, 1976 and Tim Gray, 1981, offer contrasted expositions of 'justice' in Spencer in respect of the weight attached to the element of desert in outcomes compared to the element of entitlement to opportunities. See also Weinstein, 1998: 57–61.

[34] The main direction of Sidgwick's essays of 1876 and 1899 was to a similar end.

[35] Ingold faults Spencer for seeing society as a 'resultant' not an 'emergent' (1986: 227).

[36] Thought on 'animal ethics' has sometimes echoed Calderwood's, viewing the idea as eccentric. Yet, though without reference to Spencer, Alasdair MacIntyre's recent philosophical work has lent support to some version of Spencer's ethical continuum. MacIntyre regards it as an error to suppose 'an ethics independent of biology to be possible'. He cites two reasons: 'The first is that no account of the goods, rules and virtues that are definitive of our moral life can be adequate that does not explain—or at least point us towards an explanation—how that form of life is possible for beings who are biologically constituted as we are, by providing us with an account of our development towards and into that form of life.... Secondly, a failure to understand that condition and the light thrown upon it by a comparison between humans and members of other intelligent animal species will obscure crucial features of that development' (1999: p. x).

find only natural laws, we do not find animal ethics 'even in faintest outline. The weakest life dies off; the completest survives, and contributes to the advance of the species; but the laws applicable are physical, not ethical' (1892: 358). A concept of the 'autonomous, unencumbered individual' was false, idealists argued, 'for it denied that all our aspirations and actions are embedded within a social whole' (den Otter, 1996: 151). Sidney and Beatrice Webb, sharing ground with idealist social thought (Harris, 1992), believed that the opening of the twentieth century 'finds us all, to the dismay of the old-fashioned individualist, "thinking in communities"' (Webb, 1948: 221–2). L. T. Hobhouse, sympathetic to idealism and reform, espoused a post-Spencerian version of social evolution: when the conception of the development of humanity enters into thought as the directing principle of human endeavour it can 'give consistency and unity of aim to the vastly increased power of controlling the conditions, external and internal, of life, which the advance of knowledge is constantly yielding to mankind' (1911: 155–6). In 1939 J. H. Muirhead claimed that even in the 1880s Spencer's political thought was a 'survival': state action was less an 'interference with natural liberty' but more a brake on excesses of liberty in the interest of 'a truer kind of freedom in the mass of the people' (1939: 5). Spencer's focus on 'justice' and 'beneficence' was in all cases omitted.

Idealist thinkers favoured at least some new policies and legislation to enhance society as a whole in areas including old-age pensions, education, and unemployment. By depicting Spencer's 'individual' as an unintelligible abstraction they bolstered their case. But Spencer believed he had already pulled the rug from under these critics. It was not defensible to insist on the 'special' status of man or to exempt moral or religious ideas from natural causation. Society was an organism which had evolved as its primary principle of organization for individuals in social life the law of equal freedom. Given his scientific psychology and sociology, predicated upon the inheritance of acquired characteristics cumulatively acquired in a process of adaptation to circumstances (including surrounding society), his associated concept of a 'social self-consciousness' (1859: 140–1, 1873b: 219) possessed by (non-atomic) individuals, and his denial of freedom of the will, Spencer considered idealist social analysis old-fashioned and redundant. The differences in the *content* of the moral life as understood by Spencer and the idealists were not as great as idealists usually supposed (Spencer too could have declared 'without society, no persons'). But Spencer, like Mill, would not accept that the 'common good' could be achieved by pursuing it directly (except in times of external threat): only through its indirect pursuit was it realizable since neither 'society' nor its rulers possessed a soundly superior moral authority or insight, and individuals disagreed about ends and modified their desires only through experience.

For Spencer, cherished assumptions about the authority and efficacy of moral thought and action had been grounded in a mistaken survival of faith in the supernatural. In a sense, having rendered questions of moral justification 'otiose' (by entwining normative and descriptive senses of 'nature' and 'natural'), Spencer yielded a 'moral pragmatism in which moral principles are themselves regarded as the perishable products of social evolution' (J. N. Gray, 1982: 237, 247). Consistent with his deterministic position were Spencer's minimalist expectations of the practical effects of his ideas. Incapable of changing minds directly, they at best engendered change as part of the environment to which individuals were adapting.

One revisionist interpretative approach finds in Spencer a moral theory described as 'liberal utilitarianism', in which non-defeasible rights to liberty are upheld in conjunction with consequentialism. This, though, seems to substitute a 'purified' for the 'real' Spencer

(J. N. Gray, 1982: 248). One major 'purification' involved is the omission of Spencer's denial of freedom of the will in his *Principles of Psychology*—Weinstein refers to Spencer's human beings as 'choosing' happiness, without inserting the inverted commas Spencer's analysis demands (1998: 155). However, the chief worry concerns a doubtful interpretation of what Spencer meant by 'good'. Early in the *Ethics*, Spencer declared that the conduct which is 'highly-evolved conduct, is that which...we find to be what is called good conduct' (1910: i. 44). Much weight in the revised interpretation (Weinstein, 1998: 143–4 and 151–4) is accorded Spencer's claims that the 'survival of the fittest' 'is not the survival of the "better" or the "stronger", if we give to those words any thing like their ordinary meanings' (1872: 379, see also 1897: 114). In so elucidating the meaning of 'survival of the fittest' Spencer was referring only to *Darwin's* process of natural selection (which in the *Biology* Spencer had so renamed, though he had in mind principally the struggle for existence component rather than 'variations'), and thus *not* the inheritance of acquired characteristics. He is, therefore, referring only to *one* of the mechanisms of organic change embraced by his theory of evolution. Indeed, concerning the social evolution 'of the highest of creatures, civilized men' it is this other mechanism of change, the inheritance of acquired characteristics, *never* discarded, which has for him 'become the chief factor' (1886: 462). In Spencer's view it is principally this mechanism that produces the conduct which 'is called good conduct'. The risk remains, then, that by connecting the meaning of 'more evolved' and 'good' he committed a form of the 'naturalistic fallacy' (as Moore, 1901, claimed). Whether Spencer does do this (see Flew, 1967; Richards, 1987) is not to be settled here, but to acquit him would require a denial of what he so often states and implies, that the 'normativity of nature' forms 'the heart of his evolutionary analysis' (Taylor, 2007: 126).

The traditional portrayal of Spencer as losing a battle against criticism of his theory of evolution by the 1890s contains much truth. Further comment, though, is needed on his ethical ideas in the context of Victorian thought. By the 1850s his ethical thought had slipped its moorings in theism. However, assuming that militant, or coercive, social relations remained in abeyance, he was buoyed by the prospect of new improvements arising from free individuals with a 'social self-consciousness' enjoying spontaneous cooperation in economic and social life understood as catallaxy (as encountered in Whately, and Adam Smith). Nevertheless lives thus lived remained subject to the discipline of adaptation: a Malthusian prospect persisted of demise consequent upon non-adaptation (the sign of deficiency in faculty-exercise, and 'character'). Here were ideas chiming with Boyd Hilton's portrayal of the evangelical theology of atonement, the conquest of sin through redemption, as characteristic of social thought in the first half of the nineteenth century.

This confidence on the part of Spencer that the exercise of liberty in accord with 'justice' would presage prosperity, virtue, and harmony probably peaked in the 1870s. He judged then that the power of man's egoistic and altruistic 'spontaneous cooperation', conjoined with 'the effects of fellow-feeling' (1871: 433), would 'amply suffice to originate and carry on all the activities which constitute healthy national life' (1871: 437). Social and economic life as catallaxy, in embodying wider natural principles, would enlarge to mutual benefit the worlds of producers and consumers, and conquer scarcity, disease, and ignorance, as well as sin.

By the late 1870s Spencer sensed that 'fellow-feeling' was endangered by a 'positive' and enlarged conceptualization of the state (Meadowcroft, 1995) and a revival of militancy, war, and rebarbarization. Yet his pessimism was mitigated, it should be noted, by what he saw as the tangible advances of sympathetic individuals in terms of justice and beneficence. Voluntary restraints on competition, honouring of payments due, and spontaneously-offered mutual support had become hallmarks among highly evolved persons. They pursued knowledge and culture, and engaged in public affairs, augmenting their own and others' fulfilment. They were wise parents, and attentive offspring. They were 'natural centres of happiness' (1910: ii. 423). His expectation, first stated in the *Sociology* in 1876 and gaining wider attention on its repetition in a speech in America in 1882, was that 'higher activities' would become more evident in social life 'by inversion of the belief that life is for work into the belief that work is for life' (1893: 563). We catch a scent of the later nineteenth-century theology of the Incarnation, in which man's natural goodness achieved ascendancy over his propensity for sin (Hilton, 1988). The introduction of new shades of expression and emphasis in Spencer's late-century thought implied no rupture structural continuity, but remind us that Spencer was, after all, of his time.

CONCLUSION

Spencer was an iconic figure in Victorian life, and often a shrewd critic of it. He is pivotal in the intellectual history of the natural and social sciences of Britain and America.[37] Moreover, as implied by the many translations of his writings, for few countries can histories of the biological and social sciences and political and cultural life within them be counted comprehensive unless the narrative embraces Spencer. His inclusion is not, though, a guarantee of accuracy: populist tags such as 'apologist for laissez-faire' still discourage fresh critical appreciation. Any worthwhile estimate of the legitimate authority enduring in his ideas has to be nuanced. In 1905 the Comtean positivist Frederic Harrison, who had collaborated with Spencer in lobbying for Church disestablishment and non-aggression and sparred with him over positivist humanism, gave the newly-founded annual 'Herbert Spencer Lecture' at Oxford. He quoted from Leonard Courtney's eulogy spoken over Spencer's coffin at the Golders Green crematorium,[38] but then dismissed as 'far beyond the truth' the claim that Spencer had 'evolved "one coherent conception"' (1905: 29–30). This verdict on his universal theory owed little to differences in values and much to its irremediable conceptual deficiencies. Yet his understanding of social life and individuals in terms of spontaneous cooperation and organicism, founded on an integrated continuum of analysis, biological, psychological, and sociological, retains salience today. This specific contribution exhibited defects and lacunae, but the interdisciplinary *kind of perspective* he advocated is widely accepted as essential for sound explanation in the study of individuals and social life, although the part he played is, if noted, often misread. While the applicability of a neo-Darwinian 'selectionist' explanatory paradigm to social science contexts is a growing

---

[37] Spencer founded no school of disciples. Auberon Herbert (see Offer, 2006: 9, 105–8) and Roland Wilson (1911) are examples of individuals who championed his libertarian ethics into the 20th century (on others, see Greenleaf, 1983; and Taylor, 1992).

[38] The eulogy is in Duncan, 1911: 478–81. On Harrison and Spencer see Eisen, 1968.

focus of attention (Runciman, 2009), Spencer's contribution of a 'selectionist' approach to explaining change in the *Sociology* and the *Ethics* passes almost unnoticed though warranting retrieval (Offer, 2010).

REFERENCES

Alland, A. (1974), 'Why Not Spencer?', *Journal of Anthropological Research*, 30; repr. in Offer (ed.) (2000), ii. 460–70.

Balfour, A. J. (1892), *A Fragment on Progress*, Edinburgh, David Douglas; repr. in Offer (ed.) (2000), i. 44–59.

Barton, R. (1990), '"An influential set of chaps": The X-Club and Royal Society Politics 1864–1885', *British Journal for the History of Science*, vol. 23, pt. 1, no. 76, pp. 53–81.

Barton, R. (1998), ' "Huxley, Lubbock and half a dozen others": Professionals and Gentlemen in the Formation of the X Club, 1851–1864', *Isis*, 89/3: 410–44.

Benn, A. W. (1880), 'Another View of Mr. Spencer's *Ethics*', *Mind*, os 5/20: 489–512; repr. in Offer (ed.) (2000), iii. 310–22.

Bixby, J. T. (1882), 'Herbert Spencer's *Data of Ethics*', *Modern Review*, 3; repr. in Offer (ed.) (2000), iii. 292–310.

Black, R. D. C. (2002), 'The Political Economy of Thomas Edward Cliffe Leslie (1826–1882): A Re-Assessment', *European Journal of the History of Economic Thought*, 9/1: 17–41.

Bosanquet, B. (1895/1997), 'Socialism and Natural Selection' (1895), in D. Boucher (ed.) *The British Idealists*, Cambridge: Cambridge University Press, 1997, pp. 50–67.

Bradley, F. H. (1876), *Ethical Studies*, London: King.

Calderwood, H. (1892), 'Animal Ethics as Described by Herbert Spencer', *Philosophical Review*, 1/3; repr. in Offer (ed.) (2000), iii. 352–59.

Carneiro, R. L. (1972), 'The Devolution of Evolution', *Social Biology*, 19; repr. in Offer (ed.) (2000), ii. 426–40.

Carneiro, R. L. (1973), 'Structure, Function and Equilibrium in the Evolutionism of Herbert Spencer', *Journal of Anthropological Research*, 29; repr. in Offer (ed.) (2000), ii. 441–59.

Carneiro, R. L. (1981), 'Herbert Spencer as an Anthropologist', *Journal of Libertarian Studies*, 5; repr. in Offer (ed.) (2000), ii. 563–624.

Chambers, R. [initially Anon.] (1844), *Vestiges of the Natural History of Creation*, London: Churchill.

Collins, F. H. (1889), *An Epitome of the Synthetic Philosophy*, London: Williams and Norgate.

Combe, G. (1846), *Moral Philosophy; or The Duties of Man Considered in his Individual, Domestic and Social Capacities*, Edinburgh: Maclachlan Stewart, and London: Longman.

Cunningham, S. (1994), 'Herbert Spencer, Bertrand Russell and the Shape of Early Analytic Philosophy', *Russell: The Journal of the Bertrand Russell Archives*, 14 (Summer), 7–29.

den Otter, S. (1996), *British Idealism and Social Explanation: A Study in Late Victorian Thought*, Oxford and New York: Clarendon Press.

Dewey, J. (1904), 'The Philosophical Work of Herbert Spencer', *Philosophical Review*, 13, repr. in Offer (ed.) (2000), i. 31–43.

Duncan, D. (1911), *The Life and Letters of Herbert Spencer*, London: Williams and Norgate.

Eisen, S. (1967), 'Herbert Spencer and the Spectre of Comte', *Journal of British Studies*, V7/1; repr. in Offer (ed.) (2000), ii. 227–44.

Eisen, S. (1968), 'Frederic Harrison and Herbert Spencer: Embattled Unbelievers', *Victorian Studies* (September), repr. in Offer (ed.) (2000), i. 144–65.

Elliott, P. (2003), 'Erasmus Darwin, Herbert Spencer, and the Origins of the Evolutionary Worldview in British Provincial Scientific Culture 1770–1850', *Isis*, 94: 1–29.

Elwick, J. (2003), 'Herbert Spencer and the Disunity of the Social Organism', *History of Science*, 41: 35–72.

Flew, A. G. N. (1967), *Evolutionary Ethics*, London: Macmillan.

Francis, M. (2007), *Herbert Spencer and the Invention of Modern Life*, Ithaca, NY and London: Cornell University Press; Stocksfield: Acumen.

Freeman, D. (1974), 'The Evolutionary Theories of Charles Darwin and Herbert Spencer', *Current Anthropology*, 15/3: 211–37; repr. in Offer (ed.) (2000), ii. 5–69.

Gaus, G. (2001), 'Bosanquet's Communitarian Defense of Economic Individualism: A Lesson in the Complexities of Political Theory, in Simhony and Weinstein (eds.), *The New Liberalism*, Cambridge: Cambridge University Press, pp. 137–58.

George, H. (1892), *Herbert Spencer: A Perplexed Philosopher; Being an Examination of Mr. Herbert Spencer's Various Utterances on the Land Question*, New York: Webster.

Gibbon, C. (1878), *The Life of George Combe*, 2 vols., London, Macmillan.

Gray, J. N. (1982), 'Spencer on the Ethics of Liberty and the Limits of State Interference', *History of Political Thought*, 3; repr. in Offer (ed.) (2000), iv. 234–49.

Gray, J. N. (1995), *Liberalism*, Milton Keynes: Open University Press.

Gray, T. (1981), 'Herbert Spencer's Theory of Justice—Desert or Entitlement?', *History of Economic Thought*, ii, repr. in Offer (ed.) (2000), iii. 381–403.

Gray, T. (1996), *The Political Philosophy of Herbert Spencer: Individualism and Organicism*, Aldershot: Avebury,

Green, T. H. (1883), *Prolegomena to Ethics*, Oxford: Oxford University Press.

Greenleaf, W. H. (1983), *The British Political Tradition*, ii. *The Ideological Heritage*, London: Routledge.

Guthrie, M. (1879), *On Mr. Spencer's Formula of Evolution as an Exhaustive Statement of the Changes of the Universe, Followed by a Résumé of Criticisms of Spencer's First Principles*, London: Trübner.

Guthrie, M. (1882), *On Mr. Spencer's Unification of Knowledge*, London: Trübner.

Guthrie, M. (1884), *On Mr. Spencer's Data of Ethics*, London: Modern Press.

Haines, V. A. (1988), 'Is Spencer's Theory an Evolutionary Theory?', *American Journal of Sociology*, 93; repr. in Offer (ed.) (2000), ii. 471–93.

Haines, V. A. (1992) 'Spencer's Philosophy of Science', *British Journal of Sociology*, 43/2, repr. in Offer (ed.) (2000), i. 126–43.

Harris, J. (1992), 'Political Thought and the Welfare State 1870–1940: An Intellectual Framework for British Social Policy', *Past and Present*, 135: 116–41.

Harrison, F. (1905), 'Herbert Spencer', *Herbert Spencer Lecture*, Oxford: Oxford University Press.

Hilton, B. (1988), *The Age of Atonement*, Oxford: Clarendon Press.

Hobhouse, L. T. (1911), *Social Evolution and Political Theory*, New York: Columbia University Press.

Hodgson, G. M. (2006), *Economics in the Shadows of Darwin and Marx*, Cheltenham: Edward Elgar.

Hodgson, S. H. (1872), 'The Future of Metaphysic', *Contemporary Review* (Nov.).

Hofstadter, R. (1944), *Social Darwinism in American Thought*, New York: Braziller, (rev. edn. 1955).

Huxley, T. H. (1871), 'Administrative Nihilism', *Fortnightly Review*, 10; repr. in Offer (ed.) (2000), iv. 56–74.

Ingold, T. (1986), *Evolution and Social Life*, Cambridge: Cambridge University Press.

Jacyna, L. S. (1980), 'Science and Social Order in the Thought of A. J. Balfour', *Isis*, 71: 11–34.

James. W. (1911), 'Herbert Spencer's Autobiography', in *Memories and Studies*, New York: Longmans, Green (1st published in *Atlantic Monthly*, July 1904); repr. in Offer (ed.) (2000), i. 19–30.

Jenson, J. V. (1970), 'The X Club: Fraternity of Victorian Scientists', *British Journal for the History of Science*, 5/1: 63–72.

Jones, R. A. (1970), 'Comte and Spencer: A Priority Dispute in Social Science', *Journal of the History of the Behavioral Sciences*, 6: 241–54.

Kirkman, T. P. (1876), *Philosophy Without Assumptions*, London: Longmans, Green, and Co.

Laland, K. N., and Brown, G. R. (2002), *Sense and Nonsense: Evolutionary Perspectives in Human Behaviour*, Oxford: Oxford University Press.

Leonard, T. (2009), 'Origins of the Myth of Social Darwinism: The Ambiguous Legacy of Richard Hofstadter's *Social Darwinism in American Thought*', *Journal of Economic Behavior and Organization*, 71/1: 37–51.

Leslie, T. E. C. (1879) 'Political Economy and Sociology', in his *Essays in Political and Moral Philosophy* Dublin: Hodges, Foster and Figgis, and London: Longmans, Green, pp. 383–411.

Lewis, J. (1995), *The Voluntary Sector, the State and Social Work in Britain*, Aldershot: Edward Elgar.

McBriar, A. M. (1987), *An Edwardian Mixed Doubles: The Bosanquets versus The Webbs*, Oxford: Clarendon Press.

MacIntyre, A. (1999), *Dependent Rational Animals: Why Human Beings Need the Virtues*, London: Duckworth.

MacLeod, R. (1970), 'The X-Club: A Social Network of Science in Late-Victorian England', *Notes and Records of the Royal Society of London*, 24/2: 305–22.

Marshall, A. (1925), *Memorials of Alfred Marshall*, ed. A. C. Pigou, London, Macmillan.

Meadowcroft, J. (1995), *Conceptualizing the State: Innovation and Dispute in British Political Thought 1880–1914*, Oxford: Clarendon Press.

Medawar, Sir P. (1969). 'Herbert Spencer and the Law of General Evolution' in *The Art of the Soluble* (Harmondsworth: Penguin); repr. in Offer (ed.) (2000), i. 111–25.

Miller, D. (1976), *Social Justice*, Oxford: Oxford University Press.

Moore, G. E. (1901), *Principia Ethica*, London: Cambridge University Press.

Muirhead, J. H. (1939), *The Man versus the State as a Present Issue*, London: Allen and Unwin.

Offer, J. (ed.) (1994), *Herbert Spencer: Political Writings*, Cambridge: Cambridge University Press.

Offer, J. (ed.) (2000), *Herbert Spencer: Critical Assessments*, 4 vols., London: Routledge.

Offer, J. (2003), 'Free Agent or "Conscious Automaton"? Contrasting Interpretations of the Individual in Spencer's Writing on Social and Moral Life', *Sociological Review*, 51/1: 1–19.

Offer, J. (2006), *An Intellectual History of British Social Policy*, Bristol: The Policy Press.

Offer, J. (2010), *Herbert Spencer and Social Theory*, London: Palgrave Macmillan.

Passmore, J. A. (1968), *A Hundred Years of Philosophy*, Harmondsworth: Penguin Books.

Pearce, T. (2010), 'From "Circumstances" to "Environment": Herbert Spencer and the Origins of the Idea of Organism–Environment Interaction', *Studies in History and Philosophy of Science Part C: Studies in History and Philosophy of Biological and Biomedical Sciences*, 41/3: 241–52.

Peel, J. D. Y. (1971), *Herbert Spencer: The Evolution of a Sociologist*, London: Heineman.

Perrin, R. (1993) *Herbert Spencer: A Primary and Secondary Bibliography*, New York and London: Garland.

Perrin, R. (1995), 'Émile Durkheim's *Division of Labour* and the Shadow of Herbert Spencer', *Sociological Quarterly*, 36; repr. in Offer (ed.) (2000), ii. 339–60.

Rashid, S. (1977), 'Richard Whately and *Christian Political* Economy at Oxford and Dublin', *Journal of the History of Ideas*, 38: 145–55.

Richards, R. J. (1987), *Darwin and the Emergence of Evolutionary Theories of Mind and Behaviour*, Chicago and London: University of Chicago.

Ritchie, D. G. (1900), 'Ethical Democracy: Evolution and Democracy', in D. Boucher (1997) (ed.), *The British Idealists*, Cambridge: Cambridge University Press, pp. 68–93.

Roche, M. (1973), *Phenomenology, Language and the Social Sciences*, London and Boston: Routledge and Kegan Paul.

Royce, J. (1904), *Herbert Spencer: An Estimate and a Review*, New York: Fox Duffield.

Runciman, W. G. (2009), *The Theory of Cultural and Social Selection*, Cambridge: Cambridge University Press.

Rylance, R. (2000), *Victorian Psychology and British Culture 1850–1880*, Oxford: Oxford University Press.

Secord, J. A. (2000), *Victorian Sensation: The Extraordinary Publication, Reception and Secret Authorship of 'Vestiges of the Natural History of Creation'*, Chicago: Chicago University Press.

Seth, J. (1889), 'The Evolution of Morality', *Mind*, 14; repr. in Offer (ed.) (2000), iii. 333–51.

Sidgwick, H. (1873), 'Review of Spencer's *Principles of Psychology*', *The Academy* (April), 131–4.

Sidgwick, H. (1876), 'The Theory of Evolution in Its Application to Practice', *Mind*, 1: 52–67.

Sidgwick, H. (1877), *The Methods of Ethics* (2nd edn.), London, Macmillan.

Sidgwick, H. (1880), 'Mr Spencer's Ethical System', *Mind*, 5; repr. in Offer (ed.) 2000, iii. 360–9.

Sidgwick, H. (1892), 'Critical Notices [Spencer's *Justice*]', in *Mind*, NS 1; repr. in Offer (ed.) (2000), iii. 370–80.

Sidgwick, H. (1899), 'The Relation of Ethics to Sociology', *International Journal of Ethics*, 10: 1–21.

Smith, C. U. M. (1983), 'Herbert Spencer's Epigenetic Epistemology', *Studies in History and Philosophy of Science*, 14/1 : 1–22.

Smith, G. H. (1981), 'Herbert Spencer's Theory of Causation', *Journal of Libertarian Studies*, 5; repr. in Offer (ed.) (2000), ii. 384–425.

Spencer, H. (1836), 'Poor Laws—Reply to "TWS"', *Bath and West of England Magazine*, (Mar.); repr. in Offer (ed.) (1994), pp. 179–81.

Spencer, H. (1843), *The Proper Sphere of Government: A Reprint of a Series of Letters Originally Published in 'The Nonconformist'*, London: Brittain; repr. in Offer (ed.) (1994), pp. 3–57.

Spencer, H. (1851), *Social Statics: or the Conditions Essential to Human Happiness Specified, and the First of Them Developed*, London: Chapman.

Spencer, H. (1854), 'Manners and Fashion', *Essays* (1901), iii. 1–51; 1st published in *Westminster Review* (April).

Spencer, H. (1857a), 'Progress: Its Law and Cause', *Essays* (1901), i. 8–62; 1st published in *Westminster Review* (April).

Spencer, H. (1857b), 'Transcendental Physiology', *Essays* (1901), i. 63–107; 1st published as 'The Ultimate Laws of Physiology' in *National Review* (October).

Spencer, H. (1859), 'The Morals of Trade', in *Essays* (1901), iii. 113–51; 1st published in *Westminster Review* (April).

Spencer, H. (1860), 'The Social Organism', *Essays*, i. 265–307; first published in *Westminster Review* (Jan.).

Spencer, H. (1862), *First Principles* (1st edn.), London: Williams and Norgate.

Spencer, H. (1864), 'The Classification of the Sciences', and 'Reasons for Dissenting from the Philosophy of M. Comte', *Essays* (1901), ii. 74–117 and 118–44, 1st published as a brochure.

Spencer, H. (1867), *First Principles* (2nd edn.), London: Williams and Norgate.

Spencer, H. (1870), *First Principles* (3rd edn.), London, Williams and Norgate.

Spencer, H. (1871), 'Specialized Administration', in *Essays* (1901), iii. 404–44; 1st published in *Fortnightly Review* (Dec.).

Spencer, H. (1872), 'Mr. Martineau on Evolution', *Essays* (1901), i. 371–88; 1st published in *Contemporary Review* (June).

Spencer, H. (1873a), 'Replies to Criticisms', *Essays* (1901), ii. 218–320; first published in *Fortnightly Review* (Nov. and Dec.).

Spencer, H. (1873b), *The Study of Sociology*, London: King.

Spencer, H. (1881a), *The Principles of Psychology*, 2 vols. (3rd edn.), London, Williams and Norgate.

Spencer, H. (1881b), 'Replies to Criticisms on *The Data of Ethics*', *Mind*, 6/21: 82–98.

Spencer, H. (1883), 'The Americans', *Essays* (1901), iii. 471–92; 1st published in *Contemporary Review* (Jan.).

Spencer, H. (1884), *The Man versus The State*, London: Williams and Norgate; repr. in Offer (ed.) (1994), pp. 61–175.

Spencer, H. (1886), 'The Factors of Organic Evolution', *Essays* (1901), i. 389–466; first published in *Nineteenth Century* (May).

Spencer, H. (1889), 'Preface', in F. Howard Collins, *An Epitome of the Synthetic Philosophy*, London: Williams and Norgate, 1889, pp. vii–xi.

Spencer, H. (1891), *The Principles of Sociology*, vol. ii (2nd edn.), New York: Appleton.

Spencer, H. (1893), *The Principles of Sociology*, vol. i (3rd edn.), London: Williams and Norgate.

Spencer, H. (1894), *The Principles of Biology*, 2 vols., London: William and Norgate.

Spencer, H. (1896), *The Principles of Sociology*, vol. iii, London: Williams and Norgate.

Spencer, H. (1897), *Various Fragments*, London: Williams and Norgate.

Spencer, H. (1899), 'The Filiation of Ideas', in Duncan (1911), pp. 533–76.

Spencer, H. (1900), *First Principles* (6th edn.), London: Williams and Norgate.

Spencer, H. (1901), *Essays: Scientific, Political and Speculative*, London: Williams and Norgate.

Spencer, H. (1904), *An Autobiography*, 2 vols., London: Williams and Norgate.

Spencer, H. (1910), *The Principles of Ethics*, 2 vols., New York and London: Appleton.

Taylor, M. W. (1992), *Men versus The State: Herbert Spencer and Late Victorian Individualism*, Oxford: Oxford University Press.

Taylor, M. W. (2007), *The Philosophy of Herbert Spencer*, London and New York: Continuum.

Vincent, A. (1984), 'The Poor Law Report of 1909 and the Social Theory of the Charity Organisation Society', *Victorian Studies*, 27: 343–363.

Ward, L. F. (1894), 'The Political Ethics of Herbert Spencer', *Annals of the American Academy of Political Science*, 4; repr. in Offer (ed.) (2000), iv. 75–102.

Waterman, A. M. C. (1991), *Revolution, Economics and Religion: Christian Political Economy 1798–1833*, Cambridge: Cambridge University Press.

Webb, B. (1926), *My Apprenticeship*, London: Longmans.

Webb, B. (1948), *Our Partnership*, London: Longmans, Green.

Weinstein, D. (1998), *Equal Freedom and Utility: Herbert Spencer's Liberal Utilitarianism*, Cambridge: Cambridge University Press.

Whately, R. (1832), *Introductory Lectures on Political Economy*, London: Fellowes.

Wilson, Sir R. (1911), *The Province of the State*, London: King.

Wiltshire, D. (1978), *The Social and Political Thought of Herbert Spencer*, Oxford: Oxford University Press.

Wright, T. R. (1986), *The Religion of Humanity: The Impact of Comtean Positivism on Victorian Britain*, Cambridge: Cambridge University Press.

Young, R. M. (1967), 'The Development of Herbert Spencer's Concept of Evolution', *Actes du 11 Congrès International d'Histoire des Sciences*, Warsaw: Ossolineum, vol. ii; repr. in Offer (ed.) (2000), ii. 378–83.

Young, R. M. (1970), *Mind, Brain and Adaptation in the Nineteenth Century*, London: Oxford University Press.

Zafirovski, M. (2003), *Market and Society: Two Theoretical Frameworks*, Westport, Conn.: Praeger.

CHAPTER 14

....

THE EVOLUTIONARY TURN IN POSITIVISM: G. H. LEWES AND LESLIE STEPHEN

....

MARK FRANCIS

POSITIVISM in England began when Auguste Comte's ideas on the classification of sciences became known to the wide readership of John Stuart Mill's *System of Logic*.[1] How many English positivists acquired Comte's 'positive philosophy' from the French original is unknown, but it was probably few. John Venn commented that, as far as he knew, the young Henry Sidgwick was the only man at Cambridge who studied Comte first hand, 'that is, otherwise than through the medium in Mill's *Logic*'.[2] Venn's remark that Mills's work was the medium through which positivism spread is apt because Comte's ideas were scarcely modified in the form in which they appeared in Mill's *System of Logic*—even after Mill had publicly repudiated the Frenchman's philosophy in 1865.[3] Mill saw little need to alter the basic ideas he had borrowed from Comte, because, as he ungenerously remarked, they were the same as those of Hume: the only causes that can be known are those other phenomena which are their invariable antecedents, and there are no other explanations of cause.[4] Comte had formulated his notion of causation as a historical progression that began with

---

[1] John Stuart Mill, *A System of Logic Ratiocinative and Inductive*, ed. J. M. Robson (Toronto: University of Toronto, 1973) (*Collected Works of John Stuart Mill*, vols. vii and viii). Mill's *Logic* was first published in 1843.

[2] *Henry Sidgwick, A Memoir by A.S. and E.M.S* (London, Macmillan, 1906), p. 136.

[3] John Stuart Mill, 'Auguste Comte and Positivism', in *Essays on Ethics, Religion and Society*, ed. J. M. Robson (Toronto: University of Toronto Press, 1969) (*Collected Works of John Stuart Mill*, x. 261–368). Alexander Bain (*John Stuart Mill: A Criticism, with Personal Recollections* (London, Longmans, 1882), 72–3), who was Mill's longest serving lieutenant, noted that Mill's altered estimate of Comte never extended to repudiating the latter's historical method of the three stages of knowledge or his method of social science.

[4] Mill, writing to 1865, claimed that the philosophy called positivism was not a recent invention of Comte's, but a simple adherence to the methods of all the great scientific minds which have made the human race what it is. He has merely taken his place 'in a fight long since engaged, and on the side already in the main victorious'. J. S. Mill, 'Auguste Comte and Positivism', 266, 267, and 269.

theological explanations of natural phenomena and ended with science where facts were explained in reference to invariable laws. He framed this development as a necessary historical movement through three stages—theological, metaphysical, and positive. The stages encompassed more than science, stretching out to embrace a general theory of civilization.[5] As historical entities, Comte's stages had so little basis in historical research that the positivist H. T. Buckle was regarded as a traitor by some Comteans when he offered empirical evidence to support the positivist thesis on historical change.[6]

The positivist vision, as conveyed by Mill's *Logic*, was that social progress and an increase in the scientific explanation of natural phenomena would go hand in hand. However, it was unclear how exactly this synthesis would operate. Its only support was a teleological suggestion that 'reflection, guided by history, has taught us the intimacy of the connexion of every age of humanity with every other, making us see the earthly destiny of mankind as the playing out of a great drama, or the action of a prolonged epic, wherein all the generations of mankind become indissolubly united into a single image.'[7] This image clashed with anti-teleological beliefs of English naturalism.[8] It also fitted badly with the commonplace Baconian ideas of the young English philosophers and scientists whom Mill had encouraged to take up positivism.[9] In England, positivists preferred not to explain change in the teleological fashion and space had to be found for this kind of evolutionary theory that Comte had overlooked, or spurned, when he found them in the work of scientists such as Geoffroy Saint-Hilaire and Lamarck. The mention of Lamarck's name here does not signal that mid-century English positivists engaged in a debate on the merits of Lamarck's theory of evolution compared to that of Darwin. That would falsely indicate that positivists were closely focused upon change in species, whereas their evolutionary ideas stemmed from other scientific interests. To paraphrase Peter Bowler, there were non-Darwinian revolutionary languages in Victorian England,[10] and these were co-opted into positivist discourses. That is, positivist evolutionary theory was not exclusively, nor even mainly, an adumbration of natural selection. Partly this was because positivist evolution discourse pre-dated the publication of Darwin's *Origin of Species*, and partly because it was based on investigations

---

[5] The recent Comtean scholar (Mary Pickering, *Auguste Comte, An Intellectual Biography* (Cambridge: Cambridge University Press, 1993), i. 565) draws a close parallel between Comte and Hegel, but this seems far-fetched as Comte's stages were not linked by a Hegelian dialectic. That is, if you accepted his psychology, then you might follow Hegel's ideas on how one historical movement was transformed into another. However, Comte's dislike of psychology meant that he did not care to base his stages of knowledge on the kind of introspective evidence used by Hegel.

[6] Alfred Henry Huth, *The Life and Writings of Henry Thomas Buckle* (London: Sampson Low, 1880), i. 229. Buckle's emphasis upon emotion as a cause of social change echoes Mill's views in *Considerations on Representative Government*.

[7] Mill, 'Auguste Comte and Positivism', 334.

[8] William Paley's *Natural Theology* would not allow science to reach for teleological explanations, and his influence was widespread in England.

[9] In Bernadette Bensuade-Vincent's fine discussion of the writings of positivism that were available in mid-nineteenth-century France, she makes the point that Baconianism was literally against Comte's philosophy. In other words, there was a popular variety of positivism which only adopted the most positive and verified part of science, namely the facts, and rejected the rest as conjecture. (See 'Antomism and Positivism: A Legend about French Chemistry', *Annals of Science*, 56/1 (1999), 89.)

[10] See Peter J. Bowler, *The Non-Darwinian Revolution* (Baltimore, Md.: Johns Hopkins University Press, 1992).

into traditional philosophical domains, such as the philosophy of mind and moral philosophy, where natural selection theory had less purchase than it did with questions of animal
speciation.

There was an 'evolutionary turn' in nineteenth-century positivism which modified it from
being a Comtean scientific classification based upon the succession of the sciences because
of their complexity, and because of the level of generality of their arguments,[11] to a philosophy based upon biology. The new variety of positivism retained the anti-theological rhetoric
that had attracted radicals to the original version, and it reduced the role that the human
mind had had in shaping history. Evolutionary positivism refused to allow more eminence
to the intellectual sphere than it had to the spheres of soul or spirit. For evolutionary positivists even Comte's 'humanity' was suspect; human beings were not an elevated group of
beings, but simply animals with sensory organs and a consciousness that were common to
other species in the animal kingdom.

John Stuart Mill was chiefly interested in Comte's scientific philosophy because he was
intrigued by its invention of sociology as a science, but he encouraged two of his early pro-
tégés, G. H. Lewes and Alexander Bain, to consider bringing psychological knowledge into
the positivist framework.[12] Both began to look for a positivist form of mental science, a
subject that was absent from Comte's classification. This project was part of a campaign to
support Comte. Mill had taken on the burden of raising funds for the French savant after
the latter had lost his academic position in 1843.[13] However, by the mid-1840s tensions had
arisen between Comte and Mill, so the role of organizing a subvention for Comte fell to
Lewes who, for a few years after 1847, was flattered when Comte assigned him the role of
chief English Comtist.[14] Such recognition was only fair as Comte's reputation had benefited
from Lewes's popular *Biographical History of Philosophy*—a work which did as much as
Mill's *Logic* had done for the Frenchman.[15]

Unlike Mill, Lewes stayed loyal to Comte and noted that while he was considered a heretic by most Comteans, he remained a 'reverent heretic'.[16] This heresy requires some explanation because it registers the distance between Lewes and orthodox English Comteans
from the 1850s onwards. There was a gulf—not over philosophical matters, but political
ones. Lewes, like many English liberals, had become increasingly critical of Comte's des-
potic qualities and of the utopianism in Comte's *Système de politique positive* (1851–1854)
and his *Catéchisme positiviste* (1855). This meant that his enthusiasm for positivism was
restricted to an exposition of Comte's works on the philosophy of science as these appeared

---

[11] Johan Heilbron, 'Auguste Comte and Historical Epistemology: A Reply to Dick Pels', *History of the Human Sciences*, 9/153 (1996), 155.

[12] Heilbron, 'Auguste Comte and Historical Epistemology', 72–3. And see T. R. Wright, *The Religion of Humanity: The Impact of Positivism on Victorian Britain* (Cambridge: Cambridge University Press, 1986), 50.

[13] Bain, *John Stuart Mill*, 73–4.

[14] Rosemary Ashton, *G. H. Lewes, A Life* (Oxford: Clarendon Press, 1991), 129.

[15] Ashton, *G. H. Lewes*, 49. Ashton claims that the first two volumes of the *Biographical History of Philosophy* had sold 7,000 copies by August 1845.

[16] G. H. Lewes, *The History of Philosophy* (4th edn., London, Longmans, 1871), ii. 683 (further references in the notes will be to this edition). This book is a later edition of the *Biographical History of Philosophy* mentioned in n. 15. By the time the 4th edition appeared Lewes had given up on positivism except as a historical phenomenon.

in the *Cours de philosophie positive* (1830–43). Since most English Comteans were engaged in theological debates rather than ones on philosophical issues, they found it unnecessary to focus upon scientific topics: rather than engage with Lewes it was simpler for them to condemn him for heresy.[17] The exclusion of Lewes from Comtean ranks was made easier by the fact that Comte separated himself from Lewes in 1853 for making unauthorized additions to positivism.[18] Lewes's *Comte's Philosophy of the Sciences* provided a recent gloss on subjects, such as biology, that Comte had not touched since 1838;[19] Lewes's inclusion of psychology as a scientific discipline was also difficult for Comte. Lewes treated positivism as part of a system that fell under the law of development, and he regarded this as a completion of Comte's ideas.[20] Lewes saw his stance as modernizing positivism by substituting a biologically based evolutionary theory for Comte's historical account of the growth of knowledge. To put this simply, Lewes treated human beings—together with their science and intellectual structures—as specialized organisms while Comte's positivism was a sophisticated history of ideas that was not subject to the laws of science which he thought governed all other phenomena.

Lewes's *Comte's Philosophy of the Sciences* (1853) and his *Physiology of Common Life* (1859, 1860) contained all of his positivist philosophy. His *History of Philosophy*, though becoming more technical in later editions, remained a popular exposition of the philosophical ideas of others. Though Lewes's *History* expressed enthusiasm about positivism, which it proclaimed as the eleventh and final epoch of philosophy, it contained no original ideas.

Lewes published serious philosophical work besides his *Comte's Philosophy* and *The Physiology of Common Life*, but this appeared in the 1870s when he had ceased to be a positivist. *The Problems of Life and Mind* (1874 and 1875) and *The Physical Basis of Mind* (1877) were rooted in the philosophy of Kant and Hegel, and were hostile to science.[21] In these works Lewes described his positivist work as mistaken, and objected to the notion that human mental processes could be successfully interpreted by the use of biological and neurological comparisons with animals: that would be to admit ideas of animal consciousness and sensibility into the realm of the philosophy of mind which he now believed should be

---

[17] There are two general surveys of the political English intellectuals who called themselves Comtean positivists. One is by T. R. Wright (*Religion of Humanity*) and the other by Christopher Kent (*Brains, Numbers, Elitism, Comtism, and Democracy in Mid-Victorian England* (Toronto: University of Toronto Press, 1978)).

[18] Ashton, *G. H. Lewes*, 129. Comte's attitude towards Lewes changed after he was sent a copy of Lewes's 1853 book.

[19] G. H. Lewes, *Comte's Philosophy of the Sciences* (London: Henry G. Bohn, 1853), p. iv. Lewes actually says organic chemistry and physiology are included, but since Lewes felt that the word 'biology' had been adopted by quack scientists in England it was safer to have the subjects 'organic chemistry' and 'physiology'.

[20] Lewes, *History of Philosophy*, ii. 694. This use of evolutionary language is clearly Lewes's rather than Comte's. Lewes's book on Comte is studded with evolutionary and developmental language whereas a contemporary redaction, *The Positive Philosophy of Auguste Comte*, trans. Harriet Martineau, 2 vols. (London: John Chapman, 1853), has only one reference to development in over a thousand pages.

[21] This view of Lewes's later philosophy can be found in contemporary sources. See Thomas W. Staley, 'Keeping Philosophy in Mind: Shadworth H. Hodgson's Articulation of the Boundaries of Philosophy and Science', *Journal of the History of Ideas*, 70/2 (April 2009), 300. The relationship between Lewes's Hegelianism and Kantianism and similar philosophical stances in Britain has yet to be clarified in the secondary literature.

confined to human mental processes. His revised view was that only our internal examination of mental phenomena could be faithfully studied.[22] In case anyone suspected that
some vestige of positivism lingered in his thought, he then reanalysed biology without reference to evolution,[23] and restated the laws of nature without reference to biology.[24] Lewes also
criticized his old friend, the positivist psychologist Alexander Bain, for assuming 'Nature's
uniformity'.[25] Since uniformity in nature had also been Lewes's bedrock assumption in the
1850s when he was constructing his positivist psychology, this change was almost an act of
self-abnegation. Lewes, in old age, wanted nothing to do with a scientific philosophy which
had encouraged comparative analysis between human and animal minds on the grounds
that there was no longer any reason to trust uniformity in nature. When Lewes abandoned
positivism in the 1870s, he was not just abandoning Comte's system, but the system he himself had reconfigured during the 1850s. Before Lewes had begun work upon it, positivism
had been a hierarchical classification of science headed by mathematics, and descending
through astronomy, physics, and chemistry till it reached to biology and sociology.

Comte's hierarchy of sciences had remained in Lewes's formulation of positivism, but it
served little useful function there since Lewes was not significantly interested in the problems of classification,[26] but, to reiterate, was attempting to refound sciences upon an evolutionary synthesis. Before one can appreciate the shift implied in Lewes's 1850s positivism,
it is important to recapitulate those of Comte's ideas which can be misunderstood as close
analogues to Lewes's. To begin with, it is tempting to consider Comte's system as a precursor to unity of science theories in which the life sciences were to be reduced to the physical
sciences.[27] However, Comte was emphatic that it was his duty to protect 'the scientific originality of [biology], continually exposed as it has been in the past to the encroachments of
inorganic philosophy which tends to make it a mere adjunct of its own scientific domain'.[28]
Biology was to be an independent science, and not, as it was for Lamarck, a branch of 'terrestrial physics'.[29] The mention of Lamarck's name could signal to the reader that Comte was
engaged in creating a theory of development of species, or perhaps of evolution in general,
but this would be mistaken as his intention was only to establish biology upon a secure foundation from where it could be defended against any theological and metaphysical concepts
that explained natural phenomena from the human standpoint, and attributed an arbitrary
will to them in such a way as would neglect natural processes.[30] The relics of theological and

[22] G. H. Lewes, *Problems of Life and Mind*, i (London: Trübner, 1874), pp. v and vi.

[23] Lewes, *Problems of Life and Mind*, i. 128–34.

[24] Lewes, *Problems of Life and Mind*, i. 306–13.

[25] G. H. Lewes, *Problems of Life and Mind*, ii (London: Trübner, 1875), 98.

[26] Lewes lived in a period in which the classification of sciences was a matter of intense speculation,
yet he never took issue with, nor commented upon, the philosophy of classification except once when
he noted that Herbert Spencer's objection to Comte's serial classification of the science had not been
answered. Lewes did not pay attention to the classification systems of contemporaries such as John Stuart
Mill, William Whewell, and Louis Agassiz.

[27] This sort of mistake has been soundly corrected by Johan Heilbron ('Auguste Comte and Historical
Epistemology', 134–5).

[28] *The Essential Comte, Selected from Cours de Philosophie Positive*, ed. Stanislav Andreski
(London: Croom, Helm, 1974), 111.

[29] Pickering, *Comte*, i. 588.

[30] Pickering, *Comte*, i. 589.

metaphysical explanations that particularly annoyed Comte were vitalist theories that imagined organisms were directed by a life force. For Comte, the fact that no evidence of such a
force existed showed that it was an archaic and imaginary figment.

After he had disposed of vitalism, Comte was left with no mechanism that could be used
to explain development or evolution. He simply posited that some phenomena displayed
a dynamic, rather than static, condition when undergoing change. Since he had joined his
newly invented subject sociology to biology as closely related disciplines dealing with organisms, he felt able to treat both under one general heading. However, this was not because
they were both subject to evolution. Evolutionary statements did not appeal to Comte
because they tended to be generated by empirical findings on organisms, and Comte distrusted empiricism. In addition, Comte had no need for a development theory because his
positive philosophy granted the human mind the ability to theorize in such a way as to unify
facts. What led to progress was a change in theories, not a development in the mental apparatus that employed them.[31] When it came to development, Comte was interested in social
development, not organic development in general. The study of the organic characteristics
of individual humans might be similar to the study of plants and animals, but since Comte's
philosophical theory of the mind was restricted to the collective product of all minds, their
organic characteristics did not matter to him.

Comte was preoccupied with linking the great subjects of philosophical speculation, man
and the universe, but the link between them remained in a philosophical realm, not a material one.[32] When he invoked Lamarck's theory of environmentally caused change, it was not
to refer to the animal and plant kingdoms, but was restricted to a consideration of human
mental development through socialization.[33] That is, Comte claimed that human beings
developed physical, moral, and intellectual faculties by employing them. 'Thus through
exercise, the unique characteristics of the human species—human intelligence and sociability—will eventually become more dominant with both the individual and society.'[34] Despite
his knowledge of Lamarck, and his recommendation that scientists study milieus,[35] Comte's
theory of change was a cultural, not a biological, imperative. Since he believed that he had
historical evidence on the working of the mind, he had no need to study psychology as for
him this would have been merely a study of the organic preconditions of philosophy. It was
the mind that had, over time, developed through theological and metaphysical stages to the
final scientific one.

G. H. LEWES

Unlike Comte, Lewes did not ignore the organic underpinnings of the mind: he was too
conventional a liberal to surrender the individual's psyche in exchange for a notion of

---

[31] Pickering, *Comte*, i. 337.

[32] Pickering, *Comte*, i. 590.

[33] Lewes felt that Comte could not appreciate Lamarck's contribution to science and created his
hypothesis as a mere 'philosophic artifice'. G. H. Lewes, *Comte's Philosophy of the Sciences*, 190.

[34] Pickering, *Comte*, i. 619.

[35] Pickering, *Comte*, i. 591.

a generalized mind stretching back to the ancient world. In this attitude Lewes was typically British; Comte's treatment of mind and the consequential avoiding of psychology was problematic for positivists such as John Stuart Mill and Alexander Bain from the 1840s. While they shared Comte's desire to free science from spiritual explanations that attributed volition to natural objects, they could not quite follow Comte in refusing to give psychology scientific standing on the grounds that, unlike subjects such as mathematics, its findings lacked independence from human beings. If one takes this Comtean belief as seriously as Lewes did, then the correct reply to it would be to configure psychology so that it resembled a scientific discipline that was more independent of socially constructed meanings. It would then more closely resemble those sciences that were within the Comtean canon. This is why Lewes attempted to make psychology into a positivist science by focusing upon the physiological and anatomical aspects of consciousness and sensation. For him, objective and verifiable claims about a state of mind would satisfy the Comtean demand for the independence of a scientific discipline. This, in turn, meant that the mind would no longer hold a unique place in the universe as a record of human achievement as it had with Comte. However, to offset this, Lewes felt that the method used to study mental activity should be the same scientific one that had brought progress elsewhere.

Lewes's positivist method corrected the pre-scientific presumption that the mind was seated in the part of the brain called the cerebrum. Research in neurophysiology had demonstrated that the mind was not centred in that portion of the brain, but was dispersed over the entire brain, the ganglia, and the nervous system.[36] In maintaining this Lewes was not being a reductionist and identifying the mind within the brain as a physical organ. Nor was he holding a materialist position in the manner of some nineteenth-century German psychologists.[37] Instead, he was adapting the nature of sensations and consciousness so that they were common to all animals rather than unique to human beings in particular. He imagined that since many life forms enjoyed consciousness, and that since human beings were like other animals in having sensations generalized throughout their nervous systems, he had shown that the human psyche was embedded in a living world which was neither materialistic nor mechanical in its functioning. The fact that Lewes had placed animals on the same level as humanity did not trouble him. Whereas Comte had stressed human reasoning capacity as the most essential human quality, Lewes emphasized the capacity to feel emotions as important, but this did not attribute any uniqueness to human beings as they had similar emotions to animals.

Lewes's popular exposition of positivism began in 1852 and 1853.[38] Initially he intended only to write a popular redaction of Comte's system, but this limited task rapidly

---

[36] Some historical context for English physiological psychology can be found in L. S. Jacyna, 'The Physiology of Mind, the Unity of Nature, and the Moral Order in Victorian Thought', *British Journal for the History of Science*, 14/2 (July 1981), 109–32.

[37] Peter Alan Dale (*In Pursuit of a Scientific Culture* (Madison: University of Wisconsin Press, 1989), 68 and 71) who, incidentally, rates Lewes rather than Spencer or Bain as the most eminent British psychologist of the mid-Victorian period, notes that Lewes's German sources took a reductionist approach to the relationship between mind and body.

[38] Lewes first began to speculate on Comte's philosophy in 1843, but his more systematic views on positivism only appeared a decade later when he attempted a detailed exposition of Comte. The first parts of this appeared serially in 1852 in *The Leader*, a weekly newspaper he edited with Thornton Hunt. These were reprinted in 1853 (without some of their original harshness) together with more length and some technical additions.

transformed itself into an original account of positivism because Lewes's ideas were partially rooted in a Romantic view of Man. He was enamoured with German Romantics such
as Goethe and Schelling as well as with Carlyle's version of Teutonic Romanticism. These
sources caused him to believe that Comte's notion of historical and philosophical change
had given too much weight to the intellect, and too little to heart and feeling. Nature, Lewes
believed, was a balanced uniformity composed of both intellect and passion. Unlike early
Romantics, Lewes did not imagine that man had power over nature, and he was ironically
alert for any sign that contemporaries believed that humanity was in control of the environment, or was seeking to create a Frankenstein.[39] It was obvious to him that human beings
were moved by their emotions. The intellect, Lewes proclaimed, was the servant, not the
lord, of the heart. Like Comte, Lewes found a role for religion as well as science in guiding
humanity to a better destiny, but this was based upon the needs of the individual psyche,
not, as it was with Comte, upon the need for social order.[40] While Lewes claimed it was a
Comtean strategy to subordinate the intellect to the heart, his own beliefs in the religion of
the heart reached back to his private tutelage by yet another Romantic, Leigh Hunt.[41]

Lewes's avowed Romanticism sat uneasily with the positivism that he imbibed from his
other private tutor, J. S. Mill,[42] from whom he borrowed heavily when expounding how
humanity achieved progress.[43] '[T]he evolutions of humanity correspond with the evolutions of thought—that science is the torch whereby we see our way'.[44] Mill's theory of progress—which was being summed up here—was not based upon biology. Instead it was an
orthodox Comtean notion based upon the growth of speculative beliefs and civilization. As
we shall see, Lewes abandoned this theory of the ameliorating effects of culture, and in its
place, substituted a biological evolutionary theory.

Lewes insistently used the word 'evolution' when describing Comte's three stages of history: the theological, the 'metaphysical', and the positive in which explanations of nature
are progressively ranked as supernatural, abstract, and scientific.[45] The ultimate explanation,
the scientific one, analyses phenomena by reference to the laws which are not only demonstrated by reason, but in accordance with facts.[46] So far, Lewes was an orthodox Comtean
in balancing between deduction and induction, but he also co-opted an idea from his
friend Herbert Spencer to the effect that the distinguishing characteristic of any science is
that it both sees and foresees. 'Science is prevision'.[47] This addition put tension on Comtean

---

[39] Lewes, *Comte's Philosophy of the Sciences*, 142.

[40] Lewes, *Comte's Philosophy of the Sciences*, 5.

[41] Lewes had developed his views on the religion of the heart with Herbert Spencer and Thornton
Hunt. See Mark Francis, *Herbert Spencer and the Invention of Modern Life* (Durham: Acumen and Ithaca,
NY: Cornell University Press, 2007), 119–22.

[42] Bain (*John Stuart Mill*, 76 n.) remembered Lewes 'sitting at Mill's feet' in 1842—after he had studied
in Germany.

[43] Long quotations from Book VI of Mill's *System of Logic* are included in Lewes's 1853 account
of Comte.

[44] Lewes, *Comte's Philosophy of the Sciences*, 23.

[45] Lewes refers to Comte's fundamental law as that of 'human evolution', and titles the section of his
book in which he discusses Comte's three stages of scientific explanation 'The Fundamental Law of
Evolution' (Lewes, *Comte's Philosophy of the Sciences*, 25 and 26–37.)

[46] Lewes, *Comte's Philosophy of the Sciences*, 27.

[47] Lewes, *Comte's Philosophy of the Sciences*, 27.

positivism since it refocuses science away from its historical development towards a predictive future. Comte, unlike Whewell and Mill, had provided little warrant for speculating on the development of future sciences. Instead, the essential characteristics of sciences were where they fitted on the progressive scale which started with God-centred explanations of the universe and ended with contemporary law-centred explanations that could be verified. Theologically based explanations referred to a God's will when explaining a natural phenomenon such a storm or a volcanic eruption, while 'metaphysical' explanations could be found in the work of early scientists such as Kepler where the movement of a planet was explained by assigning it to a mind that controls it.[48] Both theological and metaphysical explanations were superseded by scientific ones that referred only to the invariableness of phenomena under similar conditions. To exemplify the types of explanation Lewes invokes the basilisk which, in the theological stage of knowledge, was imagined as an invisible entity that inhabited deserted cellars, and whose glance could kill in such a way that there was no sign of violence on its victim. The later positive explanation for this phenomenon was that the person was killed by an invisible gas that had accumulated in the blocked-up cellar.[49]

Lewes treated the physical sciences in much the same way as Comte had done, but when it came to the life sciences his exposition of positivism became more novel. The variance began with biology which Comte had drawn exclusively from Blainville's lectures on comparative anatomy and physiology. From Lewes's perspective, a reliance upon Blainville was unfortunate as it left out the protean influence on biology of Geoffroy Saint-Hilaire and Lamarck who had preceded Blainville; it also omitted biological work after 1838 when Comte had ceased to interest himself in the life sciences. While Comte warned his followers against the dangers of vitalism and mechanism, the Scylla and Charybdis of biological speculation, he offered little else of value: Lewes was left to decipher the impressive early French debates on evolution by himself. For example, he consulted Saint-Hilaire's works for theoretical information about whether monsters were freaks of nature or whether they had developed from primitive germs that contained all the features which subsequently developed. This early genetic discussion helped Lewes towards an understanding of individual development of biological characteristics, but it also predisposed him to regard genetic arguments in general as a type of metaphysical explanation because they resemble theological explanations in their emphasis upon the origins of phenomena. In the place of genetics, Lewes emphasized a 'positive' conception of epigenesis as a gradual organic development in response to conditions.[50] The significance of this was that monsters were likely to be simple cases of organic deviation that could be explained by Saint-Hilaire's law of arrested development. Instead of searching for pre-existent germs, the explanation of monstrosity was to be found in the study of 'positive' embryology; and it was this science that was to become the key to explaining positivism in biology.[51]

[48] Lewes, *Comte's Philosophy of the Sciences*, 29.

[49] Lewes, *Comte's Philosophy of the Sciences*, 31. Lewes recycled the example in his *History of Philosophy* (ii. 718). He could not imagine a 'metaphysical' basilisk to place between his theological and scientific ones.

[50] Lewes, *Comte's Philosophy of the Sciences*, 32.

[51] Lewes offered examples of primitive features of developmental change: milk teeth in mammals and down in birds. Lewes, *Comte's Philosophy of the Sciences*, 32–4.

Lewes's interpolation of new theories of biology—especially that of embryology—into Comte's system had the effect of breaking down the idea that there were three specific stages in the development of scientific knowledge. Embryology suggested that development was consistent with the simultaneous presence of primitive and advanced characteristics in an organism, and Lewes suspected that this might also be the case with the development of science. This was why he endorsed the idea that the stages of knowledge might overlap, and that one could regard explanations as contemporaneous rather than successive.[52] That is, one might simultaneously hold an explanation that was, for example, metaphysical and scientific. The result of Lewes's innovations was that Comtean stages of knowledge were not handled as serious concepts, but merely useful rhetorical tools which could be used to batter orthodox religions.[53]

Lewes possessed a sense of religious awe and this went hand in hand with his suspicion that Comte's vision of humanity was excessively rational and ordered. It was like anthropomorphic images of God, except that early versions of these at least allowed for human beings to imagine that a God had passion as well as rationality. That is, Lewes preferred early or barbarian anthropomorphism to Comteanism: the former at least attributed to God an idealized totality of human nature, rather than just a part.[54] To overemphasize the rational part of human nature was simply erroneous. It did not matter to Lewes whether such an error were committed by orthodox natural theologians arguing for design in nature, or by their opponent, Auguste Comte, holding an 'unwarrantable, (strange to say) metaphysical assumption that science permits us to conceive a happier arrangement'. Lewes was incredulous at Comte's audacity here; he mockingly repeated ' "science permits it!" '[55] Lewes became outraged at Comte's naïve assumption that the natural world would have to follow edicts laid down by human reason: it was simply irritating for Comte to offer such a speculation as a scientific one. Lewes also noted with annoyance that when Comte argued that nature went from simple to complex, he did not employ an evolutionary idea, but moved inexplicably from the study of organic tissues to organic laws, then to their combination, and finally to the consideration of grouping their organs into systems.[56] Comte's ideas here, according to Lewes, were merely heuristic: organs and systems were being arranged in an intellectual framework without any reference to science. There was no hint of the empirically based 'ascending complexity' that Lewes found in the work of Liebig and Mulder and in that of his friend Herbert Spencer.[57]

Comte's positivism had not been designed to accommodate evolutionary theories; his hypothesis had been that scientific enquiry should be restricted to the study of laws rather than causes, and this meant that he discarded searches for the biological or psychological origins of phenomena: such quests were remnants of theologically inspired investigations into Man's place in the universe. In brief, for Comte, origin-hunting was primitive.

[52] Lewes, *Comte's Philosophy of the Sciences*, 51.
[53] Religion, in general, was supported by Lewes rather than attacked. He was very critical of Comte for dismissing as primitive, the awe-filled religious sensations that one experienced when gazing upwards at the starry heavens. (Lewes, *Comte's Philosophy of the Sciences*, 92.)
[54] Lewes, *Comte's Philosophy of the Sciences*, 90.
[55] Lewes, *Comte's Philosophy of the Sciences*, 91.
[56] Lewes, *Comte's Philosophy of the Sciences*, 181.
[57] Lewes, *Comte's Philosophy of the Sciences*, 135 and 170–1.

For Lewes, however, the investigations which Comte had ignored as promoting unfathomable mysteries[58] might very well be sources of serious scientific progress. Lewes saw Comte's indifference to origins as a sterile rationality which could only be corrected by examining nature in a way that was not constrained by artificial laws. On this point Lewes was sympathetic to Cuvier who believed that a 'law was too rigorous a conception to control nature',[59] and he extended this to argue against the type of development theory that relied upon a fixed and definite plan for the universe. In arguing thus Lewes was turning Comte's reliance on scientific laws against Comte himself.[60] Rather than the presence of laws always guaranteeing scientific credibility, an excessive reliance upon them created a picture of the universe that was too mechanical.[61] Since Comte himself thought that scientific explanations that displayed 'mechanism' were faulty, Lewes saw himself as triumphantly advancing a positivist position.

In any case, Lewes did not need to employ laws when analysing organic phenomena; instead, he claimed that developing organisms mirrored a natural display of the progression of life—with humanity anchored in the animal world, but having the advantages of intelligence, morality, and sociability that placed it on a higher level.[62] This appeal to the 'progression of life' as a phenomenon in nature was curious because it was a phenomenon that did not causally effect any processes or forces with which it was connected. In brief, Lewes's evolutionary positivism did not regard laws as controlling nature and man. They were merely products of development that could not stand above the very processes that changed them.

Lewes's evolutionary theory was primarily a descriptive analysis. When he wrote 'From the dawn of organic life upwards, we perceive an ascending complexity owing primarily, I believe, to the *greater multiples of the elementary equivalents*',[63] he was not expecting organic chemistry to discover the cause of evolution, but only to show that it displayed a pattern of growth. To explore the causes of development would cause the searcher to become entangled with the 'vital force' which he, like Comte, thought a phantom. As a typical example of the misuse of 'vital force' in causal explanation Lewes used the dormant seed. If, he remarked, a dormant seed sprang into life then this could be understood as: (1), the seed possessing a 'vital principle' which manifested itself under suitable conditions; (2), the seed receiving light from heat which was the 'vital principle'; or (3), the seed being a peculiar arrangement of organic molecules which, when a determined direction was given to its forces, manifested certain phenomena that we call life.[64] The first two explanations seemed circular to Lewes; the life that appeared as an abstraction was also the 'vital principle'. (This was an example of what Lewes, following Comte, called a 'metaphysical' explanation.) The third explanation was a generalized statement of what has been discovered through the observation of nature by scientists.[65] For Lewes only this sort of observation could be the

---

[58] Lewes, *Comte's Philosophy of the Sciences*, 106.

[59] Lewes, *Comte's Philosophy of the Sciences*, 53.

[60] Lewes thought that Comte's notion of law had been employed in a particularly repellent manner by some English Comteans. He suggested that Harriet Martineau had deified law and substituted it for God. (*The Leader*, 3/49 (1 March 1 1851), p. 202.)

[61] Lewes, *Comte's Philosophy of the Sciences*, 54.

[62] Lewes, *Comte's Philosophy of the Sciences*, 176.

[63] Lewes, *Comte's Philosophy of the Sciences*, 135.

[64] Lewes, *Comte's Philosophy of the Sciences*, 139.

[65] Lewes, *Comte's Philosophy of the Sciences*, 140

basis of viable scientific statements. This meant that he ruled out of contention any genetic explanations for evolution just as they were being popularized in England by Robert Chambers's *Vestiges of Creation*.[66]

Only induction based on observation was trustworthy: we should not, Lewes argued, look at acorns or eggs as 'oak-forming forces' or 'chicken-forming forces'.[67] This approach would be as insensible as imagining that there was a 'crystal-forming force' because living processes were no more mysterious than those which can be seen in the inorganic world.[68] The so-called 'vital force' was simply a special property of one form of matter.

At the centre of Lewes's non-genetic evolutionary theory was his grasp of new scientific work on the cell. These cells appeared to be universal in organisms so he ventured the question, 'What is the form which being universal may be supposed to be indispensable to organic life?'[69] Though a focus on ideas of universal forms seems Platonic,[70] its main purpose in Lewes's positivism was to allow him to construct an evolutionary theory without reference to extinct and archaic life forms. That is, Lewes simply posited that the simplest form, a single-celled organism, occupied a low evolutionary position, and then suggested an ascending order for organisms as they became more complex. This meant that the second stage of development was an association of cells, while the third was the transformation of such clusters into organic tissue.[71]

While Lewes's theory of the ascending scale of life was unaccompanied by any consideration of the actual origins of plants, animals, or Mankind such as could be found in palaeobiology or prehistory, he did adopt Spencer's early biological theory in order to provide a general explanation of evolution. This was the proposition that, as organisms advanced, they displayed an increasing power of self-preservation, and a greater tendency towards individuation. The higher an organism was on the evolutionary scale, the less likely it was to be at the mercy of the environment. Higher animals possessed 'strength, sagacity, swiftness (all of them indicative of superior strength) thus a correspondent ability to maintain life'.[72] A lower organism, however, was 'continually liable to be destroyed by the elements, by want of food, by enemies'.[73] This general Spencerian explanation that an animal's evolutionary position was based on strength and protection from the environment did not closely resemble Darwinian arguments because neither Spencer nor Lewes was interested in species, and it was not species that could be found struggling in their arguments. The purpose of Lewes's evolutionary argument was primarily to suggest that organisms higher up the scale have

---

[66] Lewes moved in the same circles as Chambers and the latter's ideas were well known to him. See James A. Second, *Victorian Sensation: The Extraordinary Publication, Reception and Secret Authorship of Vestiges of the Natural History of Creation* (Chicago: University of Chicago Press, 2000), pp. 483–4.

[67] Lewes, *Comte's Philosophy of the Sciences*, 141.

[68] Lewes, *Comte's Philosophy of the Sciences*, 163.

[69] Lewes, *Comte's Philosophy of the Sciences*, 155.

[70] Rosemary Ashton (*George Eliot, A Life* (London: Penguin Books, 1996), 162 and 104) notes that Lewes was in the habit of visiting Richard Owen in his laboratory. Since Owen was associated with a scientific variety of Christian Platonism it is possible that he lent Lewes more than his expertise in the dissection of amphibians.

[71] Lewes, *Comte's Philosophy of the Sciences*, 155.

[72] Lewes, *Comte's Philosophy of the Sciences*, 170.

[73] Lewes, *Comte's Philosophy of the Sciences*, 170.

increased functionality, and this is not an argument for natural selection as increased functionality might not aid survival.

To reiterate, Lewes's evolutionary values were not drawn from Darwin or even from Lamarck—whose work he admired. The explanatory power of their ideas was not useful to him because his scientific interests were not embedded in zoology, but in neurophysiology which seemed more specifically useful than zoology when one was interested in human progress as the centrepiece of organic evolution. The science of the brain had the advantage over palaeobiology in being experimental, and this was important to Lewes who was a keen experimenter. While Comte had been sceptical about putting a heavy reliance upon experiments, Lewes was adept at laboratory work, and had sacrificed many frogs and other animals in his search for knowledge about the workings of nervous tissue.[74] With a focus upon neurophysiology, the purpose of this evolutionary theory was not to offer a hypothesis about the adaptation of species, but to form accurate hypotheses about the functioning of the human brain in comparison with those of lower animals. These hypotheses, unlike ones about fossils, could be tested and verified.

Before Lewes could employ the results of his researches on neurophysiology, he needed to take issue with philosophers who had an aversion to the idea that sensation and thought were electrical impulses, and who were particularly irked by the statement that such things 'were secreted by the brain as bile is secreted by the liver'.[75] The basic offence here, as far as philosophers were concerned, was the notion that mental phenomena were rooted in the brain, and were materialistic in the same way as any other organic phenomena. The mind/brain debate is a perennial one, but Lewes was engaged in a particular moment of this debate which began in the 1830s, and was still going on vigorously two decades later when Lewes began speculating on the philosophy of science. While he had some sympathy with philosophers of mind, he felt that their position was untenable as it was essentially an argument that if humans were only composed of blind unconscious matter then they could not think. To Lewes this was analogous to saying that the blind cannot see or that the unconscious cannot be conscious. The only response warranted by such arguments was the experimental evidence that human beings were partly made up of matter that was conscious and sensitive, and while these qualities were not the same as thinking, they were close. Thinking, like consciousness and sensation, was a property of nervous tissue and this was something about which Lewes's contemporaries knew too much to have to rely upon a soul or spirit when explaining mental operations. 'To claim for the nervous tissues any superadded entity called thought, is to desert the plain path of observation for capricious conjecture.'[76] Lewes suspected that one might as well call strength an entity and then regard it as an immaterial principle superadded to muscular tissue. At this point, it seemed as if Lewes had joined Carl Vogt in comparing thought with bile, but he believed that he was taking a more delicate approach than that adopted by most physiologists. Rather than referring to the mind as the 'collective manifestation' of nervous tissue,[77] Lewes stressed that sensation is a special

[74] John Morley, who dined frequently with Lewes and George Eliot, was horrified more than once when he met some mutilated animal limping on the stairs after one of Lewes's vivisection experiments (F. W. Hirst, *Early Life and Letters of John Morley* (London: Macmillan, 1927), i. 41).

[75] Lewes, *Comte's Philosophy of the Sciences*, 200. In his *History of Philosophy* (ii. 751) Lewes attributes this line to Carl Vogt.

[76] Lewes, *Comte's Philosophy of the Sciences*, 201.

[77] Lewes, *Comte's Philosophy of the Sciences*, 204. Lewes it taking issue here with a well-known textbook on physiology by Todd and Baconian.

kind of material response and that positivists should avoid crude materialistic explanations. Since physiologists offering materialistic explanations employed a notion of 'vital force' as the generalized expression of all the properties of an organic being,[78] they had reverted to a 'metaphysical' and pre-scientific explanation. Lewes believed that physiologists who substituted electrical impulses for 'vital forces' were also flawed. While he thought it likely that the cause of muscular contractions was a specialized electrical impulse, there was no reason to generalize this impulse into a 'metaphysical' entity; it would always stay associated with muscular tissue, not with organisms in general.[79]

Lewes canvassed all the work of neurophysiology—back to the time of Charles Bell and Marshall Hall a quarter of a century before[80]—in order to resolve the vexed distinction between voluntary and involuntary actions, some of which may be automatic. Lewes also canvassed the problem of whether reflex or instinctive actions should be seen as truly voluntary.[81] For Lewes, the most productive discourse in neurophysiology was the subject of instinct. As far as he could discover, philosophers were treating instincts as mysterious in the same way as they treated thought. That is, they were transforming them into abstract entities that filled the same niche in the animal world as the mind did in the human one. This, Lewes argued, meant that you should refer to instinct as 'a rudimentary reason'. You should not artificially distinguish between human and animal sensibilities or human and animal consciousness as if one was more automatic than the other: they were both products of similar organic systems composed of instincts, reflex actions, and responses. There was good experimental evidence to show that the mind and instinct functioned in the same ways, and these similarities should not be overlooked by philosophers who were only interested in essentialist answers about distant causes.

Complete reductionism was avoided here because Lewes followed J. S. Mill in holding that there were some mental phenomena, such as successions of ideas, that did not admit of being deduced from a nervous organization.[82] Mill believed that psychology, like neurophysiology, should be based upon the direct study of, and experimentation on, mental phenomena (such as successions of ideas) themselves. Emphatically they should not be deduced from the laws of physiology. The point of this was to suggest that physiological laws might be induced from the laws of animal life, and that they ultimately depended upon physical conditions. In saying this in 1853, Lewes was not merely echoing Mill, but expressing dissent from Comte's dismissal of psychology as a science.

However, it was what happened after 1853 that separated Lewes's ideas from those of Mill. This gap was caused by Lewes staying faithful to Mill's teachings in the 1840s *System of Logic* about the need to put psychology on a properly empirical foundation while, at the same time, linking it to the relevant science of physiology. Mill, however, had dropped this compromise, and reverted to a conventional analysis of mental phenomena that preceded his

---

[78] Lewes, *Comte's Philosophy of the Sciences*, 206.

[79] Lewes, *Comte's Philosophy of the Sciences*, 206.

[80] G. H. Lewes, *The Physiology of Common Life*, ii (Edinburgh: William Blackwood, 1860), 26; see also pp. 47, 172, 182 and 191. Lewes's *Physiology of Common Life* was his most popular philosophical work after his *History of Philosophy*. According to Ashton (*George Eliot*, 195) the *Physiology of Common Life* was translated into several languages and was particularly influential in Russia.

[81] Lewes, *Comte's Philosophy of the Sciences*, 208.

[82] Lewes, *Comte's Philosophy of the Sciences*, 210–11.

interest in positivism. Instead of following through with the suggestion of correcting Comte by including psychology with the other sciences, Mill simply and carelessly reissued his father's rather dated work on association psychology as if his interest in science had never demanded a more rigorous treatment.[83]

The chief philosophical problem for a positivist psychology was how to stay anchored in the brain and nervous system without becoming so reductionist that you treated human beings as automatons. Reductionism would have meant that the brain was like a machine analogous to a watch or a steam engine. While Lewes considered it reasonable to consider that the brain and nervous system functioned mechanically, he insisted that this sort of functioning was a series of responses that included those that were usually called conscious and voluntary. While human beings might behave like machines, some of their functions were not instinctive nor responses to external stimuli. The mechanical analogy with the brain should not be used to rule out the role that sensation plays in the mind: sensation should be seen as acting like a mainspring in a watch or fuel in a steam engine.[84] In other words, sensation was what made living organisms act, and this animating impulse was a special property of organisms. Unlike Victorian machinery, organisms were capable of self-development and self-regulation.[85] They did not need an engineer either to plan or project-manage them.

Lewes would not permit his contemporaries to take refuge in the adage 'brutes have instinct—men have mind' because this did not recognize intelligence in the animal world.[86] He believed that mental phenomena were not truly unique to humanity and were only subsets of organic phenomena. The distinction between instinct and mind was, according to Lewes, as trivial as that between brutes with only legs and humans with arms and legs. The prominence of biology and neurophysiology in Lewes's ideas focused the role of psychology to the comparative one of looking beneath superficial distinctions to basic structures. 'Comparative anatomy shows us that all the innumerable varieties of the vertebrate structure are but modifications of one type; and comparative psychology will show that all the innumerable mental varieties are owing to various modifications of the nervous system.'[87] To Lewes the distinction between instinct and human intelligence was not a qualitative one such as would exist if men were spiritual creatures who were independent of the anatomical origins of humanity.[88] Instead, the distinction between humans and animals was a matter of degree; the small psychological differences between them were insignificant. Lewes was insistent on this point and refused to allow consciousness as a uniquely human

---

[83] See James Mill, *Analysis of the Phenomena of the Human Mind* (2nd edn., London: Longmans, 1869). This work was originally published in 1829—before J. S. Mill's venture into Comteanism, and before any advances in neurophysiology. One could argue that J. S. Mill had no need to follow his own advice on how to put psychology on a scientific basis because he could rely upon Alexander Bain to do that for him. However, in the notes both J. S. Mill and Alexander Bain added to the 1869 edition of the *Analysis*, Bain argues that James Mill did not adequately separate the emotions from the intellect (see ii. 181–2 n.) whereas J. S. Mill insists upon eliciting the emotion and the intellect in such a way as to undermine Bain's distinction (see ii. 185–6 n.). In other words, Mill undermined Bain's scientifically based observations on emotions.

[84] Lewes, *Physiology of the Common Life*, ii. 163.

[85] Lewes, *Physiology of the Common Life*. ii. 164.

[86] Lewes, *Comte's Philosophy of the Sciences*, 213.

[87] Lewes, *Comte's Philosophy of the Sciences*, 213–14.

[88] Lewes, *Comte's Philosophy of the Sciences*, 214.

characteristic.[89] Consciousness was an aspect that the human psyche shared with other animals. This proposition had extreme outcomes for philosophy. For example, there was no rationale for analysing the psychology of egoism because that would place too heavy an emphasis upon human intelligence in a way that would unnaturally separate it from the animal sensibilities that remained within human psyches.[90] More generally, Lewes's stance kept to the physiological underpinnings of psychology as long as he was a positivist; unlike his friends Spencer and Bain who shared his scientific approach to psychology, he did not engage in mental experiments to test the limits of association psychology.[91]

Lewes's physiological research led him to insist that the brain should not be treated as if it were an organ that carried out commands of the mind. Instead the mind should be regarded as including all sensation, volition, and thought and was distributed across the whole nervous system.[92] There was no particular residence for the mind; Lewes was unwilling to accept either the traditional view of the brain as a *sensorium*,[93] or the newer physiological perception that there was a centre for sensation that reduced parts of the nervous system to the minor role of reflecting impressions back to the brain as a central governor.[94] What was at stake here was Lewes's conviction that all centres in the nervous system give rise to sensation, 'and these furnish elements to the general consciousness'.[95] His arguments were supported by his own experimental work, and by the findings of German and French scientific publications. Lewes accepted as a basic proposition the fact that the brain itself was incapable of feeling a sensation while the spinal chord did possess such a capacity.[96] He also canvassed the contemporary literature for evidence about the place of the ganglia in the nervous system, and reflected carefully about the features of automatic actions that were carried out by nervous centres which were severed from the brain.[97] From this it became clear to Lewes that all nervous centres gave rise to sensation, and, therefore, furnished portions of the general consciousness.

Once Lewes had disposed of the idea that the human brain was a unique centre of consciousness, he attempted to provide a scientific explanation of the brain from an evolutionary perspective. With the help of comparative anatomy, he noted that the cerebellum, as displayed in different animals, had a progressive scale that could be charted in terms of intellectual development. However, the high place that humans had on the scale of development did not give them any special advantage. Lewes cited Alexander Bain's *Senses and Intellect* to the effect that all animal life, down to the very lowest sentient being, possessed the property of consciousness and this 'operated as the instrument for generating and supporting

---

[89] Lewes, *Comte's Philosophy of the Sciences*, 214 .

[90] Lewes, *Comte's Philosophy of the Sciences*, 216.

[91] In the philosophical writings that Lewes published in the 1870s, he did not conduct mental experiments, but by then he was no longer a positivist.

[92] Lewes, *Physiology of Common Life*, ii. 4 and 5.

[93] Lewes, *Physiology of Common Life*, ii. 5.

[94] Lewes, *Physiology of Common Life*, ii. 46.

[95] Lewes, *Physiology of Common Life*, ii. 47.

[96] Lewes, *Physiology of Common Life*, ii. 19 and 23.

[97] Lewes (*Physiology of Common Life*, ii. 277), borrowing from Herbert Spencer's *Principles of Psychology* (1855), generalized sensibility to every animal organism. According to Spencer, the only important distinction between organisms was that sensibility became more specialized as the organism became more complex.

existence'.[98] As with his notion of sensibility, Lewes's idea of consciousness was a levelling one that placed humanity on the same footing as the rest of the animal kingdom. Ascent on the organic scale only implied that an organism was superior in variety and complexity; no new properties were acquired in the process. He believed that the 'primordial tissue' that had sufficed to construct primitive organisms also worked in newer and more complex organisms such as human beings.[99] Even the human attribute of thinking did not represent a qualitative shift, but only the result of a more complex arrangement of the same sorts of specialized cells that existed in lower animals. Lewes could not understand why philosophers would not acknowledge the modest claim of animals to the same prerogatives that humans possessed in being conscious of the splendour of the universe.[100] It was his goal as a positivist philosopher to use science to demonstrate that the different varieties of animal life displayed uniformities that were subject to scientific laws. If those uniformities were studied scientifically, the mystery that surrounded mental processes would be reduced; neuroscience could not reduce all the mysteries surrounding thought, but it would reduce their number.[101]

In conclusion, the general direction of Lewes's positivism was the same as Comte's; there was an injunction that one should focus upon modern science, not traditional philosophy, when thinking about Man or the universe. However, Lewes, as he claimed, was a heretic in terms of Comteanism. This was partly due to his reliance upon the empiricism against which Comte had warned, but, more importantly, Lewes had discarded Comtean precepts in such a way as to reconfigure psychology as an evolutionary science. This was how Lewes perceived his own claim to fame: he had added 'the law of development' to Comte's great legacy which meant that he too was part of this eleventh and final epoch of philosophy.[102] The combination of theories of evolutionary neuroscience with experimental investigation allowed Lewes to remain focused upon contemporary organic processes rather than being forced to consider evolution as a problem in palaeobiology and prehistory. There was no need to guess about the place of extinct dinosaurs, mastadons, and giant hyenas in the evolutionary past. That was a speculative matter relying upon uncertain data that could not be verified, while Lewes could base his evolutionary hypotheses upon data that could be checked experimentally. His evolutionary theory was a progressive sequence produced by arranging verifiable organic data—whether neurological, anatomical, or cellular—on a scale that went from simple to complex. This progress did not mean that an organism as a whole, was, or would be, uniformly developed. There was no promise here, as there was with Spencer, that human beings would make such biological progress as to shed their primitive features, because 'primitive' did not signify an archaic characteristic that was locked into the past. Instead, 'primitive' referred to simple organic mechanisms that partially controlled individual animals and these included humans who were complex organisms. Simple and complex mechanisms existed simultaneously, and while the latter were more evolved they

---

[98] Lewes, *Physiology of Common Life*, ii. 208. Lewes borrowed the idea from Alexander Bain's *Senses and the Intellect*. It should be noted that it does not involved competition in the way Darwin's evolutionary ideas did because, in this positivist theory, all animals possess consciousness, and none, therefore, would have a competitive advantage.

[99] Lewes, *Physiology of Common Life*, ii. 74.

[100] Lewes, *Physiology of Common Life*, ii. 78.

[101] Lewes, *Physiology of Common Life*, ii. 75

[102] Lewes, *History of Philosophy*, ii. 694.

did not hold all the authority when it came to directing the human organism. Direction was not a monopoly by a mental governor because that would invoke the kind of rational mind that Lewes had painstakingly discarded. In the place of a single controller, Lewes invoked the idea of a mind controlled by a generalissimo who, if killed, would leave various generals, colonels, and captains who could function as directors of the parts of the organism that were undamaged.[103] This metaphor captured the sense of Lewes's experiments on animals and proved, at least to him, the relative independence of parts of the mind. It had the additional advantage of reminding his reader that feelings, which might be considered as primitive and located outside the cerebellum, had independent standing: emotions were not necessarily subordinate to thought. This doubt about the priority of reason in humans was directed at Comte's rather eighteenth-century view of Man as the master of the universe. For Lewes, humanity was embedded in the animal kingdom and guided by the same instincts and motivated by the same feelings.

LESLIE STEPHEN

Leslie Stephen said that had he been at Oxford he might have been a positivist,[104] but this remark was not an admission doubting the ordained tenants of positivism: it was a humorous reference to the fact that Oxford, not Cambridge, had produced 'official' Comteans such as Frederick Harrison, Richard Congreve, and J. H. Bridges. In any case, the point was moot; Stephen had been too young to become a Comtean positivist. He did not go to London to establish himself as a writer until 1865 when Comte had been dead for several years, and Mill, instead of proselytizing Comteanism, was warning the intellectually minded youth to avoid Comteans because these were sectarians.[105] Then, too, Stephen was friendly with Spencer and Huxley who condemned Comtean positivism as Catholicism minus Christianity.[106]

Like Lewes, Stephen grasped the idea that it was evolutionists who had made positivism into a workable doctrine. Instead of parroting Comte, they had brought positivism into a more thoroughly scientific condition than it had been when under his control.[107] When Stephen referred to himself as a Darwinist, as he frequently did when dramatically enunciating views on agnosticism, he was not offering allegiance to a particular evolutionary theory; he was signalling to his secular readers that he wanted to confound Christians. For him, as for many Victorians, the proclamation of faith in Darwinism was a sign that one had thrown off the shackles of orthodox religion. However, when Stephen was attempting a nuanced exposition of philosophy, he avoided talk of his agnostic mission and of the granting of souls to monkeys, and instead, claimed membership in a school of philosophy that

---

[103] Lewes, *Physiology of Common Life*, ii. 97.

[104] F. W. Maitland, *The Life and Letters of Leslie Stephen* (London: Duckworth, 1907), 172.

[105] John Morley, *Recollections* (London: Macmillan, 1917), i. 69.

[106] Morley, *Recollections*, i. 69. Also see Gillian Fenwick, *Leslie Stephen's Life in Letters* (Aldershot: Scholar Press, 1993), 145.

[107] Maitland, *Leslie Stephen*, 352.

included Hume, Bentham, James and John Stuart Mill, G. H. Lewes, and Herbert Spencer.[108] In taking up philosophy, Stephen was not neglecting Darwin; on the contrary, he doted on him as a person, and, unlike Lewes, he did not shun natural selection theory. Nonetheless, Stephen's evolutionary inspiration came from diverse sources, and he was just as likely to rely upon non-Darwinians such as Spencer and Lewes as he was upon Darwin himself.[109]

The prime source for Stephen's positivism is his *Science of Ethics*. This was a multifunctional work. Primarily, it was designed to answer Henry Sidgwick's *Methods of Ethics*, which, in attacking Spencer's *Data of Ethics*, had threatened evolutionary theory. Sidgwick had breathed new life into utilitarian ethics, and had made the evolutionary perspective look homespun. This forced Stephen into the task of reviving the kind of traditional philosophy that Spencer had brushed aside as lacking in scientific credibility. Stephen was less encumbered than Spencer in not having a general philosophy to defend, and he was quite happy to base his exposition of morals upon old ethical theories, and try 'to bring them into harmony with the scientific principles I take for granted'.[110] Secondly, Stephen was a combatant in the war against John Stuart Mill's attempt to reintroduce association psychology into English philosophical language.[111] Thirdly, Stephen was conducting a rearguard defence of positivism against his brother James Fitzjames Stephen whose attack on Mill's political philosophy threatened positivism as well as the author of *On Liberty*.[112] James Fitzjames Stephen had attacked Mill's belief that the progress of civilization was based solely on an all-embracing love of humanity which would regenerate the human race.[113] He complained that the ideal which Mill hoped to transform the world was nothing more than Comte's dated religion of humanity. This was a problem for Leslie Stephen; rather than letting his brother laugh positivism out of court as a bogus religion, he busied himself with offering a defence of the scientific rationale of ethical change. This was a necessity if he were to rescue positivism from being associated with humanity.

The arguments against utilitarianism in the *Science of Ethics* were based on the objection that it fostered too great a dependency on the role of the individual. Stephen did not concern himself with utilitarian state theory here, but only with moral philosophy. His primary question was whether an individual did, in fact, foresee the possibility of experiencing pleasure or pain before making choices. His answer was that utilitarian claims that individuals possessed foresight were only rhetorical flourishes; action did not follow rational calculations,

---

[108] Leslie Stephen, *The Science of Ethics* (London: Smith, Elder & Co, 1882), p. vi.

[109] It is necessary to make the point because Noel Annan's much-acclaimed study (*Leslie Stephen: The Godless Victorian* (New York: Random House, 1984), 192 and 198–201) offered a crude and bloated analysis of the influence of Darwin upon secular thought. The result of this was to read Stephen's evolutionary philosophy as exclusively Darwinian.

[110] Stephen, *Science of Ethics*, p. viii.

[111] Stephen took up this task again in *The English Utilitarians* (London: Duckworth, 1900), ii. 335–6 and iii. 314 and 316. To suggest that Mill 'reintroduced' association psychology implies that he had previously abandoned it. A modern view of Mill might take issue with this implication. See Fred Wilson, 'Psychology and the Moral Sciences', in John Skorupski (ed.), *The Cambridge Companion to Mill* (Cambridge: Cambridge University Press, 1998), 216) where it is claimed that Mill never 'rejected' associationism. The point stressed here is that for most of his career he did not 'defend' it either.

[112] James Fitzjames Stephen, *Liberty, Equality, Fraternity* (2nd edn., London: Smith, Elder & Co., 1874), pp. xviii–xxxii.

[113] Stephen, *Liberty, Equality, Fraternity*, 298–300.

but instinctive impulses. At first sight, Stephen's argument against utilitarianism here seems misdirected as it does not focus upon hedonistic decisions, but only foresight. However, this is because contemporary utilitarians including James Fitzjames Stephen had glossed the utilitarian calculus in a Hobbesian language when the foresight of one's own preservation mattered more than pleasure and pain. This meant that Leslie Stephen had to ask *who* was being preserved—the individual or the species to which he or she belonged. According to Stephen, this meant that the effect of actions should be seen as affecting the group, not solitary persons.[114] Showing signs of having taught Plato, Stephen referred to instinctively motivated actions as the '*essential*' qualities of Man,[115] because they were the ones that the individual shared with other members of the race. By race, Stephen could mean either 'nation' or the 'species', but here it referred to the latter. He argued that Mill's *Logic* was mistaken in viewing a species as the equivalent to a 'real kind', and it was important to correct this by introducing a Darwinian notion of species which conveyed the 'essential' aspect of Man; rather leaving Man as a mere aggregate of qualities.[116] The 'essential' qualities of Man were permanent and not a matter of choice. Since instinctive qualities could not be discarded, it was pointless to interrogate each person as if he was a Robinson Crusoe[117] rather than part of a social organism.

This social organism did not possess the frightening qualities of Hobbes's Leviathan. Stephen could find no scientific warrant for subsuming the many within one all-powerful sovereign. This caveat meant that Stephen did not perceive society as analogous to a single brain that controlled the other components of the body. Rather, he thought of society as an organism with many centres of consciousness.[118] Each part of an animal was equal to the other parts, and, in point of fact, would have no use for a supreme commander. Since Stephen was constructing a moral theory rather than a political one, he had no need to consider the monarchical or republican implications of his ideas. In any case, he was not interested in ennobling society by comparing it with notable forms of governance. His social organism was similar to a lower organism, not to a higher organism such as a human being.[119] That being the case, Stephen did not feel drawn to offer a theory of state-led morality that might have been useful in countering individualistic utility theory. Instead, he followed Spencer in arguing that the study of ethics was a matter of examining, and analysing, virtues as discrete moral qualities. Stephen wrote at length about the typical Victorian virtues of temperance, courage, and truth as these had evolved. He also speculated on how such virtues had adjusted to differing social functions depending on the level of advancement of a society. All virtues were discussed as social functions that could not exist outside a society.[120] This comment was aimed at utility arguments which weighed ethical discussions from an individual's perspective.

---

[114] Stephen, *Science of Ethics*, 95.

[115] Stephen, *Science of Ethics*, 95.

[116] Stephen, *English Utilitarians*, iii. 130–1. For Stephen the notion that Man was merely a collection of attributes made the idea of the 'uniformity of nature'—held by both Comte and Mill—extremely precarious.

[117] Stephen, *Science of Ethics*, 95.

[118] Stephen, *Science of Ethics*, 111.

[119] Stephen, *Science of Ethics*, 126.

[120] Stephen, *Science of Ethics*, 454.

Underlying Stephen's criticisms of utilitarianism was the psychological argument that, unlike virtue ethics, it fostered an excessive reliance upon the intellect at the expense of the passions. John Stuart Mill, in reviving his father's association psychology, had not placed ethics on a modern scientific foundation. Stephen's objection was that the traditional basis of ethics rested on sympathy. That is, that basis of Hume's ethics had been replicated by James and John Stuart Mill when it had no other basis than being a traditional British sentiment. However, this was a misconception. Sympathy, Stephen argued, was a basic instinct, not an additional feeling that was discovered afresh when an individual's mind reached a certain stage of development.[121] To ignore instincts was to create an elevated but thin ideal of humans as if they were only intellects. To counter this Stephen insisted that humans were automata: that many daily occupations of humans were carried out with little more consciousness than that possessed by a machine. Further, he argued, it was impossible to predict whether a given passion will, or will not, operate in certain circumstances.[122] Further, there were basic human impulses, such as those for sex and parenting, that affected morality even though their utility value accrued to the species rather than to the individual.[123] These sorts of considerations made utilitarian calculations seem implausible to Stephen.

John Stuart Mill had linked an individual's progress with social progress caused by a sense of humanity, but this was not a thesis upon which Stephen could place any reliance. To him, humanity was only a remnant of Comte's theory of civilization and was an inadequate basis for scientific laws. In place of this cultural synthesis, Stephen offered a speculative behaviouralism in which moral actions were responses to social pressures. Since societies were akin to lower organisms, Stephen's view of human beings was not a sanguine one. He had adopted Spencer's bleak belief that every part of an organic system should be understood with reference to the mutual interdependence of the other parts, and of the organic whole.[124] There was no place here for a morality based on personal choices. Nor was there a place in Stephen's positivism for a vision of humanity that had learned its lessons from civilizations of the past and used them to move towards a progressive future. Stephen had severed the ethical links that utilitarianism had forged between social progress and the pleasures and pains that supposedly had produced it. Sensations were only correlative to certain stages of development, and could not have been the motivations for social development.[125] In any case, such a development would not be of benefit to the individual, but only to the group which did not have a mind. Stephen's long-term ethical perspective was a chilly one. There was no satisfaction for the individual who behaved well. Nor would good decisions be aggregated in such a way that one could trace the path in which general benefits would accrue from good actions. Stephen's opinion was that it just so happened that there would eventually be more correspondence between the society and the environment, and that there would be an increase in moral activity. Positivism was not required to be comforting.

---

[121] Stephen, *Science of Ethics*, 230. In *English Utilitarians* (iii. 374) Stephen blames Hume's notions of causation and explanation for undermining all utilitarian speculation, and for making utilitarians overlook their need for a theory of evolution.

[122] Stephen, *Science of Ethics*, 17.

[123] Stephen, *Science of Ethics*, 91.

[124] Stephen, *Science of Ethics*, 84

[125] Stephen, *Science of Ethics*, 88.

CHAPTER 15

....

BRITISH IDEALISM
AND EVOLUTION

....

DAVID BOUCHER

For the most part the British Idealists were politically engaged and passionate social reformers, committed to transforming to their advantage the philosophical foundations of the political tendencies of the times (Boucher 2010). They notoriously intervened on questions of education, especially for women; on temperance; state intervention; natural rights; imperialism; socialism versus liberalism; and the First World War. Their contribution to the evolution debate, however, is largely ignored by historians and philosophers, who generally assume that they were hostile to it because it was a form of naturalism.[1] British Idealism came to prominence during the 1870s and was the dominant manner of philosophical thinking in Britain, Australia, Canada, and South Africa from the 1880s until the First World War. Its main targets were utilitarianism, which it regarded as failing to value any good that could not be allied to pleasure, and that form of naturalism associated with evolution.

The attitude of many philosophers these days towards evolution, with notable exceptions such as E. O. Wilson, Richard Dawkins, and Daniel Dennett, is very much like that of Wittgenstein who argued all forms of naturalism contribute nothing to philosophy. Wittgenstein dismissed naturalism because for him philosophy logically clarifies thoughts and concepts, and therefore empirical theories such as those of the evolutionists belong to a different language game (Wittgenstein 1960: iv. 112). In contemporary philosophy Thomas Nagel, for example, argues that phenomenological facts about consciousness cannot be reduced to physical facts (Nagel 2012).

British Idealism came to prominence simultaneously with the explosion of interest in evolutionary empirical theory and, unlike Wittgenstein, could not afford to dismiss it as an irrelevance. British Idealism, while seeking logical clarification of concepts, had a much

---

[1] For example, a recent history of idealism does not mention evolution (Dunham, Hamilton, and Watson 2011). Histories of the evolution debates of the nineteenth century are similarly almost silent (Bannister 1979; Crook 1994). Even the acclaimed biographies of the most celebrated evolutionists ignore the Idealist interventions (Desmond and James 1991; Desmond 1997; Francis 2007). The theme does surface from time to time, however, in William Mander's impressive history of idealism (Mander 2011).

more ambitious aspiration for philosophy. It offered a metaphysics and ontology, seeking rationally to account for all that is given in experience. The contention of naturalism is that explanations of human activity should take the same form as any other explanation of nature because humans are inextricably part of that nature (Sorley 1904: 83). The desirable method is scientific, because scientific explanation is the most appropriate way to understand the natural world. The main point at issue between naturalism and idealism is that for naturalism the facts dealt with by natural science are the only reality that is knowable. On the other hand idealists 'refuse to look upon the material process as the ultimate character of reality—so far as reality is known or knowable' (Sorley 1904: 83 and 87).

Darwin certainly intended to live up to the highest standards of scientific investigation, despite not always being able to satisfy them. Darwin's scientific method was inspired by Newton's astronomy, mediated through the empiricist astronomer John F. W. Herschel and developed in a neo-Kantian direction by the strongly anti-evolutionist philosopher of the inductive sciences, William Whewell. As their primary affiliations would suggest, the two scientists differed on metaphysical questions, and on the extent to which they agreed with Darwin. Herschel and Whewell were at one, however, in agreeing at a fundamental level what features a scientific explanation should possess. Scientific theories for them were hypothetico-deductive systems, requiring a distinction between universal laws which are fundamental, and empirical laws derived from them. The aim of the scientist must not be the discovery of contingent causes in explanation of a particular phenomenon, but, on the contrary, to explain how phenomena of different kinds are related and explicable in terms of all sufficient causes or mechanisms, quite likely reducible to some sort of force (Ruse 1993: 11).

Darwin's methodology throughout his scientific explorations attempts to explain diverse phenomena in terms of overarching causes. The hypothetico-deductive model is evident in the way Darwin presents his case supporting the hypothesis of the struggle for survival as the driving mechanism for natural selection (Ruse 1972: 311–51). Darwin's success and encouragement to apply the idea to other areas of knowledge made evolution a compelling hypothesis with which to work.

Darwin's achievement in systematically applying evolution to the natural world, based on extensive observation and scientific imagination, was widely applauded by the British Idealists. It was a hypothesis that gave credence to the fundamental starting point of the philosophy of the British Idealists, that is, the unity of existence, in that evolution posited a continuity between nature and spirit. Principally, it asserted the unity of life, and more importantly that man's mind must be continuous with animal perception, and that 'moral activity is continuous with non-moral impulse' (Sorley 1904: 34).

Like the natural scientists the British Idealists believed that all forms of enquiry require 'working hypotheses' before advances may be achieved in understanding experience (Jones 1902–3: 233, 1909: 25). A hypothesis may never be certain but may commend 'itself to our notice by the range and clearness of the light it seems to throw on the manifold data of our experience' (Jones 1893: 164). Evolution as a hypothetical conjecture constituted, for the British Idealists, an absolute postulate, or what R. G. Collingwood was later to call an 'absolute presupposition' (Collingwood 1939), exercising 'subtle dominion' in all aspects of experience. Evolution, as an absolute assumption or presupposition, if discredited would reduce the natural and historical sciences to a 'mass of contingent particulars waiting to be colligated' (Jones 1909: 22 and 196). A hypothesis is held 'only so long as the realm of reality seems to support it' (Jones 1905: 32; cf. 1922: 93). Such ideas are probably more familiar today through the work of Thomas Kuhn on paradigms. A dominant paradigm is subject to change, or paradigm shift, consequent upon a period of crisis and anomaly when there are persistent failures to account for, or explain, aberrations (Kuhn [1962] 2012).

This does not mean that the British Idealists subscribed to the same criterion of truth as Darwin and other evolutionary theorists who operated on the basis of a correspondence between the theory and the facts that support it. For the Idealists the world is not independent of our conception of it. Interpretation and what is interpreted are inseparable. Idealists reject the correspondence theory of truth. For the correspondence theory statements are propositions about the world and are tested against the reality they purport to describe. The British Idealists posit various modes or forms of experience, including the natural scientific, which fall below ultimate reality or truth, but within each domain the demarcation of what is sense and nonsense is possible. The logic is still a propositional logic, but not of discrete statements. A whole world of ideas is brought to bear on the veracity of each proposition. Truth depends on non-contradiction and coherence. H. H. Joachim, for example, argues that a discrete fact or proposition has no truth value in isolation from a whole complex of ideas and propositions. The truth of a statement such as a triangle has three angles which together add up to 180 degrees is 'true' only in relation to a whole system of facts and propositions which affirm it. In this cohering unity of ideas or 'significant whole' the 'constituent elements reciprocally determine one another's being as contributory features in a single concrete meaning' (Joachim [1906] 1939). Truths are the property of judgements in that they are implicated in a coherent unity of judgements (Mure 1954: 329). Michael Oakeshott contends that 'coherence is the sole criterion [of truth]: it requires neither modification nor supplement, and is operative always and everywhere' (Oakeshott 1933: 37).

Truth is the union of coherence and comprehensiveness. A mode, or significant whole, is the 'arbiter of fact'. This does not mean anything we conceive which is consistent is true. Bradley contends something is true within a system when its opposite is inconceivable (Bradley 1897: 218). It is what the evidence obliges us to believe. Joachim gives the clearest account of how it works. A 'significant whole' is one in which one another's being is determined by the reciprocity of the constitutive elements and which contributes to a particular meaning. The cohering elements reciprocally adjust and control each other. A centaur, for example, is imaginable, but inconceivable in reality because it fails the test of coherence. Its constituent elements resist entering into reciprocal adjustment (Joachim 1939: 68). Systematic coherence is the determining factor of a significant whole and upon it conceivability rests. Coherence is at once the test and definition of truth (Oakeshott 1933: 34–7).

In essence, then, the logic of the empirical sciences and of British Idealism is propositional. They differ, however, over the criterion of truth. Consistent with the scientific point of view, nevertheless, Idealists believed that 'Except for hypotheses, facts and events would seem to us to stand in no relation of any kind to one another' (Jones 1923: 93). In a manner prescient of Karl Popper they believed that hypotheses are never proven, but always in the process of being proved.

Evolution was the predominant form of naturalism against which idealism reacted. Yet the theory of evolution was particularly conducive to its manner of philosophizing. Like idealism, evolution challenged the conceptions that had reigned in philosophy for two thousand years, that is, the supremacy of the fixed and final, and treated as defective the ideas of origins and change. As the pragmatist John Dewey remarked: 'the "Origin of Species" introduced a mode of thinking that in the end was bound to transform the logic of knowledge, and hence the treatment of morals, politics and religion' (Dewey 1979: 305).

THE PERVASIVENESS OF EVOLUTION

From 1859 the idea of evolution began to permeate almost every facet of life, but particularly, and more perniciously, in the fields of politics, ethics, and social reform (Appleman 1979: 529–51). In typical idealist fashion, as they had done with the evaluative/descriptive concepts of natural rights, and socialism, they transformed the idea of evolution by incorporating it into the idealist world view. 'Natural Rights', while for them not naturalistic or associated with a state of nature or individualism, were so fundamental to the common good, that without them social life, as we know it, would be inconceivable (Boucher 2009: ch. 8). Socialism was rescued from the language of class conflict, and transformed into social liberalism, in which the 'right' sort of socialism afforded opportunities for self-realization and the enhancement of freedom, as opposed to dependence through state intervention (Boucher and Vincent 1993: chs. 5–6).

No manner of thinking so captured the imagination as the theory of evolution. Sorely suggests that its effect was 'revolutionary', similar to that of Copernicus, or Galileo (Sorley 1920: 267) No one person popularized it more than Herbert Spencer. He more fully drew out its implications for society and ethics than Charles Darwin (see Ruse's 'Evolution and Ethics in Victorian Britain' in this volume). Spencer was the 'acknowledged leader' of the new method in philosophy (Sorley 1920: 267). Darwin and Spencer were frequently cited not as the originators of evolutionary theory, but as those most responsible for impressing it upon the popular consciousness (Ritchie 1893: 42). Ritchie contended 'Evolution is in every one's mouth now, and the writings of Mr. Spencer have done a great deal (along with the discoveries of Darwin) to make the conception familiar' (Ritchie 1893: 42). The Idealists intervened in order to seize back the initiative and undermine the potential damage that the principle of 'the survival of the fittest' may do to the endeavour of alleviating degradation and squalor caused by the migration of rural dwellers to the cities during the Industrial Revolution.

Both Absolute Idealists, committed to the principle of monism, and Personal Idealists who differentiated themselves by putting the individual experient self at the centre of experience, embraced the concept by criticizing the naturalistic proclivities of Darwin and Spencer, while at the same time denying the apparent dualism created by Charles Lyell, T. H. Huxley, and Alfred Russel Wallace. These allies of Darwin broke ranks by positing a separate ethical evolutionary process opposed to naturalistic cosmic evolution, red in tooth and claw.

It was clear to the Idealists that evolution in all its forms needed to be confronted. Among the Absolutists Edward Caird acknowledged the force of evolutionary thinking. Caird, conceding the all-pervasiveness of the language of evolution in Victorian and Edwardian society, told the students of Balliol College: 'There is no idea which is so potent in our day as the idea of evolution, development, or organic growth' (Caird 1907: 154). W. R. Sorley, the Personal Idealist, confirms this conviction, claiming: 'There is hardly a department of thought which this new doctrine has not touched' (Sorley 1904: 33). A fellow Personalist complains that so popular has the term 'Evolution' become that its meaning has been extended beyond all reasonable bounds to apply to all phenomena universally, from gravitation to elephants (Underhill 1902: 197).

The attractiveness of such a universal manner of understanding the whole of existence was almost irresistible. Its explanatory potential was brought to bear on such diverse areas of activity as biology, geology, palaeontology, anthropology, history, philosophy, and religion. It was even a major theme of Victorian poetry. The imagery and ideas of evolution are to be found, for example, in the works of Tennyson, Browning, Matthew Arnold, Edward Fitzgerald, and Algernon Charles Swinburne (Stevenson 1979: 519).

The common convergence of so many disciplines upon the same hypotheses, indicated that knowledge was approaching more closely than ever before to the heart of reality. Darwin, although celebrated as the great champion of evolution, was elaborating ideas that had long been in currency. The success of Darwin's theory was, of course, possible because of the great strides made in geology and palaeontology which discredited the Christian view that the earth was created a little over four thousand years ago. Lamarck had propounded the notion that species change over time and that some become extinct, but the mechanism he identified as the driver was not entirely convincing. He argued that use and disuse of the organs lead to modifications in their powers to act effectively. Environmental factors could lead to physical changes and spontaneous transmutations in organisms. Lamarck suggests that various organs or features of animals are modified over time by voluntary effort, such as the giraffe having to strain its neck to reach the highest branches of a tree, or the antelope straining its limbs to become swift of flight to escape its predators. The changes, including those of moral character, were then inherited by subsequent generations. This is the doctrine of inherited characters. In Spencer's view, the 'inheritance of acquired characters becomes an important, if not the chief, cause of evolution', it is not only 'a factor', but 'an all-important factor' (Spencer 1893: 456, 1894: 608). The view that acquired characters could be transmitted by parents to their children was shared by popular opinion, and even among the Idealists Bradley appears to have subscribed to a variation of it (Collini 1978: 12).

Sir Charles Lyell, however, formulated the hypothesis of the struggle for existence in evolution, but questioned the argument supporting the doctrine of inherited characters in his famous *Principles of Geology* (1830–3). What was lacking was not the observation that the organic world evolved, but the nature of the laws and forces which caused the changes. It was Darwin's solution to this problem that made him so immediately celebrated.

In *The Origin of Species* Darwin put forward three main contentious hypotheses. The first was that new species emerge as a result of modifications that take place in other species, that is, the transmutation hypothesis. Secondly, species emerge in a manner that resembles branches of a tree, therefore at some point all species share a common ancestor in the evolutionary process. And, thirdly, the principal, but not exclusive, mechanism for change in this process was natural selection (Richards 2010: 471). Underpinning these contentions Darwin emphasized the importance of two universal features of existence. First, considerable variability within all species. No two humans, for example, are exactly alike. And second, the enormous powers of reproduction of each species. Neither played any part in Lamarck's theory. Darwin had some sympathy for the doctrine of use and disuse, but identified something far more fundamental as the principal mechanism of change, namely natural selection. Without *variation* and *rapid increase*, however, natural selection could not operate in the struggle for survival, and adaptation to the environment would not occur.

The allure of evolutionary theory for the educated public was its simplicity and accessibility in comparison with the physical and mathematical sciences. The unity of nature and spirit evolution posited held out the possibility of a common form of explanation in the natural and social sciences.

DARWIN AND HEGEL

The British Idealists in their evolutionary outlook were inspired by Hegel, and not by the naturalistic theories of Spencer and Darwin. Whereas James Hutchison Sterling, the author of *The Secret of Hegel* (1865), had placed Hegel and Darwin in an antagonistic relation, many of the British Idealists consciously conflate Hegelian philosophy and the theory of evolution in order to appropriate its favourable evaluative force. This should be no surprise because, unlike Hegel, the British Idealists in general believed that philosophy gives practical guidance for conduct. Evolution was being extensively appropriated for all sorts of political pretexts, and therefore they had to adapt it to their own ends, while remaining faithful to the spirit of Hegelian philosophy. Many Idealists were convinced, particularly Ritchie, Bosanquet, and Jones, that evolution was the key to understanding the ultimate character of the universe, and evidence of this belief was to be found in the fact that all of the separate forms of knowledge or experience were converging on the universal form of explanation. All three thinkers, but none more explicitly and forcefully than Ritchie—who overtly saw his task as applying Darwin's concepts to human society—believed that the categories of biological evolution, heredity, inheritance, natural selection, and the struggle for existence, had to be accommodated in idealist social explanation.

The tactic of the British Idealists was to argue that Hegel was a far better evolutionary theorist than Darwin, Spencer, or Huxley. Evolution was indeed completely compatible with idealism because idealism was itself an evolutionary philosophy. W. R. Sorley had no doubt that it was a theory consistent in many respects with his own Idealism because it asserted the unity of life, and the continuity between man's mind and animal perception, affirming that there is no dichotomy between moral activity and the non-moral impulse (Sorley 1904: 34). It was no coincidence, Jones suggested, that the hypothesis of evolution had become the dominant organizing principle of the day. It enabled both spiritual growth and the rational development of character to be understood in terms of an organic process, which exhibited, in turn, the Hegelian principle of unity in diversity, or identity in difference (Jones 1909: 23). Seth maintains: '*Continuity of process and the emergence of real differences*—these are, in short, the twin aspects of the cosmic history, and it is essential to clear thinking that the one be not allowed to obscure the other (Seth 1916: 103; italics in the original). The Personal Idealist Schiller concurred. The factors which comprise natural selection, such as heredity, variation, and the struggle for existence are another guise for the Hegelian identity, difference, and self-negation (Schiller [1893] 2004: 37).

William Wallace's translation of Hegel's 'lesser' logic in 1874 included a long introduction entitled *Prolegomena to the Study of Hegel's Philosophy* in which he commends Hegel's ontology as a metaphysical form of Darwinism. Wallace argued that what Darwin had done for the process of evolution in the organic world, Hegel did for the self-development of thought in philosophy (Wallace 1892: p. cx). Reason, identified as central in all life, was not for Hegel the abstract universal of ordinary thinking. The concept is a generic term for a class of objects. Reason is a concrete universal because it differentiates itself into particulars constitutive of its own nature. Starting from the same principle as the naturalistic evolutionists Hegelian Idealism assumes the unity of experience. The natural scientific evolutionary thinking of Darwin, Ritchie contended, assumes a similar premise, a monistic metaphysics, the fundamental unity of phenomena (Ritchie 1905: 22).

Biological theories of evolution were beginning to emerge when Hegel was developing his own philosophy. For Hegel we understand a part only by looking at it as part of a whole. We properly understand the early stages of something when it is viewed as the early stages of something more fully developed. This is without exception in all specialist fields of knowledge, as well in the Idealists' attempt to conceive the universe as a whole (Ritchie 1893: 47). Naturalistic evolutionary theories, however, were flawed because they failed to learn the lessons Aristotle taught, namely, the true nature of a thing is to be found not in its origin but in its end (Ritchie 1896: 44). Darwin and Spencer, for example, maintained that the higher must be explained with reference to the lower in the evolutionary process (Spencer 1978: i. 40).

The efficacy of the 'higher' evolution, or what Hegel called emanation, in the special sense widely embraced by Idealists, including T. H. Green, Bernard Bosanquet, Edward Caird, Andrew Seth Pringle-Pattison, David George Ritchie, W. R. Sorley, and Henry Jones, was that it took Aristotle seriously. While agreeing with naturalistic evolutionists that humanity is continuous with nature, the Idealists contended the lower must be explained and understood in terms of the higher. Seth, although dissenting from Hegel in many respects, is in sympathy with him in agreeing: 'Nothing can be more certain than that all philosophical explanation must be explanation of the lower by the higher' (Seth 1887: 89). The Darwinian contention, Sorley succinctly put it, is the belief that 'the higher forms are in all cases developments from simpler and lower forms' (Sorley 1904: 34). Jones contended that modern idealism refutes all theories that attribute explanatory power to origins. The last cannot be explained by reference to the first (Jones 1919: 146). The implication is that consciousness, for the idealist, is the ultimate truth of reality which entails an anthropomorphic interpretation of nature in that 'what constitutes thought constitutes things, and, therefore, that the key to nature is man' (Jones 1891: 210–11). It is at the highest stages of development that nature develops into the instruments of intelligence and morality. It is a process guided by reason, in which the explanation of morality cannot be satisfactory merely by reference to its development, but must include 'reference to the self-consciouness which makes that development possible' (Sorley 1885: 291–2).

DIVINE INTERVENTION IN EVOLUTION

Nothing better illustrates the distinctive position that British Idealism adopted in the evolutionary debate than its contribution to resolving an essential tension between those who maintained the unity of existence from a naturalistic perspective, and those who argued that moral or social development is discontinuous with nature and the result of some sort of Divine intervention. In relation to religion, evolution raised a number of issues. An avalanche of tirades emanated from Britain and Europe decrying Darwin's pernicious theories, declaiming them obnoxious, and accusing him of dethroning God and turning common sense on its head. Critics claimed that the origins of the theory were in hell, to where they should return with all of the gross creatures who profess to subscribe to them (Dickson White [1896] 1979: 362–7). Ethics, religion and evolution opened deep divisions in late Victorian Britain. Orthodox Christianity posited a distinct break between nature and spirit. Humans thus occupied a different sphere from that of animals and were distinct in possessing moral characters uniquely endowed upon them by God. Naturalistic evolution appeared to posit a fundamental challenge to this deep social convention. It postulated a continuity between nature and spirit, in which the former was explanatory of the latter.

Darwin himself initially tried to avoid becoming embroiled in religious controversy by intimating that his conclusions were consistent with what we know of the 'laws impressed on matter by the Creater' (Darwin [1859] 1979: 458). He could not, however, sit on the fence, when he thought the scientific integrity of evolution was being compromised by the introduction of unscientific concessions. Darwin believed it was his duty to discover the universal natural laws which regulated all species, including humans. His *Origin of Species*, however, deferred such discussion of human origins and evolution. His impetus to enter the fray was occasioned by what he considered to be the betrayal of the scientific calling by his closest allies, Sir Charles Lyell, Alfred Russel Wallace, and T. H. Huxley.

Lyell argued in 1863 that while evolution and natural selection explained much about the physical development of man, it could not account for the finer aspects of civilization, nor the higher faculties of the human mind. For this, he suggested, we must invoke some such explanation as Divine intervention (Lyell 1863). From the early1860s until the end of his life Wallace vehemently maintained that while not wanting to deny 'the law of continuity in physical or mental evolution', he was compelled to attribute to nature and spirit different generative capacities. The latter, he suggested, seemed to evidence the intervention of a greater power directing evolution towards special ends. He rejects natural selection as the mechanism by which morality and the higher intellectual capacities develop. In fact, he takes man to be the pinnacle of evolution, almost unchanged from the earliest evidences of his existence, and this is because the higher capacities he possesses negate natural selection. These capacities enable him to adapt his environment to his needs. Organic evolution, including the development of the human organism, is subject to different laws from the development of the civilized mind. Divine intervention, creating 'Heaven born humanity' (Wallace 1913: 102), sets man on a course that negates naturalistic evolution. It was 'by the influx of some portion of the spirit of the Diety, man became a "living soul"' (Wallace 1913: 91). He argues that the spiritual world supervenes on the natural and generates in humans ethical, mathematical, metaphysical, and aesthetic qualities. These faculties, in his view, cannot be accounted for by natural selection. In addition, this 'unseen universe of Spirit' is responsible for gravity, electricity, cohesion, chemical force and radiant force, without which the natural world would be inconceivable (Wallace 1889: 473–8). By attributing such forces to the realm of spirit Wallace significantly blurred the distinction between nature and spirit he wished to sustain.

Darwin could not accept this 'unscientific' explanation of ethical evolution attributable to the guiding hand of Divine intervention. Darwin set himself the task of re-establishing the unity of nature and spirit in his *The Descent of Man, and Selection in Relation to Sex* (1871) and *The Expression of the Emotions in Man and Animals* (1872). These two books form a continuous argument in which Darwin amasses evidence to demonstrate that there is nothing in human beings that is not a continuation of features to be found in animals. The differences that exist are differences in degree rather than kind (Cain 2009). Darwin attempted to account for the development of moral and intellectual faculties in human beings, for example, by claiming that they are to be found in rudimentary form in lower animals. He argues that 'the difference in mind between man and the higher animals, great as it is, certainly is one of degree and not of kind' (Darwin 1871: 126).

Huxley, a friend and admirer of Darwin, despite being aware of Darwin's objections to Lyell and Wallace, puts forward a more compelling rift between nature and spirit, maintaining the natural and ethical evolution are two incommensurable processes. Social existence, for Huxley, required counteracting the struggle for existence, rather than encouraging it. The pursuit of natural rights, he equated with the struggle for existence, which he understood in naturalistic terms, benefiting the individual to the detriment of society. Moral rights, in contrast, have correlative obligations and are conducive to social progress (Huxley 1890: 179–80). The idea of the survival of the fittest, in Huxley's view, is circumstantially related to the variability of nature and could not constitute an ethical standard. Ethics are not 'applied Natural History' (Huxley 1989: 132). The processes of cosmic evolution, which governs the evolution of nature and the human organism, and moral evolution are different and discontinuous. The idea of the survival of the fittest belongs to the cosmic process. The capacities required for success in this process, are inimical to existence. Fear of the opinions of others, followed by shame and sympathy, check the cosmic process by producing the first glimmerings of morality. Our feelings of approbation and disapprobation give rise to moral rules. The acquisition of the rules is the result of humans gradually becoming used to thinking about conduct in terms of them. This 'artificial personality', or conscience, counters the natural character of man. Like Wallace, however, Huxley's explanation of the disjunction introduced an ambiguity. He qualified his argument by claiming that 'strictly speaking, social life, and the ethical process in virtue of which it advances towards perfection, are part and parcel of the general process of evolution'. In addition, he argued that the 'general cosmic process begins to be checked by a rudimentary ethical process, which is strictly speaking, part of the former' (Huxley 1989: n. 20 [fn. 19 in the original]). Nature lacks the capacity for morality because it is incapable of knowing or thinking.

THE IDEALIST RESPONSE

Idealism shared with natural evolution a propensity to understand a problem or an event as it unfolded. J. B. Baillie contended: 'For a time it seemed possible to interpret all forms of experience in terms of the central fact of knowledge regarded as an evolution of thought' (Baillie 1924: 17). Green died before the full implications of evolutionary theory could be worked out, and he did not as clearly articulate the principle of continuity between nature and spirit as his followers. At times he seems to concur to a certain extent with the tentative suggestions of Lyell and Wallace in believing that the distinctiveness of man could not be attributable to the naturalistic assumption of the continuity of nature and spirit. He conceded, however: 'to deny categorically...that the distinctive intelligence of man, his intelligence as knowing, can be developed from that of "lower" animals would...be more than we should be warranted in doing' (Green cited in Neill 2003: 322).

In general, however, the Idealist response was to apply the familiar hypothesis of unity, and the spiritual nature of reality, to the problem. 'Evolution', Jones maintained, 'implies not only an unbroken identity, but also change, newness, acquisition.' Evolution involves continuity and has convinced people 'that the natural and social orders are in some way or other continuous and constitute one cosmos' (Jones 1910: 231). Andrew Seth argued that the fatal flaw in Huxley's argument is the apparent denial of the unity of the cosmos, which for the former was not so much a conclusion requiring proof, as 'an inevitable assumption' (Seth 1897: 13).

Idealism, however, while maintaining the continuity between nature and morality, was not a naturalistic philosophy and therefore felt compelled to challenge the naturalistic postulates of evolution and provide a more satisfactory theory based on Hegelian principles. The great merit of Darwinian naturalistic theories of evolutionary ethics is that they explicitly recognize the unity of the cosmos. Unity is not a proposition capable of proof: it is an inescapable assumption, a colligating hypothesis, or absolute assumption. In this respect Idealists do not go as far as to suggest that humans are so different in kind from the rest of nature that they require completely different forms of explanation.

It is nature that has to be explained in terms fitting of human beings. The contention is not that nature is intelligent, but that it is intelligible *only* to the mind that knows it, that is, the human mind. Because humans are self-conscious we should explain their behaviour in terms of values, principles, and ideas rather than instincts.

In this respect the Idealists have an affinity with Spencer and Leslie Stephen in accepting that human nature must be part of the wider cosmic nature. They differentiated themselves, however, by rejecting the tendency of Spencer and Stephen to conflate the wider cosmic process with the naturalistic laws of the non-human world. The mistake the likes of Darwin, Spencer, and Stephen made was to believe that the higher in the process of evolution could be explained in terms of the lower, that is, the effect could be explained in terms of the cause; whereas '*the true nature of the cause only becomes apparent in the effect*' (Seth [1893 and 1897] 1997: 38).

This is sometimes referred to as the higher naturalism (Watts Cunningham 1933: 155). All of humanity's enterprises require nature as their accomplice. The social organism coheres because the sinews that bind it are moral and spiritual relations. While the naturalistic evolutionists such as Darwin, Spencer, and Stephen materialized spirit, the Idealists, without denying the differences between nature and spirit, spiritualized nature. On the other hand the Idealists were bewildered as to how one could intelligibly account for human society and civilization by portraying a collision between two opposing forces, the one a purely natural process and unconscious in its operation, the other exhibiting intelligence and morality as characteristic of human processes. The Hegelian idea of evolution denies an intractable dualism between spirit and nature maintaining that 'the natural and social orders are in some way or other continuous and constitute one cosmos' (Jones 1910: 231). Without common ground between these so-called opposing forces, the ethical could not combat the cosmic process. Ritchie suggests that acknowledging the spiritual principle working its way through the universe is a prerequisite to understanding nature (Ritchie 1901: 15).

Bosanquet, Ritchie, Jones, and Seth, among others, directly address Huxley's arguments. Bosanquet believes that Huxley's distinction is a 'fatal misconception' (Bosanquet [1895] 1997: 57). Huxley gave too much credit to man and too little to nature in accounting for knowledge and morality. Ritchie rejected Huxley's dichotomy by suggesting that consciousness, reflection, and language constitute advantages in the struggle for existence, and that it is much the most reasonable hypothesis to account for them in terms of natural selection, instead of attributing them to some mysterious force (Ritchie 1895: 93).

Huxley was not completely wrong. He provided an important corrective to those theories that conflate ethical life with organic and physical processes. Idealists maintain that despite their commitment to the unity of existence, they could not ignore, nor understate, the difference between naturalistic processes and rational moral activity. Nature, on Huxley's terms, cannot know, nor think, and therefore it is not moral. But for the Idealists this is not the whole story. Knowing and thinking presuppose nature. Nature presents us with the data for intelligence to interpret. This intelligence is itself the result of nature. Knowledge, the product of intelligence, is just as much the progeny of nature as man. Nature is itself expressed through the instrument of human intelligence, without itself being intelligent. It is, nevertheless, intelligible only to mind. Mind and nature are interdependent, neither can exist without the other. Nature, is not opposed to morality, but, on the contrary, a willing partner in its development (Jones 1894: 26–30).

There are, of course, differences between organic and physical processes, and rational life, and these should not be minimized, nor should we deny the role of nature in human achievements. The principles of unity and continuity do not exclude what is equally and obviously important, that is, the emergence of significant differences among the stages within the cosmic order. Mind and nature reciprocally complement each other, and to assert that one or the other is ultimately real is to convert abstractions into realities (Watts Cunningham 1933: 155–7). Man and nature are 'indispensable factors' in that the latter is a partner in all of man's endeavours, while ignorant of all of them (Jones 1894: 27). There is a mutual reciprocity in the absence of which neither could exist. Nature is essential to man, and mind is essential to the possibility of conceiving a world. Whereas we cannot attribute love and hate to it, or any moral attributes, the progress of man depends upon its cooperation:

> The majesty of the natural world is the result of a combined endeavour. And the still more solemn majesty of the world of goodness is the product of the interaction of man with man, and of all men with nature. Hence the cosmic process which contributes to these surpassingly great ends, guiding the struggling intellect at every step, furnishing it with all it owns, casting before him all its inexhaustible wealth, is not man's foe, but his ever-constant friend, attending him in all his battles, and sharing in all his victories. (Jones 1894: 29)

SELF-REALIZATION, FREEDOM, AND EVOLUTION

Social theory was for the Idealists normative because their metaphysics conceptualized reality with reference to immanent ideals and ends. The self always projects a conception of a better self which in principle it attempts to realize. Self-realization is the attainment of a good that is common to individuals who constitute the same moral organism (den Otter 1996: 80). The ultimate purpose of each individual in society is self-realization, and the role of the state, taken in the broadest terms to include not only the apparatus of government but all that is encompassed by the terms 'nation' and 'community', is to remove the obstacles to personal self-development. Projecting such a view of humanity and of self-attainment necessarily required the Idealists to take a stance on the most fundamental of evolutionary issues. Jones rejects the naturalistic hypothesis of evolution as a competitive struggle for existence. Social progress is not the result of blind impersonal forces or structures, but cooperative and self-conscious. Spencer's parallel between the organic unity of a natural body and the body politic de-spiritualized both nature and humanity. There is no escaping the fact that social relations are moral in character, constituting a spiritual, and not a mechanistic, unity.

If society is an evolving ethical organism, how is this evolution to be conceived? Biological evolutionism and the social variants derived from it, as Ritchie observed, had a tendency to become fatalistic. Idealists, however, attribute free will to human agents struggling to emancipate themselves from fate (Ritchie 1905: 252–3). This, for Hegel, is the progress of the consciousness of freedom. Jones forcefully rejected any form of determinism in ethics, and this entailed for him the rejection of hereditary character, or acquired characteristics, but also the rejection of genetic determinism.[2] The idea of free will is incompatible with antecedent hereditary character. Consciousness mediates by converting the antecedent and external into the self, and facilitating self-determined rational action (Jones 1888: 320–6). Freedom is not a given in our character, but an achievement, which has to be attained (Jones 1922: 283). We are not born free, but are capable of becoming progressively more free by our relationships with others, and experience of life. Freedom is a power, or capability, which is not hindered by the environment, but uses it to become more free. The first signs of freedom appear when we endow facts with our own interpretation and attribute to them our own value. Just as we are neither rational, nor irrational, but in the process, or on the way, to becoming more rational, we are also in the process of becoming free (Jones 1909: 37–9, 57): 'the freedom and reason which makes us men is not realized but realizing' (Jones 1888: 321). There comes a time when every man 'ceases to be the docile medium of the traditions of his people' (Jones 1909: 54). Spirit subjects itself to self-examination in the minds of those who comprise the society it has built up, and in the process attains freedom. If morality presupposes a rational self-consciousness capable of choosing freely that which is good, then the essence of the individual and of society in their mutual implication, or inclusion, is that freedom. This means the individual conceives his or her own purposes, and in doing so realizes a social purpose. It is, to put it in Hegel's terms, 'the free will which wills the free will' (Hegel 1991: §27). The individual and the common good coincide in a unity of purpose; that is, as Bosanquet contends, freedom is the self-end of the social organism (Bosanquet 1898: 7). Freedom, as the condition of morality, and, by necessity, of the consequent system of obligations and duties, is that which gives cohesiveness to society. For Jones, 'the bond of the social organism, that which is self-differentiating, self-integrating life, is freedom', and 'freedom is the life which forms the unity of the moral organism' (Jones 1891: 200 and 207, respectively). The social organism, then, is not a mechanical, or biological, entity whose components collide, but a self-conscious unity in which the components realize themselves as ethical beings, and society realizes itself in them. In Jones's view, the welfare of the individual and of society are inseparable. The aims and purposes of the individual are inseparable from social aims and purposes.

---

[2] This is also the basis of their rejection of August Weismann's germ plasm theory and the support it gave to the eugenics movement. Weismann's theory is the beginning of the belief in genetic determinism and denied completely the idea of inherited character (Weismann [1893] 2003).

How, then does natural selection work within society and remain compatible with freedom? Both Bosanquet and Ritchie rebut the dichotomy posited by Lyell, Wallace, and Huxley. By affirming the unity of nature and spirit, and the operation of natural selection in nature and society, they insist that natural selection accounts for both organic development and moral progress. Ritchie goes as far as to suggest that natural selection is an indisputable fact (Ritchie [1900] 1997: 73). Huxley, for Bosanquet, was simply wrong in suggesting that in human society the struggle is not for existence, but for enjoyment. On the contrary, the struggle within society is for a certain conception of existence. Bosanquet argues that 'a complete discontinuity between the principles of nature and of humanity is extremely improbable, especially if we consider the latter has come into being by the process of the former' (Bosanquet [1895] 1997: 58). The improbability becomes an impossibility when considered from the point of view of the logic by which successful ideas have impressed themselves as moral upon society because of their power organically to arrange life and deal with circumstances. Within human society reason is the ultimate power, and success is often the survival of the most reasonable. Within any society there are better and worse conceptions of the common good, but the minimum criterion of excellence in the struggle for existence is the ability and capacity of the society to provide conditions for the successful maturity for its progeny, that is, 'good birth and breeding' (Bosanquet [1895] 1997: 59).

We inherit biologically the capacities for self-realization, but without an environment conducive to their flourishing our capabilities would come to nothing. Human beings inherit capacities which are capable of being developed or retarded by the social environment, or civilization, which is inherited by successive generations. Language, Ritchie argues, makes possible the transmission of experience which is not biologically inheritable. The possession of consciousness, the ability to reflect, and the use of language give human beings a tremendous advantage in the struggle for existence. The origins of these human powers or capacities are best explained, however, by the hypothesis of natural selection (Ritchie 1901: 100–1; cf. 131–2)

UNITING NATURE AND SPIRIT IN RELIGION

Darwinism revealed to the religious consciousness the brutality of nature and its manifest cruelty. Among the poets, the likes of Tennyson and Browning, attempted to escape the vision of nature, red in tooth and claw, tainting the higher conception of humanity. They envisaged the redemption of suffering in a future spiritual development. God directs evolution towards beneficent ends (Stevenson 1979: 518). The poets, as far as Henry Jones was concerned, revealed the truth of reality as clearly as philosophers, but without the endless argument. He saw in Browning's religious and philosophical temperament the idea of evolution as the immanence of God revealing Himself as the supreme intellect 'in the extreme frontier of His Universe' (Jones 1891: 207). God is no mere Creator. He reveals Himself in man (Ritchie 1905: 241).

The unifying principle that enables continuity between the higher and lower forms of naturalism, and which facilitates diversity and identity in difference, is the spiritual, which for most of the Idealists is correlative with God. The Idealists believed that the 'ordinary' or 'scientific' view, associated with Darwin, was incompatible with morality and religion because, as we saw, it attempted to account for the spiritual in terms of the material (Jones 1922: 98). Nature, understood as a dynamic, changing, unified system, is best conceived as returning to God, and evolution helps us to comprehend nature as the return of the highest to itself: 'The universe is homeward bound' (Jones 1891: 206).

For both Absolute and Personal Idealists the Absolute is manifest in finite spiritual centres. Basically it is the veracity of the finite centre to sustain itself and become completely absorbed in the Absolute that is at issue between the two camps. Nevertheless, human beings are what they are by virtue of God's presence in them. Far from being a denial of religious experience, the idea of evolution enables us to comprehend it all the better. The Divine and the human constitute the inseparable spiritual unity of the world. Christ is incarnate in the world reflecting the unity of God and man. The present and the past, instead of being divided, are united by the bridge that evolution supplies. Evolution is revelatory of the unity in the diversity of humanity in its identification of 'the one spiritual principle which is continuously working in man's life from the changing forms through which it passes in the course of its history' (Caird 1899: vol. i, p. x; cf. 24–5 and 27). For Jones: 'Evolution suggests a solution of the ultimate dualism of mind and its objects, and contains the promise of boundless help to religious faith' (Jones 1922: 98). Jones argued: 'religion, in so far as it demands a perfect and absolute being as the object of worship, is vitally concerned in maintaining the unity of the world. It must assume that matter, in its degree, reveals the same principle as that which, in a higher form, manifests itself in spirit' (Jones 1891: 183).

The rational experience of humanity is premised on the absolute postulate of the existence of God. God reveals Himself as Spirit, and knows Himself in and through the expressions of his children (Jones 1922: 356–9). Echoing Green, Sorley maintained that moral endeavour thrives on the conviction that the Divine purpose realizes itself in the moral life, and that 'in all goodness the spirit of God is manifest' (Sorley 1904: 98). In all this, man is the servant of God or even his fellow worker. The test of the morally worthwhile existence is the extent to which the individual attempts to do God's work in the world by achieving his or her own potential and contributing to the common good. Social reform and moral development were closely linked with religious self-realization (Richter 1964: 143). Religion itself could be explained and understood in terms of evolution. Just as we do not know what a seed is until we know what it develops into, religions cannot be understood by looking to their origins. We must not look for an essentialist or common element to all religions, such as the belief in a Divine Being. Some of the greatest religions have done without it. Even if there were a common element, it would be of little use because its manifestations in different religions would be so different and unconnected. We must look for a 'germative' principle, a series of phases through which any living thing passes. Evolution provides the answer. Evolution, Caird says, is 'the most potent instrument for bringing back difference to identity which has ever been put into the hands of science' (Caird 1899: 26; Jones and Muirhead 1921: 334).

Conclusion

I have tried to show that the idea and hypothesis of evolution so thoroughly permeated educated society in the Victorian era that all modes of thought had to show how they were compatible with it. Idealism cannot properly be understood without locating its arguments within the context of evolutionary debates, and to suggest that they were generally unsympathetic to evolution (Mander 2011: 261–2), disguises the extent to which they believed their own philosophy to be a more sophisticated version of evolution than either the naturalistic ideas of Darwin and Spencer, or the ethical evolutionary ideas of Lyell, Huxley, and Wallace.

Self-realization, for example, entails a view of society, which necessarily required a stance be taken in relation to the debates over heredity and its implications for free will and determinism. If its philosophy were to be compelling, idealism had to show that the principle of unity, which it assumed, was based on different principles from those assumed by naturalistic evolutionary theorists. They attempted to demonstrate that their form of evolutionary theory was both consistent with naturalistic theories, but at the same time superior to them in that it was better able to accommodate the spiritual element permeating the whole of existence. The Hegelian method of emanation enabled Idealists to explain the lower manifestations of spirit in terms of the higher, rendering evolution completely consistent with the religious consciousness.

BIBLIOGRAPHY

Appleman, Philip, 1979. ' Darwin: On Changing the Mind', in Philip Appleman (ed.), *Darwin*. New York: Norton, 305–14.

Baillie, J. B., 1924. 'The Individual and His World', in J. H. Muirhead (ed.), *Contemporary British Philosophy*. 1st ser. London: George Allen and Unwin, 15–48.

Bannister, Robert C., 1979. *Social Darwinism: Science and Myth in Anglo-American Thought*. Philadelphia: Temple Press.

Bosanquet, Bernard, [1895] 1997. 'Socialism and Natural Selection', in David Boucher (ed.), *The British Idealists*. Cambridge: Cambridge University Press, 130–41.

Bosanquet, Bernard, 1898. 'Hegel's Theory of the Political Organism', *Mind*, NS 7: 1–14.

Boucher, D., 2004. *The Scottish Idealists: Selected Philosophical Writings* (Library of Scottish Philosophy). Exeter: Imprint Academic.

Boucher, D., 2009. *The Limits of Ethics in International Relations: Natural Law, Natural Rights, and Human Rights in Transition*. Oxford: Oxford University Press.

Boucher, D., 2010, 'British Idealism: Practical Philosophy and Social Responsibility', in D. Moyer (ed.), *The Routledge Companion to Nineteenth Century Philosophy*. London: Routledge, 689–710.

Boucher, D., and Vincent, A., 1993. *A Radical Hegelian: The Political and Social Philosophy of Henry Jones*. New York: St Martin's, Cardiff: University of Wales Press.

Boucher, D., and Vincent, A., 2011, *British Idealism: A Guide for the Perplexed*. London, Continuum.

Bradley, F. H., 1897. *Appearance and Reality*, 2nd edn., Oxford: Oxford University Press.

Bradley, F. H., 1914. *Essays on Truth and Reality*. Oxford: Clarendon Press.

Bradley, F. H., 1935. *Collected Essays*, vol. i. Oxford: Oxford University Press.

Cain, Joe, 2009. 'Introduction', in Darwin [1872] 2009: pp. xi–xxxiv.

Caird, Edward, 1899. *The Evolution of Religion*, 3rd edn., vol i. Glasgow: Maclehose.

Caird, Edward, 1907. 'Spiritual Development', in *Lay Sermons and Addresses*, Glasgow: Maclehose, 151–77.

Collini, Stefan, 1978. 'Sociology and Idealism in Britain 1880-1920', *Archives européennes de sociologie*, 19: 3–50.

Collingwood, R. G., 1940. *An Essay on Metaphysics*. Oxford: Clarendon Press.

Crook, Paul, 1994. *Darwinism, War and History*. Cambridge, Cambridge University Press.

Darwin, Charles, [1859] 1979. *The Origin of Species by Means of Natural Selection or the Preservation of Favoured Races in the Struggle for Life*. New York, Avenel.

Darwin, Charles, 1871. *The Descent of Man and Selection in Relation to Sex*. London: Appleton.

Darwin, Charles, [1872] 2009. *The Expression of Emotions in Man and Animals*. London: Penguin.

den Otter, Sandra, 1996. *British Idealism and Social Explanation*. Oxford: Oxford University Press.

Desmond, Adrian, and Moore, James, 1991. *Darwin*. London: Michael Joseph.

Desmond, A., 1997. *Huxley: Evolution's High Priest*. London: Michael Joseph.

Dewey, John, [1904] 1979. 'The Influence of Darwin in Philosophy (1909)', in Philip Appleman (ed.), *Darwin*. New York: Norton, 305–14.

Dickson White, Andrew, 1979. 'The Final Effort of Theology', in Philip Appleman (ed.), *Darwin*. New York: Norton, 362–7.

Dunham, Jeremy, Grant, Iain Hamilton, and Watson, Sean, 2011. *Idealism: The History of a Philosophy*. Durham, Acumen.

Francis, M., 2006, *Herbert Spencer and the Invention of Modern Life*. Stocksfield: Acumen.

Hegel, G. W. F., 1991. *Elements of the Philosophy of Right*, ed. Allen Wood. Cambridge: Cambridge University Press.

Hutchison Sterling, James, 1865. *The Secret of Hegel*. London: Longman, Green, Longman, Roberts & Green.

Huxley, T. H., 1890. 'Natural Rights and Political Rights', *Nineteenth Century*, 25: 179–80.

Huxley, T. H., 1989. 'Evolution and Ethics', in *Evolution and Ethics: T. H. Huxley's Evolution and Ethics with New Essays on its Victorian Sociobiological Context*, ed. J. Paradis and G. C. Williams. Princeton, Princeton University Press.

Joachim, H. H., [1906] 1939. *The Nature of Truth*, ed. R. G. Collingwood. Oxford: Clarendon Press.

Jones, Henry, 1883. 'The Social Organism', in A. Seth and R. B. Haldane (eds.), *Essays in Philosophical Criticism*. London: Longmans, 187–213.

Jones, Henry, 1888. 'Morality as Freedom', *Time* (London) (March), 320–6.

Jones, Henry, 1891. *Browning as a Philosophical and Religious Teacher*. Glasgow, Maclehose.

Jones, Henry, 1893. 'The Nature and Aims of Philosophy', *Mind*, ns 6: 160–73.

Jones, Henry, 1894. 'Is the Order of Nature Opposed to the Moral Life?', an inaugural address delivered in the University of Glasgow on 23 October 1894. Glasgow: Maclehose.

Jones, Henry, 1902–3. 'The Present Attitude of Reflective Thought Towards Religion', *Hibbert Journal*, 1: 228–52.

Jones, Henry, 1905. 'The Immortality of the Soul in the Poems of Tennyson and Browning', a lecture. London: Macmillan.

Jones, Henry, 1909. *Idealism as a Practical Creed*. Glasgow: Maclehose.

Jones, Henry, 1910. *Working Faith of the Social Reformer*. London: Macmillan.

Jones, Henry, 1919. 'The Obligations and Privileges of Citizenship—A Plea for the Study of Social Science', William M. Rice Institute and Rice University, *Pamphlet 6. The Rice Institute Pamphlet*. Houston, Rice Institute.

Jones, Henry, 1922. *A Faith That Enquires*. London, Macmillan.

Jones, Henry, and Muirhead, J. H., 1921. *The Life and Philosophy of Edward Caird*. Glasgow: Maclehose.

Kuhn, Thomas S., [1962], 2012. *The Structure of Scientific Revolutions: 50th Anniversary Edition*. Chicago: University of Chicago Press.

Lyell, Sir Charles, 1830–3. *Principles of Geology*. London: John Murray.

Lyell, Sir Charles, 1863. *The Geological Evidences of the Antiquity of Man, with Remarks on Theories of The Origin of Species by Variation*. London: John Murray.

Mander, W. J., 2011, *British Idealism: A History*. Oxford: Oxford University Press.

Mure, G. R. G., 1954. 'Benedetto Croce and Oxford', *Philosophical Quarterly*, 4: 327–31.

Nagel, Thomas, 2012. *Mind and Cosmos: Why the Materialist Neo-Darwinian Conception of Nature is Almost Certainly False*. Oxford: Oxford University Press.

Neill, E., 2003. 'Evolutionary Theory and British Idealism: The Case of David George Ritchie', *History of European Ideas*, 29: 313–38.

Oakeshott, M., 1933. *Experience and Its Modes*. Cambridge: Cambridge University Press.

Pringle-Pattison, A. S., 1904. 'The Life and Philosophy of Herbert Spencer'. *Quarterly Review*, 200: 240–67.

Pringle-Pattison, A. S., 1916. *The Idea of God*. Oxford: Clarendon Press.

Pringle-Pattison, A. S. *See also* Seth, A.

Richter, Melvin, 1964. *The Politics of Conscience: T. H. Green and His Age*. Cambridge, Mass.: Harvard University Press.

Richards, Richard A., 2010. 'Darwin's Philosophical Impact', in Dean Moyer (ed.), *The Routledge Companion to 19th Century Philosophy*. London: Routledge, 689–709.

Ritchie, David G., 1893. *Darwin and Hegel with Other Philosophical Studies*. London: Swan Sonneschein.

Ritchie, David G., 1896. *The Principles of State Interference*, 2nd edn., London: Swan Sonnenschein.

Ritchie, David G., 1895. *Darwinism and Politics*. London: Swan Sonnenschein.

Ritchie, David G., [1900] 1997. 'Ethical Democracy: Evolution and Democracy', in David Boucher (ed.), *The British Idealists*. Cambridge: Cambridge University Press, 68–93.

Ritchie, David G., 1901. *Darwinism and Politics*, 4th edn., London: Swan Sonnenschein.

Ritchie, David G., 1905, *Philosophical Studies*, ed. with a memoir by Robert Latter. London: Macmillan.

Ruse, Michael, 1972. 'Natural Selection in *The Origin of Species*', *Studies in History and Philosophy of Science*, 1: 311–51.

Ruse, Michael, 1993. *The Darwinian Paradigm: Essays on Its History, Philosophy and Religious Implications*. London: Routledge.

Schiller, F. C. S. [1893] 2004. 'Review of *Darwin and Hegel* by David George Ritchie', in C. Tyler (ed.), *Early Responses to British Idealism*, ii. *Responses to D. G. Ritchie and Bernard Bosanquet*. London: Thoemmes Continuum, 35–42.

Seth, A., 1887. *Hegelianism and Personality*. Edinburgh: Blackwood.

Seth, A., [1893 and 1897] 1997. 'Man's Place in the Cosmos: Professor Huxley on Nature and Man', in David Boucher (ed.), *The British Idealists*. Cambridge, Cambridge University Press, 30–49; 1st published in 1893 and reprinted in *Man's Place in the Cosmos*. Edinburgh and London, Blackwood, 1897.

Seth, A. *See also* Pringle-Pattison, A. S. [after 1898 Pringle-Pattison was added to the name as a condition of receiving a bequest].

Sorley, W. R., 1885. *Ethics of Naturalism*. Edinburgh: Blackwood.

Sorley, W. R., 1904. *Recent Tendencies in Ethics*. Edinburgh: Blackwood.

Sorley, W. R., 1920. *A History of English Philosophy*. Cambridge: Cambridge University Press.

Spencer, Herbert, [1881] 2004. 'Professor Green's Explanations', in C. Tyler (ed.), *Early Responses to British Idealism*, i. *Responses to Jowett, T. H. Green, E. Caird and W. Walllace*. London: Thoemmes Continuum, 133–41.

Spencer, Herbert, 1893. 'The Inadequacy of "Natural Selection" II'. *Contemporary Review*, 63: 439–56.

Spencer, Hebert, 1894. 'Wiessmanism Once More'. *Contemporary Review*, 64: 592–608.

Spencer, Herbert, 1978. *The Principles of Ethics*, vol. i. Indianapolis: Liberty Press.

Stevenson, Lionel, 1979. 'Darwin Among the Poets', in P. Appleman (ed.), *Darwin*. New York: Norton, 513–19.

Underhill, G. E., 1902. 'The Limits of Evolution', in H. Sturt (ed.), *Personal Idealism*. London: Macmillan, 193–220.

Wallace, Alfred Russel, 1889. *Darwinism: An Exposition of the Theory of Natural Selection With Some of its Applications*. London: Macmillan, 441.

Wallace, Alfred Russel, 1913. *Social Environment and Moral Progress*. London: Cassell and Company.

Wallace, William, 1892. *The Logic of Hegel*. Oxford: Clarendon Press.

Watts Cunningham, G., 1933. *The Idealist Argument in Recent British and American Philosophy*. New York: The Century Co.

Weismann, August, [1893] 2003. *The Germ-Plasm: A Theory of Heredity*. Bristol, Thoemmes Press.

Wilde, Oscar, [1889] 2004. 'Some Literary Notes', in C. Tyler (ed.), *Early Responses to British Idealism*, ii. *Responses to D. G. Ritchie and Bernard Bosanquet*. London: Thoemmes Continuum, 8–9.

Wittgenstein, Ludwig, [1922] 1960. *Tractatus Logico-Philosophicus*. London: Routledge, Kegan Paul.

CHAPTER 16

···

THE EMERGENCE OF PSYCHOLOGY

···

GARY HATFIELD

FROM the standpoint of the history of philosophy, psychology is frequently seen as 'emerging' from philosophy in the latter part of the nineteenth century or the first part of the twentieth century. This conception is part of a story in which epistemology, which is concerned with normative questions of justification, finally becomes fully separated from psychology, which is concerned with causation and description. Typically, psychology is deemed to be irrelevant to epistemology, and any claim to the contrary is an instance of the 'fallacy' of psychologism. Histories of psychology frequently offer a complementary picture. Here, psychology may be seen as emancipating itself from armchair philosophy by adopting methods from physics and physiology. In this case as well, the separation is seen as a case of good-riddance.[1]

As happens with caricatures, these pictures capture and emphasize some aspects of the tangled web of relations between philosophy and psychology in the period from 1850 to 1930. Psychology has been called a 'problematic science' in the nineteenth century (Woodward and Ash 1982), in part owing to its complex relations with philosophy. Would it replace philosophy as the primary approach to understanding the human mind and human conduct (or behaviour)? Would it divide the territory, ceding logic, epistemology, ethics, and aesthetics to philosophy? Would it solve some philosophical questions (e.g. concerning mind and brain), while leaving others to philosophy as insoluble by empirical means? Would it cooperate with philosophy, each offering a distinctive perspective on shared topics concerning mind and behaviour?

The development of experimental psychology in Britain is more complex than would be expected from the cases of Germany and America. In America, the 'new' experimental psychology rapidly established itself (e.g. Scripture 1899). Its identity was consolidated by

---

[1] Standard accounts include Passmore (1957) and Boring (1950). This story has persisted (see Hatfield 2013); it informs Rorty's (1979) master narrative, in which the psychologistic fallacy arises with Descartes and Locke (Rorty avoids the term 'psychologism' but compares the problem to the naturalistic fallacy in ethics, 1979: 141). Some philosophers proclaimed not only psychology's irrelevance to epistemology, but also its impossibility as an empirical science of the normal functioning of the mind (e.g. Ryle 1949: 322–7, contending that 'psychology' cannot explain correct actions or perceptions but only mistakes; Hamlyn 1957: 20–3, making a similar point, anent perception).

the early twentieth century, so that E. G. Boring could celebrate its founders in his 1929 *History of Experimental Psychology*. In Germany, experimental psychology was well established earlier, by 1890.[2] In Britain, signs of professional consolidation were evident around 1900, with the establishment of the first psychological laboratories in 1897 (at Cambridge and London) and the founding of the British Psychological Society (1901) and the *British Journal of Psychology* (1904). But robust institutionalization was slow to come, dating to after the Second World War (Hearnshaw 1964: 168–9).

The reasons for the slow institutionalization of British experimental psychology are many and varied. In part, it reflects the slow institutionalization in Britain of laboratory science more generally, including physics (Purrington 1997: 12–16). Psychology, in claiming to provide objective knowledge of mind and perhaps physiological explanations of mind and behaviour, was slowed by more than the standard institutional inertia: before and after 1900 it was opposed by both divines and philosophers, including adherents to the newly emergent British Idealism (Hearnshaw 1964: ch. 8). At the same time, the lack of institutional consolidation around the turn of the century reflects what had been a positive condition for the growth of psychology in the second half of the nineteenth century, on both the empirical and theoretical sides: the dispersal of research and writing that addressed psychological topics among various disciplines and intellectual groups, including freelance intellectuals who saw themselves as doing psychology (Bain, Spencer, Lewes), gentleman scientists who engaged psychology (Darwin, Galton, Romanes), physiologists (Carpenter, D. Ferrier, Maudsley), Darwinian biologists (Huxley, Lloyd Morgan), and philosophers (Hamilton, J. S. Mill) or philosopher-psychologists (Sully, Ward, Stout). Psychological theorizing and debates over the foundations of psychology and theory of mind were prominent on the British intellectual scene from 1850 to 1900 and drew on an extant literature of empirical psychology that had grown throughout the previous hundred years.

Additionally, the slow process of rendering psychology as a laboratory science at its core may well reflect a British judgement that the experimental psychology of the Germans and Americans was not properly a 'new psychology' but rather the addition of new techniques to the study of an established psychological subject matter and set of theoretical conceptions, which had long been investigated by individuals who also considered themselves to be philosophers or practitioners of other sciences. This chapter first considers more closely the question of what it means to chart the 'emergence' of psychology as a discipline. It then surveys some actors' taxonomies of psychological trends or schools in Britain, looking back from the first quarter of the twentieth century. Finally, it examines connections between philosophy and psychology in the decades surrounding the turn of the twentieth century, involving the problem of the external world and the use of psychology in epistemology.

---

[2] Wundt (1896: 2); Paulsen (1906: 409), on psychology as a 'mathematical-physical' science. Ebbinghaus (1908: 23–4) dates an autonomous psychological science of experiment and measurement to the 'last decades of the nineteenth century'. Some German philosophers subsequently complained about philosophical chairs being occupied by experimental psychologists, but psychological institutes and departments forged on (Hatfield 2012).

ON THE EMERGENCE OF PSYCHOLOGY AS AN
INDEPENDENT DISCIPLINE: WHAT THIS MEANS

There are two kinds of questions involved in considering the emergence of psychology as an independent discipline. One is a historical question: when did individuals begin to engage in an intellectually autonomous activity that either they or we would call 'psychology'? For present purposes, this question can be narrowed somewhat by stipulating that we are interested in the emergence of psychology as an empirical study of mental and behavioural phenomena. The other question is conceptual: what are the criteria for identifying something as an independent discipline or as an independent intellectual practice?

These questions are of present interest for their bearing on the relation between philosophy and psychology. If psychology is to replace philosophy, it must be distinct from philosophy. Similarly, if psychology is to provide a solution, not coming from philosophy itself, to an ongoing philosophical question such as the relation between mental phenomena and the brain, or if it is to divide the territory with philosophy, or to cooperate with philosophy on some joint questions, it must be a distinct practice. The historical question is of interest in its own right, as regards the origin of experimental psychology. Some scholars favour a view of discontinuity, in which experimental psychology arises by applying experimental methods to what had been philosophical questions.[3] I favour a view that finds both continuity and change: psychology, including an empirically oriented psychology, existed prior to the latter part of the nineteenth century (indeed, had its roots in the *De anima* tradition stemming from Aristotle) and was transformed by the development of new experimental techniques.[4] Experimental psychology did not arise anew, but was empirical psychology transformed.

---

[3] Boring (1929) carefully segregates philosophical figures who 'prepared' for the 'founding' of 'physiological' or 'experimental' psychology from those who did the founding. The former include J. F. Herbart, H. Lotze, Thomas Brown, and Hamilton; the primary founders are Fechner, Helmholtz, and Wundt. Spencer and Lewes are quickly dismissed as being 'evolutionary associationists' who came too late in the tradition of 'philosophical psychology' to make ready for the new experimental science (Boring 1929: 231, 234). These authors might better be seen as evolutionary functionalists (vs. associationists), but the main point is their exclusion from 'real' psychology by Boring's historiographical determination that Fechner, Helmholtz, and Wundt mark a radical break that yields a new discipline. Although later historians of psychology regard Boring's scholarship as dated in many ways, they tend *not* to challenge this aspect of his historiography (see Hatfield 1997).

[4] In finding continuity across changes, this approach opposes work that finds a discontinuous break in the latter nineteenth century (e.g. Danziger 1990, 1997). I apply this approach to the seventeenth, eighteenth, and nineteenth centuries in Hatfield (1990, 1995, 1997, 2002, 2003). Smith (2005) and Teo (2007) challenge it. In Hatfield (2007: 431–2), I defend the continuity thesis with respect to the psychology of emotion in response to Danziger (1997) and Smith (2005)—who claim that notions such as 'instinct' and 'emotion' show a total discontinuity—by observing (1) that their arguments rely on the poorly supported metaphysical assertion that *emotion* and other psychological kinds are not natural kinds but (historically local) social constructions and (2) that they in effect essentialize the notion of *discipline* to its twentieth-century instantiation (as a specialist career path with attendant social and institutional structures). By contrast, I endorse a historical methodology that starts from actors' categories and historical institutional structures and determines actors' metaphysical positions (if any) prior to developing and applying (as needed) one's own metaphysical theories (Hatfield 1996, 2005).

The conceptual question of what counts as a discipline, a distinct 'science',[5] or as an autonomous intellectual practice,[6] may seem to be prior to the historical question in this way: criteria for what counts as a discipline are needed in order to detect the historical presence of a discipline of psychology. And indeed the conceptual question is bound up with the historical question. But I don't consider it to be independent of historical understanding. My method is to look to historical developments of intellectual practices such as empirical psychology and to identify them though (1) actors' categories and self-perceptions,[7] (2) tracing the historical process that yielded experimental psychology, and (3) considering the perceptions of connections to the past expressed by acknowledged early practitioners of the 'new' psychology. From these considerations, we may identify by ostension historical veins of the practice of empirical psychology. In connection with such veins, we can then develop notions of disciplinarity that are appropriate to earlier historical circumstances. It might be that one can be a practitioner of a discipline or a science prior to the development of present-day institutional structures of disciplinarity. Let me explain.

Those who favour discontinuity tend to have an essentialist conception of what a discipline is. On this view, disciplinary structures arise with professional specialization and its

[5] In nineteenth-century British usage, the term 'science' had something of the breadth of the German word *Wissenschaft*. The narrower usage, as connoting natural science, came later, as is illustrated by nineteenth-century British use of 'natural philosophy' to denote physics. On the word 'science' and related forms, see Ross (1962); on the terms 'philosophy' and 'psychology' in nineteenth-century Britain, see Bain (1888).

[6] Olesko (1991) analyses the terms 'discipline' and 'practice' (applied to physics as a professional calling). My analysis differs somewhat. She adopts a Foucaultian notion of 'discipline', according to which prospective professionals submit themselves to a credentialing process (Olesko 1991: 14–15). This notion is suitable to an era in which professionalization and specialization coincide (see Daston 1998), whereas in the nineteenth century (and into the first decades of the twentieth) individuals might simultaneously be practitioners of both target disciplines here: experimental psychology and speculative or systematic philosophy. They might enter a discipline through training or by simply engaging in an ongoing practice, as Wundt did with systematic philosophy (his degree was in medicine, he habilitated in physiology, and his first research was in medical physiology and then sensory psychology). I have greater affinity with Olesko's treatment of 'practice', which emphasizes the 'labor of science, its mental and material tools' (Olesko 1991: 15), although my conception is broader, extending to the intellectual work of philosophy and its branches (e.g. the 'practice' of metaphysics, mentioned later). For difficulties in treating nineteenth-century British science (mainly physics) as forging a path towards 'professionalization' in a twentieth-century sense, see Morus (2006). Finally, in focusing on self-conceptions and intellectual attitudes, I do not claim that biographical, social, 'geographic' (in an extended sense to include private and public spaces), and other material-culture manifestations (as discussed in Morus 2006) are irrelevant; rather, my aim is to insist that in the sciences and philosophy (at least), intellectual habits and attitudes can also constitute a practice.

[7] The history of science, stimulated by Kuhn (1962), teaches us not to take scientists' or philosophers' biographical, methodological, procedural, and motivational statements at face value and that such statements must be historically contextualized and checked against other sources (see also Schickore 2008). All the same, I don't know where else to begin in the history of philosophy except from a careful reconstruction of actors' categories. Caution is needed, as actors may use familiar words but express different concepts with them. Further, actors' categories aren't historical bedrock (there is none). Such categories offer a way into the intellectual worlds of past philosophers and scientists; these worlds can then be analysed using present categories as needed, including concern with social and political motivations where pertinent. On contextualism and presentism in the history of philosophy, see Hatfield (2005).

accoutrements: professional societies, intellectual specialization, journals, certificatory roles, and autonomous university departments of psychology. One applies recent criteria of disciplinehood retrospectively to determine when empirical psychology emerged as a discipline. I see this approach as 'essentialist' because it decides ahead of time what institutional structures make for disciplinarity. There are two problems with this. First, it may be useful also to consider *intellectual* criteria for disciplinehood: the articulation of a subject matter and method. Second, by essentializing the notion of a discipline it cuts off the possibility of seeing earlier social forms as constituting a form of disciplinarity from which later practices emerged. It legislates discontinuity, rather than seeking to determine continuity or discontinuity by historical means.

On the view I favour, an early notion of 'discipline' is that of a branch of learning. The division of learning into disciplines is manifest as subjects taught in school. Accordingly, psychology (*logon peri tes psyches*) was a subarea of natural philosophy in the ancient Aristotelian curriculum and its later expression in the Latin-based universities of the Middle Ages and the early modern period.[8] Divisions in this curriculum (or in the several variants of this curriculum) were established by subject matter but also by method. Thus, in medieval universities questions about God and the soul were addressed by both theology and metaphysics, but using different methods: paradigmatically, theology could appeal to revelation (which it fit into a rational structure), whereas metaphysics was to proceed by reason alone, without recourse to revelation. The same individual might practise both metaphysics and theology and distinguish the textual fruits of those practices explicitly, just as, in the early modern period, Descartes or Leibniz distinguished their metaphysics from their natural philosophy. Metaphysics was recognized as an ongoing intellectual practice[9] even as various practitioners sought to change its methods and limit its subject matter: Hume (1739–40: pp. xviii, 185, 189) and Kant (1781: pp. xx–xxi) self-identified as practising metaphysics of a new kind. William Hamilton's (1861) effort to turn metaphysics into a kind of philosophical psychology supplemented by an ontology founded in the phenomenology of consciousness had followers, including Henry Mansel (1871).[10] William James (1890: vol. i, p. vi) distinguished metaphysics from natural science and practised both.

---

[8]   Aristotelian psychology (the word is a sixteenth-century coinage to supplement the Latinized title *De anima*) covered all of the soul's powers, vegetative, sensory and motor, and rational, thus comprising fields later called biology and psychology. The cognitive powers of the soul (sensory, motor, rational) had the larger treatment. Restriction of the term 'psychology' to mental functions is eighteenth century (see Wolff, mentioned later).

[9]   The practice-view of metaphysics is distinct from an essentialist view of metaphysics, such as that of Collingwood (1940), who treats metaphysics as a set of implicit assumptions shared by the thinkers of an age. Different pictures of who engaged in metaphysics arise depending on whether one emphasizes historically situated actors' categories or projects an ahistorical conception of metaphysics (as historically local bodies of assumption) onto past figures. The latter endeavour can be legitimate, but should be done wittingly (see Hatfield 1996, 2005, for further discussion). Of course, an actor's self-description need not be given absolute authority; someone might self-apply the label 'metaphysician' but not belong to historically identified veins of metaphysical practice.

[10]   On Hamilton's reasons for making psychology the core of metaphysics, see Bain (1888: 547–8). Interestingly, Mill (1843: i. 8–9) also viewed metaphysics as a branch of 'mental philosophy' and as approaching traditional questions of ontology, concerning the existence of mind, matter, and God, through a study of the mind's 'original' furnishings and what it knows by 'intuition' concerning such entities; but, differently than Hamilton, he accorded psychology its own status within 'moral science' as an empirical science with universal laws (1843: vol. ii, bk. 6, ch. 4).

Even so, the criteria of subject matter and method do not themselves provide clean categories for disciplines across the ages, or at least cannot be presumed to do so. Conceptions of subject matter evolve (consider the changing conception of 'physics' in the seventeenth to nineteenth centuries), as do methods. In the current state of inquiry, we may need to fall back on ostensive identification of disciplinary traditions, including that of psychology. In so doing, we may also discover institutional structures prior to those of specialist professionalism. One such role is that of a professor in a university, who in the earlier period teaches and contributes to several distinct subject matters, as did Thomas Reid or William Hamilton (discussed later). Another role includes non-university intellectuals who contributed to one or another subject matter or discipline through published work.

Accordingly, psychology as a discipline existed from the time of Aristotle (see Vidal 2011). 'Psychology' as a natural science, or a branch of natural philosophy, was pronounced by Wolff (1738, 1740), Bonnet (1755), Godart (1755), and Krüger (1756). The last three, each in his own way, suggested that the techniques of observation and experiment newly prominent in the physical and life sciences should be applied in the study of the mind or of mental phenomena. The terms 'natural philosophy' and 'natural science' indicate systematic treatments of a subject matter that draw on experience to establish its explanatory principles.[11] The discipline of psychology as a natural science, defined by subject matter and method, was extant in the eighteenth century, including in Britain (see Hatfield 1995).

In Britain, the term 'psychology' was used sporadically in the eighteenth century, sometimes to mean the (often non-empirical) 'doctrine of the soul' (e.g. Broughton 1703). It occurs in Hartley's well-known work of 1749 as denoting the theory 'of the human mind' and 'of the intellectual principles of brute animals' (1749: 354). Hartley classified psychology as a division of natural philosophy, along with mechanics. In eighteenth-century Britain, mental phenomena were studied under various headings, including the 'theory' or 'science' of mind in natural philosophy and, more commonly in Scotland, as a division of 'moral philosophy' or the 'science of man' (human beings). Hume and Reid, despite their differences, rank together as the most prominent Scottish authors who self-avowedly took an empirical or observational approach to the science of mind (or of human nature). In the Scottish universities the science of mind became a fixed part of the curriculum.[12] As with Hume and Reid, theories of the senses and of belief formation were united with discussions of the

---

[11] This description draws on a historically contextualized notion of 'natural science' that comprises eighteenth-century 'natural philosophy', *Naturlehre*, or *Naturwissenschaft*. Seventeenth- and eighteenth-century concepts of 'natural philosophy' need not be identical to nineteenth- and twentieth-century notions of 'natural science' for this comparison to work; they need only to be historically homologous notions. To demand identity before retrospectively applying the term 'natural science' would (again) be to essentialize that notion to its twentieth- or twenty-first-century character. The term 'historical homology' (by analogy with biological homology) suggests that natural science evolved out of natural philosophy; on the physical sciences as evolving from the synthesis of natural philosophy with mixed mathematical sciences, see Hatfield (1996). Finally, in finding an 'empirical psychology' in the eighteenth century, I don't deny other conceptions of psychology in that century or other approaches to the mind; but I affirm a distinct disciplinary tradition of empirical psychology.

[12] Within Scottish moral philosophy, one might take a 'physical' approach to the mind (e.g. Ferguson 1773: introd, sect. 7), which did not mean reductive materialism or a foundation in mechanics, but, drawing on the etymological meaning of the term, an approach to mind as a natural power or entity. On eighteenth-century Scottish topoi for psychology and the science of soul or mind, see Hatfield (1994: 383–4); more generally, see Reed (1997) and Vidal (2011).

problem of the external world. From both our perspective and theirs, the empirically based 'psychology' (Hartley's word) in their texts was combined with consideration of problems that, by their lights and ours, were metaphysical or theological. There was in these authors an application of empirical psychology to philosophical questions. As nineteenth-century authors would later reflect, British philosophy proper had long had a psychological cast.[13]

Psychological work in Germany and Scotland from the eighteenth into the nineteenth century provided an identifiable body of observation and theory that subsequently fed into self-avowedly experimental (laboratory) psychology. Accordingly, experimental psychology arose through the addition of experimental methods to an existing discipline. My root notion of discipline, defined in terms of curricular structure and distinct combinations of subject matter and method, can be applied across this change. Coincidentally, experimental psychology became ensconced in German and American universities, and found a toehold in British universities, at a time when new social and institutional frameworks were added to existing forms of disciplinarity. These new expressions may have altered how psychologists conceived themselves—they gave rise to specialization and to specialist credentials—but such changes do not in themselves break the intellectual continuity between the extant empirical psychology and the new emphasis on experiment.

As I have mentioned, earlier disciplinary practice did not demand exclusive specialization. For example, in the eighteenth century, one might, as did Reid, (1) earn a living first as a librarian, then as a preacher, then as a professor (university professorships being a paid 'profession'); (2) lecture on a variety of topics, including mathematics, logic, natural history, natural philosophy, law, politics, the arts, and natural religion (at Aberdeen); (3) then gain a professorship in moral philosophy (at Glasgow), lecturing on the human mind and its powers, but also on the fine arts and on natural theology, while continuing to pursue writings and observations in natural history and the physiology of muscular motion (Nichols 2007: 4–8). Or, in the first half of the nineteenth century, one might, as did William Hamilton, (1) study with an eye towards the medical profession; (2) decide instead to finish with law and become a practising advocate for several years; (3) turn towards academics and accept a position as professor of civil history, lecturing on the character and history of the classic nations of antiquity; (4) engage in anatomical pursuits in opposition to the claims of phrenology; (5) become an essayist, writing on philosophy, literature, and education (Hamilton 1853); and (6) receive an appointment as professor of logic and metaphysics, focusing in teaching on those subjects, while (7) continuing to produce work against phrenology, scholarship on Martin Luther, and editions of the works of Dugald Stewart and Reid.[14] Although Hamilton was enjoined to lecture on logic and metaphysics by the title of his chair, he took metaphysics in a particular direction, placing psychology or the description of consciousness at its centre.

I have challenged the notion that psychology doesn't become a disciplinary practice until separate departments of psychology are formed. For nineteenth-century Britain, the notion

---

[13] Hodgson (1876: 228) contends that English philosophy since Locke has had a psychological cast, which he finds to be a good thing, even in the context of arguing that philosophy and psychology are independent 'sciences' (or disciplines), which should be allied but ought not to subsume one another. The American John Dewey (1886: 2) argued that 'the psychological basis of English philosophy has been its strength: its weakness has been that it has left this basis—that it has not been psychological enough'.

[14] On Hamilton's biography, see Ripley and Dana (1881) and Wolf (1970).

that disciplinary practices in the arts and sciences arise only with university institutionalization is particularly ill-suited. Darwin, Herbert Spencer, John Stuart Mill, Francis Galton, and George Henry Lewes lacked university appointments, but Darwin nonetheless was a biologist, and Spencer engaged in several disciplines, including psychology, as did Mill, Galton, and Lewes, the latter two contributing extensively to psychology.[15] Michael Faraday was a chemist and physicist who did not attend university or hold a university appointment but served at the Royal Institution of Great Britain, which was devoted to scientific education and the public understanding of science.

Because the sciences (and philosophy) were only weakly institutionalized in Britain throughout the nineteenth century, psychological activity took place in varied institutional and disciplinary contexts.[16] At university, physiological research was supported earlier than was experimental psychology, and some early psychological laboratories were extensions of physiological laboratories, as at Cambridge. That does not mean that such laboratories were not truly psychological. Moreover, physiologists of the nervous system regularly took up psychological questions, as when David Ferrier wrote his *Functions of the Brain* in order 'to present to the student of physiology or psychology a systematic exposition' of his experiments on brain function (1876: p. vii), a book that contained a chapter on 'the hemispheres considered psychologically', citing Bain and Spencer, among others. William Carpenter included 'psychological' chapters in his *Principles of Physiology* (1853) and later developed these into his *Principles of Mental Physiology* (1874), a work purporting to be consistent with dualism (1874: 26) and in which he cites Bain, Hamilton, J. S. Mill, Lewes, and Spencer, among others. The physiologist Henry Maudsley (1867) treated psychological topics from a materialistic perspective that showed no favour to the psychological works just mentioned. From 1848, physicians and physiologists published on psychology in relation to pathology in the *Journal of Psychological Medicine* and, from 1855, in the *Journal of Mental Science*. These journals published occasional articles or literature summaries on general psychology and on philosophical and metaphysical topics.

Gentlemen scientists such as Galton (1869, 1874, 1883), in his work on genius, imagination, and heredity, introduced new empirical techniques to the study of psychological questions (especially questionnaires and statistics). Darwin (1872) studied the emotions from an evolutionary perspective, and Spencer (1855), Lewes (1874–9), and George J. Romanes (1883, 1888) formulated evolutionary psychologies. Empirical investigation was widely practised in comparative (Lubbock, Romanes, Lloyd Morgan), sensory (Wheatstone, Brewster, Maxwell), and hereditary psychology (Galton) in the second half of the nineteenth century (Hearnshaw 1964: chs. 4, 6, 11). These empirical approaches made connection with the ongoing theoretical discussions stimulated by Hamilton, Bain, Spencer, Lewes, and others. In 1876, Bain founded *Mind: A Quarterly Review of Psychology and Philosophy*, with George Croom Robertson as editor, to foster work in those two 'sciences' and to secure the credentials of psychology as a 'positive' science (Robertson 1876). By that date Hamilton

---

[15] Mill also contributed to psychology, as logician and philosopher: the former, by endorsing psychology as a 'moral science' that investigates the universal laws of mind (Mill 1843); the latter, by attempting to show the relevance of psychological findings for the problem of the external world (Mill 1865).

[16] On the diversity of psychological discourses in Britain, see Rylance (2000), who places Bain, Spencer, and Lewes in context.

and J. S. Mill were dead, but Spencer, Bain, Maudsley, Lewes, James Sully, James Ward, and George F. Stout, as well as distinguished psychologists from abroad, such as Wilhelm Wundt and William James, were regular contributors to the journal.

The variety and extent of psychological activity led to claims that Britain was the leader in the 'scientific study of the mind'. Mill's early declaration (1859: 287) that 'the scepter of psychology has decidedly returned to this island' is frequently cited. Mill had in mind that, after a heyday of British psychological thought in the eighteenth century (he named Locke, Hartley, Hume, and Reid), Hamilton and Bain were now leading representatives of, respectively, in Mill's terms, the 'a priori' and 'a posteriori' branches of psychology. In this context (Mill 1859: 291), these terms denote psychologies that find the complex products of mind to be either 'original' (consciousness has an immediate power to recognize complex truths by intuition) or 'acquired' (many seemingly intuitive beliefs are the product of experience and habit).

Mill's estimation of British eminence was shared, indeed echoed, by the French psychologist Théodule Ribot. Writing in 1870, he could say that 'since the time of Hobbes and Locke, England is perhaps the country that has done the most for psychology' (1870: 41).[17] He repeated Mill's division into two 'schools', placing Hamilton, William Whewell, Mansel, and James F. Ferrier (1854) in the first (a priori) school, and James Mill, J. S. Mill, Spencer, Bain, Lewes, Samuel Bailey (1842, 1855–63), J. D. Morell (1853, 1862), and Joseph John Murphy (1869) in the second (a posteriori).[18] By 1879 Ribot revised his estimation and now credited Germany with developing a 'new' experimental and physiological psychology that surpassed the 'descriptive' psychology of Britain.

In this regard, I suggest that the strength of British psychology across the second half of the nineteenth century stems from the diversity of methods and approaches. Accordingly, theoretical perspectives as set out by Darwin, Hamilton, Bain, Spencer, Maudsley, Carpenter, Galton, Lewes, and others—as supplemented by the international literature, including Hermann Helmholtz, Wundt, Franz Brentano, and James—provide a background from which Romanes, Lloyd Morgan, Sully, Ward, Stout, and others could proceed. The earlier works provided theoretical and methodological discussions, which engaged empirical results, even if among these authors only some collected scientific data in a systematic way. The earlier authors frequently engaged with and continued yet earlier work, forming a tradition of 'general' psychology.

---

[17]   Robertson (1876: 2), perhaps referring to Ribot, noted that 'it has been said abroad that, however it be with physical science, at least in psychology and philosophy the countrymen of Locke at present are leading the van'.

[18]   The a posteriori school makes a diverse lot. Ribot included Morell and Murphy in his first edition (1870) but subsequently dropped them. Morell studied with the younger Fichte (Immanuel Hermann), was a friend of Carpenter's, and also looked to Herbart and Spencer. His works show the terminological fluidity of the time: he titled his 1853 book *Elements of Psychology* and his 1862 book *An Introduction to Mental Philosophy*. Unlike Morell, Murphy received no mention in Hearnshaw (1972) (a quite serviceable history). Murphy credited natural selection and association with some explanatory power in human psychology but argued that organismic adaptation can be explained only by a designing intelligence and that human intelligence is *sui generis* and not physiologically or psychologically explicable. Ribot's discussion of Bailey, who wrote primarily on politics and economics, was brief. Bailey is best known for his effort to refute Berkeley's theory of vision.

From a British perspective, we may be tempted to agree with the conclusion of the English experimental psychologist C. S. Myers,[19] that experimental psychology did not constitute a 'new' (discipline of) psychology, but the addition of new methods to an ongoing (discipline of) psychology. In 1909, he published the first systematic textbook on experimental psychology by an English author. In that work, he observed that

> Experimental psychology has sometimes been styled the 'new' or 'scientific' psychology. It has been spoken of as if it were quite distinct from, and independent of, the older or 'general' psychology, in which experiment finds no place. Now these are manifest errors. For experiment in psychology is at least as old as Aristotle. And scientific work is possible (*e.g.* in astronomy, geology, and natural history) under conditions which preclude experiment. We must regard experimental psychology as but one mode of studying psychological problems, not all of which, however, can be approached from the side of experiment. Far from being independent, experimental psychology has arisen as a refinement, of general psychology. Familiarity with the latter is essential to success in the former. (Myers 1909: 1)[20]

Ward (1918: p. vii) later echoed these remarks. However, *pace* Smith (2010), such remarks need not be emblematic of an attitude that psychology's subject matter is not wholly reachable by the methods of natural science but needs philosophy, too. For Myers may be seen as expanding the domain of psychological science beyond experiment, to observation, reflection, and theorizing, as opposed to restricting the 'truly scientific' to the experimental.

Nine 'Schools' of Psychology in Early Twentieth-Century Britain

By the First World War, psychology was tenuously but firmly planted in British universities. There were small laboratories at Cambridge, London, Manchester, Edinburgh, and Glasgow. Experimental psychology was especially well established at these universities and also at Aberdeen. At Oxford, William McDougall succeeded Stout in the Wilde Readership in mental philosophy in 1904. Henry Wilde, an electrical engineer who established the Readership in 1898, had specified that experimental study was not to be undertaken. Stout complied but MacDougall didn't. In 1907, he obtained three rooms in the department of physiology for a psychological laboratory. McDougall stayed at Oxford until 1920, when, after losing his laboratory space, he went to Harvard. He was productive in his Oxford years, writing books on *Physiological Psychology* (1905), *Social Psychology* (1908), *Body and Mind* (1911), and *Psychology: The Study of Behaviour* (1912), which treated purposive behaviour as the object of psychology and as a chief source of evidence, while being mentalistic in

---

[19] Myers had gone with A. C. Haddon (an anthropologist) and W. H. R. Rivers (an experimental psychologist) on the important Torres Straits anthropological expedition of 1898 and afterwards was appointed assistant to Rivers, who was university demonstrator in experimental psychology at Cambridge. Myers became director of the Cambridge laboratory in 1912.

[20] He presumably refers to Aristotle's 'experiments' on illusory localization with crossed fingers (as discussed, e.g. by Rivers 1894).

its explanatory vocabulary and allowing introspection. He had some important students, including William Brown and J. C. Flugel.

In 1921, Brown succeeded McDougall as Wilde Reader. His interests had turned to psychotherapy, but he gamely sought to establish experimental psychology more firmly at Oxford. The university hosted the Eighth International Congress of Psychology in 1923. Brown tried to establish an independent psychological laboratory and initially failed; only in 1936 did he succeed in securing funds for an Institute of Experimental Psychology— making clear that his position as its director was independent of his ongoing tenure as Wilde Reader (Brown 1936).

Also in 1923, Brown organized in his 'department' a series of lectures on 'psychology and the sciences', mainly by other Oxford faculty. The other sciences included biology (J. S. Haldane), anthropology (R. R. Marett), logic (F. C. S. Schiller), ethics (L. P. Jacks), theology (A. E. J. Rawlinson), education (M. W. Keatinge), medicine (Brown), and psychical research (T. W. Mitchell, the only non-Oxonian). Brown collected the lectures into a volume published in 1924. In his own chapter, he made a case for the independence of psychology from both philosophy and physiology. He wrote in the preface that only within the past fifty years had psychology 'achieved independence of status comparable to that of the various physical sciences' (1924: p. v), thereby dating the period of autonomy from about 1875 (as an experimental science).[21]

In his chapter on psychology and logic, Schiller differentiated the two 'sciences' by observing that logic is normative, concerning itself not with the processes but with the products of thought, while psychology is descriptive and investigates processes. This description codifies a distinction that was available explicitly in anglophone writings since Hamilton (1866: i. 17–25). Schiller observed that, while Brown presumably organized the lecture series in order to 'improve the relations between the sciences', nonetheless relations were not ideally cooperative and some of the sciences themselves 'seem to be essentially medleys of discrepant schools and points of view that carry on their intestine conflicts from age to age' (1924: 53). He named theology, ethics, and psychology to this group.

For our purposes, it is interesting to note the nine 'schools' that Schiller counted in early twentieth-century psychology, as this offers a window into how one able commentator saw the landscape. These were (1924: 53–4): faculty psychology, associationism, mechanist introspectionists, pure introspectionists, laboratory experimentalists, behaviourists, Freudian psychoanalysis, purposive psychology, and psychic research.

Schiller allowed that faculty psychology and associationism were 'antiquated' schools, which he affiliated with Aristotle, Kant, and Hume (the latter being the associationist). It is difficult to find a prominent adherent after 1850 of the view that the mind has many distinct faculties (beyond the division into intellect, emotion, and will), and nearly as hard to find a pure associationist. Hamilton is typically named as a leader of the faculty approach. There is something to this, but Hamilton (1861) offered a view in which all the powers and faculties of mind are ascribed to the mind generically, which immediately manifests these powers depending on what is at hand. Accordingly, he lists six cognitive faculties, all as 'constituted'

---

[21] Brown reports that psychology has been recognized as 'a definite branch of learning' since the ancient Greeks but was, until recently, a 'handmaid to the philosophical sciences, with but little independence of method, and none of aim or function' (1924: p. v). He credits its independence to new methods (experiment, 'deep' analysis) and the adoption of biological modes of thought.

by consciousness (1861: ii. 4, 10). Consciousness, in Hamilton's view, immediately intuits the distinction of ego and non-ego, solving by pure introspection the problem of the external world (it exists as non-ego). As to associationism, Bain was its last prominent adherent in a pure form. Leading systematic psychologists, including Spencer, Lewes, and Sully, all placed association within a larger context, whether of functional adjustment or active attentional processes. Ward (1886) made explicit the limits of association in relation to thought as an active, selective, creative process.

Schiller aligns the 'mechanist' introspectionists with Descartes and the method of the physical sciences. Perhaps the best example is the expatriate E. B. Titchener, who after graduating Oxford in 1890 trained with Wundt and then, following an unreceptive summer back in Oxford, landed at Cornell University in autumn 1892. Titchener sought by introspection to resolve consciousness into atomic elements and then to seek the laws by which these combine. Schiller's branch of 'pure' introspectionists must include Ward and Stout, who rejected the search for psychological atoms and championed the descriptive attitude towards consciousness found in Austrian phenomenologist Brentano, but also endorsed by Hamilton (with different results).

The laboratory experimentalists, who promote introspection under laboratory control but also stress the importance of behaviour as an observable expression of psychological states and processes, are ably represented by Myers, whose 1909 *Text-Book of Experimental Psychology* was the first such work by a British author. As for behaviourism, it never gained footing in Britain, being largely an American phenomenon that arose out of an originally British and German field of expertise, comparative psychology (Romanes, Lloyd Morgan, and Jacques Loeb are important background figures) as supplemented by animal learning theory (Jennings, Thorndike) and Russian reflexology (Pavlov).[22]

Freudian psychoanalysis was introduced to Britain by Ernest Jones and was represented academically at Oxford by Brown. It became for a while the face of 'psychology' among academic humanists and the public. Teleological or purposive psychology, also called 'hormic' psychology, was McDougall's province (1908, 1911). He questioned whether the manifestly purposive aspects of living systems, behaviour, and consciousness could be explained by mechanistic physiological processes; in the end, he advocated dualism. Purpose and teleology also entered into American functionalism, where these concepts were heirs of the Darwinian notion of adaptation and were not paired with dualism. Finally, psychic research was supported by some leading figures in both the US and Britain, including William James and McDougall.

Schiller's roll call of psychological schools is interesting for what it leaves out from the nineteenth-century legacy of British psychology. In particular, it does not represent the important contributions of the 'statistical' school, stemming from Galton and continued by Charles Spearman, and the strong strain of evolutionary psychology. The latter omission may befit the fact that, by 1923, Lloyd Morgan was in his waning years and the sceptre had not been passed.

Schiller's perception of how things stood in 1923 may also signal that, as it happens, British psychology was intellectually less vital in the period 1900–25 than it had been in the fifty years prior, only subsequently regaining its core power with the work of Frederic Bartlett

---

[22] On behaviourism and comparative psychology, see Boakes (1984); also, Boring (1950: ch. 24) and Flugel and West (1964: iii. 2 and iv. 5).

on memory and cognition; the various experimental studies of sense perception (Thouless, Vernon);[23] and the reinvigorating of the discussion on statistical methods by R. A. Fisher (1925, 1935). The vitality of British psychology in the latter half of the nineteenth century depended greatly on those without university appointment. In the first quarter of the twentieth century, the model of scientific research was changing, so as to become more centred in universities. The continuing hostility towards psychology at many universities, and above all, at Oxford, may help explain why British psychology was comparatively weak early in the twentieth century. Indeed, several promising or established psychologists left the field (Rivers, Hobhouse), diverted to psychotherapy (Brown), or left the country (McDougall). The hostility arose out of controversies in the latter part of the nineteenth century, including intense discussions of the respective roles of philosophy and psychology.

INTERACTIONS BETWEEN PHILOSOPHY AND PSYCHOLOGY BEFORE AND AFTER 1900

British thinkers debated and discussed the relations between philosophy and psychology throughout the last three decades of the nineteenth century. Various sides were represented. At one extreme, T. H. Green (1882) contended that a psychology of human thought is not possible, due to the normative character of thought. He argued, along lines inspired by Kant, that natural science cannot account for its own possibility, hence it must fall to philosophy to investigate thought as such. The other extreme, that theory of knowledge should be subsumed under psychology, does not have any prominent representatives in nineteenth-century Britain.[24] Even Mill is no longer regarded as obviously guilty of psychologism,[25] and his 'psychological' theory of belief in an external world (Mill 1865) appeals to 'facts' and 'laws' of psychology in the service of a philosophical argument about the status of our knowledge of an external world.

The main consensus from psychologically inclined authors in the last two decades of the nineteenth century is that philosophy and psychology are distinct disciplines (or 'sciences') that ought to be allies (Robertson 1876, 1883; Hodgson 1876; Ward 1883, 1890; Sully 1884; Bain 1888; Stout 1899). In general terms, epistemology and logic were to be regarded as distinct from psychology, as were metaphysical questions concerning the nature and existence of mind and matter and their mutual relations.[26] Many psychologists adopted psychophysical parallelism as a working hypothesis, which assumes that for every mental or

---

[23]   For references on Bartlett, Thouless, and Vernon, see Hearnshaw (1964).

[24]   Hamilton (1861) as much philosophized psychology as he psychologized philosophy (see Bain 1888: 547–8).

[25]   Skorupski (1989: 164–6) and Wilson (1998) defend Mill from the charge; Godden (2005) seeks to reinstate it in part, allowing that Mill did not intend to reduce logic to psychology but claiming that in the end he fails to provide a justificatory foundation for deductive logic. Mill himself (1843, i. 9–10) treats logic as a prescriptive science.

[26]   Bain (1888: 546–8) includes a 'Note on the Meanings of "Philosophy"' examining both 'philosophy' and 'psychology' in nineteenth-century British usage. He proposes that 'philosophy' should now embrace ontology, metaphysics, and epistemology, with logic, ethics, and psychology as distinct sciences. He was not alone in separating logic and ethics from philosophy proper (see also Ward 1890; Russell 1914c: 13–15).

psychological state there is a corresponding brain state. Within psychology, no further claims are made about the ultimate substantial basis or causal relations between mind and matter.[27] Some physiologists and their allies advocated epiphenomenalism, the doctrine that mental states have no causal powers (Huxley 1874; Clifford 1874). But psychologists tended to demur. More generally, there were border skirmishes. Thus, Ward, while granting psychology autonomy as a science (1883), became suspicious that experimental methods would be adequate for many of its main problems (1893). In essence, he advocated a phenomenological approach to central questions pertaining to the structure of consciousness. In fact, the main systematic British psychologists after 1880 acknowledged a variety of methods, including phenomenological description, and did not regard experimenting as the only method (Sully 1892: vol. i, ch. 2; Stout 1896: vol. i, introd.).

Among the most thoroughly discussed questions at the intersection of philosophy and psychology was the problem of the external world. The existence, character, and knowability of the external world had been a central theme in British philosophy from the time of Locke, Berkeley, Hume, and Reid. The question continued to be discussed by nineteenth-century authors, including Bain (1855), Hamilton (1861), and J. S. Mill (1865). From the perspective of the latter half of the nineteenth century, it was seen as a central question in 'English' philosophy, and as a question with both psychological and philosophical dimensions. One does not find, in the period from Locke to Reid, explicit discussion of which aspects of the question belong to psychology, which to philosophy. Bain's *The Senses and the Intellect* contains a lengthy section entitled 'Perception and Belief of the Material World' (1855: 370–92). After touching on 'the metaphysical disputes concerning the first origin and precise import of our notions of distance and extension', wherein he considers the origin of our *belief* in an external world, he goes on to consider 'the exact processes' by which we become aware by sight of objects at a distance with a magnitude and possessed of solidity—a more straightforwardly psychological discussion. Hamilton (1861) renders metaphysics into psychology in his own way, including his claim that the metaphysical question of the existence of a non-mental non-ego can be settled by careful attention to the deliverances of consciousness. He conjoins psychology with metaphysics. Mill (1865: ch. 11) counters with a 'psychological' theory of the origins of the belief in the external world, in which he relies on the 'facts' and 'laws' of psychology to counter what he calls Hamilton's 'philosophy'. In these authors, the relation between those parts of the question that should be answered by a scientific psychology and those that are irreducibly philosophical is not made clear, although one can find a separation of the questions in Bain and Mill.

By the last quarter of the century, the division of psychological and philosophical aspects of the question is taken up regularly, including in a set of papers delivered before the Aristotelian Society (Hodgson et al. 1891–2) and published in the *Proceedings*, which in part responded to a paper by Stout (1890) in *Mind*. Hodgson, who was president of the society, analysed the problem of the external world into philosophical and psychological issues. Here is his division:

1. Analysis of the perception of an external world, in other words, combination of its sufficient and necessary constituents (as just explained).

---

[27] These generalizations are exemplified in Sully (1884: ch. 1; 1892: vol. i, chs. 1–2) and Stout (1896: vol. i, introd.; 1899: introd., chs. 1–3). Sully was known for accurately characterizing the literature (Hearnshaw 1964: 134).

2. Epoch and conditions of its arising as an event or existent in a percipient's development (as just explained).

3. Analysis of the perception that an external world exists as the real object of the perception of it.

4. Epoch and conditions of this latter perception of reality (No. 3) arising as an event or existent in a percipient's development. (Hodgson et al. 1891–2: 26–7)

What Hodgson has 'just explained' is that (1) is the primary philosophical problem of the external world and (2) is a psychological question which is irrelevant to it; (3) depends on (1) and so is philosophical, while (4) is its psychological counterpart. Bernard Bosanquet, a respondent, observed that Hodgson's analysis of (1) drew on psychological facts concerning the spatiality of touch and vision (Hodgson et al. 1891–2: 33). Hodgson countered that the words used to describe consciousness may be ambiguous as to whether they describe 'some function of a Subject' (psychological sense) or 'some content of sensibility' (an object of philosophical analysis). The second respondent, David G. Ritchie, also found both philosophical and psychological aspects to the problem of the external world, and an upshot of the symposium was to affirm this bifurcation and to acknowledge the mutual relevance of both aspects.

The question of applying the empirical methods of psychology to philosophical topics had been raised more or less explicitly in the period from Hartley to J. S. Mill. In the latter decades of the nineteenth century, there was ever more discussion of the precise relations between philosophy and psychology (Robertson 1883; Bain 1888; Seth 1892; Mellone 1894). In these discussions, epistemology, metaphysics, and logic were distinguished from psychology in ways that twentieth-century philosophers would have found familiar: epistemology deals with justification and warrant, psychology with the causal processes of belief formation; metaphysics concerns being, psychology the subjective states by which being is perceived; logic concerns proof and the well-groundedness of belief, psychology the processes of belief formation.

I say that the distinctions would be familiar to a twentieth-century philosopher, but with one qualification. It became standard fare in the middle decades of the twentieth century to hold that psychology had been shown to be not merely distinct from but irrelevant to epistemology. Accordingly, to refer to psychological findings in the service of epistemology would be a 'mistake' (e.g. Rorty 1979). This attitude would not be accepted by many nineteenth-century figures (excluding Green). They would hold that psychology could be relevant to epistemology, without believing that psychology can on its own answer the questions of epistemology.

This attitude remained alive and well into the early decades of the twentieth century, when it was espoused by Russell. In his epistemological writings, Russell (1914a, b) allowed that epistemology was distinct from psychology but could be aided by it. He had in mind that, in epistemology (as he conceived it), one aims to find 'hard data' or very well-known propositions that could serve as the basis for other knowledge (1914b: 68–72). Along the lines of Mill's 'psychological' account of apparently intuitive beliefs, Russell held that many of the beliefs of adult human beings are logically primitive (they take them as basic) but psychologically derivative. In being psychologically derivative, they are removed from the most elemental and trustworthy psychological states. For example, he held that in perception we take ourselves to be immediately aware of objects at a distance with a shape, such as a rectangular table, but psychology tells us that this perception is causally derived from a sense datum that represents the table from a specific point of view and perhaps as smaller than it is (or with a different shape: trapezoidal). In Russell's view, the sense datum is 'hard data' and psychology can aid the epistemologist in finding sense data and making them (or immediate judgements about them) the logically primitive basis of belief. Psychology helps epistemology to resolve psychologically derivative beliefs into psychologically primitive ones that can then serve as the basis for knowledge. Psychology assists epistemology without replacing it.

THE DISTANCING OF PHILOSOPHY FROM PSYCHOLOGY

British empirical psychology arose in the eighteenth century and maintained a strong presence thereafter. Nonetheless, British psychology was especially vigorous in the second half of the nineteenth century. This psychology had strong empirical components, in physiology, animal or comparative psychology, the study of inheritance, and studies of the senses. The theoretical and systematic side of the discipline was developed with special force, including evolutionary psychology, a modified association psychology, and the phenomenology of consciousness. This overall vitality was abetted by the fact that psychological research and discussion occurred in many venues, in accordance with the weak institutionalization of British science and scholarly life in the nineteenth century.

After the turn of the century, as science became ensconced in universities, psychology suffered from a hostile reception that reduced its vitality. At Oxford, this hostility extended from the time of Green through H. A. Prichard (1907) and on to Gilbert Ryle (1949). In its 'ordinary language' guise, this hostility was root and branch of a larger antipathy towards the relevance of science to philosophy.

Russell, who held that philosophy should take science as well as common sense into account (and should give no great authority to the latter), responded to this state of affairs in the *British Journal for the Philosophy of Science* of 1953. He purports to detect a studied ignorance in the philosophy of 'common usage'. The article offers a vignette in which the professor of mental philosophy has been taken away for manifesting 'psychotic instability'. A policeman asks for a 'word' with the professor's bedmaker, who in turn asks the policeman what he 'means', as he hasn't done anything wrong; upon which the policeman asks why the bedmaker hadn't acted more quickly, seeing that the professor was 'mental'. According to Russell, the policeman and the bedmaker exhibit common usage of the words 'word', 'mean', and 'mental', but the ordinary language philosopher doesn't follow suit. Russell says of such philosophers:

> What in fact they believe in is not common usage, as determined by mass observation, statistics, medians, standard deviations, and the rest of the apparatus. What they believe in is the usage of persons who have their amount of education, neither more nor less—less is illiteracy, more is pedantry—so we are given to understand. (1953: 304)

As to the level of education, Russell complains that the focus on 'common' or 'ordinary' usage makes this sort of philosophy 'capable of excusing ignorance of mathematics, physics, and neurology in those who have had only a classical education' (1953: 303). If Russell is right, then the ongoing hostility towards psychology in some streams of British philosophy became a matter of philosophical method and style, resting on a claim that scientific psychology couldn't have authority over 'what we mean' when we use mentalistic language and that 'what we mean' is enough for philosophy. A far remove from the healthy intellectual landscape of the latter half of the nineteenth century, when there was less specialization but proportionately more knowledge.

REFERENCES

Bailey, Samuel (1842). *A Review of Berkeley's Theory of Vision*. London: Ridgway.

Bailey, Samuel (1855–63). *Letters on the Philosophy of the Human Mind*, 3 vols. London: Longman, Brown, Green, and Longmans.

Bain, Alexander (1855). *The Senses and the Intellect*. London: Parker.

Bailey, Samuel (1888). Definition and Demarcation of the Subject-Sciences. *Mind*, 13: 527–48.

Boakes, Robert (1984). *From Darwin to Behaviourism: Psychology and the Minds of Animals*. Cambridge: Cambridge University Press.

Bonnet, Charles (1755). *Essai de psychologie; ou, considerations sur les operations de l'ame, sur l'habitude et sur l'education*. London: n.p.

Boring, Edwin G. (1929). *A History of Experimental Psychology*. New York: Century.

Boring, Edwin G. (1950). *A History of Experimental Psychology*, 2nd edn., New York: Appleton-Century-Crofts.

Broughton, John (1703). *Psychologia: or, An Account of the Nature of the Rational Soul*. London: Bennet.

Brown, William (ed.) (1924). *Psychology and the Sciences*. London: Black.

Brown, William (1936). Psychology at Oxford. *British Medical Journal*, 3934 (30 May): 1121–2.

Carpenter, William B. (1853). *Principles of Human Physiology: With Their Chief Applications to Psychology, Pathology, Therapeutics, Hygiene, and Forensic Medicine*, 4th edn. London: Churchill.

Carpenter, William B. (1874). *Principles of Mental Physiology: With Their Applications to the Training and Discipline of the Mind, and the Study of Its Morbid Conditions*. London: King.

Clifford, W. K. (1874). Body and Mind. *Fortnightly Review*, NS 16: 714–36.

Collingwood, R. G. (1940). *An Essay on Metaphysics*. Oxford: Clarendon Press.

Danziger, Kurt (1990). *Constructing the Subject*. Cambridge: Cambridge University Press.

Danziger, Kurt (1997). *Naming the Mind: How Psychology Found Its Language*. London: Sage.

Darwin, Charles (1872). *The Expression of the Emotions in Man and Animals*. London: Murray.

Daston, Lorraine J. (1998). Academies and the Unity of the Sciences: Disciplining the Disciplines. *Differences: A Journal of Feminist Cultural Studies*, 10: 67–86.

Dewey, John (1886). The Psychological Standpoint. *Mind*, 11: 1–19.

Ebbinghaus, Hermann (1908). *Psychology: An Elementary Text-Book*, trans. M. Meyer. Boston: Heath. (Translation of *Abriss der Psychologie*. Leipzig: Veit, 1908.)

Ferguson, Adam (1773). *Institutes of Moral Philosophy*, 2nd edn. Edinburgh: Kincaid, Creech, and Bell.

Ferrier, David (1876). *The Functions of the Brain*. London: Smith, Elder.

Ferrier, James F. (1854). *Institutes of Metaphysic: The Theory of Knowing the Mind*. Edinburgh: Blackwood.

Fisher, R. A. (1925). *Statistical Methods for Research Workers*. Edinburgh: Oliver and Boyd.

Fisher, R. A. (1935). *The Design of Experiments*. Edinburgh: Oliver and Boyd.

Flugel, J. C. (1933). *A Hundred Years of Psychology, 1833–1933*. London: Duckworth.

Flugel, J. C., and Donald J. West (1964). *A Hundred Years of Psychology, 1833–1933*, 3rd edn. London: Duckworth.

Galton, Francis (1869). *Hereditary Genius: An Inquiry into Its Laws and Consequences*. London: Macmillan.

Galton, Francis (1874). *English Men of Science: Their Nature and Nurture*. London: Macmillan.

Galton, Francis (1883). *Inquiries into Human Faculty and Its Development*. London: Macmillan.

Godart, Guillaume-Lambert (1755). *La Physique de l'ame humaine*. Berlin: La Compagnie.

Godden, David (2005). Psychologism in the Logic of John Stuart Mill: Mill on the Subject Matter and Foundations of Ratiocinative Logic. *History and Philosophy of Logic*, 26: 115–43.

Green, T. H. (1882). Can There Be a Natural Science of Man? *Mind*, 7: 1–29, 161–85, 321–48.

Hamilton, William (1853). *Discussions on Philosophy and Literature, Education and University Reform*, 2nd edn. London: Longman, Brown, Green and Longman's.

Hamilton, William (1861). *Lectures on Metaphysics*, 2 vols. Edinburgh: Blackwood.

Hamilton, William (1866). *Lectures on Logic*, 2 vols. Edinburgh: Blackwood.

Hamlyn, D. W (1957). *The Psychology of Perception: A Philosophical Examination of Gestalt Theory and Derivative Theories of Perception*. London: Routledge and Kegan Paul.

Hartley, David (1749). *Observations on Man, His Frame, His Duty, and His Expectations*. London: Leake and Frederick.

Hatfield, Gary (1985). First Philosophy and Natural Philosophy in Descartes. In A. J. Holland (ed.), *Philosophy, Its History and Historiography*, pp. 149–64. Dordrecht: Reidel.

Hatfield, Gary (1990). *The Natural and the Normative: Theories of Spatial Perception from Kant to Helmholtz*. Cambridge, Mass.: MIT Press.

Hatfield, Gary (1994). Psychology as a Natural Science in the Eighteenth Century. *Revue de synthèse*, 115: 375–91.

Hatfield, Gary (1995). Remaking the Science of Mind: Psychology as a Natural Science. In C. Fox, R. Porter, and R. Wokler (eds.), *Inventing Human Science*, pp. 184–231. Berkeley and Los Angeles: University of California Press.

Hatfield, Gary (1996). Was the Scientific Revolution Really a Revolution in Science? In J. Ragep and S. Ragep (eds.), *Tradition, Transmission, Transformation*, pp. 489–525. Leiden: Brill.

Hatfield, Gary (1997). Wundt and Psychology as Science: Disciplinary Transformations. *Perspectives on Science*, 5: 349–82.

Hatfield, Gary (2002). Psychology, Philosophy, and Cognitive Science: Reflections on the History and Philosophy of Experimental Psychology. *Mind and Language*, 17: 207–32.

Hatfield, Gary (2003). Psychology, Old and New. In Thomas Baldwin (ed.), *Cambridge History of Philosophy, 1870–1945*, pp. 93–106. Cambridge: Cambridge University Press.

Hatfield, Gary (2005). History of Philosophy as Philosophy. In T. Sorell and G. A. J. Rogers (eds.), *Analytic Philosophy and History of Philosophy*, pp. 82–128. Oxford: Oxford University Press.

Hatfield, Gary (2012). Koffka, Köhler, and the 'Crisis' in Psychology. *Studies in History and Philosophy of Biological and Biomedical Sciences*, 43/2: 483–92.

Hatfield, Gary (2013). Psychology, Epistemology, and the Problem of the External World: Russell and Before. In Erich Reck (ed.), *The Historic Turn in Analytic Philosophy*, pp. 171–200. London: Palgrave Macmillan.

Hearnshaw, L. S. (1964). *A Short History of British Psychology*. London: Methuen.

Hodgson, Shadworth H. (1876). Philosophy and Science, II: As Regards Psychology. *Mind*, 1: 223–35.

Hodgson, Shadworth H., Bernard Bosanquet, and David G. Ritchie (1891–2). Origin of the Perception of an External World. *Proceedings of the Aristotelian Society*, 2: 26–43.

Hume, David (1739–40). *Treatise of Human Nature*, 3 vols. London: Noon and Longman.

Huxley, T. H. (1874). On the Hypothesis that Animals Are Automata, and Its History. *Nature*, 10: 362–6.

James, William (1890). *Principles of Psychology*, 2 vols. New York: Holt.

Kant, Immanuel (1781). *Kritik der reinen Vernunft*. Riga: Hartnoch.

Krüger, Johann Gottlob (1756). *Versuch einer Experimental-Seelenlehre*. Halle: Hemerde.

Kuhn, Thomas (1962). *The Structure of Scientific Revolutions*. Chicago: University of Chicago Press.

Lewes, George Henry (1874–9). *Problems of Life and Mind*, 5 vols. London: Trübner.

McDougall, William (1905). *Physiological Psychology*. London: Dent.

McDougall, William (1908). *An Introduction to Social Psychology*. London: Methuen.

McDougall, William (1911). *Body and Mind: A History and a Defense of Animism*. New York: Macmillan.

McDougall, William (1912). *Psychology: The Study of Behaviour*. New York: Holt.

Mansel, Henry Longueville (1871). *Metaphysics; or, The Philosophy of Consciousness*. New York: Appleton.

Maudsley, Henry (1867). *The Physiology and Pathology of the Mind*. London: Macmillan.

Mellone, S. H. (1894). Psychology, Epistemology, Ontology, Compared and Distinguished. *Mind*, NS 3: 474–90.

Mill, John Stuart (1843). *A System of Logic, Ratiocinative and Inductive*, 2 vols. London: Parker.

Mill, John Stuart (1859). Bain's Psychology. *Edinburgh Review*, 90: 287–321.

Mill, John Stuart (1865). *An Examination of Sir William Hamilton's Philosophy*. London: Longman, Green, Longman, Roberts, and Green.

Morell, J. D. (1853). *Elements of Psychology*. London: Pickering.

Morell, J. D. (1862). *An Introduction to Mental Philosophy, on the Inductive Method*. London: Longman, Green, Longman, and Roberts.

Morus, Iwan (2006). Replacing Victoria's Scientific Culture. *19: Interdisciplinary Studies in the Long Nineteenth Century*, 2: 1–19.

Murphy, Joseph John (1869). *Habit and Intelligence in Their Connexion with the Laws of Matter and Force: A Series of Scientific Essays*. London: Macmillan.

Myers, Charles Samuel (1909). *A Text-Book of Experimental Psychology*. New York: Longmans, Green.

Nichols, Ryan (2007). *Thomas Reid's Theory of Perception*. Oxford: Clarendon Press.

Olesko, Kathryn M. (1991). *Physics as a Calling: Discipline and Practice in the Königsberg Seminar for Physics*. Ithaca, NY: Cornell University Press.

Passmore, John (1957). *A Hundred Years of Philosophy*. London: Duckworth.

Paulsen, Friedrich (1906). *German Universities and University Study*, trans. F. Thilly and W. W. Elwang. New York: Scribner's.

Prichard, H. A. (1907). A Criticism of the Psychologists' Treatment of Knowledge. *Mind*, NS 16: 27–53.

Purrington, Robert D. (1997). *Physics in the Nineteenth Century*. New Brunswick: Rutgers University Press.

Reed, Edward S. (1997). *From Soul to Mind: The Emergence of Psychology, from Erasmus Darwin to William James*. New Haven: Yale University Press.

Ribot, Théodule (1870). *La Psychologie anglaise contemporaine (école expérimentale)*. Paris: Ladrange.

Ribot, Théodule (1879). *La Psychologie allemande contemporaine: École expérimentale*. Paris: Baillière.

Ripley, George, and Charles A. Dana (eds.) (1881). Sir William Hamilton. In *American Cyclopaedia: A Popular Dictionary of General Knowledge*, viii. 422–3. New York: Appleton.

Rivers, W. H. R. (1894). A Modification of Aristotle's Experiment. *Mind*, NS 3: 583–4.

Robertson, George Croom (1876). Prefatory Words. *Mind*, 1: 1–6.

Robertson, George Croom (1883). Psychology and Philosophy. *Mind*, 8: 1–21.

Romanes, George J. (1883). *Mental Evolution in Animals*. London: Kegan Paul, Trench.

Romanes, George J. (1888). *Mental Evolution in Man: Origin of Human Faculty*. London: Kegan Paul, Trench.

Rorty, Richard (1979). *Philosophy and the Mirror of Nature*. Princeton: Princeton University Press.

Ross, Sydney (1962). Scientist: The Story of a Word. *Annals of Science*, 18: 65–85.

Russell, Bertrand (1914a). Definitions and Methodological Principles in Theory of Knowledge. *Monist*, 24: 582–93.

Russell, Bertrand (1914b). *Our Knowledge of the External World as a Field for Scientific Method in Philosophy*. Chicago: Open Court.

Russell, Bertrand (1914c). *Scientific Method in Philosophy*. Oxford: Clarendon Press.

Russell, Bertrand (1953). The Cult of 'Common Usage'. *British Journal for the Philosophy of Science*, 3: 303–7.

Rylance, Rick (2000). *Victorian Psychology and British Culture, 1850–1880*. Oxford: Oxford University Press.

Ryle, Gilbert (1949). *The Concept of Mind*. London: Hutchinson's University Library.

Schickore, Jutta (2008). Doing Science, Writing Science. *Philosophy of Science*, 75: 323–43.

Schiller, F. C. S. (1924). Psychology and Logic. In William Brown (ed.), *Psychology and the Sciences*, pp. 53–70. London: Black.

Scripture, E. W. (1899). *The New Psychology*. New York: Scribner's.

Seth, Andrew (1892). Psychology, Epistemology and Metaphysics. *Philosophical Review*, 1: 129–45.

Skorupski, John (1989). *John Stuart Mill*. London: Routledge.

Smith, R. (2005). The History of Psychological Categories. *Studies in History and Philosophy of Biological and Biomedical Sciences*, 36: 55–94.

Smith, R. (2010). British Thought on the Relations between the Natural Sciences and the Humanities, c.1870–1910. In Uljana Feest (ed.), *Historical Perspectives on Erklären und Verstehen*, pp. 161–86. Dordrecht: Springer.

Spencer, Herbert (1855). *The Principles of Psychology*. London: Longman, Brown, Green, and Longmans.

Stout, G. F. (1890). The Genesis of the Cognition of Physical Reality. *Mind*, 15: 22–45.

Stout, G. F. (1896). *Analytic Psychology*, 2 vols. London: Swan Sonnenschein.

Stout, G. F. (1899). *Manual of Psychology*. London: Clive.

Sully, James (1884). *Outlines of Psychology, with Special Reference to the Theory of Education: A Text-book for Colleges*. New York: Appleton.

Sully, James (1892). *The Human Mind: A Text-Book of Psychology*. London: Longmans, Green.

Teo, Thomas (2007). Local Institutionalization, Discontinuity, and German Textbooks of Psychology, 1816–1854. *Journal of the History of the Behavioral Sciences*, 43: 135–57.

Vidal, Fernando (2011). *The Sciences of the Soul: The Early Modern Origins of Psychology*, trans. Saskia Brown. Chicago: University of Chicago Press.

Ward, James (1886). Psychology. *Encyclopaedia Britannica*, 9th edn., xx. 37–85. Edinburgh: Black.

Ward, James (1890). The Progress of Philosophy. *Mind*, 15: 213–33.

Ward, James (1893). 'Modern' Psychology: A Reflexion. *Mind*, NS 2: 54–82.

Ward, James (1918). *Psychological Principles*. Cambridge: Cambridge University Press.

Wilson, Fred (1998). Mill on Psychology and the Moral Sciences. In John Skorupski (ed.), *The Cambridge Companion to Mill*, pp. 203–54. Cambridge: Cambridge University Press.

Wolff, Christian (1738). *Psychologia Empirica*. Frankfurt: Renger.

Wolff, Christian (1740). *Psychologia Rationalis*. Frankfurt: Renger.

Wolf, Friedrich O. (1970). The Philosophy of Common Sense in an Age of Revolution. In William Hamilton, *Lectures on Logic and Metaphysics*, i. 5*–28*. Stuttgart–Bad Canstatt: Frommann.

Woodward, William R., and Mitchell G. Ash (1982). *The Problematic Science: Psychology in Nineteenth-Century Thought*. New York: Praeger.

Wundt, W. (1896). Ueber die Definition der Psychologie. *Philosophische Studien*, 12: 1–66.

PART IV

ETHICAL, SOCIAL, AND
POLITICAL THOUGHT

CHAPTER 17

JEREMY BENTHAM AND JAMES MILL

PHILIP SCHOFIELD

1. INTRODUCTION: A MEETING OF MINDS

IT is unclear precisely when Jeremy Bentham (1748–1832) and James Mill (1773–1836) became acquainted. The earliest surviving letter between them, sent by Mill on 27 April 1809, indicates that they were already in regular contact, with Mill taking a keen interest in Bentham's *Elements of the Art of Packing as applied to Special Juries* (printed 1810, published 1820),[1] which he was composing at the time (Bentham 1988: 25–6). A few days earlier on 8 April 1809 Étienne Dumont, Bentham's Genevan friend and editor, had drawn Bentham's attention to a favourable notice, written anonymously, of his *Scotch Reform* (1808) that had appeared in the *Annual Review* (Bentham 1988: 21–2). The author was Mill, though it is unclear whether Dumont was aware of this. The received view is that Bentham and Mill had met some time in 1808 (Bain 1882: 72), soon became intimate friends, and that Mill thereupon converted Bentham to political radicalism (Dinwiddy 1975: 684–5). As Robert Fenn (1987: 126–7 n.) has pointed out, however, there is no more evidence that Mill converted Bentham to political radicalism than that Bentham converted Mill. The fact is that by early 1809 Bentham had already concluded that sinister interest pervaded the whole of the British state and that wholesale reform was necessary. In Mill he found a like-minded collaborator. Together they provided the intellectual and practical leadership to the movement that became known as philosophic radicalism,[2] and which had a significant impact on political, legal, and ecclesiastical reform in Britain in the 1830s and beyond, while their brand of classical utilitarianism continues to have an enduring impact on moral, political, and legal philosophy.

---

[1] Bentham's texts often have a complex printing and publication history. The publication of *Elements of the Art of Packing* was delayed when Bentham was warned by his friend, the barrister Sir Samuel Romilly, that, if he did publish it, both the printer and Bentham himself would be charged with seditious libel (Bentham 1988: 60–1).

[2] The classic account is Halévy (1928).

At the time of their meeting, the contrast between Bentham's and Mill's respective situations in life was stark. Bentham, educated at Westminster School and Queen's College, Oxford, a qualified barrister, was a wealthy gentleman, owning a large house and enormous garden in Westminster, with a substantial property portfolio inherited from his father Jeremiah, a successful attorney who had practised in the City of London. He had been on familiar terms with the Marquess of Lansdowne, who (as Earl of Shelburne) had been leader of the administration in 1782–3, and had access to almost any social circle that he might have cared to join. His international reputation as a philosopher of law had been secured by the appearance of *Traités de législation civile et pénale*, a French recension of his works, edited by Dumont, and published at Paris in 1802. His ambitions had, however, suffered a major setback when in 1803 the government had effectively quashed his panopticon prison scheme, an enterprise to which he had devoted more than a decade of his life (Semple 1993). He had then turned to work on judicial evidence and procedure, where he produced a systematic account of 'sinister interest', a phrase he had first used in the 1790s in relation to the aristocratic landowners who, because of the blight they expected a panopticon prison to cast upon their neighbouring estates, had opposed its construction. Bentham argued that sinister interest infected the judicial establishment: the confusion, obscurity, and expense that characterized English law was a product of the sinister interest of lawyers, who thereby extorted large amounts of money from their clients, and denied legal redress to all but the rich. He then recognized that the political establishment was in collusion with the lawyers, and formed part of the same sinister interest that linked rulers in an alliance against the people in general. When Bentham turned to his attention to parliamentary reform in the summer of 1809, the ground for his radical critique of the British political system had already been laid (Schofield 2006: 109–36).

James Mill's father was a shoemaker in a village in Forfar, Scotland. His precocious intellect had brought him to the attention of Sir John and Lady Jane Stuart of Fettercairn, who had supported him through his studies at the University of Edinburgh. He had been licensed to preach in the Church of Scotland, but having failed to obtain a parish had moved to London in 1802, where he set to work as an author, editor, reviewer, and commentator (Bain 1882: 1–23, 36–8). At the time he met Bentham, with a young and ever-expanding family to provide for, he was struggling to make ends meet. It would not be until the publication of *History of British India* (1817) and his subsequent appointment as an assistant examiner at the East India Company in 1819 that he would become financially secure (Bain 1882: 185). For several years Bentham allowed Mill to stay at a reduced rent in one of his properties, a stone's throw from his own house (Bain 1882: 72–4). Mill was forceful, energetic, determined to translate theory into practice and hence involved in a whole range of practical initiatives, and inspired a younger generation of radically inclined politicians and writers (Bain 1882: 180–3). Bentham was jovial, contented, devoted much of his day to writing (though his self-portrayal as a reclusive 'hermit' should not be accepted at face value), but similarly determined to have a practical impact. It proved to be a powerful alliance. One of Mill's first activities was to edit Bentham's writings on judicial evidence, which led to the partial printing of 'An Introduction to the Rationale of Judicial Evidence'.[3] He became Bentham's

---

[3] The work was eventually published in Bowring (1843), vi. 1–187. Mill's eldest son John Stuart Mill's first major literary endeavour was similarly concerned with Bentham's writings on evidence: the young Mill edited the massive *Rationale of Judicial Evidence* (1827).

companion at his country retreats, initially at a farmhouse near Oxted in Surrey, and later, between 1814 and 1817, after Bentham had received £23,000 in government compensation for his expenditure on the rejected panopticon prison scheme, at the stately Ford Abbey, near Chard in Devon. They enjoyed a close and stimulating relationship at Ford Abbey, going on daily walks (or 'circumgyrations' as Bentham termed them), and discussing a range of topics, but with religion and the Church high on the agenda (Fuller 2004).[4] Bentham then lost money in a scheme to build Vauxhall Bridge and had to give up the Abbey. Mill's articles in the *Encyclopaedia Britannica*, first published in 1816–23, were in large measure a distillation of Bentham ideas, presented with a directness and simplicity of style that has not always been considered to be a characteristic of Bentham's prose.[5] Both men, however, attempted to be clear, systematic, and intellectually rigorous, and rejected as nonsense any so-called knowledge based on supernatural or metaphysical insight. Their relationship was less intense in the 1820s when Mill came to regret the influence that John Bowring, a merchant, linguist, and poet, came to have over Bentham and his affairs (John Stuart Mill 1981: 93, 135). Nevertheless their joint commitment to the greatest happiness of the greatest number as the basis for radical political reform never wavered, and while Bentham drew up his codes of law, founded the *Westminster Review* in 1824 as a radical alternative to the Whig *Edinburgh Review* and the Tory *Quarterly Review*, and immersed himself in law reform, Mill mentored not only his eldest son John Stuart but also the rising generation of young radicals—including George Grote, John and Charles Austin, Charles Buller, and John Arthur Roebuck,[6] took a major role in the founding of the University of London (now University College London),[7] and published the seminal *Analysis of the Phenomena of the Human Mind* (1829). At the same time, Mill continued to play a major role in the affairs of the East India Company where in 1830 he was eventually promoted to the position of chief Examiner.

2. BENTHAM ON THE RELATION OF PSYCHOLOGY AND ETHICS

Bentham and Mill both held the view that human beings, and sentient creatures generally, were solely motivated by a desire for pleasure and an aversion to pain. As Bentham explained, this belief was founded on experience and observation, the only basis for knowledge (Bentham 2010: 624). He began *An Introduction to the Principles of Morals and Legislation* (printed 1780, published 1789) by stating: 'Nature has placed mankind under the governance of two sovereign masters, *pain* and *pleasure*. It is for them alone to point

---

[4] For Bentham's religious views see Crimmins (1990); Schofield (1999); and McKown (2004).

[5] In contrast to the standard view, Bain (1882: 425–7) thought that Bentham's writing style was far superior to that of Mill, who was never able to free himself completely from his 'Scotticisms'.

[6] Hamburger (1965: 1–75) arguably understates the influence of Bentham both on Mill himself and on the philosophic radicals more generally.

[7] Bentham did not actively involve himself in the foundation of the university (except for an unsuccessful attempt to have Bowring appointed as Professor of English Language and Literature), though his educational ideas were an important inspiration in terms of its ethos and curriculum (see Bellot 1929: 12–13; Burns 1962).

out what we ought to do, as well as to determine what we shall do'. The sovereign masters of pain and pleasure 'govern[ed] us in all we do, in all we say, in all we think', and indicated 'the standard of right and wrong' (Bentham 1970: 11). Hence psychology (itself founded on a physiology)[8] and ethics could both be understood only in terms of their relationship to the entities of pleasure and pain. In relation to psychology, an individual was in a state of happiness or well-being when he experienced a balance of pleasure over pain; in a state of suffering or misery when he experienced a balance of pain over pleasure. As far as the individual was concerned, good consisted in the experience of pleasure, or the exemption from pain, while evil consisted in the experience of pain or the loss of pleasure (Bentham 1998: 256). When an individual anticipated the enjoyment of some pleasure (or the avoidance of some pain) from the performance of an action, he had a desire to perform that action—in other words, he had an interest in performing it. The desire or interest gave rise to a motive, which, when coupled with a belief in the power (the capacity to alter the physical world) to accomplish the action in question, led to the production of the action. Except in those cases where coercion was involved, in other words where one person's will was directed by another person's will, the will was directed by the understanding, which consisted in knowledge and judgement (Bentham 1970: 96–100; 1983b: 92–4).

The sensations of pleasure and pain were the only things that mattered, and were, therefore, the source of all value. The value of a pleasure or pain, which was equivalent to the quantity of pleasure or pain experienced, depended on six 'elements' or 'dimensions', namely intensity, duration, certainty, propinquity, fecundity, and purity. Leaving pain out of the account, the intensity of a pleasure referred to its strength; duration to the length of time for which it was enjoyed; certainty to its likelihood or probability; propinquity to its nearness in point of time; fecundity to the probability of its leading to further pleasures; and purity to the probability of its not leading to pains. There was, however, a seventh 'element', namely extent, which referred to the number of persons that were subject to the pleasurable experience. To calculate the morality of an action, one took the pleasures and pains produced in the instance of a single individual, repeated the process for each individual affected, and aggregated the results. If the balance were on the side of pleasure, the act was morally good; if on the side of pain, morally evil (Bentham 1970: 38–41). The general interest was an aggregation of the interests of all the members of the community in question. By taking extent into account, a proposition of psychology was transformed into a proposition of ethics. A right action was one that produced a balance of pleasure over pain, taking into account the pleasures and pains of every person affected by the action in question: 'An action...may be said to be conformable to the principle of utility, or, for shortness sake, to utility, (meaning with respect to the community at large) when the tendency it has to augment the happiness of the community is greater than any it has to diminish it.' A person who accepted this view was an adherent of the principle of utility (Bentham 1970: 12–13; for commentary see Postema 2006).

Each individual was motivated primarily by self-regard, that is a desire to promote his own interest. Individuals were also motivated by sympathetic regard, that is a desire to

---

[8] Mill (1829: i. 5–7) recognized that medical science had not progressed to the point where it could provide an adequate account of physiology.

promote the happiness of those towards whom they felt some friendship or affection, and by antipathetic regard, that is a desire to promote the suffering of those towards whom they felt some hostility or disaffection. Because of the predominance of self-regard, individuals could not be relied upon to promote the interest of the community as a whole where there existed a conflict between their own interest and the general interest (Bentham 1970: 116–24; 1983b: 202–4, 210–11, 277–8). The task of the legislator was to distribute sanctions, consisting of rewards and punishments—pleasures and pains—in order to discourage those actions that were detrimental to the community as a whole, and encourage those that were beneficial. In other words, actions that were detrimental to the greatest happiness should be constituted into offences (except such cases where punishment was 'unmeet' through being groundless, inefficacious, too expensive, or needless), while those that harmed no one should be left alone (Bentham 1970: 34–7, 158–64). The law was the most important means of promoting happiness, since it created security (consisting most importantly in the distribution of rights and duties that protected person, property, reputation, and condition in life), thus guaranteeing reasonable expectations, and allowing human beings to project themselves and their plans into the future (Kelly 1990: 71–136). The legislator had to attach just enough punishment to an offence to dissuade the potential offender from committing it—too little punishment would be ineffective, while anything above the minimum would be to inflict unnecessary evil. The legislator, with the happiness of the community as his objective, had it in his power to guide the behaviour of those subject to him by means of the sanctions at his disposal (Rosen 2003: 152–7). The problem that Bentham had to face, as we shall see, was how to ensure that the legislator himself was committed to promoting the greatest happiness of the greatest number, rather than his own self-interest.

In the second edition of *An Introduction to the Principles of Morals and Legislation* which appeared in 1823, having become dissatisfied with the term the principle of utility, since it did not bring to mind either the ideas of pleasure and pain or the number of the interests concerned, Bentham explained that he now preferred to speak of the greatest happiness principle or the greatest felicity principle (Burns 2005). The notion of happiness did not make sense unless it was related to the sensations of pleasure and pain, while the rightness or wrongness of an action depended more on the number of the persons affected than on any other circumstance (Bentham 1970: 11 n.) He confessed that, when originally writing *An Introduction to the Principles of Morals and Legislation*, he had not understood the implications of the principle of utility for constitutional law, and so had not appreciated the strength of the hostility manifested towards it by the then Solicitor General Alexander Wedderburn (afterwards Lord Loughborough) when he had called it 'a dangerous principle'. In particular, Bentham had not attended to 'those features of the English Government, by which the greatest happiness of the ruling *one* with or without that of a favoured few, are now so plainly seen to be the only ends to which the course of it has at any time been directed'. The principle of utility, or the greatest happiness principle, was 'unquestionably' dangerous 'to every government which has for its *actual* end or object, the greatest happiness of a certain *one*, with or without the addition of some comparatively small number of others, whom it is matter of pleasure or accommodation to him to admit, each of them, to a share in the concern, on the footing of so many junior partners' (Bentham 1970: 14–15 n.).

3. Bentham's *Plan of Parliamentary Reform*

By the time that he began to write on parliamentary reform in 1809 Bentham had come to recognize that rulers, like all other human beings, were primarily motivated by their self-interest (Dinwiddy 1975). The problem was how to organize the structure of government so that rulers promoted not their own happiness but the greatest happiness of the greatest number. In *Plan of Parliamentary Reform*, eventually published in 1817, Bentham recommended 'democratic ascendancy', which would be achieved by radical political reform. Under the existing constitution, the monarch and aristocracy joined together in order to oppress the people in general. The universal interest was thereby sacrificed to the 'conjunct yoke' of the monarchical and aristocratical interests. The King, in his role as Corruptor-General, offered money, power, and factitious dignity (titles of honour) to members of the Houses of Parliament in return for their votes. Bentham was content to allow the executive to continue in the hands of the King and his ministers, but proposed that the House of Commons should, by means of electoral reform, be made subservient to the people, and thereby act as a check upon the executive. The suffrage would be extended to males over the age of 21 who could read and sign their name. Certain classes of persons who were considered to be incapable of exercising the suffrage to their advantage would be excluded. These classes included minors, sailors and soldiers (on the grounds that they were subject to the influence of the Corruptor-General), and females (though there was no good reason in Bentham's view for their exclusion). Roughly equal electoral districts would be established, so that each person's vote had a similar value. The secret ballot would secure the freedom of suffrage, in that it would allow each person to vote according to his own judgement as to what constituted his best interest, and not according to the will of some other person, such as his landlord. Secrecy of suffrage was, in Bentham's view, the crucial measure, since where voting was open, a very small sum would be enough to bribe each voter—Bentham confessed that a few shillings would secure his own vote. Elections would take place annually at a fixed time, and compared with the existing interval of seven years would considerably reduce the value to the Corruptor-General of any bribe offered to a representative. The suffrage would, therefore, be virtually universal, practically equal, secret, and annual. In addition, government officials would be excluded from the Commons, while constant attendance would be required from the representatives themselves. Bentham envisaged that the reforms he proposed would render the members of the House of Commons dependent on the people, rather than on the King (Schofield 2006: 146–52). These measures would not have abolished the monarchy or the House of Lords. It was not until after the publication of *Plan of Parliamentary Reform* that Bentham became a republican.

4. Bentham's Republicanism

As he intimated in the second edition of *An Introduction to the Principles of Morals and Legislation*, it was not until later in his career that Bentham turned his attention wholeheartedly to constitutional law. In 1809 he began to advocate the radical reform of

Parliament, and then in 1818 republicanism. The cause of this shift is not entirely clear, but he came to recognize that in order to introduce legal reform, it would first be necessary to introduce political reform, and that meant a representative democracy, or in other words a republic (Schofield 2006: 240–9). His most important work was the monumental *Constitutional Code* (partially published 1830), on which he began work in 1822, having received an invitation from the Portuguese Cortes to draw up penal, civil, and constitutional codes (Bentham 1998: 335–6). In introductory material intended for the constitutional code, drawing on the psychological and ethical theories he had outlined in *An Introduction to the Principles of Morals and Legislation*, Bentham argued that representative democracy was the only good form of government. In an absolute monarchy, the monarch's sinister interest was 'irreconcilably opposite' to the universal interest: it was his interest that whatever act increased his own happiness should be performed, no matter how much harm resulted to the rest of the community (Bentham 1989: 152–4). The monarch operated through three 'real and corporeal' instruments, namely the soldier, lawyer, and priest, and through four 'fictitious, incorporeal, nominal' instruments, namely force, fear or terror, corruption, and delusion. The soldier, in return for his pay, used force and intimidation, mainly against foreign enemies but also against recalcitrant subjects at home. He also contributed inadvertently to delusion through military show, which perverted the judgement of the people by equating the monarch's 'power and splendor' with 'excellence, moral and intellectual'. The lawyer's principal instrument was delusion. He invented 'a sort of Divinity which he calls Common Law', which was a source of profit both to the monarch and to the lawyer himself, with money in the form of fees being exacted from those able to pay, while access to justice was denied to those unable to do so. The priest's principal instrument was also delusion, and through delusion, intimidation: 'The Divinity sprung from the brain of the Lawyer is Common Law. The Divinity sprung from the brain of the Priest is Religion.' While the lawyer confined his terrors to the present life, the priest invented a future life which he 'filled with torments in intensity and duration infinite'. According to the priest, unless an individual did the will of the monarch in the present life, no matter the amount of misery produced, he would be condemned to an eternity of torment in the future life (Bentham 1989: 183–6). The priesthood, the legal profession, and the military maintained in their various ways the authority of the monarch in return for their share in the fruits of the oppression.

In a limited monarchy or a mixed form of government, containing a legislature that purportedly represented the people, the monarch had money, power, and factitious dignity at his disposal. He consumed a proportion of these 'objects of general desire' himself, but used the remainder to corrupt the members of the legislature, typically in the form of offices, commissions, and pensions. Members of the legislature had an interest in obtaining as much of this money, power, and factitious dignity—this matter of corruptive influence—as possible. No one needed to be told that the monarch would reward any member of the legislature who contributed to increasing the number and amount of the objects of desire at his disposal: it would be as pointless as it would be for a shopkeeper to run into the street to tell passers-by that he had goods for sale. The legislature voted in favour of wars and the annexation of colonies; the additional offices, commissions, and pensions thereby created were bestowed on members of the legislature or their relations; the people were forced to pay through increased taxation imposed by the legislature. Hence a mixed form of government was a partnership in corruption, with the monarch as the leading partner and the representatives of the people as the junior partners (Bentham 1989: 195–202).

The only form of government that might be constituted in such a way as to promote the greatest happiness was a representative democracy. The key was to identify the interest of rulers with that of the people. Such an identification existed when an individual experienced good or evil in the same proportion that it was experienced by the whole community: 'As between individual and the community, identification of interests is constituted by communion in good, or by communion in evil, or by communion in both kinds.' The opposition of interests existed when the individual experienced good, but evil was experienced by the whole community (Bentham 1989: 125). Where the opposition of interests was produced by laws and institutions, 'the root of the evil is in the form of the government', and could only be remedied by changing it (Bentham 1989: 126–7). The choice was between passively accepting the situation and suffering accordingly, or else rising up and overthrowing the government and replacing it with one in which the interest of rulers coincided with that of the universal interest. There was no point merely changing the existing set of rulers for a new set of rulers. The new rulers, placed in the same situation and thus imbued with the same sinister interest, would pursue the same sinister course as the old rulers: 'The whole Official Establishment is in that case in the state of a ship infected with the plague' (Bentham 1989: 128).

In advocating representative democracy, Bentham did not adopt the traditional theory of the division of power between legislative, executive, and judiciary. He argued that when the different holders of the branches of power disagreed, government came to a standstill, and when they agreed, the division was unnecessary (Bentham 2002: 409–13). Instead he insisted on clear lines of command between the different powers of government, and invented a new terminology to represent his alternative approach. The primary distinction was between operative power and constitutive power. The operative power performed the business of government, while the constitutive power determined the persons who would exercise the operative power (Bentham 1989: 30–1).[9] Operative power was divided into legislative and executive power, with the latter divided into administrative and judicial power. The administrative department applied the general rules and ordinances sanctioned by the legislative power to particular persons and things, and had control over such resources as had been set aside for the service of the state. The judicial department likewise applied the rules and ordinances sanctioned by the legislative power, but only in those cases where there existed a dispute between two or more parties (Bentham 1989: 6–7).

In order to establish good government, Bentham argued that the natural opposition of interests that existed between rulers and subjects had to be replaced with an artificial identification of interests. In order to accomplish this, two different sets of interests had to be identified. The interest of the possessors of constitutive power needed to be identified with the universal interest, and the interest of the possessors of operative power with that of the possessors of constitutive power. In relation to the constitutive power, it was necessary to place it in the hands of every one—in other words, there should in principle be universal suffrage, but subject in practice, as we shall see, to certain exceptions. Since the universal interest was the aggregate of all individual interests, each individual should vote for the candidate whom he considered would best promote his own interest. In each electoral district,

---

[9] A further division between supreme and subordinate power will not be discussed here. A national legislature, for instance, would exercise supreme legislative power, while a provincial legislature would exercise subordinate legislative power.

that candidate would be elected who appealed to the interests of the majority of voters. Once elected to the legislature, the representative or deputy (as Bentham termed the elected candidate) would vote, in regard to any particular arrangement, in favour of the interests of the inhabitants of his own district, as would all the other deputies. The result would be that 'the arrangements which are favorable to the interests of the inhabitants of all the Districts, or at least to the majority of them,…will be adopted and carried into effect'. That part of the happiness of each individual that was not adverse to that of any other would, insofar as depended on government, be secured to him, 'while all such portions of happiness as he could not be made to enjoy without depriving others of happiness to greater amount will not be given to him' (Bentham 1989: 135–7).

In the case of the possessors of supreme operative power, an unlimited pursuit of their own interests would be detrimental to the extent that an opposition existed between their interests and the universal interest. To ensure that this power was directed towards the promotion of the universal interest, a counterforce had to be established: 'this is the power reserved or given to the creators of their power, the possessors of the supreme constitutive power, to be the annihilators of it whenever they please'. The possessors of the constitutive power would allow the possessors of the legislative power to remain in office so long as they pursued their own happiness in no other way than through their share in the universal interest. If they attempted to engage in a course of action detrimental to the universal interest, the possessors of the supreme constitutive power would remove them from office. In this way, the identification of the interests of rulers and subjects would be as complete as possible; the constitutive power would be in the hands of the subjects themselves, while the legislative power would be in hands chosen by them. In relation to the legislative power, the subjects would themselves be rulers (Bentham 1989: 132–5). In other words, the electorate, exercising constitutive power, would be sovereign (Bentham 1983a: 25). Beneath the electorate in the chain of subordination would be the legislature, and beneath the legislature, in parallel chains of subordination, would be the administrative and judicial departments, which together constituted the supreme executive power (for Bentham's democratic theory, see Harrison 1983: 225–62; Rosen 1983; Schofield 2006: 250–303).

5. SECURITIES FOR OFFICIAL APTITUDE

The purpose of Bentham's proposed constitutional structure was to promote the greatest happiness of the greatest number—the only right and proper end of government—by effecting the two subordinate ends of constitutional law, namely the maximization of official aptitude and the minimization of expense. 'The goodness of the government', explained Bentham, 'will be as the aptitude of the portions of law enacted by it and the operations performed by it', and the aptitude of the law and the operations would in turn depend upon the aptitude of those enacting the law and performing the operations: hence, the need to secure the maximization of official aptitude. Drawing again on his psychological theory, Bentham divided aptitude into three branches—moral, intellectual, and active. Moral aptitude consisted in a willingness to promote the general interest. Intellectual aptitude consisted in the knowledge and judgement required to perform the tasks associated with a particular office. Active aptitude consisted in the physical performance of those tasks. Since all expense was evil, it was also necessary to secure the minimization of expense, understood not merely in terms of monetary expense, but in terms of costs of all sorts, including taxation, punishment, remuneration, factitious dignity, and all forms of obligation (that is the imposition of constraint and restraint) (Bentham 1989: 4–5).

Viewed from another perspective, the identification of interests brought about by representative democracy provided the framework within which the securities for official aptitude could operate effectively. The detailed administrative arrangements that Bentham drew up in his writings for the constitutional code were intended to contribute to the securing of the various branches of aptitude, with particular emphasis on the members of the legislature, ministers including the prime minister and the justice minister, judges, members of the armed forces, and subordinate officials within the various sub-departments (ministries). Not all the securities were appropriate in each instance, but Bentham identified a number of securities that would apply across most of the official establishment. Of the securities for moral aptitude, the most important was the very structure of representative democracy, that is the limitation of the legislative power by its subordination to the constitutive power. This subordination would be achieved, as we have seen, by placing the power of appointment and dismissal (location and dislocation in Bentham's terminology) in the hands of the possessors of constitutive power, exercised at stated intervals. The power of dismissal was crucial, and far more important in securing subordination than the power of appointment:

> A servant whom, whatsoever be his behaviour towards you, it has been out of your power to dismiss is by that very thing made your master: your master in reality, your servant only in name. So you have but the power of dismissing him, a servant chosen though it be by an adversary will be less annoying to you than in the other case a servant chosen by yourself may be.

A second mode of limiting power was the division of the legislative power into fractions. If one person was sole legislator, elected for one year, it would be relatively easy for him to extend his power for a further year, and easier still each succeeding year. Hence, as well as annual elections, it was necessary that the power be shared among a number of individuals, each elected by a separate set of constituents, distributed into roughly equal electoral districts. The possessors of executive power would in turn be made subordinate to the possessors of legislative power by subjection to the powers of dismissal and, in cases of legal infringement, judicially exercised punishment. The legislature would also enjoy the power to prevent, both temporarily and permanently, executive acts from coming into force, and to rescind their written orders. Were it not for this subordination, the chief executive functionary (whether monarch, president, or prime minister) would be able to veto all the acts of the legislative body, and by means of the offices at his disposal, corrupt its members, and transform the government into a despotism (Bentham 1989: 30–3, 36–7, 41).

A further security for moral aptitude was of such critical importance that without it the structure of representative democracy would not of itself lead to the promotion of the greatest happiness: this security was the moral responsibility of rulers, that is their subjection to criticism at the hands of the public opinion tribunal wielding the force of the moral sanction—in short, publicity and open government. The public opinion tribunal was formed by all persons who took notice of an issue. The decision of the tribunal, while it could not be definitively ascertained, was a presumption made by 'each individual in his character of member of the tribunal of public opinion' in relation to 'the decision likely to be pronounced by the several other members' (Bentham 1989: 56–7).[10] The opinion pronounced or acted upon by each individual member of the public opinion tribunal would be determined by his conception of his own interest. The public opinion tribunal was, therefore, divided into two sections, the democratical and the aristocratical. The interest of the former was that of the majority, of the subject many, of the productive classes. The interest of the latter was that of 'the ruling and otherwise influential few', of the non-productive classes, and hence would often be in opposition to the interest of the democratical section. The members of the democratical section would attach good repute to those actions that they regarded as contributory to the universal interest, and disrepute to those that they regarded as detrimental, and apportion praise and blame accordingly. The members of the aristocratical section would attach disrepute to those actions that they regarded as detrimental to their particular interest. The will of the public opinion tribunal as a whole, however, would be determined by the interest of the majority of its members, that is by the democratical section (Bentham 1989: 68–9).

With the major exception of the legislative power, which was to be divided into fractions, official positions were to be 'single-seated', that is all functions were to be undertaken by a particular, identifiable functionary. When decisions were made by a committee, no single individual could be held responsible, and no praise or blame attached to any one by the public opinion tribunal. Without single-seatedness, it was virtually impossible to hold officials accountable for their actions (Bentham 1983a: 173–86). The implication of moral responsibility was that all government activity, and the reasons for it, should be documented, and those documents made public, unless a public case had been made for secrecy (Ben Dor 2000; Lieberman 2000).

Other securities for moral aptitude included minimizing the amount of money at the disposal of functionaries and prohibiting them from making any personal profit from it (Bentham 1989: 45); reducing the amount of salary received by functionaries, since the lower the salary, the less attractive the office as a source of corruption (Bentham 1989: 40, 47); and excluding factitious dignity, that is abolishing titles of honour artificially created and bestowed. The purpose of a title was to persuade the people that meritorious service had been performed by the person on whom it was conferred, but in practice such titles were conferred without any connection to meritorious service. The proper role of government was to make known the sort and quantity of service an individual had rendered, and allow people to decide for themselves what respect (or disrespect) they wished to give to the individual in question (Bentham 1989: 48–52).

A further security for moral aptitude consisted in the non-establishment of any religion, or more precisely in prohibiting the giving of any reward or inflicting of any punishment for making any profession of religious belief. If an individual accepted that a particular religion were true, there was no need to reward him for professing his belief. If he did not believe it to be true, such an inducement instilled a habit of insincerity and mendacity. Moreover, the reward in question could only be supplied by taxation, obtained by coercion, and hence constituted an evil in itself. To pay priests to inculcate religious belief was still worse. The priest

---

[10] Anticipating the notion of deliberative democracy, Bentham suggested that sections of the public opinion tribunal, which he termed juries, might be established in order to give a definite opinion on a particular subject-matter (Bentham 1989: 58–9).

was rendered both morally corrupt and intellectually debilitated since he concentrated on only one side of the question—that is on those arguments that tended to show, in his view, that the belief was true (Bentham 1989: 325–7). The priest, as we have seen, did not merely delude himself, but contributed to bad government by deluding the people as a whole. The advantage to rulers of an established religion was that they enjoyed the patronage of the immense mass of money, extracted from rich and poor alike, that was paid to the priests (Bentham 1989: 329). No religion had ever been established 'but for the purpose as well as with the effect of its being made an instrument of intimidation, corruption and delusion, for the support of depredation and oppression, in the hands of the government' (Bentham 1989: 331).

For the securing of intellectual aptitude, Bentham recommended examination tailored to the specific duties and powers of each office. The examination should be public, so that the public opinion tribunal could monitor the activities of the examiners, and take place orally, with each candidate encouraged to take part in the examination of his rivals, since he had an interest in bringing to light their inadequacies. The result would be 'an extraordinary supply of intellectual aptitude on the part of every one of them' (Bentham 1989: 77–84). Active aptitude required the uninterrupted attendance of the official at the place where the duty needed to be performed. With the possible exception of '[t]he periodical day of rest', each and every functionary, from the highest to the lowest, should attend the 'individual spot, if such a spot there be, in which alone the service can be rendered'. One security was to link pay to attendance (Bentham 1989: 87–9). A second security was to establish 'relish for the function'. Candidates would be required to bid in a public auction for the pay allotted to an office: they might offer to serve for reduced pay, for no pay at all, or even to give money. If a candidate was willing to pay a higher price, it could be assumed that he anticipated a greater amount of pleasure from performing, and would possess a greater degree of skill in performing, the functions attached to the office. The patron of the office—say a minister appointing an official in his sub-department—would need to take into account the results not only of the auction, but also of the public examination, indicating the degree of intellectual aptitude possessed by each candidate. The minister would choose the individual whom he considered to be the best candidate, but his choice would be subject to the scrutiny of the public opinion tribunal, who would have the same information—the results of the auction and the examination—that the minister possessed in coming to his decision. The minister would judge which candidate was the most apt, and the public would judge the minister's judgement (Bentham 1989: 89–93).

6. Bentham's Blueprint for Representative Democracy

In *Constitutional Code*, Bentham translated these principles of good government into a set of complex institutional arrangements, though only a brief outline can be offered here (for more detailed accounts see Hume 1981: 165–237; Rosen 1983: 130–67). The territory of the state would be divided into equal electoral districts, with a roughly equal number of constituents, each returning one member to the legislature, hence ensuring that each person's vote was of a similar value. Elections would be held annually, and the ballot would be secret, hence ensuring that no voter would be subject to any form of corruptive influence. The electorate would be composed of all males above the age of 21, subject to a literacy test (Bentham 1983a: 11, 27, 30). Bentham was in favour of female suffrage, and had in fact recommended it to the French as early as 1789 (Bentham 2002: 246–8), but thought that to incorporate the proposal into the constitutional code would be counter-productive until the public mind itself had become more enlightened (Bentham 1989: 99–100). Each set of constituents had the power to remove their deputy from office at any point between elections by means of a petition of a quarter of the electorate, followed by a majority vote. Several executive functionaries, including the prime minister, ministers, justice minister, and judges, were subject to the same procedure (Bentham 1983a: 31–3). The legislature would be composed of a single chamber. There would be no limits to its power—it would be 'omnicompetent', that is there would be no entrenched or immutable laws that it could not alter (see Schwartzberg 2007). It was, however, to be subject to checks in the form of the securities for appropriate aptitude (Bentham 1983a: 41–4). The deputies would be subject to a three-year period of non-relocability, so that they could not be re-elected until constituents had at least three experienced candidates from which to choose (Bentham 1983a: 72–3). In order to obviate any difficulties generated by annual elections and temporary non-relocability in relation to the continuity of policy and legislation, there would be a continuation committee attached to the legislature, consisting of outgoing members of the legislature. Members of the continuation committee had the right to make motions and speak in the legislature, but not to vote (Bentham 1983a: 67–8). The prime minister, at the head of the administrative department, would be appointed for a four-year term by the legislature, and could be dismissed by both legislature and by a petition and majority vote of the constitutive power (Bentham 1983a: 148–59). Bentham envisaged thirteen sub-departments, each headed by a minister, appointed for life by the prime minister, but removable either by the legislature, or prime minister, or petition and majority vote of the constitutive power (Bentham 1983a: 171–2, 295, 311, 365). The justice minister would be in an analogous position to the prime minister at the head of the judicial department, responsible for appointing judges, but subject to dismissal at the hands of the legislature or the constitutive power by petition and majority vote (Bowring 1843: ix. 597, 607–8, 610).

7. MILL'S *ESSAY ON GOVERNMENT*

Mill's *Essay on Government* was published in 1820, and is in many respects an exposition of Bentham's *Plan of Parliamentary Reform*, and therefore less radical than *Constitutional Code*.[11] For Mill, the role of the representatives of the people was to act as a check upon those by whom the powers of government were exercised, and hence the main division was between the people and their representatives on the one side, and the wielders of government power—the executive—on the other. This was to mirror Bentham's approach in *Plan*

---

[11] Thomas (1979: 119–46) interprets Mill's *Essay on Government* as an inconsistent compromise between Hobbesian psychology, Benthamite democratic hedonism, and Platonic paternalism. For a defence of Mill's consistency, see Wendell (1971).

of Parliamentary Reform. By the time that he began work on the constitutional code in 1822, Bentham regarded the representatives of the people (or deputies as he termed them) as themselves rulers, and drew the main line of division between the people on the one side (the constitutive power) and the deputies and all other holders of government office on the other (the operative power). This development in Bentham's thought was a product of his commitment to republicanism, and his view that the people themselves would act as a check upon an omnicompetent legislature. In *Plan of Parliamentary Reform* he had envisaged the continued existence of the monarch, who would yield executive power, and the House of Lords, and hence need to be checked by a House of Commons subject to the people. In his proposed republic, monarch and aristocrats would have no place. Mill did not follow Bentham into republicanism (Mill 1992: 35–6), and hence did not go beyond the approach outlined by Bentham in *Plan of Parliamentary Reform.*

Mill started from the same psychological and ethical assumptions as those announced by Bentham in *An Introduction to the Principles of Morals and Legislation.* He outlined his basic principles as follows:

> That the actions of men are governed by their wills, and their wills by their desires: That their desires are directed to pleasure and relief from pain as *ends*, and to wealth and power as the principal means: That to the desire of these means there is no limit; and that the actions which flow from this unlimited desire are the constituents whereof bad Government is made. (Mill 1992: 17)

The aim of government was the greatest happiness of the greatest number, namely 'to increase to the utmost the pleasures, and diminish to the utmost the pains, which men derive from one another', with happiness consisting in the balance of pleasures over pains (Mill 1992: 3–4). The great difficulty of government, instituted as it was to secure to each man the product of his labour to the greatest extent possible, was to stop rulers from exercising the powers of government badly. Just as an individual was tempted to take the objects of desire from any individual weaker than himself, so the members of government were under the same temptation in relation to the members of the community. Hence, it was necessary to establish securities against the abuse of power (Mill 1992: 6).

Mill, like Bentham, adopted the standard Aristotelian division of government into democracy, aristocracy, and monarchy for purposes of analysis. In relation to democracy, Mill repeated the commonplace argument that the people as a whole could not govern themselves, on account of both the chaos that would ensue in a mass assembly, and the fact that political questions would take up the whole of their time, and leave none for labour. In an aristocracy, the rulers would lack intellectual capacity, since they had no motive to perform the labour that was necessary to acquire that capacity, and would use their power to take the objects of desire for themselves. The same objections applied to a monarchy. Having obtained the power to take from every man what he pleased, the monarch would simply take it (Mill 1992: 17–20). Having rejected the three simple forms of government, Mill, like Bentham, rejected the doctrine of the mixed constitution, to which, it was claimed, the British Constitution owed its excellence.[12] Mill pointed out that, if any such government were established, two of the three powers would combine and 'swallow up' the third, and given the opposition between the democracy and the other two powers, it was inevitable that the

---

[12]   Bentham composed a highly ironic defence of the mixed constitution of Britain in *A Fragment on Government*, first published in 1776 (Bentham 1977: 461–73).

monarchy and aristocracy would combine in order 'to obtain unlimited power over the persons and property of the community' (Mill 1992: 17–20; compare Bentham 2002: 405–18).

The only good government was a representative democracy, where appropriate checks to the power of rulers could be instituted by means of a representative body: 'For though the people, who cannot exercise the powers of Government themselves, must entrust them to some one individual or set of individuals, and such individuals will infallibly have the strongest motives to make a bad use of them, it is possible that checks may be found sufficient to prevent them' (Mill 1992: 21–2). The representative body both needed sufficient power to check those who exercised the powers of government, and 'an identity of interest with the community; otherwise it will make a mischievous use of its power'. Each representative had two capacities: first, as a representative he exercised power over others; second, as a member of the community, others exercised power over him. The point was so to arrange matters that, 'in his capacity of Representative, it would be impossible for him to do himself so much good by misgovernment, as he would do himself harm in his capacity of member of the community'. Given that the representative needed enough power to overcome resistance from those in whom the powers of government were lodged, his power could not be diminished in amount, but only in duration: he would calculate that the profits he obtained from misgovernment would be outweighed by the suffering he experienced as a result of it. Punishing the representatives for abuse might be a further means of limiting their power, but it was often difficult to prove that a determinate offence had been committed. Hence, 'As it thus appears, that limiting the duration of their power is a security against the sinister interest of the people's Representatives, so it appears that it is the only security of which the nature of the case admits.' In contrast to Bentham, Mill did not support temporary non-relocability: a re-elected representative would be better acquainted with the business of government (Mill 1992: 22–5; for commentary, see Rosen 1983: 169–74).

The interest of the body choosing the representatives needed to be identified with that of the community as a whole, otherwise it would choose those representatives who would promote the interests of that smaller number. Mill recommended that the franchise be restricted to males over the age of 40. This would not compromise the identity of interests since these individuals had no interest distinct from that of the community as a whole. The interests of children were 'indisputably included' in those of their parents, and women in those of their fathers or husbands—and so children and women could be 'struck off' the franchise 'without inconvenience'. Mill rejected any property qualification on the grounds that, unless it were very low, it would result in an aristocracy, while a low qualification would be little different from no qualification at all. A middle course might be found, but Mill's conclusion seems to have been that it would be difficult to find a stable enough principle that would not create an aristocracy. Mill also rejected the notion that certain classes or professions should be represented, on the grounds that such classes and professions would merely pursue their sinister interests (Mill 1992: 26–35).

8. CONCLUSION

Bentham and Mill both accepted that the starting point for constitutional design was the fact that human beings were predominantly self-interested. Rulers were no different from any one else in this respect, and hence it should be no surprise that, with power in their hands, and unless subjected to some form of check, they would promote their own interests, no matter how much the community as a whole suffered as a result. A second assumption was that no one person's happiness was worth more than that of any one else: as Bentham put it, 'every individual in the country tells for one; no individual for more than one' (Bentham 1827: iv. 475). A third assumption was that each person, unless there was some special reason to the contrary, was the best judge of his own interest (Bentham 1983b: 150, 250–1). Hence, admitting every one into a share of political power by means of the franchise, providing they were not subject to corruptive influence or intimidation, would produce a representative assembly committed to the promotion of the general interest. The secret ballot was a critical measure, since it ensured that the elector could vote according to his own conception of his interest without fear of reprisal, and made futile any attempt at bribery. In his later republican writings, Bentham argued that the administrative and judicial departments of government should be directly subordinate to the legislature, and thus indirectly to the electorate, which, by virtue of its power in this respect, was sovereign. The framework created by representative democracy was supplemented by a series of securities for official aptitude, including the minimization of salaries, the abolition of titles of honour, the exclusion of established religion, public examination, pay linked to attendance, and, most importantly, publicity. By these measures, the natural opposition of interests between rulers and subjects was replaced by an artificial identification of interests. Mill's *Essay on Government* was an outline of the theory of constitutional law that Bentham proposed in his writings on parliamentary reform composed between 1809 and 1817, but did not anticipate the novel and even more radical conception of representative democracy that Bentham developed in detail in the 1820s in his writings for the constitutional code.

REFERENCES

Bain, Alexander (1882). *James Mill: A Biography*. London: Longmans, Green, And Co.

Bellot, H. Hale (1929). *University College London 1826–1926*. London: University of London Press.

Ben-Dor, Oren (2000). *Constitutional Limits and the Public Sphere: A Critical Study of Bentham's Constitutionalism*. Oxford and Portland, OR: Hart.

Bentham, Jeremy (1827). *Rationale of Judicial Evidence, specially applied to English practice*, ed. J. S. Mill, 5 vols. London: Hunt and Clarke.

Bentham, Jeremy (1970). *An Introduction to the Principles of Morals and Legislation*, ed. J. H. Burns and H. L. A. Hart. London: Athlone.

Bentham, Jeremy (1977). *A Comment on the Commentaries and A Fragment on Government*, ed. J. H. Burns and H. L. A. Hart. London: Athlone.

Bentham, Jeremy (1983a). *Constitutional Code*, i, ed. F. Rosen and J. H. Burns. Oxford: Clarendon Press.

Bentham, Jeremy (1983b). *Deontology together with A Table of the Springs of Action and Article on Utilitarianism*, ed. Amnon Goldworth. Oxford: Clarendon Press.

Bentham, Jeremy (1988). *The Correspondence of Jeremy Bentham*, viii. *January 1809 to December 1816*, ed. Stephen Conway. Oxford: Clarendon Press.

Bentham, Jeremy (1989). *First Principles Preparatory to Constitutional Code*, ed. Philip Schofield. Oxford: Clarendon Press.

Bentham, Jeremy (1998). *Legislator of the World: Writings on Codification, Law, and Education*, ed. Philip Schofield and Jonathan Harris. Oxford: Clarendon Press.

Bentham, Jeremy (2002). *Rights, Representation, and Reform: Nonsense upon Stilts and Other Writings on the French Revolution*, ed. Philip Schofield, Catherine Pease-Watkin, and Cyprian Blamires. Oxford: Clarendon Press.

Bentham, Jeremy (2010). *Writings on the Poor Laws*, ii, ed. Michael Quinn. Oxford: Clarendon Press.

Bowring, John (ed.) (1843). *The Works of Jeremy Bentham*, 11 vols. Edinburgh: William Tait.

Burns, J. H. (1962). *Jeremy Bentham and University College*. London: Athlone.

Burns, J. H. (2005). 'Happiness and Utility: Jeremy Bentham's Equation.' *Utilitas*, 17: 46–61.

Crimmins, James E. (1990). *Secular Utilitarianism: Social Science and the Critique of Religion in the Thought of Jeremy Bentham*. Oxford: Clarendon Press.

Dinwiddy, J. R. (1975). 'Bentham's Transition to Political Radicalism, 1809–1810.' *Journal of the History of Ideas*, 36: 683–700.

Fenn, Robert A. (1987). *James Mill's Political Thought*. New York: Garland.

Fuller, Catherine (2004). ' "It is the theatre of great felicity to a number of People": Bentham at Ford Abbey.' *Journal of Bentham Studies*, 7 <http://ojs.lib.ucl.ac.uk/index.php/jbs/article/view/40>.

Halévy, Elie (1928). *The Growth of Philosophic Radicalism*, trans. Mary Morris. London: Faber & Faber.

Hamburger, Joseph (1965). *Intellectuals in Politics: John Stuart Mill and the Philosophic Radicals*. New Haven and London: Yale University Press.

Harrison, Ross (1983). *Bentham*. London, Boston, Melbourne, and Henley: Routledge & Kegan Paul.

Hume, L. J. (1981). *Bentham and Bureaucracy*. Cambridge: Cambridge University Press.

Kelly, P. J. (1990). *Utilitarianism and Distributive Justice: Jeremy Bentham and the Civil Law*. Oxford: Clarendon Press.

Lieberman, David (2000). 'Economy and Polity in Bentham's Science of Legislation', in S. Collini, R. Whatmore, and B. Young (eds.), *Economy, Polity, and Society: British Intellectual History 1750–1950*, 107–34. Cambridge: Cambridge University Press.

McKown, Delos B. (2004). *Behold the Antichrist: Bentham on Religion*. Amherst, NY: Prometheus.

Mill, James (1829). *Analysis of the Phenomena of the Human Mind*, 2 vols. London: Baldwin and Cradock.

Mill, James (1992). *Political Writings*, ed. Terence Ball. Cambridge: Cambridge University Press.

Mill, John Stuart (1981). *Autobiography and Literary Essays*, ed. John M. Robson and Jack Stillinger. Toronto and Buffalo: University of Toronto Press.

Postema, Gerald J. (2006). 'Interests, Universal and Particular: Bentham's Utilitarian Theory of Value.' *Utilitas*, 18: 109–33.

Rosen, Frederick (1983). *Jeremy Bentham and Representative Democracy: A Study of the Constitutional Code*. Oxford: Clarendon Press.

Rosen, Frederick (2003). *Classical Utilitarianism from Hume to Mill*. London and New York: Routledge.

Schofield, Philip (1999). 'Political and Religious Radicalism in the Thought of Jeremy Bentham.' *History of Political Thought*, 20: 272–91.

Schofield, Philip (2006). *Utility and Democracy: the Political Thought of Jeremy Bentham*. Oxford: Oxford University Press.

Schwartzberg, Melissa (2007). 'Jeremy Bentham on Fallibility and Infallibility.' *Journal of the History of Ideas*, 68: 563–85.

Semple, Janet (1993). *Bentham's Prison: A Study of the Panopticon Penitentiary.* Oxford: Clarendon Press.

Thomas, William (1979). *The Philosophic Radicals: Nine Studies in Theory and Practice 1817–1841.* Oxford: Clarendon Press.

Wendell, Robert Carr (1971). 'James Mill's Politics Reconsidered: Parliamentary Reform and the Triumph of Truth.' *Historical Journal,* 14: 553–80.

CHAPTER 18

....

JOHN STUART MILL'S MORAL, SOCIAL, AND POLITICAL PHILOSOPHY[1]

....

DALE E. MILLER

THE renown of John Stuart Mill (1806–73) as a moral, social, and political philosopher rests largely on works that he published relatively late in life, well after *A System of Logic* (1st edn. 1843) had established him as a logician and epistemologist and *The Principles of Political Economy* (1st edn. 1848) as a political economist. The most widely read of these are *On Liberty* (1859), *Utilitarianism* (1861), *Considerations on Representative Government* (1861), and *The Subjection of Women* (1869). These works have spawned a vast interpretative literature. In keeping with the general approach of this volume, in what follows I will present a specific and therefore controversial interpretation of Mill. As much account will be taken of competing readings as space permits, but many important contributions to the secondary literature will inevitably be neglected.

1. VIEWS ON HUMAN NATURE

....

Mill's conception of human nature is the foundation on which his moral, social, and political philosophy rests. It will only be possible to discuss a few elements of this conception here, beginning with his answer to the question of what in our nature allows us to acquire knowledge. As is well known, Mill is a thoroughgoing empiricist, but at a foundational level his epistemology also draws upon the naturalistic intuitionism of the Scottish Common-Sense school. John Skorupski calls our attention to this affinity when he writes that '...Mill stands loosely in the tradition of Reid' (1998, p. 6). When a doxastic disposition is innate, with the hallmarks of innateness being that the disposition is universally shared, irresistible, and

[1] Much of the material in this article is drawn from D. Miller (2010), in which the readings of Mill defended here are developed at length. I am grateful to Ben Eggleston and Beth McHose for their comments.

impossible to acquire via experience, Mill is willing to regard the beliefs to which it gives rise as items of intuitive knowledge (see D. Miller 2010, pp. 14–18). This is clearest in his explanation of how we can know that the memory is generally trustworthy in *An Examination of the Philosophy of Sir William Hamilton* (*CW* ix. 165 n).[2]

Yet while Mill believes that we do have some intuitive knowledge, he is still critical of those philosophers generally regarded as intuitionists. He subscribes to a psychological theory known as associationism. According to associationism, mental states that we frequently experience simultaneously or consecutively become linked in our minds, so that having one summons up the other. The mental states in question may be impressions or their corresponding ideas (in Hume's senses of these terms), but they may also be feelings, desires, or volitions. Mill believes that associationism can explain how many doxastic dispositions that the intuitionists take to be founts of intuitive knowledge are actually acquired via experience. Thus while he believes that we do have *some* intuitive knowledge, he takes the intuitionists to greatly overstate how much.

Another central aspect of Mill's conception of human nature is his account of motivational psychology. Fundamentally, he shares Hume's 'belief/desire' view; strictly speaking, desires (and aversions) are our only motives. And like Hume, he recognizes the importance of sympathy in our motivational psychology. Mill departs from Hume, though, in the importance that he attaches to the motivational role of the conscience or 'internal sanction of duty' (*CW* x. 228). Mill views the internal sanction as a disposition to experience what he describes in an 1859 letter to William George Ward as 'a feeling of pain in the fact of violating a certain rule' (*CW* xv. 649). In this letter, he offers an associationist explanation of how this disposition is acquired, that is, of how a person's experiences lead to her feeling guilty about breaking certain rules (albeit not necessarily the same rules as anyone else). That our disposition to feel guilt is a product of experience is one of several reasons that Mill rejects the view that we can intuit the truth of moral rules or the moral standing of particular actions through the deliverances of the conscience.

Mill's account of motivational psychology also takes heed of our capacity to develop habitual ways of acting. In fact, he takes our capacity to develop habits—not only habitual ways of acting, but also habitual ways of thinking and feeling—to be among the most significant facts about us. A person's character is the sum total of her 'dispositions, and habits of mind and heart' (*CW* x. 7)—'dispositions' here refers to habits of the will—and habits that conduce to our doing our duty are moral virtues. While Mill is not a proponent of the sort of view that is today described as 'virtue ethics', he is a firm believer in the importance of cultivating virtue.[3] While he believes that our characters are shaped by our circumstances, Mill maintains that we have a considerable power to alter our circumstances and so to shape our own characters. In fact, he believes that, as he writes in the Hamilton volume, 'we are under a moral obligation to seek the improvement of our moral character' (*CW* ix. 466).

In the *Logic*, Mill proposes a new science of human character that he calls 'ethology' (*CW* viii. 861–74). Ethology would be concerned with the 'middle principles' of the mental sciences, in between the most general laws of psychology and the most specific and narrow

---

[2] References to Mill's works will be to the Toronto edition of his *Collected Works* (*CW*) and will include volume and page numbers.

[3] Without quite calling Mill a virtue ethicist, Wendy Donner argues that his utilitarianism is 'deeply linked' with virtue ethics (2009, p. 3).

observed regularities. While his intention was to be the founder of this science, he seems never to have felt ready to write on the subject.

2. MILL'S UTILITARIANISM: SOME PRELIMINARIES

Mill's moral theory fell into disrepute shortly after his death. This is due in no small part to the rough treatment that it received from late nineteenth- and early twentieth-century critics including G. E. Moore (Moore 1903, esp. pp. 59–109) and F. H. Bradley (Bradley 1927, esp. pp. 85–126). The second half of the twentieth century witnessed a re-examination of Mill's utilitarianism, however, and this continues today.

So much about Mill's utilitarianism is controversial that the following three sections, which deal with different aspects of his moral theory, will delve into numerous ongoing debates. Since not every interpretative avenue can be explored in a discussion of this length, though, it will be necessary to take certain things about his utilitarianism for granted even though some commentators dispute them. One point that will be assumed without argument in what follows is that Mill believes that the moral standing of actions depends in some way on how the good can best be promoted, which is to say maximized (cf. Brown 2010, pp. 15–16). Another is that Mill believes that happiness is coextensive with the good, that is, that happiness always has intrinsic value—or, as he would say, is desirable as an end—and that nothing else ever does (cf. Garforth 1980, pp. 1–14). This axiological proposition, it will further be assumed, is what Mill refers to as the 'principle of utility' (Brown 1973; cf. Wiggins 2006, pp. 147–8). A final assumption will be that Mill's essay *Utilitarianism* can offer us important insights into his own views on moral theory (cf. Jacobson 2003).

3. MILL'S CONCEPTION OF HAPPINESS

Mill's conception of happiness is the locus of some of the larger controversies in contemporary Mill studies. One fundamental question that splits scholars into opposing camps is that of whether Mill conceives of happiness in terms of mental states. Many interpreters take him to understand happiness in terms of pleasant mental states and to take these states to be the ultimate bearers of intrinsic value (e.g. Skorupski 1989, 295–9; Crisp 1997, pp. 25–8; Donner 2004, pp. 8–23; West 2004, pp. 48–73; Riley 2008, p. 258; D. Miller 2010, pp. 31–53). Others deny this, however, either because they deny that Mill ultimately identifies happiness with pleasure (e.g. Berger 1984, pp. 32–6) or because they maintain that he analyses pleasure in terms of something other than mental states—such as activities (e.g. Saunders 2010, pp. 54–6) or, more generally, 'activities, states, and abilities' (Brink 1992, p. 78)—and that he regards these as the ultimate bearers of value.

The presumption in favour of the mental-state interpretation has to be considered quite strong. It is, first, the ordinary understanding of pleasure. Second, it was the view of Jeremy Bentham and James Mill, and Mill does not contradict it even in the often-critical notes that he added to an edition of his father's *Analysis of the Phenomena of the Human Mind* (*CW* xxxi. 93–253). Third, Mill frequently refers to pleasure and pain together in a manner that suggests they share a genus, and it is hard to see how pains could be anything other than mental states (Crisp 1997, p. 27). Fourth, Mill sometimes refers to pleasures as feelings (e.g. *CW* x. 213), and he writes in the volume on Hamilton that pleasures and pains are nothing more than 'what we feel them to be' (*CW* ix. 430). While it is impossible to make a conclusive case for this reading here, a preponderance of the evidence supports the contentions that Mill conceives of happiness in terms of pleasurable mental states and that he believes that only these states have positive intrinsic value. In short, he has a hedonistic conception of happiness and he is a hedonist. (Certain passages that might seem to be inconsistent with this reading will be considered later.)

Yet even if it is correct to say that Mill shares Bentham's fundamental commitment to hedonism, it seems clear that there are some significant differences between his hedonism and Bentham's. One important difference between their views concerns the question of whether two experiences that contain equal quantities of pleasure must necessarily contribute equally to a person's happiness. Bentham famously writes that as long as the quantities of pleasure involved are equal, the parlour game pushpin is as good as poetry (Bentham 1830, p. 206).[4] In contrast, Mill equally famously claims in *Utilitarianism* that an experience of one pleasure may add more to a person's happiness than an experience of the same quantity of another, where the quantity of pleasure in an experience is the product of the pleasure's intensity and duration, and that where this is true the pleasure making the greater contribution is of a higher quality (*CW* x. 210–14). While it is not entirely clear whether he believes that there are only two grades of pleasures or many, he states that 'the pleasures of the intellect, of the feelings and imagination, and of the moral sentiments' are of a higher quality than the pleasures of the body (*CW* x. 211).

Mill's assertion that the pleasure involved in different experiences can differ in terms of quality as well as quantity has been criticized by those who, like Sidgwick, insist that for a consistent hedonist 'all qualitative comparison of pleasures must really resolve itself into quantitative', since 'all pleasures are understood to be so called because they have a common property of pleasantness' and hedonists can evaluate experiences only in terms of how much of this property they contain (Sidgwick 1981, p. 94). But this criticism misses the mark. Only if pleasure is understood to be one particular homogeneous feeling does it follow that for the consistent hedonist qualitative comparisons of pleasurable experiences must 'resolve' into quantitative ones. There is no reason to impute this view to Mill (nor does Sidgwick hold it (Sidgwick 1981, p. 127)). Mill can maintain without inconsistency that there are a variety of distinct mental states that are pleasures and that, while all contribute to our happiness, a given quantity of some contributes more than the same quantity of others.

We should distinguish here between 'internalism' about pleasure, according to which some intrinsic phenomenal quality of mental states determines whether they are pleasures, and 'externalism', according to which any subjective experience can be a pleasure for a person just if she has the right pro-attitude towards it (Sumner 1996, pp. 87–91). The form of hedonism that regards pleasure as a homogeneous feeling is the most straightforward

---

[4] The famous phrase 'pushpin is as good as poetry' is not found verbatim in Bentham; it actually comes from Mill's essay 'Bentham' (*CW* x. 113).

internalist view, but it might be possible for an internalist to maintain that there are diverse pleasures. On balance, though, the available evidence suggests that Mill is an externalist in virtue of regarding any subjective experience as a pleasure for a person if (roughly speaking) she desires it as an end, that is, for its own sake (see D. Miller 2010, pp. 78–80; cf. West 2004, pp. 54–61).

Some interpreters take Mill to believe that any quantity of a pleasure of comparatively higher quality, no matter how small, always has more value and contributes more to a person's happiness than any quantity of a comparatively lower-quality pleasure, no matter how large (e.g. Brink 1992, p. 72; Riley 2008, 2009). While this is another issue that cannot be adequately discussed here, at least three considerations militate against this reading.

First, it is implausible on its face to suggest that a brief experience of a higher quality pleasure by one person could be more valuable than any number of longer experiences of lower quality pleasures taken together. How, for instance, could ten minutes of one person's pleasurably reading philosophy possibly be worth more than all of the physical sexual pleasure to be experienced by humanity over the next thousand years? To attribute this view to Mill when there is any alternative reading available is uncharitable. Second, consider the 'decided preference' or 'competent judges' test by which Mill says that the relative quality of pleasures can be ascertained:

> Of two pleasures, if there be one to which all or almost all who have experience of both give a decided preference . . . that is the more desirable pleasure. If one of the two is, by those who are competently acquainted with both, placed so far above the other that they . . . would not resign it for any quantity of the other pleasure which their nature is capable of, we are justified in ascribing to the preferred enjoyment a superiority in quality, so far outweighing quantity as to render it, in comparison, of small account. (*CW* x. 211)

While many interpreters take the two sentences just quoted to be making the same point, it is apparent on close inspection that they are not. The first contains Mill's 'official' test for whether one pleasure is of higher quality than another. The second sentence offers a distinct and more stringent test that may not be satisfied every time that the first test is (see D. Miller 2010, pp. 58–9; Saunders 2010, pp. 64–5). Third, since this official test involves individuals' deciding which of two pleasurable experiences they would most want for themselves, it can establish at most the relative value of amounts of different pleasures that a single person's 'nature is capable of' experiencing, that is, amounts that could be enjoyed in one human life. It cannot be used to show that a finite quantity of one pleasure is more valuable than an infinite or indefinite quantity of another.

4. The 'Proof' of the Principle of Utility

Recall that for Mill the principle of utility is the axiological proposition that happiness and only happiness is desirable as an end. The case that Mill makes for this principle in chapter 4 of *Utilitarianism* has been the subject of much discussion—and of criticism that sometimes rises (or sinks) to the level of ridicule. Mill argues for three propositions from which he apparently takes the principle of utility to follow immediately:

1. Happiness is desirable as an end.
2. The 'general happiness' is desirable as an end.
3. Only happiness is desirable as an end.

The arguments for the first two propositions come quickly, in the third paragraph, with the argument for the third occupying the remainder of the chapter. It is in arguing for the first claim that Mill notoriously writes that 'The only proof capable of being given that an object is visible, is that people actually see it....In like manner...the sole evidence it is possible to produce that anything is desirable, is that people do actually desire it' (*CW* x. 234). The argument for the second step turns on the move from the claim that 'each person's happiness is a good to that person' to the claim that 'the general happiness, therefore, [is] a good to the aggregate of all persons' (*CW* x. 234). The argument for the third step is an empirical one, based on Mill's associationism. His strategy is to dispel putative counterexamples to his claim. Ostensibly, he counters the assertion that some people clearly do desire things such as money or virtue for their own sakes, not by denying it, but by contending that the assertion is consistent with the principle of utility. It is possible, Mill acknowledges, for a person to come to desire as an end something that she initially only desired as a means to happiness. But when this happens, he maintains, this object of desire has itself become a part of her happiness. Virtue, for example, 'according to the utilitarian doctrine, is not naturally and originally part of the end, but it is capable of becoming so; and in those who love it disinterestedly it has become so, and is desired and cherished, not as a means to happiness, but as a part of their happiness' (*CW* x. 235).

Each of these component arguments has been sharply criticized. The first has been roundly mocked for its apparent blindness to the fact that, however much alike they may look and sound, 'desirability' names a normative concept whereas 'visibility' does not (e.g. Moore 1903, p. 67). The second is frequently said to commit the fallacy of composition. The third has been criticized on the grounds that Mill's claim that virtue or money could be part of a person's happiness is inconsistent with his hedonistic conception of happiness. For instance, Moore writes:

> Does Mill mean to say that money, these actual coins, which he admits to be desired in and for themselves, are a part either of pleasure or of the absence of pain?...If this is to be said, all words are useless: nothing can possibly be distinguished from anything else....(Moore 1903, pp. 71–2)

At several points in *Utilitarianism*, Mill seems to warn the reader not to expect too much from his case for the principle of utility, that is, not to expect it to offer genuine proof. The title of chapter 4, for example, is 'Of What Sort of Proof the Principle of Utility is Susceptible' (*CW* x. 234). However, we must bear in mind that he says in chapter 1 that while it is impossible to prove that something is an 'ultimate end' in the 'ordinary and popular' sense of proof, considerations can still be given to determine 'the intellect to give...its assent to the doctrine', considerations that constitute proof in that word's 'larger meaning' (*CW* x. 208). Mill almost certainly takes chapter 4 of *Utilitarianism* to discharge the obligation that he accepted when he wrote in the earlier essay 'Sedgwick's Discourse' that 'Those who maintain that human happiness is the end and test of morality are bound to prove that the principle is true…' (*CW* x. 52). One aspect of the more general resurgence of interest in Mill's moral philosophy has been a spate of new charitable reconstructions of the proof. A brief sketch of one such reconstruction follows.

The proof's third step is the place to begin. One possible response to the criticism that Mill's admission that virtue or money can come to be part of a person's happiness is inconsistent with his hedonistic conception of happiness is to say that this shows that he does not have a hedonistic conception of happiness at all. However, the text does not force this extreme move upon us. Mill says that virtue, for instance, becomes part of a virtuous person's happiness when, via association, she begins to take pleasure in the consciousness of possessing it (*CW* x. 237). This suggests that it may actually be this pleasure that he considers part of her happiness, not literally the virtue itself, and that it is only this pleasure that she truly desires for its own sake. Admittedly, this would make virtue a means to happiness for her, strictly speaking. Yet perhaps we do not need to take Mill's claim that money or virtue can be more than a means to happiness absolutely literally. When Mill describes how money serves as a means to pleasure, he refers specifically to how it allows us to obtain external rewards in the form of the things that it can purchase (*CW* x. 236). It is clear that he believes that money can be more closely related to happiness than as a means to these external rewards, but not obvious that he believes that it can be more closely related to happiness than as a means—in an expansive sense of 'means' that may be peculiar to philosophers—to the 'internal reward' that a person enjoys when her consciousness of possessing money produces pleasure. A similar point can be made about virtue, whose external reward takes the form of better treatment by other people. In a popular work—*Utilitarianism* was originally serialized in *Fraser's Magazine*—it is not surprising that Mill should characterize the process by which a person comes to enjoy this internal reward in terms of virtue's or money's becoming a part of her happiness, even if when taken literally this is an inaccurate description of his view.

The first step of the proof might seem less controversial than the final one. Few would deny that happiness is desirable as an end. If the third step of the proof turns out to be successful, then this claim may be even harder to contest: it would border on nihilism to deny that the one and only thing that humans are capable of desiring as an end is worth desiring for its own sake. So Mill might easily have gotten away with it if he had not offered any reasoning at all here, but it is worth examining the reasoning that he does offer since his reputation has been so damaged by it.

The closest analogue in Mill's 'epistemology of fact' to the move that he is making in this step of the proof is his defence of the claim that the memory is generally reliable. In the Hamilton volume, Mill meets the sceptic with the 'common sense' response that we know intuitively that the memory is generally reliable, on the basis of a shared doxastic or belief-forming disposition (*CW* ix. 165 n.). Likewise, here he seems to be suggesting that our innate disposition to desire pleasure justifies us in claiming to know intuitively that it is desirable. Just as we are justified in 'trusting' that beliefs resulting from an innate belief-forming disposition are true, so too are we justified in trusting that innate desires have objects worthy of being desired. Mill does not make any explicit attempt to show that our disposition to desire pleasure is innate, but his reasoning in support of the third step of the proof suffices to show that it meets the criteria for innateness. The desire for pleasure is universally shared, it is 'primitive' rather than acquired via experience (although we can learn to find pleasure in new things), and the disposition to desire pleasure is irresistible (which does not mean that we cannot resist *acting on* desires for particular pleasant experiences).

Mill's externalism about pleasure does complicate this way of reading the proof's first step. According to his externalism, it is a person's desire for a subjective experience that makes it a pleasure for her. This leaves open the possibility that people might have entirely different pleasures, in virtue of desiring different subjective experiences. Only innate dispositions can give rise to intuitive knowledge, though, and one of the hallmarks of an innate disposition is that it is universally shared. If there are no experiences that we are all disposed to desire, then we cannot know intuitively that anything is intrinsically valuable. If we read Mill as an externalist about pleasure, then his proof can succeed only if people *do* desire the same subjective experiences for their own sakes. While not obviously true this supposition is not obviously false, either. While people certainly desire to engage in very different activities, a fact of which the author of *On Liberty* could hardly be unaware, it is conceivable that differences in their organic constitutions and prior associations might mean that two people would have very different subjective experiences while engaging in the same activity and quite similar experiences while engaging in very different ones. Thus it is possible that people who have had the same subjective experiences might have the same preferences over them but need to go about pursuing the experiences that they desire in entirely different ways.

This leaves the proof's second step. There may be no way to reconstruct Mill's reasoning here that can entirely make sense of his assertion that the general happiness is a 'good to the aggregate of all persons', but there is a reconstruction available on which it appears as a sensible piece of argumentation for the claim that the general happiness—understood as the maximization of aggregate happiness—is desirable as an end. We can take Mill to be reasoning that in seeing her own happiness as a good for her, each individual is committed to seeing happiness as desirable *simpliciter* or *tout court*; it is because happiness is desirable in this way that it is good, from a person's own point of view, for her to get some of it for herself (see Sayre-McCord 2001). So happiness is desirable regardless of who is enjoying it, and more specifically, Mill writes in *Utilitarianism*, 'equal amounts of happiness are equally desirable, whether felt by the same or by different persons' (*CW* x. 257–8 n.). Similarly, a greater amount of happiness is more desirable, regardless of whose happiness it is. Thus the most desirable state of affairs is the one that contains the most happiness. One might object here that a state of affairs can be better than another that contains more happiness if happiness is, say, more fairly distributed in it. But for this to be true, Mill might reply, fairness and happiness would both have to be desirable. Remember that he takes himself to have shown that only happiness is desirable as an end and hence that nothing can contribute to the goodness of states of affairs besides the happiness that they contain.

While the foregoing attempts to show that Mill's proof is free of the clumsy errors that have been imputed to it, it certainly falls short of establishing that Mill's case for the principle of utility is sound. Perhaps its weakest point is its third step. *Pace* Mill, the notion that people desire nothing but mental states is highly implausible. Robert Nozick's well-known 'experience machine' example is just one of several ways of illustrating this point (Nozick 1974, pp. 42–5; see also Griffin 1986, pp. 9–10; Sumner 1996, pp. 92–6).

Also, while this concern goes beyond the scope of the proof proper, there may be reason to worry about what kind of answer, if any, Mill can make to the egoist who acknowledges that happiness is desirable regardless of whom enjoys it, but who maintains that it is nevertheless rational for each individual to get as much of it as possible for herself. Sidgwick was forced to conclude that there is a 'duality' in practical reason, inasmuch as it is no less rational to promote one's own happiness exclusively than to promote the general happiness, or vice versa (1981, pp. 496–509). Limited space make it impossible to consider here whether Mill takes seriously enough the problem that drives Sidgwick to his bifurcated view. (Mill names his own theory of practical reason the 'Art of Life' and describes it all too briefly in the concluding chapter of the *Logic* (*CW* viii. 943–52; see also the essays in Eggleston, D. Miller, and Weinstein 2010; D. Miller 2010, pp. 79–90).)

5. MILL'S MORAL THEORY

While I am taking for granted that Mill believes that the moral standing of actions depends in some way on how happiness can be maximized, this is consistent with his subscribing to any of several versions of utilitarianism. The most straightforward of these is act utilitarianism, according to which an action is right if it would yield as much total net happiness as any alternative action and wrong if it would not. Another is rule utilitarianism, the most widely discussed version of which can be characterized in terms of two tenets:

(1) Whether an action is right or wrong depends upon whether the 'authoritative' set of moral rules would permit or forbid actions of that general kind.
(2) The authoritative set of moral rules is the one whose general acceptance would yield more total net happiness than the general acceptance of any other set.

These two tenets define what is sometimes called 'ideal code' rule utilitarianism. (The contrast is with 'actual' rule utilitarianism, which says in effect that existing moral rules are binding as long as their consequences are good enough.) As it is usually understood, ideal-code rule utilitarianism holds that the same moral code is authoritative for everyone within some broad group, such as a particular society or even all of humanity. The general acceptance of a set of rules then means its acceptance by everyone or nearly everyone in that group.

Until fairly recently, the act-utilitarian reading of Mill was the received one. It was generally assumed that this is what Mill means to express in chapter 2 of *Utilitarianism* when he writes that the utilitarian creed 'holds that actions are right in proportion as they tend to promote happiness, wrong as they tend to produce the reverse of happiness' (*CW* x. 210), despite the fact that the passage seems at first glance to suggest that rightness can be a matter of degree, a claim that fits uncomfortably with act utilitarianism as it is normally understood (see Norcross 2006, pp. 217–32). When J. O. Urmson proposed in the 1950s that Mill might be a rule utilitarian (Urmson 1953), J. D. Mabbott's defence of the accepted view (Mabbott 1956) seems to have been generally regarded as a satisfactory reply. Today, however, it is clear neither that the act-utilitarian reading is still the received interpretation nor that there is a received interpretation at all.

The primary factor that has unsettled the consensus that Mill is an act utilitarian is the increasing importance that has been attached to a passage in chapter 5 of *Utilitarianism* in which Mill apparently asserts that the concept of morally wrong action can be analysed in terms of the appropriateness of punishment (cf. Norcross 2006, p. 224). This passage, which appears in the chapter's fourteenth paragraph and will henceforth be labelled '5:14', reads in part:

> We do not call anything wrong, unless we mean to imply that a person ought to be punished in some way or other for doing it; if not by law, by the opinion of his fellow-creatures; if not by opinion, by the reproaches of his own conscience. This seems the real turning point of the distinction between morality and simple expediency. (*CW* x. 246)

If we take seriously the idea that in 5:14 Mill is offering an analysis of what it means for an action to be morally wrong—and the aforementioned letter to Ward offers additional evidence that we should (*CW* xv. 649)—then this complicates efforts to depict him as an act utilitarian (cf. Crisp 1997, pp. 95–133). From the act-utilitarian perspective the notion that wrong actions are always appropriately punished is very dubious. Insofar as the imposition of a punishment is itself an action, there will assuredly be actions that are morally wrong, from the act-utilitarian standpoint, but that, from this same standpoint, it would be wrong to punish. Likewise, there will be right actions that would be rightly punished.

The fact that Mill lists the reproaches of conscience among the forms of punishment in 5:14 may seem to provide an opening for someone defending an act-utilitarian reading of Mill, since this punishment is not imposed via an action. If people internalized a single rule that requires happiness-maximizing actions, then they would reproach themselves when they believed that they have done something that act utilitarianism says is wrong. To suppose that this is what Mill has in mind requires us to suppose that even though he lists several punishments in 5:14, it is really only the reproaches of conscience or guilt that he takes to have any conceptual connection with immorality. This supposition is more plausible than it might initially appear; the letter to Ward provides evidence for it, too (*CW* xv. 649). Yet the problem remains that actions make a difference to what rules people internalize, and hence to what they feel guilty about doing, and there is no reason to assume that it would be happiness-maximizing to bring it about that people internalize the rule in question, let alone that they internalize only it. Indeed, the twentieth century's leading act utilitarian, R. M. Hare, argues that it would be happiness-maximizing to instil very different rules in people, rules much closer in form and content to those of ordinary morality (Hare 1981).

The increasing attention being paid to 5:14 has resulted in a wide variety of moral theories being attributed to Mill, each of which tries in some way to do justice both to this passage and his utilitarian commitments. Some interpreters attribute hybrid views to him that, in different ways, meld act and rule utilitarianism (including, arguably, Dryer 1969, p. cv; Copp 1979; Hoag 1983; West 2004, pp. 74–95). Others take him to hold views that cannot be usefully characterized in terms of act and rule utilitarianism at all (e.g. Skorupski 1989, pp. 315–20; Gray 1996, pp. 19–48; Brown 2010) or deny that he settles unambiguously on a particular moral theory (Berger 1984, pp. 105–20; Brink 2012). Another possibility, though, is that Mill is a rule utilitarian. This is the position that will be maintained here, although of course there is no way to canvass all of the different bits of text and other considerations that bear on this question in the space of a few paragraphs.

A sophisticated form of ideal-code rule utilitarianism is the specific rule-utilitarian view to which it makes the most sense to think that Mill subscribes (cf. Donner 2009, pp. 45–54; R. Miller 2009, pp. 7–8). It is by and large the view that David Lyons argues that Mill holds (Lyons 1976). Lyons contends that in 5:14 Mill does intend to analyse what it is for actions to be wrong in terms of the appropriateness of guilt specifically. Since Mill believes that what we feel guilty about doing depends on what rules we have internalized, Lyons further maintains, this means that he must further believe that an action is wrong if and only if the agent should have internalized a rule that forbids it. And given his utilitarian views about punishment, Lyons concludes, Mill's criterion for determining what rules people should internalize must be happiness-maximization. Lyons observes that members of a given society will largely internalize the same rules, and that in addition to feeling guilty about their own violations of these rules they will tend to apply at least informal social sanctions to others who violate them, in the absence of a reason to the contrary. He therefore describes Mill's moral theory as being based on the notion of 'coercive social rules'. An action is wrong, on this view, if it would be happiness-maximizing for a rule forbidding it to be among the coercive social rules of the agent's society. It is a distinctly rule-utilitarian view. (Admittedly, Lyons himself chooses not to label Mill a rule utilitarian, but his use of the term is unusually restrictive (Gaus 1980, p. 268).)

Mill's approach here is distinctive. Most moralists would begin by offering a moral standard or criterion for ascertaining the moral standing of actions that makes no reference to the notion of guilt. Having decided which actions are wrong, they would then say that those are the actions for which guilt is appropriate. Mill, in contrast, starts with a utilitarian criterion for determining which rules it is desirable for people to internalize, and hence which actions it is appropriate for them to feel guilty about performing. He then derives his moral standard from this, via his account of what it means for actions to be wrong.

A number of passages fit this rule-utilitarian reading quite closely—certainly much more closely than they do the act-utilitarian alternative. One example is Mill's claim in *Utilitarianism* that

> In the case of abstinences indeed—of things which people forbear to do from moral considerations, though the consequences in the particular case might be beneficial—it would be unworthy of an intelligent agent not to be consciously aware that the action is of a class which, if practised generally, would be generally injurious, and that this is the ground of the obligation to abstain from it. (*CW* x. 220)

Another is Mill's contention in *Auguste Comte and Positivism* that some actions exhibit supererogatory levels of benevolence: 'There is a standard of altruism to which all should be required to come up, and a degree beyond it which is not obligatory, but meritorious' (*CW* x. 337–8).[5]

Of course, not all of the evidence is on one side. Still, one passage that might seem at first glance to clash with the rule-utilitarian reading of Mill may turn out not to do so. Mill's statement that utilitarianism 'holds that actions are right in proportion as they tend to promote happiness' may appear to be incongruent with the proposition that he is a rule utilitarian. Yet this puzzling line also fits poorly with the act-utilitarian reading. Construed in the most natural way, it implies that rightness comes in degrees, but act utilitarians deny this. While this one line might lend support to a 'scalar utilitarian' reading of Mill (see Norcross 2006), though, little else in his corpus does. So this apparently 'official' declaration does not fit well with any plausible reading. There is one way of understanding the passage, though, on which it is perfectly consistent with the reading of Mill being proposed here. If an action's tendency

---

⁵ For a more comprehensive survey of the textual evidence favouring the rule-utilitarian reading of Mill, see Fuchs 2006.

is positive, then the more pronounced the tendency the greater the likelihood that the ideal rule-utilitarian code would permit or even require it.[6] Conversely, the ideal code is likely (but not certain) to prohibit actions with pronounced negative tendencies. Therefore, Mill's meaning in the line in question may simply be that utilitarians such as himself believe that the confidence with which one can infer an action's moral standing from its tendency is proportionate to the tendency's magnitude; on this construal, 'in proportion' modifies 'hold', not 'right'.

6. Mill's Liberalism

On Liberty is Mill's most widely read work and a seminal contribution to social and political philosophy. The essay, Mill tells us, is a defence of 'one very simple principle', according to which 'the sole end for which mankind are warranted, individually or collectively, in interfering with the liberty of action of any of their number, is self-protection' (*CW* xviii. 223–4). Mill's description of this 'liberty' or 'harm' principle as 'very simple' is belied by the quantity of ink spilled in the name of explicating it. It is not even clear that it is 'one' principle; later in the essay, it is restated in the form of two 'maxims' (*CW* xviii. 292). Perhaps the single most pressing exegetical question about the essay is that of how the notion of harm is to be understood and, more specifically, how it is connected to that of interests (see Wollheim 1973; Rees 1985, pp. 137–55; D. Miller 2010, pp. 117–22, 143–5). Another critical issue, debated in the 1970s by D. G. Brown and Lyons, is that of whether the liberty principle only permits social interference with behaviour that would cause harm to someone besides the agent or whether it also permits interference with behaviour that is not itself harmful when this would help to protect someone else (Brown 1972; Lyons 1979). This issue bears on the question of whether Mill is being inconsistent when he says that we can legitimately be required to participate in harm-preventing social institutions (through serving as a witness or a juror in court, for instance) and to act as Good Samaritans by rescuing others from imminent harm on an ad hoc basis (*CW* xviii. 224–5, 276).

Mill's contemporary James Fitzjames Stephens complains that Mill nowhere offers an argument that is sufficient to establish a principle as sweeping as the liberty principle, and this objection cannot be lightly set aside (Stephen 1993, pp. 7–8). Mill does argue for the liberty principle, though, and true to his word his arguments are grounded entirely on utility, albeit utility 'in the largest sense, grounded on the permanent interests of man as a progressive being' (*CW* xviii. 224). The claim that people who enjoy individual freedom are able to make choices that better satisfy their own existing preferences does figure in Mill's case for the liberty principle. The line of argument on which he places the most emphasis, though, says that an atmosphere of liberty fosters personal development.[7]

---

[6] On Mill's understanding of actions' tendencies see Eggleston and Miller 2008.

[7] In addition, of course, in chapter 2 of *On Liberty* Mill offers his influential case for freedom of speech and expression more generally. Even here, 'ethological' considerations constitute an important line of argument, as Mill asserts that censorship breeds pusillanimous thinkers (*CW* xviii. 242). Among the key questions about this chapter that have been the subject of recent critical discussion is that of exactly how free Mill thinks speech should be. For contrasting views on this, see Skorupski 1989, pp. 369–84; O'Rourke 2001; Riley 2005.

Freedom forces people to make choices, Mill observes, and this requires them to exercise their distinctly human faculties, the faculties responsible for the higher quality pleasures. Moreover, it is only in an atmosphere of freedom that an individual can attain the harmony between her character traits and the most deeply rooted elements of her own psychology that Mill calls 'individuality' and considers to be essential to the enjoyment of a genuinely happy life (see Gray 1996, p. 45; Donner 2009, pp. 56–67; D. Miller 2010, pp. 132–7). Through choosing how to act and what environments to inhabit, a person exerts such control as she can over the constitution of her character. Mill believes no one can know better than the individual herself what sort of character is the best fit for her, and so she requires personal liberty and diverse situations in order to fashion a bespoke character for herself. Mill goes so far as to suggest that each person should consider her character a work of art with herself as artist, which implies that the appreciation of harmoniously developed characters can be a source of aesthetic pleasure (*CW* xviii. 263, 266; see also x. 95; xxi. 255). Admittedly, as desirable as Mill considers it for each person to tailor-make her own character, he does allow that there are numerous traits—the virtues, which range from cleanliness to the civic virtue or public spirit that makes citizens active and disinterested participants in public affairs—that everyone should possess (e.g. *CW* x. 393–6; see also Berkowitz 1998; D. Miller 2010, pp. 134–5, 172–6). Nevertheless, this leaves ample room for individual variation.

Some recent liberal philosophers have espoused a view according to which the state must remain 'neutral' between different ideas about what sort of life is best, over some wide range of possibilities (e.g. Dworkin 1978; Rawls 1993, pp. 190–5). Mill's liberalism, though, is not neutral in this sense. Skorupski has helpfully distinguished between 'permissive neutrality', which forbids compelling people to adopt certain forms of life and avoid others, and 'persuasive neutrality', which forbids advocating some forms of life in preference to others (Skorupski 1997, pp. 197–200). Mill's liberalism is permissively but not persuasively neutral. In the *Principles of Political Economy*, he draws a distinction 'between 'authoritative' government intervention whereby the state requires or forbids particular conduct and 'unauthoritative' intervention whereby it limits itself to activities such as 'giving advice and promulgating information' (*CW* iii. 396). The liberty principle restricts only the state's power to intervene authoritatively, leaving it free to inform, advise, and even exhort citizens to prefer a way of life that includes the development of their distinctly human faculties, the cultivation of their individuality, and the acquisition of the virtues.

7. POLITICAL AND ECONOMIC DEMOCRACY

Mill opens *Considerations on Representative Government* with a powerful, two-pronged vindication of widespread political participation (*CW* xix. 404–12). He argues, first, that people's interests are only safe from abuse or neglect if they are empowered to protect them themselves. Second, Mill describes political participation as having an improving effect on citizens' characters, helping to make them both more active and more public-spirited.

At the same time, though, Mill's theory of political democracy contains several anti-majoritarian mechanisms. He enthusiastically endorses Thomas Hare's system of proportional representation, which may not be anti-majoritarian, strictly speaking, but which is meant to ensure that minorities are represented in proportion to their size (*CW* x. 448–66). In addition, he takes the job of drafting legislation away from elected representatives and assigns it instead to a committee of legal experts (*CW* x. 428–32). The role of representatives is accordingly reduced to that of requesting that bills of particular sorts be written and voting 'aye' or 'nay' on the results. Finally, and most distinctively, Mill advocates a form of 'plural voting', in which nearly everyone receives at least one vote—he argues, albeit unconvincingly, that illiterates and anyone on public relief should be disenfranchised (*CW* x. 470–2)—but those with more education receive additional votes (*CW* x. 472–9). In an essay published two years before *Representative Government*, he ventures that university graduates might receive as many as five or six (*CW* x. 324–5).

It is worth pausing to ask precisely why Mill would support plural voting. One answer that might be given is that it is an expedient solution to the problem posed by the impending enfranchisement of the largely uneducated working class. Mill believes that it is desirable for workers and their employers to have roughly equal numbers of representatives, so that neither class can dominate the other (*CW* xix. 447). A properly calibrated plural voting scheme might accomplish this.

However, Mill makes it clear that he believes that those who know more are entitled to greater political power as a matter of moral principle. And insofar as there is a distinct group whom Mill hopes will benefit from plural voting, it is not capitalists per se. Mill believes in the existence of an intellectual elite (see e.g. *CW* xxii. 244–5). He also believes in the existence of a moral elite, characterized by their lack of selfishness and greater public spirit (see e.g. *CW* xix. 405). And incredibly, perhaps, he believes that these elites are by and large coextensive, that there are not 'two Fews but just one' (Kendall and Carey 1968, p. 34; see *CW* xix. 450). Although Mill's opinion of the formal education of his day, even at the Oxbridge universities, is too low for him to class most of the people who would benefit from plural voting as part of the elite (see e.g. *CW* i. 338), the elite would benefit. They could elect some of their number, which would let them act as swing votes when capital and labour are divided and give them a 'bully pulpit' from which to disseminate their views. And Mill believes that although the elite are in his day riven by disconsensus, their moral and political views will someday converge, and the rest of society will rightly tend to defer to them on these questions (see e.g. *CW* x. 325–6).

So Mill's nuanced theory of political democracy combines egalitarian and elitist elements, with neither clearly predominating. Interpretations that claim that Mill intends for elites to dominate the rest of society ignore the fact that he says that plural voting should never put elites in a position to outvote everyone else and that any deference shown to them is to be the 'intelligent deference of those who know much to those who know still more' (*CW* xix. 476; x. 314; cf. Hamburger 1999). On the other hand, interpretations that contend that Mill gave up his support for plural voting after discovering the Hare Plan or intended it only as a temporary measure ignore his explicit statement to the contrary (*CW* x. 477–8; cf. Baum 2000, pp. 243–5; Donner 2009, p. 101).

There is a sense in which Mill can be said to favour economic as well as political democracy, but here too his view is nuanced. Mill believes that as long as the moral and intellectual improvement of the working class that he perceives in his day continues, workers will someday no longer be willing to work for mere wages. They will demand first profit-sharing and then outright ownership of their firms (*CW* iii. 766–94). Mill considers this a welcome development, because bearing the responsibilities of ownership would accelerate their moral and intellectual development still further. However, he insists that for this transition to be legitimate workers must respect capitalists' property rights; he calls for workers to buy their firms or start their own. The state has little to do with this 'spontaneous process' (*CW* iii. 793–4; see also xx. 352–3). Mill also predicts that workers will experiment with the village-level socialism or communism described by writers like Charles Fourier and Henri de Saint-Simon; his optimism about the likely success of these experiments waxes and wanes at different points in his life (*CW* ii. 203–14; iii. 975–87; v. 7379). Mill is an implacable opponent of what he calls 'revolutionary' socialism that is managed at the level of the nation state (*CW* v. 748–9). The most socialized economy that he contemplates with any pleasure would still be one of small, internally governed enterprises that compete with one another and that workers can join or leave at their pleasure.

8. MILL AS A UTOPIAN

As a way to draw together some of the disparate threads running through this discussion, I will close by calling attention to the 'utopian' aspect of Mill's moral, social, and political philosophy (D. Miller 2010, pp. 205–11; see also Holthoon 1971).

There are two standards by which a person's life could be said to be happy, Mill suggests in the *System of Logic* (*CW* viii. 952). The lower of these is the 'comparatively humble' standard of containing more pleasure than pain. A life could be happy in this sense, Mill writes, and yet still be 'puerile and insignificant'. The higher standard is that of a life's being one 'such as human beings with highly developed faculties can care to have', which could clearly only be true of a life that involves a considerable amount of higher quality pleasure. Although the phrase is not Mill's, we could describe lives that are happy in this higher sense as being 'genuinely happy'.

Mill is a utopian inasmuch as he believes that in the future it will be possible for virtually everyone—everyone who is not the victim of some rare individual bad fortune—to lead a genuinely happy life. Bringing this day about is what we must do, he believes, if aggregate happiness is to be at a maximum. What this will take is the continuation of a process that Mill believes has already begun in the West in his day, in which people's increasing moral and intellectual development facilitates the creation of morally superior institutions and practices, which then in turn stimulate further personal development, and so on. Skorupski aptly describes this process as a 'virtuous spiral' (Skorupski 1989, p. 23). From the standpoint of social institutions and practices, its culmination would be the establishment of a 'Religion of Humanity', albeit one shorn of Comte's excesses (*CW* x. 341–68, 418–28; see also Heydt 2006). While Mill does not take this process's continuing for granted, he is optimistic. The many social reforms that he proposes are meant to show how the spiral can be made to continue to turn.

While Mill recognizes that the Religion of Humanity and the day when nearly everyone has a genuinely happy life lie in the distant future, he would no doubt be disappointed with how little we have progressed towards these ends since his day. One of the chief reasons for this lack of progress is surely the fact that we still lack a science of ethology; we still do not know much about how to make people better. But this is not to say that Mill's vision of the future is to be dismissed as fantasy; while some might consider this side of Mill excessively romantic, I do not mean to call him a utopian in this pejorative sense. And if we cannot share his optimism, then at least we can find the idea of a future peopled with highly developed individuals leading lives rich in the best sorts of pleasure to be a worthy object of hope.

References

Baum, Bruce, 2000. *Rereading Power and Freedom in Mill*, Toronto: University of Toronto Press.

Bentham, Jeremy, 1830. *The Rationale of Reward*, London: Heward.

Berger, Fred R., 1984. *Happiness, Justice, and Freedom: The Moral and Political Philosophy of John Stuart Mill*, Berkeley and Los Angeles: University of California Press.

Berkowitz, Peter, 1998. 'Mill, Liberty, and the Virtue of Individuality', in Eldon Eisenach (ed.), *Mill and the Moral Character of Liberalism*, University Park, Pa.: Pennsylvania State University Press, pp. 13–47.

Bradley, F. H., 1927. *Ethical Studies*, 2nd edn., Oxford: Clarendon Press.

Brink, David, 1992. 'Mill's Deliberative Utilitarianism', *Philosophy and Public Affairs* 21: 67–103.

Brink, David, 2012, 'Mill's Ambivalence About Duty', in Leonard Kahn (ed.), *Mill on Justice*, Houndmills: Palgrave Macmillan, pp. 21–46.

Brown, D. G., 1972. 'Mill on Liberty and Morality', *Philosophical Review* 81: 133–58.

Brown, D. G., 1973. 'What is Mill's Principle of Utility?', *Canadian Journal of Philosophy* 3: 1–12.

Brown, D. G., 2010. 'Mill's Moral Theory: Ongoing Revisionism', *Politics, Philosophy and Economics*, 9: 5–45.

Copp, David, 1979. 'The Iterated-Utilitarianism of J. S. Mill', *New Essays on John Stuart Mill and Utilitarianism, Canadian Journal of Philosophy*, suppl. vol. 5: 75–98.

Crisp, Roger, 1997. *Routledge Philosophy Guidebook to Mill on Utilitarianism*, London: Routledge.

Donner, Wendy, 1991. *The Liberal Self: John Stuart Mill's Moral and Political Philosophy*, Ithaca, NY: Cornell University Press.

Donner, Wendy, 2009. 'Mill's Moral and Political Philosophy'. Part I of *Mill*, Malden, Mass.: Wiley-Blackwell, pp. 15-143.

Dryer, D. P., 1969. 'Mill's Utilitarianism', in *Collected Works of John Stuart Mill*, vol. x, ed. J. M. Robson, Toronto: University of Toronto Press, pp. lxiii–cxiii.

Dworkin, Ronald, 1978. 'Liberalism', in Stuart Hampshire (ed.), *Public and Private Morality*, Cambridge: Cambridge University Press, Cambridge, pp. 113–43.

Eggleston, Ben, and Dale E. Miller, 2008. 'Mill's Misleading Moral Mathematics', *Southwest Philosophy Review* 23 (January), 153–61.

Eggleston, Ben, Dale E. Miller, and David Weinstein, 2010. *John Stuart Mill and the Art of Life*, New York: Oxford University Press.

Fuchs, Alan, 2006. 'Mill's Theory of Morally Right Conduct', in Henry R. West (ed.), *The Blackwell Guide to Mill's Utilitarianism*, Malden, Mass.: Blackwell, pp. 139–158.

Garforth, F. W., 1980. *Educative Democracy: John Stuart Mill on Education in Society*, Oxford: Oxford University Press.

Gaus, Gerald F., 1980. 'Mill's Theory of Moral Rules', *Australasian Journal of Philosophy* 58: 265–79.

Gray, John, 1996. *Mill on Liberty: A Defence*, 2nd edn., London, Routledge.

Griffin, James, 1986. *Well-Being: Its Meaning, Measurement and Moral Importance*, Oxford: Clarendon Press.

Hamburger, Joseph, 1999. *John Stuart Mill on Liberty and Control*, Princeton: Princeton University Press.

Hare, R. M., 1981. *Moral Thinking: Its Levels, Method and Point*, Oxford: Clarendon Press.

Heydt, Colin, 2006. 'Narrative, Imagination, and the Religion of Humanity in Mill's Ethics', *Journal of the History of Philosophy* 44: 99–115.

Hoag, Robert W., 1983. 'Mill on Conflicting Moral Obligations', *Analysis* 43: 49–54.

Holthoon, F. L. van, 1971. *The Road to Utopia: John Stuart Mill's Social Thought*, Assen: Van Gorcum.

Jacobson, Daniel, 2003. 'J. S. Mill and the Diversity of Utilitarianism', *Philosophers' Imprint* 3: 1–18.

Kendall, Willmoore, and George W. Cary, 1968. '"The Roster Device": J. S. Mill and Contemporary Elitism', *Western Political Quarterly* 21: 20–39.

Mabbott, J. D., 1956. 'Interpretations of Mill's "Utilitarianism,"' *Philosophical Quarterly* 6: 115–120.

Lyons, David, 1976. 'Mill's Theory of Morality', *Noûs* 10: 101–20.

Lyons, David, 1979. 'Liberty and Harm to Others', *New Essays on John Stuart Mill and Utilitarianism, Canadian Journal of Philosophy*, suppl. vol. 5: 1–19.

Mill, J. S., 1963–91. *The Collected Works of John Stuart Mill*, 33 vols., ed. J. M. Robson, Toronto: Toronto University Press.

Miller, Dale E., 2010. *J. S. Mill: Moral, Social and Political Thought*, Cambridge: Polity.

Miller, Richard, 2009. 'Actual Rule Utilitarianism', *Journal of Philosophy* 106: 5–28.

Moore, G. E., 1903. *Principia Ethica*, Cambridge: Cambridge University Press.

Norcross, Alastair, 2006. 'The Scalar Approach to Utilitarianism', in Henry West (ed.), *The Blackwell Guide to Mill's* Utilitarianism, Malden, Mass.: Blackwell, pp. 217–32.

Nozick, Robert, 1974. *Anarchy, State, and Utopia*, New York: Basic.

O'Rourke, K. C., 2001. *John Stuart Mill and Freedom of Expression*, London: Routledge.

Rawls, John, 1993. *Political Liberalism*, New York: Columbia University Press.

Rees, John, 1985. *John Stuart Mill's* On Liberty, Oxford: Clarendon Press.

Riley, Jonathan, 2005. 'J. S. Mill's Doctrine of Freedom of Expression', *Utilitas* 17: 147–9.

Riley, Jonathan, 2008. 'Millian Qualitative Superiorities, Part I', *Utilitas* 20: 257–78.

Riley, Jonathan, 2009. 'Millian Qualitative Superiorities, Part II', *Utilitas* 21: 127–43.

Saunders, Ben, 2010. 'J. S. Mill's Conception of Utility', *Utilitas* 22: 52–69.

Sayre-McCord, Geoffrey, 2001. 'Mill's "Proof" of the Principle of Utility: A More than Half-Hearted Defense', *Social Philosophy & Policy* 18: 330–60.

Sidgwick, Henry, 1981. *The Methods of Ethics*, 7th edn., Indianapolis: Hackett.

Skorupski, John, 1989. *John Stuart Mill*, London: Routledge.

Skorupski, John, 1997. 'The Ethical Content of Liberal Law', in John Tasoulias (ed.), *Law, Values and Social Practice*, Aldershot: Dartmouth.

Skorupski, John, 1998. 'Introduction: The Fortunes of Liberal Naturalism', in Skorupski (ed.), *Cambridge Companion to Mill*, Cambridge: Cambridge University Press, pp. 1–34.

Stephen, James Fitzjames, 1993. *Liberty, Equality, Fraternity*, ed. Stuart D. Warner, Indianapolis: Liberty Fund.

Sumner, L. W., 1996. *Welfare, Happiness, and Ethics*, Oxford: Clarendon Press.

Urmson, J. O., 1953. 'The Interpretation of the Moral Philosophy of J. S. Mill', *Philosophical Review* 3: 33–9.

West, Henry, 2004. *An Introduction to Mill's Utilitarian Ethics*, Cambridge: Cambridge, University Press.

Wiggins, David, 2006. *Ethics: Twelve Lectures on the Philosophy of Morality*, London: Penguin.

Wollheim, Richard, 1973. 'John Stuart Mill and the Limits of State Action'. *Social Research* 40: 1–30.

Zastoupil, Lynn, 1994. *John Stuart Mill and India*, Stanford, Calif.: Stanford University Press.

CHAPTER 19

....

BRITISH FEMINIST THOUGHT

....

BARBARA CAINE

DETERMINING the full extent of nineteenth-century feminist thought and the range of ideas and beliefs that should be included within it is a difficult task. The word 'feminist' only entered the language in the course of the 1890s, hence few of those nineteenth-century individuals now commonly described as 'feminist' used the term to describe themselves or their views. As a result of this, there is no functioning feminist tradition or universally accepted group of people that one can turn to in order to explore or analyse nineteenth-century feminist thought.

The difficulties in establishing such a tradition can be seen if one looks at Mary Wollstonecraft. Commonly seen as a founding figure of British feminism today, she did not occupy this place throughout the nineteenth century. Her name and the natural rights position articulated in *A Vindication of the Rights of Woman* were very important in the early nineteenth century, particularly to the radical Owenite feminists and to William Thompson and Anna Wheeler, but few mid-Victorian feminists acknowledged her significance. In part, as Rosalind Delmar (1986) has argued, this reflects differences in intellectual approach as prominent figures like Millicent Garrett Fawcett (1884) rejected any appeal to natural rights, arguing that their concern was centred on particular legal rights often connected to property. There was much more to it than that, as one can see from the ways in which mid-century feminists refrained from any public reference to Wollstonecraft, while often mentioning her in private correspondence. It is important to recognize the extent to which in dealing with Wollstonecraft, Victorian feminists were dealing rather more with a scandalous life than with a text. As Caine (1997) and Spongberg (2008) have argued, Wollstonecraft's *Vindication* might not have been so difficult to encompass had it not come to be read through the story of her life, as depicted in William Godwin's *Memoir of the Vindication of the Rights of Women*. Godwin's discussion of Wollstonecraft's intimate life had made known her passionate relationship with the American adventurer Gilbert Imlay, with whom she had an illegitimate child, her suicide attempts when this relationship came to an end, and the unorthodox nature of his marriage to Wollstonecraft in which they each kept up a separate home. His revelations about her life served to illustrate very clearly the connection, insisted on by opponents of women's rights, between feminist beliefs and sexual and emotional irregularity and excess. She was, in the eyes of Harriet Martineau, a 'poor victim of passion', and not someone who could be regarded as 'a safe example, nor as a successful champion for Woman and her Rights' (Martineau 1983: i. 401). But as this comment suggests, Wollstonecraft could not quite be ignored. Indeed, for Martineau as for many mid-nineteenth-century feminists, Wollstonecraft was a ghostly figure, haunting those seeking to stress the propriety and moderation of their cause. She was finally rehabilitated in the 1890s when 'new women' who rejected many aspects of respectable bourgeois ideals of femininity could again view her personal life and sexual rebellion sympathetically.

There was no alternate figure to whom a significant number of feminists sought to claim a connection. John Stuart Mill was very important for some women in the second half of the century. Millicent Garrett Fawcett, for example, compared him to a great artist as 'a master who forms a school and influences his successors for generations' (Fawcett 1884: 4). In support of this view, Laura Mayhall (2001) has argued recently that the ideas of Mill, especially when read alongside those of Mazzini, were of immense importance not only to mid-century but also to late nineteenth- and early twentieth-century feminists. But many of those most significant in the development of mid-Victorian feminism disputed this view, seeing Mill as a latecomer to what was already an ongoing discussion of women's rights— and moreover as one who, while important, was very narrow in his focus on married women and his lack of interest in single women or in women's work (Caine 1992).

While there was no agreed body of feminist writing in the nineteenth century, there was a broadly defined 'woman question' that was debated and discussed throughout the century. Although always couched in singular terms, the 'woman question' encompassed a range of issues including the intellectual and physical capacities, the moral characteristics, the maternal and familial duties, and the proper social role of women (Caine 1992). Underlying these specific issues was a general sense of unease about the meanings and implications of sexual difference, the nature and stability of the gender order, and the place of women in an industrializing world. Some of the formulations of this question, like some responses to it, would now be seen as distinctly feminist in their emphasis on the irrationality of prevailing ideas about women, on the injustices they faced in both private and public, and in their suggestions or demands for change. Many others would not, including as they did emphatic statements about the natural or the divine basis of women's subordination. Even these defences of the status quo, however, emanating sometimes from pulpits or from authoritative journals, were often expressed with a vehemence that suggested anxiety rather than calm assurance—and ultimately served rather to raise more questions about the position of women than to bring an end to discussion of it. But the significant point that needs to be recognized here is that there is no readily identifiable body of nineteenth-century feminist thought—and that it needs to be sought in a range of different kinds of writing, including essays, fiction, pamphlets, instruction manuals, and moral and philosophical treatises.

Fiction is particularly significant here, and particularly that of women writers. It is in novels that one finds the most extensive and nuanced discussions of the 'woman question'. This is the case from the first decades of the century when the novels of Jane Austen and Susan Ferrier explored some of the difficulties faced by women needing employment and contrasted rational and educated women with their uneducated and irrational mothers, sisters, and aunts in ways that left no doubt as to which were the more desirable. The discussion of the 'woman question' in novels continued into the mid-nineteenth century, in the work of Charlotte Brontë, Elizabeth Gaskell, and George Eliot, all of whom extended beyond the early nineteenth-century novels both in their exploration of sexual double standards and in their insistence on women's intellectual and spiritual yearning for knowledge and for the freedom to follow their own wishes and desires. The intellectual, spiritual, and emotional hunger of characters like Jane Eyre, or Maggie Tulliver or Dorothea Brooke, point very clearly to the new conception of womanhood that mid-nineteenth-century feminists endorsed, while other figures, like Mrs Transome in Eliot's *Felix Holt*, or both Gwendolen and Mrs Glasher in *Daniel Deronda*, illustrate the ways in which male sexual and financial power and female ignorance and lack of education or of worldly knowledge compound the sufferings of women. Later in the century, writers like Mona Caird, George Egerton, and Sarah Grand continued this discussion, introducing a new note of bitterness and anger into their criticism of marriage and their vision of the prison of family life. Literary discussion of the 'woman question' was not confined to women. Women's education was debated in detail in Tennyson's *The Princess*, for example, while marriage and the difficulties an intelligent and independent woman faced in having to meet the demands of wifely obedience was the subject of Trollope's *Can You Forgive Her?*. George Gissing's *The Odd Women* depicted both feminist activities and a feminist critique of marriage. This is not to suggest that all, or indeed any, of these writers could be labelled 'feminist', but rather to stress the importance to them of feminist issues and the ways in which their work raised questions about the difficulties and limitations that women faced.

The treatment of feminist issues within literature was both noted and used by nineteenth-century feminists. Emily Davies, a leading proponent of tertiary education for women, referred frequently to *The Princess* in her discussions of the need for the higher education of women, for example (Davies 1866: 10–31), while Josephine Butler drew heavily on the picture of a young, helpless 'fallen woman' depicted in Mrs Gaskell's *Ruth* in her discussions of prostitution and the sexual double standard (Butler 1909: 31). George Eliot was a particular favourite amongst many feminists who drew on her works to illustrate their arguments. From the mid-century on, the 'woman question' was almost a staple in the 'higher journals' too, with regular articles on women's literature, women's work, women's duties, appearing alongside discussions of marriage and of demands for education and political rights for women in a range of journals including the *Edinburgh, Westminster, and Fortnightly Reviews, Fraser's Magazine*, and the *Nineteenth Century*. For all its ridicule and misogyny, the *Saturday Review* also helped keep the 'woman question' in the public eye and helped to proved a backdrop and a readership for the discussion and debate about women's rights.

The value of this fictional discussion of the 'woman question' becomes all the greater because of the disparate ways in which other forms of feminist thought emerged, often in response to particular pieces of legislation or to publications of a theoretical or a very practical kind that were seen as hostile to the needs and claims of women. In some cases, it was not institutions or legislation that provoked feminist outpourings, but rather particular texts or arguments. James Mill's 'Essay on Government' for example, with its claim that 'the interest of almost all…is involved either in that of their fathers or in that of their husbands' (Mill 1828: 21), provoked extended replies from both William Thompson and Harriet Martineau. Thompson's *Appeal of one half of the Human Race, Women, against the Pretensions of the other half, Men, to retain them in political and thence in civil and domestic slaves* (1825) is a lengthy response to Mill, pointing out how his view was false in regard to every possible group of women and insisting on the need for enfranchisement to end their slavery. Harriet Martineau also addressed Mill's views in a chapter entitled 'Political nonexistence of Women' in her *Society in America*, pointing to the need for laws to protect women against their husbands and fathers as showing how worthless Mill's argument was, and arguing that, in his suggestion that women could be excluded from the vote, he was an 'advocate of despotism' (Martineau 1837: 201). James Mill ceased to be an object of interest in the mid-nineteenth century, but his place was taken by August Comte and by his major English disciple Frederic Harrison. Their suggestion that women be compulsorily excluded from paid employment and confined to presiding over a home led to eloquent and significant essays from both Josephine Butler and Frances Power Cobbe, pointing to how iniquitous an idea this was and how deleterious the consequences for women would be if anyone took note of it. In the process, they also pointed to its denial of full humanity to women (Cobbe 1869; Butler 1870).

Inevitably the absence of a widely recognized nineteenth-century definition of the feminism allows for different interpretations and applications of it by later scholars. According to the *OED*, when it first began to be used, the term 'feminist' referred to the 'advocacy of the rights of women (based on the theory of the equality of the sexes)', but later historians often define the term in a rather broader way. In her study of early nineteenth-century feminism, for example, Jane Rendall uses the term 'feminist' to 'describe women who claimed for themselves the right to define their own place in society'. Even when these women used the notion of equality, however, they sometimes interpreted it in terms of moral and rational worth, rather than in terms of labour or public roles (Rendall 1985: 1). There are different views amongst historians concerning how best to define the forms of feminist thought that were evident in the nineteenth century. Some stress the importance of concepts of autonomy and of legal and political rights, while others point rather to the ways in which some of those concerned about the position of women insisted on the need to view all social and political questions from a feminine perspective (Levine 1987: 19–23). These questions of definition affect the decision of which individuals one might label 'feminist'. The term has long been applied to those women and men advocating improved education and employment opportunities, or legal equality and political rights. More recently, however, claims have been made to extend the label 'feminist' to some of those preoccupied with the sexual double standard, or with extending women's philanthropic and public roles even when they did not wholeheartedly endorse political rights for women (Jeffreys 1985).

This broadening of the range of people and of ideas that might be labelled feminist has been accompanied by a growing recognition of the wide range of ideas on which feminist arguments drew. The importance of the natural rights tradition, of political and social radicalism, and of both political and economic liberalism to those who argued for women's political rights have long been recognized. But much recent scholarship has also stressed the importance of Evangelicalism with its emphasis on 'woman's mission' both within the domestic world and to transform or even to regenerate society (Rendall 1985: 73–100). While Evangelicals often accepted the subordination of women, the idea of their having a special religious and moral mission served both to empower them and to suggest that they needed greater access to the wider social world. Even the domestic ideology that accompanied the idea of separate spheres for men and women and justified women's confinement to the domestic world has been shown to be important in some feminist discussion (Hall 1979). Towards the end of the nineteenth century too, ideas that were once seen as antithetical to feminist interests and concerns have been shown to be helpful to them: while eugenic ideas were opposed by many because of the ways in which they emphasized the importance of women as mothers and often denied them the right to education, Lucy Bland has shown how late nineteenth-century women drew on eugenic ideas concerning the health of the race in their critique of male sexual licence and their opposition to the sexual double standard (Bland 1987b).

Just as recent historical work has suggested a wider range of influences on nineteenth-century feminist thought, so too it has raised questions about the coherence and the logical consistency of the core arguments laid down by those most closely associated with demands for the emancipation of women. Most nineteenth-century British feminists, including John Stuart Mill, saw themselves as following logical arguments of a kind entirely ignored by their opponents who relied rather on prejudice and often irrational beliefs. By contrast, many recent historians of feminism have pointed to the contradictions and paradoxes evident within the ideas and approaches of feminists themselves, in their simultaneous insistence that what passed as 'women's nature' was an artificial construction, and that many of the desirable qualities associated with femininity were innate, for example. Denise Riley (1988) and Joan Scott (1996) have both argued that these contradictions are inevitable: that there is inherently something paradoxical in feminism itself, in the ways in which at the very time that feminists are concerned to reject the limitations imposed on women and to demand that they be seen as entitled to the same rights as men and to human rights more generally, they necessarily draw on the category of women to make their claims. While the goal of feminism was to eliminate ' "sexual difference" in politics', Scott argued, it had nonetheless

> to make its claims on behalf of 'woman' (who were discursively produced through 'sexual difference'). To the extent that it acted for 'women', feminism produced the 'sexual difference' it sought to eliminate. This paradox—the need both to accept *and* to refuse 'sexual difference'— was the constitutive condition of feminism as a political movement throughout its long history. (Scott 1996: 3–4)

One can see these paradoxes in nineteenth-century British feminist thought particularly in the ways in which feminists drew on liberal political beliefs, insisting on their application to women while ignoring both the patriarchal foundations of liberalism and their own assumptions about the specific nature of women. There is a broader issue here in relation to the whole Western philosophical tradition, in which, Genevieve Lloyd argues, 'rationality has been conceived as transcendence of the feminine', and ' "the feminine" itself has been partly constituted by its occurrence within this structure' (Lloyd 1984: 11) In a more specific way, as Carole Pateman and others have argued, since the seventeenth century, liberalism has accepted, even assumed, a sexual division of labour in which women were wives and mothers living in homes and families whose male head was the political subject whose rationality required both his autonomy and his need for freedom of action. The significance of this idea of sexed citizenship was not only historical but continuous: women were not party to the original social contract and the contractual relationships they were allowed to enter were generally ones that involved relinquishing their freedom (Pateman 1988). In the nineteenth century, this was most evident in relation to the marriage contract which deprived women of their legal identity, their property, their children, and their rights over their own bodies. Hence, as the strong opposition they faced from many prominent liberals illustrated, the theoretical framework of nineteenth-century liberalism could not automatically be applied to women.

For the most part, historians tend to see nineteenth-century feminism in terms of three consecutive phases with some overlap but with marked differences between them. The first of these, which came to the fore in the 1820s and 1830s, was closely connected to the radical social and political ideas associated with the followers of Robert Owen and with the radical social and religious views of the Unitarians associated with W. J. Fox and the journal he edited, the *Monthly Repository*. For the most part, this particular feminist discussion came to an end by the late 1830s. It was followed in the mid-nineteenth century by the emergence of a rather more moderate feminism deeply committed to liberal political and economic ideas and connected with a largely middle-class women's movement which campaigned from the 1860s onwards for a number of specific political, legal, and social reforms, including women's suffrage, reform of the laws that deprived married women of their property and legal identity, and the opening of new educational and professional opportunities to women. Although there were some links through the continuation of a radical Unitarian tradition and preoccupation with abolitionism, this feminism of the mid-nineteenth century came from a different social and economic milieu and had a number of concerns very different from those of the radical feminists of the earlier decades. While this form of moderate feminism linked to specific political and social goals continued into the twentieth century, it was accompanied and sometimes came into conflict with other feminist ideas in the 1880s and 1890s. A different form of socialist feminism from that of the Owenites came to the fore, connected to trade union and labour movements and concerned with the conditions of working-class women and hence more with women's work and pay than with political rights. At much the same time there was a resurgence of radical feminist ideas, connected to the figure of a 'new woman' and often rejecting the propriety and stress on family duty of the mid-Victorian feminists, and demanding new forms of sexual freedom and of freedom from the restraints both of family life and of conventional feminine propriety.

There is considerable discussion about precisely when and how each of these phases of feminism thought developed, beginning with new debates about the extent to which the period of reaction and repression that followed the French Revolution and accompanied the Napoleonic Wars silenced all feminist voices. The conservative recuperation of the most acceptable of Mary Wollstonecraft's ideas in the novels of Jane Austen has long been recognized. Recently, however, a number of historians and literary scholars have pointed to the ways in which the writing of other women such as Mary Hays continued to stress the issue of women's rights in the early decades of the nineteenth century, insisting also on defending Wollstonecraft and presenting her life and her ideas in a very positive way (Spongberg 2010). The emergence of a new interest in women's biography and the use of women's lives as a way to recount wider historical developments has also been seen as a significant new feminist departure, bringing women's voices and interests into the writing of history (Spongberg 2005). But there is debate also about the similarities and differences of the feminist approaches of particular periods and the extent of the continuity of feminism across the whole period.

One question in which one can see both continuity and change is that concerning women's education, which was a matter of concern across the century. The growing sense of the importance of the home and of parents, especially mothers, in the education and moral development of their children made the inadequacy of women's education a matter of importance to many who had no wider interest in women's rights. Hence the late eighteenth-century insistence by both Catherine Macaulay and Mary Wollstonecraft on the need to provide women with the kind of broad and rigorous education that befitted rational creatures gave way in the early decades of the nineteenth to a demand that women needed a better education than was currently available to them to understand and fulfil their maternal and domestic duties—which included self-sacrifice and self-renunciation in the interests of husband and children. By the 1820s, however, this approach was being challenged by some women associated with radical Unitarian views, who demanded that the education of women be looked at in a slightly different way and in terms of the development of their own intellectual potential. In an article 'On Female Education' in 1822, Harriet Martineau insisted that women's education must be concerned not just with teaching them their duty but also with allowing for the development of their own intellects. Martineau accepted the domestic lot of the majority of women, and the need for a 'race of enlightened mothers' who could also be rational companions to men. But she insisted also that, until their talents and capacity for development were given free play, it was impossible to determine the relative abilities of men and women. Properly educated mothers, in her view, needed to be schooled in history, natural philosophy, and the philosophy of mind as well as modern languages— rather than the accomplishments that dominated the education of middle- and upper-class girls (Pichanik 1980). The question of women's education continued to be a major feminist concern throughout the century. But, as Tennyson anticipated in *The Princess*, it changed both form and focus in the mid-century as concerns about women's need for paid work and their entitlement and capacity to undertake the same kind of education as men, both in secondary schools and at tertiary level, took centre stage. The benefits of educating mothers continued to be extolled, but in a more and more perfunctory way after the mid-nineteenth century as the need for women to have access to universities and to professional work came to the fore.

Debates about the intellectual differences between the sexes and about the construction and meaning of femininity itself were fundamental to any significant change in the position of women; nonetheless the demand for improved education was a modest one that could quite easily be accommodated within the existing gender order. This was not so easily done with other feminist demands focusing on marriage or sexuality—which often led to discussions of the current enslavement of women in marriage and to the need for their emancipation. The political conservatism that engulfed Britain after the French Revolution and the preoccupation with wealth that accompanied industrialization, as Barbara Taylor argues, made ideas of emancipation seem impossible. It was not until the emergence of new ideas about cooperative production, social organization, and even domestic life began to emerge in the course of the 1820s that these broader questions of the emancipation of women came again to the fore (Taylor 1983). It was amongst radical circles that this question was discussed and especially amongst the interlinked circles connected with the socialist Robert Owen and the Unitarian radical W. J. Fox. Marx and Engels labelled the ideal of universal freedom that would come through the harmonizing of all human needs, communal ownership, and the transformation of the human character which Owen advocated, 'utopian'. By contrast, Owen and his followers saw their approach as one based on a scientific view of human nature and society. Owen's belief in the influence of circumstances on character— and hence on the possibilities of change—led them to argue that a new social organization based on cooperation rather than competition could produce marked changes in character and behaviour. A new social order based on cooperation would not only be more equitable and just, but also allow for a richer human development—and for the emancipation of all, including both men and women, from the constraints that currently bound them. This ideal of freedom for women was not accepted or endorsed by all of those connected with Owen, and indeed Owen himself can hardly be described as a feminist. But it became a major issue for a number of Owen's followers.

Although there were a number of women who wrote and went on lecture tours criticizing the ways in which women were oppressed and excluded from paid labour and civic life and expounding their views on the ways in which cooperative living and working patterns would emancipate them, the best known work associated with the Owenite movement remains Thompson's *Appeal.* As has already been said, Thompson's work was a critical response to James Mill's 'Essay on Government', and especially to Mill's belief that women did not need political rights in a representative system because 'the interest of almost all . . . is involved either in that of their fathers or in that of their husbands' (Mill 1821). Thomson rejected Mill's views entirely, arguing that they could be seen to be false in regard to every group of women: to married women who were more likely to be oppressed than represented by their husbands, to adult daughters living in their father's home, and to single women who had neither husbands nor fathers to protect them.

Women's relative physical weakness and their childbearing would always condemn them to an inferior position, Thompson argued, hence their emancipation and equality were possible only with a new social arrangement. But Thompson devoted much less space to arguing about possible future freedom than he did to delineating the many forms of oppression which women suffered at present. As John Stuart Mill was later to do, he devoted his greatest attention to married women, arguing that married women lived under a contract that was similar to a slave contract as 'the movable property and ever obedient servant to a husband who was also their master' (Thompson 1973: 100). Thompson's attack on marriage and on the overall situation of women echoed that of Mary Wollstonecraft in its emphasis on male sexual licence and profligacy in the degradation of women. He was scathing in his criticism of the ways in which men directed women's lives solely in order to gratify their own sexual appetites. But he moved in a rather different direction in his condemnation of the ways in which existing marriage laws and assumptions made women sexual slaves, while denying them any entitlement to sexual desire, activity, or fulfilment within marriage. 'The whole of what is called her education', he argued, trained her 'to be the obedient instrument of men's sensual gratification, she is not permitted even to wish for any gratification for herself'.

A number of the women associated with the Owenites both shared and expressed the concerns about married women and their sexual slavery that were so important to Thompson. As Barbara Taylor has suggested, several of them had left unhappy marriages and demanded personal and sexual freedom in their own lives, in ways quite similar to Wollstonecraft. But others focused attention rather more on the question of women's need for personal independence and its economic basis. While they generally agreed that the institution of private property was fundamental to women's dependence—and what was needed to end it was the transformation of the current system based on private property to one based on cooperative living and working arrangements—they also pointed to the needs of women to be able to undertake paid work that was accorded reasonable wages. Owenite women were often confronted with opposition to women's paid work and with fear of their competition from the very men most adamant in the demand for cooperation and for unionization of male workers.

It was not only those connected to socialist movements who condemned the legal and social oppression of women, but also some radical religious groups. It was amongst radical Unitarians, Kathryn Gleadle argues, especially those connected with W. J. Fox, many of whom published articles in the *Monthly Repository*, that one can find the most comprehensive understanding of the cultural basis and meaning of women's oppression (Gleadle 1995). Anticipating the argument that J. S. Mill was later to make so forcefully, they insisted not only that the origin of the position of women was to be seen in earlier forms of slavery, but also that it was the institution that most clearly resembled their current position as well. 'In what does the slavery of women consist?' asked one article in *The Crisis* in 1834:

> Does it not consist in being subjected to laws which she has been carefully excluded from all participation in forming…? Does not their slavery consist in having been systematically excluded from an education, which, however miserably defective it may be, has been an additional weapon in the hands of her tyrant?[1]

For the Unitarian radicals, as for William Thompson, there was a clear connection between women's subordinate legal status and their lack of political rights. It was only by establishing equality at the heart of the legislature, they argued, that a just and rational society might be effected. It was amongst these radicals in the 1830s, Gleadle argues, and not amongst those middle-class women demanding the right to vote in the 1860s, that the connection between enfranchisement and women's legal status was first clearly drawn. But one can see here too the disagreements over how best to analyse women's domestic roles and responsibilities that were to be so significant in the second half of the century. While some of the radical Unitarians extolled women's maternal role and insisted on the primacy and the importance of their contribution to familial and domestic life, others argued rather that, given educational limits and narrow cultural horizons, it was hard for them to do anything else. Drawing on the cooperative ideas and schemes that were quite prominent in the 1830s, some of the more utopian of Fox's followers also suggested that communal living arrangements or associated housing schemes might be the best way to set women free from ceaseless domestic drudgery. Others suggested rather that women might become family income earners, while men assumed responsibility for the domestic sphere. Others took up this broad question of women in relation to family life in different ways, suggesting the possibilities of a new model family which was more egalitarian than the norm and in which fathers played a very different role in regard both to housework and to childcare. Central to the Unitarian case, Gleadle argues, was their conception of the relationship between the family and the state. Democratic principles, many of them argued, could not be confined to the state, but had to extend to the family hearth.

These debates that had been so important amongst Owenites and radical Unitarians came to an end by the early 1840s. There was little connection, in terms either of personnel or of outlook, between the ideas of these groups and those that came to the fore in the late 1850s and 1860s. With the demise of the cooperative movement and of ideas about communal living, a radical approach to family life and domestic labour disappeared. The liberal framework of the feminist discussions of the mid-nineteenth century, with its individualism and its emphasis on the particular form of nuclear family that was evident within the British middle class, put paid to these particular ideas. Feminist debate and discussion in the mid-nineteenth century was associated primarily with a women's movement comprised of a series of specific campaigns to reform the marital laws that deprived women of their

---

[1] 'Justitia', Letter to the Editor, *The Crisis*, 3/30 (Mar. 1834), 246, cited in Gleadle (1995), 63.

property and their legal identity, to extend their educational and employment opportunities, and to gain the vote. The need for political rights and for women to become full citizens was a key concern for most mid-Victorian feminists. But this focus on legal and political reform was accompanied by a shift in approach to personal life and a greater acceptance of conventional ideas about morality and marriage. Sexual questions continued to be important, and a small number of feminists continued to insist on recognition of the sexual oppression within marriage, and for the first time to raise explicitly the issue of marital rape (Kent 1987). But what was of greater moment was the sexual double standard and most particularly the acceptance of it that underlined the regulation of prostitution through the Contagious Diseases Acts.

The one person who was involved both in some of the debates of the 1820s and 1830s and those of the mid-nineteenth century was Harriet Martineau. Martineau was a critical and in some ways radical Unitarian and published in the journal edited by W. J. Fox. She served, however, rather to anticipate the changes that came in the mid-century than to bring into this later period the radical critiques of an earlier generation. Martineau had shown little interest in the broader criticism of sexual hierarchy evident amongst Unitarian and Owenite groups or in their support for personal and particularly for sexual freedom for women. On the contrary, where those like Thompson, W. J. Fox, and Eliza Flower deplored the ways that women were tied to marriage and criticized sexual double standards, Martineau demanded absolute adherence to prevailing sexual norms, refusing to associate with any women thought to have engaged in irregular sexual conduct. She never thought to make the same demands of men. Her endorsement of domesticity for women and her concern about sexual morality went along with a great determination to ensure that she was not seen as connected to anyone like Wollstonecraft. Her sense of the possibility of making feminist demands and critiques came rather through her connection with the women engaged in the campaigns for the abolition of slavery whom she met while in America in the 1830s.

Martineau is a complicated figure in nineteenth-century British feminist thought. In the course of her long writing career, she addressed almost every aspect of women's oppression including education, social customs, marriage laws, health, clothing, paid work, and sexual exploitation both in prostitution and in marriage. But while concerned about the situation of women, she was often hesitant to advocate fundamental change or to identify herself with those demanding it. When she pointed to the limited employment opportunities available to women, for example, something which had directly affected her own life, rather than advocating for greater employment opportunities for women, Martineau contented herself with pointing to the contradictions evident between the assumption that most women were supported by their menfolk—and the vast amount of paid labour that women actually undertook. Adopting a cool and neutral stance in many of her discussions of women and the problems that they faced, she often adopted a masculine voice as well. While this stance seems to some to exclude her from the category of feminist, others have argued rather that Martineau's approach was essentially sociological, that she deserves recognition as one of the founding figures of sociology—and as one who placed women at its centre (Hoecker-Drysdale 1992). Martineau's approach changed quite markedly in the course of the 1860s when she came to recognize the importance of women raising their own voices and campaigning directly for legal and social change. The issue that brought this home to her was the Contagious Diseases Acts. As we will see, these Acts, which served to regulate prostitution in specified ports and garrison towns, were a source of very great anger and concern amongst feminists who saw them as enshrining the sexual double standard in a particularly demeaning way. Martineau too was appalled by the Contagious Diseases Acts and joined with Josephine Butler and others seeking to have them repealed. It was only when she became involved in this agitation that Martineau came to see herself as connected to the campaigns that made up the women's movement or as an advocate of women's rights. As Simone de Beauvoir was to do in the late twentieth century, Martineau became a feminist more or less retrospectively, in response to the enthusiasm and urgency of a younger genera-tion of women—who in turn offered her recognition of the work on women she had done in her earlier life.

Although there were differences in the specific views and outlooks of those associated with these various feminist campaigns of the mid-nineteenth century, all of them articulated their views within the broad framework of political and economic liberalism. There were a number of different ways in which they did this, but in all the need to recognize women as individuals was paramount. This is not to suggest that nineteenth-century feminists under-rated the centrality of women's familial role and duties; nonetheless they saw women first and foremost not as mothers, wives, or daughters, but as autonomous individuals, entitled to the same rights and freedoms as men. All the various prevailing ideas about the proper end of women, whether it be maternity or some wider civilizing mission, were based, argued Frances Cobbe, on the theory of 'Woman as an adjective' whose being should be directed towards the happiness of someone else. What was needed instead was a theory of woman as a noun whose first end of being was one proper to herself (Cobbe 1869).

One key point stressed by many mid-Victorian feminists was the need to see the cur-rent position of women, not as natural or necessary, but rather as a throwback to an earlier age. This was one of the points made most strongly by John Stuart Mill in his *Subjection of Women*. The position of women at the present time, Mill argued, bore all the signs of its origin in a primitive form of slavery and bondage. The legal and political restrictions that they faced, were 'the survivals from a state of society that has passed away'. Hence the situ-ation of women was out of kilter with all other aspects of contemporary society. The 'mod-ern conviction', Mill insisted 'is, that things in which the individual is the person directly interested, never go right but as they are left to his own discretion; and that any regulation of them by authority, except to protect the rights of others, is sure to be mischievous'—this conviction was not applied to women. They remained 'the one group in society (apart from royalty) whose opportunities and life pattern were determined solely by their birth' (Mill 1970: 136).

While Mill saw women's subordinate status as a form of slavery, others saw it in sightly different terms: as a form of legal infantilization as women were sometimes linked with chil-dren in their need of special care and protection, or worse when they were linked with crim-inals and idiots in their overall legal standing. Rather than being placed in these categories, feminists argued, women needed to be classified as adults with the same legal and political rights and economic opportunities as other adults. Frances Power Cobbe stated this view powerfully in an article entitled 'Criminals, Idiots, Women and Minors'.

> Ought Englishwomen of full age at the present state of affairs, to be considered as having legally attained majority? Or ought they permanently to be considered, for all civil and politi-cal purposes as minors? This, we venture to think, is the real point at issue between the friends and opponents of 'women's rights'. (Cobbe 1868: 778)

Cobbe was prepared to accept that at an earlier period the 'pupilage' in which women had been kept was both inevitable and sometimes even salutary. But it was no longer either necessary or viable. This point was made forcefully also by Josephine Butler and her colleagues in regard to the regulation of women's work. They strongly opposed legislation that sought to limit women's working hours or to prohibit them from undertaking particular kinds of work. There is no middle course, they argued,

> Between a system which shall map out precise duties, not only to each sex, but to every class and to every individual constituting the State, and the system which leaves to all equal freedom to work at what they choose and what they are fit for. And the principles on which modern society is based, forbid that any system should live save that of freedom of labour, a freedom which, from its nature, must be complete and universal. (Butler et al. 1870: 6)

In arguing for a removal of the many restrictions that women faced, Millicent Garrett Fawcett also summoned the arguments that were part of the case for free trade. The demand for removal of the barrier that excluded women from higher education and from many different forms of employment was, she insisted, only a 'phase of the free trade argument'.

> Free-traders argue that all artificial restrictions upon commerce should be removed, because that is the only way of insuring that each country and each locality will occupy itself with that industry for which it has the greatest natural advantages. In like manner, we say remove the artificial restrictions which debar women from higher education and from remunerative employment... and the play of natural forces will drive them into those occupations for which they have the greatest natural advantages as individuals. (Fawcett 1878: 352)

This argument was of particular importance because, while insisting that women should have opportunities for employment outside marriage (and Fawcett stressed that many of the noblest and best women remained single, devoting themselves to significant public causes), it nonetheless assumed that the majority of women would be guided into marriage—the 'occupation for which they had the greatest natural advantages'.

Although often drawing her rhetoric from a different strand of liberalism through her insistence on the ways in which organized prostitution enslaved women and hence on their need for emancipation, Josephine Butler too deployed liberal arguments in her opposition to the Contagious Diseases Acts. The Contagious Diseases Acts were first and foremost an example of the 'over-legislation', which was, in her view, 'the grand evil of the day'. She was concerned about the tendency towards central government regulation in place of local and municipal control over many community matters, including public health. She disliked the growing power of the executive and the tendency of governments to usurp what she saw as the traditional role of Parliament. But more than anything else, she was fiercely opposed to any attempt to legislate in areas of personal morality, and especially in cases like that of the Contagious Diseases Acts, which extended the powers of the police to interfere in the private lives of individuals (Butler 1879).

As we have already seen, there were many very significant men engaged in articulating and developing nineteenth-century feminist thought. The lack of legal and political rights or of a recognized public voice made women depend heavily on male support and in many cases prominent feminists were the beneficiaries of supportive fathers and husbands. While women and men often worked together, the place of men in feminism did become problematic as some women came to see the importance of women organizing and agitating for themselves. This issue came to the fore primarily in relation to the Contagious Diseases Acts and the issue of prostitution. Within this framework, in which men were not only clients, but also police, magistrates, and doctors as well as the parliamentarians who made the laws, the question of male power and privilege was inescapable. In one of her newsletters, Josephine Butler, who led the agitation against the Contagious Diseases Acts, put the case very clearly through the comments of a young prostitute she claimed to have interviewed. 'It is men, men, only men, from first to last', said the young woman.

> To please a man I did wrong at first, then I was flung about from man to man, men police lay hands on us. By men we are examined, handled, doctored, and messed on with. In hospital it is a man again who makes prayers and reads the bible for us. We are had up before magistrates who are men, and we never get out of the hands of men till we die.[2]

Butler's concerns about the specifically sexual nature of women's oppression had as a counterpoint an insistence on the importance of women campaigning themselves to end their own oppression. She became very concerned in the course of the 1870s over what she saw as a 'tendency...among men to allow women to drop out of the first ranks in this crusade' and to see the question of prostitution and its regulation as an international and scientific one with 'distinguished and learned men' as its main advocates. But men lacked the sense of urgency that she felt—and moreover, she felt that women's direct involvement in this cause of their emancipation was vital. It was the Contagious Diseases Acts that made Butler recognize the importance of women's suffrage 'as a means of self preservation'. As the franchise extended to include new groups of men, the omission of women became more and more serious. Once labourers were going to be enfranchised, Butler wrote in the 1870s,

> Our case becomes the worse; we shall be utterly sacrificed and lost, if we have no representation—if we become (tho' more than half the nation) the one unrepresented section under a government which will become more and more extended, more popular, more democratic and yet wholly masculine.[3]

While arguing that women needed to be seen as individuals entitled to the same rights as men, for the most part, nineteenth-century feminists continued to see women as very different from men in their intellectual and emotional make-up. Even those as convinced that what was generally understood to be 'women's nature' was an eminently artificial as John Stuart Mill nonetheless believed strongly that there were marked differences between the approach of men and women. Men, in his view, were far more inclined to think in terms of generalizations, for example, while women had more intuition and insight into 'present fact'. This simultaneous rejection of much that was seen as integral to femininity in the nineteenth century with a strong belief in the very particular form of sexual difference that Mill shows here has been the subject of strong criticism from twentieth-century feminist scholars. But it was easily accepted by his own nineteenth-century female counterparts, many of whom went considerably further than him in their insistence on the extent and nature of sexual difference—and on their very high evaluation of women's empathy, compassion, and capacity for nurture and on their sense of women's innate capacity for managing domestic

---

[2] Josephine Butler, 'The Garrison Towns of Kent', Third Letter from Mrs Butler, *Shield*, 9 May 1870.
[3] Josephine Butler, letter to Mrs C. M. Wilson, 12 Nov. 1803, Butler Papers, Women's Library, London School of Economics.

and familial life. When opponents of women's rights suggested that education and work and full emancipation would bring a diminution of those admirable qualities of womanhood that were so important in both social and family life, both Josephine Butler and Frances Cobbe strongly disagreed. Cobbe, who wrote at some length about the particular duties that women owed to their parents, their wider families, and to society at large, was appalled at the very idea that rights might make women less womanly. 'If women were to become less dutiful by being enfranchised less conscientious, less unselfish, less temperate, less chaste,' she expostulated, 'then I should say "For heaven's sake, let us stay where we are! Nothing we can ever gain would be worth such a loss"' (Cobbe 1881: 11–12). But she did not believe that this would be the case. Women, in her view, were innately temperate, chaste, and nurturant, capable of tender feelings towards family, friends, and the society at large that were completely unknown to men. These qualities were most evident in mothers, but they could clearly be seen in single women as well. Although very different from Cobbe in her general political outlook, and far more radical in her endorsement of suffrage reform and her preparedness to confront the sexual double standard, Josephine Butler was in agreement with Cobbe both in her horror at the possibility of any diminution in 'womanliness' and in her belief that this could not happen. 'Every good quality, every virtue which we regard as distinctively feminine', Butler argued,

> Will, under conditions of greater freedom, develop more freely… It will always be her nature to foster, to cherish, to take the part of the weak, to train, to guide, to have a care of individuals, to discern the small seeds of a great future, to warm and cherish those seed into fullness of life. 'I serve' will always be one of her favourite mottos, even should the utmost freedom be accorded her in the choice of vocation. (Butler 1868: 18)

Rather than undermining the case for political rights for women, these very differences served in the view of feminists to strengthen it because of the value of these womanly qualities to the state.

While some feminists insisted on the benefits that womanly qualities like nurturance and compassion would bestow on government and on many public institutions, others stressed rather the educative and moral benefits that women would derive from inclusion within the public and political world and in the concerns of both nation and state. John Stuart Mill was perhaps the strongest proponent of this view that women's moral and intellectual horizons would grow and expand as enfranchisement and a sense of themselves as citizens turned their attention away from family and home and towards public concerns. Mill tended to talk about political and public concerns in general terms, but for some of his more overtly patriotic contemporaries, the important connection was not just with a generalized idea of state and nation, but rather with Britain—and in many cases also with the British Empire. Millicent Garrett Fawcett included both when she proudly described herself as a 'worshipper at the inner shrine, the holy of holies, all that England stands for to her children, and to the world', and she was not alone in holding these sentiments (Fawcett 1888). She and several other feminists made clear their sense, not only that the participation of women was essential to maintain national strength, but also that 'British womanhood' was superior to any other. This view of the superiority of British womanhood was articulated first in relation to other European women: French, German, and especially Italian. Frances Cobbe's long article on 'women in Italy in 1862', for example, placed Italian women under a microscope to reveal their many failings and inadequacies: their lack of education; the impact on their intellectual and moral development of their rigid adherence to the Catholic Church; their frivolity and lack of capacity for reflection. But as imperial questions became more and more prominent in the later decades of the century, it was the superiority of British women to their colonial counterparts that was emphasized. For some feminists this sense of superiority went along with the idea of women as having a particular imperial mission to their 'little sisters'. The major target of this discussion—and indeed of British feminist campaigns to provide female doctors and teachers, to bring an end to child marriage, and to regulate prostitution—was Indian women. What is noticeable in all of these cases is the way in which 'Indian women' are seen as an undifferentiated group of absolutely helpless people, dominated over and victimized both by their own menfolk and social norms and by imperial officials. When Josephine Butler turned her attention to the Cantonment Acts which extended to India the provisions of the Contagious Diseases Acts, she never for a moment thought that Indian women might themselves take up this issue, seeing them rather as 'helpless, voiceless, hopeless'. Their helplessness appealed to the heart, she wrote,

> In somewhat the same way in which the helplessness and suffering of a dumb animal does, under the knife of a vivisector. Somewhere, halfway between the Martyr Saints and the tortured friend of man, the noble dog, stands, it seems to me, these pitiful Indian women, girls, children, as many of them are.[4]

In infantilizing and dehumanizing these colonial subjects, British feminists demonstrated their preparedness to take on a special imperial burden—something which served to show yet again their own fitness for political rights.

Many of the ideas and approaches that were characteristic of mid-Victorian feminism continued at least until the outbreak of the First World War and were evident amongst members and supporters of the largest of the suffrage societies, the National Union of Women's Suffrage Societies, led by Millicent Garrett Fawcett. But from the late 1880s and the 1890s, these ideas and approaches, and especially the insistence on the primacy of women's suffrage as the major feminist cause, were challenged on a couple of different fronts, by those who demanded a new approach to industrial legislation as a way of protecting working women, on the one hand, and by those who offered a much stronger and more militant critique of marriage and of prevailing ideals of femininity, on the other.

Both the emphasis on political campaigns and the liberal economic ideas that were so important to mid-Victorian feminists were rejected entirely by a number of women associated with the labour and trade union movements, who argued that their attack on sex-based industrial legislation reflected their complete ignorance of the lives and conditions of working women. Far from imposing unwarranted restrictions on them, industrial legislation protected women from economic exploitation. Women like Margaret Llewellyn Davies, Mary MacArthur, and Gertrude Tuckwell worked hard to increase the number of women belonging to trade unions and advocated legislative regulation of women's working hours and conditions. They regarded the liberal economic ideas of an earlier generation of feminists as outmoded, insisting that it was industrial legislation rather than its absence that secured women's freedom. 'We cannot see', Margaret Llewellyn Davies argued,

---

[4] Josephine Butler, 'Editorial', *Stormbell* (June 1898), cited in Burton (1994), 62.

How a shop-girl, standing from 70 to 80 hours a week, often in a most unhealthy atmosphere, often only allowed odd times to bolt her food, is a 'freer' woman than the mill-hand, with her legal 56 hours a week, her two hours for food, her half-holiday and her ventilated and white-washed surroundings. (Llewellyn-Davies 1897: 4)

While women connected to the labour movement and drawing on socialist and trade-union ideas provided one critique of mid-Victorian feminism, a younger generation of women who identified with the idea of a 'new woman' provided another. Here, as earlier in the century, literature played an important part in suggesting new ways of thinking about the 'woman question' and of approaching feminism. The early 1890s saw the publication of several novels dealing with a 'new woman'. This fiction and the very idea of a 'new woman' was the subject of much debate, with many well-known writers and a large number of leading feminists attacking the sexual licence and freedoms apparently demanded by this figure. But it was precisely in this fictional form, as Lucy Bland has argued, that new approaches to marriage, sexuality, and women's freedom were articulated (Bland 1987a). Unlike the writers of an earlier period, many of these novelists of the 1890s, including Olive Schreiner, Mona Caird, and Emma Brooke saw themselves as feminists and were engaged in feminist campaigns and in writing about the situation of women in non-fictional forms. They attacked prevailing ideals of womanhood, arguing both that women who were entirely dependent on their menfolk for sustenance and support were parasites and conversely that marriage and familial duties and demands destroyed not only women's independence but also their capacity to develop as full human beings.

Like the socialist women, these women also rejected the idea that it was suffrage that was the most urgent need of women. But for them it was not work, but rather questions of marriage, sexual behaviour, and family life that were of most importance. Marriage was a particular target as some 'new women' eschewed it completely, while others depicted it as a source not only of constant servitude and even slavery, but also of illness and death. Venereal disease, contracted by profligate young men and then transmitted to their innocent and ignorant wives and through them to their children, was one powerful image of the suffering that marriage imposed on women—and a number of feminists argued that the profligacy of young men was so widespread that few women were ever entirely well after marriage. The sexual double standard which feminists had long attacked was shown here as something that threatened not only individual women and families but the entire well-being of the nation and the race. But even when women were not immediately infected, marriage and family life were seen as involving the complete sacrifice of a woman's self. Both in her novel *The Daughters of Danaus* and in her collection of essays *The Morality of Marriage*, Mona Caird stressed the ways in which marriage and family life enslaved women. In her view, marriage still carried the marks of its origin involving the sale and enslavement of women and the binding of them to a man for his personal use and the procreation of his children. Women suffered not only physical abuse and humiliation, but also the loss of any capacity to engage in their own interests or to live a fulfilling life. The idea that women should devote themselves to motherhood was in her view both false and illogical: there was no more reason why women should devote their entire lives to motherhood than men should to fatherhood. But the acceptance that women should so devote themselves required nothing less than the complete sacrifice of one sex to the other (Caird 1897). The idea that women were rendered sexual slaves by marriage was not new. It was after all something that had been argued by both William Thompson and John Stuart Mill, while other early and mid-Victorian feminists had pointed to the many ways in which women could be ill-treated in marriage. What was new was the insistence on the physical, moral, intellectual, and spiritual destruction of women that accompanied all marriage, not just those in which women were explicitly ill-treated. Caird in particular also insisted on the ways in which family life, including the demands of both parents and children, sucked the lifeblood from women and destroyed them. The antagonism to marriage expressed in some of the writing of the 1890s and the insistence on the ways in which women were literally killed by it provided the framework for a much more militant form of feminism.

Critiques of marriage and of the deleterious consequences of marital sex for women did not take for granted women's asexuality or the idea that sex was imposed on them. In the 1890s, as for William Thompson, the point at issue was rather the lack of any recognition of women's own sexuality and desire—and the ways in which the sexual ignorance that was required of women prevented their being in any way prepared for adult sexual relationships. For some of those writing about the 'new woman', what women needed was the freedom to pursue emotional and sexual relationships outside marriage, rather than being completely bound within them. It is interesting to note here the ways in which the language of feminism was slowly beginning to be used in the 1890s, and in ways that linked questions of personal freedom for women with demands for legal and political rights. Some of those who labelled themselves feminists were extremely critical of the increasing emphasis on enfranchisement and on winning the vote which was the main target of organized women's campaigns, seeing the demand for suffrage as asking 'for a trifling political adjustment... rather than fighting for the full humanity and the economic, social and sexual freedom of women' (Marsden 1912: 285). As this suggests, the introduction of the turn 'feminist' did not bring unanimity amongst all those advocating the rights of women. On the contrary, one might argue that the term came into being just at the point when a mid-Victorian consensus was breaking down, bringing an unprecedented diversity of outlook and approach. The introduction of the language of feminism at the turn of the twentieth century was, however, accompanied by a new interest in the history of feminist thought and perhaps in a new sense of the significance of possible feminist traditions. William Thompson's *Appeal* was republished along with several essays on earlier feminists like Mary Astell and 'Sophia'. But it was Mary Wollstonecraft who was the subject of particular interest, with the appearance of several new and very sympathetic biographies as well as new editions of the *Vindication of the Rights of Woman*. The 'new woman', who demanded sexual freedom as well as education, work, and legal and political rights, offered an appropriate context for the re-evaluation of Wollstonecraft and a way to establish her place as a founding figure in British feminist thought.

REFERENCES

Bland, L. (1987a) 'The Married Woman, the "New Woman" and the Feminist: Sexual Politics of the 1890s', in J. Rendall (ed.), *Equal or Different: Women's Politics 1800-1914* (Oxford: Basil Blackwell), 141–64.

Bland, L. (1987b) *Banishing the Beast: English Feminism and Sexual Morality, 1885–1914* (London: Penguin).

Burton, A. (1994) *Burdens of History: British Feminists, India and Imperial Culture* (Chapel Hill: University of North Carolina Press).

Butler, J. (1868) *The Education and Employment of Women* (London, Macmillan).

Butler, J. (1879) *Government by Police* (London: Dyer).

Butler, J. (1909) *An Autobiographical Memoir*, ed. G. and L. Johnston (London).

Butler, J., et al. (1870) *Legislative restrictions on the Industry of Women considered from the Women's Point of View*, pamphlet (London: Arrowsmith).

Caine, B. (1992) *Victorian Feminists* (Oxford: Oxford University Press).

Caine, B. (1997) 'Victorian Feminism and the Ghost of Mary Wollstonecraft', *Women's Writing*, 4/2: 261–75.

Caird, M. (1897) *The Morality of Marriage and other essays on the Status and Destiny of Woman* (London: Redway).

Cobbe, F. P. (1868) 'Criminals, Idiots, Women and Minors', *Fraser's Magazine*, 78: 778–9.

Cobbe, F. P. (1869) 'The Final Cause of Woman', in J. Butler (ed.), *Woman's Work and Woman's Culture* (London: Macmillan & Co.).

Cobbe, F. P. (1881) *The Duties of Women* (London: Williams and Norgate).

Davies, E. (1866) The Higher Education of Women (London: A. Strahan).

Delmar, R. (1986) 'What is Feminism?', in J. Mitchell and A. Oakley (eds.), *What Is Feminism?* (Oxford: Basil Backwell).

Fawcett, M. G. (1878) ' The Future of Englishwomen: A Reply', *Nineteenth Century*, 4/5: 347–447.

Fawcett, M. G. (1884) 'The Women's Suffrage Movement', in T. Stanton (ed.), *The Woman Question in Europe: A Series of original Essays* (London: Sampson and Low).

Fawcett, M. G. (1888) 'Home and Politics', pamphlet published by the Central and East of England Society for Women's Suffrage.

Gleadle, K. (1995) *The Early Feminists: Radical Unitarians and the Emergence of the Women's Rights Movement, 1831–1851* (London: Macmillan).

Hall, C. (1979) 'The Early Formation of Victorian Domestic Ideology', in S. Burman (ed.), *Fit Work for Women* (London: Croom Helm), 15–33.

Hoecker-Drysdale, S. (1992) *Harriet Martineau: First Woman Sociologist* (London: Berg).

Jeffreys, S. (1985) *The Spinster and Her Enemies: Feminism and Sexuality, 1880–1930* (London: Pandora).

Kent, S. (1987) *Sex and Suffrage in Britain, 1860–1914* (Princeton: Princeton University Press).

Levine, P. (1987) *Victorian Feminism 1850–1900* (London: Hutchinson).

Llewellyn-Davies, M. (1897) *Why Working Women Need the Vote*, (London: Women's Cooperative Guild).

Lloyd, G. (1984) *The Man of Reason: 'Male' and 'Female' in Western Philosophy* (London: Methuen).

Marsden, D. (1912) 'The Woman Movement and the "Ablest Socialists"', *The Freewoman*, 2: 285.

Martineau, H. (2009 [1837]) *Society in America*, 3 vols. (Cambridge: Cambridge University Press).

Martineau, H. (1983) *Autobiography*, 2 vols. (London: Virago).

Mayhall, L. E. N. (2001) 'The Rhetorics of Slavery and Citizenship: Suffragist Discourse and Canonical Texts in Britain, 1880–1914', *Gender & History*, 13/3: 481–97.

Mill, J. (1821) *Essays on Government, Liberty of the Press, Jurisprudence and Law of Nations written for the supplement to the Encyclopaedia Britannica* (London), 21

Mill, J. S. (1970) *The Subjection of Women*, in John Stuart Mill and Harriet Taylor, *Essays on Sex Equality*, ed. A. S. Rossi (Chicago and London: University of Chicago Press).

Pateman, C. (1988) *The Sexual Contract* (Cambridge: Polity).

Pichanik, V. K. (1980) *Harriet Martineau: The Woman and Her Work, 1802–1876* (Ann Arbor: University of Michigan Press).

Rendall, J. (1985) *The Origins of Modern Feminism: Women in Britain, France and the United States, 1780–1860* (Basingstoke: Macmillan).

Riley, D. (1988) *Am I that Name? Feminism and the Category of 'Women' in History* (Basingstoke: Macmillan).

Scott, J. (1996) *Only Paradoxes to Offer: French Feminists and the Rights of Man* (Cambridge, Mass.: Harvard University Press).

Spongberg, M. (2005) 'Female Biography', in M. Spongberg, A. Curthoys, and B. Caine (eds.), *The Companion to Women's Historical Writing* (London: Palgrave).

Spongberg, M. (2008) 'William Godwin's Memoirs of the Author of the Vindication of the Rights of Woman', *Angelaki*, 13/3: 17–31.

Spongberg, M. (2010), 'Mary Hays and Mary Wollstonecraft and the Evolution of Dissenting Feminism', *Enlightenment and Dissent*, 26: 230–58.

Taylor, B. (1983) *Eve and the New Jerusalem: Socialism and Feminism in the Nineteenth Century* (London: Virago).

Thompson, W. (1973 [1825]) *Appeal of one half of the Human Race, Women, against the Pretensions of the other half, Men, to retain them in political and thence in civil and domestic slavery* (London: Virago).

CHAPTER 20

KARL MARX AND BRITISH SOCIALISM

DAVID LEOPOLD

§1

WHEN Harold Wilson famously remarked that British socialism 'owed far more to Methodism than to Marx' (1964: 1), he was articulating a widely shared view. That presumed lack of connection between the work of Karl Marx and what Wilson called 'distinctly British ideas and British traditions' is one of the things I seek to challenge here.

There are many conceptual and historical connections between Marx's writings on the one hand, and politics and culture in nineteenth-century Britain on the other. However, these connections are neither widely recognized nor well understood. In particular, there is a pervasive tendency to treat Marx's thought as a predominantly Continental creation with a limited and largely posthumous impact on British society. In what follows, I say something about that posthumous impact, but concentrate on some neglected evidence of Marx's links with British politics and culture during his lifetime.

(Note that I occasionally use the writings of Friedrich Engels—both works that he co-authored with Marx and some that he wrote alone—to illuminate my subject, but I do so, unless otherwise noted, only where it is plausible to assume a broad affinity between his views and those of Marx. In addition, I use the term 'Marx*ian*' to refer to those views shared by Marx and Engels, and not, for instance, to refer to the views of later Marx*ists*.)

§2

Marx's adult life can be told as the story of three 'exiles'. He was born and grew up in Germany but his adulthood was spent in Paris, Brussels, and London respectively. The last of these three exiles was by far the longest, with Marx having his family home in London from late 1849 until his death in 1883; living first in cramped rooms in Soho, moving later to larger accommodation in Kentish Town, and finding a final resting place in Highgate

Cemetery (Briggs and Callow 2008). Contemporary London provided both a secure haven for political refugees and a superb vantage point from which to observe and engage with the most advanced capitalist society of the day (Ashton 1986: ch. 3). Yet many traditional accounts of Marx's intellectual development leave little or no room for his work to have been influenced by, or to have impacted upon, British politics and culture during his lifetime. Two examples can be given here.

According to what might be called the 'Continental' account, Marx's intellectual development was seemingly unmarked by the accident of his geographical location in Britain. A version of this view can be found in Isaiah Berlin's well-known *Karl Marx: His Life and Environment*, which portrays Marx's intellectual formation as a wholly Continental product. Building on the philosophical foundations established during his university years in Prussia, Marx's 'final intellectual transformation' is said to have taken place in Paris, in the early 1840s, when he was still in his twenties (Berlin 1948: 80). Marx subsequently moved to London, but his links with British intellectual and political life are portrayed as always weak and those of an outsider. He is described as having few acquaintances amongst the native population, and knowing the country only superficially. His social milieu seemingly consisted entirely of German émigré communities, and his political energies had an overwhelmingly Continental focus (combating French and Russian anarchism, and building socialism in Germany). Indeed, despite living in Britain for well over thirty years, Marx is said to have 'remained almost totally unaffected by his surroundings, living encased in his own, largely German, world' (Berlin 1948: 17).

According to what might be called the 'Communist' account, the Continental picture of Marx's intellectual development needs modest revision. Whilst it accurately captures the philosophical and political dimensions of his work, the Continental account underestimates the influence of British authors in providing the starting point of Marx's economic theory. The Communist account finds a canonical formulation in Lenin's schematic sketch 'The Three Sources and Three Component Parts of Marxism'. Marx is portrayed as building on the comparative intellectual advantages (in different areas of knowledge) found in three countries in what was then the most developed region of the world. His genius brought into a 'comprehensive and harmonious' synthesis three national intellectual traditions which were previously isolated from one another: German philosophy (Hegel, of course, above all), French socialism, and British political economy (Lenin 1963: 23). On this Communist account, the influence of Britain is acknowledged, but it remains a modest one, limited to the researches into political economy that Marx conducted in the British Museum. In *Capital*, Marx is said to have 'continued' the work of Adam Smith, David Ricardo, and others; providing, in particular, a more consistent formulation and 'proof' of the labour theory of value (Lenin 1963: 25).

§3

One does not need to know much about Marx's third exile in order to be suspicious of these traditional pictures of him: either, as an insular German thinker wholly unaffected by British intellectual life; or, as primarily a Continental philosopher and revolutionary whose economic theory nonetheless reflects a modest British influence (since it starts from the work of Smith, Ricardo, and others).

Even the more generous of these traditional accounts misunderstands the one British connection that it does allow. The impact of the political economy of Smith, Ricardo, and others on Marx's economic thought is widely and rightly seen as significant. However, the influence of this British—more accurately, largely Scottish—contribution extends beyond the more technical aspects of Marxian economics to impact on both Marx's sociology and his theory of history. The writings of Adam Smith, Adam Ferguson, William Robertson, and (perhaps especially) John Millar, have plausibly been identified as a probable influence on Marx's historical and sociological theories (Pascal 1938; Meek 1967). Such claims provoked a sceptical response from critics concerned with the proper interpretation of these earlier writers, and, in particular, their view of the relation between the 'mode of subsistence'—that defines the four successive stages of hunting, pasturage, agriculture, and commerce—and the political and social arrangements that they are associated with (Skinner 1982; Haakonssen 1989: 225–6). However, the claim that this tradition of historical sociology provides part of the intellectual context in which Marx developed his theory of history, does not require us to elide (anachronistically) the differences between the Scottish 'mode of subsistence' and the Marxian 'mode of production'. Moreover, the historical connections here look reasonably straightforward. Marx read widely amongst these authors—making notes on Millar's *The Origin of the Distinction of Ranks* in 1852—and his earliest attempts at a theory of history explicitly credit these Scottish thinkers as being amongst the first to have given the study of history 'a materialistic basis' by writing histories of 'civil society, of commerce and industry' (Marx and Engels 1976b: 42).

The more serious problem with both these traditional accounts is their failure to recognize that the impact of British politics and culture on Marx's writings goes well beyond the often-acknowledged, if not always well-understood, influence of political economy. Indeed, there is scarcely room here to cover all of its dimensions. For example, I will not discuss the significant influence of British literary culture, beyond noting that anyone sampling his published and unpublished writings would soon discover Marx's evident familiarity with, and frequent utilization of, Defoe, Dickens, and especially Shakespeare, amongst other authors (see Prawer 1976). Nor will I pursue the complex influence of British political economy on Marx's thought beyond my earlier remarks. Instead, in what follows, I concentrate on some neglected evidence of Marx's sustained interest in, and engagement with, politics in Britain.

Even before moving to London, Marx had made connections with Chartism, both through Engels, who had written for the Chartist press when living in Manchester in the early 1840s, and through the Communist League, which had institutional links with the Fraternal Democrats. Marx's first speech to an audience of British workers—during his first visit to England in November 1847—was at a meeting organized by the Fraternal Democrats to celebrate the anniversary of the 1830 Polish uprising, with the Chartist *Northern Star* (2 December 1847) reporting the remarks of 'the learned Dr Marx' in full. Marx saw Chartism as representing the politically most advanced section of the British working classes, and he maintained that, given the country's class structure, the realization of their primarily 'democratic' demands would have far-reaching 'socialistic' consequences (see 1979e). This understanding of Chartism as an early stage in the unfolding struggle for socialism—rather than as part of a long-standing battle against 'old corruption' (made increasingly redundant by an evolving mid-Victorian reformism)—has been criticized (Stedman Jones 1984). However, it is the existence of Marx's engagement, notwithstanding its possible limitations, which is pertinent here. Marx read widely amongst Chartist writings, and modern historians have found evidence of Chartist influence in his analysis of British politics (Taylor 1996: 238–40). Marx also published his own work in Chartist journals including *Notes to the People*, the *Red Republican*, and the *People's Paper*. The number of articles varies but, for example, in 1853 he published some fourteen pieces in the *People's Paper*, including eight about Palmerston (discussed later in this section). Most significantly, the first English version of the *Communist Manifesto* appeared serially, throughout November 1850, in the *Red Republican*, in a little-known translation by the Chartist writer Helen Macfarlane (Black 2004). (Copies of this translation quickly became difficult to locate, and it was later eclipsed by the 'authorized' version produced by Engels and his Manchester friend Samuel Moore in 1888.) Marx knew Macfarlane and seems likely to have approved publication of her interesting version, although whether he had any further involvement in her translation is uncertain (Draper 1998: 28–30). *The Times* (2 September 1851) subsequently published two (unattributed) excerpts from the Macfarlane translation in an article warning against the spread of cheap socialist literature 'containing the wildest and most anarchical doctrines'. Marx is also known to have attended Chartist demonstrations, including the mass protests of 24 June and 1 July 1855 against proposed restrictions on Sunday trading (Marx 1980a, 1980b). Lastly, Marx came to know many Chartist leaders personally. He was friends with Julian Harney, the leader of the so-called 'physical force' wing of the movement, until 1851, but his closest Chartist connection was with Ernest Jones, a man he respected and whose advice he sometimes solicited, including, on one occasion, about whether to sue the *Daily Telegraph* (Marx and Engels 1985: 33). When Jones died, Engels wrote to Marx suggesting that 'amongst the politicians, he was the only *educated* Englishman who was, *au fond*, completely on our side' (Marx and Engels 1988: 211). Others have been less certain about the depth of the intellectual agreement here; 'Marx's mate he may have been', writes one historian, 'a Marxist he was not' (Taylor 2003: 193).

Marx's engagement with British politics was also reflected in his often disregarded journalistic career, which included a decade-long association—between August 1852 and March 1862—with the broadly progressive *New York Daily Tribune*, then the largest circulation newspaper in the world, with some 200,000 readers (Ledbetter 2007: p. xviii). Marx's *Tribune* articles have a complicated textual history; some early attributions of authorship are unreliable (the articles were typically unsigned), and there are issues about the extent to which some were rewritten (when used for editorials in particular). However, Marx wrote something like 372 articles himself, and a further 15 with Engels (who independently wrote another 147 articles which were submitted as if by Marx). Many of Marx's articles reappeared in the weekly and semi-weekly editions of the *Tribune*, and some were reprinted in Britain in the Chartist *People's Paper*. One of Marx's articles (1979d) was even mentioned in a parliamentary debate about stamp duty; praising the tone and utility of the American paper, the veteran free-trader John Bright surveyed the contents of one particular issue of the *Tribune*, noting the inclusion from Britain of 'an elaborate disquisition upon the Budget of the right hon. Gentleman [Gladstone—DL], which did him justice in some parts, but not in others, and which, so far as the Manchester school were concerned, certainly did them no justice whatever' (Hansard, 1 July 1853). Marx's *Tribune* articles sought to explain British politics and society to a North American audience, and variously covered high politics (general elections, parliamentary affairs, and the conduct of foreign policy); economic conditions (factory legislation, strikes, and economic crises); and wider social and cultural issues (capital punishment, class structure, and the role of the clergy). Marx has been criticized for exaggerating the seriousness, and likely political consequences, of contemporary economic crises, but his articles have also been credited with an acute perception of both the personalities of high politics, and the shifting character of parliamentary coalitions in Britain (Stedman Jones 1984: 125). They also confirm Marx's fierce appetite for current affairs, with his regular reading including establishment dailies such as *The Times*, *Morning Herald*, and *Morning Post*; liberal and radical weeklies like *The Examiner* and *The Economist*; and popular periodicals including *Reynolds' News* and *Punch*. Marx begrudged his financial dependence on this kind of work, and, more particularly, resented both the editorial interference with, and the amount he was paid for, these *Tribune* contributions (Marx and Engels 1983: 339). However, it would be a mistake to dismiss this journalism as either uninteresting, or unconnected with his more theoretical work. For example, one article developed a satirical contrast between the Duchess of Sutherland's charitable concern with slavery in the American South (she had recently hosted a reception for Harriet Beecher Stowe) and her family's brutal record of expropriating land from the native 'Scotch-Gaelic population'. Marx estimates that Sutherland's transformation of 'clan property into private property' had resulted, between 1814 and 1820, in some 15,000 people being violently evicted in order to create grazing for 131,000 sheep (Marx 1979c: 487, 491–2). The Sutherland case later reappeared as part of the account of 'primitive accumulation' in *Capital*, where Marx (1987a: 720) gleefully referred to his earlier *Tribune* article and the mischief it had caused at the time. The language of these *Tribune* writings should also be noted. Initially, Marx's articles were translated from German by Engels and (less successfully) by Wilhelm Pieper. However, from February 1853 onwards, Marx felt confident enough in his developing linguistic skills to write the articles in English himself. Indeed, in December 1854 he warned the commissioning editor of the *Neue Oder-Zeitung* that, since his writing for publication for the best part of the last two years had been in English, 'German may give me some trouble at the start' (Marx and Engels 1983: 507).

One of the stranger threads in Marx's contemporary journalism requires separate consideration. Marx pursued a lengthy and determined campaign against Viscount Palmerston, the foreign secretary and prime minister (Hutchinson 1969; Taylor 1996: 240–3). Marx saw Palmerston as combining a fiercely reactionary foreign policy (promoting Russian interests as a way of repressing progressive forces elsewhere in Europe), with a growing Caesarism in domestic affairs (shifting the previous constitutional balance in favour of personal power). These views brought Marx into contact with David Urquhart, a highly eccentric diplomat, independent MP, and writer whose life has proved irresistible to Marx biographers in search of 'colour'. Urquhart's own monomaniacal campaign against Palmerston was driven by a heady cocktail of Turcophilia, Russophobia, and conspiracy theory. Urquhart portrayed the whole British establishment—save, happily, the monarchy—as under malign Russian influence, but Palmerston, in particular, was identified as having a 'Russian soul', and, rather more concretely, as being in receipt of tsarist bribes (Urquhart 1866). Marx used foreign policy and diplomatic material from Urquhart's publications, and more surprisingly—and, Marx would always insist, independently—came to agree that Palmerston was in the pay of Russian absolutism (Marx and Engels 1983: 395, 440). Endorsing this historically discredited charge was scarcely the high point of Marx's journalistic career, but he did recognize that, Palmerston apart, Urquhart's views were 'diametrically opposed' to his own (Marx and Engels 1983: 455). Intellectually, Urquhart was a romantic reactionary who condemned democracy, reduced history to diplomacy, sought to return to an idealized past, and saw conspiracy everywhere (Marx 1979b: 477). Marx joked that if he had shared Urquhart's wider views he would be tempted to identify the cholera morbus, recently found in Newcastle, as despatched by the tsar 'with the "*secret mission*" to break down the last remnant of what is called the Anglo-Saxon spirit' (1979f: 326). Predictably, their one meeting was not a success (Marx and Engels 1983: 412–13). The textual history of Marx's anti-Palmerston writings is not without interest. At the time they were widely read; for example, parts of his 'Life of Palmerston' *Tribune* series appeared variously in the *People's Paper*, the *Glasgow Sentinel*, the *Sheffield Free Press*, and in Tucker's series of *Political Fly-Sheets* where they are said to have sold 15,000 copies (McLellan 1973: 265). Subsequently, however, their apparently Russophobic content led to their being omitted from, or marginalized within, certain Soviet editions of Marx's writings in the twentieth century. (For example, Marx's *Secret Diplomatic History of the Eighteenth Century* was excluded from the forty-three volumes of the *Marx-Engels-Werke* even though its authenticity was not in doubt.)

It was Marx's association with 'the International'—the International Working Men's Association (IWMA)—that most secured his reputation in Britain during his lifetime. A contemporary magazine profile confirms that it is 'as one of the foremost organizers and directors of the 'International Association' that his name is most familiar to the English newspaper reader' (Bax 1881: 349). Marx played little part in the founding of the International, but soon established a leading position within it as a result of his drafting skills, organizational abilities, knowledge of the European labour movement, and sense of purpose (Collins and Abramsky 1965). The IWMA was made up of five affiliate national groups (British, French, Italian, German, and Polish), and its history is often told in terms of Marx's evolving struggles with French anarchism (Pierre Joseph Proudhon and followers), in the period before the Brussels Congress, and with Russian anarchism (Mikhail Bakunin and followers), in the period between the Brussels and Hague congresses. However, the International was more often preoccupied with issues that had a predominately domestic focus, including free trade, the Irish Question, land nationalization (the Land and Labour League included many IWMA members), the existence of a 'wages fund', the limitation of the working day, the place of strikes, and the use of child labour. The tendency to underestimate the British dimension of Marx's involvement with the International is often reinforced by somewhat exaggerated accounts of both the insularity of the British labour movement (which, after all, had a record of support for Italian independence, the North in the American Civil War, and the Polish insurrection of 1863), and the supposedly grudging character of Marx's support for trades unions and political reforms (which he actually saw as independently valuable and establishing vital 'elbow room' for further 'development and movement' (Marx and Engels 1985: 552)). Many of Marx's writings first appeared under the auspices of the International. The 1864 'Inaugural Address', written by Marx and aimed primarily at British workers, was published as a pamphlet with a print run of 1,000, and also appeared in the *Beehive* and the *Miner and Workman's Advocate* (Collins and Abramsky 1965: 44–55). The pamphlet 'Value, Price and Profit' which anticipated certain results of *Capital* in a popular form—outlining Marx's disagreement with the Owenite socialist John Weston's 'wages fund' theory (which denied that trades unions could raise the standard of living)—was first delivered as a paper to the General Council in 1865. Marx also wrote two much-read IWMA addresses, on the Franco-Prussian War and the Proclamation of the French Republic respectively. The English version of the first of these (it was also published in French and German) was issued in leaflet form with an initial print run of 1,000, and a second edition of the same number was printed a month later. This address was welcomed by, amongst others, John Stuart Mill who (without knowing who had authored it) declared himself 'highly pleased with the address. There is not one word in it that ought not to be there; it could not have been done with fewer words' (Mill 1991: 220). The International continued to campaign for recognition of the Republic, but Marx's most important contribution to the rapidly unfolding events—following the insurrection in Paris, the short life of the Commune, and its violent repression—was undoubtedly *The Civil War in France*. Published by the General Council in pamphlet form, the first edition (June 1871) of 1,000 copies quickly ran out, a second revised edition of 2,000 copies followed shortly after, and a third edition appeared in August. (Within months it had been translated into French, German, Russian, Italian, Spanish, Dutch, Flemish, Serbo-Croat, Danish, and Polish.) This defence of, and obituary for, the Paris Commune is widely and rightly considered one of Marx's most important political works; he stresses the Commune's historical achievement—especially its anticipation of the political forms that a future socialist society might adopt—and attacks the atrocities of the Versaillese then beginning to come to light. (Estimates remain contested, but perhaps 20,000 Communards were executed, some 7,500 jailed or deported, and many thousands fled abroad.)

These various political involvements also had their personal dimensions, and Marx's third 'exile' was neither as socially isolated nor as full of rancour as often portrayed (Cohen 1991: 120–1). By way of illustration, consider Marx's friendship with Edmund Spencer Beesly, a proponent of Auguste Comte's positivism, a professor of history at University College London, and (later) the founder of the *Positivist Review* (Harrison 1959, 1965: 269–77, 1967). The political gulf here should not be exaggerated, but Marx's hostility to Comte and positivism is well known. Nevertheless, Marx and Beesly, and their respective families, became good friends. It was probably Beesly's trade union connections that initially bought him to Marx's attention; Beesly was variously an honorary member of the Amalgamated Society of Carpenters and Joiners, closely involved with the London Trades Council, and helped found the International (although he declined membership of the General Council). Marx sent Beesly a letter of support when the latter was subjected to fierce personal attacks in the press for his defence of trades unions in the aftermath of the 'Sheffield outrages' (Harrison 1959: 38–9). Marx subsequently accompanied Beesly to trade union meetings, recording, for instance, 'a really fine, very impudent speech' that Beesly gave at Exeter Hall in London (Marx and Engels 1988: 298). Marx was also impressed by Beesly's historical articles, in the *Westminster Review* and elsewhere, describing him as the only Comtist in England or France 'who deals with historical turning points (crises) not as a sectarian but as a historian in the best sense of the word' (Marx and Engels 1989: 150). Marx sent him the first volume of *Capital* in 1867 and later—and more helpfully, since Beesly did not read German—the French translation of *Capital* in fascicules as it was printed. They worked together on Beesly's authoritative history of the International in the *Fortnightly Review*, but their closest collaboration surrounded the Commune (Harrison 1981). They laboured tirelessly to help Communard refugees, organizing emergency relief, and resisting demands for their extradition. Following Marx's death, in a letter to the *Christian Socialist*, Beesly (1884) acknowledged the 'wide gulf' between their views, but noted that 'Dr. Marx and I were always good friends; to the end of his life I had great esteem and regard for him: and I am sure that he considered me to be a well-meaning person' (adding, with an insight born of familiarity, that this was more than Marx was 'willing to allow with regard to most people who differed with him'). Marx was actually less stinting than this might suggest, having earlier recorded (to a German correspondent) that 'Professor Beesly is a Comtist and is as such obliged to support all sorts of crotchets, but for the rest a very capable and brave man' (Marx and Engels 1989: 92).

<h1 style="text-align:center">§4</h1>

Whilst casting doubt on certain familiar accounts of Marx's isolation from British culture and political life, I have thus far said rather little about his engagement with British *socialism*. The present section addresses this subject more directly.

Marx acknowledged the existence of a long and distinguished tradition of British socialism, although he often inaccurately labelled it 'English' (Marx and Engels 1976b: 461). In the mid-1840s, for example, he mocked Wilhelm Weitling for imagining that socialism was a contemporary French invention. Only a German, Marx remarked, could be so insular as not to have heard of Thomas More, the Levellers, Robert Owen, William Thompson, John Watts, George Jacob Holyoake, Julian Harney, John Minter Morgan, Charles Southwell, John Goodwyn Barmby, James Pierrepont Greaves, Thomas Rowe Edmonds, Joshua Hobson, and Thomas Spence (Marx and Engels 1976b: 461). There is scarcely room here to explore all of this interesting and disparate list (which includes at least one Irishman), but I will say something about Marx's view of Robert Owen. The latter seems a suitable case study, not only because of Owen's standing—'the founder' of the modern socialist movement in Britain according to Engels (1975: 386)—but also because the connections here promise to illuminate the relation between Marxian and (certain) non-Marxian forms of socialism.

Marx admired Owen as a person, viewing him as a 'really reliable character', the kind who draws 'fresh strength' from any setback (Marx and Engels 1985: 114). This positive view is echoed in Engels's biographical sketch in *Anti-Dühring*, which begins with the familiar story of Owen's social experiment whilst manager, and part-owner, of the New Lanark Mill in Scotland; successfully transforming a 'demoralized' population into a 'model colony' by placing them in 'conditions worthy of human beings' (Engels 1987: 249) and attending to the education of the rising generation with an experimental infant school (see Leopold 2011). However, Owen's public prestige declined rapidly once he started to promote communitarian settlements based on common ownership, and openly proclaimed that religion, existing forms of marriage, and private property were the primary obstacles to social progress. Despite being banished from 'official society', and losing his fortune on unsuccessful communitarian experiments in America, Owen's commitment to working-class interests is portrayed as unwavering. He remained convinced that as long as private property arrangements obtained, the benefits of increased productivity would be directed towards the proprietors, and away from improving the character and intellect of the class who produced the wealth. Engels's biographical account of Owen has its limitations; for example, the insistence on the impeccably communist character of his middle-period communitarianism is not wholly persuasive, and there is no mention of his later spiritualist enthusiasms. However, it accurately reflects the broadly positive Marxian view of Owen's life and achievements. Owen's name is said to be linked with 'every real advance in England on behalf of the workers', including the first law limiting working hours for women and children, the first national association of trade unions, and the first wave of production and retail cooperatives (Engels 1987: 251–2).

Evidence of an interest in Owen can be found throughout Marx's adult life. Owen featured in one of Marx's earliest (subsequently aborted) projects, designed to educate German contemporaries about socialism in Britain and France. In the early 1840s, Marx and Engels—together with Moses Hess—planned to include Owen in the opening volumes of a series of foreign socialist writings in German translation, since his work was judged to be amongst those 'closest to our principles' (Marx and Engels 1982: 27). And as late as 1877, Marx was lending Owen texts to Engels for his work on *Anti-Dühring*. Among his Owen books not in storage, Marx possessed the 'very important' title *The Revolution in the Mind and Practice of the Human Race*, but reported that his two-volume *The Life of Robert Owen* was missing, with Charles Longuet (Marx's son-in-law) identified as the likely culprit (Marx and Engels 1991: 263). Engels himself once owned an extensive, even irreplaceable, collection of Owenite writings—assembled at the height of Engels's own youthful communitarian enthusiasms (see Leopold 2010; 2012) and before his partnership with Marx—which was subsequently lost in the upheavals of 1848–9 (see Marx and Engels 1989: 477, 1995: 422).

Marx belonged to a much younger generation of socialists, and did not know Owen personally. However, he appears to have heard Owen speak on at least two occasions. He attended a lecture by Owen on the latter's eightieth birthday, reporting that 'despite his *idées fixes*, the old man was ironical and endearing' (Marx and Engels 1982: 360; see also Tsuzuki 1971: 32). These *idées fixes* are most probably the two central claims about human nature repeated endlessly in Owen's writings (and rejected by Marx): that individuals do not form their own character, rather their whole character is formed for them by circumstances; and that since individuals are not accountable for their own sentiments and habits, to imagine that they merit rewards for some actions and punishments for others is a fundamental mistake (see Owen 1993b: 33–5). Some three years later, Marx heard the elderly Owen intervene, at a meeting of the Society of Arts, to oppose the idea that philanthropy could solve the problems of class-divided society (Marx 1979a: 612).

Marx associates Owen with 'utopian socialism', indeed as belonging to that movement's founding triumvirate—alongside Charles Fourier and Henri Saint-Simon. What makes the socialism of Owen, and these others, *utopian* is a moot issue, but one factor is surely their conviction that constructing detailed designs for a future socialist society is a legitimate and necessary endeavour. This suggestion distinguishes utopian from Marxian socialism, and is consistent with Marx's own association of utopianism with the drawing up of 'pictures and plans of a new society' (Marx 1986a: 499; Marx and Engels 1991: 284). Owen's inclusion in this company seems appropriate. For a large part of his life, Owen was an enthusiastic proponent of grand designs for communal living, advocating 'home colonies'—formed on the plan of a closed 'parallelogram', and containing no more than 2,500 people living and working together—as both the means of transition to, and the final institutional form of, a socialist society (1993a: 337–407).

Marx's attitude towards utopian socialism is often misunderstood. The terms 'utopian' and 'scientific' socialism are not used by Marx in an exhaustive way, as if all socialisms have to be either one or the other. In the *Communist Manifesto*, for example, utopian socialism is portrayed as one of five extant strands of non-Marxian socialism (see Leopold *forthcoming*). In addition, it is a mistake to portray Marx as having an unremittingly negative attitude towards utopian socialism. It is easy to find textual examples of him praising, as well as criticizing, utopian literature. However, that is not to imply that Marx is inconsistent, since there is an underlying structure here which renders his considered view of utopian socialism consistent (Leopold 2005).

That underlying structure can be discerned by attending to two distinctions. The first is a chronological distinction between the original generation of utopian socialists (dominated by the founding triumvirate to which Owen belongs), and subsequent generations, including the various followers of that original generation (not least, assorted Owenites). The second is a textual distinction between the 'critical' dimension of utopian writings, concerned with detailing the faults of existing society, and their 'systematic' dimension, concerned with elaborating detailed designs for the ideal society of the future. The degree of Marx's approbation broadly tracks these two distinctions. He tends to be comparatively generous about the original utopians, and comparatively disdainful of their subsequent imitators. And he tends to be comparatively generous about the critical element of utopian writings, and comparatively disdainful of their systematic dimension. Marx's view of utopian socialism is thus not only consistent, but also more balanced, less one-sidedly hostile, than often portrayed.

In what follows, I elucidate the rationale behind these two distinctions, and show how Marx's assessment of Owen embodies this interpretative framework.

The chronological distinction helps makes sense of some apparently conflicting remarks about utopian socialism found in Marx's writings. For example, his praise of the utopians' imaginative portrayal of the socialist future is explicitly restricted to the founding triumvirate, and not extended to their 'philistine' successors (Marx and Engels 1987: 326). Whilst his condemnation of utopianism as 'silly, stale and thoroughly reactionary' explicitly refers not to 'the great French and English utopians' but only to their 'ineffectual' disciples (Marx and Engels 1991: 284). The rationale behind this chronological verdict—that the more recent the utopian author, the less meritorious their contribution—rests on a historical notion of culpability. Marx does not assume that the founding generation of utopians made fewer errors than their successors, about, for instance, the nature of, and transition to, socialism. Indeed, he thinks of both the original utopians and their later followers as holding broadly the same views. However, Marx argues that the intellectual formation of the founding generation took place in a historical context which inevitably limited their understanding in certain crucial respects. On the cusp of the eighteenth and nineteenth centuries, neither the objective conditions (economic productivity) nor the subjective conditions (proletarian agency) for socialism, were sufficiently developed for misunderstandings to be readily avoidable (see Marx 1986a: 499; Engels 1987: 245). These historical circumstances were sufficiently developed to provoke socialist criticism, but not sufficiently developed for that criticism to escape serious misunderstandings (Cohen 2000: 63). Consequently, the first generation of utopian socialists were not to blame for their relevant false beliefs because a correct understanding was not yet possible. The same historical excuse is clearly not available to their subsequent disciples and epigones who 'hold fast by the original view of their masters' despite significantly changed circumstances (Marx and Engels 1976a: 516). As a result, Marx is comparatively forgiving about Owen's erroneous views, and comparatively critical of later Owenites when they subscribe to those same views.

Examples of Owen's purportedly erroneous, and paradigmatically utopian, views—in this case, about the transition to socialism—can be found in the *Communist Manifesto*. Owen is associated: first, with an 'abstentionist' view of political action, criticizing strikes and other activities associated with class struggle in particular (Marx and Engels 1976a: 515); second, with a view of the proletariat as a passive object (in need of rational reform), rather than a collective subject itself capable of 'historical initiative' (Marx and Engels 1976a: 515); and third, with a commitment to a communitarian strategy for the achievement of socialism, whereby 'home colonies' would gradually spread throughout society by the force of example alone (Marx and Engels 1976a: 516). There is insufficient space here to assess Marx's claim about their erroneous character, but the ascription of these views to Owen is certainly plausible.

Yet Marx does not consider Owen culpable for these errors, because they were unavoidable given the latter's historical context. Marx suggests: first, that it was the undeveloped state of those formative circumstances which 'causes socialists of this [utopian—DL] kind to consider themselves superior to all class antagonisms' (Marx and Engels 1976a: 515); second, that in its 'historical infancy' the proletariat did, to all intents and purposes, appear as if it were a class incapable of independent action (Marx and Engels 1976a: 515); and third, that the inevitable failure of communitarian means—the corruption of small islands of socialism by their wider non-communitarian environment—only became obvious following the dramatic collapse of Owen's own communal experiments, including the 'long since defunct' Harmony settlement in Hampshire (Engels 1988: 348).

Owen may not be culpable for his erroneous views about the transition to socialism, but the same historical exemption is not extended to later Owenites. Consequently, Marx attacks John Francis Bray, 'one of Owen's disciples', for relapsing into the very same 'abstentionist' mistakes as his master, despite the fact that by 1839—the year in which Bray's *Labour's Wrongs and Labour's Remedy* was published—working-class struggles had developed a degree of independence and militancy that was unknown in the 'not sufficiently developed' historical circumstances faced by Owen himself (Marx 1988: 394).

(Of course, this is not—as Marx himself understood—the whole story about Owen's socialist followers. In addition to repeating some of Owen's mistakes, they also developed an interesting and important body of independent work in political economy (Claeys 1987: ch. 3–5). Some of these Owenite writings appear to fall foul of Marx's scepticism about theories of exploitation resting on 'unequal exchange', but he studied them carefully and his concept of 'surplus labour' may reflect their influence (King 1983). The Owenites in question— including, alongside Bray, John Gray, Thomas Hodgskin, and William Thompson—are traditionally called 'Ricardian socialists', a label which somewhat obscures their intellectual provenance.)

I turn now to the rationale behind the second distinction which structures Marx's considered view of utopian socialism. This textual distinction runs between the utopian plans for the ideal society, about which Marx is less enthusiastic, and the utopian critique of existing society, which he judges to be of considerable value. For example, in the *Communist Manifesto*, having disparaged their 'fantastic pictures of future society', Marx describes the critical elements of utopian writings, which 'attack every principle of existing society', as 'full of the most valuable materials for the enlightenment of the working class' (Marx and Engels 1976a: 516).

The rationale here reveals an important and perplexing feature of Marx's thought. It is apparent that Owen subscribes to a plausible—but non-Marxian—view, according to which, in order to achieve their goals, socialists need to develop detailed and persuasive accounts not only of the failings of contemporary society, but also of the institutions and ethos of any future socialist society. Marx rejects the second part of this plausible view, and denies that socialists should devote time and thought to questions of socialist design (see 1987a: 17). The issues here are complex, but three kinds of argument against the need for detailed and persuasive accounts of future socialist society can be found in Marx's writings. Very briefly, Marx argues: first, that utopian plans foreclose the future in a way that is undemocratic; second, that utopian plans presuppose a degree of predictive accuracy that is unobtainable; and third, that utopian plans are redundant because optimal solutions to the social and political problems of humankind are immanent in the historical process. In the obstetric language by which Marx is often tempted, socialists should aim to play the role of the midwives of history, not *designing* solutions for a future socialist society, but rather *delivering* the 'elements of the new society with which old collapsing bourgeois society itself is pregnant' (Marx 1986b: 335). Whatever the plausibility of this position—and I do not mean to endorse these Marxian claims here—it is apparent that Marx does not primarily criticize utopian socialists for the inadequate and implausible content of their 'blueprints' for the socialist future; he criticizes them for supposing that we need 'blueprints' at all. As a result, Marx is comparatively enthusiastic about Owen's criticisms of existing capitalist arrangements, and comparatively unenthusiastic about Owen's portraits of future socialist society.

Owen's account of existing social arrangements contains a 'critical element' of great value for contemporary socialists. Marx is obviously sympathetic to Owen's identification of private property as an obstacle blocking the path to social progress. Owen criticized contemporary economic competition, not least for encouraging the 'most inferior feelings, the meanest faculties, the worse passions, and the most injurious vices' (1991: 358). Marx is also interested in Owen's discussion of the character of work in capitalist society, a discussion with obvious connections to his own account of alienation (see Leopold 2007: 223–45). In the so-called *Grundrisse*—a kind of rough draft of the project that would become *Capital*—Marx (1987b: 99) excerpts several passages in which Owen portrays workers as robbed of their health by both the monotony and exhaustion of contemporary work, and the desperation and intemperance of their snatched moments of leisure. Marx also approvingly quotes Owen on the instrumental treatment of human beings in capitalism; Owen observes that workers are treated not merely as if they were machines, but more precisely as if they were 'secondary and inferior' machines—since capitalists typically devote much less attention to the perfection of the bodies and minds of the immediate producers than to the refinement of the wood and metals of their inanimate counterparts (see Marx 1987a: 406; 1987b: 97). That Owen was himself once a manufacturer would seem to lend these claims an additional authority.

For the reasons just sketched, Marx (1987a: 17) holds that socialists should refrain from writing what he calls recipes 'for the cookshops of the future'. Nonetheless he does identify some value in Owen's vision of socialism, his contribution to 'the presentiment and visionary expression of a new world' (Marx and Engels 1987: 326). For example, Owen is credited with having recognized the need to overcome the developing 'antithesis between town and country' to which capitalist development gives rise (Engels 1987: 278). In addition, and perhaps more strikingly—since it involves a rare example of Marx speculating on the detailed content of the socialist future—Owen's experimental school in New Lanark is said to have revealed 'the germ of the education of the future', in its adumbration of an education which combines instruction, physical exercise, and, for older children, some limited participation in the world of work (Marx 1987a: 486). That said, Marx and Engels are unenthusiastic about the dry and business-like prose in which Owen elaborated his vision of the socialist future, with none of the poetry and imagination found, for instance, in Fourier's work. As Engels (1975: 386) quips: Owen was too often inclined to write 'like a German Philosopher', which is to say he was inclined to write 'very badly'.

The structure provided by Marx's considered account of utopian socialism does not exhaust his assessment of Owen's importance. Two 'supplementary' elements of that assessment might be mentioned here.

In *The Holy Family*, Marx maintains that Owen plays a significant role in the history of 'materialism'. Marx's own 'metaphysical' and 'epistemological' commitments are not usually of great philosophical interest, except insofar as they appear to bear on his social and political philosophy. However, in that context, it is striking that, in some suggestive but frustratingly brief remarks, Marx seeks to draw a connection between the standpoint of socialism and a view of scientific knowledge as drawn 'from the world of the senses and the experience gained in it'. He sketches an opaque conceptual affinity between certain forms of British socialism, which seek to make the environment more 'human', and a certain type of French 'materialism', which emphasizes the impact of the environment in shaping human beings (Marx and Engels 1975: 130–1). This conceptual affinity, he continues, is reflected in the history of philosophy. More precisely, it is reflected in the impact of Helvétius (French materialism), through the mediating influence of Jeremy Bentham, on Owen (British socialism).

In the 'Inaugural Address', Marx also insists that Owen has a significant place in the history of the cooperative movement. Marx's view of the latter is complex. He does not think that socialism could come about as a result of the gradual spread of producers' cooperatives, and he maintains that the latter will always play a marginal role in capitalist economies. However, he also insists that 'these great social experiments' are of considerable value. In particular, he suggests that by 'deed' rather than 'argument' they have demonstrated that productivity is not dependent on class division, 'that production on a large scale, and in accord with the behests of modern science, may be carried on without the existence of a class of masters employing a class of hands' (Marx 1985: 11). The crucial nature of this result for Marx's own vision of socialism will be apparent. Nor is he in any doubt about the historical origins of this momentous experiment; 'the seeds of the co-operative system', Marx insists, 'were sown by Robert Owen' (Marx 1985: 11).

Marx sometimes illustrates his understanding of the relation between utopian and Marxian socialism with the analogy of the relation between alchemy and modern chemistry. This analogy helpfully clarifies that what we have here—since modern chemistry evolved out of alchemy—is a relation not only of conceptual affinity (between elements of utopian and Marxian socialism) but also of historical development (from utopian to Marxian socialism). Utopian socialism, Marx writes, 'bore within itself the seeds of [literally "contained it *in nuce*"—DL] critical and materialist socialism' (Marx and Engels 1991: 284). This important developmental claim was also evident in the original title of Engels's famous pamphlet *Die Entwicklung des Sozialismus von der Utopie zur Wissenschaft*, but lost in its now traditional English translation as *Socialism: Utopian and Scientific*. The analogy also suggests that Marxian socialists should respect their utopian forebears. As Marx insists: 'we cannot repudiate these patriarchs of socialism [the original utopians—DL], just as chemists cannot repudiate their forebears the alchemists' (1988: 394). Without repeating their errors, Marx always defended the first generation of utopians against those who would disparage them. For example, he once explained the highly polemical tone of his earlier attack on Proudhon as a reaction (in part) to the 'coarse insults' that the latter had heaped on the utopians, a group of writers whom Marx himself had rightly 'honoured' as the forebears of modern socialism (Marx 1989: 326). A remark by Engels (1989: 459) happily captures both the attitudinal and developmental aspects of the relationship here: 'We German socialists', he writes, 'are proud of the fact that we are descended... from... Owen.'

§5

Finally, I offer some observations about the influence of Marx's ideas on British socialism in the last two decades of the nineteenth century. Since this is a less neglected topic in the literature (see Pierson 1973; Bevir 2011), and mainly takes place after Marx's death in 1883, my comments here will be brief.

There is something of a consensus in the literature about where to begin and what to include in accounts of the first posthumous generation of Marxian-influenced socialists in Britain. These accounts usually begin in the early 1880s—a period of remarkable organizational growth for European socialism—and are dominated by three figures and two organizations. Henry Mayers Hyndman is a striking character with impeccable establishment credentials, whose frock coat and top hat were far from the only things—his conservatism, enthusiasm for empire, and anti-Semitism might also be mentioned—that made him the unlikely founder of what historians have seen as 'the first modern socialist organisation of national importance in Britain' (Hobsbawm 1964b: 231). Ernest Belfort Bax is a more cerebral character (Cowley 1992), an intellectual with serious interests in German philosophy, whose engagement with socialist politics was hampered by his overly academic manner and often idiosyncratic views—of which his purportedly 'egalitarian' opposition to women's suffrage is the most glaring example (see Bax 1906: 265–319; Hunt 1996: 57–63). William Morris, the third of these figures is, of course, much better known, but not always thought of in this particular context. Indeed, it can often seem that Morris's achievements as a designer and poet have obscured his considerable stature as a socialist thinker. The two organizations in question are the Social Democratic Federation (SDF) and the Socialist League. The SDF was founded (initially as the Democratic Federation) in 1880, and has a lengthy and complex organizational history connecting it to both the Labour Party and the Communist Party in Britain (Crick 1994). In the 1880s it was essentially a sect which split in two, giving birth to the Socialist League in 1884. That schism reflected disputes about external politics (especially the SDF's hostility to trade unionism and enthusiasm for parliamentary elections) and internal structure (especially Hyndman's dominant role within the organization). Those who left (encouraged by Engels) included Morris and Bax, yet within five years the Socialist League had collapsed under the pressure of destructive internal disputes about revolutionary 'purism' and anarchism.

There is much less of a consensus in the literature about the degree and manner in which these figures and organizations were shaped by Marx's thought. Their 'orthodoxy' in this regard might not be the only, or indeed the most interesting, question about their work and influence, but it is clearly a pertinent concern in the present context.

Hyndman perhaps looks the least likely to have been significantly influenced by Marx's writings. He thought of Marx's contribution to socialism as an essentially economic one, yet his understanding of that narrowly economic theory appears limited. Not least, Hyndman seems to have retained some commitment to the 'wages fund' theory (see §3) which Marx had argued against. In 1881, Hyndman had drawn freely on *Capital* for two of the chapters of *England for All* but referred only to an unnamed 'great thinker and original writer' as one of his sources (1881: p. vi). That Marx was both a Jew and a German seems to have made Hyndman hesitate to name either him or his work explicitly (Tsuzuki 1961: ch. 3, Bax 1918: 53). Marx's consequent irritation was both predictable and justified (Marx and Engels 1992: 102–3, 162). Hyndman's wider political ambitions involved hitching Marx's economic analysis to what, at one point, Hyndman himself (1911: 282) refers to as 'a more immediate policy of my own'. Hyndman's diagnosis of social ills often articulated the concern of Tory radicalism that modernity had corroded previous systems of order and leadership without effecting their replacement (Bevir 2011: 66–70). Moreover, that Hyndman's socialism had a national focus and a commitment to state-centric and imperial solutions, also makes it hard to square with Marx's own views.

Bax (1881) wrote an article about Marx's life and ideas as part of the 'Leaders of Modern Thought' series in *Modern Thought* (he also contributed pieces on Schopenhauer and Wagner for the same series). Marx himself placed the article in the context of British critics beginning to take notice of *Capital*, linking Bax's article with Hyndman's *England for All* and what he saw as a rather condescending piece in the *Contemporary Review* by John Rae (1881). Bax's article was judged 'wrong and confused' in places, and the translations he had included were weak, but Marx welcomed the young man's enthusiasm for his economic ideas, and for the achievement of *Capital* in particular (Marx and Engels 1992: 162–3, 184–5). (Marx was especially pleased that this public recognition had cheered his wife—who was also mentioned in the biographical part of the article—in the last few days of her life.) Bax identified Marx's achievement with his contribution to economic theory, rather than to the political and religious dimensions of socialism, which, on Bax's own account, should consist of 'international Republicanism' and 'atheistic humanism' respectively (1887: 81). More generally, Bax thought of modern socialism as needing to be supplemented by an idealist metaphysics of his own development (although owing something to Schopenhauer and von Hartmann), and the philosophy of history to which it gave rise (in which the 'logical' and 'a-logical' fought for dominance). Engels would archly suggest that Bax had only ever half-digested the German philosophy to which he was so inexorably drawn (Marx and Engels 2001: 78).

Of these three, Morris is the only theorist of originality and stature whose work has significant affinities with Marx. It might be thought that such a suggestion is undermined by Morris's utopian enthusiasms, given the Marxian rejection of the need to engage in socialist design (outlined in §4). However, there are some striking structural affinities between Morris's utopian novel *News From Nowhere* and Marx's own vision of socialism. For example, 'Nowhere' has finally overcome the divide between town and country, and—perhaps more significantly—its development appears to have followed the two historical stages outlined by Marx, and organized according to the contribution principle ('from each according to his abilities, to each according to his work') and the needs principle ('from each according to his abilities, to each according to his needs') respectively (Meier 1978: 201–394). This is not, of course, to deny the existence of important differences; for example, the revival of craft labour, the marginalization of science, and the static productivity of Morris's utopia would seem to represent points of disagreement with Marx (Morris 2003). In addition, deciding whether Morris's work was influenced by, or merely shared an affinity with, Marx's writings, is extraordinarily difficult. In some cases, it appears that Morris's ideas—for instance, his insistence on both the degraded character of work in contemporary capitalism, and the importance of self-realization in work to the good society of the future—cannot reflect his serious engagement with Marx's writings because they pre-date it.

These three individuals and two organizations form the standard reference points in discussions of Marx's posthumous impact on nineteenth-century British socialism. However, those discussions are not always without their limitations.

First, influence can be negative as well as positive, and a satisfactory account of Marx's complex relationship with British socialism would have to include something on socialist critics of Marxian ideas. In the late nineteenth century these critics focused their attention on Marx's economic thought (Hobsbawm 1964a; Willis 1977). That critical reaction intensified after the appearance of the English translation of *Capital* in 1887, but had begun much earlier; the Christian Socialist J. M. Ludlow, for example, had discussed Marx's economic ideas in the *Fortnightly Review* in 1869. Fabian socialism is perhaps the central example of a socialism which is widely and rightly thought of as non-Marxian, but whose character was shaped by its interaction with Marx's ideas. There are some positive affinities here; for example, some Fabian claims about historical tendencies within capitalism have a close resemblance to Marx's own views (McBriar 1962: 62–3). More importantly, even those parts of Fabian doctrine most opposed to Marxian thought sometimes bear the latter's impress. Fabian theories of rent, for example, not only emerged out of critical discussions of Marx's labour theory of value, but were also intended to maintain some of the conclusions of his account of exploitation, not least, that 'injustice' remains even in an ideally functioning capitalist society (McBriar 1962: 29–59).

In addition, an inadequate understanding of Marx's interaction with British politics and culture during his lifetime, can distort accounts of this later period. Some of the literature is guilty of treating Marx's thought as a 'Continental' import which was only released into the 'indigenous' intellectual environment in the last two decades of the nineteenth century. The implicit suggestion is that we can examine the relationship between Marx and British socialism, in much the same way that naturalists might study the destructive, or other, impact of the (Chinese) Muntjack deer, or the (American) Signal Crayfish on the indigenous flora and fauna. I have tried to suggest in this chapter that this is a misleading framework to adopt, showing not only that Marx's own work was engaged with, and influenced by, British politics and culture, but also that his ideas had escaped into that wider environment well before the 1880s. The availability of Marx's writings in Britain during his lifetime was certainly restricted, but it was much more extensive than is often believed. That said, particular areas of Marx's thought are under-represented in those published writings, and many of the latter appeared in radical periodicals and pamphlets that quickly became inaccessible (see Marx and Engels 1995: 422).

In short, accounts of the posthumous impact of Marx's ideas on late nineteenth-century British socialism need to recognize that his own earlier engagement with British culture was serious, sustained, and significant. From amongst its various threads—economic, literary, and so on—I have concentrated here on some of its neglected political dimensions, including Marx's appreciation of the distinguished tradition of socialism in Britain.

Marx's assessment of Robert Owen—detailed in §4 and summarized here—not only confirms that claim, but also illuminates the complex relationship between Marxian and utopian socialism. Despite his rejection of utopian 'blueprints', Marx approved of certain elements in Owen's vision of socialism (including his attempts to educate the young, and to overcome the division between town and country). More emphatically, Marx thought that Owen's assessment of contemporary society was full of valuable critical materials (including his appreciation of the degraded character of work under capitalism, and his understanding of the centrality of private property as a cause of these and other social problems). Marx did think that some of Owen's views, especially about the transition to socialism (the marginal role of the proletariat and the importance of communitarian experiments, for example), were flawed, but he excused Owen of responsibility for these mistaken views since they were unavoidable in the undeveloped historical circumstances in which the latter's intellectual formation had taken place. And finally, Marx allocated Owen a significant place in both the history of 'materialism' (with which socialism had an affinity), and the history of the cooperative movement (which offered a practical demonstration that productivity does not require class division). This sympathetic and generous assessment reflects a lifelong engagement with British socialism, and is hard to square with claims in the literature about 'Marx's low esteem for Robert Owen' (Hasselmann 1971: 288). Not least, Owen was acknowledged and honoured as a distinguished representative of the utopian socialist tradition from which Marx's own views had developed, and from which, he maintained, we could still learn.

REFERENCES

Ashton, R. (1986), *Little Germany: Exile and Asylum in Victorian England* (Oxford: Oxford University Press).

Bax, E. B. (1881), 'Leaders of Modern Thought XXIII—Karl Marx', *Modern Thought*, 3/12: 349–54.

Bax, E. B. (1887), *The Religion of Socialism* (London: Swan Sonnenschein).

Bax, E. B. (1906), *Essays in Socialism: New and Old* (London: Grant Richards).

Bax, E. B. (1918), *Reminiscences and Reflexions of a Mid and Late Victorian* (London: Allen & Unwin).

Beesly, E. B. (1884), 'Letter to the Editor', *Christian Socialist* (March), 156.

Berlin, I. (1948), *Karl Marx: His Life and Environment*, (2nd edn., Oxford: Oxford University Press).

Bevir, M. (2011), *The Making of British Socialism* (Princeton: Princeton University Press).

Black, D. (2004), *Helen Macfarlane: A Feminist, Revolutionary Journalist, and Philosopher in Mid-Nineteenth Century England* (Lexington, Md.: Lexington Books).

Briggs, A., and Callow, J. (2008), *Marx in London: An Illustrated Guide* (London: Lawrence and Wishart).

Claeys, G. (1987), *Machinery, Money and the Millennium: From Moral Economy to Socialism, 1815–1860* (Cambridge: Polity Press).

Cohen, G. A. (1991), 'Isaiah's Marx, and Mine', in E. Margalit and A. Margalit (eds.), *Isaiah Berlin: A Celebration*, 110–26 (London: The Hogarth Press).

Cohen, G. A. (2000), *If You're an Egalitarian, How Come You're So Rich?* (Cambridge, Mass.: Harvard University Press).

Collins, H., and Abramsky, C. (1965), *Karl Marx and the British Labour Movement: Years of the First International* (London: Macmillan).

Cowley, J. (1992), *The Victorian Encounter with Marx: A Study of Ernest Belfort Bax* (London: British Academic Press).

Crick, M. (1994), *The History of the Social Democratic Federation* (Keele: Keele University Press).

Draper, H. (1998), *The Adventures of the Communist Manifesto* (Berkeley: Center for Socialist History).

Engels, F. (1975), 'Letters from London', in *Marx Engels Collected Works*, iii. 379–91 (London: Lawrence & Wishart).

Engels, F. (1987), *Anti-Dühring*, in *Marx Engels Collected Works*, xxv. 5–309 (London: Lawrence & Wishart).

Engels, F. (1988), 'The Housing Question', in *Marx Engels Collected Works*, xxiii. 317–91 (London: Lawrence & Wishart).

Engels, F. (1989), 'Preface (1882) to the first German edition of *Socialism: Utopian and Scientific*', in *Marx Engels Collected Works*, xiv. 457–9 (London: Lawrence & Wishart).

Haakonssen, K. (1989), *Science of a Legislator: The Natural Jurisprudence of David Hume and Adam Smith* (Cambridge: Cambridge University Press).

Hansard, 3rd ser. cxxviii (1 July 1853), 1115.

Harrison, R. (1959), 'E. S. Beesly and Karl Marx', *International Review of Social History*, 4: 22–59, 208–38.

Harrison, R. (1965), *Before the Socialists: Studies in Labour and Politics, 1861–1881* (London: Routledge).

Harrison, R. (1967), 'Professor Beesly and the Working-Class Movement', in A. Briggs and J. Saville (eds.), *Essays in Labour History*, 205–41 (London: Macmillan).

Harrison, R. (ed.) (1981), *The English Defence of the Commune* (London: Merlin).

Hasselmann, E. (1971), 'The Impact of Owen's Ideas on German Social and Co-operative Thought During the Nineteenth Century', in S. Pollard and J. Salt (eds.), *Robert Owen: Prophet of the Poor*, 285–305 (London: Macmillan).

Hobsbawm, E. J. (1964a), 'Dr Marx and the Victorian Critics', in *Labouring Men: Studies in Labour History*, 239–49 (London: Weidenfeld and Nicolson).

Hobsbawm, E. J. (1964b), 'Hyndman and the SDF', in *Labouring Men: Studies in Labour History*, 231–8 (London: Weidenfeld and Nicolson).

Hunt, K. (1996), *Equivocal Feminists: The Social Democratic Federation and the Woman Question 1884–1911* (Cambridge: Cambridge University Press).

Hutchinson, L. (1969), 'Introduction' to Karl Marx, *Secret Diplomatic History of the Eighteenth Century* and *The Story of the Life of Lord Palmerston*, 13–47 and 139–65 (London: Lawrence & Wishart).

Hyndman, H. M. (1881), *England For All* (London: Gilbert and Rivington).

Hyndman, H. M. (1911), *The Record of an Adventurous Life* (London: Macmillan).

King, J. E. (1983), 'Utopian or Scientific? A Reconsideration of the Ricardian Socialists', *History of Political Economy*, 15/3: 345–73.

Ledbetter, J. (2007), 'Introduction' to Karl Marx, *Dispatches for the New York Tribune*, in *Selected Journalism of Karl Marx*, pp. xvii–xxvii (London: Penguin).

Lenin, V. I. (1963), 'The Three Sources and Three Component Parts of Marxism', *Lenin's Collected Works*, xix. 23–6 (Moscow: Progress Publishers).

Leopold, D. (2005), 'Marx and Engels' Considered View of Utopian Socialism', *History of Political Thought*, 26/3: 443–66.

Leopold, D. (2007), *The Young Karl Marx: German Philosophy, Modern Politics, and Human Flourishing* (Cambridge: Cambridge University Press).

Leopold, D. (2010), ' "All Tell the Same Tale": The Young Engels and Communal Settlements in America and England', *Marx-Engels-Jahrbuch 2009*, 7–47.

Leopold, D. (2011), 'Education and Utopia: Robert Owen and Charles Fourier', *Oxford Review of Education*, 37/5: 619–35.

Leopold, D. (2012), 'Socialist Turnips: The Young Friedrich Engels and the Feasibility of Communism', *Political Theory*, 40/3: 347–78.

Leopold, D. forthcoming, 'Marx, Engels, and Other Socialisms', in Terrell Carver and James Farr (eds.), *The Cambridge Companion to the Communist Manifesto* (Cambridge: Cambridge University Press).

McBriar, A. M. (1962), *Fabian Socialism and English Politics, 1884–1918* (Cambridge: Cambridge University Press).

McLellan, D. (1973), *Karl Marx* (London: Macmillan).

Marx, K. (1979a), 'Blue Books', in *Marx Engels Collected Works*, xii. 606–12 (London: Lawrence & Wishart).

Marx, K. (1979b), 'David Urquhart', in *Marx Engels Collected Works*, xii. 477–8 (London: Lawrence & Wishart).

Marx, K. (1979c), 'Elections. Financial Clouds. The Duchess of Sutherland and Slavery', in *Marx Engels Collected Works*, xi. 486–94 (London: Lawrence & Wishart).

Marx, K. (1979d), 'L.S.D. or Class Budgets, and Who's Relieved by Them', in *Marx Engels Collected Works*, xii. 63–6 (London: Lawrence & Wishart).

Marx, K. (1979e), 'The Chartists', in *Marx Engels Collected Works*, xi. 333–41 (London: Lawrence & Wishart).

Marx, K. (1979f), 'The Western Powers and Turkey', in *Marx Engels Collected Works*, xii. 318–28 (London: Lawrence & Wishart).

Marx, K. (1980a), 'Agitation over the Tightening-up of Sunday Observance', in *Marx Engels Collected Works*, xiv. 323–7 (London: Lawrence & Wishart).

Marx, K. (1980b), 'Demonstration in Hyde Park', in *Marx Engels Collected Works*, xiv. 302–7 (London: Lawrence & Wishart).

Marx, K. (1985), 'Inaugural Address', in *Marx Engels Collected Works*, xx. 5–13 (London: Lawrence & Wishart).

Marx, K. (1986a), 'First Draft of *The Civil War in France*', in *Marx Engels Collected Works*, xxii. 437–514 (London: Lawrence & Wishart).

Marx, K. (1986b), *The Civil War in France*, in *Marx Engels Collected Works*, xxii. 307–59 (London: Lawrence & Wishart).

Marx, K. (1987a), *Capital*, in *Marx Engels Collected Works*, xxxv (London: Lawrence & Wishart).

Marx, K. (1987b), *Outlines of the Critique of Political Economy*, in *Marx Engels Collected Works*, xxix (London: Lawrence & Wishart).

Marx, K. (1988), 'Political Indifferentism', in *Marx Engels Collected Works*, xxiii. 392–7 (London: Lawrence & Wishart).

Marx, K. (1989), 'Note on *Poverty of Philosophy*', in *Marx Engels Collected Works*, xxiv. 326–7 (London: Lawrence & Wishart).

Marx, K., and Engels, F. (1975), *The Holy Family*, in *Marx Engels Collected Works*, iv. 5–212 (London: Lawrence & Wishart).

Marx, K., and Engels, F. (1976a), *Communist Manifesto*, in *Marx Engels Collected Works*, vi. 477–519 (London: Lawrence & Wishart).

Marx, K., and Engels, F. (1976b), *The German Ideology*, in *Marx Engels Collected Works*, v. 19–539 (London: Lawrence & Wishart).

Marx, K., and Engels, F. (1982), *Marx Engels Collected Works*, xxxviii. *Letters: October 1844–December 1851* (London: Lawrence & Wishart).

Marx, K., and Engels, F. (1983), *Marx Engels Collected Works*, xxxix. *Letters: January 1852–December 1855* (London: Lawrence & Wishart).

Marx, K., and Engels, F. (1985), *Marx Engels Collected Works*, xli. *Letters: January 1860–September 1864* (London: Lawrence & Wishart).

Marx, K., and Engels, F. (1987), *Marx Engels Collected Works*, xlii. *Letters: October 1864–March 1868* (London: Lawrence & Wishart).

Marx, K., and Engels, F. (1988), *Marx Engels Collected Works*, xliii. *Letters: April 1868–July 1870* (London: Lawrence & Wishart).

Marx, K., and Engels, F. (1989), *Marx Engels Collected Works*, xliv. *Letters: July 1870–December 1873* (London: Lawrence & Wishart).

Marx, K., and Engels, F. (1991), *Marx Engels Collected Works*, xlv. *Letters: January 1874–December 1879* (London: Lawrence & Wishart).

Marx, K. and Engels, F. (1992), *Marx Engels Collected Works*, xlvi. *Letters: January 1880–December 1883* London: Lawrence & Wishart).

Marx, K. and Engels, F. (1995), *Marx Engels Collected Works*, xlvii. *Letters: April 1883–December 1886* (London: Lawrence & Wishart).

Marx, K. and Engels, F. (2001), *Marx Engels Collected Works*, xlviii. *Letters: January 1887–July 1890* (London: Lawrence & Wishart).

Meek, R. L. (1967), 'The Scottish Contribution to Marxist Sociology', in Meek (ed.), *Economics and Ideology and Other Essays: Studies in the Development of Economic Thought*, 34–50 (London: Chapman and Hall).

Meier, P. (1978), *William Morris: The Marxist Dreamer*, 2 vols. (Brighton: Harvester Press).

Mill, J. S. (1991), 'Letter to General Council of IWMA' (after 23 July 1870), in *Collected Works of John Stuart Mill*, ed. J. M. Robson, xxxii. 220 (Toronto: University of Toronto Press).

Morris, W. (2003), *News From Nowhere*, ed. D. Leopold (Oxford: Oxford World's Classics).

Northern Star, 4 December 1847, 1.

Owen, R. (1991), 'From the Manifesto of Robert Owen', in *A New View of Society and Other Writings*, ed. G. Claeys, 358–64 (London: Penguin).

Owen, R. (1993a), 'A Development of the Principles and Plans on Which to Establish Self-Supporting Home Colonies', in *Selected Writings of Robert Owen*, ii, ed. G. Claeys, 337–407 (London: Pickering and Chatto).

Owen, R. (1993b), 'A New View of Society', in *Selected Writings of Robert Owen*, i, ed. G. Claeys, 23–100 (London: Pickering and Chatto).

Pascal, R. (1938), 'Property and Society: The Scottish Historical School of the Eighteenth Century', *Modern Quarterly* (March), 167–79.

Pierson, S. (1973), *Marxism and the Origins of British Socialism: The Struggle for a New Consciousness* (Ithaca, NY: Cornell University Press).

Prawer, S. S. (1976), *Karl Marx and World Literature* (Oxford: Oxford University Press).

Rae, J. (1881), 'The Socialism of Karl Marx and the Young Hegelians', *Contemporary Review*, 40 (October), 585–607.

Skinner, A. (1982), 'A Scottish Contribution to Marxist Sociology?', in I. Bradley and M. Howard (eds.), *Classical and Marxian Political Economy*, 79–114 (London: Macmillan).

Stedman Jones, G. (1984), 'Notes on Karl Marx and the English Labour Movement', *History Workshop*, 18: 124–37.

Taylor, M. (1996), 'The English Face of Karl Marx', *Journal of Victorian Culture*, 1/2: 227–53.

Taylor, M. (2003), *Ernest Jones, Chartism and the Romance of Politics* (Oxford: Oxford University Press).

The Times, 2 September 1851, 4.

Tsuzuki, C. (1961), *H. M. Hyndman and British Socialism* (Oxford: Oxford University Press).

Tsuzuki, C. (1971), 'Robert Owen and Revolutionary Politics', in S. Pollard and J. Salt (eds.), *Robert Owen: Prophet of the Poor*, 20–51 (London: Macmillan).

Urquhart, D. (1866), *Materials for a True History of Lord Palmerston* (London: Robert Hardwicke).

Willis, K. (1977), 'The Introduction and Critical Reception of Marxist Thought in Britain, 1850–1900', *Historical Journal*, 20/2: 417–59.

Wilson, H. (1964), *The Relevance of British Socialism* (London: Wiedenfeld and Nicolson).

CHAPTER 21

THE ETHICS OF BRITISH IDEALISM: BRADLEY, GREEN, AND BOSANQUET

ANDREW VINCENT

ONE of the most well-known dimensions of British idealist philosophy to the present day concerns its political and ethical philosophy. In fact the ethical and political can often be very difficult to disentangle at times. The three philosophers who will be examined here are F. H Bradley, T. H. Green, and Bernard Bosanquet. There is though a certain imbalance which needs to be mentioned briefly. Despite the three being key figures in the Idealist school, their respective contributions to ethical and political philosophy are dissimilar. Whereas Green's contribution to both ethics and politics is well established, Bradley's work on political philosophy is both more elusive and contentious. Bosanquet is much better known for his contributions to political philosophy; in ethics he wrote comparatively little and claimed to have largely followed Bradley's and Green's work.

Despite the commanding reputation of Idealist ethics in Britain in the later nineteenth century, there are surprisingly few core works. The key treatises on ethics for the British Idealists, between the 1870s and the 1920s, were Bradley's *Ethical Studies* (1876) and Green's *Prolegomena to Ethics* (1883). Other Idealist philosophers, such as Bosanquet, J. H. Muirhead, and J. S. Mackenzie, also wrote more synoptic works on ethics, but the former works by Green and Bradley retained an assured pre-eminence amongst both critics and supporters. Even here though the picture is somewhat cloudy. Thus, Green's *Prolegomena* was not published in his lifetime and we cannot be absolutely certain as to whether it is published in the manner Green wanted. It was put together posthumously by A. C. Bradley (the brother of F. H. Bradley) out of published and unpublished materials. It is nonetheless still seen as a crucial systematic work on Idealist philosophical ethics. Further, Bradley's *Ethical Studies* was published prior to Green's work, and for many Idealists, such as Bosanquet, was the *locus classicus* text on Idealist ethics. Bosanquet had indeed spoken of Bradley's *Ethical Studies* as 'an epoch-making event'. Yet Bradley himself retained a much more ambivalent attitude to his own work, consistently refusing to let it be republished again in his lifetime, finally relenting in the 1920s, when he began to take notes for a second edition. He died before it saw the light of day in 1927. It was edited by Marian de Glehn and H. H. Joachim.

It is also worth noting that some key critics held comparable gloomy views (if not even more damning than the author) of *Ethical Studies*. This was particularly the case with Henry Sidgwick who saw Green as the only significant writer on Idealist ethics and was particularly dismissive of Bradley's work.

The present essay will provide an overview of the contributions of Bradley Green and Bosanquet. It will then turn to some of the key linking features of British Idealist understanding of ethics. It will finally draw attention to certain philosophical problems.

F. H. Bradley

With regards to F. H. Bradley we need to take note of his own initial caution to readers. He intensely disliked the idea that his work involved any form of moral teaching; in some ways this makes him unlike T. H. Green. There is a more sceptical demeanour in Bradley, although this is not radical scepticism for its own sake, which Bradley was equally critical of in his metaphysical writings. Bradley is also certain that his views could not be summarized in one essay. The rough essay sequence of *Ethical Studies* runs through a series of constructive appraisals of moral arguments, beginning with Essay I 'The Vulgar Notion of Responsibility in Connection with the theories of Free will and Necessity', and Essay II 'Why Should I be Moral?'. Essay III 'Pleasure for Pleasure's Sake' entails a sophisticated analysis of hedonist and utilitarian theories. This is followed by Essay IV 'Duty for Duty's Sake', involving a critical assessment of Kantian theory. Essay V 'My Station and its Duties' is the most well known and most caricatured of Bradley's essays. The closest Bradley comes to a definite ethical viewpoint is Essay VI 'Ideal Morality', but even this is, in a sense, superseded by Essay VII and the 'Concluding Remarks'.

There are three issues that have often baffled critics and readers alike concerning Bradley's book. First, it is premised on metaphysical and psychological assumptions which are not spelt out in *Ethical Studies*, but are discussed in other works such as *Appearance and Reality* (1893) and *Essays on Truth and Reality* (1914). In fact there is sense of provisionality in Bradley's argumentation, which can be frustrating for the unwary reader. Second, one further reason for this provisionality is that it is a dialectical argument. The essays in *Ethical Studies* have a sequence where arguments are stated, carefully analysed, supplanted, and gradually built upon. We are watching therefore a process of continuous philosophical construction. Thirdly, Bradley is philosophically a more eclectic thinker than one might expect. There are elements of Hegel, Aristotle, Kant, Lotze, and Plato, amongst others, in his ethical thought. Hegel's presence is stronger in *Ethical Studies* than other philosophical influences. It has been argued that *Ethical Studies* is probably the closest that Bradley gets to Hegel, in comparison to his subsequent writings. However this tendency to eclecticism entails that we should try not to pin his view down to one specific ethical position, particularly not to Essay V 'My Station and its Duties'. The latter essay has become encrusted with misinterpretation to the present day.

There are certain threads in Bradley's philosophical work which are worth emphasizing: foremost, Bradley philosophical style is to discern what might be thought of as the essence of a particular argument, rather than simply trying to articulate an author's precise words or thoughts. Additionally, moral ideas are developed in terms of units of ideas or wholes. Each whole is elaborated, problems are identified and then shown to reveal an even more significant whole, which can encompass the problems of the earlier formulation. One additional thread to mention here which can again be badly misinterpreted, concerns the organic relation between the individual and society. The basic point that Bradley makes here is that the individual wholly separated from the social is a vicious and imprudent abstraction, however at the same time the individual is not solely social. It is the complex tensions between these ideas which fuel much of the dynamism of *Ethical Studies*.

Finally for Bradley the formal end of moral conduct (as it is for all the British Idealists in this essay) is overwhelmingly self-realization. All action is in fact, by definition, self-realization. In acting we realize the object we desire. This might be described as a more trivial non-moral descriptive sense of self-realization. In moral terms what we ultimately desire is the self as a comprehensive whole. For Bradley, as for most British Idealists, the individual self is real only because she is social. She can realize herself only because it is as social that she realizes herself. It is when individuals rise above their selfish or immediate concerns and try to realize themselves via more capacious social and moral ideas—ideas which incorporate the best interests of their fellow citizens—that the self can become a more comprehensive whole. This is the essence of the Idealist account of moral self-realization.

The deeper background for this theory in British Idealism lay in the work of Rousseau, Kant, and Hegel. In effect, the moral agent was not seen to be governed by any causal necessity, but conversely (in potentiality) was a self-legislating and self-determining agent. The individual was thus essentially author of the principles he or she obeys. The Idealist tradition, in the main, adopted this Kantian-inspired theory of the will. Will is realizing ideas or judgements in action. As F. H. Bradley put it, volition is 'the realization of itself by an idea, an idea…with which the self here and now is identified' (Bradley 1935: 444–5). The background to this claim was Hegel's contention that the will is literally 'thinking translating itself into existence, thinking is the urge to give itself existence' (Hegel 1991: 4, addition). Hegel calls this notion of the will a 'self-determining universality'. Moral self-realization is willing an object which truly satisfies the self in the most comprehensive manner.

The sequence of argument in Bradley's book begins (as indicated earlier) with the criteria of morality of the plain man and the vulgar notion of responsibility. Bradley initially draws attention to the problems attached to both free will and necessity. Some of the basic concepts of action and will are articulated at this point. Essay II is entitled 'Why be Moral?' The question is odd to Bradley since it suggests something outside of morality, to which morality conduces. Internally morality does constitute its own ends. Bradley proposes self-realization as the unconditional end of morality, that is, I realize myself through actions which express the stirring of the self to be something better. One realizes a self in terms of a greater more complete whole, ultimately an infinite whole. As Bradley puts it: to 'realise yourself as an infinite whole', means, 'Realise yourself as a self-conscious member of an infinite whole, by realising that whole in yourself' (*ES*, 81). As indicated earlier, it is the abandonment of selfish, more limited ideas, and the adoption (in one's willing) of the broader or more capacious social and moral ideas, that constitutes the process of realizing the self as a more complete or more infinite whole in Idealism. This is the root to moral self-realization.

This sense of realizing oneself morally in a greater whole provides the key to Essays III and IV—that is 'Pleasure for Pleasure's Sake' and 'Duty for Duty's Sake'. In a characteristic dialectic move Bradley sees hedonism as too preoccupied with a multiplicity of concrete particulars, whereas Kantianism (duty for duty's sake) is too taken up with abstract universality. Both the Kantian and Benthamite hedonistic views are seen to be one-sided structures of ideas. Pleasure and happiness are so particular that they remain utterly intangible and cannot be generalized as morality. Hedonism and utility theory thus clashes with our ordinary moral beliefs. An ordinary life includes pleasure, but pleasure is not the sole end. Virtue, as such, cannot be a means to pleasure. Hedonism to Bradley is both immoral and impractical. Pleasures are always transient and unrelated, therefore a sum of pleasures is unmeaning. How could I even have a sum of infinitely passing moments which are still proceeding and passing? It is logically impossible. In a similar way it is difficult, with regard to preference or even welfare utilitarianism, to see how one could gain clear interpersonal comparisons of utilities (whether it is preferences, pleasures, or welfare). The greatest sum of utility, in any of these formats, is surely the wildest of fictions. Can one even, minimally, compare the pleasantness of diverse transient pleasures? What would be the mechanism for such comparison? Can one actually identify a sum of pleasures? Bradley thinks these and other questions remain wholly unanswered by utilitarians.

Kantianism instead of seeking particulars, searches for a universal. For Kant the self to be realized must be equated with the good will, yet for Bradley this remains totally abstracted from any concrete particulars. The idea of purely formal abstract willing makes little sense. One cannot will nothing in particular (*ES*, 152). Bradley indicates that Hegel has said most of real significance on this argument (*ES*, 148). Both moral positions—hedonism and Kantianism—are thus viewed as abstract units of ideas (wholes) which fail to encapsulate morality.

The logical sequence of this argument leads to the most well-known Essay V, 'My Station and its Duties'. Basically utility arguments are seen to collapse into subjective particulars. Kantianism, on the other hand, ends up with a purely empty formal universalism. The philosophical resolution to this dilemma is the idea of the concrete universal. The explanation of this is as follows: as Bradley notes, 'The self so far being defined as neither a collection of particular feelings nor an abstract universal. The self is to be realised as something not simply one or the other' (*ES*, 161). The social organism *is* the concrete universal, where self-realization is embedded. As Bradley remarks, 'It is the self-realization of each member, because each member cannot find the function which makes him himself, apart from the whole to which he belongs' (*ES*, 163). He continues, 'to will we must identify ourselves with this, that, or the other; and here we have the particular side, and the second factor in volition . . . the volition as a whole . . . is the identity of both these factors, and the projection or carrying of it out into external existence . . . The unity of the two factors we may call the individual whole, or again the concrete universal' (*ES*, 72). The idea of a non-social man is a fiction; the child is born into a living world of customs and duties. Thus 'when we will morally, the will of the objective world wills itself in us' (*ES*, 180). The self is a self living in a community within a particular station and the accompanying objective duties which arise from that station.

This latter argument can be read as relativistic in temper and Bradley clearly does think that morality is historically and socially inconstant. It is also apparent that Bradley is critical of this 'station' perspective. Not all citizens are or can be fully functioning members of their state or community and most states and communities are limited by other states or communities. The state or community cannot as such provide an infinite whole for self-realization. The station and duties theory does not necessarily answer all moral problems; indeed the community or state itself may be 'confused or rotten' from within (*ES*, 203). In fact, for

Bradley the station thesis fails to account for everyday moral struggle, particularly within the individual and between the individual and a community. Thus, the fact that the 'station' argument allows killing, for example by soldiers, can for many be a serious moral issue. The underlying logic of this argument is that humans can and do regularly differentiate themselves from their station or social role. The fact that morality changes and shifts in communities undermines any secure sense of moral absolutes within any station. Additionally a community or state may require self-sacrifice from an individual, thus undermining individual self-realization. Finally, when individuals pursue creative, artistic, or scientific work it may reflect purely personal endeavours which have no communal implication, despite the fact that their work may have indirect moral implications. There is thus a system of value which can and does often exceed the social.

In essence the station and duties argument is shown to be deficient in answering the question 'what is morality?'. It provides an account of the externalities of morality, but, as a systematic unit of ideas, it does not give a sufficient account of the inner side of morality. The station argument is thus shown to be too narrowly configured. The logic of this argument leads to the Essay VI on 'Ideal Morality', which incorporates the insights of the station and duties argument (premised on customs and conventions), together with ideals of social perfection (that is, imaginative constructions of personal moral conduct which go beyond anything that custom expects of us) and non-social perfection (the pursuit of truth or beauty in the arts and sciences). All the above are still encompassed within the argument on self-realization. The non-social ideal can indirectly lead to the benefit of society and to an extent it rests on the very existence of society, but, in itself, it is not focused on morality in any ordinary manner.

Overall morality, for Bradley, exists paradoxically in the context of the inevitability of the bad self. Unless the bad self existed, there would be no possible good self. Morality thus rests permanently on a living contradiction. The reason for Bradley's pessimism here is that morality can never exist perfectly, even though it desires that perfection. The ambiguities and deep contradictions of morality, in this ideal form, are further explored in Essay VII 'Selfishness and Self-Sacrifice'. In the final analysis we are always conflicted by morality's self-contradictory nature and the unending divergence of the good and bad self. This latter argument leads to the final concluding remarks of the book. Every human being is aware that they have, put simply, a double nature, and we cannot escape this troubling 'doubleness'. Holding to something like the contradiction and complexity of the 'Ideal Morality' position is thus probably the best we can hope for. Morality cannot provide any infinite whole for self-realization. The continuing deep desire for an infinite whole—to overcome the contradiction of morality—might well lie therefore for Bradley in another sphere altogether. In this context religion provides another perspective, since morality with its contradictions cannot be final. The more perfect self, the more complete whole might therefore subsist in an invisible community. Morality always remains imperfect, incomplete, and unfinished. Morality is, ironically, an effort after non-morality. This point also figures as the prolegomena to God and religion. This is the reason why religion figures at the end of *Ethical Studies*. Religion, in effect, gives us what morality cannot.

The central argument here is that nothing that exists is perfect or good, yet morality always remains committed to moral perfection as an 'ought to be'. The individual to Bradley acts morally through a sense of this perfection. Further, he suggests that unless we divined this perfect whole, we could not have that strong sense of the contradiction. Morality leaves us with a permanent dissatisfaction. It has no finality. Yet, imperfection implies, in turn, a standard of perfection. Moral duty often sees no difference to religion. However, for Bradley, it is a failure of thought to entertain such an idea. First, the moral ideal does not exist, as such, it always remains a 'yet to be', in relation to the practical world. It is thus dissatisfying to the agent. This is not possible for religion which demands the presence of the good will within my will. Second, morality can occasionally try to make a religion of morality itself, but if it does, it regards its object as real and therefore ceases to be morality. For morality, however, the object is not real. If it becomes a worshipped object, it moves beyond morality. In sum, religion provides what morality cannot; as Bradley comments, 'The ideal self, which in morality is to be, is here [in religion] the real ideal which truly is' (*ES*, 319). Finally, morality evolves to an end (which can never be achieved without ceasing to be morality); in religion, however, the end is always there present to the agent.

T. H. Green

There are strong parallels between Bradley's *Ethical Studies* and Green's *Prolegomena to Ethics*. They do manifestly reach comparable conclusions on the nature of will, freedom, and moral action. As to who influenced who remains a moot point. As a student Bradley attended Green's lectures in Oxford; thus, clearly Green did reach his own ethical conclusions independently. Bradley, on the other hand, certainly developed his own unique, one might even say idiosyncratic, interpretations of ethics. Where they do diverge is on a range of fairly subtle issues. Green was clearly more Kantian by inclination and his tendency was to advocate a particular doctrinal teaching on morality. Bradley, as indicated, was more directly dialectically orientated (at least in *Ethical Studies*) and more intrinsically sceptical and unwillingly to be associated with any specific moral recommendations or teaching. Finally, whereas Bradley thought of religion as separate from morality, Green was less confident.

The most complete statement of Green's ethics is to be found in the *Prolegomena to Ethics*. Like Bradley Green thinks of all action as a mode of self-realization. Trivially, in any human action the subject places before itself objects which will satisfy desires. These are objects which will, in fact, satisfy a 'conceived desire'. The object which satisfies the desire is termed a good. The capacity to *conceive* desires and act upon them is described by Green as the will. The will is what Green terms (following Kant) 'free cause' or 'self-cause', namely, it is the capacity to choose to determine actions. All human action is the result of will. The will implies a motive and a motive implies, as argued, a conceived desire. This conceived desire implies, in turn, a self-distinguishing subject—namely a self which distinguishes itself from the desire.

The central ethical concept for Green is character. Moral action is the expression of character, which is a quality of the self (and will) implied in action. The good sought by the person is distinguished by Green from 'true good'. The 'true good' is that moral object (or idea) which provides a more complete and comprehensive satisfaction. This implies the full realization of the moral potentialities of the self. It follows, for Green, that the true good can be described as the endeavour to achieve the most complete form of moral self-realization. For Green this true good is equivalent to the common good and this—sequentially—has profound social and political implications. The common good embodies the more all-encompassing realization of the moral potential of the human being. Such self-realization in terms of the common good cannot be identified with pleasure. Pleasure or happiness may be a by-product of moral action, but cannot be the end of it. The self cannot be identified with discrete sensations, since the self is the presupposition to any sensations. This is a basic philosophical point in Green's rejection of utilitarian ethics.

There is a serious metaphysics underpinning Green's ethics which is spelt out in opening book of his *Prolegomena*. For Green human will, intellect, desire, and moral agency imply, transcendentally, a unifying self or subject; however, they also imply more controversially an eternal subject. This refers to the self-distinguishing eternal subject implied in human knowing and nature. Green's metaphysical method, crudely stated, is to argue that knowledge of the world and nature does *not* explain the nature of knowledge. The producer precedes the product. Knowledge of the world, including time and space, exist for the self-conscious subject, since the concepts of space and time presuppose this subject. Psychological introspection will not tell us about the nature of knowledge, because it also presupposes the conscious subject. There can be no experience of the world antecedent to consciousness. Thus, Green maintains that pure sensationalism would be speechless. Paralleling Kant's argument for the transcendental unity of apperception, Green argues that the self, the subject, relates the phenomena of perception. The unity to this system of relations that we grasp in the world, and the fact that we communicate in detail about the world, implies for Green that over and above individuals as separate particulars—rather like discrete sensations for individual minds—there is logically implied a unifying eternal subject. The eternal consciousness or subject, in Green, is analogous to a vastly expanded individual mind. Knowledge of relations implies logically a combining agency. The eternal consciousness is the final transcendental unity of apperception which makes sense of the world and moral conduct.

Green is, however, still vague on this metaphysical issue and it generated heated philosophical debates into the early twentieth century. Many philosophers, initially the personal idealists, objected to the unexplained move from the individual subject to eternal subject. They claimed that there was a notable difference between the proposition that an external world could not exist without a cognizing subject and the proposition that matter and mind are inseparable. The former is a kind of personal or subjective idealism based ultimately upon Kantian epistemology, the latter is a form of inclusive Absolute Idealism. The latter entails the kind of move that Andrew Seth criticized as the unwarranted jump from epistemology to metaphysics (Seth 1888). Whereas the major problem for subjective idealism is solipsism, the difficulties of Absolute Idealism are legion. Absolute Idealism was accused of pantheism, the negation of the individual, avoiding the problem of evil and making nonsense of any distinctions between God and man, mind and nature, and God and nature. Green never really addressed these difficulties and tended to elide the problems. Oddly, he was not seen by most personal idealists as the primary offender on this issue, partly because of his Kantian inclinations, although Seth in his core critique of Absolute Idealism certainly does not think that Green is blameless, in fact he does critically target his writings. However, Bradley and Bosanquet, in the main, came in for much more serious criticism on this issue.

In summary, Green maintains that each individual subject ultimately implies transcendentally an eternal subject or consciousness. Nature also, as the object of possible experience, that is as a connected order of knowable facts, also implies something which stretches before and after the finite human individual. Individuals, as finite centres, do not hold together this total system of relations. Nature implies something other than itself, as the condition of its being what it is. Nature and knowledge thus imply, through their uniform system of relations, an eternal consciousness, a non-natural principle independent and not reducible to the relations for which it is a precondition. This eternal consciousness, which underpins knowledge and nature, is the *same* as that which underpins history and everyday moral conduct. Thus, the quality of a good human character is underpinned by this same eternal consciousness. Moral action is 'the expression of man's character' (*PE*, 120). Character, as argued earlier, is a quality of the self which is implied in action, in that the self presents to itself objects which provide satisfaction. Abiding or more complete satisfaction is found in the true good (which is the common good), and ultimately the truly moral self. Ethical character is the ideal self incarnated in the everyday moral life of the genuine citizen. When the agent unifies their life and will with the common good then they are reproducing, as far as they are able, the eternal consciousness in their own willing. In point, the central category of Green's political philosophy is citizenship, and it is understood in the same profound metaphysical framework. Citizenship (of a reasonable civil state) implied a consciousness of the moral ends of human life, as embodied within the institutional structures of the state, in other words, a consciousness of the common good. Green's notion of moral agency underpins this concept of political citizenship and both relate intrinsically to the eternal consciousness. The state is potentially the organized body within which this eternal consciousness enables citizens to act for the common good.

Bernard Bosanquet

The present discussion will not spend as much time on Bosanquet. As he admitted on many occasions, his ideas on ethics were largely derived from Bradley and Green. Bradley's *Ethical Studies* had probably more prominence. Bosanquet has a number of discussions of morality, but nothing comparable to the two prior discussed works of Green and Bradley. Bosanquet's own more synoptic short work, *Some Suggestions on Ethics*, was in fact not published until the new century in 1918, although it still closely reflects the late nineteenth-century ethical preoccupations of Idealism. Like Bradley and Green, Bosanquet argues that moral values are be realized in and through ordinary lived experience. One *must* live and become aware of the problems and intricacies of living before making any full sense of ethics. As he comments, if you 'cut yourself loose' from the lived process 'you would be nothing'. The process of living is one of self-moulding 'whose being shall incorporate what it can of value'. To work with values and to mould oneself is not a deductive process from ethical first principles. A moral life, if anything, is inductive. No rules precondition one's actions. The more precise analogy for ethics, for Bosanquet, is with art. The self-moulding and the role of ethics are thus conceived as 'artistic creation ex nihilo' (*SSE*, 158). It is thus little surprise that for Bosanquet 'the main root of individual morals is in social function—my station and its duties' (*SSE*, 32). This is an idea which has immediate resonance with Bradley's arguments. The basic idea is that the substance of most individuals' moral beliefs' is premised upon social life. Ethical values are directed largely to the well-being of the particular group. In fact, Bosanquet suggests, much more bullishly than Bradley, that historical, anthropological, and sociological knowledge of other societies and their ethical codes continually extends and amends our own moral beliefs. Similarly, new social circumstances will also act to modify our moral sensibilities.

Unlike Bradley, Bosanquet had a much closer appreciation of and direct involvement with actual social practices. He worked, for example, intensively in the development of social work practice in London (see Vincent 1984). The social or communal life that Bosanquet is referring to here is sociologically very familiar. He is thinking of families, communities, and trades—all are considered social unities 'in which the spirit of things has taken form and grown'; in all such groups we have 'an undeniable human value of a direct and universal type' (SSE, 77). In fact, for Bosanquet, in examining ethics, every person simply starts from where they are situated at present. It is the particular situation of the individual which is crucial. There is no use seeking out timeless aphorisms or ethical texts telling one what one ought to do. All this is beside the point. One has to concentrate rather on what is personally, socially, and historically relevant and try to perfect the 'possibilities they suggest through the innumerable strains and stresses of the complex life' (SSE, 121).

However, like Bradley, Bosanquet also suggests that ethics involves something both personal and impersonal. All moral action looks beyond itself. Thus, self-sacrifice is a process of both giving up and attaining something. That which is attained for Bosanquet is 'impersonal'. The impersonality of moral acts is parallel to other value concepts such as aesthetic beauty. This has direct echoes again in Bradley's discussion of 'Ideal Morality' in Ethical Studies. We also touch here immediately a dimension of Bosanquet's philosophy of mind. Thus any value always implies a personal dimension, that is, the value only has subsistence in and through 'self-conscious beings'; however it also implies 'something more than these terms naturally express. It implies an immanent standard of perfection'. The impersonality of value is partly contained within this perfectionism, namely, values are 'notes on perfection to which persons as facts are subordinate' (SSE, 11). This contention has links with another point. In any ethical act, for Bosanquet, it is the contribution that that value makes to an impersonal more perfect order that is important. This 'perfect order' can and does go well beyond us. For example, in self-sacrifice the 'man asserts himself in something which does not die with him' (SSE, 6). In this sense, in terms of the end to which value contributes, we should, in living for others, consider our own private existence rather lightly 'in comparison with values beyond it' (SSE, 18). In living for others, it is not the personal dimension which is crucial; further, it is not our own or other's sentient existence which is intrinsically important. Acts are neither good in themselves, nor contributions to a general welfare, rather, 'our main approval is for the higher positive values and for conduct that promotes them' (SSE, 22).

Bosanquet is therefore suggesting a number of things about the status of ethical concepts which have strong parallels with Bradley's work. First, they direct us to something impersonal and more perfect. As he puts it, 'The great values draw out the powers of mind, and harmonise them in a many-sided whole' (SSE, 41). Second, there is a telos built into ethical concepts which links up with this purported perfection. Third, the most immediate of such concepts for each of us are derived from the substance of our social life, from social functions and social ideals. As Bosanquet comments, in a social whole 'All minds throughout the community give and take their colour from each other, or, more truly, partake in different degrees of the one social mind and character' (SSE, 62). Fourth, such values are not individual things, in themselves; they arise from cooperation with others. For Bosanquet, we will often directly experience this sense of unity 'when we will the preservation of our country, or ... when we will the extinction of some social evil which is a shame and a sore to the consciences of all respectable citizens' (*SSE*, 40). However, for Bosanquet, 'In principle, it would take a perfect community to elicit and harmonise the whole mind of its members' (*SSE*, 42).

Like Bradley in his concluding remarks, Bosanquet sees religion as an important way of addressing the inner contradictory character of ethics. His response to the issue of religion is, if anything, a little more blunt and secularist in temper than Bradley. For Bosanquet no one is anything unless joined to something higher; for Bosanquet this could be, for example, an artistic or scientific idea or some form of philanthropic work. This point also links in with the Idealist theory of the will. The will is crucial, namely, 'a man is good when his will is good, and bad when his will is bad. It all depends upon what kind of thing he really has at heart when he acts' (Bosanquet 1889: 109). The good will, the desire to be good, is not about some other unearthly condition. The kingdom of God is here or nowhere. The idea that it is linked to any command of a transcendent God is, for Bosanquet, a mere 'figure of speech'.

What Marks Out Idealist Ethics?

Has Idealist ethics any very specific character, such as the Kantian categorical imperative or the utilitarian maximization of happiness? As indicated earlier, one popular response to this question has been to emphasize the credo embedded in Bradley's 'station and duties' essay. This latter body of views characterizes many makeshift estimates of Idealist ethics. Henry Sidgwick, for example, in one of the first hostile reviews of Bradley's *Ethical Studies* in *Mind* (1876), complains that his Idealist ethics does not really advance much beyond a crude sociological relativism (Sidgwick 1876: 548). Sidgwick was clearly both just wrong and ill-considered in his judgement, but it nonetheless encapsulated a very pervasive cartoon version of Idealist ethics, which figures to the present day. In general the station and duties essay and the crude sociologically inspired communitarianism represent caricatured misunderstandings.

What is missing in such criticism is another broad dimension of Idealist ethical philosophy; this concerns the principles which ought to govern our moral conduct. This argument can be found—in various shapes—in Bradley, Green, and Bosanquet. A philosophical ethics worth its salt should, in this latter view, be providing rigorous justificatory reasons for specific kinds of conduct. Some critics have argued that this dimension of Idealist ethical theory is hampered by the relativist preoccupations of the former 'station' argument. There is undoubtedly a philosophical problem here but it can be, in part, resolved in terms of the argument linking the individual's will and judgement with a particular type of rational social organization.

The easiest way to look at this latter normative argument is in the context of Green's arguments on the common good where it is stated most forcefully. The underpinning for this latter argument can be clearly seen in Green's *Prolegomena to Ethics*, which tries to give the philosophical grounds for what, in a sense, we know already and indeed practise. This sense of 'already known' reflects what Green, Bradley, and Bosanquet think of as the *concrete lived process*, which precedes explicit philosophical argument. It is the extant institutions of civil society, the laws, conventions, religion, and literature, which both embody and suggest such moral ideas. Morality is not invented, but articulated from within existing lived practices.

Green's philosophical arguments here involve an extended refutation of the idea of natu-ralistic explanation of human action and morality; this refutation is common to all three philosophers. Green, like Kant, counters naturalism by arguing that experience is not a chaotic manifold, but is rather the awareness of an enduring unified subject. He differs from Kant insofar as the experiential manifold *cannot* be accounted for independently of the activity of the human mind. This is because it is only minds or consciousness that can make intellectual relationships. The self is the author of the world it knows. Mind is its own act. Without the conscious subject—presupposed in experience—any experience would be impossible.

Green has a specific moral purpose in refuting naturalism. A human driven solely by natural instincts makes little sense of morality. It is in the individual mind's activity that morality can be found. In each individual is a spiritual possibility which stands above the naturalistic claim. Humans are distinguished from animals by the ability to self-consciously think about their desires. A conscious human mind pursues ends which are not caused, but rather self-posited. For Green, Bradley, and Bosanquet the true good is the object which truly satisfies the self, that is something which constitutes a more complete realization of the self. Pleasure or happiness are possible by-products of moral action. However the self could not be identified with such by-products. The good could not be a discrete passing sensa-tion. Epistemologically this idea of a discrete passing series of sensations was associated by most Idealists with extreme forms of individualist theory. For Idealism knowledge of the world exists only in the context of the self-conscious subject. There could be no experience of things antecedent to the conscious subject. A consistent empiricist account of knowledge (characteristic of utilitarian thought) would literally be speechless unless it presupposed a conscious subject.

Morally, utilitarianism was therefore seen as a seriously problematic doctrine insofar as it was linked in the minds of most Idealists with an unsubstantiated abstract atomism. Utilitarianism was seen to treat human individuals as, more or less, self-enclosed homo-geneous moral atoms, with similar feelings which could be mechanically quantified, and among whom a quantity of pleasures could be distributed. Its demand on institutions was that they justified themselves in terms of their conduciveness to the general happiness. Utilitarianism assumed a narrow uniformity of human nature over time and place. It com-bined the abstract individualism of treating every person as a discrete unit, with the abstract universalism concerning its view of happiness, which is taken to have an existence divorced from the concrete individuals who are singularly capable of experiencing it.

In rejecting utilitarianism, Idealists argued that certain objects of will are more conducive to self-realization. Moral activity is the pursuit of an ideal set by ourselves and to which we aspire; in Green's terminology it constitutes a possible self which we could become. In the moral sphere this entails constant endeavours. Freedom is understood as motivated action which *transforms* impulses and instincts to serve ends and purposes with which one has identified one's self. Freedom is thus self-realization. The moral ideal which is the object of free endeavour is the realization of the good will, that is to say, the will which transforms and transfigures the passions and instincts. If one specified this ideal in more detail, there is then no hard and fast distinction between an individual and a public good; an individual's possible self has an intrinsic social dimension. Another way of describing this whole social dimension is the 'common good'. This social and political dimension is though much more richly developed in the writings of Green and Bosanquet than Bradley.

The common good is the more complete realization of the potential of the human being. This entails a maturity of a character which wills the good, because it is good. An individual only turns out to be good if he or she takes the perfection of character, as their central endeavour. The good is common in being the same good for all. It is therefore non-competitive. Further, the common good cannot be any material object thing which could be contended for, although there could be a conflict between a moral and material interest. Putting material goods first is, by definition, selfishness. The common good is the moral ideal which should organize and guide a person's action. It presents a motive for action and a standard to evaluate actions. The large majority of British Idealists agreed with Green on this particular line of argument.

Green also suggests that there are criteria which allow one to ascertain whether a particular action, law, or policy actually reflects the common good. Thus it should be good for all, no one should gain by another's loss, and everyone should be considered equally in terms of loss and gain. This ethical notion of the common good is, in fact, crucial to Green's philosophical theory; it provides the basis for his whole discussion of politics. Laws, institutions, and states thus only have significance insofar as they contribute to the common good. These structures do not make men moral in themselves, that requires motives and reasons, but they can provide a crucial enabling function.

In summary, despite subtle philosophical differences amongst Idealist such as Green, Bradley, and Bosanquet, there are still certain important features in common. First, they are all focused on the ordinary everyday lived aspect of ethics and human experience. It is here that we find them trying to identify the major components of our ethical sensibilities. There is nothing transcendental, speculative, or overly spiritual in such an approach. If there is a kingdom of God it is nowhere else but on earth—here and now. Many Idealists are thus intensely interested in aspects of sociological, historical, anthropological, and biological study, in so far as what it revealed about humanity. Oddly, this is also one root to why they have been severely criticized—vis-à-vis the conservative caricatures of the communitarian-orientated 'station and duties' argument. Second, Idealists see both a social and a non-social dimension to human beings. We are profoundly linked to the social and derive a great deal of our moral substance from our complex social existence; however we are, in other dimensions, more than social. Humans are not simply social automatons. The ideas of the common good and the like do not imply any sense of a social determinism. Third, in all our activity we are self-realizing creatures and moral action is the supreme form of self-realization, positing a more rational or ideal self which we judge that we ought to be. Self-realization is thus a central facet of ethics. Fourth, with varying terms to describe it—whether the common good, real will, ideal will, or general will—such Idealists consider that the key facet of 'what we consider we ought to be' refers to the common good. This is a good we share in common with others. The common good thus embodies, for most human beings, the more complete realization of the ethical potential. Bradley and Bosanquet particularly do suggest that there are humans, superlative artists or scientists, whose creative status takes them beyond ordinary moral considerations, but this is comparative rarity. Fifthly, the role of the mind and self-realization in ethics leads such Idealists to reject all forms of naturalism and realism. It also led them to a deeply sceptical stance towards utilitarian arguments. Sixthly, despite the Idealist reputation for linking ethical theory to an *ex post facto* observation of communal ethics, Idealists did utilize arguments on the common good in a great deal of contemporaneous public policy debate—as well as a guide to personal morality—at the closing stages of the nineteenth century. They focused quite intensively on prospective normative justification. In fact such normative justification is seen as a crucial dimension of their contribution to late nineteenth- and early twentieth-century political and social practice. Admittedly this latter idea is stronger in some Idealists, such as Green, than others, such as Bradley.

Some Problems with British Idealist Ethics

Certain oddities do remain within Idealist ethics. One issue concerns whether Idealist ethical philosophy is simply a form of meta-ethical reasoning and thus has, potentially, no justificatory role. There is a complex relation here between ethical theory and practice. For example, Bradley remarks in *Ethical Studies* that: 'All philosophy has to do is "to understand what is", and moral philosophy has to understand morals which exist, not to make them or give directions for making them. Philosophy in general has not to anticipate the discoveries of the particular sciences nor the evolution of history; the philosophy of religion has not to make a new religion...political philosophy has not to play tricks with the state, but to understand it; and ethics has not to make the world moral' (*ES*, 193). Philosophy looks back at the world cut and dried. Moral practice is *not* something which flows from the philosopher's premises. The alternative view Bradley caricatures as the 'moral almanac' view of the world—something which he thinks plagues utilitarians. Green unexpectedly articulates a very similar argument to Bradley. He admits, for example, that most of us suffer moral perplexity, yet philosophical theories of the good are generally 'superfluous' at such points (*PE*, § 310). The concrete lived process is crucial for morality, *not* overt philosophical arguments. As Green notes: 'Any value which a true moral theory may have...depends on its being applied and interpreted by a mind in which the ideal, as a practical principle, already actuates' (*PE*, § 311). Consequently, he contends that moral ideas 'are not abstract conceptions'. Conversely, they 'actuate men independently of the operations of the discursive intellect' (*PE*, § 317). Such ideas are deeply at work in human practices long before they are philosophically understood.

On the other hand, we should be careful not to over-interpret these arguments. There is something far more subtle at work here. As we have seen, Idealists such as Green did clearly utilize arguments on the common good to justify forms of social and political action. For Green, for example, the general principle of the common good and liberty underpinned legitimate state compulsion. This was not an abstracted sense of the common good and liberty, rather for Green the idea of the common good was derived *from* the existing practices of his own society. This argument embodies a unique blending of Kant's universalism and Hegelian *Sittlichkeit*. Consequently, for Green to force children to school, to force employers to shield their workers from dangerous machinery, or to force the restriction of alcohol, were part of the same basic pattern. Such measures were justifiable on the ethical grounds of the common good. State interference should though at all times be directed to removing barriers and providing the conditions for the realization of citizens' powers.

Nonetheless there are certain critical issues which cannot be avoided: British Idealists, rather like the German Idealists of the early nineteenth century, did tend to separate out on certain key issues. Green was, in some ways, like Hegel in generating diverse responses to specific issues. In terms of an intellectual legacy, one trajectory from Green led to figures such as D. G. Ritchie and Henry Jones who placed more emphasis on the role of ethics in justifying the collective responsibility of the state. On the other hand those, such as Bosanquet—although unquestionably *not* anti-state—nonetheless tended to stress the role of character and individual responsibility as crucial in social debate. Bosanquet's position still utilized ethical argument, but in this case to constrain the role of the state. This was particularly the case in the debate between the Majority and Minority Royal Commission reports on the Poor Law in 1909 (see Vincent 1984). It also figured prominently in debates on unemployment, health insurance, and old age pensions in the 1890s and early 1900s. In the case of Bradley there was though more of a conscious distancing of ethics from such practical debates.

One further critical point to note here is that the common good itself did create problems. Green indicates, at points, that the common good is not an overtly distributive principle. The common good was neither concerned with the equal ownership of resources nor equal distribution. Material equalities alone could not achieve a common good. Material goods are mutable, finite, and scarce. Mutual respect did not for Green require therefore a radical revision of inequalities of property. However, unquestionably this argument gave rise to a number of hostages to fortune in Idealist argument. On one count it is clear that Bosanquet derived his theory of ethical citizenship, and containment of state action, from the principles outlined in one reading of Green's account of the common good. Problematically though, the common good can—in another contested reading—be seen to be identified with the realization of the particular capacities of human selves. Thus, for example, if a person has a particular unique intrinsic capacity for, say, playing the violin, then the fulfilment of that substantive capacity could be seen in as essential for achieving that person's self-realization (and thus achieving the common good). The self-realization of that person would be via the realization of their unique personal potential. This, for a society which values the common good, could have significant distributive or redistributive implications. It follows, then, that in an environment with scare resources, such a distributive scenario, premised on the common good, could lead to potentially deep competition for resources, so that each person could realize themselves substantively.

Green is clearly extremely hesitant on this issue. As indicated earlier, Green does suggest that the common good is *not* about material resources and it is not a distributive principle. Yet he does comment, for example, in comparing Greek slavery to modern industrial work, that all humans have the exact same 'undeveloped possibility'. There is thus an underlying expectation of formal equality in civil states. He continues, more pertinently, that no one in a civilized state can enjoy their condition of life when 'the mass of men whom we call our brethren, and whom we declare to be meant with us for eternal destinies, are left without the chance…of making themselves in act what in possibility we believe them to be' (*PE*, § 270). The implication of Green's latter argument, both here and in his writings on liberalism and positive liberty, indicates that materially some citizens might have to forgo some of their property interests for the sake of others' development. It is here that we find the intellectual grounds for Green's ethical socialist legacy (see Carter 2003).

However, it is still undeniable that one of the important facets of Idealist philosophy was its attempt to address the political and social world in a very practical manner. The ideas developed on the liberalism, ethical socialism, education, poverty, social work practice and citizenship, and the like, were all intended to engage subtly with the social realities of late Victorian Britain. This was though more complex than has often been suggested and not all Idealist argument bridged or even intended to bridge theory and practice. However, for many British Idealists, with a few key exceptions—notably Bradley—philosophy was integrally related to practical life and should be directed to improve the condition of society. The bridging of theory and practice was particularly evident in the work and life of T. H. Green. Green was often seen therefore to have had a significant effect on generations of students, including many academics, churchmen, politicians, and public servants. Thus the criticisms of Idealism which are sometimes made concerning its conservatism, social quietism, and non-justificatory stance, are only partial half-truths.

Another criticism focuses on the role of religion in Idealist thought. Some have seen Idealism as too preoccupied with religion in its moral thinking. Religion for philosophers, such as Bradley, Green, and Bosanquet, certainly has an important role, although it is not an orthodox sense of religion. In one reading, for Bradley, religion provides what morality cannot. Religion functions in the context of 'faith', whereas morality functions by 'sight'. Further, morality evolves to an end (which can never be achieved without ceasing to be morality); in religion, however, the end is always there present to the agent. For Green and Bosanquet religion is much closer to what might be considered (at root) a morally and socially better life. The conception of a kingdom of God therefore implies one thing—that is the best life for human beings existing now. Consequently in examining the relation of religion and morality we need to be much clearer about what the Idealist meant by the term religion.

Conclusion

Primarily, idealistic ethics is premised on the idea of human sociality, although it is a nuanced understanding of this idea. It is neither exclusively social nor non-social, it rather focuses on the subtle interplay of these ideas. Basically sociality implies that ethics is a body of directives, to which one is obligated, which are required both by other persons and oneself, within a form of associated life. We might call this a *communal directive* account of ethics. The fundamental aim of this theory of ethics is to bring together, on one hand, the individual's own will and judgements, with, on the other hand, the laws and institutions of an organized life in the civil state. The relation of the individual to the communal directives is intricate. It is not a relativist argument, such that *any* kinds of communal directives are permissible. Rather, such directives refer to the necessary conditions for creating a moral obligation—as embedded in a rational civil state—and premised on undergirding the freedom and self-realization of its citizens. There is thus a duty imposed, but the interests and particularity of the individual are lifted above any thin or self-centred concerns. Moral obligations occur from within the associated norms of a civil community of which they are an element. This idea of a social ethics is premised against the backdrop of an Idealist ontology, namely a form of social individualism. In short, individuals are intrinsically social and ethical, but they are also at the same time, more than social.

ABBREVIATIONS

ES   *Ethical Studies* by F. H. Bradley (2nd edn., Oxford: Clarendon Press 1962).

PE   *Prolegomena to Ethics* by T. H. Green (Oxford: Clarendon Press, 1907).

SSE   *Some Suggestions in Ethics* by Bernard Bosanquet (London, Macmillan, 1918).

Some Collected Works

The Collected Works of F. H. Bradley, ed. C. A Keene and W. J. Mander (Bristol: Thoemmes Press, 1999).

The Collected Works of T. H. Green, ed. R. L. Nettleship and Peter Nicholson (Bristol: Thoemmes, 1997).

The Collected Works of Bernard Bosanquet, ed. Will Sweet (Bristol: Thoemmes, 1999).

Bosanquet: Essays in Philosophy and Social Policy 1883–1922, ed. W. Sweet (Bristol: Thoemmes, 2003).

Bibliography

Bosanquet, B. (1889). *Essays and Addresses* (London: Swan Sonnenschein).

Bradley, F. H. (1935). *Collected Essays*, vol. ii (Oxford: Clarendon Press).

Carter, M. (2003). *T. H. Green and the Development of Ethical Socialism* (Exeter: Imprint Academic).

Hegel, G. W. F. (1991). *Elements of the Philosophy of Right* (Cambridge: Cambridge University Press).

Seth, A. (1888). *Hegelianism and Personality* (Edinburgh: Blackwood).

Sidgwick, Henry (1876). 'Critical Notice of *Ethical Studies*', *Mind*, 1: 545–9.

Vincent, Andrew (1984). 'The Poor Law Reports of 1909 and the Social Theory of the Charity Organization Society', *Victorian Studies*, 27/3: 343–63.

Further General Reading

Boucher, David, and Vincent, Andrew (2011). *British Idealism: A Guide to the Perplexed* (London: Continuum Press).

Brink, David O. (2003). *Perfectionism and the Common Good: Themes in the Philosophy of T. H. Green* (Oxford: Clarendon Press).

Dimova-Cookson, Maria (2001). *T. H. Green's Moral and Political Philosophy: A Phenomenological Perspective* (Basingstoke: Palgrave Macmillan).

Dimova-Cookson, Maria, and Mander, W. J. (eds.) (2006). *T. H. Green: Ethics, Metaphysics and Political Philosophy* (Oxford, Clarendon Press).

Mander, W. J. (2011). *British Idealism: A History* (Oxford: Oxford University Press).

Nicholson, P. (1990). *The Political Philosophy of the British Idealists: Selected Studies* (Cambridge: Cambridge University Press).

Sweet, Will (ed.) (2009). *The Moral, Social and Political Philosophy of the British Idealists* (Exeter: Imprint Academic).

Thomas, G. (1987). *The Moral Philosophy of T. H. Green* (Oxford: Clarendon Press).

Tyler, Colin (2010). *The Metaphysics of Self-Realisation and Freedom: Part 1 of The Liberal Socialism of Thomas Hill Green* (Exeter: Imprint Academic).

Vincent, Andrew, and Plant, Raymond (1984). *Philosophy, Politics and Citizenship: The Life and Thought of the British Idealists* (Oxford: Blackwell).

CHAPTER 22

....

THE POLITICAL THOUGHT
OF THE BRITISH IDEALISTS

....

AVITAL SIMHONY

I. THE IDEALIST POINT OF VIEW

....

THE political philosophy of British Idealism comprises a rich tapestry of intertwining concepts. Though the different conceptual arrangements by different idealists yield a degree of diverse normative political arguments, that diversity is located within a distinctive unified approach. British Idealism numbers many thinkers, among which are T. H. Green, Bernard Bosanquet, F. H. Bradley, Edward Caird, R. B. Haldane, H. J. W. Hetherington, Henry Jones, John MacCunn, J. S. Mackenzie, J. H. Muirhead, D. G. Ritchie, and William Wallace. The British Idealists approach political philosophy from within a shared interpretative framework which I call 'the Idealist point of view'. At its core lies a project of reconciliation which is supported by the concrete/relational point of view, the developmental point of view, the moral point of view, and the metaphysical/normative point of view.

A Project of Reconciliation

British Idealists situate their account of political life in a wider philosophical context. The distinctiveness of idealism lies in the effort to develop an adequate understanding of the relationship between Subject and Object, or 'how the knowing mind relates to the world it claims to know and within which the human agent acts, whether this world is to be understood as the natural physical world or as the world of political and social institutions'.[1] As Wallace puts it: 'The central...point of Idealism is its refusal to be kept standing at a fixed disruption between Subject and Object...Its *Idea* is the identity or unity (not without the

----

[1] Raymond Plant, 'Idealism', in David Miller et al. (eds.), *The Blackwell Encyclopedia of Political Thought*, 230.

difference) of both.'² An adequate account of the Subject–Object relationship denies that they exist in opposition, separation, or in one-sided dependence, insisting, instead, on a relationship of mutual dependence.

Mackenzie appropriately describes this approach as 'the Hegelian point of view'.³ It is a point of view, Mackenzie holds, since the emphasis is not on the specific construction of Hegelian philosophy; it is rather 'the general significance of the line of thought of which he [Hegel] is the most complete and conspicuous representative'.⁴ Edward Caird clarifies that 'general significance': 'The philosophy of Hegel derives its power from the way in which it...is a philosophy of reconciliation', according to which 'in all the great controversies that have divided the world, in metaphysics and psychology, in ethics and theology, the combatants have really been co-operators'.⁵ The effort to unveil that 'the combatants have really been co-operators' is the single unifying principle that animates British Idealists' approach to 'the great controversies that have divided' their world and the modern world at large. The Hegelian conceptual vehicle of reconciliation, as Wallace stated, is idea of identity in difference. That idea, in turn, was channelled through '*the idea of organic unity*, and, as implied in that, *the idea of development*'.⁶ They, Caird held, provided the best tools of 'the work of...reconciliation' which was 'the key-note of the nineteenth-century philosophy'.⁷

The problem of modern political philosophy, for Idealists, is how to reconcile the human subject and the objective world of political and social institutions. For in the same way that 'the privilege of self-consciousness brings with it the privilege of self-deception',⁸ the world of institutions might hinder the development of human possibilities. Idealists view the modern state as the reconciling ground of the autonomous person—possessive of a sense of personal freedom, independence, and dignity—with social institutions which, while recognizing and promoting the development of individuals, also give expression to their mutual recognition and development.

British Idealists share a commitment to a vision of the good society (or polity) as a community of mutually dependent and mutually self-developing persons. It can be described as a common-good society in that membership in such a society is constitutive of the good of each member. Therefore, for a member to support the practices and institutions of such a society is to promote both his/her own good and the good of others. As a common good, the good polity contrasts with both 'private good society' and 'collective good society'. Whereas the former is formed by individuals who pursue ends which are logically independent of the ends of other individuals and hence can be enjoyed in separation from others, 'collective good society' exists beyond and above the good of its members. In a common-good society, self-development of members cannot be attained in separation from, and independently of, others; it is, rather, a joint or cooperative project.

---

² William Wallace, *Prolegomena to the Study of Hegel's Philosophy*, 148. See also Wallace, *Lectures and Essays on Natural Theology and Ethics*, 85, 118.

³ J. S. Mackenzie, 'The Hegelian Point of View', *Mind*, NS 11/41 (Jan. 1902), 54–71.

⁴ Mackenzie, 'The Hegelian Point of View', 56.

⁵ E. Caird, 'Philosophy', in Alfred Russel Wallace et al., *The Progress of the Century*, 155.

⁶ Caird, 'Philosophy', 150–1.

⁷ Caird, 'Philosophy', 155. Reconciliation of the individual and society underpins Henry Jones's writing, e.g. 'The Social Organism', in A. Seth and R. B. Haldane (eds.), *Essays in Philosophical Criticism*, and *The Working Faith of the Social Reformer*, chs. x–xi.

⁸ T. H. Green, 'Popular Philosophy in Its Relation to Life', in *Works*, iii. 105.

The main components of the good society are, first, the state conceptualized as a 'society of societies' which functions as an enabling agency. It enables all its members to make the best of themselves, to exercise freedom, by maintaining a system of rights. Second, full membership in the good society is expressed in the concept of citizenship. Citizens have an obligation of support towards the state that enables their self-development. Reciprocity of services between 'enabling state' and 'ethical citizenship' lies at the heart of the common-good society. That society, in turn, has special affinity with relational social ontology which Idealists employ to shape the boundaries of what is politically desirable.

To get a good handle on idealist political philosophy is to explore the conceptual structure that forges their ideal of the common-good society: the state, rights, political obligation, citizenship, and freedom. First, however, a brief look at the points of view which together with the project of reconciliation forge the shared 'Idealist point of view'.

The Concrete/Relational Point of View

This flows directly from the concept of organic unity. Contrasting 'concrete' with 'abstract', Idealists insist on 'relational' as the proper framework from which to approach political issues, and the need 'to learn to "think things together;" in other words, to recognize the organic relation' that connects things.[9] To do so is to explore the way in which universal ideas take shape in particular instances of human experience.

The Developmental Point of View

The idea of teleological development is, for Idealists, the twin of the organic concept and likewise functions as a tool of reconciliation. They similarly use 'evolution' which fits better with the impact Darwin has on the discourse of the time. A prime example is Ritchie's effort to wed Darwin's biological idea of evolution to Hegel's philosophical idea of development, using both to correct the abstraction and individualism of utilitarianism.[10]

The Moral Point of View

Idealists view the good polity as rooted in a rich conception of the human good which, in turn, yields a commitment to securing good-enabling institutions. They view the human good as a social good (common good) in a particular mutualist way: 'the realisation of any one individual's highest life is impossible without the co-operation of others, but... the realisation of other' lives is an essential element... in the realisation of our own'.[11] Further, the human good is perfectionist. Idealist perfectionism, however, is ethical, not political. The good, moreover, is pluralist, not monist, and teleological, but not maximizing.

---

[9] E. Caird, 'Philosophy', 164.
[10] D. G. Ritchie, 'Darwin and Hegel', *Proceedings of the Aristotelian Society*, 1/44 (1890–1), 55–74.
[11] J. S. Mackenzie, *An Introduction to Social Philosophy*, 235.

The Metaphysical/Normative Point of View

Not even Rawls denies the inevitability of metaphysics: 'Political liberalism…aims for a political conception of justice as a free standing view. It offers no specific metaphysical or epistemological doctrine *beyond what is implied by the political conception itself*.'[12] He does, however, hold that the metaphysical is politically useless. If 'useless' means that no direct inference from metaphysics to particular moral or political issues is possible, then this is hardly in contention. Nor does it entail, for Idealists, that metaphysics is practically useless. For 'man, above all the modern man, must theorize his practice, and the failure adequately to do so, must cripple the practice itself'.[13] Green's target is 'popular philosophy' which, he argues, cripples human practice by theorizing it inadequately. Indeed, Green and other Idealists tend to see their task as analogous to the task of 'the reconstruction of morals and politics' undertaken by Plato and Aristotle in face of 'the unsettlement of practical ideas' in 'the Greek age of sophistry'. In face of 'the modern "unsettlement" of practical ideas which resulted from moral and political 'popular philosophy', British Idealists set out to achieve 'the reconstruction of morals and politics' by 'a counter theory'.[14]

'A New Philosophy was Needed': A Third Way and Third Ways

With regard to normative politics, British Idealists would subscribe to 'a third way' approach. In the context of the ideological argument of their time, they reject both whole-sale laissez-faire capitalism—the 'nightwatchman' state, market model of politics and of human relations at large—and large-scale collectivism, state socialism (mechanical social-ism), and the 'social efficiency' model of human relations. A 'third way', however, does not, and cannot, occupy a single determinate normative political programme and this for two reasons: first, the valuational terms, the concepts, that make up the Idealist argument are not empirically operational, and second, the valuational concepts themselves are contested. Further, since Idealists insist on rejecting abstract, a priori political principles and on the importance of being familiar with the facts, with concrete reality, and since the facts are not divorced from the way they are perceived, the facts themselves constitute a possible source of different interpretations.

To make this point is, by no means, to undervalue the contribution of Idealist political philosophy. It is, rather, to locate it properly in 'the reconstruction of morals and politics' by 'a counter-theory', as Idealists did. The contribution of British Idealism lies in providing a distinctive conceptual framework which was capable of advancing the political argument at the time and political discourse afterwards, and this in two ways. First, the reconciling approach has the capacity to expose the futility of a discourse of dichotomies which pre-vailed at the time—individualism–collectivism—and which has continued to raise its bar-ren head in more recent dichotomous controversies, such as between communitarians and

---

[12] John Rawls, *Political Liberalism*, 10; emphasis added; see also 29, including n. 31.
[13] Green, 'Popular Philosophy in Its Relation to Life', 124.
[14] Green, 'Popular Philosophy in Its Relation to Life', 96–7.

liberals as well as between (civic) republicans and liberals. Second, Idealists provided an alternative conceptual-normative toolkit to the prevailing individualist one at the time.

Barker still makes the point best:

> Not a modification of the Old Benthamite premises [which Mill accomplished], but a new philosophy was needed, and that philosophy was provided by the idealist school.... The vital relation between the life of the individual and the life of the community,... the dependence of the individual, for all his rights and for all his liberty, on his membership of the community; the correlative duty of the community to guarantee the individual all his rights (in other words all the conditions necessary for his, and therefore for its own, full moral development—these were the premises of the new philosophy.[15]

To explore the main components of the Idealist 'new philosophy' I now turn, beginning with the idea of the state.

II. Concepts and Themes

The Nature of the 'State': The 'Society of Societies'

It should come as no surprise that Idealist thinking about the state provoked much confusion, misinterpretation, criticism, and controversy that has lingered well into the twentieth century and, to an extent, even beyond. For one thing, as Green put it, Idealists think 'of the "state" in a way not familiar to Englishmen'.[16] The Idealist conception of the state owes much to Plato and Aristotle as well as to Rousseau and Hegel. The controversy that surrounded Bosanquet's apparent glorification of the state, including what appeared to be a confusion of 'state' and 'society', has further complicated things. Moreover, 'there was not in Britain one encompassing idea (one might say 'ideal-type') of the state, incorporating moral, legal and institutional elements'.[17] Nor does it help that the Idealist conception of the 'state' encompasses a host of issues such as sovereignty, justification of political obligation, and the more specific issue of state interference. The latter issue partly explains the renewed interest in the concept of the state in the last third of the nineteenth century.

My concern here is with the nature of the state. Conceptualizing social complexity as 'state', Idealists regarded it not as an external order constraining human passions, as Burke did, but rather, in Hegelian fashion, as emanating from will and purpose which are based on the moral possibilities of human nature. They regarded the state, in turn, as the form in which human possibilities express themselves. The Hegelian underpinning of this interpretation of the state is evident in Wallace's answer to the question

---

[15]   E. Barker, *Political Thought in England from Spencer to To-Day*, 11–12.

[16]   Green, 'On the Different Senses of "Freedom" as Applied to Will and to the Moral Progress of Man' (hereafter DSF), sect. 4); emphasis added.

[17]   Cécile Laborde, 'The Concept of the State in British and French Political Thought', *Political Studies*, 48 (2000), 551.

what, according to Hegel, is the State? Not something, assuredly that lives in London, and has its holy of holies in the offices of the Treasury: not something which lives for the time being in the Cabinet, and in the upper and influential circle of the bureaucracy. The State, as Hegel conceives it, is *the completed organization, the self-contained social form, in which human life can develop its ideal activities*: it is an organization in which the family...in which the interdependence of industrial effort, commerce, and social and commercial demands and supply...while the more purely political organization itself blends[18]

Wallace explains the familiar Hegelian narrow and broad senses of 'state' as a community encompassing the whole range of human institutions and 'state' in the narrow sense of the state as 'the more purely political organization'. British Idealists focus on the 'state-as-community': 'The State, as Hegel conceives it, is *the completed organization, the self-contained social form, in which human life can develop its ideal activities.*' The italicized words express the central idea, namely that the possibility of developing the human capacity of realizing the best in oneself, lies in the integration of the modern individual with the complex network of institutions which makes up the modern state.

That the individualist conception of the state fails to provide such integration is the nub of Green's criticism of contractarian theorists. The claim that the state is 'the society of societies'[19] is uniquely suitable for the purpose of reintegration. That claim is more than a rejection of the individualist account of the state as a mere aggregate of individuals;[20] it entails much more than the sociological point that individuals are social beings. In criticizing social contract accounts of the state, Green charges that they

> make no inquiry into the development of society and of man through society. They take no account of other forms of community than that regulated by a supreme coercive power, either in the way of investigating their historical origin...or of considering the ideas and states of mind which they imply or which render them possible. They leave out of sight the process by which men have been clothed with rights and duties, and with senses of rights and duties which are neither natural nor derived from a sovereign power.[21]

Social contract theorists, Green complains, neglect the entire social fabric of the state in terms of intermediary groups—the 'societies', social institutions, and practices which function as a rich repertoire of shared values and collective achievements. The idea of the general will is clearly at work here. The point I wish to emphasize here, however, is that, with Oakeshott, British Idealists believe that social practices are not a constraint on, but really a condition of, the meaningful development and exercise of individuality.[22] Caird makes the same point in terms of social relations: 'If we regard ourselves as mere atoms, having an existence and a happiness apart from all relations with men and things into which we have been brought, these relations will seem to us so many fetters upon our liberty.'[23]

The Idealist conceptualization of the state as 'the society of societies' anticipates Rawls's argument of a social union of social unions. At the heart of his argument lies the claim that

[18] Wallace, *Lectures and Essays*, 120–1; emphasis added. See also F. H. Bradley, *Ethical Studies*, 157.
[19] Green, *Principles of Political Obligation* (hereafter *LPPO*), sect. 142.
[20] Green, *LPPO*, sect. 134.
[21] Green, *LPPO*, sect. 113.
[22] Michael Oakeshott, *Human Conduct*, 78–80.
[23] Edward Caird, *Ethical Philosophy*, 21.

no one can become a complete exemplar of humanity; for 'we are by ourselves but parts of what we might be'.[24] We need each other to complete our humanity. Hence, it is only in a social union that 'the members of a community participate in one another's nature...the self is realized in the activities of many selves'.[25] Green and British Idealists generally could not agree more.[26] The good of community of complementary human goods cannot, however, be realized without justice. As Rawls puts it: 'What binds a society's efforts into one social union is the mutual recognition and acceptance of the principles of justice; it is this general affirmation which extends the ties of identification over the whole community...Individual and group accomplishments are no longer seen as just so many separate personal goods.'[27] Setting aside Rawls's hypothetical contract, this is very much the impetus behind Green's system of rights understood as community of mutual recognition: 'the state being for its members the society of societies—the society in which all their claims upon each other are mutually adjusted'.[28]

It would be a mistake to claim, as critics of Idealists claimed at the time, that the Idealist conceptualization of the state as 'the society of societies' confuses 'state' and 'society'. Indeed, 'Positing "society" against "the state"', it has been argued, 'made little sense even for radical pluralists, as the concept of state was hardly ever formulated in mainstream political discourse as the (normative) antithesis of society. As a consequence, "anti-statism" referred to the attack on discrete aspects of the state idea or the state apparatus. When Herbert Spencer wrote his polemical *The Man Versus the State*, he targeted governmental socialism, but not the Victorian social order also represented by "the state".'[29]

The state as the society of societies captures best, I suggest, Bosanquet's own conception of the state. 'Whatever vitality there is in the reaction against the long tradition of political theory which began with Plato and has continued in the great line of his Idealist successors comes mainly from the apparent neglect by certain of its supporters of real differentiation of social structure and interest'.[30] So said Hetherington and Muirhead in 1918, acknowledging the intense criticism levelled by pluralists at Bosanquet's account of the state. Yet, as their reference to 'the apparent neglect' suggests, they believed that it is quite possible, while availing themselves of that criticism, 'to restate the essentials of the classical Idealist conception in such a way as to show that there is room in it for the utmost diversity of social functions'.

Bosanquet's defence of pluralism is a requirement of the concept of identity-in-difference. 'Difference' accounts for the essential role of multiple institutions, 'all that is "social"', namely the sphere 'Between visible activities backed by the force of the State, and the narrowest self-assertion, equally visible, of the separate, or would-be separate, human person, the whole social development—the development, that is, of man's universal nature'.[31]

Bosanquet's legacy and relevance most appropriately lies with the significant role he assigns to social institutions and groups, not with an omnipotent state, as his brief review of Follett's

---

[24] John Rawls, *A Theory of Justice*, 529.

[25] Rawls, *A Theory of Justice*, 565.

[26] T. H. Green, *Prolegomena to Ethics* (hereafter *PE*), sects. 269, 273–4, 279, 288, 360, 370.

[27] Rawls, *A Theory of Justice*, 571.

[28] Green, *LPPO*, sect. 141. See also Wallace, *Lectures and Essays*, 250, 317–18.

[29] Laborde, 'The Concept of the State in British and French Political Thought', 551.

[30] Hector J. W. Hetherington and J. H. Muirhead, *Social Purpose*, 10.

[31] Bernard Bosanquet, *The Philosophical Theory of the State* (hereafter *PTS*), introd. to 2nd edn., 12 and 11 respectively.

'very excellent book' *The New State* testifies.[32] The working of the complexity of institutions, in their various functionings and bearings on each other, sustained by 'habits, traditions, recognitions, 'is the nearest thing to an expression of the community's will'. Bosanquet calls it 'Constitution' which 'is primarily a way of co-living and co-operating'.[33] So understood, as the society of societies, the state renders moral service to its members. For it is only by participating in the many social networks that individuals enrich their life and develop their capacities.

Importantly, Bosanquet's philosophical concept of 'self-maintaining character'[34] and political concept of self-government jointly justify and take concrete shape in diverse social groups and institutions, such as the Charity Organization Society, mutual aid societies, neighbourhoods, the cooperative movement, and other participatory communities. Individual self-maintaining character and individual self-government are attainable through social cooperation in relations of mutuality and reciprocity. It is for that reason that, while rejecting state socialism, 'of practical Socialism, i.e., of the workman's ownership of the means of production', Bosanquet 'cannot have too much'.[35] It is also for the same reason that he is a less than enthusiastic supporter of state action, especially with regard to welfare provisions, insisting the essential role of non-governmental social work.

On State Action: Divisions

On two issues all Idealists agree: first, the end of the state is moral and it could be promoted only indirectly because the 'law cannot enforce morality'. Second, they reject both laissez-faire individualism (Spencer) and state socialism (the Fabians). These two issues form a shared Idealist approach to state action. This, however, is not the entire story. Within the normative space that stretches between those two poles (laissez-faire individualism and state socialism) differences over state action do emerge in the Idealist camp. Nor are these differences a mere matter of different practical implementation of shared principle and valuational concepts. Practical differences as well as different interpretations of circumstances and facts are, to be sure, clearly there. I wish, however, to highlight the possible 'theoretical' roots of differences over state action. Recall that the Idealist 'third way' does not, and cannot, occupy a single determinate normative political programme. One reason is that the valuational terms, the concepts, that make up the Idealist argument are contested. Therefore, different interpretations of the same concepts as well as the particular ways they are aligned open up the possibility of different political programmes. My argument, however, is not about actual different political programmes. It is to stress Idealists' use of their conceptual-normative language which indicates the possibility of different political directions. Two examples lend support to this claim. One concerns the issue of character and circumstances. The second example focuses on the conceptual alignment of 'positive freedom' and 'real opportunity' or 'fair chance' (see subsection 'Freedom, Rightly Understood'). Both reveal a clear difference between Bosanquet, on the one hand, and Green and Ritchie, on the other.

[32] Bernard Bosanquet, 'The New State', *Mind*, NS 28/111 (July 1919), 370.

[33] Bernard Bosanquet, 'Note on Mr. Cole's Paper', *Proceedings of the Aristotelian Society*, NS 15 (1914–15), 162–3 respectively.

[34] Bernard Bosanquet, 'The Majority Report', *Sociological Review*, 2/2 (April 1909), 114.

[35] Bernard Bosanquet, 'Individual and Social Reform', in Bosanquet, *Essays and Addressees*, 46.

The relation of character and circumstances was a central issue in the late nineteenth-century debate on social reform and state action. The essential question concerned the extent to which social and material circumstances were beyond the control of character. Whether or not 'character' is the end of social reform (and state action) is not the issue. It is important to stress this point as an anonymous contributor to *The Encyclopaedia of Social Reform* (1897) claimed: 'To-day the key-word in…economics [is] "character."…the reason why individualist economists fear socialism is that they believe that it will deteriorate character, and the reason why socialist economists seek socialism is their belief that under individualism character is deteriorating.'[36] Controversy revolved not around the goal of social reform, but the means and method of social reform. Thus, for example, though a vocal critic of Bosanquet, Hobson nevertheless agrees with Bosanquet that character normatively comes first. Chronologically, however, he claims that change in circumstances must precede change of character. And so does Ritchie. He claims that 'moral and religious influences will only raise a few above the pressure of circumstances, therefore circumstances must be altered…The economic change must come before the moral before we can know certainly what the moral change will be.'[37] Bosanquet, by contrast, claims that all social change must begin with change of character.

For Bosanquet, character is *both* the end *and* the method of social reform. Character, for him, is not only the goal of social reform; it is also the method and machinery of social reform—'a single method and organ of social therapeutics. Its principle…[is] the principle of respect for the self-maintaining character.'[38] Deeply rooted in Bosanquet's philosophy are the two essential texts 'Symposium: Are Character and Circumstances Co-Ordinate Factors in Human Life or Is Either Subordinate to the Other' (1895–6) and *The Value and Destiny of the Individual* (1913).

The following claim reveals Bosanquet's way of overcoming the 'initial dichotomy' between the self (character) and circumstances: 'The self is character, when regarded as an organised whole; it is circumstance when regarded as a congeries of details.'[39] Depending on the point of view from which one views the self, it is either character or circumstances. But what does this mean? It means that self and circumstances do not, for Bosanquet, relate as 'an "inner" self, determined by "outer" circumstance'; but rather 'a higher or larger self—relatively speaking, character—capable of re-acting to an extent which the philosopher under-estimates rather than over-estimates, on the lower or less organised self—relatively speaking, circumstance.'[40] By depriving 'circumstances' of their external status, he renders them internal to, and dependent on, character. This explains Bosanquet's rejection of 'even the simple-seeming distinction of Plato and Aristotle between "external advantage"—the social and material basis of existence including social distinction—and the moral purpose as held by the individual intellect.'[41]

---

[36] *Encyclopaedia of Social Reform*, p. 895.

[37] D. G. Ritchie, 'Memoir', in his *Philosophical Studies*, ed. Robert Latta, 48. For Hobson, see J. A. Hobson, 'The Social Philosophy of Charity Organisation', in J. A. Hobson, *The Crisis of Liberalism: New Issues of Democracy* (London, 1909), 207–8.

[38] Bosanquet, 'The Majority Report', 114.

[39] 'Symposium: Are Character and Circumstances Co-ordinate Factors in Human Life or Is Either Subordinate to the Other', *Proceedings of the Aristotelian Society*, 3/2 (1895–6), 114.

[40] 'Symposium', 114.

[41] 'Symposium', 113. See also, Bernard Bosanquet, *The Value and Destiny of the Individual* (hereafter *VDI*), 114.

The power of character over circumstances is ultimately justified, for Bosanquet, by the 'miracle of the will' which, in turn, lies with its all-powerful creative power. As 'an active unity'[42] the will creates its content by making external material its own by giving it coherence. 'The whole growth of society and civilisation, as objective mind and will, is due to a movement of this kind.'[43] On Bosanquet's account, then, 'society and civilisation' constitute 'whole second [human] nature.'[44] Bosanquet's insistence on the omnipotent power of character over circumstances becomes exceedingly evident from his analysis of 'the power of character against the so-called physical impossibility'. He challenges such impossibility: 'Physical impossibility, to a very great and indefinite extent, is relative. It is relative to the agent's or agents' strength, motive, ability, and time.'[45]

The power of character over circumstances, grounded in the 'miracle of the will', underpins Bosanquet's opposition to uniform governmental programmes to aid the poor. He celebrates social cooperation, in turn, as the vehicle of individual self-maintenance or individual self-support—individual self-maintenance through social reciprocity. Indeed, he cites 'the Co-operative movement in Great Britain' from 'the Rochdale Pioneers onwards' and trade unions as examples of transformation of circumstances by character.[46]

Back to Idealist unity. Bosanquet shares with Green and other Idealists the concept of the state as 'a moral institution', 'an institution for the promotion of a common good' of which an important function is to maintain rights.[47]

Rights that Bind

To appreciate the Idealist reconceptualization of rights, it is helpful to place it against the backcloth of the sort of dichotomous discourse of rights which Idealists strive to go beyond. On the one hand, from the old communitarianism of Marx to Sandel's new communitarianism, rights-based theories have been vilified as inimical to the ideals of community and shared goals because, conceptually, rights are atomistic and egoistic. Rights, as such, communitarian critics claim, foster egoism, separateness, and adversarial social relations. 'Thinking in terms of rights', a contemporary thinker claims, 'does more than reflect on an egoistic, atomistic situation; it creates such a situation…Because thinking in terms of rights rests on an atomistic picture of us as separate, thinking in terms of rights systematically denies the unity.'[48] This is a strong claim but not atypical of a line of criticism which can be traced back to Marx. On the other hand, rights-theorists, such as Gewirth and Margaret McDonald, seek to defend the primary normative value of individual rights against the threats posed by utilitarians and Idealists, both of whom, they claim, view rights as merely instrumental to the attainment of a social purpose.[49]

[42] Bosanquet, *VDI*, 96.

[43] Bosanquet, *VDI*, 105, n. 2; original emphases.

[44] Bosanquet, *VDI*, 97; see also 83–4, 89–90.

[45] Bosanquet, *VDI*, 117, 118 respectively.

[46] Bosanquet, *VDI*, 116 (including n. 2) and 117 respectively.

[47] Green, *LPPO*, sects. 126 and 124 respectively.

[48] John Hardwig, 'Should Women Think in Terms of Rights?', *Ethics*, 94 (1984), 448.

[49] Alan Gewirth, *Human Rights*, 155–9, and *The Community of Rights*, 86; Margaret McDonald, 'Natural Rights', in Jeremy Waldron (ed.), *Theories of Rights*.

The Idealist rights-argument merits attention precisely because it illustrates the folly of approaching normative political arguments from a narrow perspective of simple oppositions. Though Ritchie's rejection of natural rights springs to mind, it is, nevertheless, Green's reconceptualization of rights that lays bare the innovative Idealist argument. He does not deny that rights belong to individuals:

> There is no harm in saying that they [rights] belong to individuals as such, if we understand what we mean by 'individual,' and if we mean by it a self-determining subject, conscious of itself as one among other such subjects, and of its relation to them as making it what it is;…they [rights] attach to the individual, but only as a member of a society of free agents, as recognising himself and recognised by others to be such a member, as doing and done by accordingly.[50]

By connecting rights with individuals-in-relations, Green criticizes the association of natural rights with the individualist conception of political life as well as the negative image of the state. By rendering mutual recognition the conceptual core of rights, he replaces egoism of rights with mutuality of rights. Mutual recognition constitutes rights.[51] Claiming rights is not and cannot be egoistic or self-centred because claiming rights is mutual. As mutually recognized moral claims for self-development, rights equally emphasize the development of others. To recognize someone is to acknowledge his or her equal status as being an end (rather than means) in itself, to view others on a moral par with oneself; to be able to relate to them as 'I' and 'Thou' and vice versa. It is a form of communication between self-conscious persons who are aware of others as themselves and of their relation to them as part and parcel of their own awareness of themselves as persons with their own ends. Therefore, Green's basic right, 'the right to free life[,] rests on the common will of the society, in the sense that each member of the society within which the right subsists in seeking to satisfy himself contributes to satisfy others, and that *each is aware* that the other does so'.[52] Mutual awareness, however, has to result in 'practical recognition', that is in the actual practice of 'acting and being treated' as equal members of society.

Practical mutual recognition reveals that Green, like Rousseau and Marx, refuses to set up society in opposition to its individual members in order to discredit self-interested competitive individualism which he holds grounds a 'false notion of rights'. Unlike Rousseau and Marx, however, Green does not rule out the significant role of rights—divorced from the ontology and egoism and atomism—in creating cooperative social life. Far from dissolving communal ties, Green deploys rights as the internal conditions constitutive of community, for community is created by the practice of mutual recognition. Embedded in social norms and arrangements, the actual practice of mutuality of rights is at the same time the practice of mutual concern. This practice, to which Green also refers as 'distinctive social interest', forges the moral terrain of human connectedness where one's good and the good of others are intertwined. This is the stuff of which common-good society, 'a community of good for all',[53] is made of.

---

[50] Green, *LPPO*, sect. 138.   [51] Green, *LPPO*, sect. 138.
[52] Green, *LPPO*, sect. 216; emphasis added.   [53] Green, *PE*, sect. 245.

The connection that Green and Idealists forge between rights and the common good has attracted the fire of rights theorists who claim that 'there are some rights to which human beings are entitled independently of their varying social relationships'. Thus, Gewirth and Margaret McDonald insist on the need to defend such a claim since it 'has frequently been denied by utilitarian, idealist, and marxist philosophers who . . . agree in holding the rights of an individual must be determined only by the needs and convenience of *society as a whole*'.[54]

So much depends on what 'society as a whole' means. 'As a whole' might be interpreted collectively or distributively. McDonald's criticism suggests the former. Green employs 'as a whole' distributively in his important claim 'that a state is made a state by the function which it fulfils of maintaining the rights of its members *as a whole* or a system *in such a way that none gains the expense of another (no one has any power guaranteed to him through another being deprived of that power)*'.[55] Far from subordinating rights to social convenience, rights are determined by social justice as expressed in the italicized part of the quotation. Put differently, rights, for Green, are derivative of a social purpose (the common good), the end of which is self-development of each and every individual. Call it relational teleology. The intriguing nature of that claim is that it defies classification in the conventional opposition between the foundational and derivative justifications of rights. For while it is the case that they are derivative of and relative to the well-being of society (common good), the goal of society is to enable the development of all its members. Accordingly it should be 'so organised that everyone's capacities have free scope for their development'.[56] Rights, and particularly positive rights, constitute that organization.

Bosanquet's rights-argument seems more vulnerable to Gewirth's criticism of teleological rights. The problem with teleological rights, Gewirth holds, is that they lack primary normative value because they are merely instrumental to, and therefore morally subordinated to, the attainment of a social purpose. He targets both utilitarianism and the Idealist organicist tradition of which he takes Bosanquet to be a representative. On Gewirth's account of Bosanquet's rights-argument, the sequence of ends and means would be from 'social purpose' (the welfare of the social organism) to 'functions' (corresponding to social positions) as instrumental to that end, and from these to rights as instrumental to the discharge of functions. To the extent to which Bosanquet does insist that '[w]hat comes first . . . is the position', that '[t]he Position . . . is the real fact',[57] and that rights are attached to social position—and not, as with Green, to moral personality[58]—he is less immune to Gewirth's criticism.

In a similar vein, Ritchie attracts Hobhouse's criticism because his position violates relational teleology to which Hobhouse, too, subscribes. Ritchie holds that rights are 'determined by the good of society'. The problem, holds Hobhouse, 'is that he slurs the converse truth that the good of society is bound up with the recognition of the rights of its members'.[59] That recognition is, in fact, embedded in Ritchie's full argument: 'The good of a community gives us our only criterion for judging what is right for individuals to do; but the good of a

[54] McDonald, 'Natural Rights', 133; emphasis added.
[55] Green, *LPPO*, 132; emphases added.
[56] Green, *LPPO*, sect. 171.
[57] Bosanquet, *PTS*, 190 and 'Kingdom of God on Earth', in his *Essays and Addresses*, 116–18.
[58] Green, *LPPO*, sects. 27–8.
[59] L. T. Hobhouse, *The Elements of Social Justice*, 40 n.

community is itself identical with the good of its members. A healthy body is a body the parts of which are healthy, but *none of which is developed at the expense of others.*'[60] If this distributive requirement (the italicized words) is institutionalized by rights as a determinate condition of 'social health', then Hobhouse's criticism loses much of its force. Indeed, this is just how Hobhouse himself secures his own teleological justification of rights. 'Rights and duties…are not conditions limiting the common good [community] from without, but conditions constituting the common good.'[61] This rights–common good nexus plays an important role in the Idealist conception of political obligation.

Political Obligation

Green is said to have introduced the term political obligation to political discourse.

Horton holds that 'the element of Green's political philosophy which is most crucial to his theory of political obligation is his account of the common good' and concludes that Green's

'account of the common good is fundamentally flawed and in a way which crucially damages his theory of political obligation.'[62] This criticism, I claim, misses the way in which Green's account of the common good integrates a concern for justice; that is a concern for promoting the good (of self-realization, development of moral personality) of everyone.

How is the common good 'fundamentally flawed'? Primarily, 'Green's tendency to conflate within the common good all potentially conflicting values',[63] 'must address the problem…of identifying and characterising the common good; a problem which is especially daunting with respect to complex, plural and ethically diverse societies such as most modern states'.[64] Further, 'Green fails to recognise the possibility of genuine conflict between an individual's personal interest or good and the common good'.[65]

Horton's criticism does not take account of the way in which Green's theory of the common good integrates a concern for justice; that is, a concern for promoting the good (of self-realization, development of moral personality) of everyone. (Importantly, everyone is taken into account, distributively, such that no one is sacrificed to an aggregate or collective social good, and everyone shares in the good.) Integrating a concern for justice is an essential feature of common-good theories of which Thomas Aquinas's is a typical illustration.[66]

The concern for justice takes institutional shape in Green's idea of a 'system of rights'. Green employs 'system of right' normatively: 'the state is made a state by the function which it fulfils of maintaining the rights of its members as a whole or a system, in such a way that none gains

---

[60] Ritchie, *Natural Rights*, 99; emphasis added.

[61] Hobhouse, *The Elements of Social Justice*, 43; see also 106–9.

[62] John Horton, *Political Obligation*, 74.

[63] Horton, *Political Obligation*, 77.

[64] Horton, *Political Obligation*, 77.

[65] Horton, *Political Obligation*, 78.

[66] Thomas Aquinas, *Summa Theologica*, Part II: first part, questions 90–6; second part, questions 47, 58–64, 79. See also, B. J. Diggs, 'The Common Good as Reason for Political Action', *Ethics*, 83 (1973), 289–93; Aldo Tussi, 'Anarchism, Autonomy, and the Concept of the Common Good', *International Philosophical Quarterly* 17 (1977), 273–83; J. R. Lucas, *On Justice*, ch. 3, esp. pp. 53, 64–71.

at the expense of another (no one has any power guaranteed to him through another being deprived of that power)'.[67] Justice is Green's principle of moral rightness which he derives from the idea of the common good. Much as justice is the core principle of Green's theory of positive freedom (see the subsection 'Freedom, Rightly Understood'), it is, in the shape of a just system of rights, the justificatory locus of political obligation. In both the cases of positive freedom and political obligation, the principle of justice is the handmaid of the common good. Put differently, a just system of rights is the political common good. This is the missing ingredient in Horton's account of the common good.

Horton claims correctly that 'the element of Green's political philosophy which is most crucial to his theory of political obligation is his account of the common good'. His argument goes astray because he does not distinguish the moral and political dimensions of the common good. The moral (or ethical) common good—the harmonious development of human beings—is not operational politically the way Horton seems to suggest. The moral common good operates indirectly via the political common good. Therefore even if Horton is right about 'the difficulties surrounding his [Green's] conception of the common good and the idea of self-realization', his conclusion—that Green's theory of political obligation as an account of political obligation is fatally damaged—does not follow. The fundamental flaws of the moral common good are not transferable to the political common good. While Green's moral common good is perfectionist along the lines that Horton suggests, Green's political common good is not. Put differently, Green defends ethical, not political perfectionism.

There is not a direct transition from ethical common good to public policy or political programme. Moral common good is Green's ideal society in which all are self-realizing, etc. Political common good is the institutional dimension of ethical common good, not unlike the idea of a basic structure which implements justice via a system of rights. Whereas Green's account of political obligation is, ultimately bound up with ethical common good, operationally, political obligation is grounded in political common good. This claim is analogous to, and is supported by, Green's claim that 'It is not indeed necessary to a capacity for rights, as it is to true moral goodness, that interest in a good conceived as common to himself and others should be a man's dominant motive'.[68] Much the same way as 'true moral goodness' is a necessary prerequisite for exercising rights, 'a coherent, integrated and harmonious moral system' of values is not essential for Green's theory of political obligation. Justice, decidedly is. Hence,

> the moral duty, on the part of the society authorizing… punishment, to make its punishment just by making the system of rights which it maintains just. The justice of punishment depends on the justice of the general system of rights—not merely on the propriety with reference to the social well-being of maintaining this or that particular right which the crimes punished violates, but on the question whether the social organisation in which a criminal has lived and acted is one that has given him a fair chance of not being a criminal.[69]

Securing 'a fair chance', 'real opportunity of self-development' is the job of the principle of justice which is the core principle of the common good. In brief, the justificatory locus of

---

[67] Green, *LPPO*, sect. 132.   [68] Green, *LPPO*, sect. 208.   [69] Green, *LPPO*, sect. 189.

political obligation lies with a just system of rights which may be regarded as the handmaid of the common good as an ideal of the good society.

Citizenship

Discussions about citizenship revolve around the dualist construction of passive/active citizenship, rights-based citizenship versus citizenship as practice of duties. These two binary pairs are associated with what Walzer calls the 'dualist construction' of citizenship which portrays as rival the civic republican and liberal conceptions of citizenship. Whereas the former regards citizenship as practice of duties and responsibility, the latter focuses on citizenship as an entitlement, 'a right or set of rights passively enjoyed'.[70] A further dichotomy (which limits of space must exclude) concerns civil rights-centred citizenship versus social rights-centred citizenship. Associated with T. H. Marshall, the latter regards welfare rights as part and parcel of citizenship.

With civic republicans, British Idealists place civic duty at the centre of their conception of citizenship. At the same time they highlight the nexus between duties and rights.[71] Further, unlike civic republicans, they do not privilege participation in the public sphere as the way to good citizenship.

'For though to be a citizen is to possess rights—in any case, civil rights, and, in a democratic country, political rights as well—to possess rights is not to be a citizen. It is to be merely on the way to become one.'[72] To be a citizen, MacCunn insists, is to do one's duty. In a similar vein Green insists on 'active interest in the service of the state ... [which] can hardly arise while the individual's relation to the state is that of a passive recipient of protection in the exercise of his rights of person and property'.[73] Indeed, in Aristotelian fashion, Green believes that the state is 'a society of which the life is maintained by what its members do for the sake of maintaining it'.[74] However, Green concedes 'a lowering of civil vitality' in the modern state, but endorses 'the price of having recognised the claim to citizenship as the claim of *all* men'.[75]

Idealist stress on the civic duty of citizenship is not only an entailment of their ethical conception of the state. The importance of civic duty is inseparable from the urgent need to address the 'social problem' of pervasive poverty. Citizenship is made by Green a vehicle of 'social deliverance' for those who 'are left without the chance, which only the help of others can gain for them, of making themselves in act what in possibility we believe them to be'.[76] The demands of such active social service, however, are addressed only to 'persons who have exceptional opportunity of directing their own pursuits'.[77]

---

[70]   Michael Walzer, 'Citizenship', in T. Ball, J. Far, and K. L. Hanson (eds.) *Political Innovation and Conceptual Change*, 216.

[71]   Henry Jones, *The Principles of Citizenship*, ch. IV.

[72]   John MacCunn, *Ethics of Citizenship*, 69.

[73]   Green, *LPPO*, sect. 122.

[74]   Green, *LPPO*, sect. 38.

[75]   Green, *LPPO*, sect. 119.

[76]   Green, *PE*, sect. 270.

[77]   Green, *PE*, Sect. 382.

Nor does active citizenship need focus on public or political activity. 'My station and its duties' account of citizenship, which looms large in Idealist theorizing of citizenship, invests political significance in private duties. Bosanquet warns against 'the illusion that duties which deal with public matters are the only public duties. All duties are public, or at least take us beyond the ordinary self.' While Bosanquet maintains that citizenship is the prime source of a healthy political community, he stresses that 'the duties of citizenship will not necessarily drag us out of private life into politics, administration, or philanthropy'.[78]

The essential thing is that, as members of the community, individuals understand that, whatever their position and job is, if they carry it out honestly they contribute to and share in a common good. More than that, 'my station and its duties' account of citizenship has an important integrative function. Life in modern society is fragmented. The idea of citizenship helps individuals to integrate their own fragmented self into a coherent unity as well to integrate themselves into the community at large. The point of this process of integration is that, for Idealists, citizens are made, not born. Home and family, workshop, profession, trades union, church, all these are 'nurseries of citizenship'.[79]

Not only does active membership in multiple social networks make citizens, it also nurture 'a life which is "free," ' . . . . For it is fulness of life and not merely immunity from aggression, which is the test of real freedom.'[80] To the Idealist concept of freedom, I now turn.

Freedom, Rightly Understood

Context matters. Green's association with the negative–positive distinction of freedom owes much to Berlin's classic distinction between these two conceptions. Berlin's distinction, however, is an inappropriate frame for interpreting Green. The ideological context of cold war liberalism fuels Berlin's dichotomous approach to negative and positive freedom. Because he associates positive freedom with the danger of 'excessive control and interference', he is willing to discard positive freedom in favour of exclusive defence of negative freedom. Moreover, the same danger, viewed from state socialism, explains Berlin's statement that everything 'is what it is',[81] keeping equality and democracy separate from liberty. None of this sheds light on Green's reconceptualization of freedom which was fuelled by the different 'specific dangers', namely 'the evil of unrestricted laissez-faire' and 'the reign of unfettered economic individualism', to use Berlin's words.

To get a good handle on Green's reconceptualization of freedom, it is helpful to quote him in full:

> We shall probably all agree that freedom, rightly understood, is the greatest of blessings; that its attainment is the true end of all our efforts as citizens. But when we thus speak of freedom, we should consider carefully what we mean by it. We do not mean merely freedom from

---

[78] Bernard Bosanquet, 'The Duties of Citizenship', in Bosanquet (ed.), *Aspects of the Social Problem*, 11–12; MacCunn, *Ethics of Citizenship*, 77. See also Jones, *The Working Faith of the Social Reformer*, 133–4, 279.

[79] Bosanquet, 'The Duties of Citizenship', 10.

[80] MacCunn, *Ethics of Citizenship*, 72.

[81] Isaiah Berlin, 'Two Concepts of Liberty', in Berlin, *Four Essays on Liberty*, 125. All other quotations are from Berlin, 'Introduction', *Four Essays on Liberty*, xlv–vi.

restraint or compulsion. We do not mean merely freedom to do as we like irrespectively of what it is that we like. We do not mean a freedom that can be enjoyed by one man or one set of men at the cost of a loss of freedom to others. When we speak of freedom as something to be so highly prized, we mean a positive power or capacity of doing or enjoying something worth doing, and that, too, something that we do or enjoy in common with others.[82]

Rightly understood, freedom comprises three elements, each is stated both negatively and positively. First, the capacity to do—freedom involves the capacity to do things, not the mere absence of restraint; second, the value element—freedom means realizing distinctive human capacities, doing something valuable, not merely doing something we like; third, the social element—realizing one's distinctive human capacities should benefit others, and not be 'founded on a refusal of the same opportunity to other' individuals.[83] Rightly understood, then, freedom results jointly from the absence of restraint and the presence of positive capacity to do or enjoy self-realization in common with others. Call it freedom as self-realization or positive freedom or real freedom.

Unlike Berlin, Green does not separate negative and positive freedom. Nor does positive freedom replace negative freedom, but rather incorporates its two constitutive elements: freedom from restraint and freedom to choose. Though rightly understood, freedom is not merely 'freedom from restraint'; freedom, Green maintains, 'always implies…some exemption from compulsion'.[84] Indeed, Green views positive freedom as an extension of negative freedom in the 'sense of power to "do what one wills"' which, he holds, is an expression of the 'self-distinguishing, self-seeking, self-asserting principle', working its way in human development. Nor does Green devalue the capacity of self-realization which presupposes the 'power to "do what one wills"'. Self-realization, Green insists, is 'a particular kind of self-determination'.[85]

At the same time, however, Green deploys positive freedom to criticize freedom of contract, the paradigm of negative freedom, which was bound up with laissez-faire policies. Being free, on the account of this paradigm, consists in the mere absence of coercion to do whatever one like or chooses. Green's criticism is twofold: one is that absence of coercion is compatible with the lack of positive capacity to develop one's capacities of will and reason. The 'starving labourer' is an example. Though he is not coerced into a contract with his employer, the contract is only 'nominally "free"' because it is 'entered into between persons on very unequal footings'.[86] The 'starving labourer' is, therefore, in fact, powerless to do anything other than accepting a disadvantageous contract. Green's second criticism of negative freedom is that it focuses only on external obstacles: 'the mere removal of compulsion, the mere enabling a man to do as he likes, is in itself no contribution to true freedom'.[87] As the example of the drunkard reveals, internal obstacles thwart the development of human capacities even in the absence of coercion.

It is worth noting here, if only in passing, that Green places 'ability' at the conceptual core not only of positive freedom ('the positive capacity') but also of negative freedom ('the mere enabling'). And so does Bosanquet.[88]

---

[82] Green, 'Lecture on Liberal Legislation and Freedom of Contract' (hereafter LLFC), 199.
[83] Green, LLFC, 199.
[84] Green, DSF, sect. 2.
[85] Green, DSF, sect. 7.
[86] Ritchie, 'The Unseen Foundations of Society', 521–2.
[87] Green, LLFC, p. 199.
[88] Bosanquet, PTS, p. 96.

The conceptual link that need stressing, however, is the one Green forges between self-realization and real opportunity. Berlin insisted on focusing only on freedom from restraint, separating equality of opportunity from freedom. Green's concern about the 'starving labourer' leads him to link self-realization with 'positive equality of conditions' or 'real opportunity of self-development'.[89] This link joins the third social element of Green's reconceptualization of freedom. Recall: 'We do not mean a freedom that can be enjoyed by one man or one set of men at the cost of a loss of freedom to others.' Such zero-sum vision of social life, Green believes, is made real by the 'unrelenting competition' of capitalist economy. For it threatens the well-being of 'the worse-off members of society' by depriving them of 'the real opportunity of self-development'.[90] In a manner that recalls Hegel's analysis of poverty as a structural problem of capitalism, not a mere failure of character, Green states: 'Civil society may be, and is, founded on the idea of there being a common good, but that idea in relation to the less favoured members of society is in effect unrealised.'[91]

That positive freedom is 'something that we do or enjoy in common with others' means that it is a common good, the common good understood as an ideal of cooperative social life the benefits of which are enjoyed jointly, not severally. 'In common with others' contrasts with and requires that freedom should not be enjoyed by one man or one set of men at the cost of a loss of freedom to others. That requirement captures Green's principle of justice which lies at the core of his normative theory of positive freedom. If Green's idea of the good of cooperative self-realization is the common good, then social justice is Green's principle of moral rightness. Derivative of the common good, social justice is both constitutive of the common-good society and essential to its realization.

Green's freedom rightly understood turns out to be a complex conception of positive or real freedom. Using MacCallum's triadic model of freedom helps to unveil it, especially since Green himself employs such triadic structure: X (Agent) is free from Y (obstacles) to do or be Z (goals, state of character).

The obstacles can be external or internal, negative or positive. 'Positive' or 'real' in Green's 'positive freedom' or 'real freedom' is not confined to a category of 'freedom to'—only a particular kind of self-determination qualifies as self-realization. Of equal importance, 'positive' extends to the category of 'freedom from'. Realizing one's unique human capacities requires not only absence of restraint; it requires also the availability of 'real opportunity', 'fair chance', or 'positive equality of conditions'. It is, as Ritchie puts it, 'liberty in the sense of positive opportunity for self-development'.[92] Ritchie, indeed, helps to clarify Green's conception. He correctly speaks of 'Positive or real liberty' in contrast to 'the negative or merely formal liberty'.[93]

Two conceptual points merit attention. First, the intertwining of internal capabilities and external opportunities captures Green's conceptualization of freedom more adequately than the negative–positive distinction. Not that the latter is discarded; rather, negative and positive freedom are transformed into essential aspects of both internal capabilities and external opportunities. It follows, second, that Green places 'ability' at the conceptual core not only of positive freedom ('the positive capacity' and 'real opportunity') but also of negative freedom ('the mere enabling'). That he does exposes the ideological motivation behind the insistence of Berlin on negative freedom separate from 'ability' or 'positive opportunity'.

---

[89] Green, *PE*, sect. 245.   [90] Green, *PE*, sect. 245.   [91] Green, *PE*, sect. 245.
[92] Ritchie, *Natural Rights*, 139–40.   [93] Ritchie, *Natural Rights*, 138–9.

Ritchie stresses that 'Liberty in the sense of positive opportunity for self-development, is the creation of law, and not something that could exist apart from the action of the State'.[94] Recall my claim that while all Idealists reject both laissez-faire individualism and state socialism, differences over state action emerge within the normative space that stretches between these two poles. A shared Idealist 'third way' is not inconsistent with the possibility of Idealist 'third ways'. That possibility, I suggested, is implicit in Idealists' use of their conceptual-normative language to which two examples lend support. I have discussed the one concerning the issue of the relations between character and circumstances. Here I can only dwell briefly on the second example: the conceptual alignment of 'positive freedom' and 'real opportunity' or 'fair chance'.

That conceptual alignment seems to be absent from Bosanquet's analysis of positive freedom. It is particularly evident since Bosanquet employs the triadic model with greater clarity than Green.[95] However, in his account of positive freedom, 'freedom from' focuses only on internal obstacle—'the constraint of what we commonly regard as a part of ourself'. Unlike Green and Ritchie, Bosanquet does not make 'real opportunity'—the removal of external obstacles such as ill health and squalid houses—a conceptual component of positive freedom. This absence suggests a difference of emphasis between Green and Ritchie, on the one hand, and Bosanquet, on the other, on the issue of state interference. In the political discourse at the time, the conceptual link between freedom and positive or real opportunity is bound up with greater acceptance of state action on behalf of freedom. It is telling in this context that Caird associated 'socialists, or the most thoughtful of them' with wanting 'that the State should protect individuals from that hurtful and destructive competition which means the crushing of the weak by the strong; that it should do its utmost to promote the growth of individual energy and character, and to give every one *a fair chance* of living a healthful and useful life'.[96]

My point is not that Idealist unity is subverted by deep political and ideological division over the issue of state action. My point is, rather, that we ought to look for Idealist unity not in political prescriptions but in the distinctive conceptual framework, 'a new philosophy' of reconciliation, which was capable of advancing the political argument at the time and political discourse afterwards.

References

Barker, Ernest, *Political Thought in England from Spencer to To-Day* (1915; London: Williams and Norgate, 1920).

Berlin, I., 'Introduction' and 'Two Concepts of Liberty', in Berlin, Four Essays on *Liberty*, (Oxford: Oxford University Press, 1969), xxxvi–lxii and 118–72, respectively.

Bosanquet, Bernard, 'Individual and Social Reform', in Bosanquet, *Essays and Addressees* (London: Sonnenschein, 1891), 24–46.

Bosanquet, Bernard, 'Kingdom of God on Earth', in Bosanquet, *Essays and Addresses* (London: Sonnenschein, 1891), 108–30.

[94] Ritchie, *Natural Rights*, 138–9.
[95] Bosanquet, *PTS*, p. 95.
[96] Edward Caird, *Individualism and Socialism*, 6–7; emphasis added.

Bosanquet, Bernard, 'The Duties of Citizenship', in Bosanquet (ed.), *Aspects of the Social Problem* (London: Macmillan, 1895), 1–27.

Bosanquet, Bernard, 'Symposium: Are Character and Circumstances Co-ordinate Factors in Human Life or Is Either Subordinate to the Other?', *Proceedings of the Aristotelian Society*, 3/2 (1895–6), 112–15.

Bosanquet, Bernard, *The Philosophical Theory of the State* (London & New York, 1899; 2nd edn., 1910; 3rd edn., 1920).

Bosanquet, Bernard, 'The Majority Report', *Sociological Review*, 2/2 (April 1909), 109–26.

Bosanquet, Bernard, *The Value and Destiny of the Individual* (London: Macmillan, 1913).

Bosanquet, Bernard, 'Note on Mr. Cole's Paper', *Proceedings of the Aristotelian Society*, NS 15 (1914–15), 160–3.

Bosanquet, Bernard, 'The New State: Group Organisation, the Solution of Popular Government by M. P. Follett', *Mind*, NS 28/111 (July 1919), 370.

Bradley, F. H., *Ethical Studies* (London: Henry S. King & Co., 1876).

Caird, Edward, *Ethical Philosophy* (Glasgow: James Maclehose, 1866).

Caird, Edward, *Individualism and Socialism* (Glasgow: James Maclehose and Sons, 1897).

Caird, Edward, 'Philosophy', in Alfred Russel Wallace et al., *The Progress of the Century* (New York and London: Harper & Brothers Publishers, 1901), 145–70.

Diggs, B. J., 'The Common Good as Reason for Political Action', *Ethics*, 83 (1973), 289–93.

Gewirth, Alan, *Human Rights: Essays on Justification and Application* (Chicago: University of Chicago Press, 1982).

Gewirth, Alan, *The Community of Rights* (Chicago: University of Chicago Press, 1996).

Green, T. H., *Lectures on the Principles of Political Obligation and Other Writings*, ed. Paul Harris and John Morrow (Cambridge: Cambridge University Press, 1986).

Green, T. H., 'Popular Philosophy in Its Relation to Life', in *Works of Thomas Hill Green*, vol. iii, ed. R. L. Nettleship (London, 1888), 92–125.

Green, T. H., 'On the Different Senses of "Freedom" as Applied to Will and to the Moral Progress of Man', in Green, *Lectures on the Principles of Political Obligation and Other Writings*, ed. Paul Harris and John Morrow (Cambridge: Cambridge University Press, 1986), 228–49.

Green, T. H., 'Lecture on Liberal Legislation and Freedom of Contract', in Green, *Lectures on the Principles of Political Obligation and Other Writings*, ed. Paul Harris and John Morrow (Cambridge: Cambridge University Press, 1986), 194–212.

Green, T. H., *Prolegomena to Ethics*, ed. A. C. Bradley (Oxford: Clarendon Press, 1883).

Hardwig, John, 'Should Women Think in Terms of Rights?', *Ethics*, 94/3 (Apr. 1984), 441–55.

Hetherington, Hector J. W., and Muirhead, J. H., *Social Purpose: A Contribution to a Philosophy of Civic Society* (London & New York, 1918).

Hobhouse, L. T., *The Elements of Social Justice* (1922; London: George Allen & Unwin, 1965).

Hobson, J. A., 'The Social Philosophy of Charity Organisation', in J. A. Hobson (ed.), *The Crisis of Liberalism: New Issues of Democracy* (London: P. S. King and Son, 1909), 192–217.

Horton, John, *Political Obligation* (London: Macmillan, 1992).

Jones, Henry, 'The Social Organism', in A. Seth and R. B. Haldane (eds.), *Essays in Philosophical Criticism* (London: Longmans Green, 1883), 187–213.

Jones, Henry, *The Working Faith of the Social Reformer* (London: Macmillan, 1910).

Jones, Henry, *The Principles of Citizenship* (London: Macmillan, 1920).

Laborde, Cécile, 'The Concept of the State in British and French Political Thought', *Political Studies*, 48 (2000), 540–57.

Lucas, J. R., *On Justice* (Oxford: Clarendon Press, 1980).

MacCunn, John, *Ethics of Citizenship* (New York: Macmillan, 1894).

McDonald, Margaret, 'Natural Rights', in Jeremy Waldron (ed.), *Theories of Rights* (Oxford: Oxford University Press, 1990), 21–40.

Mackenzie, J. S., *An Introduction to Social Philosophy* (Glasgow: James Maclehose & Sons, 1890).

Mackenzie, J. S., 'The Relations between Ethics and Economics', *International Journal of Ethics*, 3/3 (Apr. 1893), 281–308.

MacKenzie, J. S., 'The Hegelian Point of View', *Mind*, NS 11/41 (Jan. 1902), 54–71.

Oakeshott, Michael, *Human Conduct* (Oxford: Clarendon Press, 1975).

Plant, Raymond 'Idealism', in Miller, David et al. (eds.) *The Blackwell Encyclopedia of Political Thought* (New York: Blackwell, 1987), 230–5.

Rawls, John, *A Theory of Justice* (Cambridge, Mass.: Harvard University Press, 1971).

Rawls, John, *Political Liberalism* (New York: Columbia University Press, 1993).

Ritchie, D.G., 'Darwin and Hegel', *Proceedings of the Aristotelian Society*, 1/4 (1890–1), 55–74.

Ritchie, D. G., 'The Unseen Foundations of Society by Duke of Argyll', *International Journal of Ethics*, 3/4 (July 1893), 514–22.

Ritchie, D. G., *Natural Rights* (London: Swan Sonnenschein & Co., 1895).

Thomas Aquinas, *Summa Theologica*, Part II: first part, questions 90–6; second part, questions 47, 58–64, 79.

Tussi, Aldo, 'Anarchism, Autonomy, and the Concept of the Common Good', *International Philosophical Quarterly*, 17 (1977), 273–83.

Wallace, William, *Prolegomena to the Study of Hegel's Philosophy and Especially His Logic* (2nd edn., Oxford: Clarendon Press, 1894).

Wallace, William, *Lectures and Essays on Natural Theology and Ethics*, ed. Edward Caird (Oxford: Clarendon Press, 1898).

Walzer, 'Citizenship', in T. Ball, J. Far J, and K. L. Hanson (eds.) *Political Innovation and Conceptual Change* (Cambridge, Cambridge University Press, 1989), 211–19.

FURTHER GENERAL READING

Dimova-Cookson, Maria, and Mander, W. J. (eds.), *T. H. Green: Ethics, Metaphysics and Political Philosophy* (Oxford: Clarendon Press, 2006).

Mander, W. J., *British Idealism: A History* (Oxford: Oxford University Press, 2011).

Morrow, John (ed.), *T. H. Green* (Ashgate: Imprint, 2007).

Nicholson, Peter P., *The Political Philosophy of the British Idealists: Selected Studies* (Cambridge: Cambridge University Press, 1990).

Sweet, Will (ed.), *The Moral, Social and Political Philosophy of the British Idealists* (Exeter: Imprint Academic, 2009).

Sweet, Will (ed.), *Bernard Bosanquet and the Legacy of British Idealism* (Toronto: University of Toronto Press, 2007).

CHAPTER 23

....

HENRY SIDGWICK AND THE
IRRATIONALITY OF THE UNIVERSE

....

BART SCHULTZ

I. LIFE AND SIGNIFICANCE

HENRY Sidgwick was born into what would become a remarkably accomplished family on 31 May 1838, in Skipton, Yorkshire. His brothers, William Carr (1834–1919) and Arthur (1840–1920), would become Oxford dons, and his sister Mary, known as Minnie (1841–1918), ended up marrying a second cousin, Edward White Benson (1829–96), a product of Trinity College, Cambridge, who lived with the family while he was a schoolmaster at Rugby in the 1850s. Benson would in due course become Archbishop of Canterbury, residing with Minnie at Lambeth Palace at the very centre of Victorian social and political life, but while he was at Rugby his chief accomplishment was becoming the first mentor of young Henry.

Sidgwick himself opted for Trinity College, Cambridge, where he excelled in mathematics and classics, garnering one prize or honour after another: Craven Scholar, Senior Classic, Chancellor's Medallist, and more. In 1857 he was invited to join that most famous of secret discussion societies, the Cambridge Conversazione Society, better known as the 'Apostles', which had been an intellectual incubator for such figures as F. D. Maurice, Tennyson, Erasmus Darwin, James Clerk Maxwell, and many other leading lights past and present (Allen 2010; Lubenow 1998). Discussion societies would become a large part of Sidgwick's life—beyond the Apostles, which always remained important to him as a model of intellectually liberating comradeship, such societies as the illustrious Metaphysical Society and the Synthetic Society would engage his best philosophical efforts.

But Sidgwick's Cambridge, unlike Benson's, steadily weakened his orthodox Anglican faith and steadily strengthened his Liberal reformist zeal, converting him to the utilitarianism of Jeremy Bentham and John Stuart Mill. Although upon graduation he was made a Fellow of Trinity and a lecturer in Classics (followed by a lectureship in moral philosophy), the 1860s were his self-described time of 'Storm and Stress' when in classic Victorian fashion his religious doubts steadily grew as he struggled with scientific materialism and historical biblical criticism, learning both Hebrew and German the better to engage with the textual historicity of the Bible. This would prove significant for both his philosophy and his career, since he famously decided to resign his Fellowship in 1869 because he could no longer subscribe in good conscience to the Thirty-Nine Articles of the Church of England, as the position required. However, he continued in a lectureship, and in due course, after subscription was finally eliminated, regained his Fellowship. In 1883 he was appointed the Knightbridge professor of moral philosophy, a position he would hold until just before his death on 28 August 1900.

Still, his religious concerns always shaped his life and work, inspiring his lifelong interest in 'psychical research' (parapsychology) as a possible source of evidence for the latitudinarian form of theism he found most attractive and important for purposes of philosophical ethics (Gauld 1968, 2007). He would co-found, in 1882, and serve as first president of the British Society for Psychical Research (SPR).

Sidgwick's reformist activities were wide-ranging and not invariably tied to party loyalty; as an 'Academic Liberal' he tended towards a Millian liberalism, which he did not find fully realized in Gladstone, with whom he would break over Home Rule for Ireland. In later life he could vote more as an independent, sometimes with the unfortunate shadings (and racism) of the new imperialism of the late Victorian era (Schultz 2004, 2005; Bell 2007). But he was also caught up in the Ethical Culture movement, hosting Felix Adler at Cambridge and participating actively in various progressive ethical societies (Sidgwick 1898). He served on a number of government commissions, and even considered running for office, but preferred to act in the role of public moralist and well-placed political adviser (Collini 2001).

Many of his reform efforts focused on education, especially the reorganization and professionalization of Cambridge and the expansion of educational opportunities for women (Rothblatt 1968; Harvie 1976; Brooke 1993). He is celebrated as a founding father and guiding spirit of Newnham College, Cambridge, one of the first colleges for women in England (Tullberg 1975/98; Sutherland 2006). In 1876 he married Eleanor Mildred Balfour (1845–1936), the sister of Arthur Balfour (1848–1930, prime minister from 1902 to 1905), who had been one of his students. His marriage not only brought him into one of the wealthiest and most powerful families in England and Scotland, but also secured him a key ally and collaborator. Eleanor worked with Henry on behalf of both Newnham, where she succeeded Anne Jemima Clough as principal in 1892, and the SPR, the presidency of which she assumed in 1908.

In keeping with his belief that scholars should actively contribute to new research in their disciplines, Sidgwick published extensively in his lifetime. He is best known for his first major book, *The Methods of Ethics*, which appeared in 1874 and went through five editions during his lifetime. But he also published *The Principles of Political Economy* (1883), *Outlines of the History of Ethics for English Readers* (1886), *The Elements of Politics* (1891), and *Practical Ethics, A Collection of Addresses and Essays* (1898). Singer provides an excellent collection (Sidgwick 2000) of those of Sidgwick's many essays and reviews most relevant to the *Methods*. A number of important works appeared posthumously.

Clearly, Sidgwick was not only a pre-eminent moral philosopher, but also an epistemologist, theologian, classicist, economist, political theorist, political and economic historian, literary critic, parapsychologist, and educational theorist. If he was a founder of the Cambridge school of philosophy, he was also a founder of the Cambridge school of economics (along with his colleague and sometimes nemesis Alfred Marshall) and of the Cambridge school of political theory (along with such colleagues as Oscar Browning and Sir John Seeley). He had a profound, if not always gratefully acknowledged, impact on his students and colleagues. Perhaps Balfour put it best, when he observed: 'Of all the men I have known he was the readiest to consider every controversy and every controversialist on their merits. He never claimed authority; he never sought to impose his views; he never argued for victory; he never evaded an issue' (Sidgwick and Sidgwick 1906: 311).

In recent years it has become increasingly evident just how important a force Sidgwick was in the larger cultural developments of his age. His friends included George Eliot, T. H. Green, James Bryce, William James, F. W. H. Myers, and, of special importance, John Addington Symonds, the erudite cultural historian, poet, and man of letters who was a pioneer in the serious historical study of same-sex love, and a founding father of what would become gay liberation. Many of Sidgwick's closest friends were devoted to the celebration of same-sex love on an ancient Greek or Hellenic model (Dowling 1996; Symonds 1967; Schultz 2004). Moreover, Sidgwick's sister Minnie has recently emerged as an important exemplar of Victorian/Edwardian same-sex practices (Schultz 2004; Bolt 2011).

Even more controversial has been recent work revealing the peculiar direction taken by the leaders of the Society for Psychical Research in the decades following Sidgwick's death, when Eleanor Sidgwick and her brothers and other close confidants, believing themselves to be acting on instructions from the personas of departed founders of the SPR (Sidgwick, Gurney, and Myers), conspired to bring about the birth of a 'spirit child' who would supposedly become a new Messiah. Such matters do complicate any account of Sidgwick's ethical and political thought in very unusual ways. However, the bulk of what follows will be concerned with the life and work of the Henry Sidgwick who lived from 1838 to 1900, rather than the supposed doings and communications of his surviving spirit, spouse, and relatives. To be sure, Sidgwick the man was in many ways even better and more philosophically interesting than Sidgwick the academic philosopher (Blanshard 1984). He was in fact much loved for his sympathetic conversation, and many of his deepest philosophical questions and concerns can be found in his communications with his friends, rather than in his more formal writings. But alas, his supposed posthumous communications have not to date lived up to the standard he set in his life as more conventionally conceived.

II. FROM CONFORMITY AND SUBSCRIPTION TO THE *METHODS OF ETHICS*

In 1867, when he had already been struggling with the issue of subscribing to the Thirty-Nine Articles for some years, Sidgwick sent a draft of his pamphlet on 'The Ethics of Conformity and Subscription' to Mill, in what would be their only direct exchange. Sidgwick was involved with the Free Christian Union, which was concerned to promote free and open religious inquiry, and his pamphlet eloquently reflected that commitment. Drawn to theism, which allowed for a highly latitudinarian theology emphasizing the justice, or at least non-absurdity, of the universe, he harboured considerable scepticism when it came to such matters as the Trinity, Virgin Birth, or eternal punishment. His pamphlet was in effect a brief for the type of free and open inquiry that he had absorbed from his beloved Apostles: 'I have written a pamphlet...on the text "Let every man be fully persuaded in his own mind." That is really the gist of the pamphlet—that if the preachers of religion wish to retain their hold over educated men they must show in their utterances on sacred occasions the same sincerity, exactness, unreserve, that men of science show in expounding the laws of nature. I do not think that much good is to be done by saying this, but I want to liberate my soul, and then ever after hold my peace' (Sidgwick and Sidgwick 1906: 226). Put more fully, in the published 1870 version of the pamphlet:

> What theology has to learn from the predominant studies of the age is something very different from advice as to its method or estimates of its utility; it is the imperative necessity of accepting unreservedly the conditions of life under which these studies live and flourish…we only accept authority of a particular sort; the authority, namely, that is formed and maintained by the unconstrained agreement of individual thinkers, each of whom we believe to be seeking truth with single-mindedness and sincerity, and declaring what he has found with scrupulous veracity, and the greatest attainable exactness and precision. (Sidgwick 1870: 14–15)

It is no exaggeration to say that Sidgwick devoted his life to this vision of inquiry, which informed not only his criticisms of the Church of England, but his philosophical work, educational philosophy, parapsychology, and much else besides. To his mind this form of inquiry was, especially in the ethical sphere, highly Socratic, and the needed antidote to theological orthodoxy: 'Theology has gone as far as the moral sense and natural instincts of mankind would allow (and the limit is certainly elastic), in discouraging single-minded inquiry, discouraging exactness of statement, discouraging sincerity of utterance' (Sidgwick 1870: 15). Its casuistical claims must be brought onto the more 'neutral' ground of ethics, and come before the bar 'of commonsense,—that is, of the mass of well-intentioned, intelligent, and disinterested persons', so that 'we can neutralize and dispel at once the special sophistries that tempt, and the singular scruples that beset, an individual thinker shaping his private conduct in solitude' (Sidgwick 1870: 30–1). It is noteworthy that neither Sidgwick nor Mill deemed this strategy to be inconsistent with utilitarianism, and that however critical Sidgwick may have been of common-sense morality, he treated it with great respect in certain domains.

Sidgwick's resignation crisis and struggles with the duty of truth-telling would come to define his reputation, despite his philosophical arguments (described in Section IV) on behalf of the possible justifiability of an esoteric morality, not to mention his practices of concealment on behalf of Symonds. Even his objections to the Anglican Church would largely be cast in forms unlikely to diminish, at least publicly, its authority. He took his public authority very seriously indeed, and in later life did largely 'hold his peace' rather than speak disingenuously (Schultz 2004).

But however critical he may have been of religious orthodoxy, he was deeply and sympathetically engaged with the social and philosophical attractions of a religious outlook. Indeed, he always kept one or another biblical text in his mind, as a kind of working motto for that period of his life. From 1869 to 1875, the period that saw the completion and publication of the *Methods*, his key text was in fact: 'Let every man be fully persuaded in his own mind', Romans 14:5—the epigraph of 'The Ethics of Conformity and Subscription'.

But fully persuaded he would never be. For his part, Mill had commented on the draft: 'What ought to be the exceptions…to the general duty of truth? This large question has never yet been treated in a way at once rational and comprehensive, partly because people have been afraid to meddle with it, and partly because mankind have never yet generally admitted that the effect which actions tend to produce on human happiness is what constitutes them right or wrong' (Mill 1974; Schultz 2004: 134). Sidgwick, Mill urged, should turn his 'thoughts to this more comprehensive subject'.

The *Methods* was the result, but, as the famous story related by Oscar Browning has it, Sidgwick was less than elated by his great work, commenting dejectedly upon publication of it that the first word was 'Ethics' and the last word was 'Failure'. His sense of failure was really an extension of earlier worries. He always allowed that he found the problem of whether he ought to resign his Fellowship very 'difficult, and I may say that it was while struggling with the difficulty thence arising that I went through a good deal of the thought that was ultimately systematised in the *Methods of Ethics*' (Sidgwick and Sidgwick 1906: 38). But the greater systematizing did not yield the results that he had most hoped to achieve. Ethical duty was left even more indefinite after his philosophical investigations than it had been before them.

III. Utilitarian Convergence

Sidgwick mainly considered three methods of ethics—intuitional or common-sense morality (that one ought ultimately to conform to the system of such familiar duties as truth-telling and promise-keeping), rational egoism (that one ought ultimately to act to promote one's own good), and utilitarianism (that one ought ultimately to act to promote the good of all, the greatest good). Each method, and by method Sidgwick means a way of 'obtaining reasoned convictions as to what ought to be done', receives what can aptly be called a classic treatment, but the plan of the book can make it hard to follow the thread of Sidgwick's thought, particularly on the more philosophical points having to do with intuitionism. 'Intuitionism' confusingly refers to both one of the methods of ethics—either common-sense duties or the more systematic account of them given in such works as those of William Whewell and Henry Calderwood—and, in more abstract philosophical form, to the justificatory side of all the methods, particularly when it comes to the fundamental principles they invoke.

Thus, Sidgwick denies that conscience delivers immediate judgements on particular acts. Rather, 'reflective persons, in proportion to their reflectiveness, come to rely rather on abstract universal intuitions relating to classes of cases conceived under general notions'. This leads then to intuitional or common-sense morality, which in the *Methods* covers both more deontological views and non-hedonistic teleological ones, on the ground that the latter tend to construe virtue similarly as simply the thing to be done, whatever the consequences. But the process of reflection should not stop there. Without 'being disposed to deny that conduct commonly judged to be right is so, we may yet require some deeper explanation why it is so'. Thus we reach 'philosophical intuitionism', which, 'while accepting the morality of common sense as in the main sound, still attempts to find for it a philosophic basis which it does not itself offer: to get one or more principles more absolutely and undeniably true and evident, from which the current rules might be deduced, either just as they are commonly received or with slight modifications and rectifications' (Sidgwick 1874/1907: 102).

The ascent to this philosophical intuitionism, which was rehearsed to some extent in 'The Ethics of Conformity and Subscription', is especially evident in Book III, where Sidgwick has the utilitarian demonstrating to the dogmatic intuitionist that the principles of Truth, Justice, etc. have only a dependent and subordinate validity: arguing either that the principle is really only affirmed by Common-Sense as a general rule admitting of exceptions and qualifications, as in the case of Truth, and that we require some further principle for systematising these exceptions and qualifications; or that the fundamental notion is vague and needs further determination, as in the case of Justice; and further, that the different rules are liable to conflict with each other, and that we require some higher principle to decide the issue thus raised; and again, that the rules are differently formulated by different persons, and that these differences admit of no Intuitional solution, while they show the vagueness and ambiguity of the common moral notions to which the Intuitionist appeals. (Sidgwick 1874/1907: 421)

Thus, common sense is revealed as more or less unconsciously reliant upon utilitarian calculation, or shown to presuppose something very like it, since it keeps giving way to certain more abstract formal principles (whose application is less straightforward) as the better candidates for genuinely self-evident truths. In fact, utilitarianism is derived from two more fundamental principles: 'the self-evident principle that the good of any one individual is of no more importance, from the point of view (if I may say so) of the Universe, than the good of any other; unless, that is, there are special grounds for believing that more good is likely to be realised in the one case than in the other. And it is evident to me that as a rational being I am bound to aim at good generally,—so far as it is attainable by my efforts,—not at a particular part of it' (Sidgwick 1874/1907: 382). Sidgwick also defends a universalizability principle (one must be able to will one's maxim to be a universal law) and a principle of rational prudence (or temporal neutrality, such that one should be *ceteris paribus* equally concerned with all parts of one's life), in addition to the utilitarian principle(s) of rational benevolence.

Is the *Methods* therefore a defence of the method of utilitarianism, as best representing the impartial, moral point of view?

Many have called it just that (Rawls 1971/99, 2007; Singer 2007, 2011; Singer and De Lazari-Radek 2010), and there can be no denying that Sidgwick had a great impact on the utilitarian agenda. But curiously enough, this is something that he often denied. His aim, he proclaimed at the beginning of the work, was simply 'to expound as clearly and as fully as my limits will allow the different methods of Ethics that I find implicit in our common moral reasoning; to point out their mutual relations; and where they seem to conflict, to define the issue as much as possible'. Echoing his views on theological inquiry, he confessed that 'I have wished to put aside temporarily the urgent need which we all feel of finding and adopting the true method of determining what we ought to do; and to consider simply what conclusions will be rationally reached if we start with certain ethical premises, and with what degree of certainty and precision' (Sidgwick 1874/1907: p. vi).

In fact, he would respond to critics that common-sense morality was his morality as much as anyone's, though he was perhaps more candid in his reply to Calderwood's critical review of the *Methods*, which questioned why he had not simply confined himself 'to the consideration of Intuitionism in its most philosophical form'. That gambit, he admitted, 'would have led me at once to Utilitarianism: because I hold that the only moral intuitions which sound philosophy can accept as ultimately valid are those which at the same time provide the only possible philosophical basis of the Utilitarian creed. I thus necessarily regard Prof. Calderwood's Intuitionism as a phase in the development of the

Intuitional method, which comes naturally between the crude thought of Butler's "plain man" and the Rational Utilitarianism to which I ultimately endeavor to lead my reader.' That is, allowing that the morality of common sense is his as well, he must as a philosopher nonetheless

> ask myself whether I see clearly and distinctly the self-evidence of any particular maxims of duty, as I see that of the formal principles 'that what is right for me must be right for all persons in precisely similar circumstances' and 'that I ought to prefer the greater good of another to my own lesser good': I have no doubt whatever that I do not... But I could not always have made this distinction; and I believe that the majority of moral persons do not make it: most 'plain men' would probably say, at any rate on the first consideration of the matter, that they saw the obligations of Veracity and Good Faith as clearly and immediately as they saw those of Equity and Rational Benevolence. How then am I to argue with such persons? It will not settle the matter to tell them that they have observed their own mental processes wrongly, and that more careful introspection will show them the non-intuitive character of what they took for intuitions; especially as in many cases I do not believe that the error is one of misobservation. Still less am I inclined to dispute the 'primitiveness' or 'spontaneousness' or 'originality' of these apparent intuitions. On the contrary, I hold that here, as in other departments of thought, the primitive spontaneous processes of the mind are mixed with error, which is only to be removed gradually by comprehensive reflection upon the results of these processes. Through such a course of reflection I have endeavored to lead my readers in chaps. 2–10 of Book III of my treatise: in the hope that after they have gone through it they may find their original apprehension of the self-evidence of moral maxims importantly modified. (Sidgwick 1876: 564)

Whether Sidgwick succeeded in this effort has been the subject of much debate. But some of the best textual and contextual commentary on him does take his professed stance very seriously. Thus, J. B. Schneewind's *Sidgwick's Ethics and Victorian Moral Philosophy* (1977), the most penetrating treatment of Sidgwick's ethics produced in the twentieth century, underscored how Sidgwick's work was shaped by both the utilitarian tradition and its intuitionist and religious opposition (represented in part by the 'Cambridge Moralists' William Whewell, Julius Hare, F. D. Maurice, and John Grote):

> it is a mistake to view the book as primarily a defence of utilitarianism. It is true, of course, that a way of supporting utilitarianism is worked out in detail in the *Methods*, and that there are places in it where Sidgwick seems to be saying quite plainly that utilitarianism is the best available ethical theory. From his other writings we know also that he thinks of himself as committed to utilitarianism, and that he assumes it in analysing specific moral and political issues. Yet it does not follow that the *Methods* itself should be taken simply as an argument for that position. We must try to understand it in a way that makes sense of its author's own explicit account of it. (Schneewind 1977: 192)

Before Schneewind, Brand Blanshard, long an admirer of Sidgwick, agreed that 'Sidgwick's acuteness was equaled by his sanity and moral seriousness; and for judicial detachment— the somewhat bleak, but clear, full light in which he sees things—he stands quite alone, so far as I know, in philosophic history... For those who want to know simply what ethical theories make sense and what do not, and who are bored with attempts to make the subject interesting, Sidgwick's book is supreme' (Blanshard 1961: 90–1).

IV. Critics and Chaos

To be sure, critics from T. H. Green (1883) and F. H. Bradley (1877) down to John Rawls (1971/1999, 2007), Alan Donagan (1977, 1992), Terence Irwin (1992, 2007, 2009), David Brink (2003), Thomas Hurka (2011), and Christine Korsgaard (2009) have charged that the *Methods* fails to capture in an impartial or sufficiently neutral or accurate way the best versions of the views of Aristotle, Kant, Hegel, Whewell, and/or idealist philosophers, and that the best alternative methods are either distorted or neglected out of a bias towards hedonistic utilitarianism.

One should bear in mind, however, as a necessary preliminary to considering such critiques, that Sidgwick was not claiming that he had in the *Methods* exhaustively treated all possible methods or even all methods that had been of importance historically. Indeed, his most extensive treatments of perfectionism, evolutionism, and idealism came in other works, and he was singularly appreciative, as his *Outlines* shows, of the rich diversity of historical approaches to ethics, stressing that his own work reflected the distinctively modern, more jural approach (stressing duty or the moral law) to the subject, rather than the 'attractive' forms of perfectionist egoism characteristic of the ancients (Larmore 1996). He was in key respects picking up the conversation as he found it, in what he took to be a progressive state of civilization, trying to sort out what could be taken away from the debates between Mill and Whewell.

And there is of course invariably an element of risk in following a convergence or reconciliation strategy, seeking to show how the best versions of competing approaches can be harmonized or made to coincide in their results. Just such a strategy has been followed by Derek Parfit, in *On What Matters* (2011), a work that, much like Sidgwick's, invites criticism to the effect that it has not succeeded in addressing the best versions of the views at issue. It is one thing to say that, for example, Sidgwick just got Kant or Whewell wrong; it is another matter to say that he could have reconstructed their work in better, more charitable ways. The more penetrating criticisms of Sidgwick are of the latter type, as in Donagan's attempts to show that common-sense morality can be rationalized on a more consistently Whewellian or deontological basis (Donagan 1977).

But beyond rejoinders along these lines, it must also be recognized that (1) Sidgwick was also critical of utilitarianism and transformed it in ways that radically departed from the views of Bentham and the Mills, and (2) he did not in the end hold that he had succeeded in adequately defending even the best version of utilitarianism.

Thus, on (1), Sidgwick obviously rejected the empiricism, reductionism, associationism, psychological egoism, naturalism, and generally combative anti-religious arguments of the earlier secular utilitarians. Indeed, his chief emphasis was on the sphere of personal ethics that Bentham and the Mills had largely neglected. He was profoundly influenced, not only by the Cambridge Moralists, but also by such figures as Kant, Samuel Clarke, and Joseph Butler—not to mention his great masters Plato and Aristotle. Although he deemed the metaphysical issue of freedom of the will largely irrelevant to ethics, he argued that it was a fundamental mistake to think that people were psychologically always or mostly caused to act only for their own individual pleasure or good. The earlier utilitarians, he claimed, had not succeeded either in providing a fundamental justification for their views or in recognizing the incoherence of promoting the greatest happiness as the ultimate normative standard when taking people to be hopelessly self-interested psychologically (Sidgwick 1904).

In any given situation, Sidgwick held, there is something that it is right or that one ought to do. This is the proper sphere of ethics, and this basic concept of morality is a unique, highly general notion of 'ought' or 'right' that is irreducible to naturalistic terms and *sui generis*. Moral approbation is 'inseparably bound up with the conviction, implicit or explicit, that the conduct approved is "really" right—that is, that it cannot without error, be disapproved by any other mind' (Sidgwick 1874/1907: 27). Subjectivism, emotivism, and other non-cognitivist interpretations of moral judgement misconstrue its nature, the ways in which it is simply not about one's psychological states. As Blanshard put it, summarizing Sidgwick, 'I do not call the action right because I feel in a certain way; I feel in this way because I think the action right' (Blanshard 1961: 93). With the judgement comes at least some degree of motivation, though not always sufficient motivation, to do the right thing.

Thus, Sidgwick was as much concerned to avoid the so-called 'naturalistic fallacy' as his student G. E. Moore, who in *Principia Ethica* (1903) famously challenged all attempts to define 'good' in terms of natural properties, since they left an 'open question' of whether such-and-such property really was good. Sidgwick tended to emphasize the irreducibility of 'ought' or 'right', but his account of 'good' also contained a rational element, in that, contra interpretations of him as advancing a naturalistic 'full-information' account of the good (Rawls 1971/1999), his account actually represents an objectivist view that allows that some desires, however informed, may be rejected as irrational or unreasonable (Schneewind 1977; Parfit 1984). Crisp (1990) provides perhaps the best possible defence of a full-information interpretation of Sidgwick's view, but he also admits that the objective list reading is more charitable.

At any rate, for Sidgwick there would seem to be a kind of continuum between rational judgments involving 'ought' and those involving 'good', with the latter being less tied to immediate action. But Hurka (2003) has raised some important points suggesting how close Sidgwick and Moore actually were:

> After defining the good as what we ought to desire, he [Sidgwick] added that 'since irrational desires cannot always be dismissed at once by voluntary effort,' the definition cannot use 'ought' in 'the strictly ethical sense,' but only in 'the wider sense in which it merely connotes an ideal or standard.' But this raises the question of what this 'wider sense' is, and in particular whether it is at all distinct from Moore's 'good.' If the claim that we 'ought' to have a desire is only the claim that the desire is 'an ideal,' how does it differ from the claim that the desire is good? When 'ought' is stripped of its connection with choice, its distinctive meaning seems to slip away. (Hurka 2003: 603–4)

Now, it is evident that this cognitivism figures throughout Sidgwick's reconciliation of intuitional morality and utilitarianism. But his is a particularly sophisticated, fallibilistic form of philosophical intuitionism. There are, he holds, four criteria or conditions 'the complete fulfillment of which would establish a significant proposition, apparently self-evident, in the highest degree of certainty attainable: and which must be approximately realized by the premises of our reasoning in any inquiry, if that reasoning is to lead us cogently to trustworthy conclusions' (Sidgwick 1874/1907: 338).

1. Or the 'Cartesian Criterion', demands that the 'terms of the proposition must be clear and precise'.
2. The 'self-evidence of the proposition must be ascertained by careful reflection', which

is especially important in ethics because 'any strong sentiment, however purely sub-jective, is apt to transform itself into the semblance of an intuition; and it requires careful contemplation to detect the illusion' (Sidgwick 1874/1907: 339)

3. The 'propositions accepted as self-evident must be mutually consistent', since it 'is obvious that any collision between two intuitions is a proof that there is error in one or the other, or in both' (Sidgwick 1874/1907: 341).

4. Since 'it is implied in the very notion of Truth that it is essentially the same for all minds, the denial by another of a proposition that I have affirmed has a tendency to impair my confidence in its validity' (Sidgwick 1874/1907: 341).

This last, already evident in 'The Ethics of Conformity and Subscription', adds a social dimension to Sidgwick's epistemology: 'the absence of such disagreement must remain an indispensable negative condition of the certainty of our beliefs', for 'if I find any of my judge-ments, intuitive or inferential, in direct conflict with a judgment of some other minds, there must be error somewhere: and if I have no more reason to suspect error in the other mind than in my own, reflective comparison between the two judgments necessarily reduces me temporarily to a state of neutrality' (Sidgwick 1874/1907: 341–2).

In other works, notably *Lectures on the Philosophy of Kant* (1905), Sidgwick explained that these conditions (the first two rolled into one) only afforded the best means for reduc-ing the risk of error, rather than establishing indubitable truth. These works have, unfortu-nately, too often been neglected in the large literature devoted to Sidgwick's epistemology, which has been especially shaped by debates over whether he accorded any epistemic value to common-sense morality. Some, following Rawls (1971), have found in the *Methods* some-thing akin to Rawlsian reflective equilibrium, balancing and granting some weight to con-sidered judgements, including common-sense ones, at all levels of generality (Schneewind 1977; Schultz 1992; Shaver 1999, 2011; Parfit 2011). Others, following R. M. Hare (1981) and Peter Singer (1974) have emphasized Sidgwick's critique of common-sense morality, arguing that it plays no evidentiary role in his argument (Skelton 2007, 2010a, 2010b; Deigh 2007, 2010). Much rides, however, on how tentative, dynamic, and social Sidgwick's epis-temology is taken to be, whether one reads him as finding in common-sense resources for giving bite to the coherence and consensus conditions, as he apparently did in 'The Ethics of Conformity and Subscription', and for filling out a conception of public reason/ethical code, as in such works as *Practical Ethics* (1898).

Also, given the minimal nature of Sidgwick's meta-ethics—he does not appeal to any spe-cial moral faculty or, like Moore, posit ontologically a non-natural property of 'goodness'—one could be forgiven for thinking that the very word 'intuition' may often be more trouble than it is worth, since with Sidgwick it mostly amounts, as in Parfit (2011), to the claim that there are knowable, normative object-given reasons, beliefs justified by their content, for certain acts and desires (Crisp 2002; Suikkanen and Cottingham 2009). Following Parfit's interpretation and defence of Sidgwick's intuitionism, it is also hard to see how one could avoid deploying something like the method of reflective equilibrium in some fashion, when for example comparing one apparent intuition to another.

In any event, Sidgwick's treatment of classical utilitarianism was in many respects highly reconstructive, grounding the view on a cognitivist account of moral judgement that, while metaphysically minimal, nonetheless took over much from the earlier intuitionist critics of utilitarianism.

And even on the matter of ethical hedonism, where Sidgwick is often taken as a better, more consistent representative of Benthamism than J. S. Mill, his position was in truth highly reconstructive. He did claim that the best account of ultimate goodness is a hedonistic one, and that this is an informative, non-tautological claim, though also a more controversial one than many of the others that he defends. It is on this score that critics such as Irwin charge that Sidgwick's hedonistic commitments, and his related criticisms of T. H. Green's account of self-realization, problematically presuppose that practical reason simply must be fully clear and determinate in its conclusions (Irwin 1992: 288–90). That is, Sidgwick argued that without something like the hedonistic metric it would be impossible to decisively compare, say, one virtue to another. Moreover, could one really recommend making people more virtuous at the expense of their happiness? What if the virtuous life were conjoined to extreme pain, with no compensating good to anyone? As Shaver points out, 'Sidgwick works out what it is reasonable to desire, and so attaches moral to natural properties, by the ordinary gamut of philosopher's strategies—appeals to logical coherence, plausibility, and judgment after reflection' (Shaver 2000: 270).

Naturally, on the matter of Sidgwick's hedonism there is also much debate. Sumner has maintained that Sidgwick and Mill, by contrast with Bentham,

> seemed to recognize that the mental states we call pleasures are a mixed bag as far as their phenomenal properties are concerned. On their view what pleasures have in common is not something internal to them—their peculiar feeling tone, or whatever—but something about us—the fact that we like them, enjoy them, value them, find them satisfying, seek them, wish to prolong them, and so on. (Sumner 1996: 86)

But Crisp has countered that Sidgwick's writings did not express his better inclinations on the subject: 'Sidgwick is at heart an internalist about pleasure who was misled by the heterogeneity argument into offering an externalist view which is open to serious objections' (Crisp 2007: 134).

Intriguingly, as W. J. Mander (2011) has observed, Green, an old Rugby friend of Sidgwick's, criticized Sidgwick's hedonism for being less definite as a method than the good of self-realization. Some, notably Gadamer (1988) and Irwin (1992, 2007), have found virtue in the fact that, as Blanshard put it, 'in the great mass of ethical discussion in these books [Plato and Aristotle] there is curiously little in the way of definite and solid result regarding the proper method of ethics' (Blanshard 1961: 37). But Green, in the conclusion to his *Prolegomena*, seems rather to be suggesting that he has in fact beaten Sidgwick at his own game:

> To most people sufficient direction for their pursuits is afforded by claims so well established in conventional morality that they are intuitively recognized, and that a conscience merely responsive to social disapprobation would reproach us for neglecting them. For all of us it is so in regard to a great part of our lives. But the cases we have been considering are those in which some 'counsel of perfection' is needed, which reference to such claims does not supply, and which has to be derived from reference to a theory of ultimate good. In such cases many questions have to be answered, which intuition cannot answer, before the issue is arrived at to which the theory of ultimate good becomes applicable; but then the cases only occur for persons who have leisure and faculty for dealing with such questions. For them the essential thing is that their theory of the good should afford a really available criterion for estimating those further claims upon them which are not enforced by the sanction of conventional morality,

and a criterion which affords no plea to the self-indulgent impulse. Our point has been to show…that such a criterion is afforded by the theory of ultimate good as a perfection of the human spirit resting on the will to be perfect (which may be called in short the theory of virtue as an end in itself), but not by the theory of good as consisting in a maximum of possible pleasure. (Green 1883/2003: 470)

In other words, when, with Sidgwick, one is reasoning in critical mode, not the everyday serviceable common-sense one, utilitarian calculation is just boneless, hopeless—and insufficiently respectful of individual freedom—whereas the perfection of one's capabilities is relatively clear and definite. Green, as much as Sidgwick, was sensitive to the vital importance of having a clear sense of one's duty. He simply differed over which was the more helpful and determinate account of the good for this purpose.

To be sure, Sidgwick knew full well that rational egoism was not a matter of narrow selfishness, and could take very high-minded forms, as in perfectionism or idealism. He was quite familiar with the different forms that an ethics of 'self-realization' could take, and took such views very seriously as forming a leading alternative to a hedonistic account of the good. But he could never concede that the idealists had succeeded where hedonism had not—self-realization involved too many different capabilities to be determinate, and there was nothing incoherent about the idea of a sum of pleasures.

Furthermore, it should also be stressed that Sidgwick took hedonistic utilitarianism in directions that no previous secular utilitarian had even imagined. Not only did he pose, apparently for the first time, the problem of future generations and population size, issues that bring out the difference between total and average utilitarianism. But, notoriously, he also considered, without any invocation of either God's greater wisdom or psychological egoism, how common-sense or everyday morality might have its most felicific effects if largely believed to be true, and acted upon by people who would not in any conscious way be thinking in utilitarian terms:

> Thus, on Utilitarian principles, it may be right to do and privately recommend, under certain circumstances, what it would not be right to advocate openly; it may be right to teach openly to one set of persons what it would be wrong to teach to others; it may be conceivably right to do, if it can be done with comparative secrecy, what it would be wrong to do in the face of the world; and even, if perfect secrecy can be reasonably expected, what it would be wrong to recommend by private advice or example. These conclusions are all of a paradoxical character: there is no doubt that the moral consciousness of a plain man broadly repudiates the general notion of an esoteric morality, differing from the one popularly taught; and it would be commonly agreed that an action which would be bad if done openly is not rendered good by secrecy. We may observe, however, that there are strong utilitarian reasons for maintaining generally this latter common opinion…Thus the Utilitarian conclusion, carefully stated, would seem to be this; that the opinion that secrecy may render an action right which would not otherwise be so should itself be kept comparatively secret; and similarly it seems expedient that the doctrine that esoteric morality is expedient should itself be kept esoteric…a Utilitarian may reasonably desire, on Utilitarian principles, that some of his conclusions should be rejected by mankind generally; or even that the vulgar should keep aloof from his system as a whole, in so far as the inevitable indefiniteness and complexity of its calculations render it likely to lead to bad results in their hands. (Sidgwick 1874/1907: 489–90)

Thus, although one could plausibly say that at some level Sidgwick was an 'act' utilitarian rather than a 'rule' utilitarian, and that his notion of method covered in some abstract way the decision-procedures people should deploy at least when thinking critically, he allowed such a degree of possibly justifiable indirect utilitarianism that one can envision a fully Sidgwickian ethical society in which very few people (if any) are consciously invoking the utilitarian standard at any level. Such views might accord well with a few of Sidgwick's own mature practices, but they do not accord with the familiar Kantian insistence on the necessary publicity of fundamental moral principles. Snidely allowing that this perspective allowed Sidgwick a consistent interpretation of the different 'levels' of moral thinking, critical versus everyday, Bernard Williams suggested that this was because Sidgwick was a 'Government House' utilitarian who identified the different levels with different sets of people, the colonialist rulers and the colonized respectively (Williams 1982). At the extreme, for all humanity knows, the utilitarian standard is God's standard, but the universe is made to accord with it in part by disposing humanity to believe and act on very different terms.

Yet even on this score, Sidgwick's views have attracted some forceful defenders. Peter Singer and Katarzina De Lazari-Radek attack the Kantian and neo-Kantian publicity requirement and seek to justify the indirect and esoteric strategies that Sidgwick elaborated, demonstrating, among other things, how even such supposedly alternative views as Catholic moral theology admit a 'doctrine of "mental reservation," which holds that it is permissible to say something that misleads, and yet avoid the sin of lying by mentally adding information that would, if spoken, make the response truthful' (Singer and De Lazari-Radek 2010: 36). Of course, as Sidgwick's stance on subscription suggests, he thought the greater happiness (and the moral authority of organized religion) would be better served by greater clerical transparency (Sidgwick 1870, 1898). Honest silence was better than obvious oiliness.

Now, returning to point (2), if Sidgwick gave classical secular utilitarianism a serious makeover, this turned out to be all the more poignant in that despite his best efforts he did not, to his mind, render the view fully justified.

As he explained to a friend: 'Ethics is losing its interest for me rather, as the insolubility of its fundamental problem is impressed on me. I think the contribution to the formal clearness & coherence of our ethical thought which I have to offer is just worth giving: for a few speculatively-minded persons—very few. And as for all practical questions of interest, I feel as if I had now to begin at the beginning and learn the ABC' (Sidgwick and Sidgwick 1906: 277). The 'fundamental problem' of ethics was the 'dualism of the practical reason'— such that, unlike intuitional morality, rational egoism could not be reconciled with utilitarianism. Despite all the talk of self-evident axioms, the first edition of the *Methods* concluded that 'the 'Cosmos' of Duty is thus really reduced to a Chaos, and the prolonged effort of the human intellect to frame a perfect ideal of rational conduct is seen to have been foredoomed to inevitable failure' (Sidgwick 1874: 473). As Sidgwick put it elsewhere: along with '(a) a fundamental moral conviction that I ought to sacrifice my own happiness, if by so doing I can increase the happiness of others to a greater extent than I diminish my own, I find also (b) a conviction—which it would be paradoxical to call "moral", but which is none the less fundamental—that it would be irrational to sacrifice any portion of my own happiness unless the sacrifice is to be somehow at some time compensated by an equivalent addition to my own happiness' (Sidgwick 1889: 483). Each of these convictions has as much clarity and certainty 'as the process of introspection can give' and each also finds wide assent 'in the common sense of mankind'.

In another passage from the early editions of the *Methods* he elaborated the difficulty in a singularly illuminating way:

> For, if we find an ultimate and fundamental contradiction in our apparent intuitions of what is Reasonable in conduct, we seem forced to the conclusion that they were not really intuitions after all, and that the apparently intuitive operation of the Practical Reason is essentially illusory. Therefore it is, one may say, a matter of life and death to the Practical Reason that this premiss should be somehow obtained... it seems plain that in proportion as man has lived in the exercise of the Practical Reason—as he believed—and feels as an actual force the desire to do what is right and reasonable as such, his demand for this premiss will be intense and imperious. Thus we are not surprised to find Socrates—the type for all ages of the man in whom this desire is predominant—declaring with simple conviction that 'if the Rulers of the Universe do not prefer the just man to the unjust, it is better to die than to live.' And we must observe that in the feeling that prompts to such a declaration the desire to rationalize one's own conduct is not the sole, nor perhaps always the most prominent, element. For however difficult it may practically be to do one's duty when it comes into conflict with one's happiness, it often does not seem very difficult, when we are considering the question in the abstract, to decide in favour of duty. When a man passionately refuses to believe that the 'Wages of Virtue' can 'be dust,' it is often less from any private reckoning about his own wages than from a disinterested aversion to a universe so fundamentally irrational that 'Good for the Individual' is not ultimately identified with 'Universal Good.' (1874: 470–1)

This passage, with its allusions to Tennyson's poem 'Wages', eloquently points up the larger implications of the dualism, how it might suggest that reason is an illusion and the universe absurd.

Sidgwick mainly considered two related solutions, a weakening of epistemological standards, or a theism postulating the moral government of the universe. On the first, he suggests that if 'we find that in our supposed knowledge of the world of nature propositions are commonly taken to be universally true, which seem to rest on no other ground than that we have a strong disposition to accept them, and that they are indispensable to the systematic coherence of our beliefs,—it will be more difficult to reject a similarly supported assumption in ethics, without opening the door to universal scepticism' (Sidgwick 1874/1907: 509). On the second, he explains that if 'we may assume the existence of such a Being, as God, by the consensus of theologians, is conceived to be, it seems that Utilitarians may legitimately infer the existence of Divine sanctions to the code of social duty as constructed on a Utilitarian basis; and such sanctions would, of course, suffice to make it always every one's interest to promote universal happiness to the best of his knowledge' (Sidgwick 1874/1907: 506).

Of course, Sidgwick also considered other efforts to address the dualism, such as Green's ethics of 'self-realization'. But he cogently criticized Green for waffling on the matter of whether one's own perfection could come into conflict with the common good or perfection of all, which it could do if certain capabilities figuring in one's self-realization were not simply part and parcel of the common good, but competitive. As David Brink has put it, following Sidgwick, Green waffled between a notion of perfection involving the exercise of the 'full range of an individual's rational capacities' and one involving 'the exercise of specifically moral capacities connected with the common good'. These forms of perfection are distinct, if not independent, which means that 'many sacrifices the perfection of others demands will be genuine, and not all of them will be fully compensable. And this is enough to raise the spectre that there will be a kind of dualism of practical reason, not exactly between self

and others, but between self-confined and other-regarding aspects of one's own perfection'
(Brink 2003: 122–3). Or, in Sidgwick's words, and more generally: 'It is difficult to see why
the operation of self-distinguishing consciousness is to obliterate the difference—so far as
natural desire goes—between Own good and Others' good. It would rather seem to empha-
sise and intensify it, since a self-distinguishing consciousness must distinguish itself from
other selves' (Sidgwick 1902: 78).

As with Sidgwick's epistemology, the dualism of practical reason has given rise to a vast
literature. From idealist efforts to find one's own good in the common good, to Moore's
denial that the notion of 'own good' even made sense, to Rawls's defence of the reasonable
as framing the rational, to Parfit's attempts to demonstrate that omnipersonal reasons can
be stronger than personal ones, Sidgwick's framing of the 'fundamental problem' has been
at the heart of the most important ethical philosophical discussions of the last century and
a half (Crisp 1995–6; Skorupski 2001; Bucolo, Crisp, and Schultz 2007, 2011; Smith 2009;
Phillips 2011). If most of these discussions have been framed in more limited terms than
Sidgwick's, they have nonetheless genuinely contributed to progress in ethical philosophy.
Even if we reject Sidgwick's language of personal point of view versus point of view of the
universe, it is difficult to resist the idea that, at the least, and in Parfit's words: 'When one
of our two possible acts would make things go in some way that would be impartially better, but the other act would make things go better either for ourselves or for those to whom
we have close ties, we often have sufficient reasons to act in either of these two ways' (Parfit
2011: 137).

V. Psychics, Metaphysics, Economics, and Politics

For his part, Sidgwick viewed the dualism of practical reason as more of a cosmic calam-
ity: 'In the face of the conflict between Virtue & Happiness, my own voluntary life, and that
of every other man constituted like me, i.e. I believe, of every normal man, is reduced to
hopeless anarchy' (Schultz 2004: 441). And it was precisely this shakiness at the foundations of reason and ethics that moved him to devote so much time and effort to psychical
research, which in his hands was really a form of natural theology.

Sidgwick's interest in the supernatural went back to his early years. As his faith in
orthodoxy had faded, his hopes for his 'ghostological' investigations had grown, and he
seemed to think that they might unveil the 'Unseen World' that stood behind the myths
and miracles of all the world's major religions. The most important investigation, to his
mind, concerned the possible survival of physical death, since this would open up the
way to a theistic account of how the universe might be 'friendly' in a way that the material world as known scarcely evidenced. In human history, he claimed, the postulate
of immortality 'is that of the best part of mankind: it has nearly, though not quite, the
authority of a belief of Common Sense' (Schultz 2004: 441). Moreover, as remarked, he
was profoundly convinced that the loss of the most widespread forms of religious faith
would be painful for humanity and possibly lead to moral and political chaos. As he
explained to a friend:

> In fact, the reason why I keep strict silence now for many years with regard to theology is that while I cannot myself discover adequate rational basis for the Christian hope of happy immortality, it seems to me that the general loss of such a hope, from the minds of average human beings as now constituted, would be an evil of which I cannot pretend to measure the extent. I am not prepared to say that the dissolution of the existing social order would follow, but I think the danger of such dissolution would be seriously increased, and that the evil would certainly be very great. (Sidgwick and Sidgwick 1906: 357)

Positive distaste for the prospect of survival, vividly confronting him in the shape of his friend Symonds, was something that he found utterly incomprehensible (Symonds 1967).

Unfortunately, and despite the best efforts of the Society for Psychical Research, Sidgwick never found hard proof of survival, though at the end of his life he allowed that there were some positive results from this research and grounds for hope. Within the SPR, the 'Sidgwick Group', which included Henry and Eleanor Sidgwick, the Balfour brothers, Edmund Gurney, F. W. H. Myers, Lord Rayleigh, Richard Hodgson, and others, did end up establishing to their satisfaction the reality of telepathic communication among the living (Broad 1930, 1938, 1966). But the best evidence for posthumous survival emerged only in the 1890s, with cases such as that of Leonora Piper (Gauld 2007). And by the time of the 'cross-correspondence' cases (in which separate messages to different mediums needed to be put together to make sense), the chief founders of the SPR, Sidgwick, Gurney, and Myers, were all dead—in fact, were supposedly the personas from the 'Other Side' communicating the messages that would convince Eleanor Sidgwick, the Balfours, and others of the reality of personal survival (Roy 2008a; Gray 2011). It was in this context that the—highly secret—plan to conceive a new Messiah came about. Augustus Henry Coombe-Tennant (1913–89) was the earthly child of Gerald Balfour and Winifred Coombe-Tennant (aka the medium 'Mrs. Willett'), and the supposed 'spirit child' of Gurney, but unfortunately he did not vindicate the great hopes that had been pinned on him. Nonetheless, some today still hold that 'from behind the curtain of death...came compelling evidence...that the group of seven, Myers, Gurney, Sidgwick, William Balfour, Edith Lyttelton, Annie Marshall, and Mary Catherine Lyttelton, still existed, still had an astounding agenda to be pursued, the Story and the Plan' (Roy 2008b).

It is of course possible to argue that Eleanor was thinking along lines Henry might have found congenial. After all, he had been very concerned about the decline of the religious outlook and was very sympathetic to the call for enthusiastic and inspiring ethical teachers and, in effect, a new, less superstitious, more rational religion, the better to overcome the social conflict and Machiavellianism too prevalent in the modern world. He had initially been quite enthusiastic about the Theosophical Society, until, at his behest, the SPR investigated and debunked it. There is also a rather literal esotericism about the whole scheme that makes the abstract defence of esoteric morality in the *Methods* seem eerily relevant, as though this were one way to pursue that line of thought that would have come quite naturally to Sidgwick and his circle. Sensitive mediumship and its interpretation might, like refined utilitarian calculation, be the province of the few. It is intriguing that Sidgwick's later biblical texts were, from 1875 to 1890, 'But this one thing I do forgetting those things which are behind, and reaching forth unto those things that are before, I press toward the mark for the prize of the high calling of God in Christ Jesus' (Philippians 3:13–14) and 'Gather up the fragments that remain, that nothing be lost' (John 6:12). The last refers to the aftermath of the miracle of the loaves and fishes, and suggests that he had high expectations for psychical research.

But at least in the published works of the Sidgwick who is taken to have died in 1900, there is a much more resolutely anti-metaphysical stance characterizing his ethics, economics, and politics. However obvious it may be from his psychical research that Sidgwick was profoundly critical of a materialist metaphysics, and engaged sympathetically with a complex depth psychological account of the self and personal identity that shared much with that of his greatly admired friends Frederic Myers and William James, and this much in the fashion of recent defenders of parapsychology (Tart 2009; Kelly and Kelly 2009), his academic philosophical work tended to be more by way of elaborate and very acute critiques of Spencer's evolutionism, Kantian transcendentalism, Hegelianism, the idealism of Green and Bradley, and so on. In an illustrative case, against Green's fundamental tactic for establishing a spiritual principle in nature, he argued, in a characteristic vein, that the 'argument seems to me unthinkable, because, as Green has emphatically declared, I cannot even conceive the manifold things out of the relations: and therefore I cannot even raise the question whether, if I could so conceive them, I should see them to require something other than themselves to bring them into relations' (Sidgwick 1905: 264). Sidgwick suggested that Green would never 'seriously trouble himself with Materialism', and was not therefore a source for truly effective anti-materialist arguments.

The other major treatises Sidgwick saw through publication gave very little indication of his parapsychological or metaphysical interests and talents. The *Principles of Political Economy* (1883) was an outstanding work, well informed by the latest developments in marginal utility theory coming from Jevons and others, which stressed the conceptual distinctions between normative and descriptive arguments, while steadily qualifying an individualistic, free-market account in ways that would be elaborated in C. Pigou's influential welfare economics. Indeed, the form of Sidgwick's political economy was also characteristic of his essays on economics and his third great treatise, *The Elements of Politics* (1891). He would begin with a precise statement of the 'individualistic principle'—namely, that 'what one sane adult is legally compelled to render to others should be merely the negative service of non-interference, except so far as he has voluntarily undertaken to render positive services; provided that we include in the notion of non-interference the obligation of remedying or compensating for mischief intentionally or carelessly caused by his acts—or preventing mischief that would otherwise result from previous acts' (Sidgwick 1891/1919: 42). He would then argue that the psychological assumption that each person 'can best take care of his own interest' and the sociological one that 'the common welfare is best attained by each pursuing exclusively his own welfare and that of his family in a thoroughly alert and intelligent manner'—both essential to the case for laissez-faire—can only be accepted on qualified terms allowing for numerous exceptions—including everything from education, defence, childcare, poor relief, and public works to collective bargaining, environmental protections, and protection of the interests of the mentally ill, non-human animals, and future generations.

Of course, his hope was that future generations would also represent a continued evolution in human nature, with a Millian growth of the sympathetic capabilities that would reduce social conflict and support high-minded forms of ethical socialism, such that people would be more motivated to do their part for society rather than merely advance their own interests in any narrow sense.

But Sidgwick's political philosophy admittedly assumed the utilitarian criterion as the normative bottom line, rather than arguing for it against rational egoism or other positions. And he was quite candid in owning up to the limitations of any and all attempts to outline the course of social evolution, the directions of civilization. His most extensive historical work, the posthumous *Development of European Polity* (1903), tentatively suggested only that a continued growth in federalism and large-scale state organizations was likely. If he admired the ambition of such pioneers of sociology as Spencer and Comte (whose emphasis on the 'consensus of experts' he accepted), he regarded their 'sciences' of human development as preposterous. He hoped, to be sure, that a more cosmopolitan attitude would be the wave of the future, and that the growth of international law and cooperation would decrease the likelihood of war, just as he hoped that evidence for theism might eventually be forthcoming. But he did not confuse his hopes with his evidence (Schultz 2004).

D.G. Ritchie, the idealist most disposed to reconciling idealism and utilitarianism, notoriously teased Sidgwick for having rendered utilitarianism 'tame and sleek', like a British Hegel finding everywhere the rational in the real (Ritchie 1891–2). But some, including F. A. Hayek, found in Sidgwick's political economy an alarming advance on the 'road to serfdom', the beginnings of the slippery slope that led to the 'New Liberalism' and Fabian socialism that overtook British politics in the early twentieth century (Schultz 2004). And it is true that Sidgwick countenanced a greater role for the state than the earlier utilitarians, from whom he departed on so many counts. He did not even favour the Benthamite or Austinian theory of sovereignty, which analysed law in terms of authoritative command and habitual obedience, though some have found in him certain anticipations of the law and economics approach (Medema 2004).

The political valence of Sidgwick's work has always been hard to gauge, and the debates over it are ongoing (Collini 1992 , 2001; Jones 2000; Schultz 2004, 2005; Bell 2007). Like the later Mill, he could be quite suspicious of democracy and warm to the need for a cultural 'clerisy' or vanguard of educated opinion. Unlike Mill, he was never very eloquent about the civil liberties in general; his politics tended more to reflect the anxieties that found expression in the dualism of practical reason, for example how to supply teachers or public moralists 'to correct the erroneous and short-sighted views of self-interest, representing it as divergent from duty, which certainly appear to be widely prevalent in the most advanced societies, at least among irreligious persons' (Sidgwick 1919: 213–14). But as his contributions to the Cambridge and London Ethical Societies demonstrate, he also harboured doubts about just how those public moralists might be able to perform their function, finding the common ethical ground or public reason that could render them effective; the philosophical elite may not be as helpful as one would hope:

> if we are to frame an ideal of good life for all, and to show how a unity of moral spirit and principle may manifest itself through the diversity of actions and forbearances, efforts and endurances, which the diversity of social functions render necessary—we can only do this by a comprehensive and varied knowledge of the actual opportunities and limitations. The actual needs and temptations, the actually constraining customs and habits, desires and fears, of all the different species of that 'general man' who, as Browning says, 'receives life in parts to live in a whole.' And this knowledge a philosopher—whose personal experience is often very limited—cannot adequately attain unless he earnestly avails himself of opportunities of learning from the experience of men of other callings./ But, secondly, even supposing him to have used these opportunities to the full, the philosopher's practical judgment on particular problems of duty is liable to be untrustworthy, unless it is aided and controlled by the practical judgment of others who are not philosophers. (Sidgwick 1898: 21–2)

In the end, education and ethics were always at the heart of Sidgwick's work, even when he was proclaiming their common failures as he tackled the 'deepest problems' of human life.

Bibliography

Works by Henry Sidgwick

1870, 'The Ethics of Conformity and Subscription', London: Williams and Norgate.

1874, The Methods of Ethics, London: Macmillan; repr. 1877, 1884, 1890, 1893, 1901, 1907 [referenced as 1874/1907 when the 7th edn. is cited].

1876, 'Professor Calderwood on Intuitionism in Morals', Mind, 1/4: 563–6; repr. in Sidgwick, 2000.

1879, 'The Establishment of Ethical First Principles', Mind, 4: 106–11; repr. in Sidgwick, 2000.

1883, The Principles of Political Economy, London: Macmillan; repr. 1887, 1901.

1886, Outlines of the History of Ethics for English Readers, London: Macmillan; repr. 1888, 1892, 1896, 1902.

1889, 'Some Fundamental Ethical Controversies', Mind 14: 473–87; repr. in Sidgwick, 2000.

1891, The Elements of Politics, London: Macmillan; repr. 1897, 1908, 1919.

1898, Practical Ethics: A Collection of Addresses and Essays, London: Swan Sonnenschein; repr. 1909.

1902, Lectures on the Ethics of T. H. Green, H. Spencer, and J. Martineau, ed. E. E. Constance Jones, London: Macmillan.

1902, Philosophy, Its Scope and Relations: An Introductory Course of Lectures, ed. James Ward, London: Macmillan.

1903, The Development of European Polity, ed. E. M. Sidgwick, London: Macmillan.

1904, Miscellaneous Essays and Addresses, ed. E. M. Sidgwick and A. Sidgwick, London: Macmillan.

1905, Lectures on the Philosophy of Kant and Other Philosophical Lectures and Essays, ed. James Ward, London: Macmillan.

1906, Henry Sidgwick, A Memoir, ed. E. M. Sidgwick and A. Sidgwick, London: Macmillan [referenced as Sidgwick and Sidgwick 1906].

1999, The Complete Works and Select Correspondence of Henry Sidgwick, 2nd edn., ed. Bart Schultz et al., Charlottesville, Va.: InteLex Corp.

2000, Essays on Ethics and Method, ed. Marcus G. Singer, Oxford: Clarendon Press.

Secondary Works

Allen, Peter, 2010 [1978], The Cambridge Apostles: The Early Years, Cambridge: Cambridge University Press.

Bell, Duncan, 2007, The Idea of Greater Britain, Princeton: Princeton University Press.

Blanshard, Brand, 1961, Reason and Goodness, New York: Macmillan.

Blanshard, Brand, 1984, Four Reasonable Men: Marcus Aurelius, John Stuart Mill, Ernest Renan, Henry Sidgwick, Middletown, Conn.: Wesleyan University Press.

Bolt, Rodney, 2011, As Good as God, as Clever as the Devil, London: Atlantic Books.

Bradley, F. H., 1876, Ethical Studies, Oxford: Clarendon Press.

Bradley, F. H. 1877, 'Mr. Sidgwick's Hedonism', privately published.

Brink, David, 2003, Perfectionism and the Common Good: Themes in the Philosophy of T. H. Green, Oxford: Clarendon Press.

Broad, C. D., 1930, Five Types of Ethical Theory, London: Routledge and Kegan Paul.

Broad, C. D., 1938, 'Henry Sidgwick', in Broad, Ethics and the History of Philosophy, London: Routledge and Kegan Paul, 49–69.

Broad, C. D., 1966, *Lectures on Psychical Research*, London: Routledge and Kegan Paul.

Brooke, Christopher N. L., 1993, *A History of the University of Cambridge*, iv. *The Early Years*, Cambridge: Cambridge University Press.

Bucolo, Placido, Crisp, Roger, and Schultz, Bart (eds.), 2007, *Henry Sidgwick: Happiness and Religion*, Catania: University of Catania Press.

Bucolo, Placido, Crisp, Roger, and Schultz, Bart, (eds.) 2011, *Henry Sidgwick: Ethics, Psychics, and Politics*, Catania: University of Catania Press.

Calderwood, Henry, 1876, 'Mr. Sidgwick on Intuitionalism', *Mind*, os 1/2: 197–206.

Collini, 1992, 'The Ordinary Experience of Civilized Life: Sidgwick's Politics and the Method of Reflective Analysis', in Schultz (ed.) (1992): 333-67.

Collini, Stefan, 2001, 'My Roles and Their Duties: Sidgwick as Philosopher, Professor, and Public Moralist', in Ross Harrison (ed.), *Henry Sidgwick* (Oxford: Oxford University Press, 2001), 9–49.

Crisp, Roger, 1990, 'Sidgwick and Self-Interest', *Utilitas*, 2/2: 267–80.

Crisp, Roger, 1995-6, 'The Dualism of Practical Reason', *Proceedings of the Aristotelian Society*, NS 45: 53–73.

Crisp, Roger, 2002, '*Sidgwick and the Boundaries of Intuitionism*', in P. Stratton-Lake (ed.), *Ethical Intuitionism: Re-evaluations*, Oxford: Clarendon Press, 56–75.

Crisp, Roger, 2006, *Reasons & the Good*, Oxford: Clarendon Press.

Crisp, Roger, 2007, 'Sidgwick's Hedonism', in Bucolo, Crisp, and Schultz (eds.) (2007): 104–57.

Deigh, John, 2007, 'Sidgwick's Epistemology', *Utilitas*, 19: 435–46

Deigh, John, 2010, 'Some Further Thoughts on Sidgwick's Epistemology', *Utilitas*, 22: 78–89.

Donagan, Alan, 1977, *The Theory of Morality*, Chicago: University of Chicago Press.

Donagan, Alan, 1992, 'Sidgwick and Whewellian Intuitionism: Some Enigmas', in Schultz (ed.) (1992): 123–42.

Dowling, Linda, 1994, *Hellenism and Homosexuality in Victorian Oxford*, Ithaca, NY: Cornell University Press.

Gadamer, H. G., 1988, *The Idea of the Good in Platonic-Aristotelian Philosophy*, New Haven: Yale University Press.

Gauld Alan, 1968, *The Founders of Psychical Research*, New York: Schocken Books.

Gauld, Alan, 2007, 'Henry Sidgwick, Theism, and Psychical Research', in Bucolo, Crisp, and Schultz (eds.) (2007): 160–257.

Gray, John, 2011, *The Immortalization Commission*, London: Allen Lane.

Green, T. H., 1883/2003, *Prolegomena to Ethics*, ed. D. Brink, Oxford: Clarendon Press.

Hare, R. M., 1981, *Moral Thinking: Its Levels, Method, and Point*, Oxford: Clarendon Press.

Harvie, Christopher, 1976, *The Lights of Liberalism*, London: Lane.

Hurka, Thomas, 2003, 'Moore in the Middle', *Ethics*, 113: 599–628.

Hurka, Thomas (ed.), 2011, *Underivative Virtue: British Moral Philosophers from Sidgwick to Ewing*, Oxford: Oxford University Press.

Irwin, T. H., 1992, 'Eminent Victorians and Greek Ethics: Sidgwick, *Green, and Aristotle*', in Schultz (ed.) (1992): 279–310.

Irwin, T. H., 2007, 'A "Fundamental Misunderstanding"?', *Utilitas*, 19: 78–90.

Irwin, T. H., 2009, *The Development of Ethics*, Oxford: Oxford University Press.

Jones, H. S., 2000, *Victorian Political Thought*, London: Macmillan.

Kelly, Edward, and Kelly, Emily Williams, 2009, *Irreducible Mind*, Lanham Md.: Rowman & Littlefield.

Korsgaard, Christine, 2009, *Self-Constitution*, New York: Oxford University Press.

Larmore, Charles, 1996, *The Morals of Modernity*, New York: Cambridge University Press.

Lubenow, William, 1998, *The Cambridge Apostles, 1820–1914*, Cambridge: Cambridge University Press.

Mander, W. J., 2011, *British Idealism: A History*, Oxford: Oxford University Press.

Medema, Steven G., 2004, 'Sidgwick's Utilitarian Analysis of Law: A Bridge from Bentham to Becker?', *Social Science Research Network*, 1 July, available at SSRN: <http://ssrn.com/abstract=560842> or <http://dx.doi.org/10.2139/ssrn.560842>.

Mill, John Stuart, 1974, 'Two Unpublished Letters from John Stuart Mill to Henry Sidgwick', ed. J. B. Schneewind, *Mill Newsletter*, 9/2 (summer), 9–11.

Moore, G. E., 1903, *Principia Ethica*, Cambridge: Cambridge University Press.

Parfit, Derek, 1984, *Reasons and Persons*, Oxford: Oxford University Press.

Parfit, Derek, 2011, *On What Matters*, Oxford: Oxford University Press.

Phillips, David, 2011, *Sidgwickian Ethics*, Oxford: Oxford University Press.

Rawls, John, 1971/1999, *A Theory of Justice*, Cambridge, Mass.: Harvard University Press.

Rawls, John, 2007, *Lectures on the History of Political Philosophy*, Cambridge, Mass.: Harvard University Press.

Ritchie, D. G., 1891–2, 'Review: The Elements of Politics', *International Journal of Ethics* 2: 254–7.

Rothblatt, Sheldon, 1968, *The Revolution of the Dons*, Cambridge: Cambridge University Press.

Roy, Archie, 2008a, *The Eager Dead*, Sussex: Book Guild Publishing.

Roy, Archie, 2008b 'An Interview with Professor Archie Roy', *The Searchlight*, <http://www.aspsi.org/feat/life_after/a073mt-a-Prof_Archie_E_Roy_interview.php>.

Schneewind, J. B., 1977, *Sidgwick's Ethics and Victorian Moral Philosophy*, Oxford: Clarendon Press.

Schultz, Bart (ed.), 1992, *Essays on Henry Sidgwick*, New York: Cambridge University Press.

Schultz, Bart, 2004, *Henry Sidgwick, Eye of the Universe*, New York: Cambridge University Press.

Schultz, Bart, 2005, 'Sidgwick's Racism', in Schultz and Varouxakis (eds.) (2005): 211–50.

Schultz, Bart, and Varouxakis, Georgios, 2005, *Utilitarianism and Empire*, Lanham, Md: Lexington Books.

Shaver, Rob, 1999, *Rational Egoism: A Selective and Critical History*, New York: Cambridge University Press.

Shaver, Rob, 2000, 'Sidgwick's Minimal Metaethics', Utilitas, 12: 267–77.

Shaver, Rob, 2011, 'Sidgwick's Axioms and Commonsense Morality', in Bucolo, Crisp, and Schultz (eds.) (2011): 562–91.

Singer, Peter, 1974, 'Sidgwick and Reflective Equilibrium', *Monist*, 58: 490–517.

Singer, Peter, 2007, 'Normative Ethics: Five Questions', <http://www.normativeethics.com/interviews/singer.html>.

Singer, Peter 2011, 'Philosophy Bytes: On Henry Sidgwick's Methods of Ethics', <http://philosophybites.libsyn.com/peter-singer-on-henry-sidgwick-s-ethics>.

Singer, Peter, and De Lazari-Radek, Katarzyna, 2010, 'Secrecy in Consequentialism: A Defense of Esoteric Morality', *Ratio*, 23: 34–58.

Skelton, Anthony, 2007, 'Schultz's Sidgwick', *Utilitas*, 19: 91–103.

Skelton, Anthony, 2010a, 'On Sidgwick's Demise: A Reply to Professor Deigh', *Utilitas*, 22: 70–7.

Skelton, Anthony, 2010b, 'Henry Sidgwick's Moral Epistemology', *Journal of the History of Philosophy*, 48: 491–519.

Skorupski, John, 2001, 'Three Methods and a Dualism', in Ross Harrison (ed.), *Henry Sidgwick* (Oxford: Oxford University Press, 2001), 61–81.

Smith, Michael, 2009, 'Desires, Values, Reasons, and the Dualism of Practical Reason', in Suikkanen and Cottingham (2009): 116–43.

Suikkanen, J., and Cottingham, J. (eds.) 2009, *Essays on Derek Parfit's On What Matters*, Oxford: Wiley-Blackwell.

Sumner, L. W., 1996, *Welfare, Ethics & Happiness*, Oxford: Clarendon Press.

Sutherland, Gillian, 2006, *Faith, Duty, and the Power of Mind: The Cloughs and Their Circle, 1820–1960*, Cambridge: Cambridge University Press.

Symonds, John Addington, 1967, *The Letters of John Addington Symonds*, 3 vols., ed. H. M. Schueller and R. L. Peters, Detroit: Wayne State University Press.

Tart, Charles, 2009, *The End of Materialism*, Oakland, Calif.: New Harbinger Publications/ Noetic Books.

Tullberg, Rita McWilliams, 1975/1998, *Women at Cambridge*, Cambridge: Cambridge University Press.

Williams, Bernard, 1982, 'The Point of View of the Universe: Sidgwick and the Ambitions of Ethics', *Cambridge Review*, 7 May, 183–91.

Websites

Henry Sidgwick website, maintained by Hortense Geninet, <http://www.henrysidgwick.com/ index.html>.

Henry Sidgwick, blog maintained by Hortense Geninet, <http://sidgwick.org/>.

PART V

RELIGIOUS PHILOSOPHY

CHAPTER 24

··

THE PHILOSOPHY OF JAMES
MARTINEAU

··

RALPH WALLER

THE LIFE OF JAMES MARTINEAU (1805–1900)

BORN in 1805 and brought up in Norwich, James Martineau attended Norwich Grammar School from the age of 10. He remained there for the next six years although he was not entirely happy. The major academic emphasis of the school was on classical studies, which gave him little opportunity to study his favourite subject, mathematics.

Due to the intervention of his sister, Harriet, he was moved at the age of 16 to Lant Carpenter's school in Bristol. Dr Carpenter was not only an excellent classicist with a good knowledge of mathematics, but he was also an accomplished scientist, a moral philosopher, and a trained theologian. He was a man of the world, who read the daily papers to the boys around the dinner table and kept them in touch with the Parliamentary debates. Some sixty years later, in a letter to Lant Carpenter's grandson, Martineau wrote, 'we had lessons in science, in history, in geography and in Greek Testament and smaller groups for classics and mathematics'.[1] This unusually broad curriculum widened his horizons and gave him foundations which helped him cope with the scientific revolution of the nineteenth century.

After a short period in Derby as an apprentice to an engineer, during which time Herbert Spencer also resided in Derby, Martineau entered Manchester College, York, for a five-year course, training for the Dissenting ministry. On the completion of these studies he returned to Lant Carpenter's school in Bristol as the schoolmaster, during Dr Carpenter's one-year absence through illness.

In 1828 he took up his first ministerial post at Eustace Street Presbyterian Church, Dublin, where he served for four years before moving to Liverpool in 1832 to become the minister of Paradise Street Chapel. It was in Liverpool that he formed a close association with J. H. Thom, Charles Wicksteed, and John James Tayler. These four were a constant source of

---

[1] Letter from James Martineau to Mr Carpenter about his grandfather, 20 December 1878, MS, Harris Manchester College Library, Oxford.

encouragement to one another. They were aided by Joseph Blanco White who, after leaving the Oxford Movement, was introduced by Thom into Liverpool Unitarian circles. The four friends had many things in common. They were all young, all ministers of religion, and all went on to serve their respective churches for well over a quarter of a century. They all had the same earnest desire to reconcile modern learning and religion, and were aware of influences from the Continent, having studied in Germany and Italy.[2]

For several years while editing the *Prospective Review* these four met once a month at Tayler's home. They dined together, spent the evening together, and often stayed overnight. It is difficult to trace the direct influence of any one of the four on the others, but there is no doubt from reading their correspondence and reminiscences that they interacted in a special way to stimulate and promote one another's thoughts.

While in Liverpool Martineau was caught up in the same romantic spirit as the members of the Oxford Movement, although he did not share their theology. He was soon replacing the light and airy Paradise Street Church, which reflected the rationalism of the eighteenth century, by a beautiful Gothic building in Hope Street, with a spire, stained glass windows, choir pews that were never used, and a high altar. The medieval gloom of Hope Street Church perfectly fitted the new romantic age; the carved pews, the statues, and the reintroduction of Holy Communion as a major service, all helped create a romantic atmosphere.

In 1840 Martineau was appointed as part-time Professor of Moral Philosophy at Manchester New College, now back in Manchester, in its new role as a mini-university. This was a post he held for the next forty-five years. By the time the college moved to London in 1853, the good railway service between London and Liverpool enabled him to retain both his ministerial post and his college chair. Four years later, in 1857, he took a full-time post in the college and moved his family to London.

In 1866, Augustus de Morgan resigned his Chair of Mathematics at University College London, because James Martineau, the strongest candidate for the Chair of Philosophy of Mind and Logic at University College, had been turned down by the College Council. The recommendation of the Senate to appoint him had been overturned by a coalition of those who wanted no minister of religion to be appointed and those who wanted only a minister of the Church of England. What had upset de Morgan, and the aged Crabb Robinson, was that the religious neutrality of University College meant not the exclusion of scholars and teachers on religious grounds, but their non-exclusion.

Croom Robertson, who was appointed to the chair, went on to exert a powerful influence on philosophy in England, becoming the founder and first editor of the philosophical journal *Mind*. Martineau returned to his teaching at Manchester New College, of which institution he was shortly to become principal; from there he battled with the agnosticism of Herbert Spencer and the materialism of John Tyndall. These, together with his sermons,

---

[2] Wicksteed had a knowledge of Italian, French, and some German, which had enabled him to read the works of de Wette and Paulus. He had visited Paulus at Heidelberg and had discussed at some length the great man's *Das Leben Jesu*. Tayler had studied at Bonn and Göttingen as early as 1834 and from that time onwards regularly met and corresponded with several leading German professors, including Ewald, the Old Testament scholar, who was Eichhorn's favourite pupil, and Neander of Berlin, who had been a student of Schleiermacher. Tayler also formed a close friendship with Baron Bunsen and studied his works several years before they were made famous by Rowland Williams in *Essays and Reviews* (1860). John Hamilton Thom spent almost three years studying on the Continent in the 1850s.

addresses, articles, and books, were to make an important contribution to Victorian life and thought, and cause Gladstone to rank him as the 'first among living English Thinkers', and P. T. Forsyth to place him alongside J. H. Newman and F. D. Maurice as the three outstanding contributers to English religious thought.

INFLUENCES UPON JAMES MARTINEAU

Martineau was by nature eclectic and not a follower of any one particular school of philosophy. His philosophical thinking was shaped, not by adherence to the ideas of any one individual, but rather by the experiences through which he passed and the influences of a series of thinkers who helped shape his philosophy. These included Dr James Cowles Prichard (1786–1848), Joseph Blanco White (1775–1841), Joseph Priestley (1733–1804), Jeremy Bentham (1748–1832), William Ellery Channing (1780–1842), Friedrich Adolf Trendelenburg (1802–72), Immanuel Kant (1724–1804), and Samuel Taylor Coleridge (1772–1834). It is important to note the influence of each of these in order to understand the development of Martineau's philosophical thought.

Dr James Prichard

One of the early influences on Martineau was that of Dr James Cowles Prichard MD, the author of *Researches into the Physical History of Mankind.* He was a Fellow of the Royal Society, a member of the National Institute of France, a member of the Royal Academy of Medicine of Paris, and Honorary Fellow of The Kings and Queens College of Physicians in Ireland. In 1827 Prichard kindly invited the young Martineau to the meetings of a private philosophical society of about twelve members which met regularly in Bristol. Martineau looked back on these evening meetings of the society as one of the most precious passages of life where he 'heard the ablest local men…discuss the newest questions of the time and the greatest questions of all time'.[3] He was for ever grateful to one member of the society, Samuel Worsley, whose thoughtful suggestions and accurate geological knowledge Martineau greatly admired. Such a society not only broadened his outlook but also laid the foundations for the part he was later to play in the famous Metaphysical Society, and for his defence of theism against those who propounded a purely mechanical evolutionary theory.

Joseph Blanco White

Joseph Blanco White[4] arrived in Liverpool in January 1835 from Dublin where for some four years he has been the guest of Archbishop Whately of the logic fame. He was immediately

---

[3] James Martineau, 'Biographical Memoranda', MS, Harris Manchester College, Oxford.
[4] White had been a Spanish Roman Catholic Priest, and became an Anglican who influenced the Oxford Movement through his membership of the Senior Common Room at Oriel at the same time as Pusey, Newman, Hampden, and Whately. When Whately became an archbishop, White went to live with him in Dublin, before being introduced by Thom into Liverpool Unitarian circles.

attracted to Liverpool Unitarianism and formed a friendship with James Martineau and J. H. Thom, who later became his literary executor.

There are several parallels which can be drawn between White's thought and that of the later Martineau which strongly indicate that White played an important part in shaping Martineau's subsequent ideas. It was White who encouraged Martineau to come to terms with the inner nature and discernment of religious truth. White proclaimed:

> Man must turn to the light within him, aided by its developments in Christ—the highest, the purest, the best guide he knows. He must follow that light; he must sacrifice his selfish will to the duties which conscience points out.[5]

These concepts of the inner light, of conscience, of self-surrender, and of Christ being the highest and the best known to man, were all to become intrinsic parts of Martineau's thought.

White regarded the material view of God, which existed in the common mind, as the greatest obstruction to true religion. He nourished his own religious life on the words, 'God is Spirit'.[6] In this view Martineau followed White and in 1837 preached a sermon on 'Characteristics of the Christian Theory of God' where he clearly developed the theory of God as Spirit.[7]

Martineau's debt to White did not make him uncritical of White's failings. He noted with some sadness that White's successive changes in churchmanship were produced by a series of repulsions from his current beliefs rather than by an attraction to new truth. Moreover Martineau felt that White's lack of 'moral enthusiasm' had deprived him of 'strength, and joy, and faith' in his religion,[8] which were precisely the qualities Martineau found in the American William Ellery Channing.

Martineau and Joseph Priestley

It was during his early years in Liverpool that an important shift in Martineau's thought began to occur. In 1833 he wrote a series of three articles on Priestley for the *Monthly Repository*. It was a work which showed areas of agreement between Priestley and Martineau, but it also revealed that Martineau's thought was moving along different lines. This essay painted a sympathetic portrait of Priestley, showing how in the early years of his ministry, deprived of social intercourse and friendship, he devoted himself to theological, philosophical, and scientific studies. It included the distressing picture of Priestley at the end of his time in England as 'the Pastor driven from his flock, the author despoiled of his manuscripts,...the philosopher hunted for his noble sympathy with his race'.[9] Martineau characterized Priestley as a man of truth:

---

[5] Joseph Blanco White, *Observations on Heresy and Orthodoxy* (repr. from the 2nd edn., London, 1877), p. xxxi.

[6] White, *Heresy and Orthodoxy*, p. xxxii.

[7] James Martineau, *National Duties and Other Sermons and Addresses* (London, 1903), 221–36.

[8] James Martineau, *Essays, Reviews and Addresses* (London, 1890), i. 147.

[9] *Essays, Reviews and Addresses*, i. 32.

Were we to designate Dr. Priestley in one word, that word would be 'truth'; it would correctly describe the employment of his intellect, the essential feeling of his heart, the first axiom of his morality, and even the impression of his outward department.[10]

There is a note of realism in the article in that it also depicts several of Priestley's shortcomings: his lack of memory and imagination, his notion of duty as empowered by conviction rather than by affection, and his inability to admit doubt, for he saw that all his investigations must lead to truth or falsehood. Priestley's lack of picturesque illustrations in his narratives diminished their effectiveness, and he had a tendency to oversimplify difficult and complex truths.[11] On the other hand, Martineau was clearly in sympathy with Priestley's sense of life being lived in accordance with a moral principle, a principle which was not a blind superstitious obedience but an expression of conscience. This was finally worked out by Martineau in *The Seat of Authority in Religion* almost sixty years later.

On one important issue Martineau was beginning to move away from Priestley's position, that of the necessarian theory. Priestley, following Hartley, had concluded that people simply reacted to sensations from outside themselves. Martineau noted that the same sensations produced different reactions in different people.[12] He accounted for these varying results by concluding that individuals must have differing succeptibilities to external phenomena; for him, this began to undermine the determinist position.

Martineau and Jeremy Bentham

In 1834 Martineau wrote a review of Bentham's *Deontology*. It was a straightforward critical assessment of Bentham's work which Martineau later considered of insufficient importance to be included in any of his collected writings. In this review he outlined Bentham's theory which differentiated between voluntary and involuntary acts, maintaining that voluntary acts are selected on the basis of happiness. Thus any act which increases happiness is looked upon as virtuous, and any act which brings a balance of misery is to be considered a vice. Martineau held that Bentham's system had much to commend it, but he was highly critical of Bentham for his lack of sympathy with any views contrary to his own (a healthy respect for the opinion of other was something Martineau retained all his life). Martineau made the point that just because Utilitarianism got some things right, it did not mean that different views did not also contain truth.

Thus in 1834 Martineau was willing to admit that the theories of the Utilitarians could lead to right actions. However, he went on to criticize Bentham for producing a 'selfish' system which omitted benevolence, and which was concerned only with actions rather than motives. Pleasure and pain, for Martineau, came from feelings and emotions as well as from actions. He gave the example of a fireman who might rush into a burning house to rescue a child in order to enhance his reputation or receive a reward. But an onlooker might do the same thing purely through a feeling of sympathy for the child. If the onlooker had not

---

[10] *Essays, Reviews and Addresses,* i. 36.   [11] *Essays, Reviews and Addresses,* i. 23–9.
[12] *Essays, Reviews and Addresses,* i. 40.

responded to that feeling, it would have brought him pain; if he responded, it would bring him pleasure.[13]

Martineau disapproved of Bentham's practice of evaluating every human action in terms of personal loss and gain, and for portraying human beings as exclusively motivated by views of the future and thus incapable of being influenced by the impulses and stimuli of the past. He further censured Bentham for dispensing with trial by motive and substituting it with trial by results. Martineau acknowledged that benevolence crept into Bentham's system in that he encouraged individuals to contribute to the happiness of others as this would in return promote their own happiness.

Against this position Martineau believed that true benevolence was expressed by the words of Jesus, 'If ye do good to them that do good to you, what thanks have ye?' In line with this he firmly held that thousands of kind acts were done every day which were not offered as assets in a deposit bank, but as free gifts.

It can be seen that by the mid-1830s Martineau had arrived at the basic position of his ethics, that motives, and not results, were the chief determining factor for judging a person's actions. Moreover this review of Bentham's *Deontology* revealed the beginning of Martineau's movement away from Utilitarianism (which he increasingly saw as a selfish doctrine) towards a theory of action based on inner feelings and compulsions which sprang from the conscience. The review is of additional interest because it is an indication of Martineau's continuing adherence to aspects of Hartley's philosophy in that he followed Hartley's distinction between voluntary and automatic actions, his belief that everything had a cause, and his differentiation between the cause and the external effect. Where he eventually parted company with Hartley in 1840 (as Coleridge had done previously) was on the necessarian doctrine against which Martineau asserted the free will and personal responsibility of the individual.

Martineau and William Ellery Channing

Martineau was first introduced to the writings of Channing 'through Lant Carpenter who was staying with a Mrs. Coppe of York in 1821 when she received a copy of Dr. Channing's sermon *The Evidences*':

> Dr. Carpenter read it with delight instead of taking his breakfast, for he had hardly time for both:—
> 'Aye,' said he, 'this will do, this will do indeed.'[14]

He promptly took it back to Bristol for use in the Lewins Mead Chapel and in his school where Martineau was a pupil. Some thirty years later when Martineau wrote an appreciation of Channing he noted that Channing produced no great or lasting work of history, philosophy, or art, but that his influence was 'wide and deep'.[15] Channing's impact on Martineau was considerable, as can be seen from Martineau's paper delivered to the London gathering in

---

[13] 'Review of Bentham's Deontology', *Monthly Repository*, 7 (1834), 618.
[14] Russell Lant Carpenter, *Memoirs of the Life of the Rev. Lant Carpenter* (London, 1842), 260.
[15] *Essays, Reviews and Addresses*, i. 144.

1880 celebrating the centenary of Channing's birth. In that address, Martineau set down what he considered to be the heart of the American's teaching:

> The single thought of which, from first to last, it was the living expression is this, that MORAL PERFECTION IS THE ESSENCE OF GOD AND THE SUPREME END FOR MAN; in the one, an eternal reality; in the other, a continuous possibility.[16]

Martineau then went on to outline the resultant effect of this central idea on both Channing's theology and his ethics. In his theology Channing allowed nothing to be said of God which contradicted his moral nature. In his ethics Channing affirmed that everyone had the capacity to discern right from wrong and the power to pursue the right. These were precisely the points which Martineau took up and enlarged in his article 'Five Points of the Christian Faith', written in 1841; that is, 'We have Faith in the *Moral Perceptions of Man*, and 'We have Faith in the *Moral Perfection of God*.'[17]

> Thus, by the simplest expansion of Channing's primary thought, Duty becomes supreme over the personal life; Reverence, over the social; Aspiration over the spiritual; and Love for the true, the beautiful and the good, over all.[18]

In addition to the view shared by both men, that morality was central to Christianity, there were two other areas where the ideas of Channing were sufficiently similar to those of Martineau to suggest that the older man had either influenced the younger, or at least had reinforced his religious thought.

Firstly, Channing confirmed Martineau's own view that divine goodness was intuitively known and inwardly discerned. In a letter to Martineau dated 1841 he answers Martineau's question of how God's goodness is to be reconciled with man's experience of human affairs.

> It is so long since doubts of the Divine goodness have crossed my mind, that I hardly know how to meet them. This truth comes to me as an intuitive one. I meet it everywhere. I can no more question it than I can the supreme worth of beauty or virtue.[19]

A few months earlier, Martineau had written to Mary Carpenter expressing the view that the divinity of a person or a thing is always discerned intuitively.[20] Although Martineau never systematically expounded his belief in intuition, there is little doubt that after his contact with Channing it became an intrinsic part of his theory of knowledge.[21]

Secondly, Channing played an important role in encouraging Martineau to abandon his belief in philosophical necessity, which had been a key feature of Unitarian doctrine since the time of Priestley. As early as 1831 Channing was writing to an English Unitarian, Lucy Aikin, expressing his opposition to Priestley's doctrine of philosophical necessity:

---

[16] James Martineau, 'Address to the London Meeting', in *The Channing Centenary, 1880* (London, 1880), 36.

[17] James Martineau, *Studies of Christianity* (London, 1858), 179, 184.

[18] 'Address to the London Meeting', 38.

[19] W. H. Channing, *William Ellery Channing D D* (Boston, 1980), 454.

[20] Letter from Mary Carpenter to James Martineau dated February 1841, MS, Harris Manchester College Library, Oxford.

[21] Alfred Caldecott, *The Philosophy of Religion in England and America* (London, 1901), 348–52. G. O. McCulloch, 'The Theism of James Martineau', unpublished dissertation, University of Edinburgh, 1933.

Now Priestley's system of materialism, of necessity, and of the derivation of all our moral sentiments from sensations variously modified by associations, does seem to strike a blow at our
most intimate and strongest moral convictions, whilst it robs our nature of all its grandeur.[22]

Miss Aikin's reply showed that Channing had raised doubts in her mind as to the compatibility of the Scriptures and individual moral decision with the doctrine of necessity.

By 1839 Martineau's own doubts about philosophical necessity, which he had suppressed
for some years, were surfacing; so much so that in his lecture on 'Moral Evil' delivered during the Liverpool Controversy of that year, he launched his first tentative attack against the
doctrine. On reading this paper Channing wrote to Martineau expressing his full support
and encouragement in this movement of thought:

The part of your discourse which gave me the sincerest delight, and for which I would especially thank you, is that in which you protest against the doctrine of philosophical necessity.
Nothing for a long time has given me so much pleasure. I have felt that that doctrine, with its
natural connections, was a millstone round the neck of Unitarianism in England.[23]

Friedrich Trendelenburg

In 1848 Martineau set out to Germany with his family. He spent several months studying at
Göttingen before going on to Berlin to work with Professor Trendelenburg. The year that he
spent in Germany gave Martineau an opportunity to reassess his own philosophical position. He wrote in the preface of *Types of Ethical Theory*:

I passed through a kind of second education in Germany, mainly under the admirable guidance of the late Professor Trendelenburg... The metaphysic of the world had come home to
me, and never again could I say that phenomena, in all their clusters and chains were all.[24]

He thus came to the conclusion that all phenomena owed their existence to a spiritual causality of which they were an expression. At the same time he deduced that the study of phenomena was the proper function of science, while research into the nature and character of
the invisible cause or causes of these phenomena is the prerogative of philosophy.

However, it must not be supposed that Martineau found in Germany a ready-made system of philosophy which he carefully studied and adopted. When writing from Berlin to his
old friend, J. H. Thom, Martineau maintained that German speculative thought, although
fruitful in its results, was in danger of 'developing itself into a religion wholly Pantheistic.
'Scheleiermacher's influence in so many ways good has, in this respect, I think been
disastrous.'[25]

What Martineau gained from his studies in Germany was an increased insight into
the history of philosophical thought and especially into the system of ancient Greece and

[22] Anna Letitia Le Breton (ed.), *Correspondence of William Ellery Channing and Lucy Aiken from1826
to 1842* (London, 1974), 81.
[23] Channing, *William Ellery Channing*, 447.
[24] James Martineau, *Types of Ethical Theory* (3rd edn., Oxford, 1889), vol. i, p. xv.
[25] Letter dated 25 February 1849, and quoted in James Drummond and C. P. Upton, *Life and Letters of
James Martineau* (London, 1902), ii. 331.

modern Germany. In his 'Biographical Memoranda' he describes the character of his Berlin studies:

> A short experience convinced me that, for the purpose of my special studies I should gain most by reading a good deal and hearing a little. I closely attended Trendelenburg's two courses of Logic and History of Philosophy. Beyond the references which these included, I read only two authors, Plato and Hegel…though Hegel produced in me no conviction, but rather threw me back upon the position of Kant, yet the study of him affords, I think, a discipline of great value.

Thus Martineau returned to England as an accomplished student of philosophical theology. With his knowledge of German philosophy and German biblical criticism he was one of the few people prepared to meet the challenges to religion which would be posed by the publication of Darwin's *Origin of Species*.

Martineau and Immanuel Kant

Martineau's dissatisfaction with necessarian philosophy was brought to a head in 1840 by his part-time appointment to the staff of Manchester New College, where the need to prepare and deliver lectures compelled him to harmonize the different movements of thought which had been developing in his mind since his arrival in Liverpool.

The influence of Kant on Martineau's work can be traced from this time onwards in his sermons, articles, essays, and books. In *The Study of Religion* (1888) for example, there are some sixty references to Kant, several of which are elaborate treatments of Kant's major ideas, such as his views on free will. Further evidence of Martineau's wide reading of Kant is found in *Types of Ethical Theory* (1885) where Martineau explains that he omitted to expound Kant's theory of ethics because it was too similar to his own:

> It is scarcely less a surprise to myself than it can be to my readers, that no pages in this book have been reserved for Kant. The reason, paradoxical as it may seem, is found, not in any slight of his ethical theory, but in an approximate adoption of it.[26]

His sabbatical leave in Germany during 1848-9 served to reinforce the impact of Kant upon his thinking. However the immediate influence of Kant's thought on Martineau in 1840 can be traced in an article entitled *Five Points of Christian Faith* (1841), which contains several striking resemblances to ideas propounded by Kant in his *Critique of Practical Reason*, *Religion Within the Limits of Reason Alone*, and *Lectures on Philosophical Theology*. These involve the concepts of duty, of God being the highest goodness and intelligence that can be conceived by man, and of belief in immortality.

It was in the philosophy of Kant that Martineau found the intellectual framework which enabled him to harmonize the movements of thought with which he had been wrestling. Abandoning his discipleship to Priestley and Hartley, Martineau compiled a lecture scheme which combined the critical reasoning of Kant with English empirical philosophy. Although he subsequently modified this approach by drawing on a wider variety of ideas, notably those

---

[26] *Types of Ethical Theory*, ii. 566.

of Plato, Aristotle, and the Scottish philosophers, he never gave up his adherence to some of the major insights of Kant's teaching.

Samuel Taylor Coleridge

Coleridge and Martineau never met: but in view of Coleridge's influence on the development of religious thought in the nineteenth century, it is not surprising to discover that his writings had an effect upon much of Martineau's philosophy of religion. As A. Michael Ramsey has observed, 'The importance of Coleridge becomes apparent if we ask what reading could be recommended to a layman in the eighteen-thirties who was looking for some vindication of the reasonableness of Christian belief and found the older method of "evidences" for an external and authoritative revelation no longer satisfying.'[27]

Ramsey is here referring to Coleridge's reaction against the rationalism and deism of the eighteenth century, and against the mechanical philosophy of Hartley. As the foremost religious thinker, Coleridge subsequently became the embodiment of the Romantic movement's protest against the materialism and utilitarianism of the early decades of the nineteenth century. Coleridge argued for the primacy of the imagination in religious matters, and the inadequacy of logic: 'If any reflecting mind', he wrote, 'be surprised that the aids of the Divine Spirit should be deeper than our consciousness can reach, it must arise from not having attended sufficiently to the nature and necessary limits of human consciousness.'[28]

Coleridge and Martineau had several things in common. They both aspired to become Unitarian ministers; they both abandoned their commitment to Hartley and the necessarian philosophical position; they both came under the powerful influence of Kant; they both studied in Germany and were indebted to German religious and philosophical thought. A comparison of Martineau's writings with those of Coleridge, especially *Aids to Reflection* and *Confessions of an Inquiring Spirit*, reveals not only a close relationship of ideas, but also in some cases a striking resemblance of terminology. There is however no need to prove systematically the dependence of one upon the other, for Martineau frequently acknowledged his debt to Coleridge. He quoted with approval Coleridge's view of miracles,[29] he used Coleridge's apologetics in defence of real religion, and praised Coleridge's theory of the Church and State which he considered to be vastly superior to that of Thomas Arnold.[30]

In 1856 Martineau wrote to one of his former pupils, Susanna Winkworth, expressing his appreciation of her translation of Tauler, and implying that Coleridge was one of his 'sacred guides',[31] but the most direct evidence of his debt to Coleridge can be found in an important paper entitled 'Personal Influences on Present Theology' (1856).[32]

---

[27] A. Michael Ramsey, *F. D. Maurice and the Conflicts of Modern Theology* (Cambridge, 1951), 14.

[28] Samuel Taylor Coleridge, *Aids to Reflection and the Confessions of an Inquiring Spirit* (London, 1913), 43.

[29] James Martineau, *National Duties and Other Sermons and Addresses* (London, 1903), 137.

[30] *Essays, Reviews and Addresses*, ii. 12, 31.

[31] Margaret J. Shaen, *Memorials of Two Sisters: Susanna and Catherine Winkworth* (London, 1908), 164.

[32] It was to this article that David Pym referred in *The Religious Thought of Samuel Taylor Coleridge*, when he noted that Martineau along with five other mid-Victorian theologians had published tributes to Coleridge which had helped to arouse renewed interest in Coleridge as a theologian.

In order to define more clearly the central position of Coleridge's thought, Martineau drew attention to a university sermon given by J. H. Newman, in which Newman contrasted his own thought with that of Coleridge.[33] Newman observed that there were major characteristics of religion which he and Coleridge held in common: they agreed in locating the function of belief in the conscience; in recognizing the religious nature of morality; and in making faith prior to knowledge. Martineau made the point that underlying these broad similarities there were subtle differences between Newman and Coleridge that were important. Newman portrayed the moral feeling as instinctive and to be accepted without question, whereas Coleridge saw it as a cognitive power which all people possessed. Moreover, Newman perceived no other spring of divine knowledge within the life of the individual, other than that of conscience working in the moral sphere, whereas Coleridge allowed that divine knowledge comes not only through the moral perceptions but also through the intellectual faculty. On both these issues Martineau stood with Coleridge.

In the article Martineau proceeded to discuss three major components of Coleridge's philosophical theology. Firstly, concept of duty, which Martineau shared with Coleridge, was a concept which Coleridge in his turn took from Hartley and the eighteenth-century thinkers. Secondly, Martineau argued that for Coleridge there was no such thing as 'natural religion', for all religion was both 'spiritual', springing exclusively from the supernatural element within us, and 'revealed', in so far as the primary ideas of conscience are not our own but given by God.

> All that we inadequately call our *ideals*, the gleaming lights of good that visit us, the hopes that lift again our fallen wills, the beauty which Art cannot represent, the holiness which life does not realize, the love which cannot die with death,—what are they? Not *our* higher, but a *higher than we*—the living Guide Himself, pleading with us and asking for our trust.[34]

This shows Martineau sharing Coleridge's transcendentalist philosophy, which uses the imagination to see a spiritual reality, a higher reality than the material or ordinary.

Thirdly, Martineau shared Coleridge's emphasis on 'freedom of the will' which for Coleridge distinguished a person from a thing and was a basic factor for morality[35] It was the lack of free will in the systems of Priestley and Paley which caused Coleridge to argue against them, maintaining that they portrayed a universe which excluded moral qualities. The same consideration applied to Coleridge's rejection of the Calvinistic doctrines, which he believed turned a person into an object and denied to God any moral attributes[36].

Martineau summarized what he considered to be the importance of Coleridge's religious thought in words which could be equally applied to his own philosophy of religion:

> The great strength of this school lies, we think, in its faithful interpretation of what is at once deepest and highest in the religious consciousness of men; and its recognition, in this consciousness of a living Divine person, instead of mere abstractions without authority, or the dreams of unreliable imagination.[37]

---

[33] *Essays, Reviews and Addresses*, i. 253.
[35] *Essays, Reviews and Addresses*, i. 254.
[37] *Essays, Reviews and Addresses*, i. 263.

[34] *Essays, Reviews and Addresses*, i. 260.
[36] *Essays, Reviews and Addresses*, i. 258.

The influence of Coleridge upon Martineau is reflected in their agreement upon these central principles of the Christian faith, but may also be detected in other striking similarities of thought, especially concerning the development of doctrine.

Martineau was indebted both to Coleridge and to Newman for ideas on the development of doctrine, although his early work on the subject was written before Newman's *Development of Doctrine* was published, and probably owes its origin solely to the impetus which he derived from Coleridge. As Stephen Prickett has written:

> Central to Coleridge's idea of Biblical method is his sense of doctrine and belief as a living, changing, evolving process, constantly offering new perspectives and making new connections.[38]

Martineau followed Coleridge in this idea of organic and living religion, subject to change and development, and as early as 1839 set out his own theory:

> We are warned that 'the Bible is *not* a shifting, mutable uncertain thing.' We echo the warning, with this addition, that Christianity *is* a progressive thing; not a doctrine dead, and embalmed in creeds, but a spirit living and impersonated in Christ. Two things are necessary to a revelation: its record, which is permanent; its readers, who perpetually change. For the collision of the lesson and the mind on which it drops, starts up the living religion that saves the soul within, and acts on the theatre of the world without.[39]

In 1840 Martineau cited Watts's alteration of the Jewish terminology in the Psalms in order to Christianize them, and on the basis of that precedent claimed the right to amend the hymns of Watts in order to bring them into harmony with contemporary doctrines. Martineau held the view, as did Schleiermacher, that doctrines developed in order to express, in terms more readily understood by each succeeding generation, the religious spirit which lies behind the doctrines.[40] Thus the constant factor is not the doctrine but the religious spirit which it expresses:

> In truth, the dogmatic phraseology and conceptions of every church constitute the mere dialect in which its religious spirit is expressed, and to change the technical modes of thought peculiar to any portion of Christendom into a different or more comprehensive language, is but to translate the intellectual idioms of one religious province into those of another.[41]

In 1853 Martineau was commending the Roman Catholic concept of a 'continuous thread of Divine Inspiration' which crossed the centuries and presented doctrines as maturing with time.[42] However, perhaps his most succinct exposition of his theory of the development of doctrine is found in a paper entitled 'The Living Church through Changing Creeds', written

---

[38] Stephen Prickett, *Romanticism and Religion: The Tradition of Coleridge and Wordsworth in the Victorian Church* (Cambridge, 1976), 54.

[39] James Martineau, 'The Bible: What It Is and What It Is Not', *Unitarianism Defended* (Liverpool, 1839) p.43, 43.

[40] James Martineau, *Hymns for the Christian Church and Home* (London, 1840), p. x.

[41] *Hymns for the Christian Church*, p. x. See Coleridge on the Trinity—'an absolute truth transcends any human means of understanding it or demonstrating it', *Table Talk*, 13 April 1830.

[42] *Studies of Christianity*, 233.

against fellow Unitarians who failed to recognize this continuous process of change, growth, and development of doctrine in the life of their own Churches.[43]

Both Martineau and Coleridge drew extensively from Kant as a common source. In the same way as Coleridge seized the ideas of Kant and made them his own, so Martineau was selective in what he took from Coleridge, appropriating only that which he could weave into his own consistent philosophical theology. His deviation from Coleridge's view of original sin illustrates this selectivity. Coleridge perceived of sin in terms of a deliberate divorcing of one's will from the will of God, with the consequential rejection of the true law of one's being in order to wallow in natural appetites. Original sin was a life lived solely on the plane of sense gratification: it should not be blamed on Adam as it was not a hereditary disorder, resulting from Adam's transgression and passed down through the generations; but rather Adam was the representative of all men, so that in his fall was mirrored the fall of every person.

Coleridge portrayed original sin in terms of a disease which all people have rather than as a hereditary defect originating in the first man. This disease had its origins not in an ancestor, for that would be unjust, but in the human will. Robert Barth commented that the strength of Coleridge's doctrine of original sin lay in his recognition of the communal nature of sin, in that it is due not simply to an original parent, but somehow to all humanity.[44]

Martineau also had a clear concept of sin which he defined as 'the conscious free choice of the worse in the presence of a better no less possible'.[45] This was closely linked to Coleridge's concept of sin being the deliberate divorce of one's own will from the will of God, as Martineau believed that all the impulses to choose the highest came from God. Martineau was at one with Coleridge in his locating of sin in the human will,[46] and in his opposition to the idea of a personal devil.[47]

However he went beyond Coleridge's liberal interpretation of original sin and by 1839 had rejected the doctrine altogether. Martineau dismissed the doctrine of original sin for three major reasons. Firstly he saw it as a denial of free will, which consequently undermined the very basis of morality.[48] Secondly he argued against the doctrine of original sin on the grounds of the personal origin and the personal responsibility for sin.[49] He maintained that sin and guilt could not be transferred, logically or morally, from a person in the distant past to those living in the present.[50] Thirdly he opposed the idea of original sin on the basis of scripture, arguing that neither in the Mosaic or the Christian dispensation was there any doctrinal solution to the problem of the origin of evil.[51]

---

[43] James Martineau, 'The Living Church Through Changing Creeds', *Theological Review*, 3 (1866), 296–306.

[44] Robert J. Barth, *Coleridge and Christian Doctrine* (Cambridge, Mass., 1969), 125.

[45] *Studies of Christianity*, 470.

[46] James Martineau, 'The Christian View of Moral Evil', in *Unitarianism Defended* (Liverpool, 1839), 34.

[47] 'The Christian View of Moral Evil', 30.

[48] *Studies of Christianity*, 471.

[49] 'The Christian View of Moral Evil', 35. *Studies of Christianity*, 468.

[50] *Studies of Christianity*, 474. 'The Christian View of Moral Evil', 36.

[51] 'The Christian View of Moral Evil', 15.

Thus while Coleridge tried hard to maintain a doctrine of original sin, even if an unorthodox one, Martineau found the doctrine to be incompatible with freedom, morality, duty, and scripture. He was unwilling to wrestle with the paradox of original sin and free will, which Coleridge attempted to hold together.

Martineau shared with Coleridge the desire simultaneously to achieve two things: 'to preserve the possibility of rational belief in God who was both supernatural and transcendent and... to subject such a belief to the full investigation of the educated mind'.[52]

Maurice, Newman, and Martineau all carried on different strains of Coleridge's theology through the nineteenth century. The aspect of thought which Martineau continued centred on the living God being discerned in the spirit and conscience of men and women, and when refined and developed, it enabled him to meet the challenges of Spencer, Tyndall, and Sidgwick in the second half of the nineteenth century. Against Spencer he argued that God could be known, against Tyndall he fought for the existence of an intellectual aspect in religion and for the creative activity of God, and against Sidgwick he advocated the priority of motive over action in morality.

THE RATIONALE OF RELIGIOUS INQUIRY

Martineau's main philosophical concern was with religion. In his writings he set out to explore religion philosophically and to use philosophy in his defence of Christianity. This dominant theme can clearly be seen in his book, *The Rationale of Religious Inquiry* (1836) which went into four editions and after his death was republished under a title, used for the English translation of Adolf von Harnack's famous book, *What is Christianity?*. Martineau's book made little impact in England, but in America, Joseph Henry Allen of Harvard maintained that it made an important contribution to transcendentalism amongst the American Free Churches.

> The year 1836 may be taken, as well as any, as the birth-year of the Transcendentalism which had so much to do in shaping the form of liberal opinion we have known since; at least, for its emergence in the field of theology, for it was in that year the first gun of a long battle was discharged, in a review by Mr George Ripley of Martineau's 'Rational of Religious Inquiry'.[53]

The *Rationale of Religious Inquiry* was an important attempt to examine Christianity philosophically. Martineau held that, traditionally, religion and philosophy had occupied different spheres with little contact between them, except in the field of natural history. He published this volume in the hope of providing an improved philosophical method for investigating Christianity, namely that religious truth must not be contrary to reason. Martineau was not advocating that the Christian faith must lie within the limits of reason, but rather that, although it goes beyond what reason can prove, it does not go against reason. He expressed this sentiment in the sentence, 'A divine right, therefore, to dictate a perfectly unreasonable faith cannot exist.'[54] In the development of Martineau's religious thought there

---

[52] Prickett, *Romanticism and Religion*, 69.
[53] Joseph Henry Allen, *Our Liberal Movement in Theology* (Boston, 1883), 23.
[54] James Martineau, *The Rationale of Religious Inquiry* (3rd edn., London, 1845), 26.

were two movements taking place at this time: one was towards a more critical approach to scripture and religious tradition, while the other was towards a religion based on feeling which emphasized worship and devotion to Christ. Both these elements can be found in the *Rationale* although the critical element dominates.

THE KNOWLEDGE OF GOD

Religion was central to Martineau's life and thought, with the consequence that much of his philosophy was directed to religious questions and doctrinal issues, such as the knowledge of God, the nature of God, the two natures of Christ, and the divinity and humanity of Christ. These issues combined with his opposition to the agnosticism of Spencer and the materialism of Tyndale were some of the major philosophical issues with which he wrestled.

Martineau maintained that God could be initially known through three different means; through causality in nature, through conscience, and through intuition.

He began firstly with the argument from causality because he regarded it as necessary to understand the relation of nature to God. He taught that in all causality there was a dynamic factor, consisting in the command of power necessary for the achievement of the contemplated end. The heart of causality for Martineau was that 'Every phenomena springs from something other than phenomenon, and this Noumenon is Power'.[55]

Martineau was not alone in the nineteenth century in placing so much emphasis on the argument from Cause and Design. Many thinkers accepted this argument. William Paley, Archdeacon of Carlyle was perhaps the best known nineteenth-century exponent of this idea, set out in his *Natural Theology* of 1803. Nearer Martineau's own time, the idea was again put forward in Mozley's Bampton Lecture of 1865. The argument is made one of the main pillars on which the structure of theism rests in Martineau's work *A Study of Religion* (1887). Martineau stated that this moving, living world is not yet complete, and is very different from the world in which the old argument set out to find a wise Architect.

Martineau's version of the argument from causality was simple and clear. He took up Hume's point that we never perceive the cause passing into effect. In an unpublished lecture, he wrote:

> In truth although a cause must of course precede its effect, I should imagine everyone must feel that it is not this which makes it a cause, and that the mind discriminates between a proper cause and a simple sign or symptom of a coming event.[56]

Martineau maintained that although we do not see the cause, rationally we know that it is there. He insisted that the only cause which we know are our wills, and that we are the real causes, for we are the cause of our own actions. He went on to apply this to the world by seeing evolution as a growth, a continual appearance of something new, and he held that this implied a Cause. Thus since the world needs a Cause and since Will alone is cause—there must be a divine will.

---

[55] *Essays, Reviews and Addresses*, iii. 576.

[56] James Martineau, *Unpublished Lecture on Philosophy*, transcribed by Miss Gertude Martineau from the original shorthand, p. 359, Harris Manchester College Library, Oxford.

Martineau like many other philosophers of the nineteenth century was familiar with the writings of Paley, but the attitude of the two minds, while covering much of the same ground, is distinctly different. Paley pointed to the marks of Design and called upon his hearers either to discredit them or for consistency believe in a Designer. On the other hand, Martineau started with a priori intuition of an Intelligent Cause and pointed to the marks of Design as ratifying that intuition. Moreover he believed that an examination of the range of natural history revealed intellectual purpose and intention. Martineau had a great respect for the teleological argument and portrayed God as the great Designer who bore the same relationship to the universe as an architect to his building or an inventor to his machine.[57] But he recognized that the limitation of such an eighteenth-century approach was that it presented a concept of God only as an infinitely intellectual Being; such a Being could be known only as a causal force or will, who made no demands on man's affections[58] and who displayed none of the warmer attributes which could move and win the hearts of human beings.[59] 'As revealed in the universe he remains a distant awful God'.[60]

Secondly, Martineau believed that God was revealed in the conscience of every individual, in a far deeper and more divine form than he is revealed through visible nature.[61] He saw conscience not simply as a private feeling or fancy. On the contrary he believed it was a sense of authority which came from something higher than the individual. As everyone is a person, that which is higher could only be another person, 'greater and higher and of deeper insight'.[62] Martineau identified this person with God. This moral faculty he maintained was 'the communion of God's life and guiding love entering and abiding with an apprehensive capacity in myself'.[63] Conscience reveals more than natural religion, because it is through conscience that a man knows the law of God and feels the demand of God upon his life.[64]

Martineau was by no means the first to seek for the reality of God through an argument of moral obligation. Bishop Butler, in his *Sermons* of 1726 and his *Analogy of Religion* in 1736, stated in an impressive form the argument of moral obligation. Butler's regard for the ethical factor in religious belief was a striking anticipation of Kant's position. Two contemporaries of Martineau, who took up a similar position, were A. S. Pringle-Pattison in *Two Lectures on Theism and Man's Place in the Cosmos* (1897), and Temple, whose Bampton Lecture of 1884 made the moral argument of primary importance.

Martineau was at one with Cardinal Newman in his view of conscience as the natural basis of theism. His contrast to Newman consisted in his rejecting the principle of absolute infallible dogma. Mellone, commenting on nineteenth-century leaders of religious thought, maintained that Martineau and Newman started from the same position but worked in opposite directions. Martineau rejected the historical forms of doctrine because he believed that criticism had shown them to be based solely on human invention. The way to truth, he held, was to rely on the conscience and reason and intuition of the individual person.

---

[57] *National Duties and Other Sermons and Addresses*, 230.
[58] *Hours of Thought on Sacred Things*, 2 vols. (London, 1876–9), ii. 198.
[59] *National Duties and Other Sermons and Addresses*, 231.
[60] *Hours of Thought on Sacred Things*, ii. 198.
[61] *Hours of Thought on Sacred Things*, ii. 198.
[62] *Types of Ethical Theory*, ii. 104.
[63] *Types of Ethical Theory*, ii. 105.
[64] *Hours of Thought on Sacred Things*, ii. 200.

For Martineau, the concept of God must be based on what can be discovered in the moral nature and inner feeling of man, which lies at the basis of religion. He recognized that this attitude of mind rested upon a conviction which the intellect alone exerted to its utmost power could never establish. With this went the belief that moral goodness was not merely a utilitarian convenience, or a disguised prudence, but an independent reality. Martineau made a clear distinction between prudence and conscience. The former was concerned with our welfare, the latter with our character. Prudence decides which course is wiser or more useful or more expedient, while conscience decides which cause is higher, worthier, or more noble.

Martineau put the question, from where does the inner voice of conscience come? He tried to answer this question both in the *Seat of Authority*[65] and in the *Study of Religion*,[66] by looking at the various alternatives and rejecting them, until he found one which is not against the facts of experience.

The conclusion that Martineau came to is that the voice which seems so real, is in fact, real. Thus the moral consciousness implies a dualism, a sense of right responding to a Righteousness without. Now if this hypothesis is not true, Martineau held that there would be one aspect of the dual relationship without the other, a voice where no voice speaks, a sense of duty where there is not one due, and a particular sentiment appropriate to one standing in the presence of God, and yet no God. But this dual relationship, Martineau argued, is not between conscience and a blank, but between conscience and a reality. Thus the duty within him implies one who demands that duty from him.

Martineau equated the inner voice of conscience with the voice of God, and uses it as one of the major supports of his theism. His argument was straightforward and well presented. He did not set out to prove the existence of God, but he started from a belief in the existence of God and looked for evidence to support that belief.

Thirdly Martineau held that God revealed himself directly in the hearts of men and women. Such insights are awakened by heroism, by purity, and by the word of genius that widens a persons spiritual horizons.[67]

Martineau recognized that these insights into the nature of God, from causality, conscience, and intuition were partial and liable to distortion from background and culture.[68]

What religion needed and in fact had, was a vital central focus. Martineau found such a focus in the person of Christ who, as such, was of paramount importance to his philosophy of religion.

Christ was predominantly the one who awakened the feeling for God in the individual's mind. Christ, 'in putting forth thence a transforming power upon all faithful minds...created a perception of the Internal and Spiritual God'.[69] Moreover Christ fitted into Martineau's philosophical theology as the external outward standard of all that is sacred and holy, against which individual beliefs, experiences, and interpretations can be tested. Christ is the

---

[65] James Martineau, *The Seat of Authority in Religion* (London, 1890), 5th edn. [*c*.1896], chapter 'God in Humanity'.
[66] James Martineau, *A Study of Religion*, ii (Oxford, 1900), 1–39.
[67] *Hours of Thought on Sacred Things*, ii. 215, 202.
[68] *Hours of Thought on Sacred Things*, ii. 202.
[69] *National Duties and Other Sermons and Addresses*, 235–6.

one who stops religion from being merely a private subjective belief, bringing harmony into it and reaffirming man's true inner revelation of God.[70]

In addition to this, Martineau saw Christ as the interpreter of conscience. Sometimes the conscience evokes feelings which appear as mere dreams until their reality is confirmed by the life of Christ. Christ is the one who scatters people's doubts about God and enables them to trust in their better selves.[71] Finally, it is Christ who gives to humans the complete picture of the character of God, showing his absolute holiness and selfless love without which apprehensions of God would be vague and attenuated.[72]

God As Spirit

It was because he saw God as Spirit that Martineau's Christology took on a special significance. This enabled him to portray in his writings a true union between God and man taking place in the life of Christ. Consequently, there is a multitude of references to God as Spirit throughout Martineau's publications. In his *Home Prayers*, for example, there are thirty-two references to God as Spirit. On several occasions he refers to God as being the 'Spirit of our spirits'[73] or 'Spirit of our secret life'.[74] The implication could be that God is a kind of archetypal man, but it is more likely that Martineau is emphasizing that human beings are made in the image of God, and that it is the Spirit of God which meets the spirits of people.[75] In his last letter to Estlin Carpenter, he followed this line of thought by referring to God as the 'Father of spirits' and spoke of his high regard for the Quakers, whose whole religious conviction rested on the 'inward Spirit of God'.[76]

This concern with God as Spirit was not something which developed only in his later life. In 1843 he published his *Endeavours after the Christian Life*, which has many references to God as Spirit scattered through its pages. In one of his sermons entitled 'Hand and Heart' he referred to 'God who is a Spirit'[77] and in other places he alluded to God as 'Divine Spirit';[78] in these sermons Jesus reveals the Father, not as the great mechanic of the Universe, but as 'the Holy Spirit that moves us within'.[79]

In the work of any person writing on Christian subjects one would not be surprised to find references to the Spirit of God, and yet this would not imply that the writer had any special conception of God as Spirit. In the case of Martineau, however, he clearly set down what he did mean and what he did not mean by the term 'God as Spirit'. He explained his concept

---

[70] *Hours of Thought on Sacred Things*, ii. 203, 215.

[71] *Hours of Thought on Sacred Things*, i. 73; ii. 15.

[72] James Martineau, 'The Proposition: That "Christ is God," Proved to be False from the Jewish and Christian Scripture', in *Unitarianism Defended* (Liverpool, 1839), 6.

[73] James Martineau, *Home Prayers* (London, 1892), 48, 93.

[74] *Home Prayers*, 86.

[75] *Home Prayers*, 89.

[76] Letter from James Martineau to Estlin Carpenter, 18 July 1898. Extracts are quoted by Drummond and Upton, but it is found in its complete form in MS in Harris Manchester College Library, Oxford.

[77] James Martineau, *Endeavours after the Christian Life* (London, 1843), 171.

[78] *Endeavours after the Christian Life*, 14.

[79] *Endeavours after the Christian Life*, 37.

in a closely argued sermon on the 'Characteristics of the Christian Theory of God', preached in Liverpool in 1837 and in London in 1868. He acknowledged that many religions had the concept of God as spirit and that they had often conveyed the idea of God as a universal agency. He argued that with the exception of the teaching of Christ, religion has invariably denoted a negative spirituality, with the absence of a body, or the diffusion of power and influence over a vast area.[80] Martineau maintained that Christ does not portray God as Spirit only in the sense of existing everywhere in space, or being conscious of the whole content of time, or as commanding every force and producing every movement in the universe. For if this is the sum total of his being, he would still be separated from mankind and would not be the Spirit in the Christian sense. Martineau thus saw God as Spirit in terms of

> a *Mind*, directly accessible to all other minds; seen most in the sanctity and greatness of other souls,—felt most in the secret faiths, the true remorse, the diviner aspirations our own; as an internal Deity known to immediate consciousness, and exercising that mysterious influence of spirit over spirit,... which would remain though the outward universe were cancelled.[81]

From his studies into the Jewish background to Christianity, Martineau took up what he believed to be the Jewish and Christian notion of Spirit being the common element of all that is Divine; whether it is God in his eternal essence, or the human soul that has turned to him.[82] He developed this theme further in a sermon entitled 'In him we live and move and have our being'. Here he maintained that the Infinite Spirit is not only that which makes a thing or person divine, but that it is the very source of life itself; an enveloping presence which keeps all creatures in existence:

> He is the field that holds them; he is the essence that fills them and makes them what they are.[83]

There is a danger here of the Infinite spirit being reduced to a pantheistic concept. However Martineau was aware of this and maintained that even when all the laws of movement and content of the universe have been added up, the full story of the life of God has not been told; there existed behind and beyond creation an 'infinite reserve of thought and beauty and holy love'. Thus he portrayed God as Spirit, not as a remote intellect, or as an ethical atmosphere, or simply as a presence, but as the life of all, the power that works within us; and as 'an almighty wind that sweeps wherever spirits are'.[84]

For Martineau, God as Spirit, whatever he may be in himself, shows himself to men and women, not as eternal and immutable (except towards his creation of nature, over which he has set unchanging laws) but as dynamic and ever-changing, like the 'mighty tides of nature and of history'.[85] It is in this way that he rises in the lives of men and especially in the life of Christ.[86] Martineau did however make the point that in order to be present in the life of an individual, God in no sense has to absent himself from somewhere else.

[80] *National Duties and Other Sermons and Addresses*, 233.
[81] *National Duties and Other Sermons and Addresses*, 233–4.
[82] *The Seat of Authority in Religion*, 444.
[83] *Hours of Thought on Sacred Things*, ii. 110.
[84] *Hours of Thought on Sacred Things*, ii. 108–10.
[85] *Hours of Thought on Sacred Things*, i. 13–14.
[86] *Hours of Thought on Sacred Things*, ii. 212.

From not a place, not a moment, not a creature, did the divine tide ebb to make the flood that rose within the soul of Christ.[87]

This concept of God as spirit is vital for Martineau's thought. When he spoke of the Spirit of God inspiring or filling Jesus, he was not referring to a divine hypostasis distinct from God the Father and the Son, but rather to God himself as active towards his human creation.

THE PROBLEM OF TWO NATURES

Martineau examined philosophically some of the major doctrines of the Church. He rejected the traditional doctrine of the two natures of Christ, the human and the divine, as being philosophically unsound, and replaced it with the image of Jesus the man completely filled by the Spirit of God. He thus retained, to his own satisfaction, both the divinity and the humanity of Christ. He set out in the Liverpool Controversy of 1839, his main objections to the doctrine of two natures of Christ. His essential argument was that in any such union the humanity of Christ would be lost. He maintained that in the union of two natures, the properties of Divine nature, omnipresence, omnipotence, and omniscience, would directly exclude the properties of human nature: weakness, fallibility, local movement, and position.[88] He illustrated this by saying that if any Being had the omniscience of God and the partial knowledge of man, 'it would be like saying, in addition to having all ideas he possessed some ideas'. From this illustration we can see that what is at risk is Christ's humanity, which for Martineau was a key factor in his Christology. This is Martineau's original development of Schleiermacher: he did not follow Schleiermacher's criticism that in any such union of two natures, a third would be formed, or that they would not be properly united.[89] Martineau much more anticipated modern Christological thought by objecting to such a union on the ground that the Divine nature would exclude the human nature.

In contradiction to the Athanasian Creed, Martineau reaffirmed the personal unity of God, and the simplicity of the nature of Christ.[90] In the last lecture of the Liverpool Controversy he raised some searching questions for those who held the contrary view, designed not necessarily to refute their position, but at least to point out the logical consequences of it:

What respectively happened to the two natures on the cross? What has become of Christ's human soul now? Is it separated from the Godhead like any other immortal spirit or is it added to the Deity, so as to introduce into his nature a new and fourth element?[91]

Martineau acknowledged that the doctrine of the two natures avoided some of the difficulties of biblical interpretation; but he maintained that such an approach created more

---

[87] *Hours of Thought on Sacred Things*, ii. 212.

[88] 'The Proposition: "That Christ is God" Proved to be False', 12.

[89] Friedrich Schleiermacher, *The Christian Faith*, trans. H. R. Mackintosh and J. S. Stewart (Edinburgh, 1928), 391 ff.

[90] 'The Proposition: "That Christ is God" Proved to be False', 8.

[91] James Martineau, 'Christianity without Priest and without Ritual', in *Unitarianism Defended*, 50.

problems than it solved. He was also opposed to this doctrine on the grounds that it destroyed mystery: he firmly maintained that until a person was in touch with mystery, he was not in contact with religion at all.[92] His argument against the orthodox position of the two natures was not on the grounds that it presented a mystery, but that it was a rational attempt to destroy mystery. He held that mystery did not offer an object of belief but realms of possibility to be explored, whereas in the doctrine of the two natures, people were simply told to believe both sides of the contradiction. His argument was similar to that of Maurice Wiles who suggests that 'to insist that Trinitarian symbolism is … disclosive of the essential nature of God himself embodies a claim to knowledge about the being of God that is hard to reconcile with the experiential and experimental character of faith'.[93]

Martineau's Alternative Christology: Christ Filled by the Spirit of God

According to Martineau the special position enjoyed by Christ is not due to the fact that he is from God, and that other men and women are not from God or are less so. He followed Augustine in that he believed that everything came from God, and that there are no beings or things which are not from him. In writing to Mary Carpenter in 1841 Martineau expressed this forcefully:

> In point of origin, all things, all persons, all offices, all ideas are equal and immediate derivations from the Supreme Will.[94]

He went on to argue that unless one believed in a satanic or material origin other than the Divine Will of God, which sends things into the world, one could not define divinity by means of origin except by maintaining that everything is divine. He concluded by emphasizing that he saw divinity not in origin, where all things are equal, but in 'intrinsic character and influence, eternal beauty, truth and sanctity'.

It might appear at first sight that he was advocating an adjectival divinity, but Martineau was claiming much more for Christ than that he showed in his human character glimpses of God. A constant and recurring theme throughout his writings is that Jesus has this quality of character, this divinity, because he is totally inspired and filled by the Spirit of God:

> The inspiration of Christ is … diffusive, creative, vivifying as the energy of God.[95]

In a sermon 'Christ the Divine Word' he explained the concept of the Word made flesh by asserting that in every life there is the human spirit and the Divine Spirit. It is difficult to

---

[92] 'The Proposition: "That Christ is God" Proved to be False', 8–9.
[93] Maurice Wiles, *Faith and the Mystery of God* (London, 1982), 127.
[94] Letter of James Martineau to Mary Carpenter, 10 February 1841, MS, Harris Manchester College Library, Oxford.
[95] 'What the Bible Is and What It Is Not', 7.

know where one ends and the other begins: but in Christ the Divine Inspiration spread until it covered the whole soul and

> Brought the human into moral coalescence with the Divine, then God was not merely *represented* by a foreign and resembling being, but *personally there*[96]

Martineau made the point that just once in history God entirely occupied a soul and realized the perfect relation between the human spirit and the Divine.[97]

Martineau presented a picture of the Divine character being revealed through an individual particular life. What he wished to exclude as 'antitheistic' to the personal life of God in Christ, was the Arian or Unitarian view which portrayed Christ as in imitation or mini-God.[98] In this sense he was opposed to Priestley's concept of Christ in so far as he saw it as human imitation of God, or even as a puppet worked by strings from God. Martineau was advocating not an imitation of God, which could have only limited theological implications, but the Inspiration of Christ by the Spirit of God.

Herbert Spencer and James Martineau: In Defence of Religion

Two of Martineau's major contributions to the philosophy of religion came from his controversies with Herbert Spencer and John Tyndall.

In 1862, Martineau engaged in a major debate with Herbert Spencer on agnosticism, following the publication of Spencer's *First Principles*. In October of the same year Martineau wrote an article for the *National Review* under the title, 'Science, Nescience and Faith', which was his chief criticism of Spencer's work. Martineau maintained that Spencer had extended Darwin's theory of evolution to apply to the whole natural history of the human race. Thus the world was perceived by Spencer as a training school, and the differences which separate man from the other animals were explained by a process of gradual attainment. The experiences which could not be accounted for at the individual level were attributed to collective feelings and a condensing of thought down through the ages.

Although Martineau held that the evidence for the evolutionary theory was not 100 per cent conclusive, he accepted that a case could be made out in support of it, but strongly maintained that this did not justify the sceptical attitude which the theory so often engendered towards the intellectual, moral, and religious institutions of the human mind. Martineau criticized Spencer for failing to account for important areas of human experience such as reason and conscience which he believed pointed to an authority beyond themselves.

In dealing with Spencer's idea of competition in evolution, Martineau made three observations. Firstly, that the term competition only describes a certain intensifying of powers already present. Secondly, that competition cannot exist except in the presence of some

---

[96] James Martineau, *Hours of Thought on Sacred Things*, ii. 205.

[97] *Hours of Thought on Sacred Things*, ii. 203.

[98] Letter from James Martineau to the Revd Valentine Davis, 22 August 1894, MS, Harris Manchester College Library, Oxford.

possibility of a better or a worse. Thirdly, before competition can arise there must be a desire or an instinct to lay hold of its opportunities.[99]

Martineau argued that the theist, the atheist, and the pantheist all agreed that the problem of whether there is a Supreme Being behind the world is worthy of serious consideration, and that all three embark on such an investigation in the belief that a result is possible.[100] Martineau attacked Spencer on the grounds that the positive and the theistic positions are both understandable, but that Spencer's intermediate position (that there was a first cause which cannot be known) is the least tenable of all possibilities.

Martineau criticized Spencer for maintaining that to affirm anything about the Infinite was to introduce boundaries and to close doors on other possibilities. According to Martineau, Spencer was asking 'How ... can the Infinite be the object of thought? To think is mentally to predicate: to predicate is to limit: so that under this process, the Infinite becomes the finite: and to know is to destroy it.'[101]

Martineau affirmed that to remain consistent in this process, no predicate, not even that of existence, could be attributed to the Infinite. Martineau held that to maintain the Infinite exists but is totally unknowable is a contradiction in terms.

MARTINEAU AND TYNDALE

The controversy between Professor John Tyndall and James Martineau over materialism brought Martineau to the forefront of English philosophy in the 1870s, and earned him the reputation of being a champion of theism.[102] The debate between the two men commenced with Tydall's Presidential Address to the British Association meeting in Belfast on 19 August 1874. The speech, which was reported in *The Times* of the following day and subsequently produced as a separate booklet, brought forth an immediate response from Martineau in his speech at the opening session of Manchester New College, London. This address was enlarged and published in the *Contemporary Review*, under the title 'Religion as Affected by Modern Materialism', which captured a broad readership both in the United Kingdom and America.

Martineau's 'Religion as Affected by Modern Materialism' was a clear statement of his thinking on the topic. His campaign against Tyndall's ideas was largely defensive and concentrated on two fundamental issues. He argued against matter being self-sufficient, able to create and construct out of its own necessity, and thus remove the need for God; and he vigorously opposed religion relinquishing to science the intellectual sphere and thus being confined to the emotional realm of human nature.

Martineau's general comment on Tyndall's *Belfast Address* was that it contained many true aspects of scientific investigation which were unfortunately linked together by a questionable philosophy. He attacked Tyndall's formula for ending the conflict between religion and science, which limited religion to the emotional part of human nature and assigned the

---

[99] *Essays, Reviews and Addresses*, iv. 602, 603.
[100] *Essays, Reviews and Addresses*, iii. 194.
[101] *Essays, Reviews and Addresses*, iii. 199.
[102] Arthur Stewart Eve and C. H. Creasey, *Life and Work of John Tyndall* (London, 1945), 188.

intellect to science. Martineau's own solution to the problem was to reintroduce the distinction he made in his argument with Spencer, which was that science observed what was happening in the clusters of phenomena while religion asserted that behind those clusters there was a Divine Mind at work.[103]

Martineau's major criticism of Tyndall's paper was that it gave no adequate account for the moral feelings in human beings. A careful reading of Martineau's address reveals that he was not arguing against the presence of emotion in religion, but against the portrayal of Christianity as a pleasant religious feeling which had little relation to the truth.[104]

CONCLUSION

Martineau retired in 1885 at the age of 80. Over the following thirteen years he wrote several books, including *The Seat of Authority in Religion* (1890), *A Study of Religion* (1888), *Types of Ethical Theory* (1895), and *Faith and Self Surrender* (1897). Much of his work was already dated by the time it came to print, due in part to the fact that he was reworking material and ideas contained in the essays he had published over a long time, and that he was publishing his four-year cycle of lectures.

He will be most remembered for his devotional writings rather than by his many papers on science and religion, although his contribution to philosophy of religion is still of historical importance. His two volumes of sermons, *Endeavours After the Christian Life* (1840) and *Hours of Thought on Sacred Things* (1876–9) continue to convey many important insights into the human condition. They are written in beautiful English and carry ideas and imagery that still have the power to speak to successive generations. His prayers, although steeped in traditional language, have a lasting quality. He both edited and wrote large sections of *Common Prayer for Christian Worship* (1862), and here for the first time, Horton Davies has suggested, Nonconformity produced a liturgical editor of rare genius. His *Home Prayers*, which contain beautiful expressions of the Christian faith, have often been reprinted in other anthologies, sometimes without acknowledgement.

Martineau was too broad-minded to belong to any school. He was eclectic in his nature and gathered together ideas from any source that appealed to his own intellectual and emotional character. His philosophy of religion was shaped more by his personality and the movements of the age, than by any adherence to a particular school of thought. He was born three years after the death of Kant, and lived on into the twentieth century. Across his long life, from his first article *The Duties of a Christian in an Age of Controversy* (1828), until his last book *Faith and Self Surrender* (1897), he commented on almost every philosophical and theological movement of his age, as can be seen from his four volumes of *Essays, Reviews and Addresses* (1890–1). If he had been an Anglican his influence would have been much greater, but the Church of England was too narrow for him. When told by Dean Stanley that the Church of England was progressively becoming more inclusive, Stopford Brooke asked if the Church of England would broaden sufficiently to allow James Martineau to be made Archbishop of Canterbury.

---

[103] *Essays, Reviews and Addresses*, iv. 172.   [104] *Essays, Reviews and Addresses*, iv. 168.

BIBLIOGRAPHY

Works by James Martineau

The Rationale of Religious Inquiry (London, 1836; 3rd edn., London, 1845).
'The Christian View of Moral Evil', in *Unitarianism Defended* (Liverpool, 1839).
Studies of Christianity (London, 1858).
A Study of Religion (London, 2nd edn. 1880; rev edn., 2 vols., 1900).
Study of Spinoza (London, 1882).
Types of Ethical Theory (1885), 2 vols. (3rd edn., Oxford, 1889).
Essays, Reviews and Addresses, 4 vols. (London, 1890, 1891).
The Seat of Authority in Religion (London, 1890), 5th edn. [*c*.1896].
National Duties and other Sermons and Addresses (London, 1903).
'Biographical Memoranda', Library of Harris Manchester College, Oxford.

Further Reading

Brown, Alan W., *The Metaphysical Society: Victorian Minds in Crisis, 1869–1880* (New York, 1947).
Caldecott, Alfred, *The Philosophy of Religion in England and America* (London, 1901).
Carpenter, J. Estlin, *James Martineau* (London, 1905).
Drummond, James, and C. B. Upton, *The Life and Letters of James Martineau* (London, 1902).
Eve, A. S., and C. H. Creasey, *Life and Work of John Tyndall* (London, 1945).
Hall, Alfred, *The Moral Teaching of James Martineau* (London, 1906).
Hertz, Joseph H., *The Ethical System of James Martineau* (New York, 1894).
Jones, Henry, *The Philosophy of Martineau in Relation to the Idealism of the Present Day* (London, 1905).
Knight, William, *Inter Amicos: Letters between James Martineau and William Knight* (London, 1901).
Metz, Rudolf, *A Hundred Years of British Philosophy*, trans. W. Harvey, T. E. Jessop, and Henry Stuart (1938).
Schneewind, J. B., *Sidgwick's Ethics and Victorian Moral Philosophy* (Oxford, 1977).
Sell, Alan P. F., *Commemorations. Studies in Christian Thought and History* (Calgary and Cardiff, 1993), chs. 1, 10.
Short, H. L., C. G. Bolam, Jeremy Goring, and Roger Thomas, *The English Presbyterians* (London, 1968).
Sidgwick, Henry, *Outlines of the History of Ethics*, 6th edn (London, 1931).

CHAPTER 25

....

JOHN HENRY NEWMAN

....

ANTHONY KENNY

1. Newman and Analytic Philosophy

....

In the analytic tradition the beginning of modern philosophy is often taken to be the writing by Gottlob Frege in 1879 of *Begriffsschrift*. In that essay and in later writings Frege made a great separation between logic and psychology, between the content of propositions on the one hand and our mental acts about them on the other. He separated off the logical relations between propositions themselves from the thoughts and images that might embody or accompany them. He made the distinction in order to concentrate not on the psychology but on the logic: he developed quantification theory, the kernel of modern symbolic logic, and he defended a realist theory of the philosophy of logic, and a logicist theory of the nature of mathematics. Only towards the end of his life did he return to the topic of mental acts.

Ten years before the *Begriffsschrift*, in *The Grammar of Assent*, John Henry Newman had made many of the distinctions that Frege was to make, sometimes in the same words, sometimes with a different terminology. Newman distinguished between the apprehension of a proposition and assent to a proposition, and he distinguished between the notional or logical content of a proposition and the realization of its content in the imagination. But whereas Frege disjoined logic from psychology in order to discard the psychology, Newman disjoined the two to downgrade the logic.

Unknown to Newman, the logic that he downgraded was in its last days. In his writings Frege laid the ground for a new and much more versatile logic, based on quantification theory, which has developed from that day to this. The Aristotelian syllogistic that Newman sniffed at is now seen as only a small fragment of formal logic. But post-Frege logic, however expanded, and the philosophy of logic that deals with meaning, entailment, and formal proof, still needs to be supplemented, if we are to give a philosophical account of human thought, with a theory of mental acts and states of the kind that Newman gave in his treatment of assent, knowledge, and certitude.

By 'psychology' Frege and Newman mean not the experimental science that now bears the name, but the philosophical study of psychological activity that is nowadays called 'philosophy of mind' plus the study of the justification of human belief that philosophers call 'epistemology'.

From the time of Descartes until the nineteenth century epistemology was regarded by many as the central, foundational discipline of philosophy. Frege not only originated modern logic but started a school of philosophy that replaced epistemology with the theory of meaning at the forefront of philosophical attention. His successors followed him in this. Russell and the early Wittgenstein both propounded theories of belief, but they were theories of the logical structure of belief, not of its psychological nature nor of its epistemological justification. Frege in his logical symbolism had made room for an assertion sign—a sign corresponding to the mental act of assent which is the main topic of Newman's *Grammar*. In his early *Tractatus Logico-Philosophicus* Wittgenstein criticized this: assertion belonged to psychology, he said, not to logic.[1]

Newman and Frege, then, had a common starting point, the separation of logic from psychology, but Frege explored one side of the divided territory and Newman the other. Frege's work had a great progeny in the twentieth century; Newman's had, among professional philosophers, almost none. One exception was H. H. Price, who in his Gifford Lectures *Belief* described him as the one person worth reading on the topic since Locke and Hume. But as the century progressed, analytic philosophers became interested in the topics that concerned Newman.

In his later writings Wittgenstein took seriously topics that he had earlier dismissed. His notes of his last philosophical thoughts, written just before his death in 1951, began with an explicit (if puzzling) reference to Newman. Having spent most of his life on the theory of meaning, Wittgenstein turned in his later years to the traditional problems of epistemology. To be sure, he approached them from a new angle; but his posthumously published *On Certainty* covers many of the same topics as the *Grammar*, uses many of the same illustrations, and draws some of the same conclusions.

In the second section of this essay I will address Newman's general epistemology, and in the third section I will concentrate on his application of it to questions of philosophy of religion.

2. Newman's Epistemology

As a philosopher, John Henry Newman belonged to the same British empiricist tradition as John Stuart Mill. When he argues he argues with Locke and Hume. He was nominalistic in temper. 'Let units come first and (so-called) universals second; let universals minister to units, not units be sacrificed to universals.'[2] His theory of meaning, like that of the empiricists, is strongly imagist: it is the importance that he attached to the imagination that is the driving force of his celebrated distinction between notional and real assent.

Newman was ill at ease, in his Catholic as well as his Anglican days, with scholastic philosophy, and he never really mastered the philosophical systems of the great medievals. He found even more alien the German metaphysics that was beginning to infiltrate Oxford during his last years there.[3] 'Let it be considered how rare and immaterial' he remarked 'is

---

[1] *Tractatus* 4.442.

[2] *An Essay in Aid of a Grammar of Assent*, ed. I. T. Ker (Oxford: Clarendon Press, 1985) (henceforth *GA*), p. 182.

[3] In 1844 and 1845 Benjamin Jowett paid visits to Germany to immerse himself in the study of Kant and Hegel.

metaphysical proof: how difficult to embrace, even when presented to us by philosophers whose clearness of mind and good sense we clearly confide; and what a vain system of words without ideas such men seem to be piling up, while we are obliged to confess that it must be we who are dull, not they who are fanciful and that whatever be the character of their investigations, we want the vigour or flexibility of mind to judge of them.'[4]

The only direct acquaintance we have with things outside ourselves, Newman asserted, comes through our senses; to think that we have faculties for direct knowledge of immaterial things is mere superstition. Even our senses convey us but a little way out of ourselves: we have to be near things to touch them; we can neither see nor hear nor touch things past or future. But though a staunch empiricist, Newman gives reason a more exalted role than it was allowed by the idealist Kant.

> Now reason is that faculty of mind by which this deficiency [of the senses] is supplied: by which knowledge of things external to us, of beings, facts, and events, is attained beyond the range of sense. It ascertains for us not natural things only, or immaterial only, or present only, or past or future; but even if limited in its power, it is unlimited in its range... It reaches to the ends of the universe, and to the throne of God beyond them; it brings us knowledge, whether real or uncertain, still knowledge, in whatever degree of perfection, from every side; but at the same time, with this characteristic that it obtains it indirectly, not directly.[5]

Reason does not actually perceive anything: it is a faculty for proceeding from things that are perceived to things that are not. The exercise of reason is to assert one thing on the grounds of some other thing.

Newman identifies two different operations of the intellect that are exercised when we reason: inference (from premises) and assent (to a conclusion). Assent to a proposition presupposes apprehension of its content: to apprehend a proposition is to grasp the information the predicate offers us about the subject, and to assent to a proposition is to acquiesce in it as true. Assent is an act of the intellect (because concerned with truth) but it falls within the scope of the assenter's responsibility; it is not like involuntary bodily functions.[6] It is important to keep in mind that these two are quite distinct from each other. We often assent to a proposition when we have forgotten the reasons for assent; on the other hand assent may be given without argument, or on the basis of bad arguments. Arguments may be better or worse, but assent either exists or not. It is true that some arguments are so compelling that assent immediately follows inference. But even in the cases of mathematical proof there is a distinction between the two intellectual operations. A mathematician who has just hit upon a complex proof would not assent to its conclusion without going over his work and seeking corroboration from others.

Some philosophers, for example Locke, say that there can be no demonstrable truth in concrete matters, and therefore assent to a concrete proposition must be conditional. Probable reasoning can never lead to certitude. According to Locke, there are degrees of

---

[4] *Sermons, chiefly on the theory of religious belief, preached before the University of Oxford* (London: Rivington, 2nd edn., 1844) (henceforth *US*), p. 210.

[5] *US*, p. 199.

[6] *US*, p. 185; *GA*, p. 20.

assent, and absolute assent has no legitimate exercise except as ratifying acts of intuition or demonstration.

Locke gives as the unerring mark of the love of truth: the not entertaining any proposition with greater assurance than the proofs it is built on will warrant. 'Whoever goes beyond this measure of assent, it is plain receives not truth in the love of it, loves not truth for truth-sake, but for some other by-end'.[7] Accordingly, it is always wrong to give assent without adequate evidence or argument.

Locke's doctrine is one of Newman's main targets for attack. The thesis, he says, is too idealistic and insufficiently empirical. Locke calls men 'irrational and indefensible if (so to speak) they take to the water, instead of remaining under the narrow wings of his own arbitrary theory'.

Locke was wrong, Newman maintains, to speak of degrees of assent. Assent is the acceptance of truth, and no one can hold conditionally what by the same act he holds to be true. Assent is an adhesion without reserve or doubt to the proposition to which it is given. In demonstrative matters assent excludes the presence of doubt; but even in concrete cases Newman maintains that assent never coexists with doubt. In such cases we do not give doubtful assent, nor are there instances where we assent a little and not much.

> Usually we do not assent at all. Every day, as it comes, brings with it opportunities for us to enlarge our circle of assents. We read the newspapers; we look through debates in Parliament, pleadings in the law courts, leading articles, letters of correspondents, reviews of books, criticism in the fine arts, and we either form no opinion at all upon the subjects discussed, as lying out of our line, or at most we have only an opinion about them ... we never say that we give [a proposition] a degree of assent. We might as well talk of degrees of truth as degrees of assent.[8]

Newman lists many different mental attitudes that we can take up with regard to a proposition—for instance suspicion, conjecture, presumption, persuasion, belief, conviction, doubt, moral certainty. But these, Newman claims, are not assents at all, but more or less strong inferences. We might as well talk of degrees of truth as of degrees of assent.[9]

Newman's main concern is to argue that assent on evidence short of intuition or demonstration may well be legitimate, and frequently is so. We all believe without any doubt that we exist; that we have an individuality and identity all our own, that we think, feel, and act, in the home of our own minds.

> Nor is the assent which we give to facts limited to the range of selfconsciousness. We are sure beyond all hazard of a mistake, that our own self is not the only being existing; that there is an external world; that it is a system with parts and a whole, a universe carried on by laws; and that the future is affected by the past. We accept and hold with an unqualified assent, that the earth, considered as a phenomenon, is a globe; that all its regions see the sun by turns; that there are vast tracts on it of land and water; that there are really existing cities on definite sites, which go by the names of London, Paris, Florence and Madrid. We are sure that Paris or

---

[7] *Essay on Human Understanding* IV, xvi, p. 6.

[8] *GA*, p. 115.

[9] Newman explains that assent is the mental act corresponding to assertion. His insistence that assent can only be present or absent parallels the feature of Frege's system that the assertion sign admits of no degrees: it is either there or not, just as any proposition is either true or not.

London, unless suddenly swallowed up by an earthquake or burned to the ground, is today just what it was yesterday, when we left it.[10]

Newman's favourite example of a firm belief on flimsy evidence is our conviction that Great Britain is an island.

> Those who have circumnavigated the island have a right to be certain: have we ever ourselves fallen in with anyone who has? . . . Have we personally more than an impression, if we view the matter argumentatively, a lifelong impression about Great Britain, like the belief, so long and so widely entertained, that the earth was immovable, and the sun careered round it. I am not at all insinuating that we are not rational in our certitude; I only mean that we cannot analyse a proof satisfactorily, the result of which good sense actually guarantees to us.[11]

But there are many other examples.

> We laugh to scorn the idea that we had no parents though we have no memory of our birth; that we shall never depart this life, though we can have no experience of the future; that we are able to live without food, though we have never tried; that a world of men did not live before our time, or that that world has no history: there has been no rise and fall of states, no great men, no wars, no revolutions, no art, no science, no literature, no religion.[12]

On all these truths, Newman sums up, we have an immediate and unhesitating hold, and we do not think ourselves guilty of not loving truth for truth's sake because we cannot reach them by a proof consisting of a series of intuitive propositions. None of us can think or act without accepting some truths 'not intuitive, not demonstrated, yet sovereign'.[13]

Though he denies that there are degrees of assent, Newman makes a distinction between simple assent and complex assent or certitude. Simple assent may be unconscious, it may be rash, it may be no more than a fancy. It is complex, or reflex assent, that is meant by certitude. Complex assent involves three elements: it must follow on proof, it must be accompanied by a specific sense of intellectual contentment, and it must be irreversible. The feeling of satisfaction and self-gratulation characteristic of certitude attaches not to knowledge itself, but to the consciousness of possessing knowledge. Assents may and do change; certitudes endure.

One difference between knowledge and certitude that is commonly agreed among philosophers is this: If I know p, then p is true; but I may be certain that p and p be false. Newman is not quite consistent on this issue. Sometimes he talks as if there is such a thing as false certitude; at other times he suggests that a conviction can only be a certitude if the proposition in question is objectively true.[14] But whether or not certitude entails truth, it is undeniable that to be certain of something involves believing in its truth. It follows that if I am certain of a thing, I believe it will remain what I now hold it to be, even if my mind should have the bad fortune to let my belief drop. If we are certain of a belief, we resolve to maintain it and we spontaneously reject as idle any objections to it. If someone is sure of something, if

---

[10] *GA*, p. 117.   [11] *GA*, p. 191.   [12] *GA*, p. 117.
[13] *GA*, p. 118.   [14] *GA*, p. 128.

he has such a conviction, say, that Ireland is to the west of England, if he would be consistent, he has no alternative but to adopt 'magisterial intolerance of any contrary assertion'.[15]
Of course, despite one's initial resolution, one may in the event give up one's conviction.
Newman maintains that anyone who loses his conviction on any point is thereby proved
never to have been certain of it.

How do we tell, then, at any given moment, what our certitudes are? No line, Newman
thinks, can be drawn between such real certitudes as have truth for their object, and merely
apparent certitudes. What looks like a certitude always is exposed to the chance of turning
out to be a mistake. There is no interior, immediate test, sufficient to distinguish genuine
from false certitudes.[16]

Newman correctly distinguishes certainty from infallibility. My memory is not infallible: I remember for certain what I did yesterday but that does not mean that I never
misremember.

I am quite clear that two and two make four, but I often make mistakes in long additions.

Certitude concerns a particular proposition, infallibility is a faculty or gift. It was possible
for Newman to be certain that Victoria was Queen without claiming to possess any general
infallibility.

But how can I rest in certainty when I know that in the past I have thought myself certain
of an untruth? Surely what happened once may happen again.

> Suppose I am walking out in the moonlight, and see dimly the outlines of some figure among
> the trees;—it is a man. I draw nearer, it is still a man; nearer still, and all hesitation is at an
> end.—I am certain it is a man. But he neither moves nor speaks when I address him; and then
> I ask myself what can be his purpose in hiding among the trees at such an hour. I come quite
> close to him and put out my arm. Then I find for certain that what I took for a man is but a
> singular shadow, formed by the falling of the moonlight on the interstices of some branches or
> their foliage. Am I not to indulge my second certitude, because I was wrong in my first? Does
> not any objection, which lies against my second from the failure of my first, fade away before
> the evidence on which my second is founded?[17]

The sense of certitude is, as it were, the bell of the intellect, and sometimes it strikes
when it should not. But we do not dispense with clocks because on occasions they tell the
wrong time.

No general rules can be set out which will prevent us from ever going wrong in a specific
piece of concrete reasoning. Aristotle in his *Ethics* told us that no code of laws, or moral
treatise, could map out in advance the path of individual virtue: we need a virtue of practical
wisdom (*phronesis*) to determine what to do from moment to moment. So too with theoretical reasoning, Newman says: the logic of language will take us only so far, and we need a special intellectual virtue, which he calls 'the illative sense' to tell us the appropriate conclusion
to draw in the particular case. The illative sense, he tells us, 'determines what science cannot
determine, the limit of converging probabilities and the reasons sufficient for a proof'.[18] The
word 'sense' is used as in 'good sense' or 'common sense'. It is an intellectual, not a sensory,

[15] *GA*, p. 130.   [16] *GA*, p. 145.   [17] *GA*, p. 151.   [18] *GA*, p. 232.

power—but as Newman describes its operation it does indeed sound rather like an intellectual feel for plausibility, or an intellectual nose to discriminate good evidence from bad.

> In no class of concrete reasonings, whether in experimental science, historical research, or theology, is there any ultimate test of truth and error in our inferences besides the trustworthiness of the Illative Sense that gives them its sanction; just as there is no sufficient test of poetical excellence, heroic action, or gentleman-like conduct, other than the particular mental sense, be it genius, taste, sense of propriety, or the moral sense, to which those subject matters are severally committed.[19]

Newman's epistemology has not been much studied by subsequent philosophers because of the religious purpose that was his overarching aim in developing it. But the treatment of belief, knowledge, and certainty in the *Grammar of Assent* has merits that are quite independent of the theological context, and which bear comparison with classical texts of the empiricist tradition from Locke to Russell.

None the less, there are three objections that can be made to Newman's account of assent and certitude. First, assent does have degrees: there is a difference between an assent to a proposition without fear of its falsehood, but with a readiness to examine contrary evidence and change one's mind, and an assent like Newman's certitude which contemns all objections that may be brought against it. Second, though Newman is right to emphasize that the belief that Great Britain is an island is not based on sufficient evidence, that is because it is not based on evidence at all. For evidence has to be better known that that for which it is evidence; and none of the scraps of reasons that I could produce in support of the proposition that Great Britain is an island are better known to me than the proposition itself. Thirdly, it is untrue that certitude is indefectible. Knowledge, indeed, is: if I claim to know that p and then change my mind about p, I also withdraw the claim that I ever knew that p. But 'certainty' unlike 'knowledge' is not a success-word: there is nothing odd in saying 'I was certain but I was wrong.'

3. NEWMAN'S PHILOSOPHY OF RELIGION

The great question with which Newman wrestled throughout his life—from his Anglican University Sermons preached between 1826 and 1843 to the *Grammar of Assent* written after his conversion to Roman Catholicism—was this: how can religious faith be justified, given that the evidence for its conclusions seems so inadequate to the degree of its commitment.

Some philosophers have taught that simple belief in the existence of God was amply warranted, and could be justified by apodictic proofs. Newman was not so sure of this.

'It is indeed a great question', he wrote, 'whether Atheism is not as philosophically consistent with the phenomena of the physical world, taken by themselves, as the doctrine of a creative and governing power.'[20] The source of our conviction of the reality of the divine was,

---

[19] *GA*, pp. 231–2.   [20] *US*, p. 186.

for Newman, something quite different from the physical events and processes that figure in proofs such as Aquinas' Five Ways.

In any case it was not mere belief in God's existence that Newman was concerned to justify, but specific religious faith. Faith in God is more than just belief that there is a God: Aristotle believed in a prime mover unmoved, but his belief was not faith. On the other hand, faith in God, according to the Catholic tradition in which Newman wrote, was not necessarily total commitment to God: Marlowe's Faustus, on the verge of damnation, still believes in redemption. Faith thus contrasts with both reason and love. The special feature of a belief that makes it faith is that it is a belief in something as revealed by God, belief in a proposition on the word of God.

Faith, understood as belief rather than commitment, is an operation of the intellect, not of the will or emotions. But is it a reasonable operation of the intellect, or is it rash and irrational? Newman accepts that the testimony on which faith is based is in itself weak. It can only[21] convince someone who has an antecedent sympathy with the content of the testimony.

> Faith…does not demand evidence so strong as is necessary for…belief on the ground of Reason; and why? for this reason, because it is mainly swayed by antecedent considerations…previous notices, prepossessions, and (in a good sense of the word) prejudices. The mind that believes is acted upon by its own hopes, fears, and existing opinions.

Faith is reasonable to those who already accept an antecedent probability that Providence will reveal Himself. It is wrong to think that one can be a judge of religious truth without an appropriate preparation of the mind and heart.[22]

> Gross eyes see not: heavy ears hear not. But in the schools of the world the ways towards Truth are considered high roads open to all men, however disposed, at all times. Truth is to be approached without homage. Every one is considered on a level with his neighbour: or rather, the powers of the intellect, acuteness, sagacity, subtlety and depth, are thought the guides into Truth. Men consider that they have as full a right to discuss religious subjects, as if they were themselves religious. They will enter upon the most sacred points of Faith at the moment, at their plesure—if it so happen, in a careless frame of mind, in their hours of recreation, over the wine cup. Is it wonderful that they so frequently end in becoming indifferentists?

Newman is well aware that his stress on the need for preparation of the heart may well make faith appear to be no more than wishful thinking. He emphasizes, however, that the mismatch between evidence and commitment, and the importance of previous attitudes, is something to be observed not only in religious faith, but in other cases of belief.

> We hear a report in the streets, or read it in the public journals. We know nothing of the evidence; we do not know the witnesses, or anything about them: yet sometimes we believe implicitly, sometimes not: sometimes we believe without asking for evidence sometimes we disbelieve till we receive it. Did a rumour circulate of a destructive earthquake in Syria or the South of Europe, we should readily credit it; both because it might easily be true, and because it was nothing to us though it were. Did the report relate to countries nearer home, we should try to trace and authenticate it. We do not call for evidence till antecedent probabilities fail.[23]

---

[21] *US*, p. 179.   [22] *US*, p. 190.   [23] *US*, p. 180.

Two objections may be made to Newman's claim that faith is reasonable even though acceptance of it depends not so much on evidence as on antecedent probabilities. The first is that antecedent probabilities may be equally available for what is true and for what merely pretends to be true. They supply no intelligible rule to decide between a genuine and a counterfeit revelation.

> If a claim of miracles is to be acknowledged because it happens to be advanced, why not for the miracles of India as well as for those of Palestine? If the abstract possibility of a Revelation be the measure of genuineness in a given case, why not in the case of Mahomet as well as of the Apostles?[24]

Newman, who is never more eloquent than when developing criticisms of his own position, nowhere provides a satisfactory answer to this objection.

Secondly, it may be objected that there is a difference between religious faith and the reasonable, though insufficiently grounded, beliefs to which we give assent in our daily lives. In Newman's own words, Christianity is to be 'embraced and maintained as true, on the grounds of its being divine, not as true on intrinsic grounds, nor as probably true, or partially true, but as absolutely certain knowledge, certain in a sense in which nothing else can be certain'. In the ordinary cases, we are always ready to consider evidence that tells against our beliefs; but the religious believer adopts a certitude that refuses to entertain any doubt about the articles of faith.

Newman responds that even in secular matters, it can be rational to reject objections as idle phantoms, however much they may be insisted upon by a pertinacious opponent, or present themselves through an obsessive imagination.

> I certainly should be very intolerant of such a notion as that I shall one day be Emperor of the French; I should think it too absurd even to be ridiculous, and that I must be mad before I could entertain it. And did a man try to persuade me that treachery, cruelty, or ingratitude was as praiseworthy as honesty and temperance, and that a man who lived the life of a knave and died the death of a brute had nothing to fear from future retribution, I should think there was no call on me to listen to his arguments, except with the hope of converting him, though he called me a bigot and a coward for refusing to enter into his speculations.[25]

On the other hand, a believer can certainly investigate the arguments for and against his religious position. To do so need not involve any weakening of faith. But may not a man's investigation lead to his giving up his assent to his creed? Indeed it may, but

> my vague consciousness of the possibility of a reversal of my belief in the course of my researches, as little interferes with the honesty and firmness of that belief while those researches proceed, as the recognition of the possibility of my train's oversetting is an evidence of an intention of my part of undergoing so great a calamity[26]

There is not the place to follow in detail the arguments by which Newman does his best to show that the acceptance of the Catholic religion is the action of a reasonable person. He maintains that the enduring history of Judaism and Christianity through the vicissitudes of human affairs is a phenomenon that carries on its face the probability of a divine origin. But

---

[24] *US*, p. 226.   [25] *GA*, p. 131.   [26] *GA*, p. 127.

it does so, Newman admits, only to someone who already believes that there is a God who will judge the world.

But what reason is there in the first place to believe in God and a future judgement? We have seen that Newman is chary of offering cosmological arguments in support of such a belief. Instead, he makes his celebrated appeal to the testimony of conscience.

> If, on doing wrong, we feel the same tearful, broken hearted sorrow which overwhelms us on hurting a mother; if, on doing right, we enjoy the same sunny serenity of mind, the same soothing satisfactory delight which follows on our receiving praise from a father, we certainly have within us the image of some person, to whom our love and veneration look, in whose smile we find our happiness, for whom we yearn, towards whom we direct our pleadings, in whose anger we are troubled and waste away. These feelings in us are such as require for their exciting cause an intelligent being.[27]

It is difficult for members of a post-Freudian generation to read this passage without acute discomfort. It is not the mere existence of conscience—of moral judgements of right and wrong—that Newman regards as intimations of the existence of God. Such judgements can be explained—as they are by many Christian philosophers as well as by Utilitarians—as conclusions arrived at by natural reason and common sense. It is the emotional colouring of conscience that Newman claims to be echoes of the admonitions of a Supreme Judge. The feelings that he eloquently describes may indeed be appropriate only if there is a Father in Heaven. But no feelings can guarantee their own appropriateness. Whether a feeling is appropriate or not depends on the reality and nature of the object of the feeling; and that is something that must be independently established.

---

[27] *GA*, p. 76.

CHAPTER 26

··

THE PHILOSOPHY OF SAMUEL TAYLOR COLERIDGE

··

JAMES VIGUS

But as a philosopher, the class of thinkers has scarcely yet arisen by whom he is to be judged.

J. S. Mill[1]

COLERIDGE's popular fame rests on his poetry, above all on the inspired incantations of early work such as 'The Rime of the Ancient Mariner' (1798). Coleridge maintained, however, that 'No man was ever yet a great poet, without being at the same time a profound philosopher' (*Biographia Literaria*, ii. 25–6), and it was as philosopher and theologian that he laboured at a great work that would prove he had not 'lived in vain' (*Letters*, v. 280). Philosophy and theology were never, for him, distinct pursuits: together they formed the pinnacle of an encyclopaedic quest for unified knowledge. Coleridge was influential, for instance, in the fields of what we now call biology and chemistry—but it was above all as a 'Christian philosopher' that his family and friends defended his reputation after his death in 1834.[2] Coleridge's readers, like the auditors of his inimitable philosophical monologues, were polarized in their reactions: some perceived only an 'unintelligible flood of utterance', while others experienced a spiritual awakening.[3] Yet despite this evident impact on contemporaries it remains hard to specify exactly how his thought fed into broader currents. For as Mill—himself indebted to the poetry of Coleridge (and Wordsworth) for relief from a period of depression—remarked, Coleridge's mature philosophy was too liberal for 'Tories and High-Churchmen', yet too conservative for reforming groups such as the Unitarians.[4] Reflecting the wandering characteristic of Coleridge's life, this protean complexity is also the reason for the exhilarating difficulty presented by his work. As F. D. Maurice wrote: 'I rejoice

[1] Mill, *Coleridge* (1840), quoted in *Coleridge's Poetry and Prose*, 663. I thank Monika Class, Graham Davidson, and Cecilia Muratori for valuable discussion of drafts of this chapter.

[2] See Vigus, 'Coleridge's Textual Afterlives'.

[3] The quotation is from Thomas Carlyle, *The Life of John Sterling* (1851), in *Coleridge's Poetry and Prose*, 659; contrast Ralph Waldo Emerson on p. 665.

[4] Mill, *Coleridge* (1840), in *Coleridge's Poetry and Prose*, 664. For a nuanced discussion of the political dimension of Coleridge's philosophy, see Gregory, *Coleridge and the Conservative Imagination*.

to think that those who have most profited by what he has taught them do not and cannot form a school.'[5]

That said, generations of editorial labour have put modern readers in a better position than ever before to appreciate and assess Coleridge's thought. The thirty-four-volume *Collected Coleridge* edition gathers alongside the major works a myriad fragments and informal writing, including notebooks, marginalia, and even the *Opus Maximum*, whose appearance in 2002 finally quashed rumours of its non-existence. Now that the textual situation is clarified, the way is open for Coleridge's polymathic writing to emerge from the confines of courses on English literature and theology. German contemporaries such as Friedrich Schlegel and Hölderlin who likewise composed in 'poetic' fragments have gained full recognition as post-Kantian philosophers, and Coleridge demands equivalent recognition. This is Paul Hamilton's argument in *Coleridge and German Philosophy*, and it finds a welcome echo in a recent essay collection on early German Romanticism: 'Coleridge should be included in the list of German Romantic philosophers because of his absorption in German philosophical thought.'[6] Though it begs a question about the nationality of philosophy that I will briefly address later, this remark sums up the basis of my approach in this chapter. Having considered the interesting reasons for Coleridge's textual untidiness, I will selectively sketch his philosophical development, emphasizing that the critical philosophy of Kant assisted Coleridge in the resolution of a sceptical crisis. This thesis will provide a platform for considering four key, interlocking concepts of Coleridge's mature philosophy: the distinction between reason and understanding as higher and lower mental faculties; imagination; conscience as the foundation of human consciousness; and the Trinity.

This chapter thus aims to indicate the ambitious interconnectedness of Coleridge's thought in the light of its principal impetus: the pursuit of suggestive Kantian arguments into religious ends. Thinking with—and beyond—Kant about the possibility of a rational religion constituted a great philosophical challenge of the age, and this effort pervades every aspect of Coleridge's speculation. Although Coleridge is a 'closet Kantian', and rather identifies his own philosophy as Platonism, he is in that very respect a fully-fledged *post*-Kantian.[7]

This view must contend with the fact that Coleridge's critics are traditionally embarrassed by his engagement with German philosophy. Prior to Class's important reassessment, those most broadly sympathetic to Coleridge (including Muirhead, McFarland, Hamilton, Berkeley) avoided emphasizing his engagement with Kant. This evasion owes much to the distinguished lineage of commentary on Coleridge's relationship to Kant (Wellek, Orsini, Bode), which culminates in the argument that Coleridge's religious principles are 'systematically incompatible' with the very philosophical materials he most admired as worthy of appropriation and mediation.[8] A literary-critical path beyond this conclusion would involve scrutinizing the concepts of misreading and mediation upon which it depends. More central

---

[5] *The Kingdom of Christ* (1838), dedication, quoted in Neville, *Coleridge and Liberal Religious Thought*, 36.

[6] Foley, 'Schleiermacher's Religious Views in Context', 138. Cf. Milnes, 'Through the Looking-Glass'.

[7] Class, *Coleridge and Kantian Ideas in England*, 121–40. In *German Idealism* (p. 364) Beiser writes of a 'Platonic renaissance' in Germany of the late 1790s and early 1800s; I follow Beiser's broad conception of post-Kantianism as the movement towards idealism among this generation concerned above all with the religious implications of Kant's thought.

[8] Bode, 'Coleridge and Philosophy', 610.

to the present chapter, however, is the philosophical path: Coleridge studies need to move with the sea change under way in Kant studies, signalled by Frederick Beiser's recent call 'to reassess Kant's relationship with Protestantism'. Contesting the older Anglo-American orthodoxy that the post-Kantian religious turn was a mystificatory distortion, Beiser contends that Kant 'saw his ethics as Christian doctrine'.[9] Reading Kant in this way, I suggest, highlights the timeliness of Coleridge's post-Kantian project of uniting philosophy with religion. It is against this background that Coleridge's individuality most powerfully emerges.

THE COMMUNICATION OF TRUTH

Though his vision was holistic, Coleridge's output was, as just noted, fragmentary. It was as though he were determined to live out Friedrich Schlegel's aphorism: 'It is equally fatal for the mind to have a system and to have none. It will simply have to decide to have both.'[10] Coleridge's formal untidiness to some extent reflects psychological problems. In his best-known prose work, *Biographia Literaria*, Coleridge translates from F. W. J. Schelling and others with insufficient acknowledgement, and his philosophy has inevitably attracted suspicion ever since. That is so despite various mitigating factors, including the fact that Schelling himself generously brushed aside the accusation of plagiarism. Further, Coleridge had good reason for anxiety about the reading public's insular prejudice against extensive citations of 'German metaphysics'.[11]

Yet the conspicuous ruptures and patchwork-quality of Coleridge's published prose reflect not merely anxiety or neurosis, but also the deliberate policy of a writer struggling constantly with questions of form. For Coleridge explicitly maintained a distinction between two levels of philosophical discourse, the exoteric and the esoteric. This distinction rested on the authority of the philosopher with whom he most willingly and ambitiously identified himself, 'the divine Plato'. He held this enthusiasm in common with several German Romantics, and indeed '[t]he whole bent of his mind led him to Plato and Platonism, to the English Platonic tradition and to the newer German idealism which he felt to be deeply akin to the older thought'.[12] When preparing his 1819 *Lectures on the History of Philosophy* Coleridge absorbed W. G. Tennemann's recent argument that Plato had a 'system', fully presented not in the dialogues but in the unwritten teachings. Admiring the literary qualities of the dialogues, in which Plato 'taught the idea, namely the possibility and the duty of all who would arrive at the greatest perfection of the human mind of striving to contemplate things not in their phenomena, not in their accidents or their superficies, but in their essential powers' (*Lectures 1818–1819*, i. 193), Coleridge believed that Plato elaborated on this truth orally to the early academicians. This theory supported Coleridge's natural practice, which was to adorn his published work with the rhetorical '*sweet Baits* of literature' (*Friend*, i. 23), while reserving the strictest reasoning for the inner circle who visited him for evening

---

[9] Beiser, 'Moral Faith and the Highest Good', 625, 592. I also draw on Hedley, *Coleridge, Philosophy and Religion*.

[10] *Athenäumsfragmente* [1798–1800], 53, quoted in Vigus, 'Transzendentalpoesie', 141.

[11] Ashton, *The German Idea*, 44. Bate, *Coleridge*, 131–8, offers a subtle psychological analysis.

[12] Wellek, *Immanuel Kant in England*, 67.

discussions of philosophy. The explicit motive for such a policy, outlined in the opening section of *The Friend* entitled 'On the Communication of Truth', was to avoid exposing unprepared minds to arguments that might appear religiously sceptical. Thus in *The Friend* itself, for instance, an exoteric compendium of essays designed to educate a 'promiscuous public' (i. 462) in principled political and philosophical thought, Coleridge supports conventional piety with a paean of poetic quotation on the evidences of God in the world (i. 516). In the *Opus Maximum*, on the other hand, an esoteric work with a limited audience, he reveals his conviction that the existence of God cannot be logically proved (p. 103).[13]

Moreover, there is a rhetorical motivation for the esoteric–exoteric distinction. For the notion that (Platonic) philosophy ought to culminate in a complete 'system', which nevertheless remains perpetually out of reach and thus esoteric, legitimates a poetic technique for intimating the sublime truths of a higher level of discourse than the merely propositional. In other words, Coleridge makes Plato in his own image—as a 'poetic philosopher'. But this conviction gives rise to a suggestive conflict between Coleridge's philosophical authorities. Should he follow the poetic Plato or the ostensibly prosaic Kant, who objected to the high-flown, Platonizing tone of much Romantic writing and called Plato the father of all *Schwärmerei*? And what of the ambivalence in Plato himself, who in *Republic* makes Socrates the spokesman for philosophy in its ancient quarrel with poetry?[14] Coleridge's struggle between these competing styles, evident in the difference in tone and depth of discussion between, say, the published *Friend* and the unpublished *Opus Maximum*, is a key aspect of his 'double-mindedness' (as Perry terms it): so much so that the two levels of discourse, exoteric and esoteric, or poetic and philosophical, are also reflected in his key philosophical distinction, that between reason and understanding. In order to appreciate the latter distinction, it is necessary to follow the path by which Coleridge arrived at it.

THE WILDERNESS OF DOUBT

Coleridge's voluminous reading, together with the energetic passion with which he followed first one philosophical position, then another, make it impossible to give a definitive account of his development.[15] Yet we must set out with some selective idea about it, because Coleridge was a compulsive philosophical autobiographer, noting in 1803: 'Seem to have made up my mind to write my metaphysical works, as *my Life*, & *in* my Life—intermixed with all the other events/or history of the mind & fortunes of S. T. Coleridge—' (*Notebooks*, i. 1515). One of the most striking features of the *Biographia Literaria, or Biographical Sketches of my Literary Life and Opinions* (1817) is its disclosure that Coleridge's philosophy

---

[13] Cf. *Table-Talk*, i. 262–3 (22 February 1834): 'Assume the existence of God and then the harmony and fitness of the physical creation may be shown to correspond with and support such an assumption; but to set about *proving* the existence of a God by such means is a mere circle—a delusion. It can be no proof to a good reasoner, unless he presumes his conclusion.'

[14] On this ambivalence, see Vigus, *Platonic Coleridge*, ch. 3.

[15] McFarland, *Coleridge and the Pantheist Tradition* remains the classic account, though vitiated by a wholesale division of philosophy into pantheistic and non-pantheistic (Berkeley, *Coleridge and the Crisis of Reason*, 2–6).

commenced in earnest with a modern-sounding doubt. He recounts in chapter 9 how he had wondered in the 1790s whether philosophy is possible at all:

> After I had successively studied in the schools of Locke, Berkeley, Leibnitz, and Hartley, and could find in neither of them an abiding place for my reason, I began to ask myself: is a system of philosophy, as different from mere history and historic classification, possible?

He relates that he was disposed to answer this question 'in the negative', and 'to admit that the sole practicable employment for the human mind was to observe, to collect, and to classify'.[16] The study of the philosophers just named had brought Coleridge to a crisis, which may be summed up in this way: empiricism leads to scepticism. The clue to this interpretation lies in another name that appears on the same page. If we make the empiricist assumption that there is nothing in the mind that does not derive from sense perception, notes Coleridge, then the sceptical arguments of David Hume are unanswerable. Indeed, Hume's objections must apply with 'crushing force' to *all* our 'logical forms'. For Hume had notoriously refuted proof by induction, arguing in particular that when we refer to one event as the 'cause' of another, we can mean no more than that we have repeatedly observed events of type a immediately to precede events of type b. Our imagination, says Hume, provides the link between these events: there is no absolutely certain law of causality. And if this is true, as Coleridge asks, 'How can we make bricks without straw? Or build without cement?' (*Biographia Literaria*, i. 142) This directly echoes Hume, who said that the principles of association are '*to us* the cement of the universe'.[17] Coleridge's confrontation with scepticism is much more direct than commentators generally recognize.[18]

One might ask why this mattered so much to Coleridge, given that Hume himself had absorbed the doubt and constructed probabilistic moral and social theories. But the law of cause and effect was crucial to the optimistic philosophy of David Hartley (the most important to Coleridge though nowadays the least well known of the philosophers just listed). When Coleridge declared in 1797 that 'I am a compleat Necessitarian', he invoked Hartley's *Observations on Man* (*Letters*, i. 137). Hartley was the flagship philosopher of the rational Unitarian Christianity to which Coleridge had converted as a student at Cambridge. Inspired above all by Joseph Priestley, the Unitarians' pioneering work in science, social reform, and historical critique of religious doctrine and ritual put them at the forefront of intellectual life in the wake of the French Revolution. Yet their vision of a material, mechanistic universe directed by divine providence to an inevitably happy ending for all—most eloquently expressed in Coleridge's epic poem of 1796, *Religious Musings*—threatened to founder on the kind of sceptical objections raised by Hume. From the perspective Coleridge gradually evolved from the late 1790s, there are three essential problems with Priestleyan Unitarianism and its philosophical bedfellow, necessitarianism. First, it seems incoherent,

---

[16]   *Biographia Literaria*, i. 141; compare i. 200, and the continued querying of the possibility of philosophy as late as 1818: 'Is Philosophy […] conceivable?' (*Letters*, iv. 847).

[17]   'Abstract' of *A Treatise of Human Nature*, 417.

[18]   Brice, *Coleridge and Scepticism*, for instance, follows Craig's argument as to Coleridge's suppression of Humean scepticism; yet Coleridge expounds Hume on causality at careful length in *Logic*, 181 f. (in Kantian terms: Orsini, *Coleridge and German Idealism*, 152). See, however, the very acute essay by Hort, 'Coleridge' (esp. p. 317); and for a fine account of Coleridge's use of Kantian transcendental argument in *Logic*, Milnes, 'Coleridge's Logic'.

because it depends on a 'law of association' governing chains of causes and effects, which Hume has shown to be unprovable. Second, it nevertheless denies human free will, which (as we will see shortly) now seems both epistemologically and morally unacceptable to Coleridge. Third, Coleridge, unlike Priestley, thinks it incompatible with belief in a personal God.[19]

This begins to explain Coleridge's 'presentment' around 1797 that 'all the products of the mere *reflective* faculty partook of DEATH, and were as the rattling twigs and sprays in winter, into which a sap was yet to be propelled'. Coleridge's rational Unitarianism had foundered on a sceptical crisis of reason, which resulted in 'wanderings through the wilderness of doubt'. Before he found a satisfactory solution, he relates, it was only the writings of the mystics Jakob Böhme, George Fox, and William Law that kept 'alive the *heart* in the *head*'; that 'enabled me to skirt, without crossing, the sandy deserts of utter unbelief' (*Biographia Literaria*, i. 152; cf. 200). He intimates that the pantheistic leanings of these writers enabled him to benefit from them at a time when he could not intellectually accept a personal creator-God. Coleridge ought arguably to have included Hartley himself in the list of mystics, since Hartley blends mechanistic rationality with effusions on God's presence in creation.[20] But on the other hand, this was precisely the problem: in Coleridge's view, Unitarianism strips away the divine mystery of transcendence, making God purely immanent; it thus identifies God with the world. And if God is identical with the world, if he 'rolls through all things' (as Coleridge will disapprovingly quote Wordsworth in *Aids to Reflection*, 404, and *Opus Maximum*, 113), how can we continue to talk about God at all? This explains the relentless polemic of Coleridge's later writings, in which he attacks Unitarianism, pantheism, and atheism as all of a piece (e.g. *Notebooks*, v. 6753). This equation was painfully important to Coleridge precisely because it remained so tempting and plausible: because, that is, the dreaded 'mechanical philosophy' seemed to rest on the very same ground as Wordsworthian enthusiasm about the creative power of nature.

This sceptical crisis generated by an English tradition of empiricist philosophy drove Coleridge into the arms of a parallel controversy in Germany. Coleridge developed a fascination with the alleged pantheism of Spinoza, which he may even have learned about in the early 1790s through periodical reviews of works by Friedrich Heinrich Jacobi, founder and protagonist of the German 'pantheism controversy'.[21] The main contours of the latter controversy in many respects mirror the English situation. Jacobi asserted that the Enlightenment's cultivation of reason results in Spinozistic pantheism, understood as grimly empty and nihilistic.[22] Jacobi enlisted the sceptical arguments of Hume in support of his position in a book that Coleridge annotated, *David Hume über den Glauben* (1787).[23] Coleridge essentially agreed with Jacobi's diagnosis, but responded ambivalently to the latter's solution. For Jacobi's claim was this: Hume has shown us that even those acts of the mind that we normally designate as rational really depend on indemonstrable belief (I *believe* in a law of

---

[19] See Ralph Waller's chapter on the philosophy of James Martineau, this volume.

[20] Haven, 'Coleridge, Hartley and the Mystics'.

[21] Schrickx, 'Coleridge and Friedrich Heinrich Jacobi'; Micheli, 'The Early Reception of Kant's Thought in England 1785–1805', 300–4.

[22] On the peculiarities of Jacobi's stance, see Hedley, 'Coleridge as Theologian'.

[23] Jacobi's title is usually translated *David Hume on Belief*, but there is an important ambiguity in the German *Glauben*, which also means 'faith'.

causality such that when when one ball strikes another, the second ball will move, though I cannot *prove* it). To escape the consequences of the world view that Jacobi labels 'pantheistic', we must reject reasoning in favour of one more act of belief, namely belief in the transcendent God of traditional religion. This goal was germane to Coleridge's striving, too, but he could never accept what he perceived as Jacobi's irrationalism.[24] In other words, Coleridge believed that Jacobi's diagnosis of the malaise of European philosophy was right but his cure wrong.

REASON AND UNDERSTANDING

A robuster solution offered itself in the wake of Coleridge's trip to Göttingen in 1798–9. At this fashionable university he studied the latest natural science and reported significantly that 'all are Kantians whom I have met with' (*Letters*, i. 444). Coleridge, much like his future friend Henry Crabb Robinson, who converted to 'Kantianism' while in Germany in 1801, found that Immanuel Kant's direct engagement with the British empiricists offered a new and fruitful path towards the goal of a rationally grounded religious faith.[25] It was probably in 1801 that, in Coleridge's words, Kant 'took possession of me as with a giant's hand' (*Biographia Literaria*, i. 153). It was the study of Kant that enabled him to announce grandiloquently in a letter of that year that he had 'overthrown the doctrine of association, as taught by Hartley, and with it all the irreligious metaphysics of modern infidels, especially the doctrine of necessity' (*Letters*, ii. 706). Free will is rapidly becoming Coleridge's central concern.

Coleridge's earlier-quoted reference to the 'crushing force' of Hume's scepticism in an empiricist context characteristically echoes Kant, who pursued Hume's objection regarding causality to its logical extreme: hence the epithet that Moses Mendelssohn, Jacobi's target in the pantheism controversy, bestowed on Kant, *alleszermalmend*, all-crushing (noted in *Biographia Literaria*, ii. 89). But if Kant completed the destruction of old metaphysical assumptions, he also commenced the rebuilding process, beginning with a reversal of the empiricist assumption that the human mind must conform to external objects. Kant shows instead that objects of the senses must conform to our mental faculties:[26] in short, he asserts that the human mind is active, in contrast to the passive, blank slate posited by empiricism.

Coleridge, who believed his mind had been prepared for this perspective both by the Cambridge Platonists (Ralph Cudworth considered the mind as 'senior' to the material world) and by Leibniz (see *Biographia Literaria*, i. 141), vigorously defended Kant's concept of a priori judgements against the contemporary misunderstanding that it was equivalent to the theory of 'innate ideas' long ago rejected by Locke (*Biographia Literaria*, i. 293 n.; *Logic*,

---

[24] McFarland, 'Aspects of Coleridge's Distinction between Reason and Understanding', 179; Hedley, *Coleridge, Philosophy and Religion*, 26–7; Berkeley, *Coleridge and the Crisis of Reason*, 196–7; hence Berkeley's own claim that Jacobi is the most important philosopher for Coleridge (p. 68) is implausible. Admittedly, in *David Hume über den Glauben* Jacobi denies the charge of irrationalism.

[25] Robinson's essays elucidate the philosophical problems that Coleridge likewise confronted, and his description of his conversion provides circumstantial confirmation of Coleridge's own conversion experience.

[26] *Critique of Pure Reason*, Bxvi. ('B' signifies the 2nd edn. of 1787, which Coleridge read.)

250). Coleridge needed to establish this concept because it informed the Kantian distinction between reason and understanding. And Coleridge's own philosophy, as he will declare in 1819, is precisely 'built on the distinction between the Reason and the Understanding'.[27] Essentially, the understanding is the faculty that processes sense perceptions and draws empirical conclusions in the way envisaged by Locke; whereas reason makes universal and necessary, a priori judgements (such as the propositions of geometry). The significance of this Kantian distinction is by no means merely epistemological. Rather, in the wake of Coleridge's sceptical crisis, it answered the question of how (systematic) philosophy may still be possible at all. Kant does not, as Jacobi appeared to, reject reason: rather, he redefines it as the faculty that sends us beyond the limits of experience, seeking the 'unconditioned'— a formulation that Coleridge takes up enthusiastically (*Friend*, i. 461).[28]

Later in the *Critique of Pure Reason*, Kant applies this distinction to the unsatisfactory results of all the logical analysis hitherto undertaken by traditional metaphysics. In the section entitled 'The Antinomy of Pure Reason' Kant provides proofs of equal weight both for and against propositions such as the existence of God and the freedom of the will.[29] Coleridge, appreciative of the intellectual discipline this procedure encouraged (*Biographia Literaria*, i. 153), is convinced by the rigour of Kant's demonstration in the antinomies. He also endorses Kant's 'solution'—up to a certain point. According to Kant, human reason inevitably posits certain transcendental ideas such as 'God' and 'free will', but cannot directly establish their truth. We can only do so indirectly by abandoning epistemological enquiry, and instead acknowledging the intuition we have of a moral law. We express this intuition whenever we say 'I ought'. Now, if the moral law is binding on us—as it must be, in order to be coherent in the first place—then certain conditions are necessarily in place, such as God and free will. Thus we must believe as a matter of 'moral faith' what we cannot prove. In other words, we must behave *as if* God and freedom were established. Kant, 'entangled in the snares of speculative reason, has recourse to practical reason and throws himself into the arms of faith'.[30]

Had Coleridge been straightforwardly convinced by Kantian moral faith, his philosophical development might have come to rest here. Kant's invitation to a commitment to a conditional moral faith, a faith based on an 'as if', however, was the major problem discussed by his theologically minded readers in the 1790s, and like them, Coleridge considered it unsatisfying (*Letters*, iv. 863). Could the ideas of God and immortality really be regulative only, as Kant explicitly argues, such that we can look to them only as guides to our practical conduct? Or could they not after all be constitutive, that is objects of possible experience?[31] For Coleridge, '[w]hether Ideas are regulative only, according to Aristotle and Kant; or likewise CONSTITUTIVE, and one with the power and Life of Nature, according to Plato, and Plotinus [...] is the highest *problem* of Philosophy' (*Statesman's Manual*, in *Lay Sermons*, 113–14).

---

[27] *Letters*, iv. 1049–50; also quoted in *Coleridge's Poetry and Prose*, 555.

[28] See Vigus, *Platonic Coleridge*, 133, 159 (n. 46).

[29] *Critique of Pure Reason*, B454–88.

[30] Robinson, *Essays on Kant, Schelling and German Aesthetics*, 125.

[31] On the centrality and difficulties of moral faith, see Beiser, 'Moral Faith', 604–6; on the imperative to complete Kant's unfinished system, Henrich, *Between Kant and Hegel*; cf. Hedley, *Coleridge, Philosophy and Religion*, 24–5.

In order to justify his claim that the ideas of reason are constitutive, Coleridge eventually tells the story of the antinomies in a different way: the antinomies show that the logic of the *understanding* fails when it tries to address ideas of *reason* (*Logic*, 139–40). This readjustment prepares the crucial claim: reason, which posits transcendental ideas, also gives us real *insight* into those ideas. Moreover, Coleridge conflates the ideas of reason with the things-in-themselves behind appearances, which Kant posited but denied that we can cognize. Coleridge's usual argument for the fact that we have direct, intuitive knowledge of noumena, or ideas of reason, is that it is in the nature of reason to *want* to know these things, and nature never frustrates such an 'instinct' in any other circumstances: 'Throughout animated Nature, of each characteristic Organ and Faculty there exists a pre-assurance, an instinctive and practical Anticipation: and no Pre-assurance common to a whole species does in any instance prove delusive. [...] and is it in her noblest Creature, that [Nature] tells her first lie?' (*Aids to Reflection*, 353).

This is a fragile argument, to be sure, but it supplements Kant's 'as-if' doctrine of moral faith with the optimism of an earlier idealism.[32] In thus allowing that the human mind has access to the noumenal realm, Coleridge appeals to the distinction between the 'letter' and the 'spirit' of Kant's writings. Kant is said to have provided 'hints and insinuations' that Fichte and Schelling unfolded (*Biographia Literaria*, i. 154). In developing Kant's 'hints', however, Coleridge calculatedly opens the floodgates to the kind of enthusiastic discourse that Kant had tried to banish by showing clearly the limits of our knowledge.

Even if Coleridge's philosophy is unthinkable without Kant's distinction between reason and understanding, then, his eventual definitions transgress Kant's limits on knowledge and appeal to quite different sources and modes of expression. And so we circle back to Jacobi after all. In the following passage, Coleridge invokes Jacobi's distinctively anti-Kantian description of reason—although he must then leave Jacobi behind when explaining how (intuitive) reason and (logical) understanding are mutually dependent:

> I should have no objection to define Reason with Jacobi, and with his friend Hemsterhuis, as an organ bearing the same relation to spiritual objects, the Universal, the Eternal, and the Necessary, as the eye bears to material and contingent phænomena. But then it must be added, that it is an organ identical with its appropriate objects. Thus, God, the Soul, eternal Truth, &c. are the objects of Reason; but they are themselves *reason*. We name God the Supreme Reason; and Milton says, 'Whence the Soul *Reason* receives, and Reason is her Being.' Whatever is conscious *Self*-knowledge is Reason; and in this sense it may be safely defined as the organ of the Super-sensuous; even as the Understanding wherever it does not possess or use the Reason, as another and inward eye, may be defined the conception of the Sensuous, or the faculty by which we generalize and arrange the phænomena of perception: that faculty, the functions of which contain the rules and constitute the possibility of outward Experience. In short, the Understanding supposes something that is *understood*. This may be merely its own acts or forms, that is, formal Logic; but *real* objects, the materials of *substantial* knowledge, must be furnished, we might safely say *revealed*, to it by Organs of Sense. The understanding of the higher Brutes has only organs of outward sense, and consequently material objects only; but man's understanding has likewise an organ of inward sense, and therefore the power of acquainting itself with invisible realities or spiritual objects. This organ is his Reason. (*Friend*, i. 155–6; also in *Coleridge's Poetry and Prose*, 555–6)

---

[32] Compare George Berkeley in a *Guardian* article of 1713: 'Nothing is made in vain, much less the instincts and appetites of animals', a maxim that holds 'throughout the whole system of created beings'.

So to distinguish between reason and understanding is also to distinguish human beings from animals, a leitmotif of Coleridge's thought. The 'formal Logic' exercised by human understanding (which might include the mathematical reasoning that Kant attributed to reason) is superior in degree to anything that an animal can perform because, and only because, the human mind also enjoys a difference in kind: our understanding is enlightened by the reason's perception of 'spiritual objects'.

But is there any validity to Coleridge's claim to be thus elaborating the 'hints' of Kant, or is he rather (as commentators often suppose) developing an enthusiastic mysticism discredited by the critical perspective he claimed as his starting point? This is an important question with no ready or easy answer. The fact that Fichte, Schelling, and others also believed that, in drastically departing from the Kantian critical path, they were true to its spirit, does not of itself legitimate Coleridge's method. But I wish to suggest that Coleridge drew in a coherent way on a 'hint' of Kant's that is too rarely considered in this context. This is the concept of the 'highest good', which Kant offers as a necessary aspect of 'moral faith'. Kant's view is that practical reason commands us to do that through which we will become worthy to be happy; but that this command only makes sense if we can rationally expect a world to arise in which virtue and happiness coexist proportionately (in our present world, it is only too evident that the most virtuous people are not necessarily the happiest). Such a world is 'the ideal of the highest good', and necessarily requires a 'highest will', that of God, in order to come to fruition. This world would be inhabited by a community of rational agents who, under the guidance of moral principles, would be the authors both of their own well-being and that of others. Kant refers to this community as a *corpus mysticum*.[33] This concept continues to generate scholarly controversy, and Beiser even argues that the idea of the *corpus mysticum* has constitutive status, despite Kant's explicit declaration elsewhere that the ideas of reason may be employed regulatively only. On Beiser's reading, Kant's 'chief contention is that this idea has its regulative validity, which consists in its obligatory force as a moral principle, only if we also grant constitutive status to the ideas of God and immortality; in other words, the idea of a moral world remains problematic unless we also assume the *existence* of God and immortality'.[34] This interpretation raises yet further difficulties, not least in Beiser's consequent suggestion that while the highest good is a regulative idea from the perspective of *speculative* reason, it is a constitutive idea from the perspective of *practical* reason. In his endeavour to philosophize with Kantian materials, Coleridge likewise inevitably stumbled on the problematic division between speculative and practical reason. Coleridge perhaps never escaped it entirely, but he eventually settled on a concept of unitary reason that operates in different 'spheres'. He thus maintains the Kantian primacy of practical reason, while acknowledging the fluidity of the mental faculties:

> The Practical Reason alone *is* Reason in the full and substantive sense. It is reason in its own Sphere of *perfect freedom*; as the source of IDEAS, which *Ideas*, in their conversion to the responsible Will, become Ultimate Ends. On the other hand, Theoretic Reason, as the ground of the Universal and Absolute in all Logical *Conclusion*, is rather the *Light* of Reason in the

[33] This term traditionally denotes the indwelling of all believers in Christ. In *Critique of Practical Reason*, A289 Kant speaks of the kingdom of God. Class (*Coleridge and Kantian Ideas in England*, 74–9) notes Coleridge's early exposure to Kant's principle of the highest good through an exposition by Friedrich Nitsch.

[34] Beiser, 'Moral Faith', 619.

Understanding, and known to be such by its contrast with the contingency and particularity which characterize all the proper and indigenous growths of the Understanding. (*Aids to Reflection*, 413)

However, to see how Coleridge pursued the concept of the highest good—or 'Ultimate Ends', informing a *corpus mysticum*—we need to grasp a further aspect of his dynamic faculty psychology.

IMAGINATION

So far we have considered only the supposedly 'constitutive' status of the ideas of reason, and the faculty that apprehends them. From a Coleridgean perspective, more questions remain, such as: how are ideas of reason formed, and how are they to be described? Evidently not in the propositional language of the understanding or 'formal logic', but rather in poetic language, the language of the imagination—about which Kant provided yet further pregnant hints in his treatise on aesthetics, the *Critique of Judgment*. The latter work addresses what many, including Coleridge, found problematic in the *Critique of Pure Reason*. For to elaborate the question, what is the source of our intuition of freedom, which is necessary for the coherence of the moral law, which in turn is the ground of our hope that God exists and that the world will ultimately proceed to a highest good? Kant effectively licenses Romantic speculation when he suggests that 'the imagination (as a productive cognitive power) is very powerful when it creates, as it were, another nature out of the material that actual nature gives it […] in this process we feel our freedom from the law of association'.[35] Recent commentators have linked this account of imagination to the concept of the highest good.[36] It is through imaginative play, stimulated by beautiful objects in art or nature, that we become aware of our freedom; or, romantically extending Kant's hint about the 'productive' nature of imagination, the imagination may be creative in the same kind of way that the divine intelligence is creative in producing the world.

Coleridge pursues this analogy in *Biographia Literaria*, drawing controversially on F. W. J. Schelling's *System of Transcendental Idealism*. At the end of Book I, Coleridge splits imagination into a non-hierarchical pair, the primary imagination being the means by which we perceive distinct objects (rather than a mere chaos of sensations), and the secondary the fusing power of the artist. Both are related to divine creativity:

The primary IMAGINATION I hold to be the living Power and prime Agent of all human Perception, and as a repetition in the finite mind of the eternal act of creation in the infinite I AM. The second I consider as an echo of the former, co-existing with the conscious will, yet still as identical with the primary in the *kind* of its agency, and differing only in *degree*, and in the *mode* of its operation. It dissolves, diffuses, dissipates, in order to re-create; or where this process is rendered impossible, yet still at all events it struggles to idealize and to unify. It is essentially *vital*, even as all object (*as* objects) are essentially fixed and dead. (*Biographia Literaria*, i. 304)

---

[35] *Critique of the Power of Judgment*, §49.   [36] Kneller, *Kant and the Power of Imagination*, 52.

Coleridge then provides a distinction between imagination and fancy that runs parallel to the distinction between reason and understanding. While fancy is merely a 'mode of Memory' that can *choose* to transpose its materials in different orders, but always obeying the empiricist law of association, imagination exercises a higher order of choice, a fusing (as opposed to merely juxtaposing) power.

Coleridge claims that these enigmatic definitions are the 'conclusion' of a longer discussion, nothing less than a 'transcendental deduction' of the faculty of imagination. In a typical esoteric gesture, he writes that a friend warned him against presenting so much abstruse material to the reading public. The Romantic irony of this gesture is unmistakable, since it highlights the incongruity of logically *demonstrating* a faculty whose very mode of operation consists in 'struggling' in a fragmentary way to fuse its materials.[37] At the same time, though, the abrupt dissolution of the *Biographia Literaria*'s argument manifests unease: namely the anxiety that the Schellingian imagination's omnipotent relationship to nature fails to allow enough room for distinguishing God, the mind and nature, and so implies pantheism all over again. Coleridge did not expand on his definition because he was 'blocked by his religious censor'.[38]

This explains why in 1818 Coleridge vehemently rejected the philosophy of Schelling, at least in the latter's avowedly pantheist phase around 1800. Commentators have sometimes viewed this apparent about-turn as signalling Coleridge's move away from aesthetics and literature and towards metaphysical theology; and since Coleridge's works are classified as 'English literature', this assumption has led to neglect of the post-1820 work. Yet Coleridge did continued to write poetry, to speculate on aesthetics, and still 'metaphysicised à la Schelling while he abused him'.[39] Accordingly, the imagination continued to play a key role in the various sketches that Coleridge made towards a dynamic system of faculty psychology. In the margin of a book (*Marginalia*, v. 798), he scribbled a useful diagram of the 'Order of the Mental Powers':

Reason
Imagination
Understanding.

Understanding
Fancy
Sense

The dividing line suggests a dualism between the noumenal and phenomenal realms, but the presence of 'understanding' on each side of the line indicates that the human mind is amphibious, bridging the gap. Further, the line represents a mirror: there are not six, but three powers that manifest themselves in different ways depending whether we consider them from the lower, sensual or the higher, intellectual viewpoint. The understanding processes sense perceptions (below the line), but is also responsible for logical thinking (above the line); while reason and sense, as polar opposites, are linked in the sense

[37] See Wheeler, *Sources, Processes and Methods*.
[38] Bate, *Coleridge*, 161.
[39] Henry Crabb Robinson, *Diary, Reminiscences, and Correspondence*, ed. Thomas Sadler (London, 1869), ii. 273, quoted in Hedley, 'Coleridge as Theologian', 481.

that—considered artificially in isolation—they apprehend their objects directly, without mediation.[40] Yet Coleridge adds a significant note: 'Fancy and Imagination are Oscillations, *this* connecting R. and U; *that* connecting Sense and Understanding,' the term 'oscillation' indicating the interactive dynamism of human perception and thought. Perception and cognition are imaginative acts.

In a notebook entry of 1820 Coleridge put all these elements together in a different way again, drafting a scheme of the human mind as teleological and progressive. Coleridge wants, quite simply, to synthesize everything: the philosophical and religious vocations of human beings appear in tandem, and '*Ideas*' of reason, which are (Kantian) regulative guides but also (Platonic) causal entities, constitute the raw material out of which the imagination constructs a practical '*Ideal*'. Coleridge thus attributes a cascade of verbs (creates, feels, proposes, think, form) to the imagination:

> But only as Man is capable of Ideas, is he a Philosopher by birth-right—and as far only as he is capable of an Ideal (practical product having its cause & impulse in *Ideas*, & its End, Aim, and Object in the approximate realization of the same) is Man a *Religious* Being.—But neither the one nor the other is possible except thro' the Imagination (*not* Fancy which is but the aoristus primus [...] of Memory, in the service of *Choice* [...])—neither, I say, are possible but by means of the IMAGination, by force of which the Man,
>
>   1. creates for himself, and for the use & furtherance of his *Thinking*, Representations or rather *Presences*, where *Experience* can supply no more, but had already stopt payment;
>   2. feels Wants (*pothon*, desideria) and proposes to himself Aims & Ends (*Zwecke*) that can be gratified and attained by nothing which Experience can offer or suggest, and to think of which is at the same time and by necessary involution to think and to form the notion of a higher purer Existence & a limitless Futurity. (*Notebooks*, iv. 4692)

The suggestion that imagination is necessary to make man a religious being resonates with a tradition of theology that looks to Platonic idealism for inspiration.[41] But it is no accident that the passage is also saturated with Kantian terminology—not in a way that suggests plagiarism or paraphrase, but rather reflecting Coleridge's determination to think with and beyond Kant. The subordination of the faculty of 'choice' (as being lower than 'will'; compare *Biographia Literaria*, i. 305) calls on Kant's formulation of this very distinction just prior to the discussion of the highest good.[42] His restless revisionism informs his suggestion that 'IMAGination' creates '*Presences*' rather than 'Representations' (the latter being the translation of the German term *Vorstellung*)—since 'representation' would imply the objective existence of something represented and hence lying within experience. Moreover, Coleridge uses the teleological Kantian language of *Zwecke* to denote those ideals towards which we intuitively strive. Our necessary conception of a 'higher purer Existence & a limitless Futurity' corresponds to Kant's *corpus mysticum*, especially when taken in conjunction with what Coleridge proceeds to say about the intellectual and moral development of 'the whole rational World', which is more than the development of 'one or of several Individuals,

---

[40] My commentary draws on Barfield, *What Coleridge Thought*, 96–7.
[41] Hedley, *Living Forms of the Imagination*.
[42] *Critique of Pure Reason*, B830.

but if subjective is yet universally subjective'. For 'subjective universality' is, according to Kant, a characteristic of aesthetic judgements.[43]

This entry embodies the very spirit of striving that it describes, since it is a typical fragment, a sketch for a larger projected work. As he proceeds, the rhythm and biblical allusiveness of Coleridge's prose hovers between the plaintive and the prophetic: 'if only the souls of better mould, made to live in the courts of the Sun, could be called into the Valley of Vision [...] what a new Heaven & a new Earth, would begin to reveal itself'. Such a tone strikes some commentators as unphilosophical, lacking precision and tending to a nostalgic quietism: it could be seen as a case in which 'imagination now collapses into a kind of knowledge, and so loses its discursive distinctiveness'.[44] More sympathetically interpreted, however, it is an example of how 'Kant's theory enabled entertaining the importance of creative, reflective imagination in general as a possible source for the realization of substantive changes in the world'.[45] The striving that Coleridge associates with imagination, complementing the contemplative attitude he associates with reason, informs his definition of an 'Ideal' as a 'practical product'. Coleridgean ideals are practical in the sense of being at least 'approximately' realizable; they are also practical in the Kantian sense of being founded on a moral consciousness, or conscience. There is thus a direct link between imagination and the 'will' whose moral agency is monitored by conscience. In his later writings, Coleridge tries to use these insights to change the world—to call as many souls as possible into the valley of vision.

CONSCIENCE

Coleridge is a deeply practical thinker, pursuing all the theoretical speculations so far surveyed with what he called a 'Moral Interest' (*Marginalia*, ii. 183)—without which all philosophy is in his view barren and misleading. In 1825 he published a practical guide to Christian morality, *Aids to Reflection*, a best-seller throughout the nineteenth century. Though it takes the form of a collection of aphorisms (many by the seventeenth-century clergyman Robert Leighton) with Coleridge's commentary, *Aids to Reflection* has a subtextual agenda: to assimilate and move beyond Kant's approach in *Religion within the Limits of Reason Alone*.[46] Just as Kant had appealed to our immediate consciousness of an absolutely binding moral law, so Coleridge makes this practical principle the foundational assumption of all his reasoning. In assuming that the reader can find a 'Moral Law within', insists Coleridge, 'I assume a something, the proof of which no man can *give* to another, yet every man may *find* for himself. If any man assert, that he *can* not find it, I am *bound* to disbelieve him!' (*Aids to Reflection*, 136). Coleridge does not regret the fact that his foundational premise is only an assumption that the reader is free to reject: on the contrary, this is necessary, since if it were impossible for human beings to deny the moral law, we would by definition have no free will and so would be incapable of culpability and virtue alike.

[43] Wilson, 'Coleridge's "German Absolutism"', detects Coleridge's accordance with Kantian subjective universality.

[44] Hamilton, 'The Philosopher', 178.

[45] Kneller, *Kant and the Power of Imagination*, 6.

[46] Shaffer, 'Coleridge and Kant's "Giant Hand"', 42.

Directing his exhortation to young men of university age, Coleridge reaffirms the practical imperative: 'Christianity is not a Theory, or a Speculation; but a *Life*. Not a *Philosophy* of Life, but a Life and a living Process. [...] TRY IT' (*Aids to Reflection*, 202). He thus characteristically makes far more explicit assertions of the truth of Christianity than Kant would ever allow, but nevertheless from a Kantian basis. For Kant, maintaining the rigour of the moral law, described human beings' inability to conform to it as the 'radical evil' of human nature—a concept that owes much to the tradition of Pauline, Augustinian, and Calvinist theology.[47] This is another 'hint' that Coleridge seizes upon, utilizing Kant's view that the conscience is an inner tribunal that infallibly informs us of the extent to which our will has strayed from the dictate of the moral law. But once again, in the very process of elaborating Kant's position, Coleridge radically departs from it. This is essentially because he considers Kant's stoical spirit of self-reliance to be psychologically unrealistic (*Letters*, iv. 791–2). Whereas Kant cautiously admits certain 'aids' to the renovation of the corrupt human will, such as churchgoing and prayer, Coleridge requires these to be truly efficacious. He argues once again from our needs to the expected fulfilment of those needs. The pangs of conscience inform us that we have transgressed the moral law, identified as the pure will of God; we know that our will is diseased, because we cannot avoid this transgression; therefore we need a mediating agency to reconcile us to God's will—in short, 'a redeemer'. For Coleridge, prayer begins with the recognition that we need a redeemer, the first step to surrendering our self-will. *Aids to Reflection* thus culminates in a vision of moral renovation through the agency of Christ.

Coleridge meets an objection that might be brought by orthodox Calvinists on the one hand, or Kantians on the other: if God is transcendent and unknowable and his will (expressed in the moral law) consequently unwavering, how can prayer be efficacious? In other words, are 'Objections to prayer deducible from the Perfection of the Deity & the consequent immutability of his Decrees?' Coleridge's response, jotted in the margin of a book, appeals again to the interest-driven philosophy he derived from Kant: 'Nay, Kant himself [...] supplies the answer: viz. The Idea of God is *altogether* transcendent: what therefore we are to believe concerning him must be determined by the conscience & the Moral Interest, under the *negative* condition <only> of not contradicting Reason' (*Marginalia*, ii. 183, quoted in *Aids to Reflection*, 251 n. 2). This muted tone reflects the fact that Coleridge could not banish doubts about the possibility of contact with a supersensuous realm or personal divinity even in the phase of his constructive theology (compare *Marginalia*, iii. 268).

Though the philosophical and religious questions he asked remained constant throughout his life, Coleridge's answers in the 1820s are the polar opposite of those he had given in the mid-1790s. Then, he had shared the Unitarians' necessitarianism, the denial of free will, and maintained a pantheistic identification of God with the world, which enabled him to believe that providence would gradually eradicate all the apparent evil we experience. Now he maintains, on the contrary, that conscience gives us immediate proof that we have free will; that God is transcendent; that evil exists; that in order for salvation to be possible, we must align our will with the divine will, which is only possible through supernatural aid.

In order to avoid a Jacobi-like irrationalism, or enthusiastic mysticism, however, Coleridge needed to ground his system, respecting the 'negative condition [...] of not

---

[47] Caygill, *A Kant Dictionary*, 124; Hedley, *Coleridge, Philosophy and Religion*, 244–63.

contradicting Reason'. Indeed, he proposed the chief work of philosophy as follows: '*for all that exists conditionally* [i.e. in time and space] [...] *to find a ground that is unconditional and absolute*' (*Friend*, i. 461). The 'Moral Interest' driving this apparently abstruse theological speculation is the need to show how it is possible for the finite, human will to stray from the infinite, divine will. Thus in the *Opus Maximum*, a fragmentary presentation of Coleridge's metaphysical system composed largely by dictation in the early 1820s,[48] Coleridge undertakes a theodicy. This is not a Unitarian or pantheistic theodicy in which (thought Coleridge) the reality of evil is denied, but a Trinitarian theodicy which may account for the chronic infection of the human will. The *Opus Maximum*, left by Coleridge in an almost unpublishable state, may thus be read as an esoteric accompaniment to the exoteric, polished *Aids to Reflection*.

THE TRINITY

According to Coleridge, 'It is the doctrine of the tri-unity that connects [Christiani]ty with Philosophy' (*Notebooks*, iv. 4860). The search for an unconditional 'ground' implies a foundationalist philosophy, and the *Opus Maximum* would at first sight seem to confirm this judgement. In fact, however, the work wavers between different postulations of a 'ground' or foundational certainty.[49] One reason for this is that the argument works—characteristically, as we have seen—on two mutually reflecting levels. These levels are the human and the divine; or in argumentative terms, the philosophical and the theological.[50] Post-Kantian philosophers, notably Fichte, seeking a foundational certainty on which to ground the Kantian 'system', had proposed (in various forms) self-consciousness as this absolute principle; but Coleridge argues against this approach that self-consciousness is necessarily *relational*. It is not the case, as Fichte had claimed, that the 'I' posits an 'other'; instead, an 'other' must be thought logically prior to the 'I'. In less abstract terms, an infant becomes conscious of the being of an other, the mother, before it becomes conscious of its own being. Coleridge asserts that this primal relationship between other and self is essentially a moral relationship. In Fragment I, the first step in this admittedly 'subtle' argument is as follows: 'the consciousness expressed in the term "*Thou*" is only possible by an equation in which "*I*" is taken as equal to but yet not the same as "*Thou*"', and this in turn is only possible by treating the I and Thou 'in logical antithesis, [...] as correspondent harmonies or correlatives' (*Opus Maximum*, 75). The fact that this assumption of 'equality' with another must logically occur prior to the subject's recognition of him- or herself as a distinct person supports a further striking claim (consistent with Coleridge's invocation of the moral law in all philosophical reasoning): that conscience is logically prior to consciousness. 'The conscience, I say, is not a mere mode of our consciousness, but presupposed therein' (*Opus Maximum*, 73). However, when I think 'Thou' and then think 'I', there must be some ingredient in the latter that differs

---

[48] See Barbeau, 'The Quest for System'.

[49] The plural and therefore unstable foundations of Coleridge's 'system' owe much to his love of Kantian transcendental argument, as detailed in Milnes, 'Coleridge's Logic', and align him to some extent with Friedrich Schlegel's theory of an alternating ground.

[50] The following account draws on an expanded version in Vigus, *Platonic Coleridge*, 144 f.

from the former (a difference-in-identity): and this 'can only be the Will'. In other words, consciousness of Will is the defining difference between our concept of self and that of an equal other. In insisting that there is no 'I' without an antecedent 'Thou', Coleridge echoes Jacobi (*Opus Maximum*, p. cxli); but he takes a further step in observing that these two, the I and the Thou, generate the third, the He—the third-person pronoun being unthinkable without the second and first (*Opus Maximum*, 74–5).

This argument about the foundation of human nature has its metaphysical application in Coleridge's demonstration of the logical possibility of the Christian Trinity. The first Person of the Trinity is God the Father, but in line with the reasoning just summarized, he cannot be said to exist until he has willed the existence of another—the Son. Like human parent and child, Father and Son are bound in a relation of love, by the third Person, the Holy Spirit: 'that which proceedeth from the Father to the Son and that which is returned from the Son to the Father, and which in this circulation constitutes the eternal unity in the eternal alterity and distinction—the life of Deity in actu purissima' (*Opus Maximum*, 209). Again, the first Person is identified with Will, and Will is logically prior to Being, which is identified with the second Person (*Opus Maximum*, 193 f.). Only having taken these logical steps is it permissible to consult theological tradition for an elaboration of the doctrine of the Trinity.

Differentiating the Persons of the Godhead into a Trinity, with Will first, Being second, and Love third, enables Coleridge (in Fragment 3) provisionally to explicate a mystery that the Unitarian or pantheist model could only deny (*Opus Maximum*, 218): how evil could have emerged from the perfection of God. This speculation is what Coleridge thought Plato had reserved for his esoteric, unwritten philosophy (*Friend*, i. 445), fearful of encouraging non-initiates in the misapprehension that evil is somehow within God (or, as Schelling had suggested, that it is necessary to think of a primal rupture as having occurred in the one Absolute). To begin this time at the metaphysical level: there exist 'distinct beings [...] in the plenitude of the Supreme Mind, whose essence is Will and whose actuality consists in their Will being one with the Will of God' (*Opus Maximum*, 236). There must, however, be a *potential* Will which does not coincide with the Will of God: otherwise there would be no meaning in the Idea of a Will distinct from, yet one with, God's Will. It is possible, in other words, for a Will to will its actuality in Self rather than in God. To will against God is to will the contrary of good, i.e. evil. And 'in Will alone causation inheres. To will Evil, therefore, is to originate Evil' (*Opus Maximum*, 238). In a fall which occurred prior (logically rather than temporally) to the fall of man, this potential to will evil was actualized, i.e. 'a self became, which was not God, nor One with God'. Since all actuality inheres in God, however, this was not a true actualization, but 'by a strange yet appropriate contradiction' remained 'potential' (*Opus Maximum*, 247). The self which thus became was a false self, paradoxically self-begotten, the Father of Lies. The human application of this metaphysical doctrine is that our Will is finite, and by virtue of its finitude not at one with the infinite Will of God: it is therefore radically evil. In this sense, not in the 'monstrous' sense of hereditary guilt derived from historical figures named Adam and Eve (*Aids to Reflection*, 298), Coleridge asserts the doctrine of original sin.

Yet this primal fall, an apostasy logically prior to the fall of man, remains a mystery (*Opus Maximum*, 31, 219–20; *Table Talk*, ii. 79), as it had to remain for the other post-Kantians who pursued the project of theodicy.[51] It is a mystery that requires the

---

[51] For affinities with and differences from Schelling, see Bode, 'Coleridge and Philosophy', 615–16; Berkeley, *Coleridge and the Crisis of Reason*, 179; Reid, *Coleridge, Form and Symbol*, 116 f.

imagination to dwell on mythological accounts, such as that of Genesis; and this is the imperative of Coleridge's voluminous but still little-known notebook writings in the 1820s and 1830s. Here, he speculates on the Logos, undertakes mythological-biblical criticism using a theory of the symbol, and discusses the soul's relationship to the body. In short, the later Coleridge tried to rewrite *Naturphilosophie* in a Trinitarian frame, wrestling with the topics of Schelling's work on *Human Freedom* and philosophy of mythology. The few studies so far published on these topics surely represent just the beginning of a full reconstruction of this rich phase.[52]

Conclusion

In his pioneering survey of Coleridge's philosophy, René Wellek foreshadowed many subsequent discussions in pronouncing it ultimately 'futile'. This is because Coleridge 'has built a building of no style [...] Coleridge's structure has here a storey from Kant, there a part of the room from Schelling, there a roof from Anglican theology and so on. The architect did not feel the clash of the styles'.[53] An examination of Coleridge's philosophy under the static metaphor of a building—a metaphor borrowed from Coleridge himself—could hardly reach any other conclusion. But recent developments in philosophy should encourage us to exchange this for another Coleridgean metaphor, that of a river. Constantly in flow, yet striving for an ultimate ideal, Coleridge's philosophy assimilates a main current here, a fragment there, looking back to traditional Anglican theology, but also forward to modern doubts about the whole possibility of philosophy. Coleridge's appropriation of Plato and Christian Platonism while translating the terminology of German Idealism seems less heretical than it once did, now that the appropriateness of the national epithet 'German' is being cogently challenged. The Romantics' own rhetoric of 'native' and 'foreign' should not blind us to the presence of inter-European goals and methods, most clearly evident in Coleridge's patient exposition of Kant in his *Logic* and the omnipresence of Kantian terminology in his informal, imaginative prose fragments. Finally, given that Coleridge's texts are now readily available, and given that 'the most influential recent moves in Anglo-American philosophy have involved a rejection of the empiricist assumptions on which analytical philosophy relies, in favour of a reassessment of the concerns of Kant and German Idealism, concerns which are inherently bound up with aesthetics',[54] there is reason to believe that Coleridge the philosopher's day is coming. To adapt the quotation from Mill that I took as the epigraph for this chapter, the class of thinkers may yet arise by whom he is to be judged.

---

[52] See esp. Harding, 'Imagination, Patriarchy, and Evil in Coleridge and Heidegger'; Perkins, *Coleridge's Philosophy*; Barbeau, *Coleridge, The Bible, and Religion*; Vigus, 'The Spark of Intuitive Reason'.

[53] Wellek, *Immanuel Kant in England*, 67–8.

[54] Bowie, 'Romantic Aesthetics and the Ends of Contemporary Philosophy', 213.

Works Cited

Ashton, Rosemary, *The German Idea: Four English Writers and the Reception of German Thought, 1800–1860* (Cambridge, 1980).

Barbeau, Jeffrey W., *Coleridge, the Bible, and Religion* (New York, 2008).

Barbeau, Jeffrey W., The Quest for System: An Introduction to Coleridge's Lifelong Project. In Barbeau (ed.), *Coleridge's Assertion of Religion*, 1–32.

Barbeau, Jeffrey W. (ed.), *Coleridge's Assertion of Religion: Essays on the 'Opus Maximum'* (Leuven, 2006).

Barfield, Owen, *What Coleridge Thought* (Middletown, Conn., 1971).

Bate, Walter Jackson, *Coleridge* (London, 1968).

Beiser, Frederick, *German Idealism: The Struggle Against Subjectivism* (Cambridge, Mass., 2002).

Beiser, Frederick, Moral Faith and the Highest Good. In Guyer (ed.), *Cambridge Companion to Kant*, 588–629.

Berkeley, Richard, *Coleridge and the Crisis of Reason* (Basingstoke, 2007).

Bode, Christoph, Coleridge and Philosophy. In Burwick (ed.), *Oxford Handbook of Coleridge*, 588–619.

Bowie, Andrew, Romantic Aesthetics and the Ends of Contemporary Philosophy. In Frischmann and Millán-Zaibert (eds.), *Das Neue Licht*, 213–24.

Brice, Ben, *Coleridge and Scepticism* (Oxford, 2007).

Burwick, Frederick (ed.), *The Oxford Handbook of Samuel Taylor Coleridge* (Oxford, 2009).

Caygill, Howard, *A Kant Dictionary* (Oxford, 1995).

Class, Monika, *Coleridge and Kantian Ideas in England, 1796–1817: Coleridge's Responses to German Philosophy* (London, 2012).

Coleridge, Samuel Taylor, *The Collected Works of Samuel Taylor Coleridge*, 23 vols. (Princeton: Princeton University Press) [individual volumes within the series are cited in separate entries, using the abbreviated title *CC* followed by volume no.].

Coleridge, Samuel Taylor, *Aids to Reflection* (1825), ed. John Beer, *CC* ix (1993).

Coleridge, Samuel Taylor, *Biographia Literaria; or Biographical Sketches of My Literary Life and Opinions* (1817), 2 vols., ed. James Engell and W. Jackson Bate, *CC* vii (1983).

Coleridge, Samuel Taylor, *Coleridge's Poetry and Prose*, ed. Nicholas Halmi, Paul Magnuson, and Raimonda Modiano (New York and London, 2004).

Coleridge, Samuel Taylor, *The Collected Letters of Samuel Taylor Coleridge*, 6 vols., ed. Earl Leslie Griggs (Oxford, 1956–71).

Coleridge, Samuel Taylor, *The Friend* (1809, 1818), 2 vols., ed. Barbara Rooke, *CC* iv (1969).

Coleridge, Samuel Taylor, *Lay Sermons*, ed. R. J. White, *CC* vi (1972).

Coleridge, Samuel Taylor, *Lectures 1818–1819: On the History of Philosophy*, 2 vols., ed. J. R. de J. Jackson, *CC* viii (2000).

Coleridge, Samuel Taylor, *Logic*, ed. J. R. de J. Jackson, *CC* xiii (1981).

Coleridge, Samuel Taylor, *Marginalia*, 6 vols., ed. H. J. Jackson and George Whalley, *CC* xii (1980–2001).

Coleridge, Samuel Taylor, *The Notebooks of Samuel Taylor Coleridge*, 5 vols. each in 2 pts., ed. Kathleen Coburn, Merton Christensen, and Anthony John Harding (London, 1957–2002).

Coleridge, Samuel Taylor, *Opus Maximum* (1820–3?), ed. Thomas McFarland with the assistance of Nicholas Halmi, *CC* xv (2002).

Coleridge, Samuel Taylor, *Table Talk*, 2 vols., ed. Carl Woodring, *CC* xiv (1990).

Foley, Peter, Schleiermacher's Religious Views in Context. In Frischmann and Millán-Zaibert (eds.), *Das Neue Licht*, 136–52.

Frischmann, Baerbel, and Millán-Zaibert, Elizabeth (eds.), *Das Neue Licht der Frühromantik: Innovation und Aktualität frühromantischer Philosophie* (Paderborn, 2009).

Gregory, Alan P. R., *Coleridge and the Conservative Imagination* (Macon, Ga., 2003).

Guyer, Paul (ed.), *The Cambridge Companion to Kant and Modern Philosophy* (Cambridge, 2006).

Hamilton, Paul, *Coleridge and German Philosophy: The Poet in the Land of Logic* (London, 2007).

Hamilton, Paul, The Philosopher. In Newlyn (ed.), *Cambridge Companion to Coleridge*, 170–86.

Harding, Anthony John, Imagination, Patriarchy, and Evil in Coleridge and Heidegger. *Studies in Romanticism* 35 (1996), 3–36.

Hartley, David, *Hartley's Theory of the Human Mind, on the Principle of the Association of Ideas; with Essays relating to the Subject of it*, ed. Joseph Priestley [an abridgement of *Observations on Man* (1749)] (London, 1775).

Haven, Richard, Coleridge, Hartley, and the Mystics. *Journal of the History of Ideas* 30 (1959), 477–94.

Hedley, Douglas, *Coleridge, Philosophy and Religion: 'Aids to Reflection' and the Mirror of the Spirit* (Cambridge, 2000).

Hedley, Douglas, Coleridge as Theologian. In Burwick (ed.), *Oxford Handbook of Coleridge*, 473–97.

Hedley, Douglas, *Living Forms of the Imagination* (London, 2008).

Henrich, Dieter, *Between Kant and Hegel: Lectures on German Idealism*, ed. David S. Pacini (Cambridge, Mass., and London, 2003).

Hort, F. W. J., Coleridge. In *Cambridge Essays, Contributed by Members of the University* (Cambridge, 1856), 293–351.

Hume, David, *A Treatise of Human Nature* (1739–40), ed. David Fate Norton and Mary J. Norton (Oxford, 2000).

Jacobi, Friedrich Heinrich, *The Main Philosophical Writings and the Novel Allwill*, trans. and ed. George di Giovanni (Montreal and Kingston, 1994, 2009).

Kant, Immanuel, *Critique of the Power of Judgment* (1790), trans. Paul Guyer and Eric Matthews (Cambridge, 2000).

Kant, Immanuel, *Critique of Practical Reason* (1788), trans. Mary J. Gregor (Cambridge, 1996).

Kant, Immanuel, *Critique of Pure Reason* (1781, 1787), trans. Paul Guyer and Allen W. Wood (Cambridge, 1998).

Kant, Immanuel, *Religion within the Boundaries of Mere Reason* (1793) *and other Writings*, trans. A. Wood and G. di Giovanni (Cambridge, 1998).

Kneller, Jane, *Kant and the Power of Imagination* (Cambridge, 2007).

McFarland, Thomas, Aspects of Coleridge's Distinction Between Reason and Understanding. In Tim Fulford and Morton D. Paley (eds.), *Coleridge's Visionary Languages* (Cambridge, 1993), 165–80.

McFarland, Thomas, *Coleridge and the Pantheist Tradition* (Oxford, 1969).

Micheli, Giuseppe, The Early Reception of Kant's Thought in England 1785–1805. In George MacDonald Ross and Tony McWalter (eds.), *Kant and His Influence* (London, 1990), 202–314.

Milnes, Tim, Coleridge's Logic. In *Handbook of the History of Logic*: iv. *British Logic in the Nineteenth Century*, ed. Dov M. Gabbay and John Woods (Amsterdam, 2008), 33–74.

Milnes, Tim, Through the Looking-Glass: Coleridge and Post-Kantian Philosophy. In *Comparative Literature* 51/4 (1999), 309–23.

Muirhead, John H., *Coleridge as Philosopher* (London, 1930).

Neville, Graham, *Coleridge and Liberal Religious Thought: Romanticism, Science and Theological Tradition* (London, 2010).

Newlyn, Lucy (ed.), *The Cambridge Companion to Coleridge* (Cambridge, 2002).

Orsini, G. N. G., *Coleridge and German Idealism* (Carbondale and Edwardsville, Ill., 1969).

Perkins, Mary-Anne, *Coleridge's Philosophy: The Logos as Unifying Principle* (Oxford, 1994).

Perry, Seamus, *Coleridge and the Uses of Division* (Oxford, 1999).

Reid, Nicholas, *Coleridge, Form and Symbol: or, The Ascertaining Vision* (Aldershot, 2006).

Robinson, Henry Crabb, *Essays on Kant, Schelling and German Aesthetics* (1801–4), ed. James Vigus (London, 2010).

Schelling, F. W. J., *Philosophical Investigations into the Essence of Human Freedom* (1809), trans. Jeff Love and Johannes Schmidt (New York, 2006).

Schelling, F. W. J., *System of Transcendental Idealism* (1800), trans. Peter Heath (Charlottesville, Va., 1978).

Schrickx, W., Coleridge and Friedrich Heinrich Jacobi. *Revue belge de philologie et d'histoire* 36/3 (1958), 813–50.

Shaffer, Elinor, Coleridge and Kant's 'Giant Hant'. In Rüdiger Görner (ed.), *Anglo-German Affinities and Antipathies* (Munich, 2004), 39–56.

Vigus, James, Coleridge's Textual Afterlives. In Vigus and Wright (eds.), *Coleridge's Afterlives*, 1–19.

Vigus, James, *Platonic Coleridge* (Oxford, 2009).

Vigus, James, The Spark of Intuitive Reason: Coleridge's 'On the Prometheus of Aeschylus'. In Helmut Hühn and James Vigus (eds.), *Symbol and Intuition: Comparative Studies in Kantian and Romantic-Period Aesthetics* (Oxford, 2013) 139–57.

Vigus, James, Transzendentalpoesie bei Friedrich Schlegel im Vergleich zum Begriff 'Philosophic Poem' bei Coleridge. In Klaus Vieweg (ed.), *Friedrich Schlegel und Friedrich Nietzsche: Dichtkunst mit Begriffen* (Paderborn, 2009), 133–43.

Vigus, James, and Jane Wright (eds.), *Coleridge's Afterlives* (Basingstoke, 2008).

Wellek, René, *Immanuel Kant in England* (Princeton, 1931).

Wheeler, Kathleen M., *Sources, Processes and Methods in Coleridge's 'Biographia Literaria'* (Cambridge, 1982).

Wilson, Ross, Coleridge's 'German Absolutism'. In Vigus and Wright (eds.), *Coleridge's Afterlifes*, 171–87.

CHAPTER 27

···

SCOTTISH RELIGIOUS PHILOSOPHY, 1850–1900[1]

···

ALAN P. F. SELL

A preamble is unavoidable. First, the title of this chapter is qualified by that of the part in which it appears: 'Religious Philosophy'. Thus, for example, biblical studies and doctrinal and practical theology fall outside my remit, notwithstanding that some of the philosophically minded authors to be considered could turn their hands to these and other intellectual pursuits. The age of the polymath had not yet entirely passed, the age of the disciplinary specialist was still in the making. Even with this narrowing of the theme I shall not be able to include all of those who contributed to it, and in particular I shall not be able to introduce a number of those who, with emotions varying from regret to hostility, opposed Christian intellectual positions and were answered by those who espoused them.[2]

Secondly, it will be necessary to take account of the fact that some of the writers with whom I shall be concerned outlived the nineteenth century, and published works of interest during the early years of the twentieth century.

Thirdly, the impact of what Gilbert Ryle called 'the laicizing of our culture' and 'the professionalizing of philosophy' had yet to be felt.[3] In Scotland especially the senior philosophical posts in the universities were in the hands of ministers of religion to a significant degree, and it was not unusual for appointments to be influenced by denominational considerations. To an extent hard to comprehend nowadays, Scottish society at large was occupied with biblical, doctrinal, and ecclesiastical debates. People took sides over modern

---

[1] The following abbreviations are used throughout the notes: *DECBP* (John W. Yolton, John Valdimir Price, and John Stephens (eds.), *Dictionary of Eighteenth Century British Philosophers* (Bristol: Thoemmes Press, 1999)); *DNCBP* (W. J. Mander and Alan P. F. Sell (eds.), *Dictionary of Nineteenth-Century British Philosophers* (Bristol: Thoemmes Press, 2002)); *DSCHT* (Nigel M. de S. Cameron (ed.), *Dictionary of Scottish Church History and Theology* (Edinburgh: T. & T. Clark, 1993)); *ODNB* (*Oxford Dictionary of National Biography*).

[2] For example, J. S. Mill and his interlocutors. Of those Christian authors I shall introduce here, Robert Flint, Robert Mackintosh, and James Orr appear briefly in the pages of my *Mill on God: The Pervasiveness and Elusiveness of Mill's Religious Thought* (Aldershot: Ashgate, 2004; repr. Wipf & Stock, 2012).

[3] G. Ryle, Introduction to *The Revolution in Philosophy* (London: Macmillan, 1960), 4.

biblical criticism, the status of the Scottish Church's confessional standards, and the relations between Church and State; and any of these, or all of them in combination, could
divide churches and split families. These matters coalesced in such a way as to influence
Scottish university appointments in philosophy. After more than a century of secessions
from the Church of Scotland the question of patronage came to the fore once more during
the 1830s, with many complaining that under the patronage system non-evangelical ministers were being intruded upon parishes that did not wish to receive them. Following what
became known as the Ten Years' Conflict, in 1843 the Disruption occurred when Thomas
Chalmers led one-third of the ministers and up to half of the lay representatives out of the
General Assembly. They constituted themselves as the Free Church of Scotland. Denying
that they were (like the earlier seceders) ecclesiastical voluntaries, they regarded them-
selves as the Church of Scotland, Free. They established colleges in Edinburgh, Glasgow, and
Aberdeen, and owing to their expertise in 'godly politicking'—an occupation in which the
United Presbyterian[4] John Cairns seems to have excelled—they ensured that A. Campbell
Fraser, professor of logic at the Free Church's New College, Edinburgh, and not J. F. Ferrier,
was appointed at Edinburgh University in 1856 in succession to William Hamilton; that
Alexander Bain was not appointed at St Andrews in 1858, or John Nicol at Glasgow in 1864,
or T. H. Green at St Andrews in the same year; and in 1868 the outstanding scholar Robert
Flint, who had remained with the Church of Scotland and whose spirit could not have been
less partisan, was passed over at Edinburgh in favour of the seceder Henry Calderwood.[5]
Edward Caird attributed his success in securing his Glasgow chair in 1866 to the fact that he

---

[4] Not, therefore, 'a minister of the breakaway Free Church' as stated by Alexander Broadie, *A
History of Scottish Philosophy* (Edinburgh: Edinburgh University Press, 2009), 305. One month before
the professorial election was due to be held Cairns published his *Examination of Ferrier's Theory of
Knowing and Being* (Edinburgh: Constable, 1856). According to his biographer Cairns was 'an absolute
and ruthless anti-Hegelian'. See Alexander R. MacEwen, *Life and Letters of John Cairns, DD, LLD*
(London: Hodder and Stoughton, 1895), 396. MacEwen reminds us that 'In Germany the Hegelian
philosophy had been closely connected not only with the Tübingen Schol of theology but with still
grosser rationalism' (p. 396). This did not at all appeal to the evangelicals. Letters and pamphlets flowed,
and Cairns followed up with *The Scottish Philosophy: A Vindication and a Reply* (Edinburgh: Constable,
1856). For Cairns (1811–92) see also *DNCBP, DSCHT, ODNB*.

[5] No doubt those nineteenth-century evangelicals who were conversant with the Scottish intellectual
tradition regarded these academic victories as appropriate recompense for the 'Moderate' succession
of John Simson, Francis Hutcheson, and William Leechman at Glasgow University in the eighteenth
century. Strongly confessional Calvinists regarded the more optimistic anthropology of the Moderates
as wrong in itself, for it implied that sinners had moral and epistemological abilities that their status
actually denied them—a view perceived as demeaning to Christ's saving work. See further, G. E. Davie,
The Democratic Intellect: Scotland and Her Universities in the Nineteenth Century (Edinburgh: Edinburgh
University Press, 2nd edn., 1964), ch. 14; though beware of a certain partiality which enables Davie to
describe Calderwood as 'a narrow-minded extremist' (p. 319), and to speak of Fraser, Calderwood, and
Veitch as having 'captured [their] chairs in the interests of extreme evangelicalism' (p. 328). See also
MacEwen, *The Life and Letters of John Cairns*; Arthur Thomson, *Ferrier of St. Andrews: An Academic
Tragedy* (Edinburgh: Scottish Academic Press, 1985). The following ordained persons held philosophy
chairs in Scottish universities during the second half of the nineteenth century: Henry Calderwood
(United Presbyterian, Edinburgh), William Fleming (Church of Scotland, Glasgow), Robert Flint
(Church of Scotland, St Andrews, Edinburgh), A. Campbell Fraser (Free Church, Edinburgh), and
William A. Knight (Free Church, St Andrews). As we shall see, a number of philosophically inclined
theologians held chairs in the theological colleges of the several denominations.

had 'done nothing'[6]—that is, he had not come forth as a 'party' man—least of all as a man of the 'wrong' party.

Fourthly, on the other hand, as W. R. Sorley observed of 'English' philosophy (under which rubric he, like James Seth and others, included the Scottish—the age of devolved government not having yet arrived), 'Many of its great writers have been men of leisure or men of affairs, who were not occupied with philosophy professionally but were attracted by the perennial interest of its problems.'[7] Among the latter the Scots Alexander Bain, J. H. Stirling, and James Lindsay were prominent.

Finally, how are we to construe 'Scottish' in the title of this chapter? Are we to understand 'the religious (philosophical) thought of Scots (at home and abroad)'? Or ought we to consider all who philosophized in Scotland—which would admit the Welshman Henry Jones and the Englishman A. E. Taylor? Or ought we to concern ourselves with 'religious-*cum*-philosophical thought in Scotland that was characteristically Scottish'? Not least because the Cairds and other idealists are treated elsewhere in this volume,[8] I take the last route (though reserving the right to discuss the exile Robert Mackintosh, whose professorial chair was in England). There remains the begged question, What is denoted by the term, 'characteristically Scottish religious-*cum*-philosophical thought'? The answer is, that thought which, to a greater or lesser degree, is indebted to Thomas Reid's Common Sense philosophy. The justification of this appropriately vague answer will become clearer as we proceed.

I

When Thomas Reid (1710–96) declared that 'Wise men now agree, or ought to agree in this, that there is but one way to the knowledge of nature's works; the way of observation and experiment'; and when he further remarked that 'All that we know of the body, is owing to anatomical dissection and observation, and it must be by an anatomy of the mind that we can discover its powers and principles,'[9] he was doing more than placing himself in the scientifically inductive line of Isaac Newton; he rightly understood himself as reaching back to Bacon's *Novum Organum* (1620). He also knew that 'when we turn our attention inward and consider the phaenomena of human thought, opinions and perceptions, and endeavour to trace them to general laws and first principles of our constitution, we are immediately involved in darkness and perplexity'.[10] Undeterred, he set out to advance a theory

---

[6] Caird confided thus to R. M. Wenley; see G. W. Adams and W. P. Montague, *Contemporary American Philosophy* (London: Allen and Unwin, 1930), ii. 390.

[7] W. R. Sorley, *A History of British Philosophy to 1900* (1920; Cambridge: CUP, 1965), 301. James Seth's book is *English Philosophers and Schools of Philosophy* (London: Dent, 1912).

[8] I have discussed the Cairds elsewhere. For John see *Defending and Declaring the Faith: Some Scottish Examples 1860–1920* (Exeter: Paternoster, and Colorado Springs, Colo.: Helmers & Howard, 1986), ch. 4; for Edward see *Philosophical Idealism and Christian Belief* (Cardiff: University of Wales Press, 1995, and Eugene, Oreg.: Wipf & Stock, 2006).

[9] T. Reid, *An Inquiry into the Human Mind on the Principles of Common Sense* (1764), ed. Derek R. Brookes (Edinburgh: Edinburgh University Press, 1997), 11, 12. For Reid see *DECBP, DSCHT, ODNB*.

[10] Reid, *An Inquiry into the Human Mind*, 16.

that would make good what he perceived as the deficiencies of Locke's sensationalism, Berkeley's psychological idealism, and Hume's scepticism.[11] By means of a careful analysis of self-consciousness he aspired to offer an account of those principles, both necessary and contingent, that were antecedent to experience. Whereas Oswald and Beattie appealed to the 'common sense' of humanity regarding such beliefs as those concerning the reality of the natural order, personal identity, causation, and freedom—all of which a Hume could show were epistemologically valueless and subject to illusion—Reid sought a more philosophically sophisticated and secure basis from which to launch his critique. He was as persuaded as Hume that the scientific approach of observation and experiment was the correct one, but in deriving his principles from a careful analysis of self-conscious experience he turned the tables on Hume. Far from appealing to the common sense of humanity, in the popular sense of the term, as the guarantor of truth, he argued that Hume's sensation was an abstraction that could not be dissociated from an experiencing self.[12] Negatively, Reid held that the mind is not a passive recipient of ideas that are the alleged objects of thought. Positively, he took the activist line that 'By the *mind* of a man, we understand that in him which thinks, remembers, reasons, wills'.[13] Judgement and belief, as well as simple apprehension, are, in Reid's view, integral to the operation of the senses. Thus in this natural realism self-consciousness and sense perception are brought together. Hence Andrew Seth's suggestion that 'by maintaining a theory of Immediate Perception, Scottish philosophy destroys the foreignness of matter to mind, and thus implicitly removes the only foundation of a real dualism'.[14] While it may justifiably be argued that Reid's multiplication of intuitions, and his delineation of necessary and contingent principles, leaves something to be desired, it must be conceded that his investigation of self-consciousness paved the way in Scottish religious thought for a Christian apologetic that was at the mercy neither of sensationalism nor of the vaguer types of mysticism.

The realization was not slow in dawning, however, that religious experience concerns ultimate mystery that falls outside the range of introspective self-observation. Reid and Hamilton (1788–1856)[15] could only grant the fact, and the latter, influenced by Kant's conviction that we can acquire knowledge of phenomena only, not of noumena, adumbrated his doctrine of subjective relativity, namely, that there is no way whereby we may transcend the relation of knower and known. He balanced this with the claim that there is also objective

---

[11] I am well aware of the extensive discussions that have been engendered regarding the appropriateness or otherwise of these terms as descriptive of the three writers (for example, Locke allied reflection with sensation, and was a rationalist in ethics); but this is what Reid understood himself to be doing.

[12] In an analogous way James McCosh (1811–94), who had studied under Hamilton and Chalmers, was later to turn the tables on John Stuart Mill, whose sensationalism, McCosh declared, relied upon the very intuition that Mill had ruled out. See J. S. Mill, *An Examination of Sir William Hamilton's Philosophy* (1865), ed. J. M. Robson (Toronto: University of Toronto Press, 1979); J. McCosh, *An Examination of Mr. J. S. Mill's Philosophy, Being a Defence of Fundamental Truth* (London: Macmillan, 1866). See also Sell, *Mill on God*, 52–3.

[13] T. Reid, *Essays on the Intellectual Powers of Man*, ed. Derek R. Brookes and K. Haakonssen (Edinburgh: Edinburgh University Press, 2002), 20.

[14] Andrew Seth, *Scottish Philosophy: A Comparison of the Scottish and German Answers to Hume* (1885; 2nd edn., Edinburgh: Blackwood, 1890), 76–7. Seth later added 'Pringle-Pattison' to his name in fulfilment of the terms of a will. I discuss his thought in *Philosophical Idealism and Christian Belief*.

[15] For William Hamilton see *DNCBP*, *DSCHT*, *ODNB*.

relativity in that in any known object there is a plurality of relation. At this point J. F. Ferrier (1808–64)[16] broke with his mentor and friend and, repudiating agnostic relativity, went in quest of a more rigorously rational defence of common sense. He invoked the idea of organic emergence and contended that the self that orders the several experiences of common sense remains distinct from them. That is to say, while agreeing with Reid that the several states of mind are known to self-consciousness, they are known by the self as the subject of them all. Influenced by, though not slavishly attached to, Spinoza's method, Ferrier diverged from Scottish intuitionism towards a deductive rationalism. Some found Ferrier teetering on the brink of monism; James Seth characterized his position as that of absolute idealism,[17] and Broadie justifies that label thus: 'This is a version of the doctrine of "absolute idealism", "absolute" because it concerns the character that something must have if it is to exist absolutely and is not to exist merely relatively to something else, and "idealism" because the doctrine affirms that there is no world except as an object in relation to a subject of consciousness.'[18] For all that, Ferrier regarded himself as developing, not repudiating, Scottish Common Sense philosophy, and testified that while he had read Hegel's works he had quite failed to understand them.

From our present point of view Ferrier's significance is that he exemplifies, at one extreme, the degree of definitional elasticity of which the term 'Common Sense' was capable, whilst the other extreme is represented by Oswald and Beattie who construed the term in the more popular sense of the common judgements of humanity. In between we find such an author as Henry Calderwood (1830–97),[19] himself a former student of Hamilton. In his book, *The Philosophy of the Infinite: A Treatise on Man's Knowledge of the Infinite Being, in Answer to Sir William Hamilton and Dr. Mansel* (1854), he, like Ferrier, repudiated the agnosticism he found in his teacher's work, but did so by aligning himself with the intuitionism of Reid and Stewart, and not by taking Ferrier's deductive rationalist way. The nub of his case was that it is open to human beings to have a real, though incomplete, knowledge of the infinite.

It is not difficult to understand why those who intended to uphold the tradition as adumbrated by Reid, and even by Hamilton, should have regarded Ferrier as a traitor, his protestations of fidelity to the Scottish philosophical tradition notwithstanding. His philosophy was not 'safe', and to this charge the evangelicals added their judgement that his theology was not 'sound'. They were not concerned that Ferrier turned his guns on the English Coleridge and F. D. Maurice,[20] but when he denounced the anthropological pessimism of Thomas Chalmers and other high Calvinists which led them to believe that sinful man 'can, and must, *do nothing for himself*,'[21] thereby undermining moral responsibility, this was Moderatism, and a step too far.[22] From the evangelical point of view Ferrier

---

[16] For Ferrier, see *DNCBP, ODNB*.

[17] Seth, *English Philosophers*, 239.

[18] Broadie, *A History of Scottish Philosophy*, 311.

[19] For Calderwood, see *DNCBP, ODNB*.

[20] As he did in *Blackwoods Magazine* (June 1840). For a sample, see Davie, *The Democratic Intellect*, 263–4.

[21] J. F. Ferrier, *Philosophical Works of the Late James Frederick Ferrier*, ed. Alexander Grant (Edinburgh: Blackwood, 1875), ii. 244.

[22] Many evangelicals were influenced in this matter by Ralph Wardlaw's Congregational Lecture (the first in the series, delivered in 1833), *Christian Ethics; or Moral Philosophy on the Principles of Divine Revelation* (London: Jackson and Walford, 1834). To G. E. Davie (*The Democratic Intellect*, 267) Wardlaw was 'a sectarian enthusiast'. In fact he was a distinguished Congregational divine, albeit

espoused the wrong philosophy, the wrong theology, and belonged to the wrong Church (of Scotland). When he further opposed Chalmers's idea of removing epistemology from the Scottish course in moral philosophy in favour of compulsory political science and jurisprudence, he earned a further black mark.[23] It must also be granted that, although he had earlier practised as an advocate at law, Ferrier was not always his own best advocate. Thus, following his failure to succeed to the Edinburgh chair he published a pamphlet in which he both declared his loyalty to the Scottish school of philosophy and also sardonically observed that 'It is well known that a candidate for a philosophical chair in the University of Edinburgh need not now be a believer in Christ or a member of the Established Church; but he must be a believer in Dr. Reid, and a pledged disciple of the Hamiltonian system of philosophy'.[24] This suggests that he was a very clever person who was not always very wise.

It remains only to add that the successful candidate for the Edinburgh chair, Alexander Campbell Fraser (1819–1914),[25] aroused the ire of Ferrier when in 1856 he published a paper entitled, 'Ferrier's Theory of Knowing and Being'. Ever keen to resist monistic gnosticism, Fraser branded Ferrier's rationalistic version of Common Sense theory 'a kind of Scottish Hegelianism'.[26] Ferrier replied in his *Scottish Philosophy, the Old and the New*.

Against the intellectual-ecclesiastical background all too briefly sketched, I shall introduce some philosophically inclined Scottish religious thinkers who, during the second half of the nineteenth century, tended more towards their native philosophical tradition than to the post-Hegelian idealism which became increasingly prominent, especially at Glasgow under the Cairds and Edward Caird's student, Henry Jones. By way of further placing these thinkers I shall first consider the judgements they passed upon their prominent philosophical predecessors and contemporaries;[27] I shall then discuss their contribution to apologetics and their responses to some of the particular intellectual challenges of their day. I proceed in chronological order of thinkers from Descartes onwards.

an anthropological pessimist. For a less prejudiced account see Alan P. F. Sell, *Philosophy, Dissent and Nonconformity 1689–1920* (Cambridge: James Clarke, 2004, and Eugene, Oreg.: Wipf & Stock, 2009), 154–7.

[23] For philosophy in the Scottish universities see, in addition to Davie, *The Democratic Intellect*, John Veitch, 'Philosophy in the Scottish Universities', pts. I and II, *Mind*, 2 (1877), 74–91, 207–34.

[24] J. F. Ferrier, *Scottish Philosophy, the Old and the New: A Statement* (Edinburgh: Sutherland and Knox, 1856), 7.

[25] For Fraser, see *DNCBP, DSCHT, ODNB*; Alan P. F. Sell, *Commemorations: Studies in Christian Thought and History* (Calgary: University of Calgary Press, and Cardiff: University of Wales Press, 1993; repr. Eugene, Oreg.: Wipf & Stock, 1998), ch. 10.

[26] A. C. Fraser, 'Ferrier's Theory of Knowing and Being', in *Essays in Philosophy* (a collection of his papers garnered from *North British Review*) (Edinburgh: W. P. Kennedy, 1856), 312. More than forty years later Fraser defended Hamilton against Ferrier's charges in his *Thomas Reid* (Edinburgh: Oliphant, Anderson and Ferrier, 1898).

[27] I restrict myself to thinkers from Descartes onwards, and to overall judgements passed upon them: I cannot here offer a critique of my authors' expositions as such.

II

James Iverach (1839–1922) became professor of apologetics and New Testament exegesis at the Free Church (subsequently United Free) College, Aberdeen in 1887. In 1904 his book, *Descartes, Spinoza and the New Philosophy* appeared. Descartes, we learn, went in quest of 'all the presuppositions, and all the points involved in the fact of knowledge. He did not ask Kant's question, How is knowledge possible?'[28] In the event he did not complete his analysis of the principles involved in knowledge. He stopped short, and instead offered his method of systematic doubt. Whereas his original intention was to reach universal and necessary truth, the objective of his method of doubt was certainty. He substituted 'for a process of analysis a process of abstraction',[29] whereby he separated thought from its object, the mind from the world. He thus 'introduced that dualism which spoilt the fruitfulness of his philosophy, and gave rise to that abstract rationalism which divorced philosophy from experience, and gave rise also to that empiricism which divorced experience from thought'.[30] With Descartes

> the Ego is taken to be the form of consciousness, and directly affiliated to this is the phaenominalistic spiritualism of Berkeley, the monadological spiritualism of Leibniz, and the transcendental idealism of Kant. The idea as the content of consciousness has given rise to the Ego as absolute substance of Spinoza, the Ego as absolute activity by Fichte, and the Ego as absolute reason by Schelling and Hegel, and the Ego as absolute will by Schopenhauer, and as individual will by Wundt. Taking the Ego as empirical principle, and subordinating it to its objects, we have the empirical philosophies from Locke to Herbert Spencer.[31]

In Iverach's opinion everything in Descartes's philosophy turns upon his proof of the existence of God, and his most damning criticism is that Descartes invoked God and his power to heal the dualistic breach Descartes had made between mind and body:

> he uses principles which he holds to be truths evident by the light of reason to prove the existence of God, and then he seeks to guarantee the validity of reason by the veracity of God.... [I]t is not a worthy procedure to bring in the notion of the Deity to save a system from bankruptcy.... If the consciousness of self is the first certainty, and if we cannot abstract from it, then to seek to go beyond it is futile. But Descartes did not trust his own first principle.[32]

Analytically, Descartes argues that imperfect human beings have the idea of a most perfect Being and, since they could not produce this idea themselves, it must have a cause in that Being. Synthetically, he starts from the ontological argument and contends that the idea of God is an axiom from which all else flows. Whereas Anselm's ontological argument failed to show that the idea of God is a necessary one, Descartes finds the idea given in our experience and we cannot expunge it. He is thus led to believe that our self-consciousness is inseparably

---

[28] J. Iverach, *Descartes, Spinoza and the New Philosophy* (Edinburgh: T. & T. Clark, 1904), 44. For Iverach see *DNCBP, DSCHT*; Sell, *Defending and Declaring the Faith*, ch. 6.

[29] Iverach, *Descartes, Spinoza and the New Philosophy*, 46.

[30] Iverach, *Descartes, Spinoza and the New Philosophy*, 53.

[31] Iverach, *Descartes, Spinoza and the New Philosophy*, 54.

[32] Iverach, *Descartes, Spinoza and the New Philosophy*, 62, 63.

joined to our consciousness of God. The idea of God is thus necessary, and divinely given. Descartes could not, however, answer the question, 'If God is the sum of all perfection, how can we explain the manifoldness and imperfection of the finite?'[33]

Iverach proceeds to argue that Cartesian dualism leads to the deeper dualism between 'the idealist and the mechanical schools of thought'[34] This arises from the fact that Descartes 'proceeds, not by analysis, but by abstraction, and when he limits matter to extended substance he is simply attributing reality to an abstraction, and is as scholastic as any schoolman'[35] Again,

> He left unclear the relation of will and understanding, the relation of soul to body, and the rela-
> tion of God to both;...his definition of the nature of mind and of the nature of body made it
> impossible that there should be any interaction between them.[36]

By contrast, 'the essence of the system of Spinoza' is 'the wholeness of the whole'[37] His was the quest for the highest good, human perfection. Spinoza does not seek the origin of our ideas; rather, he sets out from the conviction that true ideas are self-evident, and that 'We think truly when we apprehend things through their essential nature or through their proximate cause',[38] in other words, when we 'have in idea the real nature of the object of thought'.[39] Spinoza is concerned with concrete being, with the particularity of objects of thought, and he seeks to avoid abstractions. Whereas Hume held that distinct perceptions are distinct existences and that the mind cannot perceive any real connection among distinct existences, to Spinoza it is axiomatic that 'our fixed and necessary ideas had eternal realities correspondent to them'.[40]

To Spinoza, God, or Substance, is one, without limit or change. The problem at once arises, 'How can the concreteness of the whole and its wholeness consist with the changeableness of the *Natura naturata*?'[41] To this question Spinoza has no satisfactory answer. Again, in the interests of the inevitable necessity of things he ignores or explains away freedom and final cause: to him these are illusions prompted by human ignorance and finitude. At the same time he insists that his position poses no threat to the moral life. Indeed, he argues that 'The more the knowledge that things are necessary is applied to particular things, the greater is the power of the mind over the emotions....Universal necessity lifts us out of our isolation, and enables us to see ourselves as included in the universal Being, and one with God.'[42] At this point Iverach seems to yield to bafflement, concluding that 'it is our business to take from [Spinoza's message] as much as we find possible for us in these days of ours'.[43] It may well be, however, that he had reached the word limit of the series for which he was writing. I have elsewhere presumed to say that such was Iverach's patience

---

[33] Iverach, *Descartes, Spinoza and the New Philosophy*, 90.
[34] Iverach, *Descartes, Spinoza and the New Philosophy*, 93.
[35] Iverach, *Descartes, Spinoza and the New Philosophy*, 123.
[36] Iverach, *Descartes, Spinoza and the New Philosophy*, 130.
[37] Iverach, *Descartes, Spinoza and the New Philosophy*, 132.
[38] Iverach, *Descartes, Spinoza and the New Philosophy*, 152.
[39] Iverach, *Descartes, Spinoza and the New Philosophy*, 153.
[40] Iverach, *Descartes, Spinoza and the New Philosophy*, 161.
[41] Iverach, *Descartes, Spinoza and the New Philosophy*, 190.
[42] , Iverach, *Descartes, Spinoza and the New Philosophy*, 235.
[43] Iverach, *Descartes, Spinoza and the New Philosophy*, 242.

in laying the groundwork that 'In both book and sermon he could spend so much time on preliminaries that weighty matters were crowded together at the end, or even omitted altogether'.[44] Certainly one reviewer complained that 'The major theological part of Spinoza's writings and the main part of his political philosophy are untouched'[45] in *Descartes, Spinoza and the New Philosophy*. Elsewhere, however, Iverach did turn his attention to pantheism, albeit with reference to later writers, and I shall return to him shortly.

George Berkeley falls next to be considered, and here the authority is Alexander Campbell Fraser, whose edition of Berkeley's works is still in print, that of T. E. Jessop notwithstanding, and whose *Berkeley* (1881) remains of interest not least for the way in which Fraser relates Berkeley to other philosophers, not least to Hume and Reid.[46] We learn that by concentrating upon Berkeley's earlier works Hume is able to welcome his phenomenalist nominalism, and to present him as a sceptic superior even to Bayle. In so doing, Fraser declares, 'Hume ignores the Berkeleyan appeal to common sense on behalf of the beliefs (a) that the interpretable phenomena of sense, viewed objectively, are the real things; and (b) that in his moral consciousness of *himself*, as a free self-acting spiritual person, each of us reaches the ontological reality of substance and cause, and the spiritual basis of things—the datum universalised in "Siris".'[47] Hume thus exaggerates an aspect of Berkeley's thought, and mistakes the part for the whole. In the reaction against Hume the three elements that went to make up Berkeley's philosophy became disengaged:

> The subtle argumentative analysis and negative phenomenalism...was the Berkeley to whom Hume and afterwards John Stuart Mill avowed allegiance. The appeals to common faith or common sense, in our consciousness of self, and in connection with the favourite thought of significant and interpretable sense phenomena...forecast Reid, while they recall the *cogito* of Descartes. Lastly, the philosophical rationalism of 'Siris', which sees in the phenomenal things of sense the creative working of that *intellectus ipse* in which each separate conscious spirit shares, in its way anticipates Kant and Hegel.[48]

The upshot was that 'By the rigid application of the phenomenal criterion, the spiritual intellectualism of Berkeley was made by Hume to disappear'.[49]

Fraser grants that Hume's scepticism cannot be refuted either by Reid's appeal to the trustworthiness of our ineradicable beliefs, or by Kant's analysis of the necessities of thought, for 'To show, by means of suspected faculties, that the "experience" which has been charged with illusion, because only phenomenal, really presupposes more than phenomena, is to presume as real what the sceptic asks to be proved real. There is always an abstract possibility that our faculties may be false; but if even self-consciousness and memory must be vindicated before they can be used, we can never get to work at all.'[50] Moreover, scepticism 'is always practically refuted, by the imperishable trust which reason reposes in its own

---

[44] Sell, *Defending and Declaring the Faith*, 120.

[45] George M. Duncan, *Philosophical Review*, 14 (1905), 95.

[46] For Fraser's account of his philosophical pilgrimage see *Biographia Philosophica: A Retrospect* (Edinburgh: Blackwood, 1904).

[47] A. C. Fraser, *Berkeley* (Edinburgh: Blackwood, 1881), 214 n.

[48] Fraser, *Berkeley*, 217.

[49] Fraser, *Berkeley*, 221.

[50] Fraser, *Berkeley*, 224.

validity; so that no human mind can permanently surrender to it'.[51] Fraser concludes that Berkeley's thought

> becomes, when we pursue it further than he did, a sublime intuition of the phenomenal realities of sense, inorganic and organic, as established media for the intellectual education of finite spirits by means of physical sciences; for intercourse between individual moral agents, and for a revelation of the Eternal Spirit, in whom the merely phenomenal things of sense, and moral agents too, have their being. It includes the fundamental faith that the universe exists for an eternal moral purpose, so that our experience in it, with the conditions of thought and belief presupposed in the experience, must be practically trustworthy and reasonable.[52]

'A philosophy grounded on Faith', Fraser declares (*pace* Ferrier), 'was the highest lesson of Reid and his successors, especially Hamilton, in Scotland.'[53] We shall come to Fraser's own account of such a philosophy in due course.

First, however, we must consider the reaction of a Scottish religious philosopher-theologian to the Hegelian way of pursuing Spinoza's quest of wholeness and of joining together what Hume had put asunder, and what Kant's phenomena–noumena disjunction had, in its own way, forbidden. I summon Robert Mackintosh (1858–1931), a sharp-minded, self-styled refugee from the High Calvinism of the Free Church of Scotland, who found a congenial home in Congregationalism, and after a pastorate in Dumfries became professor of apologetics at Lancashire Independent College, Manchester.[54] His book, *Hegel and Hegelianism* appeared in 1903. I am here concerned only with his judgement on Hegelianism (itself the subject of another chapter in this book[55]), for it is the judgement of one who, like James Denney, James Orr, and others, but decidedly unlike Henry Jones, was taught at Glasgow by Edward Caird, but was finally unpersuaded by his Kant-influenced absolute idealism.

In Mackintosh's opinion, while intuitionalism 'finds its chance in the misadventures of empiricism',[56] Kant broke from intuitionalism

> by substituting *one system of necessity* for the many necessary truths or given experiences from which intuitionalism takes its start.... [Yet] Kant's idealism is incomplete. On one side, the world we know by valid processes of thinking cannot, we are told, be the real world. Or, beginning from the other side; neither the reality which ideal thought reaches after, not yet the reality which our conscience postulates, is the valid world of orderly thinking. The great critic of scepticism has diverged from idealism towards scepticism again, or has given his idealism a sceptical colour, mitigated—but only mitigated—by faith in the more consciousness.[57]

Hegel does not flinch. He boldly affirms the rationality of the universe; he strenuously denies the dualism of fact and principles and declares that all is as it must be. To the extent that he

---

[51] Fraser, *Berkeley*, 224. For Calderwood's critique of Hume, see his posthumous, *David Hume* (London: Macmillan, 1898).

[52] Fraser, *Berkeley*, 233–4.

[53] Fraser, *Berkeley*, 230.

[54] For Mackintosh, see *DNCBP, DTCBP, DSCHT, ODNB*; Alan P. F. Sell, *Robert Mackintosh: Theologian of Integrity* (Bern: Peter Lang, 1977; repr. Wipf & Stock, 2012).

[55] See William Sweet, 'British Idealist Philosophy of Religion'.

[56] R. Mackintosh, 'Theism', *Encyclopedia Britannica* (11th edn., 1910–11), xvi. 747.

[57] Mackintosh, 'Theism', 749.

rebuts Kant's scepticism, Mackintosh approved of Hegel. But he seriously questions his dia-lectical method whereby he even 'undertakes to show to candid minds that incompatible assertions not only may but must both be true'.[58] This, Mackintosh thinks, subverts the sys-tematic coherence that Hegel thought he had achieved. What Mackintosh wishes to do is to rectify the relation between the real, qua rational, and thought:

> The existence of a world of natural realities in time and space we do not think is genuinely deducible, though, when it is presented in experience, we can see that it is congruous to thought. And—what is still more important—the revelation of reality made in the philoso-phy of spirit is—to us men at least—something quite different from a set of new phases in the consciousness of an object. We must be in earnest in establishing a distinction between Divine and human consciousness. We must make the difficult assertion of the limitation of human knowledge.[59]

By contrast, Hegelianism knows too much. It 'understands all mysteries',[60] whereas Christians '*know* a love which *passes knowledge*'.[61] Thus both sceptics and philosophical dog-matists are mistaken.

Robert Flint (1838–1910)[62] was, in his judicious way, as generous as possible to abso-lute idealism. While regretting that 'The adherents of the philosophy of the Absolute must be admitted to have fallen, in their revulsion from agnosticism, into many extravagances of gnosticism', it remains the case that 'A God who is not the absolute as they understood the term, not the Unconditioned revealed in all that is conditioned, and the essential con-tent of all knowledge at its highest, cannot be the God either of a profound philosophy or a fully developed religion. The philosophy of the Absolute was, on the whole, a great advance towards a philosophical theism.'[63] Nevertheless, 'the idea of God is not one which can be rightly apprehended merely through intellect speculatively exercised or operating on the findings of science. It requires to be also apprehended through moral experience and the discipline of life.'[64] In two long sentences Flint positions himself between unmitigated intui-tionism and outright absolutism:

> Those who urge us to put all probable evidence aside, and fall back exclusively instead on intuition, or faith, or feeling, which cannot themselves at the utmost yield more than prob-able evidence, as sources of absolute certitude, ask us to abandon a practically strong and sure foundation for one which is comparatively weak and suspicious. And those who go further, and ask us to put our trust in the speculative dialectics or metaphysical hypotheses of some individual philosopher, as, for instance, of Hegel or Green, will generally be found to recom-mend us to build on what is merely a fog-bank—a process which will assuredly not lead us to a certainty that cannot be subverted or shaken.[65]

---

[58] Mackintosh, 'Theism', 750.
[59] Mackintosh, *Hegel and Hegelianism*, 287.
[60] Mackintosh, *Hegel and Hegelianism*, 290.
[61] Mackintosh, *Hegel and Hegelianism*, 290.
[62] For Flint see *DNCBP, DSCHP, ODNB*; Sell, *Defending and Declaring the Faith*, ch. 3.
[63] R. Flint, *Agnosticism* (Edinburgh: Blackwood, 1903), 586.
[64] Flint, *Agnosticism*, 599.
[65] Flint, *Sermons and Addresses* (Edinburgh: Blackwood, 1899), 333.

Positively, Flint declares that 'Complete religious certitude is reserved for those who shut their eyes against no kind of good evidence to spiritual truth; who...assent to the truth as it is in Christ...; and who...faithfully strive to act up to its demands... *Then*...we shall get the perfect certitude we seek. Until then we have no right to expect it, nor is it desirable that we should get it.'[66]

James Iverach expressed his general agreement with reference to idealism:

> To speak of the absolute and unconditioned as synonymous with God, is simply to alter the conception of God....[T]he idealistic philosophy makes religion to be simply an aspect of itself, and does not leave us a God into whose fellowship we may enter, in whose service we may find perfect freedom....We need a God who can speak to us, and if He cannot speak directly to us...the flower and fruit of religion will wither and die.[67]

He objected to the way in which Edward Caird had 'calmly annexed' revelation and brought it within the sphere of natural process, with all the pantheizing tendencies thereby entailed.[68] Not surprisingly, in Iverach's view, 'History and Fact are merely scaffolding useful for the introduction of Ideas, but as soon as the ideas are there the facts may usefully disappear.'[69]

With this we approach more decidedly theological critiques of absolute idealism—such, for example, as that for absolute idealists evil can be but a stage on the way to a greater good. But I must leave such matters and, with Flint's reference to 'probable evidence' ringing in my ears, turn to the approach of representative Scottish religious thinkers to Christian evidences and theism.

III

It is not too much to say that the second half of the nineteenth century was the golden age of Scottish apologetics; and it is equally true to say that the period marked a significant shift in apologetic style and content. To take the latter point first, the situation may be summed up under the slogan, the decline of the evidences. That is to say, it became increasingly less fashionable, because less justifiable, to appeal to biblical miracles or the alleged fulfilment of prophecy as evidence of God's existence, activity, and purpose. When Joseph Butler (1692–1752) endorsed the prevailing view that miracles and prophecy were reliable evidences of the truth of Christianity,[70] the deist Thomas Woolston (1669–1731) had already construed miracles allegorically, and the freethinker Anthony Collins (1676–1729) had already given prophecies similar treatment.[71] In the wake of Hume's devastating critique of miracles qua

---

[66] Flint, *Sermons and Addresses*, 333.

[67] J. Iverach, *Theism in the Light of Present Science and Philosophy* (London: Hodder and Stoughton, 1900), 307, 292. Among others who offered critiques of absolute idealism were Henry Calderwood in his *Handbook of Moral Philosophy* (London Macmillan, 1872; 14th edn. 1888).

[68] For a fuller discussion of Iverach and Flint on pantheism, see Alan P. F. Sell, *Enlightenment, Ecumenism, Evangel: Theological Themes and Thinkers 1550–2000* (Milton Keynes: Paternoster, 2005), ch. 7.

[69] J. Iverach, 'Pantheism', *The Expositor*, 7th ser. 4 (1907), 33.

[70] J. Butler, *The Analogy of Religion* (1736), ii, ch. 7.

[71] See Sell, *Enlightenment, Ecumenism, Evangel*, 119–21.

evidence; in the light of modern approaches to the biblical text (which prompted those who disapproved of them to mutter darkly about 'the German problem') which, inter alia, increasingly persuaded Christians that miracles were signs to believers rather than evidence for the persuasion of sceptics, and that biblical prophets were at least as concerned with forthtelling as with foretelling; given the anti-intellectual thrust of those who persisted in millenarian speculation—something that was distressing to many Christians and fodder to the increasingly vocal breed of secularists; in view of all this, many realized that older apologetic approaches would no longer work.[72] Of this Mackintosh was quite convinced: 'Would you believe *any* doctrine, whatever its moral complexion, if it had miracles enough in its train? If you would, you are no Christian. If you would not, then a certain amount of moral excellence is at any rate a *sine qua non* of revelation, and in so far its evidence is partly internal.'[73]

There is one other straw in the wind that suggested the need for a revision of apologetic method. Many Christians, among them Thomas Chalmers (1780–1847),[74] had traditionally believed that unbelief was a sin, and in their minds was the Psalmist's observation that 'the fool [that is, the immoral person] hath said in his heart, There is no God. They are corrupt…there is none that doeth good' (Psalm 14:1). The idea that unbelievers, agnostics, atheists, and secularists could be morally upright took a long time to take root, yet traditional believers were increasingly confronted by precisely such persons.[75]

Standing at the threshold of our period, Chalmers adhered throughout his life to the traditional view of the evidential value of miracles that he had propounded in *The Evidence and Authority of the Christian Revelation* (1814). There is a certain irony in the fact that the evangelical Calvinist Chalmers here adopts precisely the same method as that followed by William Leechman (1706–85), the Moderate professor at Glasgow University.[76] It is also interesting to note that James Buchanan (1804–70),[77] who succeeded Chalmers as professor of systematic theology in the Free Church (New) College, Edinburgh, published a two-volume work, *Faith in God and Modern Atheism Compared*, in which he eschewed intuitionism and concentrated on the natural, as distinct from the miraculous, evidences for the existence of God. This approach, which was indebted to Lardner and Butler, was epitomized by William Paley, of whose appeal to evidences Robert Mackintosh said, 'When such exclusively "external" arguments are urged, the contents of Christianity go for next to nothing.'[78]

As an example of one who adopted a modified view of the matter I cite William Lindsay Alexander (1808–84),[79] professor and principal of the Congregational Theological Hall,

---

[72] I do not, of course, intend to convey the impression that there was change by sudden agreement. The climate of ideas is more subject to occasional storms than to obliterating hurricanes. Moreover, exponents of the evidences are ever with us, albeit normally to be found to the right of mainline denominational and theological institutions.

[73] R. Mackintosh, *Essays Towards a New Theology* (Glasgow: Maclehose, 1889), 359.

[74] For Chalmers, see *DNCBP, DSCHT, ODNB*.

[75] Interestingly, the freethinker Anthony Collins was (early) regarded as a highly moral person, even by those who repudiated his teaching.

[76] See H. M. B. Reid, *The Divinity Professors in the University of Glasgow* (Glasgow: Maclehose, Jackson, 1923), 255. For Leechman, see *DECBP, DSCHT, ODNB*.

[77] For Buchanan, see *DSCHT, ODNB*.

[78] R. Mackintosh, 'Apologetics', *Encyclopaedia Britannica* (11th edn., 1910–11), ii. 192.

[79] For Alexander, see *DNCBP, DSCHT, ODNB*.

Edinburgh. He discusses prophecy in terms of foretelling (not forthtelling), and argues that while the fulfilment of prophecy does not prove the truth of the prophet's message directly, it does prove 'the divinity of his commission.... This proved, the truth of what he utters follows as a necessary conclusion.'[80] But the days of this taking with one hand and giving back with the other were numbered. None saw this more clearly than Flint who, in the closing year of the nineteenth century reflected thus: 'The evidentialist view...did great injustice to such a revelation as the Christian, and was, in fact, neither reasonable nor Christian. A revelation which presents mysteries as its substantive and distinctive message is a revelation which does not reveal, and belief in which is not belief in truth as such. Revelation is the manifestation of spiritual light, and spiritual light is what can be seen and felt by the spirit.'[81]

I proceed chronologically through the apologetic authors. First, brief mention should be made of William Fleming (1792–1866)[82] who succeeded James Mylne in the Moral Philosophy Chair at Glasgow, and who at the beginning of our period published a theodicy entitled, *A Plea for the Ways of God to Man: Being an Attempt to Vindicate the Moral Government of the World* (1858), in which he discussed metaphysical, physical, and moral evil, and held that 'Philosophy is not complete but in Theology';[83] William Robinson Pirie (1804–85),[84] professor in Aberdeen, who, notwithstanding his debt to the Scottish philosophical tradition, had idealistic leanings, and who in his *Natural Theology* (1867) argued (not very impressively) that since human beings have a desire for God as father and friend, there must be a God, otherwise human nature would be a delusion; and William Honeyman Gillespie (1808–75)[85] who was unusual both in being a Methodist, and also in propounding a version of the ontological argument for the existence of God in his book, *The Argument A Priori for the Being and Attributes of the Lord God the Absolute One and First Cause*, which was published in 1833 but, subsequently enlarged, reached its sixth and final edition in 1872.

In his *Biographia Philosophica* Fraser provides a revealing account of his philosophical pilgrimage. Among a number of significant remarks is the following: 'I seemed to find that in philosophy things must *at last* be "left abrupt", as Bacon puts it.'[86] He strove to find a way between what he perceived as scientific naturalism leading to the Unknowable, and the new 'gnostic Idealism, bound by its profession to eliminate all mysteries, and at last to reach infinite science of Reality'.[87] This is his account of what he did:

---

[80] W. L. Alexander, 'The Evidence to the Truth of Christianity Supplied by Prophecy', in *The Credentials of Christianity: A Course of Lectures Given at the Request of The Christian Evidence Society* (London: Hodder and Stoughton, 1880), 18.

[81] Flint, *Sermons and Addresses*, 306.

[82] For Fleming, see *DNCBP*.

[83] W. Fleming, *A Plea for the Ways of God to Man* (Edinburgh: T&T Clark; London: Hamilton Adams; Dublin: Hodges and Smith, 1858), p. vi. Fleming taught Robert Flint, and of the former R. M. Wenley wrote, 'Fleming, familiarly called "Moral Will", who had been transferred from the Chair of Oriental Languages to that of Moral Philosophy, seems to have been a hodman amidst his brethren of the Scottish school.' Quoted by Donald Macmillan, *The Life of Robert Flint, D.D., Ll.D.* (London: Hodder and Stoughton, 1914), 38.

[84] For Pirie, see *DNCBP*.

[85] For Gillespie, see *DSCHT*.

[86] A. C. Fraser, *Biographia Philosophica*, 138.

[87] Fraser, *Biographia Philosophica*, 184. Cf. his *Locke* (Edinburgh: Blackwood, 1890), 296.

I expanded Berkeley's divine language of vision into a universal sense-symbolism, and our moral consciousness of our own free agency into perfect moral agency at the heart of the Whole. Implicates of pure reason, which with Kant make human reason possible, led to implicates of moral reason, which presuppose the universe of reality to be morally constituted reality, although by us incompletely interpretable. I gradually came to think of this theistic faith, not as an infinite conclusion empirically founded in finite facts, but as the necessary presupposition of all human conclusions about anything.[88]

This is consistent with Fraser's judgement that far from being sceptical of sensation, Berkeley was a spiritual realist. At the same time, Fraser concluded that Berkeley required correction by Reid and vice versa. Berkeley failed to 'extract from the phenomena of perception the evidence of a substance different in kind from the self-conscious spirit which perceives them',[89] while 'the philosophy of Common Sense, as represented by Reid, did not rise to the conciliation of the natural order of the material with the originative freedom of the spiritual world, in which operating law in outward nature is recognised as immediate divine agency, or a part of a revelation of perfectly reasonable Will in and through a universe of things and persons'.[90] Here we have the basis upon which Fraser developed the ethical theism that is most fully adumbrated in his Gifford Lectures.[91] His position may be summed up in one sentence: 'If Nature is practically trustworthy, and fit to be scientifically reasoned about, the Omnipotent Spirit immanent in it must be perfectly good and design the goodness of all. This is final faith.'[92] Fraser fully understands that 'This is not direct argumentative proof: when we try to make it so it becomes circular reasoning. It is only the conscious expression of a postulate, without *tacit* practical assent to which human knowledge and human agency must dissolve in total doubt.'[93] As we have seen, Ferrier would not have approved of Fraser's terminus in faith, and among others who did not was James Lindsay (1852–1923),[94] who propounded a more intellectualist theism.[95] To Fraser, however, 'A philosophy grounded on Faith was the highest lesson of Reid and his successors, especially Hamilton, in Scotland',[96] and he never repudiated his conviction that 'The issue of a true philosophy is to disclose the horizon of mysteries by which the power of philosophising is bounded'.[97]

Next in chronological order comes Alexander Balmain Bruce (1831–99),[98] professor of apologetics and New Testament exegesis at Glasgow Free Church College. His oft-reprinted work, *Apologetics: or, Christianity Defensively Stated* (1892), is far from being a hard-nosed philosophically analytical study. Bruce's primary objective was pastoral. The apologist's

---

[88] Fraser, *Biographia Philosophica*, 188–9.

[89] Fraser, *Essays in Philosophy* (Edinburgh: W. P. Kennedy, 1856), 49.

[90] Fraser, *Thomas Reid* (Edinburgh: Oliphant, 1898), 125.

[91] *Philosophy of Theism* (1896; 2nd amended edn., Edinburgh: Blackwood, 1899).

[92] Fraser, *Berkeley and Spiritual Realism* (London: Constable, 1908), 84.

[93] Fraser, *Philosophy and Theism*, 176.

[94] For Lindsay, see *DNCBP*.

[95] See J. Lindsay, *A Philosophical System of Theistic Idealism* (Edinburgh: Blackwood, 1917); Lindsay, *Autobiography of Rev. James Lindsay, D.D.* (Edinburgh: Blackwood, 1924), 47.

[96] Fraser, *Berkeley*, 230. A. Seth described this book as 'the ripest and most catholic expression of the national tendency in philosophy'. See *Scottish Philosophy*, 208–9.

[97] Fraser, 'Introductory Lecture on Logic and Metaphysics', in *Inauguration of New College, Edinburgh, November 1850* (London, 1851), 179.

[98] For Bruce, see *DSCHT, ODNB*; Sell, *Defending and Declaring the Faith*, ch. 5.

vocation, he declares, 'is neither to confound infidels nor to gratify the passions of coarse dogmatists, but to help men of an ingenuous spirit, troubled with doubts bred of philosophy or science, while morally in sympathy with believers'.[99] Bruce's method is informed by two positive and two negative motives. Positively, he upholds the scientific method. This means first, that he will not countenance the 'unscientific' exclude from consideration the human being's moral sense, religious insights, and faith; and secondly, that appeal may be made to religious literatures not as authorities, but as witnesses. His second positive motive is that of speaking to his age, which includes attending to the evolutionary *themes* of development and growth (Bruce does not offer detailed critiques of evolutionary *theories*). Negatively, Bruce is dissatisfied with older theistic argumentation, whilst at the same time holding that 'If Christ's doctrine of God be true, there ought to be something in the world to verify it…The bankruptcy of natural theology is a gratuitous proposition.'[100] For all that, Bruce does not think that arguments from such external notions as motion, causation, design—or even from the idea, are valid. Rather, he starts from the assumption that God is, discusses the kind of God he is, and proceeds to our knowledge of God as revealed supremely in Jesus. Again, Bruce sets his face against all theories—agnosticism and materialism among them— that would deny what he has seen in Jesus. Working but a stone's throw from the Cairds, he is especially concerned to repudiate absolute idealism not because he has no doctrine of immanence—he does—but because the immanently ideal Christ of idealism is not the historic Christ of biblical faith. Idealism thus tends in a pantheistic direction such that humans are deprived of genuinely free action, while evil, construed as a stage on the way to a higher good, undermines all moral distinctions. Throughout, Bruce's intention is to harmonize reason and faith.

Robert Flint, who was described as 'undoubtedly the most learned man of his day in Scotland',[101] and as 'the last great apostle of Scottish moderation',[102] is Scotland's supreme apologist (as well as being an indefatigable historian and analyst of European philosophy). He is also the most comprehensive, dealing as he does with *Theism* (1877); *Anti-Theistic Theories* (1879)—a rebuttal of atheism, materialism, positivism, secularism, and pantheism; and *Agnosticism* (1903). On the one hand Flint does not think that the traditional theistic arguments conclusively demonstrate God's existence, though he believes that they have a certain cumulative force and exhibit something of God's character. On the other hand, he does not argue that the failure of the 'proofs' opens the way for faith. He doggedly seeks rational grounds for believing and, with indebtedness to Butler and Paley, holds that these may be found by inference from God's self-manifestation in causation, intelligence, and righteousness. On this basis we may, on a priori lines, affirm that our ideas of absolute being must apply to God alone. This is a philosophical and a religious necessity, for 'The heart can find no secure rest except on an infinite God'.[103] Theism might have sufficed if human beings had remained sinless, but they did not. Hence God's revelation of himself in Jesus Christ the

[99] A. B. Bruce, *The Chief End of Revelation* (London: Hodder and Stoughton, 2nd edn., 1890), p. vii. Cf. Bruce, *Apologetics* (Edinburgh: T. & T. Clark, 1892), 37.

[100] Bruce, *The Moral Order of the World in Ancient and Modern Thought* (London: Hodder and Stoughton, 1899), 351.

[101] Macmillan, *The Life of Robert Flint*, 326.

[102] Davie, *The Democratic Intellect*, 335.

[103] R. Flint, *Theism* (1877; Edinburgh: Blackwood, 11th edn., 1905), 301.

Saviour. In Christ pre-eminently is 'the truth to which all other truth tends as its centre or goal'.[104]

As well as his objection to the pantheizing tendencies he discerned in absolute idealism, Iverach paid particular attention to evolutionary thought. 'Evolution', he declared, 'is the working hypothesis of most scientific men at the present time',[105] and as such Christian apologists had to reckon with it. Darwin's theory of natural selection held no terrors for him; on the contrary, Christians should rejoice in all that science could tell them concerning God's method of creation. There is no ground for conflict between faith and science, for 'the concern of science is with the force itself and its way of working, and not with the origin and cause of it'.[106] Iverach was by no means alone, however, in regretting the way in which the evolutionary theme had been exploited by some, and in particular by Herbert Spencer. Iverach pursued Spencer relentlessly and quite regularly. Among his charges were that Spencer claims that by organic evolution the homogeneous becomes heterogeneous, but fails to explain how this happens, or could happen; that Spencer wrongly seeks to explain the higher in terms of the lower—'One has sympathy with those who labour at an impossible task',[107] he drily remarks. In passing we may note that in the light of an extensive scrutiny of comparative biology, Henry Calderwood concluded to 'the impossibility of tracing the origin of man's rational life to evolution from a lower life'.[108] In good Scottish fashion, Calderwood finds this confirmed by the deliverances of self-consciousness, the source of 'the powers of a rational life.'[109] The Living Source of all existence, he declares, is God immanent, yet transcendent also: 'we recognise the Supernatural within the Natural',[110] and the first cause is the eternal personality, 'related to the spiritual life of rational souls, as He can be related to no other type of existence within the wide sphere of Creation'.[111] As for Spencer's Unknowable, Iverach reminds us of Spencer's view that time, matter, space, and force are all forms of it and then counters, 'He...does not see that if the Unknowable is manifested, so far as it is manifested it can be known.'[112] More generally, Iverach contends that naturalistic evolutionists cannot allow for purpose in the universe, and neither can the idealistic evolutionists: 'Even Hegelian evolution, which is a greater and higher thing than Darwinism, leaves us without a future, and its outlook is bounded by the life that now is. Indeed, the highest product of evolution in the hands of Hegel seems to be a Prussian at the beginning of the present century—a respectable product of evolution certainly, but one that does not seem to have exhausted the resources of civilization.'[113]

---

[104] Flint, *Sermons and Addresses*, 312.

[105] J. Iverach, *Christianity and Evolution* (London: Hodder and Stoughton, 1894), 1.

[106] Iverach, *Is God Knowable?* (London: Hodder and Stoughton, 1884), 193.

[107] Iverach, *Theism in the Light of Present Science and Philosophy*, 94. See further Iverach, *The Philosophy of Mr. Herbert Spencer Examined* (London: Religious Tract Society, 1884).

[108] H. Calderwood, *Evolution and Man's Place in Nature* (London: Macmillan, 1893), 337.

[109] Calderwood, *Evolution*, 338.

[110] Calderwood, *Evolution*, 341.

[111] Calderwood, *Evolution*, 342.

[112] Iverach, *Christianity and Evolution*, 208.

[113] Iverach, *Theism in the Light of Present Science and Philosophy*, 237.

James Orr (1844–1913)[114] studied first at Glasgow University under Edward Caird, and then at the United Presbyterian Divinity Hall, Edinburgh, where the professor of apologetics was John Cairns. Following pastoral experience he was appointed to the Chair of Church History there and, on the union of his Church with the Free Church in 1900, he transferred to the Chair of Apologetics and Systematic Theology in the United Free Church College, Glasgow. He published on historical and theological subjects, and was skilled in popular apologetics as witness *The Faith of a Modern Christian* (1910). The full title of his major work, *The Christian View of God and the World as Centring in the Incarnation* (1893)—a work commended by Flint—proclaims his conviction that there is a Christian view of the world distinct from all others, and that at its heart is the incarnate Christ. Flint would not have disagreed with this, but Orr makes this the starting point rather than the culmination of his apologetic method. He holds that 'Christian apologetic can never be satisfactorily separated from the positive exhibition of the Christian system'.[115] As for theism, he declares that 'Proof in Theism certainly does not consist in deducing God's existence as a lower from a higher; but rather in showing that God's existence is itself the last postulate of reason— the ultimate basis on which all other knowledge, all other belief rests'.[116] For this reason, he writes, 'If I undertake to defend Theism, it is not Theism in dissociation from Revelation, but Theism as completed in the entire Christian view'.[117] This is not, in his view, to deny the fact of intellectual common ground as between believing and unbelieving rational beings. Orr stands with Flint and Iverach in regard to evolutionary and post-Hegelian idealism. He repudiates Hume's sceptical divorce of reason from faith no less than the theological presuppositions of Ritschl and his school that tend in the same direction. Underlying all is Orr's concern to oppose any who would excise the supernatural from Christianity. He was utterly persuaded that naturalistic readings of the faith entailed the overlooking of Jesus's self-consciousness as Son of God, his sinlessness, his supernatural powers, and his claims. Those who perpetrate such theologies 'are never under a greater mistake than when they imagine that it is the preaching of this old Gospel of the grace of God—old, yet ever new— which is alienating the modern world from the Churches. It is not the preaching of this Gospel which is emptying the churches, but the want of it.'[118]

Robert Mackintosh may sum up the general position taken at the end of our period by those Scottish religious thinkers who stood most obviously within the Scottish philosophical tradition. He is persuaded that Kant dealt the death blow to the classical a posteriori arguments for God's existence, by showing that they cannot 'be strung on one thread, or proved to lead up to one and the same God, unless by the use of the inconclusive ontological argument'.[119] Nevertheless a natural theology of some sort is necessary; it will always be incomplete; but it may lead people to the threshold of revelation. For example, despite

[114] For Orr, see *DNCBP*; *DSCHT*; *ODNB*; Sell, *Defending and Declaring the Faith*, ch. 7; G. G. Scorgie, *A Call for Continuity: The Theological Contribution of James Orr* (Macon, Ga.: Mercer University Press, 1988).

[115] J. Orr, *The Progress of Dogma* (London: James Clarke, 1901), 322.

[116] Orr, *The Christian View of God and the World*, 94.

[117] Orr, *The Christian View of God and the World*, 77.

[118] Orr, *The Faith of a Modern Christian* (London: Hodder and Stoughton, 1910), 234.

[119] Mackintosh, *Essays Towards a New Theology*, 365. Though Flint thought that they would gain in impressiveness, albeit not in conclusiveness, if so combined.

the inadequacy of the cosmological argument qua rational demonstration, 'If there were nothing in this world which made it look like God's world, faith would be too utterly a paradox.'[120] Moreover, humanity's knowledge of the moral law—which humanity did not institute, which it can violate, but not alter—is also suggestive of a divine inaugurator. But it is the revelation of God in Christ that is God's best word to us, and 'one cannot know what the gospel of Jesus Christ is unless one knows it from the inside'.[121] Thus, 'In nature we find suggestions of God; in conscience, the postulate of God; in Christ, the affirmation of God.... But all moral revelation is twofold—a revelation of grace and duty; a revelation of moral forces above us, and of moral obligations resting on us.'[122] Whether, like Orr, they set out from the Christian world view, or worked their way towards it, none of the Christian philosophers here discussed could keep theology at bay.

---

[120] Mackintosh, *Albrecht Ritschl and His School* (London: Chapman and Hall, 1915), 255.
[121] Mackintosh, *Essays Towards a New Theology*, 336.
[122] Mackintosh, *Essays Towards a New Theology*, 389.

CHAPTER 28

··

BRITISH IDEALIST PHILOSOPHY
OF RELIGION

··

WILLIAM SWEET

THE nineteenth century saw the birth of British Idealism—a movement which was particularly influential in Britain and its Empire in the latter third of that century through to the first two decades of the twentieth—though its roots lay in philosophical debates that go back to at least the eighteenth century. The term 'idealist' here refers to those philosophers who were influenced by Hegel and Kant and, to a lesser extent, by Fichte, Schelling, Lotze, Goethe, and the new traditions in biblical interpretation/hermeneutics of Ferdinand Bauer and David Strauss, though there has been some scholarly discussion concerning whether there were several idealist movements in Britain at the time. Principal among those who are regarded as representatives of British idealism are Edward Caird (1835–1908), Thomas Hill Green (1836–82), F. H. Bradley (1846–1924), Bernard Bosanquet (1848–1923), Andrew Seth (Pringle-Pattison) (1856–1931), and J. M. E. McTaggart (1886–1925), though others, such as J. F. Ferrier (1808–64), Benjamin Jowett (1817–93), J. H. Stirling (1820–1909), John Caird (1820–98), John Richardson Illingworth (1848–1915), Henry Jones (1852–1922), and C. C. J. Webb (1865–1954) may be included.

One of the principal subjects addressed by the British idealists was religion, and a number of their major texts discuss metaphysical and social issues that bear directly on it. The reasons for this interest are many, however, and their particular attitudes towards religion also varied. There are, arguably, three principal moments of British idealism in the nineteenth century, though there are some common features throughout. This chapter presents the major figures of British idealism who wrote on religion, identifies and discusses some of the dominant themes in their work, and discusses how they engaged in, or (through their understanding of religion) contributed to, a philosophy of religion.[1]

---

[1] For detailed discussion of many of the authors cited in this chapter, see Sweet, 2010.

1. BRITISH IDEALISM

The British idealists sought to avoid the subjective idealism of George Berkeley (where consciousness is constitutive of all existence), and proposed to follow what is often called 'objective idealism'. On this latter view, there is no rigid distinction between the material and the mental realms, and material objects cannot be described or conceived of independently of and outside the mind—or, at the very least, there cannot be an adequate account of any aspect of reality without including a reference to mind or consciousness.

This general statement does not obviate the fact that there were sometimes significant differences among the British idealists. By the end of the nineteenth century, two major currents of idealism had developed. One, an absolute idealism, saw reality as a fundamental unity called 'the Absolute'. This Absolute was maximally coherent and without contradiction. Absolute idealism sought to dissolve all dualisms, for example, between 'individual' and 'other' (e.g. society), 'nature' and 'thought', and transcendence and immanence. For absolute idealism, then, there is—strictly speaking—only one individual, and it is the basis of value and standard of good. This Absolute was said to be present in and through every existing thing, just as the life of an organism is said to be in every part of it. It was called by some the 'concrete universal'—concrete qua existent, but universal qua comprehensive.

The second major current of idealism was personal idealism, which insisted that, while there is an absolute, one must not ignore the numerical and qualitative distinctness and uniqueness of each person. Each self has value and is independent of every other. Moreover, there is a metaphysical autonomy of persons as well as a 'manifest distinctness' (and a superiority) between humanity and nature (Seth Pringle-Pattison, 1919, p. 6). The importance of persons bears on such questions as the nature of God, what it is to be a human individual, and the nature of evil and of moral struggle. Finally, wholes *depend* upon their parts as much as parts depend on wholes. Thus, while humanity needs God—for finite spirits are 'grounded in and illuminated by' it (Seth Pringle-Pattison, 1919, p. 12)—God needs humanity as well.

2. ANTICIPATIONS OF IDEALIST RELIGIOUS THOUGHT

In his survey of the origins of idealism in Britain, the idealist J. H. Muirhead wrote that 'British Idealism from the first has been in essence a philosophy of religion' (Muirhead, 1931, p. 197). Though this is at least an exaggeration if not misleading, several of the authors who influenced or who were part of the idealist movement regarded religion as a key element of experience that had to be understood and included in any account of reality.

The principal precursors to nineteenth-century idealist religious thought are Samuel Taylor Coleridge (1772–1834) and Thomas Carlyle (1795–1881). Confronted with the residual influence of Lockean empiricism and the domination of mechanistic materialism, naturalism, and utilitarian thought, as well as the impact of industrialization, Coleridge and Carlyle responded that reality is more than the empirical. While aware of the Cambridge

Platonism of the seventeenth century (see Sell, 1995, p. 25), they turned to the writings of recent German philosophers—particularly Kant, but also Fichte and Schelling—in order to elaborate an alternative, though there is some evidence that their understanding of German philosophy was rather thin (Shine, 1935). The influence of Kant, Fichte, and Schelling on Coleridge's views is evident in his autobiographical *Biographia Literaria* (1817), especially chapter 13. Carlyle similarly drew on Kant and Goethe, but also Coleridge, in articulating a 'mysticism' which proposed to bridge the gulf between the human and the divine (Carlyle, 1870, p. 64). While not usually included among the British idealists, their interest in German idealism and the fact that their writings had an influence on the work of some of the principal figures of the movement should not be ignored.

Idealist *religious* thought continues this response to the concerns of Coleridge and Carlyle: materialism and, later, evolutionary theory; ethical and metaphysical individualism; and the nature and justification of religion. By drawing on the insights and influence of the same currents of 'German thought', the British idealists sought to understand the nature of religion, and to find the right relation between religious belief and reason.

3. Early Contributions to Idealist Philosophy of Religion

James Frederick Ferrier (1808–64) is generally considered to be the first of the nineteenth-century British idealists. Educated at Edinburgh and then Magdalen College, Oxford, Ferrier was initially influenced by the Scottish 'common sense' school and the work of William Hamilton. Ferrier came to philosophy rather indirectly. Trained in law, in 1841 Ferrier was elected professor of civil history at Edinburgh. Four years later, he was appointed professor of moral philosophy and political economy at the University of St Andrews. His *Institutes of Metaphysic* (1854) articulated what was clearly an idealist metaphysics (though Ferrier denied that he had been especially influenced by Hegel). In the *Institutes*, Ferrier took a strong stand against the 'common sense' school, which he regarded as unduly favourable to religious obscurantism. For Ferrier, metaphysics simply deals with the 'necessary truths of reason' (1854, pp. 20, 24, 25, 37). He regarded self-consciousness as a necessary condition of knowledge, that 'object' and 'subject' were mutually dependent, and that there must be, in addition to a number of contingent 'absolute existences', a 'necessary' 'Absolute Existence'—in other words, 'a supreme, and infinite, and everlasting Mind in synthesis with all things'—which he acknowledges to be 'God' (1854, pp. 511–12). Though Ferrier's conclusion has a clear relation to religion, his interest, however, was not so much the analysis of or an argument *for* religion, as an argument *against* materialism.

James Hutchison Stirling (1820–1909) also came to philosophy indirectly. Influenced as a young man by the work of Carlyle, Stirling initially trained and worked as a surgeon. His earliest interests led him to challenge the then-dominant materialist theories, particularly in biology; in 1865, influenced by the work of Kant and Hegel, he published *The Secret of Hegel*. This text, which translated and commented on sections of Hegel's *Science of Logic* and *Encyclopedia of Philosophical Sciences*, presented Hegel's work as having a strong religious dimension. Stirling argued that thought enters into things—that it was impossible to talk of things without understanding them in connexion with thought—and that 'the universe is but a materialisation [of]...the thoughts of God' (1865, p. 126); he also sought to introduce a spiritual element into history. *The Secret of Hegel* was regarded by a number of younger scholars as epoch-making. T. H. Green is reputed to have said that it 'contrasted with everything else that had been published as sense with nonsense', and Benjamin Jowett wrote that Stirling's efforts had 'made the general idea of Hegelianism more plain than it has been made before in England' (Muirhead, 1931, p. 170).[2]

Stirling did not, however, present a complete analysis of religion until some twenty years later, with his selection as the first Gifford lecturer at Edinburgh in 1888. Though he never held an academic position,[3] these lectures allowed Stirling to focus on arguments in natural theology—contingency, cosmological, and particularly design arguments, from the Presocratics to Darwin. Published under the title *Philosophy and Theology* (1890), Stirling defended religion against 'Rationalism' (pp. 13–14), though he insisted that religion must become engaged with reason. The positive result of Stirling's proposal is, however, unclear. While the relation of religion and reason is a theme frequently adverted to by many of the major British idealists, Stirling's presence in that discussion—perhaps because of the opaqueness of his later writing—was negligible.

Though not its aim, the work of Ferrier and Stirling exhibits some key aspects of an idealist philosophy of religion. Not only do both emphasize the role of mind or consciousness in any account of reality, but they hold that 'thought enters into things', and that there is a mutual dependence of subject and object. There is also a suggestion of God, as Mind, in synthesis with things, and of things as manifestations of the thought of God. We find in their work, then, an evolutionary theory of consciousness, elements of a theory of the Absolute, and a tendency towards what was later called holism.

A different approach to religion, from a perspective that could nevertheless be called 'idealist', is found in Benjamin Jowett (1817–93). Jowett was, successively, a student, tutor, and fellow at Balliol College, Oxford, and a teacher or mentor to many of the major figures in British idealism, such as Green. His work, particularly his early studies, decidedly focused on religion: Christianity, its scriptures, and its doctrines.

Jowett began reading Kant, Hegel, and German biblical criticism beginning early in the 1840s, and they had a profound effect on him. Among his earliest writings are a translation and commentary on the *Epistles of St. Paul to the Thessalonians, Galatians, Romans* (1855; rev. 1859), and 'On the Interpretation of Scripture', in a volume that was a quasi-manifesto of Broad Church views, *Essays and Reviews* (1860). Here, Jowett argued that scripture must be interpreted on the basis of historical scholarship—that is, that interpretation should be scholarly rather than devotional. This proto-hermeneutical method recognized that religion was historical and the product of context, and so it needed to be subjected to rational analysis and critique. Jowett also placed the practical—in other words, ethics, social engagement, and life in community—at the centre of religion. In a letter of 1867, Jowett writes,

---

[2] Bernard Bosanquet wrote, however, 'I am convinced that Stirling never understood Hegel' (Muirhead, 1935, p. 53). Of *The Secret of Hegel*, as Stirling himself reported, it was said that he had kept the secret to himself.

[3] Stirling was consistently unsuccessful in his applications for a chair of philosophy. Edward Caird, for example, was selected over Stirling in 1865–6 for the Chair in Moral Philosophy at the University of Glasgow.

'A large proportion, some say the greater number of our Artisan Class are the enemies of religious belief. If they are to be regained and restored to religious influences at all this must be accomplished not by repeating the letter of Scripture or by insisting on their belief in miracles or on Genesis versus Science and History but by presenting to them Christianity unawares or the moral aspect of the Christian faith' (Jowett, 1965, p. 12, and the discussion in Gouldstone, 2005). This emphasis on practice over—and, in some figures, in place of—doctrine is a significant characteristic of idealist religious thought.

Jowett was criticized for his approach to Christianity. He was challenged by W. J. Conybeare for having reduced 'Christian revelation to the level of a human philosophy' (2004, p. 46). Moreover, in 1863, following the publication of the *Essays and Reviews*, Jowett was charged with unorthodoxy and brought before the Chancellor's court in Oxford (Hill, 2005). Though the charge failed, thereafter Jowett focused primarily on the translation of, and commentary on, classic texts, particularly of Plato—work that was to influence generations of students of philosophy (but see Hinchliff, 1987).

Though the influence of German philosophy, particularly that of Hegel, shows throughout his writings, Jowett's approach to religion was more theological than philosophical. Moreover, he used German thought more as a method and a guide to interpret Christian and philosophical texts than as a way of doing philosophy. Indeed, Jowett did not endorse a number of features of Hegel's philosophy, for example, Hegel's dialectic—'of all philosophies, Hegelianism is the most obscure' (1875, iv. 404)—but also his accounts of religion and of God (which Jowett believed showed an absence of the 'personal' character and which overemphasized the immanent) (see Jowett, 1875). Nor did Jowett explicitly seek to articulate a philosophy of religion, though his students T. H. Green and E. E. Smith published some extracts from his writings, collected as *Statements of Christian Doctrine and Practice* (1861), in which one finds views that fit with later idealist philosophy of religion.

Thus, while Ferrier, Stirling, and Jowett did not provide fully developed philosophies of religion, there were strong idealist influences on and in their respective views of religion, they articulated a number of positions which were characteristic of idealist philosophy of religion, and they had an important influence on later idealist philosophical and religious thought.

4. 'Transcendental' Approaches

Perhaps the first systematic attempts at articulating a distinctively idealist philosophy of religion can be found in John and Edward Caird and T. H. Green. Their respective writings reveal a similar perspective, but their views differ, and one finds a development in idealist philosophy of religion from John Caird to T. H. Green—from what one might call a philosophy of religion to a metaphysics of the Absolute.

John and Edward Caird were brought up in a devout Scottish Free Kirk atmosphere, and both went to the University of Glasgow to study divinity—John, from 1837 to 1838 and 1840 to 1845, and Edward from 1850 to 1857; Edward continued to Balliol College, Oxford, in 1860. Fifteen years older than his brother Edward, John Caird was ordained in 1845, and spent the next eighteen years of his life as a minister in city and country parishes in Scotland. He read Carlyle in the early 1850s, and soon thereafter sought out the work of 'recent'

German philosophers, such as Kant and Hegel. Edward was introduced to German philosophy in the late 1850s and, while at Oxford, fell even more under the influence of Carlyle, but also of Jowett, and became a close friend of T. H. Green who had just been appointed a fellow at Balliol. Edward's studies at Oxford obviously added to John's own philosophical interests in 'German' thought.

The two brothers were in close collaboration until John's death, and their writings complement each other's. For close to thirty years they served at the University of Glasgow; John Caird became professor of divinity there in 1863 and Edward was elected to the Chair of Moral Philosophy four years later. Nevertheless, there were important differences in their philosophies of religion.

4.1 John Caird

John Caird's 1878–9 Croall Lectures, published as *An Introduction to the Philosophy of Religion* (1880, rev. 1891), provide the first full statement of a British idealist philosophical approach to religion. The focus of the book was 'the essential rationality of religion, as against materialism and scientific agnosticism' (J. Caird, 1904, vol. i, p. cxix). Caird started from experience and 'science', not religion or faith, and the book was one of the first in English to carry in its title the term—undoubtedly borrowed from the German— 'philosophy of religion'.[4] This 'empirical' approach characterized Caird's later work as well. In his Gifford Lectures of 1893–4 and 1895–6 (posthumously published as *The Fundamental Ideas of Christianity*, 1899), Caird had no difficulty respecting the terms of the lectures, that the subject shall 'be treated as a strictly natural science like Astronomy or Chemistry'. Still, throughout, Caird's effort was to defend the rationality of Christianity.

Caird began by considering whether there can be a 'scientific treatment of religion' (1891, p. 7). He argued that there could be and, after criticizing materialist and fideistic views, particularly Herbert Spencer's notion of the 'Unknowable', Caird proceeded to a descriptive philosophical account.

Interestingly, rather than look at dogma or doctrine, Caird's focus was 'the necessity of religion', that is, how thought necessarily leads one beyond materialism to religion or, more precisely, to the 'point of view of religion' (1891, p. 87). Thought has a dynamic and expanding character—'to be ourselves we must be more than ourselves' (1891, p. 116)—and he argues that thought progresses by seeing the reciprocal relations among, and the unity of, things. It is 'driven beyond the finite' to 'the consciousness of an Absolute Intelligence, or of an Intelligence in which absolute trust is to be reposed' (1891, pp. 112, 120)—which he called 'the knowledge of God' (1891, p. 79). This approach is clearly a philosophical rather than a religious or theological one.

There are a number of distinctive points in Caird's account, enumerated principally in *The Philosophy of Religion*, but developed in *The Fundamental Ideas*.

First, for Caird, religion was the consequence of a process of thought undertaken by a self-conscious being which has, as its 'highest ideal', 'an infinite unity of thought and being' (1891, p. 312). Caird insists that this religion is a 'thing of the heart' (1891, p. 165). But while

---

[4] Caird acknowledges Pfleiderer, 1878, and 'above all' Hegel, 1840, in his Prefatory Note.

it is not something intellectual, it must have an intellectual character 'in order to elevate it from the region of subjective caprice and waywardness' (1891, p. 165). For Caird, then, his focus on religion was on religious consciousness or religious experience, and not on doctrine or dogma. Moreover, we find in Caird a suggestion that there is a development of religious consciousness towards a greater coherence and elimination of contradiction. In this way, religion has an evolutionary character that is teleological.

While Caird writes from a distinctively Christian perspective, he had some familiarity with other religions, particularly those of India—Hinduism and Buddhism (see J. Caird et al. 1882)—and he argues in *The Fundamental Ideas* that there is no rigid distinction between natural and revealed religion. Nevertheless, for Caird, Christianity was an important advance on earlier religion, and he eschewed any attempt to 'reduce' religions to something common to all of them, arguing that it is the higher stage or form of religion that explains the lower, rather than vice versa (1904, i. 25). In *The Fundamental Ideas*, he writes that 'The new element which Christianity has introduced into the thought of the world [its cardinal doctrine of the unity of God and Man] transforms, elevates, works a fundamental change in all the previous materials of religious knowledge' (1904, i. 21).

Further, since the essence of religion is an experience which is itself a product of evolution and historical consciousness, there are significant implications for religious creeds and dogmas and for scripture. In both *The Philosophy of Religion* and the Gifford Lectures, Caird reminds his readers how far religion—and particularly religious doctrine—are historical. Biblical texts need to be read by taking into account the work of philology and history. Early expressions of faith or creeds contain theological terms that are often problematic and need clarification, and should not be understood literally.

While this approach—involving the reinterpretation of doctrine and dogma—is 'theological', Caird regarded it as equally philosophical, for the root and motive of such an interpretation was to give a naturalistic, philosophical, and rational account of religion. Caird writes: 'God is not and cannot be maker or father, or ruler, or judge, in the sense in which human beings fulfil these functions; nor does the religious mind, in dwelling on such representations, accept them as exact equivalents for spiritual realities. What it does is simply to let them suggest, or in the way of imaginative indication, awaken in us conceptions of spiritual things' (1891, p. 176). The role of a philosophy of religion is not to debate but to understand the statements of believers.

Religion, then, is not a matter of assent to doctrine. It is, rather, a relation—'the elevation of the human spirit into union with the Divine' (1891, p. 159), whereby the individual surrenders itself to, and identifies its will with, the infinite. For Caird, therefore, God is manifest in finite being—that the finite is intelligible only in light of the infinite, and that the infinite has an organic relation to the finite (1891, p. 231).

Such an account has implications not only for the nature of divine personality but also for the notion of immortality. Caird's views on immortality are, however, ambiguous. In a volume of *Scotch Sermons*, he wrote an essay in which he seems to argue for 'corporate immortality' (1880, pp. 1–17), and he showed little interest in 'that notion of a mere survival after death, or of an "immortality of the soul," based on vague speculations and imperfect analogies' (1904, i. 20). Nevertheless, Caird maintained that God and finite beings remain distinct, insisting on 'the reality of nature and the individuality and independence of man' (1904, i. 80).

Finally, there is a fundamental moral character to Caird's understanding of religion. In the penultimate chapter of *The Philosophy of Religion*, Caird writes of the finite self moving towards an ideal which carries one beyond one's personal interests and focuses on life in community. It is this moral concern that leads to religion, where 'the contradiction between the ideal and the actual has vanished' (1891, p. 295). Yet while there is an evolution of religious consciousness, such a consciousness does not manifest itself in all people. For Caird, 'the reception of religious truth implies a moral and religious, and not a merely intellectual attitude of mind. It cannot be an act equally possible to the irreligious or even immoral, and to the pure and spiritually-minded' (1904, i. 36).

Throughout his work, Caird takes elements of the transcendent in traditional Christianity and shows how they are better understood as speaking of *this* world, which helps to address some of the tensions between the secular and the sacred. This approach attests to Caird's conviction that not only is religion natural (as an imperative of self-consciousness), it is rational, in that it accords 'with both the intellectual and moral needs of man' (1904, vol. i, p. cxxxi). This requires, however, rethinking what religion is, distinguishing it from doctrine and dogma, and focusing rather on experience or religious consciousness. This also understands religion as expressing not only the way in which one sees the world, but how the believer is to act. While religion goes beyond morality, its practical effect is a 'social morality', where one puts aside the 'private self' (1891, p. 265), and seeks to realize what later idealists called 'the real self'. Thus, Edward Caird writes of his brother that 'it was always a characteristic of his preaching to dwell on the ethical meaning of Christianity as all-important, and everything else as subsidiary' (E. Caird 1904, vol. i, p. xv).

It should be no surprise that John Caird was challenged by some for his views, and Edward Caird remarks that, while his brother had a strong faith in the Christian creed, was a dutiful son of the Established Church (of Scotland), and never ceased to hold what he saw as the essentials of Christianity, there were often some 'suspicions' of his orthodoxy—that he was 'not preaching Christ' (1904, vol. i, p. xviii).

4.2 Edward Caird

While there are a number of similarities between John Caird's analysis of, and philosophical approach to, religion, and those taken by his brother Edward, there are also significant differences. Despite the mutual influences, complementarities, and continuities in their respective work, Edward Caird's philosophy of religion shows a more thoroughgoing philosophical idealism. John Caird's principal interest was to understand religion and, in the process, to interpret and make sense of religious doctrines, specifically those of Christianity. Though no less interested in understanding religion, one should note that Edward came to it only after having produced studies on Kant, Hegel, and Auguste Comte, and that his interests were philosophically broader and less tied to Christianity.

Edward Caird's philosophy of religion is best seen in his two sets of Gifford Lectures (1890/1–1891/2, and 1900/1–1901/2), though some of these ideas are anticipated in his earlier work on Kant (1877 and 1889), Hegel (1883), and, particularly, Comte (1885) (which focused on Comte's attempt to articulate a 'religion of humanity' without reference to, and indeed rejecting, a 'religion of God').[5] The first set of Gifford Lectures, published as *The Evolution of Religion*, starts from where his brother John had left off in *The Philosophy of Religion*. Like his brother, Edward argued for the 'rationality' of religion. He also argued against the view that religion was best understood by looking at what all religions had in common, stripped of their cultural and linguistic specificities. Finally, like John, Edward insisted that, to understand religion, one needs to see it as essentially something that is unifying: allying man with nature, and 'joining him with his fellows in some more or less comprehensive society' (1893, i. 81). Key to that unity is mind; Edward emphasizes 'the fundamental fact of self-consciousness which unites them all to each other' (1893, i. 15). Thus, for Edward, religion is 'the more or less developed consciousness of that infinite unity, which is beyond all the divisions of the finite, particularly the division of subject and object' (1893, i. 82). This complementarity of Edward's writings on religion with those of his brother can also be seen in his second set of Gifford Lectures that, though given only after John's death, provides a background for John's posthumously published *Fundamental Ideas*.

Nevertheless, Edward developed idealist philosophy of religion in a number of ways. To begin, he presents a view only briefly referred to by John (J. Caird, 1889, p. 310)—that religion is primarily about religious consciousness and action arising out of this, and not theological doctrine. And, while John's earlier work had only hinted at the evolutionary character of religion, it was left to Edward to show this. In *The Evolution of Religion*, Edward methodically traces the development of religious consciousness, from tribal 'religions' up to the highest form of post-apostolic Christianity. Edward was, moreover, much more explicit about how religion, as a unifying principle that is present, in some form, in all peoples, is a 'consciousness of the infinite' (1893, i. 115), and was much less inclined to defend Christian teachings than his brother. (John Caird's Gifford Lectures—which follow *The Evolution of Religion*—take up this issue, by specifically identifying certain key Christian concepts—God, the relation of God to the world, the origin and nature of evil, the idea of the incarnation and of atonement, and the possibility of 'a future life'—and showing how the understanding of these concepts developed and evolved in later Christianity.)

Edward also develops a distinction, again only hinted at by his brother, between 'religion' and 'theology'. Edward's second series of Gifford Lectures, *The Evolution of Theology in the Greek Philosophers*, begins with 'the central idea of *religion*'—'the idea of God as an absolute power or principle' (1904, i. 32)—but then traces the evolution of *theology*, which he describes as 'religion brought to self-consciousness' (1904, i. 31). This provides the basis for his claim that theology and religion are opposed to each other. In *The Evolution of Religion*, Caird notes how Christianity in post-apostolic times had developed from earlier stages— that what was 'presented in the life and words of Jesus' was 'elevated to the form of reflexion by St Paul' (1893, ii. 263)—and that 'theology' continues the evolution of self-consciousness in a broadly dialectical fashion. By dialectic, Caird means the 'working out of contradiction and inconsistency', and readers need to keep in mind that he understands 'theology' in a very broad sense.

Finally, while John Caird's philosophy of religion had a strong descriptive, 'scientific' basis, it is clear that his interest in the philosophy of religion was rooted in his religious convictions, and his efforts were, consistently, in the direction of making Christianity rationally

---

[5] See also E. Caird 1999.

acceptable. This is certainly not the case with Edward. Edward's is explicitly and throughout a philosophical investigation, starting from philosophical principles. Moreover, Edward's account is a more strongly 'absolutist' one, where what was central to the philosophy of religion was not God or the gods, but what he called 'the Absolute'.

Edward Caird's more robustly idealist philosophy of religion holds, then, that what is central to religion is not the doctrines or 'eternal verities' of religion but an awareness of 'the infinite' which, even if little understood, is 'an integral element of man's mind' (1893, i. 201). Moreover, consciousness and, therefore, religious consciousness evolves, and such an evolution takes place in and through history. It is also progressive, and Caird argues that one can, much like Hegel, identify three distinct stages in the evolution of religious consciousness. Finally, it is also important to recognize that religion is not something external to the person. It is, Caird insists, a 'realisation of the self', whereby human beings are led beyond their private interests to recognize their fundamental relation with their fellow human beings. This relation may, in fact, call for self-sacrifice (1904, ii. 372).

Thus, despite the distinction between them, there is no real difference between philosophy and theology. What theology does, as already noted, is bring the original 'religious' experience to a reflective level (E. Caird 1904, i. 56–7). Caird's claim is that it is the development of self-consciousness shown in Christian religious experience that must be acknowledged, but also built on—though what this 'Christianity' means is unclear.

This account of religion has significant implications for traditional religion and religious practice.

For example, given that religion is understood as practical and social, it affirms the Christian message that one is called to build 'the Kingdom of God on earth', and that to serve God is to serve humanity (see E. Caird 1893, vol. ii, lect. 12). Moreover, when it comes to understanding religious *texts*, one's focus should be on interpretation, not the identification of doctrines—and thus it is important to be assisted by 'methods of historical and philosophical criticism' (1893, vol. i, p. ix).

What is important about Christianity, then, is not the literal signification of its teachings, but what these teachings help one to see about the development of consciousness. Christ, for example, is a model for the development of religious consciousness—Christ is 'the ideal or typical man' and 'the purest revelation of God in man' (E. Caird 1893, vol. ii, p. 233)— but Caird is wary about saying that Jesus of Nazareth was God. Instead, Caird writes of the role of Christ as 'the living realization of the nearness of our finite life to the infinite' (1907, p. 194).

On topics classically associated with the philosophy of religion—personal immortality, the relation of individual human beings to God, and the problem of evil—Caird, again, takes a different tack. For Caird, many of these debates miss what is essential in religion, and reflect an ahistorical and non-contextual understanding of what is important. Nevertheless, his account of religion does not entirely abandon orthodoxy. Caird allows that finite beings 'partake in [the eternal] as they can', and he also seems sympathetic to aspects of the Plotinian view that, in eternal 'consciousness the individuality of every particular intelligence is still preserved' (E. Caird 1904, vol. ii, p. 305). Still, the characteristics of finite being seem to be unimportant; he favours a kind of Aristotelian view, that 'living beings cannot partake in the divine and the eternal by continuing their individual existence—it being impossible for a nature which is finite and perishable to maintain forever its individuality and numerical identity' (1904, i. 289). It is doubtful, then, that Caird held that there was a robust personal immortality.

In short, for Edward Caird, religion matters and gives meaning; he alludes to Acts 17:28 when he writes that God is that 'in which we live and move and have our being' (1893, i. 166–7, 196). But it is not—as in traditional Christianity—a divine person, God, who gives meaning to existence. It is religion, understood as what is 'consistent and whole', that gives meaning, and the Absolute, which is immanent in nature but not reducible to it, serves as a philosophical principle.

Edward Caird's analysis of religion and his philosophy of religion, then, might be better described as a metaphysics of the Absolute or as a theology—in the sense of Aristotle's concept of theology—than a philosophical discipline focused on an examination of questions regarding God, religion, and religious experience. Caird's presentation of 'the Absolute' has little connexion with traditional orthodox Christianity, or with any religious system. While Christianity is a higher stage in the development of religion, Edward is less convinced than John that it is religion 'fully realized' (see 1893, ii. 324). In this and in a number of related respects, Edward Caird develops idealist philosophical thought on religion by seeing religion as part of a larger account of the development of consciousness, a development that takes place 'within' the Absolute, and that religion fits within philosophy rather than determines how philosophy ought to engage it.

4.3 T. H. Green

Thomas Hill Green was, like the Caird brothers, raised in a devout home. A child of the manse, he was also early influenced by Carlyle. Like Edward Caird, he was a student of Jowett, and their common interests led to a strong friendship. Yet there were important differences between them, and Green's philosophy of religion extends some of Edward Caird's discussion of religion in a distinctive way.

As noted earlier, the focus of both Jowett and John Caird was to uncover the message of Christianity, and thereby to show how it could engage the challenges of the modern world. By recognizing the importance of history, literary criticism, context, and the nature of self-consciousness and the role of the subject, philosophical idealism allowed one to understand religion and scripture better. Building on his brother's work, Edward Caird saw that what is central in religion is religious consciousness. Such a picture of religion, he believed, provided a more complete account both of reality and of how to act morally. More, however, needed to be said.

Though Green is best known for his political philosophy, many authors have noted the presence of questions bearing on religion throughout his writings (Tyler, 1997; Leighton, 2004; Gouldstone, 2005; Nicholson, 2006; Sprigge, 2006), and that Green saw philosophy in general as 'the reasoned intellectual expression of the effort to get to God' (letter to Holland, cited in Leighton, 2004, p. 21). His lay sermons and essays dealing with dogma and faith (several of them not published in their entirety until over a hundred years later (see Tyler 2005)), show an advance on earlier idealist thought. Like Edward Caird, Green's approach is philosophical and not creedal. The history and doctrines of Christianity contained or reflected important metaphysical and moral insights, and it was these insights—principally on the 'moral direction'—that counted most for Green. For Green, the essence of religion is faith—the 'personal conscious relation of the man to God' (1997b, p. 260). Yet this 'spiritual relation to God' (1997a, p. 179) was not religion in any institutional or doctrinal sense. Faith, then, should not be confused with theology; it is not a 'collection of propositions' (1997a, p. 161) but closer to 'an attitude or disposition' (1997b, p. 260).

Green did not write on philosophy of religion as such. There is little in Green's work that deals with the origin and development of religion, he showed no real interest in apologetics or in the philosophical issues involved in traditional religious belief, and an account of God or the divine was secondary to his principal concerns. Nevertheless, one can piece together his philosophical views on religion fairly easily.

Green held that there had to be a rational (re)interpretation of Christianity, and his interest was less in understanding historical or orthodox Christianity than in grasping the dynamics of self-consciousness and the insights that he thought Christianity contained. In his early writings, Green sought to analyse concepts central to Christianity; among his essays are texts on faith, the incarnation, justification by faith, and immortality. But Green's interest was not apologetic; it is on how these concepts are to be understood rationally. By uncovering and making explicit its reasonableness, Green holds that one can retain what is essential in religion.

For Green, the traditional doctrines of Christianity are too abstract and not reflective of the experience that gave rise to them. Dogmas, then, need to be constantly reinterpreted to grasp their meaning. Thus, for Green, Christ is properly understood as 'the ideal man' (1997c, p. 208); the Incarnation is the event whereby 'our minds must become Christ's' (1997e, p. 234); and the 'death and resurrection of Christ' should be understood as 'the surrender of the fleshly self and the substitution for it of a new man in the moral life' (1997b, p. 257). But what it means to speak of God as a person is unclear, and traditional views of God in relation to the individual leave God as a rather remote figure. Green's attitude to Christianity, then, left little room for the trappings of tradition and orthodoxy. He was critical of the institutions and doctrines that had, to his mind, deformed faith, and he became anticlerical and anti-ecclesiatical (Nettleship, 1997, p. xxxvi). Green's drift from traditional Anglican Christianity is portrayed in the 1880 novel, *Robert Elsmere*, where the author, Mrs Humphry Ward, describes the transition in belief of a Mr Grey, who was modelled on Green. Indeed, Green came to see his own religious faith as 'a modified Unitarianism' (Nettleship 1997, p. xxxv).

Nevertheless, Green sought to see where religion fits within human experience. It was the notion of 'faith' and the 'moral force' of religion that were of primary interest to him. To begin with, for Green, religion is the 'highest faith' (1997b, p. 253) that involves 'taking God into oneself'. Christianity was a model of this; Green saw faith 'represented as that which by a purely spiritual act takes Christ, as the manifestation of God, into the soul without waiting for conviction by sensible signs' (1997b, p. 253).

Moreover, this recognition of the centrality of faith requires rethinking what Christianity is—it is both a stage in the development of consciousness and a practice. Rethinking Christianity will, Green held, draw attention to matters of action and engagement, but it also will reveal deep (philosophical) truths. This rethinking involves seeing Christianity, and religion as a whole, within the larger context of the evolution of consciousness. Thus, in the *Prolegomena to Ethics*, like John Caird, Green begins with an analysis of self-consciousness and, like both Cairds, is led to a more general principle—what Green calls the Eternal Consciousness. Religion, then, rests on a metaphysics.

This Eternal Consciousness is identified with God, 'the eternal Spirit or self-conscious subject' (Green 1883, sect. 184). But this 'Eternal Consciousness' is not a *terminus ad quem* at which humanity will eventually arrive, but something already present in individual consciousness. Thus, it is an 'inward principle, not an outward restraint' (1997d, p. 196). It 'carries' individuals beyond their finite, private interests; indeed, Green writes that this 'Eternal Consciousness' is 'in full realization with what we only are in principle and possibility' (1997b, p. 268). Nevertheless, faith and religion are not constraints; this union with the divine is 'freedom'.

For Green, then, faith is not an act performed by a person, but more like a process and a 'point of view', and it is something that, like all rational processes, unfolds over time. As a point of view, faith is not based on evidence but determines what counts as evidence. Still, although it is not grounded in argument or proof, faith is not something 'intuited', but something fundamentally rational. For Christianity to be relevant it must be recognized to be at root a faith, not a doctrine, and Christianity's God must be seen not as something external to human beings and dominant over them, but immanent in the world.

As already noted, Green's account of religion and faith has implications for practice. The Eternal Consciousness is an 'ideal of a best' (1997b, p. 270). Religion, then, becomes a kind of morality. 'God has died and been buried, and risen again, and realised himself in all the particularities of a moral life' (1997a, p. 184). In the words of Green's disciple and friend, R. L. Nettleship, religion is 'the highest form of citizenship' (Nettleship 1997, p. xxv).

In several respects, then, Green's view extends earlier idealist thought on religion, and poses an even greater challenge to traditional Christianity. Green is not interested in theology—'a connected system of ideas, each qualified by every other, each serving as a middle term by which the rest are held together' (1997a, p. 164). In part, this is because he believes theology turns religion into an outside force, controlled by institutions and authorities. It is also because, when turned into dogma, the original faith and inspiration are ossified. Christian dogma and the Christian life are far from the same. It is true that Green allows that 'Christian dogma…must be retained in its completeness', but he adds that 'it must become philosophical' (1997a, p. 182), in other words, rationally expressed. Green also insists that the central concepts of Christianity be rethought. Yet if ascribing personal attributes to God is not coherent, if the content of Christianity is largely metaphorical and instead about the development of human consciousness, and if religion is no longer a matter of the transcendent, then not only does little remain of tradition, but it is unclear in what sense Green could be called a theist.

Green's account of religion is, however, not naturalistic. Religion involves a unity with the divine or the Eternal Consciousness, and is not merely a natural phenomenon subject to empirical investigation. Moreover, Green rejects those views of religion that see doctrines and dogmas as facts and not metaphors, and he notes that their proper meaning and role in the life of an individual are not those of a person who bases belief in them upon evidence (1997b, p. 258). Throughout Green's account of religion, with its development of a metaphysics of the Eternal Consciousness or Absolute, was a response to the still-influential empiricism of Hume and the contemporary challenges to faith.

Green's philosophical views on religion and faith, then, can be seen as a continuation, but also a development of earlier idealist analyses which sought to understand religion as consistent with the development of human consciousness. His account sought, as well, to articulate the 'idea' behind Christian dogma, to ground the insights of religion, and to justify these insights rationally. To have meaning and relevance, Christian dogma must, Green thought, be transformed into a philosophy. While Green continued to employ a religious terminology, he insisted that what lies at the core of religion is practice. Religion, then, is more a way of seeing and acting in the world—he describes religion as 'God-seeking morality' (1997b, p. 270)—than a set of doctrines or creeds. Nevertheless, as a defence of Christian religious belief, many believers found it lacking. If the test for what is essential to Christianity is its ability to be rationally expressed, one seems to have already assumed that religion is subordinate to reason.

4.4. Impact

There are many similarities in the 'transcendental approach' to religion of John and Edward Caird and T. H. Green, and their views on Christianity are broadly compatible. Nevertheless, one can see in their work a development in philosophical thought on religion, and there are important differences in their respective accounts. An early commentator, Alfred Caldecott, explains these differences, in part, by referring to the distinct traditions of Christianity in which the three were raised. The Cairds were influenced by Calvinist theology which emphasizes the relation of God to humanity, and by Scottish intuitionalism. Green, on the other hand, grappled with both the lengthy tradition of British empiricism and an Anglican theology that presents God as manifest 'in the Church of the Incarnate Word' (Caldecott, 1901, p. 155).

The articulation and the expression of an idealist philosophy of religion was not limited to the writings of these men. Indeed, the impact of their work—particularly of Edward Caird and T. H. Green—was largely the consequence of their roles as teachers and mentors. Many of the principal figures of the 'second generation' of British idealists, within and outside of the academy, took up, developed, and spread these views. The philosophers John Watson (see 1897), J. S. Mackenzie, and Henry Jones (see 1922), as well as churchmen such as William Temple (later Archbishop of Canterbury), were influenced by Edward Caird, and Bosanquet and Bradley were students and disciples of Green. Green's impact was particularly significant, and felt far beyond the field of philosophy—in politics, in what was to become the Labour party and New Liberalism; in social movements, such as the university settlement movement and the admission of women to universities; and in the social engagement of many religious groups.

5. Later Phases

Although British idealism was clearly in the ascendant by the mid-1880s, there were divisions in it, of emphasis and of substance. Specifically, as noted earlier, one finds two currents in the second 'moment', emphasizing divergent elements, though the differences go beyond this. There was, on the one hand, the tradition of idealism that followed from Green, and that tended to focus on a metaphysics of the Absolute. On the other hand, there was the tradition that followed from the Cairds, and that tended to retain a theism and emphasize the individuality of persons, both finite and divine. While the scholarly careers of the principal figures here—F. H. Bradley, Bernard Bosanquet, and Andrew Seth (later, Seth Pringle-Pattison)—bridge the nineteenth and twentieth centuries, all three had made significant contributions to religious thought before 1900.

5.1 Absolute Idealism

Of Green's students, the two principal figures whose work bore strongly on the philosophy of religion were Bradley and Bosanquet. Bradley is perhaps the better known, though his analysis of religion was less extensive than that of Bosanquet.

Like Green, Bradley's father was in the Christian ministry, and, as a young man, Bradley read several works dealing with Christian apologetics and the history and philosophy of religion, such as David Strauss's *Das Leben Jesu* (1835) and William Paley's *Evidences of Christianity* (1794). But Bradley was also importantly influenced by Green and, in one of his earliest works, *Ethical Studies* (1876), Bradley presents religion as a late stage in the development of morality and moral consciousness. He writes that 'Morality issues in religion' (Bradley, 1927, p. 314), which overcomes the inconsistencies and particularities within morality itself. Yet Bradley's discussion of what religion is remains at a rather general level. On substantive issues such as the nature of God, divine personality, and the immortality of the soul, Bradley is deliberately silent. Rather, religion (by which Bradley means 'religious consciousness') is simply 'the ideal self considered as realized and Real' (1927, p. 319), and 'faith' is the recognition of one's identification with that self, and the 'unity of human and divine' (1927, p. 330).

For Bradley, if religion is to have any place in contemporary thought, it cannot be as traditional doctrine. Bradley doubted whether, contra the traditional character of the divine, one could speak of God as a person, and he insisted that the fundamental unity of the universe made distinctions among persons misleading—'apart from God man is merely an abstraction', and vice versa (1930, p. 445). Though religion is not reducible to morality, it comes rather close: 'religion is essentially a doing, and a doing which is moral' (1927, pp. 316, 315). In later work, Bradley continues to insist that religion should be properly understood only in a 'practical' sense; he wrote to Samuel Alexander that 'I take 'religion' to be essentially *practical* & otherwise not to be religion (proper)' (Bradley, 1999, v. 264). And even when religious practice implies a relation to others, Bradley says little about its social character or dimension.

In his 1893 *Appearance and Reality*, Bradley returns briefly to the themes of God and religion (see 1930, pp. 439–53). Here, however, it seems that Bradley regards not only Christianity, but religion itself, as incomplete: 'religion is but appearance, and...cannot be ultimate' (1930, p. 453). Only 'the Absolute' is complete, which Bradley says goes beyond religion, and is '*in a sense* a Supreme Being, but not a personal God' (Candlish, 1996, emphasis mine). As subsequently he wrote to his brother, A. C. Bradley, 'I doubt if the religious point of view is really consistent...If the object of religion is the Absolute, then still it must be beyond the religious relation, must have that & a higher unity. Certainly in the Absolute religion as such disappears' (Bradley, 1999, iv. 39).

In some late essays, Bradley returned to write of the importance of faith, including religious faith. As in Green, faith involves 'the identification of [one's] will with a certain object'—but it is still essentially ethical (1914, p. 24). And while Bradley did write of a need 'for a new religion', what he meant was, as in Green, fundamentally metaphysics (1914, pp. 446–7).

It is, then, not surprising that Bradley did not see himself as an orthodox Christian (1999, v. 94; but see Mander 2011), and his views were not especially theistic. Bradley's account of finite individuality and the Absolute has led some scholars to see traces of panpsychism and pantheism in his writings. Moreover, while he saw religion as essentially ethical (Sprigge, 1992, p. 123), he was strongly critical of traditional Christian morality (Bradley, 1983).

In short, while one may say that religion has a place in Bradley's views, it was far from religion in a conventional sense, and his philosophical account of it is more in line with a general metaphysics of the Absolute than an analysis of the phenomenon of religion, or of religious doctrine or practice, as such. Some insist that, despite this, Bradley's views have an important bearing on religion and religious belief (see Sprigge, 1992; Mander, 1995). It is clear, however, that for Bradley, faith is, at best, a kind of feeling that hints at the Absolute. It is far from a view in which familiar theological concepts have any place.

Bradley's fellow student Bernard Bosanquet, however, wrote more extensively on religion than did Bradley, particularly concerning creedal religion, though, like Bradley, he seems to have been interested more in its 'practical' role, in the nature of religious consciousness, and in the Absolute, than in articulating a philosophy of religion as such.

Bosanquet's interest in religion was long-standing. One of his last books is titled *What Religion Is* (1920), but many of his earliest essays, in the late 1880s and early 1890s, are on religious themes as well.[6] Bosanquet's initial concern was with the (underlying) social character of religion, religious practice, and the meaning of religious texts, but also with what lies behind the key concepts of Christianity. In general, Bosanquet was sympathetic to Edward Caird's analysis of the evolution of religion and of religious consciousness (see Bosanquet, 1895), and he followed Green in the way in which he understood religion as 'faith'. Yet Bosanquet developed, in a way that neither did, a more thoroughgoing and systematic metaphysical account of religion.

In early essays, such as 'The Future of Religious Observance' and 'How to Read the New Testament', Bosanquet's primary interest is in identifying the broadly moral message that is contained in religious text and practice. Referring to the key concepts of Christianity, such as the divinity of Jesus, 'justification by faith', and 'being one with the risen Christ' (1889a, p. 151), Bosanquet finds the standard theological accounts of them wanting, and offers instead a strongly ethical, or at least non-theological, interpretation of them. In related essays from the same period, Bosanquet also focuses on experience in religion (by which he means 'religious consciousness'), rather than doctrine. For Bosanquet, religion or religious belief is 'a kind of feeling', a 'cosmic emotion' (1893a, p. 13), indicating a 'spiritual oneness of all believers' (1889a, p. 151). Anglican and Catholic theology, however, fails 'to deal with the universal and necessary nature and foundations of the religious attitude as such' (2003, i. 29). Theological doctrines and dogmas, and even some scripture, Bosanquet regards as 'superstition' (1889a, p. 153) or intellectualizations by a less than impartial authority, producing 'diminished understanding' (1889a, p. 136).

To have a place in the modern world, Bosanquet says religion has first to be interpreted and subjected to rational analysis (principally, coherence). Bosanquet clearly adopts Green's 'philosophical' approach, rather than the more 'exegetical' one of John Caird. What is most important to Bosanquet here is the moral dimension within religion. This, he holds, is what

---

[6] See Bosanquet, 1883, 1889a, 1889b, 1889c, 1891, 1893a, 1893b, 1893c, 1895.

Christian scripture emphasizes, and so it is essential to interpreting the texts properly; here the guiding principles would be the study of history and applying a rational 'lens'. But Bosanquet also argues that one needs to recognize that religious consciousness was far more than, and should not be reduced to, simple belief and assent. Thus, though Christianity has the characteristic of a 'spiritual religion', it must 'evolve' if its possibilities are to be fully fleshed out.

Despite his grave reserves about religious doctrine and traditional readings of scripture, Bosanquet recognizes religion as a source of truth and values. For example, Bosanquet holds that human beings are part of a 'spiritual organism'—a principle he finds in St Paul, but also in Plato—and so reality must be more than the purely material or naturalistic. Moreover, while religion is personal, it is not private or subjective. Like Green and Caird, Bosanquet held that at the root of religion is the recognition of a 'spiritual oneness' with others; this is what he understands by the phrase 'being one in the risen Christ'. Developing Green's view that religion is faith, Bosanquet argues that it not only expresses one's basic commitments, but also one's epistemic perspective. Thus, in a later work, Bosanquet describes religion as 'that set of objects, habits, and convictions, whatever it might prove to be, which [one] would rather die for than abandon, or at least would feel himself excommunicated from humanity if he did abandon' (2003, p. 33).

While all people are, on Bosanquet's account, 'religious', he denies that all religions are on a par. Like Edward Caird, he recognizes Christianity as an advanced stage in the develop-ment of religious consciousness but also holds that it is not the final stage, a unity between object and subject which he calls, again following Caird, 'Absolute Religion'. There is, then, an 'ultimate reality', 'the Absolute'. The precise character of this Absolute is unclear, though Bosanquet (like most absolute idealists) holds that it is 'without contradiction', contains eve-rything in itself, and is the basis of value and the standard of 'good'. While some personal idealists equated this Absolute with God, Bosanquet does not. For Bosanquet, to attribute 'infinity' to a being would deny 'every predicate which we attach to personality' (1889c, p. 325).

On Bosanquet's account, there is no 'transcendent' or 'supernatural' as such. Belief in a God who is in 'another world' is, Bosanquet says, 'heathen,' and he dismisses doctrines such as life after death as 'fancies' (1889b, p. 115). The 'Absolute' is immanent in reality in the sense that it is present in and through every living being. Nevertheless, Bosanquet allows that if by 'supernatural' one means 'the highest development of nature at the level of Spirit', he could accept such a 'refined supernaturalism' (see Sprigge, 1992).

Bosanquet's metaphysics of the Absolute has a social dimension, for the Absolute is, as noted earlier, the principle of individuality and value. Such a metaphysics, Bosanquet believes, enables one to make sense of the importance of overcoming one's attachments to oneself, and of self-sacrifice. Bosanquet does suggest, in later work (e.g. 1912, 1913, 1927), that, given the nature of this Absolute, finite individuality is 'provisional', and that religious doctrines such as personal immortality, that require the separate individuality of finite persons, are unimportant. How far this is a necessary consequence of his views has been debated, however (see Sweet 2000a, 2000b, 2007). Moreover, more than many other abso-lute idealists, Bosanquet took the fact of evil seriously, though he argued that it cannot be an ultimate feature of reality. Indeed, Bosanquet's call that evil 'cries out to be overcome' (1918, p. 96), his injunctions to build 'the Kingdom of God on earth', and his involvement with poverty relief, suggest, at the very least, that the evil in the world needs to be addressed. For

Bosanquet, then, 'the central subject-matter of the philosophy of religion' is 'the fundamental meaning of…forms of faith [such as the Incarnation and triumph through sacrifice], that is to say, the answer which they give when we ask what truth they tell us about reality' (2003a, p. 33). His focus, however, is clearly on how one is to act in this world. Though religion has a 'supersocial' character (1912, p. 379), it is still fundamentally social and focuses on life in community; 'religion and morality [are] the same in principle' (1889b, p. 125).

On Bosanquet's view, the philosophy of religion is less a matter of demonstrating or analysing particular religious beliefs, and more a metaphysical study with ethical and social implications. It is perhaps in this rather broad sense that one can allow that Muirhead is correct in holding that 'British idealism from the first has been in essence a philosophy of religion'. Nevertheless, some critics have said that what Bosanquet provides is too much of a metaphysics and a generic religion, and too abstract in its call to action in the world (see Sell 1995).

5.2 Personal Idealism

Perhaps the most thoroughgoing effort at a philosophy of religion in late nineteenth-century idealist thought, and one that seems close to theism and most open to theology, is that of Andrew Seth (Pringle-Pattison) (1856–1931).[7] Seth studied in Edinburgh under A. Campbell Fraser, and was initially influenced by Carlyle and, later, by Stirling and Hegel, but he was a disciple of neither Jowett nor Caird nor Green. Seth's interest in philosophical issues related to religion began with his earliest work and continued until the last book he published in his lifetime, his 1923 Gifford Lectures, *Studies in the Philosophy of Religion* (1930). Overall, Seth sought to defend the fundamental importance of persons, human and divine, and he is generally regarded as a 'personal idealist'. In this respect, many of his views were explicitly at odds with Green, Bradley, and Bosanquet.

Like Bosanquet and Bradley, Seth's writings in the philosophy of religion bridged the nineteenth and twentieth centuries and, like them, the core of his philosophy of religion was well established before 1900. Seth's early work challenged Kant's views on ethics and religion and, in *The Development from Kant to Hegel* (1882), he presents a broadly Hegelian account of the philosophy of religion, wherein the universe is understood to be rational and unified—a view which he held to be easily reconcilable with religious convictions. Yet shortly thereafter, in *Hegelianism and Personality* (1887), Seth began a critique of Hegel—which was an explicit attack on T. H. Green as well: that Hegel's 'conversion' of logic into metaphysics and his account of the nature and value of the individual (and, by extension, of the nature of God), were defective. For Seth, 'The real is the individual self, not the universal self'; 'the individual alone is real' (1887, p. 128). Moreover, the account of unity with the divine in Green and Hegel's views 'does not satisfy in any real sense the requirements of Theism' (1887, p. 26). This critique became even more marked in later works, though in some of his writings (such as the 1897 *Two Lectures on Theism*), Seth acknowledges the important contributions of Hegel: particularly, his conception of the divine as immanent (against deism), and his emphasis on a higher unity of God and nature, whereby God is revealed in experience.

---

[7] In 1898, Seth assumed the surname 'Pringle-Pattison' as a condition for inheriting a large country estate, The Hainings, from a distant cousin.

Seth rejected several key claims of the 'absolute idealists': for example, what he saw as Bradley's identification of the Absolute with human experience (which reduced the two to an 'undifferentiated unity'), and the emphasis on feeling as a means of access to the Absolute. Seth was also concerned that, while Hegelians recognized God's immanence, they ignored God's transcendence.

For Seth, the central problem with Hegelianism, and by extension with Green and the absolute idealists, is that they undermine the nature and value of finite (human) beings without which there is no morality. Seth held that 'I have a centre of my own—a will of my own—which no one shares with me or can share—a centre which I maintain even in my dealings with God' (1887, p. 217). Without a substantive account of finite individuals and their 'ethical independence' and freedom, there is no basis for attributing the autonomy necessary to be a moral agent. Moreover, if the individuality of persons is rejected, there can be no personal God, and the notion of a real relation to God is empty.

Nevertheless, Seth saw his views as broadly idealistic. He accepts the idealist claim that knowers are essential to the world they come to know, and that mind in some way makes nature—though much hinges on the phrase 'in some way'. To be more precise, for Seth, nature is complementary or correlative to mind. Seth is also favourable to a notion of the Absolute, though he understands this in a way that is rather different from that of the absolute idealists. He supports the view that there is a fundamental connexion among all things in the world, that God is related essentially to the world, and also that what is 'higher' is not reducible to the lower. Further—and in this he is close to Green and the Cairds—Seth allows that 'we should be able to discover in the varied manifestations [of religion] a common principle to whose roots in human nature we can point, [and] whose evolution we can trace' (Seth Pringle-Pattison 1930, p. 2). Finally, like many of the idealists, Seth is broadly concerned with the social and the ethical, and the importance of fostering a commitment to engage issues here and now. Some have described his view as an 'ethical theism', and not a creedal one (Caldecott 1901, p. 177).

Though Seth sometimes refers to scripture in his writings, his interpretation of it is far from literal or that of traditional Christianity. Moreover, his theological views are not entirely orthodox; he allows that Jesus may not have known his putative relation to God and even that the truth of the Christian message did not require Jesus to be God. Seth also did not think that one could provide a philosophical proof of the existence of God. And while he maintains that God is revealed in nature and in self-conscious life, as the Cairds emphasized, he allows that the idea of God has changed significantly over time.

Still, Seth wished to retain a number of aspects of traditional religion and religious belief. As already noted, he is concerned, for example, to preserve a notion of God and, specifically, of God as a person—and at times it seems that he is willing to say that God is the Absolute (see Seth Pringle-Pattison 1917, p. 155, though see p. 430). Moreover, he also holds that, while individuals cannot be fully understood without seeing the relations between them or their unity with the divine, selves are ultimately separate, independent of one another. Seth even seems to hold that there is a real 'problem of evil' and some kind of immortality for human beings (Seth Pringle-Pattison, 1922)—both of which were minimized by absolute idealists. Finally, while Seth would defend a strongly immanentist view of God, he rejects any attempt to eliminate transcendence altogether—to 'reduce' God to finite reality—it would mean 'the denial of any divine selfhood, any actuality of God for Himself' (Seth Pringle-Pattison et al. 1919, p. 20).

Though it is only in his later works that he attempted to present a philosophy of religion as such, it is clear throughout his work—unlike that of his idealist contemporaries—that, for Seth, the 'problem of theism is the supreme problem of philosophy' (Peterson 1898, p. 436). There is, then, resonance of Seth's view with the kind of view presented by John Caird. Nevertheless, Seth's analysis of religion is distinctive, and he attempted at length to detail what he thought was still called for, and needed to be preserved, in traditional religion.

5.3 Legacy

What we find in the later stages of nineteenth-century idealist philosophy of religion is, primarily, a development of a more rational and 'metaphysical' approach to religion, a more thoroughgoing critique of religious institutions, and less and less of a concern for classical apologetics, religious dogma, and creeds; the emphasis is on 'faith'. Religion is important, then, principally because it is 'that which carries people beyond concerns for their private interests' and is that which provides a standard of value and of ethical behaviour.

For some idealists, this leads to the view that traditional theism and a personal God are not central to religion, that the immanent is more important than the transcendent, and that the call for practical action requires nothing more than a theory of the Absolute. The doctrines of Christianity are thus transformed into a less creedal, and more rational, perspective, and philosophy of religion becomes simply a metaphysics of the Absolute (see Jones, 1922). Yet, for others such as Seth—and later figures such as James Ward and C. C. J. Webb—one finds a more personalist approach to religion, particularly Christianity. With their insistence on the irreducibility of personality and on the personality of God, they seek to remain within the Christian tradition. Even though the content of their approach is often far from popular orthodoxy, and while its emphasis is ethical, the personal idealists attempted to hold onto at least elements of a theism.

6. CONCLUSIONS

Nineteenth-century British idealist philosophy of religion—and idealist philosophical reflection on religion in general—was largely a response to a number of issues. It was a reaction to empiricism, philosophical naturalism and materialism, and utilitarian thought. It was influenced by 'German' metaphysics, logic, philosophy of religion, and biblical criticism. It also sought to understand religion in relation to new discoveries about the human mind and consciousness. It hoped, then, to provide a more accurate account of religion. In seeking to explain what religion is, its key figures moved beyond traditional creeds and doctrines to richer and more comprehensive philosophical views.

In general, the British idealists sought to provide an understanding of religion that was sensitive to the historicity of texts, to scientific (particularly evolutionary) theory, and to contemporary philosophical studies concerning the nature of consciousness and the relation of humanity to the rest of reality. They also emphasized the importance of moral life, self-realization, and engagement in the public sphere.

A central feature of idealist philosophy of religion was its view of religion and religions as historical entities—not something immutable, with unchanging doctrines and dogmas—and the product of development. Idealists insisted that religious texts needed to be read with context in mind and, more radically, with the aim of determining the 'idea' behind doctrines and dogmas—an approach which at least reconfigured, if not dissolved, many of the traditional debates (e.g. between science and religion).

A second feature in idealist reflection on religion was the effort to separate religion from theology, and to focus on religious experience, or on religion, as a kind of consciousness or as 'faith'. Rather than emphasize the content or practice of religion, idealist authors saw religion as a stage or as part of a broader evolutionary or teleological movement in consciousness. Religion, then, is not something 'external' to the individual, but 'internal', and reflects both how one sees the world and one's commitments. As a result, it was hoped that classical problems of the relation between immanence and transcendence, or the relation between the divine and the human, could be better addressed.

A further feature of the idealist understanding of religion was the conviction that religious tradition and religion as a whole have to be engaged rationally—that the aim of the philosopher is to look for, and see, reason in religion, and to show not only the rationality in the fundamental insights of religion, but also how religion is part of a rational process. The result of this approach was, often, a theory of the Absolute (regardless of whether one was a 'personal' or an 'absolute' idealist), in which traditional views and religious doctrines were re-examined and reconfigured. Personality and individuality—especially divine personality—were radically rethought.

Finally, on the idealist account, the essence of religion was practical—religion was closely related to, and is sometimes even identified with, morality and with life in community. It is in this sense that many idealists and their students and disciples took the injunction of building 'the Kingdom of God on Earth'—as a focus on social action in the 'here and now', and not as some hope for a world to come.

Despite these common features, there were important differences among the British idealists. They did not present a uniform account of religion, and there was, as argued here, a development in their analysis and understanding of what religion is. In part, this reflected each particular author's background, presuppositions, and interests; for example, those closely connected to the Christian ministry were more likely to insist on the importance of individuality and the personal character of the divine. But it also reflected the effort to understand *human* beings and not just the divine, and hence the shift from an apologetic to a more metaphysical approach.

Some have found the idealist account of religion to be at too far a distance from traditional religious belief and practice—that it either casts religion as simply an ethical approach to life or sees it as a mere feature of a larger metaphysical theory of the Absolute. Such an account also seems to have little direct bearing on the institutions and dogmas—or even the conception of deity and one's relation to it—with which most believers are familiar. Questions concerning cosmology, creation, the origin and nature of value, and human destiny seem to be superfluous or entirely beside the point. Many of the idealists regarded such attachments as basically superstitious and irrational. Nevertheless, the legacy of idealist philosophy of religion continued for some time in Britain and its Empire. It carried on well into the twentieth century, and influenced religious leaders such as Frederick and William Temple (both Archbishops of Canterbury), eminent philosophical theologians such as Alfred Caldecott and W. R. Inge, and philosophers of religion such as A. E. Taylor, C. C. J. Webb, and C. A. Campbell.

REFERENCES

Bosanquet, B., 1883. Our Right to Regard Evil as a Mystery. *Mind*, 8/31: 419–21.

Bosanquet, B., 1889a. How to Read the New Testament. In *Essays and Addresses*. London: Swan Sonnenschein, pp. 131–61.

Bosanquet, B., 1889b. The Kingdom of God on Earth. In *Essays and Addresses*. London: Swan Sonnenschein, pp. 108–30.

Bosanquet, B., 1889c. On the True Conception of Another World. In *Essays and Addresses*. London: Swan Sonnenschein, pp. 92–107.

Bosanquet, B., 1891. The Permanent Meaning of the Argument from Design. *Proceedings of the Aristotelian Society*, 2/1: 44–50.

Bosanquet, B., 1893a. The Future of Religious Observance. In *The Civilization of Christendom and Other Studies*. London: Sonnenschein, pp. 1–26.

Bosanquet, B., 1893b. Some Thoughts on the Transition from Paganism to Christianity. In *The Civilization of Christendom and Other Studies*, London: Sonnenschein, pp. 27–62.

Bosanquet, B., 1893c. The Civilisation of Christendom. In *The Civilization of Christendom and Other Studies*. London: Sonnenschein, pp. 63–99.

Bosanquet, B. 1895. The Evolution of Religion. *International Journal of Ethics*, 5: 432–44.

Bosanquet, B., 1912. *The Principle of Individuality and Value*. London: Macmillan.

Bosanquet, B., 1913. *The Value and Destiny of the Individual*. London: Macmillan.

Bosanquet, B., 1918. *Some Suggestions in Ethics*. London: Macmillan.

Bosanquet, B., 1920. *What Religion Is*. London: Macmillan.

Bosanquet, B., 1921. *The Meeting of Extremes in Contemporary Philosophy*. London: Macmillan.

Bosanquet, B., 1927. Do Finite Individuals Possess a Substantive or an Adjectival Mode of Being? In *Science and Philosophy and Other Essays by the Late Bernard Bosanquet*, ed. J. H. Muirhead and R. C. Bosanquet. London: G. Allen and Unwin, pp. 89–112.

Bosanquet, B., 2003. Religion (Philosophy of). In *Bernard Bosanquet: Essays in Philosophy and Social Policy*, ed. William Sweet, 3 vols. Bristol: Thoemmes Press, i. 29–40.

Bradley, F. H., 1914. *Essays on Truth and Reality*. Oxford: Clarendon Press.

Bradley, F. H., 1927. *Ethical Studies*. 2nd edn. London: Oxford University Press.

Bradley, F. H., 1930. *Appearance and Reality*, 2nd edn., 9th impression, corrected. Oxford: Clarendon Press.

Bradley, F. H., 1983. 'An Unpublished Note [circa 1909] on Christian Morality', ed. Gordon Kendal, *Religious Studies*, 19: 175–93.

Bradley, F. H., 1999. *Collected Works of F. H. Bradley*, vols. 1–5, ed. Carol A. Keene. Bristol: Thoemmes Press.

Caird, E., 1877. *A Critical Account of the Philosophy of Kant, with an Historical Introduction*. Glasgow: J. Maclehose.

Caird, E., 1883. *Hegel*. Edinburgh: W. Blackwood and sons.

Caird, E., 1885. *The Social Philosophy and Religion of Comte*. Glasgow: J. Maclehose and sons. (Originally published in *Contemporary Review*, 1–4, 1879.)

Caird, E., 1889. *The Critical Philosophy of Immanuel Kant*, 2 vols. Glasgow: J. Maclehose & sons.

Caird, E., 1893. *The Evolution of Religion*, 2 vols. Glasgow: James Maclehose.

Caird, E., 1904. *The Evolution of Theology in the Greek Philosophers*, 2 vols. Glasgow: J. Maclehose and sons.

Caird, E., 1907. *Lay Sermons and Addresses*. Glasgow: J. Maclehose.

Caird, E., 1999. *The Collected Works of Edward Caird*, 12 vols., ed. and introd. Colin Tyler. Bristol: Thoemmes Press.

Caird, J., 1891. *An Introduction to the Philosophy of Religion*, 2nd edn. Glasgow: James Maclehose.

Caird, J., 1899. What is Religion? In *University Sermons: Preached Before the University of Glasgow, 1873–1898*, 2nd edn., Glasgow: James MacLehose, pp. 1–26.

Caird, J., 1904. *The Fundamental Ideas of Christianity*, ed. Edward Caird, 2 vols., 2nd edn. Glasgow: James MacLehose and Sons.

Caird, J., et al., 1880. *Scotch Sermons*. London: Macmillan.

Caird, John, et al. 1882. *Oriental Religions*. New York: J. Fitzgerald.

Caldecott, A., 1901. *The Philosophy of Religion in England and America*. London: Methuen.

Candlish, S., 1996. Francis Herbert Bradley. In E. Zalta (ed.). *Stanford Encyclopedia of Philosophy*, <http://plato.stanford.edu/entries/bradley/>.

Carlyle, T., 1870. *Sartor Resartus*. In *Thomas Carlyle's Collected Works*, vol. vi. London: Chapman and Hall, pp. 1–182.

Coleridge, S. T., 1817. *Biographia Literaria; or Biographical Sketches of MY LITERARY LIFE and OPINIONS*. London: Rest Fenner.

Conybeare, W. J., 2004. The Neology of the Cloister. *Quarterly Review*, 97 (Dec. 1855); repr. in W. Sweet and Colin Tyler (eds.), *Early Responses to British Idealism*. Bristol: Thoemmes Continuum, i. 5–53.

Ferrier, J. F., 1854. *Institutes of Metaphysic: The Theory of Knowing and Being*. Edinburgh: Blackwood.

Gouldstone, T., 2005, *The Rise and Decline of Anglican Idealism in the Nineteenth Century*. London: Palgrave Macmillan.

Green, T. H., 1883. *Prolegomena to Ethics*, ed. A. C. Bradley. Oxford: Oxford University Press.

Green, T. H., 1997a. Essay on Christian Dogma. In *Works*, 5 vols., ed. R. L. Nettleship and P. P. Nicholson. Bristol: Thoemmes, iii. 161–85.

Green, T. H., 1997b. Faith. In *Works*, 5 vols., ed. R. L. Nettleship and P. P. Nicholson. Bristol: Thoemmes, iii. 253–76.

Green, T. H., 1997c. Incarnation. In *Works*, 5 vols., ed. R. L. Nettleship and P. P. Nicholson. Bristol: Thoemmes, iii. 207–20.

Green, T. H., 1997d. Justification by Faith. In *Works*, 5 vols., ed. R. L. Nettleship and P. P. Nicholson. Bristol: Thoemmes, iii. 190–206.

Green, T. H., 1997e. Witness of God. In *Works*, 5 vols., ed. R. L. Nettleship and P. P. Nicholson. Bristol: Thoemmes, iii. 230–52.

Green, T. H., 1997f. Review of John Caird's *Introduction to the Philosophy of Religion*. Academy, 18; repr. In *Works*, 5 vols., ed. R. L. Nettleship and P. P. Nicholson. Bristol: Thoemmes, iii. 138–46.

Green, T. H., 1997g. On the Different Senses of 'Freedom' as Applied to Will and to the Moral Progress of Man. In *Works*, 5 vols., ed. R. L. Nettleship and P. P. Nicholson. Bristol: Thoemmes, ii. 307–33.

Hegel, G. W. F., 1840. *Vorlesungen über die Philosophie der Religion*, 2nd edn., ed. D. P. Marheineigs. Berlin: Duncker und Humblot.

Hill, Harvey. 2005. Religion and the University: The Controversy over *Essays and Reviews* at Oxford. *Journal of the American Academy of Religion*, 73: 183–207.

Hinchliff, P., 1987. *Benjamin Jowett and the Christian Religion*. Oxford. Clarendon Press.

Holland, H. S., 1921. *Henry Scott Holland: Memoir and Letters*, ed. S. Paget. New York: Dutton.

Jones, H., 1922. *A Faith that Enquires*. London: Macmillan.

Jowett, B., 1860. On the Interpretation of Scripture. In *Essays and Reviews* by Frederick Temple, et. al., London: John W. Parker and Son. pp. 330–433.

Jowett, B., 1861. *Statements of Christian Doctrine and Practice, Extracted from the Published Writings of the Rev. Benjamin Jowett, M.A.*, extracts chosen by T. H. Green and E. E. Smith with preface by A. Stanley. Oxford: J. H. and Jas. Parker.

Jowett, B., 1875. Introduction [to Plato's *Sophist*]. In *The Dialogues of Plato*, trans. Benjamin Jowett, 2nd edn., 5 vols. Oxford: Clarendon Press, iv. 409–24.

Jowett, B., 1965. *Jowett's Correspondence on Education with Earl Russell in 1867*, ed. J. M. Prest. Oxford: Oxonian Press.

Leighton, D. P., 2004. *The Greenian Moment: T. H. Green, Religion and Political Argument in Victorian Britain*. Exeter: Imprint Academic.

Lotze, H., 1882. *Grundzüge der Religionsphilosophie*. Leipzig: S Hertzl.

Mander, W. J., 1995. Bradley's Philosophy of Religion. *Religious Studies*, 31: 285–301.

Mander, W. J., 2011. *British Idealism: A History*. Oxford: Oxford University Press.

Muirhead, J. H., 1931. *The Platonic Tradition in Anglo-Saxon Philosophy: Studies in the History of Idealism in England and America*. London: Allen and Unwin.

Muirhead, J. H. (ed.), 1935. *Bernard Bosanquet and His Friends: Letters Illustrating the Sources and Development of His Philosophical Opinions*. London: George Allen & Unwin.

Nicholson, P. P., 2006. Green's 'Eternal Consciousness'. In Maria Dimova-Cookson and W. J. Mander (eds.), *T. H. Green: Ethics, Metaphysics, and Political Philosophy*, Oxford: Oxford University Press, pp. 139–59.

Nettleship, R. L. 1997. Memoir [of T. H. Green]. In *Works* [of T. H. Green], ed. R. L. Nettleship and P. P. Nicholson, 5 vols., Bristol: Thoemmes, vol. i, pp. xi–clxi.

Peterson, J. B., 1898. Review of *Two Lectures on Theism* by Andrew Seth, *Philosophical Review*, 7/4: 434–6.

Pfleiderer, O., 1878. *Religionsphilosophie auf geschichtlicher Grundlage*. Berlin: G. Reimer.

Sell, A. P. F., 1995. *Philosophical Idealism and Christian Belief*. Cardiff: University of Wales Press.

Seth, A., 1882. *The Development from Kant to Hegel with Chapters on the Philosophy of Religion*. London: Williams and Norgate.

Seth, A., 1885. *Scottish Philosophy: A Comparison of the Scottish and German Answers to Hume*. Edinburgh and London: W. Blackwood and sons.

Seth, A., 1887. *Hegelianism & Personality*. Edinburgh and London: W. Blackwood.

Seth, A., 1897a. *Man's Place in the Cosmos*. Edinburgh and London: W. Blackwood and sons.

Seth, A., 1897b. *Two Lectures on Theism*. Edinburgh: Blackwood.

Seth Pringle-Pattison, A., 1917. *The Idea of God in the Light of Recent Philosophy*. Oxford: Clarendon Press.

Seth Pringle-Pattison, A., 1919. The Idea of God: A Reply to Some Criticisms. *Mind*, NS 27, pp. 1–18.

Seth Pringle-Pattison, A., 1922. *The Idea of Immortality*. Oxford: Clarendon Press.

Seth Pringle-Pattison, A., 1930. *Studies in the Philosophy of Religion*. Oxford: Clarendon Press.

Seth Pringle-Pattison, A. et al., 1919. *The Spirit; The Relation of God and Man, Considered from the Standpoint of Recent Philosophy and Science*, ed. B. H. Streeter. London: Macmillan.

Shine, Hill, 1935. Carlyle and the German Philosophy Problem During the Year 1826–1827. *Proceedings of the Modern Languages Association*, 50/3: 807–27.

Sprigge, T. L. S., 1992. Refined and Crass Supernaturalism. In Michael McGhee (ed.). *Philosophy, Religion and the Spiritual Life*. Cambridge: Cambridge University Press. pp. 105–26.

Sprigge, T. L. S., 2006. *The God of Metaphysics*. Oxford: Oxford University Press.

Stirling, J. H., 1865. *The Secret of Hegel*, 2 vols. London: Longman, Roberts, & Green.

Stirling, J. H., 1890. *Philosophy and Theology*. Edinburgh: T. & T. Clark.

Sweet, W., 2000a. Bernard Bosanquet and the Nature of Religious Belief. In W. J. Mander (ed.), *Anglo-American Idealism: 1865–1927*. Westport, Conn.: Greenwood Press, pp. 123–39.

Sweet, W., 2000b. Bosanquet and Bradley: Some Recent Discussions. *Bradley Studies*, 6: 63–91.

Sweet, W., 2007. God, Sprigge, and Idealist Philosophy of Religion. In Leemon McHenry and Pierfrancesco Basile (eds.), *Consciousness, Reality and Value: Festschrift in Honour of Prof. T. L. S. Sprigge*. Frankfurt and Paris: Ontos Verlag, pp. 181–210.

Sweet, W. (ed.), 2010. *Biographical Encyclopedia of British Idealism*. London: Continuum.

Tyler, C., 1997. *Thomas Hill Green (1836–1882) and the Philosophical Foundations of Politics: An Internal Critique*. Lampeter: Edwin Mellen Press.

Tyler, C. (ed.), 2005. *Unpublished Manuscripts in British Idealism: Political Philosophy, Theology and Social Thought*, 2 vols. Bristol: Thoemmes Continuum.

Ward, M. A. [Mrs Humphrey], 1888. *Robert Elsmere*, new edn. London: Smith, Elder.

Watson, J., 1897. *Christianity and Idealism*. With an Introductory Essay by George Holmes Howison. New York: Macmillan.

PART VI

THE PRACTICE OF PHILOSOPHY

CHAPTER 29

POETRY AND THE PHILOSOPHICAL IMAGINATION

LESLIE ARMOUR

THE nineteenth century opened amid a struggle for a world vision—a struggle which shows itself in the minds and works of the poets: Blake feared that sophisticated concepts were destroying our contact with reality. Coleridge wrestled with the materialism of Hartley. Wordsworth comforted himself with a vision of nature in which men and women could feel at home in a world where the revolutions of politics and industry threatened chaos. Nearly all the poets responded to the philosophical debate about the sources of values and the justification of claims about them.

Poetry was a source of vision beyond the confines of what everyone thought they knew, but it was also a way of protecting the full richness of immediate experience against the chilly analyses of science and the pragmatic need to focus awareness on the useful. Poetry could grasp the individual and break the boundaries of accepted systems. Poems express values in a way that can make them seem immediate and compelling.

A search for a clear idea of the individual in the face of a science which produced knowledge of universal laws and saw the world through abstract concepts was a constant background to much nineteenth-century thought and with it went the search for a vision of a reality in which human beings could live comfortably. Poetic creation and philosophical reflection provoked one another. Philosophers could not do what the poets did, for a poem is itself an individual and the poet invests it with the characteristics of a world of its own not to be judged by its correspondence to 'the facts'. The poet's skylark is not a contribution to ornithology. And poetry is not philosophy. But the philosopher traditionally was supposed to see beyond the confines of what the world took for granted and for that one must have a vision which breaks the bounds of the ordinary. The relation may be broken now, but throughout the nineteenth century in Britain philosophy and poetry worked together.

The nineteenth was a century of startling advance in engineering and its technological consequences which, in Britain and elsewhere, produced newly advantaged and newly impoverished classes. It was an age which fostered democratic ambitions and generated plutocracies. New kinds of knowledge encouraged speculations which suggested richer lives for human beings, but it also separated those who could share in it from those who could not, and, most importantly, led to a struggle for the human soul. At the extremes there was a battle between those who saw people as machines and those who saw them as minor gods temporarily trapped in bodies but ultimately on the road to a companionship with omniscience. The world might be Keats's vale of soul-making or it might just be a machine slowly wearing itself out, headed for the darkness of ultimate entropy.

Poetry is surely older than philosophy. Plato thought poets dangerous and in Book II of the *Republic* we are warned that poetry cannot really aspire to the truth. Aristotle was kinder than Plato and thought poetry better than history because it could deal with universals, which means, as he says in chapter 9 of the *Poetics*, that poets can grasp what is necessary or probable. By the seventeenth century even Jesuit philosophers like Pierre Le Moyne and René Rapin were writing poetry themselves and Le Moyne was probably right when he urged that, until *l'Académie* and *la Parnasse* are brought together there will be little enlightenment.[1] In nineteenth-century England it can be argued that Le Moyne's project was being realized.

There are at least two reasons for thinking that Le Moyne is right. One is that philosophy works with open concepts, concepts like truth, knowledge, and goodness which can never be fully exhausted but which cultural and political forces seek to close. It requires an act of the imagination to open them. Philosophy orders and analyses but poetry depends on creative imagination. Poetry, indeed, shows us new facets and depths to the concepts philosophers pursue. The other reason, as Gerard Case noticed in an essay on Gerard Manley Hopkins,[2] is that philosophers, beginning with Plato, sought to understand things through the discovery and application of universals while poets not only turn our minds to individuals, they create individuality. A poem is itself an individual, almost a distinct universe of its own, and from it we may learn what individuality is. Hopkins's fascination with the individual took him to Duns Scotus even while the Church he had joined was turning its face to Thomas Aquinas, a philosopher who saw knowledge as the abstraction of the universal from the flux of particulars.

William Blake epitomizes the central struggle as Peter Otto neatly explains in *Blake's Critique of Transcendence: Love, Jealousy, and the Sublime in* The Four Zoas[3] (his long and unfinished poem).[4] It opens with Tharmas being precipitated from a prelapsarian heaven and into an as-yet-unfinished world. Blake drew much from Emanuel Swedenborg who came from a wealthy mining family and had devoted himself to science and engineering, though he believed he had visited heaven and met spirits from far beyond the earth. He reported that there had been a revolution in heaven in 1757—the date of Blake's birth— in which the true believers had been separated from those who merely went through the motions, and that this great change was only beginning to have its effects on earth. Blake's poem is significantly his reflection on this. The world was upset, but the poetic imagination might begin to see through the fog, and the reality might shine through.

Blake seems centred on the eighteenth century. His 'dark satanic mills' were largely in the future: the one he had in mind is said to have been a London flour mill.[5]

---

[1] Le Moyne, 1645, vol. I, bk.II ch. i, pp. 236–7.

[2] See *The Gerard Manley Hopkins Archive*, Newbridge College (on line), <www.gerardmanleyhopkins. org/studies/philosophy.html>.

[3] Otto, 2000.

[4] British Library, Additional Manuscripts 39764 and Blake, 1963.

[5] The expression comes from a poem attached to *Milton, A Poem* made famous by the 'Jerusalem' music of Sir Hubert Parry. The original was published by Blake, the British Library thinks in 1804, though it adds (1808?). There is a modern facsimile edition published by the Blake Trust, London, 1967.

Samuel Taylor Coleridge, though he was only fifteen years younger, and died only seven years later, seems very much of the nineteenth century. Despite the wonderful—probably opium—dreams of *Kubla Khan* (a poem completed in 1797) Coleridge also seems much more worldly, a man whose feet were mostly on the ground, given to careful philosophical analysis.

It was Coleridge, however, who made the greatest claim for the poet: 'The Poet is not only the man made to solve the riddle of the Universe, but he is also the man who feels where it is not solved.'[6] In a way which recalls Blake, Coleridge adds: 'What is old and worn out, not in itself, but from the dimness of the intellectual eye brought on by worldly passions, he makes new: he pours upon it the dew that glistens, and blows round us the breeze which cooled us in childhood.'

The 'dimness of the intellectual eye' suggests a reflection on the relation of Coleridge and his friend William Wordsworth to the somewhat curious materialism of David Hartley. They were to rebel against it; but for a time it held them in its sway and with them many young British intellectuals. Hartley, who lived from 1705 to 1757, practised medicine and became something of a celebrity. His *Observations on Man, His Frame, His Duty and His Expectations*[7] became a kind of bible for rationalist thinkers.

Apart from his references to the nature of ideas which are baffling but important, Hartley was a materialist. He believed that all events had physical explanations and, in particular, that human actions—'motions' as he liked to call them—generally derived from the activity of the human brain. The human being was a fine-tuned machine. There was however one exception. Hartley admitted that there were actions properly *called* 'voluntary' but that these were caused by ideas. He did not think that determinism was thereby rendered doubtful—ideas also have causes and no one could have acted other than he did—but ideas as causes are different at least in this respect: they are internal. In his view, when I say that I am the cause of my own voluntary actions I mean that my actions are not caused by anything external to me. Hartley's moral theory was based on the classification of pleasures. Pleasures of sensation arise from external events; those of imagination from natural beauty or deformity; those of ambition from the opinions of others; those of self-interest from our self-perceptions; those of sympathy from our understanding of others; those of theosophy from God; and those of moral sense from 'moral beauty' or 'moral deformity'.[8]

Stephen Prickett in his *Coleridge and Wordsworth, The Poetry of Growth*[9] has documented the main lines of a kind of mental sea change in Coleridge and Wordsworth. The materialist theory has always been puzzling. I see clouds in the sky, but the materialist thesis is that what I am aware of are events in my brain. But my brain is not like a picture book. Contemporary materialists explain this is in several ways. Hartley himself dealt with the matter by allowing ideas to play a rather mysterious role. An idea is not exactly a physical event or, as Locke once remarked, exactly a mental substance either. But Hartley is not too helpful about what it is.

---

[6] Coleridge, 1811, 1897.

[7] Hartley, 1749, 1986.

[8] The items in the list tend to go in pairs, one with an external source and one with an internal source, with one extra (theosophy) from an external source.

[9] Prickett, 1970.

Coleridge, reflecting on Hartley, realized that imagination enters into perception because we create even while we see. Think of Wordsworth's daffodils:

> A host of golden daffodils
> Beside the lake, beneath the trees,
> Fluttering and dancing in the breeze.
>
> Continuous as the stars that shine
> And twinkle on the milky way
> They stretched in never-ending line
> Along the margin of a bay:
> Ten thousand saw I at a glance
> Tossing their heads in sprightly dance.
>
> The waves beside them danced but they
> Out-did the sparkling waves in glee[10]

Was there a 'real event' exactly like the poem? Here is Wordsworth's sister's account of the original scene: on

> a threatening misty morning...we saw a few daffodils close to the water-side. We fancied that the lake had floated the seeds ashore, and that the little cloud so sprung up. But as we went along there were more and yet more; and at last, under the boughs of the trees, we saw that there was a long belt of them along the shore, about the breadth of a country turnpike road.... They grew among the mossy stones about and about them; some rested their heads upon these stones as on a pillow for weariness; and the rest tossed and reeled and danced, and seemed as if they verily laughed with the wind, that blew upon them over the lake; they looked so gay, ever glancing, ever changing.[11]

On the materialist theory the original bits of matter were, of course, colourless and odourless. Certainly no 'jocund company' was there and no real daffodils could outdance 'the sparkling waves in glee'. Poetic imagination adds, but it also makes choices.

Coleridge, more theoretician than Wordsworth, named the thought processes in getting to 'waves in glee' primary and secondary imagination.[12] Primary imagination has to do with the actual creation of the perceived world; secondary imagination has to do with how that world is given meaning—a process we can see at work when William translates the scene witnessed by Dorothy into a poem.

Both these are to be distinguished from what Coleridge defined as 'fancy', or an elaboration for literary purposes. Do these processes falsify the 'real' world? Coleridge set himself to answer the question. He made the long journey of the mind needed to grasp Kant, Fichte, and Schelling. He also visited Germany to meet the cultural ambience in which they worked. Kant's answer was that we do not know what reality is ultimately like. We only know how our minds work and that minds systematically impose patterns on what we perceive.[13]

---

[10] From the revised version of 1815.
[11] D. Wordsworth, 1971, pp. 109–10.
[12] Coleridge, 1956, ch. XIII.
[13] Coleridge's relation to Kant is explored at length by James Vigus in his article in this volume.

This is not enough. The poet's created world has elements of vision but it also proposes a meaning. The idea of a 'real world' *transformed* by imagination is a theoretical notion distant from immediate experience. Imagination by itself is a pure abstraction but so is the idea of a world without imagination. The poetic vision requires an ideal. Coleridge insisted that there must be 'constancy' to it, an idea he expressed in 1826 in 'Constancy to an Ideal Object'.[14]

> Since all, that beat about in Nature's range,
> Or veer or vanish; why should'st thou remain
> The only constant in a world of change,
> O yearning THOUGHT! that liv'st but in the brain?
> Call to the HOURS, that in the distance play,
> The faery people of the future day—
> Fond THOUGHT! not one of all that shining swarm
> Will breathe on thee with life-enkindling breath,
> Till when, like strangers shelt'ring from a storm,
> Hope and Despair meet in the porch of Death!
> Yet still thou haunt'st me; and though well I see,
> She is not thou, and only thou art she,
> Still, still as though some dear embodied Good,
> Some living Love before my eyes there stood
> With answering look a ready ear to lend,
> I mourn to thee and say—'Ah! loveliest Friend!
> That this the meed of all my toils might be,
> To have a home, an English home, and thee!'
> Vain repetition! Home and Thou are one.
> The peacefull'st cot, the moon shall shine upon,
> Lulled by the Thrush and wakened by the Lark,
> Without thee were but a becalmèd Bark,
> Whose Helmsman on an Ocean waste and wide
> Sits mute and pale his mouldering helm beside.
>
> And art thou nothing? Such thou art, as when
> The woodman winding westward up the glen
> At wintry dawn, where o'er the sheep-track's maze
> The viewless snow-mist weaves a glist'ning haze,
> Sees full before him, gliding without tread,
> An image with a glory 'round its head;
> The enamoured rustic worships its fair hues,
> Nor knows he makes the shadow, he pursues!

The 'image with a glory 'round its head' is a Brocken-spectre, a kind of reflection sometimes seen in the Hartz mountains in which one meets, giant-sized, one's own shadow with the head surrounded by coloured rings of light. Coleridge is not the 'enamoured rustic' who 'worships its fair hues' not knowing 'he makes the shadow, he pursues'. He does know, as the title of the poem insists, that he is involved with an 'ideal object', and it is 'constancy' to the ideal object which provides the answer to the question: Do we know reality only in so far as we press the imagination to an ideal?

[14] Coleridge, 1954, 2001.

One might take Coleridge to hold that the function of the imagination is to turn nature into knowledge and knowledge into art. To what end? These words of Wordsworth from *The Prelude* might supply the answer. (Wordsworth wrote the poem specifically for Coleridge.)

> A meditation rose in me that night
> Upon the lonely Mountain when the scene
> Had pass'd away, and it appear'd to me
> The perfect image of a mighty Mind,
> Of one that feeds upon infinity,
> That is exalted by an underpresence,
> The sense of God, or whatsoever is dim
> Or vast in its own being, above all
> One function of such mind had Nature there
> Exhibited by putting forth, and that
> With circumstance most awful and sublime,
> That domination which she oftentimes
> Exerts upon the outward face of things,
> So moulds them, and endues, abstracts, combines,
> Or by abrupt and unhabitual influence
> Doth make one object so impress itself
> Upon all others, and pervades them so
> That even the grossest minds must see and hear
> And cannot chuse but feel....[15]

Wordsworth ties value, meaning, and perception together. Nature now is the reflection of Wordsworth's 'mighty mind'. Surely, as Henry Jones would later suggest, we can see Wordsworth as a harbinger of philosophical idealism in Britain.[16] To some, Wordsworth and Coleridge were dreamers. John Stuart Mill saw Wordsworth as above all the poet of 'feeling'. Feeling, he thought, should be separated from reality—a thought which drove him to deep depression (see his *Autobiography*) but he nevertheless believed the distinction must be made. What Mill proposed as an alternative philosophy to that of Coleridge and Wordsworth was not a return to Hartley and materialism but the doctrine that reality simply consists of our sensations and of the permanent possibilities for sensation.[17] To these we add our feelings.

Values are not in things but solely in feelings and the feelings which are valuable are those of pleasure. Against the project of turning nature into knowledge and knowledge into art, Mill proposed a life devoted to the search for pleasure. He had, however, to concede that not all pleasures were equal and, in the end, he became as much the champion of poetry as Coleridge and Wordsworth. And followers of Mill could argue that what gives most pleasure may well be the understanding of the enrichment of nature by art.

If the first element in the intellectual struggles of the early nineteenth century came from the scientific world picture and the passion for comparing people to machines, the second had to do with two conflicts over values. The first conflict pitted those who wanted to anchor values in nature against those who wanted to anchor values in human reactions, essentially in feelings. The second was the conflict between the individualists and the communitarians.

---

[15] Wordsworth, 1995. *The Prelude* was begun in 1798, but not published in Wordsworth's lifetime.
[16] Jones, 1922, pp. 194–5.
[17] Mill, 1865.

The battle lines tended to be drawn so that the individualists and the friends of 'feeling' tended to be on one side while the communitarians and the supporters of the idea that value was to be found in nature were on the other.

This association was imperfect but more than accidental. These conflicts, furthermore, were related to the conflict between those who accepted the view that reality was what was described by physics and those who thought there was more to be found. Those who put *all* their faith in physics tended to see values in terms of feelings and tended to be individualists. Those who thought there was more found values objectively in nature and were more likely to be communitarians. Neither side was inclined to attack science. Coleridge and Wordsworth enlisted on the side of natural value and community but, as much as Hartley and Mill, they rejoiced in scientific discovery.

The creativity of the poet for Coleridge and Wordsworth was analogous to that of God, for they added something genuinely new to the world but *only* analogous; poetry contributed to knowledge, they thought, because images and metaphors are, themselves, associated with nature in such a way that real knowledge cannot be simply conveyed in descriptive analytical sentences. Indeed, nature is itself the outcome of a creative process in which we are all actively involved. Poetry shows that the real connections between ideas are revealed in many ways, among them through striking juxtapositions and the dialectical fusions of opposites.

Wordsworth broke with the worshippers of science over technology, and particularly over the use of technology to reconstruct nature. He detested—in terms which would be recognized by any modern Green Party worker—technological interference with the environment, especially, of course, with the topography of his own Lake District. This implies a certain tension in his views, a tension which is often echoed as well in the work of Coleridge. Both are dedicated to the notion of creativity. Yet they have an attitude to nature which implies that nature itself is valuable and not to be much disturbed.

William Blake noted in his own copy of a volume of Wordsworth's poems that the poet was a damnable 'pagan' because of this attitude to nature. Nature and some aspects of traditional religion are reconciled for Coleridge and Wordsworth because human creation is to be guided by an ideal which is cosmic in scope and because there is a community of human minds of which each of us forms a part.

Wordsworth and, equally, Coleridge, supposed that there is a cosmic symphony in which we all take part and in which poets sit in the first chairs. Both thought that there was a cosmic composer, too, though they hardly conceived of him in ways which would greatly encourage most ordinary orthodox believers. The process of creation seemed to them to be obviously a shared one.

Coleridge said that he learnt very young that poetry has a 'logic of its own as severe as that of science'.[18] He insists, bluntly, that a great poet should be a profound philosopher.[19] Poetry, for him, is a balance between creativity and intellectual power. Creativity gives the poem the power of freshness which arrests the attention, but intellectual power is the power to comprehend reality. It is because of this that the great poet must be a great philosopher. The philosopher must also have a vision—disciplined by logic. Of course the philosopher can

---

[18] Coleridge, 1956, p. 3.   [19] Coleridge, 1956, ch. 15.

draw on the poet's vision and the poet can borrow from philosophers as Coleridge did. But vision and logic must balance precisely. And he thought it most powerful when they were combined in the same author. This he thinks is the greatness of Shakespeare.[20] Poetry always has to do with truth, though it is conceived to produce pleasure.[21] Pleasure and truth united are able to bond subject and object.

Coleridge is here engaged in an old debate: When we know something, do we change it? Aristotle proposed that part of the thing studied, its form, is abstracted by the mind and constitutes knowledge. But forms are universals, and the things we want to know about are often particulars. Though he changes it a bit, Coleridge actually quotes Sir John Davies (1569–1626) who wrote a little poem which largely epitomizes Aristotle's theory—and also gently lampoons its weaknesses:

> Doubtless this could not be, but that she[22] turnes
> Bodies to spirit by sublimation strange,
> As fire converts to fire the things it burnes,
> As we our meates food into our nature change.
> From their grosse matter she abstracts their forms,
> And draws a kind of quintessence from things;
> Which to her proper nature she transformes
> To beare them light on her celestiall wings;
> Thus does she, when from things particular
> She doth abstract the universall kinds,
> Which bodiless, and immateriall are
> And can be lodg'd but onely in our minds.[23]

Coleridge's solution is to paint the relation of subject to object as a creative activity from which reality itself issues. He says 'the true system of natural philosophy places the sole reality of things in…the absolute identity of subject and object'.[24] He insists, first, that 'during the act of knowledge itself, the objective and subjective are so instantly united that we cannot determine to which of the two the priority belongs'.[25] And he says that 'the theory of natural philosophy would then be completed when all nature was demonstrated to be identical in essence with that which in its highest known power exists in man as intelligence and self-consciousness'.[26] The point of the argument is that there is no abstract nature behind Wordsworth's daffodils. There is only the world in which, uniting subject and object, we perceive the daffodils.

This may suggest Hegel but Coleridge brushes off Hegel's ambition to find 'The Idea'. A good poem is a specimen of what might properly be called an idea in an older sense because it unites subject to object in an even closer way than ordinary ideas manage to do.

---

[20]   Coleridge, 1956, pp. 179–80.

[21]   Coleridge, 1956, pp. 171–4.

[22]   Coleridge says 'she' is the soul, but she might be one of the intellects or reason.

[23]   Davies, 1599, *Nosce Teipsum*, p. 24. In the version in Coleridge's text the spelling is modernized, with 'food' for 'meates' and the last two lines were changed so that 'Which bodiless, and immateriall are' becomes 'Which then re-clothed in divers names and fates'. Then 'And can be lodg'd but onely in our minds' becomes 'Steal access through our senses to our minds'. (The normal Latin of course is three words: *Nosce te ipsum*, 'know yourself'.)

[24]   Coleridge, 1956, p. 155.

[25]   Coleridge, 1956, p. 145.

[26]   Coleridge, 1956, p. 125.

A poem is not merely something which enables the self to refer to the object. The poem also engages the self in the idea. After we have read Wordsworth we stand to the daffodils in a quite different relation than we did before.

Coleridge did worry about the sources of his philosophy, and he gave a series of Monday evening lectures on the history of philosophy in a London pub, beginning on 7 December 1818.[27] He promised to show how philosophy was central to the history of man. The dominant themes were drawn from Plato, the Platonic schools, Aristotle and the Peripatetic school, Zeno and Stoicism, the effect of philosophy on the rise of the Roman Republic, Eclectic and Alexandrine philosophy, 'the degradation of Philosophy itself into mysticism and magic', and its final disappearance before its 'resumption in the Thirteenth Century, and the successive reappearance of the different sects from the restoration of literature to our own times'. These lectures came twenty years after his visit to Germany in 1798 during which he made his acquaintance with Kant and became interested in German culture and philosophy. Yet Coleridge still gives nearly all his attention to the ancients and some to the medievals. Kant is mentioned though he does not appear in the prospectus. Owen Barfield in his introduction to the lectures says that Coleridge may have been tiring by the time he came to Kant. He notes that 'though something is said about Leibniz's critique of Locke, there is no mention of Fichte nor of any other of the German school except Kant, who is accorded less space than had been allowed in earlier lectures to St. Theresa and Agrippa'.[28] Still, Coleridge does acknowledge that Kant awoke and transformed German philosophy.

This suggests Douglas Hedley's argument, based on Coleridge's *Aids to Reflection* written in 1825, that Coleridge, though he changed his mind from time to time about many things, was nearly always a Platonist of some kind. Often he seems to be a Neoplatonist, often he is not too far from Ralph Cudworth.[29] But we should note that Cudworth does not get much more attention in these lectures than Kant, though Henry More gets a better press. There is a theory about the history of philosophy in these lectures. The unfolding of mind suggested here—philosophy seen as though it were a single individual—suggests the Hegelian philosophy of spirit, but more likely the workings of the third person of the Trinity were in Coleridge's mind.

Coleridge tried to do more in these lectures: Tim Milnes says he 'finally brings down' the 'fantasy' of neutral language of description and collapses Hume's distinction between factual and evaluative claims.[30] Certainly that is what Coleridge intended. But there is no doubt that he establishes a connection between philosophy and the poetic imagination.

On the other side, the ideas of people like William Godwin, long Shelley's hero and later his father-in-law, remained in circulation. Godwin, a novelist and journalist, believed that in a small and enlightened society people would understand the natural sources of one another's feelings. Shelley for a time embraced this theory but, by 1817 when he came to write the *Revolt of Islam* in which he said he would lay down his own political theory, he had evidently changed his mind. Although 'lawless love' is still to be freely available, making feeling triumphant, he speaks in the following stanzas of bringing together 'all the cells of human thought' (notice the image of the cell, a unit which functions only in a larger whole)

---

[27] Coleridge, 2000.   [28] Coleridge, 2000, p. 874.   [29] Hedley, 2000.
[30] Milnes, 2010, p. 182.

and of 'blending all blasts of fragrance into one'. We are also told that 'Science, and her sister Poesy, shall clothe in light the fields and cities of the free' (51.5), an image which seems to conjure up not only the yet unborn Thomas A. Edison and Joseph Swan, but also to imply a good deal of cooperation, as well as a final unity of knowledge in the terms Coleridge would have accepted.

Shelley says:

> Hark! the Earth starts to hear the mighty warning
> Of thy voice sublime and holy;
> Its free spirits here assembled,
> See thee, feel thee, know thee now,
> To thy voice their hearts have trembled,
> Like ten thousand clouds which flow
> With one wide wind as it flies!
> Wisdom! thy irresistible children rise
> To hail thee; and the elements thee chain,
> And their own will, to swell the glory of thy train.
> O Spirit vast and deep as light and Heaven!
> Mother and soul of all to which is given
> The light of life, the loveliness of being,
> Lo! thou dost reascend the human heart,
> Thy throne of power, almighty as thou wert
> In dreams of Poets old grown pale by seeing
> The shade of thee:—now millions start
> To feel thy lightnings through them burning:
> Nature or God, or Love, or Pleasure,
> Or Sympathy, the sad tears turning
> To mutual smiles, a drainless treasure,
> Descends amidst us;—Scorn and Hate,
> Revenge and Selfishness, are desolate—
> A hundred nations swear that there shall be
> Pity and Peace and Love among the good and free![31]

M. Elizabeth Brocking is more cautious about Shelley and the unity of knowledge.[32] She argues that Shelley still subscribes to the Humean view that emotion motivates action. Certainly, he himself said he wanted to appeal to the 'common sympathies of the human breast'. It seems, however, that he wants emotion to stimulate reason, for he wants us to see that there is no simple conflict between good and evil. His heroic protagonists themselves, as so often in real life, show signs of tyranny in the end. There are puzzles. The religious sceptic Shelley accords Laon and Cythna personal immortality, though Ms Brocking would have us not take this too seriously.

Shelley's fondness for Plato is beyond dispute. He translated quite a lot of him for himself,[33] and his *Hymn to Intellectual Beauty* has a Platonic-sounding title. But the poem itself seems much more Neoplatonic:

---

[31] Shelley, 1975, *The Revolt of Islam*, stanzas 51.1 and 51.2.   [32] Brocking, 1985.
[33] Notopoulos, 1949, 1969, collects them.

> The awful shadow of some unseen Power
> Floats though unseen among us, visiting
> This various world with as inconstant wing
> As summer winds that creep from flower to flower.[34]

The shadow of the unseen power suggests the Plotinian 'One' which is beyond being and non-being and which structures the world without ever appearing in it.

Shelley seems also to have been moved by Berkeley. Berkeley held that reality just consists of the experiences that we have—and that God has.[35] But Berkeley also held (emphasized in *Alciphron*) that the world was 'the natural language of God'—i.e. that all natural events have symbolic significance. Thus events have a potential or real natural value and it is this natural value that Shelley, too, was trying to exhibit in many of his poems. To see Shelley as a romanticized Berkeley makes a good deal of sense, though the truth may not be so simple.

Byron, too, has been associated with Berkeley and indeed in *Don Juan* xi.1–2 he does address him:[36]

> When Bishop Berkeley said 'there was no matter,'
> And proved it—'twas no matter what he said:
> They say his system 'tis in vain to batter,
> Too subtle for the airiest human head;
> And yet who can believe it? I would shatter
> Gladly all matters down to stone or lead,
> Or adamant, to find the world a spirit,
> And wear my head, denying that I wear it.
>
> What a sublime discovery 'twas to make the
> Universe universal egotism,
> That all's ideal—*all ourselves!*—I'll stake the
> World (be it what you will) that *that's* no schism.
> Oh Doubt!—if thou be'st Doubt, for which some take thee;
> But which I doubt extremely—thou sole prism
> Of the Truth's rays, spoil not my draught of spirit!
> Heaven's brandy, though our brain can hardly bear it.

Emily A. Bernhard Jackson notices that Berkeley is the only philosopher Byron mentions.[37] One might take the *Don Juan* passage as rather ironic or even sarcastic, but Ms Jackson believes that Byron was of Berkeley's turn of mind when he wrote it, though she

---

[34] Reiman and Fraistat, 2002, 'Hymn to Intellectual Beauty'. The poem was written in 1816 while Percy and Mary were staying on Lake Geneva with Byron.

[35] Mary Shelley said Percy was a disciple of Berkeley (1840, Preface; P. B. Shelley, 1826–30, vol. v, Preface, pp. vii–x). But there is evidence that Shelley liked Hume, too, and George Brett (1931) said that in fact Berkeley came to Shelley via William Drummond. Drummond, a noted diplomat, amateur scholar, and a Fellow of the Royal Society, knew Shelley and indeed visited the Shelleys on 22 April 1819 (Notopoulos, 1949, 1969, pp. 147–51). Drummond was a sceptic and his views of religion caused a row. But whether he was a Berkeleyan or not is a question. He attacked the mechanical philosophers on many grounds and the Aristotelians on form (Drummond, 1805). Shelley certainly read him and mentions him in a note to the preface of *The Revolt of Islam* as 'very acute and powerful'. See also Liedtke, 1933; Pulos, 1963. Many disputes about these questions are reviewed in Roberts, 1997.

[36] Byron, 1988, 2009, vol. vi.

[37] Jackson, 2010.

finds his scepticism turned Humean as time went on. Philosophers, beginning with Hume himself, have often thought that from Berkeley to Hume there is a natural progression, but there seems little doubt that, even though they could both be sceptical, Shelley and Byron had very different notions of knowledge. Shelley thought that the feeling aroused in his poems led us to truth, Byron more likely was, Ms Jackson argues, a genuine sceptic. *Don Juan* is a work in praise of doubt.[38]

As the nineteenth century unfolded, science and religion regarded each another warily. Equally wary was the approach of science to history, to morals, and to the kind of knowledge which we generally know as 'the humanities'. Such thoughts must bring Keats to mind. Two lines from his *Ode on a Grecian Urn*—'Beauty is truth, truth beauty,—that is all | Ye know on earth, and all ye need to know'—and a letter on the world as a 'vale of soul-making' have provoked trunks full of attempted explanations, comments, and philosophical analyses, a paper in *Scientific American*,[39] and the title of a book by Ian Stewart on symmetry.[40] The *Ode on a Grecian Urn* was the third of the five 'great odes' of 1819.[41] The urn is speaking but whether Keats is also speaking for himself has proved a vexed question.

T.S. Eliot thought the famous lines a 'serious blemish' or 'something untrue', but mostly they have been thought either a profound insight or a dangerous error recalling Plato's fear of poets,[42] though Robert Bridges thought they saved an otherwise bad poem.[43]

Keats may not have been a dedicated student of medieval *philosophy*, but there is a lot of evidence of his interest in medieval ideas. The title of his *Belle Dame sans Merci* is taken from the medieval poet Alain Cartier. And the idea behind 'truth is beauty' can be traced back to the notion of the convertible transcendentals which had its roots in the work of Philip the Chancellor. Originally there were three transcendentals—being, goodness, and truth, properties which belonged to everything so ordered that whatever was fully in being would be fully good. 'Transcendental truth' is a complicated notion, and beauty was added later. Keats's suggestion that whatever is true must be beautiful and vice versa, is a notion which many mathematicians have taken seriously. For Keats, perhaps, it suggests that art may express the most profound truths.

One can easily think of cosmological theories as works of art, some of which succeed better than others in conveying the beauty of the world. Mathematicians see beauty in the balance of complex equations. Both can provide visions of time and eternity.

In a different way, one which is central to our enquiry here, art has often opened visions followed by science. There is an interesting relation between the increasing use of three-dimensional perspective as Renaissance art developed along with the exploration of the physics of optics. From Florence to Pisa is a short trip though the ideas may well have passed via Holland. In the nineteenth century the paintings of J. M. W. Turner cast doubts on the mechanical and fixed nature of physical reality long before the physicists began to conceptualize the alternatives. In the early part of the nineteenth century one could see how

---

[38] Jackson, 2010, esp. pp. 15–18. Ms Jackson thinks Byron was also attracted to Locke but moved on to Berkeley and Hume.

[39] Gardner, 2007.

[40] Stewart, 2007.

[41] Keats, 1973.

[42] Eliot, 1932, pp. 230–1.

[43] Murry, 1955, p. 210.

Coleridge's experiences of the poetic imagination might have made German idealism congenial to him and, later in the century, one might suggest that the struggles of the poets preceded philosophy, that British idealism, for instance, grew out of a cultural situation in the
creation of which poets had played a major part.

Trouble arises from the phrase in Keats's poem: 'all | Ye know on earth, and all ye need
to know'. Yet it does make sense in the context of Keats's world vision as it appears in a celebrated letter to George and Georgina Keats on 19 March 1819, very close to the time of the
'urn' poem. In the letter he said 'Call the world if you like the vale of Soul-making.'[44] He suggests that we start off as 'intelligences or sparks of the divinity' but 'they are not souls'. We do
live in a world of 'tears and troubles' but this all goes into soul-making, the essence of which
seems to be the certainty of a genuine individuality, 'the sense of identity'. The struggle for
self-expression in the arts seems to be an important parallel to this, and Keats speaks of the
fire in the human heart, quotes Wordsworth, and extends his thesis to other living creatures.
But he gave us no treatise to explain himself.

One might argue, however, that in Keats's letter, there is an intriguing suggestion about
the ways in which knowledge of the individual is possible. Perhaps by seeing how individuals are made we can come to understand individuality and perhaps the poetic imagination
can give us a glimmering of how this is done. Perhaps 'Looking into Chapman's Homer' and
confronting the Grecian urn offer us clues.

John Keble, who now appears in the calendar of saints in some Anglican provinces, had,
along with Edward Pusey and Newman, started a powerful movement. Keble, who was
Matthew Arnold's godfather, had taken the ideas of Wordsworth and Coleridge to a further
extreme. Keble interpreted the natural world as a collection of allegories and symbols whose
real meaning was to be found in a Platonic world beyond. For him, scientific knowledge was
secondary, essentially practical and devoid of the necessary means for the understanding
of nature.[45] He continued to have followers and, though few might go all the way with his
thesis about the relation between the two spheres, many still claimed that poetry could yield
knowledge of nature or, at least, that there is a kind of knowledge to be found in the humanities which extends into nature.

Between Keble and men like Herbert Spencer there was an impassable gulf. The idealist
philosophers later tried to fill it, though it would be hard to say whether someone like F. H.
Bradley would find Keble or Spencer the less congenial.

It was relatively rare by 1875, however, for anyone to claim the whole of real and rational
knowledge either for science or for the humanities. A gap remained. Oxford and, to a lesser
extent, Cambridge were wedded to humanistic learning while the newer universities paid
more and more attention to the 'science side'. The beginnings of what was to be the powerful Imperial College of Science and Technology were there and became a cornerstone of the
University of London.

When the dust settled, it more often than not turned out that the lines drawn between
the devotees of the humanities and the partisans of science were Cartesian. On one side the

[44] A. C. Bradley, 1909, p. 222. The letter is available at <www.mrbauld.com/keatsva.html>.
[45] Keble's writings are scattered and fragmentary—apart from his collection of poems, *The Christian
Year* (1853), and his *Lectures on Poetry*, finally translated into English from their original Latin in 1912. For
his 'two worlds' doctrine see Prickett, 1976.

physical sciences dealt with the realm of things extended in space; on the other religion and the humanities took refuge in the inner life of man.

Out of this impasse there were a number of possible escapes. Two of them interest us here. One was John Henry Newman's. His *Essay in Aid of a Grammar of Assent*[46] was a general and revisionist review of the notion of knowledge. In it, he developed the doctrine of the illative sense. Aristotle had argued that moral knowledge required a special kind of judgement which he called *phronesis*. Newman extended this doctrine to all knowledge, calling the necessary judgement 'the illative sense'. He claimed that no argument ever compels our assent. I can always call for more evidence. Or, if the argument is purely formal, as in logic or mathematics, I can always demand a new premise because I can always call in question whatever inference rules are presented to me. Personal experience does not really prove that Great Britain is an island (Newman liked this example) or that the world is round or that tomorrow will be much like today. But no one doubts these things either.

If I read Newman correctly, the realization that one is free to give or withhold one's assent puts constraints on what it is that merits assent. One cannot both hold the doctrine of free assent and be a total sceptic. One who can give and withhold assent stands at a pivotal point in the universe and has a certain dignity and responsibility. Only propositions asserting the reality of a universe which meets the conditions for the existence of dignity and responsibility are consistent with the belief in that dignity and responsibility.

It is from this, above all, that Newman builds his case for accepting the universe described by Christian doctrine. Science provides evidence which compels attention but does not compel assent. To say that it compels attention is to say that we must look for plans and maps of the universe which do justice both to the truths of science and to the status of man as a free and dignified being. The test of the picture is in part its balance. No sane man would hold any proposition which led him to deny that Great Britain was an island; but no sane man would hold any proposition which would lead him to deny the essential humanistic insights into his own being, either.

There are different kinds of assent (essentially real and notional assents), but there are not degrees of assent; and we must give our assent in order to act. Indeed, real assent differs from notional assent when we act or frame our world views.

The unity of knowledge is thus given a structure by Newman which depends on the understanding of the conditions for assent and on the tendency of real assent to structure action as well as nominal belief. These, together with the fact that conscience compels us to think of something beyond ourselves,[47] give Newman a thesis about what knowledge and knowing are, and a way of reconciling science and the humanities. In knowing ourselves, Newman thought to come to know the universe. All Newman's works, it has often been remarked, tend to be accounts of his intellectual autobiography. In knowing ourselves we know what best reveals reality.

---

[46] Newman, 1870.

[47] It is easy to write off Newman's 'argument from conscience' as a misunderstanding of the forces of one's culture, or of evolutionary psychology, but what Newman seems to suggest is that self-knowledge by its nature invokes a self-ideal which presupposes something beyond the immediate self. For our present purposes it is at least important to notice that Newman in *Gerontius* makes the old man realize that when he meets the good the light is too bright for him, but he still wants to fit himself for it. The poet if he succeeds makes us feel Gerontius' need in a way that the philosopher cannot.

Newman used his poetry to convey his world view. His *Dream of Gerontius*[48] puts forth his view of human frailty and his vision of God. *Gerontius* became famous when Elgar wrote a major work for chorus and orchestra based on it, and 'Lead Kindly Light' is sung in churches well beyond the Catholic pale.

The focal point of the reunion of knowledge is Newman's theory of ideas which he only sketches in the *Essay on the Development of Christian Doctrine*.[49] There are objective (real) ideas, and subjective (in some restricted sense, unreal) ideas. Real ideas are capable, when acted on, of generating an intelligible world and are capable of development as more and more of their aspects come to light in the course of human actions. The world is a moral arena and its point is to bring the concrete reality of this world to the ideas which have their source in another world, ultimately, Newman would say, in God.

The picture, essentially, is that science describes the background, the stage machinery, for this morality play. Statements about how the stage is made do not conflict with statements which are internal to the play itself. True, the actors have bodies and the bodies themselves are part of the stage machinery. But the Author is not bound by the laws of physics. The play is not quite like a human play because, although each actor has a part in the story, each actor also, in part at least, makes up his own lines. (Only the Author knows for sure which lines are made up by the actors, but the Author—like any other author—is omnipotent within the play and he can adapt the play as it goes along so that his own ends are served.) Newman's religious beliefs were a dominant interest and the whole story falls neatly into place in the context of a Christianity in which the Church is the vehicle through which objective ideas manifest themselves and undergo development over time.

Newman was much admired but little followed. Unbelievers and Protestants alike suspected that his road led only to Rome. Much of the Catholic hierarchy, by contrast, tended to find his modernized Christianity with its emphasis on history and development, its cheerful acceptance of the latest in science, and its insistence on the power of individual conscience, suspicious. Most Catholic scholars liked neither the hints of 'modernism' nor the Platonism which intruded on their Aristotelian beliefs. His greatest admirers continued to be literary figures who had belonged to the High Church Anglican Tractarian Movement, but they, in turn, regretted Newman's conversion to Catholicism and admired his style and diction more than his philosophical conclusions.

Oxford also produced counter-movements. In *Literature and Dogma*, Matthew Arnold replaced God by 'the eternal not ourselves that makes for righteousness'[50] which was taken for a kind of 'atheism' but which is very close in fact to Newman's God who is to be discovered through our consciences. By 1869 Arnold had already decided that all was not well and published *Culture and Anarchy* to set everyone right.[51] Twenty years earlier, social protest was the last thing one would have expected from the young Arnold, something of a dandy, a noted wit, and a young man with a taste for pranks. He had grown up along with the Industrial Revolution. Like many upper- and middle-class Englishmen, he had been kept away from overmuch direct confrontation with the reality of that revolution. His

---

[48] Newman, 1885. For all his poetry, see Newman, 1992.

[49] Newman, 1845. For Newman on ideas, see Armour, 1990.

[50] Arnold, 1873, 1889, ch. 8. The expression 'eternal not ourselves' occurs thirty-one times. (Note that a number of Arnold's religious writings have been assembled in Arnold, 1968.)

[51] Arnold, 1869, 1965, Preface.

father, Thomas Arnold, was a historian who took over a preparatory school at Laleham on the Thames when marriage forced him to give up his fellowship at Oxford. Matthew was born there in what was then a picturesque and gentle countryside. In due course, his father became headmaster of Rugby School and Matthew, after a brief spell at Winchester, became a pupil there. Thomas Arnold became a friend of Wordsworth and the family acquired a large house, Fox How, in the English Lake District. The family at Fox How became part of the Wordsworth–Coleridge–Southey culture. Though young Matthew (unlike his brother Tom) was no scholar, it was more or less assumed that he would turn out to be a poet. His school prizes were for poetry and, when he went to Oxford in his turn, he relaxed, read what he liked, and wrote more poetry.

Thus equipped, he descended on London as an assistant to various politicians and in 1850 he became a school inspector in order to persuade his prospective father-in-law that he could earn enough to support a family. The inspectorate took him into the industrial midlands and began to change his life. He could only inspect schools belonging to dissenting religious denominations. The Church of England controlled the other schools and only its clergy could act as inspectors. Arnold worked for the rest of his life among earnest dissenters, chiefly from the middle and lower parts of the middle class, who lived and worked largely in the new industrial towns and struggled for reform through education. He was in due course elected professor of poetry at Oxford, a part-time job which lasted, by custom, for ten years.

There were schools for Arnold to inspect, but schooling was not compulsory, and child labour (often necessary because of the low wages which parents earned) interfered with education. Frequently, however, the dissenting churches taught reading and writing in their Sunday schools and their pupils were not just content to read the Bible. They became the market for a prosperous industry in publishing, including cheap editions of the classics.

Arnold was in search of an authority which would prevent the breakdown of the social situation into self-destructive anarchy and would not do so at the continued expense of the already oppressed. He was also concerned to dissolve the class structure—for the nature of the class system tended to leave the aristocracy impotent, the middle class mired in Philistinism (one of Arnold's favourite words), and most of the working class doomed to drudgery and semi-illiteracy.

'Culture' was used by Matthew Arnold to cover the things of most importance—poetry and science and thoughtful religion. The aim of culture, he insisted, is to 'know the best that has been thought and said in the world'.[52] In a general way, 'culture', Arnold's superior kind or the anthropologists' kind, is whatever it is that puts meaning on human actions. We know there are two cultures involved when one act has two meanings so that people misunderstand one another's actions. Values are inescapable in such matters and we might agree that a good culture is one which makes human life meaningful in a way which is coherent and complete. Philistinism, in Arnold's sense, divided rich and poor, divided the world into oppressors and oppressed, and turned men into mere animals for whom everything was to be decided by wealth—the human equivalent, after all, of a dog's hoard of bones.

What was needed, Arnold said, was a society in which the best could be pursued for its own sake—in which science would be a search for truth and not for better guns and steam

[52] Arnold, 1968, p. 162.

engines—a society in which the pursuit of the best would not penalize the searchers. Education would create a market for the best. But Arnold had never been sure about the future:

> Time may restore us in his course
> Goethe's sage mind and Byron's force:
> But where will Europe's latter hour
> Again find Wordsworth's healing power?[53]

Wordsworth's healing power undoubtedly had something to do with the human relation to nature. Perhaps Wordsworth himself had been healed from the violence of the French Revolution not just by his life in the Lake District but by his own poetic understanding of nature, something the philosopher alone surely could not manage.

Arnold's scene in *On Dover Beach* is a gloomy one where the 'sea of faith' has run out and we are left with only human love.

> Ah, love, let us be true
> To one another! for the world, which seems
> To lie before us like a land of dreams,
> So various, so beautiful, so new,
> Hath really neither joy, nor love, nor light,
> Nor certitude, nor peace, nor help for pain;
> And we are here as on a darkling plain
> Swept with confused alarms of struggle and flight,
> Where ignorant armies clash by night.[54]

Newman had used the ignorant armies' image in a sermon.[55] They seem to have been science and religion and the result of the clash is that we are alone on the sand. The poem says, perhaps, more about the culture of the period than Arnold could manage in his essays—and says it more compellingly. It may also underline the gap between what can be said in philosophy and what the poet can convey.

Newman and Arnold are tied together by Oxford and its controversies and, as I suggested, by philosophical theologies which place emphasis on conscience[56] and what they take to be its implications for the existence of a reality greater than ourselves. Newman's God

[53] Arnold, 1850.

[54] For the text of the poem see Arnold, 1961, 1965.

[55] Honan, 1981, p. 235. The reference is to Newman's University Sermon (at St Mary's, Oxford, 6 January 1839, found in Newman, 1892, 1970). The relations between the Arnold and Newman families was complex. Matthew and John Henry Newman had respect for one another and Matthew had heard some of Newman's sermons. Arnold's father, Thomas, the headmaster of Rugby, distrusted and disliked the Tractarians on principle. Surprisingly, Matthew got along less well with Newman's younger brother Francis, once an Anglican missionary who left the Church to promote liberal reform, a very different exit from his brother's, and became a professor of Classics at the University of London. Francis Newman disapproved of some of Arnold's readings of classical authors. There are details in Honan's book.

[56] In Newman, 1969 (entry of 7 November 1859, ii. 31) the poet writes '(Some suppose) I think there is moral obligation because there is a God, but I hold just the reverse, that there is a God because there is moral obligation . . . I have a certain feeling (?) on my mind which I call conscience.' This notebook entry for 7 November 1859 is also in Newman, 1961, ch. IV, pp. 103–21.

is embedded in Catholic tradition, Arnold's eternal seems embedded in the 'high culture' which Arnold thought essential to our humanity.

Neither Newman's 'argument from conscience' nor Arnold's sense of the 'eternal' and its claims upon us has been analysed often or with sufficient care by the philosophers. The argument is that reality has goodness in—perhaps *as*—its root being, and this makes a claim on us that is personal. It creates a mixture of regret, sadness, and hope. The poet can convey this. The melancholy scene on Dover beach can be taken as a call to action, to confront the ignorant armies, and to reclaim what the receding tide has taken away. Newman's Gerontius faces the light which somehow we sense is there, from which we avert our eyes, but which like Gerontius we hope to be able to confront. Coleridge's Ancient Mariner goes through the same experience. Given the poet's vision we can perhaps take the philosophical argument seriously.

But Newman and Arnold are regarded quite differently by religious writers and, indeed, philosophers. Neither is perhaps very distant in important respects from Alfred Tennyson. But it is neither in the classical and rational culture of Arnold nor, of course, the Catholic tradition of Newman, in which Tennyson situates his philosophy but something much closer to the nature philosophy of Wordsworth. In an important way we are back with the Cambridge culture in which reconciliation with science through the understanding of nature has very often seemed pressing. Tennyson might have found the 'healing power' sought by Arnold but he would have felt himself a world away from Newman.

Tennyson outlived Arnold by four years but he was born thirteen years earlier—nearly four decades after Wordsworth and Coleridge. He was more directly interested in philosophy than any poet but Coleridge. Peter Allen says that he was regarded among the Cambridge Apostles as one of a rather Platonic band—'Maurice[57] and the gallant band of Platonic-Wordsworthian-Coleridgean anti-utilitarians'.[58] It is said he refused to meet Coleridge.[59]

Although we owe to him 'nature red in tooth and claw', *In Memoriam*, written on the death of his friend Arthur Henry Hallam, actually takes us from loss and grief to hope. It is another poetic vision of the claims of the inherent goodness of things on us. As in Coleridge, Arnold, and Newman—and indeed in Keats and his 'vale of soul making'—the message is that we become ourselves in the process of separation from some benign power and then return to a fuller understanding of reality. Perhaps this is not 'Wordsworth's healing power', but maybe it is a clue.

Tennyson was a pantheist or, rather, a panentheist as *The Higher Pantheism* suggests:

> The sun, the moon, the stars, the seas, the hills and the plains,
> Are not these, O Soul, the Vision of Him who reigns?[60]

In the poem God is in everything—the world is his vision—but God extends beyond the world, as panentheists insist. Appropriately, Tennyson had an interest in Giordano Bruno and Spinoza. His son Hallam quoted him as saying,

---

[57] Frederick Denison Maurice, 1805–72, was a liberal theologian and one of the founders of the Cambridge Apostles Club.

[58] Tennyson was elected to the Apostles in 1829.

[59] Allen, 1978, p. 76.

[60] A. Tennyson, 1870.

Bruno's view of God is in some ways mine. Bruno was a poet, holding his mind ever open to new truths, and believing in an infinite universe as the necessary effect of a divine Power; he was burnt as a heretic. His age did not believe in him. I think he was misunderstood, and I should like to show him in what I conceive to be his right colours: he was the author of much of our modern philosophy. He died the most desolate of deaths.[61]

On the same page Hallam quotes his father as saying that Spinoza was not an atheist but he 'thought joy was more real than sorrow' and he was 'Gottbetrunken'. Tennyson gives his thoughts an idealist twist: 'Matter is a greater mystery than mind. What such a thing as spirit is apart from God and man I have never been able to conceive. Spirit seems to me to be the reality of the world.'

Tennyson felt himself struggling constantly with language as lines 45–8 of *In Memoriam* suggest:[62]

> Vague words! but ah, how hard to frame
> In matter-moulded forms of speech,
> Or even for intellect to reach
> Through memory that which I became[63]

At Cambridge, Tennyson was taught to admire Locke, but he quickly moved towards philosophical idealism. Nonetheless, 'matter-moulded' seemed right to him. 'Matter' no doubt refers to the whole bodily process of speaking but it likely also refers to the fact that the objects spoken of have their own claim on the formation of what we say.

In the poem Nature is portrayed as thinking that 'spirit' means only 'wind' (a popular notion of its empirical origins) but the poet is presented as struggling against this view towards a larger and more realistic view of language and human nature. 'Nature' with a capital 'N' plays a role in all this, and T. S. Eliot remarked that Nature had become 'a real god or goddess, perhaps more real, at moments to Tennyson than God'. Eliot says that the 'hope of immortality is confused (typically of this period) with the hope of a gradual and steady improvement of this world',[64] but more likely the two are seen as connected through a benign providence.

It has been suggested that Tennyson was challenged by Charles Lyell's *Principles of Geology* which appeared in 1830–3 and which suggested that the world was very old and had been long lifeless. But he had never had a high opinion of arguments from nature to the existence of God and had voted 'no' at an Apostles' meeting when objections to Lyell were proposed.[65] The fourth line of the 'Prologue' to *In Memoriam* reads 'believing where we cannot prove'.

Though Tennyson is reported as saying that he knew of Hegel only 'through the talk of others', 'obiter and obscurely',[66] Donald Hair concludes that he did hold an idealist position in which mind is 'primary'.[67] Hair goes on to say that Tennyson regarded words as signs 'of

---

[61] H. Tennyson, 1897, ii. 424, The occasion was the gift of a book containing two addresses on Giordano Bruno by Thomas Davidson sent to Tennyson by Walt Whitman.

[62] Hair, 1991, pp. 142–3.

[63] Tennyson's poems in what follows can be found in A. Tennyson, 1891.

[64] Eliot, 1936, pp. 175–90 (quoted here from Gray, 2004, p. 136).

[65] Mattes, 1951, pp. 55–63.

[66] Staines, 1977, p. 405.

[67] Hair, 1991, p. 170.

shaping powers in the mind: the powers of perceiving likenesses and differences; of abstracting, generalizing, and classifying; of ordering experiences in ways that realize our human concerns. These ways are natural; that is they are both in us and characterize our human nature; they are God given.'[68]

Hair also maintains that Tennyson contributed to an idealist theory of grammar and took part in the 'new philology' which attacked the Aristotelian notion that speech basically consisted of sentences in which a noun precedes some form of predication. In the alternative view the pronoun, especially the first-person pronoun, becomes central in the construction of an 'all embracing Word, a logos which we apprehend partially and imperfectly when we turn back toward God (or reflect) on the power of speech which God has given us'.[69]

Language if properly understood becomes a part of a necessary system which reflects the underlying nature of the world. Experience still has a place of honour as much for Tennyson as for Locke because experience becomes clear and intelligible only when it is seen through a creative system.[70] And so, in 'The Coming of Arthur', Arthur said:

> Man's word is God in man:
> Let chance what will, I trust thee to the death.

And the line 'Man's word is God in man' is repeated later. Hair suggests that this is related to Tennyson's view of language and the philology of the time. Tennyson was evidently torn. On the one hand he saw language as developing over time, and when Benjamin Jowett sent him a copy of Hegel's *Philosophy of History* he called attention to Tennyson's lines about increasing purpose in nature (cf. *Locksley Hall*) which suggest that words are 'God in man'.[71] This view of language as a universal agent at work in humanity does not fit very well with the fact that Tennyson sometimes revelled in the 'Englishness' of English and sought to de-Latinize his work.

It is not just that Tennyson is reflecting Nicolas of Cusa's thesis that 'man is a second God' since we can create through language. It is that the underlying reality is the Word and the 'word made flesh' through experience. There are hints here about the way in which Tennyson hopes to reunify our view of nature in the face of science. Science is expressed through language too, and is itself an expression of the Word. If so, nature is not to be separated from its intelligible source.

Poetry allows us to create a new vision within which apparently clashing views can be reconciled. Tennyson's vision is that there is a reality expressed through the Word which shows itself in the patterns discerned by the sciences and in our articulations of human experience. They all testify to a unity: 'The Higher Pantheism'.

> God is law, say the wise; O soul, and let us rejoice,
> For if He thunder by law the thunder is yet His voice.
> Law is God, say some; no God at all, says the fool,
> For all we have power to see is a straight staff bent in a pool;

---

[68] Hair, 1991, p. 170.   [69] Hair, 1991, p. 171.
[70] Hair, 1991, ch. 6.   [71] Hair, 1991, p. 139.

How close is Tennyson, in the end, to Matthew Arnold? He told his son Hallam, 'Tell Mat not to write any more of those prose things like *Literature and Dogma*,'[72] but that probably was intended to urge Arnold to write more poems. Arnold's 'eternal' is always close at hand.

Hair explains the 'new philology' as a development of German language studies, first through the change from traditional classical philology which simply studied grammar and texts on their surface, to a new classical philology which wanted to see language in its role as a structure of the ancient world, and then on to the philology of German idealism which saw language as constitutive of the world.

It was coming to be accepted that language was constitutive of the world as we know it and could not be studied alone or regarded as a neutral entity, a mere object. The emphasis on classical languages in isolation had obscured the facts.

The 'new philology' with its emphasis on culture, the development of language, and the relation of language to reality became both a version of philosophy itself and source for the philosophy of history. Tennyson was not alone among the poets in being moved by it.

Hair looks in some detail at Frederick William Farrar and Baron Bunsen (C. C. J. Bunsen). Farrar did not think language was a divine revelation, but he did think there was a dialectic at work.[73] We *do* innately possess the means to language. Language, as we know it, is a continuing creation involving interaction between human beings and their environments. Thus there is an unfolding of divine providence by a kind of dialectical interaction. This suggests a Hegelian history but, rather drily, Farrar thinks linguistic progress comes about largely through the elimination of redundancy, that is, of forms which are not necessary to meaning.[74]

Baron Bunsen sought a general theory of language and history. History must be a dialectic and it involves 'antagonisms', often a subject–object tension. Out of these tensions intelligible ideas arise. He notices that Genesis says that God called Adam and waited 'to see what he would call' the animals of the world. Naming involves both things and the organized experience of the named. Things do not come ready named, but naming is not wholly arbitrary. [75]

Judith Winternitz notes that theology was at the heart of Bunsen's theses. 'Christianity was the centre of all human experience.'[76] To be such a centre there had to be a universal history. Christians had to account for the whole history of the world. But Bunsen was what Dr Winternitz calls a 'spiritual rationalist'. Reason was linked to the nature of God himself. God provided order to the world and his revelations are, therefore, conformable to reason.

Bunsen's philology had its source in the study of Sanskrit which broke with a tradition of classical philology and showed that Western languages had origins in the East. Bunsen drew on Humboldt's expansion of Herder's theory that language arises from an inner need, and, in the expression of thought, becomes universal. Yet language both forms and imprisons

---

[72] H. Tennyson, 1897, ii. 225.

[73] Farrar, 1860.

[74] Many of the issues are explored in Burrow, 1967. Burrow suggests a connection with German Idealist epistemology, though that relation, he thinks, is more distant than the direct relation to German Romanticism.

[75] Bunsen, 1854, pp. 32 ff.

[76] Winternitz, 1979. This is a splendidly complete, well-written, but unpublished thesis which, oddly, is one of the few extensive studies of a man who was very influential.

thought. So there can be frozen sections of language which emerge for Herder as national characteristics.

Bunsen was a diplomat by trade who found negotiating between the Prussian King Frederick William and the Vatican depressing. He regarded his visit to Oxford in 1838 as the 'climax' in his life. In England, he met Newman (as well as Gladstone, Macaulay, and Peel). Donald Hair thinks he influenced Tennyson's view of language. In 1848 and after he proposed a model for the multicultural societies which have become common in our time. History was evolving but not as fast as he hoped.

Bunsen's mark on English thought was increased because his political work seems to have given him influence over academic matters, and he arranged with Frederick William for Carl Richard Lepsius to become professor extraordinarius at Berlin. Lepsius was an Egyptologist who shared Bunsen's views about Christianity and the state and about the need for both a rational, liberal religion, and a coherent view of history. He was also associated with Friedrich Max Müller and together they determined to promote German philosophy in England. Bunsen secured a post at Oxford for Müller. Bunsen's *Universal History*, helped by these men, began to appear in the 1840s.

Robert Browning was an almost exact contemporary of Tennyson. Born three years later he died three years earlier, and has not infrequently been supposed to mark another step on the road to a fully developed idealism. Many thinkers have commented on him,[77] and the idealist philosopher Henry Jones took him very seriously.[78] So did George Herbert Palmer, who built the philosophy department at Harvard from a seedling in a still fairly small college into the department which, with William James, Josiah Royce, and George Santayana, dominated an emerging profession.[79]

Browning combined a scepticism about knowledge with an optimism about life and this made his philosophical idealism puzzling. A pattern which the idealist philosophers could work on had, however, clearly developed. The poets I have been discussing became a very prominent part of the British national culture and there was a range of poetic experiences which were shared by hundreds of thousands of people as public and popular education spread. There are trends and repeated ideas, but no unity of 'poetic thought', even if some poets are closer to one another than one might first think.

It would be a stretch to try to 'integrate' Gerard Manley Hopkins into any narrative of the development of nineteenth-century 'British ideas'. Newman's defection from Anglicanism was a logical result of his long reflection on the history of religion and his personal convictions about the development of Christian doctrines. Hopkins's conversion was provoked by his own undergraduate reflections on his very personal feelings. His father, a minor poet himself, was active in the Anglican Church, but Hopkins does not seem to have been reacting against his family in the way that the philosopher F. H. Bradley did. Hopkins did consult

---

[77] Mander, 2011, p. 232, cites W. Symons, 'Robert Browning as a Religious Poet', *Wesleyan-Methodist Magazine* (Dec. 1882), 943–7; John Bury, 'Browning's Philosophy', *Browning Studies* (London 1895); Josiah Royce, 'Browning's Theism', *Boston Browning Society Papers* (New York: 1897), 18–25; A. C. Pigou, *Robert Browning as Religious Teacher* (London: C. J. Clay, 1901); E. H. Griggs, *The Poetry and Philosophy of Browning* (New York: W. Huebsh 1905); and F. M. Simm, *Robert Browning; Poet and Philosopher* (New York: D. Appleton, 1924).

[78] Jones, 1891.

[79] Palmer, 1918.

Newman—who seems to have discouraged him from joining his own Oratorian Order—but his decision to become a Jesuit was his own.

Few things that Hopkins did seemed unsurprising. That was as true of his philosophy as of his religion. His Jesuit colleagues were, like most Catholics with a scholarly turn (though not Newman), devoted Thomists. But by the end of his second year of theological studies Hopkins had switched his allegiance to Duns Scotus.

He had been an Aristotelian—not unusual in Oxford undergraduates of his day—but his diary entry says the discovery of Scotus was a 'mercy of God': 'when I took in any inscape of the sky or the sea, I thought of Scotus'.[80]

'Inscape' is used by Hopkins to refer to the inner grasp of the individuality of a thing, while his use of 'instress' is associated with its essence and with our 'impressions'. In both there is 'stress'. It has to do with our relations to things as they pull towards us in our attempts at knowledge. In much that passes for knowledge, he thought, things are taken away and replaced by abstractions which 'do duty' for them in our minds. Poetry may help fill the gap. Aristotle and St Thomas believed knowledge consisted precisely in the abstraction of forms from things and in their proper ordering in the mind. Hopkins took Scotus to say that knowledge consisted of a grasp of the individual and this, according to W. A. M. Peters, is Hopkins's sense of 'inscape'.[81]

The 'thisness' of things which so fascinated Scotus is not easily captured in analysis. But look at Hopkins's poem 'Duns Scotus's Oxford':

> Towery city and branchy between towers;
> Cuckoo-echoing, bell-swarmèd, lark charmèd, rook racked, river-rounded;
> The dapple-eared lily below thee; that country and town did
> Once encounter in, here coped & poisèd powers;
>
> Thou hast a base and brickish skirt there, sours
> That neighbour-nature thy grey beauty is grounded
> Best in; graceless growth, thou hast confounded
> Rural, rural keeping—folk, flocks, and flowers.
>
> Yet ah! this air I gather and I release
> He lived on; these weeds and waters, these walls are what
> He haunted who of all men most sways my spirits to peace;
>
> Of realty the rarest-veinèd unraveller; a not
> Rivalled insight, be rival Italy or Greece;
> Who fired France for Mary without spot.[82]

Hopkins's answer to our question is surely in the line 'who of all men sways my spirits to peace'. It is, of course, the ideas of Scotus that attracted Hopkins. Scotus thought that each thing is indissolubly individual. He also developed the dialectic of the disjunctive transcendentals

---

[80] Hopkins, 1959b. The entry is for 19 July 1872 though it mentions 3 August and a post-examination holiday at Douglas in the Isle of Man. Hopkins says he found Scotus in the Baddeley Library. Edward Baddeley (d. 1868) had donated books to Stonyhurst where Hopkins was studying. (The Baddeley Library is now at Heythrop College in London.)

[81] Peters, 1948.

[82] Hopkins, 1985.

which suggests that a world of finite things must point to an infinite that provides the limits which establish their finitude. I think one sees in the poem, as well, the Scotist belief that being is unified. God comes through to Hopkins not only in the words of Scotus but even in the stones of Oxford. Not for Scotus the Thomist doctrine that we only grasp God's being as an analogy of our own. Hopkins is not so far, perhaps, as one might think from the panentheism which poets like Tennyson embraced. Above all, Hopkins had the ability to balance a massive respect for the world with an awareness of the eternal.[83]

Less noticed is Hopkins's concern with Scotus as a philosopher who could disentangle the thorny problem of grace and free will. Hopkins took Scotus to be saying that God sees the possibilities for each human being's salvation and created a world in which it is possible for each person to attain it. We must fulfil the conditions for the actualization of these possibilities and we have what he calls a 'natural pitch', our essential personality which Hopkins sometimes describes as 'prior' to existence. Our 'real self', an idea which appears in the idealist philosophers of the era, is the self of God's original vision of the possibilities. We are free to act but to lift ourselves from one level of selfhood to another, we need the assistance which is called grace.[84]

Hopkins's universe is very personal and if he is right about knowledge it is best conveyed in his poems, each of which is clearly an individual and perhaps indeed a universe of its own so that we cannot easily infer from one to another. Yet Hopkins was by his own account moved by philosophy and chose a religion with an ancient well-developed intellectual structure.

The idea of 'moment' like that of 'individual' plays a part in his thought, and Daniel Brown argues that Hopkins developed the Hegelian notion of 'moment' and the associated ideas of 'stress' from mechanics, and that Hopkins's idea of a unified universe is based on notions of unity given by the newly developed notions of conservation of energy.[85]

Brown's thesis comes essentially from very difficult questions in the interpretation of Hegel and from reading equally difficult passages in Hopkins. Hegel in the 'nature philosophy' section of the *Encyclopaedia of the Philosophical Sciences* was, among other things, trying to square his metaphysics with the physics of his time. One can certainly see how the notions of mechanical stress and the idea of thermodynamics can be developed as an account of dialectical tension.[86]

---

[83] The 'transcendentals' are properties which belong to everything—being, truth, goodness, and perhaps beauty. But Scotus argued that there are disjunctive properties—finite-or-infinite is one of them—which must belong to everything as well. The final version of Scotus' *Commentary on the Sentences* which is now generally known as the *Ordinatio*, I. 39, refers to this text (Libro I, Distinctio 39. The crucial part is Questio Unica, section 13.) The earliest text I have been able to consult is Venice: B. & B. Sessam, 1597–8. But it is not quite complete. The whole text can be found in Luke Waddington's edition (London: Lawrence Durand, 1639), 1289–1327, with the crucial discussion on 1299–1300. This version includes commentary by Waddington which was repeated in what was until recently the most used Latin text, *Joannis Duns Scoti, Opera Omnia* (Paris: Vivès, 1893, x. 610–76.) Another (abbreviated) version is in the edition of the *Commentaria Oxoniensia*, ed. Marianus Fernandez Garcia (Quaracchi: Typographia Collegii S. Bonaventurae, 1912), 1202 ff. A fuller version is included in Carl Balic's Vatican Edition (*Opera Omnia*, Typos Polyglottis Vaticanis, 1963, 401–44). The text appears there as an appendix because it is missing from the codex the editors used (against the advice of Ephrem Longpré who was the original editor of the project). A text therefore had to be imported from another codex. The Vatican edition contains long notes with all known variations of the text.

[84] Hopkins, 1959a. In Appendix II pp. 338–51, Christopher Devlin, the editor, tracks the places he has found—there seem to be four significant ones—where Hopkins lays out these views.

[85] Brown, 1997, ch. 7.

[86] Hiebert, 1966, pp. 1052–8.

Leonard Cochran, by contrast, urges that Hopkins is insisting on an organic unity.[87] Cochran says inscape, instress, scape, and stress were used 212 times in Hopkins's writings from 1886 to 1887, two years before his death. Cochran thinks, however, that Hopkins developed his views earlier, before he learned about Duns Scotus. Inscape is no doubt a psychological landscape but 'stress' bothers Cochrane. It has to do with our ability to see the universal in the particular. But he thinks 'stress may have come to be used as a synonym for being'. A good example is to be found in Hopkins's sermon of 11 January 1880 on 'God's Kingdom'.[88] Here he is talking about the commonwealth as 'the meeting of many for the common good' and he speaks of the stress of the obedience to the sovereign.

Brown asks, 'Why does Cochran borrow terms from mechanics but insist they represent only organicist ideas?'[89] The answer to Brown's question may well be that what interests Hopkins is the way in which talking about mechanics leads us to language and then that burrowing deeper into the sense of the language leads on to an organicist view. For Hopkins certainly wants to see nature not as mechanical but as developing, not through an arbitrary God, but through the God he thinks is revealed in the Christian religion. He is most likely looking for the third person of the Trinity and if one wants to find links between Hopkins and idealist philosophy one might note the parallels with the ideas of Josiah Royce. At the end of the century Royce argued that the attempt to get a nature philosophy which accords with the developing idea of mathematical physics can lead on to the infinite and the third person of the Trinity, and into the 'Church universal'.[90]

Hopkins, Newman, and Keble may seem to be exceptions, but the main thrust of the poetic imagination revealed a world vision which put conventional religion in question. The poets, equally, rejected the mechanical materialism which had a strong grip on many eighteenth-century imaginations and which also had a powerful hold on much nineteenth-century science. But the poetic vision of nature was rarely ever anti-scientific. The poetic vision suggests an integration, and Newman and Hopkins were not quite the kinds of converts who bring unalloyed joy to papal hearts.

Newman's roots were in the writings of the Platonic Church Fathers and his religious *visions* were not far from those of several English poets. Hopkins was a Scotist because he insisted on a kind of knowledge which the Aristotelian Thomists largely rejected and his poetry was very personal and not easy to integrate into the accepted system. Keble, the most orthodox poet, has faded most completely from view. The poetic visions—in the end planted in the minds of every schoolchild in the country—raised important questions both about religious experience and about religious dogmas. At their root of course was the fact that science was changing people's world views while their experiences of life—and death—demanded a response science could not provide.

The poetic imagination certainly embedded in the thought of the time powerful currents which fed the British Idealist philosophers. Idealism seemed often to provide an alternative to the established religion and to its dissenting and nonconformist rivals. In T. H. Green's case this was deliberate, and Green was immediately influential and has continued to be the most influential of the idealists on British public life. His pupil Gerard Manley Hopkins

---

[87] Cochran, 1980, pp. 143–81.
[89] Brown, 1997, pp. 199–200.
[88] Hopkins, 1959a, p. 56.
[90] Royce, 1913, ii. 430–1.

was among those influenced by him. Hopkins wrote an essay for Green in 1867 in which he suggests 'that metaphysics cannot be abolished or replaced by a materialist psychology, although there is a tendency for idealism and materialism to alternate and a danger that metaphysics might be reduced to a search for what lies beyond the empirically available'.[91]

F.H. Bradley was sceptical of those who provide a replacement for religion, but he invariably opposed Christianity. In Scotland, the Caird brothers, John and Edward,[92] were instrumental in the campaign to rescue their countrymen from the darker, hellfire, predestinationist forms of Scottish Calvinism.

'Self-realization' was the inscription on the banner under which the idealists marched. But the status of the self to be 'realized'[93] divided the idealists into two groups. The 'Absolutists', above all F. H. Bradley and Bernard Bosanquet, believed the individual must understand his natural goal, his appropriate 'self-realization', to be the enrichment of a community, something larger than himself though not the God of the established religion or its rivals.

The idealist philosophers, by and large, shared the common poetic visions of the time, for in the shared background of both there was a rationalized Neoplatonic mysticism which struggled against the focus on immediate experience which derived from Locke, Berkeley, and Hume. F. H. Bradley accepted that 'intellectual satisfaction' grasps reality only in an 'ideal form'. And the philosophers mostly sensed that the poets were not merely providers of ornaments for philosophical theory. Bradley went on to say that the intellect 'addresses only one side of our being'.[94]

Bosanquet offered a discussion of Keats's 'vale of soul-making', which runs through much of Lectures III and IV of the *Value and Destiny of the Individual*.[95] But the basic reality of the individual and the prospects for immortality were divisive ideas. In the *Value and Destiny of the Individual* Bosanquet dismisses Keats's remarks about antecedent sparks of intelligence. He also dismisses the future life, calling it 'an attractive imagination of something larger and happier than what we have; something of the same kind, but arbitrarily supposed as extended'.[96]

Keats thought the whole idea of soul-making would be set awry if the future life were to be dismissed, and Bosanquet took him to be denying that the value of the soul can be in its contribution to the universe as a whole. But Keats was actually maintaining something much more interesting about the way in which individuality comes to be and what it is.

Bosanquet insisted always that the individual must find his real life in the community. He was not in the end suggesting an immersion in the Absolute which would resemble a mystical union with God. His Absolute is not another conscious being. The community is something which has the kind of unity one finds in the British state, and the union is a union of sentiment and ideological direction of the sort which emerged in the development of the

---

[91] Hopkins, 1959b, pp. 118–21.

[92] Edward, of course, moved to Oxford where he was active in anti-war movements.

[93] The word 'realized' is troublesome. In idealist philosophies such as those of Bosanquet, it sometimes meant the appearance in individual experience of an aspect of the Absolute, finally understood only to *be* a feature of the Absolute. In philosophies like those of J. McT. E. McTaggart it meant grasping the real indissoluble self which is hidden to us by the illusions of temporal experience.

[94] F. H. Bradley, 1915, pp. 11–12.

[95] Bosanquet, 1913, pp. 63–130.

[96] Bosanquet, 1913, p. 66.

common law. Bradley may at times go even further. Both held that duties are the foundation of rights. I have rights as a citizen because I need them to carry out my duties.[97]

These views led to a debate in which Bosanquet argued with Richard Burdon Haldane (Lord Haldane), G. F. Stout, and Andrew Seth Pringle-Pattison.[98] The debate raised the curious question: 'Do finite individuals possess a substantive or an adjectival mode of being?' Bosanquet held them to be adjectival. Pringle-Pattison worried—as anyone might—about the curious terms of the debate, but clearly thought Bosanquet had not made his case. He quoted Matthew Arnold about the future belonging to 'he who flagged not in the earthly life'. Stout warned that the issue was centrally about the *value* of the individual. Lord Haldane was troubled in a way that would have interested the poets that the discussions were full of metaphors which should be taken with great care.

Readers will think Haldane was right. No one wanted to talk literally about Aristotelian substances[99] or the sort of things which people mean when they talk about noxious substances, a good substantial building, or 'a man of substance'. And, although Bosanquet did mention grammatical adjectives, he did not think his friends might be parts of speech.

The proliferation of metaphors underlines the importance of poetry. Keats's divine sparks metaphor has its evident limitations, but the words the philosophers chose to prosecute their differences tend to be miserly and one-dimensional. What it is to be a lone human being in a community when the historical tide is running out is something the reader of *On Dover Beach* can grasp. If he can relate it to Newman's sermon in which it has roots he may possibly be on the way to understanding.

Despite Haldane's question, the philosophers in the 1918 debate did not ask why it was that they were driven to metaphors or suggest that perhaps the Absolute, because it was like nothing else and must contain everything, could not actually be conceptualized. One might argue, of course, that F. H. Bradley often came close to saying just that. It might also be that individuals, as unique, present the same problems.

Throughout the heyday of idealism the pluralists, J. McT. E. McTaggart in Britain and George Holmes Howison in the United States, held firmly to the view that individuals were ultimately real. Howison conceived of a God who was simply first among equals, provoking his countryman Josiah Royce to accuse him of deifying everyone. McTaggart allowed no God but saw the world as a collection of timeless loving spirits who ultimately enjoy a mutual understanding. His universe resembled a much-expanded Trinity. Neither

---

[97] The most extreme version appears in an unpublished document in the Merton College archives available online at <http://www.anthonyflood.com/bradleyxnmorality.htm>. In it he says '(1) The individual has no rights—as an individual. His duty to self-sacrifice or self-assertion is the foundation of his rights. (2) The individual as such has no value—let alone an infinite value. The right and duty of the Whole to dispose of him is in principle unlimited.' It is as well to remember that 'the Whole' is the Absolute and not, say, a London borough council, or the French state, or even the United Nations, but in essays like 'My Station and Its Duties' (F. H. Bradley, 1876, 1927) some entities between the individual and the Absolute take on an apparent reality. In Bosanquet, 1899, the reality of such entities is made quite clear.

[98] It forms the second part of Carr, H. Wildon (ed.), 1918, and was edited from a meeting of the Aristotelian Society and the Mind Association held in London in July of that year.

[99] Such a notion would have been embarrassing for any idealist except McTaggart, though something like an Aristotelian idea of substance seems to have been floating in the background.

philosopher found favour with Royce whose view lay rather between the absolutists and the pluralists. McTaggart seems to have had little interest in poetry—though he did read novels—but in a sense he met poets like Hopkins halfway, for his theory was that, while the nature of reality was to be discovered solely by the application of pure reason and so knowledge of it consisted of universals, our actual knowledge of ourselves and others consists entirely of direct awareness, each element of which is individual. McTaggart's individual selves, unlike the Trinity, could not share natures.

The Seth brothers, James and Andrew (Andrew became Andrew Seth-Pringle Pattison), also held a kind of intermediate view. Although Andrew does not deny that there is an Absolute and he insists that God is more than man, he took a strong individualist position holding that there is a fundamental reality to individual selves and that they are in a sense *impervious*. He aroused the wrath of D. G. Ritchie in one of the longer disputes among idealists.[100]

The dispute with Ritchie came to involve the possibility of just the kind of knowledge which Gerard Manley Hopkins insisted on and Ritchie denied. Henry Jones, an admirer of Browning as we have seen, also tried to find room for compromise in the universe which he regarded as an organic whole capable of manifesting itself in complex ways through genuine individuals. He thought Browning's scepticism at least partly justified by the fact that such an organic whole can never be completely grasped by one within it, but he also thought his theory justified Browning's optimism.

Of the major challenges with which we started, one, at least, the demand for a view of nature which can accept science and yet accept the full range of the reality addressed by the humanities, produced poetry from Wordsworth through Tennyson which opened questions and surely helped stimulate developments in idealist metaphysics. There were surely particularly close connections between those poets (and some others) and idealism but poetry surely influenced the search for a wide-ranging vision which was characteristic of much nineteenth-century philosophy including the work of Mill and Spencer. Idealist metaphysics, in particular, seemed to offer then, and may still offer, hope of a positive outcome.

The larger challenge centres on how we are to understand individuals and explain the place of people, the nature and meaning of historical events, the significance of the possibility of being itself or of possible beings far beyond us on some ontological scale. Many of the poets found no conventional God or gods, but glimpsed great minds which might be the Absolute of some of the idealists or something quite different. The poets would have wanted little truck with the broken metaphors of the 1918 debate and they all glimpsed what Arnold and Newman made explicit: There is something in us which makes us think our real selves are something much more than one can find in the pages of *The Lancet*. They would have agreed that this something more makes demands on all of us.

---

[100]   For an account of the Seth brothers and their dispute with Ritchie, see Mander, 2011, pp. 356–69.

Works Cited

Allen, Peter, 1978, *The Cambridge Apostles: The Early Years*, Cambridge: Cambridge University Press.

Armour, Leslie, 1990, 'Newman's Theory of Ideas', *Paideusis*, 3 (Spring), pp. 3–16.

Arnold, Matthew, 1850, 'Memorial Verses', *Fraser's Magazine* (June).

Arnold, Matthew, 1869, 1965, *Culture & Anarchy*, London: Smith Elder (1869); ed. R. H. Super, Ann Arbor: University of Michigan Press (1965).

Arnold, Matthew, 1873, 1889, *Literature and Dogma*, London: Nelson (1873); London: Macmillan (1889).

Arnold, Matthew, 1961, *Poetry and Criticism of Matthew Arnold*, ed. Dwight Culler, Boston: Houghton Mifflin.

Arnold, Matthew, 1965, *Matthew Arnold's Poems*, ed. Kenneth Allott, London: J. M. Dent & Sons Ltd.

Arnold, Matthew, 1968, *Dissent and Dogma*, ed. R. H. Super, Ann Arbor: University of Michigan Press.

Blake, William, 1804, *Milton, A Poem*, privately circulated. There is a modern facsimile edition published by the Blake Trust, London, 1967.

Blake, William, 1963, *The Four Zoas*, manuscript is in the British Library, Additional Manuscripts 39764. There is a facsimile edition, ed. G. E. Bentley, Jr., Oxford: Clarendon Press.

Bosanquet, Bernard, 1899, *The Philosophical Theory of the State*, London: Macmillan.

Bosanquet, Bernard, 1913, *Value and Destiny of the Individual*, London: Macmillan.

Bradley, A. C., 1909, *Oxford Lectures on Poetry*, London: Macmillan.

Bradley, F. H., 1876, 1927, *Ethical Studies*, Oxford: Clarendon Press.

Bradley, F. H., 1915, *Essays on Truth and Reality*, Oxford: Clarendon Press.

Bradley, F. H., 2010, Merton archive notes in religion available at <http://www.anthonyflood.com/bradleyxnmorality.htm>.

Brett, George, 1931, 'Shelley's Relation to Berkeley and Drummond', in Wallace (1931), p. 184.

Brocking, M. Elizabeth, 1985, *Common Sympathies, Shelley's Revolt of Islam*, PhD thesis, University of Texas at Houston.

Brown, Daniel, 1997, *Hopkins' Idealism*, Oxford: Clarendon Press.

Bunsen, C. C. J., 1854, *Outlines of the Philosophy of Universal History Applied to Language and Religion*, 2 vols., London: Longman, Brown, Green and Longmans.

Burrow, J. W., 1967, 'The Uses of Philology in Victorian England', in Robert Robson (ed.), *Ideas and Institutions of Victorian Britain: Essays in Honour of George Kitson Clark*, London, G. Bell, pp. 180–204.

Byron, George Gordon, 1988, 2009, *Letters and Journals*, Newcastle upon Tyne: Cambridge Scholars Press.

Carr, H. Wildon (ed.), 1918, *Life and Finite Individuality*, London: Williams and Norgate, (edited from a meeting of the Aristotelian Society and the Mind Association).

Cochran, Leonard, 1980, 'Instress and Its Place in the Poetics of Gerard Manley Hopkins', *Hopkins Quarterly*, 6/4 (Winter), 143–81.

Coleridge, Samuel Taylor, 1811, 1897, *Lectures and Notes on Shakespeare*, ed. T. Ashe, London: George Bell.

Coleridge, Samuel Taylor, 1954, *Complete Poems of Samuel Taylor Coleridge*, London: Macdonald.

Coleridge, Samuel Taylor, 1956, *Biographia Literaria*, ed. George Watson, London: Dent. (The edition, ed. James Engell, Walter Jackson Bate, and Kathleen Coburn, published as volume lxxv in the Princeton Bollingen Series, 1983, is listed at the time of writing as 'currently unavailable'.)

Coleridge, Samuel Taylor, 2000, *Lectures 1818–1819 on the History of Philosophy*, ed. J. R. de J. Jackson, Princeton: Princeton University Press.

Coleridge, Samuel Taylor, 2001, *Collected Works of S. T. Coleridge*, xvi, ed. J. C. C. Mays and J. Crick, Princeton: Princeton University Press (in 3 parts).

Davies, John, 1599, *Nosce Teipsum*, London: Richard Field for John Standish.

Drummond, William, 1805, *Academical Questions*, London: Cadell & Davies.

Duns Scotus, John, 1597–8, *Commentary on the Sentences*, Venice: B. and B. Sessam.

Duns Scotus, John, 1639, *Ordinatio*, ed. Luke Waddington, London: Lawrence Durand.

Duns Scotus, John, 1893, *Joannis Duns Scoti, Opera Omnia*, Paris: Vivès, 1893.

Duns Scotus, John, 1912, *Commentaria Oxoniensia*, ed. Marianus Fernandez Garcia, Quaracchi: Typographia Collegii S. Bonaventurae.

Duns Scotus, John, 1963, *Opera Omnia*, ed. Carl Balic, Vatican City: Typos Polyglottis Vaticanis.

Eliot, T. S., 1932, 'Dante', in *Selected Essays*, London: Faber & Faber.

Eliot, T. S., 1936, *Essays Ancient and Modern*, London: Faber & Faber.

Farrar, F. W., 1860, *The Origins of Language*, London: John Murray.

Gardner, Martin, 2007, 'How Keats's Famous Line Applies to Math and Science', *Scientific American*, 296 (18 March).

Gray, Erik (ed.), 2004, *In Memoriam*, New York: Norton.

Hair, Donald S., 1991, *Tennyson's Language*, Toronto: University of Toronto Press,

Hartley, David, 1749, 1986, *Observations on Man, His Frame, His Duty and His Expectations*, modern edn., London: Ibis.

Hedley, Douglas, 2000, *Coleridge, Philosophy and Religion: Aids To Reflection and the Mirror of the Spirit*, Cambridge: Cambridge University Press.

Hiebert, Erwin, 1966, 'The Uses and Abuses of Thermodynamics in Religion', *Daedalus*, 95: 1052–8.

Honan, Park, 1981, *Matthew Arnold: A Life*, London: Weidenfeld & Nicolson.

Hopkins, Gerard Manley, n.d., *The Gerard Manley Hopkins Archive*, Newbridge College, County Kildare, Ireland, on line at <www.gerardmanleyhopkins.org/studies/philosophy.html>.

Hopkins, Gerard Manley, 1959a, *The Sermons and Devotional Writings of Gerard Manley Hopkins*, ed. Christopher Devlin, London: Oxford University Press.

Hopkins, Gerard Manley, 1959b, *Journals and Papers of Gerard Manley Hopkins*, ed. Humphry House, London: Oxford University Press. (Note: the two 1959 volumes constitute the revised and enlarged edition of *The Notebooks and Papers of Gerard Manley Hopkins*, ed. Humphry House, London: Oxford University Press, 1937.)

Hopkins, Gerard Manley 1985, *Gerard Manley Hopkins: Poems and Prose*, London: Penguin Classics.

Jackson, Emily A. Bernhard, 2010, *The Development of Byron's Philosophy of Knowledge*, Basingstoke: Palgrave Macmillan.

Jones, Henry, 1891, *Browning as Philosophical and Religious Teacher*, Glasgow: Maclehose.

Jones, Henry, 1922, *A Faith that Enquires*, London: Macmillan.

Keats, John, 1819, letter of 19 March, available at <www.mrbauld.com/keatsva.html>.

Keats, John, 1973, *Complete Poems*, ed. John Bernard, Harmondsworth: Penguin.

Keble, John, 1853, *The Christian Year*, Oxford: Parker.

Keble, John 1912, *Lectures on Poetry*, trans. E. K. Francis from the original Latin, Oxford: Oxford University Press.

Le Moyne, Pierre, 1645, *Les Peintures morales*, Paris: Cramoisy.

Liedtke, Hans, 1933, *Shelley durch Berkeley und Drummond beeinflust?*, Greifswald: Hans Adler & E. Panzig.

Mander, W. J., 2011, *British Idealism*, Oxford: Clarendon Press.

Mattes, Eleanor Bustin, 1951, *In Memoriam, the Way of a Soul: A Study of the Influences on Tennyson's Poem*, New York: Exposition Press.

Mill, John Stuart, 1865, *Examination of Sir William Hamilton's Philosophy*, London: Longmans.

Milnes, Tim, 2010, *The Truth About Romanticism: Pragmatism and Idealism in Keats, Shelley, Coleridge*, Cambridge: Cambridge University Press.

Murry, John Middleton, 1955, *Keats*, New York: Noonday Press.

Newman, John Henry, 1845, *The Development of Christian Doctrine*, London: James Toovey.

Newman, John Henry, 1870, *Essay in Aid of a Grammar of Assent*, London: Burns, Oates.

Newman, John Henry, 1885, *The Dream of Gerontius*, London: Burns, Oates.

Newman, John Henry, 1892, 1970, *University Sermons*, London: Longmans, Green (1892); London: SPCK (1970).

Newman, John Henry, 1961, *The Argument from Conscience to the Existence of God*, ed. Adrian J. Boekraad and Henry Tristram, Louvain: Nauwelaerts.

Newman, John Henry, 1969, *The Philosophical Notebook of John Henry Newman*, 2 vols., ed. Edward Augustus Sillam, Louvain: Nauwelaerts.

Newman, John Henry, 1992, *Collected Poems*, Sevenoaks: Fisher.

Notopoulos, James A., 1949, 1969, *The Platonism of Shelley*, Durham, NC: Duke University Press (1949); repr. New York: Octagon (1969).

Otto, Peter, 2000, *Blake's Critique of Transcendence: Love, Jealousy, and the Sublime in* The Four Zoas, Oxford: Oxford University Press.

Palmer, G. H., 1918, 'The Monologue of Browning', *Harvard Theological Review*, 11/2 (April), 121–44.

Peters, W. A. M., 1948, *Gerard Manley Hopkins*, London: Oxford University Press.

Prickett, Stephen, 1970, *Coleridge and Wordsworth: The Poetry of Growth*, Cambridge: Cambridge University Press.

Prickett, Stephen, 1976, *Romanticism and Religion*, Cambridge: Cambridge University Press.

Pulos, C. E., 1963, *The Deep Truth: A Study of Shelley's Scepticism*, Lincoln, Nebr.: University of Nebraska Press.

Reiman, Donald H., and Fraistat, Neil (eds.), 2002, *The Complete Poems of Percy Bysshe Shelley*, Baltimore: Johns Hopkins University Press.

Roberts, Hugh, 1997, *Shelley and the Chaos of History*, University Park, Pa.: Pennsylvania State University Press.

Royce, Josiah, 1913, 1968, *The Problem of Christianity*, New York: Macmillan (1913); ed. John E. Smith, Chicago: University of Chicago Press (1968).

Shelley, Mary, 1840, *Essays, Letters from Abroad, Translations and Fragments*, London: E. Moxon, 2 vols.

Shelley, Percy Bysshe, 1826–30, *The Poetical Works of Percy Bysshe Shelley*, London, William Benbow.

Shelley, Percy Bysshe, 1975, 2002, *The Complete Poetical Works of Percy Bysshe Shelley*, ed. Neville Rogers, Oxford: Clarendon Press.

Shelley, Percy Bysshe, 2002, *Shelley's Prose and Poetry*, 2nd edn., New York: Norton and Co.

Staines, David, 1977, *Notes and Queries*, NS 24, p. 405.

Stewart, Ian, 2007, *Why Beauty is Truth: A History of Symmetry*, New York: Basic Books.

Tennyson, Alfred, 1870, *The Holy Grail and Other Poems*, London: Trench & Co.

Tennyson, Alfred, 1891, *Alfred Lord Tennyson, Works*, London: Macmillan.

Tennyson, Alfred, 2004, *In Memoriam*, ed. Erik Gray, New York: W. W. Norton.

Tennyson, Hallam, 1897, *Alfred Lord Tennyson: A Memoir*, London: Macmillan.

Wallace, Malcolm W. (ed.), 1931, *Studies in English by Members of University College, Toronto*, Toronto: University of Toronto Press.

Winternitz, Judith, 1979, *Linguistic Theory of Universal History with Special Reference to C. C. J. Bunsen 1830–1880s*, Sydney University (PhD Thesis).

Wordsworth, Dorothy, 1971, *Journals of Dorothy Wordsworth: The Alfoxden Journal 1798, The Grasmere Journals 1800–1803*, ed. Mary Moorman, New York: Oxford University Press.

Wordsworth, William, 1807, *Poems in Two Volumes*, London: Longman, Hurst, Rees.

Wordsworth, William, 1995, *The Prelude: Four Texts, 1798, 1799, 1805, 1850*, ed. Jonathan Wordsworth, London: Penguin.

CHAPTER 30

THE PROFESSIONALIZATION OF BRITISH PHILOSOPHY

STUART BROWN

1. INTRODUCTION

It is possible to distinguish two senses of 'professionalization' both of which are relevant in the present context. In a broad and familiar sense 'professionalization' is a process of change in the leadership of a particular social activity: from amateurs to those who do it for a living. Professionalism is, however, linked essentially to high standards and thus to competition, achievement, and recognition.[1] And so this sense of 'professionalization' is linked to another sense in which a particular occupational group may acquire the status of a 'profession'. Professions, in this richer sense, are exclusive groups whose members not only exercise a special skill but share a common purpose and values. Typically one has to be specially qualified to join a profession and membership confers privileges and status. Members of a 'profession' are subject to a complex set of obligations and failure to meet certain minimum standards of professional conduct can typically lead to exclusion.

In the early nineteenth century the established 'professions' were a traditional few, such as lawyers, medical doctors, and the clergy. But, in what has been seen as a pervasive professionalization of British society (Perkin 1969b), an increasing number of occupations, including university teachers, sought professional status. By the 1860s it became a reformer's dream 'to erect teaching and learning, inseparably united, into a life-profession' (Pattison 1868: 204). And the project of making university teaching a regular profession was well in hand by the end of the century. In tandem with this development was the professionalization of academic subjects, including philosophy. The academic world was dividing into specialisms, with their own group identities, their own societies, and their own journals. Academics gradually ceased to be 'men of letters' who ranged over several disciplines

---

[1] The pre-eminence enjoyed by professionals derives typically from the excellence they are able to achieve through dedication by comparison with amateur standards. Good examples are to be found in the professionalization of various sports that were previously amateur.

and addressed a broadly educated laity. Their writing became more esoteric and technical, addressed primarily or exclusively to their fellow specialists.

By the end of the nineteenth century the professionalization of philosophy in Britain had in some respects only just begun.[2] Clergymen and amateurs were still prominent in promoting and administering the subject. And they naturally preferred to think of philosophy as inclusive and accessible rather than esoteric or technical. Philosophy 'finally evolved into a full-scale academic profession', according to Gilbert Ryle, during the period 1926–76.[3] And certainly for Ryle's Oxford the main dates marking this development are in the twentieth century.[4] But fundamental changes were needed, both in the wider society and in the universities themselves, to make the professionalization of academic subjects possible. Many of these took place in the late nineteenth century. Other subjects such as economics and psychology that had historically been connected with philosophy were already evolving, acquiring a distinct identity, and beginning to establish a separate institutional status. Nonetheless there were many factors holding back the professionalization of philosophy and even making it controversial in a way it was not to be in other academic areas. Amongst these factors one of the chief, as I will argue, was the absence of a single coherent and agreed view of the subject shared by those who practised philosophy for a living.[5]

Professionalization had its source not in philosophy itself, nor in other university subjects, but in large-scale social changes.[6] These changes greatly increased the size and importance of the professional classes and changed the political colour of the country. Patronage, privilege, and tradition were challenged in favour of merit and social mobility. The purpose and nature of a university education became a matter for public debate. In the second half of the nineteenth century the British university scene changed radically. University institutions were established in all the great industrial cities that had emerged during the century and, as they expanded, student numbers increased considerably. Moreover there were big changes in the backgrounds of students attending the old universities. In Oxford at the beginning

---

[2] This subject has yet to be studied in any detail, though some discussion is included in A. W. Brown 1947, Ryle 1976, and Hamlyn 1992, to each of which I am indebted. The professionalization of philosophy in America has been the subject of detailed studies, notably Kuklick 2001 and J. Campbell 2006. The American case is different but these works indicate by comparison how much remains to be done in the study of this aspect of British philosophy.

[3] Ryle 1976: 387. Ryle refers to his own 'half-century', which roughly corresponds to the first fifty years of the Royal Institute of Philosophy. Ryle's first appointment was actually in 1924, a year before the founding of what was originally called 'the British Institute of Philosophical Studies' and to whose fiftieth anniversary celebrations his lecture was a contribution.

[4] Philosophy in Oxford had been taught as part of the Classical 'Greats' curriculum. It was not until 1913 that it was established as a separate sub-faculty and not until 1920, with the establishment of the Modern Greats (Philosophy, Politics, and Economics) degree, that it could be studied separately from Latin and Greek. The emergence of the BPhil degree as a recognized qualification for teaching philosophy belongs to the period after the Second World War.

[5] See Section 3.6. I agree with what I take to be implicit in Ryle's account that it is not a coincidence that the rise of analytical philosophy to its dominance in British philosophy in the middle decades of the twentieth century happened at the same time as the subject became 'professional' to a degree that it had not been before. It would be a mistake, however, to suppose that the early stages of professionalization coincide with the origins of analytic philosophy or that no other philosophy would have served the purpose.

[6] See e.g. Perkin 1969b.

of the century, for instance, sons of clergy and landed gentry were the most prominent by background of the students matriculating. By the end of the century there were many fewer of these groups and many more undergraduates from lay professional backgrounds, both traditional and new.[7] By the end of the century university teaching was emerging as one of the new professions.

2. TOWARDS A PROFESSION OF UNIVERSITY TEACHERS

The second half of the nineteenth century was an age of reform and change for universities throughout the British Isles.[8] Many of those who wanted to see changes in the universities were inspired by the example of Germany. The unquestioned pre-eminence of German universities made them the destination of the brightest and best of students from other countries, Britain included.[9] Those who had been in Germany often joined the avant-garde of university reform when they returned. But, though academics were concerned in varying measure with reforming their institutions, much of the pressure for reform came from outside. Politicians and industrialists saw Germany increasingly as a major competitor to be emulated: the state of British universities and their need for reform became a matter of public concern and debate in a way in which it had never been before.

2.1 The Purpose of Universities

Prior to and for much of the nineteenth century universities in Britain were assumed to be basically Christian institutions that transmitted a common culture to the country's future leaders, secular and spiritual.[10] During the century this assumption was questioned as it had never been before and by its end the universities had been largely transformed into secular institutions more concerned to defend 'academic freedom' than religious or any other orthodoxy, more dedicated to teaching the best students to the highest level their abilities would admit, and more committed to specialization and to excellence in research. New subjects were emerging and there was pressure on the universities to create new chairs so that they could be taught. This is the context in which an academic profession began to emerge.

---

[7] Carthays and Howarth (2000: 579) report that these new students 'were almost equally divided between the older-established professions—law, medicine, and the armed forces—on the one hand, and new groups—sons of civil servants, journalists, university teachers—on the other'.

[8] Conditions varied considerably between the constituent countries, each of which merits much fuller treatment than is possible in a short review. For a longer review of the history of British universities and an excellent guide to the literature, see Anderson 2006.

[9] See Haines 1969: 21. It is significant that many of the leading philosophical figures, such as Green, Sidgwick, Bain, and Ferrier, spent time in this way in Germany.

[10] See Anderson 1983: esp. chs. 1 and 2.

In practice the reform of the old universities was a slow and contested process. Change was greatly facilitated by the creation of new university institutions, many of them founded on quite different lines. Of these the most controversial in its day was University College in London (UCL), established in 1827 on utilitarian[11] rather than Christian principles. University College, stigmatized as 'the godless college in Gower Street',[12] provoked a movement to found a rival college to provide 'instruction in the doctrines and duties of Christianity as taught by the Church of England as well as other branches of useful education'.[13] Such was the declared aim for King's College, which was founded in 1829 and yoked together with University College in the University of London a few years later.[14] When, in Ireland, an attempt was made to cut across religious divisions by founding a national, non-religious university,[15] the Catholic authorities responded rather as the Anglicans had done in England, first by condemning the new university as 'godless' and then by founding their own institution. Thus, in 1854, a separate Catholic University of Ireland came into existence, based in Dublin.

At that time religious orthodoxy was so important in the universities that their members were expected, and even for some purposes required, to be orthodox Christians, usually to be subscribing members of whichever was the established church. Non-Anglicans could not graduate or hold academic posts in Oxford, Cambridge, and Durham until the Universities Tests Act was passed in 1871. At King's College London, academic posts in most subjects, including philosophy, were reserved for Anglicans until 1903, when the need for public rather than Church funding made it necessary to make appointments in non-theological subjects open to those of other persuasions. Anglicans were not always on the winning side. In Edinburgh, for instance, chairs at the university were reserved for members of the established (Presbyterian) Church of Scotland until 1850 and those of other denominations could forget about academic preferment.[16] Nor did discrimination disappear by abolishing privileges for members of the established churches. The Edinburgh Town Council had the final say in the appointment to chairs at the university and, for a while, the Free Church

---

[11] Its founders included three of Bentham's supporters: Henry Brougham, George Grote, and James Mill. See Pearson 1892.

[12] A writer for the *Evening Standard* in 1828 wrote that, once King's College was established, 'there will be neither motive nor excuse for any parent to inflict upon his offspring the disgrace of education in the infidel and godless college in Gower Street' (quoted in Huelin 1978: 3).

[13] The words were those of the Duke of Wellington in proposing that such a college should be set up in London. The circumstance is narrated in Huelin 1978: 3–4.

[14] See Bellot 1929 and Huelin 1978 for a fuller account of these institutions.

[15] The colleges in Belfast, Cork, and Galway came into existence in 1845 and what was known as the Queen's University of Ireland came into being in 1850. By 1854 Dublin had three university institutions, including the Catholic University as well as the long-established (Anglican) University of Dublin (now Trinity College).

[16] A. C. Fraser, in his autobiography, had cause to lament in the 1840s that 'the rigid enforcement of the test which bound the Chairs of Philosophy in the national universities to the Church of Scotland was a bar otherwise to a professorial career' (Fraser 1905: 125). Fraser, then still a parish minister of the 'Free Kirk', was sympathetic to the project of founding a 'Free' (non-sectarian) University of Scotland.

faction used its majority to ensure preferment for its own co-religionists and thus, turning the tables, to discriminate against those of the established church.[17] And it remained difficult for those with unorthodox religious opinions to obtain or retain any academic preferment.[18]

This continued to be a problem, though an increasingly local and isolated one, for practitioners of philosophy, which had a historical role as *ancilla theologiae* that it took well into the twentieth century to shake off.[19] Clergymen with a modest exposure to philosophical instruction, as was common, were often preferred to laymen who, from a later perspective, would seem to have been better qualified. [20] This made some sense so long as it was integral to the purpose of a university education to produce Christian gentlemen fitted for a leading role in society. In that context a move from parochial work to university teaching was not the radical change of direction it might now appear but just another context for pursuing the care of souls.[21] A clergyman might even use a university chair as a stepping stone to advancement in a Church career.[22] But very gradually universities ceased to be teaching institutions concerned to produce leading citizens of orthodox opinion. Eventually they evolved into centres for research, where students learnt to cultivate an inquiring mind and were given the tools to become researchers themselves. Professors might be there to teach

[17] Fraser, by 1856 professor of logic and metaphysics at the Free Church seminary (New College), himself benefited from the change in discrimination when he was appointed to the equivalent chair at the University of Edinburgh, in preference to the better-qualified J. F. Ferrier. In 1852 Patrick Campbell, professor of moral philosophy at the 'Free Kirk' seminary, had been preferred for the other philosophy chair. See Thomson 1985: 75–6 and 91. Ferrier, as Thomson explains, went on to play an active role in lobbying Parliament to transfer the patronage enjoyed by the Town Council to the University Court, which reform became law in 1858.

[18] Alfred Momerie, professor of logic and mental philosophy at King's College London, was forced to resign his chair in 1891 because of his 'Broad Church' views. Others complained that they could not secure chairs because of their unorthodox opinions. Alexander Bain sounded out a friend in Belfast about whether it was worth his applying for the chair there in 1855 and was told that his appointment was 'out of the question' because, in spite of his 'admitted high qualifications in other repects' he was 'obnoxious to the Church party' (Bain 1904: 230–1). James Sully wrote that he gave up applying for chairs because he was 'too heavily handicapped', partly because he lacked the 'unimpeachable orthodoxy' expected (Sully 1918: 188). Sully was finally appointed to the Grote Chair of Logic and Philosophy of Mind at UCL in 1892.

[19] Many nineteenth-century British philosophers counted the philosophy of religion as their main or even exclusive interest in the subject. And of these the majority were engaged in what would nowadays be called 'apologetics'.

[20] There are many instances of such a preference, especially for chairs of 'moral philosophy', though other factors may also have come into play. The appointment of the Revd Robert Flint, then a parochial clergyman, to the Chair of Moral Philosophy at St Andrews in 1864 over Oxford's rising star, T. H. Green, may have been partly a parochial preference for a Scot. But Flint's later record shows his commitment to practise as a preacher and to use philosophy to defend religious faith. It is easy to see how Green, by contrast, would have seemed too liberal and perhaps unsound.

[21] Henry Calderwood's decision, in 1868, to give up the parochial ministry in order to accept the Chair of Moral Philosophy at Edinburgh University was explained by his son in these terms: 'he believed that, as teacher of Moral Philosophy to hundreds of youths, of whom many would yet occupy spheres of great influence, he would carry out his chief aim in life as truly as if he remained in the pastorate' (Calderwood 1900: 159).

[22] For example, R. D. Hampden, holder of the Whyte's Chair of Moral Philosophy at Oxford 1834–6, later became bishop of Hereford.

but it was now suggested[23] that they were not there primarily to teach but to pursue their special area of research.

2.2 University Expansion

In 1860 there were four universities in Scotland,[24] four in England,[25] and three in Ireland,[26] as well as a small degree-awarding college in Wales.[27] By comparison with Germany and even Scotland, England and Wales were distinctly short of university institutions and were providing a proportionately tiny percentage of their populations with a university education. In the case of England its ancient universities seemed to be in the wrong places to train the leaders of an emerging industrial economy.[28] It became a matter of national need and local pride to remedy this situation. By the end of the century the number of university institutions in England had risen dramatically as industrialists and others saw to it that there was one in every major city: Manchester (1851), Newcastle (1871), Leeds (1874), Birmingham (1875), Bristol (1876), Nottingham (1880), Liverpool (1881), and Sheffield (1897). In Wales university colleges had been founded in Aberystwyth (1872), Bangor (1884), and Cardiff (1883) and these were incorporated into the University of Wales in 1893. Student numbers in England in Wales rose from 1,128 in 1800 to 16,735 in 1899, with most of that increase occurring in the last decade or so of the century.[29]

The expansion of the university sector created many more chairs and other teaching posts for academic specialists. This expansion, moreover, was happening throughout the English-speaking world. Able academics had an improved chance of finding continuous employment in university teaching and thus of pursuing some kind of career entirely within the university world, perhaps spending time in a less desirable chair somewhere until the opportunity came up to apply for one that was to be preferred. [30]

---

[23] For instance, by Mark Pattison. See Pattison 1868.

[24] The two universities in Aberdeen were united by an Act of Parliament in that year.

[25] Two of these (London and Durham) were founded in the first half of the nineteenth century.

[26] The University of Dublin (now Trinity College) dated from 1591.

[27] St David's College, Lampeter, founded in 1828, had the power to grant BA and BD degrees.

[28] Matthew Arnold had urged that it was imperative to set up universities in 'the great centres of population' and contrasted Liverpool and Leeds unfavourably with Strasbourg and Lyons (Arnold 1868: 276).

[29] See Perkin 1969a: 23. See also Armytage 1953: ch. 2. The expansion of the universities in England and Wales continued to accelerate up to 1914. In Scotland student numbers doubled between 1870 and 1885 to a peak of 6,947 but then declined steadily for the rest of the century. This was due to a combination of factors, including the introduction of entrance examinations: Scottish universities had traditionally been 'open'. See Anderson 1983: 277.

[30] In most universities there was a career 'gap' between professors and assistants so the latter, in the middle of the century, would have had to do something else when their assistantships expired. (See Sect. 3.4.) By the end of the century the existence of additional academic posts filled this gap for many. Thus, for instance, James Seth, having served his time as assistant in logic in Edinburgh, moved to a chair in Canada in 1886 at the relatively youthful age of 26 and by 1896 was Sage professor of moral philosophy in Cornell. He was well placed to apply for the Chair of Moral Philosophy in Edinburgh when it fell vacant in 1898.

The increase in the number of academic posts in various academic specialisms made continuous careers possible for more individuals, thus helping budding academic subject professions to achieve the 'critical mass' needed for specialist societies to flourish.[31]

2.3 New Subjects, New Degrees

University courses had traditionally been offered in a limited range of subjects. In the late nineteenth century these increasingly permitted students to specialize and to study subjects that had not previously been in the curriculum. In Cambridge, for instance, it had been traditionally necessary to choose between Classics and mathematics, both subjects in which the university had a distinguished reputation. In the 1860s, however, it became possible to study either the moral or the natural sciences. The Moral Sciences tripos included logic, psychology, ethics, metaphysics, political economy, and politics. Henry Sidgwick, who had distinguished himself in the Classics tripos and begun academic life in that area, was made a lecturer in moral sciences in 1867 and was enabled to specialize in philosophy. And, thanks to the specialization allowed in part II of the tripos, students were effectively able to read for Honours in Philosophy. The moral sciences still remained a broad area, though political economy and politics were separated to form a new tripos in 1903. Eventually, some time after moral sciences had come to refer only to philosophy, Cambridge dropped what had become an archaism.

The same diversification of subject areas took place in other universities. In his history of the University of Aberdeen, for instance, John Bulloch reported that by the last decade of the nineteenth century the Faculty of Arts had been 'transformed beyond recognition' (Bulloch 1895: 207). There had been a marked move towards specialization. Instead of a fixed curriculum students were able to choose to combine a variety of subjects. New chairs had been created in English, French, German, and Education and one was contemplated also for History. Honours degrees had become available in Scotland, though until 1889 they were added on to a general degree programme.[32]

The same pattern was followed elsewhere. By 1898 separate chairs in English, Modern Languages, and History were almost universal though, in some smaller institutions, it took many years for the unsatisfactory practice of combining chairs to be discontinued.

2.4 Qualifications

In Germany the preparation of a university teacher was highly rigorous. Not only was a doctorate expected but even a postdoctoral dissertation (*Habilitationshrift*). American universities followed the German pattern, at least in making a doctorate a necessary part of

---

[31] The growth of professional societies for philosophy is traced in Sect. 3.1.

[32] The English model of honours degrees proved controversial in Scotland, where the existing broad degree structure suggested deferring specialization, in the American manner, to postgraduate study. See Davie 1961.

the qualification to be a 'professor'.[33] But, though many of the brightest and best of British graduates went to Germany to engage in further study of their chosen specialism, it was not to prepare for a doctorate.[34] 'Professional' doctorates were creeping in, even in Arts subjects, such as French and, perhaps predictably, German. But they were uncommon amongst academic philosophers in Britain at the end of the century. Henry Sidgwick is the best-known philosopher of the period who had acquired such a doctorate.[35] These were not given for research done in the years immediately after taking the first degree but only to more established scholars and only for work of some distinction.[36] Doctorates were common amongst the professoriate but these were usually honorary degrees: honours rather than qualifications. Qualifications were becoming more important for university teachers in Britain. But the qualification that had come to matter above all was not a doctorate but the class of honours gained in the first degree. Examinations that were implicitly or explicitly competitive provided the gateway to academic success.[37]

2.5 A New Profession?

By the end of the nineteenth century university teaching in Britain was well on its way to becoming a regular profession. That it had failed to be this earlier was put down to various factors: many were clergymen and so really belonged to another profession;[38] the salaries available were relatively poor;[39] and there was no clear career structure for academics.[40] The secularization of the universities resulted in a dramatic reduction in the number of clergy in university posts, especially where they had previously enjoyed a monopoly. By the end of the century a new breed of academic was emerging who not only set high standards for themselves in their research but who also took a particular pride in helping to produce the next generation of scholars in their specialism. Thus A. C. Fraser[41] expressed satisfaction as a teacher that he had helped to produce 'independent thinkers', as a result of which Edinburgh

---

[33] See J. Campbell 2006: ch. 1.

[34] See Haines 1969. James Sully, however, used his time in Germany in preparation for a London MA. (See Sully 1918: 72.)

[35] Others include Robert Latta who was awarded a DPhil by Edinburgh in 1898 for a thesis on Leibniz's *Monadology*: F. S. Granger, who was professor of philosophy at Nottingham from 1893 until at least 1935, had been awarded a London DLitt. in 1892 for work on psychology: and J. N. Keynes, then a lecturer in moral sciences at Cambridge, was awarded a ScD in 1891, for work on economics.

[36] The usual rule was that at least five years should have elapsed since taking the first degree. See Rudd and Simpson 1973: 10.

[37] As well as competitive examinations for fellowships, importance was increasingly attached to competitive scholarships.

[38] See L. Campbell 1901: 183 ff.

[39] See Sidgwick 1876: 683. Sidgwick, writing about Oxford fellowships, also cited 'the restriction of celibacy'.

[40] See Fowler 1876. See also Benjamin Jowett's 'Suggestions for University Reform, 1874', in L. Campbell 1901: 183 ff.

[41] Fraser's own career is of particular interest from the point of view of this paper, partly because it was so long, partly because he was at the centre of reforms as a dean in his own university, and partly because, to judge from his autobiography, he gradually changed from being rather a dilettante (spending his vacations in academic tourism) to being much more professional in how he viewed his own work.

had sent 'not a few professors and books of philosophy into the world, in the later decades of the nineteenth century'.[42]

It is clear that a new era of competitiveness between academic teaching institutions had begun that was to be one mark of the new professionalism. In Oxford and Cambridge the colleges compared the relative performance of their students in common examinations. Elsewhere other points of comparison were sought. For instance, in his biography of Henry Jones, H. W. J. Hetherington claimed that during Jones's tenure of the Chair of Moral Philosophy (1894–1913), Glasgow philosophy enjoyed a period of 'prosperity'. He attributed this partly to the fact that Jones's teaching style nicely complemented that of the colleagues who successively occupied the other chair (in Logic and Metaphysics): Robert Adamson from 1895 until his death in 1902 and Robert Latta thereafter. Jones saw it as his job to practise his students in 'philosophical reasoning' whereas his colleagues provided them with 'a first rate training in the technique of philosophical scholarship'. Hetherington went on to claim:

> The combination of the two methods made for a very strong school. In the competitive examinations for the various inter-university scholarships, Glasgow had far more than its share of honours, and at the present time Glasgow students of Jones's period are occupying chairs in every part of the English-speaking world. (Hetherington 1924: 81)

The expansion of the university world not only created more vacancies at the professorial level but also the need for more teaching assistance for the professors. By the early twentieth century there were many junior positions available where young academics would carry out much the same work as professors but for little reward and no obvious route to professional advancement.[43] In 1909 an association of 'junior staff' was formed and, though it initially had social aims, it soon became a pressure group. By 1919 the budding professional body came to include professors and the Association of University Teachers (AUT) was formed.[44]

Traditionally, the primary purpose of the universities had been to teach.[45] But increasingly, and certainly for professors, it became essential to engage in original research and publish its results. T. W. Heyck, in his study of the transformation of intellectual life in Victorian England, nicely sums up the new professionalism of the academic scholars and scientists of the late Victorian period:

> To them, to be a professional required certain standards and procedures in intellectual work, concentration on original research, care in the use of evidence, non-partisanship with regard to current politics and theology, valuation of work according to the idea of a 'contribution', seen as relevant to the field itself; and acceptance of the circle of fellow researchers in a field as the significant audience. (Heyck 1982: 226)

---

[42] See Fraser 1905: 205–6. Fraser detailed eleven ex-Edinburgh men in chairs in Britain and claimed 'a still greater number' in America and elsewhere in the world. This is a story, of course, not only about Edinburgh success but about the increasing opportunities of professional advancement for academics by the early twentieth century.

[43] By 1910 assistants outnumbered professors by 2 to 1. See Perkin 1969a: 23.

[44] See Perkin 1969a for a fuller account. The Scots formed their own association in 1922 and it did not merge with the AUT until 1949.

[45] Even in the late nineteenth century conservative figures like J. H. Newman denied that universities were places for promoting research and claimed that their role was exclusively to teach. See Newman 1873: ch. 1.

Instead of writing primarily for readers of the fortnightlies and quarterlies (mainly educated laity), academics addressed themselves to others working in the same specialized field to whom they looked for the validation of their own researches. This is one of the most significant developments in the professionalization of the academic world. It was encouraged by the emergence of specialist journals and specialist academic societies. Those societies were to play a crucial role in establishing a community of researchers with a common sense of subject identity and in fostering common intellectual values and shared modes of conduct, thus making the researchers into members of a profession.

3. STEPS TOWARDS THE PROFESSIONALIZATION OF PHILOSOPHY

In the late nineteenth century many subjects were establishing at least the beginnings of their modern identities. This was reflected in institutional distinctions made when new universities were created. In the University of Wales, for instance, the three original colleges at Aberystwyth, Cardiff, and Bangor each had a chair in Logic and Philosophy. Often, however, especially in small institutions or where not many students were expected, chairs were frequently combined. These sometimes surprising combinations may have made sense locally and perhaps suited the cross-disciplinary expertise of the incumbent. Thus, at Lampeter, philosophy came under the Chair of English Literature and Logic. Philosophy was usually represented in these new institutions, though the chair was often held by someone whose primary interest was in another subject, either because it was a combined chair or because the other subject was then included under philosophy, as psychology was.[46]

The trend towards professionalization affected not only university teaching generally but all academic disciplines, including philosophy. There is a separate story to tell in each case.[47] For disciplines with a clear sense of subject identity—what defines the subject and distinguishes it from others—it was relatively straightforward. But this was not how it was with philosophy. Nonetheless much was happening in the final decades of the nineteenth century to encourage the professionalization of the subject.

3.1 New Philosophical Institutions

Amateurs had traditionally[48] played a leading role in British philosophy and continued to do so right through the nineteenth century. Amateurs led the way in the forming and running of two of the leading philosophical societies that flourished towards the end of

---

[46] Economics was included under 'Moral Philosophy' or, in Cambridge, 'Moral Sciences'. Rhetoric was traditionally taught with Logic, though it shifted to English as that new subject became embedded in university institutions.

[47] See e.g. Iggers 2005 for the case of history.

[48] The 'modern' philosophy of the seventeenth century made a break with the then established university ('scholastic') philosophy, which had been accessible to a few only after long training in Latin

the century: the Metaphysical Society[49] (1869–80) and the Aristotelian Society, which was founded in 1880 and was to become in due course one of the leading professional philosophical societies of Britain.[50] Though university teachers of philosophy such as Henry Sidgwick and George Croom Robertson were also active members, and made valued contributions, they were in the minority.

The Metaphysical Society's founders included the Poet Laureate Alfred Tennyson, the architect James Thomas Knowles,[51] and the astronomer Charles Pritchard. The purpose of the society, as eventually agreed,[52] was to have free discussions of topics such as 'the logic of the sciences...the immortality and personal identity of the soul...the existence and personality of God...the nature of conscience...[and] the material hypothesis' (Knowles 1885: 178). With such an agenda it is not surprising that the membership included several senior clergymen, such as the Anglican bishop William Connor Magee, who enjoyed the cut and thrust of debate with those of persuasions opposed to his own. There were also noted scientists such as T. H. Huxley, John Tyndall, and W. B. Carpenter.

James Knowles, as well as being one of the founders, was the driving force behind the Metaphysical Society. He was a man of independent means who gave a great deal of his time to editing journals. In 1877 he took over the *Contemporary Review* and, after resigning over a disagreement about policy, he founded his own journal, the *Nineteenth Century*, in 1877. Knowles, if he was not the inventor of the philosophical 'paper', did more than anyone else to establish it as a philosophical institution by encouraging contributors to his journals to submit reasoned statements of why they held the positions they did. A. W. Brown (1947) credits Knowles with the invention of one of the characteristic institutions of modern professional philosophy in the English-speaking world: the symposium. But while again Knowles may have been the leading promoter of the symposium as secretary of the Metaphysical Society, a version of the symposium format seems to have been suggested to him by Frederic Harrison.[53]

and in methods of disputation. The new style of philosophy, which emphasized clarity of ideas and was expressed in vernacular languages, opened the subject up to amateurs, making philosophy part of the high culture of the leisured classes. John Stuart Mill stood squarely in this tradition.

[49] The original inspiration for the Metaphysical Society may have been partly, as A. W. Brown (1947) argues, the Cambridge 'Apostles', a number of whose former members were among its founders.

[50] The Scots formed their own society for professional philosophers, the Scots Philosophical Club (now Association), in 1901. The Welsh Philosophical Society was founded in 1964.

[51] Knowles (1831–1908) never presented a paper of his own to the Metaphysical Society. But he opened the inaugural meeting by reading one of Tennyson's poems.

[52] The original intention had been to have a society composed entirely of theists with the objective of strengthening their position against that of unbelievers. But some of those invited to join at the beginning made it clear that they would not join if the unbelievers could not come and present their own case. For a fuller account of the Metaphysical Society, see A. W. Brown 1947.

[53] At any rate that was the claim of Harrison himself:

> I suggested to James Knowles, our Secretary, Whip, and Editor...a mode of discussion which had no small success and might have been carried further. This was the method of *Symposium*, with the following plan. A paper on any given subject—say Future Life, Democratic Dogmas, Intuitive Knowledge, or the like, was printed and circulated to members; they were invited, in a well-arranged order, to comment in a short paper giving the threads of each writer's point of view. The papers rolled up in a snowball fashion, and then the whole set was considered in a general sitting. (Harrison 1911: 90 f.)

The Metaphysical Society did not last long, partly because it was largely composed of older men with established social positions and established beliefs to defend. But it was perhaps no coincidence that it was wound up in the same year (1880) as the Aristotelian Society was founded. The Aristotelian was also started and, in its early days, run by amateur philosophers.[54] But, though it sought to cater for a substantially amateur membership, it was transformed eventually and almost accidentally into one of the main societies in Britain for professional philosophers, where the papers presented would become increasingly hard for amateurs to follow or find interesting.

The professionalization of the Aristotelian Society was a very gradual process and indeed, though professional philosophers had taken over all the leading roles by the late twentieth century, amateurs were never excluded from membership. Like the Metaphysical Society the Aristotelian was divided into different camps largely determined by their sympathy towards or antipathy against religion. But, whereas the Metaphysical Society reached a sort of stalemate, with neither party being moved by the arguments of the other, the Aristotelian Society found a better strategy for retaining its vitality, not least through encouraging younger members. The Aristotelian also made a good choice of first president in Shadworth Hodgson, who combined wisdom in chairing discussions between members of radically different opinions with a high degree of commitment to the society. It was he who suggested that every member should take a turn to read a paper or initiate a discussion.[55] Papers would have reflected the division between those of a broadly idealist and those of a positivist persuasion, though there were also some disciples of Herbert Spencer.[56] Hodgson did not personally endorse any of these positions and, whilst willing to argue for his own idiosyncratic views, he had no wish to impose them on anybody else. Thus the Aristotelian, in its early days, lived up to its declared mission not to endorse any particular view but to welcome philosophers of any persuasion. It also lived up to its full title—the Aristotelian Society for the Systematic Study of Philosophy—by focusing for some of its early sessions on various philosophical classics.[57] This meant the members would be introducing different parts of the same book rather than merely stating and restating their positions.

In its early years the society was not well attended and was soon faced with a crisis when some of its most 'important and conspicuous members' seceded.[58] It was agreed to attempt to recruit new members from outside London. This drive was not entirely successful, but it did draw attention to the existence of the Aristotelian to philosophers elsewhere. One of the new members recruited was Alexander Bain, then professor at Aberdeen, who attended when he was in London. By 1886–7 the society was beginning to take on more of a national character with an impressive list of speakers such as D. G. Ritchie and Samuel Alexander (both then from Oxford) as well as Bain included amongst those invited.[59]

---

[54]   For an insider's account of the early years of the Aristotelian Society, see Carr 1928–9.

[55]   Carr 1928–9: 367.

[56]   Spencer declined to associate himself in person with any of these early societies.

[57]   Kant's *Critique of Pure Reason* was adopted in the fourth session and Berkeley and Hume in later sessions. See Carr 1928–9: 367.

[58]   Carr 1928–9: 369. The secession was led by a Dr Burns-Gibson.

[59]   Ritchie gave a paper on 'The Political Philosophy of T. H. Green', Alexander on 'Hegel's *Rechtsphilosophie*', and Bain on 'The Ultimate Question of Philosophy'.

In the following session the society promoted its first symposium on the subject 'Is Mind Synonymous with Consciousness?' with Hodgson himself, Ritchie, Stout, Bosanquet, and Alexander as the contributors. This was the first year that the society pre-circulated the papers to members, 'a procedure which has proved invaluable as an aid to adequate discussion' (Carr 1928–9: 373). The papers then began in 1888 to be published as part of a series of *Proceedings of the Aristotelian Society*. Moreover, because the papers were to be published, it naturally became desirable to restrict the invitation to present a paper to people who could be counted on to offer something worthy of publication. In due course an invitation to give a paper to the Aristotelian Society became a form of recognition valued by professionals, especially as the published paper would be widely read.

In 1897 an arrangement was made with the editor of *Mind*, G. F. Stout, to publish the Aristotelian Society papers in the journal and until 1900 nine or ten papers a year appeared in *Mind*. In 1900, when the Mind Association was formed expressly to assume responsibility for the journal, this informal arrangement was discontinued and the Aristotelian Society began a new series of volumes of its own proceedings, which continues to this day. The good relations between two societies were nonetheless confirmed when they held, in Durham in 1913, the first of their joint sessions,[60] which became in effect the annual conference of professional philosophers in Britain. Thus the Aristotelian Society fulfilled its ambition to be more than a local London society. It played the leading part in organizing the joint sessions: the papers were pre-circulated and published as supplementary volumes to the *Proceedings of the Aristotelian Society*. The joint sessions confirmed the symposium as one of the most distinctive institutions of professional philosophy in Britain.

The Aristotelian Society, by the turn of the century, was not only offering an impressive list of speakers but its membership included an increasing number of 'those professionally interested in the study courses in the universities'.[61] Nonetheless the society remained largely amateur well into the twentieth century. H. W. Carr, who was secretary for nearly fifty years, was a City businessman for whom philosophy was a part-time hobby, at least until 1918, when he retired from the City to become a professor at King's College London. Carr would have said that he was a true amateur rather than a professional philosopher.[62] The ethos of the society was nonetheless one in which the contribution that professionals could make was valued.

3.2 *Mind*: The First Professional Journal of Philosophy in Britain

In 1876 the first professional British journal of philosophy was inaugurated.[63] It was founded by Alexander Bain, who financed it out of his own pocket until the Mind Association was formed in 1900. Bain, himself a philosopher-psychologist, chose an editor of a similar stamp

[60] These have been held continuously since 1918.

[61] This is a phrase used by the then secretary, H. W. Carr, reporting on the early years of the society. Carr claimed that 'the real strength of the Society' was provided by the 'adhesion' of these professional teachers of philosophy (Carr 1928–9: 380).

[62] 'I had never myself thought of philosophy in the professional way as one among other pursuits. To me it has always been a natural human interest' (Carr 1928–9: 382).

[63] For an account of the early years of *Mind* see Sorley 1926. A celebratory centenary issue of *Mind* in 1976 has articles on the first two editors and the contributions they chose to include.

in George Croom Robertson, whose idea it was to call the journal *Mind: A Quarterly Review of Philosophy and Psychology*. In his editorial remarks at the outset Robertson made clear his ambition to make English philosophy more professional. In an essay on the English mind dated 1871 he had written these prophetic words:

> The representative philosophers of England[64]…have been, with hardly an exception, non-academic in position or even, many of them, anti-academic in feeling.…There was a time, long past indeed, when in England also the highest thought of the country found its utterance in the teaching of the universities, and such a time may come again. Nay, are there not signs that the day of professors is once more at hand, if not already upon us? (Bain and Whitaker 1894: 31)

The editorial policy of the journal was to publish articles without favouring one school of philosophy over another.[65] In this it was largely successful. Nonetheless, since Robertson was a professor at University College London, an institution then viewed with distrust by academics at the older universities, *Mind* was not immediately accepted by philosophers at Oxford and Cambridge. It was only under G. F. Stout, who took over in 1892 and who happily had connections with both of these ancient universities, that *Mind* gradually established its pre-eminence as an academic journal of philosophy. For many years it remained also a journal of psychology. Robertson was indeed disappointed not to have had more contributions from experimental psychologists. In reality those who worked in experimental psychology increasingly wanted to be independent of philosophy and founded their own professional organs such as the *British Journal of Psychology*, which started publication in 1904. Though it continued for many years to publish articles in psychology,[66] *Mind* became de facto an exclusively philosophical journal long before the decision to delete the reference to psychology from its title took effect in 1974.

It was still widely assumed in the late nineteenth century that a philosophical contribution of value would need the compass of a book. The success of specialist journals, however, helped to change the status an article in philosophy might have. This did not happen overnight and books continued to be written, often with the amateur at least partly in view.[67] But it is noteworthy that some of the most important philosophical publications of the early years of the twentieth century were articles in *Mind*: for instance G. E. Moore's 'Refutation of Idealism' (1903) and Bertrand Russell's 'On Denoting' (1905).

---

[64] It seems clear that Robertson means only to refer to England and not to Britain as a whole. The position in Scotland was quite different owing to the relative prominence of the universities in national life.

[65] In his editorial introduction to the first issue Robertson declared the aim of *Mind* to be 'the expression of all that is most original and valuable in current English thought, without predeliction for any special school or any department'.

[66] In 1920, for instance, all four substantial articles were psychological in theme.

[67] Many professional British philosophers in the twentieth century aspired to write in a clear and untechnical style. This indeed was part of the mission of one of its leading societies and journals, founded in 1925 and now the Royal Institute of Philosophy with its journal *Philosophy*. Their success is evidence of a continuing commitment to amateur involvement in philosophy.

3.3 Chairs in Philosophy

At the beginning of the nineteenth century there were very few chairs of philosophy in England but, by 1898, there were chairs not only in Oxford and Cambridge but in London (in both University College and King's), Birmingham, Newcastle, Leeds, Liverpool, Manchester, and Nottingham. There were new chairs also in Wales in Aberystwyth, Bangor, Cardiff, and Lampeter. In Ireland there were chairs at the long-established University of Dublin and at Queen's College, Belfast as well as in Cork.[68] In Scotland, by contrast, where there had typically been two chairs in philosophy—in Moral Philosophy as well as Logic and Metaphysics—there had actually been a contraction in the number of universities with the integration of the two rival institutions in Aberdeen in 1860.

Philosophy was, however, not very well separated from other subjects. It might be taught, as in Oxford, as a subsidiary of Classics[69] or linked, as in Cambridge, with other moral sciences such as psychology or political economy. Gradually, but only gradually, practitioners of subjects that were included in philosophy had their demands for separate status met, thus making it more likely that vacant chairs of philosophy would be filled by philosophers. In Birmingham, for instance, J. H. Muirhead was professor of political economy as well as mental and moral philosophy until the chair was split in 1900 by the creation of a separate Chair of Political Economy. By that time most philosophers would not have taken the teaching of political economy in their stride. The interconnection between philosophy and psychology, though not unchallenged, continued well into the twentieth century.[70] Sometimes, indeed, chairs in 'Mental Philosophy' or 'Philosophy of Mind' might be occupied by men whose primary interest was in experimental psychology. James Sully, for instance, who was Grote professor of logic and the philosophy of mind at University College London, from 1892 to 1903, is more celebrated by historians of psychology than historians of philosophy.[71]

The separation of strictly philosophical chairs from those that included other subjects was a precondition of the professionalization of the subjects involved. As long as subjects were combined or confused, the process of appointment to chairs would appear unsatisfactory looked at by professionals of either subject. For example, Alexander Bain, professor of logic from 1860 until 1880, included among his duties the teaching of English grammar.[72] This part of his job was sufficiently valued by the university that his chair was designated

---

[68] These colleges were then part of the Royal University of Ireland, a secular institution founded in 1880. There was at this time a separate Catholic University of Ireland, founded in 1854.

[69] In the early years of the new Oxford Greats regulations introduced in 1853, Aristotle and Plato might be studied philosophically but 'Butler, brought in as a Christian counterpart to the heathen Aristotle, was the only modern philosopher to be prescribed' (Walsh 2000: 313). Under the influence of T. H. Green, however, 'philosophy in the University acquired not only great prestige, but also a separate identity' (Walsh 2000: 318).

[70] See Sect. 3.6.

[71] It is instructive to compare Passmore 1957 with an equivalent for psychology such as Flugel 1933. Passmore, in a work generally noteworthy for its comprehensiveness, makes no mention of Sully, though this may reflect a 1950s blindness to aesthetics, Sully's main philosophical interest. Both writers give some prominence to Alexander Bain.

[72] Bain produced textbooks to supply what he saw as a deficiency in the written support offered for students: *An English Grammar* (1863; 2nd edn. 1866) and *English Composition and Rhetoric* (1866; 2nd edn. 1887–8). See Bain 1904: 272–9.

'Logic and English' when it was advertised in 1880. The vacancy attracted three very diverse candidates: the youngest, Robert Adamson, already professor of logic and moral philosophy in Manchester and one of the brightest philosophers of his generation who had already published books on Bacon and Kant: William Minto, who had assisted Bain for a few years, but whose interests and publications lay in English literature: and the oldest candidate, James Sully, who shared Bain's interests in experimental psychology and whose publications included a book on pessimism and another on psychology and aesthetics. Minto, as it happens, had made himself well known in Liberal circles and the Liberal MPs for Aberdeen were consulted about the appointment, presumably because it was a Regius chair. Minto had no interest in philosophy and it was his practice, according to Sully, to pass on to him any philosophy books that came in for review when they were both eking out a living working for journals in London.[73] Minto's appointment caused quite a stir. It was attacked by Richard Holt Hutton in *The Spectator* as a 'political job'. The other candidates were also both affronted.[74] Sully wrote scathingly about 'the mess party politicians are likely to make of it when called upon to decide such a question as a candidate's competence for teaching a highly technical subject like logic or psychology' (Sully 1918: 187).

Academic appointments were beginning to be judged by professional standards. The university world was moving on from the times when parties to the filling of a vacant chair might carry on as if it were a by-election, where the business was to identify the electorate and persuade them to vote one way or another.[75] The practice of combining chairs was on the decline. A separate Chair of English was created at Aberdeen in 1893[76] and justice was finally done to Adamson, who was appointed to the vacant Chair of Logic, from then on clearly conceived exclusively as a philosophical chair. And this trend to create separate chairs for separate subjects continued, even though there were two-subject professors at smaller universities well into the twentieth century.

3.4 Careers in Philosophy

Oxford and Cambridge provided, for some, places where students could remain after graduation and spend the rest of their lives in the academic world. As college fellowships became available quite frequently, someone who was thought good enough might have little time to wait before securing one. Bradley and Green in Oxford and Sidgwick in Cambridge are among the most distinguished of many examples of men who were able, with little hiatus, to find a suitable college fellowship to secure for them a life as an academic. Once established as a college fellow they would be well placed to apply for a chair, should one fall vacant.

---

[73] Minto, when he was editor of the *Examiner*, apparently used to pass over to Sully all the philosophical books that came to him for review so that he could concentrate on 'his proper subjects, politics and literature' (Sully 1918: 186).

[74] Sully wrote: 'To me, as also to Adamson, this bit of Crown patronage appeared to be a transparent "job"' (Sully 1918: 185).

[75] Thomson 1985 gives a detailed account of J. F. Ferrier's participation in some of these contests between candidates. See also Bain 1904.

[76] See Palmer 1965 for this separation of chairs seen as a development in English studies.

In universities where teaching was not done on a college basis, however, academic careers were unlikely to have such continuity. There were professors and they often had 'assistants', who would typically be recent graduates who had shown great promise. But, for much of the nineteenth century, there were very few academic posts in between these lowly and temporary appointees and the senior and established professors whom they were there to assist. Assistants, however brilliant, had to look for employment outside the university world once their terms of appointment had come to an end. Their best hope was to find work that was consistent with writing books and articles with which, in due course, they could hope to enhance their eligibility for a chair. Those that were clergy could find work in the parochial ministry, which for much of the century was in itself widely seen as a highly suitable background for someone who aspired to teach the young and which permitted the leisure to study and write.[77] For others there were opportunities provided in the literary world, especially by the fortnightly or quarterly journals then widely read by the educated public.[78] But, for many, their time as an assistant led nowhere.

By the turn of the century, however, a career in academic philosophy was open to an increasing number of able graduates. The creation of new universities meant that there were more chairs and someone might, as Andrew Seth (later Pringle-Pattison) did, move directly from an assistantship to a less sought-after chair and later to one for which he would by then be more eligible.[79] There were, in addition, more lectureships to which assistants might move. Robert Latta, for instance, was successively an assistant and then a lecturer in St Andrews, and was lecturer in logic and moral philosophy in Dundee, spending eight years in these positions before being appointed to his first chair in Aberdeen in 1900, making his final move to Glasgow in 1902. His steady, relatively speedy, but unspectacular progress illustrates the way in which opportunities for academics were opening up at the end of the nineteenth century.

If we contrast the career available to Latta with that of his teacher, A. C. Fraser, it is apparent that there had been big changes between the generations. Fraser was in the 'man of letters' tradition of university professors: he had no qualifications[80] and so was entirely dependent on the good opinion and influence of others.[81] Latta had not only a 'First' and studied in Germany but also took trouble to acquire a professional doctorate. Fraser's articles were addressed to a basically lay readership, mainly in the *North British Review*, of which he was editor for several years. Latta, by contrast, published in *Mind*. Fraser had been elected to the Metaphysical Society in 1871 and occasionally visited, when he happened

---

[77] Some examples of clergy who were appointed to chairs directly from parish work are: Robert Flint, previously a minister in Aberdeen and in Fife, to the Chair of Moral Philosophy at St Andrews in 1864; Henry Calderwood, a minister in Glasgow, to the Chair of Moral Philosophy in Edinburgh in 1868; Alfred Momerie, a curate in Lancashire, to the Chair of Logic and Mental Philosophy at King's College London in 1880.

[78] Amongst those who took this route were Alexander Bain, J. F. Ferrier, William Minto, and James Sully.

[79] Andrew Seth moved from an assistantship in Edinburgh to the chair in Cardiff in 1883, then to the Chair of Logic, Rhetoric, and Metaphysics in St Andrews in 1887, before being appointed to the Chair of Logic and Metaphysics in Edinburgh 1891.

[80] When he was a student the practice of graduating had lapsed at Edinburgh.

[81] His success in securing the Edinburgh chair over the better-qualified J. F. Ferrier was probably due to his good connections, as is maintained by Thomson 1985.

to be in London, though he never presented a paper. Latta, on the other hand, travelled to London expressly to present papers to the Aristotelian Society. Fraser had limited opportunities to develop his career and was fortunate to be even eligible when the chair occupied by Sir William Hamilton fell vacant in 1856 and no less fortunate in being preferred over the other candidates. Latta, by contrast, was able move up something like a ladder and enjoy a career more like that of a modestly successful twentieth-century academic.

3.5 The New Professionals

There has been a polite controversy over who was the 'first' professional philosopher in Britain. T. H. Green and Henry Sidgwick are the most prominent amongst those proposed for this honour. But others, including William Hamilton, Alexander Bain, and J. F. Ferrier, are sometimes mentioned.[82] In one way this controversy is a little misconceived, however, since, at least in a full sense, a profession needs already to exist before anyone can be a professional,[83] i.e. a member of a profession. And professions can only come about gradually, as new institutions are formed and individuals are able to pursue careers through satisfying their standards.[84] Nonetheless individuals can lead the way by personal example, in helping to establish new institutions and through their influence on the next generation. Bain, Green, and Sidgwick were indeed leaders in these ways. J. B. Schneewind has suggested they were among the first of 'a new breed of philosopher':

> unclerical, owing allegiance to no set creed, they saw philosophy as an academic discipline dealing with problems defined and transmitted by a group of experts who were the best available judges of proposed solutions. (Schneewind 1977: 6)

The creation of a philosophical 'profession' took a number of 'generations' with the profiles of successive generations gradually becoming more professional. It is instructive, particularly towards the end of the nineteenth century, to compare the career profiles of pupils with those of their teachers, as I have already done in the case of Latta and Frazer. The case of Emily Elizabeth Constance Jones is particularly interesting as she went as far as a woman then could in pursuing a career as a philosopher. She studied under Sidgwick[85] and achieved a first in the Moral Sciences tripos in 1880, though it was many more years before women could actually graduate. She was a lecturer in Girton College from 1884 till 1903, during which time she was a frequent contributor to the *Proceedings of the Aristotelian Society* as

---

[82] See e.g. Leighton 2004: 70.

[83] It is obvious that the debate is not about who was the first to do philosophy for a living.

[84] It is noteworthy that philosophers took an active part in the founding of the British Academy in 1902. A Fellowship of that body came to be widely regarded as one of the highest professional honours available to students of the humanities in Britain.

[85] The contrast between Constance Jones's career and that of Sidgwick is less marked than that between Latta and Fraser, but she was more focused on writing for a specialized group of readers. Sidgwick had very wide horizons and was as eager to be involved in the lay philosophical societies as the budding professional ones. So, although he was involved in founding the Mind Association, he was also the leading light of the Synthetic Society, a successor to the Metaphysical, whose membership was restricted to those who desired to find 'a working philosophy of religious belief'.

well as to *Mind* and to the *International Journal of Ethics*. She wrote on logic and contributed to the ongoing debate about hedonism in ethics, defending Sidgwick against his critics. As well as textbooks of logic and ethics she wrote a substantive critique of the Law of Identity. [86] She seems to have been a highly professional philosopher even though, as a woman, she had none of the prospects of academic advancement open to men with the same qualifications.

3.6 The Problem of Subject Identity

It is normally essential for the professionalization of an academic subject that it should have a distinct identity: that its practitioners should share the same intellectual values, an agreed methodology, and so on. British philosophy did not, in the nineteenth century, meet these conditions. As the century progressed, indeed, the diversity of 'schools' became more rather than less marked. One crucial division was between those in the empiricist tradition who thought of philosophy as including psychology and others who regarded them as entirely separate subjects. *Mind*, as we have seen, was conceived as a journal for both philosophy and psychology. And its first editor, George Croom Robertson, thought that psychology formed an integral part of philosophy. As he put it: the 'point of view of all modern philosophy from Descartes onwards is psychological' (Bain and Whitaker 1894: 3). This tended to be the orthodoxy in Britain, institutionalized variously in chairs of moral and mental philosophy and by the central position given to philosophy in the 'moral sciences'.[87] But others, especially those influenced by German philosophy,[88] took another view. As things turned out, psychologists were more eager to break the connection with philosophy than philosophers themselves. It was not until well into the twentieth century that, as Ryle put it, 'logic chopped both logic and philosophy free from that Mental Science or psychology into which the Two-Worlds view of Descartes and Locke had for so long glued them' (Ryle 1976: 386). Ryle's own pioneering book, *The Concept of Mind*, which deals with the mental without being psychological, was not published until 1949. The sharp sense of subject identity that the turn to conceptual or linguistic analysis brought to British philosophy in the mid-twentieth century was a further important mark of the professionalization of philosophy.[89] Then, as never before, the professionals were willing to dash the expectations of laypeople as to what philosophy was. Philosophy had become a rigorous, even technical, esoteric and professional subject worthy to take its place, if not as one of, at least alongside, the special sciences.

---

[86] See the article on her by Waithe and Cicero 1995.

[87] The orthodoxy continued in the interwar period even when it was being questioned. Beatrice Edgell, head of Mental and Moral Science at Bedford College, London, was made professor of psychology in 1927. In the following five years she was president of the four main societies in each subject, including the Mind Association and the Aristotelian Society.

[88] There was a debate in nineteenth-century German philosophy about what was called 'psychologism' (basing conclusions in logic, mathematics, or philosophy on psychological premises) that continued up to the Great War. See Kush 1995. The opposition to psychologism amongst British philosophers was not widespread: Russell, following Frege, took the lead (see Godden and Griffin 2009) but was not much followed at the time.

[89] It was important too that, though there continued to be dissenters from the dominant tradition even in prominent professional positions, they were marginalized in a way they could not have been in the heyday of the Idealist tradition.

4. THE DECLINE OF THE AMATEUR PHILOSOPHER

As philosophy became more professional so there was a decline in the status of the amateur. It is not that amateurs were excluded, as they were from some professional bodies. Amateurs continued to actively support and even hold office in the Aristotelian and other philosophical societies. But they ceased to have the influence that they had previously enjoyed. Amateurs could still write for other amateurs but not for professionals.[90] And, by and large, professionals did not attempt to write for a wider public. J. B. Schneewind rightly observed that 'Herbert Spencer was the last man to write philosophy which both excited public interest and received serious attention from the academics' (Schneewind 1977: 6). Bertrand Russell carried on the tradition of writing for both classes of reader. But, although he enjoyed the highest renown amongst both amateur and professional philosophers, he was valued by each category for quite different books. Some, such as *A Critical Examination of the Philosophy of Leibniz* (1900) and his *Principles of Mathematics* (1903), have had an enduring reputation amongst those professionals able to follow them but have no appeal to the amateur. In contrast, Russell's popular writings such as *Why I Am Not a Christian* (1927) and *Marriage and Morals* (1929) were generally ignored by professionals.

The separation of amateur and professional philosophy was largely accomplished by 1900. There were, and continued to be, professionals who thought it important to communicate their philosophy to amateurs. There were also amateurs who were more than happy to be part of an audience or readership for someone with a view of philosophy they found congenial and who could communicate to them in a way they regarded as authoritative.[91] But, though bridging the gap continued to be thought desirable and perhaps even necessary for the vitality of professional philosophy, the existence of the gap was never in question.

---

[90]   The narrowness of British academic philosophy in the mid-twentieth century created niches for amateurs to write on topics such as existentialism and Marxism and even to continue using idealism to defend religion. See e.g. the entries on Blackham, Cornforth, and Cleobury respectively in S. Brown 2005.

[91]   One philosopher who has successfully filled this role is A. N. Whitehead, whose 'process philosophy' was largely dismissed by professional philosophers, at least in Britain (though not America), including his former collaborator Bertrand Russell. Whitehead became something of a cult figure worldwide. Like Spencer before him, he fulfils a lay expectation of philosophy, that it incorporate the best science of the day into an overarching metaphysics, as Spinoza and Leibniz had done.

REFERENCES

Anderson, R. D. (1983). *Education and Opportunity in Victorian Scotland*. Oxford: Clarendon Press.

Anderson, R. D. (1992). *Studies in Economic and Social History: Universities and Elites in Britain since 1800*. London: Macmillan/Economic History Society.

Anderson, R. D. (2006). *British Universities, Past and Present*. London: Hambledon Continuum.

Armytage, W. H. G. (1953). *Civic Universities: Some Aspects of a British Tradition*. London: Ernest Benn.

Arnold, Matthew (1868). *Schools and Universities on the Continent*. London: Macmillan & co.

Bain, Alexander (1904). *Autobiography*. London: Longmans, Green.

Bain, Alexander, and Whitaker, T. (1894). *Philosophical Remains of George Croom Robertson*. London: Williams & Norgate.

Bell, Robert, and Tight, Malcolm (1993). *Open Universities: A British Tradition?* Buckingham: Society for Research into Higher Education & Open University Press.

Bellot, H. H. (1929). *University College, London, 1826–1926*. London: University of London Press.

Brock, M. G., and Carthays, M. C. (eds.) (2000). *The History of the University of Oxford*, vii. *Nineteenth Century Oxford*, pt. 2. Oxford: Clarendon Press.

Brown, Allan Willard (1947). *The Metaphysical Society: Victorian Minds in Crisis 1869–1880*. New York: Columbia University Press.

Brown, Stuart (ed.) (2005). *The Dictionary of Twentieth Century Philosophers*. Bristol: Thoemmes Continuum.

Bulloch, John Malcolm (1895). *A History of the University of Aberdeen*. London: Hodder & Stoughton.

Calderwood, W. L. (1900). *The Life of Henry Calderwood*. London: Hodder & Stoughton.

Campbell, James (2006). *A Thoughtful Profession: The Early Years of the American Philosophical Association*. Chicago and La Salle, Ill.: Open Court.

Campbell, Lewis (1901). *The Nationalization of the Old English Universities*. London: Chapman & Hall.

Carr, H. Wildon (1928–9). 'The Fiftieth Session: A Retrospect.' *Proceedings of the Aristotelian Society* 29: 359–88.

Carthays, M.C., and Howarth, Janet (2000). 'Origins and Destinations: The Social Mobility of Oxford Men and Women.' In Brock and Carthays 2000: 599–615.

Davie, George (1961). *The Democratic Intellect: Scotland and Her Universities in the Nineteenth Century*. Edinburgh: Edinburgh University Press.

Flugel, J. C. (1933). *A Hundred Years of Psychology*. London: Duckworth.

Fowler, Thomas (1876). 'On Examinations.' *Fortnightly Review*, NS 19: 418–29.

Fraser, A. C. (1905). *Biographia Philosophica: A Retrospect*. Edinburgh: Blackwood.

Godden, David, and Griffin, Nicholas (2009). 'Psychologism and the Development of Russell's Theory of Propositions.' *History and Philosophy of Logic* 30: 171–86.

Hamlyn, D. W. (1992). *Being a Philosopher: The History of a Practice*. London: Routledge.

Haines, George IV (1969). *Essays on German Influence on English Education and Science, 1850–1919*. Hamden, Conn.: Connecticut College in association with Archon Books.

Harrison, Frederic (1911). *Autobiographical Memoirs*. London: Macmillan.

Hetherington, H. J. W. (1924). *The Life and Letters of Sir Henry Jones*. London: Hodder and Stoughton.

Heyck, T. W. (1982). *The Transformation of Intellectual Life in Victorian England.* London: Croom Helm.

Howarth, Janet (2000). 'The Self-Governing University'. In Brock and Carthays 2000: 599–643.

Huelin, Gordon (1978). *King's College, London.* London: King's College.

Iggers, George C. (2005). 'The Professionalization of Historical Studies and the Guiding Assumptions of Modern Historical Thought.' In Kramer and Maza 2005: 225–42.

Knowles, J. T. (1885). Editorial Preface to 'The Metaphysical Society: A Reminiscence'. *Nineteenth Century* 18: 177–9.

Kramer, L., and Maza, Sarah (ed.) (2005). *A Companion to Western Historical Thought.* Oxford: Blackwell.

Kuklick, Bruce (2001). *A History of Philosophy in America: 1720-2000.* Oxford: Clarendon Press.

Kush, Martin (1995). *Psychologism: A Case Study in the Sociology of Philosophical Knowledge.* London: Routledge.

Leighton, Denys (2004). *The Greenian Movement. T. H. Green, Religion and Political Argument in Victorian Britain.* Charlottesville, Va.: Imprint Academic Philosophy.

Newman, J. H. (1873). *The Idea of a University Defined and Illustrated.* London: Basil Montague Pickering.

Palmer, D. J. (1965). *The Rise of English Studies.* London: Oxford University Press.

Passmore, John (1957). *A Hundred Years of Philosophy.* London: Duckworth.

Passmore, John (1976). 'G. F. Stout's Editorship of *Mind*.' *Mind*, NS 85: 17–36.

Pattison, Mark (1868). *Suggestions on Academical Organisation, with Especial Reference to Oxford.* Edinburgh: Edmonston & Douglas.

Pearson, Karl (1892). *A New University for London: A Guide to Its History and a Criticism of Its Defects.* London: T. Fisher Unwin.

Perkin, Harold (1969a). *Key Profession: The History of the Association of University Teachers.* London: Routledge & Kegan Paul.

Perkin, Harold (1969b). *The Rise of Professional Society: England Since 1880.* London: Routledge & Kegan Paul.

Rudd, E., and Simpson, R. (1973). *The Highest Education.* London: Routledge & Kegan Paul.

Ryle, Gilbert (1976). 'Fifty Years of Philosophy and Philosophers.' *Philosophy* 51: 381–9.

Schneewind, J. B. (1977). *Sidgwick's Ethics and the Rise of Victorian Philosophy.* Oxford: Clarendon Press.

Sidgwick, Henry (1876). 'Idle Fellowships.' *Contemporary Review* 27; repr. in Sidgwick, *Miscellaneous Essays and Addresses* (London: Macmillan, 1904), 320–39.

Sorley, W. R. (1926). 'Fifty Years of "Mind".' *Mind*, NS 35: 409–18.

Sully, James (1918). *My Life and Friends.* London: T. Fisher Unwin.

Thomson, Arthur (1985). *Ferrier of St Andrews: An Academic Tragedy.* Edinburgh: Scottish Academic Press.

Waithe, Mary Ellen, and Cicero, Samantha (1995). 'E. E. Constance Jones (1841–1922).' In Mary Ellen Waithe (ed.), *A History of Women Philosophers*, vol. iv. Dordrecht: D. Reidel, pp. 25–49.

Walsh, W. H. (2000). 'The Zenith of Greats'. In Brock and Carthays 2000: 311–26.

Whitaker, Joseph (1898). *An Almanack for the Year of Our Lord 1898.* London: Paternoster Row.

Index